S0-ANN-685

LETHAL VIOLENCE

A Sourcebook on Fatal Domestic, Acquaintance and Stranger Violence

LETHAL VIOLENCE

A Sourcebook on Fatal Domestic, Acquaintance and Stranger Violence

Edited by

Harold V. Hall

CRC Press

Boca Raton   London   New York   Washington, D.C.

Library of Congress Cataloging-in-Publication Data

Lethal violence : a sourcebook on fatal domestic, acquaintance, and
    stranger aggression / edited by Harold V. Hall.
        p. cm.
    Includes bibliographical references and index.
    ISBN 0-8493-7003-5 (alk. paper)
     1.Violence --United States. 2. Violent crimes--United States.
    3. Homicide--United States. I. Hall, Harold V.
    HN90.V5L48 1998
    303.6′0973—dc21   98-37992
                                                                                      CIP

No claim to original U.S. Government works
International Standard Book Number 0-8493-7003-5
Library of Congress Card Number 98-37992
Printed in the United States of America 1 2 3 4 5 6 7 8 9 0
Printed on acid-free paper

FOREWORD
Florence W. Kaslow, PhD

Perhaps we should call the last one-quarter of the 20th century *The Age of Violence.* Destructive, aggressive behaviors seem to have been unleashed in all aspects and echelons of society — the individual, the couple, the family, the schools and universities, the street scene, the workplace, the media, as well as in the worlds of gambling and drug addiction, the rackets, the criminal spheres, and the battlefields of war. No place seems like a safe haven; many people feel imprisoned in their own terror about becoming a victim of violence. This cannot be attributed to paranoia; rather, unfortunately, the high level of fear is attributable to the high level of violence that seems omnipresent in many segments of so-called civilization.

In this volume, *Lethal Violence: A Sourcebook on Fatal Domestic, Acquaintance and Stranger Aggression,* a comprehensive depiction of the many faces and facets of violence is clearly presented. It is not a pretty picture; in fact, put together in one package, the picture is so terrifying that it becomes a clarion call to everyone to take definitive action immediately to reverse the destructive forces and replace them with beliefs and behaviors that are respectful of life and hold it to be sacred, of other people's property and their right to live in peace, and of humanistically motivated means to resolve conflicts — such as mediation and arbitration instead of resorting to guns, bombs, and other weapons of murder.

The very organization of the book highlights the universality of violence and how pervasive it has become. It is true that perusing any volume on the history of civilization, one will encounter the existence of violence. But it never seems to have been this prevalent, this epidemic in its proportions, and this malevolent.

Interestingly, and noteworthy in its implications, is the fact that many people still recoil when a mother kills her child(ren). At least we still feel outrage and righteous indignation. The same is true in some segments of the community when the most horren-dous cases of child and spouse abuse come to light. But others take this in stride and almost seem to say, "So what? That's life."

The book's contributing authors refute this and describe why we must all join together to bring about a transformation in civilization to affirming life in a violence-free society, because what exists now is about torture, degradation, hurt and harm, and ultimately death — not life.

Some of the chapters indicate that the violence may be turned inward against the self, as in murder-suicide. Or it can be violence turned outward, through homicide, maiming, holding hostage, beating, knifing, robbing, and many other ways of hurting others. No matter what form it takes, this spiral of violence and destruction causes turbulence, angst, the organization of counter-force such as vigilante groups, and interferes with productive, creative efforts to enhance and enrich individual and community living. When fear is prevalent, the pursuit of happiness becomes a myth for all of those who do not relish violence and the commission of atrocities.

In many chapters, the contributors write about the violence megatrend and its lethality. Nonetheless, they conclude on an optimistic note predicting the rejection of violent sensationalism, the assertive deconstruction of the culture of violence, and the active pursuit of meaningful societal and personal values. Interventions are proposed which hold promise in reversing violent attitudes and behavior. I agree that this can and must happen. Anything else leads to the unthinkable conclusion that we will allow ourselves, our children and grandchildren, and the total fabric of our civilization to be destroyed. With this book, Dr. Harold Hall and his colleagues fill a critical niche in the literature dedicated to accurately portraying *what is* and pointing the way to *what should be.* I hope this message is heard, taken seriously, and acted upon by everyone who values the sanctity of life and believes in making the world a little safer for future generations.

ACKNOWLEDGMENTS

This volume was prepared with the unflagging help of many people. The contributors to this project uniformly produced high quality and comprehensive manuscripts. Over 500 years of collective professional experience by the contributors have yielded sound observations and helpful guidelines for the readership. At the end of each chapter, detailed author information is provided.

All of the contributors are experts in the field of violence and aggression, with most of the chapters authored by Diplomates of the American Board of Professional Psychology (ABPP). This was not planned. Numerous professionals in psychology and psychiatry were considered for authorship of chapters in *Lethal Violence*: A *Sourcebook on Fatal Domestic, Acquaintance and Stranger Aggression.* From that pool, most of those selected were ABPP certified, with renown board-certified psychiatrists also being among the contributors.

Special thanks are due to the Consulting Editors, who painstakingly reviewed every manuscript from an interdisciplinary perspective. Each chapter was reviewed by board-certified psychologists and psychiatrists, and an attorney trained in the behavioral sciences. The Associate Editors provided many valuable insights on the writing and development of *Lethal Violence.*

I wish to specifically thank the National Institute of Justice (NIJ) which generously provided staff time and access to huge datasets relevant to homicide that are cited frequently throughout the text. A quantitative system of calculating violence severity, based on the responses of 60,000 Americans, was provided by NIJ and is one of the cornerstones of the presented lethal violence typology. The National Bureau of Standards supplied the tables of the binomial probability distribution used for deception analysis in some cases of lethal violence. The U.S. Secret Service provided information on serial bombing. The Federal Bureau of Investigation, particularly the Behavioral Science Unit in Quantico, Virginia, made available valuable information on serial murder and serial rape murder.

The Editor would like to thank the following publishers for their kind permission to quote or reproduce the following copyrighted material:

The American Psychological Association for authorization to quote from the Ethical Principles of Psychologists and Code of Conduct (copyright 1992 by the American Psychological Association).

The American Psychiatric Association for allowing the reproduction of diagnostic criteria for several mental disorders from the Diagnostic and Statistical Manual, Fourth Edition (copyright 1994 by the American Psychiatric Association).

The Police S.A.F.E.T.Y. Systems, L.L.C., in Nokesville, Virginia for its permission to use "The Use of Force Model for Enforcement and Correction" (copyright by John C. Desmedt, 1995) in the chapter on police use of deadly force.

The University of Pennsylvania Press, in Philadelphia, Pennsylvania, for its permission to reproduce part of a dataset on criminal homicide victims and offenders by Marvin E. Wolfgang (1958) in his classic book *Patterns in Criminal Homicide.*

The National Academy Press, Washington, D.C., for its permission to reprint a dataset on homicide from *Understanding and Preventing Violence* (copyright 1993 by the National Academy of Sciences).

The Pacific Institute is indebted to David A. Pritchard, PhD, ABPP, a clinical-forensic psychologist in Atlanta, Georgia, who allowed his deception-detecting software to be given to every contributor. Dr. Pritchard also consented to have his software program sold to the readership at a substantially discounted price. John Monahan of the University of Virginia School of Law very graciously furnished his recent articles and papers on dangerousness prediction and risk assessment.

James I. Morrow, MGYSgt, USMC (Ret), with the Veteran's Affairs in Hilo, Hawaii, inspired much of the early interest in this book and gave many deep insights on the nature of lethal violence in humans. Pat Field, a lay expert on domestic violence, gave moral support to the book and to her, the Editor is deeply grateful. Last, but not least, Jerilynn Ono Hall, Esq, my wife, gave prodigious amounts of her time and expertise in the preparation of this volume.

Harold V. Hall
Kamuela, Hawaii

TABLE OF CONTENTS

Part I
Foundational Issues

CHAPTER 1

OVERVIEW OF LETHAL VIOLENCE

Harold V. Hall

Introduction

Clear images flash through my mind when I think about lethal violence — as a sixth grader in Las Vegas, Nevada, watching the plumes of thermonuclear blasts rise above the mountains to the north; as a platoon leader in Vietnam, spending several happy hours with the gentle Buddhist Monks in their monastery outside Nha Trang, only to hear later that the entire complex had been leveled and everyone killed in a battle; as a forensic intern at a hospital-prison for the criminally insane and sexual offenders, viewing the underbelly of human behavior in all its deviant forms; as a forensic professional, evaluating those who have killed.

I remember 31-year-old Dennis, who knifed his girlfriend to death, simultaneously stabbing himself deeply in the torso, almost eviscerating himself in the process. And 42-year-old Mark, a successful CEO of a large corporation, who drove to a secluded spot, shot his wife several times in the head and disposed of the pistol, later driving up to a police officer and claiming that a robber was the perpetrator. And 24-year-old Paul, a married man with steady employment, who used a deer rifle to shoot off the leg of a drunk acquaintance who had wandered into his

garage, then attempted to burn him with gasoline, only to be restrained from killing him by neighbors. And the Unabomber, who now approaching his mid-fifties, and despite the best efforts of countless individuals, including this writer, to accurately profile and locate him, over the span of 17 years, killed three and maimed two dozen others by his homemade bombs. And 45-year-old George, who kidnapped, tortured, sexually assaulted, and then strangled five women over the span of as many months, leaving their bodies face down near water. And 30-year-old Lucy, who repeatedly struck her child on the torso for crying, causing broken ribs which pierced his heart.

The above accounts of individual experiences pale into insignificance when compared to the magnitude of lethal violence occurring nationally and internationally. It seems that everyday, we hear chilling reports of terrorism and threats of thermonuclear destruction, sexual homicide and torture, executions of civilians by soldiers in wide-spread areas of the world, hate crimes, and racially motivated killings. The list of fatal aggression seems endless. Clearly, human lethal violence — variously referred to as "fatal aggression," "murder," "homicide," "killing," "deadly force," and "slaying" — is an important and all-too-common form of behavior. In this book, lethal violence is defined as intentionally harmful interpersonal behaviors culminating in the death of another person who does not want to die.

Violence is the paramount challenge of our times. As the other contributors to this volume have made clear, the threat and perpetration of fatal violence continue to generate increasing concern. Statistics demonstrate that no place in America is safe from murder and death:

*Over 11 **million** violent crimes were committed in this country in 1993, including over 24,000 homicides (U.S. Department of Justice, 1994).*

Most murderers have a criminal history; even in family murders, over half the defendants had a prior criminal history (U.S. Department of Justice, 1994).

Homicide is now the 10th leading cause of death in the United States, with the highest rate of any Western industrialized country (Novello, Shosky, & Froehlke, 1992). New York City has more murders each year than all of Japan in the same time period (Barnett & Schwartz, 1989). If the United States had the same homicide rate as Canada, it would have had 5,648 murders in 1993, as compared to the actual number of 24,526 (Federal Bureau of Investigation [FBI], 1993).

The chance of being a victim of a violent crime is greater than that of being hurt in a traffic accident, experiencing divorce, death from cancer, or injury or death from fire (U.S. Department of Justice, 1983).

*Serial and mass murder episodes have increased dramatically, at a rate far outstripping what would be predicted from population growth. The FBI estimates that, **at any one time**, 35 to 55 serial murderers stalk the streets of the United States (Holmes, 1989; see Cook & Hinman, Chapter 13). From 1971 to 1990, serial murder cases were reported every 39 days in this nation, an eight-fold increase compared to the period from 1940 to 1964 (Jenkins, 1992).*

The clearance rates for murder and nonnegligent homicide in this country run about two-thirds, meaning that about one-third of the killers are not even identified as likely perpetrators or arrested for their murders (Maguire & Pastore, 1994; Maguire, Pastore, & Flanagan, 1993).

During 1993, approximately 2.6% of the population of the United States — almost 5 million adults — were on parole, on probation, or in jail or prisons (U.S. Department of Justice, 1995). Over a third of those arrested for murder were in a criminal justice status (U.S. Department of Justice, 1994).

Numerous surveys have indicated that a majority of the people in this country feel unsafe from violence in their own neighborhoods. This represents a dramatic increase from previous decades.

A comparison of criminal sentences with time actually served shows that the average murderer is sentenced to about 19 years in prison, but serves only about 8 years (Famigetti, 1995).

Despite considerable technological advances and freedom from material want, children are increasingly both victimized and rewarded by violence. Children are relatively safe targets for violence. Almost a million children are victims of child abuse and neglect every year (Widom, 1989). Once entrenched, attitudes and behavior toward violence become resistant to extinction and persist into the adult years. As the contributors to this volume discuss, during a child's development, the belief is often instilled by caretakers that aggression toward others is acceptable. Instead of viewing violence as a weakness, violence in America is regarded positively, extolled, or, at the very least, tolerated, and seen as necessary. As discussed later, an aversive cycle, often intergenerational in nature, is often formed.

Representing the highest level of this century, homicide is the second leading cause of death (after auto accidents) among 15- to 24-year-olds and the leading cause of death among 15- to 34-year-old Black males (Novello, Shosky, & Froehlke, 1992). Weapons are increasingly used to kill peers. In a large survey of 11th grade students, involving half of Seattle, Washington's public schools (N = 970), about 50% of the males had easy access to handguns and 33% of handgun owners *had fired at someone* (Callahan & Rivara, 1992). As the Office of Youth Services (1994) has reported, murder arrests for youths under 18 have risen 92% since 1985, during a period when the teen population stayed the same or declined slightly (due to the "baby boomers" passing out of that age range).

Because of the pandemic of violence among those who will inherit the future, some have predicted the fall of Western society. Newt Gingrich, the Speaker of the House of Representatives, summed up this foreboding by many concerned persons in this country when he predicted: "America cannot survive with 12-year-olds having babies, 15-year-olds shooting one another, 17-year-olds dying of AIDS and 18-year-olds graduating with diplomas when they cannot read. We're at the edge of losing this civilization" (Associated Press, December 19, 1994).

This book attempts to increase our understanding of deadly aggression — why it occurs and how it can be controlled. In order to understand lethal encounters between humans — domestic partners, acquaintances, or strangers — it is important to know that all killings represent a fatal interaction between a perpetrator, victim, and context. Indeed, a slaying happens only when

all three factors occur simultaneously (see Figure 1). This simple notion means that all contributions to mortal outcomes by the perpetrator, victim, and context must be considered in order to grasp the essential features of any specific instance of killing.

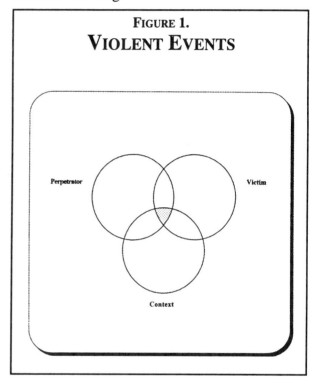

FIGURE 1.
VIOLENT EVENTS

Commonly, the input of victims and contexts is downplayed. In forensic settings, however, the database utilized to evaluate an alleged murderer for criminal responsibility must include information about the defendant, the victim, and the scene of the instant homicide. In Chapter 6, William Foote presents a multitude of data showing that the behavior of the perpetrator and the victim are often closely interlocking. Not generally known, he found that victim-precipitated homicides accounted for a substantial percentage of the killings in this country. Edwin Bixtenstine notes the same phenomenon for spousal homicide in Chapter 8. Murder-suicide, discussed by Michael Abramsky and Melissa Helfman in Chapter 10, tragically illustrates how perpetrators change roles into victims.

In an attempt to accurately describe killing by individuals, this chapter proceeds through the lethal violence sequence from baseline behavior, to the escalation stage, to the fatal aggression, to recovery, and finally, to a return to typical ways of behaving. By doing so, we can focus on the perpetrator, while not ignoring the victim and context, and thus, elucidate the factors that help explain the killing. In this book, the lethal violence sequence will be the unit of analysis for the different types of fatal aggression and ultimately a conceptual tool for developing interventions.

The main ideas discussed in this chapter — the lethal violence sequence, an applied model, and deception in killing — are based on the author's examination of several thousand violent perpetrators over a period of 25 years, over 100 appearances as an expert witness in murder and manslaughter trials, mental health-law interface activities, and a series of research investigations into human violence and aggression. This focus reflects the author's interests and values, which he will attempt to make clear. This is particularly important in the analysis of lethal violence, an area fraught with moral, ideological, legal, and methodological minefields. Such a developing field offers a variety of other possible foci for discussion and exploration.

The reader may rest assured that personal responsibility for lethal violence will not be removed by our scrutiny; no one "gets away" with murder in this analysis. Rather, a broad focus progresses toward evaluating self-control and choice on the part of the violent perpetrator toward a specific victim in a specific context, yielding varying degrees of harm. An applied model is offered, which takes into account virtually all cases of domestic, acquaintance, and stranger violence and has relevance for accurate classification and effective intervention.

Stereotyped Misconceptions Regarding Lethal Violence

To understand lethal violence, we should first examine our own thoughts and attitudes about killing. Persistent misbeliefs about fatal interpersonal encounters include the following:

Misbelief #1: Evaluator's Conclusions Are Based On Absolute Facts.

This misbelief is based on the idea that, as professionals, our conclusions about a particular killing rest on a factual basis. As a subsequent discussion of deception and distortion makes clear, our database is almost always incomplete and usually contaminated by erroneous information. Most professionals are reluctant to change their biases and values regarding fatal aggression, even in cases where data are available. A common complaint is that a proper understanding of a murder requires too much time and effort, adding to an already overloaded work schedule. Forensic professionals often present invalid conclusions when the distortions and deceptions by the defendant and significant/knowledgeable others are added to their ignorance of a case and personal bias. Fortunately, there are ways to detect and account for distortion and deception.

All evaluators of lethal violence, at some time or another, have been duped. The author would like to believe that he is not successfully deceived by assessees, given his experience and knowledge of the literature. The fact is, he would be fooled frequently without standardized testing and a time consuming search for cross-validating data.

Case Illustration. Defendant Thompson, examined for criminal responsibility for an alleged murder while burglarizing a house, stated to the examiner that the glow in the right side of his brain was noticeably unequal to that in the left hemisphere. Forces of good ("FOG") and forces of the enemy ("FOE") reportedly operated in the jail where he was incarcerated. He reported: "The police hacked off my arms and legs; it's a good thing I didn't try to get away." He claimed he heard voices, saw visions, and seemed to be responding to internal stimulation, all of which provided the basis for his schizophrenic diagnosis by the correctional facility medical staff and treatment with antipsychotic medication. Objective testing revealed elevations on scales suggesting a thought disorder, but validity scales showed results consistent with faking bad. An interview with his probation officer revealed that the defendant's mental problems had never been raised as an issue in his 100 plus burglaries and robberies over the last 10 years. His parents, upon being interviewed, pointed out that the accused had been playing the FOG and FOE story since the fourth grade, but only when he wanted to get out of serious trouble.

Misbelief #2: All Killers Are Alike.

This misbelief represents the notion that the core characteristics of those who kill are similar. Most of the media attention is paid to unusual, bizarre, or otherwise extraordinary lethal events. People tend to see killers as evil, sick, crazy, dangerous, or beyond redemption. They are seen as possessing bad traits which provide the basis for our understanding and treatment, if any.

The diversity among killers is at least as great as the similarities. For example, the conventional, over-controlled, hostile type who slays a relative usually kills only once, shows model prison behavior, and is very likely to resume a productive work life after release (Megargee, 1966, 1971). Persons of this type are typically described as mild-mannered, with no history of violence prior to the homicide. During the lethal violence sequence, this individual typically overreacts to a stimulus that has strong threat value, showing extreme violence, often taking the victim by surprise because of the murderer's normally strong

inhibitions toward any kind of violent expression.

Showing a different pattern, the sociopath who kills is maladaptive, exploitive, and manipulative generally, and is likely to recidivate violently (Toch, 1969, 1975). In nonstranger violence, this type of killer often has an impaired, conflictual relationship with the victim. Ordinarily, the sociopath's inhibitions toward violence are weak.

Misbelief #3: All Killers Are Crazy.

Related to the above is the misbelief that fatal aggression represents a radical departure from "normal" interpersonal behavior. In the author's experience, mortal outcomes usually represent the end of a continuum of maladaptive, but otherwise unremarkable, behaviors. Many killings are not well thought out. Indeed, police typically consider murder a crime of passion. Killings often represent frustrated and misguided attempts to control and dominate the victim. Such is displayed in many cases of fatal child and mate abuse, fist fights where the victim is killed by an unlucky blow to the head or striking an object, or legitimate attempts by police to control events that have gotten out of hand.

Some women kill their spouses in a passive-to-aggressive display of violence in order to free themselves from an abusive and physically powerful person. Although spouse killings should not be condoned, the motive of wanting to escape the abusive situation is normal and expected. Many persons, motivated by peer pressure, kill in gang fights and crimes where they have accomplices.

We should avoid the conceptually hazardous tendency to stereotype all killers as dangerous, mentally ill, or anything else. Risk of future harm to others depends on history, recency, and the context in which previous violence was shown (Hall, 1984, 1987; Hall, Catlin, Boissevain, & Westgate, 1984; Hall & Sbordone, 1993). A later discussion of violence prediction makes clear that other variables, such as triggers, opportunity factors, and inhibitions to aggress must be considered. The fact that a war veteran killed others in combat 20 years ago does not tell much about his possible future lethal violence. His post-discharge history of violence in the community, particularly within the last year or two, is far more important. Women who commit infanticide (e.g., see Barlow and Clayton, Chapter 7 in this volume) or kill a spouse (e.g., see Bixenstine, Chapter 8 in this volume) may be at low risk for recidivism because of the situation-specific nature of the homicide. As stated above, the overcontrolled, hostile type usually kills only once, usually a family member, and often shows good potential for rehabilitation.

A corollary of this misbelief is that perpetrators of deadly behaviors are radically different from their victims. The similarities between perpetrator and victim are striking for many types of killings. Dawson and Boland (1993) found that, for murders in large urban counties in 1988, both perpetrators and victims were often male, Black, and between the ages of 15 and 45. Most single murder victims faced a single assailant. Overall, 74% of all defendants killed a victim of the same sex; 81% of all perpetrators were male and had a male victim. Almost all Black victims (94%) were killed by someone of the same race and three-fourths of White victims were killed by White perpetrators. Over 80% of all murder defendants in the 75 counties (accounting for only 37% of the U.S. population, but 63% of the 22,680 murders reported to police) involved a victim of the same racial background.

Perpetrators are different from their victims in certain crime categories, however. In child abuse, obvious dissimilarities in terms of gender and age may emerge. Most institutional violence — particularly by the police and other public safety personnel — involves disparities in ethnicity, values, socioeconomic status, and other characteristics between perpetrator and victim. Most crimes of predation involve weaker victims of different characteristics from the perpetrator, in keeping with the general finding that predators find defenseless targets for their aggression. Some killings are based on mental aberrations: sociopathic syndromes, brain-injury, intellectual deficit, impoverished individuals, and the psychotic delusional disorders. In these cases, the differences between victim and perpetrator are usually substantial.

Misbelief #4: All Killers Are Caught.

This misbelief is that most deadly violence results in arrest and conviction. The U.S. Department of Justice (1983, 1993) has shown that murder has had a national clearance rate of 60 to 70% over the last few decades, meaning that only about two-thirds of the likely perpetrators were identified and brought into police custody. Violence between family members and acquaintances accounts for the highest percentage of persons arrested; such perpetrators are easily identified for their "crimes of passion." The one-third of perpetrators who literally "get away with murder," in the author's experience, consist of both premeditators who put some thought into their acts, and spontaneous killers who were just plain lucky.

Some perpetrators appear to murder with impunity. It is extremely difficult to apprehend a serial murderer if he (and virtually all serial murderers are male) does not wish to be caught. Serial murder suspects often have a thick police file, but few, if any, arrests. Other types of lethal violence may also carry with them a low probability of apprehension (e.g., murder for hire, gang-related killings, homicides made to look like accidents). In short, the clearance rate stands in stark contrast to our notion that heinous deeds, especially taking the lives of others, should not go undetected and unpunished. The reality is otherwise.

Misbelief #5: Evaluators Needn't Bother With Existing Theories or Data.

A common mistake, especially by forensic professionals who should know better, is the misbelief that extant theories and classification systems are not particularly helpful and should not guide the decision processes relevant to understanding lethal violence. Why make explicit something that is ultimately the result of clinical judgement and intuition? Or better yet, why not simply describe the killing act and let theory alone? In an early view, Wolfgang (1977, 1978) typified this lack of theory when he opined that most murders arose out of "trivial altercations." Daly and Wilson (1988) stated the following:

Whereas aggregate homicide rates have been studied by sociologists seeking structural explanations for variable rates, and individual homicide cases have been studied by psychiatrists seeking syndromes, hardly anyone had yet approached the analysis of homicides in the light of any sort of theory of interpersonal conflict, evolutionary or otherwise (Introduction, p. 2, emphasis in original).

Expert witnesses are often asked about their theoretical leanings while testifying, and for good cause. Our assumptions influence both the selection of data that we attend to and the conclusions we draw. All serious students of fatal aggression violence should make explicit their assumptions that act as working hypotheses and are sensitive to evolving data. Theories and classification systems are absolutely necessary for describing, understanding, planning for, and eventual controlling, lethal violence. They allow us to proceed in an orderly fashion, generate new ideas for investigation, and put into perspective the findings from the greater literature on deadly outcomes.

Theories and Classification Systems of Violence

A variety of theories and classification systems have been presented to explain violence and aggression which apparently operate on different premises and databases. Some theories have generated considerable interest and have explanatory value, although all have distinct limitations. A few have actually illuminated specific aspects of human violence to an extent acceptable to criminal courts. In reading countless transcripts of murder trials, it has become clear to this author that psychoanalytic and neoanalytic theory, for example, were more acceptable to the trier of fact in the first half of the century, whereas neurophysiological and cognitive-behavioral based assumptions appear to have gained more acceptability in the last several decades.

Unfortunately, almost all of the theories represent changing views over time, even by the same theorists, and universally fail to account for the diversity of human violence. Fatal domestic, acquaintance, and stranger interactions, the three main types of perpetrator-to-victim relationships, rarely have been encompassed by a single theory. Institutional violence is typically ignored or is the sole focus. To date, no general theory of human violence, let alone one limited to fatal aggression, has been generally accepted to the exclusion of others by the scientific community. Table 1 lists the most common theories of violence and aggression.

Theorists who see human aggression as instinctive (e.g., ethological, psychoanalytic) have presented no direct evidence of the truth of their premises. No genes relating to violent behavior have ever been uncovered. These theories typically ignore the effects of previous learning on current violence. Results from animal studies, the primary method in ethological research, are sometimes difficult to extrapolate to

TABLE 1
THEORIES OF VIOLENCE AND AGGRESSION

Theory and Source	Assumption
Psychoanalytic Freud (1920)	The death instinct (Thanatos), in strong conflict with the life force (Eros), leads to aggressive behavior through displacement.
Ethological Lorenz (1966, 1974)	Aggression stems from innate fighting instincts and is biologically advantageous to the species.
Elicited Drive Dollard, Doob, Miller & Sears (1939)	Aggression serves to terminate or reduce drives caused by deprivation or aversive stimulation.
Aggressive-Cue Berkowitz (1965a, 1969)	Frustration as one type of aversive stimulation creates a readiness for aggressive action, which is set off if aggressive cues are present.
Excitation-Transfer Zillman, Katcher & Milavsky (1972)	Combined arousal from several sources leads to the "fight or flight" response and is slowly dissipated over time.
Cognitive Neo-association Berkowitz (1983, 1988, 1989)	Aversive stimulation creates negative affect, which is then interpreted by the perpetrator, determining the nature of the violent response.
Social Learning Bandura (1973, 1983)	Aggression is acquired, instigated, and maintained like other social behaviors.

humans. Animal studies of aggression, however, have provided useful models of subclasses of violence, particularly competition-based and predatory behavior, which give us hypotheses for further investigation in humans.

Archer (1995) presented an evolutionary theoretical approach from a Darwinian perspective, concentrating mainly on homicide. He convincingly argued that sexual selection theory was better able to account for age and sex differences in homicides than non-evolutionary alternatives, such as reactions to frustrating and aversive situations. He roundly criticized psychology for skipping the descriptive stage of human aggression through which all other natural sciences have proceeded. Yet, his theory does little to explain the impact of learning on individual styles of violence, as well as why some interventions seem to work and others fail miserably.

Psychoanalytic theory does clarify how mortal outcomes are excused by perpetrators through the use of defense mechanisms. Table 2 illustrates

a variety of means to defend the ego when violent behavior is shown or contemplated. Knowing the defense mechanisms of individual perpetrators may have predictive value. Entrenched early in life, defense mechanisms are remarkably resistant to extinction and tend to show up when an individual is held to account for misbehavior. Defense mechanisms are likely to emerge when a murderer is asked who or what caused the killing, and how, looking back, he or she would put the slaying into perspective (e.g., "What would you say to the person you killed if you could?"). A perpetrator's defense mechanisms can provide clues into his or her dynamic makeup.

Case Illustration. The military court convicted Sergeant Stryker of killing his wife's lover at a bar by shooting him in the back in the presence of over 20 witnesses. The first bullet went low and to the right, ricocheting into a jukebox. The victim walked slowly towards the door. The perpetrator then assumed a "competition stance" — legs spread apart, with both hands gripping the pistol

Mechanism	Examples
	TABLE 2 **EGO DEFENSE MECHANISMS AND LETHAL VIOLENCE**
Denial of Reality	A child who witnessed her father killing her mother refuses to believe that her mother is dead until many years later.
Fantasy	During masturbation, a serial murderer imagines himself with new victims.
Repression	A mother's murderous impulse toward her dysfunctional son are denied access into her consciousness.
Rationalization	A fanatical religious leader uses ambiguous passages from the Bible to justify mass suicide.
Projection	A violent offender in prison is convinced that his cell mate is planning to kill him and murders him first.
Reaction Formation	Two men troubled by homosexual urges brutally murder homeless members of the gay community.
Displacement	A man harassed by his boss and peers for incompetent behavior kills his wife.
Emotional Insulation	A man who murders his wife's lover in a catathymic rage becomes emotionally unresponsive and apathetic.
Intellectualization	A death row inmate asks for execution by lethal injection and resists all appeals for clemency.
Undoing	A gang member who shot several rivals apologizes to the victims' families and offers them money for relocation.
Regression	A child whose self-esteem has been shattered in a dysfunctional family shoves his younger sister down the stairs, breaking her neck.
Identification	A young soldier becomes increasingly violent towards civilians in emulation of an authoritarian, brutal commander.
Overcompensation	Covering up feelings of inadequacy, a person kills by methodically arranging for murder for hire.

— and fired twice more in rapid succession. It was never determined which bullet was fired first, the one which entered slightly above the right knee, or the bullet that entered the back and tore through the heart, but the victim lurched forward with his right leg crumpling noticeably before he fell forward. Several months after the trial, Sergeant Stryker stated to this evaluator that the killing was not immoral and that the victim really caused his own death. When asked what he would say to the victim if he had an opportunity, his response was, "See, you son of a bitch, see what you made me do?"

Theories that view human aggression as an elicited drive (e.g., Berkowitz, 1965, 1969; Dollard, Doob, Miller, Mowrer, & Sears, 1939; Miller, 1948) are fundamentally flawed. Frustration does not always, as the theories predict, lead to aggression. A wide variety of other responses is possible. Drive theories would leave us facing continuous and unavoidable sources for our aggressive impulses — an outcome that does not accord with reality.

Aggression as a reaction to aversive events has, as a theory, considerable appeal (e.g., see the later writings by Berkowitz, 1984, 1988). According to Berkowitz, individuals exposed to aversive events are much more likely to be violent when compared to non-exposed persons. As others have demonstrated, the negative affect generated by an aversive event stimulates aggression (Rule, Taylor, & Dobbs, 1987). As a cognitive theorist, Berkowitz took his formulation one step further and suggested that negative affect shapes and generates thoughts that may eventually culminate in violent action. Unfortunately, like drive theories, aversive events are far too common to elucidate when and under what conditions violence will occur. Inhibitory forces which prevent the violence must be taken into account as well.

Tedeschi and Felson (1994) presented a well-validated, interactionist theory of violence which draws heavily from other social theories. Abandoning the word "aggression," these investigators focused on interactionist concepts, such as coercive action, to describe violence. Amassing a wealth of empirical data, they discussed the three goals of coercive actions: to gain compliance, to restore justice, and to assert and defend identities. Their theory of decision-making process leading to violence assumes coercion as a rational choice.

Although promising, Tedeschi and Felson's (1994) theory is incomplete. Because of its almost exclusionary emphasis on the social situation, it downplays neuropsychological/biological factors associated with violence, individual psychological differences, and the larger social structure. All of these factors have explanatory and predictive value. Their theory tells us little about severe mental disorders associated with violence, predatory violence (where perpetrator traits and history assume major importance), infanticide, some forms of institutional violence (e.g., capital punishment), and other types of violence that may not be adequately explained solely by social interactionist variables. To the ire of some, they asserted that the goal of most acts of sexual coercion is to gain sexual satisfaction.

Representing the most encompassing of the theories and reflecting the author's bias, social learning theory is sufficiently broad to incorporate most aggressive phenomena, yet has specific implications for prediction, control, and prevention. Albert Bandura (1973, 1983, 1986), who developed the theory as it applies to human aggression, focused primarily on the role of social learning factors in violence, but not to the exclusion of biological factors. According to Bandura:

[People] are endowed with neurophysiologi-cal mechanisms that enable them to behave aggressively, but the activation of these mechanisms depends on appropriate stimulation and is subject to cognitive control. Therefore, the specific forms that aggressive behavior takes, the frequency with which it is expressed, the situations in which it is displayed, and the specific targets selected for attack are largely determined by social learning factors (1983, p. 5).

In social learning theory, aggression is *acquired* through biological factors (e.g., neural systems, hormones), learning (e.g., direct experience, observation), and the interaction of the two (e.g., brain-behavior relationships). Aggression is *instigated* by the influence of models (e.g., violent parents or siblings), aversive experiences (e.g., a physical attack), incentives (e.g., praise, an anticipated increase in status for killing a policeman), instructions (e.g., in combat, capital punishment), and delusions (e.g., command hallucinations to kill). Aggressive patterns are *maintained* by external contingencies and vicarious reinforcement (e.g., peer approval, learning that a murderer was not arrested or received a light sentence) and self-regulatory mechanisms (e.g., pride in killing efficiency of military unit, feeling of control when children obey after the administration of corporal punishment).

Social learning theory has withstood research scrutiny for over a quarter of a century and is sufficiently broad to be applied to a wide variety of violence-related settings and situations (Bandura, 1973, 1977, 1986). Thus, depending on their neuropsychological makeup and past experiences, people in different cultures learn to kill in different ways — using their hands, knives, firearms, bombs, or other weapons. Through experience, primarily social in nature, they learn which persons or groups against whom it is "appropriate" to aggress, what victim behaviors justify lethal violence, and the circumstances under which killing would meet with social approval.

There is no dearth of classification schemes to account for lethal violence in humans. Early formulations were founded on a spirit or anima as the motivating force. Western religion classified killing according to the will of God ("righteous") versus that perpetrated by mortals for selfish purposes ("unrighteous"). Quickly moving to contemporary times, Megargee and Bohn (1979) cited authorities in their review of the literature, who differentiated among anywhere from 2 to 11 types of murderers — showing a clear consensus that all murderers are not alike.

In an attempt to reduce homicide to manageable proportions, law enforcement personnel classify murders according to the context in which they occur. "Homicide syndromes" include violence by intimates, youth violence, confrontational and other expressive homicides, and robbery-related and other instrumental homicides (Police Chief, 1995).

Others have classified murder and other violence by (1) the degree of dehumanization (Miller & Looney, 1974); (2) dissociative, psychotic, or ego syntonic characteristics (Tanay, 1969); (3) normal or psychopathic traits (Bromberg, 1961); and (4) endogenous-exogenous motivational stimulation (Kutash, Kutash, Schlesinger & Associates, 1978; Revitch, 1975, 1977; Revitch & Schlesinger, 1978; Schlesinger, Chapter 14 in this volume).

This last "motivational stimuli" classification scheme for homicide is particularly interesting because of its common usage by many forensic professionals in the absence of supporting empirical validation. In the writer's experience, most criminal courts do not seem especially disturbed by this typology's lack of empirical support. Based on case studies, as illustrated by Louis Schlesinger in Chapter 14 on murder and sex murder, this motivational approach draws heavily on analytically oriented concepts, but utilizes social interactionist variables as well. Schlesinger divides all types of killings into the following:

Environmentally stimulated homicides are motivated by a weakening of social controls and authority. Civil strife, murder by organized crime, undisciplined/demoralized armies returning to their home area (e.g., the South after the Civil War), urban riots, political terrorism, political assassinations, and war atrocities are examples. The common denominator is that these killings can be attributed not only to traits of the offenders, but to a general weakening of social discipline, values, and external restraints.

Situational homicides occur in response to a stressful situation, as perceived by the violent offender. These crimes are committed by individuals with minimal psychopathology, and may be either premeditated or unplanned. The idea of extreme stress or heat of passion (Hall, 1990) as a mitigation to murder has its foundations here.

Impulsive homicides occur on the spur of the moment. Due to chronically poor impulse control within a lifestyle shown by unreliable and directionless behavior, violent perpetrators of this type commit a multiplicity of antisocial acts. These offenses are diffuse, poorly structured, and largely unplanned. The Asocial Conduct Disorder or the Antisocial Personality Disorder fits into this category.

Catathymic homicides are marked by perseveration and charged emotion. Wertham (1937) offered the following: "A catathymic reaction is the transformation of the stream of thought as a result of certain complexes of ideas that are charged with a strong affect — usually a wish, a fear, or an ambivalent striving" (p. 975). He later added that a catathymic crisis involves delusional thinking, with the violence having symbolic meaning, with the victim being a part of an overpowering image, and outlined the stages of the catathymic crises as follows (1978):

1. An initial thinking disorder, which follows an original precipitating (i.e., traumatic) circumstance.

2. Crystallization of a plan, when the idea of a violent act emerges into consciousness. The vio-

lent act is seen as the only way out. Emotional tension becomes extreme, and thinking becomes more and more egocentric.

3. Extreme emotional tension culminating in the violent crisis, in which a violent act against oneself or others is attempted or carried out.

4. Superficial normality, beginning with a period of lifting of tension and calmness immediately after the violent act. This period is of varying length, from several days to months.

5. Insight and recovery, with the reestablishment of an inner equilibrium (p. 166).

Homicide without an apparent motive in a primitive expression of violence closely parallels the notion of the catathymic killing. These are sudden, senseless murders in which there were no indications of personal gain or any accompanying crime. Holcomb and Daniel (1988) compared 52 male defendants who killed without apparent motive to 154 male homicide defendants with clear motives. Defendants who killed without an apparent motive were more likely to have no history of alcohol abuse, to have claimed amnesia or denied the killing, and to have been recently released from prison.

Compulsive homicides are seen as determined completely by internal psychopathology, with no environmental contribution except for providing the opportunity to aggress. An inner need is always expressed in the killing, much as revenge is the key dynamic in serial rape murder.

In serial rape murder, fantasies usually precede the offenses by many years. Resisting the compulsion causes distress and anxiety. Most often, compulsive murders of this sort are characterized by intrusive sexual behavior involving torture or mutilation. These perpetrators carry the worst prognosis for recovery, as there is no known cure for this homicidal pattern. In Chapter 13, Patrick Cook and Dayle Hinman present an overview of serial murder based on a large database of cases collected nationally by the FBI.

Judith Chapman, in Chapter 12, discusses a variety of sexual paraphilias with compulsive features.

Empirical typologies of violence derived through statistical methods are fewer in number than heuristic, theoretically based schemes. Probably, the most accepted typology is Megargee and Bohn's (1979) Minnesota Multiphasic Personality Disorder (MMPI) Classification system, an empirical system based on several thousand subjects. This typology is broadly applicable to most kinds of violence, as well as reliable and valid. Ten groups of offenders, psychometrically defined, were identified (out of numerous possible MMPI configurations) and treatment suggestions within an institutional setting were offered. The full system will soon be revised for use with the MMPI-2. In Chapter 19, Robert Craig brings the reader up to date on this highly important area of classification.

Classification schemes should be used with caution if they (a) stem only from bizarre and unusual cases; (b) have categories which are not mutually exclusive; (c) emanate from non-verifiable theories and models; and/or (d) ignore behavioral anchors. An empirical model, presented later, can be used conjointly with an overall theory of violence that allows us to interpret new data and to provide more areas of inquiry into lethal violence.

Describing the Temporal Flow of Lethal Violence

Lethal violence is comprised of a temporal process of events for the perpetrator, victim, and context in which it occurs. No matter what type of killing was perpetrated, or why the evaluator is studying the event, it is essential to describe the evolution of the slaying over time. In this manner, we can better understand the relative contributions of deception, inhibitions, self-control, and other behaviors shown by the perpetrator and victim. A temporal description of the killing act makes comparison to other violent events in the life of the perpetrator easier. As depicted in Figure 2, any kind of violence can be described in its temporal stages.

From the vantage point of the perpetrator, Stage 1 includes history, then proceeds to the acceleration stage prior to the violence (Stage 2). The lethal act is then perpetrated (Stage 3), followed by a recovery period (Stage 4), and eventual return to typical ways of behaving (Stage 5). The following sections review the sequence for the perpetrator of lethal violence.

Baseline Characteristics

Stage 1 of the lethal sequence — the baseline

period — covers the entire history of the individual, including his or her biological makeup, early development, and attitudes formed before the killing. Societal and cultural contributions need to be taken into account to place the lethal violence into proper perspective. The actual history of violence should be scrutinized because, almost always, the instant offense bears some resemblances to past violence, if not in lethality, then in form and function.

Stage 1 information can also be utilized for the identification of the perpetrator. Disorganized serial killers, for example, often live closer to the scene of a homicide victim than their more organized counterparts (Ressler, Burgess, & Douglas, 1988). In Chapter 18, Charles Golden, Michele

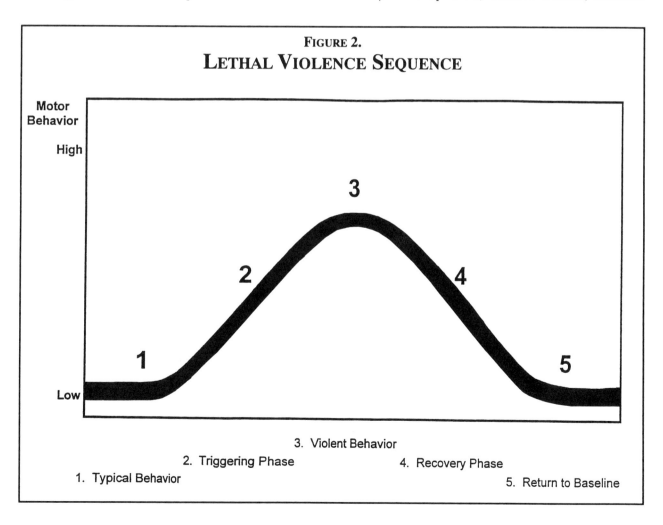

FIGURE 2.
LETHAL VIOLENCE SEQUENCE

Motor Behavior

High

Low

3

2

4

1

5

3. Violent Behavior

2. Triggering Phase

4. Recovery Phase

1. Typical Behavior

5. Return to Baseline

Jackson, Samuel Gontkovsky, and Angela Peterson-Rohne show how psychological and neuropsychological testing can yield trait data which can raise the index of suspicion for a particular suspect and may be compatible with the circumstances of a particular murder.

Second, a defense attorney may attempt to offer a pre-existing event — trauma from child abuse, impoverished living conditions, brain damage, etc. — as an element suggesting insanity or mitigation. It appears to the author that triers of fact do not hold much stock in pre-existing circumstances unless they can be causally linked to the instant murder. A comprehensive view of mitigation to murder is presented by Sandra McPherson in Chapter 16.

Third, violence during the baseline period can be used for dangerousness prediction, as previous violence is the best predictor of later harm to others. Hostage negotiation, discussed by John Call in Chapter 22, utilizes ongoing risk analysis of the perpetrators in an attempt to render hostages safe from harm.

Fourth, treatment may be geared to the background characteristics of the perpetrator. Commonly, change over time is measured by trait scales of one sort or another. Treatment for victims of attempted murder, or intervention for a family which has had a member murdered, as discussed by Mary Cerney in Chapter 20, should take into account cultural and social factors in order to make the intervention more responsive and effective. In Chapter 21, Marc Walter presents pioneering ideas on how cognitive retraining of cerebral deficits associated with violent behavior can be implemented.

Lastly, prevention strategies, discussed by this author in Chapter 17, typically target baseline characteristics in order to reduce the overall level of community violence. From both a micro and macro perspective, ways are discussed in which this concept can be applied to entire communities which are violent in nature. Prevention strategies are presented by Leighton Whitaker in Chapter 5 on countering social inducements to paralethal and lethal violence. As a means of survival, he restates and eloquently expands on the essential notion that cooperation and altruism can be taught. Essentially, a cognitive-behavioral shift from our current baseline of competition and violence is required.

Some baseline factors appear to inhibit violence as a mediating influence to a potentially lethal situation. Factors within the person (e.g., high suspiciousness) in interaction with events in the environment (e.g., presence of a police officer at a bank where a robbery is planned) act as inhibitors for most people. Inhibitors often fall into the lower range of frequency, intensity, duration, or recency of history, triggers, and opportunity to aggress.

During child development, for example, nonviolent parents inhibit violent tendencies in their children by modeling nonviolence. The child learns to think in terms of nonviolent options and, cognitively, does not consider violence a viable choice in the problem solving process. In clinical-forensic cases, a basal history devoid of violence is known to act as an inhibitor by virtue of its absence (Hall, 1987; Kozol, Boucher, & Garofalo, 1972). As Robert Eme makes clear in Chapter 3 on gender differences in juvenile violence, the sex role of females reinforces inhibition of violence. Eme clearly documents that males are a much higher risk for violence compared to females, due to a confluence of genetic, congenital, maturational, and social factors.

In general, the most powerful predictor of nonviolence is a history of nonviolence. Characteristics associated with a lower propensity to aggress include female gender, old age, high socioeconomic status, and high educational level (Kelly, 1976; Monahan, 1981; Eme, in Chapter 3). Table 3 lists common inhibitory stimuli or events for most individuals.

Developmental history. A developmental his-

TABLE 3
INHIBITIONS TO VIOLENCE

Condition or Event	Type of Variable
Nonviolent parents	Developmental
Stable home environment	Developmental
Tendency to avoid/escape confrontation	Developmental
College education	Developmental
Heroes/heroines are nonviolent	Developmental
Preference for nonviolent movies	Developmental
No serious history of violence	Historical
Pain cues from victims cause distress	Trigger
Fear of arrest/incarceration for possible misdeed	Trigger
Presence of onlookers at scene who do not approve of violence	Trigger
Anxiety over social disapproval	Trigger
High individual identifiability	Trigger
Placement in confinement	Opportunity
Stabilizing medication	Opportunity

* Compiled from the literature by Hall, 1987.

tory of aggression undeniably contributes to later violence. Generally, the literature shows that early violence begets violence, and that aggressive response sets tend to persist into later life. Early intervention leads to the best outcomes, a point reinforced by Joseph Poirier in Chapter 9 on lethal violence in the family.

Outcomes that are favorable to the perpetrator tend to maintain violent patterns. In an early study, Patterson, Cobb, and Ray (1972) reported that 80% of young normal children's assaultive behaviors across common situations produced rewarding consequences. This high level of reinforcement (and associated aggression) remained stable over time. In Chapter 4, addressing the influence of the mass media on violence, Lita Schwartz and Rosalie Matzkin make clear that vulnerable individuals who are exposed to violence on television and the movies during their development are at risk for later violence. Table 4 presents other developmental influences associated with later violence toward others.

Other investigations show that aggression tends to persist. In this country, aggression at age 8 is a good predictor of violence toward one's offspring 22 years later (Eron, Huesmann, Dubow, Romanoff, & Yarmal, 1987; Huesmann, Eron, Lefkowitz, & Walder, 1984). In a review of the international literature, Farrington (1994) cited findings from Sweden, Finland, and the United States, showing that aggression during middle childhood (about age 8) is predictive of self-reported criminal violence in adulthood (about age 30).

Widom (1992) studied 908 substantiated cases of childhood abuse or neglect, with a comparison group of 667 children, and determined that being abused or neglected as a child increased the likelihood of arrest as a juvenile by 53%, as an adult by 38%, and for a violent crime by 38%. Strikingly, victims of neglect (in the absence of physical violence) were also more likely to develop later criminally violent behavior as well. This suggests that more attention needs to be devoted

TABLE 4

DEVELOPMENTAL CONDITIONS ASSOCIATED WITH AGGRESSION

Condition or Event	Sample Reference(s)
Violent parental or sibling model (especially same-sexed)	Bandura (1973)
Physical abuse	Hoffman (1960); Goldstein (1974)
Pathological triad (pyromania, cruelty to animals, enuresis)	Hellman & Blackman (1966)
Preference for violent TV shows	Lefkowitz, Eron, Walder, & Huesmann (1977)
Alcoholism/drug abusing parents	Bach-Y-Rita, Lion, Clement, & Ervin (1971)
Juvenile record (non-violent or status crimes)	Steadman & Cocozza (1974)
Felony arrest before 15th birthday	Michigan Corrections Department (1978)
History of reinforcing results for aggression	Patterson, Cobb, & Ray (1972); Dubonowsky (1980)
Praise or reward by parents for aggression	Loew (1967)
Evidence of self-reinforcement for aggression	Bandura & Walters (1959)
Spontaneous or concussion-related loss of consciousness before age 10	Bach-Y-Rita & Veno (1974)
Relevant school problems — assault on teachers, temper tantrums, threats	Justice, Justice, & Kraft (1974)

to the families of children who have been psychologically abused or abandoned, or who have suffered severe neglect (Widom, 1989, 1992).

Because violence begets violence, the net effect of the above factors is an increase in hurtful interchanges, resulting in an "aggressive cycle" or a "violence interlock" which, once entered into, is extraordinarily difficult to resolve. The phenomenon of violent interlocks, as discussed later, is found throughout the literature on domestic, acquaintance, stranger, and institutional violence. It is made possible by any means that allow the perpetrator to seek ad lib revenge for perceived injustices. The target of aggression then seeks revenge as a response and the cycle continues.

The paradox of violent interlocks is that they can never be broken except by total obliteration or domination of one party, or by unilateral action to remove oneself from the cycle of violence. Perhaps this explains why so many abused children leave home at an early age. In the author's experience, almost all individuals who had killed others, entered into aggressive cycles with others during their developmental period.

Neuropsychological Factors. The neuropsychology/biology of the individual is part of the baseline endowment. Neuropsychological and neurological models suggest that cerebral injury can raise the risk of violent behavior in individuals (Gorenstein & Newman, 1980; Tancredi & Valkow, 1988; Weiger & Bear, 1988; Yeudall, Fedora, & Fromm, 1987).

Anatomically, brain lesions delineated as etiological factors in precipitating violent behavior include those found in the ascending inhibitory component of the reticular activating system; the limbic system, including such structures as the amygdala, hippocampus and septum; the dorsomedial and anterior thalamic nuclei; the ventromedial hypothalamus; and the baso-orbital and posteromedial frontal lobe. Discussions and empirical research relating to executive dysfunctions, commonly found in violent response patterns, are available in the neuropsychological literature (e.g., see Binder, 1983; Boll, 1985; Chusid & McDonald, 1962; Filskov & Boll, 1986; Hall & McNinch, 1988; Hall & Sbordone, 1993; House & Pansky, 1967; Lezak, 1983; Strub & Black, 1981).

The rather formidable sounding material found in this section, as well as in the other chapters in this book on the neuropsychology of violence, requires a disclaimer. Lethal violence, like everything else, is a combination of nature and nurture. *All* killings are "caused" by a differential contribution of both factors — environmental circumstances operating on hereditary predispositions. As a corollary, this means that no single factor of any sort can account completely for lethal violence.

Neuropsychological factors are most likely only an indirect cause of violence, a point emphasized by Douglas Johnson-Green and Kenneth Adams in Chapter 2. The relationship between genes and some types of killing characterized by loss of control may be due to a higher incidence of cognitive impairment. For example, a retardate may have misinterpreted reality or become behaviorally disorganized as a function of inferior intellectual status, a possibility that must be explored.

Neuropsychological/biological factors may interact indirectly with traits which then increase the chance that violence will occur. The effect of testosterone may, for example, be related to extroversion, preference for physical activity, and sociability (Schalling, 1987).

In women, between 50 and 60% of violent crimes occurs during the week preceding the onset of menstruation, but the vast majority of women do not become violent (Dalton, 1964; Morton, Addison, & Addison, 1953). The literature seems to suggest that an inherited low threshold for the activation of the brain and neurohormonal system for hostility and violence may be potentiated by psychological traits, stress, or deprivation.

Keeping the above disclaimer in mind, there is mild support for the hereditability of violence (Ghosdian-Carpey & Baker, 1987; Rushton, 1988), although no firm data exist. The differences between neurotransmitters associated with violence, however, may have an inherited basis. Eichelman (1990) found that in predatory aggression in humans, norephineprine decreases, whereas in affective violence, it increases. For both predatory and affective violence, acetylcholine and dopamine increase, and GABA and serotonin decrease. In terms of congenital influences, Reinisch (1981) found an increased risk of later violence with exposure to androgenic substances prior to birth.

Violent behaviors secondary to abnormal central nervous system functioning include, but are not limited to, acts precipitated by the following (Hall & McNinch, 1988; Langevin, Ben-Aron, Wortzman, Dickey, & Handy, 1987; Martell, 1992b; Nachshon & Denno, 1987; Silver & Yudofsky, 1987):

(a) acute confusional states;

(b) some degenerative conditions, such as Huntington's Disease, Alzheimer's Disease, and alcoholic dementia;

(c) repeated head trauma, post-concussive syndrome;

(d) toxic conditions caused by drugs, alcohol, medications, and some heavy metals;

(e) neoplastic disease processes of the central nervous system;

(f) seizure disorders, such as psychomotor, complex-partial, and temporary lobe epilepsy; and

(g) "borderland" organic mental disorders (c.f. Strub & Black, 1981) such as the episodic dyscontrol syndrome.

Neuropsychological conditions can alter the perception of reality and thus increase the risk of violence. Among the neuropsychologically impaired, for example, violence is more probable with the relatively rare delusional misidentification syndromes, with over a dozen of these types having been identified (DePauw & Szulecka, 1988).

In the Capgras Syndrome, there is a denial of the identity of familiar persons, with the delusion that they have been replaced by another person. In Subjective Doubles, the delusion is that a false double of the self exists. In Inter-Metamorphosis, the person believes that he or she has been physically transformed into another. Although DePauw and Szulecka (1988) cited literature stating that the delusional disorders and paranoid schizophrenia in particular have a higher base rate for homicide than other mental disorders, in almost all cases, the delusions existed for some time prior to the killing, implying that other factors were necessary to trigger the lethal violence.

Abnormal brain functions may impair the inhibition of violent impulses, stimulate excesses in impulsivity, particularly in combination with other risk factors, or both. Studies comparing murderers, other violent offenders, and nonviolent control subjects have shown that significant differences occur regularly on neuropsychological test batteries (Yeudall & Fromm-Auch, 1979). Langevin et al. (1987) found that murderers and assaulters showed greater cerebral impairment than nonviolent control subjects on the Halstead Reitan Neuropsychological Battery (but not the Luria Nebraska Neuropsychological Battery). One investigator found brain damage in 90% of his sample, including 100% of rapists, 94% of homicide offenders, and 87% of assaultists (Yeudall, 1977).

A summary of the literature by Martell (1992b) and the research by Fedora and Fedora (1983) showed that some violent offenders, particularly psychopathic offenders, demonstrate greater dominant (left) hemispheric dysfunction. Brain injured repeat violent offenders show significant executive deficits in organizing, monitoring, and competently implementing their behaviors. A majority of juveniles and adults on death row, in almost all cases murderers, were found to have significant brain dysfunction (Lewis, Pincus, Bard, Richardson, Prichep, Feldman, & Yeager, 1988; Lewers, Pincus, Feldman, Jackson, & Bord, 1986). If replicated, these findings may

have significance for competency to be executed, along with other forensic issues.

In sum, neuropsychological/biological deficiencies may be important only as a mediating variable, insofar as there is an existing response tendency to act violently. Hall and Sbordone (1993), after an extensive review of the literature on frontal lobe, anterior temporal lobe, and limbic/subcortical lesions as they relate to loss of executive control, argued that there are no lesions in these sites that automatically cause a violent response. No new data has changed this view.

Traits Associated with Aggression. Converging evidence suggests that traits associated with aggression, once formed during the developmental years, are generally stable throughout adulthood (Baron & Richardson, 1994). The literature suggests that traits, much like neuropsychological/biological factors, play a mediating role in aggression, interacting with other variables to cause a violent outcome. Table 5 lists some of the current operating conditions associated with violence, including traits.

As an illustration, individuals with a cluster of traits — competitive, hard driving, and time pressured — referred to as "Type A personalities," are known to engage in more child abuse and other types of violence than non-Type A persons (Baron, 1984; Baron & Richardson, 1994; Strube, Turner, Cerro, Stevens, & Hinchey, 1984). They see most situations as adversarial and are therefore at higher risk of becoming embroiled in conflict with others. As these investigators make clear, however, Type A personalities run the risk of violence only when there is environmental stress and a history of previous violence.

Traits may reveal the topography of lethal violence. Topography defines the form or style of violence when combined with other environmental factors, such as context. An example is an alienated, impulsive, hostile, substance-abusing adolescent male living in an inner-city slum, who (correctly) believes that his chances of conviction

TABLE 5	
PRESENT OPERATING CONDITIONS ASSOCIATED WITH VIOLENCE	
Condition or Event	**Sample Reference(s)**
Diffuse cerebral impairment	Volkow & Tancredi (1987)
Lesions in frontal cortex	Weiger & Bear (1988); Hall (1993)
Left hemisphere insufficiency	Krynicki (1978)
Amydala lesions (epileptics)	Eichelman (1983)
Lowered arousal	Venables (1987)
Young adult (18-29)	Kelly (1976)
Male Sex	Kelly (1976)
Race (some minority groups)	Kelly (1976)
Residential mobility	Michigan Department of Corrections (1978)
Overcrowding	Bandura (1973)
Low socioeconomic status	Monahan (1981)
No current or sporadic employment	Brenner (1977)
Marital status (single or divorced)	Michigan Department of Corrections (1978)
Subcultural acceptance of violence to solve problems	Blumenthal (1976)
Belief that certain types of violence will go unpunished (e.g., spouse, child abuse)	Monahan (1981)
Self-perception as dangerous	Webster, Slomen, Sepejak, Butler, Jensen, & Turdal (1979)
Self-mutilation (especially arm scars)	Bach-Y-Rita & Veno (1974)
Violent content fantasies	Dix (1976)
Intellectual retardation	Hirschi & Hindelang (1977)
Low frustration tolerance	Geen & Berkowitz (1967)
Feelings of helplessness and powerlessness	Webster, et al. (1979)
Elevated hostility	Webster, et al. (1979)
Overcontrolled hostility	Megargee (1966, 1971)
Deficits in verbal skills	Toch (1969)
Weak community support base	Wolfgang (1977)
Violent peers	Bandura (1973) ·
Substance abuse or dependency	Wolfgang (1977)
Hostile attribution bias	Baumeister, Stillwell, & Wotman (1990); Johnson & Rule (1986)
Proneness to irritability	Capara, Renzi, Alcini, D'Imperio, & Travaglia (1983)
External locus of control	Buss (1961); Feshbach (1970)
Type A personality	Strube, Turner, Cerro, Stevens, & Hinchey (1984); Baron (1984)
Shame-proneness	Tangney (1990); Harder & Lewis (1986)
Authoritarianism	Blass (1991); Elms & Milgram (1966)
History of undercontrolled aggression	Toch (1969, 1975, 1980)
Racial prejudice	Genthner, Shuntich, & Bunting (1975) Wilson, & Rogers (1975)

for killing a peer in a gang-related incident are slim. The form and style of his lethal violence, should it occur, are better estimated because we

are aware of topographical features of the possible perpetrator, victim, and context.

A major drawback of focusing on traits, in

addition to their indirect and oftentimes weak contribution to violence, is their covert, biasing influence on the evaluator of violence. In dangerousness prediction, for example, hostile individuals often elicit covert anxiety or anger in the examiner and may be perceived as more dangerous than they actually are (Hall, 1984, 1987). Conversely, sociopaths, some of whom are superficially charming, polite, and flattering, may be seen as less dangerous than indicated by their basal history of violence (Hall, 1987; Yochelson & Samenow, 1976).

History. Except in unusual circumstances, lethal violence does not occur without some historical precedent. As a well-established point that needs repetition, the best predictor of violence is past violence. The PROMIS Research Project (1977) showed that, with five or more arrests for violent crimes, the probability of similar future arrests *approaches certainty*. Wolfgang (1977) found that the probability of future arrest varied directly with the number of previous arrests (e.g., 80% probability with four prior arrests). Hall et al. (1984) showed that basal violence accounted for over 70% of later exhibited violence in normal young adult males. Table 6 lists previous historical events associating an individual with later violence.

In sum, the analysis of basal violence is essential to understanding the lethal act, as well as predicting dangerousness for the perpetrator. Unless the defendant raises the issue, however, past dangerousness cannot be introduced in the trial by the prosecutor. Evidence of past violence, particularly recent violence connected to the alleged murder, may be allowed in state of mind defenses at the discretion of the presiding judge. Most often, findings on dangerousness are presented at sentencing hearings, bail-setting, and in release from psychiatric hospitalization.

The Escalation Stage

The escalation stage (Stage 2) consists of behaviors and events in close proximity to the actual killing, including death threats, triggers, opportunity factors, and inhibitions. The behavior of the eventual victim and the context of the lethal violence in interaction with the perpetrator should be closely scrutinized. Criminal courts tend to pay particular attention to events that occurred during the escalation stage.

Threats of violence signal feelings and thoughts, such as anger, a dominance display, a bluff, or an intent to do violence in retaliation for noncompliance. The threat itself may constitute arrestable behavior, as in terroristic threatening, or when a firearm is brandished. Threats often precede competitive violence, and tend to be

TABLE 6
HISTORICAL FACTORS ASSOCIATED WITH VIOLENCE

Condition or Event	Sample Reference(s)
Incidents of violence are multiple	Wolfgang (1978); Petersilia (1977)
Fatal or potentially fatal violence	Steadman & Cocozza (1974)
Crime is rape, robbery, murder or aggravated assault	Michigan Corrections Department (1978)
Recency is immediate (less than one year)	Michigan Corrections Department (1978)
Firearm or other potentially lethal weapon used in aggression	Kelly (1976); Berkowitz & LePage (1967)
Past violence maintained/intensified by pain cues from victim	Ford & Beach (1951); Dubonowsky (1980)
Serious institutional misconduct	Michigan Corrections Department (1978)
Arrests for previous violence	Steadman & Cocozza (1974)
Convictions for violent crimes	Steadman & Cocozza (1974)

repeated or intensified when reinforced by the behavior of a weaker victim or by supportive onlookers. Most homicidal threats uttered during the escalation stage do not culminate in death. For criminal defendants in assault cases, the author has found that death threats that do not result in the death of the victim are not at all unusual. Typically, they serve to "pump up" the dangerous status of the contestants. The nonlethal nature of the threats is apparent when the victor opts not to kill the defeated one, but instead, stops the attack.

In a classic study, MacDonald (1968) followed 100 persons admitted to Colorado Psychiatric Hospital who had made verbal (81) or nonverbal (19) threats to kill. After a five- to six-year follow-up, he found that only three had killed another individual; four had committed suicide. *None* of the persons who had committed homicide killed the person they had originally threatened which had resulted in their involuntary hospitalization.

Death threats for noncompliance with demands of armed persons engaged in instrumental violence such as robbing a bank or hijacking a car, however, carry with them a higher risk of injury and death. If the armed perpetrator is substance intoxicated, the risk may be even higher due to the disinhibiting effects of the chemical. In the last few years, the writer has assessed armed individuals who were high on crystal methamphetamine ("ice") and other stimulant drugs who killed even when the victims complied with their wishes.

Triggers to violence during the escalation stage account for 5 to 10% of the contribution to violence in normal, young adult males (Hall et al., 1984; Hall, 1987). Although the focus of most media attention, triggers may merely represent the straw that breaks the camel's back. Triggering stimuli are precipitating causes of lethal violence, short term in duration, and tend to set violence into motion. For institutional violence, the prima-

ry trigger appears to be instructions/training to aggress. In family-intimate violence, the main trigger appears to be substance intoxication alone or in combination with interpersonal stress within the family (for minors) or breakup in a central love relationship (for adults). For criminal violence of an instrumental nature, the availability of a victim is often sufficient to set violence into motion.

Almost any kind of an aversive stimulus can trigger violence. Triggers generally set violence into motion when violence is already a prepotent response for the perpetrator (Bandura, 1977; Baron & Richardson, 1994). They often serve to intensify an individual's behavioral response to a situation. Common triggers to aggressive behaviors from the behavioral science literature are presented in Table 7.

Triggers act in a reciprocally deterministic fashion. A challenge to a fight may stimulate anger and a verbal retort which then influences the initiator of violence (e.g., a punch is thrown), which then modifies the reacting person's own responses (e.g., defensive aggression is shown). When a homicide occurs in a domestic context, there is a complex interplay of cause and effect, with an evolving set of triggers escalating and contributing to a lethal outcome.

Triggers assume inhibitory qualities when their presence suppresses or delays violence, such as the sudden arrival of onlookers, motionless victim behavior, illumination of the scene, and other events (Hall, 1987). Harking back to our evolutionary tendencies toward nonviolence, pain cues from victims normally act as a powerful inhibitor of violence (Dubonowsky, 1982). If pain from a victim maintains or even accelerates violence, the author sees it as a poor prognostic sign.

Some evidence suggests that inhibitors wear thin as a function of time during the escalation stage. The need for social approval — normally a strong inhibitor — appears to dissipate quickly (Taylor & Pisano, 1971). The erosion of inhibi-

TABLE 7
TRIGGERS TO VIOLENCE

Condition or Event	Sample Reference(s)
Central love relationship breakup	Bandura (1973)
Alcohol intoxication	Wolfgang (1978)
Drug intoxication (especially PCP, LSD, amphetamines and opiates)	Petersilia, Greenwood, & Lavin (1977)
Instructions to aggress	Milgram (1963, 1965)
Sudden pain	Bandura (1973)
Heat	Baron & Lawton (1972); Baron & Bell (1975, 1976)
Noise	Geen (1978); Mueller (1983)
Crowding	Griffitt & Veitch (1971)
Exposure to media violence	Zillmann & Johnson (1973); Geen (1990)
Unpleasant orders	Rotten, Barry, Frey, & Saler (1978)
Black color	Frank & Gilovich (1988)
Firearms	Berkowitz & LePage (1967); Caprara, Renzi, Amolini, D'Imperio, & Travaglia (1984)
Sudden worsening of financial state	Webster, et al. (1979)
Placement in incarceration	Webster, et al. (1979)
Other intense, sudden, recent stressors involving sex dominance, survival, and territoriality	Webster, et al. (1979)
Status threats in group context	Short (1968)
Insults to self-esteem	Toch (1969)
Alcohol and drugs in interaction	Pritchard (1977)
Fired or laid off from work	Webster, et al. (1979)
Unfavorable change in reward structure	Webster, et al. (1979)
Body space invasion	Kinzel (1970)
Nightmares with violent themes	Yochelson & Samenow (1976)
Elevated testosterone	Kreuz & Rose (1972); Dabbs, Ruback, Frady, Hopper, & Sgoutas (1988)
Heightened arousal	Christy, Gelfand, & Hartman (1971); Zillman, Katcher, & Milavsky (1972)

tions is explained by a model proposed by Prentice-Dunn and Rogers (1983). Here, during the escalation stage, the person has a narrow focus of attention (e.g., on his own arousal, on the thought that the victim deserves to be punished). This results in a decreased self-awareness of other private events, including inhibitions to kill. A state of deindividuation occurs, in which the killer is aware of the strictures not to harm others, but has no trepidation about carrying out the action.

To summarize, triggers are considered short term in nature and have an intense and deleterious impact upon the individual's self-control. They tend to weaken inhibitions to aggress when superimposed on a past history of violence. Decreased self-awareness during the stress and turmoil of the acceleration stage also weakens inhibitory triggers. Typical triggers for an individual can be identified by historical analysis; they tend to recur, and act in a reciprocally deterministic fashion with environmental factors and the perpetrator's own behavior during the escalation stage.

Opportunity factors must exist for lethal violence to occur. They consist of events or behaviors which make violence possible or which expand the type or severity of its expression. The opportunity afforded by firearms cannot be overemphasized. In domestic homicides, as mentioned previously, firearms are the preferred weapon. Two out of three homicides of all types involve firearms (U.S. Department of Justice, 1993). An opportunity variable may be an event as simple as release from incarceration, to more complex events, such as holding a position of authority in an institution that sanctions violence. Table 8 presents some of the more common opportunity variables associated with violence.

Opportunity variables assume an inhibitory status when the availability of victims is eliminated or reduced. Placement in solitary confinement, loss of means of transportation, an invalid physical status, forfeiture of firearms, or a regimen of tranquilizing medication are examples.

During the escalation stage, a key consideration is whether the preparation for violence was organized (i.e., self-controlled) or disorganized in nature. Factors that show self-controlled violence include the following (Hall, 1990; Hall & Sbordone, 1993): (1) lengthy time delays between triggers during the escalation stage and the violence; (2) complex chains of behaviors performed

in order to execute the violent behavior; and (3) flexibility of behavior, for example, when the perpetrator reacts with adaptable responses when faced with unexpected complications in meeting with the victim.

In regard to weapons, Hall and Sbordone (1993) also noted other factors associated with self-control during the acceleration stage. These include the possession of a weapon designed for attack (gun, knife), thus suggesting a chain of self-controlled responses (selecting, obtaining, concealing, carrying, reaching for, and later attacking with, the weapon). Chains of responses usually call for shifts in thinking and lessen the likelihood of impulsivity. The perpetrator who hides a knife in his pocket, for example, must gauge the proper time to retrieve the weapon and use it on the victim.

Killing Time

Following the escalation stage, lethal violence is expressed. Usually, the violence itself is short-lived, but may be prolonged in certain types of killing (e.g., poisoning, torture, weaponless assaults). At this stage, the characteristics of the perpetrator, victim, and context should be examined. Important parameters are duration, type of weapons utilized, wounds received, defensive

TABLE 8
OPPORTUNITY VARIABLES ASSOCIATED WITH VIOLENCE

Condition or Event	Sample Reference(s)
Availability of weaker victim	Bandura (1973)
No peaceful response possible (e.g., trapped by assailant)	Monahan (1981)
Recent purchase of firearm	Berkowitz & LePage (1967)
Possession of firearm	U.S. Department of Justice (1983)
Situation presents opportunity for instrumental aggression (e.g., beating up drunk for money)	Berkowitz & LePage (1967)
Release from preventive detainment	Stone (1975)
Cessation of tranquilizing or stabilizing medication	Stone (1975)
Vehicular transportation	Monahan (1981)

behaviors on the part of the perpetrator and victim, contextual features, such as lighting and escape routes, and the behavior of third parties. As with all of the stages and for each perpetrator who is evaluated, the examiner should construct a moment-by-moment timeline of events.

The Rogers Criminal Responsibility Assessment Scale (R-CRAS, Rogers, 1984) allows the evaluator to rate, on a Likert-type scale, behaviors or events during the lethal violence which are relevant to criminal responsibility (i.e., insanity). These include: (a) coherence and other characteristics of speech suggesting deficient or intact verbal skills; (b) intensity and appropriateness of affect, with intense expression of emotion and inappropriate affect associated with less self-control; (c) the cognitive focus of the perpetrator, ranging from nebulous to markedly specific; (d) ongoing mental conditions, such as retardation, brain damage, or schizophrenia; (e) level of substance intoxication (in most jurisdictions, all but pathological intoxication is considered inculpatory); (f) level of anxiety; (g) presence of delusions, hallucinations with bizarre behavior, or both; (h) presence of depressed or expansive mood; (i) awareness of the violence; and (j) self-reported control. Rogers provides several decision trees that yield conclusions regarding the sanity of the accused according to the test of insanity in a given jurisdiction.

The analysis of weapon usage is instructive. In general, the perpetration of violence with a weapon found at the scene of the crime indicates poor planning. Use of one's arms or legs to club, strangle, or kick a victim suggests a primitive response. An attack with certain parts of the body (e.g., biting, banging one's head against the victim) suggests an even more primitive level of aggression. Continuing to attack non-victim entities (e.g., bystanders, victim's car) suggests yet more loss of behavioral self-control.

Conversely, the perpetrator's flexibility of response and method of attack should be considered. The use of multiple weapons or shifting back and forth from one method of attack to another suggests that higher-level executive functions were utilized. In the case of firearms, the ability to reload after firing indicates the ability to recall a proper sequence (i.e., procedural memory), engage a host of sensory-perceptual skills, and short-term planning for the next shot.

In regard to mitigation to murder due to extreme emotion at the time of the homicide, Hall (1990) differentiated between self-controlled and disorganized, impulsive behavior in criminal defendants. This approach is based on the notion that predatory, instrumental, and proactive violence are more likely to involve self-control than affective, hostile, and reactive violence. These latter forms of violence are more likely to have disorganized components.

Using this approach, the evaluator looks for the behaviors associated with high self-control and choice, as well as behaviors reflecting the most impulsivity for the time before, during, and after the alleged murder. Table 9 differentiates impulsive from self-controlled behaviors along the lethal violence sequence. Self-controlled behavior is usually more competent and organized than impulsive behavior. A central assumption is that the presence of competent behavior is incompatible with extreme emotion and disorganizing response patterns. In Chapter 16, Sandra McPherson presents alternative ways of understanding mitigation to murder.

Competent performance reflects the notion that the accused may simultaneously observe and change his or her behavior in response to a fluctuating environment, all in accordance with the goal or desired object of the action sequence. Highly effectual behavior always involves reciprocal determinism, as discussed previously. Hypothesis testing is the highest form of effective performance, as when a rapist/carjacker shows behavior (e.g., threatening a victim with her life if she fails to open the locked door to her car) in order to

TABLE 9
BASIC VIOLENCE MODES

Impulsive Violence	Self-controlled Violence
1. Baseline stage	
Little or no planning for violence	Goal formulation/plans
Target is a perceived threat	Target does not represent a threat
2. Escalation (i.e., triggering stage)	
More likely public rituals	Preceded by private ritual
Intense arousal/emotion	Minimal arousal/emotion
Confused thinking	Clarity of thought
Crying, tearfulness	Subdued negative emotion
Startle reactions	Rapid habituation
Reduced verbiage/mute	Verbal interaction
Reactive and impulsive	Organized execution of plan
Heightened and diffuse awareness	Heightened and focused awareness
3. Violence	
Global, diffuse hyperactivity	Goal directed motor responses
Perseveration	Change in action principle
Goal is to reduce threat	Goal is consumption/exploitation
Rapid displacement of target	No displacement of target
Time limited	Less time limited
4. Recovery Period	
Crying, tearfulness	More likely depressed/subdued
Attempts to leave scene immediately	Attempts to hide/conceal deed
5. Return to Baseline	
More likely to experience amnesia	More likely to have recall
Post-trauma stress likely	More likely positive memories

influence a person's reaction (e.g., the victim acquiesces and opens the door; alternatively, she attempts to call for help on her cellular phone, or sits in the front seat and does nothing, or leans on the horn, or drives off), then changes his own behavior accordingly (e.g., forcing the victim in the back seat and proceeding to rape and rob the victim, attempting to break the glass and grab the phone before a call gets out, forcing the door open and rendering the victim powerless, giving up and trying another victim). Competent behavior is usually followed by planned attempts to escape identification or apprehension (e.g., killing the victim, quickly using and then disposing of credit cards, changing one's appearance or location). In essence, this skill taps the ability to show a concordance between intentions/plans and actions.

The focus on self-control and behavioral organization has led to interesting outcomes in the forensic arena. First, the percentage of favorable outcomes in mitigation to murder cases increased for the author as well as other experts. In about 80 mitigation to murder cases since the late 1970s, the author experienced favorable outcomes in the majority of the murder trials (65 to 75%). Since adoption of the criteria for self-control and behavioral organization, which are presented in detail in the following section, the percentage of favorable outcomes rose (to about 80%, all in cases involving opposing experts). An unknown portion of the increase may be due, however, to the author's heightened selectivity in taking on murder cases in the last few years.

Second, because the focus on self-control may help either the defense or prosecution, depending on the merits of the individual case, a better balancing of referrals has been achieved. In addition to an increase in the total number of requests for services, referrals come in regularly from both sides. Other experts also report about an even split of referrals from private/government defense attorneys and prosecutors.

Third, the focus on self-control and behavioral organization began to be utilized by other experts in insanity trials, at least for the state and federal courts in this jurisdiction. The federal jurisdiction's repeal of the volitional prong of the American Law Institute (ALI) test of insanity may have influenced some experts. Certainly, the underlying logic of attempting to demonstrate the existence of behaviors and events (rather than their absence, as in the ALI concern with "substantial incapacities") was appealing.

Fourth, court actors have become more focused on the concept of self-control and behavioral organization in homicide cases. From 1990 to 1995, the author collected feedback from about 40 judges, defense attorneys, and prosecutors who had previous murder cases in which mitigation was an issue. Although a small sample, they acknowledged increased concern about and interest in behavioral self-control as it relates to lethal violence. They tended to believe that extreme emotion was a regressive behavior more often occurring in bonded relationships, where one or both parties lost control of their behavior. In these types of crimes, according to the respondents, the crime scene made for ready identification and apprehension of the defendant (e.g., at home, at a party). For lack of extreme emotion, they were **uniformly impressed with the high self-control** shown by the defendant. They cited examples, including stalking, rehearsal of a slaying, and showing complex behaviors at the time of the lethal violence, such as an ability to operate, reload, and shoot the victim in vital body areas, particularly the head. Extreme emotion did not support mitigation, in their opinion, if it was due to voluntary substance intoxication.

Due to recent state supreme court rulings in Hawaii, all juries must be instructed that self-control and behavioral organization are the essential ingredients in determining whether the defendant was operating under extreme emotion at the time of the alleged murder. Further acceptability of this focus was thus generated by these rulings.

Recovery Period Behaviors

Following the attack, the victim of homicide is usually immobilized through shock or death. At this point, no victim self-control or choice is possible. The context itself may begin to exert an influence, as the enormity of the deed begins to dawn on the perpetrator. Confusion by the perpetrator and bystanders is often shown, and conflicting stories concerning what happened are the rule rather than the exception.

The perpetrator may show behaviors which can be analyzed for signs of self-control. An obvious indication of self-control is an organized escape from the scene of the crime. Other self-controlling behaviors for the recovery period include: (a) attempting to dispose of the victim's body, clothing, or the weapon used in the offense; (b) making verbal statements of crime recall (e.g., spontaneous statements to bystanders, police); (c) making nonverbal gestures indicating knowledge of what just happened (e.g., pointing to the victim's body); (d) prevaricating incompatible behavior (e.g., making up a verifiably false story); (e) cleaning one's own body or clothes in an attempt to get rid of incriminating evidence.

Return to Baseline

The final step in the killing process (Stage 5) is a return to typical behavior after the killing has taken place. The perpetrator's baseline is then changed by the killing, as well as the baselines of other involved parties. Unless a perpetrator has a significant history of violence, or is a sociopath, killing changes the person forever in his or her thoughts, feelings, and behaviors with regard to himself or herself and the world.

In the author's experience, deadly perpetrators, in retrospect, almost always try to hold themselves blameless for the killing. Those with character disorders, chronic substance abuse, or both, especially project the blame for the slaying onto the victim or others (e.g., acting in self-defense, someone slipping them an intoxicating drug, killing by accident). Inhibitions to kill in the future may thereby be reduced because the perpetrator has not accepted responsibility for the lethal act. In general, any violence, including those interpersonal interactions with deadly outcomes, makes future violence more probable, given the opportunity to aggress and availability of the right triggers. Self-controlled killers, such as robbers who kill their victims, serial murderers, and some forms of institutional aggressors, often refine methods for future lethal violence.

A Proposed Model of Lethal Violence

As stated at the beginning of the chapter, lethal violence in humans is any form of fatal interpersonal transaction during which the perpetrator purposely harms or attempts to harm another person who is motivated to avoid injury or death. Our definition purposefully excludes accidental death from socially sanctioned activities (e.g., surgery) or death when one wishes to die (e.g., as in physician-assisted suicide). Some lethal violence is socially sanctioned and not accidental (e.g., capital punishment, war, police use of deadly force); however, the focus of this book is on unlawful family and criminal violence.

Our definition leads to a model and has a number of important features. Lethal violence may involve either attempted or consummated harm. Physical harm does not have to occur before potentially lethal violence can be classified (e.g., as in attempted murder). Some crimes, such as armed robbery, carry with them an implied assumption that victims may be killed for non-compliance. Some fatal outcomes may not be intended, but arise from less injurious violence (e.g., a person fatally striking his head on a curb during a fist fight). In many cases, it is almost impossible to determine whether the perpetrator intended the fatal outcomes, or if he or she was driven out of indifference to the consequences. In our model, the full range of behaviors leading to violent acts, including but not limited to deadly outcomes should therefore be considered, rather than focusing on a narrow set of lethal acts dealing only with intended killing.

To reach the most objective conclusion in regard to classifying a behavior, one should focus on overt behavior and physical events. Intent to harm is inferred from behavior and other measurable data. The difference from more subjective approaches is more than semantics. In murder cases, the author always starts with behaviors and events that can be established for the times immediately before, during, and soon after the lethal violence. This information usually flows from a visit to the crime scene. As a homicide-specific, behaviorally oriented database grows, information about the feelings and thoughts of the perpetrator, victim, and bystanders accumulates. A time line is always constructed. In this manner, ground truth for lethal violence can be obtained. Conclusions about legal issues, such as mitigation, criminal responsibility, and dangerousness can be based on a solid foundation of cross-validated data.

This model of lethal violence events measures behavior as well as involves a judgment as to self-control and choice. Traditionally, the distinction between hostile and instrumental violence relates to the perpetrator's motive. Hostile killing applies to situations where the apparent goal of the killer is to cause the victim to suffer. Instrumental killing refers to an ostensible attempt to obtain some desired goal. Violence, in these cases, is a means to an end (e.g., shooting a security guard in a bank robbery). Another distinction is between reactive and proactive lethal aggression. Reactive aggression always involves retaliation, whereas proactive aggression involves the initiation of violence by the perpetrator without sufficient environmental provocation. Two basic types of violence — predatory and affective — involve aggression aimed at exploitation versus that characterized by charged emotion at the time of the lethal violence (e.g., competitively based aggression, defensive aggression, infanticide). All of these concepts and differentiations are inferred from behavior and events associated with the fatal interaction.

Three critical parameters of lethal violence — relationship of perpetrator to victim, degree of harm, and degree of self-control — can be incorporated into the model for better understanding, evaluation, and intervention. This model is presented in Figure 3. In terms of the relationship of the perpetrator to the victim, a lethally violent act is assigned to one and only one category. For domestic violence, the perpetrator is defined as a family member if he or she is related to the victim by blood or marriage. Intimate violence occurs within a central love relationship in a domestic context, whether or not the perpetrator and victim are married (e.g., common law marriages, long-term homosexual unions). The perpetrator is an acquaintance if there was some previous contact and interaction with the victim prior to the lethal event, excluding those perpetrators who are only "known by sight." The perpetrator is classified as a stranger if the victim could have identified the individual only as a stranger, including those individuals "known by sight."

The right side of the model shows the degree of general harm that occurred during the lethal violence sequence (with an optional rating over the lifetime of an individual). Killing a person, a specific form of lethal violence, almost always creates psychological or physical harm to others in the vicinity, to property, or to even the decedent before his or her death (e.g., intimidation by weapons, sexual assaults). The scoring system stems from the U.S. Department of Justice's National Survey of Crime Severity (1985). Based on the responses of over 60,000 Americans, this system, for the first time, provides an easily derived, quantitative score for the amount of harm to society that an individual has perpetrated during a particular act. The following sections, summarized in Table 10, demonstrate how to calculate point values.

1. *Number of persons injured.* Each victim receiving some bodily injury during an event must be accounted for. Physical injuries typically occur as a direct result of assaultive events, but can be caused by other events as well. The four levels of bodily injury are:

a. Minor harm - An injury that requires or receives no professional medical attention. The victim may, for instance, be pushed, shoved, kicked, or knocked down, and receive a minor wound (e.g., cut, bruise).

b. Treated and discharged - The victim receives professional medical treatment but is not detained for further medical care.

c. Hospitalized - The victim requires inpatient care in a medical facility, regardless of its duration, or outpatient care for three or more clinical visits.

d. Killed - The victim dies as a result of the injuries, regardless of the circumstances under

FIGURE 3.
MODEL OF LETHAL VIOLENCE

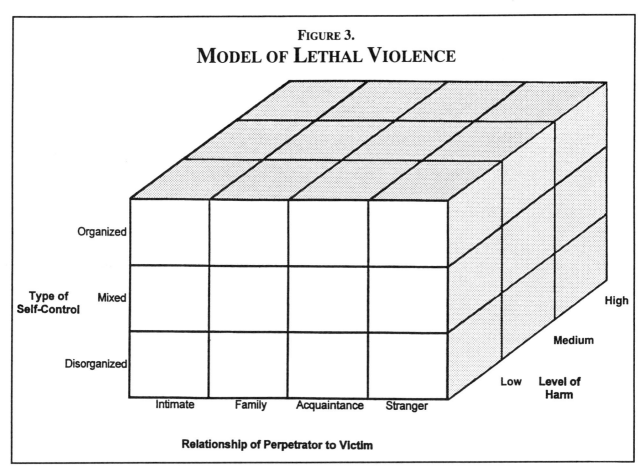

Relationship of Perpetrator to Victim

which they are inflicted.

2. *Sexual intercourse by force.* This event occurs when a person is intimidated and forced against his or her will to engage in a sexual act (e.g., rape, incest, sodomy). Such an event may have more than one victim, and the score depends on the number of such victims.

A forcible sex act is always accomplished by intimidation. Thus, the event must also be scored for the type of intimidation involved (see below). Intimidation is scored for all victims in a forcible sexual act. The victim of one or more forcible sexual acts is always assumed to have suffered at least minor harm during the event. Even when medical examination may not reveal any injuries, the event must be scored for minor harm. This level of injury should also be scored when the victim is examined by a physician only to ascer-

tain if a sexually transmitted disease has been transmitted or to collect evidence that the sexual act was completed.

3. *Intimidation.* Intimidation occurs when one or more victims are threatened with bodily harm (or some other serious consequences) for the purpose of forcing the victim(s) to obey the request of the offender(s) to give up something of value or to assist in a criminal event that leads to someone's bodily injury, the theft of or damage to property, or both. In addition to rape, robbery is a classic example. Ordinary assault and battery, aggravated assault and battery, or homicide are not to be scored for intimidation merely because someone was assaulted or injured. The event must also have included the threat of force for intimidation to have been present. With the exception of forcible sexual acts, criminal events

TABLE 10
SERIOUSNESS SCORING SYSTEM

Score sheet
Name and Identification number(s):

Component scored	Number of Victims	x	Scale Weight	=	Total
I. Injury					
(a) Minor harm	_____		1.47		_____
(b) Treated and discharged	_____		8.53		_____
(c) Hospitalized	_____		11.98		_____
(d) Killed	_____		35.67		_____
II. Forcible sex acts	_____		25.92		_____
III. Intimidation					
(a) Verbal or physical	_____		4.90		_____
(b) Weapon	_____		5.60		_____
IV. Premises forcibly entered	_____		1.50		_____
V. Motor vehicle stolen					
(a) Recovered	_____		4.46		_____
(b) Not recovered	_____		8.07		_____
VI. Property theft/damage (optional)	_____				_____
TOTAL SCORE					_____

involving intimidation are scored only once regardless of the number of victims who are intimidated. The types of intimidation are:

a. Physical or verbal - Physical intimidation means the use of strongarm tactics (e.g., threats with fists, menacing gestures). Verbal intimidation means spoken threats, not supported by the overt display of a weapon.

b. Intimidation by weapon - Display of a weapon (e.g., firearm, cutting or stabbing instrument, blunt instrument capable of inflicting serious bodily injury).

The relevance of a total severity score (net harm) for global sentencing considerations should not be overlooked. Total net harm represented by the instant offense can be linked to victim restitution criteria or to sentencing procedures, thus adding a quantitative dimension to a notoriously subjective task. Several examples of scoring follow.

A. *After sneaking up on a man and his girlfriend while they are necking at a park, a rapist forces them to exit their automobile. He shoots the man, gun whips and rapes the girlfriend (who is later hospitalized), and leaves in the automobile (which is recovered later) after taking $100 from the man. The boyfriend later dies as a result of the shooting.*

In this event, the boyfriend was killed (35.67); the girlfriend was raped (25.92), threatened with a gun (5.60) and sustained injuries requiring hospitalization (11.98). The car was stolen and recovered (4.46). The total value of the property loss was $100 (3.43). Overall, the event has a total score of 87.06.

B. *Answering a armed robbery in progress broadcast, police engage in a gun battle with three armed robbers; one of the bandits is killed and the other two captured. (No one is injured except the offenders.)*

Here, a total score of 5.60 for intimidation by weapons is awarded. As the robbers failed to carry out the offense because the police came before any property had been taken, the event is an attempt and is not scored at all within the index of crime severity. The system measures harm to victims and the community, not to perpetrators of violence.

Threshold values for various degrees of harm can be set at any level. Suggested *low* harm includes point values less than 35 and does not include the death of a victim. This level includes death threats, attempted murder, and other crimes which may have been attempted or completed at the time (e.g., robbery, burglary). *Medium* values include the death of a single victim and all point values up to 70. *High* harm includes any values beyond 70, whether or not the lethal violence sequence included one or multiple victims.

For degree of harm, the evaluator can optionally calculate point values for all acts of significant violence in a perpetrator's history. Especially important in sentencing and treatment planning, one's history of violence cannot be excluded from any serious discussion of dangerousness for a particular individual. The forensic expert should note and total all acts of previous violence that fit the above definitions. Often, knowledge of previous violence is unavailable, as when juvenile records are sealed. For this reason, the author has focused on adult violence (after age 18), although the system could theoretically be applied over the lifetime of the perpetrator.

This severity system creates a simple, quantitatively based language that has important implications for decisions relevant to sentencing, including selective incapacitation, dangerousness, victim restitution, and intervention. The beauty of the system is that it allows, for the first time, an indication of the net harm that an individual has perpetrated on society for a given act of lethal violence, or even over a lifetime.

The concept of dangerousness prediction is not held in high repute in the forensic community. Despite its frequent occurrence, lethal violence between intimates, for example, is difficult to predict accurately. A Kansas City study found a false positive rate of more than 99% in predicting domestic homicide, although police had come to the home at least once in about 90% of the cases (Sherman, Schmidt, Rogan, & Deriso, 1991).

The model presented in this book is relevant to dangerousness prediction. For an individual with frequent past violence, future acts can be predicted with promising degrees of accuracy in focused contexts and if certain guidelines are followed. (See Floud & Young, 1981; Hall, 1987; Hinton, 1983; Monahan, 1988, 1992).

A very safe prediction scheme follows from the author's clinical and research experience. First, do not predict lethal violence in particular, but violence in general, homicide being one of its possibilities. Second, in the absence of a history of violence for an individual, predict that no violence will occur in the future. Third, predict violence within a circumscribed time frame (e.g., 3 months, 1 year), as this prevents others from interpreting your prediction as interminable (in no cases does the author predict beyond 12 months). Fourth, predict violence only if there are two or more acts of violence within the last year, current triggers to aggress, and anticipated opportunity factors. Last, refuse to predict in all other cases of violence.

In clinical-forensic contexts, this writer has achieved 80 to 85% overall accuracy using the above scheme. To increase accuracy to this level, no predictions were made in about a third of the cases where knowledge was lacking. Unfortunately, this does not always please referral sources. In a research context, Hall, Catlin, Boissevain, and Westgate, (1984) achieved 75% accuracy for both true positives and true negatives with knowledge of only history (two or more violent acts) and current stress (i.e., triggers).

To increase accuracy, forensic professionals should avoid the dozen dangerousness prediction pitfalls (Hall, 1987). These are: (a) failing to perceive the relevance of violence prediction as a specific focus of inquiry in a particular case; (b) proffering conclusions with an inadequate forensic database; (c) failing to account for retrospective and current distortion; (d) predicting dangerousness in the absence of previous dangerousness; (e) falling prey to illusory correlations; (f) predicting from clinical diagnosis (e.g., Diagnostic and Statistical Manual, Fourth Edition [DSM-IV]); (g) failing to take into account triggering stimuli; (h) ignoring anticipated opportunity variables; (i) failing to note inhibitory factors which diminish the chance violence will occur; (j) ignoring relevant base rates and the anchoring strategies which follow from them (i.e., base rates for violence can be the first estimate of probability of occurrence, with later information to tailor the prediction for an individual); (k) using limited outcome measures; and (l) failing to offer circumscribed conclusions.

Shown on the left side of Figure 3, the degree of behavioral organization and self-control is the last variable to consider in the model. The traditional forensic mental health approach attempts to *rule out* self-control (e.g., by diagnosing psychosis for the time of the instant homicide). Attempting to prove the negative with this approach (i.e., that self-control did not exist) is difficult, if not impossible.

An alternative approach attempts to *rule in* self-control and behavioral organization. This tends to confine the analysis in a particular case to output (i.e., behavioral) variables. Regardless of the condition(s) that the perpetrator may be suffering from, the evaluator focuses on the effects those conditions may have had on behavior. Indications of self-control and choice, implying that impulsive behavior was not present,

include the following:

1. Preparation, as in gathering tools or weapons for the violence to follow (e.g., assembly of a rape-murder kit to carry in the car while searching for victims).

2. Rehearsal, as in practicing for the anticipated violence (e.g., shooting at a target range before a homicide with a firearm).

3. Demonstration of a variety of acts or flexibility of possible responses (e.g., use of both a knife and firearm during a homicide).

4. Ability to orchestrate multi-step, multi-task schemes (e.g., long, connected chains of behaviors to set up and carry out a killing).

5. Ability to show "change in principle" (e.g., switching from robbery to rape, or from killing to theft.)

6. Ability to show self-controlled somatic responses (e.g., sex resulting in ejaculation, eating or drinking during a violence sequence).

7. Ability to delay responses or to resist distracting stimuli.

8. Ability to monitor and self-correct ongoing behavior (i.e., hypothesis testing).

9. Ability to regulate tempo, intensity, and duration of behaviors (e.g., showing more violent behavior when people are watching, reviving the victim from unconsciousness in order to elicit pain cues).

10. Ability to stop violence after the task is complete (i.e., response cessation with no perseveration).

11. Obliteration or destruction of evidence during or after lethal violence.

The degree of self-control can be illustrated to the trier of fact in a simple chart showing the defendant's behavior for the time before, during, and after the lethal violence. On the vertical axis, the degree of self-control shown during each time period is rated on a scale of negligible, minimal, mild, moderate, and substantial. The confidence that the evaluator has in each of these ratings is presented to the court on the same scale.

In the analysis of self-control, emotional states and cognitive events should be inferred from the killer's behaviors for the time of the lethal event. The author has found that there is never only one emotion for the entire sequence of violence. Anger may be associated with fear of detection, and other emotions may wax and wane in response to internal and external stimuli. Because feelings are nonverifiable, subsequent reports of emotional states are subject to distortions and deceptions in the direction of vested interests. It is an elementary mistake to assume that particular emotions must have existed at the time of lethal violence. A person who kills does not have to be angry in order to kill the intended target. This is particularly true for many types of instrumentally motivated crimes. Many perpetrators inflict lethal violence on persons whom they claim to like and love (e.g., family violence).

Cognitive processes associated with lethal violence involve changing thoughts, self-statements, and judgments. As with emotions, they are subject to much post hoc modification. Statements made by the perpetrator during the acceleration stage of violence may involve deception and distortion in the direction of goal accomplishment. The best reflectors of cognitive processes are verbal statements, if any, uttered by the perpetrator during the violence sequence. Spontaneous statements made to police and others soon after the violence may also reflect the true thinking of the perpetrator. In the author's experience, the perpetrator's veracity tends to degrade rapidly with time, especially as he or she begins to think of the possible long-range consequences of the lethal violence. As in the case of John, the CEO who shot his wife, then frantically called the police to report a robbery, supposedly "spontaneous" statements may be part of purposeful deception.

In summary, the presented model of lethal violence allows the evaluator to place a multitude of findings regarding a particular killing into a sound perspective. A model based on the perpetrator-victim relationship is an advancement over attempting to classify types of offenders or victims outside the interpersonal context of the lethal violence. In addition, such a perspective simplifies the confusing array of perpetrator-victim relationships portrayed in the literature.

Admittedly fuzzy in its present state, the proposed model also considers self-control and choice. There is an attempt to rule in rather than merely trying to rule out this capacity, as in traditional forensic psychological/psychiatric approaches. This factor has important implications for perpetrator identification and the trial procedures themselves. The FBI, for example, initially determines whether a homicide scene is organized, disorganized, or mixed in order to profile the likely perpetrator (Ressler et al., 1988; see Table 11). Even if the perpetrator is known, the evaluator should ask whether or not the crime scene was organized or disorganized. Because self-control implies choice, trial verdicts and sentences often hinge on the perception of whether the defendant could self-control his or her behaviors at the time of the crime. Choosing to kill someone usually results in a harsher verdict (e.g., murder over manslaughter) than acting in an impulsive, disorganized manner.

Deception and Distortion in Killing

A special problem in data collection emerges from an analysis of the lethal violence sequence and model. Most acts of fatal aggression contain some degree of unintended distortion or deliberate deception on the part of the perpetrator, victim, or third parties. The reality of the lethal violence event, unobstructed by distortion, may be termed "ground truth" and is the Holy Grail sought after by forensic evaluators. Ground truth stands by itself. What really happened at the time of the killing is always, without exception and as discussed above, the result of a three-way interac-

TABLE 11
ORGANIZED AND DISORGANIZED SEX MURDER

Organized	Disorganized
First born or eldest son	Later born
Father's work stable	Father's work unstable
Inconsistent discipline in childhood	Harsh discipline in childhood
Adequate work history	Poor work history
Socially skilled	Socially immature
Average or higher intelligence	Average or lower intelligence
Sexually competent	Sexually incompetent
Lives with intimate other	Living alone
Heavy use of alcohol	Minimal use of alcohol
Significant stress triggers violence	Minimal situational stress
Victim a targeted stranger	Victim or location of crime known
Use of ruse or con to lure victim into vulnerable position	More likely direct attack and kills quickly
Controlled conversation	Minimal conversation
Restraints likely with demands for submission	Restraints not likely
Controlled mood during crime	Anxious mood during crime
Weapon brought and taken from scene	Weapon found and left at scene
Blood smearing or other unusual acts less likely	Blood smearing, cannibalism, anthropophagy more likely
Less likely insertion of items into victim's orifices	Inserts items into victim's orifices
Sexual torture before death	Sexual mutilation after death
Sexual acts before death	Sexual acts after death
Crime control reflective of obsessive	Crime disorganized reflective of compulsive lifestyle
Controlled perseveration likely (e.g., continuous choking of victim to prolong sexual assault)	Uncontrolled perseverative responses likely (e.g., slashing/stabbing, bite marks)
Less likely destruction of face	Destruction of face more likely
Alters crime scene, conceals/destroys evidence	More likely leaves crime scene intact
Scene reflects planning and overall control	Scene reflects impulsivity and disarray
Ritualistic and planned quality	Symbolic and spontaneous quality
Does not take souvenir, article, or clothing	Takes souvenir, article, or clothing
Fingerprints/footprints not likely	Fingerprints/footprints likely
Relies on own or victim's vehicle	Relies on public transportation
Body dumped at another site	Body left at scene
Hides body	More likely leaves crime scene intact
Less likely to return victim's items to grave site	May return souvenir to grave site
Keen interest in news media	Minimal interest in news media
Changes lifestyle to avoid detection	Minimal change in lifestyle
Lives/works away from crime scene	Lives/works near crime scene

tion of the perpetrator, victim, and context variables (review Figure 1). Reports of events that did not actually occur, or did occur but are denied or somehow covered over, are the result of unintentional distortion, deliberate deception, or both.

Distortion of ground truth can occur at two points of time — during the lethal violence sequence and, subsequently, when it is reported upon. Forensic evaluators, like all individuals who study a process of which they are a part, are subject to bias. When analyzing a killing, for example, evaluators often sympathize with and take the side of the victim, thus failing to consider victim provocation and characteristics of the context that were conducive to violence. More commonly, a lack of information about the perpetrator, victim, and context predisposes evaluators to reach premature conclusions. These conclusions, once formed, become highly resistant to modification.

Case Illustration. John, who had brutally sodomized and killed a tourist by shoving a bottle into her vagina and then pushing her over a cliff, all the while allegedly under the influence of PCP, was committed to the state hospital after having been found Not Guilty by Reason of Insanity (NGRI). During a court hearing on John's application for conditional release, the three examining doctors testified that this bright young man had spent two years under treatment and seemed remorseful for his deeds. No criminal history prior to the instant offense was apparent. For over a year, he had been enrolled in daytime classes in a nearby junior college with an intent to major in psychology. Release into the community was recommended with the provision that John attend Alcohols Anonymous and Narcotics Anonymous meetings, go to weekly outpatient psychotherapy, and continue his education.

At the request of the prosecutor, the author was included on the panel as a fourth examiner. Examination of state archive records revealed that the patient had had his criminal record expunged for a variety of arrests, including robbery, firearms violations, assault, extortion, and attempted murder. His unremitting history of predatory aggression suggested dangerousness since the seventh grade. Both neuropsychological and psychological testing showed strong evidence that he had malingered retardation and psychosis during his early months at the state hospital, and

then pursued a strategy of minimization and denial of his antisocial characteristics in order to obtain conditional release. Despite these findings, the state hospital pushed for his release. His petitions for discharge were denied by the courts over the next 16 years and he remains incarcerated.

Unintentional distortion diminishes our understanding of ground truth. It must be considered before a lethal event can be placed in proper perspective. Non-deliberate distortion stems from deficiencies in the (a) reporting person (e.g., because of stress, physical disability, limited intelligence, inattention, recall problems); (b) reported event (e.g., too brief, physical barriers, weak intensity, distractions, figure-ground merging, no stimulus uniqueness); and (c) evaluation methods, of which the last case is an example (e.g., unreliable or invalid measures, inadequate training, leading questions, attempting to understand a murder that occurred in the remote past). The homicide may have occurred at night, making identification difficult, or witnesses to the crime may have been hindered by obstacles that prevented them from clearly observing the killing act. The evaluator may use tests that are obsolete, with antiquated norms. The sources of non-deliberate distortion, in sum, are diverse and quite capable of rendering invalid all conclusions regarding a particular person.

Deliberate distortion must be analyzed to understand lethal violence. Many offenders interviewed by the author have remarked how easy it was to commit violence and get away with it. They usually got caught when they failed to practice conscious deception, i.e., became sloppy and impulsive through intoxication or greed which interfered with the critical mental processes necessary for successful evasion and distortion.

Almost all lethal violence involves some form of deception. In criminal violence, the dangerousness of the perpetrator is usually minimized by words or behavior prior to the lethal violence sequence. In burglaries in which a victim is killed, concealment of weapons and burglary tools is commonplace. Burglars often attempt to blend into the environment by wearing dark clothes, hiding behind visual barriers, and avoiding sudden movement, thus minimizing their presence. Robbery resulting in homicide often involves faking good, shown by seemingly innocuous approach behaviors prior to the holdup. Faking bad may be engaged in when the robber pretends to hold a pistol to the victim's back, thus ensuring compliance. Kidnapping may involve faking good, as when kidnappers who intend to kill their victims deny such motivation, or when the location or deceased status of the victim is concealed. Rape-murder frequently involves stalking, a form of concealing one's dangerousness by keeping distant from the intended victim.

In serial rape-murder of the organized type, frequently, initial statements designed to lull the victim into complacency are followed by assaultive behaviors in a safe area hidden from view. Serial rapists fake good in ways that idiosyncratically work for them. For example, Ted Bundy had victims carry his books to his car because of his "broken" arm, only to bludgeon them into unconsciousness once they arrived at the vehicle.

Those who kill may deceive after the lethal act has occurred. For example, during an evaluation, they often attempt to escape the social and legal consequences of their acts. History, triggers, and opportunity factors — the three main factors associated with dangerousness — are commonly the targets of denial and minimization (Hall, 1982, 1987). Any variables associated with violence may be targeted for denial or minimization if the perpetrator believes that they suggest dangerousness, including a history of violent acts, arrests, and convictions. Often, a perpetrator will admit to violence-related arrests that show up on a rap sheet, but not to other acts which did not culminate in arrest. Substance abuse and intoxica-tion are usually minimized, particularly if they occurred prior to the killing (most defendants know or are quickly informed by their defense attorneys that voluntary substance intoxication does not mitigate murder to manslaughter). If at all possible, the use of weapons is denied, as most perpetrators know that this suggests an intention to act aggressively.

Occasionally, perpetrators fake bad to escape the aversive consequences of their acts. A defendant may blame the instant homicide on brain damage, psychosis, or some other serious condition in order to obtain exculpation or mitigation of responsibility for the killing. Rogers (1988) estimated that about 20% of criminal defendants assessed for insanity showed suspected or definite malingering. Another 5% had non-deliberate distortion in their self-report.

Detection of faked psychosis in murderers has been the target of clinical and psychometric study. Suspicions of faked psychosis should be raised by any of the following (Hall & Pritchard, 1996):

a. Production of psychotic symptoms is apparently under voluntary control and is understandable in terms of secondary gain or environmental circumstances.

b. Psychotic symptoms worsen when being observed or when being interviewed, are bizarre for the circumstances, or involve quick shifts to non-psychotic behavior when not being observed.

c. The patient has a history of faked mental problems.

d. The patient admits faking psychosis and his or her behavior can be explained by environmental events.

e. The "psychotic" patient uses an alias, is unwilling to allow access to old records, displays evidence of a simultaneous personality disorder, or has a history of substance abuse which explains the "psychotic" symptoms.

f. Laboratory testing suggests malingering (e.g., as in voluntary blood poisoning in factitious disorders).

g. Psychological testing suggests faking bad.

h. The killing is accomplished with accomplices or the defendant has non-psychotic motives for the crime.

Feigning of memory problems by murder defendants is a fundamental concern for forensic professionals in understanding lethal violence. In the author's evaluation of murder defendants, the majority claimed a selective memory impairment sometime during the violence sequence. Approximately half were determined to have faked some aspect of their memory impairment. The loss of recall in the remaining half could be explained by substance intoxication or the emotional charge of the violent incident and was usually accompanied by disorganized behavior.

Claimed amnesia associated with lethal violence is frequent but usually short term in duration. Bradford and Smith (1979) found that 37% of their sample of 30 defendants arrested for homicide reported amnesia for a period of less than 30 minutes, with 60% claiming some sort of amnesia for less than 24 hours. They also found 44% of the subjects reporting partial (patchy) amnesia, with sudden onset and cessation. This was the largest group, followed by those who claimed no amnesia at all (37%). Only one defendant reported a complete amnestic blackout for the entire time period. Likewise, only one subject showed lack of complete recovery. Bradford and Smith concluded that malingered amnesia is most likely to be 30 minutes or less in duration.

No cases of amnesia associated with *nonviolent* crimes were found by Taylor and Kopelman (1984) in a sample of 212 incarcerated men in custody for a variety of offenses. All of the men had psychiatric disturbances of one sort or another, with substance abuse and depression the most common. Seventy percent of the victims were the perpetrator's significant others.

Parwatikar, Holcomb, and Menninger (1985) studied 105 pretrial males held on murder charges. Those who faked amnesia, but were eventually caught in their duplicity, were more intelligent than the average inmate and had more extensive criminal backgrounds. Those murderers who admitted penal responsibility, and also claimed amnesia, tended to be substance intoxicated at the time of the instant offense and scored higher on MMPI scales indicating hysteria, depression, or hypochondriasis, or all three.

Schacter (1986) suggested that genuine versus faked recall of crimes can be uncovered by first looking at the accused's behavior in general. Was the lethal violence well prepared or rehearsed? What is the nature of the claimed memory loss? Limited recall during the crime with sharply defined onset and termination is viewed with suspicion. Schacter pointed out that time confusion on the part of the perpetrator is common and not significant of anything.

The feeling of knowing is Schacter's most important construct in the deception literature. This cognitive event involves a subjective conviction that one could retrieve or recognize an unrecalled event if sufficient cues were provided. For example, the evaluator can ask murderers who claim amnesia if they could better recall or recognize violence-related events if prompted by special knowledge of circumstances of the killing (e.g., where, when and how the killing occurred). Fakers tend to discount the chance that their recall would improve.

In reviewing the neuropsychological literature on deceptive strategies, Hall, Shooter, Craine, and Paulsen (1991) found that perpetrators of violence tend to fake believable memory deficits by the following:

1. *Presenting realistic symptoms.* What seems "realistic" to an individual with no knowledge of neurology or neuropsychology may or may not seem realistic to the evaluator. The incorrect assumptions about memory (e.g., that correct recognition is no easier than free recall; that overlearned information is just as difficult to remember as new learning) tend to betray the fakers.

2. *Distributing errors.* Fakers tend to sprinkle deliberate errors throughout tests rather than miss only difficult items as a way to disguise their intentions. They try to strike a balance between missing too many items (thereby risking detection) and missing too few items (thereby failing to seem impaired). Fakers usually do not guess randomly on items to which they know the answers but instead try to control the percentage of errors.

3. *Performing at a crudely estimated fraction of actual ability.* A faker who, for example, is capable of scoring 50 on Finger Tapping deliberately slows down in order to perform at a fraction of this rate.

4. *Protesting that tasks are too difficult or feigning confusion and frustration.* Often, fakers will put on a good act but will limit their inabilities in order to seem cooperative.

Explicit Alternative Testing (EAT) is a promising forensic neuropsychological tool that attempts to measure faked sensory and recall deficits (Grosz & Zimmerman, 1965; Hall & Shooter, 1989; Hall, Shooter, Craine, & Paulsen, 1991; Pankratz, 1979, 1983, 1988; Pankratz, Fausti, & Peed, 1975; Paulsen & Hall, 1991; Theodor & Mandelcorn, 1973). Also known as forced-choice, two-alternative, or symptom validity testing, EAT involves the presentation of sensory stimuli that the testee then denies or affirms he or she can perceive. An interference period is added if memory, as opposed to sensory registration, is the object of evaluation. Almost no person should miss presented items unless a genuine impairment exists, in which case one's performance should approximate chance responding (usually one half of the items on a binary format). Deviation from chance is defined as falling outside of the common range of the binomial distribution (± 1.96 standard errors of 50% correct). The power of the method is illustrated by the fact that the (one-tailed) probability of obtaining less than 40 correct responses in 100 trials is less than 2%.

A precipitous drop to .0019 means presenting less than 36 correct answers. Usually, fakers feel that guessing correctly for 50% of the items is too high. Further, they have difficulty keeping track of their responses over 70 to 100 trials (Haughton, Lewsley, Wilson, & Williams, 1979; Pankratz, 1988). Overall accuracy rates for using EAT methodology is between 85 and 90%.

Computer software using forced-choice testing procedures is available. Pritchard (1990) obtained a 100 percent hit rate with 10 subjects instructed to fake bad and with several clinical-forensic cases in his Tests of Neuropsychological Malingering. Three functions — audition, memory, and vision — of 72 trials each use four detection rules from the binomial and normal distribution. Several dozen more cases have been added to the database since 1990, with the method retaining an extraordinary high degree of accuracy in detecting malingering (Pritchard, 1995).

Case Illustration. A 65-year-old, left-handed Filipino who was charged with the murder of his wife claimed amnesia for the alleged offense. No history of neurological problems was apparent. He presented with severe short-term visual and auditory recall deficits on the Wechsler Memory Scale-Revised and other memory testing. He obtained about 20% accurate responses on the EAT, but later admitted to exaggerating his recall deficits when confronted with the results. Analysis of the instant murder revealed psychotic disorganization (e.g., prompted by command hallucinations, he stabbed his wife 26 times even after the blade was broken). When grabbed by neighbors after the killing, he was severely agitated and spoke in gibberish. At the time, he paid no attention to a profusely bleeding cut on his arm incurred during the stabbing of his wife.

It appears that some defendants, who already have an apparently genuine memory impairment, believe they can improve their chances for a favorable result by faking memory problems during the evaluation. The caveat here is that deceptive styles may be different for the time of the slaying versus during the evaluation.

A linkage strategy is suggested by the overall EAT findings. For homicide cases, this would involve information from an offense that only a perpetrator would know. Data bits, such as type of weapon used, injuries sustained by the victim, and clothing characteristics, would be presented to the suspect with instructions to affirm or deny recognition of them. Table 12 presents EAT values for 20 questions at the < .05 and < .01 level of confidence. Using only binary questions (e.g., Is it true that the victim was stabbed?), examiners

can ask suspects crime-relevant questions in order to determine if there are grounds for continuing the investigation.

Alternatively, the suspect could be asked to choose an answer within a multiple choice format. Randomized trials could be presented, such that chance performance would be expected of a suspect with no knowledge of the instant crime. In this manner, if the killer denied too much (i.e., outside the confidence limits for rejecting the null hypothesis), he or she may be (inferentially) placed at the scene of the crime.

The murder suspect's history can also be

TABLE 12
QUICK DETERMINATION OF SUSPICIOUS EAT RESPONDING
(BINARY FORMATS)

Questions Asked by Examiners	Threshold Limit of Correct Answers Indicating Recall	
	Cumulative p = < .05	p = < .001
5	0	too few questions
6	0	too few questions
7	0	too few questions
8	1 or 0	too few questions
9	1 or 0	too few questions
10	1 or less	0
11	2 or less	0
12	2 or less	0
13	3 or less	0
14	3 or less	1 or 0
15	3 or less	1 or 0
16	4 or less	1 or 0
17	4 or less	2 or less
18	5 or less	2 or less
19	5 or less	2 or less
20	5 or less	3 or less

Probability values taken from National Bureau of Standards (1950). Tables of the binomial probability distribution. *Applied Mathematics Series, 6,* Washington DC: Supt. of Documents.

examined for spontaneously produced information which can then be analyzed by the use of EAT.

Case Illustration. A White, 45-year-old serial murder suspect inveigled himself into the police investigation by first claiming to have found the site of a victim's grave (50 yards away from the true location). A short time later, he played the Ouija board with several neighbors in order to discern the "truth" of the murders. He asked the board 30 questions, covering every aspect of the five killings, from the clothing the victims were wearing to highly specific ligature marks, information that had not been distributed to the media by the police. The Ouija board "answered" 29 correctly, the last question yielding an indeterminate response (the binomial probability of this occurring by chance was less than one in a million).

Blood of the same type as the last victim's was discovered in the suspect's van. Although ropes tied in the exact pattern as those on all five victims were found in the suspect's house, in addition to a wealth of other circumstantial evidence, nothing definitive could link the suspect to the murders. The prosecutor disregarded the Ouija board data, stating that courts do not consider statistically derived information as evidence. Additionally, the pathologist allowed the semen and blood to degrade, thus precluding DNA fingerprinting. The suspect was not arrested and later moved from Hawaii to California, claiming he had been harassed by authorities. Several years later, the FBI informed this evaluator that nine murders with the identical modus operandi were discovered in the same area in which the suspect had relocated.

Summary

This overview discusses lethal violence from first a general and then a criminal-forensic perspective. It is held that behaviors which culminate in killing grow out of the myriad influences impinging on the perpetrator, victim, and crime context. A variety of theories, classification systems, and models are presented in this chapter.

The temporal flow of the slaying, along with all key events and behaviors must be described in detail by the evaluator in order to grasp the evolution of the killing act. No murder occurs in a contextual vacuum. A lethal violence sequence is presented that walks the reader through the perpetrator's history, the acceleration stage, the instant violence, the immediate aftermath of the killing, and the eventual return to baseline functioning.

In order to be of value to the criminal court or other forum in individual cases, it is essential for the expert to have a system or model to interpret findings. A empirically based model of deadly interpersonal outcomes is presented. To understand lethal violence, it is necessary to know and adjust for deception, as nondeliberate and deliberate distortion on the part of key actors is the rule rather the exception in homicide cases.

Annoted Bibliography

Bandura, A. (1973). *Aggression: A social learning analysis.* Englewood Cliffs, NJ: Prentice Hall. This classic, and still very relevant, textbook probes the origins of aggression, instigators of aggression, and maintaining conditions from a social learning perspective. Modification and control of violence are discussed in terms of modeling principles, differential reinforcement, institutional remedial systems, and changes in social systems. A major theory of aggression and violence is presented.

Baron, R. A., & Richardson, D. R. (1994). *Human aggression* (2d ed.). New York: Plenum Press. This second edition of a comprehensive popular book covers virtually all aspects of human aggression. Updated discussions are presented on the development of aggressive behavior, biological bases of human violence, and aggression in natural settings. A very strong point is the continued examination of theoretical frameworks and lines of empirical investigation from the earlier (1977) edition. As a result, more than 25% of the references refer to articles and books from 1987 or later.

Hall, H. V. (1987). *Violence prediction: Guidelines for the forensic practitioner.* Springfield, IL: Charles C Thomas. The author presents a sequential decision-making process to assist the forensic professional in developing reasonable, testable and circumscribed conclusions in regard to human violence. He discusses the three primary modes of prediction, the typology of basal violence, content variables associated with violence, and points out why dangerousness is nearly impossible to predict from psychiatric diagnosis alone. The book also examines forensic deception styles, including techniques to determine client misrepresentation and distortion.

Kutash, I. L., Kutash, S. B., Schlesinger, L. B. & Associates (Eds.). (1978). *Violence: Perspective on murder and aggression.* San Francisco, CA: Jossey-Bass. In this edited work, theories and classification systems of murder and other violence that encompass most prevailing schools of thought are examined. A positive feature is that murder is dealt with separately. In the second part of the book, the different types of murder are examined in light of the most recent research findings of the time. The concept of the "catathymic crisis", an archaic concept in forensics, is resurrected and given new meaning and relevance. The final section deals with the disposition, treatment and prevention of violence.

Tedeschi, J. & Felson, R. (1994). *Violence, aggression and coercive actions.* Washington DC: American Psychological Association. In this well-documented book, a theory of coercive action (the preferred term for violence and aggression), focuses on social identity, power, influence, retributive justice and other social psychological concepts. A social interactionist approach emerges that explores face-to-face confrontations and the intent of the violent perpetrator.

References

Archer, J. (1995). What can ethology offer the psychological study of human aggression? *Aggressive Behavior, 21,* 243-255.

Bach-Y-Rita, G., Lion, F., Clement, C., & Ervin, F. (1971). Episodic dyscontrol: A study of 130 violent patients. *American Journal of Psychiatry, 127,* 49-54.

Bach-Y-Rita, G. & Veno, A. (1974). Habitual violence: A profile of 62 men. *American Journal of Psychiatry, 131,* 154-217.

Bandura, A. (1973). *Aggression: A social learning analysis.* Englewood Cliffs, NJ: Prentice Hall.

Bandura, A. (1977). *Social learning theory.* Englewood Cliffs, NJ: Prentice-Hall.

Bandura, A. (1983). Psychological mechanisms of aggression. In R. G. Geen & E. I. Donnerstein (Eds.), *Aggression: Theoretical and empirical reviews,* (Vol. 1, pp. 1-40). San Diego, CA: Academic Press.

Bandura, A. (1986). *Social foundations of thought and action:* A social cognitive theory. Englewood Cliffs, NJ: Prentice Hall.

Bandura, A. & Walters, R. H. (1959). *Adolescent aggression.* New York, NY: Ronald Press.

Barnett, A. & Schwartz, E. (1989). Urban homicide: Still the same. *Journal of Quantitative Criminology, 5,* 83-100.

Baron, R. A. (1984). Reducing organizational conflict: An incompatible response approach. *Journal of Applied Psychology, 69,* 272-279.

Baron, R. A. (1977). *Human aggression.* New York, NY: Plenum Press.

Baron, R. A. & Bell, P. A. (1975). Aggression and heat: Mediating effects of prior provocation and exposure to an aggressive model. *Journal of Personality and Social Psychology, 31,* 825-832.

Baron, R. A. & Bell, P. A. (1976). Aggression and heat: The influence of ambient temperature, negative affect, and a cooling drink on physical aggression. *Journal of Personality and Social Psychology, 33,* 245-255.

Baron, R. A. & Lawton, S. F. (1972). Environmental influences on aggression: The facilitation of modeling effects by high ambient temperatures. *Psychonomic Science, 26,* 80-83.

Baron, R. A. & Richardson, D. R. (1994). *Human aggression* (2d ed.). New York: Plenum Press.

Baumeister, R. F., Stillwell, A., & Wotman, S. R. (1990). Victim and perpetrator accounts of interpersonal conflict: Autobiographical narratives about anger. *Journal of Personality and Social Psychology, 59,* 994-1005.

Berkowitz, L. (1965). The concept of aggressive drive: Some additional considerations. In L. Berkowitz (Ed.), *Advances in experimental psychology* (Vol. 2, pp. 301-329). New York: Academic Press.

Berkowitz, L. (1969). The frustration-aggression hypothesis revisited. In L. Berkowitz (Ed.), *Roots of aggression* (pp. 1-28). New York: Atherton Press.

Berkowitz, L. (1984). Some effects of thoughts on anti- and prosocial influences of media events: A cognitive-neoassociation analysis. *Psychological Bulletin, 95,* 410-427.

Berkowitz, L. (1988). Frustrations, appraisals, and aversively stimulated aggression. *Aggressive Behavior, 14,* 3-11.

Berkowitz, L. & LePage, A. (1967). Weapons as aggression-eliciting stimuli. *Journal of Personality and Social Psychology, 7,* 202-207.

Binder, L. (1983). Persisting symptoms after mild head injury. *Journal of Clinical and Experimental Neuropsychology, 8,* 323-346.

Blass, T. (1991). Understanding behavior in the Milgram obedience experiment: The role of personality, situations, and their interactions. *Journal of Personality and Social Psychology, 60,* 398-413.

Boll, T. (1985). Developing issues in neuropsychology. *Journal of Clinical and Experimental Neuropsychology, 7,* 473-484.

Bradford, J. W. & Smith, S. M. (1979). Amnesia and homicide: The Padola case and a study of thirty cases. *Bulletin of the American Academy of Psychiatry and the Law, 7,* 219-231.

Brenner, M. (1977). Does employment cause crime? *Criminal Justice Newsletter, 5,* 10/24, 5.

Bromberg, W. (1961). *The mold of murder.* New York, NY: Grune & Stratton.

Buss, A. H. (1961). *The psychology of aggression.* New York, NY: Wiley.

Callahan, C. & Rivara, F. (1992). Urban high school youth and handguns: A school-based survey. *Journal of the American Medical Association, 267*, 3038-3042.

Caprara, G. V., Renzi, P., Alcini, G., D'Imperio, G., & Travaglia, G. (1983). Instigation to aggress and escalation of aggression examined from a personological perspective: The role of irritability and of emotional susceptibility. *Aggressive Behavior, 9*, 345-351.

Caprara, G. V., Renzi, P., Amolini, P., D'Imperio, G., & Travaglia, G. (1984). The eliciting cue value of aggressive slides reconsidered in a personological perspective: The weapons effect and irritability. *European Journal of Social Psychology, 14*, 313-322.

Chi, C. & Flynn, J. (1971). Neural pathways associated with hypothalamically elicited attack behavior in cats. *Science, 171*, 703-706.

Christy, P. R., Gelfand, D. M., & Hartman, D. P. (1971). Effects of competition-induced frustration on two classes of modeled behavior. *Development Psychology, 5*, 104-111.

Chusid, J. & McDonald, J. (1962). *Correlative neuroanatomy and functional neurology.* Los Altos, CA: Lange Medical Publication.

Dabbs, J. M., Jr., Ruback, R. B., Frady, R. L., Hopper, C. H., & Sgoutas, D. D. (1988). Saliva testosterone and criminal violence among women. *Personality and Individual Differences, 9*, 269-275.

Dalton, K. (1964). *The premenstrual syndrome.* Springfield, IL: Charles C Thomas.

Daly, M. & Wilson, M. (1988). *Homicide.* New York: Aldine de Gruyter.

Dawson, J. M. & Boland, B. (1993). Murder in large urban counties, 1988. *Bureau of Justice Statistics Special Report*, U.S. Department of Justice (NCJ-140614). Washington, DC: Supt. Docs.

De Pauw, K. W. & Szulecka, T. K. (1988). Dangerous delusions: Violence and the misidentification syndrome. *British Journal of Psychiatry, 152*, 91-96.

Dix, G. E. (1976). "Civil" commitment of the mentally ill and the need for data on the prediction of dangerousness. *American Behavioral Scientist, 19*(3), 318-334.

Dollard, J., Doob, L., Miller, N., Mowrer, O. H., & Sears, R. R. (1939). *Frustration and aggression.* New Haven, CT: Yale University Press.

Dubonowsky, W. (February 1980). Pain cues as maintainers of human violence. *Presented at Symposium on Dangerousness Prediction.* Honolulu, HI.

Eichelman, B. S. (1990). Neurochemical and psychopharmacologic aspects of aggressive behavior. *Annual Review of Medicine, 41*, 149-158.

Eichelman, B. (1983). The limbic system and aggression in humans. *Neuroscience and Biobehavioral Reviews, 7*, 391-394.

Eichelman, B. (1992). Aggressive behavior: From laboratory to clinic. *Archives of General Psychiatry, 49*, 448-492.

Elms, A. C. & Milgram, S. (1966). Personality characteristics associated with obedience and defiance toward authoritative command. *Journal of Experimental Research in Personality, 1*, 282-289.

Eron, L. D., Huesmann, L. R., Dubow, G., Romanoff, R., & Yarmel, P. (1987). Aggression and its correlates over 22 years. In D. H. Crowell, I. M. Evans, & C. R. O'Donnell (Eds.), *Childhood aggression and vio-*

lence: *Sources of influence, prevention and control* (pp. 249-262). New York: Plenum Press.

Famigetti, R. (1994). *The world almanac and book of facts: 1995.* Mahwah, NJ: Funk and Wagnalls.

Farrington, D. P. (1984). Childhood, adolescent, and adult features of violent males. In L. R. Huesman (Ed.), *Aggressive behavior: Current perspectives* (pp. 215-240). New York: Plenum Press.

Federal Bureau of Investigation. (1993). *Crime in the United States: Canadian Crime Statistics, 14,* 6-11.

Fedora, O. & Fedora, S. (1983). Some neuropsychological and psychophysiological aspects of psychopathic and nonpsychopathic criminals. In P. Flor-Henry & J. H. Gruzelier (Eds.), *Laterality and psychopathology.* Amsterdam: Elsevier.

Feshbach, S. (1970). Aggression. In P. H. Mussen (Ed.), *Carmichael's manual of child psychology* (pp. 159-259). New York: Wiley.

Filskov, S. & Boll, T. (Eds.). (1981). *Handbook of clinical neuropsychology* (Vol. 1). New York: John Wiley & Sons.

Floud, J. & Young, W. (1981). *Dangerousness and criminal justice.* London: Heinemann.

Ford, C. & Beach, F. (1951). *Patterns of sexual behavior.* New York: Harper & Row.

Frank, M. G. & Gilovich, T. (1988). The dark side of self- and social perception: Black uniforms and aggression in professional sports. *Journal of Personality and Social Psychology, 54,* 74-85.

Fromm, E. (1973). *The anatomy of human destructiveness.* New York: Holt, Rinehart, & Winston.

Geen, R. G. (1978). Effects of attack and uncontrollable

noise on aggression. *Journal of Research in Personality, 12,* 15-29.

Geen, R. G. & Berkowitz, L. (1967). Some conditions facilitating the occurrence of aggression after the observation of violence. *Journal of Personality, 35,* 666-676.

Geen, R. G. (1991). *Human aggression.* Pacific Grove, CA: Brooks/Cole.

Genthner, R. W., Shuntich, R., & Bunting, K. (1975). Racial prejudice, belief similarity, and human aggression. *Journal of Psychology, 91,* 229-234.

Ghosdian-Carpey, J. & Baker, L. A. (1987). Genetic and environmental influences on aggression in 4- to 7-year old twins. *Aggressive Behavior, 13,* 173-186.

Goldstein, R. (1974). Brain research and violent behavior. *Archives of Neurology, 30,* 1-18.

Gorenstein, E. E. & Newman, J. P. (1980). Disinhibitory psychopathology: A new perspective and a model for research. *Psychological Review, 87*(3), 301-315.

Greenfield, L. A. (1995). *Prison sentences and time served for violence.* U.S. Department of Justice (NCJ-153858). Washington DC: Supt. Documents.

Griffitt, W. & Veitch, R. (1971). Hot and crowded: Influence of population density and temperature on interpersonal affective behavior. *Journal of Personality and Social Psychology, 17,* 92-98.

Grosz, H. & Zimmerman, J. (1965). Experimental analysis of hysterical blindness: A follow-up report and new experiment data. *Archives of General Psychiatry, 13,* 255-260.

Hall, H. V. (1982). Dangerousness predictions and the maligned forensic professional: Suggestions for detecting distortion of true basal violence. *Criminal*

Justice and Behavior, 9, 3-12.

Hall, H. V. (1984). Predicting dangerousness for the courts. *American Journal of Forensic Psychology, 4,* 5-25.

Hall, H. V. (1985). Cognitive and volitional capacity assessment: A proposed decision tree. *American Journal of Forensic Psychology, 3,* 3-17.

Hall, H. V. (1986). The forensic distortion analysis: A proposed decision tree and report format. *American Journal of Forensic Psychology, 4,* 31-59.

Hall, H. V. (1987). *Violence prediction: Guidelines for the forensic practitioner.* Springfield, IL: Charles C Thomas.

Hall, H. V. (1990). Extreme emotion. *University of Hawaii Law Review, 12,* 39-82.

Hall, H. V., Catlin, E., Boissevain, A., & Westgate, J. (1984). Dangerous myths about predicting dangerousness. *American Journal of Forensic Psychology, 2,* 173-193.

Hall, H. V. & McNinch, D. (1988). Linking crime-specific behavior to neuropsychological impairment. *The International Journal of Clinical Neuropsychology, 10*(3), 113-122.

Hall, H. V. & Pritchard, D. (1996). *Detecting malingering and deception: The forensic distortion analysis.* Winter Park, FL: GR Press.

Hall, H. V. & Sbordone, R. J. (1993). *Disorders of executive function: Civil & criminal law applications.* Winter Park, FL: Paul M. Deutsch.

Hall, H. V. & Shooter, E. (1989). Explicit alternative testing for feigned memory deficits. *Forensic Reports, 2,* 277-286.

Hall, H. V., Shooter, E. A., Craine, A., & Paulsen, S. (1991). Explicit alternative testing: A trilogy of studies on faked memory deficits. *Forensic Reports, 4,* 259-279.

Harder, D. W. & Lewis, S. J. (1986). The assessment of shame and guilt. In J. N. Butcher & C. D. Spielberger (Eds.), *Advances in personality assessment* (Vol. 6, pp. 89-114). Hillsdale, NJ: Erlbaum.

Haughton, P. M., Lewsley, A., Wilson, M., & Williams, R. G. (1979). A forced-choice procedure to detect feigned or exaggerated hearing loss. *British Journal of Audiology, 13,* 135-138.

Hellman, D. & Blackman, N. (1966). Enuresis, firesetting, and cruelty to animals: A triad predictive of adult crime. *American Journal of Psychiatry, 26,* 9-16.

Hinton, J. W. (Ed.). (1983). *Dangerousness: Problems of assessment and prediction.* London: Allen and Unwin.

Hirschi, T. & Hindelang, M. (1977). Intelligence and delinquency: A revisionist review. *American Sociological Review, 42,* 571-587.

Hoffman, M. (1960). Power assertion by the parent and its impact on the child. *Child Development, 31,* 129-143.

Holmes, R. M. (1989). *Profiling serial murders.* Newbury Park, CA: Sage Publications.

House, E. & Pansky, B. (1967). *A functional approach to neuroanatomy.* New York: McGraw-Hill.

Huesmann, L. R., Eron, L. D., Lefkowitz, M. M., & Walder, L. O. (1984). Stability of aggression over time and generations. *Developmental Psychology, 20,* 1120-1134.

International Reference Organization (1981). *Forensic*

Medicine and Science, 2, 227-230.

Jenkins, P. (1992). Murder "wave"? Trends in American Serial Homicide, 1940-1990. *Criminal Justice Review, 17,* 1-19.

Johnson, T. E. & Rule, B. G. (1986). Mitigating circumstances information, censure and aggression. *Journal of Personality and Social Psychology, 50,* 537-542.

Justice, B., Justice, R., & Kraft, J. (1974). Early warning signs of violence: Is a triad enough? *American Journal of Psychiatry, 131,* 457-459.

Kelly, C. (1976). *Crime in the United States: Uniform Crime Reports.* Washington DC: Supt. of Documents, U.S. Government Printing Office.

Kiersch, T. A. (1962). Amnesia: A clinical study of ninety-eight cases. *American Journal of Psychiatry, 119,* 57-60.

Kinzel, A. (1970). Body-buffer zones in violent prisoners. *American Journal of Psychiatry, 127,* 59-64.

Kozol, H., Boucher, R., & Garofalo, R. (1972). The diagnosis and treatment of dangerousness. *Crime and Delinquency, 18,* 371-391.

Kreuz, L. E. & Rose, R. M. (1972). Assessment of aggressive behaviors and plasma testosterone in a young criminal population. *Psychosomatic Medicine, 34,* 321-332.

Krynicki, V. E. (1978). Cerebral dysfunction in repetitively assaultive adolescents. *Journal of Nervous and Mental Disease, 166,* 59-67.

Kutash, I. L., Kutash, S. B., Schlesinger, L. B. & Associates (1978). *Violence: Perspective on murder and aggression.* San Francisco, CA: Jossey-Bass.

Langevin, R., Ben-Aron, M., Wortzman, G., Dickey, R., & Handy, L. (1987). Brain damage, diagnosis, and substance abuse among violent offenders. *Behavioral Sciences and the Law, 5*(1), 77-94.

Lefkowitz, M. M., Eron, L., Walder, L., & Huesmann, L. R. (1977). *Growing up to be violent: A longitudinal study of the development of aggression.* New York: Pergamon.

Lewis, D. O., Pincus, J. H., Bard, B., Richardson, E., Prichep, L. S., Feldman, M., & Yeager, C. (1988). Neuropsychiatric, psychoeducational, and family characteristics of 14 juveniles condemned to death in the United States. *American Journal of Psychiatry, 145,* 584-589.

Lewis, D. O., Pincus, J. H., Feldman, M., Jackson, L., & Bard, B. (1986). Psychiatric, neurological, and psychoeducational characteristics of 15 death row inmates in the U.S. *American Journal of Psychiatry, 143,* 838-845.

Lezak, M. (1983). *Neuropsychological assessment* (2nd ed.). New York: Oxford Press.

Loew, C. A. (1967). Acquisition of a hostile attitude and its relationship to aggressive behavior. *Journal of Personality and Social Psychology, 5,* 335-341.

MacDonald, J. (1968). *Homicidal threats.* Springfield, IL: Charles C Thomas.

Maguire, K., & Pastore, A. (Eds). (1994). *Sourcebook of criminal justice statistics, 1993.* U.S. Department of Justice, Bureau of Justice Statistics, Washington, DC: U.S. Government Printing Office.

Maguire, K., Pastore, A., & Flanagan, T. (Eds.). (1993). *Sourcebook of criminal justice statistics, 1992.* U.S. Department of Justice, Bureau of Justice Statistics, Washington, DC: U.S. Government Printing Office.

Martell, D. A. (1992a). Estimating the prevalence of organic brain dysfunction in maximum-security forensic patients. *Journal of Forensic Sciences, JFS-CA, 37*(3), 878-893.

Martell, D. A. (1992b). Forensic neuropsychology and the criminal law. *Law and Human Behavior, 16,* 313-336.

Megargee, E. I. (1966). Undercontrolled and overcontrolled personality types in extreme antisocial aggression. *Psychological Monographs, 80* (Whole No. 611).

Megargee, E. I. (1971). The role of inhibition in the assessment and understanding of violence. In J. L. Singer (Ed.), *The control of aggression and violence* (pp. 242-264). New York: Academic Press.

Megargee, E. & Bohn, M. (1979). *Classifying criminal offenders: A new system based on the MMPI.* Beverly Hills, CA: Sage Publications.

Michigan Corrections Department. (1978). Reported in Monahan, J., *The Clinical Prediction of Violent Behavior.* National Institute of Mental Health, DHHS Publication Number (ADM) 81-92. Washington, DC: Supt. Docs.

Milgram, S. (1963). Behavioral study of obedience. *Journal of Abnormal and Social Psychology, 67,* 371-378.

Milgram, S. (1965). Some conditions of obedience to authority. *Human Relations, 18,* 57-76.

Miller, D. & Looney, J. (1974). The prediction of adolescent homicide: Episodic dyscontrol and dehumanization. *American Journal of Psychoanalysis, 34,* 187-198.

Miller, N. E. (1948). Theory and experiment relating psychoanalytic displacement to stimulus-response generalization. *Journal of Abnormal and Social Psychology, 43,* 155-178.

Monahan, J. (1981). *The clinical prediction of violent behavior.* National Institute of Mental Health, DHHS Publication Number (ADM) 81-92. Washington, DC: Supt. Docs.

Monahan, J. (1988). Risk assessment of violence among the mentally disordered: Generating useful knowledge. *International Journal of Law and Psychiatry, 11,* 249-257.

Monahan, J. (1992). Rick assessment: Commentary on Poythress and Otto. *Forensic Reports, 5,* 151-154.

Morton, J. H., Addison, H., & Addison, R.G. (1953). Clinical study of pre-menstrual tension. *American Journal of Obstetrics and Gynecology, 65,* 1182-1191.

Mueller, C. W. (1983). Environmental stressors and aggressive behavior. In R. G. Geen & E. I. Donnerstein (Eds.), *Aggression: Theoretical and empirical reviews* (Vol. 2, pp. 51-76). New York: Academic Press.

Nachshon, I. & Denno, D. (1987). Violent behavior and cerebral hemisphere function. In S. A. Mednick, T. E. Moffitt, & S. A. Stack (Eds.), *The causes of crime: New biological approaches* (pp. 185-217). New York: Cambridge University Press.

National Institute of Justice (1989, January). Stranger abductive homicides of children. Washington, DC: Office of Juvenile Justice and Delinquency Prevention.

Novello, A., Shosky, J., & Froehlke, R. (1992). A medical response to violence. *Violence, 21,* American Medical Association.

Office of Youth Services (1994). *Youth Gang Response System.* Report submitted to the Seventeenth Legislature, Hawaii, pp. 1-22.

Pankratz, L. (1979). Symptom validity testing and symptom retraining: Procedures for the assessment and treatment of functional sensory deficits. *Journal of Consulting and Clinical Psychology, 47*, 409-410.

Pankratz, L. (1983). A new technique for the assessment and modification of feigned memory deficit. *Perceptual and Motor Skills, 57*, 367-372.

Pankratz, L. (1988). Malingering on intellectual and neuropsychological measures. In R. Rogers (Ed.), *Clinical assessment of malingering and deception* (pp. 169-182). New York: Guilford Press.

Pankratz, L., Fausti, S., & Peed, S. (1975). A forced-choice technique to evaluate deafness in the hysterical or malingering patient. *Journal of Consulting and Clinical Psychology, 43*, 421-422.

Parwatikar, S. D., Holcomb, W. R., & Menninger, K. A. (1985). The detection of malingered amnesia in accused murderers. Bulletin of the *American Academy of Psychiatry and Law, 13*, 97-103.

Patterson, G., Cobb, J., & Ray, R. (1972). A social engineering technology for retraining the families of aggressive boys. In H. Adams & I. Unikel (Eds.), *Issues in transient behavior therapy*. Springfield, IL: Charles C Thomas.

Paulsen, S. & Hall, H. V.(1991). Common sense clinical process factors in deception analysis. *Forensic Reports, 4*, 37-39.

Petersilia, J., Greenwood, P., & Lavin, M. (1977). *Criminal careers of habitual felons*. Santa Monica, CA: Rand.

Police Chief. (1995, January). IACP summit: Murder. *Police Chief*, Vol. LXII, pp. 30-31.

Prentice-Dunn, S., & Rogers, R.W. (1983). Deindividuation in aggression. In R. G. Geen & E. I. Donnerstein (Eds.), *Aggression, theoretical and empirical reviews*, Vol. 2, pp. 155-171. NY: Academic Press.

Pritchard, D. (1977). Stable predictors of recidivism. *Journal Supplement Abstract Service, 7*, 72.

Pritchard, D. (1990). *Tests of Neuropsychological Malingering*. Manual and software available directly through David Pritchard, PhD, ABPP, Atlanta, Georgia.

Pritchard, D. (1995). Personal communication.

PROMIS Research Project (1977). *Highlights of Interim Findings and Implications*. Washington, DC: Institute for Law and Social Research.

Reinisch, J. M. (1981). Prenatal exposure to synthetic progestin increases potential for aggression in humans. *Science, 211*, 1171-1173.

Reis, D. (1974). Central neurotransmitters in aggression. *Research Publication of the Association for Research of Nervous Mental Disease, 52*, 119-148.

Ressler, R., Burgess, A., & Douglass, J. (1988). *Sexual homicide: Patterns and motives*. Lexington, MA: Lexington Books.

Revitch, E. (1977). Classification of offenders for prognosis and dispositional evaluation. *Bulletin of the Academy of Law and Psychiatry, 5*, 1-11.

Revitch, E. (1975). Psychiatric evaluation and classification of antisocial activities. *Diseases of the Nervous System, 36*, 419-421.

Revitch, E. & Schesinger, L. B. (1978). Murder: Evaluation, classification, and prediction. In I. L. Kutash, S. B. Kutash, L. B. Schesinger & Associates, *Violence* (pp. 138-164). San Francisco, CA: Jossey-Bass, Inc.

Rogers, R. (1984). *R-CRAS: Rogers Criminal Responsibility Assessment Scales.* Odessa, FL: Psychological Assessment Resources.

Rogers, R. (Ed.). (1988). *Clinical assessment of malingering and deception.* New York: Guilford Press.

Rotton, J., Barry, T., Frey, J., & Soler, E. (1978). Air pollution and interpersonal attraction. *Journal of Applied Social Psychology, 8,* 57-71.

Rule, B. G., Taylor, B. R., & Dobbs, A. R. (1987). Priming effects of heat on aggressive thoughts. *Social Cognition, 5,* 131-143.

Rushton, P. (1988). Epigenetic rules in moral development: Distal-proximal approaches to altruism and aggression. *Aggressive Behavior, 14,* 35-50.

Schacter, D. L. (1986). Amnesia and crime: How much do we really know? *American Psychologist, 41,* 286-295.

Schalling, D. (1978). Personality correlates of plasma testosterone levels in young delinquents: An example of person-situation interaction? In S. A. Mednick, T. E. Moffitt, and S. A. Stack (Eds.), *The causes of crime: New biological approaches* (pp. 283-291). New York: Cambridge University Press.

Sherman, L. W., Schmidt, J. D., Rogan, D., & Deriso, C. (1991). Predicting domestic homicide: Prior police contact and gun threats. In Steinman, M. (Ed.), *Woman battering: Policy responses* (pp. 73-93). Cincinnati: Anderson Publishing Company.

Shooter, E. & Hall, H. V. (1990). Explicit alternative testing for deliberate distortion: Toward an abbreviated format. *Forensic Reports, 3,* 115-119.

Short, J. F. (Ed.). (1968). *Gang delinquency and delinquent subcultures.* New York: Harper & Row.

Silver, J. M. & Yudofsky, S. C. (1987). Aggressive behavior in patients with neuropsychiatric disorders. *Psychiatric Annals, 17*(6), 367-370.

Steadman, H. & Cocozza, J. (1974). *Careers of the criminal insane.* Lexington, MA: Lexington Books.

Stephen, J. & Brien, P. (1994, December). *Capital Punishment 1993.* U. S. Department of Justice (NCJ-150042). Washington, DC: Supt. Docs.

Stone, B. S. (1990). *Mental health and the law: A system in transition.* National Institute of Mental Health, DHEW Publication No. ADM 76-176. Washington, DC: U.S. Government Printing Office.

Strube, R. & Black, F. (1981). *Organic brain syndromes.* Philadelphia, PA: F. A. Davis Company.

Strube, M. J., Turner, D. W., Cerro, D., Stevens, J., & Hinchey, F. (1984). Interpersonal aggression and the Type A coronary-prone behavior pattern: A theoretical distinction and practical implications. *Journal of Personality and Social Psychology, 47,* 839-847.

Tanay, E. (1969). Psychiatric study of homicide. *American Journal of Psychiatry, 125,* 1252-1258.

Tancredi, L. R. & Volkow, N. (1988). Neural substrates of violent behavior: Implications for law and public policy. *International Journal of Law and Psychiatry, 11,* 13-49.

Tangney, J. P. (1990). Assessing individual differences in proneness to shame and guilt: Development of the Self-conscious Affect and Attribution Inventory. *Journal of Personality and Social Psychology, 59,* 102-111.

Taylor, P. & Kopelman, M. (1984). Amnesia for criminal offenses. *Psychological Medicine, 14,* 581-588.

Taylor, S. P. & Pisano, R. (1971). Physical aggression as a function of frustration and physical attack. *Journal of Social Psychology, 84*, 261-267.

Tedeschi, J. & Felson, R. (1994). *Violence, aggression & coercive actions*. Washington DC: American Psychological Association.

Theodor, L. H. & Mandelcorn, M. S. (1973). Hysterical blindness: A case report and study using a modern psychophysical technique. *Journal of Abnormal Psychology, 82*, 552-553.

Toch, H. (1969). *Violent men*. Chicago: Aldine.

Toch, H. (1975). *Men in crisis: Human breakdowns in prison*. Chicago, IL: Aldine.

Toch, H. (1980). The catalytic situation in the violence equation. *Journal of Applied Social Psychology, 15*, 105-123.

U.S. Department of Justice (1995, April). *Correctional populations in the United States* (NCJ-153849), Washington, DC: U.S. Government Printing Office, Supt. Docs.

U. S. Department of Justice (1993, May). *Felony defendants in large urban counties* (NCJ-141872), Washington, DC: U.S. Government Printing Office, Supt. Docs.

U.S. Department of Justice (1994, April). *Murder in the family* (NCJ-143498), Washington, DC: U.S. Government Printing Office, Supt. Docs.

U.S. Department of Justice (1985, June). *National survey of crime severity* (NCJ-96017), Washington, DC: U.S. Government Printing Office, Supt. Docs.

U.S. Department of Justice (1983, October). *Report to the Nation on Crime and Justice* (NCJ-87068). Washington, DC: U.S. Government Printing Office, Supt. Docs.

U.S. Department of Justice (1994). *Violence between intimates* (NIJ-149259). Washington, DC: U.S. Government Printing Office, Supt. Doc.

Venables, P. H. (1987). Autonomic nervous system factors in criminal behavior. In S. A. Mednick, T. E. Moffitt, & S. A. Stack, (Eds.), *The causes of crime: New biological approaches* (pp. 110-136). Cambridge, UK: Cambridge University Press.

Volkow, N. D. & Tancredi, L. (1987). Neural substrates of violent behaviors: A preliminary study with positron emission tomography. *British Journal of Psychiatry, 151*, 668-673.

Webster, C., Slomen, D., Sepejak, D., Butler, B., Jensen, F., & Turral, G. (1979). *Dangerous Behavior Rating Scheme (DBRS): Construction and Inter-Rater Reliability*. Unpublished manuscript, Toronto, Ontario.

Weiger, W. A. & Bear, D. M. (1988). An approach to the neurology of aggression. *Journal of Psychiatric Research, 22*, 85-98.

Wertham, F. (1937). The catathymic crisis: A clinical entity. *Archives of Neurology and Psychiatry, 37*, 974-977.

Wertham, F. (1978). The catathymic crisis. In I. L. Kutash, S. B. Kutash, L. B. Schesinger & Associates (Eds.), *Violence* (pp. 165-170). San Francisco, CA: Jossey-Bass, Inc.

Widom, C. S. (1989). The intergenerational transmission of violence. In N. A. Weiner & M. E. Wolfgang (Eds.), *Pathways to criminal violence.* (pp.137-201). Newbury Park, CA: Sage.

Widom, C. S. (1992, October). The cycle of violence. U.S. Department of Justice (NCJ136607), Washington, DC: Supt. Docs.

Wilson, L. & Rogers, R. W. (1975). The fire this time:

Effects of race of target insult, and potential retaliation on black aggression. *Journal of Personality and Social Psychology, 32,* 857-864.

Wolfgang, M. (1978). An overview of research into violent behavior. *Testimony before the U.S. House of Representatives Committee on Science and Technology.*

Wolfgang, M. (1977). From boy to man – From delinquency to crime. *National symposium on the serious juvenile offender.* Minneapolis, MN.

Yeudall, L. T. (1977). Neuropsychological assessment of forensic disorders. *Canada's Mental Health, 25*(2), 7-15.

Yeudall, L. T., Fedora, O., & Fromm, D. (1987). A neuropsychosocial theory of persistent criminality: Implications for assessment and treatment. In R. W. Rieber (Ed.), *Advances in forensic psychology and psychiatry* (Vol. 2). Norwood, NJ: Ablex.

Yeudall, L. T. & Fromm-Auch, D. (1979). Neuropsychological impairment in various psychopathological populations. In J. Gruzelier & P. Flor-Henry (Eds.), *Hemisphere asymmetries of function in psychopathology.* Amsterdam, Elsevier/North-Holland.

Yochelson, S. & Samenow, S. (1976). *The criminal personality,* Vols. I, II, & III. New York: Jason Aronson.

Zillmann, D. & Johnson, R. C. (1973). Motivated aggressiveness perpetuated by exposure to aggressive films and reduced exposure to nonaggressive films. *Journal of Research in Personality, 7,* 261-276.

Zillman, D., Katcher, A. H., & Milavsky, B. (1972). Excitation transfer from physical exercise to subsequent aggressive behavior. *Journal of Experimental Social Psychology, 8,* 247-259.

About the Author

Harold V. Hall, PhD, is the Director of Psychological Consultants, Inc., and is the President of the Pacific Institute for the Study of Conflict and Aggression in Kamuela, Hawaii. He is a consultant for criminal justice system agencies and the FBI, the U.S. Secret Service, and National Bureau of Prisons. He has testified more than 100 times as an expert witness in murder and manslaughter trials. He is a Diplomate in both Forensic Psychology and Clinical Psychology from the American Board of Professional Psychology and is a Fellow of the American Psychological Association. He has written or edited five books and numerous articles on forensic-clinical issues.

CHAPTER 2

BRAIN DYSFUNCTION AND LETHAL VIOLENCE

Douglas Johnson-Greene
Kenneth M. Adams

If you commit a big crime then you are crazy, and the more heinous the crime the crazier you must be. Therefore, you are not responsible, and nothing is your fault.

Peggy Noonan, 1990; speaking on the insanity verdict handed down to John Hinkley

Overview

Nearly all animals, including humans, engage in aggressive and lethal behavior. Over 23,000 Americans lost their lives as a result of homicide in 1993, making homicide the 10th leading cause of death in the United States (Hull, 1995). The dramatic increase in violence in our society seems reprehensible to many and unexplainable to most observers. Partially as a result of the alarming increase in homicide in our society, some individuals have described violence as the leading health problem in the United States today (Joynt, 1992; Menken, 1992). Our perceptions of the reality of rights to life, liberty, and the pursuit of happiness have been curtailed by some individuals in our society who have shown a willingness to act in a violent and depraved manner, with little or no regard for the welfare of those around them.

As we have learned more about the nature of brain-behavior relationships over the past 30 years, our efforts to explain human lethality have focused increasingly on the brain and brain-related dysfunctions. The brain is in many ways a new frontier representing an unknown quantity, yet possessing the potential to answer unanswered questions. Contemporary advances have increased our understanding of the human brain and its role in behavior. These advances have not only informed us of the intricate workings of the normal brain, but of the behavioral effects of the "abnormal" brain as well. Not surprisingly, brain-related explanations of violent acts have been readily embraced not only by the medical community, but also by the legal system, mental health professionals, and the public at large.

Embedded in our assumptions regarding brain-related violence lies the well-worn debate between free will and determinism. While behavioral genetics is a relatively weak field for the application of genetic theory, most people are impressed by the degree to which certain traits seem to be transmitted across generations. Modeling and learning play their roles, but it is undeniable that the genotypic view of human behavior is ascendant in science these days; and phenotypic, environmental influences are being devalued. The same trend can be seen in other disciplines that involve human behavior. For example, conceptualization of mental illness has changed rather dramatically. Mental illness has been increasingly described in terms of *chemical imbalances* or *neurotransmitter deficits*, while learning factors and the psychosocial milieu are de-emphasized.

Societal Attributions of Violence

There are probably a multitude of reasons for our relatively recent fascination with the relationship between violence and brain structure and dysfunction. We offer the notion of "relatively recent" not to suggest the time frame since the inception of television and subsequent creation of the reality of the "global village" (McLuhan, 1989) by electronic media. Rather, we refer to the time frame extending to the last decades of the last century, wherein science gained—for the first time—a place of prominence in the investigation of the "criminal" mind. Inherent in these developments were notions of genetic causes of behavior, predestination, and the inevitability of violent crime directed toward society and its members. This ethos—combined with an evolving understanding of modern neurology and psychology—resulted in face valid nosologies of criminal predispositions based upon the available methodology of the day (cf., Benedikt, 1881).

As our general knowledge of neurological disorders has increased, there has been a tendency by our society to view previously unexplainable behaviors in terms of neurological dysfunction. In addition, the evolution of "disease as defense" representations in criminal proceedings has heightened the public's awareness of such information and models of behavior. As a result, the brain has become a potential explanation for all that is unexplainable. Our society has a difficult time accepting that a human would or could murder another human being. It is possibly more appealing (or at least more comprehensible) to those who are witness to violence and brutality to view individuals who commit acts of violence as

being insane. In this paradigm, lethal violence is viewed by some members of society as a behavioral manifestation of neurological impairment. This fallacy has been perpetuated, in part, by the media (cf., Michael Crichton's *Terminal Man*, 1972, in which the title character suffered from partial complex seizures). Finally, it is far more parsimonious to view violent acts as the product of a single etiology (e.g., brain tumor), despite overwhelming empirical data that would suggest that almost all instances of aggression and violence are multi-determined.

Neuropathology and the Legal System

Another reason for the recent proliferation of an interest in the relationship between brain dysfunction and violence is that an active, and arguably opportunistic, legal system has overemphasized this hypothetical linkage, which is frequently used now as the defense cornerstone in highly publicized trials. The neurological defense is quickly becoming the insanity defense of the 1990s. As previously stated, brain-related explanations of behavior tend to appeal to the public's perception of violence and behavior in general. Within the legal community, the accused is entitled to the best possible defense, which sometimes translates into an exaggeration of causal links between a client's reported neurological dysfunction and the crime he or she is accused of committing. Despite appeals to use new findings cautiously and to establish a clear and direct link between neuropathological findings and illegal acts (Ciccone, 1992), some expert witnesses continue to provide incomplete and misleading information, which, in turn, leads to further misuse of the neurological defense in legal proceedings.

Restak (1993) suggested that three criteria must be met in order for brain dysfunction to be considered as a mitigating factor in determining responsibility: (a) Is brain damage present and is it responsible for a behavioral deficit? (b) Is the deficit a contributing cause for a defendant's actions? Finally, (c) Can it be said that the behavior would not have occurred in the absence of the deficit? While it is fairly easy to find convincing evidence to support the first criterion, the second and third criteria are considerably more difficult to demonstrate with individuals who have committed violent acts.

The issue of *diminished responsibility* for criminal acts arising from brain dysfunction remains controversial and only minimally supported in most instances. Nonetheless, it is expected that brain dysfunction will continue to be presented as an exculpatory factor before those who judge and provide punishment for those charged with the commission of acts of violence. This is more certainly likely now in the wake of public outrage over terrorist acts and revulsion toward individual acts of violence. The legal balance has shifted away from the criminal defendant in such crimes in some subtle and not-so-subtle ways. Counsel representing those charged with such crimes may envision that there is less to lose in attempting to draw linkages between brain dysfunction and violence, however weak, as a means of providing motive and explanation for criminal behavior.

Toward a Contextual Framework

Explanation of any human behavior, including violence, must be viewed within a context of a number of cultural, sociological, developmental, environmental, and biological factors. To ignore any one aspect would result in a less than adequate explanation for the etiology of violent acts. For example, the homicide rate in the United States is roughly eight times greater than comparable Western democracies (Fingerhut & Kleinman, 1990), which suggests that biological, sociological, and environmental factors all influence violent behavior. One would have difficulty finding evidence to suggest that there is a higher

frequency of brain dysfunction among citizens of the United States. Yet, few would deny that in the United States, widespread medical technology and expert witnesses regarding these methodologies are available for legal proceedings in a greater magnitude than in other Western democracies. This seems to result in the appearance that brain dysfunction is more prevalent in the United States. Nonetheless, it is purely speculative to infer the causative factors of most acts of violence and incorrect, in most instances, to view violent acts exclusively as the product of a biological entity.

Despite the presumed overemphasis of a causal link between lethality and brain dysfunction, violence has a discrete neuroanatomical and biochemical contribution to behavioral variance that continues to be refined through ongoing research. This contribution should be considered in any model that attempts to explain aggression and violence. However, neurological explanations alone are rarely sufficient to explain human behavior (Burrowes, Hales, & Arrington, 1988; Mungus, 1983). It would be short-sighted to view acts of violence as discrete entities of either organic (structural or chemical abnormality of the nervous system) or functional (psychopathology, trauma, societal pressures) origin. In this chapter, we will attempt to highlight potential neural contributions to violence by describing neural pathways associated with aggressive behavior, characteristics of violent offenders, developmental and acquired brain disorders associated with aggressive behavior, and evaluation of potential assessment and treatments procedures for aggressive and violent behavior thought to be causally related to brain dysfunction.

Types of Aggression

Classification schemes have been established to describe different forms of aggression (Brain, 1979; Elliott, 1992; Moyer, 1968). For example, maternal aggression has been used to describe the behavior displayed by a lactating mother who is charged with the protection and care of her young. It is possible for any form of aggression to result in lethality, though some forms of aggression are more likely to result in this outcome. The available literature suggests that two forms of aggression are reliably associated with nervous system function—predatory aggression and affective aggression. Research with both non-human primates and other animals suggests that the neural mechanisms responsible for both forms of aggression are quite different.

Predatory aggression usually pertains to species-typical "instinctive" aggression, most commonly displayed by animals who are hunting for food. Therefore, this aggression typically involves attack on normal "prey" as part of an animal's foraging behavior. Affective aggression pertains to attack associated with strong feelings of anger and rage. There is a high degree of autonomic activation, along with distinctive facial expressions, posturing, and vocalizations in animals. Both forms of aggression involve the differential activation of specific neural mechanisms, as well as overstimulation of the central nervous system as a whole.

In contrast, neural mechanisms play a considerably smaller role in other types of aggressive behavior — for instance, collective aggression, as exhibited by a soldier's aggressive acts toward the enemy during time of war, the violent behavior of mentally ill and psychotic patients, premeditated homicide for secondary gain and profit, and isolated acts of aggression in a previously peaceable person. In general, brain dysfunction should be more strongly considered as an etiologic factor in those instances in which persons engage in *recurrent, sudden,* and *unexplained or unprovoked* violent acts. Naturally, individuals who engage in recurrent violent acts are usually labeled as criminals by the judicial system. In the next sections, we will review neural contributions

to violence in both the intact brain and the brains of violent offenders.

Neural Substrate of Aggression and Violence

Much of what we know, or think we know, about the neural basis of violence and aggression for humans has been inferred from animal studies. There have been more biobehavioral studies using mice than any other species. However, the applicability of these findings to human models of aggression is debatable (Blanchard, 1984; Brain & Haug, 1992). Mammalian brains are not equivalent or interchangeable in terms of both their structure and function. Still other problems arise from the lack of precision available for surgical and biochemical procedures, such as surgical ablation of finite structures deep within the cortex of a mouse brain (without damaging adjacent or surrounding tissue). Also, it has been suggested that the generalizability of findings from animal studies may be limited in terms of the inferences that are drawn between the species-typical behavior of an animal and that of a human. Obviously, some research simply cannot be performed upon humans because of the irreversible and iatrogenic potential of such studies. Fortunately for researchers, though unfortunately for those who are afflicted with neurological conditions, certain human brain disorders have allowed us to compare, in an indirect manner, how consistent animal models of aggression are with aggression in humans.

Neural Interconnections

The brain has an organizational hierarchy of inhibitory and excitatory connections that allows for interactive input from a variety of structures, each influencing the other in a maze of reciprocal connections. As a result, behavior is influenced by a number of neural pathways, each exerting its influence to modulate and control the final outcome or set of outcomes within a specific environmental context. For example, the limbic system is known to receive input from sensory systems that monitor the environment and to associate this input with emotional response. In turn, the limbic system exerts considerable influence upon the hypothalamus. The hypothalamus influences activity within the midbrain, but is inhibited and modulated by the frontal neocortex and orbitofrontal cortex. Finally, the midbrain activates motor pathways within the brain stem.

Working from the rostral (face) to the caudal (back of head) aspects of the brain, the principal neuronal components involved in aggression include the orbitofrontal cortex, septal area, hippocampus, amygdala, head of caudate nucleus,

thalamus, ventromedial and posterior hypothalamic nuclei, midbrain tegmentum, pons, and the fastigial nuclei of the cerebellum (Weiger & Bear, 1988). Aggression is most consistently associated with the limbic and paralimbic structures of the midbrain, such as the amygdala, hypothalamus, and periaquaductal gray matter (see Figure 1). These structures can be thought of as intermediaries between sensory and motor systems. Electrical stimulation and surgical ablation of various brain structures in animals, particularly structures that are part of the limbic system, have facilitated our understanding of the anatomic substrate of aggression considerably. They have also provided a great wealth of information linking brain structure and function with violent behavior.

FIGURE 1.
SAGITAL VIEW OF LIMBIC AND PARALIMBIC STRUCTURES ASSOCIATED WITH AGGRESSION

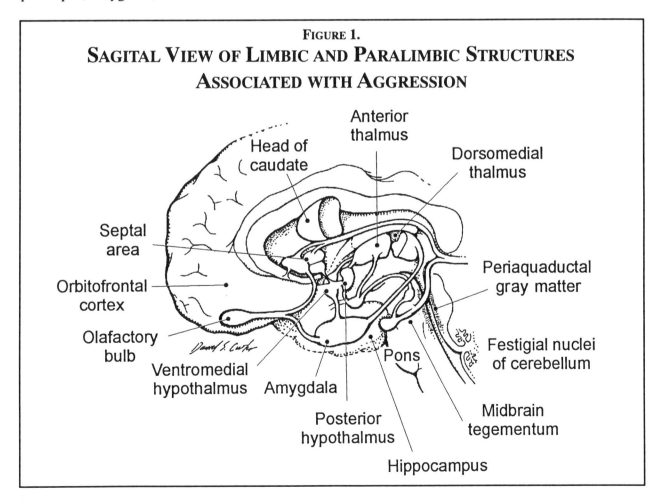

Amygdala. There are two distinct pathways that link the amygdala to the hypothalamus—the ventral amygdalafugal pathway and the stria terminalis. The amygdalafugal pathway appears to have a excitatory role, while the effect of the stria terminalis is inhibitory. Subsequent activation studies have found that electrical stimulation of specific aspects of the amygdala will produce differing effects. Stimulation of the basolateral aspects of the amygdala produces excitation, while the stimulation of the corticomedial aspects of the amygdala is inhibitory. The changes in aggression that are noted following stimulation of these areas appear to be directly related to the amygdala's influence upon the hypothalamic nuclei it innervates. The amygdala itself is innervated by multiple cortical association areas providing sensory input from auditory, visual, olfactory, tactile, and gustatory sources. Ablation of the amygdala results in the organism's inability to determine the significance of specific environmental stimuli. Consequently, stimuli that previously produced a heightened sense of arousal no longer are alarming to the organism. In other words, the amygdala is no longer able to satisfy the basic drives of the hypothalamus, such as hunger and thirst, because it fails to elicit emotional states in the presence of specific stimuli previously associated with specific emotions.

Hypothalamus. As previously described, the hypothalamus receives afferent input from the amygdala. However, it does not receive processed sensory input directly from cortical association areas. The hypothalamus functions as the "gatekeeper" for the autonomic system and is responsible for monitoring the internal state of the organism.

As with the amygdala, stimulation of different portions of the hypothalamus will produce different types of aggression. Stimulation of the medial aspects of the hypothalamus produces affective attack and stimulation of the lateral portion of the hypothalamus produces predatory attack. Aggression appears to be mediated through axons that project caudally from the hypothalamus to the periaquaductal gray matter of the midbrain (Bandler, 1988). Destruction of the hypothalamic pathways leading to the periaquaductal gray region will not produce aggression, even when the hypothalamus is stimulated.

Summary of the Neural Substrate of Aggression

The brain is a vast neural network of inhibitory and excitatory influences that operates within an environmental context. The brain structures most reliably associated with aggressive or violent behavior are part of the limbic system, particularly the amygdala and hypothalamus. Most of what we know about the neural substrate of aggression has been derived from animal models of aggression. There is concern over the applicability of animal studies, largely due to theoretical methodological, and procedural issues. Nonetheless, human neurological conditions have allowed us to confirm, in part, many of our notions concerning the neural basis for aggression.

Brain Dysfunction Among Violent Offenders

Two ways of studying the neurological contribution to violent behavior, as we learned in the previous section, include directly producing brain dysfunction in animals and studying humans who have specific neurological impairments for the presence or absence of aggressive and violent behavior, as well as determining if violent offenders have a higher incidence of brain dysfunction.

The extent to which brain dysfunction is related to criminal behavior and violence is uncertain. It has been argued that the prevalence of brain abnormalities is considerably higher among violent offenders than the public at large (Kurland, Yeager, & Arthur, 1963). However, it is unlikely that a criminal has ever learned criminal and aggressive behavior skills by virtue of having a brain dysfunction. What has been unclear is whether brain dysfunction causes acts of violence or if there is merely a correlative relationship. In all likelihood, both scenarios are true. Leading a violent lifestyle may promote some individuals to engage in behaviors that are more detrimental to the human central nervous system (CNS), such as drug and alcohol abuse, fights that result in CNS injury, and poor nutrition. These behaviors can be viewed as risk factors for the development of brain dysfunction. Similarly, brain dysfunction is thought to contribute directly to the commission of some violent acts, but almost always within the context of other contributing factors.

Individuals with brain dysfunction may, in some instances, experience a great deal of difficulty inhibiting aggressive impulses. A variety of diagnostic tools has shown increased abnormalities among individuals who have engaged in violent crimes, which has been referred to by some researchers as the "minimal brain dysfunction" hypothesis of criminal behavior (Pontius, 1973).

Incidence of Brain Dysfunction Among Violent Offenders

The abnormalities on EEG recordings of violent offenders have consistently shown two characteristic patterns. EEG recordings have shown slow brain waves that are typical of brain waves of young children. This has led researchers to suggest that the brains of violent offenders are "immature" (Hare, 1978; Pontius, 1974). EEGs of violent offenders also show "spike waves," which can be a pathognomonic sign of brain dysfunction. It has also been hypothesized, but not conclusively shown, that the spikes seen on EEG recordings of violent offenders represent dysfunction of the limbic region of the brain, the area which is most commonly associated with aggressive and violent behavior. It is possible that violent and criminal behaviors, as a function of genetic predisposition or brain injury, result from an inability to inhibit impulsive behaviors, such as aggression. Interestingly, researchers have found that as criminals age, and presumably their brains mature, there tends to be a reduction in both criminal behavior and EEG abnormalities (Robins, 1966; Williams, 1969).

Still other researchers have focused upon frontal lobe brain dysfunction, particularly the prefrontal cortex, as a neurological explanation for violent and criminal behavior (Hall & McNinch, 1988; Kandel & Freed, 1989; Raine & Scerbo, 1991; Volkow & Tancredi, 1987). Yeudall and Fromm-Auch (1979) reported on a series of studies of neuropsychological functioning that compared cognitive functioning of criminals with normal controls. The authors found that criminals were more likely than normal control subjects to demonstrate impairment on tests that are presumed to measure frontal lobe dysfunction. Their results were also found to be correlated with abnormalities on EEG recordings of the same patients. These results highlight not only the physiological substrate of aggression, but also the cognitive sequelae of frontal lobe brain dysfunction. In this instance, the criminal subjects performed more poorly on tasks that measure ability to adjust their behavior in response to feedback, to form concepts and "rules," and to anticipate the consequences of their behavior.

With the advent of Positron Emission Tomography (PET), we have been able to go far beyond measurement of structural and electrographic indices by quantifying functional aspects of the brain, such as the utilization of glucose by cells within specific brain regions. One study by Raine, Buschsbaum, Stanley, Lottenberg, Abel, and Stoddard (1994) looked at cerebral metabolic rates for glucose using PET and a task thought to reflect frontal lobe function for 22 subjects accused of murder and 22 normal controls. Their results suggested that murderers had significantly lower glucose metabolism in both the lateral and medial prefrontal cortex when compared to normal controls. Similar results have been found using PET with both violent offenders (Volkow & Tancredi, 1987) and sexual offenders (Hendricks et al., 1988).

The incidence of brain dysfunction in this population may be dependent upon the type of criminal/offender, and even the frequency and intensity of the violent acts. Fenwick (1989) found that abnormalities in electroencephalographic recordings among violent offenders ranged from 25 to 50%. Even higher percentages were found among offenders who had committed violent acts on more than one occasion. In another investigation of 15 death row inmates, all 15 had a history of mild to moderate head trauma and 10 showed evidence of neuropsychological deficits (Lewis, Pincus, Feldman, Jackson, & Bard, 1986). A subsequent study by Lewis et al. (1988) found that 14 of 37 death row inmates had committed capital crimes as juveniles. Consistent with their previous study, they found that 11 had a history of mild to moderate head trauma, 9 had electroencephalograms that were read as abnormal, but 12 also had a history of physical or sexual abuse.

Summary of Research With Violent Offenders

As a whole, researchers have found that violent offenders have a higher incidence of neurological dysfunction. Several factors may account for this increased incidence, such as engaging in high risk behaviors that are likely to result in CNS impairment. However, there are no indications that brain dysfunction caused offenders to commit violent acts. It is possible that brain dysfunction, in some instances, may play a role in the exhibition of violent behavior, possibly as a result of frontal lobe dysfunction. At best, the relationship between brain dysfunction and violence for this group remains speculative. It should be noted that the majority of violent offenders are neurologically intact. According to Vladamir Hachinski (1993), a prominent neurologist, "Brain damage may unleash violence, but it does not explain it. Most criminals are neurologically normal."

Neuropathology and Violence

As the aforementioned studies would suggest, there is a possible neurological contribution to some forms of aggression. Animal models of aggression, such as electrical stimulation or surgical ablation studies, do not always equate perfectly with human models of aggression. However, it is well known that in some instances, violent behavior can be associated with "organic mental disorders" and neurological conditions. There is an increased incidence of neurological dysfunction among violent offenders, although CNS disturbances among criminals may be partially a result of their lifestyle.

We would expect that because there is a higher incidence of CNS disturbance among criminals than in the general population, there would be support for the converse. Specifically, is there an increased incidence of aggression among individuals with known brain injury or illness? As Table 1 depicts, aggressive behavior has been linked to a variety of neurological and paraneurological disorders, including neoplastic and paraneoplastic disease, hemorrhage (Paradis, Horn, Lazar, & Schwartz, 1994), encephalitis, Huntington's chorea, Alzheimer's disease and other dementias, stroke, multiple sclerosis (Schiffer & Babigian, 1984), cardiorespiratory arrest, sleep disturbances, hypoglycemia (Benton, Kumari, & Brain, 1982), and other metabolic disorders (Elliott, 1982).

Epilepsy

Epilepsy is a disorder characterized by recurrent spontaneous seizures, sometimes unremitting, despite medication. This disorder represents

TABLE 1.
NEUROLOGICAL AND PARANEUROLOGICAL CONDITIONS ASSOCIATED WITH AGGRESSIVE BEHAVIOR

A. Trauma
B. Seizures
C. Degenerative Conditions
    1. Alzheimer's disease
    2. multiple sclerosis
    3. other dementia
D. Vascular Conditions
    1. stroke
    2. transient global amnesia
    3. cardio-respiratory arrest
    4. hemorrhage
E. Infections
    1. encephalitis
    2. meningitis
F. Mass Lesions
    1. hydrocephalus or increased intracranial pressure
    2. midline lesions
    3. neoplastic and paraneoplastic disease
G. Toxic and Metabolic Conditions
    1. endocrine abnormality
    2. alcohol withdrawal or pathological intoxication
    3. hypoxia or anoxia
    4. hypoglycemia
H. Sleep
    1. night terrors and somnambulism
    2. REM sleep disorder

one of the more common neurological conditions, affecting up to 4% of the population at some point during their lives (Hauser & Kurland, 1975). Episodic acts of aggression are not an uncommon occurrence for some individuals with epilepsy and there have been several reports of homicide in the literature (Brewer, 1971; Fenton & Udwin, 1965; Gunn, 1978; Milne, 1979; Walker, 1961). In recent years, speculation regarding a possible relationship between epilepsy and aggression has led to a flurry of research. This speculation ignores one very fundamental inequality between the probability that a person committing a violent act will have epilepsy and the probability that a person having epilepsy will commit a violent act. Despite this inequality, considerable controversy has been raised and persists concerning the biobehavioral etiology of violence for persons with epilepsy. In terms of lethal aggression, epilepsy has caught the public's attention in recent years as murder defendants have attempted to use epilepsy, almost always unsuccessfully, as their defense cornerstone.

A distinction can be made between aggression occurring during three distinct phases of an epileptic events: (a) ictal aggression, which is aggression that occurs during an epileptic event; (b) post-ictal confusional state, which is a brief period of disorientation following an epileptic event; and (c) inter-ictal aggression, which pertains to aggression that occurs between epileptic events.

Intra-ictal aggression. It is well recognized that non-directed aggression may occur during the course of a seizure. Patients will passively fight attempts to be restrained, strike another person accidentally during the course of a psychomotor seizure, or exhibit other *non-directed* behavior, such as flailing and spitting. Legitimate cases of directed violence during an epileptic seizure are highly improbable, contrary to public perceptions concerning seizures, and are, to the authors' knowledge, nonexistent in the literature. Nonetheless, highly publicized reports of possible ictal violence have increased as homicide defendants have attributed their actions to seizure activity. For example, Jack Ruby, who was eventually convicted of murdering Lee Harvey Oswald, initially used psychomotor epilepsy in the defense of his crime (Demaris & Wills, 1968). Indeed, the leading neurology textbooks of that time clearly stated that epilepsy should be considered when there is no apparent motive and the brutality of the crime transcends the typical.

In another landmark case, Brewer (1971) detailed the medical findings of a 24-year-old male from Australia who had no previous diagnosis of seizures and who was alleged to have committed two murders during a "psychomotor seizure." Following an argument with his uncle, this individual borrowed his cousin's single shell shotgun, returned 30 minutes later, and after asking his fiancee to stand clear, discharged and reloaded five shells, killing his aunt and uncle. A diagnosis of epilepsy was made after the patient was found to have a mildly abnormal EEG and pneumoencephalogram. He was subsequently acquitted on the grounds of insanity. Stereotyped and complex actions such as those described are inconsistent with known facts concerning seizures and epilepsy. This case highlights the potential misuse of attributing acts of violence

and homicide to known or suspected neurological conditions.

Despite its failure to explain violent and homicidal behavior, epilepsy is consistently more prevalent among prisoners when compared to the general population (Gunn & Fenton, 1971), which is not surprising, in view of the increased incidence of CNS disturbance among criminals in general. Again, lifestyle issues may be at least partially to blame for this finding. Criminal offenders tend to engage in activities and behaviors that lead to the development of disorders like epilepsy, particularly activities and behaviors that result in head trauma. In other words, the higher incidence of epilepsy among criminals may be an artifact of the population itself, rather than an indication that CNS disorders such as epilepsy lead to the commission of criminal behavior.

One manifestation of seizures, particularly complex-partial seizures, is the presence of automatisms. Automatisms are involuntary behaviors that can arise from a variety of conditions that affect the CNS (Mahowald, Bundlie, Hurwitz, & Schenck, 1990), including seizures. Even complex behaviors, such as disrobing or walking, can occur as an automatism. Automatisms as violent behavior complexes are exceedingly rare in epileptics. Currie, Heathfield, Hensen, and Scott (1971) studied 666 patients with partial-complex seizures and found only five who had violent outbursts, and none who had goal-directed aggressive behavior. King and Ajmone (1977) had similar findings in their study of 199 patients. In their sample, only nine patients displayed violent behavior, and none had instances of directed aggression. There have been several reports in the literature of property destruction and occasional physical aggression during an ictal event (Ashford, Schulz, & Walsh, 1980). These incidents inevitably involved disorientation, stereotyped behaviors, non-directed acts of short duration, and behaviors that were out of context with environmental activities (Benson,

1986). Rodin (1973) reviewed medical charts for 700 epilepsy patients, 34 of whom had completed aggressive acts. The profile that emerged was that of a young male with lower than average intelligence, a history of behavioral problems dating back to school age, and lack of strong religious ties. Hermann, Schwartz, Whitman, and Karnes (1980) found that chronological age was inversely related to aggression.

Treiman's (1986) exhaustive review of the literature pertaining to epilepsy and violence reviewed more than 75 crimes of violence in the United States in which epilepsy had been used as a defense, 45 of which involved murder. Nine cases occurred before EEG technology was available. Of the remaining 66 cases, Treiman reported that 26 of 60 cases were planned beforehand and 27 of 57 cases involved heavy use of alcohol at the time of the crime. In 36 of 57 cases, the violent episode was provoked, and only 12 of 50 cases had evidence of amnesia for the criminal event.

Epilepsy has been used successfully as a defense in only one of these cases. In 1966, a police officer by the name of Robert Torsney, shot and killed a 15-year-old after he slightly provoked the officer (*Matter of Torsney*, 1979). Torsney claimed at his trial to be suffering a psychomotor seizure at the time of the shooting, although he had no history of seizures prior to the shooting. He was subsequently found by the jury to be not guilty by reason of insanity, possibly as a result of conflicting testimony offered by expert witnesses.

Post-ictal confusional state aggression. Following a generalized seizure, most individuals experience a period of time lasting several minutes or more for which they will have little or no recollection. They experience confusion and disorientation, unresponsiveness, lethargy, psychosis and, in rare instances, aggression. There are several reports in the literature of individuals who became aggressive during the post-ictal confusional state.

Gunn and Fenton (1971) reviewed 17 cases in which the perpetrator experienced a seizure within 12 hours of committing the violent act. In only one of the 17 cases could the crime be directly attributed to a seizure. In that case, following a generalized tonic-clonic seizure, the individual violently attacked several members of the household where he was staying. Gunn and Fenton (1971) concluded in this instance that the patient displayed "resistive violence" in response to restraint during a post-ictal confusional state.

Rodin (1973) found that 15 of 150 epilepsy patients studied had post-ictal psychomotor attacks, which could promptly be averted by avoiding efforts to restrain the patient in all instances. Many patients who have epilepsy report that pain and dysphoria are part of their attack, which may explain why they are prone to strike out at individuals who approach them (Devinsky & Bear, 1984). In instances where directed aggression occurs in the absence of attempts to restrain, it is likely that the aggression is under the voluntary and conscious control of the patient. Also, it should be noted that over the years, many first aid instructional courses have promoted the use of physical and oral restraint for persons having epileptic seizures to prevent injury and to prevent them from swallowing their tongue. However, current thought suggests that there is usually no particular reason to restrain a person who is having a seizure.

Inter-ictal aggression. Inter-ictal aggression is more common than either intra-ictal or post-ictal aggression, yet there has been considerable skepticism regarding the possibility that recurrent seizures can produce inter-ictal disturbances of behavior. This skepticism may be due, in part, to researchers' reluctance to add to the stigma of epilepsy. Nonetheless, the relationship between inter-ictal aggression and violence is a persistent clinical hypothesis raised in many cases.

Ramani and Gumnit (1981) studied 19 epileptic patients with a history of episodic aggression, nine of whom had a history of assaultive behavior resulting in physical injury or property damage, with intensive electroencephalographic (EEG) and closed circuit television monitoring (CCTV) for an average duration of six weeks. Results of this investigation revealed that of the 15 patients who had ictal episodes following reduction of anticonvulsant medication, no patients showed evidence of directed ictal aggression during a seizure, despite the large number of seizure events recorded. Furthermore, 17 patients did not show any evidence of aggression during their hospitalization, which, according to the authors, represented a "remarkable progressive improvement over pre-hospitalization behavior." Of the two subjects who displayed aggression during their hospitalization, seizure activity could not be implicated as the causal factor. The implication of this study is that aggression among patients with epilepsy may be more related to adverse environmental factors than to neural dysfunction per se.

There are some indications that aberrant behavior during inter-ictal phases may be due to atypical mild seizures whose only observable manifestation is the behavioral abnormality (Benson, 1986; Engel, Caldecott-Hazard, & Bandler, 1986). Still others suggest that repeated stimulation of neurons leads to a progressive lowering of their threshold for discharge, a theory known as "kindling." As many patients have epileptic foci within the temporal lobe, it is possible that inter-ictal aggression is actually the result of kindling effects of the amygdala, resulting in increased aggression. While there is no strong support for either theory at present, ongoing research may help to confirm these intriguing hypotheses.

Summary of Epilepsy Research

Bona fide intra-ictal aggression is rare and involves only non-directed violence, such as being accidentally struck while attempting to restrain an individual who is having a seizure.

The perception that epilepsy can be a causative factor for homicide is vastly and dramatically overrated. The overwhelming evidence suggests that episodic aggression among individuals with epilepsy essentially represents an inter-ictal phenomenon of uncertain, or even speculative, neurobehavioral causation. Most of these individuals have shown a propensity for aggressive behavior, which is malleable given proper behavioral contingencies. Ongoing research of two recent hypotheses—the kindling phenomenon and atypical seizures—may help to explain some instances of aggression for persons with epilepsy.

Dementia and Limbic Degeneration

Wilhelmsen et al. (1994) and Sima et al. (1994) recently documented what appears to be an autosomal dominant chromosome-17 disease that is associated with increased aggressiveness, with a mean age of onset of 45 years. Clinical features included disinhibition, signs of frontal lobe dementia, withdrawal, alcoholism, and hyperphagia. Morphological findings included atrophy and spongiform change of the frontotemporal cortex, and neuronal loss and gliosis of the substantia nigra and amygdala. This disorder, termed disinhibition-dementia-Parkinsonism-amyotrophy complex (DDAPC), has a number of features consistent with frontal lobe dementia, Kluver-Bucy syndrome, and Parkinsonism. Usually, the first clinical signs of the disease are personality changes. Although DDAPC is, in all likelihood, a rare disorder, it is probable that previous cases have been incorrectly diagnosed as late onset mental disorders or early onset dementia of unknown origin.

Neoplastic and Paraneoplastic Disease

Gliomas, which represent the most prevalent form of central nervous system neoplasms, vary greatly in terms of their malignancy. Among gliomas, astrocytomas predominate as the most common cell type, although most sites within the CNS can harbor neoplastic tissue. The actual incidence of neoplastic disease within the limbic area is rare, and there are no known types of neoplasm that selectively affect the limbic system.

When neoplastic disease affects the limbic system, the effects can be as diverse as the locations and quality of the tumor itself. The effect upon an organism's behavior has been previously documented (Malamud, 1967), usually producing behavior changes resembling psychopathology, and infrequently producing violent behavior. However, there are several case examples in the literature that suggest a possible link between neoplastic disease and violence.

One of the most infamous cases is that of Charles Joseph Whitman, an ex-marine, who killed 13 persons and wounded 31 others on the afternoon of August 1, 1966, when he opened fire from a tower at the University of Texas at Austin. The night before, he had killed his mother and his wife. What appeared to be an impulsive and sudden act to many people may have been more planned than was first realized or has been documented in various textbooks. Charles Whitman kept extensive diaries prior to his death, and the contents of those diaries outlined in great detail his plan for the shootings. It has also been suggested that he had a propensity for violence. Nonetheless, results of his autopsy revealed a walnut sized malignant glioblastoma-multiforma tumor within the vicinity of the amygdala, although it has been suggested that the investigators who handled the case may have been predisposed to place the location of the tumor near this structure. As a result of the seriousness of his actions, as well as the growing problem with violence at that time, extensive research efforts were spurred concerning the nature of neurobehavioral explanations for violence. (They also closed access to the tower, giving new meaning to the phrase *closing the barn door after the horse escapes*).

Sleep Disorders

Recent literature has documented the relationship between sleep disorders and violent behavior, including homicide (Fenwick, 1986; Schatzman, 1986; Tarsh, 1986). Such behavior has been described as an automatism, which occurs during the sleep state or upon awakening, without consciousness (Mahowald et al., 1990). The etiology for this group of disorders is not clearly understood, but there are almost always indications of impaired neurological functioning.

Sleep disorders associated with violence are night terrors, sleep walking or somnambulism, rapid eye movement (REM) phase sleep behavior disorder, nocturnal seizures, and confusional arousal (Mahowald, Schenck, Rosen, & Hurwitz, 1992). The central feature of each disorder is a disturbance of the sleep-wake cycle producing increased motoric activity during normally inactive REM sleep (e.g., REM sleep behavior disorder, somnambulism, nocturnal seizures), increased confusion, disorientation, or fear upon awakening (e.g., night terrors, confusional arousal).

Episodic Dyscontrol Syndrome

Episodic dyscontrol syndrome is characterized by sudden and intense attacks of uncontrollable rage that may include alteration of consciousness. The rage attacks are typically recurrent but may, in some instances, represent isolated acts. The disorder has been hypothetically linked to several conditions, including minimal brain dysfunction (Wender, 1972), presumably because of the increased incidence of neurological soft signs found among individuals afflicted with the disorder (Elliott, 1982) and abnormal EEG recordings (Drake, Hietter, & Pakalnis, 1992). The disorder has also been linked to psychomotor epilepsy (Bach-y-Rita, Lion, Climent, & Ervin, 1971; Mark & Ervin, 1970) and undifferentiated seizure-like disorders involving a limbic ictus (Monroe, 1985) although, more recently, the relationship between episodic dyscontrol syndrome and epilepsy has been disputed (Gunn, 1981). Episodic dyscontrol syndrome has become a catch-all category that is used to describe a variety of diagnostic entities with varying degrees of psychopathology and neurological comorbidities.

One study by Stein et al. (1993) suggested that episodic dyscontrol, impulsivity, and aggression are strongly associated with neurological impairment. In their sample of 28 patients with impulsive personality disorders and 28 normal control patients, they found that patients who had impulsive personality disorders and a history of aggression had an increased incidence of right-sided (left hemisphere) neurological soft signs compared to normal control patients. An increased incidence of left hemispheric neurological soft signs among aggressive patients has also been reported by other researchers (Flor-Henry, 1976; Yeudall, 1977).

Bach-y-Rita et al. (1971) studied 130 violent patients, eight of whom had committed homicide, whose clinical symptoms were consistent with the diagnostic criteria for episodic dyscontrol syndrome. They reported that these patients had an increased incidence of abnormal EEGs, epilepsy, and impairment on neuropsychological tests of brain dysfunction. However, these patients also had a higher than usual incidence of family violence, and alcohol and drug abuse, which led the authors to conclude that violent behavior for these patients was probably multidetermined.

Other Disorders

Psychotic trigger reaction (Pontius, 1987) is the term that has been used to describe a rare, highly controversial, and as yet unconfirmed, homicidal episode presumably involving limbic system dysfunction and a "highly individualized trigger stimulus" encountered within a specific context and associated with reactivation of memory for past experiences. It is Pontius' (1987) contention that homicidal action can be evoked without alteration of consciousness in such an instance, although probably only "once in a lifetime" because of the specific contextual constellation necessary to produce the behavior. He reported a case of a man in his 20s, with no prior criminal history, who was charged with a homicide and an attempted homicide. The subject had used LSD, cocaine, and Dalmane in the days and hours before the homicide, and had not slept for four days. The victim was a stranger who reportedly resembled the subject's deceased father. He had been fly fishing in the river prior to being forcibly drowned by the subject.

Psychotic trigger reaction sounds similar to another disorder reported in the literature—reflex seizures. In reflex seizure disorder, epileptic seizures are triggered by specific stimuli or classes of stimuli, which may be explained through a learning theory model (Adams, 1976).

Guidelines for Assessment with the Population

Clearly, some individuals who have engaged in violent behavior have signs of CNS dysfunction. Conversely, some neurological conditions have been associated with occasional changes in behavior, including violent and aggressive acts. We previously stated that brain dysfunction should be considered in those instances in which an individual engages in recurrent, sudden, and unexplainable or unprovoked acts of violence. These criteria may be a useful starting point for the trained psychologist or physician who must determine if diagnostic tests should be administered to an individual who is accused of a violent crime. Other criteria to consider may include the presence of behavior problems other than violence, difficulty with basic neurologic function, such as walking, and a history of prior CNS dysfunction, such as stroke or infection.

Neurological Examination

Obviously, gross CNS abnormalities are readily apparent from a routine neurological examination. However, the vast majority of neurological abnormalities among violent offenders are considerably more subtle, hence the term "minimal brain dysfunction" (MBD). Although there is no exact definition of MBD, and the same term has been used to describe other more recently formulated disorders, such as attention deficit disorder (Wender, 1972), it is loosely defined as a brain abnormality that is of sufficient intensity to affect behavior, but not of sufficient intensity to be detected through conventional neurological examination.

Several diagnostic tools are available to those trained in their use. EEG has been discussed in other sections of this chapter as an instrument that has measured abnormalities in brain function among violent offenders. As a cautionary note, approximately 5 to 10% of individuals with no previous history of violent behavior or neurological dysfunction will have abnormal EEG recordings. Also, an absence of abnormal EEG recordings does not preclude the presence of brain dysfunction. Several studies have found that approximately 25 to 40% of epileptics have normal EEG recordings during inter-ictal episodes and that limbic and frontal seizures may be particularly hard to detect with conventional electrodermal electrodes (Goodin & Aminoff, 1984; Nousiainen, Suomalainen, & Mervaala, 1992; Salinsky, Kanter, & Dasheiff, 1987). Structural abnormalities may be detectable through the use of neuroimaging techniques, such as Computerized Axial Tomography (CAT) and Magnetic Resonance Imaging (MRI). However, it should be noted that findings from neuroimaging studies are notorious for correlating poorly with behavior.

It is useful to look at the duration and intensity of the behavioral and cognitive disturbance to assist in differential diagnosis. Sudden and intense changes in behavior are almost always associated with metabolic, infectious, or vascular changes to the CNS system. In contrast, slow, progressive changes in behavior are more indicative of a degenerative process, such as dementia. In such instances, mild to moderate changes in behavior would necessarily predate an act of violence.

Neuropsychological Evaluation

Neuropsychology is a specialized field within psychology that pertains to the evaluation of cognitive deficits associated with brain injury and illness. The diagnostic tools that are part of neuropsychology are quite useful for evaluating brain dysfunction, particularly because they can detect significant brain dysfunction even in the absence of notable neurological findings. For a number of neurological disorders discussed in this chapter, the first signs of CNS dysfunction are vague psychiatric and cognitive symptoms (Hall, 1980). It is useful, then, to be able to assess the cognitive symptoms that often represent the early stages of neurological illness.

The two general areas of the brain associated with violent behavior that have been discussed are the frontal lobes and the limbic system. Unfortunately, there are no neuropsychological tests designed to assess these specific structures. Instead, several neuropsychological tests and batteries have shown a reasonable level of predictive validity in measuring cognitive abilities thought to be subserved by these structures. For example, the Category Test from the Halstead-Reitan Neuropsychological Test Battery (HRNTB), a test that is thought to measure an individual's ability to form concepts and utilize feedback, has been found to correlate highly with known neurological impairment involving the frontal lobe (Reitan

& Wolfson, 1993). It should be noted that frontal lobe functions represent a particularly difficult ability realm to assess because of the vast array and complexity of functions subserved by this structure. Neuropsychological instruments tend to have a reasonable degree of *sensitivity* for detecting brain impairment, but the degree of *specificity* for some cognitive abilities is less strong, particularly for some sites and systems in the cerebrum. Another way of looking at this concept is that the presence of any brain dysfunction is more easily detected than is impairment of a specific structure or ability realm.

Treatment of Recurrent Violence

Recurrent violence represents a clinical chiasm for mental health providers. Violent behavior is usually refractory to traditional psychotherapy. The resiliency of this behavior as well as a historical overemphasis of the neurological contribution of violent behavior led to the development of medical interventions. However, these therapeutic interventions have limited scientific support for their efficacy and are associated with multiple iatrogenic effects. For the most part, treatments have developed as a result of desperation on the part of clinicians and because of a perceived need for some form of active treatment. Two methods of treatment that have been utilized extensively are pharmacological approaches and psychosurgery. The ongoing development of neuropsychological approaches, as discussed by Marc Walter in Chapter 21 on cognitive retraining of cerebral deficits associated with violent behavior, represents a new and exciting area of potential treatment.

Pharmacological Approaches

The premise behind the use of medication to control aggressive behavior is that by administering a pharmacological agent, one can increase inhibition of undesirable behavior, decrease activation of neural circuits responsible for aggression, or both. There are no medications that exert their influence specifically on the limbic structures. Rather, medications influence entire classes of neurons by altering their release of neurotransmitter substance. For example, gamma-aminobutyric acid (GABA), a neurotransmitter substance found in abundance within the frontal lobes, plays an important role in mediating mood states in humans. Benzodiazapines, such as Valium, exert their primary influence by affecting GABAergic neurons, which results in a calming effect for the individual.

Any medication whose primary purpose is to alter the function of the central nervous system is termed a *psychotropic* medication. Psychotropic medications have been used successfully in many instances to treat episodic aggression and violence. The actual medication administered to an individual depends upon the disorder presumed to underlie the aggressive behavior. For example, episodic dyscontrol syndrome, a disorder characterized by sudden violent outbursts, has been successfully treated with carbamazepine, which, interestingly, is classified as an anticonvulsant medication (Lewin & Sumners, 1992; Stone, McDaniel, Hughes, & Hermann, 1986). Psychotic disorders with aggressive behavioral manifestations are typically treated with a class of drugs known as neuroleptics, which are classified as major tranquilizers.

The use of medication to treat violent behavior has several drawbacks. Their effect does not tend to be localized to the specific aberrant behavior for which they were prescribed, but rather, will affect most, if not all, of a person's behaviors. For example, it may not be possible to operate machinery or drive if the medication has a sedating effect. Secondly, cognitive impairments may occur as a result of using some psychotropic medications. Learning and memory are commonly affected, sometimes to a degree that an individual would be unable to maintain gainful employment or complete activities of daily living. Thirdly, most medications lose their effectiveness after prolonged use, either through a build up of tolerance to the medication or as a result of supra-sensitivity to increased levels of neurotransmitter substance. Finally, prolonged use of neuroleptics can cause permanent brain damage. A syndrome known as tardive dyskinesia, which involves uncontrolled movement of the limbs, face, and palate, and in severe cases, affects the ability to breath and eat, may develop after prolonged use of medications.

Psychosurgery and the Control of Aggression

There is evidence that long before there was organized civilization, primitive humans performed psychosurgery in a process termed "trephining," which consisted of producing holes in the skull to allow evil spirits to exit the body. While we no longer place much stock in the capacity of evil spirits to produce aberrant behavior, we remain quite invested in ascribing aberrant behavior to the functioning of the brain. It makes intuitive sense to "fix" a brain that is presumed to be dysfunctional by either removing segments that have become defective and are presumably stimulating circuits involved in aggressive behavior, or by limiting their influence by severing their connections to other structures.

Psychosurgery was initially embraced because it provided a method of treating serious mental illness, such as psychosis and obsessive-compulsive disorder, at a time when few efficacious treatments were available for treating the seriously mentally ill. In 1949, the Nobel prize for medicine was awarded to Dr. Egas Moniz, a neurologist from the University of Lisbon, for his development of the prefrontal leukotomy surgical procedure, later referred to as a lobotomy. The applicability and interest in psychosurgery for treatment of individuals who engage in violent behavior came several years later.

Initially, animal studies provided information concerning the efficacy of psychosurgery, as well as a model of the neural contributions to violent behavior. Carlyle Jacobsen's (1936) work with the prefrontal area of monkeys and chimpanzees was perhaps the catalyst for psychosurgery in the 20th century. He noted that more excitable and aggressive monkeys became "docile, tame, and calm" following destruction of the prefrontal cortex. However, it has been suggested by some researchers that the iatrogenic effect of psychosurgery on these animals was not taken into consideration. Many of the animals subjected to this procedure exhibited a wide range of cognitive and behavioral deficits (Ward, 1948). These animals were unable to assess environmentally significant stimuli, such as social cues and fear of man, were indifferent to the presence or needs of other monkeys, and exhibited flawed problem solving. King, Lancaster, and Benitone (1970) found that monkeys who had undergone amygdalaectomies were unable to adequately use social cues in the wild, a problem which resulted in their abandonment by other monkeys and in their eventual death.

Mark and Ervin (1970) were two early proponents of the use of psychosurgery to control violent behavior. They suggested that a rather large segment of individuals who engage in aberrant behavior have brain abnormalities or "triggers" within the vicinity of limbic structures, such as the amygdala which, if properly located and excised, can result in a lessening of problematic behavior and seizures. Their unsupported link between seizures and aggressive behavior helped to promote misconceptions about individuals with epilepsy.

A case which drew international attention involving proposed psychosurgery to ameliorate interictal aggression was *Kaimowitz v. Department of Mental Health* (1973). According to Shuman (1977), the patient (John Doe) was a 36-year-old man confined to a state institution for the criminally insane under Michigan's 1948 criminal sexual psychopath statute. He had allegedly strangled to death and then raped a young nurse while he was an involuntary patient at the state hospital under treatment for sexually disturbed aggressive behavior. His offenses also included breaking and entering, and voyeurism. His childhood was an extremely troubled one, with multiple foster home placements and very substantial discipline and acting-out problems, including cruelty to animals.

John Doe's case started its road to international prominence as a result of a 1972 proposal made at the Lafayette Clinic, a premier psychiatric research facility in Detroit, connected with the Wayne State University School of Medicine. A study was proposed concerning the effects of medical or surgical treatment on patients committed to the state hospital system in Michigan for severe and recurrent aggressive outbursts. The medical treatment protocol involved cyproterone acetate. The surgical treatment involved implantation of depth electrodes as a prelude to possible amygdalotomy. The surgical plan was influenced by the work of Mark and Ervin (1970), which is described elsewhere in this chapter.

John Doe was the initial candidate for this program. His aggressive urges reportedly had a strong physiological quality. Consent was sought from John Doe to participate in the study, and a thorough preliminary set of studies was undertaken.

However, an attorney representing the Medical Committee for Human Rights, a local activist group, learned of the case and filed suit to release John Doe on a writ of habeas corpus. A great deal transpired in the legal arena thereafter and the details of the proceedings and the conflicting expert testimony are thoroughly set forth by Shuman (1977). In the end, the trial court held that free and informed consent could not be obtained from John Doe in an inherently coercive environment. The court also held that the treatment was of a sufficiently experimental nature to

maintain reservations regarding its effectiveness. Many other subsidiary findings were also set forth in the opinion, but the essential outcome was that treatment of inter-ictal aggression — even of a proven societally dangerous nature — could not be undertaken with sufficient prospect of success, particularly for individuals who are incarcerated as a consequence of such behavior. This particular case was in the public eye and figured prominently in the final recommendations of the National Commission for the Protection of Human Subjects of Biomedical and Behavioral Research.

There are a number of controversial issues that surround this form of treatment. The foremost reason that psychosurgery is controversial is that it involves intentional destruction of brain tissue, sometimes in the absence of definitive indications of brain disease (Breggin, 1975). When a person has a tumor or scar tissue that produces seizures, there is a clear and definable disease process that can, in most instances, be excised. For violent offenders, there is no well-defined disease process and, in many instances, no clear indications of brain disease at all.

One of the chief critics of psychosurgery is Elliot Valenstein (1980). He suggested that the neural circuits that underlie aggressive behavior are not readily identifiable in most instances. Additionally, he suggested that there has been an absence of well-controlled studies reporting on psychosurgery treatment outcomes for psychosurgery patients. Psychosurgery has shown promise for treating some mental illnesses, such as severe obsessive-compulsive disorder, but its effectiveness in treating individuals who engage in violent behavior is questionable. Also, it should be noted that while there are no exact figures, the current use of psychosurgery as a form of treatment for violent behavior is probably exceedingly rare in the United States and abroad. In fact, psychosurgery has been outlawed in the former Soviet Union since 1951 (Kgachaturyan, 1951).

Summary of Treatments for Aggressive Behavior

The treatments that have been developed for control of aggression have, for the most part, been born out of desperation. A lack of effective treatment in the early part of the 20th century led to the proliferation of techniques that have had limited scientific support. In particular, there is an absence of well-controlled outcome studies demonstrating both the effectiveness of these treatments and their safety. Both pharmacological and psychosurgery treatment can produce brain dysfunction as an iatrogenic effect. Since they were first developed, there has been a consistent pattern on the part of researchers and clinicians of ignoring or minimizing the unintended effects of both medication and psychosurgery. As a result, it has been suggested that these treatments have been far more useful in satisfying social goals than in providing positive benefits to those who have been treated. The use of psychosurgery has diminished greatly, leaving the pharmacological approach as the most widely recognized and used form of treatment for violence.

Future Research

There is perhaps no subject within the mental and public health domains at the present time that is more in need of further research than is violence. In general, there is a dearth of information concerning neurological dysfunction and its interaction with social, developmental, and biological factors. We have suggested throughout this chapter that scientists have been myopic in their quest to determine the causes of aggressive and violent behavior. As scientists, we have been quick to embrace neurological dysfunction as the most important factor accounting for violent behavior. But, we may be asking the wrong question. Instead of asking the degree to which brain dysfunction accounts for violent behavior, we should

be asking how brain dysfunction interacts with other factors to produce an increased potential for violent behavior.

The current research being conducted within the area of drug abuse is an excellent example of an interactionist approach for solving complex behavioral questions. One study by Fowler et al. (1993) showed that animals deprived of social contact and a stimulating environment during development are more likely to develop a preference for specific drugs, such as cocaine, over other desirable substances, presumably because of an interaction among biochemical, social, neurological, and developmental factors.

Research in this area has obvious ethical pitfalls and legal constraints. Society has attempted to balance the wider societal need for protection against the rights of individuals who, while arguably sick, can commit very violent and repugnant acts. Virtually no research in this area has been longitudinal or prospective in nature, and we are almost always in the position of attempting to sort out causes "after the fact."

The impetus for the allocation of resources to study violent behavior in the 1960s was born out of several historical incidents, most notably the Kennedy assassination and the slayings by Charles Whitman at the University of Texas. At this point, there are few resources available for conducting research in this, or any other, area. There are, however, abundant resources for the production of new prisons to house violent offenders. In a sense, we have moved further away from a biobehavioral model of violence and closer to a punishment/ moral model of violent behavior.

Summary

This chapter has focused upon the neural bases for and treatment of violent and aggressive behavior. It would be incorrect to state that violence is caused by neurological impairment. By all accounts, brain dysfunction probably accounts for a small percentage of the variance of an aggressive act in most instances. The literature suggests that there is considerable variability from one individual to the next concerning the degree to which neurological impairments are associated with a violent act. For the most part, violence is most appropriately viewed as a multi-determined biobehavioral phenomenon.

Further work is needed to create more specificity about the precise role neural influences may play in accounting for violence, particularly research that focuses upon the interaction of neurological and other factors. Once this work is completed, we believe that it will be discovered that early developmental influences interact with biological predisposition to contribute to neurological abnormalities, which, in turn, may lead to a higher incidence of violent behavior under specific social and environmental contexts.

The approaches that have been developed to treat violent behaviors have been quite controversial. Psychosurgery has lost favor to the less controversial but also potentially harmful practice of pharmacological management of violence. The changes in treatment parallel changes in society's view of violent behavior from a disorder that in some instances has a medical basis to a crime that should be punished. Unfortunately, the impetus to conduct scientific research in the area of violence has become implicitly linked with the goals of "rehabilitation" in criminal forensic settings. A moment's reflection will suggest that this is not necessarily an appropriate association. Limited resources, waning interest in conducting research in such realms, and pragmatic and ethical dilemmas will likely continue to limit investigations exploring the neural basis of violent behavior.

Annotated Bibliography

Bear, D., Reid, W. H., Appelbaum, P. S., Adamec, R. E., Mukherjee, S., Simmons, R. C., &

Harris, J. E. (1987). Neuropsychiatry and the biology of homicide. *Integrative Psychiatry*, 5, 116-139. This article provides comprehensive and timely information concerning the neural and hormonal mechanisms underlying aggression. There is a particularly strong emphasis upon limbic structures and their influence upon aggressive behavior.

Milner, J. S. (1991). *Neuropsychology of Aggression*. Boston: Kluwer. There have been few works written that deal directly with the neuropsychology of aggression. Dr. Milner's book provides the reader with an in-depth appraisal of cognitive deficits and neuropsychological conditions related to aggression. Particular emphasis is placed upon conditions affecting limbic and frontal lobe functioning and their relationship to aggression and violence.

Valenstein, E. S. (1980). *The Psychosurgery Debate*. San Francisco: W. H. Freeman and Company. Dr. Valenstein's book is a classic and definitive work regarding the use of psychosurgery. A historical perspective is offered, which highlights the possible rationales, experimental and otherwise, for the propagation of psychosurgery in the mid-20th century. This book is particularly useful for highlighting the ethical, scientific, and moral dilemmas that surround psychosurgery. Statistics are offered regarding the efficacy of psychosurgery and its prevalence.

References

Adams, K. (1976). Behavioral treatment of reflex or sensory-evoked seizures. *Journal of Behavior Therapy and Experimental Psychiatry*, 7, 123-127.

Ashford, J. W., Schulz, S. C., & Walsh, G. O. (1980). Violent automatism in a partial complex seizure,

Archives of Neurology, 37, 120-122.

Bach-y-Rita, G., Lion, J. R., Clement, C. E., & Ervin, F. R., (1971). Episodic dyscontrol: Study of 130 violent patients. *American Journal of Psychiatry, 127*, 1473-1478.

Bandler, R. (1988). Brain mechanisms of aggression as revealed by electrical and chemical stimulation: Suggestion of a central role for the midbrain periaqueductal grey region. *Progress in Psychobiology, Physiology, and Psychology, 13*, 67-154.

Benedikt, M. (1881). *Brains of criminals.* New York: Wm. Wood & Company.

Benson, D. F. (1986). Interictal behavior disorders in epilepsy. *Psychiatric Clinics of North America, 9*(2), 283-292.

Benton, D., Kumari, N., & Brain, P. F. (1982). Mild hypoglycemia and questionnaire measures of aggression. *Biological Psychology, 14*, 129-135.

Blanchard, D.C. (1984). Applicability of animal models to human aggression. In K. J. Flannelly (Ed.), *Biological perspectives on aggression.* New York: Alan R. Liss, Inc.

Brain, P. F. (1979). Dividing up aggression and considerations in studying the physiological substrates of these phenomenon. *The Behavioral and Brain Sciences, 2*, 216.

Brain, P. F. & Haug, M. (1992). Hormonal and neurochemical correlates of various forms of animal aggression. *Psychoneuroendocrinology, 17*(6), 537-551.

Breggin, P. R. (1975). Psychosurgery for the control of violence: A critical review. In W. Fields & W. Sweet (Eds.), *Neural basis of violence and aggression* (pp.

350-391). St Louis: Warren H. Green.

Brewer. C. (1971). Homicide during a psychomotor seizure: The importance of air-encephalography in establishing insanity under the McNaughten rules. *The Medical Journal of Australia, 1*, 857-859.

Burrowes, K. L., Hales, R. E., & Arrington, E. (1988). Research on the biological aspects of violence. *Psychiatric Clinics of North America, 11*(4), 499-509.

Ciccone, J.R., (1992). Murder, insanity, and medical expert witnesses. *Archives of Neurology, 49*, 608-611.

Crichton, M. (1972). *Terminal man.* New York: Alfred Knopf.

Currie, S., Heathfield, K. W. G., Hensen, R. A., & Scott, D. F. (1971). Clinical course and prognosis of temporal lobe epilepsy. *Brain, 94*, 173-190.

Demaris, O. & Wills, G. (1968). *Jack Ruby* (pp. 125-126). New York: The New American Library, Inc.

Devinsky, O. & Bear, D.M. (1984). Varieties of aggressive behavior in temporal lobe epilepsy. *American Journal of Psychiatry, 141*, 651-656.

Drake, M. E., Hietter, S. A., & Pakalnis, A. (1992). EEG and evoked potentials in episodic-dyscontrol syndrome. *Neuropsychobiology, 26*, 125-128.

Elliott, F. A. (1982). Neurological findings in adult minimal brain dysfunction and the dyscontrol syndrome. *Journal of Nervous and Mental Disease, 170*, 680-687.

Elliott, F. A. (1992). Violence, the neurologic contribution: An overview. *Archives of Neurology, 49*, 595-603.

Engel, J., Caldecott-Hazard, S., & Bandler, R. (1986). Neurobiology of behavior: Anatomic and physiological implications related to epilepsy. *Epilepsia, 27* (Suppl. 2), S3-13.

Fenton, G. W. & Udwin, E. L. (1965). Homicide, temporal lobe epilepsy and depression: A case report. *British Journal of Psychiatry, 111,* 304-306.

Fenwick, P. (1986). Murdering while asleep. *British Medical Journal, 293,* 574-575.

Fenwick, P. (1989). Dyscontrol. In E. H. Reynolds & M. R. Trimble (Eds.), *The bridge between neurology and psychiatry.* New York, NY: Churchill Livingston Inc.

Fingerhut, L. A. & Kleinman, J. C. (1990). International and interstate comparisons of homicide among young males. *Journal of the American Medical Association, 226,* 2342.

Flor-Henry, P. (1976). Lateralized temporal-limbic dysfunction and psychopathology. In H. R. Harnad, H. D. Steklis, & J. Lancaster (Eds.), *Origins and evolutions of language and speech.* New York: New York Academy of Sciences.

Fowler, S. C., Johnson, J. S., Kallman, M. J., Liou, J. R., Wilson, M. C., & Hikal, A. H. (1993). In a drug discrimination procedure isolation-reared rats generalize to lower doses of cocaine and amphetamine than rats reared in an enriched environment. *Psychopharmacology, 110,* 115-118.

Goodin, D. S. & Aminoff, M. J. (1984). Does interictal EEG have a role in the diagnosis of epilepsy? *Lancet, 8281,* 837-839.

Gunn, J. (1978). Epileptic homicide: A case report. *British Journal of Psychiatry, 132,* 510-513.

Gunn, J. (1981). *Neurology, 31,* 1204-1205.

Gunn J. & Fenton, G. (1971). Epilepsy, automatism and crime. *Lancet, 1,* 1173-6.

Hachinski, V. (1993). Brain damage and violence. *Archives of Neurology, 50,* 871.

Hall, H. V. & McNinch, D. (1988). Linking crime-specific behavior to neuropsychological impairment. *International Journal of Clinical Neuropsychology, 10,* 113-122.

Hall, R. C. (1980). Depression. In R. C. Hall (Ed.), *Psychiatric presentations of medical illness: Somatopsychic disorders* (pp. 37-63). New York: SP Medical and Scientific Books.

Hare, R. D. (1978). Electrodermal and cardiovascular correlates of sociopathy. In R. D. Hare & D. Schalling (Eds.), *Psychopathic behavior: Approaches to research.* New York: Wiley.

Hauser, W. A. & Kurland, L. T. (1975). The epidemiology of epilepsy in Rochester, Minnesota, 1953 through 1967. *Epilepsia, 16,* 1-66.

Hendricks, S. E., Fitzpatrick, D. F., Hartmann, K., Quaife, M. A., Stratbucker, R. A., & Graber, B. (1988). Brain structure and function in sexual molesters of children and adolescents. *Journal of Clinical Psychiatry, 49,* 108-112.

Hermann, B. P., Schwartz, M. S., Whitman, S., & Karnes, W. E. (1980). Aggression and epilepsy: Seizure type comparisons and high risk variables. *Epilepsia, 22,* 691-698.

Hull, J. D. (1995, January 30). The state of the union. *Time,* 53-62.

Jacobsen, C. F. (1936). Studies of cerebral function in primates: I. The functions of the frontal association areas in monkeys. *Comprehensive Psychology Monographs, 13,* 3-60.

Joynt, R. J. (1992). Make my day. *Archives of Neurology, 49,* 591.

Kaimowitz v. Dept. of Mental Health, 42 U.S.L.W. Suppl. 2063, (D. Michigan, 1973).

Kandel E. & Freed, D. (1989). Frontal lobe dysfunction and antisocial behavior: A review. *Journal of Clinical Psychology, 45,* 404-413.

Kgachaturyan, A. A. (1951). *Neuropatologiya i Psichiatriya, 20,* 18-22. Microfilmed English translation, Library of Congress, TT60-13724.

King, A., Lancaster, J., & Benitone, J. (1970). Amygdalectomy in the free-ranging vervet (ceropithecusalthiops). *Journal of Psychiatric Research, 7,* 191-199.

King, D. & Ajmone, M. (1977). Clinical features and ictal patterns of epileptic patients with EEG temporal lobe foci. *Annals of Neurology, 2,* 138-147.

Kurland, H. D., Yeager, C. T., & Arthur, R. J. (1963). Psychophysiologic aspects of severe behavior disorders. Archives of *General Psychiatry, 8,* 599-604.

Lewin, J. & Sumners, D. (1992). Successful treatment of episodic dyscontrol with carbamazepine. *British Journal of Psychiatry, 161,* 261-262.

Lewis, D., Pincus, J. Feldman, M., Jackson, L., & Bard, B. (1986). Psychiatric, neurological and psychoeducational characteristics of 15 death row inmates in the United States. *American Journal of Psychiatry, 143,* 838-845.

Lewis, D., Pincus, J., Bard, B., Richardson, E., Prichep, L., Feldman, M., & Yeager, C. (1988). Neuropsychiatric, psychoeducational, and family characteristics of 14 juveniles condemned to death in the United States. *American Journal of Psychiatry, 145,* 584-589.

Mahowald, M. W., Bundlie, S. R., Hurwitz, T. D., & Schenck, C. H. (1990). Sleep, violence-forensic science implications: Polygraph and video documentation. *Journal of Forensic Sciences, 35,* 413-432.

Mahowald, M. W., Schenck, C. H., Rosen, G. M., & Hurwitz, T. D. (1992). The role of a sleep disorder center in evaluating sleep violence. *Archives of Neurology, 49,* 604-607.

Malamud, N. (1967). Psychiatric disorders with intracranial tumors of the limbic system. *Archives of Neurology, 17,* 113-123.

Mark, V. & Ervin, F. (1970). *Violence and the Brain.* New York: Harper & Row.

Matter of Torsney, 412 N.Y.S.2d 914, reh'g ordered, 417 N.Y.S.2d 467, rev'd, 420 N.Y.S.2d 192 (Ct. App. N.Y. 1979).

McLuhan, M. (1989). *The global village: Transformations in world life and media.* New York: Oxford University Press.

Menken, M. (1992). Grappling with the enigma of violence. *Archives of Neurology, 49,* 592-594.

Milne, H. B. (1979). Epileptic homicide: Drug-induced. *British Journal of Psychiatry, 134,* 547-552.

Monroe, R. R. (1985). Episodic behavioral disorders and limbic ictus. *Comprehensive Psychiatry, 26,* 466-479.

Moyer, K. E. (1968). Kinds of aggression and their physiological basis. *Community, Behavior, and Biology, 2,* 65-87.

Mungus, D. (1983). An empirical analysis of specific syndromes of violent behavior. The *Journal of Nervous and Mental Disease, 171,* 354-361.

Nousiainen, U., Suomalainen, T., & Mervaala, E. (1992).

Clinical benefits of scalp EEG studies in intractable seizure disorders. *Acta Neurologic Scandanavia, 85,* 181-186.

Paradis, C. M., Horn, L., Lazar, R. M., & Schwartz, D. W. (1994). Brain dysfunction and violent behavior in a man with a congenital subarachnoid cyst. *Hospital and Community Psychiatry, 45,* 714-716.

Pontius, A. A. (1973). Conceptual model of minimal brain dysfunction. General Discussion, Proceedings of the MBD Conference, 1972. *Annals of the New York Academy of Sciences, 205,* 61-63.

Pontius, A. A. (1974). Basis for a neurological test of frontal-lobe system maturational lag in juvenile delinquents shown in narratives test. *Adolescence, 44,* 509-518.

Pontius, A. A. (1987). "Psychotic trigger reaction": Neuro-psychiatric and neuro-biological (limbic?) aspects of homicide, reflecting on normal action. *Integrative Psychiatry, 5,* 116-139.

Raine, A., Buchsbaum, M. S., Stanley, J., Lottenberg, S., Abel, L., & Stoddard, J. (1994). Selective reductions in prefrontal glucose metabolism in murderers. *Biological Psychiatry, 36,* 365-373.

Raine, A. & Scerbo, A. (1991). Biological theories of violence. In J. S. Milner (Ed.), *Neuropsychology of Aggression* (pp. 1-26). Boston: Kluwer.

Ramani, V. & Gumnit, R.J. (1981). Intensive monitoring of epileptic patients with a history of episodic aggression. *Archives of Neurology, 38,* 570-571.

Reitan R. M. & Wolfson, D. (1993). *The Halstead-Reitan neuropsychological test battery* (2d ed.) (pp. 85-92).Tucson, AZ: Neuropsychology Press.

Restak, R. (1993). The neurological defense of violent crime. *Archives of Neurology, 50,* 869-871.

Robins, L. N. (1966). *Deviant children grow up.* Baltimore: Williams & Wilkins.

Rodin, E. (1973). Psychomotor epilepsy and aggressive behavior. *Archives of General Psychiatry, 28,* 210-213.

Salinsky, M., Kanter, R., & Dasheiff, R. (1987). Effectiveness of multiple EEGs in supporting the diagnosis of epilepsy: An operational curve. *Epilepsia, 28,* 331-334.

Schatzman, M. (1986). To sleep perchance to kill. *New Scientist, 26,* 60-62.

Schiffer, R. B. & Babigian, H. M. (1984). Behavioral disorders in multiple sclerosis, temporal lobe epilepsy, and amyotrophic lateral sclerosis. *Archives of Neurology, 41,* 1067-1069.

Shuman, S. I. (1977). *Psychosurgery and the medical control of violence* (pp. 240-241). Detroit: Wayne State Press.

Sima, A. A. F., D'Amato, C., Defendini, R. F., Jones, M. Z., Foster, N. L., Lynch, T., & Wilhelmsen, K. C. (1994). Primary limbic gliosis familial and sporadic cases. *Brain Pathology, 4,* 538.

Stein, D. J., Hollander, E., Cohen, L., Frenkel, M., Saoud, J. B., Decaria, C., Aronowitz, B., Levin, A., Liebowitz, M., & Cohen, L. (1993). Neuropsychiatric impairment in impulsive personality disorder. *Psychiatric Research, 48,* 257-266.

Stone, J. L., McDaniel, K. D., Hughes, J. R., & Hermann, B. O. (1986). Episodic dyscontrol disorder and paroxysmal EEG abnormalities: Successful treatment with carbamazepine. *Biological Psychiatry, 21,* 208-212.

Tarsh, M. J. (1986). On serious violence during sleep walking. *British Journal of Psychiatry, 148,* 476.

Treiman, D. M. (1986). Epilepsy and violence: Medical and legal issues. *Epilepsia, 27*, (Suppl. 2), S77-104.

Valenstein, E. S. (1980). *The psychosurgery debate: Scientific, legal and ethical perspectives*. San Francisco: W. H. Freeman.

Volkow, N. D. & Tancredi, L. (1987). Neural substrate of violent behavior: A preliminary study with positron emission tomography. *British Journal of Psychiatry, 151*, 668-673.

Walker, E. A. (1961). Murder or epilepsy? *Journal of Nervous and Mental Disorders, 133*, 430-437.

Ward, A. A. (1948). The cingulate gyrus: Area 24. *Journal of Neurophysiology, 11*, 13-23.

Weiger, W. A. & Bear, D. M. (1988). An approach to the neurology of aggression. *Journal of Psychiatric Research, 22*, 85-98.

Wender, P. H. (1972). The minimal brain dysfunction syndrome in children. *The Journal of Nervous and Mental Disease, 155*, 55-71.

Wilhelmsen, K. C., Lynch, T., Neystat, M., Nygaard, T. G., Bernstein, M., Marder, K., Mayeux, R., Fahn, S., Rowland, L. P., Foster, N. L., Wszolek, Z., Koehan, K., Sima, A. A. F., & Deffendini, R. (August, 1994). *Clinical, pathologic and genetic analysis of familial disinhibition-dementia-Parkinsonism-amyotrophy-complex: A possible clue to the etiology of atypical dementias*. Fourth International Conference on Alzheimer's Disease, Minneapolis, MN.

Williams, D. (1969). Neural factors related to habitual aggression. *Brain, 92*, 503-520.

Yeudall, L. T. (1977). Neuropsychological assessment of forensic disorders. *Canada's Mental Health, 25*, 7-15.

Yeudall, L. T. & Fromm-Auch, D. (1979). Neuropsychological impairments in various psychopathological populations. In J. Gruzelier & P. Flor-Henry (Eds.), *Hemisphere asymmetrics of function and psychopathology* (pp. 5-31). New York: Elsevier/ North Holland.

About the Authors

Douglas Johnson-Greene earned his PhD in clinical psychology from the University of Mississippi in 1993. He completed his internship at the Portland Veterans Administration and Oregon Health Sciences University and postdoctoral residency in neuropsychology at the University of Michigan. He is currently a fellow in the Departments of Neurology and Psychiatry at the University of Michigan. His research interests include neuroimaging, assessment of premorbid abilities, and neuropsychological and cerebral metabolic sequelae of alcohol and drug abuse.

Kenneth M. Adams is a 1974 clinical psychology graduate of Wayne State University. He has published extensively in areas of medical psychology, including long-term effects of drugs on behavior, effects of medical/surgical interventions, and methods of assessment. Dr. Adams is President of the Division of Clinical Neuropsychology of the American Psychological Association and is the former Executive Secretary of the International Neuropsychological Society.

CHAPTER 3

SEX DIFFERENCES IN JUVENILE VIOLENCE

Overview

There is no doubt that violence in the United States is a very serious social problem. The report of the National Academy of Sciences Panel on the "Understanding and Control of Violent Behavior" indicated that in 1990, 23,438 Americans were murdered, resulting in a rate of 9.4 for every 100,000 people (Roth, 1994). This rate is nearly double that of Spain, which has the second highest rate in the industrialized world and is four times that of Canada. In addition, violent crimes short of murder are also a frequent occurrence in the United States. Rates for rape, personal robberies, and aggravated assault are among the world's highest (Roth, 1994).

Juveniles are in the forefront with regard to this problem. The homicide rate among adolescents has doubled in the last decade, while it has remained steady or declined in other age groups (Van, 1995). Adolescents are also more likely than adults to be murdered in any given year (Roth, 1994). This increase in violence is further reflected in the fact that the number of juvenile court cases involving serious crime increased 68% between 1988 and 1992 (Skorneck, 1994).

Finally, it should be noted that there is a marked sex difference in the commission of violent crime, with females accounting for only 12.5% (Gibb, 1995). This difference corresponds to a similar gender disparity in the prevalence of conduct disorder (CD). This diagnostic category is the official diagnosis of the *Diagnostic and Statistical Manual of Mental Disorders*, Fourth Edition (DSM-IV), of the American Psychiatric Association (1994) most commonly given when a juvenile presents with problems of violence. It includes the following symptoms: "often initiates physical fights; has been physically cruel to people; and, has stolen while confronting a victim (e.g., mugging, purse snatching, extortion, armed robbery" (DSM-IV, 1994, p. 90).

Conduct disorder is the most common reason for the referral of children to inpatient and outpatient treatment facilities (Abikoff & Klein, 1992; Martin & Hoffman, 1990; Robins, 1991) and is "highly predictive of later delinquency, criminality, and substance abuse in adolescence and adulthood" (Frick et al., 1993, p. 320). A decisive preponderance of conduct disordered males in both referred and nonreferred populations has been found in earlier reviews of the literature (Eme, 1979, 1984) and in more recent reviews (Baum, 1989; Hinshaw, 1992a; Kazdin, 1992, 1995; Lytton, 1990a; Martin & Hoffman, 1990; Offord, Boyle, & Racine, 1991; Quay, 1986; Robins, 1991; Schonert-Reichl & Offer, 1992). DSM-IV estimates the prevalence of this disorder for males under 18 to be between 6 and 16% and for females between 2 and 9%. Indeed, Robins

(1991) noted: "The most stable of all observations is the high rate of conduct disorder in boys as compared to girls" (p. 205). The only disagreement with the near universal acceptance of this finding comes from Zoccolillo (1993), who suggested that criteria may be biased against finding girls with conduct disorder; thus, he questioned whether or not there truly is a strong gender difference. However, as Zahn-Waxler (1993) pointed out, this reduction or elimination of the gender difference occurred as a function of Zoccolillo's selective review of epidemiological studies in which aggression, violence, and criminality were deemphasized as criteria. The validity of such an approach was therefore quite suspect. Given the striking male preponderance for violence, it is disconcerting that Robins (1991) stated: "Why this occurs, to what extent it is a biological and to what extent it is a culturally determined fact is yet to be settled" (p. 205).

In view of Robins' observation, this chapter will attempt to shed some light on the factors that contribute to the gender difference. In so doing, it will expand upon earlier efforts in this regard (Eme, 1979, 1984) and draw upon Loeber's (1990), Lytton's (1990a), Moffitt's (1993a, 1993b), Robins' (1991), and Roth's (1994) recent summaries of the various factors that contribute to the development of antisocial behavior and violence.

The National Academy of Sciences Panel on the "Understanding and Control of Violent Behavior" suggested that these factors can be conceptualized in terms of four levels (Roth, 1994):

Macrosocial: Characteristics of large social units, such as countries and communities. An example would be social values that promote or discourage violence.

Microsocial: Characteristics of encounters among people. An example would be whether or not weapons are easily accessible.

Psychosocial: An individual's characteristics that influence patterns of interacting with others. An example would be customary ways of expressing anger.

Biological: Chemical, electrical, and hormonal interactions which underlie human behavior.

This chapter, because it is from a psychological rather than a sociological perspective, will focus on psychosocial and biological factors and their interaction. Lastly, it should be noted that as with Halpern (1992) and Maccoby (1988), the words "sex," "gender," and "gender-related" will be considered synonymous and used interchangeably.

Definition

In terms of the scientific study of juvenile violence in the area of psychology, most of the research has focused on a dimension termed "undercontrolled" or "externalizing" (Baum, 1989). This dimension has been variously labeled conduct disorder, antisocial behavior, undersocialized aggressive disorder, aggressive, and delinquent. While these various categories cannot be equated and some attempts to give more precision to the various terms have been made (Hinshaw, Lahey, & Hart, 1993), the overlap is such that the major dimensions of conduct disorder can be found in all of the foregoing (Quay, 1986) and most investigations that have studied antisocial behavior classify all antisocial and delinquent behavior and conduct problems together (Lytton, 1990a, 1990b). Thus, following the lead of Lytton (1990a), we have chosen to treat conduct disorder or antisocial behavior as a unitary phenomenon and all research bearing on the factors contributing to male preponderance in conduct disorder, delinquency, antisocial behavior, and aggression will be considered as relevant to the topic of sex differences in juvenile violence.

Lastly, a consensus has recently emerged regarding a dual taxonomy of antisocial behavior proposed by Moffitt (1993a), which has been endorsed by such theorists as Achenbach

(1993), Compas, Hinden, and Gerhardt (1995), and Gottesman and Goldsmith (1994). The first category of this taxonomy is that of *adolescent limited antisocial behavior*, which is conceptualized as a temporary maturity gap that encourages teens to mimic antisocial behavior. The second category is termed *life-course-persistent antisocial behavior*, in which children's neuropsychological problems interact cumulatively with their criminogenic environments across developmental stages, culminating in an antisocial personality. It is the juveniles from the life-course-persistent category who are the most likely to engage in aggressive/violent behavior (Kazdiidzin, 1995). Moreover, the 5 or 6% of offenders who account for about 50% of the known crimes come from this group (Moffitt, 1993a). Hence, the factors that contribute to this category of antisocial behavior will be examined in this chapter because they are the most relevant to the topic of sex differences in juvenile violence (Moffitt, 1993a).

Biological Factors

The contribution of biological factors to juvenile violence has been established solidly in the literature. Moffitt (1993a, 1993b) indicated that there is strong evidence that children who ultimately become persistently antisocial suffer from deficits in neuropsychological functioning and suggested that this is one of the most robust findings in the study of antisocial behavior. Richters and Cicchetti (1993) were in full agreement with this position. The two deficits most commonly associated with antisocial behavior are deficits in executive and verbal functioning (Moffitt, 1993a, 1993b). Similarly, Gottesman and Goldsmith (1994) concluded that "the evidence for genetic influences on antisocial behavior is strong enough that developmentalists should make room for genetic concepts not only in their broad theorizing but, when feasible from time to time, in their

research programs as well" (p. 98). This conclusion applies primarily to that form of juvenile antisocial behavior which persists into adulthood (Rutter, Macdonald, Le Couteur, Harrington, Bolton, & Bailey, 1990). With regard to genes and behavior in general, it is clear that dispositions, not destinies, are inherited (Rose, 1995). As applied to antisocial behavior, Gottesman and Goldsmith (1994) indicated that there may be "*partially* genetically influenced *predispositions* for basic behavioral tendencies, such as impulsivity, that under certain experiential contexts, make the *probability* of committing certain crimes higher than for individuals who possess lesser degrees of such behavioral tendencies" (p. 72). These influences result in what Moffitt (1993a) termed *neuropsychological variation*, such as *difficult temperament*, which might constitute a risk for antisocial behavior. In summary, the biological factors relevant to the sex difference in juvenile violence will be considered under the two broad categories of *neuropsychological deficit* and *neuropsychological variation*.

Neuropsychological Deficits

That some form of neurological impairment is involved in the etiology of CD receives strong support from recent literature reviews on the neuropsychology of CD by Moffitt (1993a) and Richters and Cicchetti (1993). This neurological impairment, in turn, is hypothesized to contribute to the development of conditions such as a "difficult temperament," Attention-Deficit/Hyperactivity Disorder (ADHD), and various learning problems that place a child at risk for the development of CD.

The neuropsychological deficits that have been most thoroughly studied are deficits in executive and verbal functioning as manifested in ADHD and the various learning disabilities (primarily reading disability) that contribute to academic difficulties.

Attention-Deficit Hyperactivity Disorder

There is a consensus that childhood ADHD is a major risk factor for the subsequent development of CD (Abikoff & Klein, 1992; Loeber, 1990; Loeber & Keenan, 1994; Robins, 1991), especially when it is properly conceptualized as a disorder of *impulsivity/behavioral disinhibition* rather than motor overactivity (Barkley, 1994). Indeed, Robins (1991) indicated that we know more about hyperactivity as an early behavioral risk factor than any other behavioral predictors.

Two theories have been advanced to explain this risk. First, Abikoff and Klein (1992) theorized that ADHD and CD share a common dysfunction (such as a deficit in executive functioning, Moffitt, 1993a, 1993b; self-regulation, Douglas, 1989; or behavioral inhibition, Barkley, 1994), which maximizes interpersonal conflict, behavioral dyscontrol, etc., which, in turn, would facilitate the development of aggressive behavior. This theory has perhaps been most cogently articulated by Moffitt (1993a). She suggested that impulsivity increases the risk of long-term antisocial behavior through direct and indirect means. Deficits in impulse control can produce antisocial behavior directly by interfering with children's ability to control their behavior and to think of future consequences of antisocial acts. For example, Loeber (1990) and Loeber et al. (1993) suggested that ADHD may act as a catalyst for CD in the following ways: (a) ADHD may contribute to the persistence of conduct problems; (b) ADHD may lead to an escalation in an overt pathway to disruptive behavior, i.e., a pathway consisting of aggression, fighting, and violence in which less serious disruptive behaviors precede the onset of moderately serious and very serious behaviors; (c) ADHD may promote an escalation in the seriousness of substance use, especially as it is associated with an escalation in the overt pathway.

Indirectly, deficits in impulse control can lead to antisocial behavior by disrupting children's

success in school, thereby making it more likely that they will turn to deviant ways to achieve success. Recently, Hinshaw (1992a, 1992b) reviewed extensively the issues pertaining to the comorbidity between externalizing behavior problems and academic underachievement. The findings that are relevant to the present discussion were as follows. First, in opposition to earlier reports that posited links between aggressive behavior and underachievement, Hinshaw concluded that the specific relation in childhood pertains to ADHD. The overlap between childhood aggression and underachievement is mediated chiefly through the comorbidity of aggression with ADHD. Loeber's (1990) earlier review reached an identical conclusion. Additional support for the conclusion that it is hyperactivity rather than aggression which is the major contributor to academic difficulties in the early school years comes from a recent study by Sonuga-Barke, Lamparelli, Stevenson, Thompson, and Henry (1994). The study examined the relationship between behavior problems and intelligence in three-year-old boys and girls selected for either conduct problems or hyperactivity and found that hyperactivity, but not conduct problems, was negatively related to intelligence test scores. Hence, hyperactive children enter school already at an intellectual disadvantage and this disadvantage could interact with the demands of school to increase the risk of developing CD. Thus, the greater prevalence of ADHD in males contributes to the greater prevalence of aggression and academic underachievement in males (Eme, 1979, 1984) which, in turn, contributes to the greater prevalence of CD in males. This, of course, is not to deny that externalizing behavior can lead to academic underachievement. This pathway, however, would seem to be more probable in adolescence than childhood (Hinshaw, 1992a).

Given the importance of ADHD as a risk factor for the development of CD, it is instructive to note that current reviews of the literature

(Barkley, 1990, 1995; Hinshaw, 1992a, 1992b; Shaywitz & Shaywitz, 1988; Whalen, 1989) confirmed past reviews (Eme, 1979, 1984) in indicating a decisive male preponderance in ADHD which is most pronounced in clinic samples, but is also clearly evident in representative community populations. For example, Whalen (1989) indicated that typically, three to five males are identified for every female, with ratios as high as 9 to 1 having been reported and that the more stringent the definition, the greater the sex ratio favoring males. Hinshaw (1994) also reported that if stringent diagnostic criteria were used, prevalence estimates for ADHD (DSM-III criteria) in grade-school-aged children are 9% for boys and 2% for girls. Furthermore, the contention that the sex ratio may be a function of ascertainment bias (Berry, Shaywitz, & Shaywitz, 1985) is challenged by more current, comprehensive findings in community samples in which males appear to be more severe in their level of hyperactive-impulsive behavior than females (Barkley, 1995).

Hence, the marked sex difference in ADHD doubtlessly is a major contribution in explaining the marked sex difference in violent antisocial behavior. While a detailed examination of the reasons for the sex difference in ADHD, assuming one accepts the current consensus that ADHD and CD are independent though frequently co-occurring disorders (Abikoff & Klein, 1992; Barkley, 1990; Hinshaw, 1992a, 1992b, 1994; Loeber, 1990), is beyond the scope of this chapter, note must be taken of research on temperament by Zuckerman (1994) and Kagan (1994) which points to a possible reason for this difference.

Bates (1994) indicated that Zuckerman (1994) has made a good case for establishing a dimension of temperament termed "impulsive, unsocialized sensation seeking" as being a stable, early appearing trait with a strong biological substrate that is more characteristic of boys than girls. Similarly, Kagan (1994) reported that because he did not wish to prejudge the possibility of sex differences, he included an equal number of boys and girls in the original selection of the uninhibited and inhibited groups. Upon follow-up, both in his study and in another large study which he cited, boys were much more likely to retain their uninhibited status and girls were more likely to change from uninhibited to inhibited. Indeed, he noted that girls were more fearful than boys at every age and speculated that an unusually fearless temperament may be more prevalent in boys, observing that "biology may have some modest effect" (p. 196) in this regard. Thus, in the early developmental years, there are clear signs of a sex difference in temperament which may make a significant contribution to the decisively greater male prevalence in ADHD.

Learning Disability.

Moffitt (1993b), in her review of the neuropsychology of conduct disorder, concluded that: "Almost all of the neuropsychology studies reviewed for this article provided some evidence of deficit on language-based tests for delinquents" (p. 143). More recently, Williams and McGee (1994) found that a reading disability at 9 years of age predicted a conduct disorder at age 15 in males. Hinshaw, Lahey, and Hart (1993) suggested that deficient verbal abilities may lead to CD in the following ways:

Deficient verbal abilities may thus be linked through the proximal mechanism of deficient self-regulatory capacities or caretaker frustration in understanding the child's needs; more distally, language deficits may serve a causal role toward eventual conduct problems by fostering underachievement, which in turn exacerbates preexisting externalizing behavioral proclivities (p. 44).

Needless to say, in all of these foregoing variables, males tend to predominate.

With regard to language- and learning-disabled children, there is agreement that in referred samples, males outnumber females in ratios of

3:1 or 4:1 (Rutter & Mawhood, 1991; Wadsworth, DeFries, Stevenson, Gilger, & Pennington, 1992). However, gender ratios in research-identified samples are less consistent. While in some studies the ratio was approximately the same as it is in referred samples (Lewis, Hitch, & Walker, 1994), in others it approximated 1:1 (DeFries, Olson, Pennington, & Smith 1991; Wadsworth et al., 1992). Furthermore, in these latter studies, DeFries (1991) indicated that the gender ratio is a function of severity, with relatively more males at the extreme end of the distribution. Hence, the ratio is not truly 1:1 and there is an excess of males, especially in the severe range. Furthermore, the contention that the male excess is exclusively due to ascertainment bias (Shaywitz, Shaywitz, Fletcher, & Escobar, 1990) is flawed by the study's limited sample size and the weak statistical power of the analysis (Liederman & Flannery, 1995).

Finally, and perhaps most importantly, Shaywitz et al. (1995) have provided the first direct evidence of a sex difference in the functional organization of the brain for language. During phonological tasks, brain activation in males is lateralized to the left inferior frontal gyrus regions, while in females, both the left and right regions are activated. As deficits in phonological processing are at the core of most reading disabilities (Kamphi, 1992; Snowling, 1991; Stanovich, 1994), the finding that females devote greater hemispheric resources to the phonological tasks than do males may be the major biological explanation for females being less likely to have reading disabilities.

Thus, the question as to what extent the marked male prevalence in referred samples is due to ascertainment bias appears to be more open than Vogel (1990) would have it. Accordingly, the greater male prevalence among language- and learning-disabled children contributes to the greater male prevalence in externalizing disorders and academic underachievement, per-

haps primarily through worsening preexisting, externalizing behavior problems (Cornwall & Bawden, 1992).

In summary, Hinshaw's (1992a, 1992b) massive reviews of the literature suggest clearly that school problems in childhood are not primarily a function of aggressive behavior as Patterson and his colleagues have suggested (Patterson, DeBaryshe, & Ramsey, 1989; Patterson, Capaldi, & Bank, 1991), although this may be so in adolescence. Hence, the greater male likelihood to experience school problems because of ADHD or a verbal deficiency, etc., seems to render them more likely to develop CD. Furthermore, the interaction among all of these variables (attentional problems, aggression, and verbal/neuropsychological deficits) greatly increases the risk for males developing a delinquent disorder in adolescence (Hinshaw, 1992b).

Male Vulnerability to Biological Risk Factors

The preceding discussion established that males are more likely to be afflicted by neuropsychological deficits in executive and verbal functioning which would then increase their likelihood of developing CD. The question which then naturally suggests itself is "whence this vulnerability?"

Reviews by Loeber (1990) and Moffitt (1993a) indicate clearly that a host of pre-, peri-, and post-natal factors, such as exposure to neurotoxins (lead), low birthweight, and maternal drug use during pregnancy, can lead to neurological impairment. Kopp and Kaler's (1989) literature review on the biological risk factors that can adversely influence development during infancy offered empirical support for this conclusion, as did Rutter's (1989) review of the role of organic brain dysfunction in increasing psychiatric risk, and a recent study on pre- and peri-natal factors and the risk for hyperactivity (Chandola, Robling, Peters, Melville-Thomas, and McGuffin, 1992).

Brennan, Mednick, and Kandel (1991) have made a case for obstetrical difficulties playing a causal role in repetitive violent offending.

Thus, various biological risk factors seem to make important contributions to the development of aggression. This finding, in turn, highlights the significance of the sex difference found in earlier literature reviews (Birns, 1976; Maccoby & Jacklin, 1974; Rutter, 1970; Willerman, 1979), those of more recent vintage (Goodman, 1991; Gualtieri & Hicks, 1985, Jacklin, 1989; Zaslow & Hayes, 1986) and a recent study by Verloove-Vanhorick et al. (1994). This literature indicates that from the moment of conception, the male organism appears to be more vulnerable to a host of pre-, peri-, and post-natal stresses. For example, more males than females are conceived, but more males die before birth (Gualtieri & Hicks, 1985; McMillen, 1979) and more males experience difficulties during the birth process, resulting in more males with birth defects (Jacklin, 1989). Also, males appear to be more adversely affected by Fetal Alcohol Syndrome than females (Steinhausen, Willms, & Spohr, 1994). The biological factors that are thought to contribute to this greater male vulnerability are as follows:

Male organismic immaturity. The first factor that contributes to the greater vulnerability of males to biological risk factors is the greater organismic immaturity of the male. Taylor (1985) reported that one of the most persistent themes in male-female differentiation is the rate of development such that from the middle of the fetal period onward, the average girl is ahead of the average boy. This difference in physical maturation reaches 1 year by school entrance, 1 1/2 years at age 9, and 2 years at the onset of puberty (Garai & Scheinfeld, 1968; Tanner, 1978), and is thought to be regulated by the Y chromosome. Support for this finding is found in Tanner's (1978) observation that children with the XXY chromosome constitution (Klinefelter's syndrome) have a skeletal maturity indistinguishable from that of

the normal male, whereas children with the XO chromosome constitution (Turner's syndrome) have a skeletal maturity approximating that of the normal female constitution.

The consequence of this slower rate of development is hypothesized to be a greater likelihood of male pathology for two reasons. First, immature organisms are more susceptible to damage than mature ones (Gualtieri & Hicks, 1985). Second, the slower transcription of genomic information in males (as a function of the Y chromosome in regulating the pace of development) is postulated to allow more genomic information to be transcribed (Ounstead & Taylor, 1972). Thus, males manifest relatively more information which exists potentially in every genome. Some of this information may be misinstruction and prove disadvantageous, resulting in the greater prevalence of male pathology.

Sex-linked disorders. A second contributing factor is the greater male susceptibility to sex-linked disorders (Gaultieri & Hicks, 1985). The Y chromosome is considerably smaller than the X chromosome, thus giving the female a 4 to 5% quantitative superiority in genetic material. Because females receive two X chromosomes, they get two doses of X-chromosome sex-linked genes, one from each of their parents. Males receive only one X chromosome (from their mother) and therefore only one dose of X chromosome genes. This asymmetry in genetic material leaves males susceptible to a number of genetic defects that ordinarily do not affect females. If a daughter has a harmful recessive gene on one X chromosome, she will usually have a dominant gene on the other X chromosome to compensate for it. Thus, the recessive gene is not expressed. A male has no complementary gene to compensate for the effects of a harmful gene on his X chromosome, so the harmful gene is expressed (Cole & Cole, 1993).

Immunoreactive theory. A third factor put forth by Gualtieri and Hicks (1985) is termed the immunoreactive theory of selective male affliction. They suggested that there is "something about the male fetus that evokes an inhospitable uterine environment" (p. 427). They believe that the mother's body is stimulated to produce a kind of antibody against the male fetus (but not against a female fetus that is genetically more similar to the mother) and that these antibodies lead directly or indirectly to fetal damage. This theory recently received support from research on genomic imprinting, which suggested that paternal and maternal DNA may be in conflict with one another. This conflict then translates into maternal-fetal conflict, which may help to explain some of the medical complications of pregnancy (Haig, 1993). Additional support comes from research on the causes of schizophrenia in which it was hypothesized that influenza may play a causative role by creating maternal antibodies that then become fetal autoantibodies (Tsuang, 1994).

Fetal testosterone. A fourth factor proposed by Geschwind and Galaburda (1987) (and reviewed by McManus & Bryden, 1991) involves a model of cerebral lateralization based on the supposition that increased fetal testosterone levels modify neural development, immune development, and neural crest development by slowing brain growth during a critical period in certain areas of the left hemisphere. This modification, in turn, is then related to learning disorders, left-handedness, immune disorders, and structural anomalies. As the principal determinant of testosterone levels is hypothesized to be the H-Y antigen, determined by a gene on the Y chromosome (McManus & Bryden, 1991), males are expected to be more affected by this factor than females. Recently, this theory has undergone some modification by proposing a different mechanism for the action of testosterone; however, the theory yields the same predictions regarding brain development (Grimshaw, Bryden, & Finegan, 1995).

Male Vulnerability to Psychological Stress

In 1970, Rutter and his colleagues detected sex differences in children's responses to a number of specific family contexts, for example, parental mental illness, discord, short-term residential care, and day care participation. Rutter found then, and reaffirmed in 1985 (Rutter, 1985), the hypothesis that analogous to greater male susceptibility to biological stress, there exists a greater susceptibility to psychological stress as well. More recently, Zaslow and Hayes (1986) and Earls (1987) reviewed the literature in this regard and concluded that Rutter was correct: Psychosocial stress appears to have more serious effects on boys than on girls. The biological factors contributing to this finding and their implications for the development of CD will be discussed. A discussion of the psychosocial factors contributing to this greater vulnerability will be deferred to the appropriate section.

In a series of papers, Sackett (cited in Zaslow & Hayes, 1986) summarized the evidence of sex differences in the response of rhesus monkeys to partial and total isolation rearing. His overall conclusion was that, in comparison to males, females appeared "buffered" against permanent deficits induced by isolation rearing. Whereas females showed adaptive changes following the deprivation conditions, males rarely did. Significant differences appeared between males and females across a range of measures both in initial post-isolation testing and over a longer course of time. Zaslow and Hayes (1986) concluded that the results of these studies indicate that physiological variables must be considered in attempting to understand the basis for the sex difference in children's responses to psychosocial stress. They then discussed ways in which the aforementioned sex differences in physical vulnerability and maturity may form the basis of a sex difference in response to psychosocial stress by (a) leading to the presence of a subsample of boys with subtle neurological compromise or behavioral extremes that affect response to stress directly, or indirectly through an altered social environment (this hypothesis did not receive any support in a recent study by Breslau, 1990); (b) leading to the presence of a subsample of boys for whom psychosocial stress represents a multiple stressor, following or co-occurring with health crises; and (c) leading to overall sex differences in the ability to tolerate and recoup from arousal states. This latter possibility received support from Maccoby (1990), who indicated that there is considerable evidence suggesting that because of prenatal androgenization, males exhibit faster rise-times or higher levels of emotional arousal under conditions of stress or conflict and are slower to return to prestressor levels than females. She added that sex differences on the positive side of emotional arousal have not been studied systematically, but that there is reason to suspect that males may also be more susceptible to being aroused into states of positive excitement.

This greater vulnerability to psychological stress helps explain the finding of a disproportionately high preponderance of insecure attachments among boys in some studies (Carlson, Cicchetti, Barnett, & Braunwald, 1989), as well as the finding of a greater likelihood that insecurely attached males will develop aggressive and disruptive behaviors (Cohn, 1990; Greenberg, Speltz, & DeKlyen, 1993; Lewis, Feiring, McGuffog, & Jaskir, 1984; Renken, Egeland, Marvinney, Mangelsdorf, & Sroufe, 1989; Speltz, Greenberg, & DeKlyen, 1990; Turner, 1991).

The greater male vulnerability to psychological stress also helps to explain the greater prevalence of negative effects of nonmaternal care on males (Baydar & Brooks-Gunn, 1991; Belsky, 1988; Scarr & Eisenberg, 1993) (although this area of research is not without controversy; Belsky, 1990; Belsky & Braungart, 1991; Clarke-Stewart, 1989; Silverstein, 1991), and the consistent finding that when maternal employment in the preschool years has a negative effect, it is on males (Hoffman, 1989). A very interesting example of this negative effect was seen in a recent study by Coon, Carey, Fulker, and DeFries (1993), who found that higher maternal IQ had a negative effect on boys' but not girls' achievement scores. They attributed this surprising finding to the fact that mothers with higher intelligence tend to have more prestigious jobs and that maternal employment has been found to exert a negative effect on the achievement scores of young males.

Neuropsychological Variation

Neuropsychological variation, as defined by Moffitt (1993a), refers to the extent to which anatomical structures and physiological processes within the nervous system influence psychological characteristics, such as temperament or behavioral or cognitive development. In the scientific literature, this variation has been studied most frequently in terms of temperamental and neurophysiological correlates that index central nervous system functioning, such as neurotransmitters.

Temperament. Despite the continuing debate over the definition and measurement of individual differences in temperament, there is general agreement that temperamental differences have developmentally early biological roots (Bates, 1994) and that children with "difficult" temperaments are more vulnerable to poor developmental outcome (Bezirganian & Cohen, 1992; Maziade, Caron, Cote, Boutin, & Thivierge, 1990; Prior, 1992). Furthermore, the relationship between difficult temperaments and externalizing disorders is stronger than with internalizing disorders (Prior, 1992). This conclusion from Prior's literature review has received additional solid corroboration in two more recent longitudinal studies (Caspi, Henry, McGee, Moffitt, & Silva, 1995; Sanson, Smart, Prior, & Oberklaid, 1993).

Additionally, while gender differences in temperament appear to be minimal in the infancy period, sex-related temperamental differences emerge from toddlerhood on and increase in magnitude, with boys becoming more difficult in temperament than girls (Bezirganian & Cohen, 1992; Prior, 1992; Sanson, Smart, Prior, & Oberklaid, 1993). Thus, it may be that the tendency for males to have a more difficult temperament contributes to the greater likelihood that they will develop the coercive interaction styles typical of antisocial children (Patterson, Reid, & Dishion, 1992).

This sex difference could arise in two ways (Bezirganian & Cohen, 1992). Temperament may be different at its outset in the sexes because of biological factors. Alternately, temperament may be the same initially, but because of an interaction between temperament and parenting, socialization may mold temperament to different end products in boys and girls. Research on this latter possibility is seminal, with some indication that high mother-son punishment and control leads to an increase in difficult temperament (Bezirganian & Cohen, 1992).

With regard to the possibility that temperament is different from the outset for boys and girls, there are four biologically based factors that would contribute to gender differences in difficult temperament for which there is a respectable empirical base. Three of these — gender differences in susceptibility to psychological stress, hyperactivity, and the temperamental dimension of impulsive, unsocialized sensation seeking—have already been discussed. What remains to be examined is the possibility of a gender difference in activity level.

Activity level. Prior (1992) indicated that activity level is an almost universal factor in theories of temperament and has been hypothesized to be a precursor to higher levels of aggression (Patterson, Littman, & Bricker, 1967), most probably due to the male propensity for "rough and tumble play" (Maccoby, 1988, 1990, 1991). This propensity is clearly more typical of boys, cannot be attributed to differential socialization (Maccoby, 1990, 1991), and is a pattern that is also seen primarily in the play of nonhuman primates (Maccoby, 1991).

Furthermore, there appears to be a solid empirical basis for implicating hormonal factors in this sex difference in rough and tumble play. From approximately weeks 8 to 24 of gestation, circulating levels of testosterone are markedly elevated in male fetuses. There is also a small sex difference during the early postnatal period, testosterone being elevated in males from about the first to fifth months (after that, until puberty, there is little difference between boys and girls in the circulating level of this hormone, Maccoby & Jacklin, 1980). These periods of increased testosterone production have been found to represent critical periods for hormonal influences (Hines & Green, 1991). As articulated by Maccoby and Jacklin (1974, 1980), these hormonal influences may result in males having a lower threshold for instigator stimuli, resulting in a greater "ease of learning" of aggression than females.

Several research reviews of the animal literature have documented the contribution of androgen as a predisposition to aggression. Collaer and Hines (1995), Ehrhardt and Meyer-Bahlburg (1979, 1981), Hart (1974), Hines and Kaufman (1994), Maccoby and Jacklin (1974, 1980), Money and Erhardt (1972), Quadagno, Briscoe, and Quadagno (1977), and Tieger (1980) have all concluded that, whereas the male of the vertebrate species is the more aggressive in both laboratory and natural situations, the perinatal administration of the androgen to females (thus mimicking what typically takes place in males) results in rough and tumble play, aggression approximating that of male animals, or both.

Analogous findings have been reported in samples of fetally androgenized human females (i.e., females with the disorder of "Congenital

Adrenal Hyperplasia," CAH) for physical energy expenditure, rough and tumble play, tomboyism, and propensity for physical aggression (Berenbaum & Hines, 1992; Collaer & Hines, 1995; Ehrhardt, 1979; Ehrhardt & Meyer-Bahlburg, 1979, 1981; Hines & Green, 1991; Meyer-Bahlburg & Ehrhardt, 1982; Reinisch, 1981), although not in the study by Hines and Kaufman (1994). However, the authors of this latter study observed that their results did not necessarily contradict the prior studies because those studies were interview-based and included questions about athletics and similar activities that their study did not assess. Moreover, their study could not rule out the possibility that girls with CAH have an enhanced desire to engage in rough and tumble play, but were unable to express their desire in their experimental situation. They further noted that when their data analysis was restricted to girls with girl partners, the girls with CAH showed somewhat higher levels (albeit not statistically significant) of rough and tumble play.

The criticism that these studies can be interpreted in terms of differential parental treatment or because of illness factors (Quadagno, Briscoe, & Quadagno, 1977) is markedly weakened by the following facts. First, while it is possible that the cortisone therapy received by females whose fetal androgenization was caused by CAH may have fueled differential parental expectations and hence affected the findings, this could not account for those females whose syndrome was progestin-induced and hence not in need of such treatment (Collaer & Hines, 1995). Second, Reinisch and Karow (1977), in their review of the effects of prenatal exposure to synthetic progestins and estrogens on human development, concluded that it seemed unlikely that the fact that the parent knew the child was treated for CAH had a significant effect on the rearing of the offspring. Similarly, Berenbaum and Hines (1992) indicated that in both their study as well as the studies of others, parents reported that they

did not treat CAH girls in a "masculine" fashion. If anything, Ehrhardt and Meyer-Bahlburg (1981) indicated that parents tended to oppose, rather than encourage, those temperamental characteristics of their daughters that appeared to be the sequelae of their specific perinatal hormone conditions (e.g., if concerned about tomboyism, they tended to encourage femininity). Of course, direct observation of parental behavior would be valuable in confirming this self-report. Third, there is no relationship between the degree of virilization or illness and the degree of gender-role behavior in human or animal studies (Berenbaum & Hines, 1992) as might be hypothesized by a differential socialization theory, but which would not be expected in terms of the organizing effects on the brain of the prenatal androgen. Fourthly, objective observation has confirmed parental reports (Hines, 1993). In summary, Collaer and Hines (1995), in their exhaustive literature review on the influence of gonadal hormones on early development, concluded that the evidence is very strong for childhood play (rough, active outdoor play, athleticism) and relatively strong for tendencies towards aggression.

Neurophysiological Factors

In an extensive review of neuropsychological correlates of CD, Lahey, Hart, Pliszka, Applegate, and McBurnett (1993) concluded that although the existing literature was not strong methodologically, there was growing evidence that abnormally severe and persistent physical aggression could be linked to various neurophysiological factors. They also concluded that there was no evidence concerning possible sex differences in these factors and that nothing is known about the neurophysiological characteristics of girls with CD. However, this conclusion may be unduly pessimistic in two respects.

Brunner, Nelen, Ropers, and van Oost (1993) have found a disorder of episodic aggression in adolescents caused by a genetic mutation in a recessive gene for monoamine oxidase A (MAOA), which is located on the X chromosome. This deficiency is hypothesized to result in an excessive level of several neurotransmitters, which might cause a person to respond excessively and violently to stress. While the frequency of this deficiency in the male population has yet to be determined, the potential significance of this finding is evident in Brunner et al.'s (1993) wondering "...given the wide range of variation of MAOA activity in the normal population, one could ask whether aggressive behavior is confined to complete MAOA deficiency." Brunner et al.'s finding has received impressive confirmation in a study which used an animal model of MAOA deficiency (Cases et al., 1995). The major limitation of Brunner et al.'s finding is their failure to address the major question of how too much monoamine messenger stimulates violence (Rose, 1995), because the literature typically associates a lower level of central nervous system neurotransmitters (e.g., serotonin) with increased aggression (Lahey et al., 1993).

In addition to the prenatal organizational effects on the course of early brain development, hormones can have activational effects on specific behaviors through their contemporaneous impact on both peripheral and neural-based processes. These effects are evident in the marked increase in testosterone for males during puberty, when "concentrations can increase as much as 20 times their initial concentrations between the ages of 10 and 17" (Buchanan, Eccles, & Becker 1992, p. 65), resulting in males having approximately 17 times more circulating testosterone than females (Halpern, 1992). Prior to puberty, as has been previously noted, there is little sex difference in testosterone level as well as no difference in testosterone levels between highly aggressive and nonaggressive males (Constantino, Grosz, Saenger, Chandler, Nandi, & Earls, 1993). Buchanan et al. (1992) summarized several of the

mechanisms by which hormones could have an activating effect on behavior. Two of these mechanisms are especially relevant to the present discussion.

First, "hormone concentrations can alter discrete structures necessary for carrying out particular behaviors....During puberty, changes in a person's body may influence both ability and inclination to behave in certain ways" (Buchanan, Eccles, & Becker, 1992, p. 63). For example, the generally greater body size (which, despite the overlap of ranges, represents a mean height difference of at least two standard deviations; Breedlove, 1994), muscular strength, and speed and coordination of gross bodily movements in boys (Anastasi, 1979) can make it more likely that aggression would be used to achieve one's goals (Parke & Slaby, 1983).

Second, Buchanan, Eccles, and Becker (1992) indicated that "hormones may influence behavior and moods by acting on central nervous system structures thought to be important for affect and for perception and interpretation of sensory information" (p. 64). They then comprehensively reviewed this mechanism as applied to aggression in adolescence and concluded as follows:

Among boys...the activation effects of androgens may lead to more aggressive or rebellious behavior, especially if the higher concentrations occur in combination with environmental situations conducive to aggressive response...Data indicate that when normal adolescent boys are provoked, testosterone level may affect the aggressive response through lowering the tolerance for frustration....Among people, adolescent or adult, already having problems with rebelliousness and antisocial behavior, testosterone seems to make a difference in the degree and direction of that behavior...(pp. 93-94).

Buchanan, Eccles, and Becker (1992) reported that in contrast to males, few relations are found between hormones and girls' aggressive behavior. Among the possible reasons for this sex difference, two biologically based ones are cited. First, boys may be more susceptible to the effects of androgens due to their prenatal exposure to androgen. Second, males may have a lower threshold for androgen to have an activational effect.

Psychosocial Factors

Frick (1994), Loeber (1990), Eron, Huesmann, and Zelli (1991), and Robins (1991) agreed that the evidence is strongest for family factors in the development of a conduct disorder. These factors then provide the impetus for peer influences (Cairns & Cairns, 1991; Patterson, Capaldi, & Bank, 1991). Family factors will be considered using the tripartite model provided by Eron, Huesmann, and Zelli (1991). They indicated that parents teach children aggression by the reinforcements they provide for aggressive behavior, the models of aggressive behavior they present, and the conditions they furnish in the home that frustrate and victimize the child. These latter conditions will be considered under traditional frustration-aggression formulation.

Differential Reinforcement

Parental socialization. Patterson, DeBaryshe, and Ramsey (1989) generated perhaps the most empirically based, powerful, and comprehensive model of the development of aggressive behavior in the family. In so doing, they incorporated most of the inept management techniques that are commonly cited as characterizing families of conduct disordered children (e.g., lack of monitoring, inconsistency, parental uninvolvement) (Loeber, 1990; Perry, Perry, & Boldziar, 1990). They stated that family members directly train the child to perform antisocial behaviors through inept management techniques in which some of the reinforcement is positive. However, the most important set of contingencies for coercive behaviors

consists of escape-conditioning contingencies. Thus, many aggressive acts represent attempts by children to "turn off" irritants that are supplied by parents and siblings who are threatening, aversive, and lacking in social skills. Hence, the question becomes, is there any evidence that males are differentially reinforced in this regard?

Lytton and Romney (1991), in their meta-analysis of parents' differential socialization of boys and girls, concluded that the discouragement of aggression is directed only slightly more toward girls, and that this difference is far from significant. This conclusion is limited by the fact that the literature on differential parental socialization in general is largely restricted to children under the age of 6 and to socialization by mothers. Furthermore, since Lytton and Romney (1991) conducted their review, at least one well-designed study (Dodge, Pettit, & Bates, 1994) found that mothers of boys tended to endorse aggressive values more heavily for their sons than their daughters. Nevertheless, their review represents the data most relevant to the issue of differential reinforcement for aggression and, at the very least, there clearly is no solid, robust body of evidence for parental differential socialization of males and females for aggression. Even Hoffman (1991), whose viewpoint on differential socialization of children is the exact opposite of Lytton and Romney (1991), did not cite any research directly pertaining to parental differential socialization of aggression. Furthermore, she observed that "It is likely that gender differences in aggressiveness...evoke different parental response" (p. 195). Lytton's (1990a, 1990b) review of the effects of conduct disorder on parents and children provides strong support for this observation.

The one socialization area in North American studies where Lytton and Romney (1991) found a clearly significant sex difference was in encouragement of sex-stereotyped activities, with fathers making a somewhat larger difference than mothers. They also found a sex difference in favor of boys for stimulation of large motor behavior, with fathers again making a larger difference. Both of these differences, however, though in the direction of males, were not significant.

Peer socialization. The foregoing discussion of a differential socialization effect is radically incomplete, however, unless differential peer socialization is considered. Maccoby (1991) made a strong case for suggesting that although childhood culture is partly derivative of adult culture, it is not entirely so, and thus, makes its own distinctive, independent contribution. Her research suggested that beginning in preschool, a cluster of play behaviors in boys (rough and tumble, along with an assertive-dominant interaction style) is a central element in the spontaneous segregation of children into same-sex play groups. Furthermore, her research indicated that this segregation into same-sex play groups is indeed spontaneous, is not primarily a function of adult pressure, and is not closely linked to involvement in sex-typed activities. This sex segregation then results in a divergence of interactive styles for the sexes (Maccoby, 1990). Boys, in their groups, are more likely than girls in all-girl groups to interrupt one another; use commands, threats or boasts of authority; refuse to comply with another's demand; heckle a speaker; call another child names; etc. This differential peer socialization for a rough-and-tumble, assertive-dominant interaction style clearly seems to predispose males to being more aggressive, less compliant, more oppositional, more defiant of rules and, thus, more likely to develop a conduct disorder.

Modeling

Patterson, DeBaryshe, and Ramsey (1989) reported that there is a high degree of intergenerational similarity for antisocial behavior, such that having an antisocial parent places a child at risk for antisocial behavior and that many aggressive children come from homes in which at least one parent is exceptionally violent (Perry, Perry, & Boldziar, 1990). Additionally, Robins (1991) reported that children of criminal and alcoholic parents have a greatly increased risk of conduct disorder. Eron and Huesmann (1990) also provided evidence for an intergenerational transmission of aggression. These clear findings can, in part, be explained from a social learning theory perspective which suggests that aggression between family members provides a likely model for the learning of aggressive behavior as well as the appropriateness of such behavior within the family (Widom, 1989). As there are ample opportunities for children to learn from a variety of sources that aggression is regarded as a masculine activity (Eagly & Steffen, 1986; Huston, 1983; Hyde, 1984, 1986; Parke & Slaby, 1983), this modeling obviously has a greater socialization effect on males than females, because children are clearly more likely to imitate same-sex models if an action is modeled by several models of the same sex (Maccoby & Martin, 1983). Furthermore, Hyde (1986), in her meta-analysis of gender differences in aggression, confirmed Maccoby and Jacklin's (1974) conclusion that "boys consistently exhibit more aggression following exposure to a model" (p. 229).

Gender schema theory. In addition to traditional modeling theory, social-cognitive learning theory suggests that boys and girls develop sex-role-related cognitive standards for seeking, interpreting, and responding to aggressive stimulation (Parke & Slaby, 1983). This information processing of aggressive stimuli through the optic of sex-role-related cognitive standards could operate in a number of ways.

First, based upon the finding that aggression is more stable for males than females, Eron and Huesmann (1990) suggested that males are more likely to develop a cognitive script that includes an aggressive strategy. As a result, they are more likely to seek out and create aggressive situations, as well as to become exquisitely sensitive to aggressive cues in the environment. Thus, although an individual's environment and learning conditions may change radically, aggression can persist.

Second, Dodge (1986, 1993) outlined a social information processing model which suggests that biases or deficits at any of the steps in the model (encoding, mental representation, response access, response evaluation, enactment) can lead to aggressive behavioral responses. There is now considerable empirical evidence to support this claim (Dodge, 1986, 1993). Regarding cue encoding, aggressive children have been found to search for fewer social cues before making attributions about another's intent than do nonaggressive children and are also more likely to focus on aggressive cues in their environment than are their less aggressive peers. At the mental representation step of processing, aggressive children display a bias toward making attributions of hostile intent regarding the behavior of others. In studies of response access, aggressive children have been found to generate more aggressive responses and fewer assertive responses than nonaggressive children, and to value aggressive responses more and assertive responses less than do their peers. In terms of response evaluation, aggressive children have been found to evaluate aggression more positively, to expect that aggression will come easily for them, and to feel that inhibiting aggression will be especially difficult. The usefulness of this model receives strong support from the social interactionist theory of aggression (Tedeschi & Felson, 1994), which primarily views aggression as a decision that is made to use coercion to influence others, express grievances, or assert social identity. With regard to enactment, the few studies that have been conducted have found aggressive children to be less skilled at enacting competent peer group entry behaviors than other children (Dodge, 1993).

What, then, is the evidence for sex differences in the foregoing pattern of cognitive biases and deficits that may influence male children to behave aggressively? The answer depends, in part, upon whether the biases are the cause or the consequence of aggressive behavior. At this juncture, the reformulated model allows for both processes (Crick & Dodge, 1994). To the extent that these biases are the consequences of aggressive behavior (which may represent justifications for aggressive behavior; Richters & Cicchetti, 1993), a clear sex-difference seems to be present. Because boys clearly tend to be more aggressive (Block, 1976, 1978, 1979; Eagly & Steffen, 1986; Hyde, 1984, 1986; Parke & Slaby, 1983), they would then be more likely to manifest the pattern of cognitive biases and deficits which, in turn, increases the likelihood that they would behave aggressively. To the extent that this pattern of cognitive biases and deficits is essentially a primary cause and not a derivative of aggressive behavior, evidence for a gender difference in children is essentially unexamined, although there are two intriguing possibilities which suggest such a difference.

Encoding and mental representation stage. Evidence for the possibility that boys are more likely to encode their social interactions in a way that is conducive to aggression comes from studies of the role of physical abuse and early harsh discipline in the development of child aggression. These studies suggested that the effects of physical abuse and harsh discipline may be mediated, at least in part, by maladaptive social information processing that develops in response to abuse/harsh discipline (Dodge, Bates, & Pettit, 1990; Weiss, Dodge, Bates & Pettit, 1992), as well as exposure to aggressive models and insecure attachment (Dodge, 1993). Thus, as Ledingham (1991) indicated, proponents of a social-cognitive model of aggression, such as Dodge, have clearly acknowledged the role of early negative emotion as a historical determinant of the cognitive appraisal process. If one accepts this analysis, the prior discussions on modeling and the greater male vulnerability to insecure attachments become relevant, as these factors would make it more likely that males develop knowledge structures of the world as a hostile place that requires coercive behavior to achieve desired outcomes (Dodge, 1993). Furthermore, the following evidence that males are more likely to be exposed to harsh discipline/conflict provides additional support for the hypothesis that males are more likely to develop a maladaptive social information processing approach.

In their meta-analytic review of the social psychological literature, Eagly and Steffen (1986) reported that subjects tended to aggress more against men than women. Lytton and Romney (1991) reported that in North American studies, there is a slight tendency to apply more disciplinary strictness to males. Males are more often the target of physical abuse (Cummings, Hennessy, Rabideau, & Cicchetti, 1994), and are at somewhat greater risk for injury than females (Knutson, 1995).

Also, males appear to be exposed to more conflict both before and after their parents' divorce (Hetherington & Camara, 1984; Hetherington, Stanley-Hagan, & Anderson, 1989) and to their parents' marital conflict in general (Emery, 1982). Thus, in their current review of marital conflict and its effects on children, Fincham and Osborne (1993) indicated that boys may act out more than girls when exposed to marital conflict because parents enmeshed in marital conflict may come to resent an opposite-sexed child, who is perceived as reminiscent of the spouse. As the mother is usually the primary caretaker of both sexes of children, this sort of resentment may be experienced more frequently by boys. Research support for this theory is found in a study by Kerig, Cowan, and Cowan (1993), in which fathers who were lower in marital satisfaction were more negative toward their daughters, whereas mothers who were lower in marital satis-

faction were more likely to reciprocate their son's negative affect.

Huston's (1983) literature review reported that direct observation of teacher behavior in both preschool and elementary classes indicated that boys receive more disapproval and scolding and that this occurred even when the behavior of boys and girls was similar. She attributed this higher rate of teacher disapproval and scolding to generalized expectations that boys will misbehave, which are based partly on objectively observable patterns and partially on stereotypical beliefs about the sexes.

Huston (1983) observed that this uneven exposure to more negativity may, in part, be due to the fact that males are less responsive to disciplinary measures prior to the onset of any antisocial precursors and hence precipitate a harsh response. Support for such an interaction comes from Maccoby (1990), who reported the fascinating finding that preschool males gradually become unresponsive to "polite suggestions" from female peers. Furthermore, she concluded that neither differential socialization nor observational learning can account for this phenomenon, and, that at this point in time, it is essentially inexplicable. Similarly, Serbin, Sprafkin, Elman, and Doyle (1984) reported that girls found it difficult to influence boys, but that the reverse was not true. One can then easily hypothesize that this resistance to being influenced by female peers generalizes to adult females (mothers, teachers), thus precipitating more severe treatment. The previously discussed study of sex differences in the interaction between temperament and parents by Bezirganian and Cohen (1992) provided support for this possibility. They interpreted their finding of high mother-son punishment and control leading to an increase in difficult temperament as due to males interpreting their mothers' attempts to discipline, control, and punish as a form of aggression to which the males responded negatively.

The foregoing helps explain the conclusion of Masten, Best, and Garmezy (1990) that there is a general tendency for boys, rather than girls, to respond to stress with an externalizing pattern. A major reason for this externalizing tendency in boys was revealed in a study by Cummings, Davies, and Simpson (1994), which found that the emotional insecurity generated by marital conflict was reflected in different psychological processes for boys and girls, with boys more prone to feelings of threat, which predicted adjustment problems, and with girls more prone to self-blame, which predicted internalizing problems.

In summary, a major reason why boys appear more likely to encode and represent social information in a hostile fashion is that they are exposed to more abuse, conflict, harsh discipline, etc. In addition, they are more likely to react to these stressors with an externalizing pattern which, in turn, generates even more conflict.

Response evaluation stage. There may be a gender difference in the response evaluation stage. This possibility comes from the social psychological literature which suggests that sex differences in beliefs about the perceived negative and positive consequences of aggression mediate to a significant extent the sex differences in aggressive behavior. In their review, Eagly and Steffen (1986) suggested that the female gender role increases the likelihood that women more so than men will perceive negative consequences of aggression (guilt and anxiety, harm to others, and danger to oneself). Campbell, Muncer, and Coyle (1992) suggested that the male gender role increases the likelihood that men more so than women will perceive positive consequences of aggression. Thus, they suggested that women tend to view aggression as a result of loss of self-control resulting from a build-up of stress. As such, it represents a personal failure to adhere to standards of behavior which they set for themselves and, consequently, they view it negatively.

Men, by contrast, tend to view aggression as the exercise of control over others triggered by challenges to their self-esteem or public integrity and, as such, they view it positively. Thus, in essence, women view aggression as a loss of control, while men see aggression as a regaining of control.

Support for this theory is found in a study by Davis and Emory (1995) of first and third grade children, which demonstrated that boys displayed greater negative affect than girls when they received a disappointing gift, even when trying hard not to do so. Girls also displayed higher levels of social monitoring (attempts to control their negativity) and tension (anxiety over expressing negativity). The author theorized that girls are more socialized to "act nice" and to control their negative feelings.

This theory dovetails very nicely with Block's (1973) theory of sex-typing. In the first stage of this theory, very young children of both sexes are viewed as "agenic" (the tendency to be individualistic, self-assertive, expansive). At the next stage, however, when conformity to rules and roles becomes important, there is a critical bifurcation of the sexes due to different socialization pressures. Girls are encouraged to suppress assertiveness and aggression for the sake of "communion" (tendency to focus on harmony with the group), while boys are allowed to remain "agenic," but are encouraged to control and suppress tender feelings. This theory received strong support from Eagly's (1993, 1995) comprehensive literature reviews as she concluded that "thematic analysis of demonstrated sex differences in social behavior suggests that they conform to stereotypic expectations that women are communal and men are agenic" (p. 154). Similarly, in a meta-analysis of gender differences in personality, Feingold (1994) concluded that women were higher than men in anxiety, trust, and, "especially tender-mindedness" (p. 429).

Adopting this theory, one can easily see how

females can come to view aggression as a "loss of control," as it represents a violation of the socialization for communion at the expense of agency. Similarly, one can easily see how males can come to see aggression as a means of regaining control as it is an extension of their continuing socialization for "agency." When this latter socialization is combined with a socialization to suppress tender feelings, it is small wonder that aggression toward another may be viewed more positively by males than females. This analysis has essentially been adopted in the reformulated model, which posits that gender may moderate the relationship between social information processing and behavior through cognitions that are more interpersonally related for girls (e.g., more prosocial or cooperative and more concerned about social approval) and more instrumentally related for boys (e.g., more concerned about controlling external events and more dominating toward peers) (Crick & Dodge, 1994).

Frustration-Aggression

The foregoing findings of greater exposure of males to stress/conflict could also increase the likelihood of male aggression through another mechanism — frustration-aggression. This hypothesis is a traditional major theoretical formulation (Johnson & Fennell, 1992) that has its most current, comprehensive statement in the work of Leonard Berkowitz (1989, 1992), in which he posited two systems of aggression. The first system he proposed is what he calls reactive/emotional aggression. Along with the classic formulation, he maintained that there is an innate biological predisposition for the organism to impulsively attack the source of frustration. Its goal is to inflict harm or injury. However, aggression can subserve other goals, such as an attempt at coercion or an effort to preserve one's power, dominance, or social status. He termed this aggression "instrumental" because it is carried

out for an extrinsic purpose, rather than simply for the pleasure of doing it (as is reactive aggression). For Berkowitz, though, the focus is primarily on establishing the validity of the reactive/emotional aggression and how it serves as the basis for the learning of instrumental aggression. It is precisely this focus that will be taken in the present discussion.

Berkowitz (1992) accounted for the failures of the classic formulation to explain why this innate, organismic reaction is not always evidenced in two ways. First, learning can modify the frustration-aggression relationship, so that people can learn to respond nonaggressively to thwartings. Second, and most importantly, experiencing frustration depends to a great extent on how the person interprets the event in terms of past and present cognitions and attributions. Hence, events are likely to be experienced as frustrating only when there are "barriers to the attainment of expected goals" (p. 46) or when frustrations are viewed as arbitrary or illegitimate.

In summary, the best statement of his theory for our purposes is as follows:

Many conditions can determine how unpleasant the failure to attain the desired goal may be. Obviously, we will be more unhappy about not getting what we want if we had anticipated great pleasure than if we had expected only small satisfaction....It is because of this felt displeasure, I hold, that a frustration produces an instigation to aggression. The negative affect is the fundamental spur to the aggressive inclination (p. 44).

In applying his theory to the development of aggression (even if frustration only facilitates rather than instigates aggressive behavior as Tedeschi and Felson's [1994] critique of Berkowitz would have it), Berkowitz indicated that parental mistreatment can be a potent source of the unpleasant feelings/negative affect which serve as a primary instigator to aggression. No better example of this exists than in the families of antisocial children which produce a good deal of frustration by their harsh and inconsistent discipline and little positive parental involvement with their children (Patterson, DeBaryshe, & Ramsey, 1989). Thus, Rutter (1994) indicated that "There is now abundant evidence that serious family discord is a good risk indicator for conduct disorder in children" (p. 181). Furthermore, there is evidence that boys are more likely than girls to be exposed to certain types of parental mistreatment.

First, as previously discussed, boys are more often the target of physical abuse than girls (Crittenden, Claussen, & Sugarman, 1994), and rather than habituating to others' hostility due to their history of exposure to family violence, become more aroused and angered by it (Cummings et al., 1994). Furthermore, it appears that boys may be less able to respond to the buffering role of a major caretaker than girls because they appear to be less attuned to the caretaker's internal experiences and emotional expressions which would mediate such buffering (Wolfe & McGee, 1994).

Second, if, as previously indicated, males are more exposed to frustrating parenting in the form of marital conflict, they can be expected to have a greater likelihood to develop the negative affect that generates aggressive inclinations and undergirds instrumental aggression.

In addition, if Zaslow and Hayes' findings (1986) of support for the hypothesis that boys are more adversely affected by psychosocial stress are correct, there is an interaction between male gender and susceptibility to stress which suggests that males are more likely than females to become aggressive when exposed to the same levels of frustration. Among the avenues of investigation of this interaction between sex and psychosocial adversity, research on parental divorce stands out as the one area in which this hypothesis has been discussed most widely (Zaslow, 1988). This literature has been the subject of several recent comprehensive reviews which have yielded the following conclusions.

Reviews by Zaslow (1988, 1989) as well as the one by Grych and Fincham (1992) support the hypothesis that sons show more adverse responses (the most consistent finding being higher levels of externalizing problems, such as aggression and conduct disorder) to parental divorce than daughters, both immediately and over a period of years if, as preadolescents, they are living with an unremarried mother. As this circumstance occurs approximately 90% of the time (Hetherington et al., 1989), at least one third of male children born in the late 1970s and early 1980s (Grych & Fincham, 1992) can be expected to experience a highly frustrating situation that may last for years. Additional support for this finding comes from studies which indicated that this sex difference is not simply restricted to clinical samples of individuals involved in divorce (Zaslow, 1989), and from studies which show that males are more adversely affected by marital conflict in general (Fincham & Osborne, 1993). Moreover, in a meta-analysis of parental caregiving and child externalizing behavior in nonclinical samples, Rothbaum and Weisz (1994) concluded that there were stronger caregiving-externalizing associations for boys than girls, but only in studies of preadolescents and only in analyses of mothers. Thus, it would appear to be a robust finding that males are more adversely affected by marital conflict/divorce.

The reasons commonly cited by reviewers for the greater male vulnerability to divorce are as follows (Cummings, Davies, & Simpson, 1994; Fincham & Osborne, 1993; Fincham, Grych, & Osborne, 1994; Herzog & Sudia, 1973; Hetherington, Stanley-Hagan, & Anderson, 1989; Rothbaum & Weisz, 1994; Rutter, 1994; Zaslow, 1988). First, father absence has a more adverse affect on males because of the absence of a male role model. Second, males appear to be exposed to more conflict and are likely to model fathers who are more aggressive than mothers during marital conflict. Third, because boys may be more likely than girls to respond to marital conflict with externalizing, noncompliant, antisocial behaviors, firm, consistent, authoritative control may be more essential in the parenting of boys. During and following divorce, however, the discipline by custodial mothers often becomes erratic, inconsistent, peremptory, and punitive. Fourth, parents enmeshed in marital conflict may come to resent an opposite-sexed child who is perceived as reminiscent of the spouse. As the mother is usually the primary caretaker of the children, this sort of resentment may be experienced more frequently by boys and mothers may react more negatively to aggressive behavior displayed by sons than daughters. Finally, in times of stress, boys are less able than girls to disclose their feelings and to solicit and obtain support from parents, other adults, and peers. It should also be noted that these aforementioned differences in parental treatment of boys are also in evidence prior to parental separation (Shaw, Emery, & Tuer, 1993).

Peers

Peer influences, especially during adolescence (Hartup, 1983), appear to be a very important factor in the greater likelihood of males developing a conduct disorder for several reasons. First, Patterson's coercion model (Patterson, 1993; Patterson, DeBaryshe, & Ramsey, 1989; Patterson, Capaldi, & Bank, 1991; Patterson, Reid, & Dishion, 1992), as well as the social cognition and social network model of Cairns and Cairns (1991) suggested that training for antisocial behavior in the home results in aggressivity that is rejected by the normal peer group, which then provides the basis for peer groupings based upon deviance. This theory finds strong support in Reid's (1993) literature review which showed clearly that the aggressive child is at high risk for rejection by the normal peer group, and for an intensification of aggressive behavior through the

retaliations and provocations elicited by the aggressive behavior. This deviant peer group membership then becomes a major training ground for delinquent acts. Peers are thought to supply the adolescent with attitudes, motivations, and rationalizations to support antisocial behavior as well as to provide opportunities to engage in specific delinquent acts.

Second, as previously discussed, Maccoby's research (1988, 1990, 1991) has shown how same-sex peer groups provide males with powerful socialization experiences in competition, dominance, and assertiveness. The implications of this differential peer group socialization for antisocial behavior are twofold. First, "groups of a given sex vary in how much they encourage the display or inhibition of borderline antisocial behaviors" (Maccoby, 1986, p. 275). She offered examples of factors in male groups which are more likely to promote antisocial behavior, including: a greater likelihood of male retaliatory fighting, a greater probability of competitive and risk-taking behavior, and a greater likelihood of "male play" in large groups on streets and playgrounds where they will not be supervised and monitored by adults. Second, she indicated that "[i]ndividual temperament may lead certain boys who like rough play to seek out other like-minded boys" (p. 275). Hence, given the greater male prevalence in ADHD and the attendant impulsivity and low frustration tolerance this disorder implies, it can easily be seen how males with this disorder might have these characteristics amplified by the culture of male groups (analogous to the type of magnification of male rough-and-tumble play seen in same-sex groups in non-human species; Breedlove, 1994) and thus brought closer to the borderline between social and antisocial behavior.

Evidence for the efficacy of this kind of socialization in male groups comes from a recent, fascinating study of female delinquency. Caspi, Lynam, Moffitt, and Silva (1993) found that early puberty in females is associated with behavior problems only for girls enrolled in mixed-sex educational settings. Their interpretation was that the presence of boys in mixed-sex educational settings served to dilute school norms for tolerable conduct with the resultant adverse impact on females. Thus, males, from preschool on, are more exposed to such norm dilution, which then becomes maximized in deviant peer groups, gangs, etc.

Gangs, in turn, make a considerable contribution to the remarkably consistent inverse relationship between socioeconomic status and antisocial behaviors in men, such that lower socioeconomic status is correlated with a greater prevalence of male antisocial behavior and severe delinquency (Dodge, Pettit, & Bates, 1994; Dohrenwend et al., 1992; Johnson & Fennell, 1992).

Conclusion

Perhaps one of the more useful ways to summarize the major points of this chapter would be to integrate its findings with a modified version of Loeber's (1990) ordering of the different manifestations of the *life-course-persistent* type of antisocial behavior in childhood and adolescence that results in violence (see Figure 1). In so doing, the sex differences will be considered in the developmental stage (i.e., preschool, school age, adolescence) in which they would appear to be most relevant.

With regard to preschool, Loeber reported that the earliest post-natal manifestations are usually noted in terms of the infant's difficult temperament, with activity level being one dimension

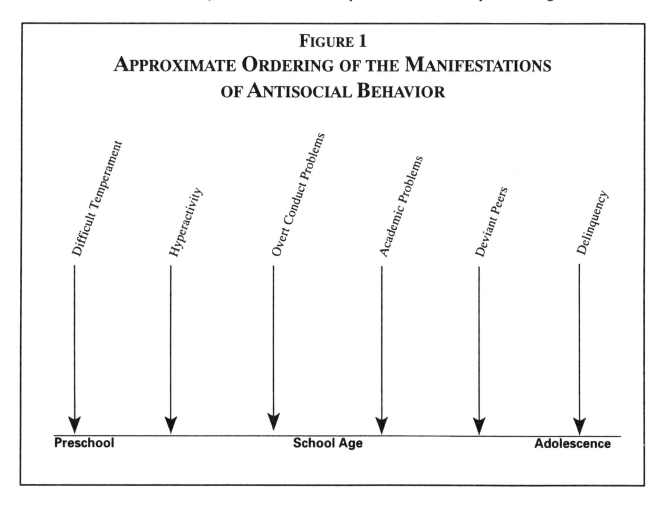

FIGURE 1
APPROXIMATE ORDERING OF THE MANIFESTATIONS OF ANTISOCIAL BEHAVIOR

Difficult Temperament

Hyperactivity

Overt Conduct Problems

Academic Problems

Deviant Peers

Delinquency

Preschool   **School Age**   **Adolescence**

of temperament. Hyperactivity itself becomes more apparent in the later preschool years. The author of this chapter found a significant sex difference in difficult temperament, in hyperactivity/impulsivity, and in male vulnerability to physical and psychosocial stressors. These differences would make males more likely to develop the neuropsychological deficits which would then begin to interact cumulatively with environmental adversity across development. In addition, the greater male propensity for being "difficult" and for "rough and tumble play" seems to be accentuated by the encouragement of sex-stereotyped activities (perhaps more so by fathers) and by spontaneous segregation into same-sex peer groups which then markedly increases the likelihood that males adopt an assertive-dominant interaction style.

In the school-age child, this assertive-dominant style, along with the neuropsychological deficits, clearly seem to predispose males to becoming more aggressive, less compliant, more oppositional, more defiant of rules, and thus, more likely to become violent. This takes place in a number of ways.

First, as Loeber (1990) noted, there would be a continuity between preschool and school-age disruptive behaviors in that the assertive-dominant style becomes diversified and develops into the overt symptoms of CD. Secondly, this style receives an even heavier dose of differential socialization as sex-segregated peer influences become even more powerful and as boys model ever more closely the cultural stereotypes of male aggressivity, dominance, and antisocial behavior. Thirdly, problems begin to "stack" (Loeber, 1990) in two major ways to the detriment of males. First, the greater male vulnerability to academic difficulties (due to ADHD and learning disability) makes it even more difficult for males to find satisfaction in an interpersonal style and identity that is not heavily laden with assertive-dominant-aggressive characteristics. Secondly, both the greater male vulnerability to psychological stress (e.g., parental divorce) and the greater likelihood that they will be exposed to psychosocial adversity (e.g., males are more exposed to marital conflict and physically abused) make it even more probable that their propensity to "act out" and externalize their problems would be magnified.

Finally, in adolescence, the markedly male prevalence in antisocial behavior continues its diversification into delinquency and is aided and abetted by the following mechanisms. First, on a biological level, the huge increase in testosterone level and the decisively greater body size further amplify both the ability and inclination of males to engage in aggressive behavior. Secondly, on an intrapsychic, cognitive level, social information processing has become structured for males in ways that enhance both the likelihood and desirability of engaging in antisocial conduct. Thirdly, on a social level, the greater male propensity to develop the antisocial trait serves more clearly as a determinant for a host of new problems, such as peer rejection, academic failure, and depression (Patterson, 1993). This, in turn, makes association with a deviant peer group all the more likely, resulting in training in antisocial behavior that is all the more intensive.

Thus, the confluence and interaction of the foregoing factors help to explain the marked sex difference in juvenile violence. By taking them into account, programs designed to prevent and treat juvenile violence can hopefully become more effective.

References

Abikoff, H. & Klein, R. G. (1992). Attention-deficit hyperactivity and conduct disorder: Comorbidity and implications for treatment. *Journal of Consulting and Clinical Psychology, 60*(6), 881-892.

Achenbach, T. (1993). Taxonomy and comorbidity of conduct

problems: Evidence from empirically based approaches. *Development and Psychopathology, 5,* 51-64.

American Psychiatric Association. (1994). *Diagnostic and statistical manual of mental disorders* (4th ed.). Washington, DC: Author.

Anastasi, A. (1979). Sex differences: Historical perspectives and theoretical implications. *Catalogue of Selected Documents in Psychology, 10* (2), Ms. No. 1999.

Barkley, R. A. (1990). *Attention deficit hyperactivity disorder.* New York: Guilford Press.

Barkley, R. (1994). Impaired delayed responding. In D. Routh (Ed.), *Disruptive behavior disorders in childhood.* New York: Plenum Press.

Barkley, R. (1995). Sex differences in ADHD. *The ADHD Report, 3*(1), 1-5.

Bates, J. E. (1994). Introduction. In J. E. Bates & T. D. Wachs (Eds.), *Temperament: Individual differences at the interface of biology and behavior* (pp. 1-6). Washington, DC: American Psychological Association.

Baum, C. (1989). Conduct disorders. In T. Ollendick & M. Hansen (Eds.), *Handbook of child psychopathology* (2nd ed.), (pp. 171-196). New York: Plenum Press.

Baydar, N. & Brooks-Gunn, J. (1991). Effects of maternal employment and child-care arrangements on preschoolers' cognitive and behavioral outcomes: Evidence from the children of the national longitudinal survey of youth. *Developmental Psychology, 27*(6), 932-945.

Belsky, J. (1988). The "effects" of infant day care reconsidered. *Early Childhood Research Quarterly, 3,* 235-272.

Belsky, J. (1990). Parental and nonparental child care and children's socioemotional development: A decade in review. *Journal of Marriage and the Family, 52,* 885-903.

Belsky, J. & Braungart, J. M. (1991). Are insecure-avoidant infants with extensive day-care experience less stressed by and more independent in the strange situation? *Child Development, 62,* 567-571.

Berenbaum, S. A. & Hines, M. (1992). Early androgens are related to childhood sex-typed toy preferences. *Psychological Science, 3*(3), 203-206.

Berkowitz, L. (1989). Frustration-aggression hypothesis: Examination and reformulation. *Psychological Bulletin, 106*(1), 59-73.

Berkowitz, L. (1992). *Aggression: Its causes, consequences and control.* New York: McGraw Hill.

Berry, C. A., Shaywitz, S. E., & Shaywitz, B. A. (1985). Girls with attention deficit disorder: A silent minority? A report on behavioral and cognitive characteristics. *Pediatrics, 76,* 801-809.

Bezirganian, S. & Cohen, P. (1992). Sex differences in the interaction between temperament and parenting. *Journal of the American Academy of Child & Adolescent Psychiatry, 31*(5), 790-801.

Birns, B. (1976). The emergence and socialization of sex differences in the earliest years. *Merrill-Palmer Quarterly, 22,* 229-250.

Block, J. H. (1973). Conceptions of sex role: Some cross-cultural and longitudinal perspectives. *American Psychologist, 28,* 512-526.

Block, J. (1976). Issues, problems and pitfalls in assessing sex differences: A critical review of "the psychology of sex differences." *Merrill-Palmer Quarterly, 22,* 283-308.

Block, J. (1978). Another look at differentiation in the socialization behaviors of mothers and fathers. In F. Denmark & J. Sherman (Eds.), *Psychology of women: Future direction of research*. New York: Psychological Dimensions.

Block, J. (1979, September). *Socialization influences on personality development in males and females*. Paper presented at the meeting of the American Psychological Association, New York.

Breedlove, S. (1994). Sexual differentiation of the human nervous system. In L. Porter & M. Rosenzweig (Eds.), *Annual review of psychology*. Palo Alto, CA: Annual Reviews Inc.

Brennan, P., Mednick, S., & Kandel, E. (1991). Congenital determinants of violent and property offending. In D. J. Peppler & K. H. Rubin (Eds.), *The development and treatment of childhood aggression* (pp. 81-92). NJ: Lawrence Earlbaum Associates.

Breslau, N. (1990). Does brain dysfunction increase children's vulnerability to environmental stress? *Archives of General Psychiatry, 47*, 15-20.

Brunner, H., Nelen, X., Ropers, H., & van Oost (1993). Abnormal behavior associated with a point mutation in the structural gene for monoamine Oxidase A. *Science, 262*, 578-580.

Buchanan, C. M., Eccles, J. S., & Becker, J. B. (1992). Are adolescents the victims of raging hormones? *Psychological Bulletin, 111*(1), 62-107.

Cairns, R. B. & Cairns, B. D. (1991). Social cognition and social networks: A developmental perspective. In D. J. Pepler & K. H. Rubin (Eds.), *The development and treatment of childhood aggression* (pp. 249-278). NJ: Lawrence Erlbaum Associates.

Campbell, A., Muncer, S., & Coyle, E. (1992). Social representation of aggression as an explanation of gender differences: A preliminary study. *Aggressive Behavior, 18*, 95-108.

Carlson, V., Cicchetti, D., Barnett, D., & Braunwald, K. (1989). Disorganized/disoriented attachment relationships in maltreated infants. *Developmental Psychology, 27*(1),108-118.

Cases, O., Seif, I., Grimsby, J., Gaspar, P., Chen, K., Pournin, S., Muller, U., Aguet, M., Babinet, C., Shih, J., & De Maeyer, E. (1995). Aggressive behavior and altered amounts of brain serotonin and norepinephrine in mice lacking MAOA. *Science, 268*, 1763-1766.

Caspi, A., Henry, B., McGee, R.O., Moffitt, T.E., & Silva, P.A. (1995). Temperamental origins of child and adolescent behavior problems: From age three to age fifteen. *Child Development, 66*, 55-68.

Caspi, A., Lynam, D., Moffitt, T. E., & Silva, P. A. (1993). Unraveling girls' delinquency: Biological, dispositional, and contextual contributions to adolescent misbehavior. *Developmental Psychology, 29*(1), 19-30.

Chandola, C. A., Robling, M. R., Peters, T. J., Melville-Thomas, G., & McGuffin, P. (1992). Pre- and perinatal factors and the risk of subsequent referral for hyperactivity. *Journal of Child Psychology & Psychiatry, 33*(6), 1077-1090.

Clarke-Stewart, K. A. (1989). Infant day care. *American Psychologist, 44*, 266-273.

Cohn, D. (1990). Child-mother attachment of six-year-olds and social competence at school. *Child Development, 61*, 152-162.

Cole, M. & Cole, S. (1993). *The development of children*. New York: W. H. Freeman and Company.

Collaer, M. & Hines, M. (1995). Human behavioral sex differences: A role for gonadal hormones during early development? *Psychological Bulletin, 118,* 55-107.

Compas, B., Hinden, B., & Gerhardt, C. (1995). Adolescent development: Pathways and processes of risk and resilience. In L. W. Porter & M. R. Rosenzweig (Eds.), *Annual Review of Psychology* (Vol. 46, pp. 65-93). Palo Alto, CA: Annual Reviews Inc.

Constantino, J., Grosz, D., Saenger, P., Chandler, D., Nandi, R., & Earls, F., (1993). Testosterone and aggression in children. *Journal of the American Academy of Child and Adolescent Psychiatry, 32,* 1217-1222.

Coon, H., Carey, G., Fulker, D., & DeFries, J. (1993). Influences of school environment on the academic achievement scores of adopted and nonadopted children. *Intelligence, 17,* 79-104.

Cornwall, A. & Bawden, H. N. (1992). Reading disabilities and aggression: A critical review. *Journal of Learning Disabilities, 25*(5), 281-288.

Crick, N. & Dodge, K. (1994). A review and reformulation of social information-processing mechanisms in children's social adjustment. *Psychological Bulletin, 115,* 74-101.

Crittenden, P. Claussen, A. & Sugarman, D. (1994). Physical and psychological maltreatment in middle childhood and adolescence. *Development and Psychopathology, 6,* 145-164.

Cummings, E. M., Davies, P. T., & Simpson, K. S. (1994). Marital conflict, gender, and children's appraisals and coping efficacy as mediators of child adjustment. *Journal of Family Psychology, 8*(2), 141-149.

Cummings, E., Hennessy, K., Rabideau, G., & Cicchetti, D. (1994). Responses of physically abused boys to interadult anger involving their mothers. *Development and Psychopathology, 6,* 31-41.

Davis, M. & Emory, E. (1995). Sex differences in neonatal stress reactivity. *Child Development, 66,* 14-27.

Davis, T. (1995). Gender differences in masking negative emotions: Ability or motivation. *Developmental Psychology, 31,* 660-667.

DeFries, J. (1991). Discussion. In E. E. Duane & D. B. Gray (Eds.), *The reading brain: The biological basis of dyslexia* (p. 163). Parkton, MD: York Press.

DeFries, J., Olson, R. K., Pennington, B. F., & Smith, S. D. (1991). Colorado reading project: An update. In D. D. Duane & D. B. Gray (Eds.), *The reading brain: The biological basis of dyslexia* (pp. 53-63). Parkton, MD: York Press.

Dodge, K. A. (1986). A social information processing model of social competence in children. In M. Perlmutter (Ed.), *Eighteenth Annual Minnesota Symposium on Child Psychology,* (pp. 77-125). Hillsdale: Lawrence Erlbaum Associates.

Dodge, K. A. (1993). Social-cognitive mechanisms in the development of conduct disorder and depression. In L. W. Porter & M. R. Rosenzweig (Eds.), *Annual review of psychology* (Vol. 44, pp. 559-580). Palo Alto, CA: Annual Reviews Inc.

Dodge, K. A., Bates, J. E., & Pettit, G. S. (1990). Mechanisms in the cycle of violence. *Science, 250,* 1678-1683.

Dodge, K., Pettit, G., & Bates, J. (1994). Socialization mediators of the relations between socioeconomic status and child conduct problems. *Child Development, 65,* 649-665.

Dohrenwend, B. P., Levav, I., Shrout, P. E., Schwartz, S.,

Naveh, G., Link, B. G., Skodol, A. E., & Stueve, A. (1992). Socioeconomic status and psychiatric disorders: The causation-selection issue. *Science, 255,* 946-951.

Douglas, V. (1989). Can Skinnerian theory explain attention deficit disorder? A reply to Barkley. In L. Bloomingdale & J. Swanson (Eds.), *Attention deficit disorder: Current concepts and emerging trends in attentional and behavioral disorders of childhood* (Vol. IV, pp. 235-254). Oxford: Pergamon Press.

Eagly, A. (1993). Sex differences in human social behavior: Meta-analytic studies of social psychological research. In M. Haug, R. Whalen, C. Aron, & K. Olsen (Eds.), *The development of sex differences and similarities in behavior* (pp. 421-436). Boston: Kluwer Academic Publishers.

Eagly, A. (1995). The science and politics of comparing men and women. *American Psychologist, 50,* 145-158.

Eagly, A. H. & Steffen, V. J. (1986). Gender and aggressive behavior: A meta-analytic review of the social psychological literature. *Psychological Bulletin, 100,* 309-330.

Earls, F. (1987). Sex differences in psychiatric disorders: Origins and developmental influences. *Psychiatric Developments, 1,* 1-23.

Ehrhardt, A. (1979, September). *Biological sex differences: A developmental perspective.* Paper presented at the meeting of the American Psychological Association, New York.

Ehrhardt, A. & Meyer-Bahlburg, F. (1979). Prenatal sex hormones and the developing brain: Effects on psychosexual differentiation and cognitive functioning. In W. Creger (Ed.), *Annual review of medicine* (Vol. 30). Palo Alto, CA: Annual Reviews Inc.

Ehrhardt, A. & Meyer-Bahlburg, F. (1981). Effects of prenatal sex hormones on gender-related behavior. *Science, 177,* 1312-1318.

Eme, R. (1979). Sex differences in childhood psychopathology: A review. *Psychological Bulletin, 86,* 574-595.

Eme, R. F. (1984). Sex-related differences in the epidemiology of child psychopathology. In C. S. Widom (Ed.), *Sex roles and psychopathology* (pp. 279-308). New York: Plenum Press.

Emery, R. R. (1982). Interparental conflict and the children of discord and divorce. *Psychological Bulletin, 92,* 310-330.

Eron, L. D. & Huesmann, L. R. (1990). The stability of aggressive behavior — even unto the third generation. In M. Lewis & S. M Miller (Eds.), *Handbook of developmental psychopathology* (pp. 147-156). New York: Plenum Press

Eron, L. D., Huesmann, L. R., & Zelli, A. (1991). The role of parental variables in the learning of aggression. In D. J. Pepler & K. H. Rubin (Eds.), *The development and treatment of childhood aggression* (pp. 169-188). NJ: Lawrence Earlbaum Associates.

Feingold, A. (1994). Gender differences in personality: A meta-analysis. *Psychological Bulletin, 116,* 429-456.

Fincham, F. D., Grych, J. H., & Osborne, L. N. (1994). Does marital conflict cause child maladjustment? Directions and challenges for longitudinal research. *Journal of Family Psychology, 8*(2), 128-140.

Fincham, F. D. & Osborne, L. N. (1993). Marital conflict and children: Retrospect and prospect. *Clinical Psychology Review, 13,* 75-88.

Frick, P. (1994). Family dysfunction and the disruptive behavior disorders. In T. Ollendick & R. Prinz

(Eds.), *Advances in clinical child psychology* (Vol. 16, pp. 203-226). New York: Plenum Press.

Frick, P., Lahey, B., Loeber, R., Tannenbaum, L., Van Horn, Y., Christ, M., Hart, E., & Hanson, K. (1993). Oppositional defiant disorder and conduct disorder: A meta-analytic review of factor analyses and cross-validation in a clinic sample. *Clinical Psychology Review, 13*, 319-340.

Garai, J. & Scheinfeld, A. (1968). Sex differences in mental and behavioral traits. *Genetic Psychology Monographs, 77*, 169-229.

Geschwind, N. & Galaburda, A. M. (1987). *Cerebral lateralization: Biological mechanisms, associations, and pathology.* Cambridge: The MIT Press.

Gibb, W. (1995, March). Seeking the criminal element. *Scientific American*, 101-107.

Goodman, R. (1991). Developmental disorders and structural brain development. In M. Rutter & P. Casaer (Eds.), *Biological risk factors for psychosocial disorders* (pp. 26-44). New York: Cambridge University.

Gottesman, I. & Goldsmith, H. (1994). Developmental psychopathology of antisocial behavior: Inserting genes into its ontogenesis and epigenesis. In C. Nelson (Ed.), *Threats to optimal development* (Vol. 27, pp. 69-104). Hilldale, NJ: Lawrence Erlbaum Associates.

Greenberg, M., Speltz, M., & DeKlyen, M. (1993). The role of attachment in the early development of disruptive behavior problems. *Development and Psychopathology, 5*, 191-213.

Grimshaw, G., Bryden, M., & Finegan, J. (1995). Relations between prenatal testosterone and cerebral lateralization in children. *Neuropsychology, 9*, 68-79.

Grych, J. H. & Fincham, F. D. (1992). Interventions for children of divorce: Toward greater integration of research and action. *Psychological Bulletin, 111*(3), 434-454.

Gualtieri, T. & Hicks, R. E. (1985). An immunoreactive theory of selective male affliction. *The Behavioral and Brain Sciences, 8*, 427-441.

Haig, D. (1993). Genetic conflicts in human pregnancy. *The Quarterly Journal of Biology, 68*, 495-525.

Halpern, D. F. (1992). *Sex differences in cognitive abilities* (2nd ed.). NJ: Lawrence Earlbaum Associates.

Hart, B. (1974). Gonadal androgen and sociosexual behavior of male mammals. *Psychological Bulletin, 81*, 383-400.

Hartup, W. W. (1983). Peer relations. In P. H. Mussen & E. M. Hetherington (Eds.), *Handbook of child psychology* (Vol. 4, pp. 104-174). New York: Wiley.

Herzog, E. & Sudia, C.E. (1973). Children in fatherless families. In B. M. Caldwell & H. N. Ricciuti (Eds.), *Review of child development research* (Vol. 3, pp. 141-232). Chicago: The University of Chicago Press.

Hetherington, M. & Camara, K. (1984). Families in transition: The processes of dissolution and reconstitution. In R. Parke (Ed.), *Review of child development research* (Vol. 7, pp. 398-439). Chicago: The University of Chicago Press.

Hetherington, M., Stanley-Hagan, M., & Anderson, E. R. (1989). Marital transitions: A child's perspective. *American Psychologist, 44*(2), 303-312.

Hines, M. (1993). Hormonal and neural correlates of sex-typed behavioral development in human beings. In M. Haug, R. E. Whalen, C. Aron, & K. L. Olsen

(Eds.), *The development of sex differences and similarities in behavior* (pp. 131-149). Dordrecht: Kluwer Academic Publishers.

Hines, M. & Green, R. (1991). Human hormonal and neural correlates of sex-typed behaviors. *Review of Psychiatry, 10*, 536-555.

Hines, M. & Kaufman, F. (1994). Androgen and the development of human sex-typical behavior: Rough-and-tumble play and sex of preferred playmates in children with Congenital Adrenal Hyperplasia (CAH). *Child Development, 65*, 1042-1053.

Hinshaw, S. P. (1992a). Academic underachievement, attention deficits, and aggression: Comorbidity and implications for intervention. *Journal of Consulting and Clinical Psychology, 60*(6), 893-903.

Hinshaw, S. P. (1992b). Externalizing behavior problems and academic underachievement in childhood and adolescence: Causal relationships and underlying mechanisms. *Psychological Bulletin, 111*(1), 127-155.

Hinshaw, S. P. (1994). *Attention deficits and hyperactivity in children*. Thousand Oaks, CA: Sage Publications.

Hinshaw, S., Lahey, B., & Hart, E. (1993). Issues of taxonomy and comorbidity in the development of conduct disorder. *Development and Psychopathology, 5*, 31-49.

Hoffman, L. W. (1989). Effects of maternal employment in the two-parent family. *American Psychologist, 44*(2), 283-292.

Hoffman, L. (1991). The influence of the family environment on personality: Accounting for sibling differences. *Psychological Bulletin, 110*, 187-203.

Huston, A. C. (1983). Sex typing. In P. H. Mussen & E. M. Hetherington (Eds.), *Handbook of child psychology* (Vol. 4, pp. 388-432). New York: Wiley.

Hyde, J. S. (1984). How large are gender differences in aggression? A developmental meta-analysis. *Developmental Psychology, 20*, 722-736.

Hyde, J. S. (1986). Gender differences and aggression. In J. S. Hyde & M. C. Linn (Eds.), *The psychology of gender: Advances through meta-analysis* (pp. 51-66). Baltimore: The Johns Hopkins University Press.

Jacklin, C. H. (1989). Female and male: Issues of gender. *American Psychologist, 44*(2), 127-133.

Johnson, J. H. & Fennell, E. B. (1992). Aggressive, antisocial, and delinquent behavior in childhood and adolescence. In C. E. Walker & M. C. Roberts (Eds.), *Handbook of clinical child psychology* (2nd ed., pp. 341-358). New York: Wiley.

Kagan, J. (1994). *Galen's prophecy*. New York: Basic Books.

Kamphi, A. (1992). Response to historical perspective: A developmental language perspective. *Journal of Learning Disabilities, 25*, 48-52

Kazdin, A. E. (1992). Child and adolescent dysfunction and paths toward maladjustment: Targets for intervention. *Clinical Psychology Review, 12*, 795-817.

Kazdin, A. E. (1995). Conduct disorder. In F. Verhulst & H. Koot (Eds.), *The epidemiology of child and adolescent psychopathology*. Oxford: Oxford University Press.

Kerig, P., Cowan, P., & Cowan, C. (1993). Marital quality and gender differences in parent-child interaction. *Developmental Psychology, 29*, 931-939.

Knutson, J. (1995). Psychological characteristics of maltreated children: Putative risk factors and consequences. In J. Spence, J. Darley, & D. Foss (Eds.), *Annual review of psychology*, (pp. 401-431). Palo

Alto, CA: Annual Reviews Inc.

Kopp, C. B. & Kaler, S. R. (1989). Risk in infancy: Origins and implications. *American Psychologist, 44*(2), 224-230.

Lahey, B., Hart, E., Pliszka, S., Applegate, B., & McBurnett, K. (1993). Neurophysiological correlates of conduct disorder: A rationale and a review of the research. *Journal of Clinical Child Psychology, 22,* 141-153.

Lahey, B. B. & Loeber, R. (1994). Framework for a developmental model of oppositional defiant disorder and conduct disorder. In D. K. Routh (Ed.), *Disruptive behavior disorders in childhood* (pp. 139-180). New York: Plenum Press.

Ledingham, J. E. (1991). Social cognition and aggression. In D. J. Pepler & K. H. Rubin (Eds.), *The development and treatment of childhood aggression* (pp. 279-285). NJ: Lawrence Erlbaum Associates.

Lewis, C., Hitch, G., & Walker, P. (1994). The prevalence of specific arithmetic difficulties and specific reading difficulties in 9- to 10-year old boys and girls. *Journal of Child Psychology and Psychiatry, 35,* 283-292.

Lewis, M., Feiring, C., McGuffog, C., & Jaskir, J. (1984). Predicting psychopathology in six-year-olds from early social relations. *Child Development, 55,* 123-136.

Liederman, J. & Flannery, K. A. (1995). The sex ratios of families with a neurodevelopmentally disordered child. *Journal of Child Psychology and Psychiatry, 36*(3), 511-517.

Loeber, R. (1990). Development and risk factors of juvenile antisocial behavior and delinquency. *Clinical Psychology Review, 10,* 1-41.

Loeber, R. & Keenan, K. (1994). Interaction between conduct disorder and its comorbid conditions: Effects of age and gender. *Clinical Psychology Review, 14*(6), 497-523.

Loeber, R., Wung, P., Keenan, K., Giroux, B., Stouthamer-Loeber, M., Van Kammen, W., & Maughan, B. (1993). Developmental pathways in disruptive child behavior. *Development and Psychopathology, 5,* 103-133.

Lytton, H. (1990a). Child and parent effects in boys' conduct disorder: A reinterpretation. *Developmental Psychology, 26*(5), 683-697.

Lytton, H. (1990b). Child effects — still unwelcome? Response to Dodge and Wahler. *Developmental Psychology, 26*(5), 705-709.

Lytton, H. & Romney, D. M. (1991). Parent's differential socialization of boys and girls: A meta-analysis. *Psychological Bulletin, 109*(2), 267-296.

Maccoby, E. (1983). Socialization in the context of the family: Parent-child interaction. In P. H. Mussen & E. M. Hetherington (Eds.), *Handbook of child psychology* (Vol. 4, pp. 1-87). New York: Wiley.

Maccoby, E. (1986). Social groupings in childhood: Their relationship to prosocial and antisocial behavior in boys and girls. In D. Olweus, J. Block, & M. Radke-Yarrow (Eds.), *Development of antisocial behavior in boys and girls* (pp. 263-284). New York: Academic Press.

Maccoby, E. (1988). Gender as a social category. *Developmental Psychology, 24*(6), 755-765.

Maccoby, E. (1990). Gender and relationships: A developmental account. *American Psychologist, 45*(4), 513-520.

Maccoby, E. E. (1991). Gender and relationships: A

reprise. *American Psychologist, 46*, 538-539.

Maccoby, E. (1992). The role of parents in the socialization of children: An historical overview. *Developmental Psychology, 28*(6), 1006-1017.

Maccoby, E. & Jacklin, C. (1974). *The psychology of sex differences.* Stanford, CA: Stanford University Press.

Maccoby, E. & Jacklin, C. (1980). Sex differences in aggression: A rejoinder and reprise. *Child Development, 51*, 964-980.

Maccoby, E. & Martin, J. A. (1983). Socialization in the context of the family: Parent-child interaction. In E. M. Hetherington (Ed.), *Handbook of child psychology* (Vol. 4, pp. 1-87). New York: Wiley.

Martin, B. & Hoffman, J. A. (1990). Conduct disorders. In M. Lewis & S. M. Miller (Eds.), *Handbook of developmental psychopathology* (pp. 109-116). New York: Plenum Press.

Masten, A., Best, K., & Garmezy, N. (1990). Resilience and development: Contributions from the study of children who overcome adversity. *Development and Psychopathology, 49*, 547-555.

Maziade, M., Caron, C., Cote, R., Boutin, P., & Thivierge, J. (1990). Extreme temperament and diagnosis: A study in a psychiatric sample of consecutive children. *Archives of General Psychology, 47*, 477-484.

McManus, I. C. & Bryden, M. P. (1991). Geschwind's theory of cerebral lateralization: Developing a formal, causal model. *Psychological Bulletin, 110*(2), 237-253.

McMillen, M. (1979). Differential mortality by sex in fetal and neonatal deaths. *Science, 204*, 89-91.

Meyer-Bahlburg, H. & Ehrhardt, A. (1982). Prenatal sex hormones and human aggression. *Aggressive Behavior, 8*, 39-62.

Moffitt, T. (1993a). Adolescent-limited and life-course-persistent antisocial behavior: A developmental taxonomy. *Psychological Review, 100*, 674-701.

Moffitt, T. (1993b). The neuropsychology of conduct disorder. *Development and Psychopathology, 5*, 135-151.

Money, J. & Ehrhardt, A. (1972). *Man and women, boy and girl.* Baltimore, MD: Johns Hopkins University.

Offord, D. R., Boyle, M. H., & Racine, Y. A. (1991). In D. J. Pepler & K. H. Rubin (Eds.), *The development and treatment of childhood aggression* (pp. 31-54). Hillsdale, NJ: Lawrence Earlbaum Associates.

Ounstead, C. & Taylor, D. (1972). The Y chromosome message: A point of view. In C. Ounstead & D. Taylor (Eds.), *Gender differences: Their ontogeny and significance* (pp. 241-261). London: Churchill Livingstone.

Parke, R. D. & Slaby, R. G. (1983). The development of aggression. In P. H. Mussen & E. M. Hetherington (Eds.), *Handbook of child psychology* (Vol. 4, pp. 548-605). New York: Wiley.

Patterson, G. (1993). Orderly change in a stable world: The antisocial trait as a chimera. *Journal of Consulting and Clinical Psychology, 61*, 911-919.

Patterson, G. R., Capaldi, D., & Bank, L. (1991). An early starter model for predicting delinquency. In D. J. Pepler & K. H. Rubin (Eds.), *The development and treatment of childhood aggression* (pp. 390-410). Hillsdale, NJ: Lawrence Erlbaum Associates.

Patterson, G. R., DeBaryshe, B. D., & Ramsey, E. (1989). A developmental perspective on antisocial behavior. *American Psychologist, 44*(2), 329-335.

Patterson, G., Littman, R., & Bricker, W. (1967). Assertive behavior in children: A step towards a theory of aggression. *Monographs of the Society for Research in Child Development, 44*(4, Serial No. 113).

Patterson, G., Reid, J. & Dishion, T. (1992). *Antisocial boys*. Eugene, OR: Castalia.

Perry, D. G., Perry, L. C., & Boldziar, J. P. (1990). Learning of aggression. In M. Lewis & S. M. Miller (Eds.), *Handbook of developmental psychopathology* (pp. 135-142). New York: Plenum Press.

Prior, M. (1992). Childhood temperament. *The Journal of Child Psychology and Psychiatry and Allied Disciplines, 33*(1), 249-279.

Prior, M. (1993). Sex differences in psychological adjustment from infancy to 8 years. *Journal of the American Academy of Child and Adolescent Psychiatry, 32*(2), 291-304.

Quadagno, D., Briscoe, R., & Quadagno, J. (1977). Effect of perinatal gonadal hormones on selected non-sexual behavior patterns: A critical assessment of the non-human and human literature. *Psychological Bulletin, 84*, 62-80.

Quay, H. (1986). Conduct disorders. In H. Quay & J. Nerry (Eds.), *Psychopathological disorders of childhood* (3rd ed.) New York: John Wiley & Sons.

Reid, J. (1993). Prevention of conduct disorder before and after school entry: Relating interventions to developmental findings. *Development and Psychopathology, 5*, 243-262.

Reinisch, J. (1981). Prenatal exposure to synthetic progestins increases potential for aggression in humans. *Science, 211*, 1171-1173.

Reinisch, J. & Karow, W. (1977). Prenatal exposure to synthetic progestins and estrogens: Effect on human development. *Archives of Sexual Behavior, 6*, 257-288.

Renken, B., Egeland, B., Marvinney, D., Mangelsdorf, S., & Sroufe, A. (1989). Early childhood antecedents of aggression and passive-withdrawal in early elementary school. *Journal of Personality, 57*, 274-284.

Richters, J. & Cicchetti, D. (1993). Mark Twain meets DSM-III-R: Conduct disorder, development, and the concept of harmful dysfunction. *Development and Psychopathology, 5*, 5-29.

Robins, L. N. (1991). Conduct disorder. *The Journal of Child Psychology and Psychiatry and Allied Disciplines, 32*, 193-209.

Rose, R. (1995). Genes and human behavior. *Annual Review of Psychology, 46*, 625-54.

Roth, J. (1994, February). Understanding and preventing violence. *National Institute of Justice Research in Brief*, 1-20.

Rothbaum, F., & Weisz, J. (1994). Parental caregiving and child externalizing behavior in nonclinical samples: A meta-analysis. *Psychological Bulletin, 116*, 55-74.

Rutter, M. (1970). Sex differences in children's responses to family stress. In E. Anthony & C. Koupernik (Eds.), *The child in his family*. New York: Wiley.

Rutter, M. (1985). Resilience in the face of adversity. *British Journal of Psychiatry, 147*, 598-611.

Rutter, M. (1989). Isle of Wight revisited: Twenty-five

years of child psychiatric epidemiology. *Journal of the American Academy of Child & Adolescent Psychiatry, 28,* 633-653.

Rutter, M. (1994). Family discord and conduct disorder: Cause, consequence, or correlate? *Journal of Family Psychology, 8,* 170-186.

Rutter, M., Macdonald, H., Le Couteur, A., Harrington, R., Bolton, P., & Bailey, A. (1990). Genetic factors in child psychiatric disorder-II. Empirical findings. *Journal of Child Psychiatry and Psychology, 31,* 39-83.

Rutter, M. & Mawhood, L. (1991). The long-term psychosocial sequelae of specific developmental disorders of speech and language. In M. Rutter & P. Casaer (Eds.), *Biological risk factors for psychosocial disorders* (pp. 233-259). New York: Cambridge University Press.

Sanson, A., Smart, D., Prior, M., and Oberklaid, F. (1993). Precursors of hyperactivity and aggression. *Journal of the American Academy of Child and Adolescent Psychiatry, 32,* 1207-1216.

Scarr, S. & Eisenberg, M. (1993). Childcare research: Issues, perspectives, and results. In L. W. Porter & M. R. Rosenzweig (Eds.), *Annual review of psychology* (Vol. 44, pp. 613-644). Palo Alto, CA: Annual Reviews Inc.

Schonert-Reichl, K. & Offer, D. (1992). Gender differences in adolescent symptoms. In B. B. Lahey & A. E. Kazdin (Eds.), *Advances in clinical psychology* (Vol. 14, pp. 27-54). New York: Plenum Press.

Serbin, L., Sprafkin, C., Elman, M., & Doyle, A. (1984). The early development of sex differentiated patterns of social behavior. *Canadian Journal of Social Science, 14,* 350-363.

Shaw, D., Emery, R., & Tuer, M. (1993). Parental functioning and children's adjustment in families of divorce: A prospective study. *Journal of Abnormal Child Psychology, 21,* 119-134.

Shaywitz, S. & Shaywitz, B. (1988). Attention deficit disorder: current perspectives. In J. F. Kavanagh & T. J. Truss, Jr. (Eds.), *Learning disabilities: Proceedings of the national conference* (pp. 369-389). Parkton, NJ: York Press.

Shaywitz, S., Shaywitz, B., Fletcher, J., & Escobar, M. (1990). Prevalence of reading disability in boys and girls. *Journal of the American Medical Association, 264,* 998-1002.

Shaywitz, B., Shaywitz, S., Pugh, K., Constable, R., Skudlarski, P., Fulbright, R., Bronem, R., Fletcher, J., Shankweller, D., Katz, L., & Gore, J. (1995). Sex differences in the functional organization of the brain for language. *Science, 373,* 607-609.

Silverstein, L. B. (1991). Transforming the debate about child care and maternal employment. *American Psychologist, 46*(10), 1025-1032.

Skorneck, C. (1994, July 25). Serious crimes up among juveniles. *Chicago Sun Times,* p. 9.

Snowling, M. (1991). Developmental reading disorders. *Journal of Child Psychology and Psychiatry, 32,* 49-73.

Sonuga-Barke, E. J. S., Lamparelli, M., Stevenson, J., Thompson, M., & Henry, A. (1994). Behaviour problems and pre-school intellectual attainment: The association of hyperactivity and conduct problems. *Journal of Child Psychology & Psychiatry, 35*(5), 949-960.

Speltz, M., Greenberg, M., & DeKlyen, M. (1990). Attachment in preschoolers with disruptive behavior: A comparison of clinic-referred and non-problem children. *Development and Psychopathology, 2,* 31-46.

Stanovich, K. (1994). Annotation: Does dyslexia exist? *Journal of Child Psychology and Psychiatry, 35,* 579-595.

Steinhausen, H., Willms, J., & Spohr, H. (1994). *Journal of Child Psychology and Psychiatry, 35,* 323-331.

Tanner, J. (1978). *Fetus into man: Physical growth from conception to maturity.* Cambridge: Harvard University Press.

Taylor, D. (1985). Developmental rate is the major differentiator between the sexes. *The Behavioral and Brain Sciences, 8,* 459-460.

Tedeschi, J. T., & Felson, R. B. (1994). *Violence, aggression, and coercive actions.* Washington, DC: American Psychological Association.

Tieger, T. (1980). On the biological basis of sex differences in aggression. *Child Development, 51,* 943-963.

Tsuang, P. (1994). Genetics, epidemiology, and the search for causes of schizophrenia. *American Journal of Psychiatry, 151,* 3-6.

Turner, P. J. (1991). Relations between attachment, gender, and behavior with peers in preschool. *Child Development, 62,* 1475-1485.

Van, J. (1995, February 18). Murderous statistic: Teens blamed for soaring U. S. homicide rate. *Chicago Tribune,* p. 15.

Verloove-Vanhorick, S., Veen, S., Ens-Kokkum, M., Schreuder, A., Brand, R., & Ruys, J. (1994). Sex difference in disability and handicap at five years of age in children born at very short gestation. *Pediatrics, 93,* 576-579.

Vogel, S. A. (1990). Gender differences in intelligence, language, visual-motor abilities, and academic achievement in males and females with learning disabilities: A review of the literature. *Journal of Learning Disabilities, 23,* 44-52.

Wadsworth, S. J., DeFries, J. C., Stevenson, J., Gilger, J. W., & Pennington, B. F. (1992). Gender ratios among reading-disabled children and their siblings as a function of parental impairment. *Journal of Child Psychology & Psychiatry, 33*(7), 1229-1239.

Weiss, B., Dodge, K. A., Bates, J. E., & Pettit, G. S. (1992). Some consequences of early harsh discipline: Child aggression and a maladaptive social information processing style. *Child Development, 63,* 1321-1335.

Whalen, C. (1989). Attention deficit and hyperactivity disorders. In T. Ollendick & M. Hersen (Eds.), *Handbook of child psychopathology* (2nd ed.). New York: Plenum Press.

Widom, C. S. (1989). Does violence beget violence? A critical examination of the literature. *Psychological Bulletin, 106* (1), 3-28.

Willerman, L. (1979). The effects of families on intellectual development. *American Psychologist, 34,* 923-929.

Williams, S. & McGee, R. (1994). Reading attainment and juvenile delinquency. *Journal of Child Psychology and Psychiatry, 35,* 441-459.

Wolfe, D. & McGee, R. (1994). Dimensions of child maltreatment and their relationship to adolescent adjustment. *Development and Psychopathology, 6,* 165-181.

Zahn-Waxler, C. (1993). Warriors and worriers: Gender and psychopathology. *Development and Psychopathology, 5,* 79-90.

Zahn-Waxler, C., Radke-Yarrow, M., & Wager, E. (1992). Development of concern for others. *Developmental Psychology, 28*, 126-136.

Zaslow, M. J. (1988). Sex differences in children's response to parental divorce: Research methodology and postdivorce family forms. *American Journal of Orthopsychiatry, 58*(3), 355-378.

Zaslow, M. J. (1989). Sex differences in children's response to parental divorce: Samples, variables, ages, and sources. *American Journal of Orthopsychiatry, 59*, 118-141.

Zaslow, M. J. & Hayes, C. D. (1986). Sex differences in children's response to psychosocial stress: Toward a cross-context analysis. In M. E. Lamb, A. L. Brown, & B. Rogoff (Eds.), *Advances in developmental psychology* (Vol. 4, pp. 285-333). London: Lawrence Erlbaum Associates.

Zoccolillo, M. (1993). Gender and the development of conduct disorder. *Development and Psychopathology, 5*, 65-78.

Zuckerman, M. (1994). Impulsive unsocialized sensation seeking: the biological foundations of a basic dimension of personality. In J. E. Bates & T. D. Wachs (Eds.), *Temperament: Individual differences at the interface of biology and behavior* (pp. 219-245). Washington, DC: American Psychological Association.

About the Author

Robert F. Eme, PhD, teaches at the Illinois School of Professional Psychology, Meadows Campus, in Rolling Meadows, and is also in private practice. He is a Diplomate in Clinical Psychology from the American Board of Professional Psychology. His interests lie in the areas of adolescent development and sex roles/differences. Dr. Eme has special expertise in conduct disorders associated with juvenile violence.

CHAPTER 4

VIOLENCE, VIEWING, AND DEVELOPMENT: DOES VIOLENCE IN THE MEDIA CAUSE VIOLENCE IN YOUTH?

Lita Linzer Schwartz
Rosalie Greenfield Matzkin

The Contemporary Picture

Vignette: The Laurie Show case

At approximately 6:30 a.m. on a December morning in 1991, three young people arrived by car at the home of 16-year-old Laurie Show. Two of them, Michelle Lambert and Tabitha Buck, both aged 17, got out of the car, while the driver, Lawrence Yunkin, headed for a nearby McDonald's. There, he ate breakfast, and then returned to the street where Show lived to pick up Lambert and Buck. By the time he arrived, Buck and Lambert had entered the Show home, brutally stabbed Show numerous times, strangled and mutilated her, and were already outside the house waiting for Yunkin in order to make their getaway. Laurie died a few minutes later in her mother's arms, having uttered the first few syllables of her murderer's name.

Yunkin and Lambert dropped Buck off at her high school, then went home, gathered up their laundry, and went to a nearby laundromat where they watched a detective show on television while the machines did their work. Later in the day, *they visited family, and then went bowling with Buck in the evening (Schwartz & Matzkin, 1993).*

Laurie Show's murder is not an isolated instance of lethal violence committed by youths. A few examples: In 1993, two 10-year-olds in Liverpool kidnapped and killed a two-year-old boy (Davies, 1993; Schmidt, 1993). Also in 1993, a 13-year-old boy in upstate New York brutally choked, head-bashed, and sodomized a 4-year-old neighbor (Dobbin, 1994). In the space of a few days in early Fall 1994, two 11-year-olds dropped a 5-year-old to his death from a 14th-story window in Chicago ("Boy, 5," 1994), and three 6-year-old boys stomped and kicked a 5-year-old female playmate in Norway, leaving her to freeze to death in the snow (Fornell, 1994). In another recent case in Utah, a 17-year-old was accused of murdering his stepmother and half-sister after allegedly becoming "obsessed" with the film "Natural Born Killers" (Assoc. Press, 1994).

Among dozens of incidents of inexplicably violent teenage murders, one recent case, which made national headlines, seemed particularly disturbing. In a Philadelphia neighborhood bordering a suburb, a senseless brain-bashing by baseball bat-wielding mid-adolescent youths seeking vengeance for an alleged rape that had not occurred left an accused but innocent youth dead, hundreds of his peers in shock, and several families with ruined lives — the result of several days of one-option-only planning (Gammage, Gibbons, & Marder, 1994). Early the following week, many of the assailants were reported to be "high-fiving" each other in the halls of their high school. Many of their classmates were aware of who had participated in this crime; none reported the perpetrators to school officials or the police (or their own parents). This did not occur in an inner city community acknowledged to have high crime rates by youthful offenders.

One stunning element that runs through all of these acts of violence is the fact that in none of these cases or thousands of others, were there any indications of remorse, regret, or guilt on the part of the child murderers. To the rational adult, the horror of these murders is almost equaled by the horrors of no display of affect on the part of these young murderers. Furthermore, there appears to be no recognition of the devastation wrought on the families of the victims or those of the killers by these acts.

A second factor in lethal violence by children and youth today is their desire for immediate gratification. Accordingly, they make no effort to control impulsive behavior arising from the situation immediately at hand. In the case of the 5-year-old's death in Chicago, his killers were allegedly angered by his refusal to steal candy for them. In the case in Norway, the little boys simply decided to be "mean" to the little girl.

A third element of today's scenes of violence by children and youth is their perception (and that of many adults) that their acts are the fault of everyone else...that *they* are victims. It is true that children of drug addicts, alcoholics, or mentally ill parents tend to be abused and/or neglected, but there *are* invulnerable children (see Jenkins, 1991) who "make it" despite a host of such negatives in

their backgrounds. Violence is not inevitable.

On the other hand, an apparently functional middle-class family background is no guarantee that adolescent children will not become murderers. The Laurie Show murderers and their victim came from middle-class families in suburban Lancaster, Pennsylvania. This is also true in the even more recent homicides in the Allentown, Pennsylvania, area, where two sets of parental murders by teens in a three-day period stunned the entire community. In the first case, two of three sons, both skinheads, murdered their parents and 11-year-old brother (Miller, 1995); in the second, a 16-year-old described as a "clean-cut churchgoing youth," ambushed and shot both of his parents (Bauers, 1995).

Equally disturbing is the fact that so many of our young people see weapons and death all around them, and that too few of them even blink. In fact, the subhead of an article in *Newsweek* on "Kids who kill" read "Disputes once settled with fists are now settled with guns. Every 100 hours, more youths die on the street than were killed in the Persian Gulf" (Witkin, 1991, p. 26). Is there a new and more generalized callousness affecting our youth, making it possible for them to participate in lethal aggression, or to witness it, or to have knowledge of it with less humanity or concern?

The Laurie Show case is significant because it encompasses so many elements common to these cases: (1) its murderers are adolescents who typically watched a lot of television and programs of a particular kind; (2) following the murder, they expressed and exhibited no remorse or regret or guilt whatever; (3) some members of the community knew of the plan in advance, were involved in earlier assaults or murder plots, and witnessed repeated acts of cruelty, both physical and mental, to the victim in the months prior to the actual murder; (4) the murder victim never protected herself by taking violent action against the stalker/abuser/murderer and was not considered an abusive person; and (5) the case aroused much publicity, and one of the murderers, Michelle Lambert, has appeared several times on network broadcasts including *A Current Affair* (Schwartz & Matzkin, 1993).

Statistics indicate that murder among young people rose during the 1980s in the United States:

In 1990 the homicide rate in Boston increased by 45% over the previous year; in Denver by 29%; in Chicago, Dallas and New Orleans, by more than 20%.... Across the country, 1 out of 5 teenage and young adult deaths was gun related in 1988 — the first year in which firearm death rates for both Black and White teenagers exceeded the total for all natural causes of death combined (Richters & Martinez, 1993, p. 7).

Statistics also indicate that the number of homicide victims ages 10 to 19 increased 48% from 1984 to 1989, as did the number of juveniles (age 17 years and under) arrested for murder, from approximately 1,500 in 1987 to more than 2,674 in 1990, an increase of 55% (Henkoff, 1992, p. 63).

There is no question that a gun, especially a semiautomatic like the AK-47, the Uzi, or the Cobray M11/9, gives its holder power — or the illusion of power — to eliminate others indiscriminately, to be "somebody" in a gang, to be private and unassailable. Firing the gun and hitting a target, any target, provides an instant rush of excitement.

"For young people who can boast that 'human life means nothing,' the gun has lost its deadly mystique and mystery" (Sanders, 1994, p. 159). And indeed, guns are fast becoming the possession of choice among youngsters who do *not* have to live in inner cities to find them attractive. In an op-ed column in *The New York Times*, Herbert (1994) observed that although the gun industry in the United States is doing well both in terms of manufacturing and gun sales, there is a continuing need for new markets. He quoted directly from the "Editor's Note" in *S.H.O.T. Business,* a trade publication for the firearms

industry: "An important mission of this magazine is to show our readers how they can expand their customer base, especially to women and children" (Herbert, p. A23).

Has the Media Become the Scapegoat for Explaining Violence?

The fact that there are incontestable statistics confirming increases in violent and lethal acts by and to young people, and most reprehensibly, by and to children, has alarmed the public. And, as the public, the academic world, the police authorities, and others respond by considering the causes and links among these troubling trends, the media appears to bear ever-increasing scrutiny by these groups and other institutions.

Historically, but with greater and more focused publicity today, the public blames "the media" for increases in fatal crimes. Because the problem of increased youthful violence is a world-wide issue, responses and solutions are sought everywhere. European expressions of concern over the effects of the media have led to more protective measures by government, most of which have somewhat closer ties to media industries than do those in the United States. The immediate Scandinavian response to the tragedy in Trondheim, Norway, was to drop a popular children's television show that allegedly highlights interpersonal (or inter-character) violence (Mellgren, 1994). Even in the United States, the issue of media effects has been making more consistent and negative headlines in consumer publications as well as academic journals over the past several years.

During Senate hearings in October 1993, Attorney General Janet Reno warned the television industry that "unless it moved immediately to stem the tide of shootings, stabbings and other mayhem beamed daily into the nation's homes, the White House and Congress would seek laws to do it for them" (Wines, 1993). According to

Wines, "it was the bluntest government condemnation of broadcast violence since the Surgeon General linked television to aggressive behavior 21 years ago. And it drew anguished protests of innocence from some of the industry's most visible executives" (Wines, p. A1).

This has forced American commercial networks, which tend not to respond as quickly to outcries against violence as programmers elsewhere, to undertake some efforts to reschedule programs that might be inappropriate for young children. Many say this is not enough. Indeed, financial cutbacks during the 1980s have been identified as one of the factors leading to increases in violent programming during prime time, because the cutbacks included personnel who were in charge of program screening (Auletta, 1991). While Hollywood film-makers are instructed by the film industry to label their films, which *may* exclude youths from seeing certain films in movie houses, this does not affect their accessibility once on videotape and available for rental or television.

The Problem For Social Science Research

If we look at the risk factors that seem to coalesce during children's pre-puberty and adolescent years, we can observe the interaction of genetic, environmental, and individual personality factors which, when not outweighed by protective factors, present the frightening possibility that individuals will engage in activities destined to compromise their well-being and even lives (Jessor, 1992).

The American public appears to believe that media violence plays a role in the spiraling societal violence we are experiencing. According to one article, "About 68% of Americans believe that the most influential force shaping young people's values is popular entertainment — movies, TV, music videos — and they are not happy about it (Rankin, 1995, p. E1). A *Times Mirror* poll

reported that "80% of the public believes that TV violence is harmful to society, up from 64% 19 years ago. And a *USA Weekend* poll found 96% of the public believes that TV glorifies violence" (Rankin, p. E8).

This becomes somewhat ironic because some critics of social science research refuse to accept the findings of much of the research which does indicate a relationship between violent behavior and media programing. As noted by Zillmann, Bryant, and Huston (1994):

To date the social sciences have largely failed to convince leaders and legislators that particular mass-media messages may cause measurable harm and ultimately be in the public disinterest. The methods currently extant in the social sciences seem incapable of incontrovertible "proof" of harm from consumption of specific media-disseminated messages (p. 15).

In this same article, Zillmann et al. expressed concern over the dilemma this creates for social scientists because, they admonished, the critics of studies on the effects of media violence have raised the criteria for acceptable "proof" beyond "those characteristics of the social sciences in general" (1994, p. 15). The authors cited several studies which underscored the point, including Freedman (1992) and Milavsky, Stipp, Kessler, & Rubens (1982) (p. 15).

Another important and disturbing consequence of this unreasonable demand for unequivocal agreement and "incontrovertible evidence" is that the critics have managed to create the (inaccurate) impression that "social scientists are in irreconcilable disagreement and lack reliable answers. Indeed, the inconsistencies in research findings are to be found in the bulk of research efforts" (Zillmann, et al., 1994, p. 15).

Actually, there are areas of very strong agreement among social scientists on some issues regarding the role of media in violent behavior by the young. For one thing, it is in the main accepted that excessive viewing of intensely violent programming over time can contribute to an increase in lethal violence by children and youth *if* those young people are already vulnerable because of other influences in their lives.

In its 1993 report on "Violence and Youth," based on extensive research, the American Psychological Association's Commission on Violence and Youth included in its summary report a number of items relevant to children's exposure to violence in the mass media. Some of its key statements are:

• There is absolutely no doubt that higher levels of viewing violence on television are correlated with increased acceptance of aggressive attitudes and increased aggressive behavior.

• Children's exposure to violence in the mass media, particularly at young ages, can have harmful lifelong consequences.

• In addition to increasing violent behavior toward others, viewing violence on television changes attitudes and behaviors toward violence in significant ways.

• The concept of reality and how others live is also affected by the viewing of television programming and commercials.

However, there is still little conclusive evidence that patterns of violent behavior result *directly* from viewer exposure to video, film, television violence, or all three, despite thousands of studies.

The Desensitization Issue

What seems increasingly clear is the need to address a number of troubling issues related to media programming because of their long-term implications. The most significant of these is the pattern of desensitization to media images of violence, inhuman acts, aggression, and cruelty about which families as well as educators and others are complaining and insisting they are seeing reenacted in dramatically increasing numbers. Of equal concern are increasing attitudes of cyni-

cism and disengagement or callous indifference by children and youths from virtually every socio-economic, regional, and racial group toward real-life situations in the community, society, and the world. An alarming number of young people seem to experience palpable pleasure in their media encounters with violent entertainments, and express unabashedly insatiable demands for more of the same. Responses by media entertainment producers anticipate these appetites. Using media hype to seduce their young audiences, the trailers for these offerings which simulate reality effectively, whether on film, video, or computer, feature as much graphic violence as possible.

Worried parents, teachers, and other interested adults who anxiously query youngsters about such entertainment proclivities are universally scoffed at by these youngsters who claim their encounters with media violence "do not affect" them. This unquestioning acceptance of their media interests is a source of concern for many parents, teachers, and social scientists.

That the problem is widespread seems clear. Here are a few examples:

• Shortly after it opened in Los Angeles, a center city movie theater had to cancel a showing of *Schindler's List* while it was in progress. The reason? The disruptions caused by the screaming, clapping, and cheering young audience members, who were responding to scenes in which Jews were being rounded up, shot,or sent to extermination camps. Explanations given to the press regarding these behaviors during the movie suggested that the youngsters had not been given any advance preparation for seeing the film (i.e., that it was based on true events).

• The most targeted film audiences for movies in commercial release are those between the ages of 12 and 25, for whom most American films are produced. Overall, these movies tend to include a good deal of danger and violence (acceptable enough, however, to be able to obtain a PG-13 rating) and are variations on the action/adventure genre, which put virtually no emphasis on character development or plot, but much emphasis on derring-do and special effects.

• The sensationalizing of the O. J. Simpson case, among others, and its "entertainmentalization," again seems to put the issue of life and death into some tinseltown world of unreality. We have, for example, the case of the curiosity seekers filmed following Simpson during his confused and confusing drive around Los Angeles, while technically a fugitive. These people, mainly young, seemed, on the whole, when seen on television, less emotionally concerned about the tragic events than about having their faces shown on television.

• In an all-state teachers' workshop held at Delaware State University during the summer of 1991, teacher-participants, *without exception* spoke at length and with great passion about noticeable and dramatic increases in aggressive behavior and violent interactions between and among pupils at all levels of schooling, from preschoolers to high school students. Those attending the conference came from a diversity of regions in the state — rural, suburban, and urban. The participants also complained about the students' lack of remorse or any meaningful affect after such acts of aggression.

Among teenagers in some communities, there is a concomitant sense of hopelessness, a belief that they will not live to celebrate their 21st birthday. Such attitudes, as well as the continued soaring success of violent media entertainment targeted at children and youth, encourage researchers to ponder the roles of marketing, competition, and product as they may be impacting on childhood affect.

An Interactive Perspective

The world of the 1990s is a very different one from that of the 1890s. It is also very different from the 1950s or even the 1960s. The rapidity of technological change has influenced lifestyles and helped to shape the attitudes, values, and beliefs of the last generation of youth in ways that would have been unforeseeable just a few decades ago. The acceleration of change has been brought about largely by the institutionalization of modern mass media, which has then precipitated for mass media-oriented societies exposure to a wide variety of events — real and imagined — including an exposure to various authentic and imaginary uses of lethal violence. As noted above, the impact of mass media on children and on family life is the subject of much research, and, indeed, of this chapter.

In her classic article, "The Mass Media: New schoolhouses for children," Selma Fraiberg's (1987) description of her own childhood offers an eloquent contrast with the childhood of today's media-oriented environment.

Many, many years ago when I was a child, a home was a shelter against the dangers outside. I had heard, as a child, that there was savagery in the world, that men committed murder, that homes were burglarized, that a child had been kidnapped and ravished, and that in far off lands there were revolutions and wars. But all these things happened in another world. Murderers, kidnappers, and burglars lived on another planet — not so far away as dragons, witches, and monsters, but almost as far — and in any case that had not much more reality for me than the creatures of the fairy tales (p. 573).

Fraiberg pointed out later in her article: "For today's child, a home is no longer a shelter against the dangers outside. The child is a fascinated spectator of the whole world" (1987, p. 574). While traditional familial, religious, and psychosocial dimensions of life still play large and influential roles in the dispositioning of human beings, all variables, including those of our contemporary and continually expanding multi-mediated encounters, must also be considered.

It is our position that lethal violent behavior by the young results from an interaction of many variables, and that it may be impossible, in most cases, to determine which variables carry the most weight in any given interaction. Huesmann and Eron (1986) support this view, stating that "in order for aggression to become a serious problem, it is necessary that a number of factors be present to increase a child's aggression. No one factor would probably be sufficient" (p. 64). This is illustrated in Figure 1, which shows the many personal and social variables that interact to cause violent behavior. To clarify our position, we will discuss psychosocial development, changes in society, and the changing role of film and television in our lives. Then we will show how these factors are interwoven in the fabric that is today's world rather than being discrete factors affecting the individual.

The Role of Development

Many people believe that, with certain exceptions relevant to severe physical problems, most babies born in the United States are in roughly equal positions at the starting gate of life and that developmental theories propounded by mental health professionals about stages of

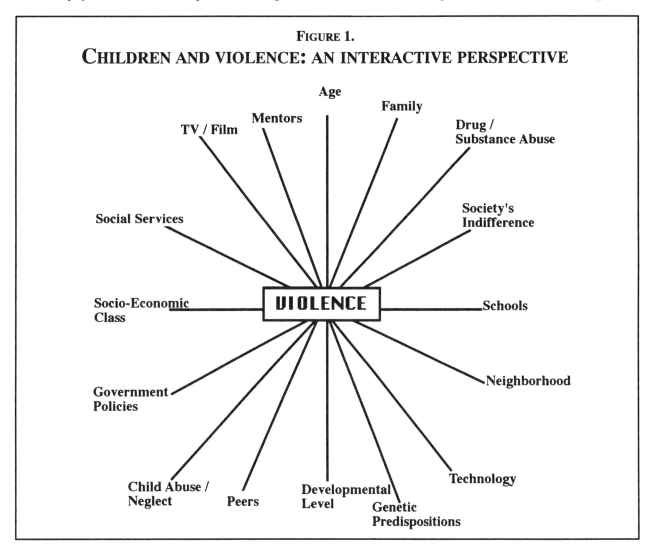

FIGURE 1.
CHILDREN AND VIOLENCE: AN INTERACTIVE PERSPECTIVE

development describe them all with reasonable accuracy. Others believe that there are clear genetic differences present at birth among children of different ethnic backgrounds that are virtually unmodifiable by postnatal events (notably Murray & Herrnstein, 1994). Neither position has total validity.

In fact, at birth, neonates have already been affected with respect to their physical, cognitive, and emotional development by genetic combinations, their mother's prenatal diet and intake of any harmful substances, and the uterine environment. All except the genetic matter must be

they are of the same sex or not, and whether they are White, Black, Hispanic, Asian, Native American, or a mixture of two or more of these racial lines.

Theoretical Perspectives

Psychosocial development, as delineated by Erikson (1950), provides a guideline to the paths children may follow as they move through the stages from infancy to adulthood (as shown in Table 1), with each later stage tending toward one end of a continuum or the other while build-

---

TABLE 1.
PSYCHOSOCIAL DEVELOPMENT:
Infancy to Young Adulthood (after Erikson)

Developmental Stage	Psychosocial Stages	
Young Adulthood	Intimacy _____	Isolation
Adolescence	Identity _____	Role Confusion
Middle Childhood	Industry _____	Inferiority
Late Preschool (4-5 yrs.)	Initiative _____	Guilt
Early Childhood (2-3 yrs.)	Autonomy _____	Shame & Doubt
Infancy	Basic Trust _____	Mistrust

Based on Erikson, E. H. (1950). *Childhood and Society.* **New York: W.W.Norton.**

---

considered environmental influence, as is everything that happens to and around them postnatally. Even biological siblings who share some genetic heritage as well as the same parents are affected in different ways by environmental influences due to their unique psychophysiological makeup, birth order, and changes within the family over time. One may stand a month earlier than the other, while the latter is quicker to verbalize, with both functioning within the normal parameters of infant development. As they continue to develop, one may prove to be more resistant than the other to negative events in daily life, or one may respond by withdrawal and the other by aggression. This is true whether

ing on the resolution of those that came earlier. Critical to healthy psychosocial development in Erikson's eyes is the development of a sense of basic trust by infants in those who care for them. If this does not occur, because the parents are unable or unwilling to meet the infant's basic needs, a pattern tends to be set for wariness in future interpersonal relationships, perhaps culminating at the extreme in a totally defensive and hostile posture toward all of society — a sociopathic individual. At the time of Erikson's second stage, the continuum of Autonomy to Shame and Self-Doubt, the toddler learns the power of "No!" and begins to exercise some control over his or her actions. If a toddler finds himself or herself powerless, on the other hand, perhaps the victim of child abuse, the unspoken inner question may become "Why?" and the pattern of self-image as victim may begin to emerge. Similarly, lack of freedom to explore at the next stage, or to measure up to his or her peers in the outcome of effort in the middle childhood years, may direct future efforts toward gaining attention and acceptance by any means as a child approaches adolescence.

According to Ashbach (1994), on middle childhood's continuum of a sense of industry to a sense of inferiority:

The mastery of skills, different for each gender, and the acquiring of new capacities loom very large. These children want to watch how older youths and adults handle life. . . .

Their need for mastery produces a love of repetitiveness. This accordingly makes latency-aged children prone to slogans and ideal targets for advertising. The hunger for brightness and activity exposes such children to the danger of advertising images penetrating deeply into the self-concept. This means that instant gratification, the expectation of action and excitement, and a perceptual apparatus accustomed to short, choppy imagery and information becomes internalized in the core of the self (p. 125).

Maslow's (1987) hierarchy of needs parallels Erikson's perspective in some ways. His view that basic physiological, security, and shelter needs must be met before positive self-esteem can be attained has ties to Erikson's sense of trust. How secure or trusting can a neglected child, an abused child, a hungry child feel? To what degree can a child focus on learning or following rules when that child has witnessed or been the victim of abuse before leaving home in the morning, or has not eaten so that the rumbles of an air-filled digestive system are louder than the teacher's voice?

Similarly, peer pressure is, in part, associated with the needs for acceptance and belongingness as prerequisites for self-esteem and self-actualization and is related to the elementary school child's needs to see himself or herself as capable in comparison with his or her peers and as acceptable to them, needs which continue into the adolescent years. If these middle-level needs in the hierarchy are not met, again, the child may strike out in frustration and anger.

Cognitively, one can be guided by Piaget's theories (1936, 1952) as to how children process incoming stimuli at various ages. Young children, particularly, need time to interpret and internalize their perceptions — to "digest" what they see and hear. As the Singers (1990) have noted, the slow pace of Fred Rogers of *Mr. Rogers' Neighborhood* is designed to permit such activity by his preschool viewers. Cartoons are not so paced, however, as their rapid and repeated visual and auditory sequences are directed toward maintaining the viewer's attention. The preschool viewer in this situation resembles the myopic grizzly bear whose attention is drawn to a moving target, but not a static one, and who responds accordingly.

In what Piaget calls the preoperational stage, roughly ages 2 to 7 years, children can perceive changes in one dimension of a situation (e.g., height but not width), but not the way in which one variable interacts with another, nor can children in this preschool/primary level group usually perceive events or objects from any perspective other than their own. As we shall suggest, however, parents can introduce alternative perspectives to young children to good effect.

In the next stage, termed concrete operations, children in the middle childhood years can begin to manipulate more than one variable or factor at a time, but, according to Piaget, are still tied to concrete objects/data to do so. They cannot, in his view, wrestle mentally with options, alternatives, and the potential consequences of each until they reach Piaget's stage of formal operations at about age 12 years. If children have an impulse to act at age 6, then, it is unlikely, from a Piagetian view-point, that they will anticipate the long-term outcome or irreversibility of their behavior. (There are exceptions to this age-based view.) The same appears to hold true for those older children who have either not attained the stage of formal operations or who have not been made aware of the possibility of varying options and alternatives to handle immediate situations.

Adolescence and the Role of Peer Acceptance

Peer acceptance, defining one's identity, and disengaging from the family are major Eriksonian tasks of adolescence, and clearly, in an era of mass media advertising, conspicuous consumption, and two-income families, the importance of peer acceptance is evident for young people. There are still emotional ties to family members

FIGURE 2.

LIFE-SPACE OF THE ADOLESCENT — THE WORLDS WITHIN WHICH THE ADOLESCENT FUNCTIONS AND WHICH AFFECT THE ADOLESCENT'S LIFE

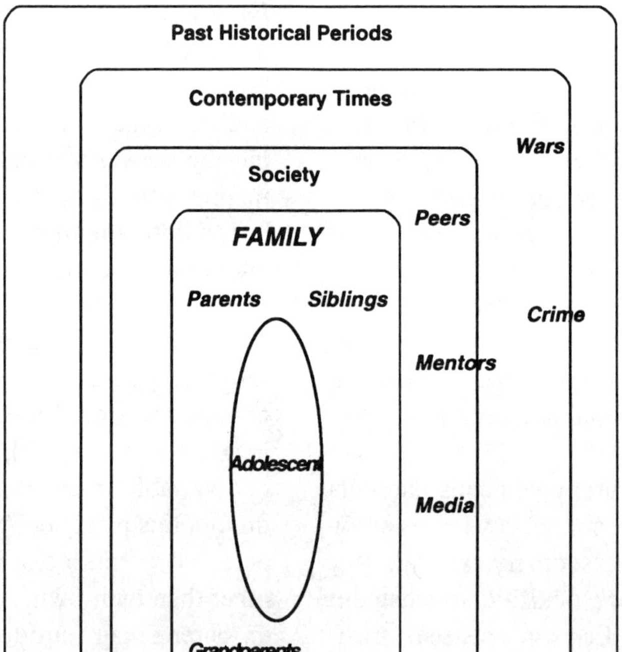

Past Historical Periods

Contemporary Times

Society

FAMILY

Wars

Peers

Parents   Siblings

Crime

Mentors

Adolescent

Media

Grandparents

Extended Family   Education

Socio-Economic Class

in the healthy family, but dress, behavior, and expressed attitudes increasingly reflect the influence of peers and the larger society. All of these elements are present in the life-space of the adolescent, as seen in Figure 2. Assuming that the adolescent has worked through the earlier stages on the healthier end of each continuum, and has developed an appropriate sense of fantasy vs. reality, he or she can watch violent films or television programs without incorporating the techniques shown into his or her behavioral repertoires.

The gore of some films, such as *Friday the 13th* (and its sequels), however, can "act to overstimulate and destabilize the ego of the viewer.... Intense experience without symbolic meaning can lead to an inner world of chaos, impulse, and anxiety" (Ashbach, 1994, p. 126). In such a mental state, and wanting to maintain accepted status with peers, a *vulnerable* adolescent may well act out that inner world in a lethally violent way. For those urban youth who live in communities where violence and aggression occur daily, the impact of such cumulative exposure, when tied to media reinforcement, can be fatal.

Criminal violent behavior among urban youth may be easily modeled during a developmental period when many adolescent youth struggle to achieve individuation and identity, and typically seek counter-culture expressions. According to Barrett (1993), conformity and peer pressure of gangs and "posses" appear to be significant in explaining violent behavior among urban youth.

As we have noted all along with some of the recent and sensational murder cases, peer pressure — the feeling or need to belong to a gang — is not simply, however, an "urban" problem. Children and adolescents watch what their contemporaries watch. Even if they do not initially prefer certain kinds of programming, they will conform to peer standards, especially if they are brought together for a birthday party, or a sleep-over, for which violent or horror videos are rented as "entertainment."

Fantasy, Imagination, and Reality

Adults who were children in the pre-television era listened to the sound effects on radio programs and imagined what was happening. Similarly, they visualized the descriptions of their heroes. Singer and Singer (1990) have emphasized the role of fantasy and imagination within the realm of the child's cognitive development. As children were frightened by what they heard, sensitive parents of the pre-television era taught them the difference between the "stories" they heard and the real world. Those who were avid readers as children may say that they still "see" places and costumes as they read a novel or historical text as adults. Singer and Singer (1990) averred that reading and listening to the radio were both found to stimulate imagination more than television and to be more active processes according to a number of studies that compared the effects of all three media experiences. "The fast pace of television programs and their entertainment function may interfere with the process of reflection needed for reading comprehension and creative thinking" (Singer & Singer, p. 191). Signorielli (1991) similarly asserted that "A sizable body of research evidence supports the position that television viewing has a negative impact upon children's imagination and creativity" (p. 43).

The relevance of imagination to lethal behavior is made clear in Biblow's (1973) studies, also summarized by the Singers. "Imaginative children can use a variety of vicarious fantasy experiences to moderate their anger, while children who lack these inclinations are not only basically more aggressive but show an increase in anger and aggression following exposure to a violent film" (Singer & Singer, 1990, p. 258). In other words, those children who have richer fantasy lives have the potential — the options — to find more alternative reactions than those children who have not developed their imaginations. The more imaginative children are less likely to respond to stimulation with reflexive aggression.

Gratification: Instant and Quasi-Passive

Ashbach (1994) supported the view that media images, particularly certain kinds of animations, commercials, and violent programming, can trigger dangerous impulses, inhibit positive imaginative development, or both, in children. He referred specifically to the problem that arises when the "slow and accumulating process of thought and fantasy being integrated with the... increase in the growth of the personality that seems to suffer the most inhibition when the consumption of media images becomes excessive or defensive" (1994, p.120). He pointed especially to the danger or threat of death that serves as the basis for many animated cartoons, even though the dangers and threats are somehow magically overcome by the intended "victim." The part that concerned him was that *"there are no real consequences* [emphasis added] attendant to the use of massive aggression and force. Magically, all characters reappear in the next cartoon and the cycle of conflict and resolution, gratifying the child's wish to overcome limitation and smallness, is repeated once more" (Ashbach, 1994, p. 120). No wonder six-year-olds, rarely as it may happen, can brutally, or accidentally, kill another child without feeling remorse; they do not see the permanence of their act.

Similarly, violent computer games, which tend to be sexist both in content and attraction, excite children, especially boys, and use a number of their psychomotor skills (such as reaction time). What they do *not* do is evoke imagination or innovation (Sanders, 1994).

Adding to the acting-out behavior without consideration of consequences, according to Ashbach (1994), are television commercials. Like cartoons, "they too 'mimic' the form of unconscious fantasy. They are powerfully seductive little 'daydreams' that bring the dreamer (the viewer) the image of fulfillment and gratification of their wishes, and most importantly, without effort or delay" (p. 122). Rather than working out conflicts or desires through imagination, the message is received — even perceived as encouraged — to "go for" what you want when you want it, whether "it" is a thing or a person.

Sanders (1994) asserted that television *delivers one of the most debilitating psychological blows in denying the youngster the chance to turn inside himself or herself and to have a silent conversation with that budding social construct, the self. The TV short-circuits the developmental process, replacing emotional and psychological needs and desires with consumer values. Instead of listening to his or her own inner voice, the young person pays attention to the loudest commercial or the noisiest cop show (pp. 43-44).*

Even in the realm of sports, so often touted as a positive influence and certainly pervasive on the television screen, the message transmitted is one of instant gratification. Football coach Vince Lombardi is supposed to have said, "Winning isn't everything... it's the only thing!" Philadelphia's hockey team, the Flyers, for example, were proudly called the "Broad St. Bullies" for years because of their aggressiveness toward other teams during games. More recently, the world — including children and youth — witnessed the attacks on Olympic ice-skater Nancy Kerrigan, designed to enhance a competitor's chances of winning the 1994 Gold Medal.

The school world cannot compete with such exciting audio-visual images. Learning to read takes more effort than many of the young are willing to expend, even with the advent of computer-based reading instruction.

The Concept of Death

Does television provide a resource for helping children prepare for the reality of death? Or has it led to a desensitization about death?

According to Speece and Brent (1992), the concept of death is composed of a set of largely distinct components including:

(a) universality, defined as the understanding that all living things die;

(b) irreversibility, defined as the understanding that once a living thing dies, its physical body cannot be made alive again; and

(c) nonfunctionality, defined as the understanding that all life-defining functions cease at death" (p. 211).

Children usually acquire the concept of death between the ages of 5 and 12 years of age, but Speece and Brent's research with a group of White, lower middle-class, rural kindergarten through third graders (N=91) suggested that most children do not attain a mature understanding of all three key components until at least age 10. Universality seemed to be easier to understand than either irreversibility or nonfunctionality, with a combination of sequential and concurrent acquisition processes leading ultimately to the mature level of comprehension. Irreversibility posed some difficulties especially relevant to our concern with children and lethal violence stemming both from some religious traditions about miraculous revivals and, as Speece and Brent pointed out, death often being "depicted in children's books and television cartoons as reversible" (p. 227).

In actuality, newspaper and television reports of violent or particularly tragic deaths of adolescents frequently mention that psychological counselors were called into the school to help students work through their grief, and that classmates often attended the peer's funeral as a group. Small group discussions among the deceased's friends, with or without adult guidance, appear to help the young (as well as their elders) deal with this personal loss. These aids to handling grief and shock seem to occur in neighborhoods where youthful or adolescent death is a rarity, and murder even more rare.

In studies by Wass and her colleagues (1989), gifted and heterogeneous student samples, both of which report high proportions of violent death on their favorite programs and on the news,

perceive television's portrayals of death as realistic and, thus, see television as an important part of a child's preparation for life. At the same time, many other students view television's depiction of death as distorted and the young children's exposure to violent death on television as having adverse effects on their feelings, thoughts, or behavior (Wass, Raup, & Sisler, pp. 170-171).

Waas et al. found that adolescents have a more mature perception of death than younger children and have a keen awareness of its pervasive presence in the media. More than 700 rural and urban Florida students, ages 12 to 18 years, from all socioeconomic levels, both White and Black, chose action/detective type programs as their *second* favorite program (after sitcoms/cartoons/funny movies) but they reported nevertheless "approximately two-fifths of the deaths on their favorite programs as violent" (Wass, et al., 1989, p. 165). When questioned about whether young children should be allowed to watch violent death on TV, of the 47% who answered "no" and 53% who answered "yes," only 11 to 20% gave a qualified "yes" if the child could distinguish between the real world and the world seen on television (p. 166). Of greater interest here, though, is the concern of more than a quarter of those who said "no" because they believed "that a child might copy violent acts or become a violent person" (p. 168).

Asked how frequently they discussed death with parents or friends after having watched television programs presenting death, "Eighty percent of the students reported that they 'never' or 'seldom' talk to their parents about death...." (Wass, et al., 1989, p. 169). They reported not liking to think about death, being uncomfortable with the topic, feeling able to handle the concept, or being fearful that others would think they were "crazy" if they wanted to discuss it. Indeed, from a clinician's point of view, an adolescent's desire to discuss death might suggest a pre-suicidal state of mind. On the other hand, as might be expected of adolescents, more of them felt more comfortable having such discussions with their peers in such a discussion than with their parents.

Although the adolescents in the Waas et al. study were split in their feelings about younger children watching violence on television, there are studies by social scientists that suggest, sometimes quite strongly, that even toddlers' behavior is affected by the models they see on TV, and that crime increases as television is introduced into remote communities. Signorielli (1991) asserted, furthermore, that "children must learn to distinguish between fantasy and reality on television and it is not until the age of seven that the average child can make these distinctions" (p. 42). This appears to conflict somewhat with the Speece and Brent study of young school-age children above. In her review of major studies, including her own, Signorielli joined the growing number of researchers who are inclined to give more credence to the notion that media exposure shapes behavior, including aggressive behavior, as well as shaping attitudes and values. Signorielli stated:

First, viewers will imitate the violent behaviors that they see on television. Second, viewing violence will make people insensitive to the issue of personal violence as well as violence in society. Third, exposure to violence on television will help to shape and mold people's values, that is, will cultivate violence-related conceptions about the world (p. 95).

In a documentary video on children and television, this theme is elaborated upon by a number of researchers. They explain how the images of sex, violence, and anti-intellectualism that are so pervasive on programs seen by children "contribute to aggressive behavior, lessened attention spans, and diminished cognitive abilities among our young" (Adelman, 1993).

The Vulnerable vs. the Resilient

Media violence has been shown to be apparently more damaging to youngsters who come from abusive homes, and who additionally tend to spend many hours watching violent media programming. According to Greenbaum's (1994) long-term study of 4000 youths in Denver, Pittsburgh, and Rochester (NY):

Greater risks exist for violent offending when a child is physically abused or neglected early in life. Such a child is more likely to begin violent offending earlier and to be more involved in such offending than children who have not been abused or neglected. Children who are victims of or witnesses to multiple acts of violence in the home are two and one-half times more likely to commit subsequent acts of violence than children who are spared such domestic violence (p. 4).

Huesmann (1986) also believed that there is a close association between violent behavior and academic performance. Huesmann stated:

The more aggressive child becomes the less popular child and the poorer academic achiever in school. These academic and social failures may become frustrators instigating more aggressive responses. In addition, however, children who are less successful in school and less popular become the more regular television viewers. Perhaps they can obtain the satisfactions vicariously from television that they are denied in school and in their social life. They may also be better able to justify their own previous aggression after seeing more aggression in the media (pp. 135-136).

On the other hand, there is a substantial body of research that shows a higher rate of illiteracy (or below-grade level reading ability) among children and adults today. Sanders (1994) tied this finding to the increase in antisocial behavior, stating as follows:

Illiteracy leaves behind shells of people —

ghosts who take to the streets in a terribly dangerous state. They are unable to feel remorse or sorrow or guilt about their actions, even those of the most violent and gruesome kind. Society needs to fear ghosts who feel no more real than the shimmering of an image on a computer screen. For them, others are no more real than they are. Under those conditions anything can happen and does happen. Behavior becomes literally antisocial (p. 78).

Those children and youth who explode in lethal violence as well as other crimes grab the headlines. Such incidents are frequent enough to make it appear that the great majority of children, mostly male, from inner-city or very poor neighborhoods, and of varying ethnicity, are prone to violence. Federal statistics for 1976 to 1991 showed that 0.3 out of 100,000 offenders age 13 years or younger committed murder or nonnegligent manslaughter in 1976; the rate in 1991 was 0.2 out of 100,000. In the 14- to 17-year-old range, however, the rate more than doubled from 7.6 out of 100,000 in 1976 to 15.7 out of 100,000 in 1991 (Maguire, Pastore, & Flanagan, 1993, p. 394).

An increasing body of research evidence suggests that violent youths' perception of themselves as victims is not entirely baseless (Barrett, 1993). Dysfunctional families, not necessarily "broken" ones, and overburdened educational and social service systems fail children and youth by not providing a solid support base, positive interaction models, constructive options for problem resolution, and fulfilling learning opportunities in the educational sector. Continuing frustration in one area of life-space or another, coupled with such lacks of support, easily propels youths to striking out against anyone (many murders have random targets), anywhere (in the home, on the street, at school).

There are many children in these same circumstances, however, who avoid drug use, delinquency, and murder. Longitudinal observation

sheds light on their resiliency. Researchers have found that parental supervision, attachment to family, and consistency of discipline were the most important barriers to delinquency and drug use. Commitment to school and, in particular, avoidance of delinquent and drug-using peers were additional protective factors (Greenbaum, 1994, p. 6).

Jenkins (1991) mentioned the importance of a mentor in the life of those who are *invulnerable* to the deprivations of family and society. The mentor may merely be the only adult who takes an interest in the youth, but more often is able to suggest to him or her that the youth's abilities can be directed toward personally and socially acceptable goals. The combined efforts of the youth and mentor, then, are focused on constructive behaviors. The mentor may be able to direct the youth toward peer groups similarly focused so that the need for peer acceptance is also met.

The Role of Mass Media: A Brief Look Backward

Most of us take our electronic media — movies, television, cable — very much for granted, even as we condemn its influence. We don't recall often enough what life was like before the media gained such a dominant role in our lives. Once upon a time, for example, going to a movie was a social experience that people engaged in by and large for escape, entertainment, and emotional release. Parents and young children attended together. For teenagers and young adults, by the late 1920s and 1930s, certain moviegoing conventions had been established: news of the week, two full-length movies, cartoons, coming attractions, popcorn, and a chance to sit next to someone and hold hands in the dark — their chance to escape into privacy.

Early motion pictures were criticized in their time with regard to their content and presumed negative impact on recreation and reading. Many social critics, criminologists, educators, women's groups, and religious groups continued to take exception to the rapid and growing sophistication of theme and content that movies were providing by the 1920s. In fact, the post-World War I period saw rapid changes in the social, moral, and fashion conventions of the United States (Matzkin, 1984). According to Mast (1986), as criticisms mounted:

Such notoriety brought the film business to the attention of the United States Congress and the edge of federal censorship — the last thing any producer wanted. The industry decided once again to clean its own house, to serve as its own censorship body.... In 1922, they found Will H. Hays, President Harding's campaign manager, Postmaster General of the United States, Presbyterian elder, and Republican. Hays became president of the Motion Picture Producers and Distributors of America, an organization supported and financed by all the major film companies in America, known colloquially as the Hays Office, which he headed for twenty-five years (p. 107).

During the 1920s, Hays helped to develop a "Purity Code," which some in Hollywood called the "Don'ts and Be Carefuls" (Cook, 1991, p. 229). However, following publication of the Payne Fund research on children and the movies between 1933 and 1935 (Charters, 1933), which indicated that movies had profound effects on children, there was a great public outcry for more stringent Hollywood regulation, which led to the "Production Code."

The Production Code that dictated the content of American films from the mid-1930s to the mid-1950s and even later, reflected religious views of what constituted indecent content. Anything sexually suggestive was prohibited, including a shared marital bed, nudity, excessive kissing, rape, and adultery. Cook (1991), addressed this issue as follows:

But the Code's most labyrinthine strictures were reserved for the depiction of crime. It was forbidden to show the details of a crime, or to display machine guns, submachine guns, or other illegal weapons, or to discuss weapons at all in dialogue scenes. It was further required that law enforcement officers never be shown dying at the hands of criminals, and that all criminal activities within a given film were shown to be punished. Under no circumstances could a crime be shown to be justified. Suicide and murder were to be avoided unless absolutely necessary to the plot, and the suggestion of excessive brutality or wholesale slaughter of any kind was absolutely prohibited. The antiviolence strictures of the Code seem positively civil in this age of the cinema of cruelty, but the Code as a whole was obviously restrictive and repressive (pp. 298-299).

Television Changes American Lifestyles: Media as Social Context

The introduction of television to the public at large in the late 1940s had a strong negative impact on the film industry and changed lifestyles worldwide. Television's early entertainment programming emerged largely from the format of radio drama and sit-coms, and maintained many of the rules of the motion picture Production Code. Initially, people used the new medium as they had first used radio. Families watched programs together, and often invited neighbors to join them in this novel experience. Gradually, television began to take on more importance and more time in the lives of users/viewers. As the medium branched out, changed formats, added more sophisticated programming, beefed up its advertising, expanded its genres, and most of all, expanded its viewing hours virtually around the clock, television's role in daily American life not only became routinized, but changed many other aspects of American lifestyles. More and more people stayed at home to watch sports programs, which were tied to media contracts. That American television is advertiser-driven is almost an oxymoron, and one that is virtually unique in the entire world.

Television's influences on the American way of life have been far more profound and pervasive than those of the earlier American film and radio industries. For one thing, as compelling as a movie might be, most people went to the movies once or twice a week. For another, that encounter was usually two to four hours in duration. By contrast, not only do we have 24-hour-a-day programming, with options up to nearly 100 different channels at present, but there are options of 500 cable stations looming within the next few years. Gradually, television has assumed the role of arbiter of our popular culture for a large proportion of Americans.

Television Content: Its Relation to Business and Children's Programming

With the Hays Code's demise by the end of the 1950s and the new emphasis in the 1960s on a movie ratings system, television and commercial film production have turned increasingly to marketing techniques to target their somewhat more narrow audiences. By the 1970s, the controversies surrounding the broadcasting of televised violence began to resonate for larger numbers of educators, parents, and other groups. The Surgeon General's report (1972) in the last years of the Carter Administration, indicated there was much to be concerned about. The report stopped short of indicting television as a source of youthful violence, but expressed deep concern about the cumulative impact of television on children.

However, during the early 1980s, the Reagan Administration insisted on moving toward both media and business deregulation, and explosions in both technology and cable operations intensified the competition for market shares. By "narrowcasting" to specific demographic consumer

audiences, the media industries, including television, video, cable and others, have been waging an intense struggle for time, audience share, and advertising dollars.

The early 1980s brought not more violent programming to prime time, but more explicit and open depictions of sex and violence. To some extent, this new openness can be attributed to the volatile changes at the networks brought about by corporate buyouts of the three major networks during the first half of the decade. (Again, this does not mean that the number of violent acts per hour went up, however.) Until then, NBC, CBS, and ABC original networks had been owned and operated by organizations that included all three of the network founders — individuals who had been with the industry for almost 40 years (Auletta, 1991, p. 7). The new corporate network owners were helped in their audience ratings wars in part because they no longer had to be concerned about previously existing FCC regulations. In this way, they put the final nail in the coffin of responsible programming, especially for children.

It is in the areas of children's programming and cable television that increases in acts of violence and aggression are deemed to be most significant, as noted below. To cut costs, however, the networks' new owners fired personnel and encouraged expansion of cheaper programming such as talk shows and tabloid news magazines, and cut back their program practices departments (Auletta, 1991, pp. 224-225). They also encouraged the modeling of network programming to utilize some of the conventions of local news and entertainment broadcasting. These changes represented the thinking of the time, and reflected the "clash between the public interest and the corporate interest" as suggested years earlier by Edward R. Murrow (Auletta, 1991, p. 333). The results and implications, some of which were evolving even before the 1980s, were nonetheless accelerated:

• By the age of 12 or 13, or by graduation

from elementary school, the young viewer will have witnessed approximately 8,000 murders and more than 22,000 assorted acts of violence — more than 30,000 violent acts before he or she hits the schools and streets of our nation as a teenager (Murray, 1988, pp. 1, 12).

• The average child logs in about five hours of commercials during an average week of television viewing. During those five hours, children see approximately 1,000 commercial messages. Before entering school, young children will have seen about 240,000 commercials, and by the end of high school, these young children will have seen about 1 million commercials. About 100,000 of those commercials will have been for beer products (Postman, 1987, p. 8).

Deregulation's impact on children's programming has been enormous. It has also been controversial, as noted by the critics from a variety of societal sources and interest groups. In unprecedented numbers, programming for children and young people has been initiated, created, produced, and promoted by sponsors who are coincidentally creating coordinated products which are being marketed for television sales and are often available in various retail outlets. Children are clearly being turned into consumers and, at a very young age, with obvious effects on, among other things, the family budget.

Because children's programming is also ratings-oriented, programs intended for boys are more numerous than for girls. Allegedly, girls will watch male-oriented television programs, but boys will not watch (or be permitted to watch) programs oriented toward girls. The case of "My So-called Life," an evening television sitcom created in the mid-1990s and particularly popular with teenage girls was not renewed for another year because the audience was too narrow, too female.

The Impact of Television on the Family

By 1980, ownership of television sets had virtually reached saturation level in American households. Today, it is very unusual to find a family without a television set, and most have more than one (DeFleur & Dennis, 1991, p. 210).

Researchers have found that:

• Between the ages of three and adolescence, children spend more time with television than they do in school (Huston, Donnerstein, & Fairchild, 1992).

• In most households, the television is on at least 7 hours a day (Liebert & Sprafkin, 1988, p. 4).

• The average person watches almost 30 hours of television each week, about four and a quarter hours each day (Nielsen, 1990).

• "Children between the ages of two and five watch almost four hours each day (27 hours and 49 minutes each week); those between ages six and eleven watch three and a third hours each day. Older people (over 55) watch the most and teenagers the least, but even teens watch a little more than three hours per day" (Signorielli, 1991, p. 48).

• In many homes, the television is not turned off when guests arrive in the house. Instead, it is simply left on or turned down in many homes.

• More than one television in the home makes it likely that people do not watch television together. Members of the same household can turn to television rather than to each other for companionship or entertainment. Even spouses may choose to watch programming separately rather than have to compromise or share a leisure time activity. If people do not watch the same programs, they cannot actually share the same experience. This can create isolation and separation as opposed to shared activity.

The use of remote control devices promotes constant channel switching for many people. Particularly among men, "channel surfing" appears related to some kind of masculine notion of dominance (Kolbert, 1993; Schlain, 1993). The remote control has also had an hysterical effect on advertising, forcing commercials to become more rapid, more dramatic, and more eye-catching than ever before (DeFleur & Dennis, 1991). The ubiquity of the VCR has also encouraged patterns of "zipping and zapping" (Merrill, Lee, & Friedlander, 1994, p. 224).

Additionally, the use of a remote control channel changer influences the fantasies of the young viewer. As stated by Ashbach (1994):

With just a flick of the finger the child is able to gratify his or her every desire, or at least this is the impression. The child can move from cartoons, to sport, to horror movies or science fiction, to drama or sexual soap operas without having to think or engage the mind. Like Adam in the Garden of Eden, the child is king of all he or she surveys and is able to control and change everything based on his or her whim. The frequent outcome of this process is paradoxically an inflated sense of omnipotence and grandiosity as well as a heightened sense of passivity....

The child has acquired the use of Merlin's "magic wand" but is unable to anticipate or control the consequences (p. 122).

Television as a babysitter for young children often allows young or inexperienced paid caregivers to put infants and children in front of programming for which they are not ready emotionally, with no notion of the impact that such programming may have on very young children. Because commercial television is ratings-driven, more attention, time, and money may be spent on television commercials than on programming content.

One does not have to wax sentimental about the early days of movies, radio, or television to acknowledge disturbing trends in entertainment content today, or to acknowledge that, as in the past, entertainment media industries are still profit driven. A return to the kinds of movies and television that allowed for and standardized taboos and limitations, that denied social, political, and economic realities and inequities, that supported and almost standardized the myth of the American Dream and "the Bitch Goddess of Success" would be no panacea at all. On the other hand, the Hays Code, for all of its controls and rigid adherence to narrow conventions, did help to protect children from being exposed to excesses of violence and cruelty.

If we believe that people can be influenced cumulatively over time by the media to modify their attitudes, beliefs, and values, then it seems reasonable to be concerned about the influence of today's more graphic violence on viewers, especially young viewers. Much of the graphic and explicit violent programming to which young viewers are exposed seems to have no meaningful intellectual, artistic, ethical, or humanistic underpinnings, but instead introduces all viewers to simplistic stereotypical and cartoonish characters and thinking.

Violence and Media Effects Research

For those of us old enough to recall the beginnings of the television era, it is not difficult to observe the different conventions that exist today for our contemporary technological entertainment. It may be worth reminding ourselves of and noting those earlier times for those who are too young to remember. Understanding the cumulative long-term consequences of these changes is rather more amorphous, and more difficult to pin down. In part, that is because there are so many differences in emphasis in the research world.

Numerous communications theories have emerged over the last half century which attempt to understand and explain peoples' experiences with the various mass media. Beginning with the long discarded "magic bullet" theory, which inaccurately suggested that a cause and effect (or stimulus/response relationship) existed in media communications interactions, there have been other theories offered and rejected. One other such concept is the Catharsis Theory, which actually has its origins in early Greek theater and in the Aristotelian conception of Greek tragedy. Among the conventions which Aristotle insisted were necessary to the definition of a tragic play was that of catharsis, or the purging of emotions of pity and fear in the audience through the audience's identification with the tragic hero and events being explored on stage. Some early media researchers suggested that viewers might achieve such purging, or release from their anger, pity, frustration, or other feelings through exposure to the media.

How media needs differ for different individuals and groups, and whether the expectations are indeed met (gratified), have been the subject of research and discussion since the early 1950s when the theory of Uses and Gratifications first came into prominence (see Davison & Yu, 1974; Blumler & Katz, 1974). While there are important distinctions amongst newer theories that have emerged since the early days of Uses and Gratifications, including social learning, modeling, disinhibition, arousal, and cultivation theories, there are also important areas where research efforts and conclusions overlap.

Signorielli (1991) reviewed the literature, cited, and summarized some of the more recent and salient theories:

Observational or social learning theory posits that children (or viewers in general) imitate the behavior of television characters in much the same way that they learn social and cognitive skills — by imitating parents, siblings, and peers.... Social learning theory was proposed by Bandura and Walters (1963) and focuses upon the role of modeling in the child's social development. The original laboratory experiments (often called the Bobo doll experiments) revealed how children could model behaviors exhibited by live models as well as those seen on film (Bandura, 1965; Bandura, Ross, & Ross, 1961, 1963).... Disinhibition theory postulates that television viewing may lower inhibitions about behaving

aggressively (Comstock, 1989).... Arousal Theory (Zillmann, 1982) examines how violence on television may instigate aggression (pp. 85-86).

From this last perspective, television viewing, especially of action-adventure programs, can be physiologically arousing which, in turn, may influence other behaviors that may take place while the viewer is in a state of increased arousal. This theory suggests that increases in aggression occur because of arousal, rather than from modeling.

During the last several years, the separate researches of Gerbner, Friedlander, and Centerwall seem to be associated most strongly with reclaiming the belief that violent media programming contributes to violent behavior, especially by and to the most vulnerable — the young. Bernard Friedlander (1993) addressed this clearly:

Nothing in the intricate web of relationships suggests that television's instrumental role in the problem of community violence is negligible. In fact, there are two [aspects] at the flashpoint threshold of violent behavior — where mass media influence and especially television may be closer to the action than has been recognized. The first of these is the component involving **release of violence and disinhibition of behavioral control.** *The second is the component involving* **provocation** *to violence in such cases as sexual challenge, personal or group challenge to esteem, gang rivalry, ethnic rivalry, interpersonal quarrel, craving for possession, power or control (p. 75).*

Friedlander (1993) stated further "that these components are represented in media with exceptionally high intensity and exceptionally high redundancy in the media lifestyle of affluent materialism and in the imagery of power and control portrayed by media heroes" (p. 76). He continued his explanation, asserting that:

It is plausible to maintain that the factor of **addictive disinhibition** *is one of the most funda-*

mental elements in the operating realities of mass media, most especially television, where the principal objective of entertainment programs and advertising is to overcome whatever inhibitions might deter the viewer from watching the programs and buying the products. In this respect, mass media contribute mightily to a culture of disinhibition. Television does not set out to cultivate violence, but to cultivate disinhibition behavior. Violence is simply one of the ways in which the disinhibition and disregard of internalized behavioral restraints manifest themselves (p. 76).

This would seem to resonate for young people who feel alienated from the mainstream, who live in economic hopelessness or isolation, or who feel or are unemployable, but who can turn on the television and have their despair reinforced by commercials (and programs) that appear to dictate what they must possess or look like, or that promise them that if they possess this or that product, or can adopt a particular look or style, the world will be theirs.

Similarly, arousal theory accentuates and reinforces feelings of aggressiveness. Programming such as Music Television (MTV), targeted at teenaged males, often suggests or depicts images of violence — violence that is being inflicted on women. Using the most sophisticated and rapid editing techniques, the MTV images do not necessarily create images that match the music, lyrics, or both. They do place emphasis on images of power or sexuality, and the trappings of power. Power is shown to be about possessions and beauty, and about manipulating, often violently, people who get in the way of the subject's dreams, fantasies, or desires (Jhally, 1990).

Gerbner's studies in Message and Cultivation Analysis, begun more than 25 years ago, are the "most long term and extensive content analysis of television programming that include the study of violence...." (Signiorelli, 1991, p. 87). The research, begun in 1967 to 1968, involved "the annual content analysis of a week-long sample of prime-time and weekend daytime network dramatic programming,... and... conceptions of social reality that television viewing may tend to cultivate in different groups of viewers" (Signorielli, 1991, p. 88). Results have continued to show small but accumulating influences of television viewing on aggression (Gerbner, Gross, Morgan, & Signorielli, 1980; Signorielli & Morgan, 1990). The Gerbner studies suggest that heavy viewers of television are more likely to perceive the real world in ways that reflect the most common and repetitive messages and lessons they are getting from the television world than people who watch less television but are otherwise comparable in important demographic characteristics (Gerbner et al., 1980).

Gerbner's work suggests that children's programming contains the highest levels of graphic and lethal violence. The studies found that "since 1980, when children's television programming was deregulated (meaning that the codes pertaining to violence were dismantled), the average number of violent actions per hour have increased from 18.6 acts per hour before 1980, to 26.4 per hour since 1980" (Signorielli, 1991, p. 94). This compares to approximately five acts of violence per hour on prime time television programming (Huston et al., 1992).

Results of recently published polls and studies illustrate the public's mood regarding links between media and behavior and support Gerbner's cultivation analysis. *The Philadelphia Inquirer* selected a Page One banner headline to underscore the reports: "'The more they watch, the more they fear,' announced the results of a study by the Survey Research Center" (Seplow, 1994, p. A1). The article announced that "23.6% of heavy television viewers believe there is a very *serious chance* that they will be victimized, while 16 percent of light viewers share that fear.... Sixty-four percent of heavy viewers, but 51.6 percent of light viewers, say one can't be too careful when it comes to trusting people" (Seplow, 1994, p. A21).

that heavy viewers of television, particularly of violent programming, including local news broadcasts, tend to have a darker view of the world, to feel less safe, and to be more pessimistic than those who are considered light viewers. How one's view of the world may affect one's desire, for example, to own a gun, to join a gang, to engage in aggressive behavior, may not be clear cut, but that such media uses encourage a climate of callousness and disengagement seems obvious.

Rural, Suburban, and Urban Violence

The advent of television to remote communities in recent years has eradicated the innocence of their youth with respect to what happens elsewhere, and has done it in living color. Brandon Centerwall's seminal study (1989) concluded that

following the introduction of television into Canada and the United States — and its exclusion from South Africa — white homicide rates remained stable in South Africa, whereas homicide rates in Canada and white homicide rates in the United States doubled. There is an observed 10-15-year lag between the introduction of television and the subsequent doubling of the homicide rate (p. 7).

The Centerwall study took into account several factors, including definitive changes in homicide rates (expansion in most cases), of the number of television households, age distribution, urbanization, economic conditions, alcohol consumption, capital punishment, and availability of firearms. Centerwell stated that "the behavioral effects of exposure are primarily exerted upon children" (1989, p. 15). While the Centerwell study took into consideration the effects of alcohol on violent behavior, it did not speak directly to the more current problem of drug addiction and its impact on violent crime.

It is well documented that millions of children in our cities are being exposed to community violence, drug violence, child abuse, hopeless social and familial conditions, and inadequate educational opportunities. It is also well documented that the urban poor are among the highest users of mass media and violent mass media programming (Huston et al., 1992, p. 15). Exposed both inside their homes and in the little boxes some use for escape, as well as outside of their homes, they face daily dangers that make survival a constant dilemma.

It is important to note that there are dangers operating in the suburbs as well, where dysfunctional families live more privately behind beautifully kept homes and lawns, and where abuse and aggression are also practiced, if more privately. In addition, in the 1990s scene where two incomes are either required or desired, many youngsters are left at home alone, or with siblings or housekeepers and babysitters who do not monitor what the children are watching day after day. Television is a place of learning, including incidental learning. Children find themselves learning about how to act, speak, dress, flirt, and fight from their encounters with this medium. The suburbs are no guarantee against the problems of aggression and violence, especially by children who may feel undervalued, neglected, lonely, isolated, or frightened. Among the examples of lethal violence we mentioned at the very beginning of this chapter were several which were perpetrated by youngsters who lived in suburban areas, were aggressive, and used television as a clear form of disinhibition.

As noted by Friedlander (1993):

It is also sadly true that the rural countryside can be as hazardous for children as the urban slum. I discovered this by direct encounter during the summer of 1990 when I taught a workshop on developmental psychology at the University of Wyoming. Wyoming is perhaps the most rural and "whitest" of all 50 states in the Union, and it claims the reputation of having the highest per capita rate in the country for unwed school-age pregnancies.

I was appalled at the frequency with which my informants reported the plight of children in remote communities far out in the thinly populated countryside who were trapped in settings dominated by assaultive and murderous clan conflicts, feuds, property disputes, political antagonisms, brutal and often alcoholic families, vehicular homicides and suicides (p. 71).

Direct Effects of Exposure to Violent Media

The preponderance of research regarding media effects and violence appears to conclude that for most young people, the long-term direct effects of violent media exposure are minimal. Most young people have the skills to utilize their selective processes, or other coping mechanisms or protective reflexes to protect themselves from, or to enable them to withstand, the constant visceral assaults that violent media offer, even as they choose to watch them.

Eron and his associates (1971) and Huesmann and his associates (1984, 1986) discussed results and implications of 20-year longitudinal studies which indicated that children who were aggressive at age eight, and who were heavy viewers of brutal and violent media programming, were also likely to be aggressive and violent individuals 20 years later.

There are others, as we have noted earlier, who are more vulnerable, or who are clearly more aggressive or who find in media violence a particular kind of resonance or personal triggering mechanism or some other meaning, modeling, motivation, and even method. These are children, for the most part, who can be characterized as aggressive because of emotional, environmental, genetic, or drug and alcohol related disorders that have been part of their lives since their earliest years, and perhaps even before their birth.

The non-clinical evidence about which parents, teachers, and others are increasingly concerned cannot be dismissed. The fact that so much of the public believes they are seeing evidence of heightened aggression in their own schools and homes, directly following the viewing of such shows as "Teenage Mutant Ninja Turtles" and "Power Rangers," which they are linking to television viewing, seems to indicate that the problem may have something to do with cumulative and increasingly graphic depictions of violence. And so ubiquitous are these trends — from commercials for MTV to the uses of the language of war to describe political campaigns — that we may even be losing our own critical awareness of the crucial impact of such programming on children and on adults.

Indirect Effects: The Consequences of a Climate of Violence

Exposed as they are today to expanded media programming, intended and unintended for their viewing, are our children losing their childhood? And if they are being exposed to experiences for which they are not really emotionally or intellectually prepared, do they have the internal resources to protect themselves? How are children to be protected from those experiences for which they are not developmentally ready? How closely can we link child development, growth, feelings, attitudes, aggression with the "electronic box" to which they attend with such fervor and frequency?

If we consider how willing advertisers and sponsors are to pour billions of dollars into media promotion because they believe that commercials will influence people to buy their products, it seems reasonable to examine other influences and conventions that may also be promoted indirectly. Television commercials are created for 30- or 60-second spots. Cumulatively, one can argue that programming, created and viewed for lengthier time slots, potentially creates predispositions, beliefs, and stereotypes.

Like direct effects, indirect effects of increased media violence are also multifaceted. Youthful demands for more violent and more graphically violent programming seem to indicate a higher level of tolerance for violence. The producers who encourage, incite, and initiate by continually raising the ante — with better and more sophisticated special effects and editing techniques creating ever more explicit, more realistic, and more bloodcurdling images — create a disturbing vicious cycle, and thus the phenomenon of a new level of callousness and disengagement. Because so many teenagers insist that they are not bothered by the violence, and seem to believe that movies and television are only reflecting the darker impulses of modern society, it may be that our young people are moving away from the kinds of humanitarian impulses so necessary to a democratic society.

Two 1990 studies of youth summarized in a *New York Times* article "paint a portrait of a generation of young adults, from 18 to 28 years of age, who are indifferent toward public affairs...." (Oreskes, 1990, pp. A1, D21). People for the American Way and the Times Mirror Center for the People and Press characterize the present youthful generation as plagued by an "apathy and alienation" in which "the disengagement runs deeper... setting them apart from earlier generations" (Oreskes, 1990, p. D21).

It is a generation that, according to a report by the Times Mirror Center for the People and Press,

knows less, cares less, votes less and is less critical of its leaders and institutions than young people in the past.... The indifference of this generation — to politics, to government, to news about the outside world — is beginning to affect American politics and society, helping to explain such seemingly disparate trends as the decline in voting, the rise of tabloid television, and the effectiveness of negative advertising.... At the conclusion of the 1988 campaign, Times Mirror's research showed that young voters who began the

campaign knowing less than older voters, were every bit as likely to recall (negative) advertised political themes such as pollution in Boston Harbor, Willie Horton and the Flag.... Sound bites and symbolism, the principal fuels of modern political campaigns, are well suited to young voters who know less and have limited interest in politics and public policy (Oreskes, 1990, p. D21).

This may well be influencing the growth of the politics of hate.

As Signorielli (1991) concludes,

while some might be concerned about the few children who will imitate the violence, concern should also focus upon the majority of children who may become more fearful, insecure, dependent upon authority, and who may grow up demanding protection and even welcoming repression in the name of security. This is the deeper problem of violence-laden television both for us and our children (p. 98).

Remedies: Proactive and Reactive

According to Kubey and Czikszentmihalyi (1990), television does not necessarily produce active audiences, even when there is homogeneity in responses to viewing. Most people have the capacity for two important experiential tools — recognition and perception. Viewers of most television programming are simply using their recognition skills — identifying, observing, noticing shapes, and sets. These are more or less scanning activities or abilities, and are relatively passive. However, the degree of activity of very young children or of teenagers, and the role of incidental learning as well as role modeling and social learning are also important considerations that need to be addressed in future studies of the relationship between children and the media. "The more complex experience of perception requires far more complex interpretation of information and experience. Thus it requires more training to be useful" (Kubey, 1990, pp. 209-210).

Ultimately, we believe that vulnerability must precede the influence of television programs or films, that the media may legitimate a crime in the mind of the vulnerable, or may demonstrate a method of murder, but that these visual and aural stimuli do not, in isolation, cause the increase in lethal violence by the young. It is more likely that there is a circular effect, as Huesmann and Eron (1986) have suggested, in that vulnerable children who are heavy television viewers and who identify with the aggressive characters tend to "encode in memory the aggressive solutions they observe" (p. 77), behave accordingly with outcomes desirable to them reinforcing the aggressive behavior, which leads to social and academic failure, which leads to increased television viewing from which they gain vicarious satisfaction.

The first line of prevention, as we have already suggested, is in the home, with parents supervising their children's exposure to television programs and discussing with them what is seen. Clearly that will not solve the problems in neglectful, overburdened, or dysfunctional families. Other preventive measures might include reducing aggressive resolution of conflicts in the home, substituting alternative dispute techniques, resisting the pleas to purchase toys that promote violence (from toy guns to "Power Rangers"), and teaching even young children that words and actions have consequences that might not always be what they expect.

If children watch television without supervision or parental comment, they may have questions that go unanswered and experiences that are unassimilated. Parents must assume much more responsibility, and should be encouraged to do so by the schools. If the parents can be encouraged to *impose rules for television use and mediate television viewing, they promote "scaffolding:" children begin to see the world through the perspective of "the other" and to consider alternative viewpoints and interpretations.... Parents can even help a child express concern and empathy for a character on TV who may be treated unfairly by another character in the story. A child begins to understand, then, that television stories and characters are fictional, that television writers exaggerate negative personality traits, and that plots are designed to make us laugh, sometimes at any cost. When adults mediate, children begin to view television more actively and critically (Singer & Singer, 1990, p. 183).*

As children get older, they can learn to appreciate just how special effects are used to enhance the speed of the chase or the trauma of a scene. They can be asked to consider other ways in which a situation might have been resolved, or whether a conflict might have been prevented by proactive behavior. Unfortunately, not even all adults watch television or films with such a critical eye, savoring instead the opportunity to be a passive viewer, the familiar "couch potato." Some may "interact" with the program being viewed, yelling "Go get 'em!" at the screen, or feinting fist jabs at the villain or the victim on screen. Such behaviors do little to teach the children present about the difference between reality and fantasy.

School personnel and, through them, the students also need to be taught the techniques and value of alternative dispute resolution techniques. We must find ways to make non-violent actions the only mode acceptable to peer groups of all ages and backgrounds.

We submit as well that sponsors and creators of programs, films, and video games should promptly assume responsibility for the content of their products, indicating their awareness of potential impact on the young, before pressure groups push for enactment of highly restrictive codes. Such proactive action, if practiced universally by the media, and if tied to more constructive story content, could at least be preventive for those who are now very young or yet unborn.

Where parents are unable or unwilling to

teach their children critical thinking skills, especially with regard to media viewing, it may fall to the schools to add yet another task to their overburdened curricula. For example, "Since 1987, the province of Ontario — Canada's largest — has required media literacy instruction for all students from Grades 7 to 12. Media literacy is also well developed in regions of England, Scotland, and Australia, as well as in many European countries" (Kubey, 1990, p. 68).

In Conclusion

While this chapter has focused specifically on some of the most disturbing elements of mass media exposure, it is important to stress that there are a myriad of ways in which the mass media enrich and inform our lives, and the lives of children. The amount of creativity, joy, useful information, and just old-fashioned laughter and amusement which media can provide for so many billions of people across this planet cannot be dismissed. Amidst the criticism of media these days, thoughtful and positive scholars are also embracing the media and suggesting ways in which the media, especially television, can be made better and more useful (Bianculli, 1992; Perkinson, 1995; Siano, 1995). The criticism may be seen as offering hope for reform in the future.

Nonetheless, it appears from all of the foregoing that television and youthful lethal violence may be related to some degree, with variations according to the vulnerability of the individual. Proactive and reactive measures that we have suggested will not reduce youthful violence by themselves. Much more has to be done in terms of providing hope to the hopeless, meaningful education to the young, jobs at respectable wages, as well as eliminating drugs from the American scene, ridding the streets of guns, and solving a variety of social and economic problems.

We must teach children as early as possible that actions have consequences, some of which may be unforeseen, and that their lives, as well as those of others, have value. We must teach children to think critically, reflectively, and independently, rather than to be passive, governed by others and led like sheep. We may not be able to keep adolescents from seeking peer approval, but it should be possible to change what merits such approval.

References

Adelman, L. (1993). Violence on television: Teach the children. American Educational Research Association, Division E (Counseling and Human Development) *Newsletter, 12* (1), p. 3.

American Psychological Association Commission on Violence and Youth (1993). *Violence & youth: Psychology's response*, Vol. I. Washington, DC: American Psychological Association.

Ashbach, C. (1994). Media influences and personality development: The inner image and the outer world. In D. Zillmann, J. Bryant, & A. C. Huston, (Eds.), *Media, children, and the family: Social scientific, psychodynamic, and clinical perspectives* (pp. 117-128). Hillsdale, NJ: Lawrence Erlbaum Associates.

Associated Press (1994, November 4). Police seize suspect obsessed by a movie. *The New York Times*, p. A25.

Auletta, K. (1991). *Three blind mice: How the networks lost their way.* New York: Random House.

Bandura, A. (1965). Influence of models reinforcement contingencies on the acquisition of imitative responses. *Journal of Personality and Social Psychology, 1,* 585-595.

Bandura, A., Ross, D., & Ross, S. A. (1961). Transmission of aggression through imitation of aggressive models. *Journal of Abnormal and Social Psychology, 63*, 575-582.

Bandura, A., Ross, D., & Ross, S. A. (1963). Imitation of film-mediated aggressive models. *Journal of Abnormal and Social Psychology, 66*, 3-11.

Bandura, A. & Walters, R. H. (1963). *Social learning and personality development*. New York: Holt, Rinehart, & Winston.

Barrett, R. K. (1993). Urban adolescent homicidal violence: An emerging public health concern. *Urban League Review, 16*, 67-76.

Bauers, S. (1995, March 6). Slain couple's son arrested in Missouri. *The Philadelphia Inquirer*, pp. A1, A10.

Bianculli, D. (1992). *Teleliteracy: Taking television seriously*. New York: Continuum.

Biblow, E. (1973). Imaginative play and the control of aggressive behavior. In J. L. Singer, (Ed.), *The child's world of make-believe* (pp.104-128). New York: Academic Press.

Blumler, J. & Katz, E. (Eds.). (1974). *The uses of mass communication: Current perspectives on gratification research*. Beverly Hills: Sage Publications.

Boy, 5, is killed for refusing to steal candy. (1994, October 15). *The New York Times*, p. 9.

Centerwall, B. S. (1989). Exposure to television as a cause of violence. In G. Comstock (Ed.), *Public communication and behavior*, Vol. 2, (pp. 1-58). New York: Academic Press.

Charters, W. W., Ed. (1993). *Motion pictures and youth: The Payne Fund Studies*. New York: Macmillan.

Comstock, G. (1989). *The evolution of American television*. Newbury Park, CA: Sage Publications.

Cook, D. (1991). *A history of narrative film* (2nd ed). New York: W. W. Norton.

Davies, K. (1993, February 27). Two young suspects in a toddler's slaying have had tough lives. *The Philadelphia Inquirer*, p. A5.

Davison, W. P. & Yu, F. T. C. (Eds.). (1974). Mass communication research: Major issues and future directions. New York: Praeger.

DeFleur, M. D. & Dennis, E. E. (1991). *Understanding mass communication*, (4th ed.). Boston: Houghton Mifflin.

Dobbin, B. (1994, October 8). Jail term for teen in boy's slaying. *The Philadelphia Inquirer*, p. A3.

Erikson, E. H. (1950). *Childhood and society*. New York: W.W. Norton.

Eron, L. D., Walder, L. O., & Lefkowitz, M. M. (1971). *Learning of aggression in children*. Boston: Little, Brown.

Fornell, P. (1994, October 18). 6-year-olds suspected in death of girl, 5. *The Philadelphia Inquirer*, p. A-16.

Fraiberg, S. (1987). The mass media: New schoolhouses for children. In L. Fraiberg (Ed.), *Selected writings of Selma Fraiberg* (pp. 573-587). Columbus: Ohio State University Press.

Freedman, J. L. (1992). Television violence and aggression: What psychologists should tell the public. In P. Suedfeld & P. E. Tetlock (Eds.), *Psychology and social policy* (pp. 179-189). New York: Hemisphere.

Friedlander, B. (1993). Community violence, children's development, and mass media: In pursuit of new insights, new goals, and new strategies. In D. Reiss, J. E. Richters, M. Radke-Yarrow, & D. Scharff (Eds.), *Children and violence* (pp. 66-81). New York: Guilford.

Gammage, J., Gibbons, T. J., Jr., & Marder, D. (1994, November 16). Three charged in mob beating death of Fox Chase teen. *The Philadelphia Inquirer*, pp. A1, A12.

Gerbner, G., Gross, L., Morgan, M., & Signorielli, N. (1980). The "mainstreaming" of America: Violence profile No. 11. *Journal of Communication, 30* (3), 10-29.

Greenbaum, S. (1994). Drugs, delinquency, and other data. *Juvenile Justice, 2* (1), 2-8.

Henkoff, R. (1992, August 10). Kids are killing, dying, bleeding. *Fortune*, pp. 62-69.

Herbert, B. (1994, December 7). Targeting women for guns. *The New York Times*, p. A23.

Huesmann, L. R. (1986). Psychological processes promoting the relation between media violence and aggressive behavior by the viewer. *Journal of Social Issues, 42*, 125-139.

Huesmann, L. R. & Eron, L. D. (1986). The development of aggression in American children as a consequence of television violence viewing. In L. R. Huesmann & L. D. Eron (Eds). *Television and the aggressive child: A cross national comparison*. Hillsdale, NJ: Lawrence Erlbaum Associates

Huesmann, L. R. & Eron, L. D. (Eds.). (1986). *Television and the aggressive child: A cross national comparison* (pp. 45-80). Hillsdale, NJ: Lawrence Erlbaum Associates.

Huesmann, L. R., Eron, L. D., Lefkowitz, M. M., & Walder, L. O. (1984). Stability of aggression over time and generations. *Developmental Psychology, 20*, 1120-1134.

Huston, A., Donnerstein, E., Fairchild, H., et al. (1992).

Big screen, small world. Lincoln: University of Nebraska Press.

Huston, A., Zillmann, D., & Bryant, J. (1994). Media influence, public policy, and the family. In A. Huston, D. Zillmann, & J. Bryant (Eds.), *Media, children, and the family: Social scientific, psychodynamic, and clinical perspectives* (pp. 3-18). Hillsdale, NJ: Lawrence Erlbaum Associates.

Jenkins, R. L. (1991). Socializing the unsocialized delinquent. In W. A. Rhodes & W. K. Brown (Eds.), *Why some children succeed despite the odds* (pp. 141-148). New York: Praeger.

Jessor, R. (1992). Risk behavior in adolescence: A psychosocial framework for understanding and action. In D. E. Rogers & E. Ginzburg (Eds.), *Adolescents at risk: Medical and social perspectives*. Boulder, CO: Westview Press.

Jhally, S. (Writer, Director, Producer) (1990). *Dreamworlds: Desire/sex/power* (video). Northampton, MA: Media Education Foundation.

Kolbert, E. (1993, December 26). The remote control avenger. *The New York Times*, Sec. 9 (Styles of the Times), p. 8.

Kubey, R. (1990). Media implications for the quality of family life. In D. Zillmann, J. Bryant, & A. C. Huston, Eds. (1994). *Media, children, and the family: Social, scientific, psychodynamic, and clinical perspectives* (pp. 61-69). Hillsdale, NJ: Lawrence Erlbaum Associates.

Kubey, R. & Czikszentmihalyi, M. (1990). *Television and the quality of life: How viewing shapes everyday experience*. New York: Lawrence Erlbaum Associates.

Liebert, R. M. & Sprafkin, J. (1988). *The early window: Effects of television on children and youth* (3rd ed.).

New York: Pergamon Press.

Maguire, K., Pastore, A., & Flanagan, T. J. (1993). *Bureau of Justice Statistics Sourcebook of Criminal Justice Statistics — 1992*. Washington: U. S. Department of Justice.

Maslow, A. H. (1987). *Motivation and personality.* New York: Harper & Row.

Mast, G. (1986). *A short history of the movies* (4th ed.). New York: Macmillan.

Matzkin, R. G. (1985). The film encounter in the life-world of urban couples: A uses and gratifications study. (Doctoral dissertation, Teachers College, Columbia University).

Mellgren, D. (1994, October 19). Horrified Scandinavians react to killing. *The Philadelphia Inquirer*, pp. A1, A9.

Merrill, J. C., Lee, J., & Friedlander, E. J., (1994). *Modern mass media*, (2nd ed.). New York: Harper Collins.

Milavsky, J. R., Stipp, H. H., Kessler, R. C., & Rubens, W. S. (1982). *Television & aggression: A panel study.* New York: Academic Press.

Miller, K. E. Q. (1995, March 6). Mother's love was not enough to save family. *The Philadelphia Inquirer*, pp. A1, A10.

Murray, C., & Herrnstein, R. J. (1994). *The bell curve.* New York: Free Press.

Murray, J. P. (1988, Summer). On tv violence. American Psychological Association Div. 29 (Child, Youth, and Family Services) *Newsletter, 16* (3), pp. 1, 12.

Nielsen Media Research. (1990). *Report on television.*

New York: A. G./ Nielsen Co.

Oreskes, M. (1990, June 28). Profiles of today's youth: they couldn't care less. *The New York Times*, p. A1.

Perkinson, H. (1995). Getting better: Television and moral progress. In A. Alexander & J. Hanson (Eds.), *Taking sides: Clashing views on controversial issues in mass media and society* (3rd ed.) (pp. 9-16). Guilford, C T: Dushkin Publishing.

Piaget, J. (1936). *The language and thought of the child.* New York: Harcourt, Brace, and World.

Piaget, J. (1952). *The origin of intelligence in children.* New York: International Universities Press.

Postman, N. (1986). *Amusing ourselves to death: Public discourse in the age of show business.* New York: Penguin Books.

Rankin, R. (1995, March 16). No crusade by Clinton on violence in the movies. *The Philadelphia Inquirer*, pp. E1, E8.

Richters, J. E., & Martinez, P. (1993). The NIMH community violence project: I. Children as victims of, and witnesses to violence. In D. Reiss, J. E. Richters, M. Radke-Yarrow, & D. Scharff (Eds.), *Children and violence* (pp. 7-21). New York: Guilford Press.

Sanders, B. (1994). *A is for ox: Violence, electronic media, and the silencing of the written word.* New York: Pantheon Books.

Schlain, B. (1993, April). Channel surfing — strictly male turf: Overuse of the television's remote control. *Cosmopolitan*, p. 110.

Schmidt, W. E. (1993, February 23). 2 boys arraigned in abduction and killing of British toddler. *The New York Times*, p. A3.

Schwartz, L. L., & Matzkin, R. G. (1993) [Transcripts of proceedings in cases of *Comm. of Penn. vs. Tabitha Buck, Lisa Michelle Lambert, and Lawrence Yunkin* for the murder of Laurie Show.] Unpublished raw data.

Seplow, S. (1994, December 2). The more they watch, the more they fear. *The Philadelphia Inquirer*, pp. A1, A21.

Siano, B. (1995). Frankenstein must be destroyed: Chasing the monster of television violence. In *Taking sides: Clashing views on controversial issues in mass media and society* (3rd ed.) (pp. 28-35). Guilford, CT: Dushkin Publishing.

Signorielli, N. (1991). *A sourcebook on children and television.* Westport, CT: Greenwood Publishing.

Signorielli, N., & Morgan, M. (1990). *Cultivation analysis: New directions in media effects research.* Newbury Park, CA: Sage Publications.

Singer, D. G., & Singer, J. L. (1990). *The house of make-believe: Children's play and the developing imagination.* Cambridge, MA: Harvard University Press.

Speece, M. W., & Brent, S. B. (1992). The acquisition of a mature understanding of three components of the concept of death. *Death Studies, 16,* 211-229.

Surgeon-General's Scientific Advisory Committee on Television and Social Behavior (1972). *Television and growing up: The impact of television violence.* Washington: United States Government Printing Office.

Wass, H., Raup, J. L., & Sisler, H. H. (1989). Adolescents and death on television: A follow-up study. *Death Studies, 13,* 161-173.

Wines, M. (1993, October 21). Reno chastises TV networks on violence in programming. *The New York Times*, p. A1.

Witkin, G. (1991, April 8). Kids who kill. *Newsweek*, pp. 26-32.

Woenstendiek, J. (1993, March 28). Grim data on teens in U.S. *The Philadelphia Inquirer*, pp. A1, A6.

Zillmann, D. (1982). Television viewing and arousal. In D. Pearl, L. Bouthilet, & J. Lazar (Eds.), *Television and behavior: Ten years of scientific progress and implications for the eighties*, Vol. 2, Technical reports (pp. 53-67). Washington: United States Government Printing Office.

Zillmann, D., J. Bryant, & A. C. Huston, Eds. (1994). *Media, children, and the family: Social, scientific, psychodynamic, and clinical perspectives.* Hillsdale, NJ: Lawrence Erlbaum Associates.

About the Authors

Lita Linzer Schwartz, PhD, is Distinguished Professor Emerita of Educational Psychology and Professor Emerita of Women's Studies at The Pennsylvania State University, and is a Diplomate in Forensic Psychology of the American Board of Professional Psychology. She is a graduate of Vassar College (AB), Temple University (EdM), and Bryn Mawr College (PhD).

Rosalie Greenfield Matzkin, EdD, is a Lecturer in Films and Communication at The Pennsylvania State University. She is a graduate of Syracuse University (BA), and Teachers College, Columbia University (MA, MEd, and EdD). Both authors can be reached at The Pennsylvania State University, Ogontz Campus, Abington, PA 19001.

CHAPTER 5

SOCIAL INDUCEMENTS TO PARALETHAL AND LETHAL VIOLENCE

Leighton C. Whitaker

As long as people believe in absurdities they will continue to commit atrocities.
Voltaire

The purpose of this chapter is to develop an understanding of social and interpersonal inducements to our society's megatrend to violence in order to counter and replace violence with respect for and nurturance of life. My thesis is that both the individual and society must be held accountable if we are to reduce murder and other criminal violence.

First, we must understand the nature of the violence megatrend: what it consists of, what influences have formed it, how it is sustained, and where it is headed. Second, we have to motivate our society to stop denying the actual causal influences by exposing the absurdities behind the denials and illusions. Third, we must counter and undermine the actual causal forces: the kinds of influences which, acting in concert with one another, conjointly result in various forms of morbidity capped by lethal violence. Fourth, we have to actively promote a societal orientation that is more nurturing, respectful, and life-enhancing.

The Violence Megatrend

The fateful question for the human species seems to me to be whether and to what extent their cultural development will succeed in mas-tering the disturbance of their communal life by the human instinct of aggression and self-destruction.
Sigmund Freud (1930/1961)

By this criterion of cultural success, the United States is becoming a failure. We have become a world leader in both externalized and internalized forms of violence. Our externally directed violence leadership is epitomized by a higher murder rate than the vast majority of other Western or industrialized nations, and by our being the world's leading exporter of cigarettes, violence entertainment movies, and weaponry. Our internally directed violence leadership is manifested in high rates of suicide, eating disorders, and drug dependencies. Our youth outdo the youth of most other nations in both externalized and internalized violence.

It may seem that not all of the phenomena just listed should appear in the category of violent behaviors, but violence practitioners aid and abet one another by acting out and modeling morbidity. Accepting violence, however culturally acceptable the medium, means acceptance of violence simultaneously toward oneself and others. For example, "Although intense aggression toward others and suicide are often considered to represent very different problems, there is a surprisingly strong relationship between the two; violence-prone and assaultive adolescents are at much greater risk for suicidal behaviors" (Lore & Schultz, 1993, p. 16). The two forms of violence — external and internal — are so closely intertwined that it is difficult to imagine how self-destructiveness cannot hurt others and vice versa. They must be considered together.

Although homicide rates in the United States have not been increasing overall in the past decade, they were already very high compared to other industrialized nations. Isaac Asimov (1981) reported that "Forty million Americans are murdered, maimed, raped, mugged, or robbed every year" (p. 223). Our "civilized West" is the civilization in which a human being has been killed by others every 20 seconds in the half century up to 1979, illegally or legally. This is three times the rate of the century preceding these 50 years (Asimov, p. 222).

The likelihood of being murdered in that part of the civilized West called the United States is 7 to 10 times higher than most European nations (Lore & Schultz, 1993). Furthermore, we are experiencing an ominous acceleration in the development of the "violencing of America" among the youth of our nation. Lethal violence has increased rapidly among youth during the past decade, as shown by the numbers of murderers and victims. According to the National Centers for Disease Control (Butterfield, 1994), whereas homicide arrest rates among males ages 15 to 19 went up 127% between 1985 and 1991, the rates for males ages 25 to 29 dropped 1%, and for ages 30 to 34 dropped 13%. Consequently, males from ages 15 to 19 have become more likely than those in any other age group to be arrested for homicide. During the same period, 1985 to 1991, the annual rate at which 15 to 19 year old males were being killed increased 154%, far exceeding the rate change for any other age

group. Virtually all of this increase in youth homicide, 97%, has been directly associated with the use of guns.

Significantly, Black youths are more likely to be perpetrators and at least 10 times more likely to be victims, a fact the Centers for Disease Control hesitated to emphasize, perhaps to avoid fueling prejudicial interpretations. But, understanding causes requires disclosure of at least the major factors, of which racism is surely one.

Thus, the widely perceived "violencing of America" during the past decade is based largely on the social megatrend of youth violence, most blatantly expressed in enormously increased youth homicide rates attributable to guns. In turn, this major increase in youth gun violence has been attributed to the coming of crack cocaine in the mid-1980s, when drug dealers put guns in the hands of teenagers assigned to enforce drug deals, especially in Black inner city ghettos characterized by poverty, poor education, and fatherlessness. But, as will be documented later in this chapter, our gun culture has been growing rapidly for many decades. Clearly, the gun culture has been appealing to our society overall, and is self-reinforcing as more guns are "needed" to protect us from "criminals with guns."

In addition, hate crimes, which include attacks on gays and various ethnic minorities, and often result in lethal violence, have been increasing rapidly overall. A study by the New York City Gay and Lesbian Antiviolence Project showed an overall increase of 8% in reports of antigay attacks from 1993 to 1994, with 274 injured victims, including 9 homicides (Dunlap, 1995). In Pennsylvania, hate crimes increased by 130% from 1988 to 1993 — from 181 in 1988 to 1989, to 417 for 1992 to 1993, and preliminary data showed further escalation through 1994 (Moran, 1995). Youth were disproportionately represented, with 56% of the accused offenders and 37% of the victims being in the 11- to 20-year-old age group. And although Blacks comprise only 9% of the state's population, they comprised 46% of the hate crime victims.

If American society at large is not suffering a greater homicide rate overall, why is there such public concern? The concern is well founded. Considering that youth violence has been reaching ever younger age groups, and based on projections from currently available data, youth violence per se will continue to increase and the violent youth will enter adulthood, thereby probably spawning greater numbers of dysfunctional people. By 1988, 1 in 12 high school students had already attempted suicide and 1 in 4 had carried a weapon (Centers for Disease Control, 1992), and weapon carrying has increased since then. As the future of any country is largely determined, sooner as well as later, by its youth, and the youth of our country are so inclined to violence, we can expect still higher rates of violence in our future. Violent youths tend to be violent adults and to raise violence-prone children.

Our society is not only affected by the enormous increase in homicides, representing the most extreme morbidity, but by the vastly broader, more pervasive, and causally significant but less blatant phenomenon of what I shall call "paralethal" violence. Paralethal violence comprises all those behaviors and influences and their conjointly determined effects that discourage the constructive, affirming, and nurturing orientations essential to a civilized society and to life itself. It represents the replacement of patient, hard-earned, personal and social development, with facile destruction of our society for now, for the near future, and for generations to come, *or not to come*.

Denials and Some "Solutions" that Contribute to Violence

Can't we safely avoid the admittedly arduous endeavor to understand the complexity of violence causation? Can't we react effectively by putting more money and effort into apparently simple "solutions" already at hand? No, because, as we shall see, the mentality behind the simple-minded solutions is too much like the fatally limited mentality of murderers themselves.

Consider, for examples, five reactive "solutions" to lethal violence: more and longer imprisonments; more death penalties; putting more police on the streets; allowing qualifying citizens to carry concealed weapons to protect themselves; and increasing use of corporal punishment, including as public spectacle.

More prisoners. By 1995, we have already incarcerated nearly 1.5 million United States citizens, including over 1 million in prisons, and the others in jails and holding cells, a total of more than double the number of inmates just a decade before. While most inmates are males, female imprisonment rates rose 359% between 1974 and 1991 (Conn & Silverman, 1991). In contrast, Canada has only one-fourth the U.S. imprisonment rate, while England and Wales have one-fifth and Japan one-fourteenth (Holmes, 1995). By 1991, the prison system had become the fastest growing sector of U.S. government employment and the cost of building a maximum security cell had risen to $50,000, nearly the cost of the most expensive four-year college education that year, and yet, the chances that a murderer would never appear in a courtroom, let alone be imprisoned, were 1 in 3 (Conn & Silverman, 1991).

What will happen if this trend continues? California provides an instructive example. In 1995, for the first time, our most populated state will spend more on prisons than on its university systems, which have been the pride of the state. Since 1980, it has built 17 new prisons and more than quintupled the number of prisoners from 23,511 to 126,140, and now plans to build 15 more prisons by the year 2000. By the year 2002, according to a **Rand Corporation study (Butterfield, 1995b), the** "three strikes" law implementation (mandating a prison sentence of 25 years to life for third-time offenders) means the Department of Corrections will consume 18% of the California state budget, with only 1% left for the universities. At this rate, according to correction agency predictions, by the year 2027, California will have 401,000 convicts, more than the present convict population of all of Western Europe, Australia, Canada, Japan, and New Zealand combined.

Meanwhile, neither crime rates nor costs are diminishing and only lack of prison and jail space is preventing even more rapid escalation of incarceration rates. What is our society's response thus far in the face of this failure? Arrest more criminals, build more prisons, hire more guards. In September 1994, President Clinton signed a $30 billion crime bill, including more than $10 billion to build new state and federal prisons. Has such a policy been effective in other countries? Russia, which has a similar incarceration policy and the same incarceration trend and current rate of incarceration has also failed to reduce its escalating crime.

More death penalties. Advocates of the death penalty are managing to get legislatures to increase death penalty rates. Presumably, more applications of the death penalty will not only get rid of violent criminals but will make potential violent criminals think twice. But does the death penalty demonstrably reduce lethal violence? Not so far. Besides being enormously expensive, with an average of $20 million per case spent to kill the killer, the death penalty is hopelessly ineffective psychologically as a deterrent because those who commit lethal violence are almost never attuned to distant consequences.

Furthermore, the death penalty is suspect in terms of fairness and justice as related to race. Though half of all citizens murdered each year in the United States are Blacks, an overwhelming 85% of convicted murderers executed since 1977 (the year of initiation of the modern era of capital punishment) had killed a White person, while only 11% had killed a Black person (Eckholm,

1995). The General Accounting Office in Washington, D.C. reported in a 1990 review of 28 studies on race and the death penalty, that 82% of the studies found that the race of the victim influenced the likelihood of the murderer being charged with capital murder or receiving the death penalty. "Other things being equal, the studies show, killers of white people are more likely to receive death sentences than killers of blacks" (Eckholm, 1995, p. B4). Thus, we appear more ready to kill killers if they have killed Whites than if they have killed Blacks. The resultant message is that White peoples' lives are more precious than the lives of Blacks.

Despite evidence that the death penalty is not a deterrent, more states are enacting it into law. Governor Pataki, in March of 1995, made New York the 38th state with capital punishment. He declared in signing the death penalty bill, "It is a solemn moment because this is something aimed at preventing tragedy. And we've seen too many tragedies in the past" and stated that the new law is "the most effective of its kind in the nation" (Dao, 1995, p. A1). "The law takes effect Sept. 1, 1995 giving the state's district attorneys, most of whom have never handled death penalty prosecutions, six months to prepare for the enormous costs and technical problems of such cases" (Dao, 1995, p. A1). The governor's claim that the death penalty will prevent tragedy may be politically expedient but oxymoronic: will it be the most effective of the ineffective measures? Even if it outstrips the other capital punishment laws by actually having at least some deterrent effect, can it possibly be cost-effective?

Many death penalty supporters are not focusing on or claiming deterrence effectiveness. They are talking "justice," meaning revenge. As one supporter said, "I'm a mother who's suffering every day. I have children at home who are suffering all the time for the loss of their brother. No. 1, there has to be justice, and we talk about deterrence later" (as cited in Dao, 1995, p. B5). While it is easy to empathize with this mother's feelings, when will our society, after such expense in time, money, and concern, get around to actual prevention instead of merely humoring popular but mistaken opinion? As Winston Churchill put it, "Revenge is, of all satisfactions, the most costly and long drawn out; retroactive persecution is...the most pernicious" (Humes, 1994, p. 83).

More police. Surely, however, one can depend on the traditional tactic of "putting more cops on the street" to curtail crime. Police departments were established in this country more than 150 years ago. But no studies have shown convincingly that adding police officers lowers crime rates. Rather, the evidence from studies of this relationship in our cities show no effect, except perhaps to instill a false sense of security. A 1981 analysis of police beats in Newark, New Jersey, the most thorough study ever done, showed that foot patrols had virtually no effect on crime rates (Moran, 1995).

This is not to say that police forces do no good; but, merely adding still more police will not help. We cannot expect the police, who are increasingly at risk as violence victims themselves, to solve a massive problem that cannot be attributed to them or their numbers. No matter how good a job they do, they cannot, by themselves, address the root causes of violence. They are kept mainly in reactive, instead of preventive, positions but are expected somehow to offset an ever increasing supply of violent offenders who are obtaining more and more lethal weapons. Perhaps putting police into the community as part nurturers and part enforcers, rather like good parents, will be of some help.

Our violence problem, however, is not really the fault of police who are increasingly "out-weaponed." According to the Federal Bureau of Investigation (FBI, 1995), 76 law enforcement officials were killed while on duty in 1994, six more than in 1993. All but one of the 1994 slayings was committed with a firearm, six officers were killed with their own weapon, and 33 of the officers were wearing body armor at the time they were slain.

More guns. By now, a large segment of our citizenry has concluded that police are not the answer, and has advocated not only arming themselves, but carrying concealed weapons. As Verhovek (1995) puts it: "A powerful movement to allow ordinary citizens to obtain permits easily for carrying concealed weapons is taking hold across the country, a product of both the new Republican control of many state governments and of increasing fears that the police are incapable of protecting citizens from criminals" (p. A1). Sixteen states now have such legislation pending, and Texas, which already leads the states in guns per capita, has now passed such a bill. It looks like the United States will rapidly add to its current supply of 222 million guns already in circulation by 1994. We do not know for certain the outcome of such legislation, but we do know the results of past relaxations in gun control.

We know that the rapid rise of guns in circulation thus far is highly correlated with the rise of key forms of violence, especially youth violence and hate crimes, including murder and suicide. Just as the rise in murders among youth is highly correlated with gun availability, so is the rise of "successful" suicides in the young in contrast to the number of attempts, which is much more constant (Leary, 1995).

Furthermore, homicides have increased overall where concealed weapon restrictions have already been relaxed. Four out of five urban areas studied by the University of Maryland showed increases in killings by guns after laws were passed making it easier to carry concealed weapons (Killings said to rise, 1995). In Florida, after weapons laws were relaxed, the average monthly homicides committed with guns increased 3% in Miami, 22% in Tampa, and 74% in Jacksonville. Florida continues to have the highest crime rate in the nation and all of the cities studied there showed higher rates of homicide with guns since the relaxed legislation took effect.

Of course, the theory is that only good citizens will be allowed to carry concealed weapons, but those weapons are likely to be as easily obtainable as a driver's license, which is obtainable by most violent and potentially violent persons, and the "good citizens" may include many who, having such a lethal weapon, will be more likely to react violently. If nothing else, will this further arming of our citizenry promote a despairing message, that all we can do as a society is to become armed and expect the worst from one another? Surely that will lead to an escalating war of nerves and greater societal distress.

The assumption that we can only rely on our own concealed weaponry has already been popularized in our youth culture. High school students have experimented with weapon carrying, including for "self-protection," and it doesn't work. According to the Centers for Disease Control (Newman, 1995) 1 in 10 high school students has carried a weapon to school and 1 in 14 has been threatened or injured in school. What is the mentality behind our persistent advocacy of freer access to weapons? Consider the following paragraph from reporter Maria Newman (1995): "At first, the two dozen or so students milling about outside Theodore Roosevelt High School in the Bronx agreed that schools need to be made safer. But in a few moments, swift as switchblades, the students produced a gleaming assortment of weapons" (p. A1). Now envision the photograph that appeared beside it. Students are gathered around smiling and gleefully showing off their weapons, which they easily smuggled into school. All of their weapons, they were proud to point out, were smuggled right through the school's metal detector. Isn't the message here that each and every expensive repressive measure will be met by successful undermining?

Now consider the above paragraph again, this time substituting adults for teenagers: "At first, the many legislators and the thousands of adult citizens lobbying in their legislatures agreed that society needs to be made safer. But in a few weeks, with hair trigger swiftness, they produced a gleaming assortment of weapons." Now imagine a picture of a sample of such adults grinning with satisfaction as they display their vast assortment of guns for the camera, especially because they were able to smuggle them past the new weapon detectors developed by U.S. Justice Department grants from 1995 through 1997 (Butterfield, 1995a). Of course, the weapons in this case are not going to be mere switchblades, brass knuckles, or box cutters. They will be far more lethal and their carriers, licensed to conceal them on their persons, able to avoid surveillance, or both, will be far more numerous and mobile.

Meanwhile, inevitably, devices already invented during the Cold War with the U.S.S.R. and now being adapted to surveillance uses in our own country, are about to be marketed. Soon, pending permitting legislation, all concealed guns will be easily detectable using these devices. We continue to produce an endless series of reactive countermeasures, all predicated on the despairing assumption that we cannot trust one another not to maim and kill. Thus have we become a nation at war with itself.

More beatings. Sensing that present measures are not working, United States citizens and their legislators have mounted a growing movement at both state and local levels to institute beatings for convicted criminals, including making such corporal punishments into public spectacles (Copeland, 1995). Twenty-three states already allow corporal punishment. Now, more severe versions are being suggested. Tennessee would command the county sheriff to administer floggings of from 1 to 15 strokes on the courthouse steps with a cane of a size and length determined by the state Supreme Court. Although such spectacles might entertain, much like public hangings used to and current television and movies do in growing abundance, and they might satisfy revenge thirst, there is no evidence that they would have a deterrent effect. Perhaps most importantly, society would be sending yet another message to the effect that, like the criminal, it does not wish to take real responsibility for thinking through the violence problem indigenous to its own influence but, instead, will continue to act impulsively and to inflict violence much like ordinary violent criminals.

More imprisonments, death penalties, police, guns, and corporal punishment are measures sharing certain characteristics: They are emotionally appealing, simple-minded reactions already shown by studies to be far more likely to contribute to rather than resolve the violence megatrend. They mirror, mimic, and magnify, rather than counter, killers. If pursued further into our nation's future, they are likely to be ever more expensive financially, psychologically, and spiritually, and they will distract even more time, money, and energy which could be used constructively.

As distractions, the simple-minded reactive measures provide immediately gratifying diversions; they provide narcotic-like, illusory forms of relief from anxiety and anger that short-circuit needed understanding, planning, and truly helpful action. And, because they are so inadequate, expensive, and misleading, they result in more distress each year, adding to hopelessness and despair as we spend more, worry more, and perceive — correctly — that our society is continuing to deteriorate at a rapid rate.

Causal Influences

Why do we doggedly persist in devising and implementing measures that are disastrously counterproductive? What accounts for their immense popularity in the face of failures? The answer is not on the surface. We must look at these failures in terms of our deeper motivations. Do we design for failure?

Psychiatrist Karl Menninger's (1968) words of wisdom from three decades ago still apply:

The inescapable conclusion is that society secretly wants crime, needs crime and gains definite satisfactions from the present mishandling of it! We condemn crime; we punish offenders for it; but we need it. The crime and punishment ritual is part of our lives. We need crimes to wonder at, to enjoy vicariously, to discuss and speculate about, and to publicly deplore. We need criminals to identify ourselves with, to secretly envy, and to strictly punish. Criminals represent our alter egos — our "bad" selves — rejected and projected. They do for us the forbidden, illegal things we wish to do and, like scapegoats of old, they bear the burdens of our displaced guilt and punishment — "The iniquities of us all" (p. 153).

Individuals who are guilty of outright criminal acts, but who deny that they have done wrong, are aided and abetted by a society which, neglectful of the nurturance needs of the young, is entertained by and often profits monetarily from murder and other crimes, but denies its facilitating role. Unless we cease our denial that disidentifies us with our criminals, we will surely never have enough jails, prisons, guards, security officers, locks, alarm systems, judges, lawyers, probation officers, emergency rooms, or as many or as destructive guns as we are told we need.

The O.J. Simpson feeding frenzy. The United States and much of the world were enthralled by the endless merchandising of the trial of athlete/actor/celebrity O.J. Simpson, who was accused of the brutal murders of his exwife and her male friend. Although such extreme attention was due, in part, to wanting to understand the law and how our courts work, the overwhelming interest had to be explained otherwise.

"The trial of the century," as it was touted, was immensely popular violence entertainment on television, in the press, and in books, and sure-ly movies to come. Great amounts of money were spent out of public coffers, and great amounts were garnered commercially. The trial and its off-shoots became a vast public spectacle, a feeding frenzy for millions of spectators and at least thou-sands of entrepreneurs who cashed in by provid-ing further titillation. The O.J. circus exceeded the wildest desires of a citizenry hungry for vio-lence entertainment. As the "Arts and Entertain-ment" channel of cable television titled their spe-cial program about the O.J. case, the United States is "Merchandising Murder" (1995) with endless supplies of merchants and customers. A few other nations, at least, are reluctant to join in. Canada, which has only a fraction of our gun pos-session and murder rates banned a popular tabloid type television showing of "A Current Affair," which exploited the Simpson case. Perhaps we should emulate our "backward" neighbor to the north! Apparently, our neighbor doesn't buy the standard tabloid mentality disclaimer: "We don't cause these things. We just reflect them." If the tabloid type "reporters" were to view themselves in a mirror, they would see that their tabloid reflecting mirror is actually a magnifier of murder to the extent of at least 1 million portrayals to one actual murder, as is documented later in this chapter. Thus, as Menninger insisted, the causes of crime, lethal violence included, lie largely in our desires for it, our revels in it, and our denials that we have anything to do with its causes.

Definitions and denials of responsibility. Lethal violence takes various forms, defined legally by the extent to which the form involves intent and justification. Vehicular homicide does not usually involve manifest intent to kill. War is usually justified as a societal decision and played out, rather like a game, within a certain set of rules. The forms are seldom pure, however. Sometimes, vehicular homicides or, more broad-ly, "accidental homicides," have conscious intent or at least an unwitting or unconscious motive.

War typically is "justified" as a necessary expedi-ent to avoid some greater destructiveness, but readily invites murder-minded participants moti-vated by ego-mania, greed, and destructiveness. Generally, however, murder is the paramount example of lethal violence because it is consid-ered both clearly intentional and unjustified.

Murder, defined legally as the unlawful killing of a human being by another with malice aforethought, is produced by an interplay of social, situational, and personal factors, none of which by themselves can explain it. Even a very defective or deranged person bent on murder must be aided and abetted by an opportune situa-tion and a facilitating social context. Furthermore, the murderous tendency itself is the developmen-tal culmination of paralethal interpersonal or social influences. Conversely, even an opportune situation and powerful social facilitation together do not guarantee a murderous act unless the would-be murderer has a personal proclivity to take another's life. For example, many coura-geous persons living under the Nazi regime risked their own lives to save Jews despite enor-mous social pressure and situational opportunity to kill them. In essence, lethal violence is typical-ly the end result of a momentous concerted com-ing together of destructive forces comprising social, situational, and personal influences, none of which by itself is adequate to cause it.

But, both murderers and society at large almost always disavow responsibility. In my experience as a forensic psychologist interview-ing and testing about 200 murderers, I have not seen any who really acknowledged responsibility or wrongdoing (And Dr. Harold Hall, the Editor of this volume, tells me that none of the several thousand violent offenders he has evaluated thought he or she was "bad" because of their vio-lence; most thought they did the right thing, or had no other choice.).

In the vast majority of cases, the murderer talks about his or her crime in the third person as in, "I'm sorry it happened," rather than "I'm sorry I did it." Disavowal often goes even further, as in the case of the New York subway gunman who killed several people and injured many more, but insisted at his trial in 1995 that he was "a humanitarian." (Perhaps this is the kind of person Mark Twain had in mind when he said that, if a man came to his door claiming he just wanted to do him good, he would run for his life). Even when murderers acknowledge that they were actually agents in the murderous acts, they deny their real motivation and the actually destructive consequences in favor of attributing virtue to themselves. For example, hate crimes and even entire wars are usually buttressed with claims to save society, whether the agents are "Christian" skinheads saving us from the "Jewish menace" or an entire nation waging war to perform "ethnic cleansing."

At the very least, murderers do not acknowledge that they themselves did wrong. Even the murderer who expresses sorrow for *the* wrongdoing does not act as though it is his wrongdoing. For example, a young man called Adam, featured on the Sally Jesse Raphael (1995) television show, was quite clearly contrite about a brutal murder. But his attribution of causality in recalling his mental state at the time of the crime cleared him of a mindful, intentional responsibility. Referring to his murderous beating of a man until his brains began to disgorge from his skull, Adam said, "It just happened." This typical explanation or, more accurately, lack of explanation, expresses a deep-seated denial representative of the extremely passive, simple-minded, reactive mentality common to murderers and much of our societal propagation of violence. It represents our general agreement on a principle adhered to by those engaging in violent and paraviolent behaviors: lack of acknowledgment of causal responsibility coupled with simple-minded, not genuinely thinking responses of a reactive, rather than reflective, nature. And, as previously discussed,

the denial is frequently topped off by rationalizations attributing virtue to the murderers. The murderer and society aid and abet one another in this shared mentality of denial and pretentious claims to virtue.

Legal inducements to violence. Contrary to popular perception, most inducements to violence are perpetrated legally. For example, pushers of legal drugs, including alcohol and tobacco, are responsible for vastly more deaths than "crack" cocaine pushers who are themselves notorious dealers in lethal drugs. Like the legal drug pushers, violence entertainment merchandisers disavow any harmful consequences of their actions. The following excerpt from Alexander Solzhenitsyn's 1978 Harvard University commencement speech is even more applicable today than when it was delivered:

Society has turned out to have scarce defense against the abyss of human decadence, for example against the misuse of liberty for moral violence against young people, such as motion pictures full of pornography, crime and horror. This is all considered to be part of freedom and to be counterbalanced, in theory, by young people's right not to look and not to accept. Life organized legalistically has thus shown its inability to defend itself against the corrosion of evil (Solzhenitsyn, 1978).

It's the rage: A gun is fun. In the United States, gun promotion has proceeded at an ever more frenetic pace in recent decades, greatly outstripping gun possession rates in other nations. From 54 million guns in 1950, the number grew to 104 million in 1970, to 160 million in 1980, to 200 million by 1992 (Hollman & McCoy, 1992), and 222 million by 1994. At this rate, we are close to, if not past, the point by now of having at least one gun for every man, woman, and child in this country.

Guns are widely and effectively advertised in direct fashion in regular advertising media, including magazines, and we see guns publicized by movies, television, newspapers, and novels. Even more strikingly, gun sales are also greatly stimulated by real-life news accounts of their destructive accomplishments. Such gun publicity spurs gun sales in a way that clearly shows the nature of their appeal. Violent entertainment models violent behaviors in fictional fashion while news accounts of actual, especially egregious, crimes, provide real-life models. These real-life criminals who commit lethal violence quickly become heroes of a sort and the sales of whatever guns they used soar. Erik Larson (1993), noted:

After the assassination of President John F. Kennedy, sales of the otherwise undistinguished Mannlicher-Carcano rifle used by Lee Harvey Oswald soared. Even the murder of schoolchildren can increase sales. After Patrick Edward Purdy opened fire on a school yard in Stockton, California, with an AK-47, sales of the gun and its knock-offs boomed. Prices quadrupled, to $1,500. Guns Unlimited felt the surge in demand. "I didn't sell an AK until Stockton in California; then everybody wanted one," James Dick said in a deposition (p. 72).

Our movies and TV shows do far more damage than simply enhancing the appeal of exotic weapons, however. They teach a uniquely American lesson: When a real man has a problem, he gets his gun. He slaps in a clip, he squints grimly into the hot noon sun, and then he does what he's gotta do (p. 74).

Manufacturers, distributors, and sellers of guns have been supported enormously by money interests, including the lobbying of legislators. Larson (1993) has documented this collusion from his standpoint, that of a gun dealer. In showing how a gun became a murder weapon, he "provides a clear example of the culture of non-responsibility prevailing in America's firearms industry; it is but one example of how their commercial ethos governed the gun's progress from conception to its use as a murder weapon in a Virginia Beach classroom" (Larson, p. 50). The gun,

the Cobray M-11/9, was advertised by its producer as "The gun that made the 80s roar."

During the 1990s, the gun industry, together with the movie and television industries, has begun special efforts to put guns in the hands of women and children. The gun merchants are now massively producing, promoting, and marketing guns for women, including special guns designed to appeal especially to women (Herbert, 1994). Women have been especially active in lobbying for legislation permitting them to carry concealed weapons, and target ranges catering especially to women are prospering, all with considerable support from the gun industry and violent entertainment. Although males were committing 88% of violent crimes in the United States (Miedzian, 1991), females have become more violent, a trend reflected and seemingly endorsed by television. Women "in jeopardy" TV films and series are now being abetted by women who try to and do kill. According to CBS Vice-president Peter Totorici, "...these programs were being produced in part because of success of reality-based shows coupled with the fact that women are the principal viewers of prime-time television" (Killer women, 1992). The term "reality-based" is a euphemism for violence entertainment, similar to the euphemism "action picture." Meanwhile, gun merchants now see a future in emphasizing marketing guns to youth, including through public relations ploys, such as promoting target ranges especially targeted, as it were, at youth.

The media and violence entertainment. Our society directly and indirectly fosters violence and helps develop violence prone individuals in a great many direct (by commission) and indirect (by omission) ways that we deny. Most blatantly, our popular media culture spawns ubiquitous and innumerable sensational portrayals of violence which serve to train their audiences directly in paralethal and lethal violence. Television, movies, video games, sensationalistic magazines and newspapers, and many best-selling books sell themselves to consumers by appealing to violent proclivities. These wares are usually concocted to fit a well-known formula for commercial success: violence sells. The traditional tabloid newspapers follow the maxim, "If it bleeds, it leads," meaning that gory violence is sure to be printed up in headline stories. In recent years, violent entertainment formulas have become more sophisticated, as will be discussed later.

But, like murderers, the commercial violence pushers deny responsibility for contributing to violence, and often claim, much like the "humanist" New York mass murderer, that they are performing a socially valuable service. Their principal motivation, by far, is money. They know that "Violence is Golden" (Whitaker, 1993a).

Whereas television producers often claim that their shows merely reflect real-life violence and therefore are "reality-based," consider that the average 18-year-old has already seen 200,000 portrayals of murder on television, but only about one in three 18-year-olds has witnessed an actual murder. Thus, youths experience a ratio of 600,000:1 or a rate of 600,000 television show murders for every real-life murder directly experienced. Now add to the left-hand side of this equation, television news of murders, news of homicides "justified" by war, movie murder portrayals, publications of newspaper and magazine accounts of murder, mystery and war stories, and, not least, the murders depicted in video games. Then, the ratio is probably at least 1,000,000:1 or an average of 1 million portrayals of murder for each murder experienced in real life by the age of 18. Yet, even this equation does not take into account the considerable trend toward more gruesome kinds of murder or include the far more numerous paralethal violence behaviors, short of murder, that are portrayed. These and many other considerations, to be discussed in this chapter, lead to the conclusion that popular culture, especially in the form of violence entertainment, fosters, rather than merely reflects, lethal violence.

We are confronted with violence portrayals nearly everywhere everyday. We see violence sensationalized and therefore promoted in most large and small screen presentations, throughout newspapers and magazines, on billboards, in a large percentage of best-selling books, and in the continuing proliferation of gun stores, and we hear it in the lyrics and strident beat of popular music. Meanwhile, the violence entertainment promoters deny any causal link between their commercial wares and our society's violence megatrend, just as the cigarette industry denied — and still denies — any causal link between cigarettes and the diseases and early deaths with which they are so intrinsically associated. Their denial may or may not be witting, but that leaves only two possibilities. Either they know they are lying or they are deluded themselves. A previous spokesperson for the tobacco industry, now dying of lung cancer and backing the nation's toughest anti-smoking bill (Moss, 1995) asserted in a television interview that people in the tobacco industry actually do not believe in the vast aggregation of scientific evidence that cigarettes kill. In either case, it remains imperative to persist in disabusing as many people as possible of the insupportable claim that cigarettes are not addictive and lethal.

The combination of ubiquitous big and little screen violent entertainment heroes and publicity about actual murder heroes, all brandishing guns in macho exhibitionistic displays of power, trains impressionable young people especially to obtain and use guns, all the while telling them it's desirable behavior. Thus, our society supplies massive amounts of violent entertainment, drugs, guns, and various other methods for aggressing against others and oneself. These supplies must be in great demand by great masses of consumers. Otherwise, how can we explain the fact that, while society is manifestly strenuously objecting, the violence megatrend shows little or no signs of abating? The next section of this chapter is offered to provide a sample of the voracious demand.

A night at the movies: Popcorn, soda, and splattered brains

"OVER 70 CRITICS AGREE 'PULP FIC-TION' IS THE BEST FILM OF THE YEAR!" reads a *New York Times* ad that I saw for many days (e.g., March 14, 1995). The ad boasts that this film has received seven Academy Award nominations, including for best picture. Critic Janet Maslin calls it "A stunning vision of destiny, choice and spiritual possibility!" and "A work of depth, wit and blazing originality." As a picture, it was nominated in the "comedy" category.

My wife and I went to a local showing of this "hilarious adventure" on a Saturday night in March, me with my clipboard and pad in an effort to experience the movie and audience reactions first hand. Here's a condensed account of my experience.

Theater crowded but got good seats. Older woman by herself on my left. Each seat is equipped with a drink holder for sodas and most patrons have a soda and/or popcorn by now. The entertainment begins with a preview of "Tank Girl," consisting entirely of scenes of a woman who sadistically relishes perpetrating various sensational acts of violence. (I am reminded of the initiative taken by the television and movie industries in the summer of 1994 "to put more weapons in the hands of women").

Pulp Fiction begins. Setting is Los Angeles (same as O.J. trial). Dictionary definition given on the screen: pulp fiction means it is lurid and the paper it is printed on is crude. Hatred of Jews, it's us or them, and readiness to risk others' lives and their own are the orientation of a man and a woman in early restaurant scene where he talks about the anticipated ease of holding up people there in contrast to the difficulty of robbing banks.

Quickly, a shift to actors John Travolta and

Samuel Jackson, the latter playing a bullying African American with a big gun. He casually kills one young man while questioning another (loud laughter response from many people in the audience) and further directly terrifies another man. Two other men are then killed. (Meanwhile, the older woman to my left says, in a voice loud and distinct enough to be heard by a dozen or so people around us, "Get a vocabulary!" which is her reaction to the preponderance of s — and f — words in the admittedly limited vocabulary of Travolta and Jackson. My strong impulse 10 minutes into this movie is to leave with or without a refund. But I stay with this self-chosen assignment and continue writing in the dark).

Next, a boxer (played by Bruce Willis) near the end of a career in which he almost made it to the top of his brain damaging "sport," is told threateningly that he must "go down in the fifth" so that bets can be rigged.

Next, we see a drug dealer and his girlfriend in residence, she proud that her erogenous zones, including lips, nipples, and clitoris, are pierced to hold jewelry. Casual morbidity is clearly the sustaining theme by now, with no relief in sight. John Travolta (nominated for best actor in this role) is there to purchase "high quality" cocaine, which he administers to himself right there. He leaves to keep an obligation to take care of a woman (played by Uma Thurman) at the request of her husband. At her suggestion, they go to dinner at a restaurant/club featuring personnel who impersonate entertainment celebrities. She uses cocaine in the ladies room and they then win a dance contest and go to her place. While Travolta is in the bathroom, she gives herself more cocaine, bleeds, and is immediately near death. Travolta takes her, against the drug dealer's protests, to the latter's apartment, where the dying woman is viewed with no caring whatever by two women there, but comes back to life when Travolta stabs her in the heart with adrenaline. Arriving back at her place, she is non-emotional, except she does want to tell him a joke about a mama tomato who squeezes one of her little tomato children, because the child is lagging behind, whereupon the child turns into ketchup, get it!

Butch the boxer lays bets that he will win, then beats his opponent, who soon dies. He escapes in a cab driven by a pretty young woman from Columbia who repeatedly, sadistically, wants to hear how it feels to beat a man to death. On arriving at a motel to pick up his girlfriend, he learns that the watch handed down to him via his grandfather and father has been left behind. Butch goes to retrieve it, sees Vincent (Travolta) emerging from the bathroom and blows him away with Vincent's own huge gun.

Butch, still using his girlfriend's car, runs over the hit man looking for him, then totals the car, and goes into a firearms store emblazoned with a confederate flag and is caught prisoner, together with the injured hit man, by the owner who calls a police officer who turns out to be even more actively sadistic than the owner. The officer forcefully sodomizes the Black hit man who is then saved by the escaped Butch, who then collects his girlfriend, who can only have sex if the television is turned on loud to a war film.

For quite a while now, the 20-or-so-year-old man sitting right behind me has been laughing uproariously at each sadistic event and pressing his knees spasmodically against the back of my seat. By this time, he is joined in loud laughter by the young woman sitting next to him and many, but not a majority, of the audience. Lots of popcorn and sodas have been consumed throughout the theater. I try to take on a Zen-like orientation suited to observing without reacting as I ordinarily would, i.e., say something to the man behind me. I have given up hope that the movie will have any comic richness.

Hawkins is driving a car with Travolta in the front passenger seat, holding his big gun casually pointed at a young Black man in the back seat.

Mistake. The gun goes off and the young man's head is blown apart, splattering his brains throughout the back seat area. Travolta says that they may have hit a bump, causing the gun to go off. They proceed anxiously to disengage themselves from possible detection, soon enlisting a man who specializes in getting rid of unwelcome bodies in a car graveyard run by his woman friend. The man is very clever and efficient, thereby exciting admiration in Travolta and Hawkins, despite the unpleasant cleanup work he has them do. Hawkins discovers an injustice in that he, rather than Travolta, is cleaning up the brain-splattered back seat area, while Travolta only has to clean up other forms of blood and flesh in the front seat area.

Finally, about two hours into this movie, we are back at the original restaurant scene with the young man and woman about to rob the customers and manager. It ends with an epiphany. Hawkins manages to use his gangster talents to abort the robbery and sends off the couple with $1,500 of his own (illicitly gained) money, this after a personal, spiritual revelation of the true message contained in a Bible passage he has used many times previously to terrorize people. Thus, we have a happy ending, complete with blazing message of free choice and redemption.

The theater lights go on. The popcorn and sodas have been consumed along with an orgy of violence entertainment made more innocent by a Hollywood style saving grace. I do not have the impression that anything constructive has been learned by the audience although I am assured by critic Janet Maslin that "Quentin Tarrantino's film refutes the idea that drifting passively is a good way to fulfill one's destiny and to get through life" (a frequently repeated ad in the New York Times in 1995).

I am puzzled as to how Travolta, once killed, is alive and active at the end, but this is just a flashback. The woman on my left is also puzzled and she asks me how that can be. I tell her it is an earlier scene presented at the end. (I realize that this flashback gives the impression that Travolta is really alive, despite having been killed. It reminds me of the childhood game: "Bang, you're dead. Now, get up." In other words, death is not for real and such violence is harmless).

The woman on my left now says she is 67, the mother of five, and a grandmother. She looks much younger. She says she came to this movie because she likes John Travolta and likes to go to the movies and had recently enjoyed the movie "Roommates" with Peter Falk. She found it "strange" that people laughed during the violent scenes in Pulp Fiction and said, "In my day people were taught to love, but it's different now." I replied "Yes it is."

On March 26, 1995, CNN television featured interviews with various people associated with *Pulp Fiction.* No one found anything objectionable about the film. After all, it won the best picture award at the Cannes Film Festival, and is making enormous amounts of money for everyone associated with it. It is called "utterly original and humorous." Writer-director Tarrantino proudly talked of his ability to get the audience to like the male protagonists even though they are introduced right at the beginning of the film killing other men in cold blood, men "who weren't threatening them," Tarrantino emphasizes. Yet, the audience likes these men; they even "love" them throughout the film. The artistic achievement, apparently, is to get people to like or even love evil people, and probably to model themselves after these ego ideals.

The newest movie genre fits a formula that studiously melds sex, violence, and "humor" so that one inevitably evokes the others. There is no sex without violence and no sex-violence without a pass at humor. It's sado-masochism presented "with a light side" and, often, no longer even with a claim to any saving grace, unless "artistic" cleverness qualifies as a compensating accomplish-

ment. **It's just for fun.** *Naked Killer* **is another** example, incorporating women as the sadistic protagonists. Consider a reviewer's description:

Naked Killer, an amusing action-adventure spoof from Hong Kong, unfolds on territory that is way beyond the "Valley of the Dolls." Imagine the erotic world of "Basic Instinct" exaggerated into a kung-fu cartoon of sexy lesbian avengers executing quadruple leaping somersaults in a deadly assault against the opposite sex. Their campaign of assassination involves not only murder, but castration and genital mutilation as well....It must be counted as some sort of accomplishment that Naked Killer can treat its subject so lightly that the sex and violence seem as innocent and playful as an extended pillow fight (Holder, 1995, p. C8).

Since when is it harmless to treat murder and genital mutilation as "an artistic triumph," as if these atrocities were nothing more than a pillow fight? When does nothing but style matter? Isn't this the ancient art of sophistry, an argument that is correct in form and appearance, but is actually invalid, especially an argument used for deception and the display of intellectual brilliance? Isn't this old-fashioned con artistry slickly done with modern means? And isn't the result much more insidious than if we were lied to less expertly?

I had written about the two movies discussed above just before going to bed for the night, wondering about what effects such material really has on peoples' psyches. Ostensibly, both movies are harmless spoofs. Maybe other people have very different deep affective consequences from mine. The following dream made mine clear.

I was on a crude field-like area. Long columns of men and women, two or three abreast, were walking like prisoners along the rim of a long ditch wide enough to hold their bodies should they fall or be pushed in. They appeared drab, resigned, and nearly lifeless, about 10 or 15 to a group, each group in a column like the people along the ditch. But, apart from these long columns, I saw small groups of men who were not yet fully arranged, as it were; they were merely sitting or standing idly, instead of forming a long, trudging column like the men and women along the ditch. These men were talking casually among themselves, their ranks still askew in relation to the prisoners.

Then, a lone, official-looking man appeared, prepared to shackle the men whose group I was closest to. I advised the men in this group that they were going to lose their freedom if they conformed to the demand made on them. I knew that if they resisted, the official would summon his confederates, who would try collectively to shackle one group at a time. But these men were apathetic and let themselves be shackled by the lone official. I now considered escaping from the field and finding allies to help me return to the field in a further effort to free the now newly shackled men. But then I saw that the men had no apparent desire to be free. I woke up with a sense of despair.

The question remains. Is our culture now really so pervaded with the lurid tabloid mentality that there are no safe havens? Two weeks after seeing *Pulp Fiction*, my wife and I searched hard and successfully for a film that was life-enhancing. We went to a select theater in Philadelphia and saw *The Secret of Roan Inish*, a film made in Ireland that features an orphaned 12-year-old girl's experience as related to a Gaelic folk myth based on a children's novel. It was really about love, that four-letter word which has a substance usually avoided now by Hollywood, although *Forrest Gump* did win the Oscar for best picture. When *The Secret of Roan Inish* "...was shown at the Philadelphia Festival of World Cinema last May, the children in the audience seemed to be mesmerized. Even the adults were quiet and well-behaved" (Ritz Film Bill, 1995, p 15).

The same Film Bill, however, gleefully announced the revival of *Faster, Pussycat! Kill! Kill!*, a 1966 "masterpiece" of "a Gothic melodra-

ma centering around a gang of three psychotic go-go dancers and their thirst for violence..." and featuring their atrocities against "a young all-American couple who try to make friends." One of the lithesome threesome kills the young man after humiliating him and the threesome then go off, with his girlfriend as hostage, committing more atrocities featuring "a series of amazing scenes of seduction, scheming and action...culminating in a hellacious climax of catfights, rage and revenge, and one of the most entertaining B-movies ever made" (Schut, 1995, p. 30). Thus, even the best of the movie houses merchandise morbidity.

Although this movie ran at only one theater, it was given a full newspaper review and a three-star rating (Rickey, 1995). "The virtue of the film is that [it] can be enjoyed either as the embodiments of male sexual fantasy (tough women built like marshmallow-soft centerfolds) or as female power made flesh. Or both" (p. 5). "This movie leaves you so giddy it should be a controlled substance" (p. 14). Yes, violence can become addictive.

Parties to the Sado-Masochistic Violence-Addiction Contract

It should be no surprise that other countries are not only buying violence entertainment films from the United States, but are making their own versions and selling them to the United States. Thus, films like *Naked Killer*, made in Hong Kong, follow the Hollywood formula precisely. Nor is our dedicated, incessant cultivation of the violence mentality, now emphatic for women and children as well as men, limited to the tabloids, television, and movie making. What goes around does come around. We have made violence fashionable. As stated by Spindler (1995):

Paris, March 15 — An underground fashion newspaper being passed out on the first day of the fall '95 women's ready-to-wear shows here opens with a chart listing the six most popular films in Paris: Natural Born Killers, Pulp Fiction, Interview with the Vampire, True Romance, Serial Mom, and Reservoir Dogs. Calling attention to their shared violence, the newspaper, called F (for freedom), asks: "New reality or fashionable attitude?" (p. C13).

Like the columnist, Amy Spindler, I think both. The new Paris fashion designers for women propose tough, masculine, dangerous-looking clothes that look indistinguishable from men's "to affect a camaraderie like that among gangsters. [T]hose sadomasochistic trappings have become such a common touchstone in fashion that they no longer shock" (Spindler, 1995, p. 13). Meanwhile, what has happened to the Paris famous as a world center of high culture?

Product formulation. How can our violence entertainment industries be so effective? How have we achieved leadership in drug use, violence entertainment, and lethal violence? What formulas, overt or covert, might there be for addicting people to sado-masochistic violence? The knowledge base for addicting people to violence is extensive and has proven formulas. Let's begin with a modern version that sells "action movies."

As the United States simultaneously neglected its youth in recent decades, massively modeled violence and drug addictions for them, and complained of the results, we also rapidly escalated the national debt and the foreign trade deficit. Not coincidentally, as we became the world's greatest debtor nation, we resorted to tactics well known to drug pushers. We strove hard to addict others, as well as ourselves, to whatever we could sell, with little or no thought about the moral and physical violence we have been perpetrating and are continuing to perpetrate. The theme common to these phenomena is living impulsively in the present and thinking little about the future, particularly for our neglected youth, who are becoming saddled with the growing national debt and adult-inculcated spiritual bankruptcy.

As Anne Thompson (1988), speaking of the escalation of "action films," put it, "The actioner — once strictly a B-flick staple — has been jazzed up, studio-style for mass consumption" (p. 1F). According to James Jacks, a Universal Studios acquisition executive, "Action pictures play perfectly to the TV generation" (as quoted by Thompson, p. 1F). These movies became hot exports as well as pleasers of the masses in this country, and were enormously profitable, despite their extreme cost, as exemplified by *Rambo III*, costing nearly $60 million.

The close relationship between our violence culture and the drugging of America is evident in the fact that violence, like drugs, must be provided in ever larger doses to satisfy the consumer addict. In the words of James Glickenhaus (as quoted in Thompson, 1988), who directed *The Exterminator* and *The Soldier*:

No one has ever seen anything like this. When we were kids, we played cops and robbers, cowboys and Indians. In an action picture you get to live out your fantasy — wreck a lot of stuff and shoot people like you can't in real life. You have to end with a bang. If the beginning of a film is exciting, you have to top that. The more people get, the more they want (p. 1F).

Serial killer Ted Bundy, who sadistically murdered more than 20 innocent women, gave eloquent testimony to the power of criminal training in the perverse monomaniacal contamination of sexuality with violence in our popular culture (Bundy says, 1989):

And it happened in stages, gradually. My experience with...pornography that deals on a violent level with sexuality is once you become addicted to it...I would keep looking for more potent, more explicit, more graphic kinds of material...you begin to wonder if maybe actually doing it would give you that which is beyond just reading it or looking at it (p. 4A).

Although Bundy's particular childhood experiences inevitably account for much of his adult personality, he found added inspiration from our culture's violence panderers. Most people exposed to pornography (the contamination of sex with violence) will not become killers, but they may tend to become more disrespectful and thus contribute to the mountain of para-violence attitudes and behaviors that are capped by lethal violence.

Beguiling the buyer. To take full effect, however, the sadomasochistic contract has to be agreed upon by all parties. The contract comes with a solid deathtime guarantee: if fully executed according to instructions, the contract ensures destruction of all of the parties, whether they have been actively or passively agreeing. Those who do not die physically, die spiritually.

Obtaining passive, non-thinking agreement is crucial for selling the contract. I thought about Erich Fromm's 1941 book, *Escape from Freedom* (1969), which shows with deep insight how evil emanates from man's failure to accept responsibility for freedom. Fromm's initial purpose was to understand how the Nazis could tyrannize the world. The answer was that Hitler had not only powerful, active help but, just as importantly, deep-seated passive collusion from people everywhere, at least until they woke up. Hitler appealed to the worst in people and there was plenty of that.

Hitler knew just what to do. His methods were based on an already sophisticated psychological science of propaganda, including what was known about hypnotism. He studied the tried and true propaganda methods to propagate his own credo. For example, he assembled great masses of people toward the end of the day, kept them standing when or until they were tired and ready to be passive, addressed them stridently while they were all facing him instead of one another, and then appealed to their weakness in the name of power, inducing and seducing them into manic idolatry: "Heil Hitler, Heil Hitler, Heil Hitler." His audiences grew, as even whole nations gave in and other nations wavered, tempt-

ed by the easy pleasures of scapegoating their "inferiors" so as to feel powerful and virtuous themselves. Yet, how could he have made so many intelligent people believe such great lies? Hitler knew his lies had to be huge and uncompromising, the opposite of the humble truths that the people did not want to believe. He declared, "The great masses of the people...will more easily fall victims to a big lie than to a small one" (Kaplan, 1992, p. 676).

Winston Churchill, that most indomitable enemy of tyranny in general, and of Hitler in particular, sized up his enemy well. Churchill understood that Hitler had to not only be produced by social and interpersonal influences but, to be successfully demonic on a large scale, had to fill a big power void. Churchill (as cited by Humes, 1995) stated:

Into that void strode a maniac of ferocious genius of the most virulent hatred that has ever corroded the human breast...Corporal Hitler. This wicked man, the repository and embodiment of many forms of soul-destroying hatred, the monstrous product of former wrongs and shames (p. 154).

People who do not feel they are leading meaningful, empowered lives are ready to be drawn into cult forms of behavior that easily deteriorate into violence. As psychiatrist Arthur Deikman (1990) explained in his book, *The Wrong Way Home*, cults are not limited simply to what we are used to calling cults. They exist in often subtle group allegiances characterized by compliance with the group, dependence on a leader, devaluation of the outsider, and avoidance of dissent. Whether expressed as membership in the Nazi party, street gangs, the Ku Klux Klan, college fraternities, or even business and professional groups, members may be called upon to commit atrocities in the name of group allegiance, and for what the group calls virtue. Even more broadly, suggestible individuals do not even have to be members of an organization as such to be persuaded by group pressure to buy into clearly self-destructive and other-destructive practices in conformity with social myths, especially if the propaganda is expertly engineered by advertisers or public relations professionals.

Trickery, in one form or another, is a necessary method to employ at the very beginning to sell addictions, whether to cigarettes, alcohol or other drugs, memberships in gangs and other cults, or directly violent behaviors. For example, in March 1995, the Japanese cult Aum Shinrikyo (Supreme Truth), was found to possess vast supplies of death-dealing nerve gas ingredients, but denied responsibility for the mass nerve gas attack on Tokyo subway system. Then, Supreme Truth was found to advise supreme lying.

Indeed, Japanese press reports say a secret recruitment handbook recovered from Aum outlines the ideal way to rope in somebody they want. First, an Aum member befriends a potential recruit — without letting on the Aum affiliation — and then a third person acting as an Aum representative invites them both to a sect program.

The covert Aum member responds enthusiastically, and the "friends" go together to a few Aum activities. All the time, the secret Aum member suggests that they both become more involved in the sect (Kristof, 1995).

All addiction cultivation, and the violence toward oneself and others that it inevitably brings, is predicated on lies. Atrocities do arise from absurdities, as the French philosopher Voltaire insisted. Many perfectly legal, well-educated, "respectable" groups of people can and do play these cheap tricks. Such legal evil, expertly executed, and so incalculably insidious, is vastly profitable to the pushers who reap money, prestige, and power.

But how, exactly, do even "otherwise intelligent and thoughtful" people buy into addictions? The pushers do their best to get the buyer not to think, to try to ensure that actual active thinking will be preempted, much as it is in schizophrenic disorders (Whitaker, 1980, 1992). Schizophrenic

thought disorder is simultaneously illogical, unwitting, and impaired. But, whereas false premises and illogicality tend to occur in schizophrenic persons without someone trying right then and there to induce it, the bypassing or short-circuiting of rational thinking is deliberately induced by pushers. The pusher's mission is to get the potential buyer's attention while making sure to short-circuit the buyer's tendency to think, especially to think critically. Usually, therefore, the buyer is approached on the simpler cognitive levels of sensation or perception, that is, below the level of thinking.

Thus, impulsive cognitive style represents the opposite of the responsible educational process which teaches the entire cognitive sequence that deserves the name "thinking," the active, critical process enabling both inhibiting, unwarranted actions and taking *deliberate, actively wished for actions.* As Shapiro noted, impulsive cognitive style is captured in the doer's non-explanation: "I just did it — I don't know why" (Shapiro, 1965, p. 135). In this style, thinking per se is short-circuited. The person really wasn't thinking. The common motto in impulsive cognitive style is simply accepting the impulse to "Just do it!" In other words, "Don't think; just act!" The denial of the need to think is conveyed by the beer ad: "Why ask why?"

The Social Structure and Dynamics of Paralethal Violence

Now, let us examine the social and dynamic structure of paralethal violence and then, within the causal paradigm, the nature of current youth culture and its determiners, with a view to how we, as a society, have produced and continue to produce it and, in the last section of this chapter, how we can counter and reverse the megatrend to violence.

Lethal violence causality and the second cybernetics. Lethal violence is the end result of many interacting, often synergistic, personal, social, and situational factors, each of which by itself is insufficient to produce lethal violence. Indeed, these factors, considered individually, are never enough to produce any form of violent behavior, let alone lethal violence. Each, by itself, can be excused readily by its defenders who serve to benefit at the expense of its victims.

For example, consider the situational factor defined as availability of a gun, which is necessary, but not sufficient in murders committed with a gun; a gun cannot by itself explain any violent act, let alone lethal violence. But it is, of course, a powerful potentiating factor in violence, and a gun makes possible a lethal degree of violence. The well-known aphorism offered by people who would protect "the right to bear arms," that "Guns don't kill people, people do," recognizes that guns by themselves never have and never will kill anyone, while implicitly denying that guns are an extremely potentiating and enabling factor in the necessary mingling of paralethal influences.

Similarly, consider the factor of violence entertainment. Those who would deny its influence claim, with some supporting evidence, that violence entertainment in movies, television, videos, magazines, books, and other communication media cannot (fully) explain why murders are committed. Yet, a serial killer such as Ted Bundy (Whitaker, 1990) has explained the important role violence depictions played in his increasingly murderous personal development. Thus, it is true, as its defenders claim, that violence entertainment definitely cannot (by itself) explain murder, that, in fact, only individuals who are already of a murderous personality proclivity would relate to violence depictions by behaving murderously. How can we conceptualize the causality of lethal violence in terms of this evident reality of mutually causative factors, in contrast to denying their causal influence by compartmentalizing them and taking them out of context?

We can consider any pattern of causally relevant factors as a gestalt: a structure or configuration of physical, biological, or psychological phenomena so integrated as to constitute a functional unit with properties not derivable from its parts in summation (Webster's Third New International Dictionary, 1966). A gestalt or functional unit may have, at any given time, equilibrating or deviation-enhancing causality. Such causality can be understood in terms of cybernetics: the comparative study of the automatic control system formed by the nervous system and brain and by mechanoelectrical communication systems and devices (as computing machines, thermostats, photoelectric sorters) (Webster's Third New International Dictionary, 1966).

We usually think of cybernetics as a science of self-regulating systems that are equilibrating, such as thermostats, which maintain a constant temperature by registering and countering deviations from that temperature. But a particular gestalt or system of mutually causative factors may be deviation-amplifying, as in the processes loosely called "vicious cycles" and "compound interests." Maruyama (1963) conceptualized these deviation-amplifying processes in terms of the "second cybernetics."

The first cybernetics helps to explain some phenomena pertinent to the causal structure and dynamics of paralethal and lethal violence, such as the maintenance of poverty, racism, poor education, and unemployment, because these four conditions tend to mutually maintain themselves. The second cybernetics helps to explain the deviation amplification that characterizes acceleration toward lethal violence. In these cases, an increase in factor A tends to increase factor B which, by being increased, increases factor A.

A simple exercise illustrates the difference between the first versus second cybernetics. Your task is to stand on one foot. First, try to maintain this position while fixing your gaze precisely on a nearby reference point, e.g., 5 feet away. If you carefully maintain this reference, e.g., the exact corner of a table, you will probably find it relatively easy not to lose your balance. Now, standing on only one foot again, try to keep your balance while shifting your gaze about, e.g., from the table corner to an armchair, and then to the wall, so that your reference point varies in distance and location. You will probably find it much more difficult to keep your balance this time. Changing one factor induces change in a second, which then induces further change in the first.

Deviation amplification may be favorable or unfavorable in terms of violence. It may be favorable, e.g., when a positive father becomes involved in his family and in child-rearing. The more nurturing and dependable the father, the more inclined the child may be to pursue education. In turn, the father can now respond with further nurturance as he rewards the child's effort. Or, using this simple configuration again, a father's withdrawal may cause his child to lose interest in school, whereupon the father may retreat further and so on.

The factors involved in lethal violence causation are usually more numerous. Consider the common gestalt of: fatherlessness, protest masculinity, drug use, violence entertainment, and gun availability. Applying the second cybernetics, we would envision a pattern of mutual reinforcement of deviation amplification. Not only would fatherlessness tend to induce protest masculinity, which would tend to induce use of drugs, violence entertainment, and guns, but this causal "loop" would feed back on itself, further amplifying the lethal violence potential.

The second cybernetics model depicted here also lends itself to strategies to break out of the "vicious circle." One may see clearly where and how to intervene positively in such a gestalt of otherwise self-reinforcing causal lethal violence factors. For example, providing positive father figure role models, and making unavailable guns, drugs, violence entertainment, or all three, can be effective means of incapacitating the vicious cycle.

Institutional factors in the violence culture. Consider the role alcohol plays in violence. While often associated with lethal violence via drunk driving and use of guns, alcohol is also a major co-determiner of violence even when cars and guns are not available. For example, guns are not allowed in institutions of higher education and, in contrast to many high schools, the no gun rules at universities and colleges are generally effective, which probably helps to account for both lower suicide and homicide rates on college campuses (Schwartz, 1990; Schwartz & Whitaker, 1990; Whitaker & Pollard, 1993b). But, college and university campuses have become much more dangerous in recent years. One causal factor, probably, is the influence of the increasingly violent surrounding culture's influence; as youth in the United States have become more violent, so have college students. Another contributor to violence on college and university campuses is that heavy underage consumption of alcohol is often tolerated on campus.

As many college personnel have observed, the much publicized phenomenon of campus "date rape" rarely, if ever, occurs without the use of alcohol by the rapist, or victim, or both; usually, both have been drinking (Rivinus & Larimer, 1993). The attitudes of male students toward rape are predisposing or co-determining also. Thirty-five percent have said they might commit rape if there was no chance of being caught, and 84% have said "some women look as though they're just asking to be raped" (Conn & Silverman, 1991, p. 6).

While not receptive to the weapons industry, colleges and universities are very vulnerable to the alcohol industry and its oxymoronic pairings of alcohol and wholesome fun, even though most college students are under age 21 and their alcohol use violates state laws. Furthermore, colleges and universities usually receive some federal funding and are required thereby to assure the government that their campuses are kept drug free, but considerable illicit alcohol and other drug use continues on the vast majority of campuses. Thus, legal restrictions on alcohol and other drug use appear to have minimal effect at colleges and universities. College students are much less likely to use guns than their non-college peers, but far more likely to drink alcohol, and are quite subject to alcohol-related violence.

Protest masculinity. Many authors have elaborated on the close relationship between morbidity-infused images of masculinity and the much higher rates of homicide, suicide, and paraviolence behaviors in men (e.g., Cousy, 1975; Daniell, 1984; Gerzon, 1992; Mailer, 1984; Whitaker, 1987, 1990). "Real men," according to the popular mythology, show "strength" by dominating women and other men, and not showing emotional needs, except to act out anger. Their toughness is shown in being able to hold their tobacco, alcohol, and other drugs, and acting as though they are not afraid of killing or dying.

Rosemary Daniell (1984) coined the word "macha" to represent the female equivalent of the macho male. Like macho men, macha women are more prone to morbidity. Their numbers are increasing, as is especially evident in the acceleration of violent crimes committed by females and the greatly increased number of female prisoners. For example, the number of women prisoners increased 359% from 1974 to 1991 (Conn & Silverman, 1991).

Protest masculinity is a kind of false masculinity, an attempt at compensation for the lack of adequate fathers and father figures. This lack and the resultant internal void is illustrated by Mark Gerzon (1992) in his book, *A Choice of Heroes*, in which he states: "I recognized that what is missing in typical male macho behavior is not just the feminine but, even more important, the deep masculine" (p. 272). Lacking genuine masculine role models, boys submit to the relentless barrage of false masculine images thrust at them by the vast popular media and advertisement industries, and become eager to emulate the "powerful" caricatures of "men" wielding huge guns positioned at crotch level. It is then but a short step to getting a gun, or "hitting on a girl," or both. The script has no provision for fatherhood except the act of intercourse.

Large and small screen entertainment, video games, and much popular music present macho imagery every day and night as heroic. None of this macho heroism has value for would-be functional people unless they can join the presenters in making money from it. But, the relentless, sensational role-modeling thus inculcated has far greater influence than the careful cultivation of respect for one's own and others' lives, because the latter is reliant on non-sensational personal examples in family, neighborhood, and school settings. After all, television is the prime baby and child sitter, and movies and television continue to play highly influential roles through all of the most formative years.

While an alarming number of high school graduates are illiterate on the whole, most prisoners in our society have not only failed to complete high school, but have been infused with protest masculinity and thus, lack both education and genuine masculine confidence. The lack of education and, thereby, job opportunities, tends to increase protest masculinity which, in turn, tends to make boys deride education.

The destructiveness inherent in protest masculinity has an especially strong appeal for spectators who, not measuring up to the real or fancied toughness of the gladiator-hero or his opponent, can feel superior to the opponent by identifying with the "hero." Such was the pleasure in watching Roman gladiators. And such is the pleasure in boxing spectacles. Today's boxing spectator tries to deny his own fear and inadequacy by identifying with the "heroism" of the winning boxer-mutilator. The boxers themselves are typically minority males who can be more readily exploited and sacrificed in the ring, due to bigotry and their otherwise impoverished condition. *The Selling of Mike Tyson* is a newspaper article that captures the essence of the social, physical, and psychological morbidity inherent in machismo:

Mitch Green brought a menacing facade and an ominous reputation with him. He had earned the nickname "Blood" while a gang leader in Queens. Very quickly, however, Green's glower turned to genuine fright.

Tyson smacked him in the mouth with such force in the second round that Green's mouthpiece flew out of the ring. In the third, the mouthpiece was sent flying again, along with a bridge and two teeth (Lyon, 1986, pp. 1D, 4D).

When Green, in an attempt to survive, frantically clasped Tyson to his body, the crowd booed its displeasure. As the newspaper columnist observed, "People are anxious to worship a gladiator once more" (pp. 1D, 4D). The fact that boxer-gladiators both cruelly inflict and are cruelly inflicted with brain damage was compensated for with enormous profits, in this case, $2 million of television rights catering to many millions of sadistic viewers, who thereby made the contracts possible. Now, as this chapter is being written, Tyson is out of prison, having served a term for rape, and is about to engage in the next highly lucrative match, which is eagerly anticipated as more gladiator heroism. Some spectators worry that he may no longer be "Iron Mike," especially because he apparently had some spiritual guidance in prison.

In contrast, consider the following letter printed in the same newspaper on the same day, from a man who may be deviant, but is not morbid at all:

Dear Ann Landers: I am a 30-year-old male with a steady girlfriend and a normal sex life. When "Sara" does not spend the night with me, I sleep with my Teddy bear. She is the one who gave me the Teddy, but she doesn't know I sleep with it.

When I was little, I didn't sleep with any stuffed animals. This just started a year ago, when Sara gave me this wonderful little Teddy. Do you think I should see a psychiatrist? I worry about this regression to childhood. Please give me your opinion —The Bear Facts in Bayside.

Dear Bay: Not to worry. If the Teddy is a comfort to you, go ahead and sleep with it. Obviously, the symbolism is clear. Teddy is a substitute for Sara (Landers, 1986).

This apparently normal man, Bay, who is very "deviant" in terms of the prevailing macho culture, is reaching out for help, while truly morbid men who are not deviant are seldom motivated or able to do so, because of their macho orientation.

Fatherlessness, poverty, and race. As noted previously, fatherlessness, a rapidly escalating phenomenon in our society, tends to cause more protest masculinity. When nurturing and disciplining fathers are absent, male children are especially vulnerable to the relentless macho role modeling in violence entertainment. Furthermore, fatherless boys are increasingly surrounded in our society by other fatherless boys and are thus subject to a young peer culture that, on the whole, has little masculine guidance. Marshaling considerable evidence for this claim, David Blankenhorn (1995) asserted that "...if we want to learn the identity of the rapist, the hater of women, the occupant of jail cells, we do not look first to boys with traditionally masculine fathers. We look first to boys with no fathers" (p. 31). From 1960 to 1990, the percentage of births outside marriage rose from 5.3 to 28.0 and the percentage of children living apart from their fathers rose from 17.5 to 36.3. This trend is having a cumulative detrimental effect. We may, therefore, expect that even the more than doubled percent of males in prison from 1980 to 1990 will be exceeded from 1990 to 2000.

A 1990 study commissioned by the Progressive Policy Institute showed that the "relationship between crime and one-parent families" is so strong that, when it is taken into account, the relationship between race and crime as well as between low income and crime is erased (Blankenhorn, 1995, p. 31). However, it is important to understand the close relationships among fatherlessness, poverty, and race as a kind of causal gestalt of factors that is worsening. Fatherlessness typically results in the mother having to — not necessarily choosing to — leave her children in order to work outside of the home. Thus, the children are not only without their father, but their mother is less available. Furthermore, such fatherless families are usually much poorer than families with fathers, even when the mothers get outside jobs. Thus, the job of being a mother is neglected, often in favor of poor quality day care, the family is poorer economically, *and* the father is absent.

More, rather than fewer, United States citizens are becoming disadvantaged. Our poverty-fatherlessness-minority culture appears to be increasing. We have become the Western world nation with the greatest gap between the rich and the poor (Bradsher, 1995). Economic inequality has risen since the 1970s. Presently, 1% of United States households — having a net worth of at least $2.3 million each — own nearly 40 percent of the nation's wealth.

Noting that society is all too willing to rationalize the deterioration of the family, Blankenhorn (1995) posited that "A good society celebrates the ideal of the man who puts his family first" (p. 5). Compare this ideal with that presented by the typical sensational "action movie" hero, who represents protest masculinity at its worst.

Writing on the enormous rise in the United States of what has been diagnosed as "Attention-Deficit-Hyperactivity Disorder" (ADHD), Peter and Ginger Breggin, in their book, *The War Against Children* (1994), argued persuasively that children's "attention deficits" are better termed "Dad Attention Deficit Disorder" (DADD) or "Teacher Attention Deficit Disorder" (TADD). Whereas such children, mostly males, are seen as

early delinquents who have a brain deficit and need psychiatric drug treatment, usually with Ritalin, neurologist Fred Baughman, Jr. (1993) noted that studies have failed to confirm any definite improvement from drug treatment. However, such children often improve quickly if given more nurturing adult attention, including when discipline is nurturantly applied. Yet, the numbers of children and adolescents on Ritalin has at least doubled from 1991 to 1995 (Breggin, 1995).

The nurturing process we call education has also deteriorated in recent decades, especially in economically and socially disadvantaged inner city schools where even high school graduates are often illiterate. Several indices reflect this decline. For example, between 1977 and 1991, the number of American children diagnosed as having learning disabilities increased 142%; between 1945 and 1991, the average number of words in the written vocabulary of a 6-to-14-year-old American child decreased from 25,000 to 10,000; in 1991, 36 million adult Americans read below the 8th grade level (Conn & Silverman, 1991). The vast majority of prisoners, not coincidentally, are especially poorly educated.

Defenders of paralethal violence. Arguments by deniers of the destructive influence of various relevant factors, including guns, violence entertainment, alcohol and other drugs, fatherlessness, poverty, racial prejudice, and early experiences of brutality, can successfully defend the factor of their choice on the limited basis of its being neither necessary nor sufficient to explain any violent act. (A common rationalization, for example, is "He didn't need a gun to do it; he would have found a way"). Yet, it is clear that all of these factors play roles in determining and facilitating outright lethal violence and paralethal violence. Thus, I call them paralethal factors.

The misleading nature of arguments by violence factor defenders is illustrated by a scene with Peter Sellers in a Pink Panther movie. Sellers is at a hotel desk, where he sees a dog standing peacefully by the hotel clerk, and asks the clerk, "Does your dog bite?" The clerk says, "No." Then Sellers reaches out to pet the dog and is bitten. In shock, Sellers says "I thought you said your dog doesn't bite?" The clerk answers, "But it's not my dog."

In this instance, as in all instances when violence factor deniers help determine violent behavior, the abettor (the clerk) has misled his customer (Sellers). He has contributed to the violence both by having the dog there and not advising of the danger, but he can facilely excuse himself. After all, he was not required by law to look after the well-being of his fellow human being.

How We Can Counter and Replace Our Violence Culture

Criticizing and understanding our society's innumerable inducements to violence implies innumerable ways to counter and replace such morbidity. Clearly, fostering nurturing, rather than abusive and neglectful, child-rearing practices is key. By becoming a more nurturing society, we can hold youth and ourselves more accountable, just as constructive parents provide a foundation upon which discipline can be based. We will then produce fewer people who, by neglect, coupled with training to be violent, are disenfranchised and then express their anger, sense of entitlement, and power needs through violent behavior. People who act as though they have nothing to lose have seldom been given much to begin with.

We need to redefine power as the ability to nurture, recognizing that whereas anyone can destroy the fruits of nurturance, only genuinely powerful people can create meaningful lives. Whereas violence entertainment promotes a destructive orientations, we need to be constructive and to nurture constructive orientations.

Beyond observing and promulgating these general truths, what can we do specifically to counter the presently increasing violent culture we have given the youth of our country? The possibilities for practical, constructive programmatic actions are seemingly limitless, are usually much less expensive even in the short run than most current revenge measures, and are enormously preventive of future expense. A few are listed here.

Improve parenting. Our finest but most neglected art is parenting. Our society has left far too much of it to people who are exploiting rather than nurturing. Encouraging men to be real fathers, rather than mere biological fathers, is probably our single greatest social challenge. But it can be performed by almost any man willing to try.

My own favorite example is "The Bicycle Man" from Belmont, North Carolina (Kuralt, 1985), who supplied and maintained youngsters with bikes they would otherwise never have had. This genuine hero, Jethro Mann, grew up without a bike and so he found special meaning and satisfaction in spending tremendous time and personal care, and his quite limited financial resources, teaching kids fun, caring, and responsibility. Mr. Mann fit stereotyped notions of being disadvantaged: he was Black, poor, and old. But he was really quite spiritually rich, living out his own powerful personal philosophy. Mr. Mann said: "I look at it this way. I have had a good life myself and I'm not apt to have much more. But whatever I do have, I hope it will contribute to someone else's welfare. And that is what I try to do" (Kuralt, p. 13). Mr. Mann is a real man!

Blankenhorn (1995) offered 12 proposals for improving the fathering parental orientation, including grass roots neighborhood actions and government incentives to encourage active parenting. For example, he suggested forming fathers' clubs devoted to good fathering and cited already active community groups.

Arthur Ashe (1993), the great athlete, scholar, and father emphasized the crucial importance his father had for his personal development, especially after the death of his mother. Ashe stated:

My father was a strong, dutiful, providing man. He lived and died semi-literate, but he owned his own home and held jobs that were important to him and to people in the community where we lived. His love and caring were real to me from that Sunday morning in 1950 when he sat on the bottom bunk bed between my brother Johnnie and me and told us between wrenching sobs that our mother had died during the night. From that time on he was mother and father to us. And the lesson he taught us above all was about reputation (p. 4).

James Michener (1992), bereft of both parents at birth, emphasized how father figures, such as an "uncle" and other men in the community were essential in enabling him to avoid not only cigarettes and alcohol but a criminal lifestyle.

Any parent or parent figure, male or female, can perform an enormously helpful nurturing service to children by being affectionate and caring, reading to them, listening to and talking with them, and telling them stories. Reading to a child from the time they can begin to recognize words not only gives them a head start on becoming literate and invested in education, but can create an affectionate, mutually respectful bond between parent and child. Children are strengthened thereby both cognitively and socially and will develop confidence in their own growing powers to understand themselves and the world around them. In the process, they develop a security base which will help them resist the omnipresent commercial inducements to disrespect and commit violence toward themselves and others. The positive, caring attention they get from being read to, listened to, and being told stories will very likely prevent the kinds of "attention disorders," hyperactivity, and delinquent behaviors increasingly targeted as symptomatic of "chemical imbalances" needing drug treatment. Similarly, children taught to care for pets, to appreciate nature, and to learn about themselves and others without commercial pressures will become more independent and creative thinkers.

Recreational and sports activities can be enormously helpful also, depending on the spirit of engagement. Children can be taught to compete fairly, to be gracious winners and good losers, to take joy in the process, and to train to become more physically fit and respectful of their bodies.

Parents should be careful to keep harmful intruders out of the home, particularly in the form of violence entertainment emanating from television sets and VCRs, and their induction of passive mindlessness. Screen out these otherwise ubiquitous baby-sitters. Make sure that children's (and adults') exposures are limited to constructive programming in the home and at movie theaters.

Teach critical thinking. Mindlessness is not a natural condition; it has to be learned through violent enforcement because all children, otherwise, are naturally endlessly curious until they are forced to stop being curious and to give up their capacity to be imaginative, thoughtful, and creative.

While impulsive cognitive style and its obliviousness to harmful consequences may characterize much of infantile behavior, children of even elementary school age show an eagerness and ability to develop critical thinking. In fact, some of the most effective deterrents to cigarette smoking have been created by children. For example, Melissa Antonow of Our Lady of Hope School in Queens, New York, produced the "Come to Where the Cancer Is" cartoon, a takeoff on the Marlboro Country cigarette ads. Her cartoon showed a skeleton of a man riding a horse alongside tombstones marked variously "lung cancer," "heart disease," and "emphysema." Melissa's "ad" appeared in all New York City subway cars. Similarly, Caheim Drake of Public School 112 in the Bronx produced an anti-smoking ad showing a "Pack of Lies" — a cigarette pack with each cigarette bearing a label such as "Fun," "Relaxation," "Safe," "Cool," "Mature," and "Popular" (Howe, 1992).

If children, with the aid of their adult teachers, can cut through denial and engage in effective critical thinking which gets to the truth, formal education can serve to immunize children from the adult-instigated propaganda that exploits all consumers. This nurturing educational process requires that we, the adult teachers, engage in the critical thinking processes we have been trained to abnegate in our own commercialized upbringings. We will need to stop being so suggestible as to smoke cigarettes, to drink alcohol to the point of intoxication, and to participate actively or acquiesce passively in externally directed, as well as internally directed, mindless violence. We, as adults, will have to *actively criticize* all aspects of the cigarette, alcohol, weapons, and violence entertainment industries, instead of passively accepting them.

Some communities have demonstrated how adults can decrease the gross intrusion of destructiveness training. A largely Black community within the city of Philadelphia found itself targeted by an advertising campaign designed to addict Black people specifically to a new brand of cigarettes that was given a suave, cool image. Their protest resulted in the cigarette advertisers, i.e., drug pushers, calling off the campaign.

In Perth Amboy, New Jersey, a neighborhood group sent its young people out on the streets to demonstrate how easy it was for persons under 18 to buy cigarettes (Teltsch, 1992). The underage young people were able to make cigarette purchases in 63 of the 94 stores they visited. The community of Perth Amboy was selected for such a drive against child and teenage smoking because it was saturated with billboards urging tobacco and alcohol use for Black and Hispanic residents. The advertisers know whom to prey on just as the regular, more obviously disrespectable street drug pushers do: target those with less power. But those with apparently less power, including minorities and the young, can protest effectively, as in these cases. And it so happens that Black youth are taking up cigarette smoking at far lower rates than their White peers.

Counter racism. Considered individually, fatherlessness, gun availability, commercial exploitation, including violence entertainment, lack of education, and poverty play obviously enormous roles in violence propagation. So does racism. When Arthur Ashe (1993) was asked if AIDS was the heaviest burden he had ever had to bear, he replied, "Race has always been my biggest burden" (p. 126). People of color are often held in lower esteem across innumerable situations in our society, ranging from country club membership exclusions to automatic assumptions of intellectual inferiority. Clearly, children should be taught to respect persons of all ethnic backgrounds and to resist absurd, oxymoronic pairings of race and religion with this or that supposed inferiority.

Racism and other ethnic prejudices also take the form of expecting less from minorities, in keeping with judgments of lower capacity. But, as many education experiments have shown, Hispanic children, given encouragement, may prove quite superior in calculus, Black children in chess, and so on. We do a disservice by expecting and encouraging less. Everyone needs nurturance and encouragement and everyone should be held accountable.

Probably, any field of endeavor made really open to minorities will lead to excellence by many. I have often thought, for example, about what would happen if Blacks were discouraged from entering any occupation but medicine. I predict that, within two generations, most of our best physicians would be Black, just as most professional basketball players now are Black, because that occupation opened up wide during the past couple of decades.

Reform education. As discussed earlier, our schools have been turning into armed camps, where teachers are preoccupied with trying to establish a sufficiently secure environment for education to have a chance. Often, however, school is education in name only. Not only high school, but often college graduates are illiterate, as well as undisciplined. Part of the problem, as exemplified in the California dilemma, is that schools have been stripped of adequate financing, largely because of astronomically increasing spending on more prisoners and punishments. Commercial enterprises are filling the void both outside and inside the classroom. For example, whereas commercial-free textbooks ordinarily would cost hundreds of dollars per student per year, in 1993, public school spending for textbooks containing advertisements, averaged only $45.91 per student (Consumer Reports, 1995). What is happening to fill the great gap in ad-free education funding?

In addition to the 30,000 commercial messages sent to children every day by ads on TV, radio, billboards, and the like outside of schools, school properties themselves are now filled with commercials on radios, ads on walls, and even on school buses and, most importantly perhaps, in their study materials, according to an 18-month research project by Consumers Union's Education Services Department (Consumer Reports, 1995). Among the 160 examples of such ads was: "There are no endangered species, maintains the Council for Wildlife Conservation and Education, which turns out to be affiliated with the National Shooting Sports Foundation — an organization that has the same address as the National Rifle Association" (p. 327).

Actually, hundreds of species of life are already extinguished, and many more are endangered, one of which is the human being. Communities and their governments need to retake fiscal and programmatic responsibility for their school systems, and to disallow the same lying and deception that plague life outside the schools.

Fill the spiritual void. We have a compelling urge in our society to resort to legalistic solutions which are usually partial and temporary; they do not get at the heart of the matter, and they do not address the spiritual problem. Legalism cannot fill the void of disrespect.

Inherent in most, if not all, acts of violence, whether legal or not, is a failure of empathy. The only possible exception is when violence is truly needed to stop a greater violence, though this situation usually reflects earlier grave oversights. For example, the world stood by too long as the Nazis came to power (by filling a spiritual void in Germany), in large part because of lack of caring and empathy for Jewish people.

No list of ways to understand and counter social inducements to violence would be adequate without emphasizing the universal human need to find meaning in life. Of course, not just any meaning will do. The meaning has to be life affirming and infused with respect for all human beings. Many supposed spiritual quests, often in the guise of a particular religion or cult, achieve the opposite. By positing the inferiority of outsiders, they become exclusive rather than embracing, threatening instead of comforting, and ultimately destructive instead of constructive. A truly spiritual orientation means that others' lives and one's own are sacred. In this sense, spiritual development means cultivation of a broad mindedness that spans the universe of life rather than shrinks one's awareness. It means a sensitive awareness of oneself together with an empathic identification with others, rather than a blind conformist following in the authoritarian tradition of mindlessness. Teaching and learning mindfulness, caring, and empathy are ways all of us can contribute every day to a better, non-violent society. We can counter the current barrage of social inducements to violence by becoming a spiritually determined nation and world of mindful, wholesome misfits.

Why be so "optimistic?" As I write this, the richly varied citizenry of the fundamentally great country called the United States, led by our President and First Lady, have reached out with their hearts and minds in empathic response to the

Oklahoma City mass murder bombing. And people from all over the world are also responding in recognition of the value of life everywhere and our being in this together. Let us continue to wake up to the opportunity in this crisis to respect ourselves and our fellow beings. And let us all practice this spiritual wisdom and let it be our legacy:

I expect to pass through this life but once.
If therefore there be any kindnesses I can show,
or any good thing I can do to any fellow beings,
let me do it now. Let me not defer or neglect it,
for I shall not pass this way again.

A. B. Hegeman

Summary

This chapter outlines, analyzes, and illustrates powerful social inducements to our society's violence megatrend in order to replace violence with respect for and nurturance of life. The megatrend is defined as a rapid rise in both internalized and externalized violence by youth, as determined by neglect, together with programming for violence addictions. Lethal violence is depicted as the capstone of a mountain of paralethal factors, including the worsening of parenting, education, and poverty, and the growth of commercial violence cultivation and gun availability.

Denial of the nature of the inducements are linked with the popularity of expensive, reactive "solutions" that aren't working: more prisoners, death penalties, police, guns, and corporal punishments. Criminals' disavowals of responsibility are likened to our society's disavowals of its contributions to violence in the media, entertainment, and weapons industries, and in the "pushing" of harmful legal, as well as illegal, drugs.

The role of the avid consumer of violence is illustrated by the "O.J. feeding frenzy," sensational television and movie portrayals inculcating sadomasochism, and in the readiness to join cults combining compliance with the group, dependence on a leader, devaluation of the outsider, avoidance of dissent, and consequent readiness to harm. Psychosocial methods for cultivating violent proclivities are analyzed and illustrated in terms of propaganda, public relations, and advertising methods, all of which rely on and cultivate passive cognitive style when trying to sell to violence addicted customers.

Suggestions for reversing the violence megatrend include improving parenting and our educational systems, teaching critical thinking, and filling the spiritual void with dedication to the sacredness of one's own and others' lives. Illustrations depicting the nature of these needs and how to meet them are given.

I predict greater public awareness of our shared denial and responsibility with increasing grass roots, spiritual, and governmental efforts to reverse the neglect and violencing of our society, with particular attention to nurturing and protecting our youth. I see many current efforts that are promising and foresee that people will feel truly empowered by the active development of emotional nurturance and the rejection of violence sensationalism. I think that most people are fed up with violence and ready to acknowledge what is now deeply wrong with our society. I believe that our anger about the present situation can be turned to excellent advantage in the assertive deconstruction of our violence culture and in the active pursuit of meaningful societal and personal values.

Annotated Bibliography

Blankenhorn, D. (1995). *Fatherless America: Confronting Our Most Urgent Social Problem*. New York: Basic Books. Focusing on a crucial aspect of the psychosocial basis of the dissolution of the family and the accompanying youth violence megatrend, Blankenhorn posits a powerful argument. He integrates theory and considerable research evidence to show how the continuing demise of real fatherhood, as distinct from procreation, leaves boys especially with a great void in their identities, a void filled by a false "hypermasculinity" defining masculinity largely as abilities to dominate and destroy.

Gerzon, M. (1992). *A Choice of Heroes: The Changing Faces of American Manhood.* Boston: Houghton Mifflin Co. Gerzon provides an insightful perspective on the quick-to-violence hero images that have most influenced young men over the last few decades. He combines his own investigative travels with recent cultural history to explain how our youth adopt and are constricted by ill-fitting stereotypes. The frontiersman, soldier, and even the expert and the breadwinner are too often obsolete, so the author suggests new kinds of masculinity.

Whitaker, L. C., & Pollard, J. W. (Eds.). (1993). *Campus Violence: Kinds, Causes, and Cures.* New York: The Haworth Press. College students, who represent the future leadership of our society, have increasingly perpetrated and been victims of violence, phenomena that colleges and universities have tended to downplay. This volume frankly addresses the kinds and causes in terms of the surrounding culture, alcohol and other drugs, race relations, lesbian and gay students, and male role models. It gives special attention to actual lethal violence events on campuses and what to do to alleviate and prevent them.

References

Ashe, A., & Rampersad, A. (1993). *Days of grace: A memoir.* New York: Knopf.

Asimov, I. (1981). *Isaac Asimov's book of facts.* New York: Bell Publishing Co.

Baughman, Jr., F. A. (1993, May 12). Treatment of attention-deficit hyperactivity disorder. *Journal of the American Medical Association, 269*: 2368.

Blankenhorn, D. (1995). *Fatherless America: Confronting our most urgent social problem.* New York: Basic Books.

Bradsher, K. (1995, April 17). Gap in wealth in U.S. called widest in west. *New York Times*, pp. A1, D4.

Breggin, P. R., & Breggin, G. R. (1994). *The war against children.* New York: St. Martins Press.

Breggin, P. R. (1995, April 13). Personal communication.

Bundy says porn fueled violent fantasies. (1989, January 25). *Philadelphia Inquirer*, p. 4A.

Butterfield, F. (1994, October 14). Teen-age homicide rate has soared. *New York Times*, p. A22.

Butterfield, F. (1995a, March 10). Justice department awarding grants to develop gun detectors. *New York Times*, p. A22.

Butterfield, F. (1995b, April 12). New prisons cast shadow over higher education. *New York Times*, p. A21.

Centers for Disease Control (1992, October 16). Behaviors related to unintentional and intentional injuries among high school students — United States, 1991. *MMWR 41*(41), 760-772.

Conn, C., & Silverman, I. (Eds.). (1991). *What counts: The complete Harper's index.* New York: Henry Holt & Co.

Copeland, L. (1995, March 10). Caning criminals? It gains advocates. *Philadelphia Inquirer*, pp. A1, A20.

Cousy, R. (1975). *The killer instinct*. New York: Random House.

Daniell, R. (1984). *Sleeping with soldiers*. New York: Holt, Rinehart, and Winston.

Dao, J. (1995, March 8). Death penalty in New York restored after 18 years; Pataki sees justice served. *New York Times*, pp. A1, B5.

Deikman, A. J. (1990). *The wrong way home*. Boston: Beacon Press.

Dunlap, D. W. (1995, March 8). June '94 produced a record for antigay attacks. *New York Times*, p. B2.

Eckholm, E. (1995, February 24). Studies find death penalty tied to race of the victims. *New York Times*, pp. B1, B4.

Freud, S. (1930/1989). From Civilization and its discontents. In P. Gay (Ed.), *The Freud reader*, p. 772.

Fromm, E. (1969). *Escape from freedom*. New York: Avon Books. (Original work published 1941).

Gerzon, M. (1992). *A choice of heroes: The changing faces of American manhood*. Boston: Houghton Mifflin Co.

Holden, S. (1995, March 17). Mutilating, murderous lesbians, with a light side. *New York Times*, p. C8.

Hollman, L. & McCoy, C. (1992, August 2). The growing urban arsenal: Are rising handgun sales only a reflection of the problem, or a cause too? *The Philadelphia Inquirer*, pp. E1, E4.

Holmes, S. A. (1995, October 28). Ranks of inmates reach one million in a 2-decade rise. *New York Times*, pp. A1, A25.

Howe, M. (1992, June 17). M.T.A. panel approves cut in cigarette advertisements. *New York Times Metro*, p. B3.

Humes, J. C. (1994). *The wit and wisdom of Winston Churchill*. New York: Harper Perennial.

Kaplan, J. (Gen. Ed.). (1992). Adolph Hitler. In *Familiar quotations*, 16th edition, John Bartlett, p. 676. Boston: Little, Brown and Company.

Killer women on TV (1992, October 12). *New York Times*, p. C20.

Killings said to rise after gun laws are relaxed (March 15, 1995). *New York Times*, p. A23.

Kristof, N. D. (1995, April 4). With cult under cloud, its still his guiding star. *New York Times*, p. A4.

Kuralt, C. (1985). *On the road with Charles Kuralt*. New York: Ballantine Books.

Landers, A. (1986, May 22). Letter from the bear facts in Bayside. *Philadelphia Inquirer*.

Larson, E. (1993). The story of a gun. *The Atlantic Monthly, 271*, 48-78.

Leary, W. E. (1995, April 21). Young people who try suicide may be succeeding more often. *New York Times*, p. A15.

Lore, R. K., & Schultz, L. A. (1993). Control of human aggression. *American Psychologist, 48*, 1, 16-25.

Lyon, B. (1986, May 22). The selling of Mike Tyson. *Philadelphia Inquirer*, pp. 1D, 4D.

Mailer, N. (1984). *Tough guys don't dance.* New York: Random House.

Maruyama, M. (1963). The second cybernetics: Deviation-amplifying mutual causal processes. *American Scientist, 51,* 164-179.

Merchandising murder (1995, March 31). "Arts and entertainment" channel of cable television. (Philadelphia area channel 29, 9-10 p.m. EST)

Michener, J. (1992). *The world is my home: A memoir.* New York: Random House.

Miedzian, M. (1991). *Boys will be boys: Breaking the link between masculinity and violence.* New York: Doubleday.

Moran, R. (1995, February 24). Hate crimes increasing in Pa. *New York Times,* p. B2.

Moss, D. (1995, March 3). Md. snuffs out smoking in nearly every workplace. *USA Today,* p. 3A.

Newman, M. (1995, March 10). Weapons at school: Box cutters escape detection. *New York Times,* pp. A1, B4.

Rickey, C. (1995, April 2). Once an adult movie, now a hoot. *Philadelphia Inquirer,* pp. 5, 14.

Ritz Film Bill (1995, March/April). John Sayles changes course. Philadelphia: Entropy Design, pp. 15-17.

Rivinus, T. M., & Larimer, M. E. (1993). Violence, alcohol, other drugs, and the college student (Chapter 4, pp.71-119). In L. C. Whitaker & J. W. Pollard (Eds.), *Campus violence: Kinds, causes, and cures.* New York: The Haworth Press. Published simultaneously in *Journal of College Student Psychotherapy, 8,* 1/2, 3, 1993.

Sally Jesse Raphael (1995, March 3). National Broadcasting Company (Philadelphia area Channel 2, 10 a.m.)

Schneider, K. (1995, March 13). Hate groups use tools of the electronic trade. *New York Times,* p. A12.

Schut, E. (1995, March/April). Faster, Pussycat! Kill! Kill! *Ritz Film Bill,* p. 30. Philadelphia: Entropy Design.

Schwartz, A. J. (1990). The epidemiology of suicide among students at colleges and universities in the United States (Chapter 2, pp. 25-44). In L. Whitaker & R. Slimak (Eds.), *College student suicide.* New York: The Haworth Press. Published simultaneously in *Journal of College Student Psychotherapy, 4,* 3/4, 1990.

Schwartz, A. J. & Whitaker, L. C. (1990). Suicide among college students: Assessment, treatment, and intervention (Chapter 12, pp. 303-340). In S. Blumenthal & D. Kupfer (Eds.), *Suicide across the life cycle: Risk factors, assessment, and treatment of suicidal patients.* Washington, DC: American Psychiatric Press.

Selling to school kids. (1995, May). *Consumer Reports,* pp. 327-329.

Seventy-six in law enforcement slain in '94 F.B.I. says. (1995, April 3). *New York Times,* p. A14.

Shapiro, D. (1965). *Neurotic styles.* New York: Basic Books, Inc.

Solzhenitsyn, A. I. (1978, June 8). *Solzhenitsyn on Western decline* (Harvard University commencement address).

Spindler, A. M. (1995, March 16). In Paris, clothes that look tough, masculine and dangerous. *New York Times,* p. C13.

Teltsch, K. (1992, August 18). Keeping teenagers smokeless. *New York Times*, Metro Section, pp. B1, B4.

Thompson, A. (1988, May 1). Action! The films that win audiences. *Philadelphia Inquirer*, p. 1F.

Verhovek, S. H. (March 6, 1995). States seek to let citizens carry concealed weapons. *New York Times*, p. A1.

Whitaker, L. C. (1980). *Objective measurement of schizophrenic thinking: A practical and theoretical guide to the Whitaker Index of Schizophrenic Thinking*. Los Angeles: Western Psychological Services.

Whitaker, L. C. (1987). Macho and morbidity: The emotional need vs. fear dilemma in men. *Journal of College Student Psychotherapy, 1*, 4, 33-47.

Whitaker, L. C. (1990). Myths and heroes: Visions of the future. *Journal of College Student Psychotherapy, 4*, 2, 13-33.

Whitaker, L. C. (1992). *Schizophrenic disorders: Sense and nonsense in conceptualization, assessment, and treatment*. New York: Plenum Press.

Whitaker, L. C. (1993a). Violence is golden: Commercially motivated training in impulsive cognitive style and mindless violence. *Journal of College Student Psychotherapy, 8*, 1/2, 45-69. Published simultaneously in L. C. Whitaker and J. W. Pollard (Eds.), *Campus violence: Kinds, causes, and cures*. New York: The Haworth Press.

Whitaker, L. C., & Pollard, J. W. (Eds.). (1993b). *Campus violence: Kinds, causes, and cures*. New York: The Haworth Press. Published simultaneously in *Journal of College Student Psychotherapy, 8*, 1/2, 3.

About the Author

Leighton C. Whitaker, PhD, ABPP, is in private practice and teaches at the Widener University Institute for Graduate Clinical Psychology, where he is Adjunct Clinical Professor. Dr. Whitaker is Editor of the *Journal of College Student Psychotherapy* and Consulting Editor for Mental Health of the *Journal of American College Health*. He has authored, 65 articles, book chapters, and books, including the *Whitaker Index of Schizophrenic Thinking* (Western Psychological Services, 1980) and *Schizophrenic Disorders* (Plenum Press, 1992).

His previous positions include Associate Professor and Director of Adult Psychology for the University of Colorado Health Sciences Center, Professor and Director of the University of Massachusetts Mental Health Services, and Director of Swarthmore College Psychological Services. He has done forensic work for many years and has been consultant to the U.S. Department of Labor's Job Corps Programs. His work with youth has been featured on local and national television and in newspapers.

Acknowledgments

The author thanks The Haworth Press of New York, London, and Norwood (Australia) for permission to excerpt portions of three articles he authored for the *Journal of College Student Psychotherapy*, all listed in the References, as follows: Macho and Morbidity: The Emotional Need vs. Fear Dilemma in Men; Myths and Heroes: Visions of the Future; and Violence is Golden: Commercially Motivated Training in Impulsive Cognitive Style and Mindless Violence.

CHAPTER 6

VICTIM-PRECIPITATED HOMICIDE

William E. Foote

Introduction

As behavioral scientists have evaluated the phenomenon of homicide, their primary emphasis has been upon the perpetrators who commit the acts (Cornell, 1993; Daly & Wilson, 1988; Daniel & Robins, 1985; Goetting, 1989a; Lester, 1977; Mann, 1992; O'Brien, 1987; Poussaint, 1983) and upon the social and economic factors that may predicate the killing of one person by another (Brooks & Harford, 1992; Hsieh & Pugh, 1993; Smith, Devine, & Sheley, 1992; Ullah, 1988). This emphasis has largely ignored the other actor in the homicide drama—the victim. This chapter examines factors that contribute to homicidal victimization generally, with specific emphasis on those victims who somehow initiate or contribute to the sequence of events that result in their deaths.

Hans von Hentig (1940) was the first to observe "that the behavior of culprit and injured are often closely interlocking..." (p. 303). In his analysis of victim-perpetrator interactions, he conceded that a large proportion of victims fall prey to criminals through no fault of their own. However, others, particularly victims of "bunco games" (swindles built around gaining the confidence of victims), enter into the victim role with some intention of gaining something for themselves. While they may not intend the final result

(e.g., losing money), they nevertheless voluntarily involve themselves with the offender. With homicides, von Hentig saw different sorts of people entering into the homicidal dyad, all of whom somehow made themselves more vulnerable to homicidal victimization. His distinctions will be discussed later in this chapter.

Von Hentig worked as a criminologist in the 1930s and 1940s, a time when experimental methodology, especially in large scale epidemiological research, was not well-developed. In spite of that, his observations of human relationships bear reevaluation at the end of this century. His work not only helped define the sub-discipline of victimology, but also may have been accurate in analyzing the people who initiate their own demises.

Nearly two decades later, Wolfgang (1958) built on von Hentig's observations in his seminal study of 588 homicides that occurred in Philadelphia between 1948 and 1952. Wolfgang coined the term "Victim-Precipitated Homicide" (VPH) to describe a specific group of cases. This term is applied

to those criminal homicides in which the victim is a direct, positive precipitator in the crime. The role of the victim is characterized by his having been the first in the homicide drama to use physical force directed against his subsequent slayer. The victim-precipitated cases are those in which the victim was the first to show the use of a deadly weapon, strike a blow in an altercation - in short, the first to commence the interplay and resort to physical violence (Wolfgang, p. 252).

Wolfgang (1958) expanded and illustrated this definition in a series of examples. These included a case in which an intended robbery victim "initiated, frightened or alarmed the felon by physical force so that the robber, either by accident or compulsion, killed the victim" (Wolfgang, p. 252). His other examples included instances of an abused wife killing an attacking husband, which could have been classified as a case of self-defense, and other less equivocal instances in which the offender killed the victim in a direct attempt to prevent serious injury or death to herself or himself. Wolfgang also cited cases in which the victim dared the offender, or cases of an argument in which the victim initiated blows. To expand the scope of time in which victim precipitation may occur, Wolfgang discussed instances in which one person quarreled with or beat upon another person. The one who was beaten then returned to kill the ultimate homicide victim. Wolfgang's research also evaluated a host of demographic, personal, and situational variables that provided parameters for the VPH phenomenon.

Overview of the Literature

Wolfgang's research evaluated 588 cases of homicide that occurred in Philadelphia between 1948 and 1952. From this sample, he delineated a group of 150 cases he defined as VPH. These were compared to 438 Non-Victim-Precipitated Homicides (NVPH). In all, he determined that 26% of the homicides in his sample were victim-precipitated. Since 1958, these variables have been evaluated in research focusing on homicide generally, and in a small number of studies designed to specifically replicate most or part of Wolfgang's original research.

For example, Voss and Hepburn (1968) repli-cated Wolfgang's (1958) research with a sample of homicides in Chicago in 1965. Using Wolfgang's definition, they found that 28% of the 429 homicides were VPH. Similarly, Curtis (1974) examined reported crimes from across the country for the year 1967. Curtis found that, of the cases for which there was sufficient information to determine who initiated the violence, 39% were VPH.

Goetting (1989b) reviewed cases involving individuals accused of marital homicide in Detroit in 1982. Goetting found that 60% of these killings met the criteria for victim precipitation. Mann (1989) also examined a sample of homicides perpetrated by women in six large cities across the U.S. This research determined that a substantial 83% of homicides committed by these women in domestic situations were VPH, compared to 49% of those occurring in non-domestic contexts.

As this subsequent research suggests, the proportion of VPH in a given sample may vary depending upon the specific situational or demographic context. However, as will be evident in the balance of this chapter, Wolfgang's (1958) original findings are robust and valid, even when examined in light of research done in the last 50 years. His research examined VPH on the basis of the race of the victim, the age of both offender and victim, the gender of both victim and offender, the domestic context, the impact of alcohol, the method of homicide, and individual psychopathological and historical variables. This section of the chapter will examine the impact of those demographic and personal variables upon homicidal deaths generally, with specific emphasis on VPH research.

Race and ethnicity

The race of both the homicide offender and victim has been the focus of considerable research. Research has demonstrated that Blacks, especially Black males, are overrepresented as victims of violent death (Holinger, Luke, Montes, Perez, & Sandlow, 1987). These researchers evaluated violent death rates in the U.S. from 1900 through 1980. Overall, the rates of violent death for non-Whites have been consistently higher than those for Whites. Non-White males had the highest violent death rates, followed by White males, non-White females, and White females. These rates include deaths caused by suicide, homicide, and accident. Of these, motor vehicle accidents accounted for the largest number of deaths, followed by other accidents, suicide, and homicide. This research demonstrated, however, that for non-White males, homicide has recently risen to the second highest cause of death.

Pokorny (1965) reviewed homicide files from Houston for the years 1958 though 1961. His analysis of 425 victims included figures for "Latin Americans,"[1] as well as for non-Hispanic Whites, and Blacks. In line with the bulk of research on the topic, Blacks were again grossly overrepresented as victims of homicide. With figures expressed as a function of the number per 100,000 of that group in the overall population, Blacks had a rate of 32.26, compared to 12.07 for Latin Americans and 5.26 for "Other Whites."

In a similar study spanning the years 1958 through 1974, Rushforth, Ford, Kirsch, Rushforth, and Adelson (1977) reviewed homicides in the Cleveland area. They found that the rates for

homicides increased over that interval for all racial groups. Table 1 illustrates their findings. The rate for Blacks in the earliest interval, 1958-1962, was 15 times that of Whites, a ratio that remained generally constant over the intervals studied.

More recently, Kellermann et al. (1993) conducted a well-controlled study of homicide across a number of American communities. This study focused upon homicides in the home and found that Blacks, compared to their proportion of the population, were more likely to be homicide victims (62%)[2] than Whites (33%).

In addition, a recent examination of homicides in a single Alabama county between 1978 and 1989 (Fine et al., 1994) found that the homicide rate for Blacks (41.4 per 100,000) was more than five times that for Whites (7.1 per 100,000). This study found that homicidal violence is generally an intra-racial phenomenon, as demonstrated by other studies (Mann, 1989; Rogers, 1993). That is, Blacks are much more likely to kill Blacks (96% of their cases). Although Whites kill mostly Whites (77%), they commit a larger number (23%) of inter-racial killings (see O'Brien, 1987 for exploration of this issue).

Wolfgang's (1958) original research also indicated that, in general, Blacks were disproportionately represented as victims of homicide. In a city where only 18% of the population was Black, 73% of the homicide victims were Black. However, among VPH victims, Blacks constituted 79%

TABLE 1			
MALE HOMICIDE RATES (PER 100,000)			
	Years		
Race	**1958-1962**	**1963-1968**	**1969-1974**
Whites	2.6	5.1	10.5
Blacks	39.4	64.8	135.7
Note: This data is taken from Rushforth et al., 1977			

1. His group described as "Latin Americans" most likely included people we would describe today as "Latinos," "Hispanics," or "Chicanos."
2. For purposes of simplicity, percentages have been rounded off to the next higher or lower number.

of the VPH sample compared to 70% of the NVPH group. These findings were replicated by Bloch and Zemring (1973), although they encountered a startlingly larger proportion of younger (aged 15 to 24) Black victims.

In a direct replication of Wolfgang's study, Voss and Hepburn (1968) examined the files of the Homicide Division of the Chicago Police Department for one year—1965. From this data, information concerning 394 victims and 415 offenders was reviewed for a host of variables. As might be expected, the largest number of these victims (81%) were Black males. Of these cases, 118, or 37%, were classified as VPH.

The issue of race as a factor in VPH may be reevaluated in light of recent research which brings into question associations between racial group and homicide. In their large scale epidemiological research examining the role of mental illness in violence, Swanson, Holzer, Ganju, and Jono (1990) carefully assessed socioeconomic level along with race. They found that when socioeconomic status was controlled, race was not related to the commission of violent acts. Given the intra-racial nature of homicide, we might expect that the impact of race on homicide victimization may be more related to the victim's socioeconomic status. That is, a large proportion of Black people are poor, so it is poverty that contributes to the high rate of homicide victimization in this group, not the victim's racial identity, per se.

Support for that hypothesis was provided by Hsieh and Pugh (1993), who found a moderate, but positive correlation (.58) between poverty and homicide rates. The relationship between poverty and violence is also supported by Braucht, Loya, and Jamieson (1980), who reviewed a number of studies which located a high proportion of urban homicides within a relatively small part of a city. In almost every case, this part of town was the poorest, with low quality housing and few economic opportunities.

However, socioeconomic level may not account for cultural differences between Blacks and other racial groups. For example, Poussaint (1983) observed that Black males have a very low suicide rate as compared to White males. He posited that Black-on-Black homicide may be a substitute for suicide among Black males. The experience of low self-esteem and high degrees of self-hatred lead young Black males to engage in high risk lifestyles which place them at higher risk for homicidal perpetration and victimization. Support for this hypothesis is gained indirectly from a recent study of post-traumatic stress disorder (PTSD) among a large sample of urban dwellers (Breslau, Davis, & Andreski, 1995). They found that experiences which may lead to emotional distress are more often part of childhood for poor Blacks than for Whites. Among poor, ill-educated Blacks, the incidence of exposure to early misconduct (which may have found sanction within their neighborhood) and family members with mental illness was much higher than exposure to those experiences for Whites.

Poussaint's (1983) thinking may help us understand one aspect of VPH. If it is assumed that some VPH victims intend to die in the homicidal interaction, then the notion of substituting homicide for suicide becomes quite viable. Initiating an attack that has a high probability of resulting in one's own death may be for some a way of accomplishing self-destruction while maintaining respect in the eyes of their peers and family. If it is also assumed that some portion of VPH victims are more prone to depressive illness because of an inherited predisposition for mental illness (Breslau, Davis, & Andreski, 1995), then the intentionally self-destructive attack on another may be an expression of risk factors normally associated with suicide (Moscicki, 1995). A later section of the chapter will discuss this hypothesis in more detail.

Age

The chances of being killed in a homicide are greater for younger people than for older ones (Holinger, 1979, 1980; Kellerman et al., 1993; Tardiff, 1985). For example, Fine et al. (1994) found that for all racial groups, individuals between the ages of 25 and 34 had the highest death rate, with the second highest falling in the 35 to 44 age range, and the third highest among those between the ages of 15 and 24. These findings are similar to those of a Canadian study (Maxim & Keane, 1992), in which the homicide rate peaked at age 30 for the mostly White sample. A similar age-related pattern was seen in homicide offenders (Rizzo, 1982).

Both Wolfgang (1958) and Voss and Hepburn (1968) found a similar pattern in their overall data. The largest age group of victims was between the ages of 25 and 29, and the next largest in the next older (30 to 34) category.

However, VPH victims appear to be older than the NVPH victims. Wolfgang (1958) found that the highest proportion of VPH victims fell between the ages of 30 and 34, and the next largest group in the 35 to 39 category. In Wolfgang's study, the impact of age on homicide rate differences between VPH and NVPH was not large enough to be statistically significant. Voss and Hepburn's (1968) findings were similar, but were statistically significant.

The bulk of research indicates that young adults are the most frequent victims (and perpetrators) of homicide. This may be related to the overall high violence rate of younger people (see Dietz, 1987; Felson, Ribner, & Siegel, 1984), and the fact that young people spend most of their time in contact with other young people (Massey & McKean, 1985). The finding that the VPH appears to be more of a phenomenon among older people may be related to differences in gender among VPH perpetrators and the incidence of VPH in domestic contexts.

Gender

Most homicides occur between male offenders and male victims. A recent review of 34 studies from the United States and a host of other countries (Daly & Wilson, 1988) found that the proportion of male-on-male versus female-on-female homicide was a consistent ratio of 9:1 or 10:1. If it is the case that men kill mostly men, it is also the case that women kill mostly men.

For example, Pokorny (1965) noted that across all races, in male-perpetrated homicides, 80% of the victims were male. Likewise in female-perpetrated killings, 84% of their victims were male. In addition, because men account for such a large proportion of homicide perpetrators (see Braucht et al., 1980; Daly & Wilson, 1988), the largest number of female victims are killed by men. For example, in the Pokorny (1960) study, of the 82 women killed, 80% were killed by men and only 20% by women.

In a somewhat smaller study reviewing 145 cases taken from the homicide records for six U.S. cities, Mann (1989) compared instances in which women killed in a domestic context to those in which women killed in a non-domestic interaction. Males were almost exclusive victims in domestic contexts (96.6%), compared to only 65.5% in non-domestic contexts.

Similarly, in a large-scale study involving all homicides committed in the U.S. in 1980, Wilbanks (1983) examined 21,002 cases. Of all the cases, males killed males in 63%, males killed females in 20%, females killed males in 12%, and 5% of the total deaths resulted from females killing females. For both male and female offenders, arguments (which may be a VPH context) accounted for a substantial proportion of cases. For male offenders, 60% of cases occurred during some sort of brawl or argument. For female offenders, 71% of the homicides were tied to interpersonal conflict. Because men predominate as both offenders and victims of homicide, one might expect men to be more frequent VPH victims than women. This expectation was borne out in Wolfgang's (1958) sample, where 95% of VPH victims were male. Later, Voss and Hepburn (1968) found that of their VPH victims, 89% were male.

In another study of domestic homicides, Goetting (1989b) reviewed the cases of 84 individuals (28 male and 56 female) arrested for homicide in Detroit in 1982 and 1983. In this unusual sample, in which females predominated as offenders, almost 90% of both victims and offenders were Black. Two-thirds of the offenders in Goetting's sample were females, and one-third of the victims were women. Of the cases for which she had sufficient data, Goetting found that 60% were victim-precipitated. A much higher proportion (71%) of the homicides that women committed were VPH, as compared to only 10% of those perpetrated by males.

In a review of data gathered from a clinical population, Langevin, Paitich, Handy, and Russon (1982) assessed the circumstances of 106 cases. Although this study did not examine victim precipitation, per se, the researchers did gather data concerning the acts of the victims. Most of their sample was male (71%) and the largest group of victims (35%) was either spouses or paramours of the perpetrators. In this context, the offenders reported that prior to the killing, 32% of the victims tormented the offender and 41% directly threatened the offender.

In summary, across a broad range of research, men are the most common victims of homicides committed by both men and women. That situation is exaggerated in the VPH cases, where women are more likely to be offenders and men are still more likely to be victims.

Domestic Context

As discussed above, men are most likely to kill and when they kill, they most often kill other men. Women are much less likely to kill, but when they kill, they also most often kill men. However, when family members kill each other, the proportions change. For example, Pokorny (1965) found that of the 100 homicides that occurred between husbands and wives (including Black, White, and Hispanic subjects), the percentages of wives killed by husbands (53%) and husbands killed by wives (47%) were about equal. Similarly, in a sample of Black couples, Plass (1993) found that the rate (per 100,000) of husbands killing wives was 6.28 while that of wives killing husbands was 6.08. This finding is not uniform, however, as recent research involving a review of data from all racial groups determined that, of cases involving intimate partners, 61% of the victims were women and only 39% were men (Browne & Williams, 1993).

Wolfgang (1958) compared victim-precipitated to non-victim-precipitated contexts. He found that in the VPH group, 86% of the cases involved the killing of a spouse. The NVPH group had only 65% spouse victims. Of the spouses killed in VPH cases, 85% were husbands killed by wives and only 15% were wives killed by husbands. In contrast, the NVPH group consisted mostly (72%) of wives who were killed by their husbands. Voss and Hepburn (1968) did not discriminate between husbands and wives, but found that 42.1% of the VPH homicides were of a member of the family or a friend.

In her review of 145 cases of female-perpetrated homicide, Mann (1989) compared domestic to non-domestic contexts. Her research indicated that 84% of the domestic killings could be considered VPH, while only 49% of non-domestic homicides were VPH.

In exploring why the domestic context produces such a high percentage of victim-precipitated homicides by women, it must first be noted that domestic homicide is the most severe form of domestic violence. Generally, the research indicates that the overall rates of violent acts occurring between marital partners are approximately equal (Bachman & Pillemer, 1992). Also, in many cases the more severe violence is initiated by the woman (Stets & Straus, 1990).

However, a fight between a man and a woman is usually not fair because men are generally bigger and more familiar with fighting. According to one study, women are two to three times more likely to suffer from serious injury in domestic disputes than are men (Brush, 1993). This higher risk of injury for women makes self-defense by women an adaptive and perhaps life-saving strategy. In a domestic conflict in which the male strikes the first blow, the woman may be forced to defend herself by killing the male. For that reason, it is not surprising that many domestic homicides committed by women are judged to be VPH. Goetting (1989b) found that 81% of domestic homicides committed by wives were VPH, while only 10% of those committed by husbands fell into this category.

However, it is not just self-defense that gives rise to these domestic killings. Spousal quarrels account for a somewhat higher proportion of VPH than NVPH. Wolfgang (1958) found that 20% of the VPH cases occurred in domestic altercations, while only 12% of the NVPH cases were in the context of fights. Mann (1989) found that although 59% of the female perpetrators in her sample claimed self-defense as a motive, the data indicated that these women were actually "the victors in the domestic fight" (p. 22). As evidence, Mann noted four features of the perpetrators in her sample. First, a majority of her offenders were single and from Mann's perspective, "(at least theoretically) could have left their abuser..." (p. 23). Second, she found that 56% of the homicides studied involved premeditation by the offender. This challenges the notion that these women reacted in self-defense to an immediate threat. Third, nearly half (49%) of the female offenders in her sample had previous arrests. Of her overall sample, 38% had misdemeanor

arrests, and 29% had between 1 and 13 prior felony arrests. Fourth, 30% of the killers in Mann's sample had violent offense histories. In this group, half claimed self-defense. While most would recognize our obligation not to "blame the victim" (Pleck, Pleck, Grossman, & Bart, 1978), it is also critical to examine each player in the domestic drama without assumptions about who is the victim and who is the offender.

Impact of Alcohol

The relationship between alcohol ingestion and homicide has been well-established (Abel, 1986; 1987; Abel & Zeidenberg, 1985, 1986; Blount, Silverman, Sellers, & Seese, 1994; Budd, 1982; Combs-Orme, Taylor, Scott, & Holmes, 1983; Goodwin, 1973; John, 1977; Klatsky & Armstong, 1993; Lester, 1993; Pernanen, 1991; Tardiff, 1985; Welte & Abel, 1989). Goodwin (1973) found that as many as 75% of all homicide victims had alcohol in their systems at the time of death. In a study of psychiatric patients, Langevin et al. (1982) found that 20% of the homicide victims had been drinking at the time of the offense. However, in a recent review of the topic, Collins and Messerschmidt (1993) noted that although a substantial proportion (50%) of homicide offenders reported that they had been drinking at the time of the offense, only 13% thought the alcohol was causal and only 28% thought alcohol contributed to the offense.

Given the pervasiveness of alcohol as a concomitant to homicidal violence, it should be no surprise that it appears as a factor in victim-precipitated cases. In Wolfgang's (1958) VPH group, 78% of both victims and offenders were drinking at the time of the offense, while only 60% of the NVPH group showed similar levels of inebriation. If only victims are assessed for alcohol use, 69% of the VPH victims were drinking, while 47% of the NVPH group had alcohol in their systems at the time of death.

In a replication of Wolfgang's (1958) study, Voss and Hepburn (1968) indicated that 61% of their VPH sample included homicides in which alcohol was present in the situation as compared to only 52% of their NVPH group. Although the Mann (1987) study provided no cross-tabulation of alcohol use and victim-precipitation, she found that alcohol was used prior to death by 58% of the women's victims. Of these, 22% would have met the legal standard for intoxication during that interval. In cases of homicide between marital partners, Goetting (1989b) found that 93% of the victims had ingested alcohol prior to death. As noted above, this is the group that had a VPH rate of 60%, so that virtually all of the VPH victims would have been using alcohol.

Still, the apparent relationship between VPH and alcohol should be viewed with some caution. In the review cited above (Collins & Messerschmidt, 1993), the authors noted that the use of incarcerated offenders as subjects may be an unsound research practice because these offenders may not be representative of the general population in their alcohol use, or, for our purposes, in the frequency of their contact with those who use alcohol. Incarcerated offenders may also overstate the extent of both their own and the victim's alcohol intake as a means of diminishing their responsibility for the offense. Research may also fail to discriminate between different levels of alcohol intake and the relationship of the time of alcohol ingestion to the time of the offense.

As a partial control for some of these problems, Kellermann et al. (1993) enlisted households comparable to those in which homicides occurred. They found the incidence of alcohol consumption in these homes in which homicides occurred (73%) to be higher than that in which no killing occurred (55%). These researchers also found that homicide offenders were more likely to have used alcohol (63%) than were individuals in less violent homes (42%). Moreover, indications of more severe alcohol use were disproportionately evident in the homes where homicides occurred. Thus, it is not just the use of alcohol that contributes to an increased probability of homicidal victimization, but the presence of severe abuse that contributes to the danger.

In summary, the use of alcohol by both offenders and victims increases the probability that a homicide will occur. In cases of VPH, a higher proportion of victims had been drinking at the time of death. Why alcohol users are more vulnerable to homicidal victimization is a question that has been studied extensively (Collins, 1981; Pernanen, 1991). A number of variables have emerged.

First, victim-precipitation is defined by the initiation of violence by the ultimate victim. Thus, the propensity for violence by the victim is an important variable. Pernanen (1991) noted that, in combination with situational and individual factors, there is a complex relationship between how much alcohol a person has ingested and the chances that the person will engage in violent behavior. At low intoxication ranges, there is a lower rate of violence. However, as blood alcohol levels increase, the chances of violent behavior increase until the blood alcohol levels are very high, when the violence rate decreases (although Pernanen's data also indicated a high violence rate among those who had ingested a large amounts of alcohol, e.g., over nine bottles of beer).

Second, Pernanen (1991) noted that one of the reasons for a higher violence rate among people who drink is that drinking often takes place in locales in which violence is more likely to occur. It may be the case that violent people drink to be around other violent people, and not just for the chemical impact of the liquor. Thus, a potential VPH victim may actually make three separate decisions. First, the decision is to choose to go to the "Biker Bar." The second decision may be to drink to a state of violent intoxication. The third decision may coincide with actually starting the fight.

Finally, alcohol affects the victim's judgment (Blum, 1981). For example, a male victim is likely to misjudge the danger inherent in the potentially homicidal situation. Moreover, because of the alcohol, he is also likely to underestimate the impact of the alcohol upon his own functioning. It is when a weapon is involved that judgment becomes a much more important variable than when the potential violence is accomplished by fists (Kellermann et al., 1993).

Method of Homicide

Indeed, over the last 50 years, people who kill each other have been increasingly more likely to use firearms than other weapons. In Wolfgang's (1958) original sample, more victims died as a result of stab wounds than by gunshot injuries. However, later research by Pokorny (1965), Voss and Hepburn (1968), and Abel (1986) found higher rates of death by gunshot.

(1993) found 26% from stabbing, 50% from firearms, and the balance (24%) from a combination of blunt instrument, strangulation, burns, or other trauma. These researchers also found that the mere presence of a firearm in the home, especially a firearm that was unlocked or loaded, added to the probability of death.

In victim-precipitated cases, the picture changes somewhat. Table 2 depicts selected data from three large studies of both overall samples, comparing VPH and NVPH samples. As is evident from this data, more stabbings occurred in VPH cases than NVPH cases. The higher rate of stabbings in VPH cases may be related to the domestic context of VPH and the higher frequency of women perpetrators. Women are typically less familiar with firearms than men, so they may resort to using firearms less readily. As many of these homicides occur in the home, a knife may be a more accessible weapon (Goetting, 1989b).

Because the use of firearms in domestic homi-

TABLE 2
METHOD OF HOMICIDE AND HOMICIDE RATES

Method	General			Victim-Precipitated/ Non Victim-Precipitated			
	Wolfgang	Pokorny	Voss & Hepburn	Wolfgang		Voss & Hepburn	
				VPH	NVPH	VPH	NVPH
Stabbing	39	25	28	54	34	33	23
Shooting	33	64	50	26	35	57	46
Beating	21	6	15	17	23	8	18
Other	7	5	7	3	8	2	13

Note. The values represent percentages of total deaths in that group. Data taken from: Wolfgang(1958), pp. 256-257; Pokorny (1965), p. 481; Voss and Hepburn (1968), pp. 503-507.

In domestic homicides, the rates are not dissimilar to the overall picture. Goetting (1989b) found that the rates in domestic homicide were 32% by stabbing and 58% by shooting, with the remaining 10% unclassified. Kellermann et al.

cides is increasing (Kellermann et al., 1993), it may be expected that the incidence of death by gunshot in VPH samples will increase. As many VPH cases occur in the context of domestic violence, the use of a firearm may escalate the level of lethality of an argument. A firearm may also allow the less physically powerful, as women typically compare to their mates, to make it an even fight.

Individual Psychological Variables

If it is assumed that the VPH victim somehow initiates the chain of events leading to his or her demise, a possible fertile area for inquiry would be the psychiatric history of the victim. While the major studies of VPH have not inquired about psychiatric history, other research has examined the general topic.

Hillard, Zung, Ross, Holland, and Johnson (1985) followed 3,284 patients evaluated in a psychiatric emergency room between the years 1971 and 1979. Twenty-two of these patients died by homicide. Patients with affective disorders comprised more than half (12) of this small group. Substance abusers made up one-third (7) and three were schizophrenic.

In a similar study, Herjanic and Meyer (1976) reviewed the cases of 214 homicide victims and found that 15% of these victims had psychiatric histories. For about one-half of this group, alcoholism and drug addiction were the diagnoses. Sociopathy accounted for about one-fourth of the homicide victims. Fewer than one-tenth received an Axis I, or mental illness diagnosis.

In a very large scale study, Keehn, Goldberg, and Becke (1974) reviewed the cases of almost 10,000 men who served in World War II and had been treated for "psychoneurosis," compared to a similar number of normal controls. These men were followed over 24 years to determine death rates for both groups. Homicide death rates for the psychoneurosis group were 2.61 times those of the control group. While the psychoneurosis group was undifferentiated as to specific diagnosis, the researchers suggested that this homicide victim group may coincide with the 20% of psychoneurotic servicemen who had some sort of pre-service personality disorder.

In all, the evidence that mental illness contributes to susceptibility to homicide is not well-established in non-victim-precipitated cases. However, it appears that the victim's substance abuse or antisocial tendencies may enter into the homicide equation. In addition to diagnosis, these tendencies may also be expressed in direct antisocial behavior.

Prior Criminal History

Victims of homicide, as noted above, are more likely to abuse alcohol and to be involved in domestic violence. Given this pattern, one would expect that criminal behavior would also be more prevalent in this group. Several studies of domestic homicides demonstrated a history of prior antisocial or violent conduct by the victims. Mann (1989) found that when women killed their mates in the domestic homicides, a high proportion of those victims (77%) had a prior arrest record, compared to only 46% of people killed in non-domestic settings. Overall, victims of domestic homicides also had a higher proportion of a violent history (55%), compared to their non-domestic controls at 34%).

Kellermann et al. (1993) compared individuals who were killed in domestic homicides to those who survived in similar households. They found that about twice as many homicide victims (36%) had an arrest history as compared to the surviving controls (15%). In addition, in homes where homicides occurred, the chances that a family member had received injuries severe enough to require medical attention were about 10 times more likely than in non-homicidal households. In all, this research suggested that both criminal activity and severe violence may predicate a potentially homicidal encounter. In the Wolfgang (1958) study, fewer than one-half (47%) of the homicide victims had prior arrest histories. However, if these are divided along VPH and NVPH lines, 62% of VPH victims had been arrested, compared to only 42% of NVPH victims. Of the offenses committed by each group, the VPH contingent committed more (60%) violent offenses than the NVPH group (50%).

In summary, homes where people get killed are ones in which there is more violence. VPH victims are themselves more violent than the average homicide victim, and are more likely to have a history of criminal arrests and of violent offenses.

Preliminary Summary and Base Rates

Wolfgang (1958) observed that his sample of 150 VPH victims had some features which differentiated them from their NVPH counterparts. The research on VPH in the past 50 years has not been extensive, but work has been done with special populations, such as women offenders, or within special contexts, such as domestic homicides. The data generated from these studies echo Wolfgang's earlier observations.

Table 3 allows for a comparison of the data from the two large scale VPH studies, those of Wolfgang (1958) and Voss and Hepburn (1968). Wolfgang (1958) observed that his VPH cases had the following characteristics:

1. Negro[3] victims;
2. Negro offenders;
3. Male offenders;
4. Female offenders;
5. Stabbings;
6. Victim-offender relationships involving male victims of female offenders;
7. Mate slaying;
8. Husbands who are victims in mate slaying;
9. Alcohol in the homicide situation;
10. Alcohol in the victim;
11. Victims with a previous arrest record;
12. Victims with a previous record of assault (Wolfgang, 1958, pp. 264-265).

An examination of Table 3 reveals that, for those variables evaluated in both studies, Wolfgang's original conclusions were supported. VPH is more likely to be an intra-racial, inter-gender domestic killing in which both the offender and victim are likely to have been drinking. The VPH victim is more likely to show some significant signs of antisocial behavior in a higher arrest rate and a more significant history of violent behavior. The tendency of VPH victims to be older than NVPH victims was one finding that appeared to be a trend in Wolfgang's research, but did not meet statistical standards. However, this trend did prove statistically significant in Voss and Hepburn's research. The base rates outlined above help us to generally predict who will be VPH victims. If one is a Black male, and married (or in common-law relationship), his chances increase. If he has a drinking problem and a history of criminal activity, especially violent criminal activity, the chances are increased even more. If he keeps a gun around the house, he places himself in a dangerous situation indeed.

However, these base rates do not help us predict the individual case with much certainty because it is likely that VPH victims may be more different from each other than the above picture would suggest.

Need for New Definitions

In his defining work on victim-precipitation, von Hentig (1940) delineated four types of people who are more likely to be victims of homicide victims: *the depressive, the greedy for gain, the wanton*, and the *tormentor*. The *depressive* may be entering into the homicidal interaction as a means of suicide. The *greedy for gain* type may be a person who is engaged in theft, but enters into a risky situation in pursuit of that goal. Simi-

---

3. Given the use of terms for racial differences at the time that Wolfgang did his research, he used the term Negro for people we now call Black or African American. For the same reasons, he included people we would now describe as Latin American, Latino or Hispanic into his "White" group.

TABLE 3

COMPARISON OF RATES OF VICTIM-PRECIPITATED HOMICIDES (VPH) AND NON VICTIM-PRECIPITATED HOMICIDES (NVPH) ON DEMOGRAPHIC AND SITUATIONAL VARIABLES

		Wolfgang		Voss & Hepburn	
Variable		VPH	NVPH	VPH	NVPH
Victim Race:	Black	79	70	91	79
	White	21	30	9	21
Victim Gender:	Male	94	70	89	76
	Female	6	30	11	24
Offender Gender:	Male	71	79		
	Female	29	21		
Relationship of victim and offender:	Spouse	87	68		
	Non-Spouse	13	32		
Alcohol:	Present	74	60	61	52
	Absent	26	40	39	48
Victim arrest record:	Present	64	42		
	Absent	36	58		

Note: Data taken from Wolfgang (1958), pp. 256-257 and from Voss and Hepburn (1968), p. 507.

larly, von Hentig described the *wanton*[4] as usually a woman, who, overborne by lust, ignores signs that she is in personal peril. Although we cannot accept von Hentig's portrayal of women, this classification does recognize that people may, in pursuit of another, non-criminal goal, place themselves at risk. The tormentor is an abusive person who becomes the victim of homicide as a result of self-defense or retaliation by the victim for the tormentor's actions.

Unfortunately, Wolfgang (1958) and Voss and Hepburn (1968) did not attempt to distinguish between different classes or kinds of VPH. Rather, they used a simple distinction: the VPH victim is the first one to strike blows or use a weapon. The data reviewed above indicates that this distinction tells us very little about the individual VPH case. In fact, the sorts of cases reviewed are quite heterogeneous. Some are male-versus-male or bar fights. Many are domestic disputes in which the wife killed the husband. A smaller number are not well-defined at all, and leave open to speculation both the persons involved as offenders and victims and the situation in which the homicide occurred. The range of alternatives was suggested by Wolfgang himself as he indicated that VPH victims may be brought into the homicidal interaction by their own acts or by mere chance.

This heterogeneity of person and circum-

---

4. At the time von Hentig wrote this paper, women were often stigmatized for sexual behavior. Rape victims were often blamed for the offense and were questioned carefully about what they did to "entice" the offender to attack them. As subsequent research has indicated (see recent review by Koss, Goodman, Browne, Fitzgerald, Keita & Russo, 1994), the dress, physical attractiveness, and behavior of rape victims usually have little to do with the risk of rape.

stance provides a limited basis for further analysis. Without an understanding of the types of people brought into VPH, it is far more difficult to develop more effective research or focused treatment interventions.

An examination of the VPH literature yields at least three dimensions that could be used to distinguish among VPH victims: risk-taking, aggressiveness, and intentionality. Farley (1991) has developed the concept of risk-taking in the context of his research on the "Type-T Personality." He described the "Type T personality" as an individual who takes risks in benign, legal contexts and the "T-Negative personality" as one who seeks risks in antisocial ways. Unfortunately, the dimension of risk-taking would not be effective as a single explanatory principle for VPH because most VPH victims are relatively high on this factor. Thus, the continuum of risk-taking would allow little room for description or prediction.

Another possible dimension would be that of aggressiveness. This is a well-studied aspect of behavior and can be inferred from behavioral data (see Meloy, 1988). Again, however, most VPH victims demonstrate higher than average levels of aggressiveness, so that this concept does little to distinguish between individuals.

A third dimension of VPH is intentionality. This concept was first developed in research on suicide (Mayo, 1992) to allow professionals conducting psychological autopsies to determine whether the equivocal death was an accident or a suicide (by definition, an intentional death). In suicide, the victim wants to die. This distinction is related to suicide method (McIntosh, 1992), as a person who uses a gun for a suicide attempt is generally seen to use a more lethal or intentional method than one using an overdose of drugs.

While the most comprehensive model of VPH could use some combination of three (or more) factors including risk-taking, aggressiveness, and intentionality, the explication of such a complex typology would be beyond the scope of this chapter. However, the concept of intentionality does provide sufficient breadth for the development of a theoretical dimension of VPH that would serve heuristic purposes. This dimension allows for the differentiation of both persons and situations in which VPH occurs on the basis of the extent to which the potential victim actually desires to expose himself or herself to a potentially lethal situation. A visual representation of this continuum is shown in Figure 1.

Hetero-suicide[5] (HS)

At one end of the continuum is the individual who clearly wants to die, like the depressive in von Hentig's (1940) typology. This person, however, in contrast to the modal suicidal person (Motto, 1992; Moscicki, 1995), has chosen to die at the hand of another, rather than by his or her own hand. I will call this person the Hetero-Suicide (HS), one who commits suicide by causing another person to commit the act. This category includes people who enter into confrontations with opponents who are bigger, have more fighting experience, or are better armed than the potential VPH victim.

Within this category are those who seek death in a confrontation with police, labeled by law enforcement officers as "suicide by cop" (Geberth, 1993; Van Zandt, 1993). Those who become "suicide by cop" victims may engage in detailed planning for the confrontation with police which results in their death. These plans may include the deliberate killing of another person, perhaps a hostage, as a means of eliciting the self-killing shot from the police. Others appear to

---

5. The term hetero-suicide is an oxymoron. If the Latin elements are evaluated, "hetero" means "other or different," while "sui" means "of one's self" when applied to the root -cide, meaning to kill (Webster's Dictionary, 1991). However, the contradictions inherent in the term may capture the contradictory qualities of the behavioral phenomenon.

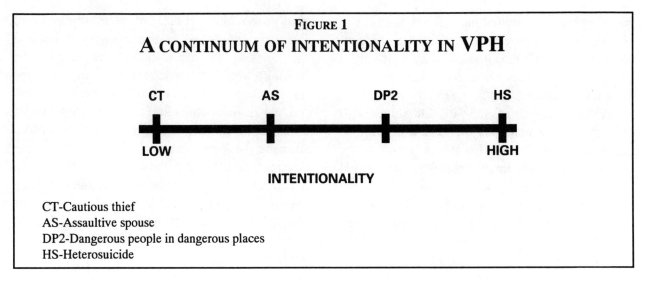

FIGURE 1

A CONTINUUM OF INTENTIONALITY IN VPH

CT   AS   DP2   HS

LOW   HIGH

INTENTIONALITY

CT-Cautious thief
AS-Assaultive spouse
DP2-Dangerous people in dangerous places
HS-Heterosuicide

be more impulsive and situation-specific. In these cases, the homicidal situation may evolve more suddenly after the police have entered the equation. The case of Paul Myrick[6] falls into this latter category.

Paul Myrick was a 46-year-old, White construction worker. He had a history of several psychiatric hospitalizations, heavy alcohol use, multiple drunk-driving arrests, and prior arrests for assaulting his common-law wife, Arlene. They had two young boys. One Sunday, they took the boys, along with Arlene's teenage daughter, Shana, to the nearby mountains on a fishing outing. While there, Paul drank about a six-pack of beer, but appeared normal to his family, because they usually saw him with about this much alcohol in his system. They drove home and by late afternoon, Paul and Arlene were in the midst of a full-blown argument about Shana. One of the boys, with a recognition that this parental argument, like earlier conflicts, could come to blows, called 911, summoning the police to the home. When he heard the sirens, Paul left the house and returned to the family van which was parked in front of their home. He retrieved his fishing knife from his fishing gear in the van. When the police arrived, he was standing in the front yard with the fishing knife in his hand. He was partially surrounded by the police, who repeatedly told him to drop the knife. He responded to this command by telling the police, "Kill me. I'd rather die than go to jail." One officer approached Paul, and when the officer was within six feet, Paul lunged at him with the knife. Although he was still about three feet from the officer at the time of this action, other officers responded with a volley of shots, killing Paul on the spot.

This is a case of "suicide by cop," but differs from the accounts provided by Van Zandt (1993) and Geberth (1993) because the whole episode was not intended by the victim to result in his death, as it was in most of their cases. In contrast, the case of Paul Myrick began as a common family pattern, but was interrupted by the arrival of police. While the confrontation with his killers may have been a product of chance, his actions once they arrived were not. He clearly expressed his intent to die. He initiated actions (lunging at the officer) which insured that he would be killed.

In this conceptualization, "suicide by cop" would be seen as a special case of the HS phenomenon. That is, when persons initiate situations

---

6. In this case example, as in the others in this chapter, the client's name and other specific features of the events in the case have been altered to protect the privacy of the client's family. Also, these cases are composites of several cases, combined to provide a coherent behavioral sequence.

in which the police kill them, it is probably not the only situation in which HS occurs. It is conceivable that other situations could be arranged that would have the same essential elements.

Research suggests that there may be an overlap of HS victims with murder/suicide cases. That is, people who "first commit homicide, and then inflict death upon themselves" (Wolfgang, 1958, p. 269). This group of offender/victims has been studied extensively (Allen, 1983; Berman, 1979; Buteau, Lesage, & Keily, 1993; Coid, 1983; Danto, 1978; Palmer & Humphrey, 1980; Rosenbaum, 1990) and a picture emerges of the typical case. These offender/victims are usually male and usually kill their spouse (women who kill their children constitute much of the balance of the cases). While a small proportion of the murder-suicides are planned (Berman, 1979), many of them appear to be impulsive, and arise out of a domestic conflict. A substantial number of the offenders/victims are mentally ill, with evidence of severe mental illness, such as a psychosis, or a personality disorder with a strong depressive and impulsive component, such as a Borderline Personality Disorder. As many of the "suicide by cop" cases involve a murder/suicide scenario, many of these may make up a portion of the HS group.

Definitions and risk factors for the HS case. The HS case is defined by several features. First, the victim shows a clear desire to die at the time of the confrontation with the potential killer. The HS victim may arrange the situation so that the killer has no choice but to kill the HS victim. For example, the HS victim may point a weapon at the police or threaten a family member while another person has a gun on the potential HS victim. Alternatively, the HS victim may directly express a desire to die to the potential killer, as in the Paul Myrick case.

Second, the HS victim may resort to committing a serious crime, including the killing of another to accomplish the hetero-suicide. Third, the HS victim may engage in considerable pre-meditation and planning prior to the homicidal incident.

As for risk factors, in accordance with the data from murder/suicide cases, it is my hypothesis that the HS victim would share at least some characteristics with people who simply kill themselves without having to bring anyone else into the scenario. The most recent discussion of these factors is provided by Moscicki (1995), who observed that among the main risk factors for adult suicides are: (a) the presence of psychopathology in the form of a mental disorder, usually some combination of mood disorder, like depression, with a personality disorder; (b) the presence of a substance abuse disorder; (c) a history of suicide or serious disruption in the victim's family; and (d) when a stressful event occurs in the context of a highly lethal method for death, like a firearm.

As a second group of risk factors, HSs are not typical suicides because another person is enlisted to assist in the death. Because of that feature, the HS victim should show signs of either grandiosity (feeling more powerful, smart, capable, etc. than others) or paranoia (assuming that others are out to get him or her). From either of these bases, the HS victim would see herself or himself as a "victim" and may set up the situation to prove it. The HS victim may express fantasies involving being killed by another person (Van Zandt, 1993).

In summary, the HS is a person who clearly wants to die and probably resembles other suicides in history, personality, mental disorder, and the situational factors that predicate the HS event. The HS victim may have premeditated the HS event, and if so, is more likely to have grandiose or paranoid personality features. If it is not premeditated, features of depression and impulsivity may predominate. Because of the similarity to murder/suicide cases, the HS victim may be more dangerous to others than the usual suicide case, and may not hesitate to kill another to accomplish his or her own death.

Dangerous People in Dangerous Places (DP2)

On the continuum of intentionality for VPH victims, the next in line would be the person who does not express any intent and may not have a clear intent to die. Rather, this person is entering into a situation in which some probability of injury or death is present. Usually, there is also a chance that the DP2 person will be able to injure or kill another person in the potential confrontation. While von Hentig (1940) did not suggest all of the aspects of this scenario, it is closest to the wanton type, in that both of these populations involve people who take risks. These cases include many victims of gang violence (Rogers, 1993), who recognize that as a result of usual gang activities, there will be a probability of killing and of being killed. Another group would be those who habitually spend time in contexts in which violence occurs (Massey and McKean, 1985). The case of Denton Rogers illustrates the DP2 pattern.

There weren't many Friday or Saturday nights when Denton Rogers wasn't down at his favorite bar, the Rusty Spur. He was a 30-year-old, short-haul truck driver. Along with his brother, Billy, Denton worked for his father, who owned the trucking company. Denton had a wife and several children, but did not seem to spend much time with them because of his work during the week and his partying over the weekends. He got home from work and showered, put on his Levis and cowboy shirt, donned his best hat and headed for the country-western bar that was his second home. Billy came along most of the time and they developed a group of friends which was usually in attendance at the rail of the Rusty Spur. At least once a weekend, someone had a little too much to drink and a fight broke out in the club. In fact, the Rusty Spur had been the scene of a number of homicides, and had a reputation among local police officers as a "rough joint." The owners, rather than discourage violent customers

from coming to the establishment, merely hired a crew of large, surly bouncers to keep the customers in line. Denton had been a participant in a number of these fights, and had come home with black eyes and a broken nose. Once, he had even been arrested for drunk and disorderly behavior.

The night of his death was not that different from his usual weekend routine. On this occasion, it was nearing closing time at the Rusty Spur and Denton had been drinking heavily all evening. He and Billy had argued throughout the evening. At one point, the bouncer had been called to separate them, but this intervention merely caused Denton and Billy to lower their voices and continue the argument. At closing time, they left the Rusty Spur, and as they neared their pickups in the parking lot, their argument intensified. Denton pulled out his pocket knife, and Billy drew his as well. A knife fight ensued. At the end of the fight, Denton lay face up in the parking lot with Billy's knife in his chest, and the tip of the blade in his heart. He later died as a result of this wound.

The DP2 pattern has as its essential elements a combination of people with a proclivity for violent behavior and places where violence occurs. I will not discuss the situational context of violence as a general issue, as another chapter of the book will discuss that in more detail. However, a number of researchers have observed that situational elements often have a profound effect upon the commission of violent acts (Gulotta, 1980; Luckenbill, 1977; Massey & McKean, 1985; Monahan & Klassen, 1982).

Other people make up part of this situational context. The degree to which those people are also violent may have a significant impact upon the probability that one person will attack another and the intensity of that violence once it occurs. Felson et al. (1984) found "that the aggressive actions of significant others indicate that violence is appropriate for the major antagonists" (p. 460). Observers may also serve as an audience that demands that the antagonists act more violently.

The presence of alcohol may also set the occasion for violence, as was evident in the review of the research on that topic. Collins and Messerschmidt (1993) contended that most people believe that drinking increases the likelihood of violence, and thus, people may behave in accordance with that expectancy. The researchers also suggested that the use of alcohol changes the rules of the potentially violent situation because individuals believe they will not be held to the same standard of accountability as sober persons.

Some places where alcohol is served may be places where violence is expected. In his Canadian sample, Pernanen (1991) observed that 22% of the severe assaults occurred in drinking establishments.

Definitions and risk factors for the DP2 case. The Dangerous Person Dangerous Place category is defined by two elements. First, the DP2 victim must show some history of violent behavior. This may be related to an arrest record for violent offenses, or may be evident in the statements of friends and family. Second, the DP2 victim has to be in a place that a reasonable person would describe as "dangerous." That is, the place must be one that is associated with a high homicide rate or one that is understood by the community as a place where violence occurs.

Hypothesized risk factors for the DP2 case center around the DP2 victim. First, the DP2 victim is likely to have a criminal history, most likely a history of violent offenses. Second, the DP2 victim is likely to have a history of episodic heavy drinking. The pattern is most likely to coincide with weekends, paydays, or holidays. Third, the DP2 victim is likely to be part of a social group in which violence is condoned or may be a prerequisite for membership. This expectation of violence from the social group may be formalized (as in some gangs) or may be a more casual norm in which violence is a frequent topic of conversation and in which the most violent individuals

have the highest status. Fourth, a component of the DP2 personality is a tendency to take risks. Farley (1991) examined the Type T personality and a variant of that personality, the T-Negative, individuals who are prone to involvement in high-risk criminal activity. DP2 cases may fit with the T-Negative pattern of seeking socially disapproved stimulation.

In summary, DP2 cases arise as a result of a mix of two volatile ingredients: violent people and places where violence occurs. The people are likely to have criminal histories which include violent offenses, and are likely to be heavy episodic drinkers. The places are likely to serve alcohol or are places where people drink. In those places, it is likely that there will be people who will condone or expect violence.

The Assaultive Spouse (AS)

Next on the continuum are people who are bound up in a violent relationship with a spouse or a common-law partner or are in a relationship with no formal structure. In these relationships, violence has become part of how both people in the dyad relate to each other. As suggested by von Hentig's Tormentor category, it may be a relationship of oppression of one partner by the other (see Koss et al., 1994, for this perspective) or may be a relationship in which both partners are violent (see Steinmetz, 1978 and Yllo & Straus, 1981). As noted above in the section on domestic context, many VPH cases occur between spouses. This group includes more female perpetrators than are usually found in homicides. Domestic contexts also include more victims with criminal histories than one might expect on the basis of large population studies.

In contrast to the other kinds of VPH on the intentionality continuum, it is my contention that the degree of intentionality for AS cases is lower than that of the other two groups. The AS victim may know that he or she is in a dangerous place (a home where domestic violence occurs), but the AS victim may prefer safer places. The domestic context of the AS case differs from the DP2 context because it is not always, or even usually, violent. It is one, however, where there is a finite risk over the long run of injury or death. The AS case differs as well because more is known about both the victim and the offender in domestic settings than in the other cases. The case of Charles Romero provides an example of the AS homicide.

No one would have called the marriage between Charles and Elaine Romero a happy one. Charles worked as a packer for a local computer firm, and Elaine worked at an elementary school as a teacher's aide. From the beginning of their relationship, and even while they were dating, friends and family observed Charles striking Elaine. After the marriage, the family saw Elaine appear at family gatherings with black eyes, bruises, and, on one occasion, a broken arm. Charles drank more than most other people in the family, and had a reputation among the extended family for becoming rowdy at weddings, christenings, and funerals. His drinking was an everyday activity, and the amount he drank stayed fairly constant over the course of their relationship. Charles had a habit of going out with his friends, and returning in the early morning hours. Elaine's sister told her that she had seen him with other women on several of his nights out. It was not unusual for Charles to beat Elaine the day after these outings. He would accuse her of being unfaithful to him, and would bring up instances when he believed she was either looking at other men in an inviting way or days when she could not account for her time with the kind of specificity he demanded. The battering started in the midst of these allegations, and typically did not end until Elaine was cowering on the floor in an attempt to protect herself, or Charles became exhausted from pulling her hair, punching her, kicking her, and throwing her into the walls of their small house. After the beating, he would

usually go to bed. The next day Charles was contrite, remorseful, and would shower Elaine with gifts and promises that it would never happen again.

On the day of the homicide, Charles had come home in the early hours, having stayed out from the night before. He continued to drink during the day, and his mood deteriorated as the day passed. He started his often repeated diatribe about Elaine's unfaithfulness, but this time he pulled his pistol out of his bedside stand and placed it in his belt. This was the first time he had ever had the weapon out in Elaine's presence and she became frightened. She got a steak knife from the kitchen and held it point down in her right hand. When he saw her with the weapon, Charles approached her, saying he was going to kill her this time. As he came within arm's length, Elaine stabbed him near his neck between the bones of his collar bone. He stumbled outside and died of his wound.

This case captures several critical aspects of the AS case. Usually, there is a long history of severe abuse that precedes the homicide. Also, Elaine, the offender in this case, had a reasonable belief that Charles might kill her because he had not only signalled the beginning of an abusive incident by his diatribe, but also had a gun. For any reasonable person, the presence of that weapon would have signalled that the chances of Elaine suffering serious injury or death seriously increased.

Definition and risk factors for the AS case. The Abusive Spouse case is defined by both historical and situational factors. First, there must be a history of more than one incident of battering by the AS victim upon the AS offender. Second, to distinguish the AS from the DP2 case, the AS victim is not usually involved in a high-risk lifestyle and does not usually place himself or herself at risk. Third, the AS victim does not perceive the actual homicidal context as a high-risk situation. The history of spousal violence by the

AS victim may give that person a sense of mastery and safety in the battering situation. Fourth, the AS case is most likely to occur at a time interval immediately before, during, or after an incident in which the AS victim battered the AS offender.

The risk factors for the AS victim follow the pattern recognized by researchers in the area of domestic violence. First, the AS victim is likely to be a man. As noted above, males perpetrate more severe violence than women and are more likely to injure partners in a battering incident. Second, the AS victim is likely to be Black. The research explored above includes a high number of Black men killed by Black women in domestic contexts. Third, AS victims would be expected to have characteristics commonly noted in abusive men. These include the following elements: (a) abusive men have a frequent history of either witnessing or experiencing abuse as a children (Waldo, 1987); (b) abusive men are more likely to be dependent and have low self-esteem (Murphy, Meyer, & O'Leary, 1994); (c) abusive men are likely to share significant characteristics with persons with Borderline Personality Disorder (Dutton, 1994), including an intolerance of being alone, intense anger, demandingness, and impulsivity; (d) the AS victim is likely to drink alcohol, but the role of alcohol in the circumstances of the offense and in the coincident battering is likely to be less important than in the other cases noted above; (e) the AS victim may have a criminal history, but it is likely to consist mostly of domestic violence convictions; and (f) the AS offender is more likely to have an arrest history, with about one chance in three of a violent offense in that history.

In summary, the AS victim is typically a Black male in a domestic relationship with a Black woman. While he does not usually lead a high-risk lifestyle, he does drink alcohol. A person of unstable moods, the AS victim tends to be dependent upon the partner and fears abandonment by the partner. The AS victim has battered

the partner (the offender) on at least one previous occasion. The killing of the AS victim usually occurs in proximity to a beating, often one in which the offender has reason to fear for his or her life.

The Cautious Thief (CT)

At the end of the intentionality continuum is the Cautious Thief (CT). The CT victim may not be a full-time professional felon, but may pursue theft as an alternative to a more demanding or less lucrative vocation, much as the *greedy for gain* type of von Hentig's (1940) typology. This person usually engages in theft in objectively safe situations. The CT victim may use a gun to intimidate the burglary victim, the elderly woman in the parking lot, or the store clerk. It is in this latter context that Albert Lopez met his demise.

Albert was a 26-year-old who didn't have much to do in the way of conventional work during most days. Playing video games, using drugs with his friends, or just hanging out in his car demanded most of his time. When money started running low, he burglarized a house and sold the stolen items to a "fence," or used his 9mm semi-automatic pistol to rob someone on the street or a convenience store. He had been arrested on a number of occasions for these offenses, and had spent five years in the state penitentiary for one of them.

On this occasion, he had a big weekend planned, and knew some ready cash would allow him to party longer and with a better quality of drugs and liquor. On Thursday night, he entered a convenience store at 2:25 a.m., when no customers were present. As was his usual practice, he pulled the 9mm out of his pants and stuck it in the clerk's face. The clerk, a veteran robbery victim, readily turned over the cash from the register. This seemed to satisfy Albert, and he turned to leave the store. However, the clerk opened a drawer next to the cash register, pulled out his own .45 caliber semiautomatic pistol, and shot Albert in the side, head, and back. Albert died at the scene.

This case illustrates several important aspects of the CT case. Albert, aside from the use of a weapon, did not behave in an aggressive or brutal way. The use of the weapon was instrumental in gaining his goal, robbing the store. Also, Albert did not anticipate that this was a dangerous situation. Previous similar robberies had occurred without incident, and he had no reason to believe this would be any more complicated.

Definition and risk factors for the CT. The Cautious Thief (CT) case has several defining characteristics. First, the CT victim is involved in the commission of another crime at the time of the CT incident. Second, the CT victim does not define the situation as one in which he or she will be hurt. Third, in most CT incidents, the CT victim's use of force is designed to accomplish some goal, but violence is not a goal in itself.

A number of risk factors may be associated with CT victimization. First, the CT victim is most likely to have an extensive history of theft crimes. These probably date back to the person's teen years. Second, in part because of this criminal history, the CT victim usually meets the criteria for an Antisocial Personality Disorder. Third, the CT victim may be a user of illicit drugs, such as heroin or crack cocaine. The high monetary demands of such habits may drive the theft activities. Fourth, the CT victim is unlikely to be using alcohol at the time of the CT incident, as the CT victim is, after all, at "work."

In summary, the CT victim usually dies in the commission of an offense in which he or she is carrying a weapon. Having some experience with this means of making a living, the CT victim has little expectation that the theft will be dangerous to him or her, but has little compunction about using the weapon, if the occasion demands it. The CT victim usually has a drug habit, a criminal history, and an antisocial personality disorder.

The incident in which the CT victim is killed usually comes as a fatal surprise.

Treatment Recommendations

Treating VPH victims is impossible, as VPH victims are usually defined posthumously. However, the concept of VPH and our accumulated knowledge on the topic does give mental health professionals an opportunity to treat potential victims, a group of people who normally do not receive psychological or psychiatric interventions. The most fruitful approach would be to make recommendation according to each category of VPH victim. As these groups differ significantly from each other, treatment recommendations are geared for each category of VPH victim.

The Hetero-Suicide (HS) may be approached as one would generally approach a suicidal patient (Litman, 1995). Interventions directed at relieving depression are critical. If substance abuse is present, achieving sobriety may lower the probability of HS. Although therapists treating suicidal clients are unaccustomed to addressing these components, focused interventions dealing with the grandiose or paranoid components of the picture may be helpful. As many of these components have psychotic features, it may be necessary for a physician to provide antipsychotic medications. Hospitalization may be necessary in the most severe cases, especially following a situational stressor, such as an interpersonal loss. As family members are likely victims if the HS picture includes a murder-suicide component, family therapy can help alert other family members to the developing danger. To the extent that the potential HS victim premeditates, it may be possible to intervene in the behavioral sequence leading up to the HS scenario.

The person with a potential to be a Dangerous Person in a Dangerous Place (DP2) has a number of features that would allow for intervention. First, the prominent alcohol problem may be treated through an array of alcohol treatment strategies (Flavin, Franklin, & Frances, 1990). Second, the potential DP2 victim can benefit from interventions to help deal with anger control (see Novaco, 1975). Third, potential DP2 victims may benefit from cognitive interventions directed toward defusing potentially dangerous situations, and avoiding those situational contexts likely to evoke maladaptive behavior (Marlatt, 1985).

More research has been done on the topic of treatment with victims of spousal violence than with the perpetrators (Geffner & Pagelow, 1990). Because the spouse abuse victim is the perpetrator in Abusive Spouse (AS) cases, treatment of the victim/offender would be well-advised. Interventions centered around anger management, as discussed above, may be appropriate, or therapy directed toward empowering the abused partner to leave may be most effective (Browne & Williams, 1989). More recently, attention has shifted to the treatment needs of AS (see Dutton, 1995). Interventions directed toward management of emotional shifts, depression, anxiety, and impaired self image have been critical. Recognition of the contribution of personality disorders to the behavior of AS has allowed for specific treatments directed to these disorders (Dutton, 1994). Dutton (1995) emphasized the importance of holding the AS responsible for his or her violence, as well as helping the client deal with needs for dependency and a sense of powerlessness. In general, making the AS less dangerous should have the impact of reducing the incidence of AS victim-precipitated homicide.

The Cautious Thief (CT) is probably the least treatable of all of these types. By definition, most CT cases involve antisocial personality disorders. Antisocial people are notoriously difficult to treat (Rosenbaum & Maiuro, 1990). In part, this difficulty arises because potential CT victims do not see anything wrong with their lifestyle, and may, in fact, find it quite satisfying. Correctional interventions focused upon developing alternative employment strategies may reduce these homicides. Cognitive interventions directed at developing more effective problem-solving capacities may also prove beneficial, but it is critical to engender motivation to change. As Prochaska, Di Clemente, and Norcross (1992) suggested, this is not a simple process.

Summary

Homicide is a drama played out by at least two actors. When we focus our attention on only one actor—the offender—we run the risk of failing to understand what the drama is about. This chapter examined Victim-Precipitated Homicide (VPH). VPH victims constitute the one-quarter to four-fifths of homicide victims who somehow set into motion the events that result in their own demise. Men make up the majority of VPH victims and a large portion of those men are Black. Although women are only rarely homicide offenders, women, especially Black women, are the offenders in almost a third of victim-precipitated cases. A high proportion of these crimes occur in the home and evolve from domestic conflicts. Women who kill their mates often do so as a means of self-defense, but some kill for retaliation or because they are angry and out of control.

Although researchers in the area have not attempted to define different types of VPH victims, this chapter contains a four-component model which evaluates VPH on the basis of the extent to which the VPH victim demonstrates the intent to die. One group, the Hetero-Suicide (HS), fully intends to die, but wants someone else to pull the trigger. The killer in HS cases may be a police officer, which would make the HS case a "suicide by cop." However, HS cases can involve family members, acquaintances, or strangers.

A less-intentional victim is the one who may be habitually violent and seeks out high-risk environments. The Dangerous Person in Dangerous Places (DP2) victim spends time in the company of other violent people in places where violence is a predictable and common occurrence.

The Abusive Spouse (AS) does not view the domestic conflict as a dangerous place for him or her. Rather, the AS may believe that the advantage of physical power is in the AS victim's hands. Although it is possible for the less powerful victim of domestic violence to resist or retaliate, that is not the expectation of the AS individual.

The Cautious Thief (CT) believes that the situation is almost completely under his or her control. When the CT begins a crime, because the CT has a weapon or is bigger and stronger than the potential theft victim, from an objective standpoint, the CT has little to fear. However, the circumstances may shift suddenly when the CT is killed by the victim or potential victim of the CT's own crime.

Recommendations for Future Research

The most comprehensive research on VPH was done at least a quarter century ago. Subsequent study has not focused on VPH alone, but on other variables, such as domestic homicide, with VPH as a sidebar. Over the last 50 years, the nature of homicide has changed. Firearms are a more prominent feature of homicidal death. A larger portion of the U.S. population is now Hispanic, which may alter our current assumptions concerning VPH as it relates to ethnicity and socioeconomic level. Drugs, especially crack cocaine and crystal methamphetamine, have increased the rate of homicides in some populations, especially poor Blacks. VPH research that comprehends these variables will be much more applicable to current clinical and public policy decision-making.

Similarly, the research methods used in most VPH research lack the sophistication of current epidemiological and psychopathological research. Researchers now view socioeconomic level as a variable that must be controlled in research involving race. Researchers now better recognize gay men and lesbian women as distinct research populations. Methodologies utilizing interview techniques have been developed to allow for the provision of specific diagnoses to research subjects, even in large scale studies. The epidemiologic catchment area studies (see Swanson et al., 1990) and the techniques of psychological autopsy (Hazelwood, Dietz, & Burgess, 1982), provide methods whereby the individual's history, family context and, perhaps psychological processes at the time of death may be assessed.

I hope that the hypotheses discussed in this chapter will stimulate and guide new research in VPH. Further, that clinicians will evaluate their patients to determine not only if the patients pose a danger to others, but also if the patients themselves have a potential to become victims of homicides.

Annotated Bibliography

Dutton, D. G. (1995). *The Domestic Assault of Women.* Vancouver: University of British Columbia Press. This book presents a reasoned perspective on domestic violence. Dr. Dutton achieves a balance in his discussion of both abused women and their abusers. His exposition of treatment strategies for abusive men brings together state-of-the-art research and clinical experience to provide practical guidance for the treating clinician.

Johann, S. L., & Osanka, F. (Eds.). (1988). *Representing... Battered Women Who Kill.* Springfield, IL: Charles C Thomas. This edited volume provides a wide range of papers on psycholegal issues in homicide arising from domestic contexts. I especially recommend Dr. Mann's chapter in that volume, as it represents a thorough examination of homicide in a specific population of women in domestic contexts. Also, Dr. Mann does her work with a sense of real-world pragmatism and ideological neutrality that is refreshing in domestic violence research.

Wolfgang, M. (1958). *Patterns in Criminal Homicide.* London: University of Oxford Press. Because of its primacy and thoroughness, this work should be required reading for any student of Victim-Precipitated Homicide. This large study provides not only a comprehensive picture of homicidal violence in Philadelphia in the late 1940s and 1950s, but represents a thoughtful examination of all of the players in the homicide drama.

References

Abel, E. L. (1986). Guns and blood alcohol levels among homicide victims. *Drug and Alcohol Dependence, 18,* 253-257.

Abel, E. L. (1987). Drugs and homicide in Erie County, New York. *International Journal of Addictions, 22*(2), 195-200.

Abel, E. L., & Zeidenberg, P. M. (1985). Age, alcohol and violent death: A postmortem study. *Journal of Studies on Alcohol, 46*(3), 228-231.

Abel, E. L., & Zeidenberg, P. M. (1986). Alcohol and homicide: A comparison between Erie County, New York and Los Angeles County, California. *American Journal on Drug and Alcohol Abuse, 12,* 121-129.

Allen, N. H. (1983, Fall). Homicide followed by suicide: Los Angeles, 1970-1979. *Suicide and Life-Threatening Behavior*, pp. 155-564.

Bachman, R., & Pillemer, K. A. (1992). Epidemiology and family violence involving adults. In R. T. Ammerman & M. Hersen (Eds.), *Assessment of family violence A clinical and legal sourcebook* (pp. 108-120). New York: John Wiley & Sons, Inc.

Berman, A. L. (1979, Spring). Dyadic death: Murder-suicide. *Suicide and Life-Threatening Behavior*, pp. 15-23.

Bloch, B. & Zemring, R. E. (1973). Homicide in Chicago. *Journal of Research in Crime and Delinquency, 10,* 1-12.

Blount, W. R., Silverman, I. J., Sellers, C. S., & Seese, R. A. (1994). Alcohol and drug use among abused women who kill, abused women who don't and their abusers. *Journal of Drug Issues, 24*(2), 165-177.

Blum, R. (1981). Violence, alcohol and setting: An unexplored nexus. In J. J. Collins (Ed.), *Drinking and crime* (pp. 110-142). New York: Guilford Press.

Braucht, G. N., Loya, F., & Jamieson, K. J. (1980). Victims of violent death: A critical review. *Psychological Bulletin, 87*(2), 309-333.

Breslau, N., Davis, G. C., & Andreski, P. (1995). Risk factors for PTSD-related traumatic events: A prospective analysis. *American Journal of Psychiatry, 152*(4), 529-534.

Brooks, S., & Harford, T. (1992). Occupation and alcohol-related causes of death. *Drug and Alcohol Dependence, 29,* 245-251.

Browne, A. & Williams, K. R. (1993). Gender, intimacy, and lethal violence: Trends from 1976 through 1987. *Gender & Society, 7*(1), 78-98.

Browne, A. & Williams Kirk R. (1989). Exploring the effect of resource availability and the likelihood of female-perpetrated homicides. *Law & Society*

Review, 23(1), 71-94.

Brush, L. D. (1993). Violent acts and injurious outcomes in married couples: Methodological issues in the national survey of families and households. In P. B. Bart & E. G. Moran (Eds.), *Violence against women* (pp. 240-251). Newbury Park: Sage.

Budd, R. D. (1982). The incidence of alcohol use in Los Angeles County homicide victims. *American Journal of Drug & Alcohol Abuse, 9*(1), 105-11.

Buteau, J. M., Lesage, A. D., & Kiely, M. C. (1993, October). Homicide followed by suicide: A Quebec case series, 1988-1990. *Canadian Journal of Psychiatry,* pp. 552-556.

Coid, J. (1983). The epidemiology of abnormal homicide and murder followed by suicide. *Psychological Medicine, 13*, 855-860.

Collins, J. J. (1981). *Drinking and Crime.* New York: Guilford Press.

Collins, J. J. & Messerschmidt, P. M. (1993). Epidemiology of alcohol-related violence. *Alcohol Health & Research World, 17*(2), 92-100.

Combs-Orme, T. P., Taylor, J. R., Scott, E. B., & Holmes, S. J. (1983). Violent deaths among alcoholics: A descriptive study. *Journal of Studies on Alcohol, 44*(6), 938-949.

Cornell, D. G. (1993). Juvenile homicide: A growing national problem. *Behavioral Sciences and the Law, 11*, 389-396.

Curtis, L. A. (1974). Victim precipitation and violent crime. *Social Problems, 21*, 594-605.

Daly, M. & Wilson, M. (1988). *Homicide.* Hawthorne, NY: Aldine De Gruyter.

Daniel, A. E., & Robins, A. J. (1985, September). Violent women. *Psychiatry in Family Practice,* pp. 96-108.

Danto, B. L. (1978). Suicide among murderers. *International Journal of Offender Therapy & Comparative Criminology, 22*(2), 140-143.

Dietz, P. E. (1987). Patterns in human violence. In R. E. Hales & A. J. Frances (Eds.), *American Psychiatric Association Annual Review, Vol. 6* (pp. 465-490). Washington, DC: American Psychiatric Press, Inc.

Dutton, D. G. (1994). Behavioral and affective correlates of borderline personality organization in wife assaulters. *International Journal of Law and Psychiatry, 17*(3), 265-277.

Dutton, D. G. (1995). *The domestic assault of women.* Vancouver: University of British Columbia Press.

Farley, F. (1991). The type-t personality. In L. Lipsitt & L. L. Mitkin (Eds.), *Self-regulatory behavior and risk taking: Causes and consequences* (pp. 371-382). Norwood, NJ: Ablex.

Felson, R. B., Ribner, S. A., & Siegel, M. A. (1984). Age and the effect of third parties during criminal violence. *Sociology and Social Research, 68*(4), 452-562.

Fine, P., Roseman, J. M., Constandinou, C. M., Brissie, R. M., Glass, J. M., & Wrigley, J. M. (1994, May). Homicide among Black males in Jefferson County, Alabama 1978-1989. *Journal of Forensic Sciences,* pp. 674-684.

Flavin, D. K., Franklin, J. E., & Frances, R. J. (1990). Substance abuse and suicidal behavior. In S. J. Blumenthal & D. J. Kubfer (Eds.), *Suicide over the life cycle* (pp. 177-204). Washington, DC: American Psychiatric Press.

Geberth, V. (1993, July). *Suicide by cop.* Law and Order,

pp. 105-108.

Geffner, R. & Pagelow, M. D. (1990). Victims of spouse abuse. In R. T. Ammerman & M. Herson (Eds.), *Treatment of family violence* (pp. 113-135). New York: John Wiley & Sons.

Goetting, A. (1989a). Patterns of homicide among children. *Criminal Justice and Behavior, 16*(1), 63-80.

Goetting, A. (1989b). Patterns of marital homicide: A comparison of husbands and wives. *Journal of Comparative Family Studies*, 341-354.

Goodwin, D. W. (1973). Alcohol in suicide and homicide. *Quarterly Journal for the Study of Alcoholism, 34*, 144-1-56.

Gulotta, G. (1980). Victimization and interpersonal misunderstandings in dyadic systems. *Victimology: An International Journal, 5*, 110-114.

Hazelwood, R., Dietz, P., & Burgess, A. (1982). Equivocal deaths: Accident, suicide or homicide? In R. Hazelwood, P. Dietz, & A. Burgess (Eds.), *Autoerotic fatalities* (pp. 139-153). Lexington, MA: Heath.

Herjanic, M. & Meyer, D. A. (1976, June). Psychiatric illness in homicide victims. *American Journal of Psychiatry*, pp. 691-693.

Hillard, J. R., Zung, W. W., Holland, J. M., & Johnson, M. M. (1985). Accidental and homicidal death in a psychiatric emergency room population. *Hospital and Community Psychiatry, 36*(6), 640-643.

Holinger, P.C. (1980). Violent deaths as a leading cause of mortality: An epidemiological study of suicide, homicide and accidents. *American Journal of Psychiatry, 137*(4), 472-475.

Holinger, P. C., Luke, K. W., Montes, P., Perez, S., &

Sandlow, J. (1987). Synthesis: Violent deaths in aggregate. In P. C. Holinger (Ed.), *Violent deaths in the United States* (pp. 138-158). New York: Guilford Press.

Hsieh, C. & Pugh, M. (1993, Autumn). Poverty, income inequality, and violent crime: A meta-analysis of recent aggregate data studies. *Criminal Justice Review*, pp. 182-202.

John, H. W. (1977). Alcoholism and criminal homicide: Overview. *Alcohol Health and Research World*, 8-13.

Keehn, R. J., Goldberg, I. D., & Beebe, G. W. (1974). Twenty-four year mortality follow-up of Army veterans with disability separations for psychoneurosis in 1944. *Psychosomatic Medicine, 36*(1), 27-46.

Kellermann, A. L., Rivara, F. P., Rushforth, N. B., Banton, J. G., Reay, D. T., Francisco, J. T., Locci, A. B., Prodzinski, J. B., Hackman, B. B., & Somes, G. P. (1993). Gun ownership as a risk factor for homicide in the home. *The New England Journal of Medicine, 329*(15), 1084-1091.

Klatsky, A. L. & Armstrong, M. A. (1993). Alcohol use, other traits, and risk of unnatural death: A prospective study. *Alcoholism: Clinical and Experimental Research, 17*(6), 1156-1162.

Koss, M. P., Goodman, L. A., Browne, A., Fitzgerald, L. F., Keita, G. P., & Russo, N. F. (1994). *No safe haven: Male violence against women at home, at work, and in the community*. Washington, DC: American Psychological Association.

Langevin, R., Paitich, D. O., B, Handy, L., & Russon, A. (1982). The role of alcohol, drugs, suicide attempts and situational strains in homicides committed by offenders seen for psychiatric assessment. *ACTA Psychiatry of Scandinavia, 66*, 229-242.

Lester, D. (1977). The prediction of suicide and homicide rates cross-nationally by means of stepwise multiple regression. *Behavior Science Research, 1*, 61-69.

Lester, D. (1993). Restricting the availability of alcohol and rates of personal violence (suicide and homicide). *Drug and Alcohol Dependence, 31*, 215-217.

Litman, R. L. (1995). Suicide prevention in a treatment setting. *Suicide and Life-Threatening Behavior, 25*, 134-142.

Luckenbill, D. F. (1977, December). Criminal homicide as a situated transaction. *Social Problems*, pp. 176-186.

Mann, C. R. (1989). Getting even? Women who kill in domestic encounters. In S. L. Johann & F. Osanka (Eds.), *Representing...battered women who kill* (pp. 8-26). Springfield, IL: Charles C Thomas.

Mann, C. R. (1992). Female murderers and their motives: A tale of two cities. In E. C. Viano (Ed.), *Intimate violence: Interdisciplinary perspectives* (pp. 73-81). New York: Hemisphere Publishing Corporation.

Marlatt, G. A. (1985). Cognitive factors in the relapse process. In G. A. Marlatt & J. R. Gordon (Eds.), *Relapse prevention* (pp. 128-200). New York: Guilford Press.

Massey, C. R. & McKean, J. (1985). The social ecology of homicide: A modified lifestyle/routine activities perspective. *Journal of Criminal Justice, 13*, 417-428.

Maxim, P. S. & Keane, C. (1992). Gender, age, and the risk of violent death in Canada, 1950-1986. *Canadian Review of Sociology and Anthropology, 29*(3), 329-354.

Mayo, D.L. (1992). What is being predicted? Definitions of "suicide." In R. W. Maris, S. L. Berman, J. T. Maltsberger, & R. I. Yufit (Eds.), *Assessment and Prediction of Suicide.* (pp. 88-101). New York: Guilford Press.

McIntosh, J. L. (1992). Methods of Suicide. In R. W. Maris, A. L. Berman, J. T. Maltsberger, & R.I. Yufit (Eds.), Assessment and Prediction of Suicide. (pp. 381-397). New York: Guilford Press.

Meloy, R. (1988). *The psychopathic mind: Origins, dynamics and treatment.* Northvale, NJ: Aronson.

Monahan, J. & Klassen, D. (1982). Situational approaches to understanding and predicting individual violent behavior. In M. E. Wolfgang & N. A. Weiner (Eds.), *Criminal violence* (pp. 292-319). Beverly Hills, CA: Sage Publications.

Moscicki, E. K. (1995). Epidemiology of suicidal behavior. *Suicide and Life Threatening Behavior, 25*(1), 22-35.

Motto, J. A. (1992). An integrated approach to estimating suicide risk. In R. W. Maris, A. L. Berman, J. T. Maltsberger, & R. I. Yufit (Eds.), *Assessment and Prediction of Suicide* (pp. 625-239). New York: Guilford Press.

Murphy, C. M., Meyer, S., & O'Leary, K. D. (1994). Dependency characteristics of partner assaultive men. *Journal of Abnormal Psychology, 103*(4), 729-735.

Novaco, R. (1975). *Anger control: The development and evaluation of an experimental treatment.* Lexington, MA: Lexington Books.

O'Brien, R. M. (1987). The interracial nature of violent crimes: A reexamination. *American Journal of Sociology, 4*, 817-835.

Palmer, S. & Humphrey, J. A. (1980, Summer). Offender-victim relationships in criminal homicide followed by offender's suicide, North Carolina, 1972-1977. *Suicide and Life-Threatening Behavior*, pp. 106-118.

Pernanen, K. (1991). *Alcohol in human violence*. New York: Guilford Press.

Plass, P. (1993, June). African American family homicide: Patterns in partner, parent, and child victimization, 1985-1987. *Journal of Black Studies*, pp. 515-538.

Pleck E., Pleck, J. H., Grossman, M., & Bart, P. B. (1978). The battered data syndrome: A comment on Steinmetz' article. *Victimology, 2*(3-4), 680-684.

Pokorny, A. D. (1965). A comparison of homicides in two cities. *Journal of Criminal Law, Criminology and Police Science, 56*, 479-487.

Poussaint, A. F. (1983). Black-on-Black homicide: A psychological-political perspective. *Victimology, 8*(3-4), 161-169.

Prochaska, J., DiClemente, C., & Norcross, C. (1992). In search of how people change: Applications to addictive behaviors. *American Psychologist, 47*(9), 1102-1114.

Rizzo, N. D. (1982). Murder in Boston: Killers and their victims. *International Journal of Offender Therapy and Comparative Criminology, 26*(1), 36-42.

Rogers, C. (1993). Gang-related homicides in Los Angeles County. *Journal of Forensic Sciences, 38*(4), 831-834.

Rosenbaum, A. & Maiuro, R. D. (1990). Perpetrators of spouse abuse. In R. T. Ammerman & M. Herson (Eds.), *Treatment of family violence* (pp. 280-310). New York: John Wiley.

Rosenbaum, M. (1990). The role of depression in couples involved in murder-suicide and homicide. *American Journal of Psychiatry, 147*(8), 1036-1039.

Rushforth, N. B., Ford, A., Hirsch, C., Rushforth, N. M., & Adelson, L. (1977). Violent death in a metropolitan county. *New England Journal of Medicine, 297*, 531-538.

Smith, M. D., Devine, J. A., & Sheley, J. F. (1992). Crime and unemployment: Effects across age and race categories. *Sociological Perspectives, 35*(4), 551-572.

Steinmetz, S. (1978). The battered husband syndrome. *Victimology, 2*(3-4), 499-509.

Stets, J. & Straus, M. (1990). Gender differences in reporting marital violence and its medical and psychological consequences. In M. G. Straus, R. (Ed.), *Physical violence in American families* (pp. 151-166). New Brunswick, NJ: Transaction Publishers.

Swanson, J. W., Holzer, C. E., Ganju, V. H., & Jono, R. T. (1990). Violence and psychiatric disorders in the community: Evidence from the epidemiologic catchment area surveys. *Hospital & Community Psychiatry, 41*, 761-77.

Tardiff, K. M. (1985). Patterns and major determinants of homicide in the United States. *Hospital and Community Psychiatry, 36*(6), 632-639.

Ullah, P. (1988). Unemployment and psychological well-being. In J. G. Howells (Ed.), *Modern perspectives in psychosocial pathology* (pp. 247-267). New York: Brunner/Mazel.

Van Zandt, C. R. (1993). Suicide by cop. *The Police Chief, LX*(7), 24-30.

von Hentig, H. (1940). Remarks on the interaction of

perpetrator and victim. *Journal of Criminal Law and Criminology, 31*, 303-309.

Voss, H. L. & Hepburn, J. R. (1968). Patterns of criminal homicide in Chicago. *Journal of Criminal Law, Criminology and Police Science, 59*, 499-508.

Waldo, M. (1987). Also victims: Understanding and treating men arrested for spouse abuse. *Journal of Counseling and Development, 65*, 385-388.

Webster, M. (1991). *Webster's ninth collegiate dictionary.* Springfield, MA: Merriam Webster, Inc.

Welte, J. W. & Abel, E. L. (1989). Homicide: Drinking by the victim. *Journal of Studies on Alcohol, 50*(3), 197-201.

Wilbanks, W. (1983). Female homicide offenders in the U.S. *International Journal of Women's Studies, 6*(4), 302-310.

Wolfgang, M. (1958). *Patterns in criminal homicide.* London: University of Oxford Press.

Yllo, K. & Straus, M. A. (1981). Interpersonal violence among married and cohabiting couples. *Family Relations, 30*, 339-347.

About the Author

William E. Foote, PhD, is a forensic psychologist in private practice in Albuquerque, New Mexico. He was reared and educated in New Mexico, receiving his PhD from the University of New Mexico in 1978. He completed a pre-doctoral forensic internship at Atascadero State Hospital in California in 1976-1977, and was licensed to practice in New Mexico in 1979. His practice centers around consultations and evaluations for both criminal and civil (largely tort) cases. He has been a consultant to the Indian Health Service, the Social Security Administration, the Department of Energy, and the Disciplinary Counsel for the New Mexico Supreme Court. He has been a Diplomate in Forensic Psychology from the American Board of Professional Psychology since 1984. Dr. Foote has served in a number of roles in the New Mexico Psychological Association, including President, Ethics Committee Chair, and APA Counsel representative. He holds faculty appointments and teaches in the University of New Mexico Department of Psychology, Medical School, and School of Law.

Questions and comments may be addressed to William E. Foote, PhD, 3200 Central Avenue, SE, Suite 3200, Albuquerque, NM, 87106-4811.

Part II
Family and Juvenile Violence

CHAPTER 7

WHEN MOTHERS MURDER: UNDERSTANDING INFANTICIDE BY FEMALES

Sally H. Barlow
Claudia J. Clayton

The sanctity of life and consequent protection of neonatal life are considered by many to be intrinsic to civilization. This strong belief about our essential humanness is, however, countered by cultural anthropologists' claims that large numbers of primitive societies practice infanticide, reportedly as an effort to ensure their very survival. Evidence from Federal Bureau of Investigation (FBI) Uniform Crime Reports suggests that industrialized societies practice infanticide as well (although these statistics are not clearly separated from homicide rates).

Infanticide is a social reality that has existed without regard for temporal, geographic, or economic barriers. In Roman Britain, archeological digs have revealed that the likely explanation for infant burial sites outside known cemetaries is infanticide (Mays, 1993). Infant exposure apparently was practiced regularly in ancient Athens (Thurer, 1994). Accounts of infanticide in Victorian England (Higginbotham, 1989) are even more reliable, as these facts come from a number of corroborating sources. Such practices are evident in all parts of the globe and throughout history, although the reported incidence varies enormously, depending upon the historian. For example, DeMause (1976) indicated that infanticide was quite prevalent, while Hanawalt

(1977), Helmholtz (1975), and Wrightson (1975) reported smaller rates. More recent data (Hrdy, 1992) suggest that the range of infanticides is somewhere between zero and 40% of live births. While the range is variable, the fact remains that whether primitive or civilized, ancient or present day, parents are quite capable of killing their young. In fact, initial findings (d'Orban, 1979; Resnick, 1969) suggested that mothers are at least as likely as fathers to accomplish the deed.

The Search for a Definition

The major advantage of formulating definitions of infanticide and related concepts is that clear conceptualizations allow both professionals and nonprofessionals to (a) increase awareness and vigilance, (b) understand underlying psychological mechanisms, (c) formulate possible cause and effect models, and (d) encourage research to expand our knowledge base.

The word infanticide is from the Latin for "child murder." No standard definition exists, however (Hoffer & Hull, 1981; Piers, 1978). Some scientists have proposed a broad definition that includes "any form of lethal curtailment of parental investment in offspring brought about by conspecifics" (Hausfater & Hrdy, 1984). This definition would include abortion, contraception resulting in gamete destruction, and nutritional or other neglect of an infant, as well as direct killing of an infant (Hausfater & Hrdy, 1984). Langer (1974) defined infanticide as "the willful destruction of newborn babies through exposure, starvation, strangulation, smothering, poisoning, or through the use of some lethal weapon" (p. 353). Although contraception and abortion are important issues, they will not be dealt with here.

It is important to note that medical and legal definitions vary and do not include many definitions used in the general literature (see Table 1). For instance, the term "neonaticide," which refers to the killing of an infant within the first 24 hours of life, is not used consistently in the literature. "Filicide" is the killing of a child of any age by one or both of the natural parents. In Bourget and Bradford's 1990 article, *Homicidal Parents*, distinctions were proposed among pathological filicide (including altruistic motives and homicide-suicide), accidental filicide (including battered child syndrome), retaliating filicide, neonaticide (including unwanted children), and paternal filicide. Bourget and Bradford did not delineate which of the previous headings include maternal filicide or maternal neonaticide. Although promising, their work, which drew upon the previous work of Resnick (1970) and d'Orban (1979), does not provide clear, agreed-upon, non-overlapping definitions. As yet, no such definitions exist in the literature. Additional changes have been proposed in some definitions.

In the released *Encyclopedia of Bioethics* by Reich (1995), the section on infanticide distinguishes between active and passive forms of infanticide. Some argue that such a distinction comes up against legal barriers and also weakens the moral basis of medicine as a life-preserving enterprise.

Questions Raised by the Non-Human Primate Data

It is inappropriate to make a blanket assumption that behavior of other primate species is directly analogous to human behavior. Each species has evolved its own set of behaviors that should be appreciated apart from those of other species as well as in comparison to them. However, consideration of the behavior of non-human primates in addition to that of various human cultures, past and present, may lead to questions that might otherwise be overlooked (Masters, 1990). Following are some brief examples of infanticidal behavior in non-human primates. (Lower mammals will not be addressed here as extrapolations to human behavior may be even more problematic, and space does not allow adequate exploration of the issues.)

The killing of unweaned infants by adult males has been observed in many primate species. In mountain gorillas of the Parc des Virungas, Zaire, most infanticide was perpetrated by unfamiliar males on infants whose mothers were not accompanied by mature males of their own group. Infanticide has been observed only rarely in encounters between adult males within the group. Using known cases of infanticide, a rate of 1 per 22.7 group-years is estimated. The rate increases to 1 per 17 group-years if suspected cases are included (Watts, 1989).

Seven cases of within-group infanticide were observed during 15 years of monitoring the "M-group" of approximately 90 chimpanzees in the Mahale Mountains National Park, Tanzania (Hamai, Nishida, Takasaki, & Turner, 1992). The killings were perpetrated by adult males and usually occurred during the morning feeding period, when hunting most frequently occurred. The victims were cannabalized. Indeed, it seemed "as if once an infant fell into the hands of an adult male, it suddenly changed to a lump of meat rather than a conspecific, even though it was still

	TABLE 1 LEGAL AND MEDICAL DEFINITION OF TERMS 1914 TO PRESENT	
Term	**Definition**	**Source**
Infanticide	In medical jurisprudence, the murder of a new-born infant. It is thus distinguishable from abortion and "foeticide," which are limited to the destruction of the life of the fetus in utero.	Bouvier, J. (1914). *Bouvier's law dictionary and concise encyclopedia, Vol. 1*. St. Paul: West Publishing Co., p. 1561-1562.
Infanticide	The killing of a young child shortly after its birth. (Infant is defined as one who has not yet reached the age of majority, usually 21.)	Ballentine, J. (1969). *Ballentine's law dictionary, 3rd ed*. San Francisco: Bancroft-Whitney Co., p. 618.
Infanticide	The murder or killing of an infant soon after its birth. The fact of the birth distinguishes this act from feticide or procuring abortion, which terms denote the destruction of the fetus in the womb.	Black, H. (1990). *Black's law dictionary: Definitions of the terms and phrases of American and English jurisprudence ancient and modern. 6th ed.* St. Paul: West Publishing Co., p. 778.
Prolicide	A word used to designate the destruction of the human offspring. Jurists divide the subject into feticide, or the destruction of the fetus in utero, and infanticide, or the destruction of the newborn infant.	Black, H. (1990). *Black's law dictionary: Definitions of the terms and phrases of American and English jurisprudence ancient and modern. 6th ed.* St. Paul: West Publishing Co., p. 1213.
Infanticide	The taking of the life of an infant.	Dorland, W. A. (Ed.) (1988). *Dorland's illustrated medical dictionary, 25th ed.* Philadelphia: W.B. Saunders Co., p. 833.
Infanticide	No definition listed.	Duncan, A., Durstan G., & Wellbourn, E. (Eds.) (1977). *Dictionary of medical ethics.* London: Darton, Longman & Todd Pub.
Infanticide	Yet to be released by publishers. According to preliminary reports, passive and active forms of infanticide are included.	Reich, W. T. (Ed.) (1995). *Encyclopedia of bioethics.* New York: Macmillan Publishing Co.
Neonaticide and filicide are not specific terms found in medical or legal definitions. According to the Library of Congress, the above constitute all the available references.		

alive" (Hamai et al., 1992, p. 159). Mothers of victimized infants had mated mostly with immature males, rather than the alpha male or other high ranking males, whereas the infants of females who mated exclusively with the alpha male were not killed. When females whose

infants had been killed came into estrus, the higher ranking males were more likely than others to mate with them (Hamai et al., 1992).

In her studies of chimpanzees at the Gombe Stream Reserve, Goodall (1986) documented 17 attacks on stranger females with infants, usually by adult males. The objects of the attacks were the adult females, but the infants often were injured or killed, and sometimes eaten, by the males. Goodall (1986) also observed a rare case of infanticide by females. Passion, an adult female, aided by her daughter, Pom, was seen killing and devouring three infant chimpanzees over a period of four years. The pair was suspected in the disappearance of seven other infant chimpanzees during that time. Infant deaths or disappearances, and numerous nonlethal attacks on infants, have occurred in some single-male troops of Hanuman langurs during takeover of the troop by a new male (Mohnot, 1971; Vogel, 1979; Vogel & Loch, 1984).

Several explanations have been proposed to explain infanticide in non-human primates. A common view is that it is to the male's reproductive advantage to destroy infants the male did not sire, and to do so before the infant is weaned, thus causing the mother to come into estrus sooner than normal, and be available for mating. The data on mountain gorillas presented by Watts (1989) indicated that all but one of the mothers whose infants were killed transferred to the group to which the infanticidal male belonged. Interbirth intervals were indeed shortened for these females, and there was a high probability that they would mate with the infanticidal male(s). Similar reasoning has been applied to the langur troops, except that males take over groups, rather than females transferring to different groups.

Hamai et al. (1992) suggested that within-group infanticide in chimpanzees serves to coerce females into copulating less promiscuously and with higher ranking adult males, an evolutionary strategy of male-male competition similar to that mentioned above for gorillas and langurs. Hiraiwa-Hasegawa (1987) suggested that feeding is the major function of infanticide in this species. The two theories are not mutually exclusive, but the fact that not all infants are consumed indicates that nutrition may not be the primary motivation.

Goodall's observations at Gombe suggested a slightly different evolutionary hypothesis: The attacks of stranger males upon mothers may aid in recruiting the adolescent daughters, who often travel with their mothers, into the group. The killing of the infants is only incidental to the attacks on the mothers (Goodall, 1986).

Several non-evolutionary explanations also have been suggested. Crowding or other stressful conditions may increase irritability (Burke, 1984), although primates have relatively sophisticated behaviors for conciliation and avoidance of conflict in crowded situations (de Waal, 1989). Goodall (1986) suggested chimpanzee xenophobia as an explanation for attacks on mothers by stranger males. Eibl-Eibesfeldt (1989) suggested that cases of infanticide in non-human primates are too infrequent to be regarded as an evolutionary adaptation. He also noted that the small number of deaths that were directly observed were accomplished by only a few animals, and that inferred incidents actually may have been due to other causes, such as dogs chasing langur troops in research areas.

Eibl-Eibesfeldt (1989) and Masters (1990) regarded primate infanticidal behavior as pathological (as contrasted to an evolutionary adaptation). Masters cited Harlow and Harlow's (1962) data on mother monkeys who were themselves raised without mothers. Harlow and Harlow found that disruption of the relationship between mother and infant can cause severe behavioral aberrations in the infant even after it has grown to maturity. Passion was a poor mother (Goodall, 1986), and Masters speculated that because of this, Pom formed an unusually dependent attachment to her, even to the extent of participating in Passion's pathological behavior toward other infants. Masters' oblique suggestion was that Passion herself was a victim of poor mothering. She also suggested that such a possibility should be investigated for infanticidal males.

Eibl-Eibesfeldt (1989) wrote of chimpanzee

"temper tantrums," that is, their tendency to lose control when they are in a state of strong emotional arousal. Such situations may occur during feeding and competitive male displays, and the aggression may be displaced toward females or infants.

Implications of the Non-Human Primate Findings

Why is infanticide in non-human primates committed almost exclusively by males who are unrelated to the infant, while in humans it is committed by females as well as males, who are usually members of the victim's family? Masters (1990) argued that:

the atypical behavior of the infanticidal chimpanzee females and the motherless monkey mothers most closely resembles family-based infanticide among contemporary Western humans. I argue further that the infanticidal behavior of non-human primate males emerges in human life on the one hand in male efforts to control certainty of paternity by controlling women, on the other, in the overt and covert infanticidal behavior of powerful dominant groups and states (p. 106).

This view seems somewhat simplistic overall, given the cognitive complexity of humans, although Hrdy (1992) argued that most classes of infanticide that occur in animals have been documented at least anecdotally in humans. (She noted, however, the deplorable lack of accuracy of incidence rates in humans, which data might allow us to make more reliable comparisons between the two literature domains.)

At least two aspects of the non-human primate observations are suggestive of significant categories of human infanticide. Controlling the certainty of paternity may emerge in humans as a possible basis for the disproportionately high rate of abuse and murder of stepchildren in industrialized nations (Daly & Wilson, 1988). Child abuse

culminating in death may be analogous to the loss of control in chimps suggested by Eibl-Eibesfeldt (1989), to abusive behavior due to poor parenting of the abusive animal as suggested by Masters (1990), or both.

Animal models obviously lack adequate explanatory power for the entire range of infanticidal behavior in humans. Nevertheless, a possible and important extrapolation from this literature is that infanticide may not be instinctual in human mothers. Awareness of history, personal memories, the ability to judge the impact of present acts on future situations, complex social relationships, and cultural awareness influence human decisions. Psychopathology, sometimes physiologically based, may also contribute to human behavior.

The ongoing and impressive research of Daly and Wilson (1980, 1983, 1984, 1988) and Hrdy (1976, 1977, 1979, 1987, 1990, 1992) provides possible bridges between comparative and human research. These authors suggested that parents' behaviors toward their children are shaped by a number of factors which influence parental investment. Hrdy (1992) implied that a reasoned, rather than moralistic approach based on empirical data of human and non-human primates, will enable us to better understand this phenomenon. The actual impact of these authors' works and how they expand our understanding of human infanticide remains to be seen.

Human Infanticide: Seven Possible Reasons

A number of authors contend that infanticide exists presently for the same reasons it has always existed in human history: lack of food supply to ensure survival of the group, problems of deformity and sickliness in newborns, manipulation of family composition, and questionable paternity (Horan & Delahoyde, 1982; Hrdy, 1992; Miller, 1981; Piers, 1978; Rose, 1986).

Lack of food supply appears to be a particularly compelling reason for human infanticide. Whenever infanticide has been an economic necessity for an entire community's survival, it has apparently become so ordinary as to not be worth recording (Lagaipa, 1990; Thurer, 1994). However, it is a problematic reason, given the number of societies in which infanticide has taken place where economics (and its direct connection to food supply) were not at issue. (See Hrdy, 1992, for a detailed account). DeMause (1990) suggested a method allowing one to detect genuine accounts of infanticide due to demographic characteristics, such as lack of food and money. He proposed an assessment of sex ratios, wealth, and level of civilization to determine if true demographics are the motive for infanticide. For instance, if parents kill their children because they fear the children will eventually starve to death if allowed to live, the ratio of male to female deaths will parallel that particular culture's birth ratios. If lack of sufficient wealth is offered as a motive, fewer infanticides will occur in the wealthy as opposed to the poor classes. Finally, if scarce resources are proposed as a motive, the civilization with fewer resources will commit more infanticides than the civilization with more resources (DeMause, 1990, p. 3).

Several accounts in history allow this method to be applied.

Thurer (1994) documented the known historical data regarding three concurrent cultures: the Egyptians, Jews, and Phoenicians from approximately 5th to 1st centuries B.C.E. Based on archeological findings, the Jews and Egyptians rarely engaged in infanticide and if they did, it was likely due to one of the three reasons listed above. The Phoenicians, on the other hand, engaged in wholesale slaughter of infants in ritual sacrifice (sometimes 100 infants in one year). One could argue that this infanticide was indirectly related to food supply, as these sacrifices often had to do with appeasing their Gods and ensuring a rich harvest, but the Phoenicians were a relatively prosperous people and this reasoning could only be used inversely and indirectly. One could not legitimately offer demographics as an explanation. Rather, this suggests an additional reason for infanticide: ritualized sacrifice, in which fear about food supply is raised to a societal and religious level justifying such deaths and, in the case of the Phoenicians, programmed into their community activities for hundreds of years.

In seeking other motives which go beyond demographics, Thurer (1994) also suggested that misogyny plays a powerful role in determining the prevalence of infanticide in particular cultures. This notion was substantiated by a number of authors (Freed & Freed, 1989; Krishnaswamy, 1984; Kusum, 1993; Lester, 1985; Shalinsky & Glascock, 1988), and is sometimes referred to euphemistically as "population control" or "maximizing long-term reproductive success" (Hawkes, 1981).

While a deep-seated hatred of women could be subsumed within one or more of the original reasons for infanticide, its impact is likely pervasive enough to warrant its own category. It accounts for a complex picture regarding the treatment of women, values about mothering, and resources allocated for childrearing that create a context within which infanticide can and does occur.

A final category must be added: mental illness of the mother, whether temporary, as might occur in postpartum depression, or long-standing, as reported in serial infanticides among those with serious personality disorders or debilitating psychotic disorders.

These seven reasons — (a) inadequate parenting skills coupled with loss of control, (b) lack of food supply, (c) questionable paternity, (d) presence of deformity/sickliness, (e) ritualized practices, (f) misogyny, and (g) mental illness — fashion for us a lens through which we might view infanticide. This lens will serve as an aid in determining the level(s), from the personal to the societal, at which infanticide might occur: individual, dyad, small group, or large group, as well as the parallel underlying motive(s): psychological, physiological, sociological, and their combinations. We will need all of these to comprehend and treat infanticide.

Infanticide: Incidence

Systematic documentation regarding infanticide is still scarce. Certainly, perspective has something to do with the inattention or lack of focus afforded this topic. For instance, the estimated incidence rates of infanticide, even if severely underreported, do not approach the numbers in other areas of lethal violence which seriously warrant our attention. Still, failure to track infanticides as a specific crime category is a strong statement about society's ambivalence regarding this subject.

While overall deaths of children under 15 years of age have decreased dramatically during the past 30 years in the United States, homicide rates in this age group have increased significantly, are currently among the highest in the world, and more than tripled between 1958 and 1982: 235 neonates and children up to 14 years of age were killed in homicides (Van Biema, 1994). Homicide rates for children younger than 5 were highest, with women committing most of the murders. Almost 72% of these infants were killed by relatives (Saunders, 1989). Also, some confusion exists in the reporting of data, as there are few cases where filicide, neonaticide, and infanticide in general are separated from child homicide. These data may also be underreported, given the changes in the International Classification of Diseases and the revision of the standard certificate of death following 1968 (see Table 2).

The FBI's most recent statistics (1992) indicate that 662 children under the age of 5 were murdered that year. Ernest Allen, president of the National Center for Missing and Exploited Children, estimated that about two-thirds of those victims were killed by one or both parents. The U.S. Department of Health and Human Services calculated that, in 1992, about 1,000 children died from abuse or neglect (Van Biema, 1994). "Far more common than the sensational murders in Union County are the smaller deceptions practiced by mothers who claim that abused or neglected children died of Sudden Infant Death Syndrome (SIDS) or accidents" (VanBiema, 1994, p. 50). Many experts estimate that only half of the country's abuse deaths are uncovered. According to recent statistics from a Department of Justice study, of the 8,063 homicides in urban areas in the United States in 1994, parents were charged in 57% of the murders of children under age 12 and, in 55% of those cases, the killer was the mother ("Depression, Stress," 1994).

According to Richard J. Gelles, the director of the Family Violence Research Project at the University of Rhode Island (Smith and Mehren, 1994), "an estimated 650-700 mothers kill their children every year. That represents more than half of the 1,300 children killed by parents or caretakers on average each year since 1976." An extensive review of the available scholarly books and articles as well as popular press (i.e., within one week of the Susan Smith confession, newspapers in the United States alone carried nearly 400 stories referring to infanticide) still indicates that infanticide is not a well-researched topic. Of these scholarly works, many are anecdotal. Of the few empirical studies which examined female homicide rates, one of the most thorough was conducted by Totman (1978). Her subjects were women who had committed spouse (N=36) or child (N=14) murders and were incarcerated in California in 1969. Weisheit (1986) studied a somewhat larger sample of women (N=39) who had murdered their children and were imprisoned in Illinois

TABLE 2
ESTIMATED INCIDENCE RATES OF HOMICIDES, INFANTICIDES U.S.A.

Number	Target	Time Period	Act	Source	Possible modification of data
235	0-14 yrs	1958-1982	Homicide	FBI	Likely underreported statistics
662	0-5 yrs	1992	Homicide (filicide, neonaticide, infanticide, not separated out)	FBI	National Center for Minority and Exploited Children estimate 2/3 of these were killed by one or both parents.
1,000	children (unspecified)	1992	Abuse or neglect	U.S. Department of Health and Human Services	Some claims of SIDS, etc. may well have been infanticides. Most experts estimate only half of country's abuse deaths are uncovered.
650-700	children (unspecified)	yearly since 1976	Infanticide by mother	Family Violence Research Project	This represents more than half of the 1300 children killed by parents or caretakers on average, every year.
8,063	all ages, urban areas	1994	Homicide	Department of Justice	Of these homicides, parents were charged in 57% of the murders of children under age 12. In 55% of these cases, the killer was the mother.

during two time periods — 1940 to 1966 and 1981 to 1983. Both studies were confined to narrow ranges of subjects. The findings suggested that mothers killed most often with their hands (beating, strangulation, suffocation), were in general, young and unemployed, and had a low level of education. Silverman and Kennedy (1988) conducted a study based on Canadian crime statistics, comparing female homicide rates for a 23-year period. Their findings confirmed other findings regarding infanticides: 69% of these women who had committed infanticide were under 21 years of age, 30% were under 17, and almost 70% were single. A majority of the women used their hands, rather than other means, to kill. The authors noted the possible complications involved in comparing

infanticide to noninfanticide murders, as infanticide is a technical/legal definition in Canada. Still, when both groups were combined, Canadian women killing their young children were considerably younger than other female homicide categories. In addition, the motive was more likely labeled as mental illness. While these studies are partially helpful in broadening our understanding of infanticide, clear incidence rates for certain segments of the population do not exist. The above statistics do not contain sufficient data to calculate rates. If we were able to do so, this might enable us to better understand rural versus urban rates, younger versus older killers, impoverished versus unimpoverished killers, as well as other pertinent demographics. The proportion of variance attributable to societal influence versus mental illness also would be an important concern.

Four Types of Infanticide: A Preliminary Categorization

Infanticide by mothers, a complex phenomenon, might be provisionally understood as occurring within one of four contexts: societal infanticide; infanticide by a young, unmarried mother; infanticide by an older mother; and filicide. A description of each proposed type follows, with accompanying case histories, treatment proposals, and assault cycle (see Figures 1 through 4). These categories are meant to be provisional and clearly are not discrete units, as overlapping variables across categories exist.

Cycle 1: Societal Infanticide

The first category of infanticide we propose deals with governmental pressures and cultural traditions stemming directly or indirectly from inadequate basic resources, such as food or water. An understanding of these matters will be introduced with a sampling of societal/political accounts, followed by a plausible case history and possible assault cycle.

Brazil. According to Scheper-Hughes (1989), the average woman in Alto, Brazil, experiences 9.5 pregnancies, 3.5 child deaths, and 1.5 stillbirths. Sixty percent of all child deaths there occur in the first 6 months of life. Apparently, Alto women distinguish among natural child death (disease), those resulting from sorcery or

---

FIGURE 1
ASSAULT CYCLE OF SOCIETAL INFANTICIDE: CHINA AND INDIA*

2. Female infants are born to families in which there is already a female child.

1. Governmental pressures to limit family size (i.e., prior to 1986, China's one-child policy) or environmental pressures such as lack of food lead to pressures of family composition which influences the destruction of female rather than male infants.

3. Institutional decisions and other cultural sanctions are already strongly in place which encourage emotional distance between mother and child.

4. Options such as fostering out, boycotting the governmental policy, abandonment, sex-selective abortion are either culturally, economically, or individually unavailable. The infant is killed.

5. The cycle repeats itself if governmental pressure continues to influence family size and composition.

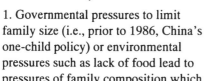
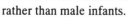
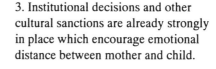
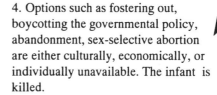
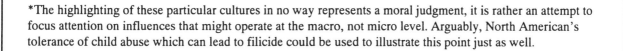

---

*The highlighting of these particular cultures in no way represents a moral judgment, it is rather an attempt to focus attention on influences that might operate at the macro, not micro level. Arguably, North American's tolerance of child abuse which can lead to filicide could be used to illustrate this point just as well.

evil eye, and those deaths which are fated or inevitable, according to their folk beliefs, as "child sickness or child attack." Allowing nature to take its course is seen as allowing the will of God. The real pathogens in this environment, according to Scheper-Hughes, are "poverty, deprivation, sexism, chronic hunger, and economic exploitation. If mother love is a natural script, what does it mean for these women whose hearts have turned to stone?" (p.14). She contended that these circumstances, also prevalent in northern India (as supported by Miller, 1981) and Bangladesh, where a 30% to 40% mortality rate in the first year of life is common, lead to delayed attachment. She also compared these experiences to those she encountered in battlefields and emergency rooms in over-crowded inner-city public hospitals where a "lifeboat ethic exists...the morality of triage" (p.16), which she believed explains these mothers' reluctance to "anthropomorphize" their infants.

Shalinsky and Glascock (1988) conducted a study of 60 nonindustrial societies and corroborated, on a much larger scale, the findings from Alto. In their work, they highlighted the concept of "liminal" (transitional) people — infants and the elderly. These were the first of the tribe to be killed, as they were seen as non-human. According to these researchers, the deed of infanticide, found in high percentages ranging from 53% to 91%, was viewed as "nontraumatic" because the infants were viewed as not real.

Romania. As reported in the *Economist* ("Misery in the Maternity Wards," 1990), in Ceausescu's Romania, the state-sanctioned demand to increase the population from 22 to 30 million by the end of the century included tactics such as banning contraceptives and making abortion punishable by up to five years in prison. The result was one of the highest infant-mortality rates in Europe, contributed to by what some doctors called passive (and likely some active) infanticide — infants were left to die by mothers who had nowhere to put them in their crowded apartments, and no food with which to feed them. Ceausescu went so far as to suspend international medical protocol in 1987 by imposing a 30-day delay in registering births. Some speculated that this enabled Romania to cover up their sky-rocketing infant mortality rate.

China. The *New York Times* reported in June 1991 that 5% of girl infants are unaccounted for in China (McGowan, 1991). According to a recent report in the Chinese newspaper *China Information News,* nearly half of 2,300 fetuses examined by ultrasound were aborted once the sex (female) was known. Estimates of female fetus abortions run from the thousands to the millions. Until 1986, China's one child per family policy was enforced, although international censure, among other things, brought the Government to end this policy.

India. Poverty appears to dictate a similar preference in India. The writer Elisabeth Bumiller found one Indian woman equating infanticide with abortion, saying "instead of killing the child in the womb, I killed the child when it was born. If that is accepted, why can't I do this?" ("Issues for," *Audubon,* 1994, p. 56). In a recent chapter by Kusum (1993), controversy surrounding prenatal diagnostic techniques was examined. The author noted that while advances such as amniocentesis were intended to detect various diseases and disorders, they more recently have been misused in India "solely for detecting the sex of the unborn child" (p. 150) in order to abort the female fetuses. While female infanticide was banned in India by an Act in 1870, the practice still exists. This practice, along with increasing rates of the above-mentioned feticide, combine to create one of the world's highest rates of sex-selection in favor of males (Kusum, 1993, p. 151).

Hrdy's (1992) astute account placed this argument of societal influences into stark relief as she examined additional cross-cultural data. Her findings indicated that food-related reasons for infanticide might be better understood within the larger context or "web of fitness tradeoffs" which include such issues as "culturally imaginable, economically or institutionally available" options to the mother (Hrdy, p. 409-411). In an effort to show that infanticide is one of many choices open to parents as they consider possible ways to deal with the enormous demands of parenting, she reported data from four different cultures — two present-day and two past.

West African mothers rarely, if ever, choose infanticide as an option to curtail parental investment and choose fostering-out instead. Hrdy compared the present-day West Africans with their 18th century European mother counterparts who utilized a similar strategy by hiring wet-nurses. Present-day Amazonian and Papuan tribes, where 20% to 40% of live births end in infanticide, are compared with their pre-modern European counterparts who utilized abandonment at approximately the same rate — 20% to 40%. Hrdy documented that abandonment meant almost sure death, and that parents knew this, thus making these forms of infanticide (one active, one passive) equivalent (p. 427). Although it is impossible to determine the proportion of infanticide attributable to such societal influences and fitness trade offs, it is clear that these operate at the cultural level as customs and are important determiners of maternal-infant attachment.

Amighi (1990) reminded us that much of our understanding of societal infanticide is based on Western perspectives. She suggested that these are flawed, ethnocentric measures that attempt to understand attachment and bonding from only one point of view. Two aspects of the mother-infant bond are apparent, according to her research, involving first, a mother's concern for her child's physical survival, and second, maternal warmth and concern for her child's emotional well-being. What we may have labeled maternal detachment may, in fact, be "maternal ambiva-

lence" (p. 132). This explains, for instance, the cases in which a mother may kill one infant and nurture another, or a mother who may neglect an infant who fails to thrive, then devote herself to another.

Case History 1, Societal infanticide. The name "Mei Mei" in Chinese or "Mui-Mui" in Indian means "little girl dying," "saved from the grave," and a "little sister." This case history, though hypothetical, is based on the actual accounts of thousands of female newborns unaccounted for in India and China, and was brought to our attention in an article by Jo McGowan (1991).

Mei Mei was born to Chinese parents who already had one daughter and were hoping desperately for a boy child. A number of reasons form the foundation for this preference: (a) until 1986, their government strictly enforced a policy of one child families; (b) a secure future is often based on the birth and rearing of a productive son; and (c) a daughter only means increased expenses because they will need to provide a dowry for her and once she is married, she will not likely make financial contributions to them. As McGowan (1991) related, "village mid-wives were often instructed to draw a bucket of water when a woman went into labor. If the newborn had the misfortune to be a girl, she was plunged into the bucket before she had a chance to draw her first breath" (p. 481).

This story is similar to the story of Mui Mui in India, as illustrated by the words of the Indian physician, Dr. Datta Pai (reported in Kusum, 1993), who stated, "Today a woman with more than one daughter has a gun pointed out at herself and her progeny. How can you deny her the right to have a son instead of a third or fourth daughter. You can't wish away centuries of thinking by saying that boys and girls are equal" (p. 163).

Treatment. At the recently held United Nations Fourth World Conference on Women in Beijing, China, a number of important issues relevant to this topic were addressed. While ostensibly appearing ethnocentric, the delegates' recommendations bear directly on treatment issues for societal infanticide:

• Expand human rights awareness to all countries.

• Develop alternative strategies to population control — no longer to include female feticide and female infanticide.

• Ease specific immigration procedures enabling infants from other countries to be adopted by adults in the United States.

Cycle 2: Neonaticide by a Young, Unmarried Female

While only covering one particular time in history, a review of Victorian England provides a glimpse of Cycle 2 issues at work in shaping the forces that lead to the killing of an infant within the first 24 hours of birth. Arguably, this set of circumstances could be reviewed for ancient Greece, modern Rome, 15th century France, or 18th century Australia with the same result. Victorian England provides a particularly interesting backdrop against which to understand the complex forces because of the available scientific as well as literary information. One need only turn to the legal records detailing the evolution of laws governing this particular type of murder, read Dicken's *Oliver Twist* or Elliot's *Adam Bede,* or turn to the numerous diaries of the period to understand these forces at work.

From 1800 to 1850, an unprecedented population explosion, due ironically to a decrease in the overall infant death rate, occurred in England and Wales, which doubled the populace from 9 to 18 million. (The explosion took place across Europe with a similar results, and was partially attributed to improved living conditions, including the year-round availability of cow's milk.) The average number of surviving births per household was six. The death rate for 0- to 1-

year-olds had declined sharply to 11% for the upper classes, while infant mortality rates for the same age group remained at 35% for the working classes and was somewhere between 60% to 90% for illegitimates (Rose, 1986). Of these deaths, the younger the child, the more disproportionate the risk. The statistics from 1863 to 1887 illustrate this: deaths of children under 1 year old totalled 3,225, whereas deaths in the 2- to 3-year-old group totalled only 70 (Rose, 1986). All the available cow's milk in the world could not account for this change in survival rates for children older than 12 months. What else might account for these deaths especially at a time of overall decline in infant mortality? Victorian medical records list "wasting diseases," i.e., congenital defects, injury, and lack of food (Rose, 1986, p. 8) as the leading cause of death. There was also a category for violent deaths, including death from burns, falls, or opiates. Surely, murder was among these (Higginbotham, 1989; Moseley, 1978), especially because infanticide was thought to be the most frequently "committed crime in all of Europe" as recently as 1800 (Horan & Delahoyde, 1982, p. 1). Alarmists charged that several hundred infants died each year in London, while other reports suggested as few as 10 cases of murder or concealment. The actual number of deaths due to infanticide lies somewhere between these two extremes and is likely due, in part, to the increased population pressures, a consequent decrease of resources, and the society's attempt to rectify this problem through the enactment of the New Poor Law, which changed the relief available to the poor and limited a woman's right to seek support from the father of her child (Piers, 1978; Rose, 1986).

The New Poor Law had an impact on large numbers of women, both married and unmarried, although it was clearly more harmful to the latter group. The economic exigencies placed upon these unmarried women in Victorian England were enormous, as they had very few occupation-

al positions available to them (prostitute and servant were two). In addition, the most societally
legitimate position at the time, that of wife, was
in serious jeopardy. Bachelorhood had become
more popular (as high as 45% by some accounts;
Rose, 1986). Women seeking other forms of
employment, with marriage seemingly unattain-
able, could, if fortunate, become servants to upper
class households. They still ran the risk of becoming pregnant through a relationship with a
boyfriend, an "indiscretion," or even rape,
according to the unwritten rule of "droit du
seigneur" (Piers, 1978, p. 57), which gave the
man of the house the right to deflower any female
who was his social inferior. While Victorians publicly eschewed such behavior, it nevertheless
occurred with regularity (45% of all illegitimate
births occurred to servants). These young women
were then dismissed without letters of recommendation for future employment, suitable only for
the poor house, if that, as many poor houses
would not accept them if their pregnancies were
discovered.

The fate of those women working in the poor
houses initially or simply starving in the streets
was far worse. The image of a servant girl hiding
her newly born infant under the linen in her room,
or the malnourished prostitute stuffing her newborn down a drain illustrates some of the underlying conditions which contributed to this particular
form of infanticide: economic distress, paternity
issues, possible mental disorder, and mysogyny.
As Piers (1978) stated, "we are unable to admit
the lethal discrimination against women — primarily poor women — and their unwanted children" (p. 122). The birth of a deformed or sickly
infant only added to the mother's motive to murder. Women of well-to-do families, married or
not, certainly had unwanted, often illegitimate
pregnancies as well, but had more resources
available to them, such as abortion (although this
was illegal, as well as considered to be immoral).
The back street abortionist-butchers available to

women of fewer means were legendary in London and for this reason, often avoided. Infanticide
was preferrable. Only one death would result, not
two.

The English society's sensibilities rallied
around what it perceived to be a terrible evil
inflicted upon good people by "mad women" or
women of "easy virtue" who, through lack of
proper moral education, or worse, through the
"encouragement of immorality" brought on by
the establishment of foundling homes, had
become pregnant (Rose, 1978). The English people did not consider that the economic retrenchment inherent in the New Poor Law severely cut
the funds available for such unfortunate women.

The larger proportion of infanticides was
attributable to the women of limited resources
who, through isolation and desperation, often
concealed the birth of their child, killing the
infant within the first 24 hours through exposure
or other means. Clearly, a crime closely associated with infanticide was concealment of birth, in
which a secret childbirth resulted in death, even if
no evidence of murder existed, and which was
considered a capital offense. Similar laws had
been enacted in Australia (Thearle & Gregory,
1988), France (Moseley, 1978), Canada, and other countries. In America, a 1643 Massachusetts
law duplicating the English statute was entitled,
"An act to prevent the destroying and murdering
of bastard children" (Saunders, 1989, p. 369).
Just as these other countries grappled with the
enforcement of these laws, so did England, which
eventually reduced the punishment to a two year
sentence in 1803 as it became clear that the law
was impossible to enforce. Difficulties of convict-
ing led to pressure to change the law, as medical
evidence was hard to find, and the creation of a
new category of crime for mothers accused of
infanticide occurred, one that would not be a capital offense and would not require medical evidence. (This was suggested in 1860, but did not
become law until the 20th century.) Lenient

judges and confused jurors were unable to determine who was the true victim, although this was not so in cases where mothers murdered older children. An illuminating account of this can be found in Higginbotham's (1989) *Victorian Studies* article detailing the period from 1839 to 1906 using court records of charges, verdicts, and sentences for women in London who had murdered their infants.

What is most troubling about the Victorian era was its apparent duplicity. England was a major world power with enormous resources. This was a period in history when "the sun never set" on English soil, given the vast colonization that had occurred during the previous century. Yet, the way the British chose to deal with this sticky problem at home was to ignore it, and when evidence of it became undeniable, to enact stringent laws to further divide the classes. When dead infants littered the streets, as some historians believe, and Victorians could no longer ignore the problem, they provided a way to avoid the deeper social ills — the role of the state, parental responsibilities, allocation of resources — by focusing on the obvious perpetrators: those "murdering mothers." The public outcry regarding these women served to focus energy on that part of society which was mentally disturbed, immoral, or both.

Victorian England provides the modern-day industrialized world with what the historian Barbara Tuchman might have referred to as a "distant mirror." It is sobering to note that perfectionistic parents in the United States have been dubbed by some as the present-day Victorians (Piers, 1978). The current political climate has fostered an inordinate amount of attention on the "pregnant teen problem" and its concomitant problems — suspected abuse, concealment of birth, unsafe abortions, and possible murder — murder whose motive is not unlike that of a young servant girl in Victorian England.

Hrdy (1992) offered several reasons for this

form of parental retrenchment which apply to Victorian England as well as to modern-day America: "high reproductive value of the mother combined with poor current prospects, low potential for paternal support in environments where support is critical; or poor prospects of either productive or reproductive returns from investment in the infant" (p. 428). In other words, a young mother who has many years ahead of her during which to be impregnated and bear offspring, but who currently has almost no support for the present pregnancy, especially support of the father where that support is essential, may be more likely to engage in destruction of the infant rather than other options such as fostering out, etc. An actual case history follows.

Case History 2, Neonaticide by a Young, Unmarried Female. J.T., a 16-year-old high school student, was admitted to a psychiatric hospital in Canada by order of the police. She had been charged with the attempted murder of her newborn (See Cherland & Matthews, 1989, for complete details). She had no previous psychiatric history, and upon questioning, related the following:

She became pregnant when she and her 18-year-old boyfriend began having sexual relations. They used no contraception. J.T. was aware that she was pregnant, however, she was terrified of telling anyone because she thought she was too young. She did tell her boyfriend, but stated they did not discuss the pregnancy after that and did not make any plans. She received no pre-natal care and gained only 10 to 15 pounds during her pregnancy. She had no difficulty concealing the pregnancy from her friends and family. Nor did she have any difficulties with her studies or regular activities. She denied feeling depressed or suicidal during her pregnancy. Her mother asked her about a month prior to delivery if she was pregnant and the patient stated that she had the urge to be honest but was fearful and therefore denied it. A few hours before the baby was born, she began to experience labor pains. She went into the bathroom and delivered the baby in the bathtub. She stated that when the baby was born, she was overwhelmed with a terrible panicky feeling and began to stab the baby with the scissors she had used to cut the chord, (p. 337).

Fortunately, her mother intervened when J.T. realized that she did not really wish to kill the baby and called out to her. The mother, aware of the seriousness of the situation, called the authorities. Once in the hospital, J.T. was assessed using the Minnesota Multiphasic Personality Inventory (MMPI) and the Thematic Apperception Test (TAT). Her MMPI profile was characteristic of a person who maintains emotional distance and utilizes the defense mechanisms of denial, avoidance, and projection to "under-control impulses and act without sufficient deliberation." Her TAT responses were typical of people whose emotional needs as children were not met, with common defense mechanisms of "denial, avoidance, and regression" (p. 338). In addition, a family assessment was conducted, as J.T.'s wish to keep her child necessitated her parent's help. After 12 days of hospitalization, J.T. was released to face a criminal trial for attempted infanticide (the legal term used in Canada). At an interim custody hearing, J.T. was found not to be criminally responsible. (Unfortunately, the report does not specify the basis for this decision, only that the court accepted the physician's arguments for temporary insanity.) The infant, having been placed with social services, was returned to J.T. several months later on the condition that she receive counseling. At a one-year follow-up, J.T. had graduated from high school, was working part-time, and was living in the home of her parents. The father of the child visited the baby three or four times a month. A social worker met regularly with J.T. and the baby. J.T.'s future goals included moving out of her parents' home and obtaining training as a legal secretary once her child was five years old.

Resnick's (1970) extensive review of neonaticide revealed that it is clinically different from other forms of child murder by parents in that it is usually committed by a younger, unmarried woman who has denied the pregnancy and often hides the infant's body. He suggested that two subgroups exist: premeditators, who exhibit little moral concern; and those who, fearing parental disapproval, panic after the birth and murder the infant. These findings have been replicated by Wilkie, Pearn, and Petrie, (1982).

The notion of detachment is the most likely underlying mechanism explaining infanticide, especially neonaticide, in those mothers who have few resources, who have denied the pregnancy, concealed the birth, and murdered the infant within the first 24 hours, before "it" means anything (see Figure 2). These mothers deny the humanness of the child, the potential for relatedness, and concentrate instead on the burden and terror that ensues from the birth. Piers (1978) suggested that it is this fluctuating nature of attachment in humans which provides the circumstances for infanticide to occur. When a mother does not bond with her infant, she is experiencing "basic strangeness...the opposite of empathy...[the infant is] an inanimate thing" (p. 37-38). It is infinitely easier to discard an inanimate thing as opposed to a living human person. It is perhaps the industrialized nation's form of "liminal."

J.T.'s case history illustrates two important elements: an attempted, rather than successfully completed, killing of a newborn and the possibility of rehabilitation. The medical and mental health communities have become more involved in assessing the likelihood of adequate maternal care for such cases.

J.T.'s case also raises legal issues which are different from country to country, although often based on similar legal precedent. For instance, England's Infanticide Act of 1939, still in place, applies to the killing of a child under the age of 12 months by a mother who is not fully recovered

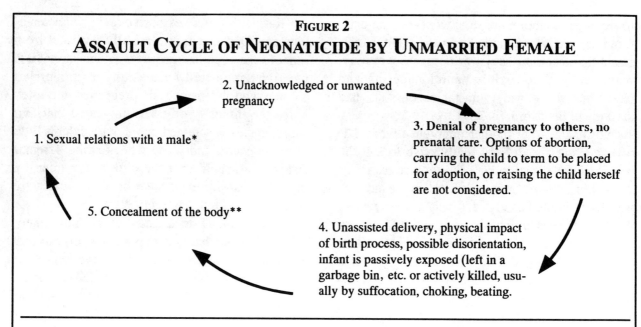

FIGURE 2
ASSAULT CYCLE OF NEONATICIDE BY UNMARRIED FEMALE

1. Sexual relations with a male*

2. Unacknowledged or unwanted pregnancy

3. Denial of pregnancy to others, no prenatal care. Options of abortion, carrying the child to term to be placed for adoption, or raising the child herself are not considered.

4. Unassisted delivery, physical impact of birth process, possible disorientation, infant is passively exposed (left in a garbage bin, etc. or actively killed, usually by suffocation, choking, beating.

5. Concealment of the body**

* If the woman has not resolved the issues of continuing sexual contact with a partner or partners and does not use birth control methods, she risks repeating the cycle again. Often young women report that by acknowledging the need for birth control, they must likewise acknowledge their sexual activity which they would prefer not to do.

** Concealment of the body does not ensure escape from legal recourse. If detected and indicated, she will begin an entirely new cycle where she might herself become the victim of other assault cycles, as "baby killers" are not accepted by fellow inmates.

from the aftermath of pregnancy, birth, and lactation, and suffers from some kind of mental disorder because of this. At most, she will be convicted of "infanticide," akin to manslaughter, rather than murder. A very similar Infanticide Act exists in Canada (Silverman & Kennedy, 1988). The reasoning apparently is that no woman in her "right mind" would kill her infant. In the United States, no such assumption is made. Cases of child murder by mothers are often prosecuted where murder convictions are sought, even when the mother is obviously psychologically impaired, although a number of these cases include women who are found not guilty by reason of insanity (Goldstein, 1989). As many attorneys and psychiatrists know, employing the insanity defense requires a vigorous test of a defendant's knowledge and appreciation of the wrongfulness of the criminal act. The

M'Naghten Rule, the broad base upon which the insanity defense rests, is not precise and has resulted in a divergence of legal opinion regarding wrongfulness. The American Psychiatric Association (Insanity Defense Work Group, 1982), attempting to raise awareness surrounding this issue, issued a statement regarding the insanity defense, suggesting that psychiatric diagnoses used in such cases be sufficiently severe to warrant a diagnosis of psychosis, and carefully delineated that many levels of psychopathology did not necessarily rise to that level, including hallucinations, gross disorganizations of behavior, and extreme affective disturbance. The formulation and use by most states of the Model Penal Code has also clarified some of the problems inherent in the M'Naghten Rule by expanding wrongfulness to include a deeper understanding of the act, including an affective awareness.

It could be argued that the insanity defense of the postpartum mother in the United States is somewhat akin to the infanticide acts in England, Australia, Ireland, Canada, etc. In such cases, the Diagnostic and Statistical Manual of Mental Disorders, Fourth Edition (American Psychiatric Association, 1994, DSM-IV) diagnosis of Postpartum Depression, specifically labeled as "Postpartum Onset Specifier" (p. 375) to be considered along with the relevant mood disorder, includes similar conditions: hormonal changes, altered body image, activation of conflicts related to pregnancy.

Sometimes referred to as the "baby blues," postpartum depression also includes such symptoms as insomnia, loss of appetite, withdrawal from relationships, self-doubt, difficulty concentrating, ambivalence toward the baby, and thoughts of death. Nearly two-thirds of new mothers experience such baby blues for a brief period just after the birth of their child. But, for 10% of these women, depressive symptoms are far more severe and prolonged. Approximately two out of every 1,000 cases evolve into psychosis. That psychosis may or may not result in infanticide. According to some authors (Appleby & Dickens, 1993), not enough is known about postpartum depression. They suggest, however, that this becomes a critical issue, as large numbers of medical and mental health practitioners are asked to assess a mother's ability to care for her child.

A recent study (as reported in Brody, 1994) stated that postpartum depression was as common in rural Africa as in the industrialized West, indirectly implying a biological substrate, although reliable data do not exist to confirm this.

Treatment. Planning intervention for this type of infanticide will require a number of strategies aimed at the societal and individual level. The following list illustrates this point:

• Sex education aimed at the schools and community that includes information about the consequences of being sexually active, and appropriate forms of birth control, including abstinence.

• Public Service Announcements offering information about alternatives (carrying a baby to term, skills required to keep the infant, or adoption procedures).

• All-out efforts to stem the tide of unmarried teenage pregnancy, possibly including economic and legal sanctions against fathers, and governmentally sponsored legislation.

• Personal counseling for young women who have acknowledged their pregnancies; subsequent after-birth counseling and training for the women who choose to keep their infants.

Cycle 3: Infanticide by an Older Female

According to our preliminary categorization, the older mother who kills her child manifests different characteristics. She does not kill the child within the first 24 hours of birth and is often married. She may or may not be suffering from postpartum depression or another major mental disorder (see Figure 3).

Case History 3, Infanticide by an Older Female. Five cases will be presented: Elizabeth Diane Downs, an example of a woman who had a peculiar relationship with a male, as well as a personality disorder; Medea, an example of a revenge infanticide; Lucrezia Gentile and Patricia Zile, examples of postpartum depression infanticide, and the recently sensationalized case of Susan Smith.

In May 1983, Elizabeth Diane Downs, a Springfield, Oregon, mother, claimed that a stranger waved down her car on a deserted road and shot her and her three children, killing her seven-year old daughter, Cheryl Lynn. Based primarily on the testimony of one of the children who lived through the ordeal, Elizabeth Downs is serving a life sentence for murder. She was apparently willing to "discard" her three children

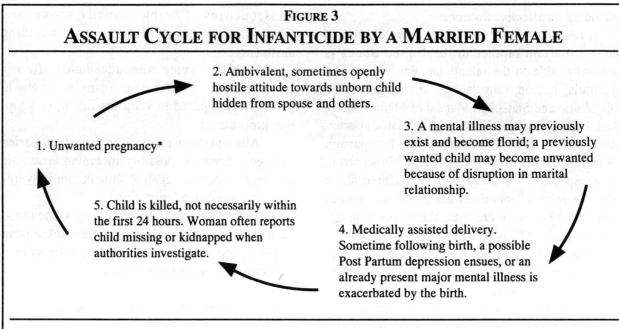

FIGURE 3

ASSAULT CYCLE FOR INFANTICIDE BY A MARRIED FEMALE

1. Unwanted pregnancy*

2. Ambivalent, sometimes openly hostile attitude towards unborn child hidden from spouse and others.

3. A mental illness may previously exist and become florid; a previously wanted child may become unwanted because of disruption in marital relationship.

4. Medically assisted delivery. Sometime following birth, a possible Post Partum depression ensues, or an already present major mental illness is exacerbated by the birth.

5. Child is killed, not necessarily within the first 24 hours. Woman often reports child missing or kidnapped when authorities investigate.

* If original stressors which caused the woman to become ambivalent about her infant initially are not ameliorated and/or major mental illness, if persistent is not treated, it is possible the cycle could start again with a subsequent pregnancy and later death. An example in the extreme of just such a circumstance is a case where an Atlanta woman smothered four of her children, one each time her husband threatened to leave her. Originally, the authorities thought the deaths were caused by SIDS.

because they were getting in the way of her relationship with her boyfriend. According to author Rule, who wrote a true crime novel based on the story, in such premeditated crimes, three elements exist: (a) an anti-social personality, (b) histrionics — the actress taking over, and (c) narcissism — "I deserve whatever I want because I'm special" (as reported in Smith & Mehren, 1994).

The legend of Medea, immortalized by Euripides in approximately 400 B.C.E., is the story of a woman who discovered that her husband, Jason, was having an affair with another woman. She was so enraged that, in an act of revenge, she killed the two things which mattered the most to him — his children.

In the true case of Pauline Zile, a 24-year-old housewife, she had reported to police that her seven-year-old daughter had been abducted from a shopping mall. A massive hunt for the girl ensued. Both Pauline and her husband were indicted for murder when blood was found in their apartment. Later, it became evident that they had participated in killing their daughter and had then hidden the body in a shallow grave (Van Biema, 1994).

In the case of Lucrezia Gentile, a Brooklyn housewife, she told police that her two-month-old baby had been kidnapped. Later, she confessed that she had drowned her two-month-old son in the bathtub. When questioned, she told the police that she couldn't stand his incessant crying. Doctors believed it was the result of a temporary mental breakdown, which they diagnosed as postpartum depression (Toufexis, 1988).

Finally, there is the horrifying case of Susan Smith, the South Carolina woman who allowed her automobile to roll into a lake on October 25, 1994, drowning her two young sons who were still strapped into their car seats.

The facts of the case are similar to the Downs case in that Smith had a relationship with a boyfriend who did not want children. Whether or not Smith could be diagnosed as a Narcissistic Personality Disorder is questionable, however. She was found guilty of murder, the jurors rejecting the lesser charge of involuntary manslaughter, and was sentenced to life in prison.

Treatment. Intervention strategies will need to include prevention based on adequate detection.

• Training for health care professionals who will be in contact with the mother during and after the birth process to accurately diagnose a major mental disorder, if present.

• Follow-up care for those mothers and newborns who are at risk.

• Lobbying for legislation to pressure insurance companies to extend maternity coverage so that all mothers can expect at least 48 hours post-birth care, with 72 hours for problematic births.

• Development of a medically sanctioned, empirically based protocol which gives physicians, nurses, and other medical personnel a tool to determine level of risk and treatment strategy.

As summarized by Tucker (1994), "For years to come, the name Susan Smith will be shorthand for many painful subjects: deteriorating family structures, the loss of innocence in small-town America, infanticide" (p. B11). Perhaps each of the above accounts — Downs, Zile, Gentile, and now Smith — reminds us that these recommendations for treatment require our serious consideration.

Cycle 4: Filicide Controversy about the state of childhood may be relevant to an understanding of filicide. While it is suggested that childhood has been relatively nonexistent until recently, others believe that it has always been a protected state, quite like it is now (Pollack, 1983). Much of the information culled from research of diaries and autobiographies suggests that children and parents felt mutual affection and attachment in Britain and America from the 16th to 19th centuries, as well as at other times in human history.

It is likely that the wish to cherish childhood has always been an important one held by most adults. Placing filicide within this context may shed light on our response to child beating. "How can this happen?" ask some. Others suggest that a measured examination of parental investment, available resources, and parental retrenchment will allow us to more accurately assess and treat the problem (Daly & Wilson, 1988; Hrdy, 1992). Childrearing is a very demanding task. "It is a wonder more kids are not battered, beaten, drowned or killed," stated Mills, a UCLA forensic psychologist, (as reported by Smith and Mehren in *The Los Angeles Times,* 1994). In the same article, Charles Ewing, the author of the book *Fatal Families*, is also quoted as follows: "[Filicide] may disabuse us of our naive notion that people don't hurt the ones they love. Not only do they hurt the people they love, they also kill them" (p. A1).

The notion of children as inanimate objects that might explain neonaticide does not explain the murders by parents of children ages 2 to 5, as these children have distinct characteristics and possess a certain relatedness. Does intermittent attachment explain such murders? This type of infanticide requires the additional explanations drawn from the empirical literature which suggest that child abuse has likely preceded the act of murder, but that the murder itself was not intended (see Figure 4). The abuse occurred for the first, and tragically last, time at a lethal level. As the anthropologist Korbin stated, "murder is usually not the first assault on the child" (Van Biema, 1994, p. 50). Based on her research of women incarcerated for deadly child abuse, she also stated that many of these crimes are preventable. "These women often let others know about incidents of abuse prior to the fatal incident."

Societal influences indirectly and directly impact filicide rates as well. In Britain in the 1980s, it was not an accident that assaults on young children increased along with the level of

FIGURE 4
ASSAULT CYCLE FOR FILICIDE BY FEMALE*

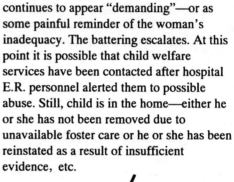

2. Stress of parenthood, adulthood and motherhood combine with limited resources and little or no social network to cause seemingly unbearable pressure. An infant or child, usually vulnerable for some reason, begins to be battered.

1. Sometime in the woman's life, usually as a child herself, she was battered by her parents or parent surrogates.

3. As pressures increase, the battered child continues to appear "demanding"—or as some painful reminder of the woman's inadequacy. The battering escalates. At this point it is possible that child welfare services have been contacted after hospital E.R. personnel alerted them to possible abuse. Still, child is in the home—either he or she has not been removed due to unavailable foster care or he or she has been reinstated as a result of insufficient evidence, etc.

5. Incarceration occurs if found guilty, released if found innocent. Either way, cycle may begin again.

4. During a beating, the woman accidentally batters the child to death.* This act is more likely to come to the attention of the authorities if there are previous incidents of record. Whether she will be indicted will depend on a number of variables.

* It is also possible that if there is a man in the home (father, stepfather, boyfriend, etc.) he may be participating as well.

unemployment (Rose, 1986). Similar circumstances have occurred in America and Europe.

Case History 4, Filicide. An analysis of 104 cases of suspected and/or confirmed fatalities of infants and young children ages 0- to 5-years old was conducted by Schloesser, Pierpont, and Poertner (1992) in an attempt to understand the phenomenon by utilizing existing records and matching birth and death certificates. They concluded that some form of "active surveillance" would enhance the quality of investigation. The

first step is the establishment of a policy that each child death be reviewed by a state level group representing the various departments that have access to relevant information. Schloesser et al. (1992) suggested that this policy focus on all child deaths. By examining all deaths, the problem of deciding whether to study the suspicious death of a child is avoided, and determining whether it is a child abuse death, a homicide, or a natural death becomes a standard part of the review process. It needs to be clear that the purpose of such a review is the establishment of an epidemiological data base that can be used to link characteristics of the child and family to the death, not to affix blame or to determine if a professional or an agency failed to follow policy or procedure. The authors assert:

At a minimum the agencies that keep birth and death certificate information, the state child protection agency, the income maintenance agency, the state law enforcement agency, and the state attorney general should all take part in the information gathering and review process....This method would make each child abuse fatality a relatively unambiguous event, amenable to definition and study, making it useful as a measurement standard between states and between nations (pp. 8-9).

Treatment. The ability to intervene at the various critical stages requires a number of broad-based and specific intervention strategies. The following list highlights some of those.

• Initiating legislation and educational programs to increase parents' investment in their offspring, either by accessing available community resources or offering new ones.

• Instigating an active campaign to increase parents' options — fostering out, adoption, and birth control.

• Intervening in the battering cycle sooner and more firmly — developing a protocol based on empirical data which more accurately predict batterers.

• Changing policies to include "active surveillance" methods nationwide.

Infanticide: A Moral Imperative or Aristotelian Dilemma?

James Q. Wilson (1993), in a presidental address to the American Political Science Association, utilized the topic of infanticide to demonstrate the idea of a "moral sense." He suggested that moral behavior is more likely to occur when a sense of utility or usefulness combines with a

sense of duty, in other words, an exchange of advantage and obligation. This is perhaps an apt portrayal of the mutual interplay of parent and child as well as government and individual citizen. According to the research, infants and parents are actually predisposed to attachment. If not, civilization would have ceased long ago, given the inordinately long period of dependency in humans.

Our brains make possible the imagining of such commitments through a sophisticated higher mental process that allows us to project ourselves into the future and to imagine the rewards as well as obligations of childrearing. Ironically, we may possess the capacity to imagine that we are attached or loyal to a fictional group (i.e., watching a movie) or to a real but not present group (networking on a computer), and still may not imagine ourselves loyal or attached enough to a newborn infant to ensure his or her survival. This detached object status actually may be the necessary prerequisite to murder. In this sense, a moral sentiment can expand half-way across the world on the internet, yet stop where the cradle begins. How can this be so? How does the "maternal instinct" go awry? Hrdy (1992) suggested an approach for dealing with these questions. If we as a society are more willing to search for the predictors of parental retrenchment based on the real and present constraints that prevent parents from choosing alternative "tactics for reducing parental effort we [will] go a long way towards understanding the proximate causes of infanticide" (Hrdy, 1992, pp. 428-429). We must examine the impact of societal practices, cultural attitudes, and demographics. Perhaps the most pertinent is the examination of our peculiar beliefs about parenting, not the least of which is our stubborn adherence to the myth of "mother love" as a cultural imperative.

In a study of mothers of handicapped infants (Childs, 1985), 40% of the mothers admitted to entertaining thoughts of infanticide. This is an understandable response to the circumstances.

Just as some women fear deformity in infants, so too might they fear infants themselves and the "deformity" these infants represent to their so-called mothering. Is it possible that a random survey would uncover a similar percentage — that 40% of all mothers at some time or another have thoughts of infanticide? We allow the mothers of handicapped infants to express grief, rage, and fear. What if the fears of the "deformed mother" and "handicapped mother" reside in some women to such an extent that they too are at risk. There is a strong ethic not to acknowledge parenting failures, especially "maternal instinct" failure. For many women, the magic moment of bonding does not occur after the birth of a child. These women, assured of societal opprobrium should they admit such a thing, are far less willing to acknowledge their lack of ability, because it appears to them to be a lack of morals, and are therefore less willing to seek assistance.

One of the myths of motherhood is that only mothers create families. It is more likely that families create mothers, and that fathers or spouses, the networks of neighbors, extended families, and other resources are all necessary in the raising of our children.

Aristotle's explanations of human behavior might serve us well. He never reduced complex human interactions to one fundamental principle, e.g., self preservation or utility. In order to fashion a morality regarding infanticide, perhaps the most we can hope for is to rely on Aristotle's teleology and to acknowledge that there are several partially consistent moral principles operating (Halliwell, 1987). We are seeking, as Aristotle did, "a grasp of what is good in human life and a rough ranking of those goods" (Wilson, 1993, p. 9).

Annotated Bibliography

Rule, Ann (1988). *Small Sacrifices: A True Story of Passion and Murder*. London: Corgi Press. In May 1983, Elizabeth Diane Downs, a Springfield, Oregon, mother, claimed that a stranger waved down her car on a deserted road and shot her and her three children, killing her seven-year old daughter, Cheryl Lynn. Primarily based on the testimony of one of the children who lived through the ordeal, Diane Downs is serving a life sentence for murder. She was apparently willing to discard her three children because they were getting in the way of her relationship with her boyfriend. According to author Rule, in such premeditated crimes, three elements exist: (a) an antisocial personality, (b) histrionics — the actress taking over, and (c) narcissism "I deserve whatever I want because I'm special." Rule, who is a particularly adept crime writer, reveals the elements of the case in spine-chilling detail that reads as much like a novel as it does a true crime story.

Straus, Murray (1994). *Beating the Devil Out of Them: Corporal punishment in American families*. New York: Lexington/Macmillan. Together with his co-workers at the Family Research Lab of the University of New Hampshire, Straus details the consequences of continuing to use physical punishment in the disciplining of our children. He presents data showing that adults who were hit by their parents as teenagers are more likely to be depressed as adults in proportion to how frequently they were hit. While this and other data are at times unclear, the bottom line is not: we ought to stop hitting our kids. He presents the countries who have passed laws against corporal punishment (Sweden, Norway, Finland, Denmark, Austria), and challenges us to do likewise.

References

American Psychiatric Association (1994). *Diagnostic

and statistical manual of mental disorders, 4th ed. Washington, DC: Author.

Amighi, J. (1990). Some thoughts on the cross-cultural study of maternal warmth and detachment. *Pre and Perinatal Psychology Journal, 5*(2), 131-146.

Appleby, L., & Dickens, C. (1993). Mothering skills of women with mental illness: Not enough known about the postpartum period. *British Medical Journal, 306*(6874), 348.

Ballentine, J. (1969). *Ballentine's law dictionary* (3rd ed.). San Francisco: Bancroft-Whitney Co.

Black, H. (1990). *Black's law dictionary: Definitions of the terms and phrases of American and English jurisprudence ancient and modern* (6th ed.). St. Paul: West Publishing Co.

Bourget, D., & Bradford, J. M. W. (1990). Homicidal parents. *Canadian Journal of Psychiatry, 35*(3), 233-237.

Bouvier, J. (1914). *Bouvier's law dictionary and concise encyclopedia* (Vol. 1). St. Paul: West Publishing Co.

Brody, J. (1994, November 6). Battling the baby blues: Research brings understanding, help for postpartum depression. *Star Tribune,* p. 3E.

Burke, B. (1984). Infanticide: Why does it happen in monkeys, mice, and men? *Science, 84*(5), 26-31.

Cherland, E., & Matthews, P. C. (1989). Attempted murder of a newborn: A case history. *Canadian Journal of Psychiatry, 34,* 337-339.

Childs, R. E. (1985). Maternal psychological conflicts associated with the birth of a retarded child. *Maternal-Child Nursing Journal,* 175-182.

Daly, M., & Wilson, M. (1980). Discriminative parental solicitude: A biological perspective. *Journal of Marriage and Family, 42,* 277-288.

Daly, M., & Wilson, M. (1983). *Sex, evolution and behavior* (2nd ed.). Boston: Willard Grant Press.

Daly, M., & Wilson, M. (1984). A sociobiological analysis of human infanticide. In G. Hausfater & S. B. Hrdy, (Eds.), *Infanticide: Comparative and evolutionary perspectives* (pp. 487-502). Hawthorne, NY: Aldine de Gruyter.

Daly, M., & Wilson, M. (1988). *Homicide.* Hawthorne, NY: Aldine de Gruyter.

DeMause, L. (1976). *The history of childhood.* London: Souvenir Press.

DeMause, L. (1990). The history of child assault. *The Journal of Psychohistory, 18*(1), 1-28.

Depression, stress can trigger moms to kill. (1994, November 5). *Star Tribune,* p. 14A.

deWaal, F. (1989). *Peacemaking among primates.* Cambridge, MA: Harvard University Press.

d'Orban, P. T. (1979). Women who kill their children. *British Journal of Psychiatry, 134,* 560-571.

Dorland, W.A., (Ed.). (1988). *Dorland's illustrated medical dictionary* (25th ed.). Philadelphia: W. B. Saunders Co.

Duncan, A., Durstan, G., & Wellbourn, E. (Eds.) (1977). *Dictionary of medical ethics.* London: Darton, Longman & Todd Pub.

Eibl-Eibesfeldt, I. (1989). *Human ethology.* Hawthorne, NY: Aldine de Gruyter.

Freed, R. S., & Freed, S. A. (1989). Beliefs and practices

resulting in female deaths and fewer females than males in India. *Population and Environment: A Journal of Interdisciplinary Studies, 10*(3), 144-161.

Goldstein, R. L. (1989). The psychiatrist's guide to right and wrong: Part III: Postpartum depression and the "appreciation" of wrongfulness. *Bulletin of the American Academy of Psychiatry and Law, 17*(2), 121-128.

Goodall, J. (1986). *The chimpanzee of Gombe: Patterns of behavior.* Cambridge, MA: The Belknap Press of Harvard University Press.

Halliwell, S. (1987). *The poetics of Aristotle: Translation and commentary.* Chapel Hill: University of North Carolina Press.

Hamai, M., Nishida, T., Takasaki, H., & Turner, L. (1992). New records of within-group infanticide and cannibalism in wild chimpanzees. *Primates, 33*, 151-162.

Hanawalt, B. (1977). Childrearing among the lower classes of late medieval England. *Journal of Interdisciplinary History, 8*(1), 1-22.

Harlow, H., & Harlow, M. (1962). The effect of rearing conditions on behavior. *Bulletin of the Menninger Clinic, 26*, 213-224.

Hausfater, G., & Hrdy, S. B. (Eds.). (1984). *Infanticide: Comparative and evolutionary perspectives.* New York: The Aldine Publishing Company.

Hawkes, K. (1981). A third explanation for female infanticide. *Human ecology, 9*(1), 79-96.

Helmholtz, R. H. (1975). Infanticide in the province of Canterbury during the fifteenth century. *History of Childhood Quarterly, 2*, 379-90.

Higginbotham, A. R. (1989, Spring). Sin of the age: Infanticide and illegitimacy in Victorian London. *Victorian Studies*, 319-337.

Hiraiwa-Hasegawa, M. (1987). Infanticide in primates and a possible case of male-biased infanticide in chimpanzees. In Y. Itso, J. L. Brown, & J. Kikkawa (Eds.), *Animal Societies: Theories and Facts* (pp. 125-139). Tokyo: Japan Scientific Societies Press.

Hoffer, P., & Hull, N. E. H. (1981). *Murdering mothers: Infanticide in England and New England.* New York: New York University Press.

Horan, D., & Delahoyde, M. (1982). *Infanticide and the handicapped infant.* Provo: BYU Press.

Hrdy, S. B. (1976). The care and exploitation of nonhuman primate infants by conspecifics other than the mother. *Advances in the Study of Behavior, 6*, 101-158.

Hrdy, S. B. (1977). The puzzle of langur infant-sharing. In *The langurs of Abu: Female and male strategies of reproduction.* Cambridge: Harvard University Press.

Hrdy, S. B. (1979). Infanticide among animals: A review, classification, and examination of the implications for the reproductive strategies of females. *Ethology and Sociobiology, 1*, 13-40.

Hrdy, S. B. (1987). Sex-biased investment in primates and other mammals. In R. Gelles & J. Lancaster (Eds.), *Child abuse and neglect* (pp. 97-147). Hawthorne, NY: Aldine de Gruyter.

Hrdy, S. B. (1990). Sex bias in nature and in history: A late 1980's re-examination of the "biological origins" argument. *Yearbook of Physical Anthropology, 33*, 25-37.

Hrdy, S. B. (1992). Fitness tradeoffs in the history and evolution of delegated mothering with special reference to wet-nursing, abandonment, and infanticide. *Ethology and Sociobiology, 13*, 409-442.

Insanity defense work group: American Psychiatric Association statement on the insanity defense (1982). *American Journal of Psychiatry, 140*, 681-688.

Issues for the September 1994 United Nations international conference on population and development (1994). *Audubon, 96*(4), 56.

Krishnaswamy, S. (1984). A note on female infanticide: An anthropological inquiry. *The Indian Journal of Social Work, 45*(3), 297-302.

Kusum, (1993). The use of pre-natal diagnostic techniques for sex selection: The Indian scene. *Bioethics, 7*(2/3), 149-165.

Lagaipa, S. J. (1990). Suffer the little children: The ancient practice of infanticide as a modern moral dilemma. *Issues in Comprehensive Pediatric Nursing, 13*, 241-251.

Langer, W. (1974). Infanticide: A historical survey. *History of Childhood Quarterly, 1*, 353-365.

Lester, D. (1985). The relation of twin infanticide to status of women, societal aggression, and material well-being. *The Journal of Social Psychology, 126*(1), 57-59.

Masters, A. L. (1990). Infanticide: The primate data. *The Journal of Psychohistory, 18*, 99-108.

Mays, S. (1993). Infanticide in Roman Britain. *Antiquity, 67*, 883-888.

McGowan, J. (1991). Little girls dying: An ancient and thriving practice. *Commonweal, 118*(14), 481-482.

Miller, B. D. (1981). *The endangered sex: Neglect of female children in rural North India*. Ithaca, NY: Cornell University.

Misery in the maternity wards. (1990, January 20). *The Economist, 52.*

Mohnot, S. M. (1971). Some aspects of social changes and infant-killing in the Hanuman langur *Presbytis entellus* (Primates: Cercopithecidae) in Western India. *Mammalia, 35*, 175-198.

Moseley, K. L. (1978). The history of infanticide in Western society. *Issues in Law and Medicine, 1*(5), 345-361.

Piers, M. (1978). *Infanticide*. New York: W. W. Norton & Co.

Pollack, L. (1983). *Forgotten children: Parent-child relations from 1500-1900*. Cambridge: Cambridge University Press.

Reich, W. T. (1995). *Encyclopedia of bioethics*. New York: Macmillan Publishing Co.

Resnick, P. J. (1970). Murder of the newborn: A psychiatric review of neonaticide. *American Journal of Psychiatry, 126*, 1414-1420.

Resnick, P. J. (1969). Child murder by parents: A psychiatric review of filicide. *American Journal of Psychiatry, 126*(3), 325-334.

Rose, L. (1986). *The massacre of the innocents: Infanticide in Britain 1800-1939*. London: Routledge & Kegan Paul.

Rule, A. (1988). *Small sacrifices: A true story of passion and murder*. London: Corgi Press.

Saunders, E. (1989). Neonaticides following "secret"

pregnancies: Seven case reports. *Public Health Reports, 104*(4), 368-372.

Scheper-Hughes, N. (1989, October). Death without weeping: Has poverty ravaged mother love in the shantytowns of Brazil? *Natural History,* 8-16.

Schloesser, P., Pierpont, J., & Poertner, J. (1992). Active surveillance of child abuse fatalities. *Child Abuse and Neglect, 16,* 3-10.

Shalinsky, A., & Glascock, A. (1988). Killing infants and the aged in nonindustrial societies: Removing the liminal. *The Social Science Journal, 25*(3), 277-287.

Silverman, R. A., & Kennedy, L. W. (1988). Women who kill their children. *Violence and Victims, 3*(2), 113-127.

Smith, L., & Mehren, E. (1994, November 5). Why does a mother kill her child? *Los Angeles Times,* pp. A1, A4.

Thearle, M. J., & Gregory, H. (1988). Child abuse in nineteenth century Queensland. *Child Abuse and Neglect, 12,* 91-101.

Thurer, S. L. (1994). *The myths of motherhood: How culture reinvents the good mother.* Boston: Houghton Mifflin.

Totman, J. (1978). *The murderess: A psychological study of criminal homicide.* San Francisco: R & E Research Associates.

Toufexis, A. (1988, June 20). Why mothers kill their babies. *Time, 131,* 81-83.

Tuckman, C. (1994, November 17). The legacy of Susan Smith. *The Denver Post,* B-11.

Van Biema, D. (1994, November 14). Parents who kill. *Time, 50.*

Vogel, C. H. (1979). Der Hanuman-Langur (*Presbytis entellus*), ein Paradeexemplar fur die theoretischen Konsepte der "Soziobiologie"? Verhandl. *Deut. Zool Ges.,* 73-89.

Vogel, C. H., & Loch, H. (1984). Reproductive parameters, adult-male replacements, and infanticide among free-ranging langurs (*Presbytis entellus*) at Jodhpur (Rajasthan), India. In G. Hausfater & S. B. Hrdy (Eds.), *Infanticide: Comparative and evolutionary perspectives* (pp. 237-255). New York: Aldine.

Watts, D. P. (1989). Infanticide in mountain gorillas: New cases and a reconsideration of the evidence. *Ethology, 81,* 1-18.

Weisheit, R. (1986). When mothers kill their children. *The Social Science Journal, 23*(4), 439-448.

Wilkie, I., Pearn, J., & Petrie, G. (1982). Neonaticide, infanticide and child homicide. *Medicine, Science and the Law, 22,* 31-34.

Wilson, J. Q. (1993). The moral sense. *American Political Science Review, 87*(1), 1-10.

Wrightson, K. (1975). Infanticide in early seventeenth-century England. *Local Population Studies, 15,* 10-21.

About the Authors

Sally H. Barlow, a graduate from the University of Utah in 1978, earned her ABPP Diplomate in Clinical Psychology in 1991. She has published in the areas of individual and group psychotherapy research, has received numerous grants, among them an NIMH grant to study common and specific factors in short-term group psychotherapy, and has presented papers at national and international conferences.

As an associate professor, she teaches graduate courses in assessment, psychodynamic treatment, group theory and intervention, and diversity at Brigham Young University, where she received the Excellence in Teaching Award. Her recent interests include the regulation of psychology as a profession, as well as the education of future psychologists.

Claudia J. Clayton is an assistant professor of psychology at Brigham Young University.

She holds a PhD in anatomy, with emphases in neuroscience and pharmacology, from the University of Utah School of Medicine, and a PhD in clinical psychology from Brigham Young University. She received post-doctoral training at the University of Rochester School of Medicine and Dentistry and the University of North Carolina at Chapel Hill. Her interests include developmental psychology, biological psychology, personality disorders, and family dynamics.

CHAPTER 8

SPOUSAL HOMICIDE

V. Edwin Bixenstine

Introduction

Among violent crimes, homicide is rare. Intuitively, it strikes us as an event reserved largely for the outlander, the actions of a menacing stranger. Our topic in this light is counter-intuitive. It is the *cross-gender killing, often in anger and fear, of a spouse, a lover, or a former spouse or lover*; in short, the killing of someone toward whom we are assumed to have or to have had a tender and protective, rather than a murderous, regard. Confounding intuition all the more is that this form of homicide, among other forms, is not rare. Indeed, as we shall see, in some countries where criminal violence and murder are low compared to the United States, it is the major expression of that rare violence in which humans kill humans.

Overview and Base Rate Information

We have no good record of spousal homicide throughout history. Feminists—those men and women who focus their energies on advocating and championing the rights and welfare of women—believe that wives have always borne the brunt of lethal spousal abuse. Dickstein and Nadelson (1989) reported that paleopathologists at the Virginia Commonwealth University's Med-

ical College of Virginia have detected spouse abuse in the mummified remains of 2000- to 3000-year-old Pre-Columbian men and women in Chile and Peru. Women suffered more skull fractures than men, and 45% of them died when no known war was in progress. Some sense of proportion in recent history is revealed in the efforts of Frances Power Cobbe, a "propagandist" and feminist reformer of 19th century England (Bauer & Ritt, 1988). Her study of court records for England and Wales in 1877 revealed that 1,500 women each year were victims of "brutal assault." How many of these resulted in death is not reported.

Wolfgang (1958), however, learned that 487 homicides were committed by men in England and Wales between 1886 and 1905; one-half of the victims were female intimates, about equally represented by wives and mistresses or sweethearts. Between 1900 and 1949, 20% of 1,080 male murderers killed their wives. By comparison, only 13 of 130 women murderers had killed their husbands. Such numbers tend to confirm feminist views.

This kind of wife-directed mayhem may have its roots in ancient customs. The right of the husband to chastise his spouse and heir comes down from ancient Rome, where "family law" was distinct from criminal and civil codes. The Roman male head of the family had the authority to administer punishment *including capital punishment* (Mancuso, 1989). By the 19th century, British common law began to curb male authority by removing the right to inflict capital punishment and limiting the "instrument of restraint" to a rod no thicker than the man's thumb—the "rule of thumb" (Stacey, Hazlewood, & Shupe, 1994). By the 1850s, Parliament further restricted male prerogatives in a series of laws mandating fines and imprisonment for wife beating. Frances Power Cobbe, thus, rode a tide already underway when, in 1878, she lobbied Parliament to advance laws permitting court-ordered separation, child custody to wives, and child support, remedies still very much current, but previously available only to upper class women (Bauer & Ritt, 1988).

Reform was in the air on this side of the Atlantic as well. Maryland, in 1882, prescribed 40 lashes or one year in prison for wife beaters. By 1910, divorce for reason of cruelty was available in all but 11 states. The reform tide receded over two World Wars to reappear in the 1970s under the "rights" movements spawned by the Vietnam war (Stacey et al., 1994).

In the United States, homicide rates in general have always been far higher than in most other countries. Figure 1 presents a graph generated by Reiss and Roth (1993) from data supplied by the World Health Organization. Rates are extremely low for many countries—Greece suffers only one homicide per year for every 100,000 persons, and "bloody" Ireland about one-half of that. Noteworthy is that countries with low rates suffer higher proportions of family homicides. The Danes, for example, kill family members twice as often as non-family persons (Straus & Gelles, 1990).

In recent years, the United States has recorded between 8 and 10 homicides annually for every 100,000 persons (see Figure 2). Rates may have been at about this same level in the later 19th century (Wolfgang, 1978), but were at the lowest level as this century opened, at a rate of a little more

than one homicide for every 100,000 persons annually (Daly & Wilson, 1988). Rates climbed to a high point in the early 1930s, then fell to a low of about 4.8 persons annually per 100,000 in 1962, before again rising to recent levels.

The Federal Bureau of Investigation (FBI) **only began in 1977 to publish homicide frequency by relationships** (husband, wife, mother, etc.). However, several studies of family and spousal homicide exist for earlier years, though not for the whole country. Wolfgang (1958) used Philadelphia, Pennsylvania, police records of homicides occurring during the years 1948 to 1953. Table 1 was adapted from Wolfgang (1958, p. 66) and introduces two features not previously considered: race and age.

We note from Table 1 that 5.7 persons per 100,000 were killed annually (1948 to 1953). Men succumb at more than 3 times the rate of women. But startling is the huge rate difference by race: 11.8 Black persons were killed for every White; 12.7 Black men for each White man; and 9.6 Black women for every White woman. Offender rates echo these proportions, e.g., there were 23.2 Black for every White woman offender. Highest offender rates were in the 20 to 24 age group, though women were most lethal in the 25 to 29 age group.

These proportions are reflected in spousal/lover homicides. Wolfgang (1958) found 80 women and 74 men killed; 64 Black men compared to 59 Black women were slain, while only 10 White men died compared to 21 White women. Still, American White women in this sample were about 8 times, and Black women 18 times, more aggressive than were the English and Welsh women.

Bourdouris (1971) studied 6,389 homicides in Detroit, Michigan, occurring between 1926 and 1968. He did not report his results as comprehensively as Wolfgang and pooled spousal and other family relations. However, it is clear that homicide rates in Detroit were comparable to those in

FIGURE 1.
HOMICIDE RATES FOR SELECTED COUNTRIES

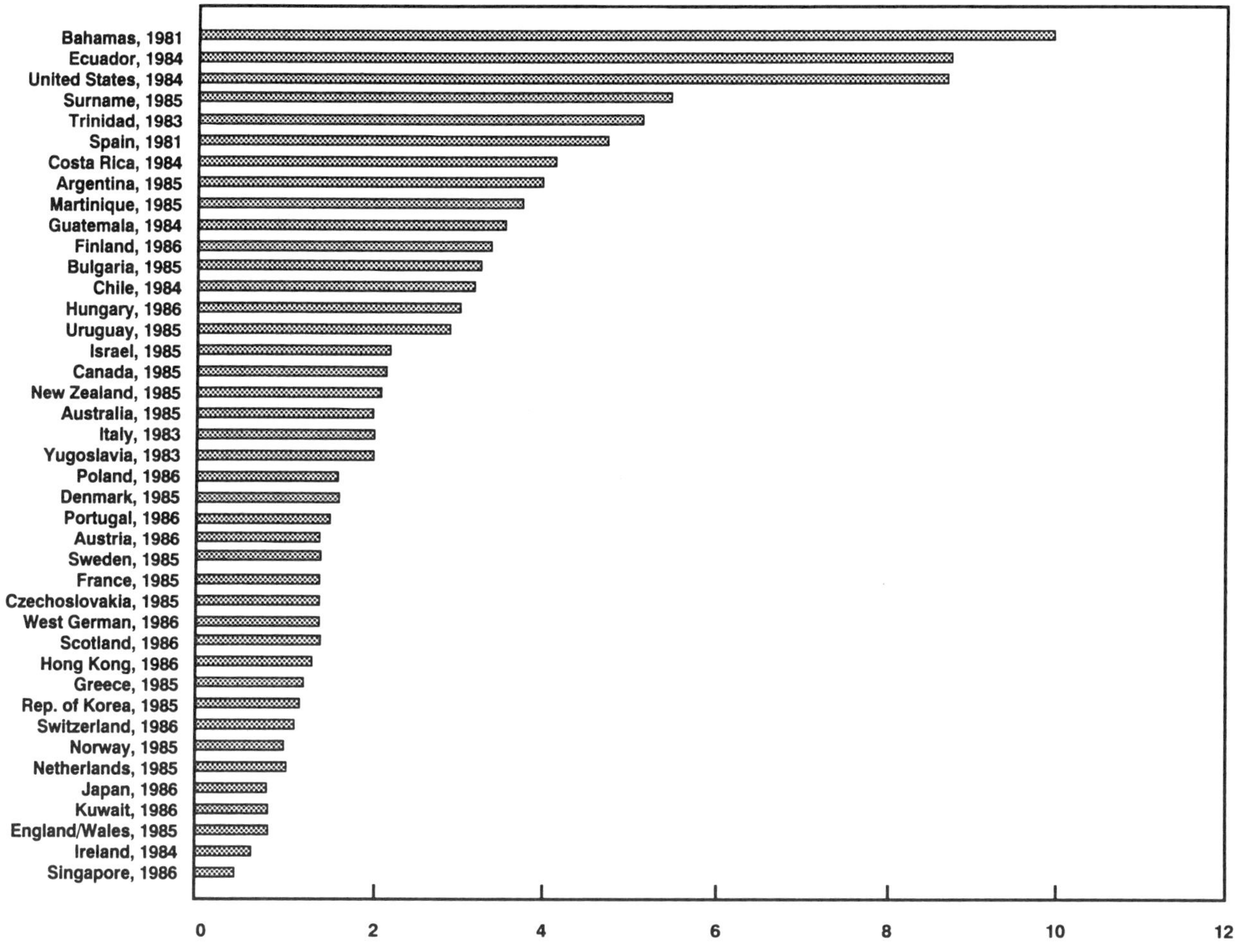

Homicide rates for selected countries. Reprinted with permission from Understanding and Preventing Violence by Reiss and Roth. Copyright 1993 by the National Academy of Sciences. Courtesy of the National Academy Press, Washington, DC.

Philadelphia. White men were more frequent offenders than White women, while Black men and Black women were about equal to each other. Meanwhile, Black rates overall exceeded White rates by ratios larger than Wolfgang reported.

Kratcoski (1988) examined 2,600 homicides between 1970 and 1983 in Cuyahoga County, Ohio, which includes Cleveland. In 1980, 82% of the County was White (56% for Cleveland). Thirty-one percent of the homicide victims were White, 68% Black. Kratcoski examined gender and race against relationship to victim in three broad classes: family, acquaintance, and stranger. White men killed family (about 70% spousal) at more than twice the rate White women did. Black males were 37% more lethal with family than Black women, a departure from Wolfgang and Bourdouris above. Again, however, the greatest variance was not sexual, but racial. Overall, Blacks committed murder at more than 18 times

FIGURE 2.
HOMICIDE RATE PER 100,000 POPULATION

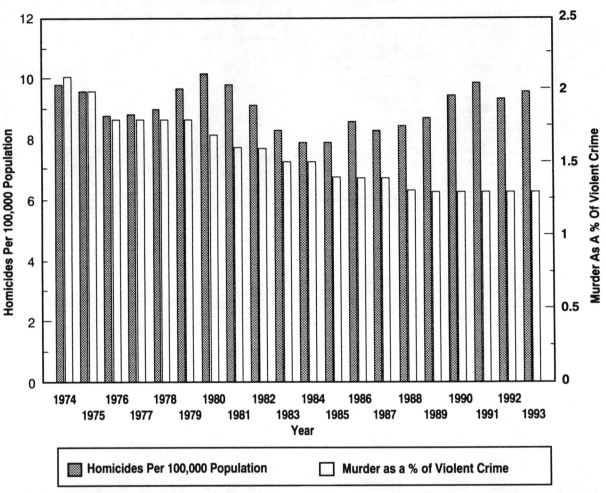

Homicide rate per 100,000 population and as a percentage of violent crime (murder, forcible rape, robbery, and aggravated assault combined). Composed from data presented in the Uniform Crime Reports (1993).

White rates. Blacks killed strangers 17 times, acquaintances 20 times, and family 14 times the rates at which Whites killed these categories of persons.

The Uniform Crime Reports (UCR) of the FBI do not break down relationships by race. In 1993, the latest available report, 335 husbands and 928 wives were victims of murder. Additionally, 256 men and 603 women died at the hands of girlfriends and boyfriends. These 2,122 spouses/lovers killed were a markedly lower proportion of all those murdered than Wolfgang found, being only 9.1% each year compared to 26.2%, and represented a rate under .9 per 100,000 persons annually. The UCR (1993) provided figures for race-on-race, sex-on-race, and sex-on-sex homicides. As has been true for some time, Blacks predominantly kill Blacks (86%) and Whites kill Whites (92%). Whites kill Blacks less (6%) than Blacks kill Whites (13%). Females kill more than 11% of

TABLE 1
HOMICIDE RATES FOR BOTH VICTIMS AND OFFENDERS
BY RACE, SEX, AND AGE

Victims

	Both Races			Blacks			Whites		
	Total	M	F	Total	M	F	Total	M	F
Rates Per 100,000, All Ages	5.7	9.0	2.6	22.5	36.9	9.6	1.9	2.9	1.0
Rate Per 100,000 For 5-Year Age Group With Highest Rate	10.4 (25-29)	15.7 (35-39)	6.9 (25-29)	41.0 (25-29)	69.4 (35-39)	28.2 (25-29)	3.1 (30-34)	4.6 (55-59)	2.3 (30-34)

Offenders

	Both Races			Blacks			Whites		
	Total	M	F	Total	M	F	Total	M	F
Rates Per 100,000, All Ages	5.7	9.0	2.6	22.5	36.9	9.6	1.9	2.9	1.0
Rate Per 100,000 For 5-Year Age Group With Highest Rate	12.6 (20-24)	22.7 (20-24)	5.4 (25-29)	47.4 (25-29)	92.5 (20-24)	22.3 (25-29)	4.6 (20-24)	8.2 (20-24)	1.2 (20-24)

*Note. Adapted with permission from Table 4 in **Patterns in Criminal Homicide** by Wolfgang. Copyright 1958 by the Trustees of the University of Pennsylvania. Courtesy of the University of Pennsylvania Press, Philadelphia, PA.*

those slain, and about 12% of all men killed.

Men kill 90% of all women slain. Blacks kill males at 10 times the rate Whites kill males, but they kill females at only 6 times the rate Whites kill females. The current Black offender murder rate is 40.2 persons per 100,000 annually, which is about 18 persons or 79% higher than Wolfgang's sample. White offender murder rates (4.8 persons per 100,000) have also increased nearly 3 persons per 100,000, a 153% increase over Wolfgang's sample. Of course, rates for cities, such as Philadelphia, have soared to 30 and 40 per 100,000 (Rosenfield, Decker, & Kohfield, 1993).

Spousal homicide has been a historic feature of human experience. The American experience has three distinctive developments. First, American homicide rates overall have grown, with some periods of reprieve, throughout the century to a high of about 10 persons per 100,000, the highest among the world's industrial countries. Spousal rates follow the general homicide rates, but neither fall as far nor rise as high.

Second, while women are killed more frequently by intimates than they kill intimates, the proportion in America has been less extreme than elsewhere. Over the 17 years on record, however, proportions of women to men killed have steadily increased from 1.2 to 1 in 1977 to 2.6 to 1 in 1993. (See Daly & Wilson, 1988, for figures on other countries.)

Third, racial differences in America are remarkable. Currently, Blacks kill and are killed at more than 8 times the rate of Whites. Homicide is the leading cause of death of Black men and women ages 15 to 34 (Campbell, 1992), and the steady attrition of Black men, rated at 4,100 per 100,000 over a lifetime (Reiss & Roth, 1993) has helped reduce their numbers to only 83% of Black women. Females kill Black men at a rate 9.4 times greater than they kill White men (UCR, 1993). As the great bulk of men killed by females are of the same race, this ratio speaks to the higher rates at which Black females kill male intimates. Over all, in real numbers, more Black men and women, representing 12.3% of the population, than White men and women, representing 84.7% of the population (Estell, 1994), commit and suffer murder each year. Moreover, these differences have been present at least since the 1920s. Reiss and Roth (1993) reported that fragmentary data suggest that Black rates were 2 to 3 times White rates in post Civil War times and that the pattern for Black homicides differs from that of other "immigrant" groups, which ordinarily are high with the first generation and become insignificant in subsequent generations. The general impression that high Black rates are relatively recent, a function of post-World War II migration and urbanization, is without basis. It is difficult to imagine how any understanding and effective treatment of homicide, including spousal homicide, can be addressed without serious attention to factors promoting and sustaining Black and White differences.

Literature and Clinical Lore

Studies of spousal homicide are relatively scarce. They indicate, however, that spousal homicide rarely occurs in cold blood (Browne, 1987; Campbell, 1992; Chimbos, 1978; Walker, 1989a). Coates (1988) found that 2% of women and 25% of men who engaged in physical violence with intimates admitted trying to kill them. This progression from physical violence to homicide makes it reasonable to examine research on violence to augment our understanding of homicide. Unfortunately, we go from rags to riches, as violence has become a celebrated topic. A reference list for spousal violence reveals 52 domestic journals, 28 emerging in the last 20 years and 9, including *Violence and Victims, Journal of Family Violence,* and *Journal of Interpersonal Violence,* in the past 10 years. Additionally, a tide of edited books has complemented this explosive exposition. The result is that we have both not enough and too much.

Beginning with studies of homicide, let us ask where, how, when, and why? Spousal homicide occurs largely in the home. Cazenave and Zahn (1992), sampling eight U.S. cities, confirmed Wolfgang's (1958) findings: Women are killed more often in the bedroom, men in the kitchen. Black women kill at home (76%), but half the time on the porch, driveway, or street fronting the house (Mann, 1990). However, being killed at home does not mean spouses were living together. Goetting (1989) found that 85% of the victims in her study were killed at home, but only 48% of the men were residing there. Cazenave and Zahn (1992) and Stout (1993) found that one-half or more of their female victims were separated from their killers at the time of their death. Wilson and Daly (1993) believe that this and other evidence show that women universally run an elevated risk when estranged over that when co-residing.

Women more often use knives to kill. Men, by comparison, use their hands. In recent years, however, the use of guns by both sexes has risen. Goetting (1989), Mann (1990, 1992), and Walker (1989a) reported gun usage in between 48 and 75% of their various samples. The UCR (1993) reported that 70% of homicides are caused by gunshot. An analysis by Farley (1986) attributed this shift to the availability of cheap and plentiful handguns. Four hundred thousand new handguns were purchased yearly in the 1950s, rising to over 2 million yearly in the late 1960s and 1970s, in step with a surge of almost 100% in homicide rates. Farley also found a higher use of guns by Blacks than Whites.

Goetting (1989) observed that spousal "[h]omicide is a leisure-related activity..." (p. 292). It occurs more often in the vacation months and on weekends, although Mann (1990) found that the largely unemployed, Black females in her study killed more frequently during the week, as weekends provided no greater leisure than weekdays. Finally, half of all homicides occur during after-work hours—8 p.m. to 2 a.m. Gelles and Straus (1988) observed that, in late evening and early morning, neither party to a passionate dispute may easily break off and leave the house. Stores are closed. Friends and family are not conveniently accessible. The bedroom and kitchen, places ordinarily of intimate commerce, become fields of battle with no easy retreat.

At last, we come to the question most fraught with controversy and uncertainty. *Why do men and women, intimate partners and lovers, kill each other?* And why do American intimates kill at rates 5 times those in most other countries, and Black Americans at rates 4 or 5 times that?

While estimates vary (Myers et al., 1984), conservatively, 2% of us (5,160,000) yearly suffer a serious psychological pathology. If 1% of this group is homicidal, we have 51,600 potential murderers among us. Even if half are children or unmarried and unattached, we still have 25,800 disturbed, homicidal men and women living in close consanguinity with others, sufficient to account for 2,200 spouse/lover homicides and enough to spare for the 22,000 non-intimate homicides occurring yearly. This logic suggests examining whether killing intimates arises from homicidal psychopathology.

Danto (1982) assembled the psychiatric lore regarding the ways in which murderers are distinct. Their fantasies actually have less anger, fear, and aggression. They are "emotionally dull." They cope with tension by either repressing or exploding. They are interpersonally shallow. Male murderers often feel guilty, inferior, and view women as dangerous. Most (70%) have defective superegos, 10% suffer dissociative reactions, and 13% become psychotic after killing, but only 7% are psychotic at the time.

Most of these differences do not represent "serious" psychopathology. "Dissociative reactions" for 10% sounds serious, and the 7% who murder while psychotic definitely qualify for suffering from serious psychopathology. The 13% who become psychotic are ambiguous. Was this state present before the homicidal act or the result of terrible realization after the act? In any case, if Danto's lore is apropos, then either our logic exaggerated the numbers of homicidally disturbed or the seriously pathological managed to restrain homicidal mania better than persons free of serious pathology. We would conclude that serious mental disturbance is *not* a prerequisite for murder.

However, Daniel and Harris (1982) studied women charged with murder and referred for pre-trial psychiatric evaluation. Women charged with other crimes served as a comparison. Both groups had high prior psychiatric hospitalizations (77% and 64%, respectively), and both suffered a high incidence of at least one "primary psychiatric disorder" (85% and 93%, respectively). Seven of eight women who killed children were found to be psychotic, but only 1 of 8 women who killed husbands was psychotic. Six of the eight spousal killers reported physical abuse by their husbands. No killer of a non-intimate was psychotic. Of course, psychiatric labeling has been long debated. Did the foreignness of the act or the killer's mental state determine the psychotic label? Also, what cases were sent for pretrial evaluation, and what triggered such referrals?

Batterers are often subjects in research on psychopathology. If we have 3 million batterers (Straus & Gelles, 1990) and 2,200 spousal murderers yearly, even if physical assault accompanies all homicides, only a tiny percentage kill (.07%). While illuminating the hazards of predicting homicide from assault history, it remains reasonable to assume that psychopathologies in batterers may instruct us about murderers.

Hotaling and Sugarman (1986) identified risk markers for violent husbands in an analysis of 52 case-comparison studies. Consistent characteristics were: *Sexual aggression toward a partner, violence toward their children, witnessing violence as a child,* and *alcohol usage.* The only consistent marker for the spouse victim was *witnessing violence as a child.* Hotaling and Sugarman (1990) later pursued their analysis, assisted by 2,143 subjects drawn from the National Family Violence Survey (Straus & Gelles, 1990). They generated an updated list of markers. The resulting six factors were quite similar for both men and women. Only two factor scores based on the women's judgments differentiated assaults on women: *(low) socioeconomic status* and *marital conflict,* neither of which were characteristics of the female victim. However, four factor scores based on the men's judgments differentiated assaults on women: *(low) socioeconomic status, marital conflict, witnessing parental violence as a child,* and *experiencing parental violence as a child.* This supports the assertion that the man's character, not the woman's, determines assaults on women.

Hastings and Hamberger (1988) compared alcoholic and non-alcoholic batterers with non-batterers. Fewer batterers were well-educated, employed, and in intact relationships. They more frequently witnessed and experienced abuse as children. Elevated measures of personality disorder, dysphoria, and nonconformity were found,

with alcohol acting to amplify differences with non-batterers.

Hamberger and Hastings (1988), Rosenbaum and Mauero (1990), and Vaselle-Augenstein and Ehrlich (1992) offered extensive reviews of studies done since Hotaling and Sugarman's (1986) survey. A number of batterers' features converge: low self-esteem, poor verbal skills, elevated dependency, poor impulse control, antisocial tendencies, and poor assertion skills. They and others (see Murphy, Meyer, and O'Leary, 1993) agree, however, that there is no single "Batterer's Syndrome." There may be at least two "types," one severe and the other mild, a distinction recently confirmed by Pan, Neidig, and O'Leary (1994). Hamberger and Hastings (1988) proposed eight types defined by three independent factors they generated. They labelled these factors *borderline/schizoid, narcissistic/antisocial,* and *passive-dependent/aggressive.* A person high on the first two factors would be distant, suspicious, unempathic, and hostile; the ingredients most identified in the *severe* abuser. A person high only on the third factor might be the mild abuser. Barnett and Hamberger (1992) compared batterers with maritally discordant and maritally satisfied men, and concluded that violent men are distinctive in three general areas: *impulsiveness, blunted intimacy,* and *poor problem solving skills,* which, though different, are not incompatible with Hamberger and Hasting's three factors.

Less attention has been paid to women's or victims' characteristics. Hotaling and Sugarman's (1990) survey found women victims consistently *to have experienced abuse in the family of origin, to have witnessed abuse in the family of origin, or both and to suffer low self-esteem.* The latter characteristic may be an outcome of chronic partner assault rather than a precursor to it. However, Perog-Good (1992) found that dating females, not yet into long-term relationships, who inflict sexual abuse on and sustain sexual abuse from males show low self-esteem. This characteristic may help explain why women choose, and do not easily escape, batterers.

Feminists oppose "pathologizing" assaultive and homicidal men and oppose even more "pathologizing" women. Pathologizing men helps them avoid personal responsibility. Pathologizing women paradoxically accomplishes the same end: it transforms reasonable self-defense against assault into irrational acts of disordered persons, which puts blame on women and, once again, exonerates men (Browne, 1987; Dobash & Dobash, 1990; Horsfals, 1991; Koss, Goodman, Browne, Fitzgerald, Keita, & Russo, 1994; Walker, 1989a, 1989b).

Walker (1989a) has testified in defense of 150 women spousal murderers. She does not believe that a psychological disorder explains why women remain with abusers or kill them. "There is plenty of strong, sane rationale behind the battered woman's apparent passivity in the face of acute violence" (Walker, 1989a, p. 44). She has called that rationale "the Battered Woman Syndrome" (Walker, 1984). Women become locked into cycles where calm gives way to gathering tension which, in turn, ultimately explodes in an acute battering incident. Tension collapses and remorse and loving contrition persuade the woman to "join with the batterer in sustaining the illusion of bliss. She convinces herself too...the illusion of absolute interdependence is firmly solidified in the woman's psyche...she for his caring behavior, he for her forgiveness" (Walker, 1989a, p. 45).

Walker rejected the insanity plea. The Battered Woman Syndrome leaves women no alternative but to remain, even under threat of death, where "batterers are violent for their own personal reasons, not because of anything their women do or don't do" (Walker, 1989a, p. 46). In the end, trapped and assaulted, women kill in self defense. "[N]early all of them kill not out of anger, jealousy, or other emotions, but out of terror" (Walker, 1989a, p. 65). Their act is aberrant and with

the freedom gained by murder from chronic assault, they become the normal women they have actually always been. And the "personal reasons" batterers brutalize mates? The short answer: Power and dependency. "The batterer would often rather kill, or die himself, than separate...he is always more terrified of abandonment than of violence" (Walker, 1989a, p. 65).

Walker attended little to racial differences. Although her sample was predominantly White, she referred to Black women at one point. Women who are convicted appear angry and "[m]any of those who appeared angry were also Black. Their palpable fear and terror were somehow obscured" (Walker, 1989a, p. 217). Walker admonished that "[i]t is essential to explain to [the client] how dangerous it would be to express anger during a trial" (Walker, 1989a, p. 203). This revelation came after Walker chided male jurors and judges for believing that anger, and not fear, explains a woman's fatal actions. Walker (1989b) strongly defended advocacy research, but her assertion that all women kill spouses out of terror may be based more on an advocate's wish to advance the welfare of her clients than on objective observation.

Ewing (1987) assembled a sample of women murderers who had also been brutally abused, but many of his subjects overlapped with those of Walker (1989a) and Browne (1987), an associate of Walker, so there is a question of independence. Browne (1987) studied intensively 42 of Walker's sample, comparing them with 205 abused, non-homicidal women. Browne's sample was also mostly White (22% Black) and, presumably, her comparison group as well. Her homicide group was of somewhat higher socio-economic status than the victims or comparison women. Victim husbands, thus, suffered an unfavorable status in comparison with their wives, which may have contributed to their abusiveness. Browne sketched cases of chronic, shockingly brutal attacks on women, with little provocation or reason. These men threatened death more frequently than comparison men.

Browne found that homicidal women are not distinctive from other women and that the character and actions of the men explained the tragic end of the women. She concluded that batterers have been conditioned to violence by their families of origin and *"feel* as though they are constantly victimized....This sense of threat, coupled with an inability to trust, seems to underlie many of the perceptions that trigger their anger" (Browne, 1987, p. 34). Her "transgenerational" violence finds wide support. Hotaling and Sugarman (1986) found the witnessing of parental violence in the family of origin associated consistently with wife abuse. This relationship continues to be documented (Murphy et al., 1993; Ney, 1992; Rosenbaum & Mauero, 1990; Stout, 1993).

Walker explained why women do not leave abusers. Browne (1987) explained why essentially normal women form such unions. Most of the women in her study agreed that their victims made a first impression of "the most romantic and attentive lovers they'd ever had" (Browne, 1987, p. 40). These men were superattentive and seeking instant commitment. They were *needy* and "neediness can be a charming quality..." (Browne, 1987, p. 41). So bedazzled were many women that they knew almost nothing of their mates before becoming involved with and committed to them. Ominously, the feature the women found so appealing soon revealed a dark side. Lacking confidence, these men turned what had appeared to be sensitive involvement into control, isolation, possession, and jealousy.

Walker's and Browne's impassioned but well-documented presentations paint the innocent, victimized woman and the flawed, vicious man. Yet, they, and other feminist advocates, stop short of asserting that these men are pathological. Instead, these men express the patriarchal character of our society. As long as we subjugate women to men, define maleness through separation and contest,

and define femaleness through attachment and nurturing, we will generate male assaultive control over women. This feminist perspective is widely embraced and has the advantage of unifying disparate, fragmentary data. It has its detractors. Hotaling and Sugarman (1986) found that "Traditional sex role expectations turned out to be the only consistent nonrisk marker" (p. 114). This led them to conclude: "This review does not find support for a sex role inequality interpretation of male violence" (p. 119). Their conclusion has not deterred feminists from advancing the patriarchal thesis.

Other researchers have not found quite the same picture as did Walker and Browne. Chimbos (1978) studied Canadian men (29) and women (5) spousal killers (presumably White). Nearly one-third (mostly men) reported there had been no previous physical violence, although 4 of the 5 women killers had been abused. However, case excerpts create a different picture than those presented by Browne and Walker. Men killers generally described mates who demeaned them, flaunted affairs, and humiliated them. Even 2 of the 3 excerpts of the women's statements keyed on verbal humiliation and accusations of disloyalty as precipitating factors.

Totman (1978) also drew a different picture from her 36 women (10 Black) spousal killers in a California prison. Five were convicted of first degree murder motivated by the woman's involvement with another man and four of these killed additionally for insurance benefits. Excerpts from interviews of the remaining women did not conform with the image of a helpless woman killing in self-defense. Totman observed that women "wanted to be loved by their men" (p. 55). They tolerated flirtation and affairs poorly. They also tolerated abuse, not from helplessness, but for "two kinds of sentiment: 'When you make your bed, you have to lie in it' and 'I just thought that's what women were supposed to do. Most of my friends (or my mother) had it the same way'" (p. 54).

In one regard, the women in Totman's study were like those in Browne's and Walker's studies. All denied conscious consideration of murder as an alternative. Although not clearly in danger, 20 claimed self-defense or defense of their children; the remainder claimed that the killing was accidental (2 persons) or that they suffered clouded or absent consciousness, a state repeatedly found by Walker (1989a). Totman, however, asked the women why they had not chosen or had rejected another solution. "Most respondents reiterated their ambivalence about their situation—that it was indeed destructive but that it was also attractive" (p. 52).

Other studies have not provided the case descriptions of those just reviewed. Several reinforced the considerable, although not inevitable, presence of prior physical abuse of women murderers (Barnard, Vera, Vera, & Newman, 1982; Campbell, 1992; Cazenave & Zahn, 1992; Wilbanks, 1983). Others tended to confirm Chimbos' (1978) depiction of the part women play in promoting their deaths. Barnard et al. (1982) and Showalter, Bonnie, and Roddy (1980) found that homicides by males are precipitated by the mate's rejection, leaving, or engaging in affairs. All 11 of Showalter et al.'s (1980) female victims had engaged in affairs, 10 quite openly so.

Some recent publications have studied male spousal murderers. Campbell (1992), studying 28 Dayton, Ohio, men; Goetting (1989), studying 46 Detroit men; and Stout (1993), studying 23 Missouri prisoners found a number of common features: considerable use of alcohol, high levels of estrangement, low socioeconomic indicators, and a history of crime. Campbell additionally found excessive violence accompanying the murder and jealousy as a prominent motive. Campbell, Goetting, and Cazenave and Zahn (1992), while not explicitly acknowledging it, were studying predominantly Black samples (79% to 86%). Cazenave and Zahn's group of 42 men and 41

women from eight U.S. cities confirmed features noted above: low socioeconomic indicators, estrangement, substantial use of alcohol, and excessive violence with female victims. They also report that most of the subjects lived in common-law marriages.

Mann (1990, 1992), Plass (1993), and Rose and McClain (1990) explicitly focused on Black homicides. Plass utilized FBI reports for 1990, and Rose and McClain canvassed St. Louis, Atlanta, and Detroit. Their works were essentially epidemiologic and brought forth little not already considered. Both works, however, advanced speculations about Black violence and lamented the absence of research into its roots.

Mann's (1990) report, based on 296 female murderers (78% Black) drawn in 1979 and 1983 from six cities, compared Black with White offenders. Partial data elicited an estimate that 70% of the Black women were unemployed. Most (64%) of the Black killers were unmarried, significantly more than Whites. Blacks had more records of crime (58% to 38%) and of violent crimes (36% to 27%). Blacks and Whites victimized family equally (67%), but Black women were more likely to kill mates. Their victims were less often (31% to 50%) "helpless" (e.g., young, sick, asleep, intoxicated), and they acted alone more often than Whites (87% to 66%). Murder by Black women was more often (70% to 49%) victim-precipitated compared to Whites.

Hawkins (1986a) edited a work devoted exclusively to homicide among Black Americans. He believed research has failed to illuminate the patterns of Black homicide, the etiological factors, and the situational correlates. One contributor (Wilbanks, 1986) asserted that most "treatises on Blacks and crime do not address the issue of racial disproportionality in offender rates...or seek to explain that difference..." (p. 43). Other contributors (Humphrey & Palmer, 1986) stated, "Violence among Blacks is particularly little understood" (p. 57). These representative observations converge to form the conclusion that, in spite of bustling publications about domestic violence, we have failed to address the center of gravity — why do Black Americans fatally attack others, mostly Black family and acquaintances, at such alarmingly high rates?

Description of the Composite Spousal Murderer

Before drafting a composite of the spousal murderer, some observations should be briefly brought forth. Murder rates, including spousal murder, vary among regions, with southern rates being highest (Browne & Williams, 1989; Hawkins, 1986b; Parker & Toth, 1990), leading to the speculation that Black rates may be connected to Black southern origins. No clear explanation of this thesis has been forthcoming, however.

While the mostly White female murderers of Browne (1987) and Walker (1989a) were free of prior criminal charges, Mann (1990), Totman (1978), and Wolfgang (1958) found half or more of their female offenders had prior police records. Mann (1990) also found that the arrest record of the Black women in her study were mere percentage points ahead of White women (55% to 53%). Wolfgang (1958) found 68% of Black and 56% of White male murderers had prior records. The substantial presence of prior criminal arrests for largely Black male samples was confirmed by Campbell (1992) and Goetting (1989). Whites may have fewer prior arrests but more incidents of calling on police to intervene in domestic disturbances, as Blacks are wary of involving police (Plass, 1993).

Feminists hold that courts are biased against women. "[J]udges are often unwilling to treat male aggression against women, including life-threatening aggression" (Koss et al., 1994). Walker (1989a) chafed at "ignorant, old, white, male judges" (p. 68) who are too lenient with homicidal men and too strict with women. Browne

(1987) asserted that women "are frequently sentenced to longer prison terms than are men" (p. 11). These assertions may be true, but the implication that women are punished more than men, is contrary to the evidence.

What is striking is the degree to which both sexes serve no or only brief sentences for murder. Wolfgang (1958) found that 69% of White women, 41% of White men, 29% of Black women, and 15% of Black men who were "available for prosecution" were not sentenced. This represents a bias against both Blacks and males. Still, of those sentenced, half (51%) were sentenced for manslaughter and received less than 9-year terms, two-thirds of these were less than 2 years. Seventy percent of females were sentenced for manslaughter, with 83% of these given sentences of less than 2 years. Wilbanks (1983) reported that of 47 women arrested for murder, only 32% were sentenced, receiving 5 years or less as the most frequent (41%) sentence. Mann (1990) found that only 43% of females arrested for murder went to prison. She reported that most of these women (67%) received prison times of 9 years or less with a mean of 3.3 years and that the final sentence dispositions of Blacks and Whites were similar. Finally, Rose and McClain (1990) found (for the year 1975) that 17% of Detroit's family homicide defendants were dismissed by the Grand Jury, particularly in the cases of wives, and an additional 25% were given probation. In Atlanta, 44% of family homicide defendants were dismissed and 10% were given probation, while in St. Louis, an "overwhelming majority" of family homicide defendants were dismissed by the Grand Jury, and no family related members were convicted of murder.

Proceeding with our composite outline of the spousal murderer requires invention and selective attention in view of the fragmentary and contradictory information available. We start with the most hard-formed and reliable observations which may be advanced. We build on that skeleton, as might an archeological anthropologist, to flesh out a composite picture. Many may find the bones of our skeleton hardly more than cartilaginous, if not frankly "soft" tissue, but let us begin with the "hardest" skeletal features of the spousal murderer and progress to those least durable.

The Skeletal Base

1. The murderer is more likely a Black man or woman.

2. The male murderer may be somewhat younger than the woman murderer though both are between 20 and 40 years of age.

3. The murderer is probably an urban dweller, often of the Southern region.

4. The murderer is probably unemployed or employed in a low paying jobs.

5. The murderer usually has children.

6. The male murderer is probably estranged from his victim spouse.

7. The female murderer is probably living with her victim spouse.

8. The murderer and victim usually live in unmarried cohabitation (common law marriage).

9. The male or female murderer is likely to use a gun in the execution of murder and may fire several shots into the victim's body.

10. The male or female murderer is likely to have witnessed and experienced violence in his or her family of origin.

11. The male or female murderer may use alcohol, drugs, or both, but is not necessarily under the influence at the time of the homicidal event.

12. The male murderer probably has a police record of prior crimes, often violent in nature.

13. The female murderer may also have a police record, less violent in nature.

14. If the male or female murderer is White, there would more likely be less of a record of prior offenses but more of a record of police calls for domestic disturbance.

15. The female murderer probably shoots her victim spouse after an argument in which blows are exchanged, in which she is assaulted, or in which the spouse threatens to kill her or himself.

16. The male murderer is likely to shoot his victim spouse after an argument in which the spouse threatens separation or, having already separated, declines to return.

17. The male murderer usually believes, often with reason, that the victim was intimate with another man or men, and the man is jealous.

18. The female murderer is usually less jealous of her victim mate than worried that he does not love and respect her.

19. The male murderer is more likely unemployed, while his spouse works, or holds a position of lesser status than his victim spouse.

20. The female murderer is usually unemployed or marginally employed and feels dependent on her victim spouse for her and her children's support.

21. Following the murder, male and female murderers, if undergoing psychological evaluation, would probably show evidence of a personality disorder.

22. Following the murder, the female murderer often claims clouded or absent consciousness for the homicidal event.

23. Following the murder, the female murderer is probably acquitted, placed on probation, or serves a short sentence of about 3 years.

24. Following the murder, the male murderer is probably also acquitted, but less often than the female murderer, placed on probation or serves a relatively brief prison sentence of about 5 years.

25. If psychologically evaluated before the homicide, the male murderer would probably be ascribed a personality disorder diagnosis (showing impulsivity, blunted empathy, passive/aggressive tendencies, poorly formed ego identity, hostility).

26. If psychologically evaluated before the homicide, the female murderer would probably evince evidence of a borderline personality disor-

der (showing unstable interpersonal relationships, poor sense of self, impulsivity, affect instability, transient dissociative symptoms).

Case Illustration:

We go from composite and hypothetical to a particular and real murderer. In the case to be presented, murder was definitely attempted twice, although, by some quirk of fate, somehow averted in each instance.

Shawn and Kristi, both White, sought help from a counselor in the author's practice in August 1990. Shawn, 18 years old, had dropped out of the 11th grade and was seeking work in order to support Kristi, 15 years old, his pregnant wife. Shawn had moved out of his home at age 16 because of conflicts with his stepfather and had taken residence with his grandmother. Kristi had lived with him there briefly before returning to her mother's home. She expressed discontent with her circumstances and hoped they might find an apartment.

They were seeking counseling because of frequent arguments. Kristi objected in anger to Shawn's physically restraining her from leaving when she wished. Shawn was frustrated at not being able to communicate and reason with Kristi. He was particularly frustrated at their physical separation. What troubled him about Kristi was her habit of leaving whenever they disagreed. He felt that they would never work out their differences unless she stayed, thus, his efforts to restrain her. Shawn professed his love for Kristi frequently, but also professed his inability to understand her. Kristi, still in school, did not understand Shawn's jealousy of her friends, classmates, and family.

The counselor endeavored to help this young couple learn basic communication and conflict resolution skills and agree to certain basic behavioral rules. One of these was for Shawn to avoid hitting or restraining Kristi. Shawn also agreed to honor a "cooling off" time, permitting Kristi time

away to compose herself. Both agreed to remain at a formal distance when arguing. These steps were followed with some success for a period, but Kristi's mother was urging her to stay at her home until the baby was born, contrary to Shawn's desire. As the sessions wore on, Shawn's frustrations grew, and so did the frequency of arguments. Shawn began to threaten divorce which, however, seemed not to be a serious concern to Kristi.

Kristi did not believe they were getting anywhere in counseling and did not believe she needed it for herself. "I follow my own counsel," she said. Shawn wanted them to continue, but was not interested in working individually. They discontinued counseling in September 1990.

Late at night on June 10, 1991, Kristi filed charges against Shawn for domestic violence. The next morning, she visited with Mark, a male friend home on leave from the Army. Mark had met her at a popular plaza at 1:30 a.m. that morning, had accompanied her to her home, and had stayed there until 12:30 p.m., when he prepared to leave. They were walking to his car when Shawn came out from behind the house next door. Kristi and Shawn began arguing, and Kristi told Shawn to leave. Shawn, 10 feet away, raised a small-caliber hand gun and pointed it at Kristi. He shot her twice, in the front and back of the head. Then he shot Mark above the left eyebrow. Mark later claimed the attack was unprovoked and that there had never been words between them.

Both victims survived and were conscious when police arrived. Kristi told police that Shawn had beaten her some months ago, causing her daughter's premature birth and subsequent death. She claimed that Mark was only a friend but that Shawn was jealous. Shawn had threatened to kill her when she told him that she was ending their marriage. She had not believed him.

Shawn fled the scene but gave himself up the next day in the company of his lawyer. He was charged with attempted aggravated murder, felonious assault, and breaking and entering. A guilty plea resulted in a sentence of 7 to 25 years. With good behavior, he may be free at the time of this writing.

Could we have predicted Shawn's murder attempts at the time of counseling? We have seen many battling, occasionally battering, couples. None, including Shawn and Kristi, have set off alarm bells regarding lethal outcomes. Our review brought out only one distinguishing feature: the youth and personal immaturity of this couple. They lacked the capacity to empathize with each other, to identify the elements of their conflicts, and to tolerate anything other than compliance with their own wishes. But while most of the couples we counsel are older and more competent, many suffer the very same failings.

Guidelines to Assessment

On May 4, 1970, a squad of the Ohio National Guard turned in unison and fired on students at Kent State University, killing four. Demonstrations against the Vietnam War were under way at campuses across the country. Could we have predicted such a tragedy occurring somewhere, prompted by student demonstrations, macho posturing of politicians, and frustrated police/soldiers with loaded guns? Yes. Could it have been predicted at a low-key, conservative university like Kent State? No. That the shooting by the National Guard occurred at Kent State magnified the enormity of the fact that it occurred at all. These homicides arose from the intersection of multilayered, circumstantial forces that, absent any single ingredient, would have never come to pass.

Might all murder, except for a few premeditated "felony murders," arise from the same improbable confluence of circumstances? Yes, and that explains the dilemma for assessment and prediction. Improbable events do not lend themselves to predictive control. Monahan (1978)

reviewed studies attempting to predict criminal behavior. False positives averaged more than 72%. In one study of 7,000 parolees, for every correct identification of a repeat offender, there were 326 false positives. Earlier, we calculated that, every year, .07% of batterers kill their spouses. Knowing that a person batters would improve a prediction of murder by about 80 times the base rate, yet, we would be wrong 9,993 times for every 10,000 such predictions. Adding other ingredients (such as sex, race, age, income, marital status), we might improve our prediction by many factors and still be more often wrong than right.

To advise family members or authorities that someone is prepared to commit murder places a grave burden on all concerned, including a possible suit for defamation and damages risked by the clinician. Failure to notify potential victims or authorities embraces a different set of costs, including a risk of charges of malpractice against the clinician by survivors. It is vexing to know enough about correlates of lethal violence to believe we can improve on chance, yet not know whether that improvement is by a factor of 100 or less, or 10,000 or more. Recognizing these limitations, let us set forth in Table 2 what we can to provide guidelines for an assessment of the risk of murder. Table 2 draws on risk marker research already discussed, as well as works by Browne (1987), Campbell (1993), Daly and Wilson (1988), Reiss and Roth (1993), and Straus and Gelles (1990).

Intervention

If intervention should ever assume a prevention mode, it is in regard to spousal homicide (Tifft, 1993). Once it occurs, the victim is beyond treatment and the offender becomes the subject of the criminal justice system. As such, perhaps half are acquitted or placed on probation, and the remainder serve relatively brief sentences. Courts

---

TABLE 2
RISK OF LETHAL SPOUSAL ABUSE CHECK LIST

(Listed in descending order of judged risk.)

1. Prior life endangering actions toward mate (choking, burning, stabbing, discharging a weapon).
2. Prior life endangering actions toward family or others.
3. History of multiple acts of severe physical violence to mate.
4. Increasing frequency of physical violence to mate.
5. History of injury sustained from mate violence.
6. History of assault on others.
7. Gun(s) in the home or carried.
8. Threats to kill mate.
9. Threats with a weapon.
10. Black.
11. Male, if White.
12. 20 to 40 years of age.
13. Regular alcohol or drug use.
14. Prior criminal record.
15. Cohabitating, non-married.
16. Recently divorced or estranged.
17. Recent extra-mate sexual affair(s).
18. Belief that mate is having or may have affairs.
19. Threat of suicide.
20. Forced sex or marital rape.
21. History of violence observed or experienced in family of origin.
22. Age difference of 9 years or more between mates.
23. Unemployed or marginally employed.
24. Less than high school education.
25. Lacking employable work skills.
26. Living in urban inner city.
27. Repeated verbal abuse and humiliation.
28. Approval of physical violence against mate under some circumstances.
29. Fantasies of homicide or suicide.
30. Social isolation.
31. One mate (usually male) controlling the other.
32. For women, leaving and returning to the home.
33. History of repeated mild physical violence (slapping, pushing, grabbing).
34. Destroying mutual or mate's property.

(The following may be assessed by psychometrics.)

35. Low self esteem.
36. Poor self concept.
38. Passive-aggressive/dependent tendencies.
39. Affect instability (mood swings, temper outbursts).
40. Anti-social/hostile attitudes.
41. Depressed affect.
42. Poor impulse control (acts on impulse).
43. Paranoid ideation.
44. Poor verbal, problem solving skills.
45. Lack of empathy (blunted intimacy).

---

routinely specify treatment as a condition of probation and parole, but no publications were found which addressed post-homicide treatment of spousal murderers. Walker (1989a) held that battered women find homicide liberating and self-treating. According to Walker, such women needed little more than support and encouragement.

The feminist focus on the patriarchal features of society lends itself to a primary prevention approach. A program to change society through laws which neutralize male controls and protect women should foster a reduction in the prevalence of male perpetrated spousal murder. Since the later 1970s, women have pursued this program by introducing a handful of statutes, somewhat unevenly and not in all states, designed to accomplish this end. These statutes provide for civil injunctive relief, temporary injunctive relief, defining abuse as a criminal offense, warrantless arrest on probable cause, requiring state agencies to collect and report data on family violence, and establishing funds for shelters or establishing standards of operations for shelters. Many feel that the events of the last 15 years have confirmed the value of this program and vindicated the feminist position.

Browne and Williams (1989) and Stout (1992) examined the effects of these statutes and the resources created by them for women by comparing states with and without these changes. Both researchers found some evidence of reduced female victim rates in states enjoying the changes compared to states not adopting them. However, Browne and Williams (1989) found that *male* vic-

tim rates were most beneficially affected. Indeed, the effect appears to be evident in country-wide statistics based on FBI reports since 1977, see Figure 3, where a decline appeared to be well underway before the 1980s. Figure 3 reveals that whereas wives experienced a modest rate decline, husbands enjoy a dramatic decline. Conversely, rates for non-married couples actually increased,

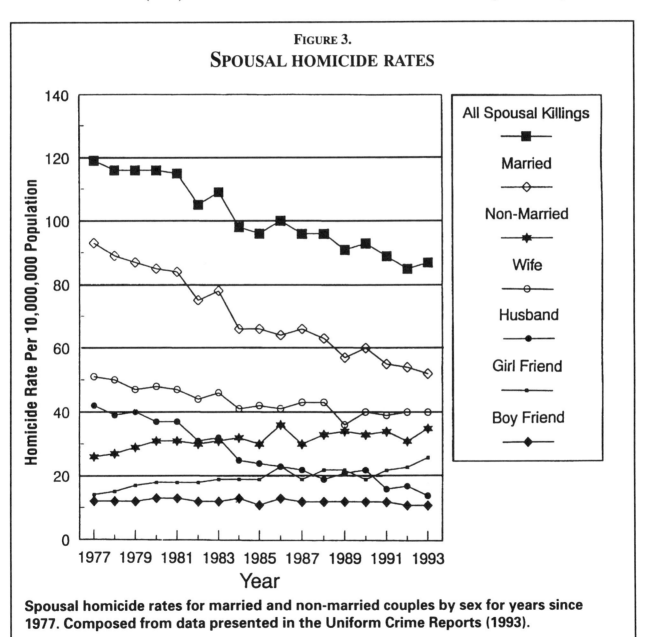

FIGURE 3.
SPOUSAL HOMICIDE RATES

Spousal homicide rates for married and non-married couples by sex for years since 1977. Composed from data presented in the Uniform Crime Reports (1993).

entirely as a function of risk to non-married women. Still, the reduction in domestic homicides may have helped hold murder rates relatively constant and made murder a shrinking proportion of violent crimes, which have increased 62% (shown in Figure 2).

We shall return to this matter. Meanwhile, few (under 2%) severely and repeatedly battered women yearly call on about 1,500 shelters (Johnson, Crowley, & Sigler, 1992), which would suggest services provided to 12,000 women (Gelles & Straus, 1988). Initially focused on providing safe haven and counseling to women, shelters have sponsored treatment for abusers, largely through all-male abuser groups led by professionals. Family service agencies also offer group counseling to abusers and have encouraged Batterers Anonymous as an auxiliary modality. In addition, agencies conduct couples and family sessions directed at teaching effective communication and conflict management skills. These efforts constitute *secondary* prevention programs as they seek to reduce the duration of abusing behavior and to interrupt it short of a fatal conclusion. We are beginning to see research on the efficacy of these programs, some (Markman, Renick, Floyd, Stanley, & Clements, 1993; Stacey et al., 1994) were rather positive, while others (Jacobsen & Addis, 1993; Tolman & Bhosley, 1991) were less so (see Edleson, 1990 for a review).

Advocates for women have been reluctant to endorse couples and family counseling for fear that women would be exposed to their batterers and because empowerment of battered women via separation and independence is preferable to reconciliation with their batterers (Ellis, 1992; Geffner & Pagelow, 1990). Unfortunately, it appears that most battered women return to their men (Johnson, Crowley, & Sigler, 1992). It is unlikely that effective revision of *interpersonal* behaviors can take place without the involvement of both parties. A program sensitive to risk, outlined by Hanks (1992), seeks to integrate a variety of interventions for the specific couple. Here, couples counseling, same-sex group work, drug/alcohol counseling, or separation ("empowerment") advising are recommended based on an assessment of the chronicity and psychopathy of the batterer. Stacey et al. (1994) also advocate matching treatment steps with types of problems in a similar fashion.

Another focus for intervention should be the violent actions of women. Numerous researchers (e.g., DeMaris, 1992; Gelles & Straus, 1988; Kim & Cho, 1992; Lloyd, 1990; Straus & Gelles, 1990) have found that women, both in dating and spousal relationships, are more frequently physically abusive than their male partners. These findings are criticized by feminists who ridicule the idea of the "Battered Husband" (Avis, 1994; Dobash, Dobash, Wilson, & Daly, 1992; Koss et al., 1994). Considerable energy has gone into rebutting such findings by showing that when men and women fight, women are injured much more often (Brush, 1990; Cantos, Neidig, & O'Leary, 1994; Koss & Haslet, 1992; Stets & Straus, 1990). It seems obvious to the dispassionate observer, however, that women have no more business hitting men than men have hitting women. It is an unfair fight from either perspective. But more to the point, women's violence may contribute to the risk of fatal outcomes to both.

Stacey et al. (1994) described a program designed for abusive men. In spite of initial disbelief, they found a substantial part played by abusive women. They were constrained in directly addressing this matter because the local shelter "stridently resisted all attempts during the 1980s to involve female victims of [our] clients...and denied that women's own violence was even a problem worth acknowledging" (Stacey et al., p. 124). Colorado has written this view into a law prohibiting couples treatment as inimicable to battering defined as a crime (O'Leary, 1993). These restraints fly in the face of research on women's violence and should be abandoned or undone in the interest of effective intervention.

Barriers to Intervention

A primary barrier to intervention is our ignoring of and ignorance about Black spousal homicide. For a case example, let us return to Figure 3. Why are husbands "sheltered" from murder 2.2 times more then women over the years? Browne and Williams (1989) suggested that this is because resources provided to women have created an *alternative* to "self-defense murder." Meanwhile, the risk to non-married women has *increased* by a factor of 1.9, while that to non-married men remains essentially constant. Why have the resources not worked to lower non-married couples' risk?

By considering the part played by Blacks, we may develop an entirely different explanation of these phenomena. Black population size correlates negatively (-.62) with resources for abused women, a correlation Browne and Williams (1989) employed as a covariate. The direct implication is that *these resources are not as available to Black as to White women.* Moreover, there is reason to believe that Black women make less use of shelters, even where available, as they view them as places that are run for and by White women (Plass, 1993).

Consider further that married Blacks make up only 48% of all Black families, down from 78% in 1950 (Estell, 1994). Mann (1990) found that only 28% of the Black homicide offenders in her study who were mothers were married. Recent widely publicized estimates are that 68% of Black births are to non-married mothers. Keeping in mind the fact that Black homicides equal or exceed White homicides and that non-married Blacks constitute somewhere between 52 and 72% of all Black families, we may infer that *most non-married homicides involve Blacks, while most married homicides involve Whites.* Next, as the proportion of non-married Black couples has

risen steadily over the last 40 years, *the proportion of Blacks represented in the married category has fallen steadily.* This Black migration from the married to non-married ranks could explain the increase in non-married homicide, the reduction in married rates, and the puzzling advantage in rate reduction enjoyed by husbands since 1977. As Blacks withdraw from the ranks of married persons, the married class approaches the lower homicide rates characteristic of Whites as well as the customary ratio of about two White wife homicide victims for every White husband victim. There may not be a true rate reduction in spousal homicide at all.

Certain questions remain. If domestic Black homicides are increasingly between non-married couples, why aren't non-married rates as high or higher than married rates? Secondly, in view of the lethal offender balance between Black men and women, why are only non-married female rates ascending? Perhaps, police often misclassify Black couples as "acquaintances" or "friends," categories that contained 8 times as many homicides (7,076) in 1993 as "boyfriend" and "girlfriend" (859). Blacks kill "acquaintances" as opposed to "family" proportionately more than do Whites. Is this variance due to ambiguities in classifying non-married Black relationships? Perhaps, also it is easier for police to identify the relationship of the Black male offender because he conspicuously advances his possessive claim on the female victim, while the Black female offender may exert no similar possessive claim to help police identify the spousal relationship (Daly & Wilson, 1988). But, by now, we are stringing one speculation to another. Obviously, these are questions which should be researched. Lacking data supporting or rejecting these suppositions raises doubts as to whether we have a true spousal homicide reduction since 1977 and whether resources valued by feminists have been the prevention success so widely hailed.

This much is clear: The massive contribution

of Blacks to spousal murder makes imperative the advent of new approaches to prevention. Many researchers proceed as if no color differences exist, or assign the differences to socio-economic factors (O'Carroll, 1986). While poverty and crime correlate, the high murder rate among Black intimates cannot be assigned solely to this factor. Wolfgang (1958) demonstrated this nearly 40 years ago. Others (Hampton & Gelles, 1994; Staples, 1986) also concluded what is apparent in the arithmetic of figures already reviewed. If Blacks, at 12.3% of the population, account for half the homicides (more than 8 times the rate of Whites), but exceed Whites in poverty only by a factor of 3 (Estell, 1994), then Black homicides have an unexplained residual. Moreover, being poor, per se, does not determine crime or homicide, as witness the many impoverished countries with low rates. Nor can we settle on "racial" differences. African countries, often impoverished, when not at war or under civil strife, have had low murder rates (Humphrey & Palmer, 1986; Kruttschnitt, 1993). And, American Blacks serving in the armed forces have homicide rates which are only 9% of civilian rates (Reiss & Roth, 1993).

Nor can solutions be found if the White community washes its hands of the problem of prevention by concluding that it is up to Blacks to solve their own problems. The Black "subculture of violence" may be descriptively accurate yet misleading because, in the final analysis, that subculture, as the term implies, is cradled within, and is an expression of, an ecological whole in which we all play a part.

Asian immigrants are poor, live in ghettos, are "racially" distinct and discriminated against. What about our social ecology promotes the absorption of these peoples so that in two generations, they are indistinguishable as far as crime is concerned? Jews, for ages, have been the object of discrimination, repression, pogroms, and bitter exclusion, yet seem, in this country and others, to

survive and flourish without exceptional crime rates. We very much need to study how these accommodations emerge and why they have not occurred for our Black citizens. These are not questions Blacks face alone, although they are likely not to be understood or resolved unless Blacks take leadership in addressing them.

Summary and Conclusion

Questions as to why Black Americans kill intimates at exceptionally high rates and why Americans generally lead the world's industrial countries in this grim race have not been answered. We have many suppositions—the American culture with its credo of individual freedom, the Black "subculture of violence," the unique availability of handguns, the breakdown of the family, the stress of ethnic diversity—but we have no confident answers. The reason is that we have simply neglected to research these questions sufficiently.

Research into homicide is difficult and time consuming. Researchers cannot expect their large introductory classes in psychology or sociology to conveniently provide samples of murderers as they do samples of date rapists or people from dysfunctional homes. The inconvenience of this research would be a fordable barrier even if a governmental policy existed which facilitated the collecting, effectively detailed cataloging, and ready accessing of information on spousal murder. The modern computer makes implementing such a policy quite feasible. Why, then, has such a policy not been implemented? Why have we built so little on Wolfgang's (1958) excellent beginnings?

Two reasons emerge, both political. First, either Blacks as a voting block would take umbrage at a searching analysis of Black homicide and its causes, or policy makers, including those who set goals for grants in support of research, believe serious political repercussions would occur. Quite likely, until influential Blacks unite to call for research into Black homicides, the reality or its perception will remain in force.

The second reason rests in the women's movement and the contest for the finite pool of public monies available. Gelles and Straus (1988) lament years of watching factional fighting for limited funds.

An example of this kind of competition is the radical feminist argument that there is no such thing as a battered husband. That concept flies in the face of logic and empirical data. Yet, radical feminists believe that if we acknowledge the existence of battered husbands, then the funding designated for programs to assist battered women will be cut further because monies will be directed at programs for battered men...(p. 188).

The almost universal silence among feminists regarding Black homicide suggests that a similar concern for the diversion of resources might be at work. An additional disincentive to feminists may be that Black women are an "embarrassment." They kill spouses at rates which make it difficult to maintain the image of the woman as the universal victim. The "angry Black woman" picture, which Walker (1989a) attempted to dispel, may once more divert resources to men.

Feminists seem to have captured the high ground in the struggle for what Stacey et al. (1994) call a "Social Movement Industry." Certainly, violence has been a "growth industry" for social scientists, not to mention social service agencies and law enforcement organizations. The problems of crime and homicide are not, however, partisan. They belong to all. It is time to address the problem with this reality in mind.

Annotated Bibliography

Daly, M., & Wilson, M. (1988). *Homicide.* Hawthorne, NY: Aldine de Gruyter. These authors present a general theory of homicide. Their *evolutionary* thesis is that nature moves all to protect reproductive access and survival of our "genetic stuff." Women are assured their offspring carry their genetic code; men are not, and therein the fundamental tension. Spouse killing is mostly wife killing, not out of animus, but from miscalculation in an effort to secure reproductive rights. Not an easily sold theory, but Daly and Wilson are elegant and skilled in their attempt to do so.

Stacey, W. A., Hazlewood, L. R., & Shupe, A. (1994). *The violent couple.* Westport, CN: Praeger. This latest book outlines a program designed to intervene in and promote resolution of family violence. The research findings are valuable, but the book stands out because the authors reveal great sophistication about the socio-political climate in which such endeavors exist. Their analysis of the organizational and self-serving features of the helping "industry" is knowledgeable and revealing.

Straus, M. A., & Gelles, R. J. (1990). *Physical violence in American families.* New Brunswick, NJ: Transaction Publishers. These prolific scholars bring integrity and balance to their research and interpretations. Here, they continue to analyze the voluminous data generated by their second survey of 1985, in which they interviewed 6,002 families. While they did not study homicides, their survey acts as a valuable reference to the seed-bed of domestic violence from which homicide springs.

Walker, L. E. (1989a). *Terrifying love: Why battered woman kill and how society responds.* New York: Harper & Row. This book imparts the sense of impatience and injustice women feel and makes understandable their actions.

In all likelihood, however, Walker's repudiation of objective empiricism in favor of advocacy research is a message more for the converted than the uncertain.

Wolfgang, M. E. (1958). *Patterns in criminal homicide*. Philadelphia: University of Pennsylvania Press. This classic is still the most frequently referenced work on domestic homicide. This is not a comment on Wolfgang's writing style, which although quite lucid, is somewhat dry and scholarly. It is instead a tribute to the clarity and orderliness of his analysis and the timeless relevance of the information he has assembled in this book.

Case Readings

Browne, A. (1987). *When battered women kill*. New York: Free Press. Browne presents the case of Molly and Jim under the heading "Typical Violence" (pp. 56-58, 89-93, 131-134, 187). It is a shocking expose of a man's cruelty and a woman's agonizing forbearance. Browne has many other cases, most of which illustrate Walker's Battered Woman's Syndrome—the cycles of tension building, explosion, tension release, contrition and remorse.

Chimbos, P. D. (1978). *Marital violence: A study of interspousal homicide*. San Francisco, CA: R & E Research Associates. Chimbos presents six cases in detail, four of them of male murderers. Five of these cases revolve around alcohol use, usually by both parties. Case 1, beginning on page 62, is probably typical, based on Chimbos' general observations of the male wife killer. The man, Sam, is intoxicated. His wife, also drunk, proceeds to taunt Sam by dancing and kissing a male visitor. Sam's request for propriety is ignored, and he stabs her to death.

Ewing, C. P. (1987). *Battered women who kill: Psychological self-defense as legal justification*. Lexington, KY: D. C. Heath. This author presents in the Appendix (pp. 99-142) 100 brief case descriptions of battered women who killed. The descriptions were gathered from newspapers, magazines, articles, books, and trial and appellate court opinions published between 1978 and 1986. They provide a kaleidoscopic snap shot series of women spousal murderers from across the nation. It appears that most of the women sampled in this manner were White.

References

Avis, J. M. (1994). Advocates versus researchers—a false dichotomy? A feminist, social constructionist response to Jacobson. *Family Process, 33,* 87-91.

Barnard, G. W., Vera, H., Vera, M., & Newman, G. (1982). Till death do us part: A study of spouse murder. Bulletin of the American *Academy of Psychiatry and Law, 10,* 271-280.

Barnett, O. W. & Hamberger, L. K. (1992). The assessment of maritally violent men on the California Psychological Inventory. *Violence and Victims, 7,* 15-22.

Bauer, C. & Ritt, L. (1988). A Victorian indictment of wife beating. In G. W. Russell (Ed.), *Violence in intimate relationships*. New York: PMA Publishing.

Bourdouris, J. (1971). Homicide and the family. *Journal of Marriage and the Family, 33,* 667-676.

Browne, A. (1987). *When battered women kill*. New York: Free Press.

Browne, A. & Williams, K. R. (1989). Exploring the effect of resource availability and the likelihood of female-perpetrated homicides. *Law and Society Review, 23,* 75-94.

Brush, L. D. (1990). Violent acts and injurious outcomes in married couples: Methodological issues in the National Survey of Families and Households. *Gender & Society, 4,* 56-67.

Campbell, J. C. (1992). "If I can't have you, no one can:" Power and control in homicide of female partners. In J. Radford & D. E. H. Russell (Eds.), *Femicide: The politics of woman killing.* New York: MacMillan.

Campbell, J. C. (1993). The Danger Assessment Instrument. Risk factors of homicide of mate by battered women. In C. Block & R. L. Block (Eds.), *Questions and answers in lethal and non-lethal violence. Proceedings of the first annual Workshop of the Homicide Research Working Group.* Washington, DC: U.S. Department of Justice, National Institute of Justice Research Report.

Cantos, A. L., Neidig, P. H., & O'Leary, K. D. (1994). Injuries of women and men in a treatment program for domestic violence. *Journal of Family Violence, 9,* 113-124.

Cazenave, N. A. & Zahn, M. A. (1992). Women, murder, and male domination: Police reports of domestic violence in Chicago and Philadelphia. In E. C. Viano (Ed.), *Intimate violence: Interdisciplinary perspective.* Washington, DC: Hemisphere Publishing Corp.

Chimbos, P. D. (1978). *Marital violence: A study of interspousal homicide.* San Francisco, CA: R & E Research Associates.

Coates, C. J. (1988). A psychosocial approach to family violence: Application of Conceptual Systems Theory. In G. W. Russell (Ed.), *Violence in intimate relationships.* New York: PMA Publishing.

Daly, M. & Wilson, M. (1988). *Homicide.* Hawthorne,

NY: Aldine de Gruyter.

Daniel, A. E. & Harris, P. W. (1982). Female homicide offenders referred for pretrial psychiatric examination: A descriptive study. *Bulletin of the American Academy of Psychiatry and Law, 10,* 261-269.

Danto, B. L. (1982). A psychiatric view of those who kill. In B. L. Danto, J. Bruhns, & A. H. Kutsher (Eds.), *The human side of homicide.* New York: Columbia University Press.

DeMaris, A. (1992). Male versus female initiation of aggression: The case of courtship violence. In E. C. Viano (Ed.), *Intimate violence: Interdisciplinary perspective.* Washington, DC: Hemisphere Publishing Corp.

Dickstein, L. J. & Nadelson, C. C. (1989). Conclusion. In L. J. Dickstein & C. C. Nadelson (Eds.), *Family Violence: Emerging Issues of a National Crisis.* Washington, DC: American Psychiatric Press.

Dobash, R. E. & Dobash, R. P. (1990) How theoretical definitions and perspectives affect research and policy. In D. J. Besharov (Ed.), *Family violence: Research and public policy issues.* Washington, DC: The AEI Press.

Dobash, R. P., Dobash, R. E., Wilson, M., & Daly, M. (1992). The myth of sexual symmetry in marital violence. *Social Problems, 39,* 71-91.

Edleson, J. L. (1990). Judging the success of intervention with men who batter. In D. J. Besharov (Ed.), *Family violence: Research and public policy issues.* Washington, DC: The AEI Press.

Ellis, D. (1992). Woman abuse among separated and divorced women: The relevance of social support. In E. C. Viano (Ed.), Intimate violence: *Interdisciplinary perspective.* Washington, DC: Hemisphere Publishing Corp.

Estell, K. (Ed.). (1994). *The African American Almanac.* Detroit, MI: Gale Research Inc.

Ewing, C. P. (1987). *Battered women who kill: Psychological self-defense as legal justification.* Lexington, KY: D. C. Heath.

Farley, R. (1986). Homicide trends in the United States. In D. F. Hawkins (Ed.), *Homicide among Black Americans.* New York: University Press of America.

Geffner, R. & Pagelow, M. D. (1990). Victims of spouse abuse. In R. T. Ammerman & M. Hersen (Eds.), *Treatment of family violence: A sourcebook.* New York: John Wiley & Sons.

Gelles, R. J. & Straus, M. A. (1988). *Intimate violence.* New York: Simon & Schuster.

Goetting, A. (1989). Men who kill their mates: A profile. *Journal of Family Violence, 4,* 285-296.

Hamberger, L. K. & Hastings, J. (1988). Characteristics of male spouse abusers consistent with personality disorders. *Hospital and Community Psychiatry, 39,* 763-770.

Hampton, R. L. & Gelles, R. J. (1994). Violence toward Black women in a national representative sample of Black families. *Journal of Comparative Family Studies, 25,* 105-119.

Hanks, S. E. (1992). Translating theory into practice: A conceptual framework for clinical assessment, differential diagnosis, and multi-modal treatment of maritally violent individuals, couples, and families. In E. C. Viano (Ed.), *Intimate violence: Interdisciplinary perspective.* Washington, DC: Hemisphere Publishing Corp.

Hastings, J. & Hamberger, L. K. (1988). Personality characteristics of spouse abusers: A controlled comparison. *Violence and Victims, 3,* 31-48.

Hawkins, D. F. (1986a). Black homicide: The adequacy of existing research for devising prevention strategies. In D. F. Hawkins (Ed.), *Homicide among Black Americans.* New York: University Press of America.

Hawkins, D. F. (1986b). Black and White homicide differentials: Alternatives to an inadequate theory. In D. F. Hawkins (Ed.), *Homicide among Black Americans.* New York: University Press of America.

Horsfals, J. (1991). *The presence of the past: Male violence in the family.* North Sydney, Australia: Allen & Unwin.

Hotaling, G. T. & Sugarman, D. B. (1986). An analysis of risk markers in husband to wife violence: The current state of knowledge. *Violence and Victims, 1,* 101-124.

Hotaling, G. T. & Sugarman, D. B. (1990). Prevention of wife assault. In R. T. Ammerman & M. Hersen (Eds.), *Treatment of family violence: A sourcebook.* New York: John Wiley & Sons.

Humphrey, J. A. & Palmer, S. (1986). Race, sex, and criminal homicide offender-victim relationship. In D. F. Hawkins (Ed.), *Homicide among Black Americans.* New York: University Press of America.

Jacobson, N. S. & Addis, M. E. (1993). Research on couples and couple therapy: What do we know? Where are we going? *Journal of Counseling and Clinical Psychology, 61,* 85-93.

Johnson, I. M., Crowley, J., & Sigler, R. T. (1992). Agency response to domestic violence: Services provided to battered women. In E. C. Viano (Ed.), *Intimate violence: Interdisciplinary perspective.* Washington, DC: Hemisphere Publishing Corp.

Kim, K. & Cho, Y. (1992). Epidemiological survey of spousal abuse in Korea. In E. C. Viano (Ed.), *Intimate violence: Interdisciplinary perspective.* Washington, DC: Hemisphere Publishing Corp.

Koss, M. P., Goodman, L. A., Browne, A., Fitzgerald, L. F., Keita, G. P., & Russo, N. F. (1994). *No safe haven: Male violence against women at home, at work, and in the community*. Washington, DC: American Psychological Association.

Koss, M. P. & Haslet, L. (1992). Somatic consequences of violence against women. *Archives of Family Medicine, 1*, 53-59.

Kratcoski, P. C. (1988). Families who kill. *Marriage and the Family Review, 12*, 47-70.

Kruttschnitt, C. (1993). Violence by and against women: A comparative and cross-national analysis. *Violence and Victims, 8*, 253-270.

Lloyd, S. A. (1990). Asking the right questions about the future of marital violence research. In D. J. Besharov (Ed.), *Family violence: Research and public policy issues*. Washington, DC: The AEI Press.

Mancuso, P. J., Jr. (1989). Domestic violence and the police: Theory, policy, and practice. In L. J. Dickstein & C. C. Nadelson (Eds.), *Family violence: Emerging issues of a national crisis*. Washington, DC: American Psychiatric Press.

Mann, C. R. (1990). Black female homicide in the United States. *Journal of Interpersonal Violence, 5*, 176-201.

Mann, C. R. (1992). Female murderers and their motives: A tale of two cities. In E. C. Viano (Ed.), *Intimate violence: Interdisciplinary perspective*. Washington, DC: Hemisphere Publishing Corp.

Markman, H. J., Renick, M. J., Floyd, F. J., Stanley, S. M., & Clements, M. (1993). Preventing marital distress through communication and conflict manage-

ment training: A 4- and 5-year follow-up. *Journal of Counseling and Clinical Psychology, 61*, 70-77.

Monahan, J. (1978). The prediction and control of violent behavior. In *Research into violent behavior: Overview and sexual assaults*. Hearings before the Subcommittee on Domestic and International Science Planning, Analysis, and Cooperation of the Committee on Science and Technology, U.S. House of Representatives. 95th Congress, Second session.

Murphy, C. M., Meyer, S., & O'Leary, K. D. (1993). Family of origin violence and MCMI-II psychopathology among partner assaultive men. *Violence and Victims, 8*, 165-176.

Myers, J. K., Weissman, M. M., Tischler, G. L., Holzer, C. E., III, Leaf, P. J., Orvaschel, H., Anthony, J. C., Boyd, J. H., Burke, J. D., Kramer, M., & Stoltzman, R. (1984). Six-month prevalence of psychiatric disorders in three communities. *Archives of General Psychiatry, 41*, 959-967.

Ney, P. G. (1992). Transgenerational triangles of abuse: A model of family violence. In E. C. Viano (Ed.), *Intimate violence: Interdisciplinary perspective*. Washington, DC: Hemisphere Publishing Corp.

O'Carroll, P. W. (1986). Patterns and recent trends in black homicide. In D. F. Hawkins (Ed.), *Homicide among Black Americans*. New York: University Press of America.

O'Leary, K. D. (1993). Through a psychological lens: Personality traits, personality disorders, and levels of violence. In R. J. Gelles & D. R. Loseke (Eds.), *Current controversies on family violence*. Newbury Park, CA: Sage.

Pan, H. S., Neidig, P. H., & O'Leary, K. D. (1994). Predicting mild and severe husband-to-wife physical aggression. *Journal of Consulting and Clinical Psy-*

chology, 62, 975-981.

Parker, R. N. & Toth, A. M. (1990). Family intimacy and homicide: A macro-social approach. *Violence and Victims, 5*, 195-210.

Perog-Good, M. A. (1992). Sexual abuse in dating relationships. In E. C. Viano (Ed.), *Intimate violence: Interdisciplinary perspective*. Washington, DC: Hemisphere Publishing Corp.

Plass, P. S. (1993). African American homicide: Patterns in partner, parent, and child victimization, 1985-1987. *Journal of Black Studies, 23*, 515-538.

Reiss, A. J., Jr. & Roth, J. A. (1993). *Understanding and preventing violence*. Washington, DC: National Academy Press.

Rose, H. M. & McClain, P. D. (1990). *Race place and risk: Black homicide in urban America*. Albany, NY: SUNY Press.

Rosenbaum, A. & Mauero, R. D. (1990). Perpetrators of spouse abuse. In R. T. Ammerman & M. Hersen (Eds.), *Treatment of family violence: A sourcebook*. New York: John Wiley & Sons.

Rosenfield, R., Decker, S., & Kohfield, C. (1993). Different levels, common causes: St. Louis homicide rates in national perspective. In C. R. Block & R. L. Block (Eds.), *Questions and answers in lethal and non-lethal violence. Proceedings of the first annual Workshop of the Homicide Research Working Group*. Washington, DC: U.S. Department of Justice, National Institute of Justice Research Report.

Showalter, C. R., Bonnie, R. J., & Roddy, V. (1980). The spousal-homicide syndrome. *International Journal of Law and Psychiatry, 3*, 117-141.

Stacey, W. A., Hazlewood, L. R., & Shupe, A. (1994). *The violent couple*. Westport, CN: Praeger.

Staples, R. (1986). The masculine way of violence. In D. F. Hawkins (Ed.), *Homicide among Black Americans*. New York: University Press of America.

Stets, J. E., & Straus, M. A. (1990). Gender differences in reporting marital violence and its medical and psychological consequences. In M. A. Straus & R. J. Gelles (Eds.), *Physical violence in American families*. New Brunswick, NJ: Transaction Publishers.

Stout, K. D. (1992). "Intimate femicide" Effect of legislation and social services. In J. Radford & D. E. H. Russell (Eds.), *Femicide: The politics of woman killing*. New York: MacMillan.

Stout, K. D. (1993). Intimate femicide: A study of men who have killed their mates. *Journal of Offender Rehabilitation, 19*, 81-94.

Straus, M. A. & Gelles, R. J. (1990). *Physical violence in American families*. New Brunswick, NJ: Transaction Publishers.

Tifft, L. L. (1993). *Battering of women: The failure of intervention and the case for prevention*. Boulder, CO.: Westview Press.

Tolman, R. M. & Bhosley, G. (1991). The outcome of participation in a sheltered-sponsored program for men who batter. In D. Knudsen & J. Miller (Eds.), *Abused and battered: Social and legal responses to family violence*. New York: Aldine de Gruyter.

Totman, J. (1978). *The murderess: A psychosocial study of criminal homicide*. San Francisco, CA: R and E Research Associates.

Uniform Crime Reports for the United States, 1993. Federal Bureau of Investigation, U.S. Department of Justice, Washington, DC: U.S. Government Printing Office.

Vaselle-Augenstein, R. & Ehrlich, A. (1992). Male batterers: Evidence for psychopathology. In E. C. Viano

(Ed.), *Intimate violence: Interdisciplinary perspective*. Washington, DC: Hemisphere Publishing Corp.

Walker, L. E. (1984). *The battered woman syndrome*. New York: Springer.

Walker, L. E. (1989a). *Terrifying love: Why battered woman kill and how society responds*. New York: Harper & Row.

Walker, L. E. (1989b). Psychology and violence against women. *American Psychologist, 44*, 695-702.

Wilbanks, W. (1983). The female homicide offender in Dade County, Florida. *Criminal Justice Review, 8*, 9-14.

Wilbanks, W. (1986). Criminal homicide offenders in the U.S.: Black vs. White. In D. F. Hawkins (Ed.), *Homicide among Black Americans*. New York: University Press of America.

Wilson, M. & Daly, M. (1993). Spousal homicide risk and estrangement. *Violence and Victims, 8*, 3-16.

Wolfgang, M. E. (1958). *Patterns in criminal homicide*. Philadelphia: University of Pennsylvania Press.

Wolfgang, M. E. (1978). Overview of research into violent behavior. In *Research into violent behavior: Overview and sexual assaults*. Hearings before the Subcommittee on Domestic and International Science Planning, Analysis, and Cooperation of the Committee on Science and Technology, U.S. House of Representatives. 95th Congress, Second session.

About the Author

V. Edwin Bixenstine, PhD, ABPP, is Emeritus Professor of Psychology at Kent State University and currently in private practice in Kent and Cuyahoga Falls, Ohio. His research focus has been interpersonal conflict and resolution. His practice is 40% marital and family counseling, with about 10% of these cases involving physical violence, usually mild and by both parties. Correspondence may be sent to Dr. Bixenstine at 407 Wilson Avenue, Kent, Ohio, 44240.

CHAPTER 9

VIOLENCE IN THE FAMILY

Joseph G. Poirier

Introduction

This chapter explores the complex problem of lethal violence in the domestic setting. Lethality connotes violence that results in death or that has the potential to be deadly. Unlike stranger-to-stranger violence, the reality of domestic violence cannot be captured in merely recording deaths of family members. This is because domestic violence occurs within a fundamental social institution: the family. The institution has emotional bonds, it has a history, and it has a future. Domestic violence can only be meaningfully understood within that context.

Like stranger-to-stranger violence, some domestic violence is premeditated and willful, while some occurs without premeditation and is the tragic result of anger between family members over sometimes incidental circumstances. Any professional who has worked with troubled family situations can describe families that have maintained a torrid, anger-laden stability for weeks, months, and even years. Unlike stranger-to-stranger violence, most family violence occurs in a context of seething anger between two or more family members. At some point, that anger is catapulted into a violent act by dynamics that are often not well understood.

Violence in the domestic setting can involve an infinite combination of family members as players and at various times, the same family members can play the roles of perpetrator, victim, or active or passive witnesses. Violent behavior can assume many patterns and all family members are at least passively affected by any domestic violent act and by the underlying dynamics.

No single source of data comprehensively documents the problem of domestic violence. Therefore, attempting to organize the array of data that is available can become very confusing. Research, however, provides us with five predominant forms of domestic violence: physical and sexual assault of spouses or intimate others, physical and sexual abuse of children, and physical abuse of the elderly. This chapter will review these five forms of domestic violence, each of which carries its own implications for lethality. In the author's experience in conducting thousands of court-ordered assessments of family matters, violence in the domestic context is always potentially lethal, if not presently, then in the future.

Overview and Epidemiology

Domestic violence is perhaps the ultimate expression of violence because, in whatever form, it violates the integrity of the family, the most precious social institution in our culture. Violent behavior in the domestic setting is especially troublesome because, by social definition, the family should be a caring environment combined with the evolving dynamics of human bonding. Although family violence has always been a facet of human history, it has only been in the last three decades that society has become willing to allow the study of the hallowed institution of the family. Previously, our sentiment as a culture was to regard the family setting as private and something to be protected from the probing inquiry of the public. With the public's increasing awareness of the pervasive nature and the devastating impact of domestic violence, this attitude has changed (Family Violence Working Group, 1994).

For all the interest in the phenomenon of family violence over the last 30 years or so, there has been little change with respect to the prevalence of family violence. A historical increase in incidence data regarding domestic violence seems to have begun to level off. This statistical plateau, however, is probably more an indication of the gradual sophistication of measurement techniques, as opposed to any actual reduction in domestic violence. Researchers may have refined data collection procedures and developed sampling error adjustments so that current (demographic) estimates are more accurate, but in reality, as a society, we have not yet begun to decrease the extent of domestic violence. At best, we are running in place with the overall problem. In recent years, there has been some interest in prevention efforts with domestic violence as opposed to mere collection of demographics. Likewise, there have been some advancements in the development of treatment strategies, but much work remains to be done.

In the review that follows, an emphasis has been maintained on more recent research and on studies that work with larger population samples. There are two databases regarding the prevalence of family violence that are most commonly cited by investigators (Koss, Goodman, Browne, Fitzgerald, Kieta, & Russo, 1994): the National Family Violence Survey (NFVS) and the National Crime Victimization Survey (NCVS). There have been two NFVSs: the first occurred in 1975 (Straus, Gelles & Steinmetz, 1980) and the second in 1985 (Gelles, 1987; Gelles & Pedrick, 1985; Straus, 1990; Straus & Gelles, 1986, 1988).

The NCVS is a body of data that was collected for more than 20 years by the United States Department of Justice (Bureau of Justice, 1994a, 1994b). It was a compilation of criminal victimization information based on household surveys. Because the household members' self-reported members' data were not cross-checked against actual law enforcement or court records, there was sampling error. The NCVS data were statistically manipulated to accommodate this problem (Bachman, 1994a).

Family members were asked to describe violent behavior inflicted by other family members. Such a format raised an obvious index of caution regarding the data. The expectation would be significant underreporting by victims of domestic violence. Apart from these limitations, the NCVS data were time-tested and voluminous. The NCVS data were described in many reports by the Bureau of Justice, and included annual bulletins that provided year-to-year data comparisons in an attempt to capture evolving trends.

A benchmark year for NCVS data was 1981. That year represented a peak year for all NCVS categories of crime. The most recent NCVS report (Bureau of Justice, 1994a) reflected data from 1992. The survey collected data only on victims age 12 or older. These data showed that the rate of all household crime for 1992 had remained stable or had decreased slightly.

In the 1992 data, the violent crime category did not reflect any significant change and this had been true also for the 1991 data. In 1992, approximately 36% of attempted violent crimes were completed. During 1992, a total of 33.6 million crimes against persons were committed and of these 33.6 million crimes, 14.8 million occurred in the household. Twenty percent of all of these crimes met the criteria for threatened or actual violence. The violent crime rate was 32 victimizations for every 1,000 persons. Family violence, defined by the survey as crimes by one family member against another, accounted for 7% of all of the reported violent crimes. This figure represented 9% of all completed crimes and 6% of all attempted crimes. The 1992 NCVS data further reflected that 86% of all relative-committed serious crimes were assaults. Of the reported family-violence incidents, 59% were simple assaults and 27% were aggravated assaults.

Literature and Clinical Lore

Violence is a complicated behavioral phenomenon, no matter in which setting it may occur. Roth (1994a, 1994b) described violent behavior as being devised of *diverse* acts and *complex* causes and proposed a helpful two-dimensional framework for organizing violence risk factors. The first dimension — temporal proximity — refers to the elapsed time by which the risk factor precedes the violent act. There are three levels of temporal factors: (1) *predisposing,* which can increase the risk of violence for months or even years in advance; (2) *situational,* which surrounds an interpersonal situation disposed to violence; and (3) *activating,* which immediately triggers a violent act.

The second dimension of the framework comprises the observable levels of the violent act. There are four observable levels: (1) macro social, which is broad social and economic forces; (2) micro social, which is encounters between people in particular settings; (3) psychosocial, which is individual behavioral development from childhood through adulthood; and (4) neurobehavioral, which is biological

processes that underlie all human behavior (Roth, 1994b).

The outcome of domestic violent behavior, when viewed in the context of domestic violence, must also be understood as having a reverberating effect throughout the social system in which it occurs. Domestic violence induces "post traumatic" sequelae not only for the victims, but also for perpetrators, observers, and the entire social matrix of the affected family. Post traumatic effects can be apparent across many parameters for perpetrators and victims. These parameters include the physical, psychological, spiritual, interpersonal, social, financial, and political. In the family context, domestic violence has an ongoing temporality that can be multi-generational. It is for this reason that violence in the domestic situation produces lasting consequences. These effects can be immediate or have a late onset, but they are always disruptive and usually harmful to family stability.

The review of estimates of the occurrence of domestic violence is an endeavor complicated by several variables. To begin with, domestic violence is a sensitive topic and laden with many fundamental taboos. Acknowledging violent circumstances is often very difficult for family members, especially when they are immediately caught up in a web of violent behavior. Another complicating factor is that estimates of domestic violence vary from one research effort to the next because researchers investigate different behavioral parameters. Additionally, researchers employ different research methodologies, study different populations or segments of population, and collect data at different times.

Moreover, the notion of violence is inseparable from its legal definitions and implications, which often vary from jurisdiction to jurisdiction. Legal definitions of violent behavior are based ultimately on the values and mores of society. Certain aggressive acts in the domestic setting, such as murder and child abuse, capture near universal agreement as being egregious. Other forms of domestic violence, however, are more controversial in definition, significance, and implication. Spouse abuse and psychological/emotional abuse of children are two salient examples of domestic violence that lack conceptual clarity.

In summary, finding a standardized definition of domestic violence is difficult. Engaging family members to acknowledge domestic violence is a significant hurdle and there are complex methodology problems. In the literature review that follows, the reader will appreciate that nearly 30 years of collective effort have created an impressive array of research data. The reader will also realize that the expanse of data can be difficult to assimilate. As one group of researchers described, "Family violence is difficult to measure; no consensus exists as to what constitutes family violence, it most often occurs in private, and victims are often reluctant to report incidents of family violence to anyone else because of fear of shame or from fear of reprisal" (Zawitz, Klaus, Bachman, Bastian, DeBerry, Rand, & Taylor, 1993, p. 24). The following sections present the research findings from the literature for the five predominant types of domestic violence.

Physical Assault of Spouses/Intimate Others

Based on the 1975 NFVS data, Straus, Gelles, and Steinmetz (1980) reported that 12% of the spouse respondents in the study acknowledged at least a single incident of violence during their marriage. We can infer from this that approximately two million women were physically abused during the year of the study. More recent Bureau of Justice (1993) data estimated that female family members were victims of domestic violence at a rate three times that of male family members. Gillespie (1989) suggested that in the United States, one female was subjected to domestic violence every 20 seconds. Twenty years of spouse abuse data have yielded approxi-

mates that fall widely within these estimates.

The first NFVS (Straus et al., 1980) involved face-to-face interviews of randomly selected married couples, while the NFVS resurvey (Straus et al., 1990) involved telephone interviews with randomly selected households. The initial survey reflected 12% of married couple respondents who reported at least a single incident of physical assault and 16% of the respondents who reported the occurrence of physical violence in the year just preceding the survey (Straus et al., 1980). In the 1985 NFVS resurvey, one out of six American couples surveyed, or 16% of all couples, reported at least one incident of physical assault during that year.

Straus and Gelles (1988) also reviewed other studies utilizing the NFVS data. The marital violence prevalence rates from these studies ranged from 121 to 510 incidents per 1,000 for any type of husband/wife violence (14 studies). Severe husband/wife violence prevalence rates ranged from 287 to 603 per 1,000 (three studies). Prevalence rates for severe violence inflicted by husbands varied from 8 to 102 per 1,000 (seven studies); the same data, but for wife perpetrators, ranged from 25 to 59 per 1,000 (four studies). When these combined rates were applied to the estimated 54 million couples in the United States in 1975, a projected 8.7 million couples experienced violent incidents which carried a risk of personal injury. For every 1,000 couples, 116 reported violent acts perpetrated by the husband for the year of the study. "Severe violence by the husband" was reported by 3 out of every 100 wives. Severely violent acts included such behaviors as threats with a weapon, (e.g., gun or knife), beating, punching, kicking, choking, and striking with objects. Extrapolating from the estimate of "severe" incidents, 1.8 million women were severely assaulted by their husbands in the survey year. The authors observed, however, that the estimate of 3 out of every 100 wives who were beaten severely should be regarded as an underestimate (Straus & Gelles, 1988).

Other investigators (Browne, 1987; Davidson, 1978; Douglas, 1987; Fagan, 1988; Langhan & Innes, 1986; Novello, 1992; Stark, Flitcraft, Zuckerman, Grey, Robinson, & Frazier, 1981) estimated that between 1.5 and 4 million women each year experience violence within the marital relationship. Walker (1989) estimated that 50% of all women have been battered in their lifetime. Wilson (1993) estimated that 28% of all women in relationships have been domestic violence victims. The same authors reported that every year, at least 1 in every 10 women was abused by her male partner and that there was repeated, severe violence in 1 out of every 14 marriages.

The NCVS report for 1992 (Bureau of Justice, 1994a) showed that the rate of violent crimes against women was 3.8 per 1,000, compared to 0.8 per 1,000 for men. In comparison to women, men were significantly more likely to be victimized by a casual acquaintance. The male-to-female rates were comparable when offenders were well known to the victims, but not relatives.

A significant majority of all family violent crimes in the NCVS data was committed by spouses or ex-spouses (53% of 489,460 domestic violent crimes). Violent crimes were most likely to be committed by the victim's spouse when compared with other perpetrator categories, including the victim's ex-spouse, parents, or children. Violent crimes involving relatives occurred between parents and children 14% of the time and 33% of the time between the victim and other relatives. Annually, women experienced more than 10 times as many incidents of violence by an intimate as compared to men (Bachman, 1994a, 1994b). Family-based violence accounted for 5% of all violent incidents against men, compared to 33% for women. Men were far more likely to experience violence by an acquaintance (35%) or a stranger (31%).

Bachman (1994a, 1994b) analyzed data on violence against women from the NCVS. She found that women were significantly less likely to be victims of all types of violent crime in comparison to men. In contrast to men, however, women were more likely to be victimized by intimates, such as husbands or boyfriends. Marital status was a variable in the probability of a family member being victimized. Married individuals were the least likely, and never-married individuals were the most likely among all groups, to be victimized by a casual acquaintance. The highest probability for violent crime to be committed against relatives by relatives occurred when the offenders were divorced or separated (Gelles, 1987; Harlow, 1991; Bureau of Justice Statistics, 1988; Bureau of Justice, 1992). Data also consistently reflected that any overt effort by a woman to leave an abusive relationship was a factor in domestic violence (Jones, 1980; Sonkin, Martin, & Walker, 1985; Browne, 1987).

Bachman (1994a) found that women with lower educational levels and lower family income levels were most likely to be violently victimized. One non-significant variable for family-based violence was residence in a central city, suburban, or rural area. In the same data, the reporting of violent victimizations by women to police authorities did not vary by victim-offender relationship. The reasons for not reporting did, however, depend on victim-offender relationship. If offenders were strangers, the most frequent reason for not reporting was the expectation that the incident may not have been reportable as a crime. If offenders were intimates, the reason for not reporting was most typically fear of reprisal by the offender (Bachman, 1994a).

The female victims in Bachman's study described that they reported their victimization because they wanted the offender to be punished. Women victimized by men whom they knew were more likely not to report; these women said that they believed the matter to be private or personal (Bachman, 1994a). Another significant finding by Bachman was that if a woman victim reported a violent incident as perpetrated by a stranger, police responded more quickly (less than five minutes) than if the perpetrator was reported as known to the victim.

According to FBI statistics (Bureau of Department of Justice, 1994a), 22,540 murders occurred nationwide in 1992. About 15% of those murders were committed by an intimate other (defined as spouse, ex-spouse, boyfriend, or girlfriend). Dawson and Langan (1994) reviewed the Bureau of Justice statistics and reported that the most frequent type of lethal family violence involved husbands and wives. The second most frequent type of lethal family violence involved offspring as the victims and the parents as the perpetrators. These authors determined that murders of offspring by parents represented 21% of the total pool. In contrast, only 12% of the total victim pool involved offspring murdering parents. The study found that sons (82%) were more often the perpetrators than daughters (18%). The group of offspring accused of murdering their parents was the youngest group of all family murder assailants; two-thirds of the offspring accused as murderers were under the age of 30.

Sexual Assault of Spouse/Intimate Others

Many researchers who have reported on demographic data regarding the occurrence of rape have relied on NCVS data (Bureau of Justice, 1985, 1989, 1992a, 1992b, 1992c, 1993, 1994a, 1994b). The term "rape" is a prime example of the problem of definitions with domestic violence data. Legal definitions of rape vary widely. To the average person, rape is an emotionally laden term, and in the family context, it carries a particularly onerous connotation. When collecting data, researchers will usually avoid direct reference to rape with family members and instead make oblique inquiries about "unwanted" or "forced" sexual overtures (Finklehor & Yllö, 1983a, 1983b; National Victims Center, 1992;

Pagelow, 1984; Walker, 1984).

In an early study, Russel (1982) conducted a study in which more than 900 randomly chosen women were surveyed. This research employed conservative criteria to define rape and found that of the women who had been married, 14% reported at least one rape incident by husbands or ex-husbands. Russel's definition of rape excluded sexual fondling and included aggressive sexual acts only if self-reported.

The NFVS data from 1987 to 1991 showed that every year, 133,000 women (age 12 or older) were victims of rape or attempted rape. Most of these rapes (55%) were committed by someone known to the victim (Koss, Goodman, Browne, Fitzgerald, Keita, & Russo, 1994). These data did not identify the percentage of domestic sexual abuse of women that resulted in death.

According to Koss et al. (1994), all rapes were most likely to be committed between the hours of 6:00 p.m. and midnight. Also, similar to physical violence, most rape was perpetrated by intimates as opposed to strangers or acquaintances (Koss et al., 1994). Based on the reports of victim-respondents, non-stranger rapists were most likely (70%) to be under the influence of alcohol or drugs at the time of the victimization when compared with strangers (Bachman, 1994a, 1994b).

Pagelow (1984) suggested that the more intimate the relationship between the victim and the assailant, the greater the likelihood of more serious violence in sexual assaults. Bachman's (1994a, 1994b) more recent research, however, found that women rape victims incurred more frequent and more severe physical injuries when the assailant was a stranger than when the assailant was an intimate. Also, according to Bachman's data, women who were rape victims reported knowing the perpetrator more frequently (55%) than those who reported the perpetrator as a stranger (44%).

Rape is a form of behavior that combines

aggression and deliberate transgression of inti-mate body space. Perhaps it is because of that combination of factors that the impact of sexually assaultive behavior in the domestic context is so devastating. There is no clear data as to the num-ber of rapes in the domestic setting that are lethal. Likewise, data is not available as to the number of domestic rape incidents also associated with domestic physical violence. Furthermore, the number of domestic physical violence cases resulting in death and involving sexual assault is undetermined in available data. These are areas of data collection that will hopefully be a focus of research in the future.

Koss et al. (1994) observed that "[t]he effect that violent sexual assault by an intimate has on a woman's perception of self, of alternatives, of entrapment, and of danger cannot be overestimat-ed" (1994, p. 47). So profound is the impact of sexual violence within the family setting that the marital relationship is usually irreversibly tainted. There is no data that reflects the number of mari-tal relationships that are terminated because of marital rape. The marital relationship damaged by domestic rape, in turn, forecasts poorly for any children who may be involved.

Physical Abuse and Neglect of Children

The classic statement of the problem of child abuse was presented by Kemper in a brief 1962 article entitled *"The Battered Child Syndrome"* (Kemper, Silverman, & Steels). Since Kemper's original description, the problem of child abuse and neglect has received considerable attention. Collecting demographic data about battered chil-dren, however, presents the unique problem of not being able to accept at face value a child's self-report. Moreover, the reliability of a child's self-report is dependent on the child's age, emo-tional maturity, and other factors (West, 1988).

Historically, establishing criteria for child abuse and for determining the role of child wel-fare agencies has been part of state statutes for more than 200 years (McCurdy & Daro, 1994). In 1974, the Federal government adopted a more direct role in child abuse policy with the passage of the Child Abuse Prevention and Treatment Act (P.L. 93-247). The passage of this legislation established a set of uniform operation standards with respect to the identification and management of child abuse cases. Individual states, however, continue to decide definitions of maltreatment, investigative procedures, service systems, and data collection procedures (McCurdy & Daro, 1994, p. 1). These differences in jurisdictional definitions, in turn, create difficulties when police authorities, protective service workers, and public and private sector clinicians attempt to coordinate effective services. One early estimate of the rate of child physical abuse was offered by Straus, Gelles, and Steinmetz (1980). Based on the NFVS data, they estimated that, in 1975, 2 mil-lion children in the United States were abused. This estimate was based on 4% of the parent respondents who had acknowledged inflicting severe abuse on their children and, therefore, was an obvious underestimate of the problem.

In the 1985 NFVS follow-up survey, Straus and Gelles (1988) presented data showing that 1.5 million children were physically abused per year. Their working definition of abuse was a child being "...kicked, bitten, punched, beaten up, burned or scalded, or...threatened or attacked with a knife or gun" (p. 31). When the authors added "hitting a child with an object" to the definition, the rate for abused children increased to 110 per 1,000 per year or 6.9 million children being phys-ically abused each year. These data reflect the scope and gravity of the child maltreatment prob-lem; the impact of child abuse on the victim's overall development is well established (Finkle-hor & Browne, 1985; Jaffe, Wolfe, & Wilson, 1990; McCurdy & Daro, 1993).

In 1986, the National Committee for the Pre-vention of Child Abuse, along with state child welfare agencies, began conducting annual surveys and gathering demographics regarding child abuse and neglect. The latest Committee report was for 1993. These data were fraught with interstate definition and classification differences but were the only available estimates of nationwide incidence information. According to the National Committee for the Prevention of Child Abuse data, in 1993, almost 1,300 children died due to abuse and neglect (McCurdy & Daro, 1994). This number reflected an average of three children per day who died of maltreatment. It is important to note that "maltreatment" in this report included physical and sexual abuse and the neglect of children. The available format of the data, however, did not permit further differential analysis, for example, of deaths identified by categories of child physical abuse, sexual abuse, or neglect. Deaths were simply logged under the generic category of child maltreatment. The same data source also reflected that, in 1992, there were more than 3 million reports of child maltreatment nationwide. These data were based on a study of state-by-state polling of protective service investigations. Nationwide, children's protective service agencies confirmed more than 1 million reported cases of child abuse and neglect. Of the substantiated cases, 15% (more than 150,000) involved sexual abuse. The 1993 National Committee to Prevent Child Abuse survey data reflected a decrease in the rise of deaths of children secondary to maltreatment when compared with earlier years.

Dawson and Langan (1994) reviewed Bureau of Justice family murder data and they found that mothers were generally the most frequent perpetrators of child abuse. When a child abuse victim was under age 12, a family member was the most frequent statistical suspect and parents were the perpetrators 57% of the time. For murder victims under age 12, death was preceded 79% of the time by physical child abuse inflicted by the parental figure who eventually inflicted the lethal abuse.

McCurdy and Daro (1994) addressed the problem of childhood maltreatment fatalities being mistakenly perceived as accidental deaths or sudden infant death syndromes (SIDS). These authors noted that variations in how state agencies report such data make it very difficult to document the actual extent of the problem. Their research reflected that younger children were most at risk for lethal outcomes from maltreatment. For the years 1991 to 1993, fatalities from maltreatment accounted for 86% of the deaths for children under the age of five years. For children less than one year of age, 46% of deaths were identified as due to maltreatment (McCurdy & Daro, 1994).

Maternal substance abuse as a form of child maltreatment affects prenatal and postnatal development. In the 1993 National Committee to Prevent Child Abuse survey, 12 states were systematically collecting data regarding the problem and reported almost 7,000 drug-exposed babies (McCurdy & Daro, 1994). The fact that only 12 states collected and reported data was an obvious reflection of less than committed interest in the problem.

Sexual Abuse of Children

Finklehor et al. (1988) suggested that child sexual abuse did not become a significant area of interest to child health professionals until the mid-1970s, when there was an increase in government funding which, in turn, led to a significant increase in data collection. Several federal agencies, including the National Institute of Mental Health, the National Center on Child Abuse and Neglect, the U.S. Department of Justice, and the Office of Juvenile Justice and Delinquency Prevention joined in a massive effort to collect reliable demographic data. This interest led to a surge of public attention on the problem, along with an unprecedented increase in the number of complaints of child maltreatment to authorities.

Researchers (Finklehor et al., 1988; Widom, 1989) began to emphasize that the fundamental problem of elusive definitions with domestic violence matters was especially applicable to child sexual abuse. To begin with, variations in definitions of abuse and in age cutoffs contributed to wide variations in estimates of child abuse prevalence data.

In an effort to highlight the problem, Finklehor et al. (1988) compared differences in reported child sex abuse prevalence rates across 19 studies, with the differences in self-reported rates ranging from 6 to 62% for females and from 3 to 30% for males. A similar review by Whitcomb (1992) across seven studies reflected a range of difference from 12 to 38% for women and from 3 to 16% for men.

The author has participated in the evaluation of more than 1,800 matters of suspected child sexual abuse. Less than 160 of these cases have involved women as the alleged perpetrators. These observations are consistent with nationally reported data in which more than 90% of all reported sexual offenders were men (Finkelhor, 1984; Finkelhor & Hotaling, 1983). Sgroi (1982) estimated that the actual number of female perpetrators was much higher and that the stronger cultural taboo for women accounted for the suppressed number of reported cases.

Of the approximately 3 million cases of child maltreatment that were reported in 1993, 11% involved allegations of child sexual abuse (McCurdy & Daro, 1994). These data were based on nationwide incidence reports from state departments of social services. Approximately 34%, or 1 million, of the reported cases were deemed confirmed by investigating protective services workers. Of the confirmed cases, 15% involved child sexual abuse circumstances (McCurdy & Daro, 1994). Prorating these data reflect that, for every 1,000 children in the United States, approximately 15 were maltreated and that approximately 3 of these 15 maltreated children per 1,000 were sexually abused.

Incest refers to inappropriate sexual activity between family members, relatives, or both. When incest involves a child participant, the circumstance is child sexual abuse. Meiselman (1978) provided a comprehensive, early historical review of incest. She described formal research efforts with incest behavior that began in the late 19th century. More recent reviews of the incest problem were completed by Russell (1986) and Courtois (1988). Russell's study (1986) was limited to female respondents, but it remains one of the more definitive statements of the incest problem. Russell's data reflected that approximately 20% of the respondents acknowledged at least a single incest victimization that had occurred before the age of 18. Moreover, according to Russell's findings, at least two-thirds of all child sexual abuse involved incest circumstances. Incest occurred among all combinations of family member partners, both immediate and extended. Incest did not always involve a child victim nor was all incest necessarily regarded as abusive by the participants (Courtois, 1988). The most common patterns of incest are parent to child and sibling to sibling and the single most prevalent incest pattern is father/stepfather to daughter. Any caveats regarding the collection of research data with domestic violence are only magnified with incest due to the powerful and essentially universal taboos associated with incest.

Early efforts to identify a "sexually abused child syndrome" were abandoned due to the lack of empirical data (Whitcomb, 1992). When child sexual abuse began to come to the attention of the public some 20 years ago, there was a corresponding surge of cases reported to authorities. Through the 1980s, child sexual abuse cases entered the courtrooms in unprecedented numbers. One aspect of this phenomenon was the appearance of expert witnesses who professed to be able to describe a syndrome picture that identified a sexually abused child. Two factors appeared to have contributed to these overzealous claims. The first factor was the high sensitivity of child sexual abuse circumstances. The second factor was the inability of children to function in the courtroom as reliable witnesses. Opposing experts quickly challenged the unfounded assertions and the courts reacted with decisions that recognized the limitations of the clinical art of assessing and predicting the problem of child sexual abuse. Myers, Bays, Becker, Berliner, Corwin, and Saywitz (1989) provided an excellent review of these legal/medical/mental health interface issues in legal proceedings that deal with child sexual abuse.

Studies showed that there are different risk factor considerations for child sex abuse in comparison to child physical abuse (Finklehor & Baron, 1986). In contrast to child physical abuse, impoverished financial circumstances have not been identified as a risk parameter with child sexual abuse. As with child physical abuse, marital conflict, distressed mother/child relationship(s) and the natural father being absent from the home were high risk parameters for child sexual abuse. The troubled mother/child relationship factor could be due to the mother being physically or psychiatrically disabled or emotionally unavailable. This latter factor could serve as an influence because the mother would not be available to monitor the child's status, and also because the spouse/intimate other relationship might be stressed. A stressed marital relationship is a risk parameter in that it can serve as a catalyst for the perpetrator to seek need fulfillment in an abusive sexual relationship with a child family member. The absent father factor carries particular increased risk when there is a stepfather figure in the home (Finklehor & Baron, 1986).

Research efforts to demonstrate a link between the impact of child sexual abuse and the degree of force used by the perpetrator have been inconsistent (Finklehor et al., 1988). In the author's experience, the idiosyncratic sensitivities

of the child victim as well as the victim's emotional maturity are more important. That is, the child victim who is mature enough to be aware of moral implications and the social taboos associated with child sexual abuse is usually more vulnerable to trauma.

Physical Abuse of the Elderly

In Western culture the welfare of the elderly as a social concern is a recent phenomenon. The elderly are the fastest growing segment of our population and this statistical reality has spawned considerable interest in the plight of the elderly. Vetch and Garrett (1992) suggested that if child abuse was discovered in the 1960s, then elder abuse was discovered in the 1970s. These authors also concluded that initial attempts to apply definitional content from child abuse research to elder abuse research were imprudent. Likewise, early efforts to mimic child abuse data collection procedures were not appropriate with the elderly. The elderly, for example, were often autonomous in their living status and were not victims in the characteristic passive or silent way that children usually are. Unlike child victims, elderly victims may be abused because of financial or other forms of control that they may have over their perpetrators. As adults, the elderly can be more clever and manipulative in not revealing abuse. According to Vetch and Garrett (1962), for these reasons, many early efforts to collect elderly abuse data with procedures developed for child abuse led to incorrect conclusions as to the actual extent of elder abuse.

Stein (1991) described a recent effort to assemble a group of 10 researchers from a variety of disciplines in order to establish a national research agenda for elder abuse. According to Stein, in spite of extensive preparation by the program participants, they could not arrive at a consensus regarding even basic definitions of elder maltreatment. Stein concluded that the struggle to arrive at basic, consistent working definitions as reflected in the futile effort of these researchers was indicative of a broader problem with collecting meaningful data regarding elder abuse.

Bachman (Bureau of Justice, 1992b) reviewed violent crime victimization rates from the period from 1987 through 1990. She found that the elderly were less likely than younger age groups to be victims of crime and, in particular, violent crime. For violent crime victims under the age of 25, the rate was 64.6 per 1,000, and for violent crime victims over the age of 65 the rate was 4.0 per 1,000. When the elderly were victimized, however, they were more likely to incur serious injuries. Bachman's study was based on data from the NCVS and on data from the Federal Bureau of Investigation's (FBI) Comparative Homicide File (CHF). The NCVS data has been previously described. The CHF was an FBI statistical research tool that was based on adjusted reports of homicide incidences. The CHF reflected lethal victimizations by age groups calculated from information collected from 1980 through 1987.

Bachman's findings (Bureau of Justice, 1992b) reflected that, as a group, elderly victims were more likely than other age groups to report perpetrators as strangers. The death rate of the elderly due to felonious assault reflected their greater likelihood to suffer a lethal outcome by stranger assailants; the data, however, did not explain why. Presumably, the typical isolated living circumstances of many elderly and their more fragile physical health were two factors. Bachman's data did not provide specific information regarding a lethal outcome during domestic abuse of the elderly. In reviewing statistics reflecting annual domestic violence homicide rates, Bachman found that, as a family member aged, the statistical likelihood of homicide death by another family member diminished. In comparison, with younger family members, there was a greater likelihood of homicide death by acquaintance than by either a family member or by a stranger.

Base Rates

The following data, summarized in Table 1, provides a sampling of baseline incidence and prevalence data for the five areas of domestic violence. Use of the table format permits quantitative comparisons of data from different resources. The tabled data illustrate the problem of different data formats across studies; accordingly, attempts to compare data among studies must be approached with care.

The statistical recording of behavioral data from a population is reported as *incidence* and *prevalence* statistics. *Incidence* refers to the rate of occurrence of an event. Typically, incidence will be expressed as the number of occurrences for a specific length of time, for example, 24 per year. Incidence can also be reported as an occurrence rate for a number of subjects, for example, 24 per 1,000 adolescent girls. *Prevalence* data reflects how often a behavior occurs and is usually expressed as a percentage, for example, 24% of the 1,000 adolescent males in the study. The notions of incidence and prevalence are thus straightforward; in practice, however, the concepts are used in less than standardized ways across different studies.

The data in Table 1 reflect that spouse/intimate physical abuse is a highly prevalent form of domestic violence. Females are the more frequent victims in such abuse, averaging a 60% greater abuse rate in comparison to male victims. The prevalence of spouse/intimate physical abuse is exceeded, however, by reports of both child maltreatment (see Table 3) and elder abuse (see Table 5). Table 2 reflects the well-established statistic that significant others perpetrate most sexual abuse, particularly rape. There is little empirical data that documents sexual abuse of men by significant others; this assuredly is due, in part, to cultural issues of male bravado and the predictable reluctance by male victims even to acknowledge that such a prob-

TABLE 1
SPOUSE/INTIMATE OTHER PHYSICAL DOMESTIC VIOLENCE BASELINE DATA

Researcher(s)	Research Date(s)	Data/Statistic
Bachman	1994	5% of all male victims of violent assault perpetrated by intimates or other relatives; 33% of all female victims of violent assault perpetrated by intimates or other relatives
Benson	1992	One woman abused in less than every 20 seconds
Dawson & Langen	1994	Husband and wife violence is most frequent form of family violence
Jaffe, Wolfe & Wilson	1990	Severe violence in one of every 14 marriages
National Crime Survey	1994a, 1994b	53% of all violent family crime is perpetrated by spouse or ex-spouse
Straus & Gelles	1988	1.8 million victims of domestic violence, 34 out of every 1,000 wives
Walker	1989	50% of all women are battered in their lifetime
Wilson	1993	28% of all women are domestic violence victims in their life time

TABLE 2
SPOUSE/INTIMATE OTHER SEXUAL ASSAULT BASELINE DATA

Researcher(s)	Research Date(s)	Data/Statistic
Bachman	1994	Rape injuries more severe when assailant is stranger than if assailant is intimate
Koss et al.	1994	Most sexual assaults against women inflicted by intimates
National Crime Survey	1994a, 1994b	133,00 women raped annually, 55% by non-strangers, not necessarily a family member
Pagelow	1984	The more intimate the victim-assailant relationship, the more likely injury in sexual assault
Russel	1982	14% of women respondents reported at least a single rape by husband or ex-husband

lem might exist.

Tables 3 and 4 depict the widespread reporting of child maltreatment. The extent of the problem of child maltreatment is horrific in its commentary on the status of the well-being of children in contemporary society. The problem is even more overwhelming in its implications for the future functioning of victims. The data in

Tables 3 and 4 are based on legal definitions and, therefore, the information is inclusive of youngsters from birth to age 18 years. It is important to note that, from the clinical perspectives of conducting assessment or providing treatment, the child/adolescent distinction is immensely important. The child-to-adolescent developmental periods are ones of enormous and rapid change. The ability of a youngster to comprehend environmental events depends on his or her chronological age and level of cognitive awareness. Likewise, the ability of a child to cope with the trauma of neglect and abuse

of 7 million reports of domestic violence each year in the United States.

The Domestic Violence Assault Cycle

A family violence cycle can be understood on multiple levels. Most domestic violence circumstances have a history of disturbed dynamics between the family members involved. Based on the author's clinical experience with families, a cycle of domestic violence may begin with an isolated episode of conflict that goes unresolved. With each additional episode, the momentum of a

TABLE 3
PHYSICAL CHILD ABUSE AND CHILD NEGLECT BASELINE DATA

Researcher(s)	Research Date(s)	Data/Statistic
Dawson & Langen	1994	Second most frequent type of family violence is parent to child or murder victims under age 12; death was preceded by parental inflicted child abuse (79% Incidence)
McCurdy & Daro	1994	In 1993, 3 million reports of child maltreatment nationwide; this is a rate of 5 children per 1,000
National Crime Survey	1994a, 1994b	14% of all family crime is parent to child
National Committee for the Prevention of Child Abuse	1994	In 1993, 1,300 children nationwide died of child abuse or neglect; this is a rate of three children's deaths per day
Straus, Gelles & Steinmetz	1980	In 1975, 2 million children abused in the United States based on a study of parental self-report
Widom	1992	Child with abuse or neglect history has 53% increased risk of arrest as a juvenile, 58% increased risk of arrest as an adult

depends on the child's developmental status and emotional integrity.

The reported 1.5 to 2 million cases per year of elder abuse (see Table 5) can be compared to 3 million reports of child maltreatment (see Table 4) and to 1.8 million reports of spouse/significant other physical abuse (see Table 1). According to the data across the five tables, there are just shy

cycle escalates. The circumstances of the subsequent episodes may or may not be related to the original conflict. The feelings of the affected family members fester, resentment escalates, and feelings of anger gradually begin to build, while the original precipitants are often long forgotten by family members. With the passage of time, however, there can be a progressive accumulation

TABLE 4
BASELINE CHILD SEXUAL ABUSE DATA

Researcher(s)	Research Date(s)	Data/Statistic
Finklehor et al.	1989	Across different studies, child sexual abuse prevalence ranged from 6% to 62% for females and 3% to 30% for males
Gomes-Schwartz et al.	1988	Average age of first abuse is 9.1 years; majority of child victims subjected to repeated assaults over a period of months; 23% of cases resulted in physical injury
McCurdy & Daro	1994	In 1993, of the 3 million nationwide reported cases of child maltreatment, 11% involved child sexual abuse; of the 1 million confirmed cases, 15% involved child sexual abuse allegations
Whitcomb	1992	Child sex abuse self-report incidence across different studies ranges from 12% to 38% for women and 3% to 16% for men

of unresolved issues. Seemingly inexplicable alliances among different family members may form regarding areas of conflict. Such alliances can be based on unrelated issues or on different areas of interest or conflict. By such processes, a family can have simultaneous cycles of lethal violence operating at any given time; cycles can occur within cycles. For example, a family can be struggling with an abusive spouse/intimate relationship and, simultaneously, the angry father becomes involved in a physical or sexual child abuse dynamic.

One well-known example of a domestic violence cycle was described by Walker (1979, 1988) as the "the battered woman syndrome." This syndrome involves three repetitive and predictable stages of abuse of the female partner by her husband or significant other. Walker's (1984, 1988) battered woman syndrome is now a classic description of the domestic physical assault cycle between spouses and intimate others. Initially, there is a phase of progressive tension-building in the couple's relationship. In the second phase, there is a progression of untoward interspouse

acts that leads to a triggering of the battering event. Finally, in the third phase, a period of calm and reduced tension occurs, during which the perpetrator is kind and remorseful. Walker explained: "These patterns lead to an intensity in the relationship, with participants always expecting to be overwhelmed by the rapidity of the abusive acts, yet also reinforced by the rewards in the third phase of the cycle" (1988, p. 141). It is the latter dynamic that maintains the troubled and abusive relationship. In spite of the trauma of the battering event(s), the very process of the battering behavior inexplicably sustains itself.

Summit (1983) described a domestic violence cycle that involves child sexual abuse. Summit proposed an "accommodation syndrome" that could be characteristic of child sexual abuse. The syndrome involved a cycle in which, following disclosure, the child sexual abuse victim succumbs to the insensitive reactions of family members and professional investigators. The victim may respond by "accommodating" to this pressure and recanting the original accusations. Following the disclosure, the victim must withstand

TABLE 5
ELDER ABUSE BASELINE DATA

Researcher(s)	Research Date(s)	Data/Statistic
Aravanis et al.	1993	1.5 to 2 million elder victims of abuse or neglect per year in the United States
Bachman	1992	Elderly less at risk than younger age groups but more serious injuries when abuse occurs
		Average annual homicides per year by family member perpetrator, 1.0 per 100,000
McCallum	1993	International data suggest elderly victim maltreatment prevalence base rates of 30 per 1,000
Pillemar & Finklehor	1989	32 elderly victims per 1000; 58% of abuse perpetrated by spouses
Zawitz et al.	1993	Twenty-year survey shows elderly are significantly less likely than younger age groups to be crime victims, elderly victim rate for violent crime is 4 per 1,000

the rigors of ongoing investigation and legal proceedings. Finally, Summit suggested a third and probably most damaging level of impact for victims. This level of impact involves family members and ill-advised professionals responding to the victim as though he or she had somehow contributed to the abuse. The victim is regarded as traumatized, but also mysteriously perceived as becoming sophisticated and, in some way, tainted by the abuse. Due to his or her exposure to the taboo elements of child sexual abuse circumstances, victims are viewed with a subtle sense of awe that only serves to distance the victim from loved ones.

The more one delves into the problem of maltreatment of children, the more complex the problem becomes. The scope of the problem extends far beyond the immediate impact of the physical or sexual abuse or the neglect of the child victims. Child maltreatment occurs due to a wide range of circumstances. For example, parenting or caretaking figures can be immature, disturbed emotionally, stressed beyond emotional and/or

physical resources, involved with intoxicants, or a combination of these factors (Milner, 1995). Moreover, parenting figures or caretakers may have characterological problems with anger control.

Child abuse and neglect circumstances pose many challenges to detection and intervention. The child victim is typically less likely to complain on his or her own behalf. Even if a child discloses maltreatment, the parenting figures will often bond in a defensive alliance to deny any wrongdoing in order to protect the marital relationship and the family unit. In addition, there are the problems of psychological abuse and children's deaths that on the surface seem accidental. Investigators and clinicians may be very experienced and very skilled, but the detection of these more subtle forms of child maltreatment are far from a scientific pursuit.

Whenever a domestic violence incident occurs, reactions ripple throughout the immediate and extended family system. An incident of violence may also set the stage for additional and different forms of domestic violence. McCay (1994), for example, suggested that marital violence may be a precursor to child abuse. Depending on the nature of the domestic violence disclosure, reactions to the violence can reach further into the extended family. Patterns of reaction can then reverberate to the community, back again to the family, and so on. Naturally, this cycling of reactions to domestic violence can only further contribute to the trauma of the original incident.

The possible cyclic relationship between exposure circumstances of child abuse and later manifestations of acting-out behavior in children and adolescents has been addressed in the literature for many years. As summarized at a recent research conference (U.S. Department of Justice, 1984), "we replayed some of the historical disputes between the psychologist, the physiologist, and the sociologist in trying to explain the causality of child abuse and neglect and juvenile delinquency. Perhaps it should not be a goal to resolve these different perspectives, but rather to apply the most useful contribution of each" (pp. 21-22).

Widom (1992) hypothesized a domestic violence cycle that linked childhood exposure to maltreatment with later aggressive behavior when the victims become adults. Widom suggested that a childhood history of physical abuse predisposes the child survivor/witness to violence in later years. According to Widom's data, even childhood victims of neglect are as prone as child physical abuse victims to later violent criminal behavior. This finding challenged the traditional view of approaching child victims of neglect in a manner different from child victims of abuse. Furthermore, it showed that a history of neglect or abuse increases the odds of adult criminal aggressive behavior by 40%. This was clearly an important finding. Widom's data implicated childhood exposure to neglect or abuse as a factor in generating cycles of intergenerational repetition of domestic violence.

Widom's findings were based on the National Institute of Justice (NIJ) research, in which the official court records of neglected and abused children were tracked for more than a 20-year period. A second phase of the research was undertaken in which the researchers conducted interviews with the subjects. Multiple parameters which were being explored in the interviews included mental health concerns, educational problems, health issues, and occupational difficulties as manifested by child victims.

One compelling finding from Widom's preliminary data was that maltreated youngsters who were removed from their homes of origin and placed in foster care situations as a remedial measure fared no better on adult measures of arrest or violent criminal behavior than their counterparts who were left in their homes of origin. This finding had significant implications for interventions directed at removing such youngsters from their homes.

Proposed models of the cycle of child physical abuse and neglect abound. Tzeng, Jackson, and Karlson (1991) offered a review of approximately 25 such models which operate from different theoretical perspectives. The National Committee to Prevent Child Abuse data identified three primary factors as contributing to domestic maltreatment of children. These factors are (a) parental substance abuse, (b) family needs for support services, and (c) economic stresses. Factors less frequently reported are lack of knowledge of good parenting, domestic violence, and family fragmentation (McCurdy & Daro, 1994).

The cycle of domestic violence with the elderly is similar in some respects to the cycle for spouse and child abuse. Domestic abuse of the elderly can include both physical and sexual violence; most of the reported data, however, reflect physical abuse. The American Medical Association (AMA, 1992) provided a handbook which addresses diagnostic and treatment guidelines for elder abuse, particularly with the elderly who are cognitively incapacitated and not able to adequately speak for themselves. The AMA guidelines encourage care-providers to the elderly to watch for observable medical injuries but also to be alert for more subtle signs of psychological abuse. The elderly who are not able to be assertive about abusive circumstances may be hospitalized, reside in nursing care facilities, or in partial-care situations. According to Vetch and Garrett (1992), the elderly who still reside at home with spouses engage in more mutually instigated patterns of abuse that are typical of spouse abuse with younger partners.

The general effects of abuse on elderly victims are similar to those of child or spouse victims. "These effects include a lowering of the self-esteem and coping skills of the victim, a sense of a stigma and associated attitudes of self-blame, and the isolation of the victim from peers and the general community" (Finkelhor & Pillemar, 1988, p. 247). Likewise, elderly victims can manifest a similar array of psychiatric symptoms observed with other victims of domestic violence.

Case Example of Domestic Violence

Contrary to the impression sometimes created by traditional psychology texts, an actual mental health case history that matches textbook criteria is unusual. The following example of domestic violence depicts the complex intertwining of dynamics that is more typical of case situations. This is especially true as one moves beyond the case history of an individual into the infinitely more complex realm of the family. The following family history portrays only one of the myriad scenarios that can lead to actual or potentially lethal behavior for family members. The case highlights risk factor data identified in this chapter.

The G. Family: One of the most volatile domestic circumstances that unfortunately is increasingly common, is that of disputed custody (Poirier, 1991). When custody of children

becomes an issue, the emotions of the two parents, which are already bitter because of the dissolution of the marital relationship, are only intensified by the pending loss of parental custodial ties for one side. The G. family consisted of three children and the parents. After years of marital discord, a separation occurred. Mr. G left the marital home following a particularly bitter marital argument that involved the sincere, but misguided, intervention efforts of the maternal in-laws.

Mr. G. came from a blue-collar family background. His father worked in an industrial mill and was heavy-handed in disciplining his children, particularly Mr. G. The father also abused Mr. G.'s mother. During the current evaluation effort, Mr. G. observed that his father's severe discipline constituted child abuse by contemporary definition and caused him trauma. Mr. G. stated, "My father taught me about life. My father taught me to be a man." As an adolescent, Mr. G. excelled in academics, although he candidly acknowledged, "I think I was kind of a nerd." Eventually, Mr. G. attended law school, but in his last two years, he encountered severe conflicts with his professors. He was to suggest later in marriage counseling that he realized his conflicts with the professors were somehow related to unresolved issues with his father, but he was nonetheless unable to control his impulses with his professors.

Mr. G. met his wife in law school. Mrs. G. was one of few women students in her class and she was regarded by faculty and fellow students as a superior scholar. Mrs. G. was described as quiet but friendly and having a very warm disposition. The courtship was driven by an impetuous and demanding Mr. G. Mrs. G. related that she was aware that Mr. G.'s assertive social manner was an attraction to her. She completed her law degree and passed the bar on a scheduled course. Mr. G. was forced to withdraw from school because of his abrasive manner. Mrs. G. began practicing administrative law with a private law firm. From the beginning, she commanded an excellent salary.

The couple married a year after Mrs. G. became employed. Mrs. G. suggested during marital counseling that Mr. G. had never forgiven her for outshining him in completing law school and going on to practice law. She stated, "Although we lived comfortably on my income and my job benefits, he made it feel like I should be ashamed of what I had accomplished because somehow I was the reason he never passed the bar." Mr. G. eventually completed law school, with Mrs. G. paying his tuition. After several futile efforts, Mr. G. stopped taking the bar exam; he rationalized that his "legal thinking" was too superior for the simplistic sophistication of the exam. Mr. G. found employment with a small law firm. When he was hired, his agreement with his employer was that he would pass the bar within a year. When this did not happen, Mr. G. was valuable enough to the firm to be continued as a "senior law clerk." Dissatisfied, Mr. G. eventually left the firm and continued in an endless search for a job.

With the passage of time, the couple had three children, a boy and two girls. As the youngsters grew older, and as the parents became unable to parent collaboratively, longstanding conflicts in the marital relationship intensified. At first subtle, these conflicts eventually found Mr. G. imposing demands on the children to side with him. As preteens, the children enjoyed strong bonds with their mother. Although Mrs. G. was the parent working outside the home, the youngsters responded to her warmth and consistency as a caring parent. The children also enjoyed their father, but they had become appropriately wary of his moodiness and increasing temper displays. Initially, Mr. G.'s temper was expressed in unkind and angry words directed toward his wife over inconsequential events and this was followed by temper fits and throwing of household objects. Eventually, the children also became targets of Mr. G.'s verbal

and physical expressions of temper.

Mr. G. indulged himself with large, expensive purchases. Mrs. G. passively permitted this to mollify her husband. Mr. G.'s outbursts escalated to include swatting at Mrs. G. and angrily engaging in menacing tirades toward the youngsters when they misbehaved. At other times, trying to curry the favor of the children, Mr. G. indulged the children with gifts and favored activities. In family therapy sessions, the children pointed out the inconsistencies in their father's interest in them. For example, when flying kites and playing video games, Mr. G. always took over the activities himself and essentially left the children as passive observers. The two older children described their father as more like a competitive playmate. The older children observed that, "he does not act like other fathers."

Following a series of angry outbursts, Mrs. G. proposed and then insisted on a marital separation. Mrs. G. decision was supported by her parents, a factor that predictably only infuriated Mr. G. even more. A rejected but still defiant Mr. G. left the family home. To the dismay of Mr. G., the children flourished in the new-found peaceful atmosphere of the home. Mrs. G. adapted her schedule and established a routine that included her regular participation in the youngster's academic and extracurricular activities. Mr. G. attempted to woo the youngsters with other activities, but the inconsistency of his attentiveness produced the same response in the children as it had previously. Mrs. G. and the children settled into a comfortable and mutually rewarding lifestyles. Mr. G. became increasingly morose, complaining, and blame-avoiding. The youngsters became increasingly resistant to visitation and eventually refused contact with their father.

The domestic situation entered angry and protracted litigation, with Mr. G. representing himself. A judge responsible for the case ordered couple and family therapy with the goal of reinitiating visitations. Months of therapy, character-

ized by a bitter, angry, and vindictive Mr. G., were modestly effective in reestablishing limited visitations. The children and Mrs. G. complained every step of the way. Just before the start of unsupervised visits, Mrs. G. was murdered in a shopping mall parking lot. The incident was not witnessed.

The G. matter was very tragic. Emotion-driven ferocity was suggested in the death of Mrs. G. She died of multiple fatal gunshot wounds. The spent ammunition of a full clip of cartridges from a semiautomatic military assault weapon was found. Almost every spent cartridge struck Mrs. G. Most of the wounds were in her upper torso. To investigators at the crime scene, the victim's death was clearly premeditated. Subsequently, Mr. G. was convicted of first degree murder and incarcerated. The children, who were functionally orphaned, were placed by the court in foster care.

Assessment of Domestic Violence

The involvement of mental health workers in domestic violence matters will usually fall into one of three distinct areas of responsibility. These are *investigation, assessment,* and *treatment.* It is very important for clinicians working with domestic violence to keep these three responsibilities as separate as possible. Each role imparts a different mandate for the clinician.

Investigation is most often the statutory mandate of social workers employed with protective service or child welfare agencies. The primary goal of investigation is the accurate collection of evidence for adjudication. The "client(s)," therefore, for the investigating clinician are the prosecutor's office and the court. Family members must not be lulled into perceiving that investigating clinicians are primary advocates for the family. Investigation is for the primary purpose of aiding the jurisdiction (usually the state) in the collection of evidence to prosecute a domestic violence incident that violated statutes.

Assessment is the clinical evaluation of a fam-

ily circumstance. Assessment, which will occur usually after the investigation phase is completed, can be court mandated. Family members must be fully advised of the situation in which a clinician is conducting a court-ordered assessment. The confidentiality rights of family members are limited in such circumstances. The usual objectives of assessment are understanding the family dynamics and generating treatment goals.

Treatment within a domestic violence situation may or may not be court-ordered. With treatment, however, the working presumptions are that the clinician is an advocate for the family and that the clinician will work to create a healthier family environment. In practice, the distinctions among these areas of responsibility frequently become ambiguous. Such ambiguity can lead to different individuals in a case circumstance presuming a role(s) for the clinician that may or may not be accurate. The clinical roles of investigator, diagnostician, and therapist all have different ethical and legal implications and this must not be forgotten.

As suggested above, the answer to the clinician's question, "who is the client?" (Monahan, 1983), varies with the clinician's defined role in a domestic violence case. Is the clinician's client a specific family member, the marriage, the family unit, the judge ordering the evaluation, or is it the community at large? In most situations the answer is, all of the above, although with different priorities, depending on how the clinician becomes involved. It is the clinician's responsibility to be clear as to his or her role and to explicitly inform all parties involved of such. When a misperception occurs regarding the clinician's role, the clinician will stand accountable.

Clinicians need to be especially clear about their role in domestic violence matters when criminal charges are likely. When domestic violence results in serious injury or death, criminal charges will be lodged. Criminal charges may or may not involve the consequence of capital punishment. In any event, criminal charges move the matter into the highest level of legal evidence and procedural requirements. Involved clinicians will, almost assuredly, be part of these legal proceedings. The time for the clinician to begin anticipating involvement in the adversarial process is from the very beginning. It is heedless to wait until a subpoena is received.

The initial disclosure of suspected domestic abuse can occur in a variety of ways. The settings can include the home, day care centers, nursing homes, shelters, schools, private clinical offices, hospital emergency rooms, etc. Individuals who make the discovery or to whom the disclosure is made can include parents, extended family members, caretakers, clergy, school and police officials, health professionals, and the like. Depending on local statutory requirements, the initial investigation of suspected cases will usually be the responsibility of police officials, protective services workers, or both. Medical personnel will conduct collateral evaluations to document medical findings, as applicable, regarding cause of death or physical or sexual abuse (Witwer, 1994). Mental health clinicians will then become involved in the psychological assessment of the perpetrator, victim, and family status.

Victims and perpetrators of domestic violence can present with the entire spectrum of recognized psychiatric symptoms. The symptoms can be acute or chronic and range in intensity from minimal to severe. One widely used system of psychiatric nomenclature is the *Diagnostic and Statistical Manual-IV, Fourth Edition* (DSM-IV) of the American Psychiatric Association (1994). One should note the DSM-IV disclaimer statement (p. xxvii) in that the DSM-IV disorders were developed for clinical purposes and the fit between clinical applications and forensic objectives is often disharmonious. A lack of consistency is frequently apparent when clinical diagnoses are construed as necessarily conveying a forensic determination, or vice versa. A clinical diagnosis

of personality disorder, for example, does not necessarily convey anything about a perpetrator's complicity in a crime. Likewise, a person being legally convicted of a serious sexual crime does not necessarily justify a clinical diagnosis of sexual disorder (i.e., paraphilia).

Commonly observed DSM-IV diagnostic categories for victims might include reactive symptoms, encompassing the anxiety disorders or the mood disorders. In some situations, the criteria for Post Traumatic Stress Disorder (PTSD) diagnosis may apply. According to current criteria, a diagnosis of PTSD must involve actual or threatened death or serious injury.

For perpetrators of domestic violence, common DSM-IV diagnoses include impulse control disorders, substance abuse disorders, and personality disorders. Perpetrators may present with bona fide major psychiatric disorders, such as thought disorders, bipolar disorders, or paranoid conditions. Such diagnoses may bear on the issues of the perpetrator's competency to stand trial or criminal responsibility. It is important to note that no particular diagnostic category is predictive of, or causally associated with, victims or perpetrators of domestic violence. Recognizing that abusive circumstances are always cause for clinical concern, DSM-IV established special coding categories for physical and sexual abuse for adults and children and for victims and perpetrators (p. 682).

Researchers have identified numerous domestic violence risk factors that can be useful in assessment efforts (Finklehor, 1983). Research has not, however, determined identifiable family circumstances or perpetrator profiles that are causally linked to domestic violence risk. Thus, while risk factor data may have inferential usefulness, the presence of a given factor within a given family situation can always produce "false positive" or "false negative" expectations.

One risk factor that researchers agree is common to many forms of domestic violence is substance abuse by family members. Substance abuse causes and maintains domestic violence. The role of alcohol abuse, in particular, is well-documented as a factor in both physical and sexual domestic violence toward women. With men, alcohol is associated with a social expectation of sexual aggressiveness (Koss et al., 1994). Due to these attributes, the role of alcohol in domestic violence is generally predictable in its potential to induce aggressive behavior with men.

According to Roth (1994a), the one consistent research finding linking violence and psychoactive substances was that alcohol consumption increased aggressive behavior. Roth found that the relationship of alcohol consumption and violent behavior was based on alcohol's pharmacological effects combined with the psychological/social set that alcohol ingestion and aggressive behavior were acceptable in certain settings. This was an important observation, particularly regarding both physical and sexual spouse abuse. Roth also described the role of illicit substance abuse in inducing violence. Of particular note was widespread abuse of cocaine, phencyclidine, and marijuana as precursors to violent behavior. Murphy, Jellinek, Quinn, Smith, Poitrast, and Goshko (1991) described that in a study of 206 cases of serious child abuse and neglect, 46% of the parents had documented substance abuse difficulties. Roth's (1994) data reflected that parental substance abuse was the most prevalent finding with child physical abuse.

In their review of violence against women, Koss et al. (1994) concluded that the single most distinguishing factor of violence perpetrated against women was that most perpetrators were male. This finding was ironic in its simplicity and suggested an important caution. The caution was that the search for predictive personality and other risk factors may be a misguided quest. Still, studies have identified generic personality disorder characteristics such as narcissism, antisocial behavior, schizoid features, and borderline traits

as common features of spouse abusers (Koss et al., 1994). Likewise, generic factors such as poor socialization, irresponsibility, macho-oriented behavior, and compulsivity have been associated with spouse abusers by a variety of studies (Burgess & Youngblood, 1988).

Several risk factors have been described as being characteristic of parents who are prone to child maltreatment. These include low family income, parents who are teenagers, single parents, parents with unwanted children, children with special needs, isolated family circumstances, and problem parenting styles (Finkelhor, Hotaling, & Yllö, 1988). There has also been a growing body of data that has suggested that children who have been exposed to family violence are at higher risk for the development of patterns of acting-out behavior (National Committee for Prevention of Child Abuse, 1986; Roth, 1994b; Whitcomb, 1992). Still other data have supported an increased propensity to violent behavior by adults who were exposed to violence as children (Koss et al., 1994; Widom, 1989, 1992).

In 1984, the Department of Justice formed the Attorney General's Task Force on Family Violence. The Task Force concluded, "A great portion of those who assault both strangers and loved ones were raised themselves in violent households. This is learned behavior. To tolerate family violence is to allow the seeds of violence to be sown into the next generation" (Family Violence Working Group, p. 3).

Attempting to go beyond the limitations of assessment of child sexual abuse based on a risk factor approach, Finklehor et al. (1986) proposed assessment based on a *traumagenic dynamics* model. The authors pointed out that risk factor data did not show the extent of trauma with a given situation. They suggested that the appropriate question was not, "Was it more or less serious," but "What are the specific injurious dynamics that were present?" (p. 194). Four specific areas of inquiry were suggested with the traumagenic model. These questions were, "What was the degree of sexual traumatization?" "How stigmatizing was the experience?" "What were the circumstances of betrayal?" and "What were the powerlessness dynamics?" The authors suggested that the answers to these inquiries would provide a more realistic assessment of the extent of trauma, as well as what type(s) of treatment may be indicated.

In most domestic violence matters, the first challenge of assessment is usually to gauge the "dangerousness" potential of the identified perpetrator and, in turn, the level of risk that exists for the family. The clinical assessment of dangerousness is a complicated clinical effort and one that does not bear strong empirical validity (Campbell, 1995; Melton, Petrila, Poythress, & Slobogin, 1987; Monahan, 1981; Tardiff, 1992). The limits of the clinical prediction of dangerousness are also well recognized by the courts (*Barefoot v. Estelle*, 1983; *Tarasoff v. Regents of University of California, 1976*). The clinical limits of assessing dangerousness potential pose an even greater problem when assessing the risk that exists for the family. With family circumstances, the issue of risk is complicated by the number of family members and by the embedded history of family dynamics. In the end, the single most accurate predictor of violence potential with an individual is a history of violent behavior (Melton et al., 1987).

Initial assessment of family violence potential must begin with an extensive family history. It is astonishing sometimes how patterns of domestic violence behavior are transmitted across generations, which is why the author recommends gathering a family history that extends back at least two generations. There should be detailed inquiries regarding any history of familial substance abuse, mental illness, and violent behavior, domestic or otherwise. The inquiries regarding prior domestic violence should include any history of stalking, menacing, and threatening behavior. Such family history is often layered by strong

familial codes of loyalty and taboo. Family members should each be questioned about developmental hallmarks regarding anger expression, anger management, and the family's response to such circumstances. Leading inquiries such as, "What was the most violent domestic behavior you have ever engaged in?" or "What was the most violent domestic event you have ever witnessed?" can yield useful clinical information.

The history-taking should include specific inquiries regarding family members, cultural backgrounds, and applicable social values that may in some way have a bearing on domestic lifestyles. The author has evaluated family situations, for example, where the still viable attitudes of forebearers with regard to child discipline or the domestic roles of women were quite out of step with contemporary views. There have been situations where a family member's death occurred because of perceived clashes between traditional family values and more modern attitudes. The family history-taking should also be sensitive to any neurological findings with family members that may be associated with aggressive domestic behavior. Inquiries about family history of unusual deaths or illness can sometimes uncover circumstances of familial violence that have been covered over by polite attempts to preserve family honor or to cope with shame. Significant changes in family traditions or in family modes of celebration can be markers of tragedies, perhaps associated with violence.

Mental illness associated with violent behavior should be explored. This would specifically include schizophrenia, major affective disorders, paranoid disorders, personality disorders, conduct and impulse disorders, attention deficit disorders, and depressive disorders. Of the many challenges posed for the clinician in assessing domestic violence, perhaps none is more formidable than penetrating family defensiveness. The family defenses can be laced with efforts to falsify or malinger. More often than not, however, such efforts are motivated by feelings of familial self-preservation, pride, and loyalty. The particular mix of family motivations is usually based on the family's history of using healthy or unhealthy coping strategies. Understanding and working with this interplay of sensitive family dynamics is one form of the true art of assessing and treating circumstances of domestic violence.

Frequently, family members will not appreciate the significance of a domestic violent event until the clinician deftly probes the situation. One strategy is to pose analogous domestic violence events outside the family situation. One example could be, "Gee, if I were to do that, my daughter would...." Another example could be, "If that were my property that you damaged, my reaction would be...."

Due to the complexity of domestic violence, assessment and treatment should always be conducted by a multidisciplinary team. The disciplinary makeup of the team is not critical. No one discipline has a monopoly on understanding or working with the problem of domestic violence. The makeup of a team will usually vary with the availability of personnel.

Another factor that can complicate domestic violence assessment is the involvement of multiple other outside players. Depending on the circumstances, factions within the family may be already formed. Legal interests will not usually coincide completely with clinical goals (Mock & Crawford, 1994). The realities of the adversarial process will pit professional roles one against the other. Clinicians must be knowledgeable of these circumstances and anticipate the inevitable problems they create.

Aside from the domestic violence situation itself, it is usually the necessary interface with the judicial system that will present the area of most difficulty for clinicians. Most mental health clinicians are exposed to years of training directed at instilling sensitivity and empathy in working with others. The thrust of this training is not entirely

compatible with the responsibilities of engaging in forensic work. The death of a family member, flagrant circumstances of neglect, or physical and sexual abuse can instigate the compassion of the mental health worker. Intense emotions can induce professionals to fail to maintain professional objectivity.

A common forum for these problems is the courtroom. Expert witnesses have opposing views and may testify in disparaging ways against each another. Experts can also fall prey to the antics of an opposing attorney during cross-examination when an attorney attempts to discredit the clinician's credibility and professionalism. When this occurs, the credibility of the entire mental health profession is compromised. Furthermore, the family situation for which the expert is advocating is not enhanced in the eyes of the court. Expert witnesses must present their views and opinions vigorously, while adhering to empirical data. The effective expert is also able to convey respect for the fact that others can interpret the same data differently.

Clinicians are prone to becoming zealous advocates for family members with whom they are working. Such advocacy can motivate clinicians to move imprudently into an investigatory role against other family members in order to bolster the clinician's advocacy interest. The clinician working with victims can portray perpetrators in a biased light in order to foster the victims' plight. Clinicians working with perpetrators can minimize the victim's assertions against the perpetrators. When clinicians function as expert witnesses in domestic violence cases, opposing attorneys will attempt to disparage their credibility by preying on their intentions to be compassionate.

Once a therapeutic alliance is established, the clinician's objectivity becomes intertwined with patient advocacy. Attempts in the courtroom by clinicians to justify their objectivity are usually flashpoints for challenges by attorneys. A more effective strategy is to understand the adversarial process and work with it. The adversarial process will always pit an advocacy view against the opposing view, despite objectivity. Clinicians from traditional mental health settings are quite familiar with the transition from diagnostician to therapist with the same patient or families. Legally, however, these are two distinct responsibilities and crossing the respective boundaries may cause problems. Clinicians who are involved therapeutically with family members may be asked to function as expert witnesses. In doing so, they should candidly acknowledge the evolving nature of their professional involvement. The principle is the same as the open acknowledgment to an opposing attorney that the expert witness is being financially compensated. This does not necessarily mean the clinician is a "hired gun." Rarely is the point made that the attorneys, and for that matter even the judge, are similarly being compensated for their time and expertise. Alas, this is one vagary of the legal realm for clinicians who venture into the courtroom.

Clinicians who become involved in domestic violence work must appreciate that rarely does any domestic violence matter resolve itself to the satisfaction of all the family members. For this reason, domestic violence matters are fertile ground for ethical complaints or civil liability suits against involved professionals. It therefore behooves clinicians to adopt appropriate risk management strategies when working with domestic violence situation.

Treatment Considerations in Domestic Violence

As with any major health or social problem, the ultimate intervention with domestic violence is primary prevention. Effective primary prevention can forestall domestic violence (Friedman, 1994). It can also serve to interrupt the cycling dynamics that are often characteristic of domestic violence. Primary prevention efforts are restrict-

ed, however, by our lack of a clear understanding of the causes of domestic violence. As Finkelhor, Hotaling, and Yllö aptly observed, "Family violence is easier to count than explain" (1988, p. 22).

In very recent years, mental health treatment efforts with domestic violence have been enhanced by the courts becoming more responsive to the intolerable plight of domestic violence victims. In the past, the courts would do little until a domestic violence incident occurred and family members were harmed. Many jurisdictions have enacted legislation allowing concerned family members to petition the courts for emergency relief from threatened or actual domestic violence. Typically, the courts are empowered to stipulate temporary "no contact" or restraining orders in justified situations with relaxed hearing procedures. Such interim court interventions will take place pending formal hearings of the complaint with all involved parties.

Treatment with all domestic violence victims must be protective initially and supportive and nurturing throughout. There has been important germinal work in treatment approaches with spouse/intimate victims of domestic physical abuse and with sexual abuse victims, both adults and children (Finklehor et al., 1988; Kashani et al., 1992; Koss et al., 1994). The development of specific treatment techniques with elder abuse victims, however, has not received widespread attention (Vetch & Garrett, 1992). Intervention with abused spouses and intimate others is initially a case management challenge. In an effort to prevent further violence, the abused spouse/intimate other must often be referred to a shelter. The victim will also often require support with self-help needs. Some shelters offer a sophisticated array of services beyond temporary shelter. Such services can include educational formats providing skill development in financial management, child care, accessing resources, and legal advocacy. Additional supportive services are designed for abusers and include anxiety-reduction and anger management workshops. The latter treatment modalities for abusers focus on helping perpetrators learn to act responsibly for their own behavior, change sexist beliefs, and replace aggressive behavior with self-assertiveness (Kashani et al., 1992).

Domestic violence matters present with unique treatment issues that are different from traditional individual and group psychotherapy efforts with violent behavior. This is due to the individual and familial dynamics that result in domestic violence acts going far beyond mere impulse or uncontrolled rage.

Effective treatment of domestic violence must incorporate family therapy as the focal treatment modality. In every family situation, there is a delicate balance between family dynamics of caring and feelings of anger. Unless adult family members manage this balance with maturity, domestic violence is a common result. A primary goal of family therapy is helping family members achieve such a balance and deal effectively with circumstances that create unbalance.

One common problem in initiating treatment with domestic violence matters is the resistance of family members to enter treatment even when they can acknowledge that a problem exists. This often occurs because the family is apprehensive about the reaction of the perpetrator. This is one circumstance where the court can be of assistance to the clinician; the court can order that the family participate in treatment and, if necessary, impose appropriate "restraining" measures for the perpetrator.

Recovery from mate violence is a lengthy process that may require a variety of interventions. Empirical data identifies factors that are conducive to a positive response to treatment with rape victims. The victim's age, level of education, and pre-trauma self-esteem are important such variables (Koss et al., 1994). The same authors also identified cultural and religious values carrying taboo implications as important factors in victim response to domestic rape that must be incorporated into treatment.

In addition to the use of peer group psychotherapy, which is a recognized and effective mode of treatment with rape victims, psychotherapists employ behavioral and cognitive techniques or a combination of the two. The common treatment approaches include graduated exposure to fear-provoking stimuli and anxiety management strategies (Koss et al., 1994). Therapists utilize fear stimuli that range from "imagined" (covert) stimuli to elaborate, staged in vivo reenactments. Anxiety management strategies include anti-anxiety medication, relaxation techniques, and role playing.

In the writer's clinical experience, there are unique differences from traditional treatment methods when providing treatment to perpetrators of domestic violence. Treatment with perpetrators should be structured, demanding, vigilant, and, when appropriate, confronting. Expectations by perpetrators to quickly re-normalize their relationship with the family need to be realistically managed.

Treatment efforts with perpetrators may often be complicated by the reality of the perpetrator's involvement with the court system. The perpetrator may be pending arraignment, on bond status, in preliminary detention, incarcerated, or on probation or parole. In some instances, perpetrators who have caused injury or death to family members may be deemed psychiatrically dangerous to themselves or to others and require inpatient care. Each of these circumstances engenders different treatment considerations for the clinician. The treatment plan must contain provisions on behalf of all of the family members.

One novel approach in dealing with sexually aggressive perpetrators was addressed in research conducted by Abel, Becker, Mittleman, Cunningham-Rathner, Rouleau, and Murphy (1986). These researchers conducted structured interviews with 561 non-incarcerated males with paraphilia (i.e., sexual disorder) diagnoses. The subjects were drawn from several cities and were matched in demographic characteristics so that the sample would reflect a profile of the general population. The range of sexual acting out behaviors (paraphilias) acknowledged by the subjects covered the clinical spectrum. Incest offenders were a focus in the study. Of the 561 subjects, 159 (28%) admitted to female-target incest, for a total of 45.2 acts per victim. These subjects acknowledged 286 female victims, with a total of 12,927 incest incidents. Forty-four (8%) subjects cited male-target incest, with a total of 36.5 acts per victim; they acknowledged 75 male victims, for a total of 907 incest incidents. These figures were compelling testimony as to the gross underestimation of reported incidents by victims of actual incest. The subjects recruited for this study were promised the opportunity of treatment and this led to another significant finding. Apart from the startling data regarding the extent of incest acts, the apparent willingness of the subjects to acknowledge candidly their behavior clearly underscored their hope for treatment.

Treatment for child abuse victims is a complex process and must begin with steps to ensure that the sexual abuse will not continue (Gomes-Schwartz, Horowitz, & Cardareli, 1988). Child abuse victims often require intensive psychotherapy to restore their pre-trauma psychological integrity. At some point, family therapy will emerge as a critical modality to address the abuse at the family level. Depending on the circumstances, the perpetrator will or will not be a participant in the family therapy. First, the treatment objective is to cope with crises. Later, a mending of the family matrix and the instilling of a realistic sense of family optimism become the foci. The long-term treatment process involves an interweaving of modalities designed to accommodate the needs of the individual family members and the family as a system.

Treatment efforts with children who are victims of domestic abuse must focus on the abusing parents. Older children, who can intellectually and emotionally appreciate the meaning of an abusive home environment, will often require individual psychotherapeutic intervention. All of the family members, including the perpetrator, must experience quick and decisive intervention to reduce the threat of further abuse and to communicate explicitly that there will be no tolerance for domestic violence. Kashani, Daniel, Dandoy, and Holcomb (1992) identified three areas of initial intervention with child victims of domestic violence. These were interventions to enhance areas of parental strengths, steps to decrease environmental stress for the family, and finding alternative placements for children at risk.

Treatment of the problem of domestic elder abuse must recognize the unique aspects of the elderly lifestyle. Historically, there has been a tendency to view the problem of elder abuse as essentially similar to the problem of child abuse. This is due, in part, to the common perception that the elderly are childlike in both their dependency and their demeanor. Because they are older, the elderly are often inaccurately perceived as being infirm or psychologically limited. This, of course, is not always true. Many elderly are not as effectively self-assertive as they may have once been. The elderly can exhibit blunted emotional energy as well as cognitive and memory deficits in comparison to their prior psychological status. On the other hand, most seniors remain legally autonomous and most live their lives functioning quite independently. Unlike most child victims, the elderly can also be perpetrators of abuse and many elderly abuse scenarios involve spouses who reciprocally perpetrate abuse on each other (Vetch & Garrett, 1992).

Family therapy nourishes the continuation of the family as a unit and assists in maintaining an emphasis that the family itself can offer the most curative influences to cope with violence trauma.

One initial treatment strategy is to explore family circumstances that may engender aggressive behavior. The use and availability of alcohol and illicit substances, as well as the availability of weapons and related implements, should be carefully reviewed with the family. Furthermore, interests in certain activities, such as cults, weapons-oriented social organizations, and various activist groups, should be probed. Each family situation must be reviewed for sources of stimulation that may instigate aggressive behavior.

In developing a treatment plan, therapists need to take into account what is characteristic for the nuclear family as to its ethnic, cultural, spiritual, and family history. These family factors may or may not coincide with established community values. Nevertheless, the unique styles of functioning within given families must be recognized and incorporated into treatment plans. Treatment objectives must also address any physical health needs of family members, especially health issues that have a direct bearing on the potential for aggressive behavior.

One important adjunctive treatment method with domestic violence situations is drug therapy. The use of drugs in treatment always involves ethical issues of informed consent and the patient's rights to refuse treatment. The problem becomes especially thorny when the target behavior is aggression. The use of medication to control aggression has received considerable attention by clinicians and remains a controversial management modality (Kashani et al., 1992; Tardiff, 1992). A major basis for this controversy is the problem of selective effectiveness with the use of drugs. The use of medications with management of aggressive behavior, however, will assuredly continue as an important area of research.

Treatment work with domestic violence circumstances is very demanding and potentially traumatizing for caregivers (Uriquiza, Wirtz, Peterson, & Singer, 1993). Therefore, treatment services for domestic violence cases must also include consideration of the needs of caregivers. Routine caregiver support services can include special supervisory and consultant sessions, rotation of caseload responsibilities, and establishment of caregivers' support groups. Moreover, multidisciplinary teams are also a useful means of buffering the problem of caregiver stress. Another important support service for caregivers is the providing of training and supervision for them to cope with the rigors of being participants in the adversarial process. Domestic violence matters offer a unique opportunity for clinicians and legal professionals to develop cross-training and collaborative models of supervision.

Ultimately, domestic violence is a complex interplay of genetic, social, psychological, and environmental factors (Egeland, Stroufe, & Ericson, 1983). Our cultural inattention to the problem of domestic violence is a subtle, but potent, maintenance factor of the problem. The social system response, from disclosure to resolution, is a critical variable in whether or not a domestic violence cycle will be interrupted and for how long. Interruption of a domestic violence cycle will not occur with mere police intervention or necessarily with the arrest of a perpetrator (Hirschel, Hutchison, & Dean, 1992). The intervention process must persist through protective service involvement, family support services, litigation, formal treatment services, and ongoing follow-up.

Summary

The topic of family violence continues to receive considerable attention and study, but it remains a social problem of overwhelming consequence. Although advances have been made, a tremendous amount of work remains in order to alter the extent of the domestic violence problem. In reviewing the domestic violence research effort, Finklehor, Hotaling, and Yllö concluded, "These are not 'discoveries' that add up to a 'cure.' But they are achievements that show promise. As the field gains momentum, adds investigators, and conquers some problems of methodology, the possibility is great that further research will contribute measurably to the reduction in the toll of family violence" (1988, p. 31).

Commendable progress has been made in system response following initial disclosure of domestic abuse. Investigation of reported domestic violence is far from being a sophisticated or consistent process, but statistical data has begun to suggest that investigatory efforts, at least with reported domestic violence, has become effective.

There are significant shortcomings in the clinical assessment and treatment of domestic violence. Part of the problem is the incompleteness of our understanding of the etiological factors of domestic violence. Another significant problem is the lack of a societal commitment to the problem of domestic violence. Without that commitment, there is no political mandate to address the domestic violence with public funding of prevention and intervention.

We do not understand very well how some family situations can maintain themselves for lengthy periods suffused with dynamics of actual or potentially violent behavior. What are the dynamics that maintain such family situations just short of a lethal outcome? Could an understanding of these dynamics be used therapeutically with troubled families? Could clinicians teach families to use these dynamics prophylactically until healthier and more permanent changes were realized? Would the understanding of such family processes improve our ability to help troubled families to prevent lethal events?

Finally, more research is needed regarding intergenerational transmission of the effects of domestic violence. Is there a hereditary component or perhaps a biochemical component to intergenerational transmission of domestic violence potential? If the transmission mechanism is primarily due to environmental factors, then

we do not understand these factors or the interaction of these factors very well. In spite of these circumstances, the social institution of the family continues as the nucleus of our society. The meaning and role of the family continue to undergo a fundamental evolution that is often difficult to comprehend, except that it has never lost its proclivity for violent manifestations.

Annotated Bibliography

Finkelhor, D., Araji, S., Baron, L., Browne, A., Peters, S. D., & Wyatt, G. E. (1986). *A source book on child abuse*. Newbury Park, CA: Sage Publications. This is a superb, widely referenced little volume. Its proposed intent is to be a "source book" regarding child sexual abuse. As indicated in the title, the book surveys and comments on pertinent research data.

Finkelhor, D., Hotaling, G. T., & Yllö, K. (1988). *Stopping family violence: Research priorities for the coming decade*. Newbury Park, CA: Sage. This is a compact resource that summarizes briefly the history of family violence research. The book outlines priority areas of needed research regarding child physical abuse, child sexual abuse, and spouse abuse. Research parameters are identified, research designs are described and time frames and projected costs are suggested. This thoughtful and provocative little text raises questions regarding societal and political priorities.

Hotaling, G. T., Finkelhor, D., Kirkpatrick, J. T., & Straus, M. A. (Eds.). (1988). *Family abuse and its consequences: New directions in research*. Newbury Park, CA: Sage. This book contains a series of articles that were originally presented at the Second National Conference of Family Violence in 1984. More than 160 papers were presented at the conference; the book contains 21 selected papers organized into major sections and covering such topics as the prevalence of family violence, physical violence against children, wife abuse, elder abuse, and sexual abuse. The sexual abuse articles also cover date and courtship abuse. This book is an excellent basic resource on family violence.

Koss, M. P., Goodman, L. A., Browne, A., Fitzgerald, L. F., Keita, G. W., & Russo, N. F. (1994). *No safe haven: Male violence against women at home, at work, and in the community.* Washington, DC: American Psychological Association. This is a recent, comprehensive resource published by the American Psychological Association that addresses violence perpetrated against adult women. The authors have provided a superior review of the literature. The final chapter (Chapter 12 entitled, "Common Themes and a Call for Action") proposes a series of initiatives at multiple levels to begin to address the problem.

The interested reader is also referred to the following journals: *International Journal of Child Abuse and Neglect, Journal of Elder Abuse and Neglect, Journal of Family Violence, Journal of Interpersonal Violence and Violence and Victims.*

References

Abel, G. G., Becker, J. V., Mittleman, J., Cunningham-Rathner, J., Rouleau, J. U., & Murphy, W. (1987, March). Self-reported sex crimes of non-incarcerated paraphiliacs. *Journal of Interpersonal Violence*, pp. 3-25.

American Medical Association (1992). *Diagnostic and treatment guidelines in elder abuse and neglect.* Chicago: Author.

American Psychiatric Association (1994). *Diagnostic and statistical manual of mental disorders* (4th ed.). Washington, DC: Author.

Bachman, R. (1992). *Elderly victims* [NCJ-138330]. Washington, DC: U.S. Department of Justice.

Bachman, R. (1994a, January). *Violence against women* [NCJ-145325]. A national crime victimization survey report. Washington, DC: U.S. Department of Justice.

Bachman, R. (1994b, July). *Violence against women* [A National Crime Victimization Survey Report]. Washington, DC: U.S. Department of Justice.

Barefoot v. Estelle, 463 U.S. 880 (1983).

Browne, A. (1987). *When battered women kill.* New York: The Free Press.

Bureau of Justice. (1985, March). *The crime of rape* (NCJ-96777). Washington, DC: U.S. Department of Justice.

Bureau of Justice. (1988, March). *Report to the nation,* 2nd edition [Bureau of Justice Statistics]. Washington, DC: U.S. Department of Justice.

Bureau of Justice Statistics. (1989). *Criminal victimization in the United States, 1987.* Washington, DC: U.S. Department of Justice.

Bureau of Justice. (1992a, December). *Criminal Victimization in the United States* [Bureau of Justice Statistics]. Washington, DC: U.S. Department of Justice.

Bureau of Justice. (1992b, December). *Criminal victimization in the United States: 1973-1990 trends*

[Bureau of Justice Statistics]. Washington, DC: U.S. Department of Justice.

Bureau of Justice. (1992c). *Criminal victimization in the United States, 1990.* Washington, DC: U.S. Department of Justice.

Bureau of Justice. (1993). *Highlights from 20 Years of Surveying Crime Victims* [Bureau of Justice Statistics]. Washington, DC: U.S. Department of Justice.

Bureau of Justice Statistics. (1994a, March). *Criminal victimization in the United States: 1992* (NCJ-145125). Washington, DC: U.S. Department of Justice.

Bureau of Justice Statistics. (1994b, July). *Criminal victimization in the United States: 1972-92* (NCJ-147006). Washington, DC: U.S. Department of Justice.

Burgess, R. L., & Youngblood, L. M. (1988). *Social incompetence and the interpersonal transmission of abusive parental practices.* In G. T. Hotaling, D. Finklehor, J. T. Kirkpatrick, & M. A. Straus (Eds.), *Family abuse and its consequences: New directions in research* (pp. 38-60). Newbury Park, CA: Sage.

Campbell, J. (1995). *Assessing dangerousness: Violence by sexual offenders, batterers and child abusers.* Interpersonal Violence: The Practice Series. Thousand Oaks, CA: Sage.

Courtois, C. A. (1988). *Healing the incest wound: Adult survivors in therapy.* New York: Norton.

Davidson, T. (1978). *Conjugal crime.* New York: Hawthorn Books.

Dawson, J. M., & Langan, P. A. (1994). *Murder in Families* [Special Report]. Washington, DC: Bureau of Justice Statistics.

Dawson, J. M., & Langan, P. A. (1994, July). *Murder in Families* [Bureau of Justice Special Report]. Washington, DC: U.S. Department of Justice.

Douglas, M. (1987). The battered woman syndrome. In D. J. Sonkin (Ed.), *Domestic violence on trial* (pp. 6-39). New York: Springer Publishing.

Egeland, A., Stroufe, & Ericson, M. (1983). The developmental consequences of different patterns of maltreatment. *Child Abuse and Neglect, 7,* 299-305.

Fagan, J. (1988). Contributions of family violence research to criminal justice policy on wife assault: Paradigms of science and social control. *Violence and Victims, 3*(3), 159-186.

Family Violence Working Group. (1994, June). *A report to the Assistant Attorney General for the Office of Justice Programs* [Justice Programs on Family Violence]. Washington, DC: National Institute of Justice.

Finkelhor, D. (1983). Common features of family abuse. In E. D. Finkelhor & R. J. Gelles (Eds.), *The dark side of families: Current family violence research.* Beverly Hills: Sage.

Finkelhor, D. (1984). *Child sexual abuse: New theory and research.* New York: Free Press.

Finkelhor, D., Araji, S., Baron, L., Browne, A., Peters, S. D., & Wyatt, G. E. (1988). *Sourcebook on child sexual abuse.* Beverly Hills, CA: Sage.

Finklehor, D., & Baron, L. (1986). *Risk factors for child sexual abuse.* Beverly Hills, CA: Sage.

Finklehor, D., & Browne, A. (1985). The traumatic

impact of child sexual abuse: A conceptualization. *American Journal of Orthopsychiatry, 55*, 530-541.

Finkelhor, D., & Hotaling, G. (1983). *Sexual abuse in the national incidence study of child abuse and neglect* [Report to the National Center on Child Abuse and Neglect].

Finkelhor, D., Hotaling, G., & Yllö, K. (1988). *Stopping family violence: Research priorities for the coming decade*. Newbury Park, CA: Sage.

Finklehor, D., & Pillemar, K. (1988). Elder abuse: Its relationship to other forms of domestic violence. In G. T. Hotaling, D. Finkelhor, J. Kirkpatrick, & M. D. Straus (Eds.), *Family abuse and its consequences: New directions in research* (pp. 244-254). Newbury Park, CA: Sage.

Finkelhor, D., & Yllö, K. (1983a). *License to rape: Sexual abuse of wives*. New York: Holt, Rinehart & Winston.

Finkelhor, D., & Yllö, K. (1983b). Rape in marriage: A sociological view. In D. Finkelhor, R. Gelles, G. Hotaling, & M. A. Straus (Eds.), *The dark side of families*. Beverly Hills, CA: Sage.

Friedman, L. (1994, November). Adopting the health care model to prevent victimization. *National Institute of Justice Journal*, pp. 16-19.

Gelles, R. (1987). *Family violence*. Newbury Park, CA: Sage.

Gelles, R. J., & Pedrick, C. C. (1985). *Intimate violence in families*. Beverly Hills CA: Sage.

Gillespie, C. (1989). *Justifiable homicide: Battered women, self defense and the law*. Columbus, OH: Ohio State University Press.

Gomes-Schwartz, B., Horowitz, J., & Cardareli, A. P.

(1988, July). *Child sexual abuse victims and their treatment* [National Institute of Juvenile Justice and Delinquency Prevention]. Washington, DC: U.S. Department of Justice.

Harlow, C. (1991). *Female victims of crime* [Bureau of Justice Statistics]. Washington, DC: U.S. Department of Justice.

Hirschel, D., & Hutchison & Dean, C. (1992, February). The failure of arrest to deter spouse abuse. *Journal of Research in Crime and Delinquency*.

Hotaling, G. T., Finkelhor, D., Kirkpatrick, J. T., Straus, M. A., (Eds.) (1988). *Family abuse and its consequences: New directions in research*. Newbury Park, CA: Sage.

Jaffe, P. A., Wolfe, D. A., & Wilson, S. K. (1990). *Children of battered women*. Newbury Park, CA: Sage.

Jones, A. (1980). *Women who kill*. New York: Fawcett Crest.

Kashani, J. H., Daniel, A. F., Dandoy, A. C., & Holcomb, W. R. (1992, March). Family violence: Impact on children. *Journal of the American Academy of Child and Adolescent Psychiatry*, pp. 181-189.

Kemper, C., Silverman, F., & Steels, B. (1962). The battered child syndrome. *Journal of the American Medical Association, 181*, 1.

Koss, M. P., Goodman, L. A., Browne, A., Fitzgerald, L. F., Kieta, G. P., & Russo, N. F. (1994). *No safe haven: Male violence against women at home*. Washington, DC: American Psychological Association.

Langan, P. A., & Innes, C. A. (1986 August). *Preventing domestic violence against women*. Washington, DC: U.S. Department of Justice.

McCay, M. M. (1994, January/February). The link between domestic violence and child abuse. *Child Welfare*, pp. 29-39.

McCurdy, K., & Daro, D. (1993). *Current trends in child abuse reporting and fatalities: The results of the 1992 annual fifty state survey* (Working paper number 808). Chicago, IL: National Center on Child Abuse Prevention Research.

McCurdy, K., & Daro, D. (1994, April). *Current trends in child abuse reporting and fatalities: The results of the 1993 annual fifty states survey* [(Working paper number 808)]. Chicago, IL: National Center on Child Abuse Research.

Meiselman, K. (1978). *Incest.* San Francisco: Jossey-Bass.

Melton, G., Petrila, J. Poythress, N., & Slobogin, C. (1987). *Psychological evaluations for the courts.* New York: Guilford.

Milner, J. S. (1995). Physical child abuse assessment: Perpetrator evaluation. In J. T. Campbell (Ed.), *Assessing dangerousness: Violence by sexual offenders, batterers and child abusers* (pp. 41-67). Thousand Oaks, CA: Sage.

Mock, L. F., & Crawford, C. A. (1994, November). Health and criminal justice: Strengthening the partnership. *National Institute of Justice Journal*, pp. 2-7.

Monahan, J. (1981). *Predicting violent behavior: An assessment of clinical techniques.* Beverly Hills, CA: Sage.

Monahan, J. (Ed.). (1983). *Who is the client?* Washington, DC: American Psychological Association.

Murphy, J., Jellinek, M., Quinn, D., Smith, G., Poitrast, F., & Goshko, M. (1991). Substance abuse and serious child mistreatment: Prevalence, risk, and outcome in a court sample. *Child Abuse and Neglect,*

15, 197-211.

Myers, E., Bays, J., Becker, J., Berliner, L., Corwin, D., & Sawitz, K. (1989). Expert testimony in child sexual abuse litigation. *Nebraska Law Review, 68*(1 & 2), 1-145.

National Committee for Prevention of Child Abuse. (1986, September). *Child abuse: Prelude to delinquency? Findings of a Research Conference Conducted by the National Committee for Prevention of Child Abuse.* Washington, DC: Office of Juvenile Justice and Delinquency Prevention.

National Victims Center. (1992). *Rape in America: A report to the nation.* Arlington, VA: Author.

Novello, A. (1992, June). From the Surgeon General, U.S. Public Health Service, a medical response to domestic violence. *Journal of the American Medical Association*, p. 3132.

Pagelow, M. D. (1984). *Family violence.* New York: Praeger.

Pillemar, K., & Finkelhor, D. (1988). The prevalence of elder abuse: A random sample survey. *The Gerontologist, 28*(1), 51-57.

Poirier, J. (1991). Disputed custody and concerns of parental violence. *Psychotherapy in Private Practice, 9*(3), 7-23.

Roth, J. A. (1994a, February). *Psychoactive substances and violence* [Research in Brief]. Washington, DC: U.S. Department of Justice.

Roth, J. A. (1994b, February). *Understanding and preventing violence* [Research in Brief]. Washington, DC: U.S. Department of Justice.

Russel, D. E. (1982). The prevalence and incidence of forcible rape and attempted rape of females. *Victi-*

mology: An International Journal, 7, 81-93.

Russel, D. (1986). *The secret trauma: Incest in the lives of girls and women.* New York: Basic Books.

Sgroi, S. (1982). *Handbook of clinical intervention in child sexual abuse.* Lexington, MA: Lexington Books.

Sonkin, D., Martin, D., & Walker, L., (Eds.). (1985). *The male batterer: A treatment approach.* New York: Springer.

Stark, E., Flitcraft, A., Zuckerman, D., Grey, A., Robinson, J., & Frazier, W. (1981). *Wife abuse in the medical setting: An introduction for health personnel* [monograph series no. 7]. Washington, DC: U.S. Government Printing Office.

Stark, E., & Flitcraft, A. (1988). Violence among intimates: An epidemiological review. In V. B. Van Hasselt, R. L. Morrison, A. S. Bellack, & M. Hersen (Eds.), *Handbook of family violence* (pp. 293-317). New York: Plenum.

Stein, K. F. (1991). A national agenda for elder abuse and neglect research: Issues and recommendations. *Journal of Elder Abuse and Neglect, 3*(3), 91-108.

Straus, M. A. (1990). The national family violence surveys. In M.A. Straus & R. J. Gelles (Eds.), *Physical violence in American families: Risk factors and adaptation to violence in 8,145 families* (pp. 3-16). New Brunswick, NJ: Transaction.

Straus, M. A., & Gelles, R. (1986). Societal change and change in family violence from 1975 to 1985 as revealed by two national surveys. *Journal of Marriage and the Family, 48,* 465-479.

Straus, M. A., & Gelles, R. J. (1988). How violent are American families? Estimates from the National Family Violence Resurvey and other Studies. In G. T.

Hotaling, D. Finklehor, J. T. Kirkpatrick, & M. A. Straus (Eds.), *Family abuse and its consequences: New directions in research* (pp. 1-35). Newbury Park, CA: Sage.

Straus, M. A., Gelles, R. J., & Steinmetz, S. (1980). *Behind closed doors: Violence in the American family.* Garden City, NY: Anchor.

Summit, R. (1983). The child sexual abuse accommodation syndrome. *Child Abuse and Neglect, 7,* 177-193.

Tarasoff v. Regents of University of California, 131 Cal. Rptr. 14 (1976).

Tardiff, K. (1992, June). The current state of psychiatry in the treatment of violent patients. *Archives of General Psychiatry,* pp. 493-499.

Tzeng, O., Jackson, J., & Karlson, H. (1991). *Theories of child abuse and neglect: Differential perspectives, summaries and evaluations.* New York: Praeger.

Uriquiza, A. J., Wirtz, S. J., Peterson, M. S., & Singer, V. A. (1994). Screening and evaluating abused and neglected children entering protective custody. *Child Welfare, 73*(2), 155-171.

U.S. Department of Justice. (1984). *Family violence: interventions for the justice system* [Program Brief]. Washington, DC: U.S. Department of Justice.

Vetch, M. R., & Garrett, R. R. (1992, September). Elder and child abuse. *Journal of Interpersonal Violence,* 418-428.

Walker, L. E. (1979). *The battered woman.* New York: Harper & Rowe.

Walker, L. E. (1984). *The battered woman syndrome.* New York: Springer.

Walker, L. E. (1988). The battered woman syndrome. In G. Hotaling, D. Finkelhor, J. Kirkpatrick, & M. A. Straus (Eds.), *Family abuse and its consequences: New directions in research* (pp. 139-147). Newbury Park, CA: Sage.

Walker, L. E. (1989). *Terrifying love: Why battered women kill and how society responds.* New York: Harper & Row.

West, I. (1988). *Study findings: Study of national incidence and prevalence of child abuse and neglect.* Washington, DC: U.S. Department of Health and Human Services.

Whitcomb, D. (1992, March). *When the victim is a child* (2d ed.). [Issues and Practices in Criminal Justice]. Washington, DC: U.S. Department of Justice, National Institute of Justice.

Widom, C. S. (1989). Child abuse, neglect, and adult behavior: Research design and findings on criminality, violence, and child abuse. *American Journal of Orthopsychiatry, 59,* 355-367.

Widom, C. S. (1992, October). *The cycle of violence* [Research in Brief]. Washington, DC: National Institute of Justice.

Wilson, A. (1993). Introduction. In A. Wilson (Ed.), *Homicide: The victim/offender* (p. 3). Cincinnati, OH: Anderson Publishing Co.

Witwer, M. (1994, November). Doctors focus on the threat to health from violence. *National Institute of Justice Journal,* p. 8.

Zawitz, M. W., Klaus, P., Bachman, R., Bastian, L. D., DeBerry, M., Rand, M., & Taylor, B. (1993, October). *Highlights from 20 years of surveying crime victims: The National Crime Victimization Survey, 1973-92* [NCJS-144525]. Washington, DC: U.S. Department of Justice.

About the Author

Dr. Poirier is a clinical psychologist with a specialty in forensic psychology. He is the Clinical Director of the Child and Adolescent Forensic Evaluation Service (CAFES) with the Montgomery County Maryland Government. CAFES is a multidisciplinary team that conducts evaluations on juveniles and their families for the Juvenile Court. Dr. Poirier is also the Co-Director of the Prince George County Maryland Circuit Court Mental Hygiene Service (CCMHS). CCMHS conducts forensic assessments of criminal, juvenile, civil and domestic matters. Dr. Poirier holds separate board certifications from the American Board of Professional Psychology in the specialty areas of forensic, clinical, and family psychology. His mailing address is: 10620 Georgia Avenue, Suite 209, Silver Spring, MD, 20902. Dr. Poirier can also be contacted by E-mail: jpoirier@cap.gwu.edu.

CHAPTER 10

MURDER-SUICIDE

Michael F. Abramsky
Melissa Helfman

Psychologists who study aggressive-lethal behavior divide such actions into two categories: predatory and affective violence (Meloy, 1992). Predatory violence is characterized by dispassionate aggression against individuals with whom the aggressor has no intimate relationship. Serial killings and incidental violent behaviors where the aggressor's actions complement another goal, e.g., robbery, are examples of predatory aggression.

Affective violence involves a heightened state of arousal and destructive actions committed against an individual with whom the aggressor is intimately involved. Murder followed by suicide is one subcategory of affective violence.

Murder followed by suicide occurs primarily in three situations.

1. Spousal. This is by far the most common instance of murder followed by suicide. In these cases, the perpetrator, a spouse, common-law spouse, or lover, kills his or her significant other and then takes his or her own life. Generally, there are a number of precursory acts that precede the killings. Arguments and spousal batterings are characteristic of the relationship and the final action usually occurs when one spouse tries unequivocally to terminate the relationship.

2. Offspring homicide. This category of murder followed by suicide involves a parent who kills a child and then takes his or her own life.

3. Workplace homicide. This category of murder followed by suicide generally involves an employee who kills a boss or supervisor. Often, there is a context of conflict between the two and the final act may be triggered by an imminent or feared demotion or termination.

There are other aggressive situations which begin with a homicide and end with the perpetrator's suicide. However, they are so rare that studying and writing about them is most difficult and has little heuristic value. Mass homicide where a perpetrator enters a crowded facility, opens fire, and then kills himself or herself is an example of this phenomenon. It may also be argued that certain violent actions, such as that of Charles Whitman, who barricaded himself in a Texas tower, then opened fire on passersby before he was ultimately killed by the police, is an example of a homicide carried out in a way that invites the perpetrator to be killed. There are also suicide pacts where an individual may kill another with the victim's prior agreement, then takes his or her own life. While these unusual examples touch our intellectual curiosity and beg for explanation, they are so rare and the methodological problems involved in studying them so immense, that they have been excluded from the current study. This chapter will focus on the three major categories of homicide followed by suicide that have been most studied in the literature.

Epidemiology of Murder-Suicide

Murder followed by suicide represents a **unique hybrid** that transcends the usual dichotomy of murder versus suicide. Discussing early theories of aggression, Litman (1967) summarized Freud's fundamental position that aggressive behavior was either directed inward as suicide or outward as homicide. However, over time, Freud's theories became more complex and this simple dichotomy was discarded. In his later writings, Freud acknowledged that aggression toward the self could easily spill over into murderous actions toward others or that hostility directed outward could reverse itself, causing self-destructive behavior.

West (1966) has provided the most complex study of murder followed by suicide. Studying a population in Great Britain, West found that suicidal murderers were more often female, were older, killed victims who were close relatives, and had fewer previous criminal convictions than non-suicidal murderers. Coid (1983) summarized the epidemiological data on murder-suicide in 17 major cities, and the rate of homicides committed by mentally ill offenders in those same cities (See Tables 1A and 1B).

In analyzing the data, two measures are isolated: First, the rate of murder-suicide which tracks the number of such occurrences per 100,000 people in the population. Second, the percent of murder-suicide is shown. This refers to the number of murder-suicides compared to the overall number of homicides and is repre-

TABLE 1A
COMPARATIVE RATES OF ABNORMAL HOMICIDE
PER 100,000 POPULATION

Country	Source	Years	Rate in population	% mentally abnormal	Rate of mentally abnormal offenders
USA, Philadelphia	Wolfgang (1958)	1948-52	6-10	2.7	0-16
Israel Non-Jews	Landau (1975)	1950-64	4-00	2.6	0-10
USA, Albany Co.	Grunberg et al. (1977)	1963-75	3-50	6.5	0-22
Bermuda	Coid (1982)	1920-79	2-35	3-8	0-09
Canada	Schloss & Giesbrecht (1972)	1961-70	1-63	7-7	0-12
Japan	Criminal Statistics Japan (1980)	1978	1-60	8-35	0-13
Hong Kong	Wong & Singer (1973)	1961-71	1-57	7-0	0-11
Scotland	Criminal Statistics Scotland (1979)	1978	1-50	8-9	0-14
Israel Oriental Jews	Landau (1975)	1950-64	1-07	17-6	0-18
England & Wales	Criminal Statistics (1980)	1970-79	0-88	21-2	0-18
Iceland	Gudjonsson & Petursson (1982)	1940-79	0-72	18-6	0-13
Israel Western Jews	Landau (1975)	1950-64	0-59	20-0	0-11
Scotland	Gibson & Klein (1969)	1957-68	0-45	8-2	0-11
England & Wales	Morris & Blom-Cooper (1967)	1900-49	0-40	21-4	0-08
England & Wales	Morris & Blom-Cooper (1967)	1950-59	0-39	26-5	0-09

(Coid, 1983)

TABLE 1B
COMPARATIVE RATES OF MURDER-SUICIDE
PER 100,000 POPULATION

Country	Source	Years	Rate in population	% mentally abnormal	Rate of mentally abnormal offenders
USA, Philadelphia	Wolfgang (1958)	1948-52	6-10	3-6	0-21
USA	West (1965)	1959-60	4-50	4-0	0-18
Israel Non-Jews	Landau (1975)	1950-64	4-00	6-6	0-26
Bermuda	Coid (1982)	1920-79	2-35	5-5	0-13
Canada	Schloss & Giesbrecht (1972)	1967-70	1-90	10-5	0-19
Australia	West (1965)	1959-60	1-70	22-0	0-36
Hong Kong	Wong & Singer (1973)	1961-71	1-57	5-0	0-07
Canada	Greenland (1971)	1968	1-50	18-0	0-27
Canada	Schloss & Geisbrecht (1972)	1961-66	1-36	15-6	0-21
Israel Oriental Jews	Landau (1975)	1950-64	1-07	25-6	0-27
England & Wales	Criminal Statistics (1980)	1969-79	0-88	8-2	0-07
Iceland	Gudjonsson & Petursson (1982)	1940-79	0-72	8-5	0-06
Israel Western Jews	Landau (1975)	1950-64	0-59	67-8	0-40
Scotland	Gibson & Klein (1969)	1957-68	0-45	9-2	0-04
England & Wales	Morris & Blom-Cooper (1967)	1900-49	0-40	29-1	0-11
England & Wales	Morris & Blom-Cooper (1967)	1950-59	0-39	33-3	0-12
Denmark	West (1965)	1959-60	0-27	42-0	0-22

(Coid, 1983)

sented as a percentage. Analyzing the rate of murder-suicide shows a remarkable lack of cross-cultural and temporal variation. The rate of suicide-homicide averages about 0.19 per 100,000 population. Given the problems in defining the act and in cross-cultural data collection, there is a remarkable conformity of results.

It appears that there is a rather constant base rate of murder-suicides in all populations. Coid (1983) has suggested that these rates reflect the similar prevalence of mental illness in all countries. This assumption is supported by looking at the rate for offenders diagnosed as mentally abnormal by country. The rates of murder-suicide and the rates of mentally abnormal offenders are similar, lending support to the hypothesis that murder-suicide is committed more frequently in the heat of mental deterioration or psychotic breakdown.

Coid's conclusion is partially supported by West (1966), who found that a large proportion of individuals who killed and then took their own lives, had a history of major depressive illness. Selkin (1976) has echoed this view, as has Rosenbaum (1990).

When we turn to the data reflecting murder-suicide as a percent of the overall homicide rate, a very different picture emerges. The proportion of murderers who commit suicide varies widely from country to country: 4% in the U.S. (West, 1965); 5% in Hong Kong (Wong and Singer, 1973); 8% in Finland (Virkkunen, 1974); 16% in Iceland (Hansen and Bjarnason, 1974); 33% in

Great Britain (Morris and Blom-Cooper, 1967); and 42% in Denmark (West, 1966).

A summary interpretation of this data shows that as the rate of homicides goes up, the proportion of murder-suicides declines. In countries which have a high homicide rate, such as the United States, there is a low percentage of murder-suicide. In countries like Denmark, where there is a low homicide rate, the percentage of murder-suicides is quite high.

This data suggest that murder-suicide is a constant, reflecting a form of gross pathology in the dyad. Coid (1982) speculated that murder-suicides reflect gross pathology in the aggressor. In contrast, Wolfgang (1959) suggested that the victims were often provocative and hypothesized "victim-precipitated murder" in his murder-suicide sample. Further studies should concentrate on the pathological dynamics between aggressor and victim to explain this unique phenomenon.

As homicides increase, they seem to come from different categories of murder, e.g., arguments, predatory, and incidental homicides, which are largely orthogonal to murder-suicide rates. These rates seem to vary widely from country to country as compared to murder-suicides, which are constants. The studies point to murder-suicide as a unique and constant phenomenon inherent in the human condition of dyadic relationships.

The Cycle of Violence

Workplace homicides and spousal murders show a common pattern, but different object choices. The psychodynamic pattern was first described by Maier (1912, 1923) and was summarized by Meloy (1992) as catathymic homicide, derived from the Greek words *kata* and *thymos*, meaning, "in accordance with emotions."

Catathymic homicides follow a progression (Revitch & Schlesinger, 1978; Schlesinger, Chapter 14; Wertham, 1937), which may be summa-

rized as follows:

1. The future perpetrator suffers a traumatic blow, generally characterized as a rejection or narcissistic wound. In spousal homicides, this is usually initiated by the woman threatening to leave, or actually leaving, the relationship. In workplace homicides, an individual may be fired or demoted. In one case examined by the senior author, the murderer lost a hotly contested union election.

2. The trauma is internalized as an extreme disequilibrium or psychic tension. The masculine experience is usually one of emasculation or an assault on the sense of self, while in women, this is usually experienced as a sense of incompleteness, emptiness, or feelings of abandonment.

3. The perpetrator projects all blame onto the offending party, psychologically denying any personal responsibility for what has gone wrong.

4. An incubation stage follows (Revitch & Schlesinger, 1978). During this stage, tension escalates and virtually all psychic energy is focused on the traumatizing event and the devastation it has caused the perpetrator.

5. On the perpetrator's part, the blow to self-esteem becomes all consuming, unambiguous, and magnified to an almost cosmic level. Due to projection, the offending party is then seen as an embodiment of evil, malignant, and without redemption. Primitive psychic splitting occurs. During the initial phase of the incubation stage, the psyche of the perpetrator is characterized by obsessive, compulsive preoccupations with the initial traumatic event. Paranoid ideation emerges, with the perpetrator misinterpreting events or exaggerating them. For example, pathological jealousy is a common precursor to spousal homicide, with the perpetrator convinced that his wife is "cheating" on him or laughing at him in concert with a new lover. In workplace homicides, it is common for the future perpetrator to believe that figures in authority have singled out the perpetrator and

continue to plot against him or her. The perpetrator takes on the role of the victim and is on the defense, manifestly fearful of a future attack.

During the later phases of incubation, concrete precursors to the violence begin to appear. A Michigan teacher who explosively killed a school superintendent had begun to be more threatening toward his wife, to be more verbally explosive at work, and to sadistically kill stray animals on his country property. A union official of the United Auto Workers who had lost an election, began carrying a gun to work, keeping it loaded, fearing a future attack. Later stages of incubation show more behavioral changes clustered around a rehearsal for violent action.

6. A behavioral trigger sets off the homicide. The trigger is the last straw; an unequivocal sign that there is imminent danger. In the case of the teacher, he discovered at a disciplinary hearing that the superintendent was keeping a "second file" documenting his past misbehavior. The union official became aware of a meeting from which he had been excluded and became convinced that union members were talking and plotting against him.

7. The perpetrator then carries out the violent act.

8. In most cases, catharsis is achieved. Following the act, the perpetrator achieves a state of normality, often for several months. With distance, they are often baffled as to why they committed the criminal acts in question.

9. In some cases, the homicide is followed by a suicide or a serious suicide attempt.

The following three sections of this chapter discuss the most frequent subcategories of affective homicides. These are spousal murders, offspring murders, and workplace homicides.

Each section discusses general data concerning the frequency and parameters of the particular homicide, the frequency and parameters of homicides in their respective categories which are followed by a suicide of the perpetrator, hypotheses concerning the psychological motivations and triggers which activate murder suicides, and a clinical vignette which illustrates a documented case.

Spousal Homicides

Spousal homicides constitute the most frequent subcategory of affective murder. This is not surprising as, for most people, the relationship to a spouse or lover is the most intimate, passionate, and conflictual form of relationship.

The extent of this conflict is reflected in the high incidence of spousal battery. Domestic violence has become commonplace in American life. Browne (1987) quoted several surveys that documented spousal abuse as occurring at least once in 20 to 25% of American households. Spousal abuse is a psychological syndrome evidenced by escalating episodes of violence characterized by beatings, and occasionally by the use of weapons. Sometimes, fatalities occur.

When homicides do occur, two patterns are common. First, when a man kills his wife it is usually because he "crosses the line," loses control, and a beating results in an unintended homicide. When a wife kills her husband, it is generally in retaliation for a pattern of being battered. Browne (1987) classified these homicides as self defensive. In two-thirds of the spousal homicides, the victim was a woman and in one-third, a man. Among Black couples, 47% of the victims were husbands and 53% were wives (Dawson and Langan, 1994).

Studies support the notion that spousal murders occur in a context of more general domestic violence. Detroit and Kansas City police records revealed that in 85 to 90% of spousal murders, police had been called for episodes of domestic violence at least once prior to the murder, and in 54% of the cases, they were called five or more times (Sherman & Berke, 1984). Overall, spousal homicides accounted for 6.5% of the total number of homicides in the United States. Of all the murders which occurred in American families (about 16% of the total homicides), 40.9% occurred between husbands and wives (Dawson and Langan, 1984). Table 2 illustrates the patterns of family homicides.

Silverman and Mukherjee (1987) reported a higher rate of spousal homicides compared to total homicides in their Canadian sample. They found that spousal homicides comprised 20% of the total homicides in that country. When homicidal actions between common-law couples were

the victims.

Berman (1979) studied murder-suicide in the cities of Philadelphia, Baltimore, and Washington, D.C. Berman narrowed his sample to "dyadic deaths," where offender and victim are played by the same person. A total of 972 dyadic homicides were isolated and 1.5% were found to have resulted in murder followed by suicide.

Palmer and Humphrey (1980) found that the rate of murder followed by suicide in North Carolina from 1972 to 1977 was 0.9 per 100,000 population. They did not calculate the percent of

TABLE 2
PATTERNS OF FAMILIAL HOMICIDES

Relationship of Victim to Assailant	Family Murder Victims and Defendants	
	Number	Percent
All	2,592	100.0%
Spouse	1,059	40.9
Offspring	543	20.9
Parent	304	11.7
Sibling	244	9.4
Other	442	17.1

(Dawson & Langan, 1994)

also factored in, the rate jumped to 30.4%. When previously married couples, now separated or divorced, were factored in, the rate jumped to 40.8%. Overall, their Canadian data suggested a higher portion of spousal homicides than occur in the United States.

Only a small proportion of domestic homicides are followed by a suicide of the perpetrator. The Canadian data of Silverman and Mukherjee (1987) revealed that spousal murder-suicides constituted 10% of the total domestic homicide incidents. Allen (1983) studied murder-suicide in Los Angeles from 1970 to 1979. She found that spousal murderers committed suicide following their actions in 1.1 to 3.5% of the cases, varying by year. Seventy-one percent of the murder-suicide perpetrators were husbands or boyfriends of

murder-suicides compared to the overall homicide rate in the state and over these years.

All researchers have found that murder-suicide is a relatively rare phenomenon, even in spousal homicides. Even in this most horrific and personal crime, the number of individuals who kill themselves following a murder is quite small.

The small proportion of domestic murder-suicides compared to the overall domestic homicide rate suggests that a unique psychological dynamic fuels these crimes. While good empirical and survey data are lacking, case studies compiled by the senior author suggest that a catathymic pattern generates most domestic homicide-suicides.

The catathymic pattern is precipitated by a spouse threatening to leave or actually leaving the relationship. The incubation phase is characterized by the perpetrator becoming obsessed, often stalking or following the victim, demanding reconciliation. Pathological jealousy and outright paranoia are common. The perpetrator shows general decompensation in his or her day-to-day life, often characterized by tempermentality and outbursts toward others. Substance abuse is frequent, as are bouts of depression and suicidal preoccupation. Ultimately, following a "final" rejection, the perpetrator prepares and then explosively kills the spouse. The perpetrator then turns the same weapon on himself or herself.

General domestic homicides appear to occur in the context of domestic battery. Between the warring couple, an argument ensues, violence escalates, and the murder is disorganized and unintended.

In contrast, catathymic murder-suicides appear to be characterized by an irrevocable rejection, an incubation-decompensation phase, a preparatory phase, more characterized by suicidal preoccupation than homicidal intent, and an explosion where both lives are taken.

The important variables which may separate domestic murders from domestic murder-suicides are the triggers which set the sequence into motion, the length of time between insult and action, the marital history of the couple, the crime being organized or disorganized, and individual psychological factors, such as the perpetrator's acute state of depression and perhaps the parties' structural personality flaws.

Clinical Vignette: A Murder Triad

Livonia, Michigan, is a clean, tidy suburb on Detroit's west side. Its ranch style homes were built mostly in the 1960s and are peopled by blue and white collar workers who work in auto industry plants nearby. Sandra and Michael Brattin lived on one of these streets.

They were the stereotypical "perfect couple." Neighbors described them as working on their home together, doing their lawn, and spending time with their two pre-teen daughters.

Both Michael and Sandra worked at a Ford plant, where 1,600 workers made air conditioners and heaters. The Brattins worked the same shift and on the same assembly line. They even took their breaks together.

No one knows when or how, but problems began to appear in their marriage. Arguments shattered the peaceful air of their home. Michael began to suspect that Sandra was romantically involved with Michael O'Brian, a fellow worker. The Brattins took a trip to the Bahamas to heal their marriage. Things got better for a while, but by Thanksgiving 1994, they separated.

Michael Brattin grew morose. Things became tense at work among the triangle. Supervisors sensed a problem developing. Sandra Brattin was to be reassigned.

On January 4, 1995, Michael Brattin bought a 12-shot .40 caliber semi-automatic pistol. Like a good citizen, he registered the gun. Years before, Michael Brattin had been a hunter, but had given away his guns, as he feared his children would find them and a tragedy result.

On January 9, 1995, a Saturday, Michael Brattin entered the plant and shot his wife three times in the legs. When Michael O'Brian intervened, Mr. Brattin shot him six times in the chest and head. He then turned the gun on himself, putting a single bullet in his brain.

Offspring Homicides

Offspring homicides are another variant of familial murder, with the perpetrator being a parent and the victim a child. Offspring murders constitute 20.9% of familial murders and 3.5% of the overall homicide statistics. Unlike all other categories of homicide, in offspring murders, a majority of the murderers are female, with 55% of these crimes being committed by women. When a child is killed, it is more likely to be a son (64%)

than a daughter (36%; Dawson and Langan, 1994).

In some ways, offspring murders show a similar context to spousal murders. A major portion of offspring homicides occurs in a context of battering and abuse. Some 79% of the children killed by a parent showed a history of prior abuse, while 6% had been raped or sexually assaulted.

Only a few studies have empirically explored murder-suicide in offspring homicides. Palmer and Humphery (1980) found that perpetrators kill themselves 66% of the time after murdering a child. Unfortunately, the study did not separate the sex of the offender. The sex of the offender variable appears to be very important in offspring murders because of the uniquely disproportionate number of female murderers involved in this type of crime.

In her Los Angeles sample, Allen (1983) found that only 2% of the women who killed then suicided had murdered their children first. Most had killed their spouse, not children, before taking their own life. Offspring murders and suicide were higher for males at a rate of 3.4 percent.

The most intensive study of offspring murder was conducted by West (1966). Gathering his statistics in England, West found that 91.7% of the females in his sample killed their child prior to committing suicide. Furthermore, 53 of the 55 women sampled killed a child who was under six years of age. In studying men, West found that 17.1% of the males murdered only a child before taking their own life. Males who committed familial homicides more often killed both spouse and children before committing suicide.

Overall, the few empirical studies which have explored offspring homicide-suicide suggest strong cross-cultural variations in this phenomenon and perhaps regional differences, and disparate patterns depending on the sex of the offender and the sex and age of the child victim. For a general taxonomy of types of child murder see Table 3.

In generalizing from homicide patterns, it is hypothesized that males kill children in a context of battering and rage, similar to the general pattern of spousal homicides. Typically, such offspring homicides occur when a child is disobedient. The father strikes out at the child and, in a loss of control, kills. Children may also be secondary victims. West's 1966 data suggested that in many cases, the primary homicide target may be a female spouse and that in an ongoing rage, the father completes a spousal homicide by killing children.

The pattern of offspring homicide may be very different for women. In general, women commit far fewer aggressive acts than men and are less prone to physically abuse their children. Therefore, it is unlikely that most female offspring murders occur in a context of battering and rage.

Females, we hypothesize, kill their children for perceived altruistic reasons. They believe that the child is better off dead because he or she is unloved, cannot be cared for, or is abandoned by the father. West's data show that most children are under the age of six when murdered by their mother. This lends credence to the hypothesis that it is the very helplessness and fragility of children which make them victims.

Children are probably seen as an extension of the mother, who herself feels alone, unwanted, or abandoned by a male.

Selkin (1976) has described a dynamic he referred to as "murder by proxy." Murder by proxy occurs when victims are chosen because they are identified with a primary target. By analogy, a modal murder-suicide occurs when a despondent mother kills her children, as she sees them as an extension of her own pain and then consecutively takes her own life. In this case, the mother has an intimate self-object bond with her children. Despondency in her life generalizes to their lives as well. Death is seen as a humane solution for all.

Little empirical research has been found in

TABLE 3
PARENTAL MURDER OF OFFSPRING UNDER AGE 12

Prosecutors' files contained information on reasons why a parent murdered an offspring under age 12. One or more reasons were given for 62 of the total 84 offspring murder victims under age 12. The following presents reasons and the number of victims:

- Unspecified forms of child abuse (18)
- Victim's behavior, such as crying or misbehavior (15)
- Parent's emotional instability or retardation (9)
- Unwanted newborn baby (8)
- Unintended consequence of the commission of another crime (lethal conflict between the parents) (6)
- Neglect (5)
- Difficulty handling the responsibility of child rearing (3)
- Child held hostage (1)

Examination of the details concerning the method of killing covered all but three of the victims. By far the most frequent method of murder was beating: punching with fists, kicking, throwing, pushing, slapping, hitting (with belts, hammers, or wooden brushes), and striking body against furniture (shower head or walls). With five of the victims counted under two or three methods of murder, specific methods and the number of victims were as follows:

- Beating (35)
- "Shaken baby syndrome" (10)
- Arson (6)
- Newborn disposed of in toilet or trash can (6)
- Drowning in bathtub (6)
- Firearm (5)
- Suffocation/strangulation (5)
- Neglect (dehydration, starvation, and failure to use infant heart monitor) (4)
- Stabbing (3)
- Starvation (2)
- Other methods, including poisoning with carbon monoxide, lethal doses of drugs, running over with a car, boiling, and putting in freezer (5)

Of the five victims who were shot to death, three died because the assailant accidentally fired a gun while committing another crime; therefore, two offspring victims under age 12 were intentionally killed with a firearm.

(Dawson & Langan, 1994)

---

this area and such research is desperately needed. Offspring homicides appear to be a more heterogeneous phenomenon than the other forms of affective violence studied in this chapter. Offspring homicide-suicides may differ in pattern and motive, depending on the sex of the perpetrator, the age of the children, and the context in which it occurs.

Clinical Vignette: The Abandoned Mother

Grand Rapids is the heart of Western Michigan. It was settled by Dutch Protestants with very conservative political and moral views.

Mary Hoekstra (not her real name) was 32 years old and had two children—a six-year-old boy and a four-year-old girl. She had married David when she was 22. Theirs was a cold and distant relationship. However, she endured the silence and lack of affection as she had been reared to do by her rather stern Dutch Reform family.

In her mid-20s, Mary began hearing rumors that David saw other women. She denied this, as it conflicted with her personal and cultural views of the sanctity of marriage.

However, one day, David came home and stated he wanted a divorce and abruptly left after packing his bags. Soon after, he was seen in the company of one of Mary's best friends.

David refused to talk of reconciliation and stopped seeing Mary and the children. Under Michigan's no-fault law, the divorce proceeded over Mary's objections. Mary grew despondent. She had few work skills and two small children to care for. She felt ridiculed in the community and an outcast. She was plagued by suicidal preoccupation, but feared talking to her family or to a professional. She saw her despondency reflected in her children. They were lonely, uncared for, and abandoned.

Finally, Mary saw her family doctor. Alarmed at her pale and withdrawn look, he prescribed a tranquilizer which allowed her to sleep. On the day before the final divorce hearing, she took the remaining tranquilizers prescribed by her doctor and put them in her children's milk. After they fell asleep, she carried them to her car in the garage. She turned on the engine, held her children, and waited to die.

A passerby noticed the smoke coming from the garage and called the police. When they arrived, both children were dead. Mary was revived.

She was arrested, went to trial, and an unsympathetic jury found her guilty of second degree murder. She is currently serving 25 years in one of Michigan's state penitentiaries for her crime.

Workplace Homicide

Workplace homicides include a broad range of violent acts tied together by the location in which these acts occur. The National Institute of Occupational Safety and Health reported that 750 lives are claimed each year by workplace homicides. Such homicides are the third leading cause of occupational deaths behind vehicular and machine related fatalities.

Fox and Levin (1993) estimated that a majority of victims of workplace violence are not acquaintances of the offender, but are incidentally caught up in a primary violent act, e.g., robbery being the primary motive, with murder being incidental. This belief is reinforced by studying the occupations of victims. The most frequent occupations of victims are retail clerks, taxi drivers, and public and private police officers. Common to all of these occupations is that the individuals often work alone, work at night, and encounter strangers in the performance of their duty.

Other categories of victims are coworkers who are killed in the course of arguments, or coworkers with whom the perpetrator has a grudge fostered by an outside contact, such as a love triangle. The data gathered by Fox and Levin point to one-third of violent offenders in the workplace being employees or former employees. Most workplace homicides do not result in the subsequent suicide of the perpetrator. Murder-suicides appear to occur most frequently in respect to employees killing supervisors or authority figures. Nationally, such supervisor murders occur about twice a month.

Figure 1 illustrates the frequency of workplace homicides committed by employees against employers or supervisors. Figure 1 shows that there has been a dramatic rise in such occurrences, with only six incidents occurring in 1976 and 24 incidents occurring in 1988. Data are not available for the proportion of killers who then killed themselves.

The killers of employers studied by Fox and Levin rarely displayed histories of mental illness.

Only 11 of 125 killers studied had a past history of documented mental health problems. However, Fox and Levin's data may be an underestimation of the frequency of mental illness in the offenders. (See chapter by Feldmann and Johnson in this volume.)

Employer murders followed by suicides appear to be a unique subset of general workplace homicide. Dynamically, such murder-suicides involve an intense, conflicted transference to an authority figure. The employee appears to have a love-hate relationship with this figure—needy of approval and, conversely, experiencing extreme rage and disappointments when such approval is not forthcoming.

The employee-employer conflict shows a pat-

tern of escalation which usually involves censure or termination of the employee. This sets the catathymic pattern in motion.

The employee becomes obsessed with his or her own victimization. The employee projects his or her hate and disappointment onto the authority figure. Paranoid and obsessive qualities begin to dominate the personality structure from moderate to intense, from rational to irrational. The perpetrator often shows peak precursive behavior, such as verbalizing threats or showing firearms to fellow employees. Sometimes he or she becomes openly more belligerent in the workplace or outside of work. Following this incubation period, the perpetrator concretizes the plans for murder and carries it out. The employee's actions are

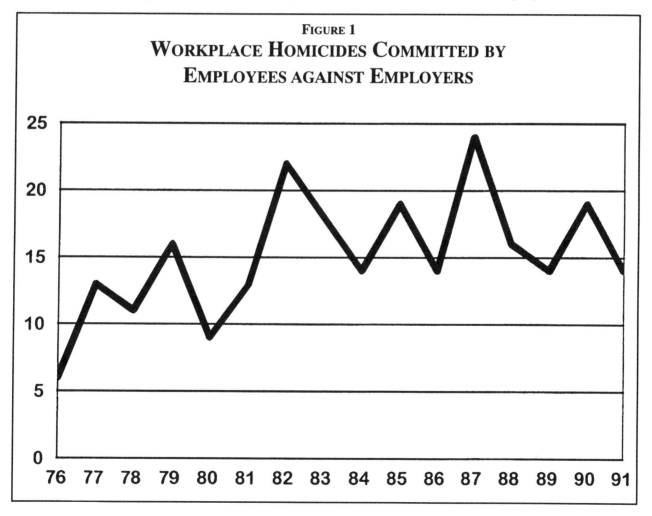

FIGURE 1
WORKPLACE HOMICIDES COMMITTED BY
EMPLOYEES AGAINST EMPLOYERS

selective, not random. The offending supervisor or employer is targeted, while "benign" fellow workers are generally spared. Suicide is frequent, but some perpetrators, especially those who are caught in the act, give themselves up. The perpetrators of such crimes tend to be middle-aged and White. Ninety-two percent are male.

Fox and Levin have isolated two patterns common to workplace killings. First are employees who show a long history of frustration and disappointment. Their jobs have been a constant source of trouble or personal devaluation. Often, they have suffered from domestic tragedies, such as divorce or family illness. Job conflicts are the "final straw" which sets off a murderous rampage.

A second pattern is the "entitlement profile." This involves basically good, longstanding workers who perceive that they have given everything to the company. Job trauma results in feelings of betrayal and ultimately revenge.

In both cases, it is usually the older workers who explode. Such workers are more involved in their careers. Unlike the shorter term, younger workers who see themselves as less anchored and more mobile, the middle-aged workers see the job disappointments as a small death. Termination of employment is experienced as a termination of life.

While specific personality characteristics of such offenders have not been isolated, anecdotal evidence suggests obsessive-paranoid qualities dominating or activated by trauma in these individuals. These persons are generally externalizers. They persistently project blame onto others, who are seen as accountable for the misery in their lives.

Murderers tend to lack support systems. They are loners without family, who literally have little to lose after their jobs are threatened.

Fascination with alcohol and firearms also appears to be an important variable, with most studies finding the perpetrator having an escalating drinking problem prior to the killing. Seven-

ty-five percent of deaths are caused by firearms and 14% are caused by piercing weapons, such as knives (Fox & Levin, 1993).

The rise of such crimes also appears to have sociological implications. The 1950s and 1960s were boom times, with an expanding economy. Poorly educated workers and workers with low skill levels easily found and kept jobs. There was little anxiety, as even a job loss was quickly compensated for by a job replacement.

However, as the economy has shrunk and more jobs require theoretical and technical expertise, middle-aged workers find themselves being edged out by younger and better educated replacements and, as a result, live in a constant state of anxiety about their futures. Such a generalized shift appears to have forced an increase in the situational determinants of workplace killings.

Clinical Vignette: The Royal Oak Post Office Murders

Royal Oak was a small farm community outside of Detroit. As the city grew, Royal Oak was swallowed, and its farmland gave birth to neat middle class homes. It remained, however, a peaceful place.

Adjacent to its small downtown area, sat the Royal Oak Post Office. In contrast to the city, it was known for its tension. Workers called it a sweatshop, where they were driven to constantly increase production. Spying on employees was alleged and management was seen as harsh, vindictive, and rabidly anti-union.

Thomas McIlvane was a letter carrier who worked out of the Royal Oak Post Office. He had a checkered career. An ex-Marine, he had been demoted in the service several times for insubordination. Eventually, he was given a "General Discharge," military parlance for an inability to adjust. Reports described him as volatile and anti-authority.

Pathologically, he was drawn to the post

office, which, like the military, was an autocratic organization. Paradoxically, for all of its selective screening procedure, the post office failed to do a background check on the kind of man they were hiring. It was only a matter of time before the autocratic power structure and the troubled ex-Marine clashed.

On April 8, 1990, McIlvane was terminated. This followed years of constant disputes, ranging from allegations of fraud on McIlvane's part to unfair union practices on the part of management. It was a constantly stormy and contentious relationship.

Subsequently, McIlvane filed an appeal grievance. While the appeal worked its way through the slow legal process, McIlvane began his own form of grievance. There were 21 documented reports of McIlvane making threats to management. He was arrested several times, but was found not guilty for lack of evidence.

On his own, he practiced with his guns and developed his kick boxing skills in controlled aggression. He was rehearsing for his final act of retribution.

The grievance he filed was turned down; his termination stood. Again, as in the military, and perhaps like his entire life script, Thomas McIlvane was not wanted.

On November 14, 1991, McIlvane entered the Royal Oak Post Office wearing a long coat. His hand was in his coat pocket and gripped a sawed off shotgun. McIlvane went straight to Christopher Carlisle's office. Carlisle had been his division head and was perceived as his chief tormentor. McIlvane killed him in cold blood. He then systematically went through the building, killing two more supervisors and wounding five others, before shooting himself.

A psychological autopsy performed after the killings revealed McIlvane's troubled past, his constant conflicts with authority, and his volatility. He was a loner, a gun freak, and a kick boxing champion who blamed the post office for all of

his problems.

At the time of the killing spree, the Royal Oak Post Office was being investigated because of numerous employee complaints. Workers interviewed after the shootings were not surprised. The destructive actions of post office supervisors were exposed. McIlvane had made explicit threats, bragging to anybody who would listen. Nobody did.

Psychodynamics

Murder followed by suicide presents significant methodological difficulties in trying to understand the causes of the act. Because the offender is also a victim, post violence interviews are impossible and explanatory concepts are thus generally inferential.

Research regarding murder-suicide generally occurs via the method of a "psychological autopsy." In this approach, data are collected from a variety of previously existing sources, such as interviews with acquaintances and family, reviews of personal writings, and other related information. The small sample of these acts also makes generalizing trends difficult.

Theorists who have focused on murder followed by suicide have centered on two possible explanatory dynamics. First, murder followed by suicide may be viewed as a type of altruism. In such cases, the perpetrator is seen as morbidly depressed (West, 1966). This severe mood disorder shapes and distorts the thinking process to the point where life is seen as hopeless and this view generalizes to intimates. The perpetrator feels that he or she is helping the victim by taking the victim's life and rescuing that person from a world that is beyond repair.

A variation on this theme was espoused by Selkin (1976), who hypothesized that a rescue fantasy permeates such actions. In Selkin's scenario, the perpetrator feels that he or she is saving the victim from a worse fate at the hands of a third party. In spousal killings, the perpetrator may feel that he or she must kill the spouse to free the spouse from the ravages of another predatory party. Similarly, a mother may kill her children to protect them from an abusive father.

Both authors see depression as the major etiological factor to murder followed by suicide. There is empirical support for this view, with West (1966) finding that one-half of his sample was either psychotically or severely neurotically depressed at the time of the murder-suicide.

The second explanatory dynamic also postulates the role of depression in the phenomena of murder followed by suicide. In accordance with Freud's early formulations of depression as primarily an aggressive phenomenon, this hypothesis suggests that the perpetrator is already struggling with aggressive impulses directed toward the self. Such impulses are guided by or stem from a sense of worthlessness and guilt. Because of dominating aggression, the perpetrator is primed to self destruct. A triggering event then occurs and the affect is murderously displaced to another. Once released, the aggression-guilt complex takes over and the perpetrator turns the aggression on himself or herself in a destructive manner.

Studies which compared homicides with homicide-suicides found that there are clear differences in these phenomenon. Perpetrators who commit only homicides demonstrate higher levels of psychopathy, are younger, and are less likely to manifest traditional forms of psychopathology, such as depression. All view murder followed by suicide as a subset of suicidal behavior. The primary purpose is destruction of the self.

The concept of depression, however, does not appear to have full explanatory power to describe all the parameters of murder followed by suicide. Our understanding is increased when murder-suicide is viewed within the framework of self psychology.

The act of murder followed by suicide is inherently paradoxical. We naturally think of aggressive actions occurring either toward oneself or toward others and indeed, empirically, this is the case.

Older theories aimed at explaining either homicide or suicidal actions, but more modern psychoanalytic theories, falling under the rubric of object relations, are promising in explaining murder followed by suicide.

Object relations theorists (Kernberg 1975, 1984; Kohut, 1978) posit that early stages of development are characterized by a lack of differentiation between self-representations and object representations. Cognitively the infant's psychic structure is incapable of separating and integrating self and object representations.

Furthermore, this primitive psychic organization causes the infant to reflect the affective state of the maternal care taker. Kernberg (1984, 1989), following Jacobson (1964), hypothesized that antisocial personalities and narcissistic personalities with antisocial traits have, to varying degrees, sadistic and predatory maternal introjects derived from real parental abuse or severe neglect. This results in a very primitive, sadistic superego. These sadistic introjects are normally projected onto the external world, and result in an image of people as nasty, brutish, and cruel.

As adults, narcissistic and antisocial personalities bifurcate the world into cruel, exploitive people (projected object-representations) and a grandiose, entitled, and perfect self. Concomitantly, when there is a narcissistic wound to the self, such as a rejection, projection causes the wounded individual to devalue the other or attack in order to maintain a stable sense of self. This aggression protects the homeostatic balance between self and others.

In the true psychopath or antisocial personality disorder, aggressive acts are committed against others in a predatory fashion. Psychopaths will aggress against or exploit others because the targets deserve it and at the same time, feel entitled, peaceful, or happy in propagating such terrible acts. Their separation from others is complete. They act without guilt and, in fact, this is a major reason why such individuals can perform horrendous acts and get away with them.

Kernberg (1989) also diagnosed a less pathological group of personality disorders called narcissistic personalities with antisocial features. Such individuals are capable of more long-term commitments in relationships and tend to experience some genuine guilt. They do form attachments, but have primitive superego development and a more unstable balance between self-representations and object-representations. We would hypothesize that murder followed by suicide is committed by narcissistic personality disorders with antisocial traits, and suggest the following scenario as modal:

A narcissistic personality disorder becomes primitively attached to another individual, such as a wife, child, or employer. The valuation of the narcissist by the other is the central mechanism in maintaining the narcissistic sense of self or internal stability. It is only through the love of the other that the narcissist can feel grandiose, whole, and worthwhile. This is similar to what Kohut described as a merger transference. This is a highly ambivalent, volatile relationship with slight insults from the other resulting in the narcissist experiencing major mood swings, depression, and aggression.

A major insult may occur, such as a marital rejection, an affair, a work termination, or a child wishing to break away. The quality and quantity of these narcissistic wounds destabilize the narcissist's sense of self, and a major regression occurs. The regression takes the narcissist back to a very primitive level of psychic organization. The distinction between self and other is destroyed and, affectively, a primitive superego expression of rage dominates.

The loss of self-object differentiation and the primitive superego rage collaborate to produce a

murder followed by suicide. In such a regressed state, the murder of the other, and the destruction of the self are not separate psychological acts, but an expression of a primitive relationship without differentiation. In a sense, killing the other is killing the self and murder followed by suicide simply concertizes this primitive psychic expression.

By factoring in both the narcissistic insults from the other and the personality vulnerability of the perpetrator, a tenable theory of murder followed by suicide is offered. Empirical research is needed to support this theory.

Warning Signs

Explosive murders and murder-suicides are not always predictable. However, there are some common factors that define most of these events. Historically, perpetrators come from families where there was abuse, abandonment, or parental dysfunction. Premorbidly, they show a history of violent, angry, volatile relationships and only marginal adjustment in areas of their life, such as work. A fascination with weapons is common. As personalities, they generally show themselves to become easily emotionally wounded and hurt. Such wounds activate acute depressions, obsessions, and paranoid ideation. Problems are resolved by aggressive acting out, threatening others, or substance abuse.

Proximately, perpetrators are under great stress. These stressors usually involve a potential separation or abandonment in their work life or relationships. Violence is usually preceded by a general deterioration in habit and hygiene patterns. Violent and aggressive actions begin to appear. Often, there are explicit threats to kill others or themselves. Actions are planned, not spontaneous. Consequently, precursors are often noticeable to others and include the purchasing of weapons, verbal aggression, openly aggressive acts, insubordination, obsessions with victimization, suicidal threats, and major changes in habit patterns. Active interventions by employers or mental health professionals may defuse the situation. Ignoring the problem enhances the possibility of violence occurring.

References

Allen, N. (1983). Homicide followed by suicide: Los Angeles, 1970-1979. *Suicide and Life-Threatening Behavior, 13*(3).

Berman, A. (1979). Dyadic death: Murder-suicide. *Suicide and Life Threatening Behavior, 9*(1).

Browne, A. (1987). *When battered women kill.* New York: Macmillan.

Coid, J. (1982). *Homicide in Bermuda.* M. Phil. Thesis: University of London.

Coid, J. (1983). The epidemiology of abnormal homicide and murder followed by suicide. *Psychological Medicine, 13*, 855-860.

Criminal Statistics England & Wales (1980). CMND, HMSO: London.

Dawson, J., & Langan, P. (1994). *Murder in families* (Special Report, Bureau of Justice Statistics), Washington, DC: U.S. Department of Justice.

Fox, J. A., & Levin, J. (November 30, 1993). Firing back: The growing threat of workplace homicide. *The Annals of the American Academy of Political and Social Science, 5*, 119-137.

Fox, J. A., & Levin, J. (May 12, 1993). Postal violence cycle of despair turns tragic. *USA Today*, 13a.

Gibson, E., & Klein, S. (1969). Murder 1957 to 1968. HMSO: London.

Greenland, C. (1971). Evaluation of violence and dangerous behavior associated with mental illness. *Seminars in Psychiatry, 3*, 345-356.

Gudjonsson, G., & Petursson, H. (1982). Some criminological and psychiatric aspects of homicide in Iceland. *Medicine, Science and the Law, 22*, 91-98.

Hansen, J., & Bjarnason, O. (1974). Homicide in Iceland, 1946 1970. *Forensic Science, 4*, 107-117.

Jacobson, E. (1964). *The self and the object world.* New York: International Universities Press.

Kernberg, O.F. (1975). *Borderline conditions and pathological narcissism.* New York: Aronson.

Kernberg, O.F. (1984). *Severe personality disorders: Psychotherapeutic strategies.* New Haven: Yale University Press.

Kernberg, O.F. (1989). The Narcissistic Personality Disorder and the differential diagnosis of antisocial behavior. *The Psychiatric Clinical of North America, 12*, 553-570.

Kohut, H. (1978). *The search for the self.* New York: International Universities Press.

Landau, S.F. (1975). Pathologies among homicide offenders: Some cultural profiles. *British Journal of Criminology, 15*, 157 166.

Litman, R. (1967). Sigmund Freud on suicide. *Psychoanalytic Forum, 1*, 205-221.

Maier, H. (1912). Ueber einige arten catathyme wahnbildung und paranoia [On types of catathymic formations in psychosis and paranoia]. *Ztschr F.d. Ges. Neurol U Psychiat., 13*, 555.

Maier, H. (1923). Ueber einige arten der psychogenen mechanismen [On types of psychogenetic mechanisms]. *Ztschr F.d. ges Neurol U Psychiat, 39*, 116-120.

Meloy, J.R. (1992). *Violent attachments*. Northvale, NJ: Aronson.

Morris, T., & Blom-Cooper, L. (1976). Homicide in England. In M. E. Wolfgang (Ed.), *Studies in Homicide* (pp. 24-35). Harper & Row: New York.

Palmer, S., & Humphrey, J. (1980). Offender-victim relationships in criminal homicide followed by offender's suicide. *Suicide & Life-Threatening Behavior, 10*, 106-118.

Revitch, E., & Schlesinger, L. (1978). Murder: Evaluation, classification, and prediction. In I. Kutash, S. Kutash, and L. Schlesinger (Eds.), *Violence: Perspectives on murder and aggression* (pp. 138-164). San Francisco: Jossey-Bass.

Rosenbaum, M. (1990). The role of depression in couples involved in murder-suicide and homicide. *American Journal of Psychiatry, 147*, 1036-1039.

Schloss, B., & Giesbrecht, N. (1972). *Murder in Canada. A report on capital and non-capital murder statistics, 1961-1970*. Centre of Criminology: University of Toronto.

Selkin, J. (1976). Rescue fantasies in homicide-suicide. *Suicide Life-Threatening Behavior, 6*, (2).

Sherman, L., & Berke, R. (1989). The specific deterrent effects of arrest for domestic assault. *American Sociological Review, 49*, 261-272.

Silverman, R., & Mukherjee, S.K. (1987). Intimate homicide: An analysis of violent social relationships. *Behavioral Sciences and the Law, 5*(1), 37-47.

U.S. Department of Health and Human Services (1993). *Preventing Homicide in the Workplace* (NIOSH Publication No. 4-5). Rockville, MD: Author.

Virkkunen, M. (1974). Suicide linked to homicide. *Psychiatric Quarterly, 48*, 276-282.

Wertham, F. (1937). The catathymic crisis: a clinical entity. *Archives of Neutology and Psychiatry 37*, 974–978.

West, D.J. (1966). *Murder followed by suicide*. Cambridge: Harvard University Press.

Wolfgang, M. (1958). An analysis of homicide-suicide. *Journal of Clinical and Experimental Psychopathology, 19*, 208-217.

Wolfgang, M. (1959). Suicide by means of victim-precipitated homicide. *Journal of Clinical and Experimental Psychopathology, 20*, 335-349.

Wong, M. & Singer, K. (1973). Abnormal homicide in Hong Kong. *British Journal of Psychiatry, 123*, 295-298.

About the Authors

Michael Abramsky received his doctorate from SUNY at Buffalo in 1973. He is a Diplomate of the American Board of Professional Psychology. Dr. Abramsky is in private practice in Birmingham, Michigan. In addition to a general clinical practice, Dr. Abramsky is a Forensic Consultant. He has served as a Forensic Examiner in a number of high-profile murder cases in Michigan, including the Highland Park Serial Killer and the murder of a contestant following the Jenny Jones talk show. Dr. Abramsky has lectured and published in the areas of psychological trauma, violent behavior, the relationship between alcohol and violence, and forensic assessment.

Melissa Helfman received her Masters Degree in Clinical Psychology in 1992 from the Center for Humanistic Studies in Detroit. Following graduation, she worked as a diagnostician in the criminal justice system and in a local correctional facility with Inmate Services. Currently, she is a Senior Clinician at Psychological Rehabilitation Services in Birmingham, Michigan. She is pursuing doctoral studies in the area of forensic psychology.

Part III
Criminal Violence

CHAPTER 11

WORKPLACE VIOLENCE: A NEW FORM OF LETHAL AGGRESSION

Theodore B. Feldmann
Phillip W. Johnson

Introduction

In recent years, a new form of lethal criminal activity has emerged in the United States; the workplace has become fertile ground for assaults and homicide. Historically, crime in the workplace has been limited largely to robbery attempts. With the exception of those employed in fields where violence is considered an occupational hazard, such as police officers or prison guards, most American workers have felt relatively immune from crime on the job. Injury or death at work was more likely to result from some type of industrial accident than from the intentional infliction of harm by another. In recent years, however, a trend has developed for disgruntled employees, customers dissatisfied with goods or services, and individuals who bring personal grudges or disputes into the workplace from outside, to utilize violence as a problem-solving technique. This shift represents a radical change in perspective regarding violence in America; aggression is now viewed as a viable solution for all of life's ills.

These acts of workplace aggression have created a climate of fear and insecurity for employers and employees alike. Thus, management of the potentially violent person has become an increasing concern for workplace managers. The inherent level of danger and tragedy associated with these crimes has resulted in a new and destructive source of stress for corporate America.

It is clear that attacks in the workplace represent a serious form of lethal violence. Many incidents are on record in which massive loss of life has occurred, as exemplified by the following:

Case Illustration: On September 14, 1989, Joseph Wesbecker, a 47-year-old former employee, entered the Standard Gravure Printing Plant in Louisville, Kentucky. Wesbecker was armed with an AK-47 assault rifle, two MAC-11 assault weapons, a .25 caliber pistol, and a 9mm pistol. He roamed throughout the plant, randomly firing his weapons, killing eight people and wounding 12 others. He then killed himself with a single gunshot to the head.

Mr. Wesbecker had a long history of mental illness, and was under the care of a psychiatrist. At the time of the incident, he was taking lithium carbonate, a mood stabilizing drug, and Prozac, an antidepressant. As a result of the psychiatric condition, he had been on disability leave from work since March 1989. It is alleged that he blamed the company for many of his personal and emotional problems. During the attack, Wesbeck-

er seemed to target many of the company officials he felt were responsible for his difficulties.

Case Illustration: On June 19, 1990, a 42-year-old unemployed construction worker killed eight people and wounded five others before killing himself. The individual entered a car loan office in Jacksonville, Florida, at 10:45 a.m., and opened fire. The apparent precipitant was the repossession of his 1988 Pontiac Grand Am by the finance company in January of that year. The attacker was armed with a .30 caliber semiautomatic rifle, a .38 caliber revolver, a 9mm pistol, and a .357 magnum revolver. A few days earlier, the suspect apparently shot and killed two other people following a dispute over the services of a prostitute. He had no known psychiatric history, but did have a criminal record. In 1968, he was arrested for "dangerously displaying a weapon," and in 1971, was charged with manslaughter in the shooting death of a man, for which he received five-years probation on a reduced charge of aggravated assault.

In order to better understand this form of lethal violence, this chapter reviews the phenomenon of workplace violence, and presents the results of an on-going empirical study of these incidents. Case illustrations from the workplace violence database are also presented to better depict the nature of these violent acts.

An Overview Of Crime In The Workplace

Workplace violence has escalated dramatically in the last 15 years. Virtually unheard of prior to 1980, workplace violence has increased to the point where the National Institute for Occupational Safety and Health (NIOSH) now estimates that 1,400 people are murdered in the workplace each year (1992). Homicide is now the second leading cause of death in the workplace, behind work-related accidents. It has become the leading cause of death for women in the workplace, and is the third leading cause of work-related death for men.

In 1993, the U.S. Bureau of Labor Statistics reported that homicide accounted for 17% of all occupational fatalities. Clearly, such a trend would have been difficult to predict in 1980.

Other forms of crime in the workplace, such as physical and sexual assaults, as well as verbal threats and intimidation, have also risen at alarming rates. A study by the Northwestern National Life Insurance Company (1993), for example, reported that an estimated 2.2 million workers were the victims of some type of attack in the workplace between July 1, 1992 and June 30, 1993. According to this study, 6.3 million workers were threatened and 16.1 million were harassed.

It has been shown that workplace violence can occur in a variety of settings. Duncan (1995), in a study of 39 incidents, reported that government buildings were the most frequent site for workplace violence (38% of the cases), with factories the second most common setting (18% of cases). No occupation or work setting is immune from violence, however, as the following vignette demonstrates.

Case Illustration: On July 28, 1993, a 52-year-old man shot and killed a physician in his office after the doctor refused to refill a prescription for pain medication. The assailant then drove two blocks to another doctor's office and fatally shot a physician's assistant and wounded a nurse. The perpetrator used a 9mm pistol; during the attack he apparently accidentally shot himself in the hand. He was apprehended by police as he attempted to flee the second office.

In addition to the cost in human life and suffering, workplace violence exerts a tremendous financial impact. The National Safe Workplace Institute (1993) estimated that in 1992, the total cost to employers of workplace violence was approximately $4.2 billion. The financial impact of a single incident of workplace violence can be seen from the following case.

Case Illustration: On August 3, 1990, in Sonoma County, California, Christina Appelton, *a 20-year-old winery worker, was stabbed to death outside the plant by a co-worker who had been fired for "poor work habits." The perpetrator, who had been placed in the winery by a temporary employment agency, had a history of violent criminal behavior. The temporary agency had failed to conduct a background check or review his work references. On November 24, 1992, a Sonoma County jury awarded the victim's estate $5.5 million in damages.*

The impact of workplace violence can be summarized as follows: (1) a climate of fear is created in the workplace; (2) employee morale is damaged; (3) productivity is diminished; (4) liability risk is increased; (5) consumer confidence is damaged; (6) insurance rates increase; and (7) as demonstrated in the case illustration above, a major incident of workplace violence can literally put a small company out of business.

Finally, the psychological damage imposed on survivors of workplace trauma is staggering. It has been reported by the Federal Bureau of Investigation (FBI, 1993) that survivors who received therapy or counseling immediately after exposure to workplace violence returned to work, on the average, within 12 weeks, and only 13% chose to pursue litigation. On the other hand, those survivors who delayed treatment, on the average, returned to work in 46 weeks, and 94% pursued litigation. Clearly, the first 24 hours after the traumatic incident are the most critical for debriefing and initiating the recovery process.

Much has been written and presented in the popular media about workplace violence (*Time Magazine*, 1994). Likewise, legal and professional publications have focused on the impact and consequences of violent acts (Law Firm of Littler, Mendelson, Fastiff, Tichy, & Mathiason, 1994; White & Hatcher, 1988). To date, however, little has appeared in the psychiatric or psychological literature on the phenomenon of workplace violence. The lack of empirical data has led to many generalizations about workplace violence which have not been confirmed; the potential exists for these generalizations to contain a number of myths and misconceptions.

Commonly held beliefs about workplace violence include the following: (1) most workplace violence is narrowly defined as those acts perpetrated by disgruntled employees (Fox & Levin, 1993); (2) the typical profile of this disgruntled employee fits the stereotype of the "Workplace Rambo," who demonstrates excessive interest in weapons, as well as characteristics of the "avenger personality" described by Depue (1993) and others; (3) assault weapons are the most commonly used weapons in these incidents; (4) most perpetrators are older, with a mean age of 38.2 years reported by Duncan (1995); and (5) stalking occurs frequently in association with these acts. While some of these generalizations are confirmed by the data in this chapter, others find little or no support to date.

In order to further investigate this problem, a workplace violence database was developed in 1994 by the Department of Psychiatry and Behavioral Sciences at the University of Louisville School of Medicine. This chapter presents the results from 252 cases of workplace violence contained in the database to date. Case illustrations from the database are included to further demonstrate the nature of workplace violence.

The Workplace Violence Database: Methodology and Results

The phenomena of workplace violence, although not entirely new to the culture, appears to have radically increased in the last few years. Sadly, it is no longer uncommon to hear of shootings in post offices, businesses, hospitals, or even health clubs. Often, such incidents result in the heavy loss of life or serious injury to numerous individuals. Despite the increasing frequency of these tragedies, the personal motivations of the perpetrators remain shrouded in mystery. Their primary intent appears to be the infliction of as much damage to as many people as possible in a limited period of time. Escape may or may not be a goal; many incidents end with the perpetrator taking his or her own life, or provoking law enforcement officers into shooting (the phenomenon of "suicide by cop"). Some symbolic statement or position appears to frequently be the purpose of the violent act. This chapter examines a variety of demographic, psychosocial, and psychiatric factors in order to better clarify the motivations for workplace violence and the profiles of the perpetrators.

Methodology

Through June 1, 1995, data were collected on 252 incidents of workplace violence from across the United States. Information on each incident was initially collected from two primary sources: (1) news media reports and (2) businesses, companies, or agencies which contacted the authors for consultation regarding a specific threat or individual. Examples of the latter sources include the authors' consultations with the U.S. Postal Service and U.S. Census Bureau, as well as work with businesses in the private sector. This initial information was then supplemented by telephone contact with the law enforcement agencies in whose jurisdiction the incident occurred. Further information was obtained from employers, victims, witnesses, and family members. Whenever possible, attempts were made to conduct clinical interviews with the perpetrators and perform psychological testing.

For the purposes of this study, workplace violence was defined as any incident which met the following criteria: (1) the incident must have occurred in a work environment; (2) an act of violence or aggression occurred which was of sufficient severity to merit reporting to a law enforcement agency; (3) if the incident was not reported to police, some action to address the situation was taken by the employer (e.g., disciplinary action, counseling, restraining orders, use of outside consultants, etc.); and (4) if no actual violence occurred, a threat occurred which was either reported to police or dealt with internally by company authorities (Feldmann, 1995a). Professions in which the threat of violence might be considered an occupational hazard (e.g., police officers, correctional officers, etc.) were excluded from this study. Likewise, assaults against physicians or staff by psychiatric patients were not included in the database, although assaults by non-psychiatric patients and others in medical settings were recorded.

Variables examined in this study included the setting in which the incident occurred, the motivation for the violent act, weapons used, military history, excessive weapons interest, number of persons killed or wounded, whether warning signals of the attack were observed, the presence of stalking, and whether hostages were taken. Psychiatric variables included primary and secondary diagnosis, alcohol or drug use at the time of the attack, psychotropic medications used, and suicide. All psychiatric diagnoses were recorded according to criteria in the Diagnostic and Statistical Manual of Mental Disorders, Fourth Edition (DSM-IV, 1994). For those subjects who were diagnosed prior to 1994, the current equivalent DSM-IV terminology was used. This information was then entered into a computer in the format illustrated in Table 1. Individual variables will be discussed further in the sections below.

Data from incidents within the past five years have been collected. Information on earlier events was also collected when available. In addition, new reports of workplace violence are added to the database as they occur.

Categorization of Incidents

In this study, the category of workplace vio-

TABLE 1
WORKPLACE VIOLENCE DATABASE

1. Incident Title	10. Psychiatric Diagnosis	18. Hostage-Taking During Incident
2. Date and Location	11. Weapons	19. Precipitant
3. Subject's Name/Age	12. Number Killed	20. Suicide
4. Sex	13. Number Wounded	21. Psychotropic Medications Used
5. Race	14. Setting	22. History of Excessive Interest in Weapons
6. Marital Status	15. Alcohol Use at Time of Incident	23. History of Military Service
7. Education	16. Drug Use at Time of Incident	24. Narrative Summary of Incident
8. Occupation	17. Stalking During Incident	
9. Category		

lence refers to the primary identity and motivation of the perpetrator. Seven categories have been identified: (1) disgruntled employees; (2) disgruntled customers or clients; (3) persons involved in personal or domestic disputes which were carried into the workplace; (4) mentally ill persons for whom no other motivation was determined; (5) criminals for whom the workplace was a target of opportunity; (6) disgruntled students or trainees; and (7) abusive supervisors.

The largest category in the study consisted of criminals engaged in robbery attempts, gang-related activities, and physical or sexual assaults in which the victims were chosen randomly. It should be noted that this group had no connection with the work setting except for it being the target of criminal activity. The criminal group accounted for 69 incidents (27.38%). Within the criminal group, robbery was the most commonly encountered motive, occurring in 53 of the 69 cases (76.81%). Gang-related activities accounted for 10 incidents (14.49%) in the criminal category. Physical assaults occurred four times (5.8%), and sexual assaults took place in two incidents (2.9%).

Disgruntled employees represented the second most common group, with 49 incidents out of 252 (19.44%). The next most frequently encountered group was the mentally ill, with 47 cases (18.65%). Personal and domestic disputes

brought into the workplace represented 45 incidents (17.86%). Customers or clients who were displeased with products or services accounted for 20 cases (7.94%). Disgruntled students or trainees were identified in 13 incidents (5.16%). Included in this group were individuals ranging from high school students, college and graduate students, and physicians in training, to persons in on-the-job training programs. Finally, physically abusive supervisors accounted for nine incidents (3.57%).

While disgruntled employees are most often associated with workplace violence, the study has found that over 71% of workplace violence is committed by persons who come from outside the work environment. Table 2 summarizes these findings.

Settings for Workplace Violence

Table 3 describes the settings in which the violence occurred. Seven broad groupings have been identified: (1) public or government facilities; (2) restaurants and bars; (3) offices and businesses; (4) plants and factories; (5) medical facilities; (6) schools; (7) and convenience or food stores. The results indicated that workplace violence is divided fairly evenly across all workplace environments. It appeared, however, that persons working in professional and service-oriented

TABLE 2
CATEGORIES OF WORKPLACE VIOLENCE

Category	Number	Percent
Criminals	69	28.75%
Disgruntled Employees	49	19.44%
Mentally Ill	47	18.65%
Personal/Domestic Disputes	45	17.86%
Disgruntled Customers/Clients	20	7.94%
Disgruntled Students/Trainees	13	5.16%
Abusive Supervisors	9	3.57%
Total # of Incidents	240	100%

TABLE 3
WORKPLACE VIOLENCE SETTING (N= 252 INCIDENTS)

Setting	Number	Percent
Office/Business	47	18.65%
Public/Government Facilities	44	17.46%
Restaurants/Bars	38	15.08%
Medical Facilities	35	13.89%
Schools	34	13.49%
Convenience/Food Stores	28	11.11%
Plant/Factory	26	10.32%
Total # of Incidents	252	100%

fields (e.g., businesses, restaurants, government, and medical) are at greater risk for workplace violence than persons working in manufacturing and industrial fields.

Number of Workplace Violence Offenders

A total of 314 individuals took part in the 252 cases reported here. In most cases, the perpetrator acted alone — 211 incidents (83.73%). Incidents involving two or more people occurred 41 times: 21 cases (8.33%) had two perpetrators, 18 cases (7.14%) involved three people, and two incidents (0.79%) consisted of four or more persons acting together. Thirty-three of the multiple-subject incidents were in the criminal category, primarily

robbery attempts or gang-related acts of violence. The remaining seven cases were equally divided among the other categories. Table 4 breaks down the total number of persons involved in workplace violence across the categories.

Offender Demographics

The mean age for workplace violence offenders in this study was 29.7 years, with a range of 14 to 71 years. (Table 5 summarizes the age ranges for those persons whose age was known.) The results indicated that workplace violence is an overwhelmingly male activity (95.54% of subjects) (see Table 6). In only 14 of the 252 incidents studied was the perpetrator female. Slightly

TABLE 4
NUMBER OF PERSON BY CATEGORY (N=252 INCIDENTS)

Category	Number of Persons	Percent
Criminals	119	37.90%
Personal/Domestic Disputes	53	16.88%
Disgruntled Employees	50	15.92%
Mentally Ill	45	14.33%
Disgruntled Customers/Clients	23	7.32%
Disgruntled Student/Trainees	14	4.46%
Abusive Supervisors	10	3.18%
Total # of Persons	314	100%

TABLE 5
AGE RANGE (N=299 SUBJECTS)

Age Range	Number	Percent
10-14 Years	2	0.67%
15-19 Years	54	18.06%
20-24 Years	64	21.40%
25-29 Years	53	17.73%
30-34 Years	36	12.04%
35-39 Years	28	9.36%
40-44 Years	25	8.36%
45-49 Years	23	7.69%
50-54 Years	8	2.68%
55-59 Years	2	0.67%
60-64 Years	2	0.67%
65-69 Years	1	0.33%
70-74 Years	1	0.33%
Total # of Subjects	314	100%

more than half (53.50%) of perpetrators were White, 39.17% were Black, and 5.41% were Hispanic (see Table 6).

Information on marital status was obtained for 286 of the 314 people studied. Fifty-one percent were married, 23% were divorced, 11% separated, 9% single, and 6% were widowed at the time of the violent attack. Educational background can be summarized as follows: (1) some high school — 20%; (2) high school graduate — 41%; (3) some college — 13%; (4) college graduate — 19%; (5) graduate or professional school — 7%. Thirty-nine percent of the sample were unemployed at the time of the incident; these persons fell mainly in the criminal and disgruntled employee groups.

The final demographic variable examined was military history (see Table 7). Fifty-three persons (16.88%) had served in the armed forces (three of whom were on active duty at the time

TABLE 6
SEX AND RACE OF WORKPLACE VIOLENCE OFFENDERS

Sex (N = 314 Subjects)	Number	Percent
Male	300	95.54%
Female	14	4.46%
Total # of Subjects	314	100%
Race (N = 314 Subjects)		
White	168	53.50%
Black	123	39.17%
Hispanic	17	5.14%
Asian	2	0.64%
Unknown	4	1.27%
Total # of Subjects	314	100%

TABLE 7
MILITARY SERVICE

Served in the Military	Number	Percent
Yes	53	16.88%
No	253	80.57%
Total # of Subjects	314	100%
Branch of Service	**Number**	**Percent**
Army	31	58.49%
Marine Corps	13	24.53%
Navy	5	9.43%
Air Force	4	7.55%
Total # of Subjects	53	100%
Combat Experience	**Number**	**Percent**
Yes	16	30.19%
No	31	58.49%
Information Not Available	6	11.32%
Total # of Subjects	53	100%

of the incident), primarily in the Army and Marine Corps. Of those persons with military experience, 16 had combat experience (30.19%). Fourteen individuals served in Vietnam, one in the Korean War, and one in Operation Desert Storm.

Precipitant

This variable was defined as either *acute* or *insidious*. Acute precipitants included those for which there was little or no indication of the impending violence. A situation occurred in which the perpetrator acted spontaneously, with a minimum of planning or premeditation, or with few, if any, warning signals. Insidious precipitants, on the other hand, built up over time and culminated in some violent action. These were usually the result of long-standing conflicts or grievances. Warning signals of impending violence were usually noted and interventions to defuse the situation were either unsuccessful or not attempted.

In 251 of the 252 incidents examined, some type of precipitant was identified. Acute precipitants were found in 92 cases (36.51%), while insidious precipitants were identified in 159 cases (63.10%). The majority of the insidious cases were related to the disgruntled employees, personal/domestic disputes, and mentally ill cate-

gories. Most of the acute cases involved criminal acts, such as robbery, where the violence was clearly secondary to an attempt to obtain money or property.

Weapons

A variety of weapons have been used in workplace violence. Many subjects carried and used multiple weapons during the event. Thus, the total number of weapons used in workplace violence incidents was examined (see Table 8), as were the primary weapons which appeared to inflict the greatest number of injuries and fatalities (See Table 9). The following case vignettes provide examples of multiple weapons used in workplace violence incidents or threats.

Case Illustration: In February of 1988, a 39-year-old computer software engineer who had been fired from his job in 1986, returned to his place of employment in Sunnyvale, California, armed with two bandoleers of ammunition, three handguns, a rifle, and a shotgun. He killed seven

TABLE 8
TOTAL WEAPONS (N= 252 INCIDENTS)

Total Weapons (N = 252 Weapons)	Number	Percent
Handguns	273	62.33%
Rifles/Shotguns	46	11.14%
Physical Force	30	6.85%
Knives	29	6.62%
Assault Weapons	22	5.02%
Bombs/Grenades	22	5.02%
Hammer/Blunt Objects	3	0.68%
Other Explosives	2	0.46%
Bottle/Broken Glass	2	0.46%
Mace	2	0.46%
Motor Vehicle	2	0.46%
Hatchet	1	0.23%
Shovel	1	0.23%
Baseball Bat/Stick	1	0.23%
Stun Gun	1	0.23%
BB Gun	1	0.23%
Total # of Weapons	438	100%

TABLE 9
PRIMARY WEAPONS USED (N= 252 INCIDENTS)

Primary Weapon Used (N = 286 Weapons)*	Number	Percent
Handguns	183	63.99%
Physical Force	29	10.14%
Knives	21	7.34%
Rifles/Shotguns	19	6.64%
Assault Weapons	14	4.90%
Bombs/Grenades	7	2.45%
Hammer/Blunt Objects	2	0.70%
Other Explosives	2	0.70%
Bottle/Broken Glass	2	0.70%
Motor Vehicle	2	0.70%
Mace	1	0.35%
Hatchet	1	0.35%
Shovel	1	0.35%
Baseball Bat/Stick	1	0.35%
Stun Gun	1	0.35%
Total # of Weapons Used	286	100%

*Weapons Actually Used to Inflict Injury/Death

people and wounded four others.

Case Illustration: In March of 1993, a 46-year-old soon-to-be-laid-off employee was arrested for allegedly threatening to kill 30 of his co-workers. When police searched his house, they found 12 guns, including revolvers, semi-automatic pistols, rifles, and large quantities of ammunition.

The results of this study indicated that handguns were used in the majority of incidents (63.99% of primary weapons). The next most frequent weapon category was physical force, defined as fist fights, kicking, choking, or other forms of assault in which the human body was the primary instrument used to inflict injury; this category accounted for 10.14% of the weapons used. Other frequently used weapons included knives (7.34%), rifles/shotguns (6.64%), and assault weapons (4.90%). These weapons accounted for injuries or fatalities in 216 of the 252 cases (85.71%).

In spite of the predominance of "traditional" weapons, such as handguns, physical beatings, rifles, and knives, many offenders in this study utilized weapons of opportunity, such as tools, sticks, or bottles. Others committing workplace violence employed more unusual weapons, such as bombs, other explosives, mace, stun guns, and even motor vehicles. The following vignette represents a case of an unusual weapon.

Case Illustration: On March 9, 1995, a 36-year-old man entered the headquarters of the International Federation of the Red Cross in New York City and doused himself with gasoline. He then set himself on fire. The man spoke broken English and made statements about human rights violations in Poland. He was dead on the scene when EMS personnel arrived. Two employees of the office were seriously burned during the incident.

The lethal nature of workplace violence can be illustrated by examining the number of persons killed or injured in each incident. The weapons described above resulted in a total of 382 deaths (1.51 deaths per incident), and 574 injuries (2.27 wounded per incident). The categories accounting for the highest rates of injury or death were disgruntled customer clients, mentally ill, disgruntled employees, and personal/domestic disputes.

Excessive interest in weapons was defined as an on-going preoccupation with weapons and their use, or extreme fascination with military or paramilitary activities. Characteristics of persons in this group included large weapons collecting, frequent wearing of camouflage fatigues or other military attire, extensive reading of gun publications and other periodicals with a military or paramilitary theme to the exclusion of other reading material, and frequent boasting about prowess with weapons or the martial arts. In the study, 121 people (38.54%) demonstrated an interest in weapons that was deemed to be excessive in nature.

Stalking and Hostage-Taking

Stalking may be defined as the unwanted or surreptitious following of another person for the purpose of harassment or some other criminal activity. This is the definition most commonly used by those states that have enacted anti-stalking laws. Stalking of victims occurred in 79 of the 252 incidents presented here (31.35%). The categories in which stalking occurred most frequently were personal/domestic disputes, disgruntled students/trainees, and disgruntled employees. Stalking of a victim was associated with an extremely high fatality rate (91%). Interventions for stalking victims include support and understanding for the victim, notification of law enforcement agencies, and restraining or emergency protective orders. In addition, adequate workplace security is extremely important. This includes limited access to the workplace, and parking lot security. Do not allow the victim to be alone; utilize a "buddy system" and escorts until the threat has passed. The following case is typical of stalking in the workplace.

Case Illustration: A former colleague stalked

and shot a Northwestern University professor on March 9, 1995. The assailant believed that the victim had stolen research from him that led to the assailant's dismissal from the University of Minnesota, where the two men had worked several years before. Following the shooting at the Evanston, Illinois campus, the suspect returned to Minneapolis, entered the administration building at the University of Minnesota Medical School, and fatally shot himself.

Hostages were taken in 38 incidents (15.08%). Data on both stalking and hostage-taking are presented in Table 10. The motivations for hostage-taking include: (1) to escape from an interrupted criminal act; (2) to elicit sympathy for radical causes; (3) to embarrass governments, forcing a change in domestic or foreign policy; or (4) to gain retribution for a real or perceived wrongful act (Feldmann & Johnson, 1993; Fuselier, 1981).

The taking of hostages occurred most often among disgruntled students/trainees, criminals, usually during foiled robbery attempts, and personal/domestic disputes. It is essential to remember that the management of hostage situations requires the presence of trained law enforcement officers who are experienced in hostage negotiation techniques. Employers should never attempt to deal with these situations on their own.

Case Illustration: On September 6, 1990, a 17-year-old armed high school sophomore, described as an academic underachiever who had trouble getting along with peers, held classmates hostage for more than five hours before surrendering to authorities. The incident occurred at South Forsyth High School in Forsyth County, about 40 miles northeast of Atlanta. The student carried a large duffle bag which he said contained a science project; the bag actually carried a rifle, a shotgun, and two handguns. The incident started at 8:30 a.m. when the student pulled a rifle on two teachers outside a classroom. At one point, he held two classrooms with about 40

TABLE 10
STALKING AND HOSTAGE-TAKING

Stalking (N = 240 Incidents)	Number	Percent
Yes	79	31.35%
No	170	67.46%
Total # of Incidents	252	100%
Hostage Taking (N = 252 Incidents)	**Number**	**Percent**
Yes	38	15.08%
No	214	84.92%
Total # of Incidents	252	100%

students at gunpoint. During the morning, most of the students were gradually released, some in exchange for food.

The demands made by the student were for a school bus and $3,000. He wanted to be taken to Savannah, where he planned to get a boat and sail to an unidentified Caribbean island. He also requested and received a bottle of No-Doz sleeping tablets. The incident ended about 1:45 p.m. when he began to get dizzy from the medication. He gave one of his weapons to a hostage, then the other hostages forced him against a wall. At that point, police entered the room and apprehended the student.

Psychiatric Diagnoses

Psychiatric diagnoses were found in 280 of the 314 persons studied (89.17%). This large number suggests that mental health assessment and intervention may greatly reduce the number of incidents. Both primary DSM-IV diagnoses (see Table 11) and secondary diagnoses (see Table 12) were recorded. In addition, primary and secondary psychiatric diagnoses were categorized according to broader diagnostic groups (e.g., affective disorders, personality disorders, psychoses, etc.); this is presented in Tables 13 and 14.

The most common primary psychiatric diag-

noses encountered were antisocial personality disorder (20.71%), depression (18.93%), and borderline personality disorder (12.50%). The antisocial personality diagnosis occurred primarily in the criminal group, and was uncommon in the other categories. A surprising number of adolescents were found in this study, many of whom met diagnostic criteria for conduct disorder (7.50% of primary diagnoses); in most instances these adolescents were in the criminal or the disgruntled student/trainee categories. The most commonly encountered secondary diagnoses were alcohol abuse/dependence (30.65%), polysubstance abuse/dependence (13.71%), and alcohol intoxication (11.29%).

Due to the large number of primary and secondary diagnoses, it is more useful to examine the diagnostic groups into which the perpetrators fell. Personality disorders accounted for the most frequent primary diagnosis (40.71%). As indicated above, antisocial personalities were most commonly found in the criminal group. For all other categories in the study, the borderline personality was the most frequently encountered personality disorder. The personality disorders were followed in frequency by affective disorders (20.71%), substance abuse disorders (13.93%), and psychotic disorders (10.36%). Among the secondary diagnoses, substance abuse disorders were most

TABLE 11
PRIMARY PSYCHIATRIC DIAGNOSES (N= 252 INCIDENTS)

Primary DSM-IV Diagnosis (N = 280 Subjects)	Number	Percent
Antisocial Personality Disorder	58	20.71%
Depression	53	18.93%
Borderline Personality Disorder	35	12.50%
Conduct Disorder	21	7.50%
Alcohol Abuse/Dependence	15	5.36%
Alcohol Intoxication	13	4.64%
Schizophrenia	11	3.93%
Psychotic Disorder NOS	8	2.86%
Delusional Disorder, Paranoid Type	6	2.14%
Personality Disorder NOS	6	2.14%
Polysubstance Abuse/Dependence	5	1.79%
Paranoid Personality Disorder	5	1.79%
Bipolar Disorder	5	1.79%
Pedophilia	5	1.79%
Narcissistic Personality Disorder	4	1.43%
Cocaine Abuse/Dependence	4	1.43%
Sexual Sadism	4	1.43%
Schizoaffective Disorder	3	1.07%
Schizoid Personality Disorder	3	1.07%
Adjustment Disorder	2	0.71%
Post-Traumatic Stress Disorder	2	0.71%
Attention Deficit Hyperactivity D/O	2	0.71%
Dependent Personality Disorder	2	0.71%
Oppositional Defiant Disorder	2	0.71%
Organic Delusional Disorder	1	0.36%
Avoidant Personality Disorder	1	0.36%
Delusional Disorder, Grandiose Type	1	0.36%
Amphetamine Abuse/Dependence	1	0.36%
Marihuana Abuse/Dependence	1	0.36%
Delirium	1	0.36%
Total Subjects with Diagnosis	280	100%
No Diagnosis	14	
No Diagnostic Information	20	
Total # of Subjects	314	

common (58.87%), followed by personality disorders (25.81%).

Psychotropic medication use at the time of the incident was found in only 38 subjects (12.1%); the majority of persons taking medication were in the mentally ill group. Antidepressants were the most commonly encountered drugs

(40.43%), followed by antipsychotics (21.28%), and mood stabilizing agents, such as lithium carbonate (12.77%).

Alcohol and Drug Use

Alcohol use at the time of the incident was

TABLE 12
SECONDARY PSYCHIATRIC DIAGNOSES (N= 252 INCIDENTS)

Secondary DSM-IV Diagnosis (N = 124)	Number	Percent
Alcohol Abuse/Dependence	38	30.65%
Polysubstance Abuse/Dependence	17	13.71%
Alcohol Intoxication	14	11.29%
Borderline Personality Disorder	12	9.68%
Personality Disorder NOS	11	8.87%
Depression	9	7.26%
Paranoid Personality Disorder	6	4.84%
Cocaine Abuse/Dependence	3	2.42%
Pedophilia	2	1.61%
Organic Personality Disorder	2	1.61%
Bipolar Disorder	1	0.81%
Schizotypal Personality Disorder	1	0.81%
Psychotic Disorder NOS	1	0.81%
Conduct Disorder	1	0.81%
Adjustment Disorder	1	0.81%
Obsessive Compulsive Disorder	1	0.81%
Antisocial Personality Disorder	1	0.81%
Dependent Personality Disorder	1	0.81%
Sexual Sadism	1	0.81%
Hallucinogen Abuse	1	0.81%
Total Secondary Diagnoses	124	100%

TABLE 13
PRIMARY PSYCHIATRIC DIAGNOSES BY GROUP
(N= 252 INCIDENTS)

Primary DSM-IV Diagnosis (N = 314 Subjects)	Number	Percent
Personality Disorders	114	40.71%
Affective Disorders	58	20.71%
Substance Abuse Disorders	39	13.93%
Psychotic Disorders	29	10.36%
Disorders of Childhood/Adolescence	25	8.93%
Psychosexual Disorders	9	3.21%
Adjustment Disorders	2	0.71%
Organic Mental Disorders	2	0.71%
Anxiety Disorders	2	0.71%
Total Subjects with Diagnosis	280	100%
No Diagnosis	14	
No Diagnostic Information	20	
Total # of Subjects	314	

TABLE 14
SECONDARY PSYCHIATRIC DIAGNOSES BY GROUP
(N= 240 INCIDENTS)

Secondary DSM-IV Diagnosis (N = 124)	Number	Percent
Substance Abuse Disorders	73	58.87%
Personality Disorders	32	25.81%
Affective Disorders	10	8.55%
Psychosexual Disorders	3	2.42%
Organic Mental Disorders	2	1.61%
Psychotic Disorders	1	0.81%
Disorders of Childhood/Adolescence	1	0.81%
Adjustment Disorders	1	0.81%
Anxiety Disorders	1	0.81%
Total Secondary Diagnoses	124	100%

documented in only 91 perpetrators of workplace violence (28.98%). Drug abuse at the time of the incident was found in 31 subjects (9.87%). Cocaine was the most frequently abused drug in this study (15 subjects). It is interesting to note that alcohol and drug use occurred less frequently than might be expected. There may be some underreporting in this area due to the reluctance of many subjects to disclose information or the inability of witnesses to recognize signs of intoxication. It is obvious that a person being assaulted or victimized may not have the opportunity to recognize indicators of intoxication.

Case Illustration: On October 14, 1993, a 19-year-old weightlifter, described as an "angry loner dedicated to pumping iron," opened fire with a shotgun at a San Diego health club where he worked out. Four people were killed before the subject returned to his car and killed himself. Two others were wounded. The subject used a 12 gauge shotgun, which he reloaded several times during the attack. The perpetrator had a history of drug abuse and steroid use. Witnesses said that he was "obsessed" with developing the "perfect body," and had been using anabolic steroids more frequently to attain his goal.

Suicide

A *completed suicide* followed 43 workplace violence incidents (13.69%), while *suicidal threats or ideation* were present in 56 additional cases (17.83%). Of interest is the observation that in this population only 10 *suicide attempts* (3.18%) were identified. This is likely due to the lethal nature of the weaponry used; in other words, most suicide attempts were successful. No evidence of suicide was found in 202 subjects (64.33%). The following example is typical of suicide in the workplace.

Case Illustration: A 27-year veteran of the Baltimore Police Department shot two supervisors and then killed himself at police headquarters in July 1991. The perpetrator had been suspended from duty the night before, pending an investigation of charges that he had sexually molested a 10-year-old relative. He did not impress co-workers as a discipline problem or a long-simmering threat.

Reassessing the Nature Of Workplace Violence

The findings of this study indicate that workplace violence should be defined more broadly than just acts committed by disgruntled workers. The personality types involved in these incidents are also more complex than previously thought. For example, the data indicated that criminals engaged in robbery attempts are responsible for the largest number (27.38%) of workplace violence acts, while disgruntled employees comprise the second largest group (19.44%). In addition, significant risk exists from other sources; over 53% of cases consisted of persons falling into the five remaining categories. In over 71% of cases, factors external to the workplace contributed to the violent acts (disgruntled customers/clients, personal/domestic disputes, mentally ill, and criminals).

Clearly, criminals, customers dissatisfied with products or services, personal disputes carried into the workplace, and random acts influenced by mental illness represent an equal or greater threat than the disgruntled employee. These external threats are significant because employers have less control over them than they do with disgruntled employees. This observation has important implications for workplace security in that identification and intervention become more difficult as employers face danger from sources about which they have little or no information. This poses a most difficult dilemma for business and industry: How do you provide adequate workplace security without imposing a barrier between you and the people with whom you do business? Many of the guidelines given to employers emphasize the need for pre-employment screening for potentially violent individuals (Littler et al., 1994). While this activity is of obvious benefit for the disgruntled employee category, how does a business or employer identify a potential customer or spouse/partner of an employee as dangerous?

Another interesting outcome of this research concerns the issue of weapons in the workplace. While much attention has been focused on the role of assault weapons in workplace violence, they are used infrequently in most incidents. Handguns, which are easily concealed and therefore harder to detect, pose a far greater threat. Furthermore, small semi-automatic pistols with magazine capacities of 14 to 16 rounds can be at least as lethal as larger assault weapons. Many such weapons are currently available in 9mm, and .380 and .45 calibers. The ease and speed at which these guns can be reloaded gives them firepower approaching that of assault weapons. Even when firearms are banned from the workplace, knives, physical assaults, and other weapons of opportunity (e.g., tools) may be used to carry out violent acts. This is aptly shown in the following vignette.

Case Illustration: On January 8, 1994, a dental assistant was beaten to death with a hammer by her estranged husband at the dental office where she worked. The dentist she worked for had arranged escape routes for her should her husband appear, but the subject attacked her before she could escape. The victim had filed for divorce and had obtained a restraining order to keep him away.

The data also revealed interesting findings with respect to the personality types and psychopathology of workplace violence offenders. It has been widely held that most persons involved in these acts display paranoid, often delusional, behavior accompanied by poor interpersonal skills, few friends, a tendency to hold grudges, and generally poor work performance over time (White & Hatcher, 1988). Although some elements of this profile are confirmed by the data, a more complicated picture of the violent individual in the workplace begins to emerge. The notion of the "crazed killer" appears to be overstated, in that relatively few of the subjects in the study demonstrated psychotic features (slightly more than 10%).

Individuals with unstable personality disorders who are prone to conflicted relationships and poor tolerance of stress represented a much larger proportion in the study than previously expected. This group, coupled with depressed persons displaying suicidal ideation, made up the majority of individuals engaging in workplace violence. Drug and alcohol use contributed relatively little to workplace violence, with the exception of those persons falling into the personal/domestic dispute category. Job performance for the disgruntled employee category in the sample ranged from unsatisfactory to outstanding, with considerable variation in between.

It appears that the profile of the "avenger personality" may hold up for those in the disgruntled employee and disgruntled student/trainee groups, but fails to identify the disgruntled customer/client, the personal/domestic dispute, mentally ill, and criminal groups. The one factor that does seem common to all groups is sensitivity to *narcissistic injury* and the narcissistic rage that usually follows. This term refers to the intense feelings of anger that arise from a perceived wrongdoing that threatens a person's underlying sense of self-esteem and identity (Kohut, 1978). It encompasses much more than the anger or disappointment that accompanies the loss of a promotion, dissatisfaction with a product or service, or some other workplace conflict. Narcissistic injuries threaten the entire personality to such an extent that a massive retaliation (narcissistic rage) must be carried out to restore the cohesion of the self. This formulation bears many similarities to the catathymic cycle of violence and homicide (Meloy, 1992; Revitch & Schlesinger, 1978).

Individuals with severe depressions and personality disorders are particularly vulnerable to narcissistic injury and rage. It is, therefore, not surprising that they constitute the two largest diagnostic groups in the study. Even persons in the criminal group show this sensitivity to narcissistic injury, which is often manifested by grandiose fantasies and feelings of entitlement (Meloy, 1988). Reactions to narcissistic injury tend to escalate over time, and this study supported the idea that, in many cases, clear warning signals can be identified

before the violent act occurs.

A variety of settings are at risk for these types of incidents. The widespread nature of workplace violence indicates that no environment is immune; seemingly, there are no safe havens from acts of aggression. White-collar workers, professionals, and those in service-oriented fields are at as much risk, if not more, than blue-collar and unskilled workers. People working in service-oriented activities, such as stores and restaurants, are clearly at the greatest risk for violence from disgruntled customers/clients and criminals. Robbery attempts in restaurants, bars, and convenience stores carried the second highest risk of injury or death in this study, behind personal/domestic disputes.

Finally, the study found that stalking occurred in about one-third of the cases of workplace violence, but carried an extremely high fatality rate. Nearly all of the cases presented here, in which stalking occurred, resulted in the murder of the victim. Although many states have adopted anti-stalking laws, it appears that these have little deterrent effect on violent offenders as currently utilized. Although only 79 confirmed cases of stalking were found in the sample, stalking was probably underreported. This occurred, in part, because victims may have been unaware that they were being followed.

In this sample, stalking occurred most often in the personal/domestic dispute, disgruntled student/trainee, and disgruntled employee categories. The tragic consequences and fatal shootings associated with stalking in these categories can be understood in the context of the extremely high affect levels that occur in conflicted relationships, such as the loss of a spouse or significant other, and the narcissistic injury that often accompanies the loss of a promotion or dismissal from a job. Persons experiencing rejection in a significant relationship or facing unemployment for whatever reason may develop a pathological fixation on the person they blame for the situation (Meloy, 1992). When this occurs, stalking may take place,

TABLE 15
COMPARISON OF WORKPLACE VIOLENCE CATEGORIES

	Disgruntled Employees	Personal/ Domestic	Disgruntled Customers	Mentally Ill	Criminals	Students/ Trainees	Abusive Supervisors
Mean Age	40.15	29.28	34.81	33.55	23.83	21.07	43.44
Sex							
Male	98%	88.68%	95.65%	91.3%	98.32%	92.86%	90.91%
Female	2%	11.32%	4.35%	8.7%	1.68%	7.14%	9.09%
Race							
White	68%	58.49%	56.52%	78.26%	29.41%	78.57%	90.91%
Black	20%	32.08%	21.74%	17.39%	67.23%	14.29%	0.00%
Hispanic	4%	9.43%	17.39%	2.17%	3.36%	7.14%	9.09%
Asian	2%	0.00%	4.35%	0.00%	0.00%	0.00%	0.00%
Weapons Interest	48%	28.3%	47.83%	41.3%	38.66%	35.71%	27.27%
Setting							
Office/Business	12.24%	20.00%	35.00%	10.42%	28.99%	0.00%	10%
Public/Government Facility	34.69%	13.33%	15.00%	25.00%	4.35%	0.00%	40%
Plant/Factory	34.69%	11.11%	0.00%	0.00%	4.35%	0.00%	0%
Medical Facility	6.12%	11.11%	25.00%	29.17%	1.45%	30.77%	40%
School	6.12%	22.22%	0.00%	20.83%	1.45%	69.23%	10%
Restaurant/Bar	6.12%	17.78%	25.00%	10.42%	24.64%	0.00%	0%
Convenience/ Food Store	0.00%	4.44%	0.00%	4.17%	34.78%	0.00%	0%
Warning Signs Present	83.67%	82.22%	65%	83.33%	15.94%	69.23%	90%
Stalking	34.69%	66.67%	15%	12.5%	15.94%	38.46%	40%
Hostage-taking	6.12%	17.78%	5%	12.5%	23.19%	30.77%	0%
Weapons Used							
Handguns	65.12%	65.31%	72.73%	50.00%	80.51%	37.50%	0%
Rifles	2.33%	6.12%	9.09%	14.81%	5.08%	0.00%	0%
Assault Weapons	6.98%	4.08%	9.09%	9.26%	2.54%	0.00%	0%
Knives	9.30%	12.24%	4.55%	1.85%	4.24%	25.00%	0%
Bombs	4.65%	2.04%	4.55%	3.70%	0.00%	12.50%	0%
Physical Force	2.33%	6.12%	0.00%	9.26%	5.93%	25.00%	100%
Number Killed/Incident	1.65	1.11	3.05	2.43	1.07	0.23	0
Number Wounded/Incident	4.06	0.95	2.9	4.10	0.73	0.46	2.3
Diagnostic Group							
Affective Disorders	52%	20.75%	25%	21.74%	0.84%	28.57%	11.11%

continued on following page

	Disgruntled Employees	Personal/ Domestic	Disgruntled Customers	Mentally Ill	Criminals	Students/ Trainees	Abusive Supervisors
TABLE 15, CONTINUED							
COMPARISON OF WORKPLACE VIOLENCE CATEGORIES							
Personality Disorders	26%	37.74%	20%	8.7%	57.14%	21.43%	22.22%
Psychotic Disorders	2%	0.00%	5%	56.52%	0.00%	14.29%	0.00%
Substance Abuse Disorders	2%	28.30%	40%	4.35%	9.24%	0.00%	0.00%
Psychosexual Disorders	2%	0.00%	0%	2.17%	0.84%	0.00%	66.67%
Disorders of Adolescence	0%	1.89%	5%	2.17%	15.97%	21.43%	0.00%
Suicidal Intent Observed	60%	48%	43%	60%	5%	50%	18.18%
Alcohol Use During Incident	28%	58.49%	52.17%	15.22%	19.33%	14.29%	9.09%

accompanied by violent fantasies of retaliation. At some point, the anger connected with the rejection becomes so intense that fantasy no longer provides a sufficient outlet, and violent behavior becomes the only way of dissipating the rage.

Profile of the Workplace Violence Offender

The general characteristics of workplace violence can be summarized as follows:

(1) workplace violence is usually committed by males under the age of 35;

(2) offenders usually act alone;

(3) external threats (outside the workplace) are greater than internal threats (e.g., employees);

(4) service industries are at greater risk than manufacturing industries;

(5) handguns are the weapons of choice in workplace violence, with assault weapons playing only a limited role;

(6) over 89% of offenders have psychiatric diagnoses;

(7) personality disorders comprise the largest diagnostic group;

(8) suicide is less common than previously thought;

(9) alcohol and drug use are relatively uncommon; and

(10) warning signals are apparent in about two-thirds of cases.

While the features outlined above are common to all incidents of workplace violence, considerable variation existed from one occurrence to another. Within the categories of workplace violence, significant differences were found. Thus, in order to fully understand the type of person who engages in these acts, it is necessary to examine the unique features of each type of workplace violence (see Table 15).

Disgruntled Employees

This group consisted of older individuals, with a mean age 40.15 years. Sixty-eight percent were White, and 98% were male. Nearly 50% of this group had served in the military, with 40% of those persons having had combat experience. Forty-eight percent of persons in this category had an excessive interest in weapons.

Disgruntled employees were most likely to commit their crimes in either a plant/factory or public/government facility (34.69% each). Warning signals prior to the attack were observed in 83.67% of cases. Stalking occurred 35% of the time. Hostage-taking was relatively uncommon, occurring in only 6% of incidents. Handguns were the primary weapon of choice (65.12%), followed by knives (9.3%), and assault weapons (6.98%). Injuries or death occurred in 73.46% of cases, with an average of 1.65 persons killed per incident and 4.06 persons wounded per incident.

Eighty-six percent of persons in this group had a psychiatric diagnosis. Affective disorders, usually in the form of depression, were found most commonly (52% of subjects). Personality disorders, most often of the borderline or paranoid type, were the next most frequent diagnostic group (26%). Evidence of suicidal thought or intent was present in 60% of individuals. Alcohol use was found in 30% of persons, while drug abuse was extremely rare (2%).

Personal/Domestic Disputes

The mean age for persons in this group was 29.98 years. Eighty-eight percent of this group were male, and 11.32% were female; this category had the largest number of female offenders. Fifty-eight percent of offenders were White, 32% Black, and 9.4% were Hispanic. A history of military service was found in only 13.21% of the subjects. Twenty-eight percent had an excessive interest in weapons.

Workplace violence associated with a personal/domestic dispute was most likely to occur in schools (22.22%), offices/businesses (20%), restaurants/bars (17.78%), or public/government facilities (13.33%). Clear precipitants and warn-

ing signs were found in 82.22% of cases. The victim was stalked in two-thirds of the cases, the largest percentage found in the study. Hostages were taken in 17.78% of incidents. Handguns were used in 65.31% of cases, followed by knives (12.24%), rifles/shotguns (6.12%), and physical force (6.12%). Injuries or fatalities occurred in 91% of cases. An average of 1.1 persons were killed in each incident, and 0.95 persons wounded per incident.

Slightly over 90% of persons in this group had a psychiatric diagnosis: most common were the personality disorders (37.74%), followed by substance abuse disorders (28.3%), and affective disorders (20.75%). Alcohol use was found in 58% of subjects, representing the largest percentage in the study. Drug use occurred in only 9.4%. Suicidal ideation or attempts occurred in 49% of the subjects.

Criminals

Criminals represented the second youngest group of workplace violence offenders, with a mean age of 23.83. As with other groups, males far outnumbered females (98.32% were male). Unlike other categories, however, Blacks were the most commonly encountered racial group (67.23%). Only 1.68% of the subjects had military service, and none of those individuals had combat experience. Thirty-eight percent of the persons in this category displayed an excessive interest in weapons.

Nearly 85% of people in this group had a psychiatric diagnosis. Personality disorders were most common (57.14%), consisting primarily of antisocial personality disorder. Conduct disorder of adolescence (15.97%) was the next most frequent diagnosis, followed by substance abuse disorders (9.24%). It is interesting to note that less than 1% of this group had evidence of depression. Accordingly, less than 4% of subjects reported suicidal ideation. Alcohol use was found in

19.33% of offenders, and drug use occurred in 13.45%.

As with other categories of workplace violence, handguns were the weapon of choice. The percentage of handgun use (80.51%), however, was higher than for other groups. Stealth and escape may have been primary goals among the criminals as compared to other groups. Injuries or fatalities occurred in 88.41% of incidents, resulting in 1.07 deaths and 0.73 injuries per incident. The most common settings for these crimes were convenience/food stores (34.78%), offices/businesses (28.99%), and restaurants/bars (24.64%). Warning signals were found in only 15.94% of cases; thus, criminal acts appeared to be more random and spontaneous than other forms of workplace violence. Stalking of victims occurred in 16% of cases, and hostage-taking occurred in 23.19%.

Disgruntled Customers/Clients

Persons falling into this category had a mean age of 34.81 years. Ninety-five percent of offenders were male. Whites accounted for 56.52% of the sample, followed by Blacks (21.74%), Hispanics (17.39%), and Asians (4.35%). A history of military service was found in 21.74%, but only 20% of these people had combat experience. An excessive interest in weapons was found in 47.83% of the sample.

Eighty-seven percent of subjects had psychiatric diagnoses, with substance abuse disorders found most frequently (40%). Other common psychiatric problems included affective disorders (25%) and personality disorders (20%). Some form of suicidal preoccupation was present in 43% of the subjects. It is interesting to note that 52.17% of the perpetrators were intoxicated with alcohol at the time of the incident. In contrast, only 8.7% of offenders used drugs at the time of the incident.

These incidents occurred most often in

offices/business (35%), medical facilities (25%), restaurants/bars (25%), or public/government facilities (15%). Handguns were used in 72.73% of cases, followed by rifles/shotguns (9.09%), assault weapons (9.09%), bombs/grenades (4.55%), and knives (4.55%). In two-thirds of these cases, some warning sign was present. Injuries or fatalities occurred in 90% of incidents; 3.05 persons were killed and 2.9 persons were wounded per incident. Stalking occurred in 15% of cases and hostage-taking in 5%.

Mentally Ill

The mean age for persons in the mentally ill group was 33.55 years. Over 91% of person in this group were male. Whites accounted for 78.26% of the sample, Blacks for 17.39%, and Hispanics for 2.17%. A history of military service was found in 23.91% of the subjects, of whom 9.09% had combat experience. Excessive weapons interest was present in 41.3%.

This was the only group in the study in which substantial numbers of psychotic individuals were found (56.52%). Affective disorders were identified in 21.74% of the subjects. Some form of suicidal intent was identified in 63% of the subjects. Alcohol and drugs were used by 15.22% of the offenders.

The most common settings for mentally ill incidents were medical facilities (29.17%), public/government facilities (25%), and schools (20.83%). Warning signals were present in only 16.67% of cases. Weapons used by the mentally ill group were somewhat different than for other categories. Handguns were used in 50% of the incidents. This was followed by rifles/shotguns (14.81%), assault weapons (9.26%), physical force (9.26%), bombs/grenades (3.7%), and motor vehicles (3.7%). Injuries or fatalities occurred in 91.67% of cases, resulting in 2.43 deaths per incident and 4.1 injuries per incident. Stalking occurred in 22.92% of the cases and hostage were taken in 12.5% of cases.

Disgruntled Students/Trainees

This was the youngest group in the sample, as might be expected, with a mean age of 21.07 years. Ninety-two percent of offenders were male. Whites accounted for 78.57% of the sample, followed by Blacks (14.29%), and Hispanics (7.14%). One subject (7.14%) in this category had served in the military, without combat experience. An excessive interest in weapons was found in 35.17% of the sample.

Eighty-six percent of subjects had psychiatric diagnoses, with affective disorders found most frequently (28.57%). Other common psychiatric problems included conduct disorders (21.43%), personality disorders (21.43%), and psychotic disorders (14.29%). Some form of suicidal preoccupation was present in 50% of the subjects. Fourteen percent of the perpetrators were intoxicated with alcohol at the time of the incident, while none of the offenders used drugs.

These incidents occurred exclusively in schools (69.23%) and medical facilities (30.77%). Warning signs were observed in 69.23% of incidents. Handguns had the lowest frequency of use in this category (37.5%). Other weapons used included knives (25%), physical force (25%), and bombs/grenades (12.5%). Injuries or fatalities occurred in 61.54% of incidents. These were the "safest" incidents in terms of injury or loss of life: 0.23 persons were killed per incident and 0.46 persons were wounded per incident. Stalking occurred in 38.46% of cases and hostage-taking in 30.77%.

Abusive Supervisors

This was the oldest group in the study, with a mean age of 43.44 years. Ninety percent were White males. Thirty-six percent of this group had served in the military, with 50% of those persons having combat experience. Twenty-seven percent of persons in this category had an excessive interest in weapons.

Abusive supervisors were most likely to commit their crimes in either a medical facility or public/government facility (40% each). Warning signals prior to the attack were observed in 90% of cases. Stalking occurred 40% of the time. No incidents of hostage-taking were reported. All of these incidents involved the use of physical force, most often in connection with a sexual assault. Injuries occurred in 90% of cases, with an average of 2.3 persons wounded per incident; no deaths resulted from these acts.

Eighty-two percent of persons in this group had a psychiatric diagnosis. In keeping with the frequency of sexual assaults in this group, psychosexual disorders were the most commonly encountered diagnostic group (66.67% of subjects). Personality disorders were the next most frequent (22%). Suicidal thought or intent was rare in this group, occurring in only 18.18% of individuals. Alcohol use was found in one case; no cases of drug use were identified. It is likely that alcohol use was underreported, particularly in light of the high base of alcoholism found in combat veterans.

Implications For Workplace Security

As workplace violence becomes more common, it is likely that forensic psychiatrists and psychologists will be consulted with increasing frequency by business and industry. These consultations may include forensic evaluation of a threatening employee or the profiling of a specific external threat (e.g., a spouse/partner who is stalking or threatening an employee). Selection of forensic consultants should be based on impeccable academic credentials and training, a long professional history of working with violent individuals, and an established record of success in workplace violence intervention. It should be remembered that, in the event of a tragedy and the inevitable civil or criminal litigation that follows, employers will have to justify the basis for selection of their forensic consultants.

Workplace violence consultations should be carried out in conjunction with the company's security consultants and legal counsel. The goal of such collaboration is to protect lives and make the workplace secure without interfering with normal business activities. Threats, both internal and external to the work environment, must be evaluated. Programs aimed at improving employee relations should be instituted. These include stress management, recognition of the impaired employee, effective communication skills between employer and employee, as well as between the business and its customers, and helping both employees and management deal effectively with anger. It is also important that an employee manual be developed which contains, among other things, a clear proscription against threatening statements and behavior, as well as a clearly stated policy banning weapons of any kind from the workplace.

Most importantly, it is imperative that every business have a *crisis management plan* that can be implemented should a violent or threatening incident occur (Feldmann, 1995b). In the past, these strategies have usually been restricted to disaster plans in the event of fire or natural disasters. As the climate of violence increases, however, these plans should be modified to include incidents of workplace violence. Essential components of the crisis management plan (see Table 16) should include designated escape routes for all employees. Code words can be utilized to alert everyone of a potential threat. For those businesses in which employees often work alone in offices or other settings, regular check-in times can be easily established to ensure that all personnel are safe and accounted for. A resource directory should be housed on-site which includes all important telephone numbers, referral sources,

and consultants. Along with this directory, a clearly defined chain of command must be established to guarantee that the proper people are notified in the case of emergency. Crisis situations are always very chaotic; a pre-planned response unit of management and security personnel can help to overcome this tendency.

One common question with respect to planning for workplace violence is, "How do we make adequate preparations without frightening our employees?" Increased employee awareness and training are the best ways to overcome fear. Thus, violence drills and simulations should be incorporated into other safety training programs. This can be accomplished by using scripted scenarios developed by forensic and security consultants. All employees and supervisors should participate, utilizing role-playing techniques. In this manner, the crisis management plan can be practiced until everyone is familiar with his or her assigned duties. Following these exercises, debriefing sessions should be held, during which all of the participants have an opportunity to discuss both cognitive and affective reactions to the exercise. The consultants must assume an active role in this critique process. Through these training activities, workers and managers will become increasingly comfortable with all of the crisis management procedures. These sessions will also help to assure that when an actual crisis occurs, the management and response plan is carried out rather than ignored.

Didactic in-service programs and small-group discussions with security and forensic consultants will also serve to increase employee awareness and decrease fear. Such programs ultimately reassure employees that management has taken adequate steps to insure their safety. Essential components of these training sessions include: (1) recognition of the factors that contribute to workplace violence; (2) the assessment of threatening situations; (3) stress management techniques; (4) the warning signals of impending violence; and

---

TABLE 16

COMPONENTS OF THE WORKPLACE CRISIS MANAGEMENT PLAN

1. Designated escape routes for all employees

2. Utilization of code words to alert personnel of a threatening situation

3. Regular check-in times for employees/supervisors who work alone or in isolated areas

4. Development of a resource directory, which is housed on-site, containing all important telephone numbers, referral sources, consultants, and emergency procedures

5. Implementation of a clearly defined chain of command to ensure that the proper people are notified in the case of emergency

6. Pre-planned response units of management and security personnel

7. Violence drills and simulations incorporated into all safety training programs; included are in-service programs with security and forensic consultants designed to both increase employee awareness and decrease fear

---

(5) interventions to defuse hostile or threatening situations (Feldmann, 1995b).

A variety of factors may lead to workplace violence. Familiarity with these will assist both supervisors and employees in gaining a better understanding of the dynamics that lead to workplace violence. Common factors which should be stressed during training sessions include: (1) interpersonal conflicts; (2) harsh or extreme demands; (3) communication problems; (4) lack of input into decision-making processes; (5) repetitive tasks and boredom; (6) unresolved grievances; (7) feelings of helplessness; (8) ambiguous expectations; (9) family/marital dysfunction; (10) drug and alcohol abuse; and (11) emotional disturbances.

It should be emphasized that when stress occurs over a prolonged period of time, the threshold for frustration, anger, and eventually violence, is significantly lowered. Thus, stress management programs are extremely important in the prevention and early intervention of violence.

The recognition of impending violence is stressed extensively in psychiatric settings (Hall, 1987). Government agencies, businesses, and industrial facilities, however, rarely address this issue. Training sessions must examine the personal and situational factors which contribute to violence. These factors include: (1) statements about violence and previous violent behavior; (2) history of mental illness and drug/alcohol abuse; (3) legal history, with special attention to violent crimes; (4) socioeconomic status and employment stability; (5) the degree of social approval of violent behavior in the person's culture and family environment; (6) availability of weapons; (7) current mental status; (8) fantasies about aggressive behavior; (9) delusions, especially of a paranoid, grandiose, or aggressive nature; (10) auditory hallucinations, especially of a command type; (11) on-going stressors in other areas of the person's life; (12) the degree of acknowledged personal responsibility for creation of the conflict situation; (13) ability to discuss or develop strategies for the resolution of the conflict; and (14) the degree of appreciation for the consequences of verbalized threats and aggressive fantasies.

Interventions to prevent or deal with workplace violence may occur on many different levels. Good relations with employees and customers provide a solid foundation for dealing with conflicts. Stress management programs are useful in defusing potential disputes and improving employee morale. Employee assistance programs are of benefit in the recognition and management of impaired employees. These programs should also be made available to spouses/partners of employees in order to reduce the potential of domestic violence being brought into the workplace. Training in effective communication skills and the management of anger are also of benefit.

Signals of potential risk for violence from employees or customers include: (1) verbal abuse and threats to employees or supervisors; (2) physical assaults on employees, co-workers, or supervisors; (3) abuse of alcohol/drugs while working; (4) angry complaints of unfair working conditions or treatment; (5) uncharacteristic absenteeism or tardiness; (6) decreased work performance; (7) odd, peculiar, or bizarre behavior; (8) radical change in personal appearance; (9) withdrawal from friends and family; (10) rumors of rage and planned retaliation; (11) destruction of property in the workplace; and (12) stalking.

Obviously, some acts of violence cannot be avoided because they are conceived, planned, and implemented in secrecy. Often, however, indicators of impending violence may be identified before violence actually occurs. This study found that two-thirds of workplace violence was preceded by such warning signals. When these signals are identified, the company and its consultants must be prepared to take positive action.

Data on these warning signals may be gathered from supervisors, co-workers, union stewards, family members, and personnel files. Once sufficient information has been collected regarding an individual's psychological stability or potential for violence, active intervention is warranted.

When a potential threat is identified, the business or agency must work closely with forensic mental health consultants and risk management professionals within the company to thoroughly assess the situation. All sources of potentially helpful information must be explored. These include direct discussion with the threatening or violent individual. A comprehensive psychiatric evaluation is mandatory, if the person consents. Contact with collateral sources of information are also invaluable. Discussion with these individuals will not only reveal much personal information

about the patient, but will also activate the individual's support system, thus diffusing his or her destructive potential.

Intervention with the potentially violent individual may occur in either a *subtle* or *confrontational* manner (Feldmann, 1995b). The goal in either approach is to alleviate the threat. In the subtle approach, the individual is engaged directly and his or her assistance is sought in resolving the situation. A thorough discussion may resolve the situation, and will provide valuable clinical data. The goal of these discussions is to defuse the conflict, assess personality structure, and gain insight into the propensity for violence.

The confrontational approach is resorted to when discussion and negotiation have failed and the situation escalates. Disciplinary actions, a leave of absence, dismissal, the filing of criminal charges, or initiation of civil commitment proceedings should be carefully reviewed with the company's legal counsel.

In general, a subtle approach is usually preferable to confrontation because it attempts to open a dialogue between the parties involved. Such discussions allow for the ventilation of frustration and narcissistic rage. Empathic acknowledgment of the person's complaints, even if not objectively justified, lays the foundation for eventual compromise. Such an approach is most useful in dealing with individuals over time. A more confrontational approach through the criminal or civil justice systems may thwart a tragedy, but may also further polarize and isolate the violent individual. Thus, long-term management is not enhanced and, in fact, may be eroded.

In dealing with potentially violent people, the following guidelines should be observed:
(1) The most important initial consideration is to remain calm if at all possible;
(2) Potentially violent individuals may have difficulty controlling their feelings/behavior, or may use the threat of violence as a tool to obtain their goal;

(3) Uncontrolled demonstrations of anxiety may antagonize either of these dynamics;

(4) It is imperative to do nothing that might threaten or provoke a potentially violent person;

(5) Behavior construed as threatening or demeaning will complicate any attempted resolution, and may elicit overt aggression;

(6) The goal should always be to defuse a potentially violent situation by an empathic and non-threatening approach;

(7) An employer may be firm in his or her position and still exhibit these qualities. A "tough" approach is not likely to de-escalate a potentially violent situation, and in fact is more likely to bring it about;

(8) Always treat the threatening person with respect and dignity, even if it is not your natural inclination in the situation;

(9) Acknowledge that you understand their frustration and anger, and express the hope that by working together the situation can be resolved;

(10) Attempt to enlist his or her input on how the situation can be remedied;

(11) Let the individual know that his or her concerns have been heard; and

(12) Express your concerns about the situation, but do not be artificial or contrived. The projection of a cold, unfeeling view of the situation will only inflame the rage.

The presence of a crisis management plan and adequate employee training in all of these areas will lessen the risk of liability on the part of the employer if a violent incident does occur (See Table 16).

Summary

Incidents of workplace violence are becoming more frequent and more lethal. They tend to attract intense media coverage which may result in a contagion effect. The cost of workplace violence to both business and society is enormous. Lost wages, hours, and productivity represent only the superficial impact of a workplace violence incident. Extreme emotional trauma also accompanies these acts for surviving victims, witnesses, and families. Civil litigation is another likely outcome of such incidents. It is imperative, therefore, to better understand the origins of workplace violence and to improve identification of the at-risk individual. A more thorough understanding of these incidents also allows for improved interventions to prevent violence and better crisis management when an incident occurs. It is hoped that the research findings presented here can be translated into useful proactive techniques to make the workplace environment safer and more productive.

Suggested Reading

Feldmann, T. B. & Johnson, P. W. (1993). Hostage situations and the mental health professional. In P. Blumenreich & S. Lewis (Eds.), *Management of the Violent Patient: A Clinician's Guide*. New York: Brunner/Mazel.

Hall, H. V. (1987). *Violence Prediction: Guidelines for the Forensic Practitioner*. Springfield, IL: Charles C Thomas.

Meloy, J. R (1992). *Violent Attachments*. Northvale, NJ: Jason Aronson.

National Safe Workplace Institute. (1993). *Breaking Point: The Workplace Violence Epidemic and What to Do About It*. Washington, DC: Author.

White, S. & Hatcher, C. (1988). Violence and trauma response. In *Occupational Medicine: State of the Art Reviews*, Vol. 4. Philadelphia: Handley and Belfus.

References

American Psychiatric Association. (1994). *Diagnostic and Statistical Manual of Mental Disorders*, Fourth Edition. Washington, DC: Author.

Bureau of Labor Statistics. (1993). Washington, DC: U.S. Department of Labor.

Depue, R. L. (1993). *Violence in America: In our communities and in our workplaces.* Paper presented at the FBI National Academy Conference, Birmingham, AL.

Duncan, T. S. (1995). Death in the office: Workplace homicides. *FBI Law Enforcement Bulletin, 64*(4), 20-25.

Federal Bureau of Investigation (1993). *Response and Management of Critical Incidents.* Special Operations and Research Unit. FBI Academy. Quantico, VA.

Feldmann, T. B. (1995a). *Workplace violence: An examination of 240 incidents.* Paper presented at the annual meeting of the American College of Forensic Psychiatry, San Francisco.

Feldmann, T. B. (1995b). Workplace violence: Origins and interventions. *Clinical Advances in the Treatment of Psychiatric Disorders, 9*(1), 6-12.

Feldmann, T. B. & Johnson, P. W. (1993). Hostage situations and the mental health professional. In P. Blumenreich & S. Lewis (Eds.), *Management of the violent patient: A clinician's guide.* New York: Brunner/Mazel.

Fox, J. A. & Levin, J. (1993, November 30). Firing back: The growing threat of workplace homicide. *The Annals of the American Academy of Political and Social Sciences.*

Fuselier, G. D. (1981). A practical overview of hostage negotiations. *FBI Law Enforcement Bulletin, 50*(6), 2-11.

Hall, H. V. (1987). *Violence prediction: Guidelines for the forensic practitioner.* Springfield, IL: Charles C Thomas.

Kohut, H. (1978). Thoughts on narcissism and narcissistic rage. In P. Ornstein (Ed.), *The search for the self*, Vol. 2. New York: International Universities Press.

Law Firm of Littler, Mendelson, Fastiff, Tichy, & Mathiason. (1994). *Terror and violence in the workplace.* San Francisco: Author.

Meloy, J. R. (1988). *The psychopathic mind: Origins, dynamics, and treatment.* Northvale, NJ: Jason Aronson, Inc.

Meloy, J. R (1992). *Violent attachments.* Northvale, NJ: Jason Aronson, Inc.

National Institute for Occupational Safety and Health (1992). *Report on traumatic occupational fatalities.* Washington, DC: U.S. Department of Health and Human Services.

National Safe Workplace Institute (1993). *Breaking point: The workplace violence epidemic and what to do about it.* Washington, DC: Author.

Northwestern National Life Insurance Company (1993). *Fear and violence in the workplace.* Minneapolis, MN: Author.

Revitch, E. & Schlesinger, L. (1978). Murder: Evaluation, classification, and prediction. In I. Kutash, S. Kutash, and L. Schlesinger (Eds.), *Violence: Perspectives on murder and aggression.* San Francisco: Jossey-Bass.

White, S. & Hatcher, C. (1988). Violence and trauma response. In *Occupational medicine: State of the art reviews*, Vol. 4. Philadelphia: Handley and Belfus.

Workers who fight firing with fire (1994, April 25). *Time Magazine, 144*, pp. 35-37.

About the Authors

Theodore B. Feldmann, MD, is an Associate Professor in the Department of Psychiatry and Behavioral Sciences at the University of Louisville School of Medicine. He has several clinical positions at local hospitals and clinics and is in private practice in psychotherapy and forensic psychiatry in Louisville, Kentucky. He has been board certified in psychiatry since 1986. He has numerous publications in clinical and forensic psychiatry.

Robert W. Johnson, PhD, is an Assistant Clinical Professor in the Department of Psychiatry and Behavioral Sciences at the University of Louisville School of Medicine. He is also in private practice in clinical forensic psychology. His interest areas include terrorism, aircraft hijackings, hostage negotiation, and violence in the workplace. He is a Diplomate in Forensic Psychology from the American Board of Professional Psychology.

CHAPTER 12

VIOLENCE AND THE SEXUAL PARAPHILIAS

Judith Boczkowski Chapman

Homicides linked to deviant sexual acts make for good copy. Although horrified and disgusted, ordinary Americans were drawn in large numbers to watch a television reenactment of Ted Bundy's spree of sex-related murders and were eager to buy up magazines which offered psychological profiles of the late Jeffrey Dahmer. Unlike the commonplace crimes of nonsexual assault or gun-related murders, these incidents seemed so aberrant in nature that the population could comfortably peruse the details of such heinous acts without a concomitant sense of heightened anxiety. The crimes seemed too rare, too incredulous, to present much threat to the average citizen. In fact, the majority of mental health professionals never encounter a violence-prone paraphiliac in their practices.

Paraphilia, as defined by the most recent edition of the Diagnostic and Statistical Manual for Mental Disorders, Fourth Edition (American Psychiatric Association, 1994, DSM-IV), refers to recurrent sexually arousing fantasies, urges, or behavior that involve either (a) nonconsenting partners or children, (b) objects or animals, or (c) the suffering or humiliation of oneself or another. Paraphilias are distinguished from nonpathological fantasies and behavior by the distress they cause the individual or the level of functional impairment that results. Unlike the sexual dysfunctions which identify problems related to erot-

ic desire or the sexual response cycle, the paraphilias refer specifically to deviant sexual arousal. These disorders are rarely diagnosed in women.

Only eight categories of paraphilias are given diagnostic codes in the DSM-IV (See Table 1). These disorders have been specified because of their relative frequency of occurrence. Many of the less commonly reported paraphilias are described in detail in other sources (Krafft-Ebing, 1886/1965; Levine, Risen, & Althof, 1990; Tollison & Adams, 1979) and can be diagnosed using the DSM-IV label "not otherwise specified" (NOS). Even within the identified categories of paraphilias, many subtypes exist and disagreement occurs between researchers as to how the focus of a paraphilia should be grouped. For example, De Silva (1993) asserted that fetishism should include attraction to specific textures, items of clothing, or body parts (partialism), while the DSM-IV limits fetishism to nonliving objects, excluding partialism from this category.

Another controversial classification is that of rape. Bradford, Boulet, and Pawlak (1992) reported that while the diagnosis of "coercive paraphilic disorder" was seriously considered as a separate disorder for the last DSM revision, it did not appear in DSM-IV. This seems, at least in part, to reflect the various theories of motivation for the act of rape. Currently, the act of coercing a nonconsenting partner to engage in sexual

---

TABLE 1

SPECIFIC PARAPHILIAS AS LISTED IN DSM-IV

Diagnostic Category	Sexual Focus
Exhibitionism	Exposure of genitals to unsuspecting other
Fetishism	Use of inanimate objects
Frotteurism	Touching/rubbing nonconsenting partner
Pedophilia	Victim 13 years old or younger
Sexual Masochism	Humiliation or suffering of self
Sexual Sadism	Humiliation or suffering of others
Transvestic Fetishism	Cross-dressing
Voyeurism	Observing naked, disrobing other or sex act
Not Otherwise Specified	Paraphilias not listed above
Overcompensation	Covering up feelings of inadequacy by methodically arranging for murder for hire

---

activity may fall under a specified paraphilia, such as sadism or pedophilia, or it may not be considered a paraphilia at all. The choice of diagnosis is based on whether or not the rapist is driven primarily by sexual urges and to which victim characteristics he is responding. Others have suggested that rape would be inappropriately categorized as a paraphilia because it occurs infrequently in combination with other commonly reported paraphilias and consequently, may have a different developmental course (Abel & Osborn, 1992).

Epidemiology

Paraphiliacs rarely seek treatment for their disorders and the incidence of such pathology in the general population has been difficult to ascertain with any degree of confidence. When found in mental health settings, these individuals have typically come in at the urging of a distressed significant other or in response to a recent arrest. In an effort to avoid social ostracism or the law, paraphiliacs generally attempt to shroud their predilections in secrecy. For these reasons, even persons seeking treatment or convicted of sexual offenses are likely to minimize past misdeeds.

Data from various sources suggest that guarantees of confidentiality may be of some benefit in obtaining a more accurate estimate of the incidence and frequency of sexual acts. Self-reports of convicted pedophiles when interviewed in the parole office by a parole officer and in a Sexual Behavior Clinic by a psychologist were compared (Kaplan, Abel, Cunningham-Rathner, & Mittleman, 1990). In the clinic setting, where perceived confidentiality was greater, these offenders admitted to a mean number of molestations which was 28 times greater than the number of molestations reported in the parole office. Abel et al. (1987) reported on data gathered from 561 paraphiliac subjects who were recruited through sexual disorder treatment programs in which confidentiality was assured. Because many of the subjects had multiple paraphilic diagnoses, a total of 1,170 paraphilias were diagnosed in this group. Of these, approximately 19% were pedophiles targeting girls outside the home, 13% targeted boys outside the home, 13.4% targeted girls within the home, and 3.7% targeted boys within the home. Many engaged in more than one type of pedophilic activity. Other represented paraphilias included exhibitionists (12.1%), voyeurs (5.2%), frotteurs (5.2%), transvestites (2.6%), sadists (2.4%), fetishists (2%), and masochists (1%).

To fully understand the epidemiology of paraphilias, these authors also examined the striking differences in frequency of the paraphilic act reported by individuals representing each type of disorder. There, of course, can be great variation in the number of acts committed by persons with the same diagnosis. This may reflect individual differences as well as opportunity. However, Abel et al. (1987) suggested that certain types of paraphiliacs are more likely to commit a greater frequency of sexual acts than other types. This difference appears unrelated to risk. For example, transvestites, who presumably could engage in cross-dressing in relative privacy, reported engaging in paraphiliac acts at half the median frequency of exhibitionists.

Abel et al. (1987) subdivided data gathered from pedophiles, the most commonly reported paraphiliacs, by gender of victim and whether or not the act occurred within the family (i.e., incest). The median number of paraphiliac acts for this category included 1.4 for non-incest female victims, 10.1 for non-incest male victims, 4.4 for female incest victims, and 5.2 for male incest victims. These data, contrary to expected findings (Marshall, Barbaree, & Butt, 1988), certainly suggest that boys are at greater risk for victimization by a pedophile than are girls. Although more pedophiles report molestation of girls, those molesting boys apparently engage in this activity at a much higher frequency. Further, it appears that exhibitionism and public masturbation are the paraphilic acts performed with the greatest frequency (approximately 50 median acts per offender), while sadistic acts (3.0) and rape (0.9) occur relatively infrequently. Undoubtedly, one is far more likely to be the victim of a crime of exhibitionism than of sexual assault.

Most researchers working in sex offender treatment programs suggest that self-report data on paraphilic behavior likely underrepresent the actual occurrence of deviant acts. Accurate estimates of this pathology are further complicated by the reluctance of victims to come forward with their experiences. Russell's (1984) random sample of San Francisco households suggested that only 2% of incest victims and 6% of non-incest paraphiliac victims ever reported the abuse. Others have contended that only about half of all rapes are ever reported (Dormanen, 1980). With both victim's and perpetrator's disinclination to disclose, base rates of paraphilic acts have remained rather speculative.

Cross Diagnoses and Paraphilic Behavior

It was not until the DSM-III (American Psychiatric Association, Third Edition, 1980) that paraphilias were first recognized as a major classification of psychosexual disorders with distinct operational definitions for each category. Previously, sexually deviant behavior was subsumed under the personality disorders. This was based on assumptions that paraphilias developed prior to adulthood, persisted throughout life, and were frequently not associated with feelings of guilt or anxiety (Adams & Chiodo, 1984). The DSM-III was believed to offer an improvement over previous classifications because it limited the characteristics of paraphilias to an individual's sexual behavior rather than presuming a relationship between personality factors and deviant acts.

With the advent of the new nosology, paraphiliacs came to be regarded as individuals who responded to only a narrowly defined range of sexual stimuli, compulsively sought out these stimuli, and were generally unable to experience arousal in other situations. Although DSM-III acknowledged that multiple paraphilias could occur, there was no presumption that multiple paraphilias were more likely to be found than isolated paraphilias. Some continued to assert that multiple diagnoses were indeed rare (Money, 1984).

This perspective is illustrated in an earlier textbook on sexual disorders (Tollison & Adams, 1979) as the authors discussed the dilemma of diagnosing a paraphiliac who entered a home for voyeuristic observation and later committed a rape. They debated whether such an individual should be considered a voyeur who attempted rape secondary to his voyeuristic arousal or a rapist who peeped prior to physical assault. In current clinical practice, paraphilias are less likely to be viewed as mutually exclusive. Since DSM-III-R (American Psychiatric Association, 1987), multiple coexisting paraphilic disorders are regarded as a more probable occurrence.

In a study by Bradford et al. (1992) adult males who had been admitted to a Sexual Behaviours Clinic for forensic psychiatric assessment were questioned regarding their history of sexually deviant behavior. Despite the fact that no absolute safeguards were offered for confidentiality, the paraphiliacs admitted to multiple sexual aberrations. Among the exhibitionists, for example, 20% admitted to heterosexual pedophilia (defined by the authors as a preference for prepubertal victim), 20% to heterosexual hebephilia (preference for victims between 12 and 16 years of age), 10% to homosexual pedophilia, 8% to homosexual hebephilia, 21% to obscene phone calling, 30% to frotteurism, 13% to attempted rape, and 6% to committed rape.

Abel and Osborn (1992) reported similar findings, although they also obtained data on many additional categories of deviant behavior. They concluded that most paraphiliacs did have a secondary paraphilic diagnosis, with sadism being the diagnosis most likely to extend into other paraphilias. It is because of this commonly observed crossing-over phenomena that the authors proposed that inadequate behavioral control, rather than specific learning experience, may be a more likely explanation for the development of paraphilias. Consideration of personality variables, such as impulsivity, as an etiological factor seems oddly reminiscent of earlier views of paraphilia as a type of character pathology.

Paraphilias and Lethality

Most paraphilic acts involve a victim. These behaviors, however, can run the gamut from nuisance crimes (such as voyeurism, exhibitionism) to those with potentially deadly outcomes (e.g., sadism, masochism). Sexual homicides can be the outcome of a well-rehearsed murder fantasy or may occur spontaneously when a victim responds in an unexpected manner, a sex offender is in danger of being found out, or a paraphilic act gets out of control.

Various sources have described the range of sexual activities associated with harmful or lethal outcomes (Eckert, Katchis, & Donovan, 1991; Hucker & Stermac, 1992; Rosman & Resnick, 1989). Table 2 offers a list of criminal activities and other documented high risk sexual behaviors. Not all activities described in Table 2 necessarily imply the presence of a paraphilia. In many cases, sociopathy alone can account for the perpetrator's behavior. Certain clearly harmful paraphiliac activities, such as pedophilia, are not listed in Table 2 because they are not typically associated with a lethal outcome. It is when sadistic activities cross over into pedophilia that they become potentially life threatening.

Sexual homicides generally refer to murders which occurred during the commission of a sexual offense (Roberts & Grossman, 1993). As with paraphilias, accurate statistics have been difficult to ascertain. To a large extent, this seems to be a matter of varying definitions as to what constitutes a sexual offense. It has further been suggested that current data are misleading because of inadequate dissemination of findings among investigative agencies, the occasional lack of conventional evidence of a crime's sexual nature, and a failure of investigators to recognize the sexual dynamics leading to seemingly nonsexual homicides (Burgess, Hartman, Ressler, Douglas, & McCormack, 1986). Even when evidence found at the crime scene obviously indicates a sexual act, it may be impossible for the investigators to determine the motive behind the killer's behavior (i.e., driven by paraphilic motive versus antisocial

<table>
<tr><td colspan="2">TABLE 2
LETHAL AND POTENTIALLY LETHAL SEXUAL PRACTICES</td></tr>
<tr><td>Sexual Activity</td><td>Postmortem Activity</td></tr>
<tr><td>Asphyxia/Ligature Use
Foreign Objects for Anal/Vaginal Penetration
Flagellation (Whipping)
Necrophilic Homicide
Fisting
Piquism
Rape
Bondage
Necrophilic Homicide</td><td>Necrophilia
Mutilation
Preserving Body Parts
Necrophagia (Consuming flesh)
Vampirism (Drinking Blood)</td></tr>
</table>

stimulus seeking).

Although descriptions may vary, it is clear that the incidence of sexually related crimes remains quite low. Federal Bureau of Investigation (1989) data indicate that just 1% of all U.S. homicides involves sexual offenses. Sex crimes also accounted for only about 1% of all arrests. Roberts and Grossman (1993) reported that only 4% of all Canadian homicides occurring between 1974 and 1986 had been classified as sexual homicides and that the annual percentage remained relatively stable over the period examined. Further, when describing the number of Canadian sexual homicides as a percentage of the reported number of Canadian sexual assaults, the resulting figure was less than 1%.

Despite the many problems with the lack of a reliable data base, it appears that the commission of violent paraphilic acts remains a relatively rare phenomena. The next section will describe in greater detail three categories of paraphilic behavior that could potentially result in lethal violence. These include the range of sadistic, masochistic, and necrophilic acts. Brief case examples from the author's clinical practice are included. In reviewing these paraphilias, the reader is urged to keep in mind paraphilic cross diagnosis. Even individuals presenting with a primary paraphilia that has minimal risk for violent behavior should be assessed thoroughly for possible multiple diagnosis of a more dangerous nature.

Sadism

Violence is the cornerstone of sexual sadism. The focus of the paraphilia is sexual arousal from observing the psychological or physical suffering of another. The mildest form of this disorder may involve only fantasies of sadistic behavior which never evolve into a behavioral enactment. Sadism may also involve milder forms of abuse, such as paddling or restraint, frequently with a consenting partner. Inclusion of a masochistic partner may allow for greater experimentation in the range of violent behavior. Hazelwood, Warren, and Dietz (1993) have suggested that some partners of violent sexual sadists repeatedly consent to be victimized, but unlike masochists, seem to derive no sexual pleasure from the activities. They have proposed that a combination of victim personality variables and sadist manipulation leads to the development of a highly dependent relationship quite similar to "battered woman syndrome."

Other sadists require a nonconsenting partner in order to feel arousal from complete dominance and control over another's suffering. Certainly, when arousal to suffering is combined with indifference to the consequences of sadistic pursuits (as in antisocial personality), the paraphilic acts become increasingly dangerous.

Fedora et al. (1992) compared the penile circumference responses of "sexual aggressive offenders," "sexual nonaggressive offenders," and normal controls when presented with a battery of deviant and non-deviant sexual stimuli. The sexual aggressive group had a significantly greater penile response to sadistic slides than did the other groups. However, penile circumference responses did not correlate with the extent of physical harm inflicted. That is, it did not appear to be a good predictor of dangerousness. Interestingly, 5% of the control subjects demonstrated a significant penile response for sadism.

Sadistic fantasies are actually believed to be quite common (Haeberle, 1978). Several studies point to the powerful impact fantasies can have on sexual arousal and behavior. Dekker, Everaerd, and Verhelst (1985) found that individuals can learn voluntary control of sexual arousal through the use of daydreams and masturbation fantasies. Arousal can be enhanced by one's capacity for vivid imagery and there is no evidence that habituation occurs in either physical or psychological responding to a stimulating erotic fantasy repeated over time (Smith & Over, 1987). Although fantasies are not necessarily precursors to sadistic behavior, individuals who have engaged in sadistic criminal activity in all probability began with a recurrent sadistic fantasy (MacCulloch, Snowden, Wood, & Mills, 1983). In a study of 36 men convicted of sexual homicides, 82% of the subjects reported engaging in daydreaming and compulsive masturbation as children and 81% reported these behaviors as adults (Burgess et al., 1986). Characteristically, their daydreams took on aggressive and sexualized themes. These often socially isolated men reportedly slipped quickly into vengeful fantasies when frustrated or offended, as a means of gaining control over situations.

Etiology. Sadistic behavior typically begins in early adulthood and may occur as a secondary paraphilia (Abel & Osborn, 1992). Frequently, such men come from troubled home environments in which parents may have been largely unavailable to them because of their own difficulties with substance abuse, psychiatric disorders, or aggressive behavior (Burgess et al., 1986; Langevin et al., 1988). Some were abused by their poorly functioning parents. Fisher and Howells (1993) have suggested that a repetitive pattern of early victimization can lead to certain expectations regarding relationships. One such cognitive scheme can be illustrated by the following case:

A 29-year-old former high school wrestling champion had sought an evaluation for homosexual pedophilia at the advice of his lawyer. He revealed during the assessment that he had usually threatened to strangle his victims as a way of keeping them quiet. Eventually, he came to realize that his arousal was enhanced by observing intimidation and fear in the faces of the boys. In recounting his own history of sexual abuse, he reported having been molested several times as a child by an older cousin and two uncles. The patient rationalized his own paraphilic behavior in disclosing his world view that men could be dichotomized into "those that take" and "those that get taken." He believed that he had languished in the latter group as a child, but indicated that as he grew in height and physical strength he began to realize that he could "do some taking of my own."

Marshall (1993) observed that the failure to develop close parental bonds in childhood was often later associated with feelings of poor self-esteem and underdeveloped social skills. Certainly, these qualities can limit the facility with which individuals form close friendships and relationships. Consequently, those who commit severe sadistic acts often report significant social isolation and feelings of intense loneliness.

Biological differences have also been proposed to account for the behavior of sexually aggressive individuals. Although Langevin et al.

(1988) were unable to consistently find differences on endocrine measures, subtle differences in the anatomical structure of the temporal lobes were noted. A statistically significant percentage of sexual sadists were observed to have a right temporal horn dilatation when compared with non-sadistic sexual offenders and control subjects. Although only 41% of the 22 sadists examined showed this abnormality, the authors suggested that this may represent a certain subtype of sex offender who may be more prone toward severe violence or recidivism.

Behavioral Facilitation. Several triggers for sadistic acts have been proposed. Malamuth and Spinner (1980) have suggested that exposure to pornographic materials, particularly those depicting violent acts, may have disinhibitive and modeling effects on certain males. Substance abuse is frequently associated with the commission of sexual offenses. However, Hucker and Stermac (1992) observed that intoxicant use is high among most criminal offenders and research has not consistently demonstrated greater use among sexually aggressive offenders.

Men with a history of sadistic fantasies or acts may be more likely to engage in such behavior or intensify the severity of the act when experiencing periods of stress (Adams & Chiodo, 1984). As suggested earlier, a stressor may likely be in the form of a negative interpersonal experience. This is not to suggest that most sadistic acts are performed impulsively in response to a stressor. Dietz, Hazelwood, and Warren (1990) reviewed descriptive data from 30 sexually sadistic criminals studied by the National Center for the Analysis of Violent Crime. In 93% of cases, the sadistic offenses had been carefully, often elaborately, planned in advance. Social withdrawal, intoxication, and compulsive masturbation with the use of violent imagery or erotic materials may all occur prior to the commission of a sadistic act.

The Act. Deaths resulting from sadistic acts are rare and can be accidental. Lethal asphyxia, although not usually the aim of such behavior, can occur as the result of ligature compression of the carotids during sexual acts. Dietz et al. (1990) reported that a majority of sadistic murderers in their study asphyxiated their victims. However, the authors noted that most murderers made an effort to keep their victims conscious for as long as possible, even resuscitating them if necessary, in order to prolong their suffering. Unexpected asphyxia can also occur during some methods of bondage (asphyxia as a paraphilic focus is discussed further in the section on Masochism). When the victim is a child or elderly person, forceful rapes or beatings can lead to varying degrees of injuries and death. Similarly, the use of foreign objects for penetration, such as rods or bottles, can cause serious injuries to internal organs.

Some sadistic acts involve preparation on the part of the partner in order to avoid great harm. Eckert et al. (1991) described the practice of *fisting* as the forceful thrusting of one's fist high up into the descending colon of another. Deaths have occurred when this act is performed on an unprepared or nonconsenting partner. For a partner who has relaxed the anal sphincter with dilatation, lubrication, use of muscle relaxants, or local anesthetics, such behavior may have less dangerous consequences. Deaths from hemorrhaging have also occurred in response to vaginal fistings.

Piquerism (or *piquism*) as described by Wilber (1985) involves sexual arousal in response to cutting, slashing, or stabbing. He suggested that milder forms of this behavior pattern may begin with the mutilations of photographs of people, progress to the cutting and slashing of undergarments, later evolving into the mutilation of a victim. Some reports have described the carving of words or patterns (e.g., tic-tac-toe, satanic symbols) into the bodies of victims (Eckert et al., 1991).

Research on behavior patterns of sadistic criminals suggests that most use some kind of ruse to con their victim into initially cooperating with or assisting the offender (Dietz et al., 1990). Victims are usually bound, gagged, or blind-folded during the sexual act and many offenders keep their victims captive for extended periods of time. Victims' reports or taped recordings of the event have shown that offenders tend to maintain a cool, detached affect during the sadistic activity.

Other researchers have suggested that sexual murderers can usually be characterized by either an organized or disorganized behavior pattern (Ressler, Burgess, Douglas, Hartman, & D'Agostino, 1986). In their study of convicted sexual murderers, the organized killer was described as (a) higher functioning, (b) planful, (c) likely to identify a precipitating stressor prior to the murder, and (d) likely to be emotionally distressed at the time of the murder. Such men are more likely to use restraints and commit sex acts with the living victim. This pattern is more characteristic of the sexual sadist. The disorganized murderer, by contrast, is likely to (a) come from a less stable home, (b) report sexual aversions or inhibitions, (c) experience fear or confusion at the time of the crime, and (d) know his victim. The disorganized killer may be more likely to position a body at the murder, keep the body, or engage in sexual acts with the corpse.

The infliction of pain and the pleading of a terrified victim have been associated with a substantial decrease in the reported sexual tension of a sadist even when no genital stimulation occurs. Orgasm is not necessary for sexual gratification and semen is frequently absent from such crime scenes (Baik & Uku, 1988; Wilber, 1985). Dietz et al. (1990) reported that sadistic criminals frequently seek to acquire a "souvenir" of their crime. A majority of the offenders they studied kept detailed written descriptions of the offense or made audiotape or videotape recordings. Similarly, many kept personal items of their victims. Any of these objects could be used as a stimulus for later arousal, facilitating a vivid re-experiencing of the sadistic event.

Masochism

In sexual masochism, the paraphiliacs are the victims of their own sexual urges. Arousal occurs in response to fantasies or acts of being humiliated or physically abused. Like sadism, sexual arousal may be limited to masochistic fantasies which never culminate in related acts. Occasionally, masochistic acts involve being forced to engage in demeaning behavior that does not necessarily involve physical harm (e.g., crawling, begging, being urinated upon). When a partner is involved, the fantasy accompanying the act is that of being completely overwhelmed and rendered helpless by a more powerful, often ruthless, other. Arousal may occur to both physical pain as well as the perception of being dominated by another. For almost all sadistic acts previously described, there are willing masochistic partners. The goal of masochism, however, is sexual gratification, not annihilation. In the absence of other coexisting psychopathology, the masochist does not desire to be killed during the sexual act. Nevertheless, this outcome may, in fact, occur.

Quite often, the masochist will prefer to engage in risky sexual activity without a partner. Such acts have included shocking, self-mutilation, the use of machinery for stimulation, and autoerotic asphyxia. When equipment malfunctions or others fail to appear as planned, serious injuries or deaths have occurred (O'Halloran & Dietz, 1993).

Sexual masochism is the paraphilia most likely to be diagnosed in females. Men, however, still outnumber women in this category at a ratio of 20:1 (American Psychiatric Association, 1994).

Etiology. Masochism closely parallels sadism in its age of onset (Abel & Osborn, 1992) and presumed course of development. Much of the theory for etiological factors related to this disorder comes from the psychoanalytic literature. An abusive or emotionally distant parent may be the model for future significant relationships. Unlike the sadist, who becomes increasingly aggressive to cope with victimization or negligence, the masochist opts to embrace the pain. Bach (1991) suggested that a masochist tends to idealize the parent and take responsibility for the parent's psychiatric problems or aggressive behavior. In the role of victim, the masochist can "be there" for an abusive or sexually disordered parent who needs a tension release. Self-injurious behavior, such as hair-pulling, head-banging, or eating disorders, may also occur in childhood (Novick & Novick, 1988). Although not essential to the diagnosis, some have suggested that masochistic drives are not limited to an erotic focus, but also pervade the self-concept (Levine et al., 1990). Dependent or puerile behavior can be part of that concept as in this example:

A 57-year-old man was referred by his urologist for an evaluation of erectile dysfunction. Medical records were significant for a diagnosis of schizophrenia, an old conviction for child molestation, and recurrent treatment for anorectal injuries. The patient appeared for his appointment dressed completely in black leather. He reported being a member of a "S & M church" in a major nearby city. The patient referred to himself as the "devoted love slave" of the "high priestess" of this cult and described episodes of whipping, beating, and humiliation at the hands of this woman. Other than such sexual activities, he admitted that his only other pleasure was in watching videos of "The Muppets." In reviewing his early history, the patient spoke fondly of a "sainted grandfather" who had sexually abused him in childhood and taught him the joys of his current lifestyle.

Behavioral formulations for the development of masochistic behavior suggest that it is the consequence of early experience in which the individual learned to pair pain or humiliation with arousal (Tollison & Adams, 1979). This inclination may be further reinforced through masturbation fantasies. The following is a case example of a paraphilia which evolved out of a negative rein-forcement experience:

A Viet Nam veteran was referred by a post-traumatic stress treatment program when the staff learned of a paraphilia which was recently discovered by his wife. The patient described a 20-year history of compulsive masturbation while wearing a diaper he had freshly soiled. He also detailed a history of substantial abuse during childhood. His stepfather had frequently locked the patient, clad only in a diaper, in a closet for long periods of time to punish him for "bad behavior." The patient described the terror and physical discomfort he experienced in the closet and reported that he would plead incessantly to be released. When the stepfather eventually liberated the boy, he would demand sexual favors as payment for his freedom.

Behavioral Facilitation. As detailed in the section on sadistic acts, masochistic acts may involve elaborate preparation and planning. For some who secretly engage in autoerotic activities, the exodus of family members may provide a window of opportunity to arrange for self-hangings or electric shock. Drugs, in addition to having a disinhibiting effect, may be acquired for specific purposes during the paraphilic act (Eckert et al., 1991; Hucker & Stermac, 1992). Anesthetics are sometimes used to help the masochist endure the physical stress of certain forceful activities. Other substances, such as cocaine or volatile nitrites, are used to heighten the perceived intensity of a sexual response.

The Act. Autoerotic activities may often involve dangerous, and sometimes deadly, methods of producing sexual arousal. Of these methods, acts specifically designed to produce asphyxia are commonly the cause of masochistic-related deaths. In this practice, the victim intentionally induces a state of cerebral hypoxia during masturbation in order to intensify the sensations associated with ejaculation. Frequently, this is done by hanging a rope over the rafters to form a ligature and using a cloth under the rope to prevent abrasions. Usually, the victim arranges for a release mechanism that can be activated prior to loss of consciousness. Plastic bags, anesthetics, self-drowning, and chest compressions are additional methods which have been used (Hucker & Stermac, 1992). Two reported deaths from autoerotic asphyxia have involved the use of hydraulic shovels on tractors (O'Halloran & Dietz, 1993). In Blanchard and Hucker's (1991) study of 117 accidental fatalities from autoerotic asphyxiation, a large number of cases involved transvestism and occasionally involved the use of mirrors or cameras for self-observation.

Other unusual dangerous activities have involved the use of equipment such as vacuum cleaners or exhaust pipes for masturbation (Eckert et al., 1991) and masturbation combined with self-induced blood letting and ingestion of blood (McCully, 1964).

Necrophilia

Sexual attraction to the dead, or necrophilia, is certainly the rarest of the sexual paraphilias described in this chapter. In a comprehensive analysis of the 122 known cases of reported necrophilic fantasies and behavior, Rosman and Resnick (1989) were able to identify certain cognitive themes and behavioral patterns that were recurrent among the many single case studies. These authors identified true necrophiliacs as those who reported sexual fantasies or a series of sex acts with corpses. They distinguished these individuals from "pseudonecrophiles" who did not appear to be acting out of necrophilic drive, but who may have reported having had sexual activity with a corpse because of opportunity or aggressive urge. Among the true necrophiles, some limited themselves to necrophilic fantasies, others to sexual activity with a dead body ("regular necrophilia"), and another subset actually committed murder in order to obtain corpses for sexual activity ("necrophilic homicide").

Etiology. Rosman and Resnick (1989) observed that the mean age of onset for necrophilic behavior was the early 30s. This is considerably later than the believed onset for most paraphilic behaviors. If the behavioral formulation for the development of paraphilias is considered (Barlow, 1974), it is possible that younger individuals would be less likely to have the specific conditioning experiences (for example, arousal while preparing a body for embalming) that lead to deviant arousal to corpses. It is also likely that such persons may have already had another diagnosable paraphilia. Rosman and Resnick reported that more than half of their sample of true necrophiles had a prior history of sadistic behavior. Approximately half also appeared to be personality disordered (83% of homicidal necrophiles). Although it has been suggested that necrophilic activity is likely related to schizophrenic disorders (Prins, 1985), these authors found only 11% of their sample to be psychotic.

Rosman and Resnick (1989) suggested that necrophiliacs can be characterized as virtually lacking in self-esteem and being extremely avoidant of rejection, particularly by women. Their desired sexual object therefore becomes someone who is incapable of rejecting them. Possession of such a sexual partner was the most frequently cited reason for engaging in necrophilic behavior.

Behavioral Facilitation. Although alcohol use has been associated with most criminal offenses, those performing necrophilic acts seem less likely to have been intoxicated than sadistic offenders (Ressler et al., 1986). In the Rosman and Resnick (1989) report, those committing necrophilic homicide were more likely to have consumed alcohol than the regular necrophiles. The authors hypothesized that alcohol was more likely to have been used to overcome inhibitions about murder than necrophilia.

A more probable facilitator for the commission of necrophilic acts is simply being in a position where one has access to corpses. Fifty-seven percent of the necrophiliac sample had selected occupations which allowed for access to dead bodies (Rosman & Resnick, 1989).

The Act. A majority of the murders by disorganized sexual killers described by Ressler et al. (1986) appeared to be necrophilic homicides. Approximately three-quarters of this group engaged in sexual activity with the corpse and 76% performed post-mortem mutilation. Facial disfigurement or disembowelment were the acts performed most frequently. These data are similar to Rosman and Resnick's (1989) description of necrophilic behavior. In their review, vaginal intercourse, mutilation, and kissing were the acts most frequently performed. Not surprisingly, homicidal necrophiles were more likely to carry out post-mortem mutilation than were the regular necrophiles. The latter were more likely to engage in sexual activities that would not be considered unusual with a living partner, such as kissing, fondling of breasts, or oral sex. Necrophagia and vampirism described by Prins (1985) seem to be performed in only a minority of cases; however, a third of one group of subjects kept the body (Ressler et al., 1986). As in sadism, sexual gratification from necrophilic activity does not necessarily involve ejaculation.

Case Report

The following case report illustrates the developmental course of multiple paraphilic behavior. This particular case was selected because the presenting problem, exhibitionism, is commonly seen in sexual disorder clinics. The reader will observe that as the patient's sexual focus became modified over time to include other victim characteristics, the behaviors evolved into increasingly sadistic acts.

Identifying Problem

This 44-year-old male sought treatment at a mental health clinic following arrest for an incident in which he approached a woman whom he believed to be a prostitute and offered her money to watch him masturbate. The patient was placed on probation by the court and ordered to seek counseling. The initial clinical interview and psychological testing failed to reveal any psychopathology other than the paraphilias.

Social History

The patient was the eldest of four children. He had been an anxious child and experienced problems with bed-wetting until the age of 13. This problem was discussed openly within the family with some ridicule of the patient. His father's occupation necessitated that he was frequently away from the family for extended periods of time, leaving the mother as the primary disciplinarian. The patient indicated that his mother effectively used guilt-inducing strategies to influence his behavior rather than punishing him for bad behavior. He reported feeling much closer to his mother emotionally, but resenting the perceived control she had over him. The family did not have a significant religious affiliation.

He was an average student who was uncoordinated in sports and awkward with girls. He entered the military after high school and completed a tour of duty in Viet Nam. He met his wife several years after his military discharge.

At the time of the evaluation, the patient had been married for about 20 years and had a teenage daughter. He was a successful businessman and reported great personal satisfaction in his relationships with his wife and child. The recent arrest had caused the couple significant distress. Another continuing source of distress for this patient was the poor relationship between his wife and mother. Both seemed to vie for his attention and used guilt to influence his behavior. The onset of this interpersonal conflict dated back to the time of his engagement.

Sexual History

The patient's earliest erotic memory was of an event that occurred at the age of 13. While camping in the backyard, he followed through on a dare to run naked down the street at night. He did not believe that anyone had seen him, but experienced delight in the thought that he had "gotten away with something." Although the patient denied masturbatory experiences prior to the age of 18, he described a "recurring wet dream" in adolescence. In this fantasy, he would appear naked in a large box through which he could see out but no one could see in. He would masturbate in the box while watching unsuspecting women.

The patient denied any sexual experience prior to age 20, when he was stationed at a military base outside Saigon. A Vietnamese prostitute had entered the base that night and he reported being the "fourth in line" to have sexual intercourse with her. This occurred in a semi-public location on the compound within view of a couple of his fellow soldiers. Until his return to the U.S., the patient continued to have sexual contacts with prostitutes.

He described only one other relationship with a woman prior to his marriage and indicated that sexual contacts with her were infrequent. Although he reported satisfaction with the frequency and type of sexual activity within his marriage, the patient first began masturbating in his car within the first few months of his marriage. His wife described the patient as quite conservative sexually. She stated that he seemed to have low sexual desire, occasional problems with impotence, and always insisted that she take a passive role.

When the patient first began masturbating in his car, he used the sight of attractive women as a stimulus for his arousal without intending to be observed. Soon, however, he was noticed and found that the startled expressions of his victims enhanced his arousal. The arousal was much more intense when the victim appeared too fearful to respond. At such times, the patient reported feeling as if he had emotionally overpowered his victim.

This response frequently occurred when he was observed by an older woman. Eventually, he was specifically seeking out women over 70 years of age. Most often, he would frequent supermarkets and offer rides to potential victims. He indicated that he was startled and abandoned his pursuit on one occasion when a victim responded with interest to his gesture. He became extremely frightened by another woman's loud protestation and this curtailed his activity for awhile.

Shortly after the patient's exhibitionism began, he also began making obscene phone calls. This behavior developed similarly in that the patient first dialed numbers of non-English speaking women. Typically, he would select Asian names at random from the phone book. He used the female voice as a stimulus for his arousal while he masturbated. Initially, he seemed unconcerned that the victim failed to understand his propositions. However, as the patient's exhibitionistic activity with older women grew, he began seeking out the phone numbers of women in retirement communities who could react to him. His masturbation fantasies during these calls involved the act of physically and psychologically overpowering an aging female.

Prior to the patient's arrest, he had been masturbating in locations outside his home several times each week and having three to four multiple phone calling sessions per week. The patient reported that he was more likely to engage in these activities following a disagreement with his wife. He also taped a television program about dementia and used this tape of older women as a masturbatory stimulus. More frequently, he found himself pursuing Asian elders on the street. When he was unable to find older women as victims, he sought out prostitutes. He acknowledged significantly less arousal when masturbating before younger, consenting females.

Eventually, the patient began making visits to nursing homes. He was then having a recurrent fantasy about tying up an elderly woman and holding a toy gun to her head while he masturbated in front of her. He in fact described in considerable detail a dream in which he had engaged in this behavior with a 90-year-old nursing home resident who then "passed out" in response to him. The patient expressed feeling great fear that she had died. Although the patient denied that this dream was a description of an actual event, he did admit to having the rope and gun in his car.

Assessment

A complete evaluation of the scope and severity of a paraphilic disorder includes assessment of sexual arousal, social-sexual behavior, and cognitive schemas (Claire, 1993). Behavior therapists have traditionally also included gender role behavior (Barlow, 1974). A variety of methods can be utilized to obtain this information. Given the reluctance of many paraphiliacs to provide specific details about their disorder, it may be useful to evaluate for consistent responding when multiple approaches are used to measure one parameter (e.g., both self-report and physiological indices to assess for deviant arousal).

Sexual arousal includes both subjective and objective measures of interest. Occasionally, physiological arousal and an individual's report of sexual interest will be closely correlated. *Social-sexual behavior* involves an assessment of social skills, as well as sexual knowledge and experience. A *cognitive* evaluation provides information about a paraphiliac's belief system, including motivation for acting on sexual urges and barriers to change.

Self-report

The paraphiliac's description of his sexual urges, fantasies, and behaviors will usually first be obtained in the clinical interview. In addition to an overview of the problem, a sexual history may offer some insight into the development of deviant behavior. This typically includes an assessment of early sexual interest, parental views regarding sex, religiosity, and a sequential history of the types of sexual activities experienced from childhood through adulthood. Included in this evaluation are inquiries about masturbatory fantasies (McAnulty & Adams, 1992). Some clinicians may even require individuals to maintain an ongoing journal of sexual urges, their antecedents and consequences, and masturbation fantasies throughout the treatment period.

When obtaining data about the actual paraphilic act, victim characteristics must be fully assessed. For example, if the patient is a pedophile, gender and age range of victims should be determined, as well as exclusionary characteristics (e.g., body hair on boys; early breast development on girls). Victim behavior is an important aspect of arousal. The paraphiliac may report changes in sexual arousal in response to fear, shock, or struggle.

The clinical interview can also provide information about cognitive distortions the paraphiliac maintains. Such beliefs may help the patient to rationalize his behavior and continue to act on urges without censorship and with minimal threats to self-esteem. Examples include "Kids need adults to teach them how to have sex" or "Every women secretly fantasizes about being raped." Murphy (1990) described an approach to the assessment of cognitive distortions in paraphiliacs and the role of cognitive distortions in maintaining aggressive behavior.

Questionnaires and card sorts have also been developed to ascertain sexual interests. The Clarke Sexual History Questionnaire (Langevin, Handy, Paitich, & Russon, 1983) evaluates not only reported normal and deviant sexual behavior, but also urges and fantasies. Other questionnaires, such as the Derogatis Sexual Functioning Inventory (Derogatis & Melisaratos, 1979), primarily assess non-deviant sexual interests and behavior, but also tap into sexual attitudes and knowledge. For persons in a significant relationship, questionnaires which evaluate relationship satisfaction can provide relevant information about interpersonal behavior. For others, measures of social anxiety and dating behavior, such as the Survey of Heterosocial Interactions (Twentyman & McFall, 1975), provide some information about social competence.

Physiological Measures

An individual's response to erotic stimuli can be assessed through the use of transducers designed to measure changes in penile tumescence. Both circumferential strain gauges and volumetric devices have been used for this purpose with equivalent efficacy (Wheeler & Rubin, 1987).

Paraphiliacs are assessed in a laboratory setting which is typically in an adjoining room to the clinician and the recording instruments. The clinician, through the use of a speaker system, can instruct the patient in the procedure for attaching the transducer to the penis and direct his attention to each set of stimuli. Deviant and non-deviant sexual stimuli are subsequently presented in the form of photographs, slides, videotapes, or audiotapes. The patient is often asked to subjectively rate his arousal as physiological measures are taken. This evaluation can also be repeated at periodic intervals throughout treatment to assess for changes in sexual arousal. Although repeated exposure to the same sexual stimuli has been shown to produce decrements in arousal, ratio measures used to reflect sexual preference have appeared to remain stable (Eccles, Marshall, & Barbaree, 1987). Therefore, patients should be exposed to the entire set of deviant and non-deviant stimuli on repeated assessments in order to accurately evaluate progress in therapy.

Unfortunately, even a high correlation between subjective and objective measures is no assurance of accuracy. It is not possible to confidently ascertain whether the paraphiliac is, in fact, attending to presented stimuli or his own fantasies during physiological assessments. Hall, Proctor, and Nelson (1988) measured physiological indices of arousal in 122 prison inmates while they were exposed to a series of non-deviant and pedophilic tapes. Eighty percent of this group reported being able to voluntarily and completely inhibit their arousal during penile plethysmography. Certainly, an individual's motivation for distortion of data must be considered.

Behavioral Observation

Access to police reports or victim testimony may occasionally provide an eyewitness report of the paraphiliac's behavior. In most cases, however, behavioral observations of sexual deviants are limited to assessments of social, rather than sexual, skills and behavior. Behavioral checklists, such as the one designed by Barlow, Abel, Blanchard, Bristow, and Young (1977), assess for both verbal and nonverbal social functioning. This instrument has been used successfully with paraphiliac patients (Hayes, Brownell, & Barlow, 1983).

Treatment

Approaches to the treatment of paraphilia must be tailored to the individual's sexual focus and needs. In general, therapies are designed to (a) decrease inappropriate sexual arousal, (b) enhance arousal to appropriate sexual stimuli, (c) improve sexual and social competence, (d) expand sexual knowledge, (e) challenge maladaptive cognitions, and (f) prevent relapse. The majority of publications on the treatment of paraphilic behavior have focused on the techniques used to reduce arousal to inappropriate stimuli because this is often viewed as the first link in the behavioral chain leading to the commission of a paraphilic act. These approaches have been used with paraphiliacs who have engaged in violent or potentially violent sexual behavior. There is, however, no treatment currently known to be effective for sex murderers.

Decreasing Deviant Arousal

Behavioral interventions directed toward decreasing sexual arousal have involved various forms of aversion therapy. An unpleasant stimulus is paired with the sexual stimulus in an effort to weaken the conditioned arousal response. Obviously, the success of this technique is dependent on the paraphiliac's willingness to attend to deviant stimuli during sessions. Some form of aversion therapy has been used in the treatment of all the major categories of paraphilias. Frequently a combination of aversion techniques is implemented.

In *faradic*, or electrical, aversion, the paraphiliac receives mild shocks to the forearm while engaging in paraphilic imagery or while exposed to paraphilic stimuli. This technique has been shown to result in decreased penile tumescence to deviant stimuli in a variety of paraphilic disorders, including masochism (Abel, Levis, & Clancy, 1970). *Olfactory* aversion involves the use of unpleasant odors, such as valeric acid or ammonia, to decrease arousal. This technique can more easily be self-administered by a motivated patient. For example, a paraphiliac may be asked to uncap a vial of valeric acid and inhale when fantasizing about exposing himself or while beginning to dial a number for the purpose of making an obscene phone call. Laws, Meyer, and Holmen (1978) were able to significantly reduce arousal to sadistic stimuli when using only this technique in the treatment of a sexual sadist.

Covert desensitization (Cautela, 1967; Hayes, Brownell, & Barlow, 1978) is a cognitive aversion technique in which the paraphiliac learns to focus on aversive imagery while experiencing deviant fantasies. Initially, the therapist will construct a sensitization scene based on details obtained in the assessment. The aversion component involves detailed suggestions of unpleasant imagery, such as nausea and vomiting, arrest, public ridicule, or embarrassment. This too can be a self-administered therapy, but obviously requires good imaginal abilities.

Masturbatory satiation is a mildly aversive technique in which the paraphiliac is required to continue masturbating for 30 to 40 minutes after orgasm, while describing aloud deviant imagery (Marshall, 1979). Compliance may be problematic, as this approach is often regarded as quite boring and tedious by the patient.

A less frequently used approach is that of *shame aversion* (Serber, 1970; Wickramasekera, 1976). This approach has primarily been applied in the treatment of exhibitionists who are lacking in sociopathic symptomatology. The paraphiliac is actually asked to engage in a paraphilic act in front of an audience that is similar in characteristics to his usual victim. The therapist aides who make up the audience are asked to either stare blankly at the exhibitionist or express ridicule. For obvious reasons, this is not a technique which can be utilized with violent sex offenders.

In fact, more drastic measures, such as surgical castration or pharmacologic interventions, have been proposed for the violent sex offender. Bradford (1989) reviewed the use of cyproterone acetate and methoxyprogesterone acetate for decreasing sexual arousal in paraphiliacs. The former is an antiandrogen treatment which works through competitive inhibition of androgens at the receptor. A high rate of success, dependent on an adequate dose and length of treatment, has been reported with a number of different paraphilias. This drug does seem to produce a dampening effect on sexual behavior in general. Also, aggression that was not associated with sexual drive seems to remain unaffected by cyproterone acetate. Methoxyprogesterone acetate is a female hormone which interferes with the production of testosterone and increases its metabolic clearance. This drug appeared to be less effective in decreasing aggressive behavior. However, it was associated with a decrease in sexual fantasies and perceived increased control over paraphilic urges.

Enhancing Non-deviant Arousal

This aspect of treatment may be more complex. A paraphiliac may have little arousal to appropriate adult sexual situations because of minimal or negative experiences in this area. By contrast, the paraphiliac has had many years of reinforcement from masturbation to deviant fantasies and engaging in paraphilic acts. Through the assessment, the clinician can determine whether non-deviant sexual acts are a neutral stimulus or are actually aversive. For example, a sexual sadist who had been ridiculed and humiliated by women because of awkward social skills and clumsy sexual technique may feel extremely anxious in any situation in which he is not completely dominating his partner. In this case, arousal to appropriate sexual situations will not occur until the sadist has overcome his conditioned heterosexual anxiety. *Imaginal desensitization* is a behavioral approach to the treatment of specific fears (Wolpe, 1958). This involves gradually exposing the patient to a hierarchy of increasingly anxiety-provoking heterosexual scenes while offering relaxation induction.

Aversion relief (Abel et al., 1970) and fading (Barlow & Agras, 1973) are other means of gradually increasing the positive valence of previously neutral appropriate stimuli during or after exposure to deviant stimuli. A similar technique is *orgasmic reconditioning* (Marquis, 1970). This requires that the paraphiliac use any fantasy necessary to obtain a full erection, but then switch to appropriate imagery (i.e., adult, nonviolent), often with the help of explicit photographs, immediately prior to ejaculation. With repeated sessions, the paraphiliac is asked to begin using the appropriate fantasy earlier in the process, until only that stimulus is being used during masturbation.

Lastly, sex therapy may be necessary when the paraphiliac or his partner is experiencing a sexual dysfunction. Frequently, the spouse of the paraphiliac may complain of her husband's lack of sexual desire, occasional bouts of erectile dysfunction, or "prudish" attitudes about their sexual activities.

Education and Skill Training

Increased interest in non-deviant sexual behavior is ill-fated if the individual continues to lack the social or sexual skills necessary to successfully act on his urges. With improved social competence, a paraphiliac may have more appropriate sexual opportunities and greater likelihood of reinforcement for non-deviant sexual arousal (Hayes et al., 1983; Marshall & Barbaree, 1988).

Social skills training programs usually offer a combination of instruction, modeling, rehearsal, feedback, and reinforcement. When appropriate, assertiveness training and anger management may also be added to help the paraphiliac learn more adaptive modulation of affect (Lang, 1993).

Sex education may be necessary when the paraphiliac displays a poor understanding of basic reproductive anatomy, physiology, and normal sexual behavior. This intervention may also have an impact on the overly restrictive sexual attitudes sometimes held by the paraphiliac and may help to expand his sexual repertoire, thereby increasing the likelihood of experiencing reinforcement for engaging in non-deviant acts.

Cognitive Therapy

People rely on their personal belief system to help them understand events and to influence the behavioral course they take in coping with certain stressful events. When that belief system is distorted, their choice of coping may also be maladaptive. The first step in cognitive therapy, therefore, is assisting the paraphiliac to recognize the often dysfunctional nature of his cognitive schema. The second more labor intensive step is helping him to challenge these beliefs, adopt new beliefs, and learn adaptive coping strategies. Lang (1993) suggested that group therapy may offer an effective approach to confronting a paraphiliac's cognitive distortions. Role plays within this setting may be instructional as a paraphiliac learns to see how others view him, assumes greater empathy, and gains a deeper understanding of the impact abuse has on the victim.

Relapse Prevention

As with any behavioral change, successful treatment does not imply a life-long cure without risk of recurrent deviant urges or behavior. Many sexual disorder treatment programs prepare patients for this eventuality with the hope that one error will not lead to an abandonment of all self-management and coping skills. Paraphiliacs are taught to recognize both stressful life events and prodromal behaviors as danger signals. These behaviors can include a return to masturbation with deviant fantasies or engaging in any number of "trigger" activities, such as drinking, buying pornography, or placing oneself in a high risk situation (e.g., a pedophile agrees to babysit for a neighbor). Paraphiliacs are taught to use danger signals as a cue to invoke some of their previously learned skills to seek out their former therapist for "booster" sessions.

Recidivism

The true measure of treatment success for paraphilic disorders is in recidivism rates. Determination of accurate recidivism rates for para-philiacs, with or without treatment, currently seems nearly an impossibility because of methodological limitations. Many studies of recidivism rates lump together all sex offenders, combining exhibitionists with those committing violent sexual crimes. Some studies define recidivism by later criminal conviction (sex-related or not), others use self-report, and a small portion use physiological data. Furby, Weinrott, and Blackshaw (1989) observed that many studies of untreated sex offenders actually have lower recidivism rates than treated offender studies. They hypothesized that these results are likely due to differences in sample size, offender type, and recidivism measure used. Their review noted recidivism rates ranged from 0 to 52% for untreated sex offenders who may or may not have also been paraphiliacs.

Pedophiles constitute the largest proportion of paraphiliacs and much interest has been focused on the efficacy of treatment programs for this group. Paraphilic characteristics and recidivism rates at a one year follow-up were compared for 200 child molesters who had undergone a multicomponent treatment for pedophilia (Abel, Mittleman, Becker, Rathner, & Rouleau, 1988). Pedophiles who had multiple target types of victims were shown to be more likely to recidivate. That is, those who committed both hands-on (e.g., fondling) and hands-off (e.g., exhibitionism) offenses or assaulted both boys and girls within and outside the home appeared more likely to engage in pedophilic activity after treatment than pedophiles who reported greater specificity in their targeted victim. The frequency of past molestations or the number of victims molested prior to treatment appeared unrelated to recidivism. In general, the treated pedophiles had an impressive 95% reduction in the frequency of child molestations committed after treatment. The authors noted that re-arrest records were not helpful in assessing recidivism because none of their repeat offenders were arrested. Their data were based on self-report.

As paraphiliacs are by definition driven by recurrent deviant urges and behavior, arrests or incarceration without treatment would not be expected to have a significant impact on future offending. However, a comparison of recidivism rates of treated versus untreated paraphiliacs is insufficient for the evaluation of the efficacy of a treatment intervention. Meaningful studies of recidivism rates should provide a comparison between exposure to specific treatment regimens and the frequency of post-treatment paraphilic acts at follow-up in an adequate sample size. This does not describe most of the currently available literature. A majority of treatment studies involve small sample sizes or single case reports. Control groups are seldom included and follow-up data are often unavailable or of insufficient length. Several paraphiliac categories are often lumped under one nonspecific label, such as sex offender or sexual aggressive. Few studies control for sociopathy as a confounding variable in treatment response. Because most treatment studies offer multi-component approaches, the relative efficacy of specific treatment interventions remains elusive.

In Perkin's (1991) review of the clinical treatment of sex offenders, he acknowledged these concerns, but also urged that violent paraphiliacs who receive treatment in a secure setting need other interventions after their release. He noted that while behavior therapy appeared to be effective in producing desired behavior change in a controlled environment, better follow-up through community programs may help to minimize recidivism.

Summary

Although there is ample room for improvement in much of the current empirical research in this area, it is important to consider that paraphilia as a diagnostic category has only existed since 1980. The incidence of this disorder in the general population is unknown. Even less is known about the nature of violent paraphiliacs because they represent only a small portion of sexual deviants and remain mostly outside mental health settings unless coerced by the legal system. As sexually aggressive behavior is more often viewed as a criminal act rather than a behavioral disorder, judicial dispositions of paraphiliacs seem to take priority over psychological referrals. When treatment is recommended, many receive nonspecific therapies because few clinicians are experienced with this population. All specific treatments require a high level of patient motivation and cooperation for success. Often, paraphiliacs refuse treatment or remain minimally invested in this process. Undoubtedly, few seem aware that efficacious therapies exist for this disorder. Perhaps this problem could be remedied by greater education of the public, as well as personnel in the criminal justice system, about the availability of programs and clinicians with expertise in this area.

This chapter presented a review of the literature in the area of sexual paraphilias with a particular emphasis on those disorders which have been associated with lethal violence. Key points to consider include the following:

(1) Although paraphiliacs are reluctant to disclose details about their disorder, perceived confidentiality of information improves the accuracy of self-reports.

(2) Most paraphiliacs have two or more paraphilic disorders.

(3) Violent paraphilic behavior is unusual; lethal violence is even more rare.

(4) Factors associated with violent paraphilic behavior include a history of abuse, previous sexual violence as a perpetrator, poor parental bonds, impaired social skills, social isolation, and poor self-esteem.

(5) Severity of violence in a paraphilic act often increases over time or in response to stress.

(6) Murders associated with paraphilic behaviors are often noteworthy for their brutality.

(7) Assessment must be multifaceted to ascertain the multiple factors which maintain the current maladaptive behavior pattern.

(8) Treatment interventions should target all deviant conditioned physiological responses, problematic cognitions, and skill deficits identified in the assessment.

(9) Instruction in relapse prevention and follow-up is recommended for most paraphiliacs, but is essential for violent-prone individuals.

Annotated Bibliography

Hollins, C. R. & Howells, K. (Eds.). (1991). *Clinical approaches to sex offenders and their victims*. West Sussex, England: Wiley. This text reviews theories of offending, assessment methods, and clinical work with offenders and victims. Special topic areas included research on child testimony, work with offenders in secure settings, and prevention programs.

Marshall, W. L., Barbaree, H. E., & Laws, D. R. (Eds.). (1990). *Handbook of sexual assault: Issues, theories, and treatment of the sex offender*. New York: Plenum. This entire volume is dedicated to the study of the sex offender by well-known researchers in the area of sexual deviance. Chapters review specific treatment interventions for this population and offer pragmatic recommendations for clinicians.

Tollison, C. D. & Adams, H. E. (1979). *Sexual disorders: Treatment, theory, and research*. New York: Gardener. Although now somewhat dated, this comprehensive reference book offers detailed descriptions of the full range of paraphilic disorders. The many case reports are particularly well worth reading.

They are invaluable in providing a complete impression of the nature and scope of specific paraphilias.

Other Case Readings

Dietz, P. E., Hazelwood, R. R., & Warren, J. (1990). The sexually sadistic criminal and his offenses. *Bulletin of the American Academy of Psychiatry and Law, 18*(2), 163-178. This article presents a descriptive study of 30 sexually sadistic criminals. Included are common behavioral patterns of sex offenders prior to, during, and following commission of a crime. The data source is the National Center for the Analysis of Violent Crime.

Moes, E. (1991). Ted Bundy: A case of schizoid necrophilia. *Melanie Klein and Object Relations, 9*(1), 54-72. This is for those interested in a psychoanalytic perspective on serial sexual murder and necrophilia. Included is a psychobiography of Ted Bundy, which reviews his early history, character, and murders.

Ressler, R., Burgess, A., Douglas, J., Hartman, C., & D'Agostino, R. (1985). Sexual killers and their victims. *Journal of Interpersonal Violence, 1*(3), 288-308. This includes an overview of the behavior pattern of organized and disorganized sexual killers. Case vignettes by survivors of each type of sexual murderer provide a greater understanding of lethal violence associated with paraphilic drive.

References

Abel, G. G., Becker, I., Mittleman, M., Cunningham-Rathner, J., Rouleau, J., & Murphy, W. (1987). Self-reported sex crimes of nonincarcerated **paraphiliacs**. *Journal of Interpersonal Violence, 2*(1), 3-25.

Abel, G. G., Levis, D. J., & Clancy, J. (1970). Aversion therapy applied to taped sequences of deviant behavior in exhibitionism and other sexual deviations: A preliminary report. *Journal of Behavior Therapy and Experimental Psychiatry, 1*, 59-66.

Abel, G. G., Mittleman, M., Becker, J. V., Rathner, J., & Rouleau, J. (1988). Predicting child molester's response to treatment. *Annals of the New York Academy of Science, 528*, 223-234.

Abel, G. G. & Osborn, C. (1992). The paraphilias: The extent and nature of sexually deviant and criminal behavior. *Psychiatric Clinics of North America, 15*(3), 675-687.

Adams, H. E. & Chiodo, J. (1984). Sexual deviations. In H. E. Adams & P. Sutker (Eds.), *Comprehensive handbook of psychopathology* (pp. 777-806). New York: Plenum.

American Psychiatric Association. (1980). *Diagnostic and statistical manual of mental disorders* (3rd ed.). Washington, DC: Author.

American Psychiatric Association. (1987). *Diagnostic and statistical manual of mental disorders* (3rd ed., revised). Washington, DC: Author.

American Psychiatric Association. (1994). *Diagnostic and statistical manual of mental disorders* (4th ed.). Washington, DC: Author.

Bach, S. (1991). On sadomasochistic object relations. In G. Fogel & W. Myers (Eds.), *Perversions and near-perversions in clinical practice* (pp. 75-92). New Haven: Yale University.

Baik, S. & Uku, J. (1988). Ligature strangulation of a woman during sadomasochistic sexual activity. *The American Journal of Forensic Medicine and Pathology, 9*(3), 249-251.

Barlow, D. H. (1974). The treatment of sexual deviation: Toward a comprehensive behavioral approach. In K. S. Calhoun, H. E. Adams, & K. M. Mitchell (Eds.), *Innovative treatment methods in psychopathology* (pp. 121-147). New York: Wiley.

Barlow, D. H. & Agras, W. S. (1973). Fading to increase sexual responsiveness in homosexuals. *Journal of Applied Behavioral Analysis, 6*, 355-367.

Barlow, D. H., Agras, W. S., Abel, G. G., Blanchard, E. B., & Young, L. D. (1977). A heterosocial skills behavior checklist for males. *Behavior Therapy, 8*, 229-239.

Blanchard, R. & Hucker, S. (1991). Age, transvestism, bondage, and concurrent paraphilic activities in 117 cases of autoerotic asphyxia. *British Journal of Psychiatry, 159*, 371-377.

Bradford, J. (1989). The organic treatment of violent sex offenders. In A. J. Stunkard & A. Baum (Eds.), Perspectives in behavioral medicine: *Eating, sleeping, and sex* (pp. 203-221). Hillsdale: Erlbaum.

Bradford, J., Boulet, J., & Pawlak, A. (1992). The paraphilias: A multiplicity of deviant behaviors. *Canadian Journal of Psychiatry, 37*, 104-108.

Burgess, A., Hartman, C., Ressler, R., Douglas, J., & McCormack, A. (1986). Sexual homicide: A motivational model. *Journal of Interpersonal Violence, 1*(3), 251-272.

Cautela, J. (1967). Covert sensitization. *Psychological Reports, 20*, 459-468.

Claire, I. C. (1993). Issues in the assessment and treatment of male sex offenders with mild learning disabilities. *Sexual and Marital Therapy, 8*(2), 167-180.

Dekker, J., Everaerd, W., & Verhelst, N. (1985). Attending to stimuli or images of sexual feelings: Effects on sexual arousal. *Behavior Research and Therapy, 23*(2), 139-149.

Derogatis, L. R. & Melisaratos, N. (1979). The DSFI: A multidimensional measure of sexual functioning. *Journal of Sex and Marital Therapy, 5*, 244-281.

De Silva, P. (1993). Fetishism and sexual dysfunction: Clinical presentation and management. *Sexual and Marital Therapy, 8*(2), 147-155.

Dietz, P. E., Hazelwood, R. R., & Warren, J. (1990). The sexually sadistic criminal and his offenses. *Bulletin of the American Academy of Psychiatry and Law,* 18(2), 163-178.

Dormanen, S. (1980). Statistical patterns of victimization. *Evaluation* (Special issue), 12-13.

Eccles, A., Marshall, W. L., & Barbaree, H. E. (1988). The vulnerability of erectile measures to repeated assessments. *Behavior Research and Therapy, 26*(2), 179-183.

Eckert, W., Katchis, S., & Donovan, W. (1991). The pathology and medicolegal aspects of sexual activity. *The American Journal of Medicine and Pathology, 12*(1), 3-15.

Federal Bureau of Investigation (1989). *Uniform Crime Reports for the United States.* Washington, DC: Department of Justice.

Fedora, O., Reddon, J., Morrison, J., Fedora, S., Pascoe, H., & Yeudall, L. (1992). Sadism and other paraphilias in normal controls and aggressive and nonaggressive sex offenders. *Archives of Sexual Behavior, 21*(1), 1-15.

Fisher, D., & Howells, K. (1993). Social relationships in sexual offenders. *Sexual and Marital Therapy, 8*(2), 123-136.

Furby, L., Weinrott, M., & Blackshaw, L. (1989). Sex offender recidivism: A review. *Psychological Bulletin, 105*(1), 3-30.

Haeberle, E. (1978). *The sex atlas.* New York: Seabury.

Hall, G. C., Proctor, W. C., & Nelson, G. M. (1988). Validity of physiological measures of pedophilic sexual arousal in a sexual offender population. *Journal of Consulting and Clinical Psychology, 56,* 118-122.

Hayes, S. C., Brownell, K. D., & Barlow, D. H. (1978). The use of self-administered covert desensitization in the treatment of exhibitionism and sadism. *Behavior Therapy, 9,* 283-289.

Hayes, S. C., Brownell, K. D., & Barlow, D. H. (1983). Heterosocial skills training and covert desensitization effects on social skills and sexual arousal in sexual deviants. *Behavior Therapy, 21*(4), 383-392.

Hazelwood, R. R., Warren, J., & Dietz, P. E. (1993). Compliant victims of the sexual sadist. *Australian Family Physician, 22*(4), 474-479.

Hucker, S. & Stermac, L. (1992). The evaluation and treatment of sexual violence, necrophilia, and asphyxiophilia. *Psychiatric Clinics of North America, 15*(3), 703-719.

Kaplan, M. S., Abel, G. G., Cunningham-Rathner, J., & Mittleman, M. (1990). The impact of parolees' perception of confidentiality of their self-reported sex crimes. *Annals of Sex Research, 3,* 292-303.

Krafft-Ebing, R. von (1965). *Psychopathia sexualis.* (E. S. Klaf, Trans.). New York: Stein & Day. (Original work published 1886).

Lang, R. (1993). Neuropsychological deficits in sexual offenders: Implications for treatment. *Sexual and Marital Therapy, 8*(2), 181-200.

Langevin, R., Bain, J., Wortzman, G., Hucker, S., Dickey, R., & Wright, P. (1988). Sexual sadism: Brain, blood, and behavior. *Annals of the New York Academy of Science, 528*, 163-171.

Langevin, R., Handy, L., Paitich, D., & Russon, A. (1983). A new version of the Clarke Sexual History Questionnaire for Males. In R. Langevin (Ed.), *Erotic preference, gender identity, and aggression* (pp. 287-305). Hillsdale: Erlbaum.

Laws, D. R., Meyer, J., & Holmen, M. L. (1978). Reduction of sadistic sexual arousal by olfactory aversion: A case study. *Behavior Research and Therapy, 16*, 281-285.

Levine, S., Risen, C., & Althof, S. (1990). Essay on the diagnosis and nature of paraphilia. *Journal of Sex and Marital Therapy, 16*(2), 89-102.

MacCulloch, M., Snowden, P., Wood, P., & Mills, H. (1983). Sadistic fantasy, sadistic behavior, and offending. *British Journal of Psychiatry, 143*, 20-29.

Malamuth, N. & Spinner, B. (1980). A longitudinal content analysis of sexual violence in the best-selling erotic magazines. *Journal of Sex Research, 17*, 226-237.

Marquis, J. (1970). Orgasmic reconditioning: Changing sexual choice through controlling masturbatory fantasies. *Journal of Behavior Therapy and Experimental Psychology, 1*, 263-271.

Marshall, W. L. (1979). Satiation therapy: A procedure for reducing deviant arousal. *Journal of Applied Behavioral Analysis, 12*, 10-22.

Marshall, W. L. (1993). The role of attachments, intimacy, and loneliness in the etiology and maintenance of sex offending. *Sexual and Marital Therapy, 8*(2), 109-121.

Marshall, W. L. & Barbaree, H. E. (1988). The long-term evaluation of a behavioral treatment program for child molesters. *Behavior Research and Therapy, 26*(5), 499-511.

Marshall, W. L., Barbaree, H. E., & Butt, J. (1988). Sexual offenders against male children: Sexual preferences. *Behavior Research and Therapy, 26*(5), 283-391.

McAnulty, R. D. & Adams, H. E. (1992). Behavior therapy with paraphilic disorders. In S. M. Turner, K. S. Calhoun, & H. E. Adams (Eds.), *Handbook of behavior therapy* (2nd ed.) (pp. 175-201). New York: Wiley.

McCully, R. S. (1964). Vampirism: Historical perspective and underlying process in relation to a case of auto-vampirism. *Journal of Nervous and Mental Disease, 139*, 440-452.

Money, J. (1984). Paraphilias: Phenomenology and classification. *American Journal of Psychotherapy, 38*(2), 164-179.

Murphy, W.D. (1990). Assessment and modification of cognitive distortions in sexual offenders. In W. Marshall, H. E. Barbaree, & D. R. Laws (Eds.), *Handbook of sexual assault: Issues,theories, and treatment of the offender* (pp. 331-430). New York: Plenum.

Novick, K. K. & Novick, J. (1987). The essence of masochism. *Psychoanalytic Study of the Child, 42*, 353-384.

O'Halloran, R. & Dietz, P. (1993). Autoerotic fatalities with power hydraulics. *Journal of Forensic Sciences, 38*(2), 359-364.

Perkins, D. (1991). Clinical work with sex offenders in secure settings. In C. R. Hollins & K. Howell (Eds.), *Clinical approaches to sex offenders and their victims* (pp. 151-177). West Sussex: Wiley.

Prins, H. (1985). Vampirism: A clinical condition. *British Journal of Psychiatry, 146*, 666-668.

Ressler, R., Burgess, A., Douglas, J., Hartman, C., & D'Agostino, R. (1986). Sexual killers and their victims. *Journal of Interpersonal Violence, 1*(3), 288-308.

Roberts, J. V. & Grossman, M. G. (1993). Sexual homicide in Canada: A descriptive analysis. *Annals of Sex Research, 6,* 5-25.

Rosman, J. & Resnick, P. (1989). Sexual attraction to corpses: A psychiatric review of necrophilia. *Bulletin of the American Academy of Psychiatry and Law, 17*(2), 153-163.

Russell, D. E. H. (1984). *Sexual exploitation: Rape, child sexual abuse, and workplace harassment.* Beverly Hills: Sage.

Serber, M. (1970). Shame aversion therapy. *Journal of Behavior Therapy and Experimental Psychiatry, 1,* 213-215.

Smith, D. & Over, R. (1987). Does fantasy-induced sexual arousal habituate? *Behavior Research and Therapy, 25*(6), 477-485.

Tollison, C. D. & Adams, H. E. (1979). *Sexual disorders: Treatment, theory and research.* New York: Gardener.

Twentyman, C. T. & McFall, R. M. (1975). Behavioral training of social skills in shy males. *Journal of Consulting and Clinical Psychology, 43,* 384-395.

Wheeler, D. & Rubin, H. B. (1987). A comparison of volumetric and circumferential measures of penile erection. *Archives of Sexual Behavior, 16,* 289-299.

Wickramasekera, I. (1976). Aversive behavior rehearsal for sexual exhibitionism. *Behavior Therapy, 7,* 167-176.

Wilber, C. G. (1985). A case of lust murder. *The American Journal of Forensic Medicine and Pathology, 6*(3), 226-232.

Wolpe, J. (1958). *Psychotherapy by reciprocal inhibition.* Stanford: Stanford University Press.

About the Author

Judith Boczkowski Chapman, PhD, ABPP, was a staff psychologist at the Department of Veterans Affairs Medical Center at Livermore, California during the writing of this chapter. She received her doctorate in Clinical Psychology from the University of Georgia. Dr. Chapman is a Diplomate in Clinical Psychology from the American Board of Professional Psychology and is a Fellow of the Academy of Clinical Psychology. She first began treating patients with paraphilic disorders in graduate school under the supervision of Dr. Henry E. Adams. She has continued her work in this area at both the V.A. and in her private practice. Dr. Chapman has presented seminars on this topic to psychology interns, medical students, and psychiatry residents. Currently, she is a staff psychologist at the Palo Alto V.A.

CHAPTER 13

SERIAL MURDER

Patrick E. Cook
Dayle L. Hinman

Overview and Epidemiology

This chapter focuses on the behavior of those statistically rare humans who engage in repeated (serial) acts of homicide. Serial murder is a type of violence that has occurred throughout history, and has been well known during the 20th century (Jenkins, 1989, 1992). An opinion piece in *The New Yorker* described the serial killer as "an icon of pop culture" who has no apparent motivation for his crimes except gratification of desire, whose connections with his victims are fantasized, who is difficult to apprehend, and whose "entire outward life has been constructed as a means of satisfying the forbidden" ("A Riddle," 1994, p. 45). Serial murders, in various portrayals, none more ingenious or grotesque than the real thing, provide plot lines for countless novels and screen plays. According to Robert Ressler, who was one of the original Federal Bureau of Investigation (FBI) profilers of serial murderers, the serial killers in popular fiction "are rendered more ritualistic, cunning and strangely charismatic than they truly are" (quoted in Bruni, 1994).

Real-life practitioners of serial murder captivate the interest of the press and the public alike. They often become celebrities, and may be elevated to the status of cult heroes. They are given nicknames, e.g., "Jack the Ripper" (unknown), "the Boston Strangler" (Albert DeSalvo), "the Night Stalker" (Richard Ramirez), "the Son of Sam" (David Berkowitz), and "the Green River Killer" (unknown). People even buy their "art." In 1980, John Wayne Gacy was convicted on 33 counts of murder of young men in Illinois. Until his execution in 1994, Gacy sold the pictures he painted while in prison. Gerard Schaefer, a South Florida deputy sheriff who abducted, mutilated, and murdered at least 20 young women in the 1970s, sells the "killer fiction" he writes in prison.

Serial murder and *mass murder* are sometimes confused with each other. Mass murder refers to multiple homicides (four or more victims) committed during a relatively short period of time (one event), at one location. Colin Ferguson is a recent example of a mass murderer. In March 1995, Ferguson was convicted of killing six passengers and wounding 19 in a hail of gunfire on a Long Island Rail Road commuter train.

In this chapter, we utilize the most recent definitions developed by the Critical Incident Response Group (CIRG) of the FBI. The CIRG operates the Investigative Support Unit, which oversees the programs of the National Center for the Analysis of Violent Crimes (NCVAC) and the

Abducted Children and Serial Killers Unit at the FBI Academy in Quantico, Virginia. These definitions were developed as a result of in-depth, long-term studies of serial murderers and their crimes. According to the CIRG, serial murder involves multiple acts of homicide (two or more victims) occurring on more than one occasion or at more than one location. Serial murders can be classified as either the *spree* type or the *classic* type.

In the spree type of serial murder, there are homicides of multiple victims at two or more locations. A significant classifying factor is that there is no "cooling off" period between homicides. The spree killer maintains a high level of excitation, perhaps to the point of frenzy.

On August 1, 1966, the first author's last day on campus as a graduate student at the University of Texas at Austin, Charles Whitman murdered his wife and mother, then went to the top of the University of Texas Tower. From that vantage point, Whitman shot and killed 13 people and wounded 31 others. Whitman is often cited as an example of a mass murderer (Time-Life Editors, 1992). Under current definitions used by the CIRG, Whitman would be classified as a spree serial killer because he killed at three locations. In many instances, spree killers may already be fugitives from justice. In rare cases, there may be more than one perpetrator. As we began writing this chapter, the authorities apprehended two young men who were killing people and stealing their cars to continue their trip across the country.

In the classic type of serial murder, there are two or more separate homicide events which occur over a period of time (hours, days, weeks, or even years). There is a cooling off period between episodes. These crimes are predatory. The offender frequently stalks his victims. The motive is clearly psychological. The offender's behavior and the crime scene evidence typically indicate sexual and sadistic features, and may involve torture and mutilation of the victim. Ted Bundy was one of the most notorious examples of the classic serial killer. Intelligent, manipulative, and elusive, he killed at least 30 female victims from coast to coast. He was finally apprehended in Florida during a traffic stop. His trial was one of the first in which forensic odontology (bite mark evidence) played a major role in a conviction. Bundy was executed by electrocution in 1989.

A number of law enforcement experts believe that the incidence of serial murder may be increasing. Until recently, a person was at greater risk of being killed by a family member, friend, or acquaintance, than by a stranger. According to the Uniform Crime Reports (UCR; FBI, 1994), strangers and unknown persons committed 53% of the 23,271 reported murders in the nation in 1993. This was an all-time high. Table 1 presents the numbers and percentages of total homicide victims murdered by family members, acquaintances, strangers, and unknown others in 1993.

According to the UCR, "Every American now has a realistic chance of murder victimization in view of the random nature the crime has assumed" (FBI, 1994, p. 287). Suggested causes for the shift in homicide patterns include the proliferation of handguns, the breakdown of the family unit, and the increase in violence associated with illicit drugs, gangs, and juvenile crime.

It is difficult to determine the percentage of homicides between strangers that are the work of serial killers. Estimates range from a possible underestimation of 2 to 3% of annual homicides to a probable overestimation of thousands of victims. There are problems in using data from crime reports, vital statistics records, unidentified bodies, and missing persons reports to estimate serial murder rates (Kiger, 1990).

Jenkins (1992) compiled a list of serial murder cases reported in the press and other sources from 1940 to 1990. He concluded that there was an increase in serial murders over that period of time which cannot be attributed solely to increased reporting. He argued that social/envi-

TABLE 1
SUMMARY OF NUMBER AND PERCENT OF MURDER VICTIMS
BY RELATIONSHIP, 1993 (N = 23,271)

	Relationship of Victim to Offender			
	Family	**Acquaintance**	**Stranger**	**Unknown**
Number	2,725	8,142	3,259	9,145
%	11.7%	34.9%	14%	39.2%

Note. Data from Crime in America. Uniform Crime Reports 1993. Federal Bureau of Investigation, 1994, Washington, DC: U.S. Government Printing Office.

ronmental factors, such as the youth culture (greater access to target victims) and changes in the mental health system (deinstitutionalization), have contributed to the trend.

Serial murder is not unique to modern times, and is not exclusively a North American phenomenon. Newton (1990) estimated that the United States could claim the highest percentage of known serial killers (74%), followed by England (7%), Germany (6%), and France (2%). Data are simply not available for many countries.

In the sections which follow, we summarize what is known about serial murder, present several cases, and discuss "assessment" of serial murderers by means of criminal investigative analysis or "profiling." We conclude with discussions of interventions for serial murderers who have been apprehended and the conditions which allow serial killers to avoid apprehension. This chapter demonstrates the value of studying identified serial murderers, as the FBI has done, and the absolute necessity of sharing crime information through the FBI's Violent Criminal Apprehension Program (VICAP) and other programs developed to track and apprehend serial offenders.

In *Hunting the Devil,* a book about Russian serial killer Andrei Chikatilo, author Richard Lourie observed: "Fame is a killer's last crime" (1993, p. 270). In this chapter, we refer to serial killers by name for purposes of illustration and pedagogy. Otherwise, we would prefer to memorialize their innocent victims and to honor the law enforcement professionals who work to bring serial killers to justice.

Literature and Clinical Lore

There are a number of ways to categorize and conceptualize serial murder. The primary goal of this chapter is to communicate concepts, descriptive information, and examples that help to explain the phenomenon of serial homicide. This is information that can aid in the investigation of serial murders and lead to the apprehension of serial killers by focusing on particular types of individuals and eliminating others from the pool of potential suspects.

The literature contains a variety of definitions of serial murder. Egger (1990a) reviewed the literature on serial murder. Egger's definition characterizes many, but certainly not all, serial murders. According to Egger, a serial murder is one in which one or more individuals (most often males) commit two or more murders of victims with whom they have no relationship. The murders occur at different times, usually at different locations, and appear to have no connection with each other. The motive involves power over the victims, rather than material gain. The victims have symbolic value to the perpetrator(s) and may be seen as prestigeless and unable to defend themselves. According to Egger, the victims may be "perceived as powerless given their situation in time, place, or status within their immediate surroundings (such as vagrants, prostitutes, migrant workers, homosexuals, children, and single often elderly women)" (1990a, p. 4).

Characteristics of Serial Murderers

There is no typical serial killer. Most people's ideas about what a serial killer is like have been influenced by the most recent, most publicized serial killers or by the villains in best-selling novels or hit movies. Jeffrey Dahmer's crimes and trial were widely reported in the media. Dahmer became a household name. Not many serial killers do what Dahmer did: kill young men in his apartment while attempting to make them into sexual zombies for his own pleasure. Richard Trenton Chase, who was psychotic, ate body parts and drank the blood of his victims (anthropophagy). Chase believed that he needed the nutrient value of his victims' blood and tissue in order to survive. One cannot explain his crimes with the same set of factors that apply to a cunning psychopath like Ted Bundy.

Information accumulated in studies of identified serial killers and their crimes does suggest that there are some commonalities and types of serial killers:

Age. Most serial killers are in their 20s when they begin to kill.

Race. Most serial killers in North America are White. There have been exceptions. Wayne Williams, a Black, is thought to have killed 29 boys and young men in Atlanta, Georgia, between 1979 and 1981. Williams was convicted on two counts of murder in February 1982.

Sex. Most serial killers are male. Female serial killers are more likely to be custodial killers, such as babysitters, nurses, and serial spouse killers. Christine Fallings smothered three of the children she babysat between 1978 and 1982. She is suspected in the deaths of three other children. Aileen Wournos, a prostitute, was convicted of killing seven men along interstate highways in Florida. As is often the case with serial murderers, she is also a suspect in other murders. Wournos is atypical for a female serial killer. She fits the description of a classic serial killer. It is also unusual for a prostitute to be a serial killer, rather than a victim of one.

Single versus multiple offenders. Most serial killers operate alone. Multiple offenders may occasionally be involved in spree killing. It is even less common for pairs of offenders of the same or different sexes to be involved in classic serial murder. In those cases, one offender is usually the dominant actor, and one is submissive. Their crime scenes usually reflect the dynamics of two different offenders. Ottis Toole and Henry Lee Lucas were serial killers who killed individually and also as a team.

Relationship to Victim. Most serial killings are homicides of strangers. Exceptions include some spree homicides of acquaintances, custodial/caretaker homicides (e.g., nurse-patient, babysitter-child), and serial murders of spouses ("black widow or widower" murders).

Powerless Victims. Serial killers frequently target "powerless" victims: children, vagrants, and the elderly. They very often prey on prostitutes, who are society's "throw-aways." Prostitutes are readily available and easy to pick up. They may not be missed. They may be difficult to identify. Their murders may not produce the same kind of community outrage as a string of murdered coeds. Importantly, killing prostitutes may often have symbolic sexual importance for the killer. Other serial killers target more challenging prey. Ted Bundy sought victims he considered worthy of his attention.

Location. Serial killers can be classified as

geographically transient or *geographically stable* (Holmes & DeBurger, 1985). Some serial murderers put many miles on their cars as they search for new victims. They attempt to avoid detection by operating in far-flung jurisdictions. Ted Bundy left a string of victims from one corner of the country to another. He was a highly mobile murderer. Local murderers operate in the same community. Arthur Shawcross was a local serial killer and also a recidivist. After serving a 14-year sentence for raping and strangling an eight-year-old girl, and admitting to killing a young boy in his hometown, Shawcross moved further west in New York State. He murdered 11 prostitutes in and around Rochester. Jeffrey Dahmer, who killed 17 boys and young men between 1978 and 1991, was a place-specific murderer for most of his homicides.

Use of Weapons. Most serial killers use weapons to exert control over their victims. Serial killers want contact and interaction with their victims. Few use guns, explosives, or poison to kill. They use knives, ligatures, blunt objects, and their hands. Victims are most often stabbed, strangled, or beaten to death.

Mental illness. Most serial killers are not mentally ill. The public may have an image of a mentally deranged serial killer because that is how they are portrayed in movies. It is easy to assume that only a "crazy" person would do such evil deeds. Many people believe that there is a link between mental illness and violence. Recent research has shown that mental illness is only a modest risk factor for violence, and then only for actively psychotic (e.g., hallucinating, delusional, or both) individuals (Monahan, 1992).

Few serial killers commit their crimes in response to psychotic symptoms (Dietz, 1992). Rarely do they meet the legal criteria for insanity. One serial killer examined by the first author tried to feign mental illness. He tried to convince examining psychologists and psychiatrists that an angel had ordered him to kill hitchhiking teenagers. He hoped to be found not guilty by reason of insanity. Instead, he was found competent to stand trial, sane at the time of his offenses, and guilty of murder.

Estimated Number of Serial Killers

Serial killers are the "outliers" at the upper extreme of the distribution of human aggression and violence. They are statistically rare. Realistic estimates are that there may be approximately 50 or 60 serial killers operating in the U.S. at any given time.

The National Center for the Analysis of Violent Crime (NCAVC) at the FBI Academy has developed a data base on mass, spree serial, and classic serial murderers from 1960 to the present. A computer search identified wire service reports of mass and serial murders. The reports were analyzed and victims were categorized as killed, attempted, or suspected. Table 2 presents a summary of the ages at the time of first and last murder and the numbers of victims of the serial murderers in the NCVAC data base (NCAVC, 1994).

From Table 2, it can be seen that the 526 spree and classic serial killers in the data base were responsible for the deaths of over 2,400 victims. They were suspects in almost 1,700 additional homicides.

Organized Versus Disorganized Serial Murderers

One of the most useful typologies of serial murderers distinguishes between *organized* and *disorganized* serial killers. In 1986, Ressler, Burgess, Douglas, Hartman, and D'Agostino described the FBI's development of and rationale for categorizing sexual murders and crime scenes as either organized or disorganized: "The premise for this dichotomy is that facets of the criminal's personality are evident in his offense. Like fingerprints, the crime scene can be used to aid in iden-

TABLE 2

AGES AT FIRST AND LAST MURDER AND NUMBER OF VICTIMS OF SERIAL KILLERS IN THE NCVAC DATA BASE

Characteristic	Spree (n=126)	Classic (n=400)
Mean age time time of crime	28.7[a]	
Mean age first murder		27.9[b]
Mean age last murder		32.5[b]
Victims killed	510	1,916
Victims attempted	160	303
Victims suspected	67	1,630

Note.

[a]n=104.

[b]n=266.

Adapted from Serial, mass, and spree murderers in the United States: Search of major wire services and publications: Offenders operating from 1960 to present. National Center for the Analysis of Violent Crime. 1994, Quantico, VA: FBI Academy.

tifying the murderer" (pp. 290-291).

Organized murderers are characterized as those who plan their murders and leave fewer clues at the crime scene because they control the activity at the scene. Disorganized murderers act more spontaneously. Their lack of planning and control, and their behavior at the crime scene more often result in the presence of evidence. Detailed descriptions of these two types based on research and accumulated investigative experience appear in later sections of this chapter. The typologies are general in nature and were developed to serve as an investigative guide. Obviously, it would be unrealistic to try to fit every serial murderer into one of only two categories.

Organized offenders sometimes deteriorate and become disorganized. Ted Bundy's early crimes were typical of the organized offender. His later crimes, especially the murders at the Chi Omega sorority in Tallahassee, were characteristic of a disorganized killer. It is much more likely for an organized serial murderer to decompensate

and appear to be disorganized than for a disorganized serial killer to suddenly behave in an organized manner. Factors that could influence organized offenders to behave in a disorganized fashion might be the influence of intoxicants or the panic they feel when they are in danger of imminent apprehension. Offenders characterized as disorganized could learn through experience and become more organized as they gain cumulative crime experience (practice).

The Serial Killer's Motives

While there may be similarities among some types of serial killers, there is nothing that is typical. The known serial killers are a very heterogeneous group. It is important to understand serial killers' motivations and fantasies and to know the way that they have operated in the past and may operate in the future during each phase of their acts of violence. For example, recognizing the characteristics of the types of serial killers who repeatedly return to the scenes of their crimes could be instrumental in their apprehension.

What is the motivation for a person to commit serial homicides? A combination of biological factors (e.g., heredity, brain injury, mental illness, substance abuse, etc.) and psychological factors (e.g., childhood physical abuse, sexual abuse, or both, learned associations between violence and pleasure, etc.) causes the serial murderer to have higher than normal *instigation to aggression* and deficient *inhibitions against aggression*. These concepts are part of the conceptual framework for analyzing violent behavior proposed by Megargee (1993).

According to Megargee, instigation to aggression is "the sum of all forces that motivate an individual to commit a violent or aggressive act" (1993, p. 620). Instigation includes both biological and psychological sources. The psychological sources for instigation to aggression include *extrinsic* and *intrinsic* motivation. In extrinsic or instrumental motivation, the primary motive for the violent behavior is some outcome other than injury of the victim. Injuring the victim is secondary. An example would be an armed robber who kills a convenience store clerk and a customer to eliminate witnesses and to facilitate his escape.

In contrast, intrinsic motivation for aggression involves the conscious or unconscious desire to cause physical harm to the victim, the "target" (Megargee, 1993). Intrinsic motivation has sometimes been referred to as angry motivation. For many acts of violence perpetrated by serial murderers, "angry motivation" does not seem a strong enough term, nor does it convey the sexual aspects of these crimes of violence. As is well known for lust murderers (Hazelwood & Douglas, 1980), sexual sadists (Dietz, Hazelwood, & Warren, 1990), serial rapists, and other kinds of sex offenders, the lines between anger, power, sex, and violence are always blurred.

Some spree killers and others who kill multi-ple victims may have primarily extrinsic motivation, (e.g., profit, escape, rape murder). For most serial murderers, the motivation is intrinsic — there are personal psychological motives for the crime. Spree serial killers and classic serial killers want to kill. They choose to kill. They like to kill. For many serial murders, as for other crimes of violence, there may be a combination of intrinsic and extrinsic motivations, and the extrinsic motives may actually be secondary.

Robert Rodriguez, one of the serial killer we studied, was a former police officer. He confessed that in 1984, he set out to find a girl to rape. When she resisted, he killed her with a knife. In 1992, he again set out to rape someone. He found two teenage girls on a fairly isolated stretch of beach on the Gulf of Mexico. He shot them, but did not rape them. He demonstrated intrinsic motivation to murder his victims. He consciously or unconsciously intended to kill them from the outset. He was a "classic" type serial killer because of the cooling off period between the two incidents. We question whether his cooling off period was really eight years. We suspect that there may have been other victims in the interim. We may never know. Rodriguez killed himself when the investigation was closing in on him. His confession was contained in a suicide note. He wrote: "After a 1984 killing, I told myself I could live normally and not repeat and that if I did, I would take my own life in return, and to prevent my causing further misery." What is more likely is that he killed himself to avoid prosecution, incarceration, and execution.

The motivation for serial murder is often something other than sex. For the serial killer, according to Geberth, "the experience is one of great pleasure in exerting power and control over his victim including the power of life and death" (1990a, p. 73).

Working to oppose instigation to aggression is a set of factors — inhibitions against aggression. According to Megargee (1993), these are the reasons why a person would not perform an aggressive act against a particular target person. Inhibitions include moral prohibitions against violence and practical considerations, such as the likelihood of being apprehended and punished. According to Megargee, "Internal inhibitions, or taboos, include learned moral injunctions that stipulate that aggression in general is wrong, that particular aggressive acts are forbidden, or that aggressive acts directed at certain individuals or under certain circumstances are reprehensible" (p. 630).

Obviously, serial killers lack sufficient inhibitions against repeated violence toward others. In those instances of disorganized serial killers who are actively psychotic, the lack of inhibition may be a product of the mental illness. Most other serial killers appear to believe that the normal social taboos do not apply to them. In addition, they lack consciences and have no empathy for their victims. These are both characteristics of individuals with severely antisocial personality disorders (also called "psychopaths" and "sociopaths"), "sexual psychopaths," and sexual sadists.

Causes of Serial Murder

All manner of biological, psychological, and sociological causes for serial murder have been suggested. In a death row interview, Ted Bundy blamed pornography for his crimes. This was what his interviewer wished to hear, but an unlikely etiological factor in his crimes. In contrast, Heilbroner's (1993) article in Playboy suggested that our culture and sexual repression are causative factors in the occurrence of serial murder.

Many serial killers experienced some form of abuse as children. Child abuse often sets the stage for adult relationship problems, the perpetuation of child abuse in the next generation, and other forms of violence. Not all abused children grow up to be child abusers themselves. The majority of abused children do not kill anyone when they grow up. Fewer become serial killers. As with other types of criminals, when apprehended, serial killers may offer the "abuse excuse." Independent verification of their alleged history of abuse is essential for accurate assessment of the dynamics of the offender's individual case.

Ex post facto assessments of causative factors are typically done by forensic psychologists and psychiatrists to obtain information for use at trial or for sentencing purposes. The underlying causes of serial homicide vary from case to case. They are not different from the causes of other forms of extreme violence. Information on causes of violence appears elsewhere in this book. The reader can also refer to Megargee's (1993) chapter on aggression and violence for an excellent overview of this topic.

To date, social, behavioral, and biological sciences have not contributed a great deal to our understanding of serial murder. True crime accounts of serial murder outnumber scientific works in the literature. Other types of violence (e.g., child abuse, spouse abuse, rape) have received more attention from academic researchers than has serial homicide. As a consequence, there is a relative paucity of scientific information about serial murder.

Most of what is known about serial murder has been the result of the studies done by the FBI. The goal of the FBI research has been to understand the behavior of the serial killer. As a practical matter, investigative concern is not on why particular individuals become serial killers — it is on why they do what they do to their victims. The variables of primary interest are those that can lead to the identification and apprehension of the perpetrator.

The Assault Cycle: Phases of Serial Murder

Just as there is no typical serial killer, there is

no typical script by which the violent events of serial homicide occur. Each one is different. As we have indicated, there are some patterns that are typical of organized offenders, and some that are typical of disorganized offenders. The differences in these patterns are seen through the five phases of the assault cycle: the *fantasy phase*, the *triggering phase*, the *violent event*, the *post-offense phase*, and *recovery and return to baseline*.

Phase One: Fantasy

One of the things that help organized serial killers to be organized is that they plan their crimes. They fantasize, visualize, research, and mentally rehearse their crimes over and over. There is pleasure for them in the anticipation of the total violent event. One experienced investigator likened this to a person planning a vacation trip to Hawaii (or Florida, a state that has attracted more than its share of serial killers). The individual studies travel brochures and day dreams about the sunny beaches, blue sea, and warm breezes. The person has pleasurable mental images of being there. The more he or she fantasizes, the stronger the drive to experience the event becomes.

Disorganized serial killers are like persons who step off a plane only to discover that they have somehow lucked out and landed in Hawaii (or Florida). They may have fantasized about being in paradise, but they have no well thought out plan. They have no travelers' checks, swim suit, or itinerary. They frantically try to enjoy the unexpected vacation amid confusion and reckless abandon.

Phase Two: Triggering

Organized offenders always have a fantasy (or purpose) for their acts of violence. Their crimes are premeditated to the extent that they have planned them. They may stalk their victims. A triggering event, such as a major life frustration or other precipitating stress factor, may occur which increases instigation. A suitable target, often a stranger of a particular type, may present herself or himself (a victim of opportunity) and serve as a trigger for the violent event.

By contrast, disorganized offenders rarely plan. They commit a spontaneous assault without any premeditation. They select a victim of convenience and opportunity in a random fashion, usually near their "comfort zone." There may be triggering events in their life that increase their instigation or diminish their inhibitions, e.g., an argument with a spouse, getting fired from a job, or a mental health crisis. If they have a fantasy, it is likely to be infantile and regressed, or patently psychotic.

The serial killer's selection of a victim reflects the needs, fantasies, and means of the offender. *Victimology*, the study of the role and characteristics of the victim in a specific crime, is important to understanding a particular serial killer. Was the victim helpless or infirm? Was the victim young or old, attractive or unattractive? Are the serial victims similar in any way?

Some victims have escaped death at the hands of serial killers. There is little that a potential victim can say or do to escape imminent violence once a serial killer has targeted him or her. The killers have already made up their minds to kill when they confront their victims. How can one avoid becoming the victim of a serial killer? There is not much one can do except to follow the tenets of crime prevention. Don't go to unsafe places. Don't trust strangers or let them into your home. Serial killers look just like everybody else. And, of course, lock your house and car doors.

Phase Three: The Violent Event

The differences between organized and disorganized serial killers become manifest when the killer encounters the victim. These differences are played out in the violent event and its aftermath.

During the violent encounter, organized offenders are likely to:

1. Bring a weapon or "murder kit" (weapons, restraints, gloves, etc.) with them, and take them from the scene.

2. Use guile to obtain access to the victim.

3. Use restraints (handcuffs, rope, tape, etc.) which may be part of their murder kit.

4. Possibly transport the victim to another location to play out their violent fantasies, before or after the murder.

5. Personalize their victim (e.g., leave the victim's face exposed).

6. Commit aggressive and sexual acts, experiment with living victims, or both.

7. Display control of the victim through manipulation or threats, and want the victim to show fear.

8. Show controlled rage in the assault.

9. Use a vehicle (Geberth, 1990b; Ressler, Burgess, Douglas, Hartman, & D'Agostino, 1986).

During the violent event, disorganized murderers are likely to:

1. Commit spontaneous assaults without any planning or premeditation.

2. Use a weapon of opportunity and leave it at the scene.

3. Select a victim randomly, usually near the killer's "comfort zone."

4. Experiment sexually with unconscious or dead victims.

5. Depersonalize their victim (e.g., cover the victim's face).

6. Use a "blitz" attack to disable the victim.

7. Commit the murder in a careless fashion, often leaving considerable evidence.

8. Commit the assault and leave the body at the same site.

9. Show uncontrolled rage, which is reflected in the crime scene.

10. Position the body for symbolic purposes or to depersonalize the victim (e.g., face down).

11. Make no attempt to conceal the body.

12. Not use a vehicle. (Geberth, 1990b; Ressler et al., 1986).

The decisions made by the serial murderer, and the methods and means used in the execution of a murder reflect his or her fantasy, needs, personality, abilities, and resources.

The FBI Crime Classification Manual (Douglas, Burgess, Burgess, & Ressler, 1992) defines *modus operandi* (MO) as the actions taken by the offender to perpetrate the offense successfully. MO is learned behavior that evolves as the offender becomes more sophisticated and confident. *Signature* or *personation* is repetitive ritualistic behavior by a serial offender, usually displayed at every crime scene and having nothing to do with the perpetration of the crime.

The MO more specifically relates to the commission of the crime, the protection of the offender's identity, and escape. The signature involves the acting out of a fantasy on the part of the offender. It is unnecessary to the commission of the crime, but may be of essential importance to the murderer. The MO is constantly changing and dynamic. It depends on such factors as the location of the crime, the actions or reactions of the victim, and what the perpetrator has learned from his or her past crimes and mistakes. An offender who has been arrested in the past based on his or her identification from fingerprints at the scene will surely learn to use gloves during his or her next offense. Similarly, a rapist who has been identified based on DNA will take measures to remove serological evidence from future scenes. Loss of control over a victim may change the offender's approach or cause the perpetrator to add the use of restraints or a more threatening type of weapon in his or her next crime. Likewise, some elements of the signature may change over time as the killer's fantasies are realized or frustrated by his or her violent encounters with the victims.

Phase Four: Post-offense Behavior

As we have already indicated, the disorganized offender typically leaves the body at the scene "DRT" ("dead right there"). This type of killer frequently takes a souvenir, a personal item (e.g., panties) from the victim, or something from the scene to use later for fantasy purposes. An organized offender may either discard the body after the crime, or expend great energy concealing it. He or she may take some item from the victim that has more meaning to the killer than just a souvenir. This trophy might be a piece of jewelry or perhaps even a body part. The trophy can serve as a symbol of the perpetrator's conquest.

After committing a murder, disorganized offenders usually act in a very rigid manner. There may be changes in their demeanor that are noticeable to their associates. Organized offenders go about their business as usual.

Phase Five: Recovery and Return to Baseline

Serial killers have a "murder clock" that determines when they feel the desire to kill again, much like our "hunger clock" tells us when it is time to eat. After a murder, the time it takes the killer to "recycle" and have a desire to kill again varies from individual to individual. The cycle is affected by how much enjoyment the killer derived from his or her last murder, whether or not it went as planned, and other factors which increase or decrease instigation and inhibitions.

Serial killers tend to escalate their killing over time. Geberth (1990a) attributed this to their need to maintain an equilibrium, and to the fantasy and psychological "high" that can produce more frequent and bolder crimes.

Two Case Examples

The second author was involved in investiga-

tions of murders committed by the two serial killers discussed in this section. These cases illustrate many of the points we have made in previous sections. The case summaries show examples of the MOs and signatures of these serial killers.

Danny Rolling

Over a four-day period in August 1990, Danny Rolling, a drifter and sometimes armed robber, stabbed, raped, and mutilated five young people in Gainesville, Florida, the home of the University of Florida. Four young women and one young man were found murdered. The first crime scene probably did not raise the specter of a serial killer. The number and nature of subsequent crime scenes convinced the authorities that a serial killer was at work in their college town.

Serial killer Ted Bundy had been executed by the State of Florida the previous January. The anxious public readily associated the Gainesville murders with the horror Bundy had wrought in Tallahassee near the Florida State University campus in 1978. For many people, it was unthinkable that there could be another serial killer preying upon Florida college students. Some, confusing Ted Bundy with horrific movie serial killers with supernatural powers (e.g., Jason, Freddie Krueger), suggested that Bundy might not be dead, and could be on the loose in Gainesville.

It was the signature of Danny Rolling's violent acts that indicated that there was a serial murderer at work in Gainesville. Rolling was a "fan" of Ted Bundy. In fact, he bought the knife he used in the Gainesville murders in Tallahassee at the Army-Navy store across from the Florida State University campus. Rolling's signature would not have been mistaken for Bundy's by the trained investigators who comprised the Gainesville task force.

In the first case, Rolling approached an apartment located in a large complex on a busy street.

The apartment had been rented by three female University of Florida students. Only two of the girls had moved in. Rolling brought gloves, a pry tool, a large knife, and duct tape with him to the scene. He pried open a back door that faced a wooded area and entered the two-story apartment. He bound the mouth, wrists, and ankles of the young woman he discovered in the living room. He sexually battered (raped) her, stabbed her in the back, and removed her nipples. She was later discovered nude, lying on her back with her legs spread. A towel containing dish washing liquid had been placed under her buttocks. The contents of her purse had been scattered on the floor next to her body and cash had been taken. The tape that had been used to bind the victim had been removed and taken away from the scene.

The body of another young woman was found in an upstairs bedroom. She had been stabbed numerous times through her right side, breast, and arm, and had a gaping incised wound on her left thigh. She had been dragged to a position at the end of the bed. She was lying on her back with her legs spread apart and her feet on the floor. Her panties had been removed, but she had not been sexually assaulted. There was evidence that her personal belongings had been searched and that items were missing. It appeared that the offender had consumed food at the apartment.

The second crime scene was a small, single-story duplex apartment on a quiet residential street. The female victim lived alone and was a student at the community college. Rolling entered her apartment by prying a sliding glass door open. The victim was discovered sitting on the side of her bed with her legs spread and her body bent forward at the waist. She was nude except for shoes and socks. She had been sexually battered and stabbed in the back. Her head had been removed and placed on a shelf that had been positioned nearby. Her nipples had been removed and she had been cut open from her chest to her pubic area. The apartment had been searched and cash

was missing from her purse. It appeared that food had been eaten at the apartment.

Crime scene three was a large three-story apartment complex located near the first crime scene. Two university students — a male and a female — shared the two-bedroom apartment. Rolling entered the apartment from the rear by prying the sliding glass door open. He stabbed the young woman in the back and sexually battered her. Her nude body was later dragged to the hall and positioned with her legs spread apart. Her wrists had been bound together with duct tape, which was later removed and taken from the scene. She had been washed and a towel that contained dish washing liquid had been placed under her buttocks. The young man's body was discovered on his bed. He was clad in a t-shirt, underwear, and socks. He had been stabbed multiple times in the chest, hands, neck, leg, and face, and there was a large incised wound on his abdomen.

The victims' nipples had been removed at two of the three crime scenes. All of the victims who had been sexually battered had also been stabbed in the back. Money had been taken from each of the three scenes and it appeared that food had been consumed at each scene. No common fingerprints were identified at the three separate scenes. However, the serological evidence obtained in the sexual assault kits was identical. A common factor in the crimes was the long amount of time that would have been required for the offender to commit the crimes at the three locations.

The MO of the offender in the commission of the crimes demonstrated the sophistication and planning of an organized offender. Approaching from the woods at night limited the view of potential witnesses. Prying open a rear door provided quiet access and an element of surprise. The perpetrator did not have to formulate a ruse to gain entry. Wearing gloves prevented the discovery of latent fingerprints. Using tape to restrain the victims provided control of the situation. Taking the tape with him when he left prevented the recovery of latent prints, hair, or fiber evidence. Using a large knife ensured control and death of the victims and the elimination of any witnesses who could identify him. In the two cases where a second person was present, Rolling killed them first in order to spend more time with the targeted victims.

In contrast, washing the victims' genital areas, leaving towels under the victims' buttocks, positioning the victims to degrade them and shock the persons who discovered the crimes, cutting off the victims' nipples, removing the victim's head, taking photographs as trophies, and eating snacks at the scenes were all elements of Danny Rolling's signature. All of these actions arose from his fantasies. These commonalities demonstrated that a single perpetrator was responsible for the crimes. But, what if the crimes had taken place hundreds of miles apart, and over a period of years?

Danny Rolling pleaded guilty to killing the five students and received five death sentences. He is currently on death row in Florida.

Michael Lee Lockhart

Serial killer Danny Rolling broke into his victims' residences through the back doors. A different kind of serial killer talked his way in through the front door.

In an interview, Michael Lee Lockhart said, "It's very scary. I could be so smooth and lovable one minute and be the devil the next minute." Lockhart, dubbed the "Romeo Killer" by the press, came to Florida sporting his youthful good looks, an abundance of confidence and charm, driving a stolen late model red Corvette. In broad daylight, he smooth-talked his way into the suburban Pasco County residence of a 14-year-old girl who knew well that she was never allowed to let a stranger into her home when her parents were at work. He must not have looked like the dangerous man she had been warned about by her parents and teachers when he parked the shiny red car in the driveway of a nearby house for sale. He motioned to her as she jogged around the cul-de-sac and asked to use her phone to call the realtor.

She could not have sensed his evil intentions as she unlocked the door and invited him to use the kitchen telephone. We can only imagine the horror she must have felt when he armed himself with a knife from her mother's kitchen and chased her through her home. She attempted to barricade herself in her brother's room. Lockhart, who only seconds before seemed to be a handsome stranger and possible future neighbor, kicked the door from the frame. He savagely choked her, raped her vaginally and anally, and stabbed her multiple times. Her partially nude body was discovered by her little brother a short time later, her organs protruding from a gaping wound in her abdomen.

Lockhart was prosecuted for this crime, and for a remarkably similar murder of a 16-year-old Indiana teenager. He was also prosecuted for the murder of a Texas Police officer. Michael Lee Lockhart is currently on death row in Texas.

Initially, Lockhart bragged that he killed between 20 and 30 people in a crime spree in three states, but later he claimed, "I don't remember none of it, the blood or the place, or the pictures. I just don't remember. I've put it out of my mind because I don't want to remember." Regarding the evil inside him, Lockhart said, "It's something I have no control over, something that turns off and on when it wants to turn off and on."

Assessment (Profiling) of Serial Killers

After the release of the highly successful movie based on Thomas Harris's (1988) novel *Silence of the Lambs*, young women inquired about how they might train to become "profilers" of serial murderers, like Clarice Starling, the FBI trainee portrayed by actress Jodie Foster in the movie. *Criminal investigative analysis*, as psychological profiling is now called, is not a professional expertise that is acquired easily or quickly.

Criminal Investigative Analysis and Profiling

Psychological profiling began as a pilot project at the FBI in 1978. Articles generated by the NCAVC researchers soon began to appear in the professional literature (e.g., Ressler, Douglas, Groth, & Burgess, 1980). Articles about profiling soon followed in the popular press (e.g., Porter, 1983).

It has been said that the goals of science are to understand, predict, and control. The goals of criminal investigative analysis are to understand, identify, and apprehend.

Most of what is known about serial killers has been developed by law enforcement professionals who have had the opportunity to study many of the serial killers who have been apprehended and to work on numerous violent crime investigations. The research done by law enforcement specialists has been empirical in nature, designed to accumulate practical information about serial murderers and their offenses. By identifying commonalities, they have been able to develop typologies, understand the link between crime scenes/offenses and characteristics of the offenders (Douglas, Ressler, Burgess, & Hartman, 1986), and develop information which is useful in investigations. In this chapter, we have presented information that has been "field-tested" in numerous violent crime investigations in this country and abroad.

Some investigators have claimed that something magical happens as a result of the profiling process. Criminal investigative analysis (profiling) is not magic. The profiler's tool box does not contain tarot cards, a ouija board, or fairy dust. (The second author does have a crystal ball on her desk, but it is there only for dramatic effect). Profiling is simply a process that is based on log-ic, intuition, crime scene experience, and years of shared investigative experience. Investigators use profiling techniques in cases every day without calling it profiling. The process of sitting down and reviewing case information and brainstorming often leads to a suggestion or new idea that yields positive results.

The FBI defines profiling as an investigative technique by which to identify the major personality and behavioral characteristics of the offender based upon an analysis of the crime(s) he or she has committed (Douglas & Burgess, 1986). It is important to clarify that investigators use this process to analyze what has happened in the crime scene for what it may reveal about the type of person most likely to have committed the crime. In other words, we profile all of the activity, not the person. Suspect information is not presented during the profiling process because the group could unconsciously attempt to match the scene to the suspect.

The profile process is similar to that used by clinicians to formulate a diagnosis and a treatment plan. Data are collected and assessed, the situation is reconstructed, hypotheses are formulated, a profile is developed and tested, and the results are reported (Douglas et al., 1986). It has been our experience that a small profiling group yields the best results. When individuals from different specialized disciplines and backgrounds join together to discuss a case, the crime scene data are analyzed from each member's unique perspective. A team composed of a forensic pathologist, a blood spatter expert, a forensic psychologist, and experienced investigators and profilers can often make investigative sense out of information that emerges from the crime scene. They attempt to determine what happened, why it happened, and what type of person did it. Suggestions regarding possible motives and investigative strategies then can be provided to the investigators.

Geberth (1990b) devoted a chapter of his book on homicide investigation to offender profiling, with special emphasis on serial murder. An advocate of profiling, he acknowledged the unpredictability of human behavior, and advised against "putting all of your investigative eggs into the psychological basket" (p. 536).

In a recent survey of police psychologists, Bartol (1995) found that 2% of the work time of in-house psychologists, and 3.4% of the time of part-time consulting psychologists were involved in "criminal profiling." Interestingly, Bartol also found that 70% of the police psychologists surveyed did not feel comfortable doing profiling and were skeptical about its validity. Unfortunately, what many mental health professionals think of as profiling is merely opining about the characteristics of an offender based on theory or a reading of the research literature. Criminal profiling done by psychologists, psychiatrists, or criminologists without the appropriate training and experience in investigating violent crimes frequently is useless. Worse, it may misdirect investigations.

Criminal investigative analysis requires special training and a great deal of investigative experience. This experience is important because, as one seasoned investigator put it, "It is easier to recognize something you have seen before."

Criminal Investigative Analysis and Investigations

Ressler, Burgess, Douglas, Hartman, and D'Agostino (1986) discussed the usefulness of profiling serial killers using the distinction between organized and disorganized offenders. In contrast to more traditional psychological analyses, this approach is based on specific testable concepts and behavior of offenders which can be related to crime scene evidence. Rather than relying on hypotheses developed from psychological theories of motivation, which cannot be verified until the offender is identified and studied, attention is given to the MO and signature aspects of serial murders. According to Ressler et al.,

"Analysis of these data from the crime scene may be useful in understanding the psychosocial nature of the murderer and lead (it is hoped) to his capture" (p. 306).

Knowing a serial murderer's level of preparation helps in understanding his or her motivation and fantasy. For example, an ordinary burglar "cases" a house and enters when no one is home. A burglar who enters knowing that people are home is looking for a thrill, or for contact with a victim. Bindings and murder weapons are not burglary tools. When a perpetrator brings these things to the scene, his or her fantasy about what may happen is not limited to burglary and escape.

The maxim of profilers is: *The crime scene tells the tale*. From a detailed analysis of the crime scene, the trained profiler can often suggest a variety of factors that may help to focus the investigation on the most likely target and eliminate others from immediate consideration. The degree of sophistication necessary to perpetrate a crime, and the killer's ability to control the victim, can suggest the killer's criminal arrest history and level of intelligence. The method of approach to the victim speaks to the offender's personality style and demeanor. Specific types of sexual activity, or the lack of sexual activity, may reveal information regarding sexual experience, sexual perversions, and dating or marital status. The time of the crime, preparation, and attention to detail, may suggest work habits or employment type. Items taken from the victim or the scene may relate to the offender's lifestyle or socioeconomic status. The type, number, and location of injuries to the victim, such as facial battery or multiple stabs to the heart, may suggest a previous relationship between the victim and offender. The method of disposal of the victim's body, and the care given to clean or alter the crime scene, can also provide possible relationship information. The type, location, and number of wounds can also provide a clue to the race and gender of the offender. In the Wournos investigation, profilers suggested that the perpetrator was a female. They were ultimately proven to be correct.

The most difficult factor for the profiler to interpret is the age of the offender. The selection of the victim, preparation for the crime, and the elements of the actual offense, can provide the basis for an estimation of the social/emotional age of the offender, which may be different from his or her actual chronological age. Offenders who have been incarcerated or institutionalized for a significant period of time may be described as younger than their actual age because they suffer from what we call "arrested development."

Information about serial murderers developed by investigative profilers can be used in interviewing suspects and planning prosecutorial strategies for serial killers who have been apprehended.

Earlier in this chapter, we discussed the offense and crime scene characteristics of organized and disorganized serial killers. What do profilers know about the personal characteristics of these two types?

Personal Characteristics of Organized and Disorganized Serial Murderers

Based on the FBI research, we know that organized offenders are more likely to be described as:

1. Intelligent.
2. Socially competent.
3. Sexually competent.
4. Skilled workers.
5. Likely to have been reared with inconsistent discipline.
6. Psychopaths (i.e., sociopaths or antisocial personalities), or sexual sadists and not psychotic.

Disorganized offenders are more likely to be described as:

1. Average or below average in intelligence.
2. Socially immature.
3. Sexually inexperienced or incompetent.
4. Having a poor work history.
5. Having experienced harsh discipline as a child.
6. More likely to be actively psychotic (Geberth, 1990b; Ressler et al. 1986). Not many are psychotic.

VICAP and New Technology

Law enforcement officers traditionally have not been known for their willingness to share information with other agencies. With increased utilization of computer tracking through the FBI Violent Criminal Apprehension Program (VICAP), this is changing. It has become possible to identify similarities in crimes that occur in different locations and jurisdictions. As a consequence, it is becoming somewhat easier to identify and track the operations of serial murderers. VICAP is a national data center designed to collect, collate, and analyze information on violent crimes across the country. Investigators complete a short form and forward it to the NCAVC at the FBI Academy. The information is input into the computer. VICAP staff members look for similarities in MO, signature characteristics, victimology, physical evidence, suspect description, and suspect behavior. Investigators are notified of possible matches.

Several states have developed similar programs (Florida: VICIS; New York: HALT; New Jersey: HEAT; Washington: HITS; Canada: ViCLAS) designed to fit their individual needs. They also participate in the VICAP program by forwarding data forms to the FBI Academy.

One of the most important technological developments in the apprehension and prosecution of serial murderers is the use of DNA data bases. Several states have enacted legislation mandating submission of blood samples for DNA-typing from all offenders adjudicated guilty of violent crimes, regardless of their sentences. Now, blood, semen, and some hair evidence can be used to identify offenders in unsolved violent crimes.

Treatment

There is no known treatment for serial murderers. By definition, they are repeat offenders. It is well known that the best predictor of future behavior is past behavior. The nature of serial murderers' psychopathology is that they have strong intrinsic motivation to harm other humans, and in many cases, they achieve great pleasure from doing so. They kill other human beings because they like to kill.

Many people in the criminal justice system advocate the death penalty for serial killers. They point out that execution is certain to stop the serial killer's series of homicides. Arguments for and against the death penalty aside, execution does do this.

We were involved in the investigation of a possible serial killer. His history indicated that he had attempted to kill a woman he had raped. He served a prison sentence and was released. He subsequently killed a female clerk unnecessarily during a robbery. At trial, he was sentenced to death, but the judge overruled the jury's verdict. While in prison, the defendant wrote a novel revealing themes of serial murder. After serving 17 years, he was released. Several years later, he came to our attention as the prime suspect in the disappearance of another female clerk. This case points to the need for people at all levels of the criminal justice system to recognize the signs of serial murder dynamics in repeat violent offenders.

An alternative that offers the same degree of safety to the public is lifetime imprisonment without parole. Clearly, there is no way to certify a serial killer rehabilitated, cured, or safe to return to the community. Incarceration offers the opportunity for intensive study of those serial killers who are willing to cooperate. Some refuse to cooperate altogether. Others try to "cut a deal" by revealing information about other crimes or blatantly lie to try to con the authorities. Some serial killers cooperate to a fair degree. Studies of these individuals have contributed to our knowledge about serial killers, their motives, and their operations. Some would argue that the opportunity to study serial killers is potentially of greater value to society than their execution. Given the lengthy time between sentencing and execution due to the appeals process, most serial killers who wish to cooperate are available for years of study.

Serial killers who are found not guilty by reason of insanity are involuntarily committed. If their mental health improves as a result of psychiatric treatment, should they be released? We think not. The chance of recidivism is extremely high. There is no guarantee that they will comply with a treatment regimen once they are released from the hospital.

One reason for studying serial killers who have been incarcerated is to elicit information about additional crimes they have committed. Locating the bodies of missing persons and solving unsolved cases is humanitarian because it gives some degree of closure to the family members of missing victims. So does prosecuting serial killers on additional charges, even if they already are facing a death sentence. For similar reasons, we participated in the post mortem investigation of Robert Rodriguez, whom we mentioned earlier. If he could have been tied to other victims, other cases might have been closed. Other loved ones might have felt closure.

Maintaining Conditions and Difficulties in Interventions

Serial murder is chronic. While some serial killers may stop killing for a period of time, most want to kill and enjoy the experience enough to recycle and kill again. And again. To the extent that they are smart, cunning, and careful, they may continue without apprehension. They may study the careers of other killers, read the law enforcement manuals, and do other things to perfect their evil craft.

Too frequently, detectives fail to link cases that have been committed by the same offender because they expect the MO to be exactly the same. Another major impediment to the apprehension of serial killers who move about is *linkage blindness*. Egger wrote that linkage blindness occurs when "Law enforcement investigators do not see, are prevented from seeing, or make little attempt to see beyond their own jurisdictional responsibilities" (1990b, p. 164). There are numerous documented instances of linkage blindness in serial murder investigations across the country.

We had the opportunity to interview a serial murder suspect who was in police custody on unrelated charges. The detective in charge of the case was working with state and federal law enforcement agencies to determine whether the suspect could be linked to any unsolved cases. He was ordered off the case by his supervisor, who justified his action by stating that the suspect had not killed anyone in their agency's area of jurisdiction! The suspect was released. His present whereabouts are unknown.

What can be done to reduce the linkage blindness that delays the apprehension of serial murderers? If all agencies will participate in the VICAP program, that will be a giant step in the right direction. It is of utmost importance that individuals with responsibilities at all levels of the criminal justice system be educated about serial murder and understand that serial murderers can be identified as such early in their violent careers. Professional organizations for violent crime investigators need to continue to provide training in this area. Every time violent crime investigators network and share case information, there exists the possibility that a violent criminal will be taken off the street. Because of the high risk of lethal violence, it is essential to identify serial killers as quickly as possible.

Summary

In this chapter, we presented the current definitions of serial murder and discussed much of what has been learned about this phenomenon. We have emphasized information that has practical significance for the apprehension of serial killers.

There is no one cause or known cure for the individuals who commit serial murder. Studies of serial murderers have given us insight regarding their motives and behavior. Hopefully, this type of knowledge can help us identify and apprehend these violent offenders earlier in their homicidal careers. There remains a great deal more to learn about the causes of serial murder, as well as all other types of lethal violence.

Case Readings

There is no shortage of available reading material on serial murder cases. One of the better compendiums of cases is *Serial Killers* (Time-Life Editors, 1992). New York: Time-Life Books.

One of the best documentary videos on this topic is a CNN Special Report, *Murder by the numbers* (1993). Atlanta: CNN Video.

References

Bartol, C. (in press). Police psychology: Then, now, and beyond. *Criminal Justice and Behavior*.

Bruni, F. (1994, September 4). Hack by popular demand: Serial killers are hot in fiction, films. *Tallahassee Democrat*, p. 4E.

Dietz, P. E. (1992). Mentally disordered offenders: Patterns in the relationship between mental disorder and crime. *Psychiatric Clinics of North America, 15,* 539-551.

Dietz, P. E., Hazelwood, R. R., & Warren, J. (1990). The sexually sadistic criminal and his offenses. *Bulletin of the American Academy of Psychiatry and Law, 18*(2), 71-86.

Douglas, J. E. & Burgess, A. W. (1986). Criminal profiling: A viable investigative tool against violent crime. *FBI Law Enforcement Bulletin, 55,* 9-13.

Douglas, J. E., Burgess, A. W., Burgess, A. G., & Ressler, R. K. (1992). *Crime classification manual: A standard system for investigating and classifying violent crimes.* New York: Lexington Books.

Douglas, J. E., Ressler, R. K., Burgess, A. W., & Hartman, C. R. (1986). Criminal profiling from crime scene analysis. *Behavioral Sciences and the Law, 4*(4), 401-421.

Egger, S. A. (1990a). Serial murder: A synthesis of literature and research. In S. A. Egger (Ed.), *Serial murder: An elusive phenomenon.* New York: Praeger.

Egger, S. A. (1990b). Linkage blindness: A systemic myopia. In S. A. Egger (Ed.), *Serial murder: An elusive phenomenon.* New York: Praeger.

Federal Bureau of Investigation (1994). *Crime in America. Uniform Crime Reports 1993.* Washington, DC: U.S. Government Printing Office.

Geberth, V. G. (1990a, May). The serial killer and the revelations of Ted Bundy. *Law and Order,* 72-75.

Geberth, V. G. (1990b). *Practical homicide investigation: Tactics, procedures, and forensic techniques (2nd ed.).* New York: Elsevier.

Harris, T. (1988). *Silence of the lambs.* New York: St. Martin's Press.

Hazelwood, R. R. & Douglas, J. E. (1980, April). The lust murderer. *FBI Law Enforcement Bulletin,* 103-107.

Heilbroner, D. (1993, August). Serial murder and repression. *Playboy, 78,* 147-150.

Holmes, R. K. & DeBurger, J. E. (1985). Profiles in terror: The serial murderer. *Federal Probation, 49*(3), 29-34.

Jenkins, P. (1989). Serial murder in the United States 1900-1940: A historical perspective. *Journal of Criminal Justice, 17,* 377-392.

Jenkins, P. (1992). A murder "wave"? Trends in American serial homicide 1940-1990. *Criminal Justice Review, 17*(1), 1-19.

Kiger, K. (1990). The darker figure of crime: The serial murder enigma. In S. A. Egger (Ed.), *Serial murder: An elusive phenomenon.* New York: Praeger.

Lourie, R. (1993). *Hunting the devil.* New York: Harper.

Megargee, E. I. (1993). Aggression and violence. In H. E. Adams & P. B. Sutker (Eds.), *Comprehensive handbook of psychopathology (2nd ed.).* New York: Plenum.

Monahan, J. (1992). Mental disorder and violent behavior: Perceptions and evidence. *American Psychologist, 47*(4), 511-521.

National Center for the Analysis of Violent Crime (1994). *Serial, mass and spree murderers in the United States: Search of major wire services and publications: Offenders operating from 1960 to present.* Quantico, VA: FBI Academy.

Newton, M. (1990). *Hunting humans: The encyclopedia*

of serial killers (Vol. 1). New York: Avon Books.

Porter, B. (1983, April). Mind hunters: Tracking down killers with the FBI's psychological profiling team. *Psychology Today*, 162-170.

Ressler, R. K., Burgess, A. W., Douglas, J. E., Hartman, C., & D'agostino, R. (1986). Sexual killers and their victims. *Journal of Interpersonal Violence, 1*(3), 288-308.

Ressler, R. K., Douglas, J. E., Groth, A. N., & Burgess, A. W. (1980, September). Offender profiles: A multidisciplinary approach. *FBI Law Enforcement Bulletin*, 157-161.

A riddle wrapped in a mystery inside an enigma (1994). *New Yorker, 70*(41), 45-46.

Time-Life Editors. (1992). *Mass Murderers*. New York: Time-Life Books.

About the Authors

Patrick E. Cook received his PhD from the University of Texas at Austin. A Diplomate in Clinical Psychology, he practices clinical, forensic, and police psychology in Tallahassee, Florida. He performs pre-employment, special duty, and fitness for duty evaluations for three police departments. He is the psychologist for the Tallahassee Police Department Tactical Apprehension and Control Team. Dr. Cook is a consultant to the Florida Department of Law Enforcement on violent crime investigations, and is a member of the Florida Homicide Investigators Association. His interests in serial murder and pre-employment screening of police officers began over 20 years ago when he had the opportunity to evaluate a prolific serial murderer. The killer had been hired by a law enforcement agency that did not do psychological screening of applicants, after having been screened out by one that did. Dr. Cook may be contacted at 2027 Thomasville Rd., Suite 102, Tallahassee, FL, 32312, telephone: (904) 386-8116.

Dayle L. Hinman is a Special Agent for the Florida Department of Law Enforcement, and is the State-wide Coordinator of the Criminal Assessment Profile Program. She consults with law enforcement investigators and offers assistance in the analysis of homicide crime scenes. She has been associated with the task force investigations of such serial murderers as Danny Rolling, Aileen Wournos, and Oscar Bolin. With over 20 years of law enforcement experience, she instructs at numerous police academies in the areas of serial murder investigation and profiling through crime scene analysis. Special Agent Hinman received a B.S. degree from Florida State University and is currently working on a Master's degree. She was the recipient of a year-long fellowship in the Behavioral Science Unit at the FBI Academy and is one of only 33 graduates of the program. She currently serves on the education and training committee that has established the criteria for understudies in this program. She was a founding member and is a past president of the Florida Homicide Investigators Association. She continues to promote the exchange of homicide information among law enforcement agencies. Special Agent Hinman may be contacted at the Florida Department of Law Enforcement, P. O. Box 1489, Tallahassee, FL, 32302.

CHAPTER 14

MURDER AND SEX MURDER: PSYCHOPATHOLOGY AND PSYCHODYNAMICS

Louis B. Schlesinger

In spite of its significance as a major cause of death, murder has been neglected as an object of serious scientific study. Sex murders (that is, homicides motivated primarily by underlying sexual conflicts) constitute a small percentage of all homicides, but the tragedy they cause and the potential for repetition make them too important to be neglected. Unfortunately, in the Federal Bureau of Investigation's (FBI) *Uniform Crime Reports*, sex murders are not categorized separately. Assaults with distinct manifestations of genitality (for example, rape) are classified, but definite sex murders are not. As a result, the exact prevalence of such cases remains unknown.

There have been many previous attempts at classifying murder, crime, and violent behavior for a variety of purposes, including that of prediction. Brancale (1955), for example, classified crime simply into administrative and psychiatric groupings, whereas Clark (1971) postulated six specific categories of social offenses. Halleck (1971) regarded crime as either adaptive (motivated by some type of logical or purposeful notion) or maladaptive (a result of psychopathology where the motivations are not always apparent). Similarly, in Tanay's (1969) classification system, homicide is categorized as dissociative, psychotic, or ego-syntonic. Tanay's ego-syntonic homicide is comparable to Halleck's adaptive

crime; his dissociative and psychotic categories correspond to Halleck's maladaptive crime. Miller and Looney (1974), in their study of adolescent offenders, regarded the presence of "episodic dyscontrol and dehumanization" as a major predictor of adolescent homicide.

The problems of how to evaluate an individual who has committed or may commit a murder are well illustrated by the varying interpretations of the fictional character Raskolnikov, in Dostoyevsky's novel *Crime and Punishment*. Dostoyevsky provided a motive for Raskolnikov's murderous deed: personal gain bolstered by the idea of "great men daring to cross ethical barriers." Florance (1955), in her analysis of this case, argued that Raskolnikov's act was the result of unresolved Oedipal and incestuous conflicts. If a present day general clinical psychologist were to evaluate Raskolnikov, he would probably diagnose him as depressed. A forensic psychologist would be preoccupied with his criminal responsibility and "sanity." Yet, such evaluations do not really explain Raskolnikov's behavior and offer little guidance for assessment of his future dangerousness. Revitch and Schlesinger (1981) argued that Raskolnikov knew what he was doing but did not know why he was doing it. The act was clearly premeditated, yet it had a compelling element to it.

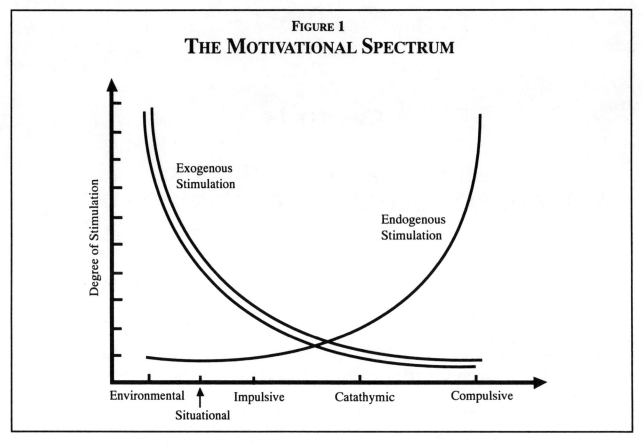

FIGURE 1
THE MOTIVATIONAL SPECTRUM

Reliance on psychiatric diagnosis per se — except where the offense was a direct outgrowth of a paranoid condition, an organic disorder, or a toxic state — proves unrewarding as a means of predicting future violence. The majority of the research, however, has emphasized the role of psychosis, various demographic factors, family history of violence, certain personality traits, or other signs and symptoms — all with varying degrees of success (Dershowitz, 1973; Hellman & Blackman, 1966; Rubin, 1972; Smith & English, 1978).

In search of a common denominator to use as a basis for classification, Revitch and Schlesinger analyzed the dynamics of the antisocial (homicidal) act and, as a result of that analysis (based solely on clinical experience as opposed to systematic empirical research), developed the concept of motivational stimuli (Revitch, 1977;

Revitch & Schlesinger, 1978, 1981, 1989). These stimuli are spectrally distributed, with purely external (sociogenic) on one end and purely internal (psychogenic) on the other. In moving from the external to the internal, they specified five separate categories of offenses: (a) sociogenic or environmental, (b) situational, (c) impulsive, (d) catathymic, and (e) compulsive. In compulsive offenses, the endogenous pressures are paramount, and external factors play a minimal role. The reverse is true for the environmental offenses. The other categories of offenses have a mixture of endogenous and exogenous factors, depending on their position in the spectrum (see Figure 1). Organic, toxic, and paranoid cases form a group of their own, distinct from our system of classification. Specific criteria used to categorize cases are detailed throughout this chapter and are illustrated by descriptive case studies.

Organic, Toxic, and Paranoid Murders

Murder associated with psychiatric conditions most commonly occurs in the organic, toxic, and paranoid states, and sometimes in the state of psychotic depression (Bourget & Bradford, 1987; Good, 1978, Rosenbaum & Bennet, 1986). Among the organic conditions, epilepsy stands out as a major cause of sudden attacks of violence and aggression. The epileptic seizure itself, or violence as a manifestation of postictal confusion, is often cited as the cause of attacks that are goalless, chaotic, and mainly unprovoked. Various encephalopathies, brain injuries, and brain tumors have all been regarded as possible causes of murder, temper tantrums, and acts of aggression. Mark and Ervin (1970) reported a case where homicidal violence was linked to a tumor in the limbic system; after the tumor was removed, the overt aggression was substantially reduced. In numerous other cases cited in the literature, all of the above organic pathologies have been regarded as directly contributory to various types of violence.

The most common substance associated with aggression is alcohol (Yarvis, 1990). In Wolfgang's classic 1958 study of homicide, 54% of the offenders and 53% of the victims were under the influence of alcohol at the time of the offense. Among the various other drugs, phencyclidine (PCP or "Angel Dust") is the most dangerous (Petersen & Stillman, 1979), resulting in the most assaultive or extremely aggressive behaviors. Lysergic acid diethylamide (LSD) also may produce violent behavior if the subject develops paranoid delusions and responds to them. Similarly, amphetamine abuse often gives rise to paranoia with resultant acts of aggression. Heroin is not directly a cause of violent crime, but it is a major indirect cause, because many individuals will engage in criminal activities to obtain money to buy the drug.

Paranoid schizophrenia and the various para-
noid states and disorders are frequently the cause of violent, antisocial, and homicidal acts. Swanson, Bonhert, and Smith (1970), in their extensive review of the paranoid conditions, concluded that pathological jealousy and paranoid delusions are major causes of homicide. Lanzkron (1963) found that 37.3% of 150 mental patients charged with murder had paranoid delusions and that 20% displayed pathological jealousy and delusions of infidelity.

The most classic example of an individual whose homicidal act was motivated directly by delusions of persecution is the case of Daniel M'Naghten, from which the legal test of insanity — the M'Naghten Rule — arose. M'Naghten was tried in March 1843 for the willful murder of the private secretary to Sir Robert Peel. Actually, Sir Robert was the target and the secretary had been killed by mistake. M'Naghten was diagnosed as a case of "homicidal mono-mania." Two years before the murder, M'Naghten had had persecutory delusions, believing that he was being followed by spies who laughed in his face, shook their fists at him, or made other motions of ominous significance. He tried to escape his persecutors by leaving his native Scotland for England, but returned to Scotland because he believed that the same malevolent group of people had followed him abroad. A year before the murder, he had requested protection from the Provost of Glasgow. The English court was puzzled by the seeming sanity of M'Naghten when he spoke about subjects unrelated to his delusions. This case would not present much difficulty in diagnostic formulation at the present time, in spite of the impression of "general sanity" independent of his delusional system.

The following is a case of murder committed by a paranoid schizophrenic whose total personality was disorganized:

Case Illustration 1: C.R., a 32-year-old male, was seen for evaluation to aid in the determination of sanity and competency to stand trial. He was charged with murdering his 51-year-old mother by bludgeoning her with his fists and a door. The autopsy revealed that the victim died of multiple skull fractures and had been repeatedly struck in the neck and face.

According to the police reports, the victim was found dead by her husband, who telephoned the police. When the police arrived at the home, they found, according to their report, "blood on the walls...broken furniture...broken windows... blood in the bathroom, a broken and bent door of the medicine cabinet, etc." C.R. was arrested that evening while riding his bicycle a few blocks away from the scene of the murder. He was described by the authorities as being "soaked with blood."

Once under arrest, C.R. readily admitted to killing his mother. He stated, "I hit her with anything I could get my hands on — I hit her with furniture." He further stated that he told his mother he wanted to kill her as "fast as I could." While at the police station, C.R. "kept yelling as loud as he could 'I'm glad she's dead.' "

For several years prior to the tragedy, C.R. had had numerous psychiatric contacts and hospitalizations. There were four separate hospitalizations the year before the murder. On one occasion, C.R.'s father pleaded with the judge to keep C.R. in custody because he was afraid that C.R. would kill his mother. The psychiatric opinion was that C.R. was not potentially dangerous despite his violent behavior and threats, and the judge released him. About one month later, the murder occurred.

According to newspaper interviews, C.R.'s neighbors evaluated him as dangerous. One resident who had warned his own children to stay away from C.R. stated, "A real concern of a few neighbors was that he would do something serious. He was always a loner. A few years ago C.R., had long hair and then one day he shaved himself bald."

C.R. was seen by a mental health examiner on

two occasions in the county jail. On the first visit, he was extremely agitated and questioned the examiner in great detail about his credentials and the purpose of the visit. He inspected all notes that the examiner took. After about ten minutes, C.R. made a fist and refused to continue the examination, stating, "I'm as sane as you are. They're trying to make me a mental case and I'm not." The examination was terminated.

One month later, C.R. was more cooperative but clearly psychotic and paranoid. He was unable to concentrate and stated that noise and telephones bothered him. His thoughts drifted, and his conversation was bizarre. Frequently, he stared into space for long periods of time, repeating one or two words. He made statements such as, "I can't think, how can a dead man think, I'm dead." "People are on me conspiring. I'm the center of everyone's conversation, I'm the nucleus, they say things like it's only a disease and they talk about me." "People don't act the way they should, everyone's out to make a buck and they want to destroy me. A secret society is doing it, they want to get rich and start a world war."

When asked why he killed his mother, C.R. said that she was a member of this secret society. Because his mother went to her native Poland during the summer without C.R., he became convinced that she was going to attend a meeting with the Communists and the secret society. He stated that his mother was trying to destroy him and voices said that he should kill her.

Comment: This homicide was obviously a direct outgrowth of paranoid delusions and command hallucinations. C.R. was a disorganized paranoid schizophrenic, and his psychosis and dangerousness were obvious to almost everyone, including his father and neighbors. Unfortunately, prior to the homicide, the courts and attending physicians could not recognize the implications of C.R.'s illness. Unlike Daniel M'Naghten, whose personality was seemingly intact except for his delusion, C.R.'s behavior was bizarre and deteriorated, and even the murder itself was chaotic and confused. C.R. was committed to a mental hospital after he was deemed fit to stand trial but found not guilty of the charges by reason of insanity.

Classification of Motivational Dynamics

There has been a trend in recent years, particularly among those of a purely humanistic orientation, to devalue classification. However, without a structure by which to order events, the world would appear chaotic and without relationships. Admittedly, complex phenomena such as human behavior are difficult to classify; rigid boundaries cannot be established because of fluid borderline cases. Furthermore, different examiners may stress different facets of behavior and levels of consciousness, as illustrated by the case of Raskolnikov cited above, and therefore may present different evaluations of the same event (Perr, 1975). The legal definition and approach deal with motivational factors, but because only the most superficial and seemingly logical phenomena are considered; what seems to be premeditation may actually be a compelling, irrational need with reasons obscure to the offender. In the classification system outlined in the preceding section and described in detail in the following sections, motivational stimuli are emphasized and distinguished between environmental and endogenous influences.

Sociogenic or Environmental Offenses

The present rise in crime in general, and violent crime in particular (*Uniform Crime Reports*), is in large part due to the breakdown of social order and social stability. Rapid social change, feelings of alienation, and strained economic conditions for the poor, and more recently for the middle class, provide a background for stimulating various offenses. There are numerous histori-

cal examples of increased violence, crime, and murder in times of great social upheaval. Both Wedgwood's (1957) book on the Thirty Year's War and the various accounts of Nazi atrocities illustrate the point. In addition, classic experimental studies by Haney, Banks, and Zimbardo (1973) and Milgram (1963) illustrate the effects of context in inducing fairly normal undergraduate college students to participate in very aggressive acts.

A typical case of an individual committing homicide, for example, with motivation derived chiefly from a social environment is that of the professional hit man. Many semiprofessional criminals with various personality makeups, regardless of the presence or absence of psychopathology or psychosis, have in common environmental influences as their main stimulus to crime. Sutherland's (1947) concept of differential association — criminal behavior learned in interaction with others — generally applies to this group. Most cases of violence, murder, and antisocial behavior committed by individuals for some specific and gainful purpose rarely come to the attention of psychologists.

The following case is illustrative of the typical professional criminal.

Case Illustration 2: A man in his late 40s was evaluated for his participation in a bank robbery and kidnapping of a high-ranking bank employee. This man, who was friendly and spoke freely and volubly, said that he viewed criminal activities as a job that was completely separate from his private life and his ethics. He had typical middle-class ambitions for his children and did not want them to be connected with the organization. He himself, he explained, had become involved with organized crime because he wanted to make his life richer and brighter, even if he had to accept a different set of values: "As a kid I was deprived. My father worked hard for a living. There was no money in the house. Other kids ate steak but we ate cereal." At the age of 14, he was induced to steal cars and to perform other services for petty neighborhood gangs. He then graduated to bigger jobs, and later murdered on orders from his superiors.

Situational Offenses

Situational offenses are essentially reactions to stressful situations (see Steadman, 1982). They may be committed by individuals with little or no psychopathology; however, all types of personalities may be involved. About 70% of all homicides (*Uniform Crime Reports*) are situational in nature and usually stem from domestic disputes or barroom arguments. Theodore Dreiser's novel, *An American Tragedy*, illustrates a typical situational murder committed to eliminate a companion who interfered with the protagonist's future plans. Most of the situational murders and acts of violence one sees have an element of impulsivity, fear, anger, and despair, and occasionally a paranoid tinge to the thinking processes. The following case illustrates a typical situational murder.

Case Illustration 3: J.G., a 53-year-old year old businessman charged with murdering a customer of one of his stores, was evaluated to aid in the determination of sanity. J.G. owned about 10 dry cleaning stores in a blighted inner-city area that had deteriorated markedly in the prior 15 years. His business had been established under a different set of conditions, but he could not move away because it seemed almost impossible, at his age, to start over.

He reported that he was constantly called in the middle of the night for some type of break-in or assault on an employee. Crime in the neighborhood of his business became so serious that he had to erect a bulletproof glass wall separating the customers from the cashiers or he could not get employees to work for him.

One week prior to the murder, a man assaulted J.G.'s wife in one of the stores and attempted to rape her. The attempt was foiled when she was aided by one of the employees. Also during the week preceding the murder, one particular customer continually appeared at several of the locations, demanding refunds, complaining, making harsh accusations of improper treatment, and the like.

On the day of the murder, J.G. was called to settle an argument between this customer and a female cashier. The argument escalated, and J.G., wearing a licensed gun that was visible, could not calm the irate customer. As tension increased, the customer threw an adding machine at J.G. and began to climb over the counter to jump at him. At this, J.G. drew his gun, shot the man, and killed him. Another customer was injured as the bullet ricocheted.

J.G. showed no evidence of significant psychopathology — either clinically on the psychological tests, or by history. He was a stable, middle-class individual who only wore the gun at the recommendation of the police, as did other merchants in the area. The background of tremendous stress, fear, and intimidation contributed to this situationally induced homicide. If it were not for the generalized stress of his business and the specific stress of the events of the week prior to the incident, in all likelihood, this murder would not have occurred.

Impulsive Offenses

Impulsive individuals react to situations in a diffuse, stimulus-response manner. These people, whose life pattern is characterized by lack of direction and unpredictability, tend to drift into and out of difficulties (Schlesinger, 1980). Their offenses are diffuse, poorly structured, and unpremeditated or only partially premeditated. Impulsive offenders are differentiated from situational offenders by the multiplicity of their antisocial acts and by their poor impulse control. Psychological evaluation reveals looseness of personality integration as the main characteristic.

The offenses may be aggressive (including murder), nonaggressive, or a combination of both. Such individuals usually are easily led and excessively influenced by external circumstances. They may be recruited into semiprofessional crime (see Gibbons, 1968), but they lack the purposefulness and the know-how of professionals. Their involvement, in essence, is casual. Their antisocial acts are fueled by the mere prospect of money or by chronic feelings of anger and revenge, low self-esteem with compensatory strivings for recognition, or various combinations of these factors. The following case is illustrative.

Case Illustration 4: A.D., a 25-year-old-year male, stabbed two people, one of whom died as a result. On the day of the incident, A.D. had had an argument with the owner of a tavern, who allegedly threatened A.D. with a hammer. In anger, A.D. left the tavern and returned with a knife to show that "no one could just walk all over me." At his return, the argument resumed and resulted in the impulsive stabbings of the victims.

When interviewed, A.D. tended to gloss over and minimize his various past aggressive acts, presenting them as purely incidental, unrelated, and of little importance. He had a history of fighting, gambling, arrests for arguments with police officers, domestic disputes, and the like. The police were frequently called to his home to quell heated arguments precipitated by suspected infidelity on the part of his wife.

Psychological tests found him to be of low-average intelligence, while projective tests elicited suspiciousness, emotional instability, and very poor self-concept. He was a drifter who worked at unskilled jobs, and his entire life was characterized by lack of direction.

Catathymic Offenses

The concept of catathymic crisis was originally introduced into the field of criminal psy-chopathology by Wertham (1937) and was used as an explanation for various unprovoked episodes of severe violence without organic etiology. Wertham defined catathymic crisis as "a transformation of the stream of thought as a result of certain complexes of ideas that are charged with a strong affect, usually a wish, a fear or an ambivalent striving" (p. 975). Gayral and his colleagues (1956) described emotional outbursts under the name "catathymic paroxysms;" and Revitch (1964) labeled severe emotional outbursts in a prison population as "catathymic attacks," differentiating these outbursts from psychomotor epilepsy.

It was Hans W. Maier, however, who in 1912, first used the term *catathymia*, which is derived from the Greek "cata" and "thymos," translated most appropriately as "in accordance with emotions." In his original paper, Maier apparently regarded catathymia as a psychological process or a reaction activated by tenacious affect, which, when stimulated, overwhelms the psychic equilibrium and disrupts logical thinking. Revitch and Schlesinger (1978, 1981, 1989; Schlesinger & Revitch, 1980; Schlesinger, 1996) defined catathymic crisis not as a diagnostic entity, as did the earlier authors, but rather, as a psychodynamic process frequently accompanied by disorganization and characterized by an accumulation of tension released through the violent act. They divided this process into two types: acute and chronic (see Table 1). The acute process is essentially a sudden, unprovoked murder or violent act without apparent motivation. This process should be differentiated from situational murders and assaults committed in an explosion of anger, fear, or jealousy or under the influence of paranoid delusions, drugs, or alcohol. Deeper sources of emotional tension are tapped and release an overwhelming affect attached to "complexes of ideas" that are disturbed. In fact, the perpetrator of the assault cannot give a reasonable explanation for the act and, in many cases, can only partially

TABLE 1
DIFFERENTIATING CHARACTERISTICS OF ACUTE AND CHRONIC CATATHYMIC PROCESS

Activation of Process	Incubation Period	Feeling	Victim	Memory of Events
Acute				
Triggered by a sudden overwhelming affect attached to ideas of symbolic significance	Several seconds or longer	Usually a flattening of emotion	Usually a stranger	Usually poor
Chronic				
Triggered by a buildup of tension, a feeling of frustration, depression, and helplessness	Days to years	Usually relief	Usually close acquaintances and family members	Usually preserved

recall the event. Satten, Menninger, and Mayman (1960) described a classic case of an acute catathymic attack when a soldier drowned a preadolescent girl without any obvious provocation and with partial amnesia for the event. Ruotolo (1968) believed that an injury to the pride system is instrumental in precipitating such rage.

The chronic catathymic process is itself divided into three stages: incubation, violent act, and relief. Depressed mood, loose schizophrenic-like thinking, and obsessive preoccupation with the victim characterize the incubation period, which may last for weeks, months, or even up to a year in some cases. The individual comes to believe, for some reason, that the only solution to his or her state of tension is through violence. In retrospect, the act itself seems ego-alien and of a dreamlike quality. A vivid description of this process can be found in Yukio Mishima's (1956) novel, *Temple of the Golden Pavilion*. Here, the central character was obsessed with the beauty of a temple — which acted as an irritant to his psychic equilibrium — and was compelled to destroy it by setting it on fire. In the early stages of this condition, such individuals often will seek attention through various mental health channels

(Revitch & Schlesinger, 1981, 1989). Too frequently, however, expressed ideas of violence are dismissed as mere fantasy (Schlesinger & Kutash, 1981), and the patient is treated solely for depression. The following two cases illustrate the acute and chronic catathymic process, respectively.

Case Illustration 5: S.C., an 18-year-old youth, while working as a gasoline station attendant, strangled a female nightclub entertainer to death under the following circumstances. Shortly before closing time, the victim entered the station requesting a dime to make a telephone call. S.C. loaned her the dime, and when he looked into the telephone room, the woman had her dress lifted and invited S.C. to have sexual relations with her. He was unable to effect an erection, prompting the woman to taunt, "Go home to your mother." S.C. then grabbed a piece of rubber tubing, wrapped it around her neck, and strangled her. He placed the body in his car, drove to a vacant lot, and left the remains there. He slept well that night and went to school the next day without any recollection of the event.

While he was attending classes, fragments of the offense intruded into his consciousness and resulted in some anxiety and panic. S.C. looked

into the trunk of his car, found the woman's eyeglasses, and at this point believed he might have actually committed a murder. Previous to this, he woke up feeling that the murder was a bad dream that he had had. After finding the glasses, S.C. went to the lot and saw police officers there who discovered the body. He then turned himself in and confessed.

Comment: In this case, the memory for the event was preserved to the minutest detail, although the incident seemed unreal and dreamlike to S.C., and he spoke about it without emotional display and in an objective, quasi-clinical way. Flattening of affect and the unreal aspect of the event in similar cases are not indications of schizophrenia or callousness, as thought by some, but are understandable defense reactions against an unpleasant event. The emotional stress leading to the ego disintegration in this case, at least on the surface, is an injury to his pride system. After all, the victim mocked him when he could not get an erection. The very character of the victim's approach was ego threatening and rendered him confused and helpless. His fragile makeup could not deal logically with the situation, and the killing was without obvious or experienced anger; it was, instead, a primitive reaction to a noxious stimulus where his logic was overwhelmed by the strong affect attached most likely to unresolved conflicts regarding his sexuality.

Case Illustration 6: G.W., a 29-year-old male charged with murdering his wife, was evaluated in the county jail to aid in the determination of sanity. G.W. was employed steadily as a salesman and had a good work record and no prior involvement with the law. He stated that when he met his wife (the victim), he felt uncomfortable because she was "overly protected as a child; she was weak-minded. Her parents were very dominant." He further stated, "She always went back to her parents when we had an argument or a problem."

Prior to the commission of the murder, there

was a period of approximately nine months of extreme marital discord that left G.W. feeling depressed and helpless. His wife threatened him with divorce and returned home on numerous occasions to live with her parents. Finally, his wife chose to separate permanently, and her departure exacerbated his depression and precipitated vague suicidal ideas.

G.W. sought treatment at a local clinic, but the depression did not abate; unfortunately, his ideas of violence were not taken seriously by the treating psychiatrist. He bought a gun and went to his wife's place of employment and showed it to her. He stated, "I purchased the gun. I thought of suicide. I talked to her for a final time with the gun in my car, and then I put the gun to my head and told her 'I'm going to kill myself.'"

The wife brought charges against him for this incident, and G.W. served 30 days in jail before being released on bail. When released, he bought another gun, and again had some suicidal impulses. He did maintain hope, however, that his wife would some day return home.

The approaching Christmas season apparently made G.W. feel worse. On Christmas Eve, he followed his wife and her parents to midnight mass and then back to their house. When they pulled into the garage, he "went up behind them and I asked to speak to my wife. I pulled out the gun and I put a lot of shots into my wife. I wanted them to know I meant business." Fatally wounded, the victim tumbled out of the passenger side, and G.W. began kissing her on the lips, expressing his love and devotion to her. The parents called the police. G.W. dropped the gun and was arrested without any resistance.

Comment: In this case, the incubation phase for the catathymic process was preceded by depression and suicidal preoccupation, later mixed with, and finally dominated by, homicidal drive. Unfortunately, G.W.'s therapist ignored his patient's statements about violence. The patient's marital difficulties emanated from his own conflicted relationship with his wife (see Meloy, 1992), which was graphically illustrated in his protestations of love while killing her. The marital relationship created such a state of confusion and helplessness that he could release the catathymic tension only by eliminating the source of the tension through homicide or by removing himself from the source through suicide.

Compulsive Offenses

The compulsive (recently referred to as serial) murders occupy the extreme endogenous end of the motivational spectrum and are the least influenced by external or sociogenic factors. The need to commit the act is very compelling, and there is a strong potential for repetition. In some cases, the urge to commit a sex murder is so strong that the offender's attempt to resist it will bring on anxiety and somatic manifestations. Krafft-Ebing (1886/1934) reported the case of a 21-year-old man who attacked and stabbed young girls in the genitals: "For a while he succeeded in mastering his morbid craving, but this produced feelings of anxiety and a copious perspiration would break out from his entire body" (p. 111). William Hirens, famous for his saying "Catch me before I kill more, I can't help myself," developed headaches and sweated profusely when he tried to resist the urge (Freeman, 1956). Revitch and Schlesinger (1981) described the case of an offender who prayed at bedtime that he would not wake up, so that he would not have to commit a sex murder the following day.

Compulsive sex murders are frequently committed in a ritualistic and similar manner, but sometimes the compulsive urge may be manifested in other forms, yet stimulated by the same psychodynamics. The murders may be frequent or isolated, or repeated after long intervals. Frequently, fantasies may precede the homicidal act by many years; and even after years of imprisonment, the compulsion may persist. In one case,

reported by Revitch (1957), a man's fantasies about tying female legs persisted for more than 30 years before he actually acted out his fantasy.

The vast majority (but perhaps not all) of the compulsive homicides have an underlying basis of sexual conflict (Grubin, 1994; see also Meloy et al., 1994). Men are far more frequently involved in compulsive sex murder than women, and women are most likely to be the victims. In some cases, however, the compulsion to kill is so strong that the sadistic murderer may attack men, women, children, and even animals. Wilson and Pitman (1962) described an individual who stabbed sheep while abusing them sexually; the same individual also choked and mistreated women while dating them, and also sadistically murdered and mutilated women, men, children, and various animals. Compulsive sex murder also has been associated with necrophilia (attraction to dead bodies) (see Smith & Brown, 1978), as well as with vampirism, cannibalism, mutilation of the body, and other bizarre and primitive associated behaviors.

Not all compulsive sex murders are accompanied by overt expressions of sexuality, and many sexually motivated assaults or murders (see Banay, 1969) may be interpreted as common crimes (such as mugging or robbery). In many cases, intercourse does not occur (Abel, Becker, & Skinner, 1981); the act of aggression itself satisfies the sexual component. In some of these cases, the sexual dynamics can be recognized by certain signs, such as the excessive amount of force used. Banay (1969) confirmed the general impression that hidden sexual forces frequently lie at the root of many apparently nonsexual crimes. Thus, the sexual element in homicide may be hidden, implied, or overt.

In most of the cases in our clinical experience, the compulsive sex murderer has had an unhealthy and disturbed emotional relationship with his mother (Meyers, 1994). The mothers may be rejecting and punitive or, at times, seductive, overprotective, and infantilizing. The offenders frequently may know about, or actually witness, the mothers' sexual promiscuity, which is extremely disruptive to the psychological development of males. These men frequently develop the defense mechanism of splitting: viewing women as pure and all good or as evil and all bad. The case of a 26-year-old male who brutally killed an 18-year-old girl after she "quickly agreed" to have sex with him is illustrative. Repressed incestuous feelings seem to be the main stimulus to gynocide. The offender displaces emotion from the mother to other women; in other words, sexually motivated murders are displaced matricide. (See Table 2.)

with multiple stab wounds. The first woman was stalked by E.F. in a shopping mall. Witnesses reported that he shouted obscenities to her while he was stalking her. He stated that he had a strong urge to kill her because she was Oriental (Korean); for years, he had been fantasizing about killing Oriental women. After abducting her, he took her to a reservoir and killed her, inflicting numerous stab wounds.

The second victim was driven off the road by E.F., forced into a field, and stabbed several times. When she no longer moved, the offender had intercourse with her (necrophilia) and then left her. When he was asked why he had killed the second victim (who was not Oriental), he said

---

TABLE 2
THOUGHT CONTENT OF COMPULSIVE SEX MURDERS

1. Hostility to women
2. Preoccupation with maternal sexual conduct and indiscretion
3. Overt or covert incestuous preoccupation
4. Feelings of sexual inferiority, weakness, and inadequacy
5. Need to completely possess the victim (a lifeless body is not threatening)

In sadistic sex murder, there may be a fusion of sex and aggression. Freud (1905/1938) believed that the sexual instinct has many components, "some of which detach themselves to form perversions. Our clinical observation thus calls out attention to fusions, which have lost their expression in the uniform normal behavior" (p. 572). Additionally, a neurological substrate may underlie compulsive sex murder. According to MacLean (1962), the limbic structures governing feeding and aggression are interconnected with the structures governing sexual functions. As an example, MacLean pointed to the display of genitals in the male squirrel monkey during a fight (see also Pontius, 1993).

Case Illustration 7: E.F., a 36-year-old male, was found guilty of the murders of two women, both of whom he had abducted and then killed

that she looked Oriental at night. He also explained that he had not killed the second victim in the same vicious manner as the first one, describing the first woman as "really butchered up with a bayonet." He also cut off the ear of the first victim, because he had heard that Vietnam veterans treated their victims in the same way.

E.F. spoke of his fascination with Oriental women and his collection of Oriental pictures. He also reported that he enjoys killing people and watching them die — especially if they urinate or defecate "for the last time. I want to watch them die, the slimy bastards."

Comment: This is a classic and typical case of a (serial) compulsive murderer with sexual dynamics. The sexual element is obvious in the murderer's need to kill women. However, the compulsion has a diffuse quality, so that killing anybody may sometimes satisfy the urge to some extent. E.F.'s history included witnessing his mother's sexual promiscuity with numerous boyfriends. He felt ashamed of the way his mother behaved, and believed that other schoolchildren knew of her conduct. E.F.'s prognosis for being able to control his strong urge to kill is extremely poor. He kills because he has a need to kill, not because of any rational or logical motive. He will remain an extremely dangerous person who, in all probability, would kill again if he were ever released from prison.

Case Illustration 8: M.M., a 23-year-old male, murdered a 17-year-old female and described the crime in the following manner. He met the victim at an arcade. She was by herself, and they started talking. They went for a ride in his truck and he pulled over while they were still talking. She said that she had a boyfriend and did not want him to know that she was out with M.M.

After a few hours, M.M. took her home, but dropped her off about 100 yards from her house, so that her parents would not know that she was out with him. They planned to meet again the following evening at the arcade. They met, bought some beer, and went to a motel room, where they drank, watched television, got into bed.

M.M. could not explain why he suddenly grabbed her by the neck and pulled her on the floor: "I was real angry now; I was real angry, man. I put my belt around her neck and [the belt] broke. She passed out but didn't die; she was dizzy. I helped her get dressed. She kept saying 'Let's go back to my girlfriend's and get high.' I didn't think I did anything wrong; she didn't leave when I left her to return the hotel key." He did indicate, however, that he was worried about her saying something.

M.M. then drove the victim to a remote area for the purpose of "wanting to hurt her again. I was real angry. It had nothing to do with her. It was my whole life. I beat her up, I kicked her, I left her. Nothing affected me at this time. I had no feelings at the time for nobody."

Following the brutal beating, which resulted in the girl's death, he went to a gas station and "they saw blood on my pants." He then went to a bar and got cleaned up. After that, he went to Tracy's (his girlfriend's) house, where he was living. He had a conversation with her, but lied to her about the assault and homicide. He made up a story about cocaine because "if I told her the truth, there would have been another body." He stated further: "The reason was that Tracy didn't accept me for what I am. Instead of hurting her, I hurt someone else." He went to bed that evening but could not sleep because he was thinking of what happened.

The following day, M.M. went to work, but "Nothing much happened." He told Tracy of the assault later in the day, but "I didn't tell her we had sex." He also went back to the crime scene because "I was curious." He found the dead victim and covered her: "I didn't want to move her. If I didn't say nothing, I wouldn't be in here; I'd be there doing it again."

Apparently, Tracy called the police after M.M. confessed to her, and he was subsequently arrested. When asked why he had killed the girl, he referred to his disturbed relationship with Tracy. He also spoke of a long history of emotional abuse by foster parents and said that his biological mother was promiscuous and rejecting. He also emphasized that he had killed the victim because she "had sex with me too easily" and that upset him.

A year before this homicide, M.M. had been charged with rape, but was found not guilty at trial, although he admitted to the examiner that the rape actually had occurred. (He would not go into the specifics of it.) There were three prior incidents of choking women, which began while he was in the military. Once he choked a woman after he picked her up at a bar; he did not kill her because someone interrupted, but she was hospitalized for a brief period of time. On another occasion, he almost killed a prostitute; again, she did not die, but was severely injured.

Because of his behavioral difficulties, M.M. had gone to numerous psychiatrists and psychologists, but he never really connected emotionally with any of them. He felt that they did not care: "Nobody ever took notes; they just listened to what I said and never wrote anything down."

M.M. was of dull-normal intelligence and performed poorly in school. Clinical assessment and psychological tests revealed evidence of severe characterological disturbance, probably falling within the borderline spectrum, but with strong antisocial traits.

Thematic Apperception Test (TAT) stories were filled with depressive themes: "looking how messed up the world is, the world is so rotten the way they treat him, he didn't like the world, he is waiting for something to happen — maybe suicide or jump out. He's got a problem, something hurt him in the past and he can't handle it. He can't talk to anyone; he closed his mind; no one cares. He will take his life or conquer other people to show 'em things are bad and people don't care." "Something bad happened — the loss of a friend, divorce of his parents. They are no good, they mistreated him, they didn't care about him, they ignored him. His mother wasn't a caring person. He grows up feeling hate and anger for his being ignored. She was rotten; she left him. He stuck up for something he thought was right to help him deal with the past. He started fighting with people who had hurt him. He was used. A friend, the girlfriend, she competed against him, wanted to run him, wanted to be in control, made him feel rotten; he couldn't handle it."

To another TAT card, he responded that two men were having an argument "over a girl — he went out with his girlfriend. He found out and shot him. Anger — he made him feel angry; he wanted to kill him. Relationships are strong, and sometimes you kill people because they are so strong. He didn't care about him; he is nothing to

him. He kills him so he can have that girl to himself. He doesn't get caught because he planned it so he wouldn't."

One final TAT excerpt probably describes the dynamics that relate directly to the current murder: "This is a woman in bed. Something happened. She is dead. Something happened. He killed her. She used him. I don't know. All he was good for was to go to bed with. He went off and killed her with a weapon. He choked her to death. There was emotional hurt and anger. He was being treated like she didn't care. Most women don't care when it comes to relationships. When you love someone, you don't get it back. You get hurt and offended by it. He put all feelings into another girl; she hurt him. He wanted to go out and do something to another girl. He loves the other one too much. He would hurt her. He didn't care. He didn't plan it. He is just so angry it all broke up and it came out on the wrong person — a one-night stand. He met her in a bar. He didn't want to hurt the one he loved, but he wanted to show how hurt and angry he was. He is only human and could only take so much. His girlfriend didn't treat him with respect. She had a jealousy problem. He takes off and leaves her."

Comment: This is another case of compulsive sex murder, with all the elements of a repetitive serial murder. One cannot understand M.M.'s behavior if one simply diagnoses some type of overt mental illness, such as psychosis or depression. At the same time, one should not try to create a logical, easy to understand motive to explain the assaults and the homicide, because there is no simple logical motive. In this case, there is a combination of hostility toward women, preoccupation with maternal sexual conduct, overt and covert incestuous preoccupation, guilt over and rejection of sex as impure, and a feeling of sexual inferiority. M.M. has almost all the elements of a compulsive offender, as listed by Revitch and Schlesinger (1981). He reported, even without direct questioning, his preoccupation with his biological mother's sexual indiscretions. He was not able to describe exact or specific dynamics or fantasies regarding his mother, because everything was very confused to him; but he did emphasize his belief that she was promiscuous, and he harbored great rage at her because she gave him up for adoption. He also described intense anger at various foster parents, particularly one family that "got rid of me because I wet the bed." When apprehended by the police, M.M. said that he killed the victim because he "wanted to teach her a lesson for having sex with a person that she did not know on the first time." This statement is illuminating, because it shows how the victim's immediate willingness to have sex upset M.M.'s defenses and resulted in an overpowering urge to kill her.

Prediction and Treatment Issues

Previously, the consensus was that dangerousness prediction was tenuous and unreliable (Cocozza & Steadman, 1976; Dershowitz, 1973; Monahan & Cummings, 1975; Rubin, 1972; Smith & English, 1978). Admittedly, such prediction cannot be made with absolute accuracy; however, it is a mistake to claim that some sort of prognostic evaluation is totally impossible (see also Sendi & Blomgren, 1975). Tanay (1975) was correct when he stated that "the description of a tendency is frequently confused with prediction of the occurrence of a future event like homicide and suicide" (p. 23). In other words, the prediction of dangerousness should be based on the evaluation of a tendency and a possibility. More recent investigation suggests that dangerousness prediction can be made with promising degrees of accuracy, if certain guidelines are followed (Hall, 1987).

One of the major mistakes in predicting future violence is the equating of dangerousness with psychosis (Frederick, 1976; Slovenko, 1977). Kozol, Cohen, and Garafolo (1966) sup-

ported this view: "We have found that general diagnostic categorization of patients in terms of conventional psychiatry offers only limited assistance" (p. 82). Moreover, one's predictions about the repetition of a psychotic episode may diverge from similar predictions concerning an antisocial act.

The concept of the motivational spectrum — seen in the context of the offender's personality integration, inner resources, social network, and empathic capacity is of help in prognostication. Thus, situational offenders should have the best prognosis. The future of environmentally or socially influenced offenders will depend largely on their value system, opportunities, associations, and maturity. Impulsive offenders who commit a violent act may continue in antisocial activities of all sorts, but these activities will not necessarily be homicidal or severely aggressive. The catathymic offenses are usually limited to a single episode, unless the individual is extremely disturbed and poorly integrated. The compulsive offender, who kills because of a compulsion to kill, is the most dangerous. Prediction of antisocial behavior, then, is the prediction of a possibility in some cases, a probability in others, and, at times, a very high degree of probability in sexually motivated compulsive offenders. Compulsive, catathymic, and many impulsive crimes are clearly pathological and ego dystonic; thus, purely legal action will not deter or rehabilitate but, on the contrary, will fail to reduce the danger to society. These cases should be handled in specialized institutions, with Herstedvester in Denmark serving as a model (Sturup, 1968).

It is hoped that the preceding method of evaluating and classifying antisocial individuals will be of help to the clinical/forensic psychologist in making some type of prognostic evaluation of such individuals in daily practice (and may also serve to encourage empirical evidence gathering as well). The following ominous clinical signs, if found in a patient in combination, should also alert the psychologist to the strong probability of severe dangerousness despite the absence of overt psychosis: (a) history of unprovoked assaults and mistreatment of women; (b) breaking and entering, committed solo and under bizarre circumstances; (c) stalking victims; (d) fetishism of female underclothing and destruction of female clothes; (e) expressions of hatred, contempt, or fear of women; (f) violence against animals, particularly against cats; (g) violent and primitive fantasy life; (h) confusion of sexual identity as elicited on the projective tests; and (i) sexual inhibitions and moral preoccupation with sexual conduct (see Table 3). Threats to kill should be taken seriously, especially if a catathymic process is suspected.

institution. Other individuals, such as family members, who are involved with the offender must be made aware of his or her problems and the provision of such information should not be considered a breach of confidentiality. Frequently, the offender welcomes such control, as the offender also wants to control his or her own behavior. An understanding of the signs and dynamics of murder is very important, as many of these individuals are in treatment before a homicide actually occurs. Additionally, many such individuals — except perhaps for the most notorious cases — are eventually released from prison. Treatment failures are attributable primarily to the therapist's inability to recognize important prognostic signs prior to the offense and to establish

---

TABLE 3
OMINOUS CLINICAL SIGNS (SEEN IN COMBINATION) PREDICTIVE OF SEX MURDER/SEX AGGRESSION (DESPITE ABSENCE OF PSYCHOSIS)

1. Unprovoked assaults and mistreatment of women
2. Breaking and entering committed solo and under bizarre circumstances
3. Fetishism of female underclothes and destruction of them
4. Expression of hatred, contempt, and fear of women
5. Violence against animals (particularly cats)
6. Violent and primitive fantasy life
7. Confusion of sexual identity
8. Sexual inhibitions and moral preoccupation

There are no specific psychotherapeutic techniques for treating sex murderers, nor are there any specific medications (Schlesinger & Revitch, 1990). Any of the various psychotherapeutic approaches may be relevant and useful in a given case, and psychopharmacology can also help to reduce various symptoms. Therapeutic rapport and support cannot be overemphasized. Insight is important, but so are expressions of feelings and emotions because of the cathartic effect. The issue of control is also central in treating such an individual in an outpatient setting, or even in an

and maintain rapport and support after the offender has been released from an institution.

Annotated Bibliography

Revitch, E., & Schlesinger, L. B. (1981) *Psychopathology of Homicide.* Springfield, IL: Charles C Thomas. In this book, the authors consider and explain the psychopathology and psychodynamics of various forms of homicide. The emphasis is on homicide, not as a homogenous phenomenon, but as a complex behavior with distinct and varying etiology, clinical course, and prognosis. The concept of "motivational spectrum," developed by the authors, is presented with chapters on socially and environmentally stimulated homicides, situational homicides, impulsive homicides, catathymic homicides, and compulsive (sexually motivated) homicides. Murder as a result of organic, toxic, and paranoid causes constitute a separate group and are examined in a section by themselves. This text also discusses the issues involved in prediction and disposition of homicidal offenders.

Revitch, E., & Schlesinger, L. B. (1989). *Sex Murder and Sex Aggression: Phenomenology, Psychopathology, Psychodynamics and Prognosis.* Springfield, IL: Charles C Thomas. The authors discuss sexually motivated murders as well as sexually aggressive behavior. Cases involving sudden explosive homicides triggered by unresolved sexual conflicts are compared with compulsive (serial) homicides whereby the perpetrator seeks out a victim (usually a woman to kill, thus satisfying underlying sexual drives. Rich case material is presented to illustrate various points.

Schlesinger, L. B., & Revitch, E. (1983). *Sexual Dynamics of Antisocial Behavior.* Springfield, IL: Charles C Thomas. In this edited book, 15 chapters on the sexual motivation of various antisocial behaviors are presented. The first section of the book examines acts that are reluctantly condoned, such as prostitution, pornography, nymphomania, sexual permissiveness, and problems of gender dysphoria. In the second section, sexually motivated acts that are both illegal and socially condemned are the focus, with topics such as female genital exhibitionism, kleptomania, rape, sexually motivated burglaries, as well as pyromania. In the final section of the book, rare and bizarre disorders involving sexual and aggressive elements are dealt with, including chapters on necrophilia, vampirism, eroticized repetitive hangings, sex murders, and sadomasochism.

References

Abel, G. G., Becker, J. V., & Skinner, L. J. (1981). Aggressive behavior and sex. *Psychiatric Clinics of North America, 3,* 133-151.

Banay, R. S. (1969). Unconscious motivation in crime. *Medical Aspects of Human Sexuality, 3,* 91-102.

Bourget, D., & Bradford, J. M. W. (1987). Affective disorder and homicide: A case of familial filicide, theoretical and clinical considerations. *Canadian Journal of Psychiatry, 32,* 222-225.

Brancale, R. (1955). Problems of classification. *National Probation and Parole Association Journal, 1,* 118-125.

Clark, R. (1971). *Crime in America.* New York: Pocket Books.

Cocozza, J. J., & Steadman, H. J. (1976). The failure of psychiatric prediction of dangerousness: Clear and convincing evidence. *Rutgers Law Review, 29,* 1084-1101.

Dershowitz, A. M. (1973). Dangerousness as a criterion for confinement. *Bulletin of the American Academy of Psychiatry and the Law, 11,* 172-179.

Florance, E. C. (1955). The neurosis of Raskolnikov: A study in incest and murder. *Archives of Criminal Psychodynamics, 1,* 344-396.

Frederick, J. C. (1976). Determining dangerousness. In *Paper victories and hard realities.* Washington, DC:

Health Policy Center, Georgetown University.

Freeman, L. (1956). *Catch me before I kill more*. New York: Pocket Books.

Freud, S. (1938). Three contributions to a theory of sex. In *The basic writings of Sigmund Freud*, trans. A. Brill. New York: Modern Library, 1938. (Original work published 1905.)

Gayral, L., Millet, G., Moron, P., & Turnin, J. (1956). Crises et paroxysmes catathymiques. *Annales Medico-Psychologiques, 114*, 25-50.

Gibbons, D. C. (1968). *Society, crime and criminal careers*. Englewood Cliffs, NJ: Prentice Hall.

Good, M.I. (1978). Primary affective disorder, aggression and criminality: A review and clinical study. *Archives of General Psychiatry, 35*, 954-960.

Grubin, D. (1994). Sexual murder. *British Journal of Psychiatry, 165*, 624-629.

Hall, H. V. (1987). *Violence prediction: Guidelines for the forensic practitioner*. Springfield, IL: Charles C Thomas.

Halleck, S. (1971). *Psychiatry and the dilemmas of crime*. Los Angeles: University of California Press.

Haney, C., Banks, C., & Zimbardo, P. G. (1973). International dynamics in a simulated prison. *International Journal of Criminology and Penology, 1*, 69-97.

Hellman, D. S., & Blackman, N. (1966). Enuresis, fire-setting and cruelty to animals: A triad predictive of adult crime. *American Journal of Psychiatry, 122*, 1431-1435.

Kozol, H. L., Cohen, M. I., & Garafolo, R. F. (1966). The criminally dangerous sex offenders. *New Eng-land Journal of Medicine, 275*, 79-84.

Krafft-Ebing, R. von. (1934). *Psychopathia Sexualis*, trans. F. J. Rebman. Brooklyn, NY: Physicians and Surgeons Book Co., 1934. (Original work published 1886.)

Lanzkron, J. (1963). Murder and insanity. *American Journal of Psychiatry, 119*, 754-758.

MacLean, P. D. (1962). New findings relevant to the evolution of the psychosexual functions of the brain. *Journal of Nervous and Mental Disorders, 135*, 289-301.

Maier, H. W. (1912). Uber katathyme Wahnbildung und Paranoia. *Zeitschrift fur die gesamte Neurologie und Psychiatrie, 13*, 555-610.

Mark, V. M., & Ervin, F. R. (1970). *Violence and the brain*. New York: Harper & Row.

Meloy, J. R. (1992). *Violent attachments*. Northvale, NJ: Jason Aronson, Inc.

Meloy, J. R., Gacono, L. B., & Kenney, L. (1994). A Rorschach investigation of sexual homicide. *Journal of Personality Assessment, 62*, 58-67.

Meyers, W. C. (1994). Sexual homicide by adolescents. *Journal of the American Academy of Child and Adolescent Psychiatry, 33*, 962-969.

Milgram, S. (1963). Behavioral study of obedience. *Journal of Abnormal and Social Psychology, 67*, 371-378.

Miller, D., & Looney, J. (1974). A prediction of adolescent homicide: Episodic dyscontrol and dehumanization. *American Journal of Psychoanalysis, 34*, 187-198.

Mishima, Y. (1956). *Temple of the golden pavilion*.

Berkeley: University of California Press.

Monahan, J., & Cummings, L. (1975). Social policy implications of the inability to predict violence. *Journal of Social Issues, 31,* 153-164.

Perr, I. N. (1975). Psychiatric testimony and the Rashomon phenomenon. *Bulletin of the American Academy of Psychiatry and the Law, 3,* 83-98.

Peterson, R. C., & Stillman, R. C. (1979). Phencyclidine: A review. *Journal of the Medical Society of New Jersey, 76,* 139-144.

Pontius, A. A. (1993). Neuropsychiatric update of the crime "profile" and "signature" in single or serial homicides: Rule out limbic psychotic trigger reaction. *Psychological Reports, 73,* 875-892.

Revitch, E. (1957). Sex murder and sex aggression. *Journal of the Medical Society of New Jersey, 54,* 519-524.

Revitch, E. (1964). Paroxysmal manifestations of non-epileptic origin: Catathymic attacks. *Diseases of the Nervous System, 25,* 662-669.

Revitch, E. (1977). Classification of offenders for prognostic and dispositional evaluation. *Bulletin of the American Academy of Psychiatry and the Law, 5,* 41-50.

Revitch, E., & Schlesinger, L. B. (1978). Murder: Evaluation, classification and prediction. In I. L. Kutash, S. B. Kutash, & L. B. Schlesinger (Eds.), *Violence: Perspectives on murder and aggression.* San Francisco: Jossey-Bass.

Revitch, E., & Schlesinger, L. B. (1981). *Psychopathology of homicide.* Springfield, IL: Charles C Thomas.

Revitch, E., & Schlesinger, L. B. (1989). *Sex murder and sex aggression.* Springfield, IL: Charles C Thomas.

Rosenbaum, M., & Bennett, B. (1986). Homicide and depression. *American Journal of Psychiatry, 143,* 367-370.

Rubin, B. (1972). Prediction of dangerousness in mentally ill criminals. *Archives of General Psychiatry, 27,* 397-409.

Ruotolo, A. (1968). Dynamics of sudden murder. *American Journal of Psychoanalysis, 28,* 162-176.

Satten, J., Menninger, K. A., & Mayman, M. (1960). Murder without apparent motive: A study in personality disorganization. *American Journal of Psychiatry, 117,* 48-53.

Schlesinger, L. B. (1980). Distinctions between psychopathic, sociopathic, and anti-social personality disorders. *Psychological Reports, 47,* 15-21.

Schlesinger, L.B. (1996). The catathymic process: Psychopathology and psychodynamics of extreme aggression. In L. B. Schlesinger (Ed.), *Explorations in criminal psychopathology: Clinical syndromes with forensic implications.* Springfield, IL: Charles C Thomas.

Schlesinger, L. B., & Kutash, I. L. (1981). The criminal fantasy technique: A comparison of sex offenders and substance abusers. *Journal of Clinical Psychology, 37,* 210-218.

Schlesinger, L. B., & Revitch, E. (1980). Stress, violence, and crime. In I. L. Kutash & L. B. Schlesinger (Eds.), *Handbook on stress and anxiety.* San Francisco: Jossey-Bass.

Schlesinger, L. B., & Revitch, E. (1990). Outpatient treatment of the sexually motivated murderer and potential murderer. *Journal of Offender Counseling, Services, and Rehabilitation, 15,* 163-178.

Sendi, I. B., & Blomgren, P. G. (1975). A comparative study of predictive criteria in the predisposition of homicidal adolescents. *American Journal of Psychiatry, 132,* 423-427.

Slovenko, R. (1977). Criminal justice procedures in civil commitment. *Hospital and Community Psychiatry, 28,* 817-826.

Smith, J. T., & English, M. J. (1978). Alternatives in psychiatric testimony on dangerousness. *Journal of Forensic Science, 23,* 588-595.

Smith, S. N., & Brown, E. (1978). Necrophilia and lust murder. *Bulletin of the American Academy of Psychiatry and Law, 6,* 259-268.

Steadman, H. S. (1982). A situational approach to violence. *International Journal of Psychiatry and Law, 5,* 171-186.

Sturup, G. K. (1968). Treatment of sexual offenders in Herstedvester, Denmark. *Acta Psychiatrica Scandinavia,* Supp. 204, 44.

Sutherland, E. H. (1947). *Principles of criminology.* Philadelphia: Lippincott.

Swanson, D. W., Bonhert, P. J., & Smith, J. A. (1970). *The paranoid.* Boston: Little, Brown.

Tanay, E. (1969). Psychiatric study of homicide. *American Journal of Psychiatry, 125,* 1252-1258.

Tanay, E. (1975). Dangerousness and psychiatry. *Current Concepts in Psychiatry, 1,* 17-26.

Wedgwood, C. V. (1957). *The Thirty Years War.* Harmondsworth, Middlesex, England: Penguin Books.

Wertham, F. (1937). The catathymic crisis: A clinical entity. *Archives of Neurology and Psychiatry, 37,* 974-977.

Wilson, C., & Pitman, P. C. (1962). *Encyclopedia of murder.* New York: Putnam.

Wolfgang, M. E. (1958). *Patterns of criminal homicide.* Philadelphia: University of Pennsylvania Press.

Yarvis, R. M. (1990). Axis I and axis II diagnostic parameters of homicide. *Bulletin of the American Academy of Psychiatry and Law, 18,* 249-269.

About the Author

Louis B. Schlesinger, PhD, is a clinical and forensic psychologist in private practice, as well as on the faculty of John Jay College of Criminal Justice, City University of New York. A Diplomate in Forensic Psychology of the American Board of Professional Psychology, he has testified in numerous forensic cases and has published many articles, chapters, and books on this topic. Dr. Schlesinger has written another book entitled *Explorations in Criminal Psychopathology: Clinical Syndromes with Forensic Implications.*

CHAPTER 15

AIRCRAFT HIJACKING IN THE UNITED STATES

Theodore B. Feldmann
Phillip W. Johnson

Introduction

Since the mid-1960s, aircraft hijacking has represented a unique form of violent crime in America. A variety of motivations, including political, personal, and criminal, have influenced hijackers. These incidents have been the source of great public concern and have attracted extensive media coverage. Aircraft hijackings have also posed complex and difficult problems for law enforcement agencies and airline security personnel. Due to the large number of victims of these crimes, the potential for loss of life and tragic outcome has been great. As a result, aircraft hijackings merit special consideration in any discussion of violent crime.

Attacks against commercial aircraft represent a serious form of lethal violence. Many incidents of aircraft hijacking are on record in which massive loss of life occurred. In the Fall of 1985, for example, the Abu Nidal terrorist group seized an Egyptair flight and diverted it to Malta. Once on the ground, the aircraft was stormed by Egyptian commandos. During the ensuing gun battle, 57 people were killed and another 23 wounded. In 1986, Pan American Airways was the target of several hijacking incidents, which resulted in 50 passengers and airline employees being killed. Another example of the lethality of aircraft hijacking occurred in San Diego, where a fired

Pacific Southwest Airlines employee smuggled a pistol aboard a flight carrying his former boss. The hijacker forced his way into the cockpit and fired his weapon at the flight crew. This act caused the plane to crash, taking the lives of all 43 passengers and crew members on board.

In order to better understand this form of lethal violence, this chapter reviews the phenomena of air piracy and hostage-taking and presents the results of a three-year study of all hijackings involving U.S. registered air carriers. Case illustrations from the aircraft hijacking database are also presented to better depict the nature of these violent acts.

Historical Overview Of Hijackings

The first recorded incident of air piracy hijacking occurred in Arequipa, Peru, on February 21, 1931 (Arey, 1972). The hijacking involved a Ford Trimotor aircraft operated by Pan American Grace Airways. The flight was on a mail delivery route among a number of small villages in Peru. The incident occurred during a period of political unrest in Peru, and involved a group of disgruntled soldiers who wanted to use the aircraft to distribute propaganda leaflets throughout the countryside. The hijackers also wanted to use the aircraft to transport soldiers to various areas where fighting was in progress. The plane, piloted by Captain Byron D. Rickards, was seized shortly after landing in Arequipa. Of interest is the fact that Captain Rickards would later be involved in a second hijacking in the same geographic area.

No additional aircraft hijackings occurred between 1931 and 1947. From 1947 to 1961, however, 47 other hijackings occurred worldwide (Crenshaw, 1987). The majority of these took place in Eastern Europe, Cuba, South America, and Asia. During this period, 22 hijackings occurred in the Soviet-bloc countries of Rumania, Czechoslovakia, Poland, Hungary, and Yugoslavia. All of these incidents involved persons desiring to flee to the West.

The first hijacking of an American registered air carrier occurred on May 1, 1961. A lone Hispanic male, armed with a handgun, hijacked a National Airlines Convair 440 to Havana, Cuba. The plane, on a scheduled flight from Miami to Key West, carried seven passengers and a crew of three. The hijacker's stated demand was to return home to his family in Cuba. This incident was the first of 306 hijackings of U.S. air carriers, involving a total of 442 hijackers. During the 30 years since that first hijacking, over 19,000 passengers and 1,700 crew members have been involved in cases of air piracy. No estimates exist on the number of relatives and friends who were also touched or traumatized by these events.

Aircraft hijacking is only the latest manifestation of a long historical trend toward acts of piracy. Since at least the 16th century, piracy has occurred on the high seas. Although acts of piracy date back to ancient times, recorded acts occurred most frequently in the 1700s and 1800s. In the modern era, episodes of train robbery and armored car hijackings have occurred with regularity. In almost all of these crimes, the primary goal was robbery.

While aircraft hijacking is the most recent form of an age-old phenomenon, air piracy is unique due to the complexity of the underlying motivations involved in this act. The acquisition of money or property is no longer the primary goal of the aircraft hijacker. Although many hijackings have involved extortion, the majority have been motivated by political, social, or personal concerns. A variety of mental illnesses also complicate many contemporary incidents of hijacking. Thus, the earlier profile of the pirate as a criminal and robber manifesting unbridled psychopathic traits no longer applies exclusively to the aircraft hijacker. This chapter will examine the motivations, personality types, and profiles of the contemporary aircraft hijacker.

Historical Overview Of Hostage-Taking

The phenomenon of hostage-taking may be endemic to the history of mankind, but has reached epidemic proportions over the past 25 years. A hostage situation may be defined as one in which a person or persons are held against their will, with their release contingent upon certain demands being met (Feldmann & Johnson, 1993). Essential to the hostage situation is the presence of demands; without demands, a hostage situation does not exist. This is in contrast to a barricade or potential suicide situation in which an individual holds himself, and perhaps others, but makes no demands. In such an instance, there is no leverage or bargaining point around which release of those held can be obtained.

The motivations for hostage-taking are many, but can be summarized as follows: (1) to effect an escape from an interrupted criminal act; (2) to elicit sympathy for radical causes; and (3) to embarrass governments and force a change in domestic or foreign policy (Federal Bureau of Investigation [FBI] Special Operations and Research Unit, 1981; Fuselier, 1981; Stratton, 1978).

Jenkins, Johnson, and Renfeldt (1977) have defined two basic types of hostage situations. The first is the traditional kidnapping in which a hostage is taken to a secret location and held for ransom. The other type is the hostage-barricade situation in which one or more persons are seized, but no attempt is made to reach a hideout. Rather, the hostage-takers allow themselves to be surrounded in a public place where negotiations are conducted.

A review of case studies by law enforcement officers reveals four categories of persons who take hostages (Fuselier, 1981; Gray, 1981). These include: (1) persons with mental disorders; (2) criminals without mental disorders who planned to take hostages in the commission of a crime, or who take hostages because they were interrupted during the crime; (3) prisoners in penal institutions who take hostages in order to escape or effect some change in the penal system; and (4) terrorists who take hostages in order to secure retribution or alleviation of disturbing social conditions.

It has generally been believed that the mentally ill group comprises over 50% of all hostage-takers (Fuselier, 1981). These persons are thought to represent four traditional diagnostic groups: (1) schizophrenia; (2) depression; (3) antisocial personality disorder; and (4) inadequate personality disorder. This latter group corresponds to an outdated Diagnostic and Statistical Manual, Second Edition (American Psychiatric Association, 1968, DSM-II) diagnostic category which is characterized by low self-esteem and inept responses to stress (American Psychiatric Association, 1968; Strentz, 1983). The inadequate personality may be viewed as related to several of the DSM-IV (1994) personality disorders which are marked by a high degree of impulsivity and low self-esteem; these include the borderline, histrionic, avoidant, and narcissistic personalities. It has traditionally been thought that the taking of hostages represents an "irrational, mindless, ineffective, or necessarily perilous" activity (Jenkins et al., 1977). In a study conducted by the Rand Corporation, however, Jenkins et al. found that these acts actu-

ally have a very high rate of success. In virtually all cases, the hostage-takers receive extensive publicity; this is often a major objective for the perpetrators. Furthermore, the hostage-takers have nearly an 80% chance of escaping apprehension, punishment, or death. Thus, hostage-taking is an extremely effective and successful type of criminal activity.

The Phenomenon Of Aircraft Hijacking

Up until recently, hijackings and hostage-takings were fairly distinct and separate phenomena. Hijackings were restricted almost entirely to robbery attempts involving armored cars, ships, and trains. Hostages, on the other hand, were usually taken for money (e.g., kidnapping) or to ensure escape (e.g., bank robberies or prison escape attempts). Over the past 30 years, however, two additional criminal activities have emerged in which hostage-taking plays an important role: terrorism and aircraft hijacking. With the increase in air piracy, however, there is a merging of hijacking and hostage-taking into a unique criminal activity. By definition, a person who sets out to hijack an aircraft intends to take hostages. From another perspective, the taking of hostages is not the accidental by-product of some other criminal goal. Thus, as contrasted to other criminal acts, aircraft hijacking provides an excellent vehicle by which to study the phenomenon of hostage-taking.

As mentioned earlier, the first incident of aircraft hijacking occurred in 1931 in Peru. Since then, a total of 849 hijackings have occurred worldwide. Of these, 306 have involved U.S. registered air carriers, representing 36% of all hijackings. Many of these cases, such as TWA Flight 847 (to be discussed later), have attracted global attention and resulted in tragic outcomes.

In spite of the scope of this problem, until recently, no organized research had been conducted to examine the phenomenon of aircraft hijacking. In 1987, however, a comprehensive study of aircraft hijacking in the United States was undertaken by the University of Louisville and the FBI. This project created a database on all 306 incidents involving U.S. air carriers. The findings presented in this chapter are based on this research effort.

The Aircraft Hijacking Research Project: Origins and Methodology

In order to study aircraft hijacking in a systematic manner, the Department of Psychiatry and Behavioral Sciences at the University of Louisville School of Medicine and the FBI submitted a proposal to the National Institute of Justice (NIJ) to create a database examining all hijackings of U.S. registered aircraft occurring between 1961 and 1989 (Bell, Lanceley, Feldmann, Johnson, Cheek, Lewis, & Worley, 1989). This study, entitled "The Aircraft Hijacking Research Project," NIJ Grant #87-15-CX-0037, was conducted between 1987 and 1990. It brought together a unique group of professionals from the University, the FBI Field Office in Louisville, and the Special Operations and Research Unit at the FBI Academy in Quantico, Virginia. The goals of the study were to identify the motivations for aircraft hijacking, develop a comprehensive profile of the aircraft hijacker, explore the factors that influenced the outcome of these incidents, and improve the negotiation strategies and crisis management procedures used by law enforcement agencies during hijackings.

A major component of the research project was to assess and evaluate those factors of a situational, psychosocial, and behavioral nature which influence hostage situations. This was accomplished by examining two levels of data. The first was on an incident level. Each hijacking incident was examined with respect to date, location, type of aircraft, number of hostages, number of persons killed and/or injured, duration, weapons used, law enforcement response, and outcome.

The second level of analysis was of the hijacker. Demographic information, demands made, psychiatric history, criminal history, and psychosocial factors were evaluated.

Data were obtained from a variety of sources. A list of all U.S. registered air carrier hijackings was obtained from the Federal Aviation Administration (FAA) and the FBI. The research team then traveled to FBI Headquarters in Washington, D.C., to review all FBI case files on the incidents. Whenever possible, hijackers were interviewed using the Diagnostic Interview Schedule (DIS), the Minnesota Multiphasic Personality Inventory (MMPI), the Sixteen Personality Factor Questionnaire (16-PF), and the Shipley Institute of Living Scale as a measure of intellectual functioning. Police identification records were also obtained for those subjects who had criminal histories. Standardized case history forms were developed to systematically analyze each incident and each hijacker.

The result of this endeavor was the development of a research database covering all U.S. hijackings from 1961 through 1989. This is the only database of its kind in existence covering the psychological and psychosocial factors associated with aircraft hijacking.

Basic Characteristics Of Aircraft Hijacking

A total of 306 hijackings of American air carriers occurred between 1961 and 1989. These crimes involved 442 hijackers. The occurrence of aircraft hijacking is obviously not limited to the United States. The American hijackings account for only 36.04% of all incidents. International air carriers have been hijacked 543 times, representing 63.96% of the world total. The United States, however, has experienced more hijackings than any other country. When compared to the 306

American incidents, the next most frequent countries are Colombia (53), Russia (31), and Poland (28). Tables 1 and 2 illustrate the scope of the problem of aircraft hijacking.

Aircraft Hijacking by Year

The peak years for aircraft hijacking in the U.S. and worldwide occurred between 1968 and 1972. During this five-year period, 38.3% of all hijackings took place. The largest number of incidents occurred in 1969 and 1970, with 87 and 83 hijackings, respectively. A significant decline in hijacking occurred between 1973 and 1976. The incidence of aircraft hijacking increased again between 1977 and 1985, when slightly more than 34% of all hijackings were committed. During

this second span, the peak years were 1980 (41 incidents) and 1985 (36 incidents). A sharp decline in the number of incidents then followed. The total numbers of aircraft hijackings by year are presented in Table 3 and Figure 1.

Destinations

On a manifest level, the most obvious reason to hijack an aircraft is to obtain transportation to some desired location. Although there are many other variables involved in aircraft hijacking, it is of interest to look at where hijackers wanted to go. Cuba was the most frequent destination for the U.S. hijackings, accounting for 148 of the 306 incidents (48.37%). As will be discussed later in the chapter, many of these incidents involved

TABLE 1
WORLD HIJACKINGS BY COUNTRY OF REGISTRATION (1931-1989)

Country of Registration	Number of Hijackings	Percentage
United States	306	36.04%
Colombia	53	6.24%
Russia	31	3.65%
Poland	28	3.30%
Cuba	22	2.59%
Czechoslovakia	22	2.59%
Iran	18	2.12%
Brazil	16	1.88%
Japan	15	1.77%
Mexico	15	1.77%
Venezuela	14	1.65%
India	13	1.53%
France	12	1.41%
Canada	11	1.30%
Germany	11	1.30%
Philippines	11	1.30%
Argentina	10	1.18%
Ecuador	10	1.18%
Lebanon	0	1.18%
Turkey	0	1.18%
Others/Not Known	211	24.85%
Total	849	100.00%

TABLE 2
NUMBER OF AIRCRAFT HIJACKINGS BY CARRIER OF REGISTRY 1931-1989

Carrier of Registry	Number of Hijackings	Percentage
U.S. Air Carriers	306	36.04%
International Air Carriers	543	63.96%
Total	849	100.00%

Cuban refugees who wished to return home (61 hijackings). A great many other hijackers, however, including the mentally ill, terrorists, and others with political motivations, as well as criminals attempting to escape the American criminal justice system, have demanded to go to Cuba.

Canada was a destination that also occurred with some regularity, involving primarily persons who wished to avoid the draft during the Vietnam War. Although hundreds of destinations around the world were recorded, in general, the destination of the hijackers appeared to be related closely to their underlying motivation. These will be discussed further in the sections on demands and categories of hijackers.

Number of Hostages Taken

As mentioned earlier, over 21,000 people have been taken hostage in the 306 U.S. incidents. This figure includes 19,875 passengers and 1,756 crew members. When the outcomes of the hijackings are taken into consideration, 11,421 passengers and 1,018 crew members were held during successful hijackings. Unsuccessful hijackings involved 8,454 passengers and 738 crew members. A more extensive discussion of hijacking outcomes is found later in the chapter.

Fifty-six incidents resulted in injury and/or loss of life. This represents 18.3% of the total number of hijackings. Forty-five deaths occurred, including 26 hostages, 15 hijackers, 1 law enforcement officer, and 3 bystanders. The total number of persons injured was 233. This figure

breaks down to 204 hostages, 23 hijackers, 4 law enforcement officers, and 2 bystanders. When the number of persons involved in these incidents, over 21,000, is taken into consideration, the number of injuries and deaths is surprisingly low. The potential for loss of life during a hijacking, however, remains great.

Types of Aircraft Hijacked

The study showed that the Boeing 727 was the most frequently hijacked aircraft. One explanation for this finding is the frequency with which this aircraft was in service during the peak years of aircraft hijacking. A total of 1,831 B-727s were produced, with 1,658 being used by commercial airlines. When compared with all other types of planes produced, the ratio of B-727s hijacked to those produced is quite high. Another factor may also have been in operation, however, which made the B-727 a frequent target. For example, there are many cases in which hijackers appeared to choose the type of aircraft they attacked. The choice of aircraft seized was often related to specific escape plans devised by the hijackers. The B-727 possesses one unique characteristic that made it a likely target. All of these planes were equipped with retractable rear stairs that could be lowered in flight. Thus, a hijacker intending to use a parachute to escape, such as D. B. Cooper and others, could exit the aircraft more easily than from other types of planes.

The B-727, however, was by no means the only type of aircraft hijacked. The DC-8 and DC-

TABLE 3
NUMBER OF AIRCRAFT HIJACKINGS BY YEAR (1931-1989)

Year	Number of Hijackings	Percentage
1931-1949	15	1.77%
1950-1959	23	2.71%
1960	9	1.06%
1961	11	1.30%
1962	3	0.35%
1963	1	0.12%
1964	2	0.24%
1965	5	0.59%
1966	4	0.47%
1967	6	0.71%
1968	35	4.12%
1969	87	10.25%
1970	83	9.78%
1971	58	6.83%
1972	62	7.30%
1973	22	2.59%
1974	26	3.06%
1975	25	2.94%
1976	18	2.12%
1977	32	3.77%
1978	31	3.65%
1979	27	3.18%
1980	41	4.83%
1981	32	3.77%
1982	32	3.77%
1983	35	4.12%
1984	28	3.30%
1985	36	4.24%
1986	16	1.88%
1987	14	1.65%
1988	16	1.88%
1989	14	1.65%
Total	849	100.00%

9 were the next most frequently hijacked, again due to the large number of such planes in service. Nearly all types of commercial planes in service, from jumbo jets to twin-engine propeller driven planes, were targeted by hijackers. Likewise, many small private aircraft and helicopters were used in hijackings. The helicopter, in particular, was the aircraft of choice for prison escapees. The following case illustrates one of the more unusual incidents involving a private plane.

Case Illustration: Jack R. Johnson was 19 years old when he attempted to commandeer a small single-engine aircraft while over southwestern Indiana. The subject went to Tri-State Airways in Evansville, Indiana, on November 11, 1975, to hire an aircraft, a Cessna 152, for a

FIGURE 1
NUMBER OF AIRCRAFT HIJACKINGS BY YEAR (1931-1989)

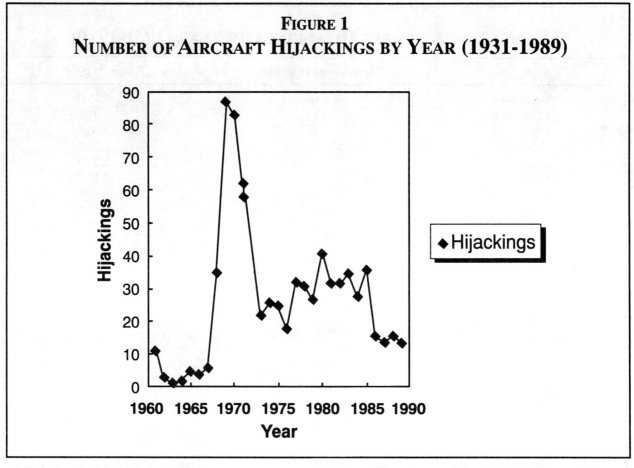

sightseeing and instructional flying course.

Shortly after takeoff, the pilot leveled off at 4,000 feet. At that time, Johnson pulled a handgun and threatened the pilot's life. Johnson then ordered the pilot to put the aircraft into a steep dive and crash into the ground. The pilot began a series of violent maneuvers that were intended to throw Johnson off balance. During these maneuvers, the pilot attempted to wrestle the gun away from Johnson. While in the midst of a struggle, the door to the aircraft came open. When the pilot saw this, he pushed Johnson out of the aircraft. The subject fell approximately 3,500 feet to his death in a cornfield.

Duration of Hijackings

Aircraft hijackings tend to be relatively brief events. The shortest hijacking in the sample lasted only three minutes, after which the hijacker was subdued by passengers and crew of the aircraft. The longest hijacking lasted 44 hours. The mean length, however, was 4 hrs 18 min. Over 95% of all hijackings had a duration of between 3 hrs 17 min and 4 hrs 47 min. In general, the longer a hijacking lasted, the more likely it was to be successful. For example, only 20% of hijackings with a duration of less than 38 minutes were successful. On the other hand, when the hijacking lasted one hour or more, the success rate was 80%.

The duration of aircraft hijackings can be compared with other types of hostage incidents. Terrorist kidnappings, for example, have an average length of 38 days, while hostage-barricade situations not involving aircraft have an average duration of 47 hours (Jenkins et al., 1977).

Outcome

In this study, outcome was defined as either successful or unsuccessful, according to the following criteria. An aircraft hijacking was judged to be successful if: (1) the hijacker took control of the aircraft; (2) at least some of his demands were met; and (3) he avoided arrest or apprehension by authorities during the period of time immediately following the hijacking. In those cases in which the hijacker was arrested some period of time after the incident, as often occurred, the hijacking was considered successful. An unsuccessful hijacking was an incident that failed to meet any of the three criteria outlined above.

A total of 164 (53.59%) of U.S. hijackings were successful. One hundred forty-two (46.41%) incidents were unsuccessful. Overall, aircraft hijackings are less successful than other types of hostage situations, which have success rates ranging from 60% to 77% (Jenkins et al., 1977). Many variables influence the outcome of air piracy, including the number of hijackers, weapons used, mental status, and psychiatric history. Specific factors affecting outcome will be discussed in the sections below.

Number of Hijackers

Hijackings were attempted by 442 individuals. The number of hijackers involved in a particular incident becomes very interesting and important when outcome is taken into consideration. Of the 306 American hijackings, 237 incidents (77.45%) involved a single hijacker. Individuals acting alone, however, were successful only 46% of the time. Incidents involving multiple hijackers, in contrast, were successful over 75% of the time (see Table 4).

Where the Hijacker Took Control of the Aircraft

In nearly two-thirds of the incidents studied,

the aircraft was commandeered in flight. Many different scenarios were found, however, in which the hijacker took control at other times. The aircraft was seized at the gate in 38 incidents (12.42%). In 19 incidents (6.21%), the hijacking took place during the landing approach, implying that either the hijacker had not made up his mind or did not have sufficient opportunity to act until very late in the flight. Twenty-eight incidents involved seizure of the aircraft on the ground just before takeoff, during taxi, or while parked.

Only four incidents involved unusual settings. In two incidents, the hijackers took control of the aircraft at the ticket counter when they brandished guns; both incidents occurred at small airports where the ticket counters and the gates were located in the same area. Another hijacker, suffering from a mental illness, tried to take control of an out-of-service aircraft in the hanger. The fourth announced the hijacking after the plane had landed and arrived at the gate. He then refused to allow the passengers to de-plane. This data is presented in Table 5.

Who Hijacks Aircraft? Demographics

Aircraft hijacking has involved people of all ages and backgrounds. The mean age for all hijackers in the study was 30.3 years. Ages ranged from 10 to 73 years. A number of children and adolescents are included in the database; in most cases these were individuals who accompanied their parents during hijacking attempts. Surprisingly, there were a number of cases in which adolescents hijacked aircraft on their own. In most instances, these cases occurred in connection with some personal problem or underlying mental illness.

Case Illustration: *Thomas Marston was a 17-year-old from Georgia, who hijacked a National Airlines Boeing 727 on March 8, 1971. His primary motivation for the crime was to escape from his mother, whom he perceived as overly critical*

412 Lethal Violence

TABLE 4
NUMBER OF HIJACKERS AND OUTCOME (1961-1989)

Number of Hijackers	Successful		Unsuccessful		Total
Col. %	N	Row %	N	Row %	N
1 77.45%	109	45.99%	128	54.01%	237
2 11.11%	26	76.47%	8	23.53%	34
3 5.23%	15	93.75%	1	6.25%	16
4 2.61%	6	75.00%	2	25.00%	8
5 1.31%	3	75.00%	1	25.00%	4
6 1.31.%	3	75.00%	1	25.00%	4
7 0.33%	1	100%	0	0%	1
8 0.33%	1	100%	0	0%	1
9 or More 0.33%	0	0%	1	100%	1
Total 100.00%	164	53.59%	142	46.41%	306

and demanding. Marston had been a poor student and also had many disciplinary problems at school. He also had a history of running away from home, often traveling great distances.

On the day of the hijacking, he had gotten into trouble at school for cutting classes. He realized that he would once again be punished by his mother, so he decided to flee the country. After seizing the aircraft, Marston demanded to be taken to Canada. His rationale for this demand was that since many people attempting to avoid the draft fled to Canada, he would be safe from his mother in such a haven. In addition to his academic and personal problems, Marston met the diagnostic criteria for conduct disorder of adolescence.

Overall, aircraft hijackers represent an older class of criminal than those committing other crimes, as reported in the FBI Uniform Crime Reports (1993). Table 6 lists hijackers by age group.

As with most violent crime, aircraft hijacking is a predominantly male activity. Four hundred four hijackers (91.4%) were male, while 38 (8.6%) were female. Male hijackers tended to be older, with a mean age of 30.5 years and a range of 10 to 73 years. The mean age of female hijackers was 28.4 years, with a range of 16 to 57 years.

Race and ethnicity were identified for 413 hijackers; no data were available for those individuals who fled to other countries and never returned, or for fugitives who were not apprehended. Whites, Hispanics, and Blacks dominated the

TABLE 5
WHERE THE HIJACKER TOOK CONTROL OF THE AIRCRAFT (1961-1989)

Location	Number	Percentage
In Flight	198	64.71%
At the Gate	38	12.42%
Approach to Landing	19	6.21%
On Takeoff	12	3.92%
Parking Ramp	11	3.59%
Taxi to Takeoff	5	.63%
At Ticket Counter	2	0.66%
Aircraft Serviced in Hanger	1	0.33%
On Helipad	1	0.33%
After Landing at the Gate	1	0.33%
Not Known	18	5.88%
Total	306	100.00%

TABLE 6
HIJACKER AGE GROUPS (1961-1989)

Age Range	Number	Percentage
10-19	35	8.84%
20-24	99	25.00%
25-29	93	23.48%
30-34	60	15.15%
35-39	37	9.34%
40-44	33	8.33%
45-49	19	4.80%
50-54	9	2.27%
55-59	6	1.52%
60 and over	5	1.26%
Total	396	100.00%

* No Data Available on Age for 46 Hijackers

database as the most frequent hijackers. Sixty-two percent of the hijackers were U.S. citizens. Table 7 lists all groups according to race and ethnicity.

A prior criminal history was often difficult to elucidate. At least 40% of hijackers had been arrested previously. This number may be higher, however, due to the frequent use of aliases or uncertainty about the true identity of some hijack-ers. This represented a particular problem with respect to fugitive hijackers who were never apprehended.

The educational background of hijackers can be summarized as follows: (1) grade school only, 17.77%; (2) some high school — 24.37%; (3) high school graduate — 23.35%; (4) some college, 22.34%; (5) college graduate — 5.08%; and

TABLE 7
HIJACKER RACE/ETHNICITY (1961-1989)

Race/Ethnicity	Number	Percentage
White	187	45.28%
Black	72	17.43%
Hispanic-White	128	30.99%
Hispanic-Black	14	3.39%
Arab-White	7	1.69%
Arab-Black	2	0.48%
American Indian	2	0.48%
Asian	1	0.24%
Total	413	100%

* No Data Available on 29 Hijackers

(6) post-graduate education — 7.11%. Thus, aircraft hijackers appear to be better educated than other criminals.

Most hijackers (49.19%) were unemployed at the time of the incident. Twenty-eight percent worked full-time when the hijacking occurred, and only 2.61% were employed part-time. The remaining hijackers were prisoners (7.49%), students (6.51%), disabled (2.28%), retired (1.95%), or family members (1.3%).

Information on marital status revealed that slightly over 50% of hijackers were married at the time of the incident. Clearly, fewer subjects were married than would be expected in any random sample of the adult population. One explanation for this finding is the fact that many hijackers were mentally ill, socially disenfranchised, criminals with antisocial personality disorders, or members of fringe groups. Common to all these individuals were problems with interpersonal relations or a desire to avoid long-term commitments.

Motivations For Aircraft Hijacking: Categories

One of the primary goals of the research into aircraft hijacking was to categorize incidents into distinct types at both the incident and hijacker levels. A cursory review of the data indicates readily that hijacking is a heterogeneous event; many of the incidents bear little resemblance to one another. For some cases, the only common denominator is that an aircraft was seized. The development of discrete categories has significance for the management of hijackings because intervention strategies that work with one type of hijacker may not work with another.

In order to arrive at the categories presented below, a number of factors were examined. The stated demands of the hijackers, their membership in political and religious groups, history of mental illness, and psychosocial stressors yielded the most valuable information in determining the motivation for the hijacking. Analysis of this data led to the creation of six categories of aircraft hijacker: (1) the mentally ill; (2) extortionists; (3) terrorists and/or politically motivated; (4) prison escapees; (5) personally discontented; and (6) Cuban refugees returning home. Using this system of motivational categorization, all but five incidents could be explained. Tables 8 and 9 list the categories of aircraft hijackings and hijackers.

Mentally Ill

This group was defined by the presence of a significant mental illness. For incidents in this category, mental illness was the driving force behind the hijacking. Other factors, such as political beliefs or attempts to obtain financial compensation, were either absent or clearly secondary to the illness. Thus, the hijackers in this group were operating under the influence of significant psychopathology, such as delusions, paranoid or grandiose thinking, or impulsive/unstable emotional states that led directly to the hijacking attempt. A case illustration best exemplifies this category.

Case Illustration: Oranetta Mays was a mentally ill individual who seized an aircraft at the gate at Cleveland-Hopkins International Airport. She carried a diagnosis of chronic paranoid schizophrenia, and had a long history of psychiatric treatment.

On the day of the hijacking, she was experiencing visual and auditory hallucinations as well as paranoid delusions. One of her delusional beliefs was that she was being followed and persecuted by Prince Charles and his security guards.

The incident began when she "heard" a voice tell her that she must flee from her home to avoid being killed. She then "saw" a sign instructing her to "go to Brazil." In response to these auditory and visual hallucinations, she proceeded to the airport. She had in her possession a handgun and, in spite of her psychosis and disorganized thinking, was able to smuggle the gun through the security checkpoint.

She then boarded a Pan Am flight bound for New York and announced her demand to go to Brazil. While she was on the plane, local and federal authorities attempted to begin negotiations with her. During the negotiation process, she continued to experience both auditory and visual hallucinations. At one point, she looked in the back

of the plane and "saw" Prince Charles and his men. At that point she realized that her efforts to escape them would be unsuccessful.

A psychiatrist was consulted during the incident. At some point late in the hijacking, Mays stated that she was tired and wanted to take a nap. She indicated that she would surrender after she got some rest. She then said "this will all be over soon." That statement was misinterpreted by the psychiatrist and law enforcement officers as a reference to suicide.

As a result of that misunderstanding, a decision was made to assault the aircraft. When the assault took place, Mays opened fire, wounding one police officer. She was also wounded in the attack. After the incident was resolved, it was discovered that she had never contemplated suicide, but was simply very fatigued. She was eventually found not competent to stand trial and was subsequently hospitalized in a psychiatric facility.

The mentally ill group consisted of 104 incidents, representing 33.99% of the 306 total incidents. All of the mentally ill hijackers acted alone, accounting for 23.53% of the 442 hijackers studied. Schizophrenia was the most common diagnosis in this group (27.7%). Other frequently encountered diagnoses included personality disorders (25.4%), mostly of the borderline type; mood disorders such as depression and bipolar disorder (20.0%); psychoactive substance-use disorders (11.5%); and non-schizophrenic psychoses (7.4%).

Among the mood disorders, depression was found much more commonly than bipolar disorder. This finding was somewhat unexpected because the traditional profile of the aircraft hijacker was thought to include large numbers of manic-depressive individuals. Suicidal ideation was common in this group: 49.8% experienced thoughts of suicide, 14% stated that they intended to kill themselves during the hijacking, and 9% had prior histories of suicide attempts.

Hijackings in the mentally ill category tended

TABLE 8

CATEGORIES OF AIRCRAFT HIJACKING BY INCIDENT (1961-1989)

Category	Number	Percentage
Mentally Ill	104	33.99%
Terrorist/Politically Motivated	62	20.26%
Cuban Refugees	61	19.93%
Extortionists	38	12.42%
Prison Escapees	22	7.19%
Personally Discontented	14	4.58%
Unspecified Hijacking	5	1.63%
Total	306	100.00%

TABLE 9

AIRCRAFT HIJACKERS BY CATEGORY (1961-1989)

Category	Number	Percentage
Terrorist/Politically Motivated	115	26.02%
Cuban Refugees	108	24.43%
Mentally Ill	104	23.53%
Extortionists	53	11.99%
Prison Escapees	35	7.92%
Personally Discontented	14	3.17%
Unspecified Hijackers	13	2.94%
Total	442	100.00%

to be more dangerous than other hijackings. While in most cases of aircraft hijacking, weapons were never actually discharged, in the mentally ill group, 24% of incidents involved rounds being fired. The majority of injuries and deaths occurred in the mentally ill and terrorist hijackings.

Ninety-three percent of mentally ill hijackers were male. Eighty-three percent were White and 17% were Black. Most were U.S. citizens (84%). At the time of the hijacking, 42% were single, 19% married, 19% divorced, 5% separated, and 3% widowed. Most were unemployed (59%) and 85% were in psychiatric treatment at the time of the incident. Finally, this group tended to be younger than other hijackers, with a mean age of 27.8 years.

Extortionists

In this group, the primary motivation for the hijacking was the exchange of the aircraft and hostages for money. Thirty-eight extortion hijackings occurred during the study period, representing 12.42% of the total. These incidents involved 53 hijackers (11.99% of all hijackers).

As a group, the extortion hijackings were the least successful, with only eight of the extortion hijackers (15.1%) achieving their goal. There are several possible explanations for this outcome.

First, these hijackings usually involved making at least one stop during the incident to pick up the money demanded. Authorities would generally inform the hijacker that a period of time was needed to obtain the money; this obviously also provided law enforcement agencies with a much-needed interval to develop intervention strategies. Finally, complicated escape routes had to be developed by the hijacker. In most cases the subject elected to make his escape by parachuting from the aircraft, a clearly dangerous undertaking. These factors made the extortion hijackings much more complicated than other attempts. With the increased complexity came greater potential for something to go wrong, leading to a low success rate.

Extortion hijackings became more frequent during the period between 1968 and 1972. The peak year for this type of hijacking was 1972, when 20 incidents occurred. The frequency then dropped off considerably until 1979 and 1980, when another smaller peak occurred. By the mid-1980s, this type of hijacking had virtually disappeared. The reasons for the decline in extortion attempts most likely lie in improved security, coupled with the low rate of success of these incidents. Well-publicized successful hijackings, such as the D. B. Cooper incident, were the exception rather than the rule.

Case Illustration: D.B. Cooper, whose real name remains unknown, was the first successful extortion hijacker. He demanded and received $100,000 when he hijacked a Boeing 727 on November 24, 1972. He parachuted out of the aircraft over the Rocky Mountains. Extensive searches of the area where Cooper jumped uncovered some of the money and gear used in his escape, but Cooper was never found. It is unclear whether he survived the incident or not.

An investigation into Cooper's background failed to reveal any significant information; it is thought that he used an alias, but no clues as to his true identity were ever found. Cooper apparently purposely chose the 727 because it was a

part of his escape plan; the rear stairs of the aircraft could be lowered in-flight, which allowed a convenient means of escape via parachute.

The notoriety of the D.B. Cooper affair, however, did lead to a contagion effect. Throughout the 1970s, a number of "copy cat" hijackings, modeled on Cooper's, took place. In spite of the publicity that Cooper received, his was not the first extortion hijacking, as illustrated below.

Case Illustration: Arthur G. Barkley, who seized an aircraft on June 4, 1970, had worked as a delivery truck driver for a baking company in Phoenix, Arizona. Initially, Barkley was well-liked by co-workers and viewed as "just like everyone else" at the company. For unknown reasons, however, things began to change for Barkley in the years that preceded the hijacking. The most noticeable change was the emergence of marked paranoid ideation. Barkley began to believe that the company and his immediate supervisors were discriminating against him with respect to job assignments. He also believed that others were making fun of him and plotting against him. These beliefs led him to file a lawsuit against the company for damages, back pay, and worker's compensation. When the suit was unsuccessful, Barkley then tried to sue the IRS for reasons which were unclear.

On the day of the hijacking, Barkley went to Washington, D.C., ostensibly to argue his suit against the IRS in federal court. When he was denied access to the courthouse, Barkley became agitated and more irrational. He then proceeded to Baltimore-Washington International Airport and hijacked an aircraft, demanding $100 million. Authorities responded by giving him $125,000, and Barkley allowed the plane to take off. He instructed the pilot to fly north to an unknown destination.

Once the plane was airborne, Barkley counted his money; he was surprised and angered to find that he was given only $99,875. He then ordered the pilot to return to Baltimore to pick up *the rest of his money. At this point, the aircraft was over upstate New York. While en route back to Baltimore, Barkley decided that he would "reprimand the President and the director of the IRS for not being able to count accurately," according to a statement he later give to law enforcement officers.*

Once the plane had returned to Baltimore, authorities decided that they would not allow the aircraft to depart again. Plans were made to disable the plane by shooting out its tires. The plan went smoothly until Barkley saw police on the runway. At that time, he ordered the pilot to take off again. The pilot distracted Barkley while police boarded the aircraft and evacuated most of the passengers. Barkley started shooting indiscriminantly, but the pilot and other crew members were able to subdue him.

Barkley was the first hijacker in U.S. history to seize an aircraft for purposes of extortion. His initial monetary demand for $100 million is the highest on record.

As with other hijacking categories, most of the subjects in the extortion group were men; there were 48 male hijackers and 5 females. The mean age of extortion hijackers was 34.7 years, somewhat older than other groups of hijackers. The majority of these individuals was single. Most of the hijackers in this group (73%) had prior criminal histories. Fifteen extortion hijackers (28.3%) had psychiatric diagnoses which included: (1) schizophrenia — six hijackers; (2) personality disorders — four hijackers; (3) unspecified psychoses — three hijackers; and (4) depression — two hijackers. In addition to these psychiatric diagnoses, 24 hijackers (45.3%) had histories of drug or alcohol abuse. Thus, 39 of the 53 hijackers in the extortion group (73.6%) had some history of mental or emotional problems.

Terrorists/Politically Motivated

The FBI has defined terrorism as the unlawful use of force or violence against persons or property to intimidate or coerce a government or civilian population in furtherance of political or social objectives (FBI, 1988). It may be useful, however, to expand the definition of terrorism to include the use of violence or fear to further some cause which may be political, social, religious, racial, cultural, or even economic in nature. A review of world terrorism indicates that any grievance may be felt to warrant the use of force, with the end justifying the means. As a result of this mindset, innocent citizens may be attacked as a way of influencing governments because attacks against individuals or public institutions may be viewed as more effective and more convenient than attacks against military targets. Terrorist acts are also highly symbolic, with the statement sometimes being more important than the actual consequences of the act.

In this study, membership in the terrorist or politically motivated group was based on either: (1) the affiliation of the hijacker with a group or organization that was characterized as radically active or extremist; or (2) statements made by the hijacker that indicated the hijacking was being carried out to make a political statement. The political affiliation or statement was perceived as the driving force behind the hijacking. Examples of terrorist groups from the study include the Black Panthers, the American Nazi Party, Croatian independence groups, and many little-known fringe groups. The more widely known Middle Eastern and European terrorist groups have had little impact on American hijackings to date, probably because of the difficulty these groups have operating within the United States.

Sixty-two hijackings fell into the terrorists/politically motivated group. These incidents involved 115 hijackers. In this category, 83% of hijackers were male and 17% were female; this category contains the highest number of female subjects. Forty-six percent were Black, 34% White, and 18% were of Arabic ethnicity. Seventy-four percent were U.S. citizens. The terrorist hijacker group also was relatively young, with an average age of 28. Forty-nine percent of terrorist hijackers were unemployed. Fewer terrorist hijackers were married (32%) than in other groups.

The incidence of mental illness and substance abuse was relatively low in this group. Forty hijackers (35%) in this group had psychiatric or substance use diagnoses; this represented a smaller percentage than in other groups. The most common was a personality disorder (31%), followed by schizophrenia (22%), depressive disorders (13%), and alcohol abuse/dependence (9%). It is likely that terrorist groups were more selective in their membership than other groups. Persons with emotional or drug problems represented liabilities to the group due to their instability and were, therefore, excluded.

Case Illustration: Anthony Bryant was a member of the Black Panthers who hijacked an aircraft to Havana in 1969. The purpose of the hijacking was to impress the Cuban government so that it would provide financial support for the group's activities in the United States. Because the goal of the incident was to raise money for the party, Bryant decided on his own to rob the passengers and turn that money over to the party leadership. In this manner, Bryant believed that his own position within the group would be improved.

Unknown to Bryant, however, was the fact that one of the passengers, carrying a large sum of money, was a Cuban diplomat returning from the United Nations in New York. Once the plane landed in Havana, the diplomat quickly conferred with the police and identified Bryant as the hijacker and robber. Rather than receiving the hero's welcome that Bryant expected from his revolutionary comrades, he was arrested and imprisoned for stealing from the Cuban government. Bryant was eventually released and returned to the U.S., only to be arrested and tried in Miami on the federal charge of air piracy.

It is interesting to compare the frequency of politically motivated hijackings to that of other aircraft hijackings. The politically motivated hijacking represented 20.26% of all hijackings of U.S. registered air carriers between 1961 and 1989. While the image of a terrorist most frequently comes to mind when news of an aircraft hijacking is reported, the data showed this not to be the case. The chronological relationship of terrorist hijackings to all aircraft hijackings is also of note. The largest number of aircraft hijackings occurred in the years between 1968 and 1972, and in the early 1980s. Most of the politically related hijackings in the U.S. occurred between 1969 and 1971. Since that time, terrorist hijackings have been relatively infrequent, in spite of incidents like TWA Flight 847, which received intense media coverage.

These findings have a number of significant implications. First, although the threat of terrorist incidents has increased worldwide, the number of politically related hijackings in the United States suggests that the risk here is significantly lower. Since 1980, terrorist attacks have escalated sharply on a global scale, while terrorist hijackings in the U.S. have remained relatively stable and infrequent. This observation reflects the success of counter-terrorist measures by U.S. law enforcement agencies, the difficulty terrorist groups have operating within the U. S., and the effectiveness of airport security procedures (Busby, 1989). The threat nevertheless remains for U.S. air carriers that operate overseas and for U.S. airports that serve as international gateways.

A second area of significance is the fact that, although infrequent to date, politically motivated hijackings are very successful when they occur. These hijackers were successful 81% of the time, compared to the overall hijacking success rate of just over 50%.

Success in hijacking may be related to several variables. One of obvious importance is the type of weapon used in the hijacking. Of the politically motivated hijackers, 56% had handguns, 24% had explosives, 17% had knives, 4% had automatic weapons, 1% carried an incendiary device, 1% had shoulder weapons, and 2% had miscellaneous weapons. In addition, this group contained a large number of multiple-hijacker incidents. As indicated earlier, the success rate for hijackings rose as the number of hijackers increased.

These findings have significance for law enforcement agencies in terms of planning and responding to a terrorist hijacking. It can be assumed, for example, that terrorist hijackings will involve more hijackers than other types of aircraft hijacking. Further, these individuals will be better armed and more likely to possess a real weapon than a fake or alleged weapon (see "Weapons" section below). Thus, the chances of a successful tactical assault on an aircraft held by terrorists are likely to be decreased, while the risks of injury or loss of life will be increased. In these situations, then, a negotiated resolution to the incident becomes even more desirable. In addition, law enforcement officers may assume that terrorist hijackers are less likely to be suffering from mental illness, as compared to other categories of hijackers. This fact will have important impact on the conduct of negotiations. As personal and psychological factors are less likely to be influencing terrorist hijackers, different negotiation strategies will be required as contrasted to those utilized with other groups.

Prison Escapees

Escape attempts from prison accounted for 22 hijackings involving 35 individuals. Eighty-five percent of the hijackers were male and 15% were female. Of these 35 hijackers, 94% were White, 3% were Black, and 3% Hispanic. Eighty-three percent of the subjects were either single, divorced, widowed, or separated. Only 17% were married at the time of the incident.

In this group of hijackers, six individuals (17%) had formal psychiatric diagnoses. All persons in this category had personality disorder diagnoses, which consisted of four antisocial personalities and two borderline personalities.

An interesting observation is the fact that only 18 people (52%) in this group were actually incarcerated at the time of the incident. The remaining 17 individuals involved in prison hijackings were civilians who were assisting in the escape attempt. Five of these 17 civilians were female.

Unlike other hijackings, the prison escape attempts utilized either small private aircraft or helicopters, as contrasted to larger vehicles. In most instances, the aircraft was chartered for other purposes and then diverted to the escape attempt. Only one commercial aircraft was seized in these attempts. It should be noted that none of the prison escape hijackings were successful.

This group also contained the only three-time hijacker in U.S. history. Garrett Trapnell initially attempted to hijack an aircraft in an extortion attempt. He was apprehended and convicted on air piracy charges. Twice during his incarceration, Trapnell organized hijackings designed to gain his freedom. Both were unsuccessful. The first involved his girlfriend, who seized a helicopter and attempted to land it inside the prison; she was killed during the incident. It is interesting to note that this escape plan was inspired by a movie that Trapnell had watched. Seven months later, the woman's teenage daughter attempted to hijack a TWA flight in Springfield, Illinois. Her demand was for the release of Trapnell in exchange for the hostages. Today, Garrett Trapnell remains incarcerated at the U.S. prison in Marion, Illinois.

Personally Discontented

This category is defined by a hijacking attempt which was the result of some personal issue or motivation that was not readily apparent to outside observers. While mental illness may have played a prominent role in these events, the overriding factor behind these hijackings was some type of personal problem or concern. The act of air piracy tended to be viewed as either a means of resolving the problem or a way of escaping some personally unpleasant situation. Common precipitants in this category were family, marital, or relationship problems, work-related problems, or financial difficulties.

The personally discontented category consisted of 14 hijackers, each of whom acted alone in seizing an aircraft. Thirteen of these individuals were White males who were U.S. citizens. The remaining person in this category was a Black female. Six hijackers in this group were single, five were married, and three were widowed or divorced. The mean age for these hijackers was 34 years, somewhat older than other hijacker groups.

Nine of these offenders had psychiatric histories, while 11 had indicators of substance abuse problems. Three-fourths of the people in this group had positive suicidal ideation. In summary, members of this group displayed a significant level of psychiatric impairment which laid the foundation for aberrant behavior. Various psychosocial stressors, however, served as the trigger or spark for the implementation of the criminal act. In short, the hijacking attempt was a result of the stressor rather than a product of mental illness.

Cuban Refugees

This group consisted of Cuban immigrants who hijacked aircraft as a means of returning home. Sixty-one incidents occurred, involving 108 hijackers. Persons who hijacked aircraft to Cuba for other reasons, such as terrorists and extortionists, are not included in this category. Within this group, 96% were male and 92% were White or Hispanic. Slightly over 50% were married. Nearly 60% were unemployed at the time of

the hijacking. Only 11 hijackers (10.3%) had psychiatric diagnoses. The Cuban hijackers had the highest success rate of any group of hijackers, 80.3%, and involved multiple hijackers more often than other groups.

This group can be best understood by examining the motivations for their hijackings. The majority of persons in this group initially came to the United States in the years following Castro's takeover. Most came here to escape Communist oppression, to rejoin family members who had come here earlier, or to seek improved financial opportunities. In spite of large and supportive Cuban communities in many American cities, the immigrants faced a number of hardships. Language and cultural differences, isolation from family and friends who remained in Cuba, and inability to find employment all led to dissatisfaction with life in America. Out of this dissatisfaction, a desire to return home arose in many Cubans. Due to a variety of factors, including the U.S. embargo imposed during the Kennedy administration, aircraft hijacking became a convenient means of returning home.

Cuban hijackings were further facilitated by the fact that through the mid-1970s, the Castro government welcomed such hijackers. Their return home was used for political purposes as proof that the Cuban society was preferable to life in America. It was only in the late 1970s, as a result of intense international pressure, that the Cuban government shifted its stance and viewed hijackers as criminals.

Problems Encountered in Categorizing Hijackers

One of the most difficult problems encountered in categorizing hijackings and hijackers was the degree of overlap that existed among the groups. Areas such as demands and destination crossed category lines. For example, demands for money were made by persons in the extortion, mentally ill, and terrorist groups. Likewise, Cuba as a destination was found among these same three groups. As indicated earlier, the categories were determined by examining all variables in each case and deciding upon the primary motivation for the hijacking.

The problem of overlap was particularly true with respect to mental illness. While the mentally ill constituted an entire category unto themselves, some evidence of mental illness was present across all groups. In the study, it was often difficult to determine if mental illness was the primary cause of the hijacking, a contributing factor, or an unrelated finding. In order to clarify this issue, the researchers examined not only formal diagnoses but also psychiatric history and indicators of mental illness observed or reported during each incident, including the presence of psychosis (see Table 10), delusions (see Table 10), suicidal ideation (see Table 11), and alcohol or drug use (see Table 12).

Mental illness clearly played an important role in all hijackings, as indicated by the fact that 209 hijackers had formal psychiatric diagnoses.

Personality disorders comprised the largest diagnostic group across all categories, with 63 hijackers (30.14%) meeting DSM-IV criteria. Schizophrenia constituted the next largest group, with 51 hijackers (24.4%). Substance use disorders (17.22%), affective disorders (12.44%), and adjustment disorders (8.61%) were the next most frequent diagnoses (see Table 13).

Slightly more than 25% of hijackers had histories of psychiatric treatment (see Table 14). This finding was complicated, however, by the fact that no information was available about prior treatment in 38% of the cases. It is likely, therefore, that previous treatment occurred more often than the findings suggested.

The same ambiguity occurred when indicators of mental illness during the hijacking itself were examined. Seventy-nine individuals (17.87%) displayed behavior that was clearly suggestive of a psychiatric disorder (see Table 15). Over 70% (313 hijackers) had no indications of mental illness, while insufficient information about mental illness was present for 50 hijackers (11.13%) (see Table 15). Suicidal ideation or

TABLE 10
PSYCHOSIS AT TIME OF HIJACKING (1961-1989)

Psychosis	Number	Percentage
Yes	54	12.22%
No	314	71.04%
Unknown	4	16.74%
Total	442	100.00%

Nature of Delusions at Time of Hijacking (1961-1989)

Paranoid	20	37.04%
Grandiose	19	35.19%
Mixed	6	11.11%
Religious	4	7.41%
Somatic	1	1.85%
Unknown	4	7.41%
Total	54	100.00%

TABLE 11
SUICIDAL HIJACKERS (1961-1989)

History of Prior Suicide Attempts	Number	Percentage
Yes	54	12.22%
No	171	38.69%
Unknown	237	49.10%
Total	442	100.00%
Indications of Suicidal Intent During Hijacking	**Number**	**Percentage**
Yes	62	14.03%
No	331	74.89%
Unknown	49	11.09%
Total	442	100.00%

TABLE 12
HIJACKER DRUG AND ALCOHOL USE (1961-1989)

Past History of Alcohol Abuse	Number	Percentage
Yes	71	16.06%
No	128	28.96%
Unknown	243	54.98%
Total	442	100.00%
Past History of Drug Abuse	**Number**	**Percentage**
Yes	61	13.80%
No	139	31.45%
Unknown	242	54.74%
Total	442	100.00%
Alcohol Used During Hijacking	**Number**	**Percentage**
Yes	79	17.87%
No	247	55.88%
Unknown	116	26.24%
Total	442	100.00%
Drugs Used During Hijacking	**Number**	**Percentage**
Yes	33	7.47%
No	277	62.67%
Unknown	132	29.86%
Total	442	100.00%

TABLE 13
PSYCHIATRIC DIAGNOSES (1961-1989)

Diagnostic Group	Number	Percentage
Personality Disorders	63	30.14%
Schizophrenia	51	24.40%
Substance Use Disorders	36	17.22%
Affective Disorders	26	12.44%
Adjustment Disorders	18	8.61%
Other Psychotic Disorders	8	3.83%
Anxiety Disorders	3	1.44%
Organic Mental Disorders	2	0.96%
Attention Deficit Disorder	1	0.48%
Dyslexia	1	0.48%
Total # of Hijackers	209	100.00%

TABLE 14
HISTORY OF PSYCHIATRIC TREATMENT (1961-1989)

Psychiatric Treatment	Number	Percentage
Yes	114	25.79%
No	156	35.29%
Unknown	172	38.91%
Total # of Hijackers	442	100.00%

TABLE 15
INDICATIONS OF MENTAL ILLNESS DURING THE HIJACKING (1961-1989)

Indicators Present	Number	Percentage
Yes	79	17.87%
No	313	70.81%
No Information	50	11.31%
Total	442	100.00%

intent during the incident was found in only 62 persons (14%) (see Table 11).

Several major difficulties were encountered when trying to examine the indications of mental illness during a hijacking. First, this information came largely from statements given by passengers and flight crew. For the most part, these witnesses were not trained in the recognition of psychiatric disorders and, therefore, were likely to miss all but the most obvious manifestations. Law enforcement officers, who may be better trained at recognition of mental illness, often viewed the hijackers from a great distance and, thus, may have missed critical signs. The hijackers themselves tended to be poor historians when interviewed after the fact about their mental state during the incident.

A second difficulty with these observations concerned the stress level inherent in hijacking incidents. Behaviors that might readily be seen as bizarre or erratic were often not noticed because of the high level of anxiety associated with the incident. Hostages have often described a high level of chaos during these incidents which obviously interferes with their ability to observe behavior. Complicating the situation even more was the fact that during some hijackings, passengers and even some members of the crew were unaware that a hijacking was in progress. All of this implies that signs of mental illness were probably underreported in these incidents.

Criminal activity is frequently influenced by alcohol and drug use. Studies have suggested that as much as 80% of violent crimes occur in connection with substance abuse (FBI, 1993). It is logical to assume, therefore, that aircraft hijacking might also be associated with high rates of alcohol abuse, drug abuse, or both. In fact, alcohol use during the incident was reported in only 79 hijackers (17.87%), while drug use was even less common (7.47%). Clear histories of alcohol and drug abuse were found in 16% and 13.8% of hijackers, respectively. Once again, substance abuse was probably underreported due to difficulties in observation, failure of witnesses to recognize signs of intoxication, and the reluctance of hijackers to disclose information.

What was clear from the data, however, was the fact that mental illness was often found in aircraft hijackers across all categories. This finding has significant implication for profiling and screening, and for the management and negotiation of hijackings by law enforcement agencies. The presence of a psychiatric disorder adds to the complexity and unpredictability of a hijacking, and increases the risk of a tragic outcome. The

potential benefit of utilizing well-trained psychiatric and psychological consultants is underscored.

An Analysis Of Hijacker Demands

Demands are of critical importance in any hostage situation; without them, there is no common ground around which to negotiate a settlement. A stated demand gives police negotiators a starting point from which to begin efforts to gain the release of the hostages.

It was possible to determine whether or not demands were made in 295 of the 306 American hijackings; information about demands was unavailable for 11 incidents. Clearly stated demands were made in 283 incidents (95.93%). Only 12 incidents occurred in which no demands of any kind were made (4.07%). In examining the types of demands made, five general categories were identified. During many hijackings, multiple demands were made, which varied in priority over time. For the aircraft hijacking study, however, the researchers identified the primary demand that was stated most often during the incident and appeared to be most directly related to the motivation for the hijacking.

Not surprisingly, the most frequent demand was for transportation to some specified location. This demand occurred in 204 incidents (66.67%). Often, the location had direct relevance to the purpose of the hijacking; Cuban immigrants, for example, hijacking a plane and demanding to go to Havana. Monetary gain was a distant second in terms of stated goals or demands. Hijacker demands are listed in Table 16.

Weapons Used In Aircraft Hijacking

A wide variety of weapons has been used in aircraft hijacking, ranging from handguns, rifles, bombs, and other common weapons, to

TABLE 16
HIJACKER DEMANDS (1961-1989)

Demand Type	Number	Percentage
Transportation	204	66.67%
Money	38	12.42%
Political	31	10.13%
Prisoner Escape/Release	22	7.19%
Personal	11	3.59%
Total	306	100.00%

exotic homemade weapons and devices. In addition, many hijackers possessed fake or inoperable weapons which nevertheless created enough fear in the flight crew to enable the hijacker to gain at least temporary control of the aircraft. Finally, some hijackers claimed to have weapons, but their existence was never verified during the incident. Table 17 summarizes this data.

For the purposes of this study, weapons were grouped into one of three categories. Real weapons were defined as any instrument that was clearly seen by witnesses and had the capacity to inflict injury or death. Examples of this category include guns, knives, and bombs. Fake weapons were any items that the hijacker had in his possession that appeared to be a weapon, but in reality proved to be harmless. Toy guns and starter pistols, for example, were used in several incidents. Another example of this category was a

TABLE 17
WEAPONS USED IN AIRCRAFT HIJACKING (1961-1989)

Weapon Type	Real	Fake	Alleged
Handguns	179	6	24
Knives	58	1	3
Bombs	41	32	68
Incendiary Devices	22	10	2
Rifles/Shotguns	20	0	0
Assault Weapons	11	0	0
Others	47	0	0

Real Weapons Used in Successful Hijackings

Handguns	122
Knives	30
Bombs	30

Real Weapons Used in Unsuccessful Hijackings

Handguns	57
Knives	28
Bombs	11

box with wires protruding which the hijacker said was a bomb. Alleged weapons consisted of those that the hijacker claimed to have in his or her possession, but were never proven to exist. It should be pointed out that in the case of aircraft hijackings, even fake and alleged weapons carried enough risk for the safety of passengers and crew that they were taken seriously by all concerned.

In the study, the most commonly used real weapons were handguns (179), knives (58), bombs (41), incendiary devices (22), rifles and shotguns (20), and assault weapons (11). The most commonly found fake weapons were bombs (32), incendiary devices (10), and handguns (6). Alleged weapons most often consisted of bombs (68) and handguns (24).

The presence of a real weapon greatly increased the chances of success in aircraft hijacking, as would be expected. At the same time, however, a handgun, bomb, or knife was no guarantee of success. For example, real handguns were used in 57 unsuccessful hijacking attempts. Likewise, real bombs were used in 11 unsuccessful attempts and real knives in 28. Factors that seemed to exert more influence on success than weapons status included the presence of mental illness. Overall, mentally ill hijackers tended to have less success than other groups regardless of the weapons used. Disorganization at a cognitive, affective, or behavioral level may be the single most important factor for decreasing the chances of a successful hijacking.

Handguns as the most frequent weapon used can be explained by examining four factors. First, handguns are easily available to the public. Second, handguns obviously possess a greater lethal threat than do weapons such as knives. Third, even the threat of a handgun preserves physical distance between a hijacker and others, thus decreasing the chances of him or her being physically overpowered by the hostages. Finally, handguns are easily concealed and may be smuggled aboard the aircraft more readily than larger weapons. This was particularly true in hijackings that occurred prior to 1972 to 1973, when metal detectors went into service at all U.S. airports. Of the handguns used, the .38 caliber revolver was the most frequently encountered.

It is a commonly held belief that assault weapons play a large role in violent crime. This assumption persists in spite of statistics which indicate that they are used in a relatively small number of criminal acts. Their role in aircraft hijacking was also limited. Only 31 incidents involved the use of these weapons. Clearly, their size made them more difficult to get aboard an airplane, and the cost of assault weapons, in comparison to handguns, may also have decreased the popularity of their use. In the research sample, assault weapons were used primarily by terrorist groups which stormed the aircraft while it was still on the ground.

The Impact of Metal Detectors and Weapons Screening

The installation of metal detectors in all U.S. airports in 1972 and 1973 had a dramatic effect on aircraft hijacking in a number of ways. First, hijackings decreased in frequency. Although the phenomenon remained relatively common until the mid-1980s, it did not approach the peak numbers seen from 1969 through 1972. The success rate for hijacking also decreased in the post-metal detector years. Although it was anticipated at the time that metal detectors would ultimately prevent the hijacking of aircraft, this unfortunately has not been the case. In response to the screening for metallic weapons, hijackers began to utilize bombs and incendiary devices more frequently. These weapons could be constructed of materials not identified by metal detectors, and could easily be contained in common items, such as radios and tape players. The use of fake and alleged weapons also increased in frequency after 1972.

Implications for Development of Security Strategies

It has often been said that criminals remain one step ahead of law enforcement officers when it comes to ingenuity in committing crimes. This is certainly the case with aircraft hijackers. Although it was not a hijacking, the case of Pan Am Flight 103, which was bombed over Lockerbie, Scotland, illustrates how lethal weaponry can be smuggled aboard aircraft in spite of security measures. Furthermore, no method of airline security is foolproof (Moore, 1976). The database contained incidents of hijacking in which handguns were taken on board aircraft even after metal detectors came into service. The recent introduction of semi-automatic pistols manufactured from plastic and other composite materials once again increases the risk of firearms being secreted aboard aircraft. As weapons technology advances, the risk of violence on aircraft likewise grows. Because the risk of loss of life is so great in these incidents, any reference to a weapon must be taken seriously no matter how thorough the security measures are. Thus, the problem of weapons screening will remain a major concern for airlines and governments well into the 21st century.

Aircraft Hijacking: The Threat To Life And Property

As mentioned earlier, the most frequently hijacked aircraft has been the Boeing 727. As these planes cost millions of dollars, the financial impact of this form of criminal activity can easily be appreciated. Aircraft hijacking also has a significant impact on the victims (Simon & Blum, 1987). Both physical and psychological sequelae to passengers and crew result from these incidents. The psychological effects of being held hostage are myriad and varied. Fear, anxiety, and depression are common reactions to being held hostage. As many hostages are blindfolded or kept in isolation, sensory deprivation plays an important role, especially if the hostage situation extends over a period of time. Identification with the hostage-takers, such as the Stockholm Syndrome, may also be seen. Finally, psychological effects, such as post-traumatic stress disorder, may be encountered long after the hostage situation is resolved.

Case Illustrations: Hijackings Resulting In Loss of Life

By their very nature, aircraft hijackings carry the potential for a tragic outcome. Although most hijackings have been resolved successfully through negotiation, several dramatic examples demonstrate the great risk for loss of life.

Case Illustration: *One such incident was the hijacking of TWA Flight 847 on June 14, 1985. The plane, a Boeing 727, left Athens at 10:00 a.m. local time bound for Rome. One hundred fifty-three passengers and crew were on board, 135 of whom were American. Shortly after take-off, two Arab hijackers, Mohammed Ali Hamadi and Hasan 'Izz-al-Din, acting under instructions from the Hezbollah, took over the plane and demanded to go to Algeria. During the incident, the hijackers used the names "Castro" (Hamadi) and "Said" ('Izz-al-Din).*

The plane instead went to Beirut because of fuel constraints. During refueling in Beirut, 19 passengers (women and children) were released. The plane then took off for Algiers, where 21 additional passengers were released. Following the stopover in Algeria, the plane once again departed for Beirut.

When the plane landed in Beirut, the hijackers demanded that other Arab terrorists be allowed to board the plane. When these requests were initially denied, Hamadi shot and killed American serviceman Robert Stethem. Following that, the other terrorists were permitted to board.

The leader of the new group of terrorists was

Imad Mugniyah, a prominent member of the Hezbollah. Seven passengers were then taken off the plane and sent to a terrorist stronghold in Beirut. The plane then departed again for Algiers and subsequently returned to Beirut. Because of the movement back and forth between Algeria and Lebanon, a planned assault on the plane by the U.S. Delta Force was not possible.

Once back in Beirut, Nabih Berri, leader of the Shiite Amal militia in Lebanon, agreed to represent the hijackers in negotiations. Berri ordered that the remaining passengers be taken off the plane and housed in a building in Beirut. The hostages were then taken by bus to Damascus, where they were freed on June 30, following intervention by Syrian President Assad.

On January 1, 1986, Hamadi was apprehended by West German authorities for attempting to smuggle liquid explosives at Frankfurt airport. He was convicted and sentenced to life in prison by a West German court.

Case Illustration: Another example of the inherent risk in these situations was Pan Am Flight 73, which was hijacked to Karachi, Pakistan, on September 6, 1986. This hijacking was carried out by the Abu Nidal terrorist group with assistance from the Libyan government. Once on the ground in Karachi, negotiations with the hijackers were undertaken.

During the course of the negotiation, a power failure occurred on the plane, resulting in the loss of all lights and communications. The hijackers reacted to what they perceived as an assault on the aircraft, and opened fire. Pakistani troops surrounding the aircraft then stormed the plane, killing 18 passengers and crew, as well as three hijackers.

Case Illustration: Finally, TWA Flight 840, en route from Rome to Athens, was hijacked and bombed on April 2, 1986, by a group calling itself the Arab Revolutionary Cells, led by Mohammed

Abdel Labib ("Colonel Hawari"). Hawari's bomb-makers were trained by Abu Ibrahim, a well-known Palestinian terrorist.

A one-pound charge of plastic explosives was placed under a seat cushion and triggered by a change in cabin pressure as the plane descended, at an altitude of approximately 15,000 feet. The explosion tore a hole in the plane's fuselage through which four passengers (all Americans) were sucked out. The bomb was apparently carried on board by a Lebanese woman during an earlier leg of the flight. The terrorist group claiming responsibility said that the bombing was in retaliation for American military maneuvers in the Gulf of Sidra, during which several Libyan missile sites and patrol boats were destroyed. This bombing was one of the events that led to the April 15, 1986 American bombing raid on Libya.

Why Do Aircraft Hijackings "Go Bad?"

One of the most striking aspects of aircraft hijackings is the fact that most are resolved without injury or loss of life. According to data collected by the FBI (1988), over 95% of incidents are resolved peacefully when negotiations with the hijackers occur. In spite of this observation, the risk still exists for loss of life on a large scale. A number of factors can be identified that are associated with a tragic outcome for hijackings.

These incidents are obviously complex events influenced by many variables. Unpredictable or chance occurrences often lead to the deterioration of a hijacking. The power failure during the Karachi incident described above illustrates this point. Failure of communication equipment during negotiations will also increase the chances of fatalities. Other types of mechanical failures have also been observed in those hijackings where loss of life has been sustained. The common theme in these examples is that variables over which no one has control may adversely affect the outcome.

An even more serious issue concerns the unpredictable nature of human behavior. In the study of aircraft hijackers, researchers found that the chances of injury or death to someone involved was the highest in those incidents that were accompanied by alcohol or drug use. This results from the disinhibiting effects these substances have on behavior, and their tendency to impair judgment. The effects of stress on behavior also exert an influence. Everyone involved in a hijacking experiences tremendous stress. As stress levels increase, whether from physical or psychological sources, behavior becomes more unstable. Prolonged hijackings, for example, place stress on the hijackers, flight crew, and law enforcement officers through fatigue and sleep deprivation. Incidents of long duration involving single hijackers carry greater risk than those with multiple hijackers because the single hijacker literally has no backup; he or she must attend to many issues simultaneously, often in a sleep deprived state. As stress escalates, the potential for impulsive behavior increases.

Two distinct time periods are associated with increased stress on the hijacker. The first occurs when the hijacker takes control of the aircraft. This period is associated with the greatest risk for injury or death. Many of the hijackers interviewed said that their anxiety level was highest at that time. The display of a weapon is often necessary in order to successfully gain control of the aircraft. That weapon may be discharged either intentionally or accidentally as a result of fear, anger, or the chaos of the moment. The second dangerous time is immediately prior to landing or surrender. Once again, affect levels are higher due to concerns about escape, apprehension, or unexpected developments. The hijacker may act violently out of desperation or fear.

Hostages also experience stress during these incidents. Feelings of anger, helplessness, or vulnerability ensue frequently. When this stress results in impulsive behavior, the risk for injury is increased greatly. One example of this is when the hostages attempt to overpower and subdue the hijackers. While a few cases exist in which the hostages were successful in regaining control of the aircraft, a more frequent outcome is gunfire in which passengers or crew members are wounded. Structural damage to the aircraft is another obvious risk of such attempts. The law enforcement axiom that hostages should not attempt to resist is clearly borne out by the data. Passengers are safer when they do exactly as the hijacker says and make no attempt to resist.

The lack of adequate intelligence about the situation places law enforcement officials in difficult situations during hijackings. The formulation of effective negotiation strategies and the planning of tactical interventions are dependent upon accurate information about the number of hijackers, their weapons, their demands and motivations, and conditions aboard the aircraft. When decisions are made based on faulty or inadequate intelligence, the risk of injury or death increases. The case of Oranetta Mays, cited earlier, illustrates this point. A decision was made to assault the aircraft based on a misinterpretation of the subject's statements. This resulted in a shoot-out between police and the hijacker, with two people being wounded.

In addition, three hijacking categories are associated with increased risk for loss of life: mentally ill incidents, prison escapes, and terrorist hijackings. Incidents involving mentally ill hijackers are marked by impulsivity, unpredictable behavior, and the risk that the hijacker may seriously misinterpret events taking place. The presence of psychosis or suicidal ideation further increases the threat because the hijacker may have poor contact with reality or may be prepared to die.

Hijackings committed by prison escapees are more dangerous because the subjects usually have histories of violence. The convicts often experience subjective feelings of desperation and may perceive that they "have nothing to lose." Thus, the threshold at which violence occurs is significantly lowered. Prison guards and law enforcement officers also appear to be more willing to assault an aircraft held by prisoners. This is due in part to their judgment that negotiations are less likely to be successful with this group.

Finally, terrorist hijackings are associated with several unique factors that increase the risk of injury or death. In many such incidents, violence is the primary goal of the hijackers. Many terrorist groups feel that the killing of hostages is the only way to effectively make their statement (Kupperman & Kamen, 1989). There also exists among members of these groups a commitment to die for their cause. If expectations for personal survival are low, then the value of other human life diminishes greatly. This is particularly true for many Islamic terrorist groups in which "death for the cause" is associated with martyrdom. The group "Islamic Jihad," responsible for the 1983 bombing of the Marine barracks in Beirut, exemplifies this philosophy (Martin & Walcott, 1989).

Characteristics of Incidents With Successful Outcomes

The term "successful outcome" has two distinct meanings, depending upon the perspective used to view an aircraft hijacking. From the hijacker's point of view, a successful hijacking is one in which the aircraft is seized, demands are met, and escape is carried out. From a law enforcement perspective, however, successful resolution is defined by the safe release of all hostages, apprehension of the hijackers, and the absence of injury to law enforcement personnel. In each of these instances, distinct characteristics of the hijacking can be defined.

A great many factors are implicated in the success of an aircraft hijacking attempt. Incidents involving multiple, heavily armed hijackers tend to be more successful from the hijacker's point of

view. Other factors associated with success include a longer duration of the incident. As the duration of the incident increases, hijackers often develop an attachment to the hostages. The formation of a personal bond decreases the likelihood that hostages will be harmed. A destination receptive to the hijackers also increases the chances of success. Examples include those flights to Cuba in the late 1960s and early 1970s, as well as terrorist hijackings to Libya and other states supportive of terrorism. Finally, the absence of mental illness greatly increases the chances for success.

From a law enforcement viewpoint, single hijackers who are free of mental illness and in possession of fake or alleged weapons comprise the "safest" type of incidents in terms of potential for loss of life. Longer incidents also are safer in that they allow adequate time for authorities to establish contact with the hijackers as well as to develop effective intervention strategies. The presence of extortion demands also increases the chances for a peaceful resolution, because the hijacker knows that harming the hostages will lessen his chances of receiving the money he demands. Furthermore, because escape is crucial to the extortion hijacker, keeping the hostages safe helps avoid an armed confrontation with authorities.

Perhaps the single most important variable, however, is the presence of negotiations. Over 95% of incidents in which negotiations occurred were resolved without injury or death. This area will now be discussed in more detail.

The Significance of Hostage Negotiation Strategies

In response to the phenomenon of hostage-taking, strategies for hostage negotiation were developed. The main impetus for developing negotiation protocols was the terrorist action against Israeli athletes during the 1972 Munich

Olympics (Schrieber, 1972). As a result, law enforcement agencies around the world have been forced to address the problem of hostage-taking and develop strategies to establish meaningful contact with hostile, desperate, or mentally ill individuals (Vandiver, 1981). In weighing the demands of the hostage-takers versus the welfare of the hostages, there is a delicate balance between decisions that involve active and empathic listening and those which eventuate in tactical options (Fuselier, 1986). A constructive and harmonious equilibrium between these occasionally competing viewpoints may be difficult to achieve. Because of the high potential for a tragic outcome, a thorough understanding of the dynamics of hostage situations and negotiations is essential.

The basic goals of hostage negotiation may be summarized as follows: (1) to establish contact with the hostage-takers; (2) to elicit specific information about the event, including number of hostages and hostage-takers, demands, illness of or injury to the hostages, and motivations for the incident; and (3) to conduct a meaningful dialogue with the hostage-takers which will result in surrender of the subjects and safe release of the hostages (Feldmann & Johnson, 1993). This dialogue may involve a mutual "give-and-take" in which some demands are met in exchange for the safe release of the hostages (e.g., trading food for the release of hostages). It may be speculated that the establishment of the give-and-take dynamic is of paramount importance in decreasing the likelihood of violence and bringing about the resolution of a successful negotiation. On the other hand, certain demands, such as for weapons, alcohol or drugs, or a getaway car, are not met under any circumstances; granting these demands will be likely to escalate or unnecessarily prolong the situation. The overall objective of the negotiations is to obtain release of the hostages without any injuries to the hostages, law enforcement officers, or hostage-takers, and without the use of

tactical personnel (e.g., SWAT). These strategies have been described extensively in the literature (Feldmann & Johnson, 1995; Fuselier, 1981;).

Many variables complicate the management of a hostage incident. These include impulsive or irrational behavior on the part of the hostage-takers, the effects of stress and anxiety on both criminals and negotiators, unpredictable behavior on the part of the hostages, media intrusions, and communications or technical problems. The nature of the relationship between the negotiator and the hostage-taker will also exert a strong influence on the outcome. The interventions provided by the negotiator must be designed not only to obtain release of the hostages, but also to psychologically stabilize the hostage-taker as well as the situation in order to prevent rash or impulsive acts which may result from stress, fatigue, or impaired judgment.

Alcohol and drugs are frequently implicated in hostage situations. When present, they complicate the situation and significantly increase the risk of a tragic outcome. Both substances cause a general increase in the level of impulsivity and aggression in the hostage-taker. They also cause impairment in judgment, resulting in the hostage-taker being unable to realistically evaluate the nature of his or her actions and their consequences. A false sense of confidence or bravado may ensue, which influences the hostage-taker to behave in ways he or she might ordinarily resist. This further increases the risk of injury or death to the hostages, law enforcement officers, and the hostage-taker.

In many hostage incidents, depression and suicidal ideation also complicate the situation. The taking of hostages may result from feelings of hopelessness or desperation associated with depression. The suicidal hostage-taker may consciously or unconsciously hope that police will eventually kill him or her, and may even attempt to provoke police into shooting. Fortunately, law enforcement professionals have become increasingly aware of the phenomenon of "suicide by cop," and take protective measures to prevent its occurrence.

Finally, hostage situations may be complicated by the attachment that sometimes develops between hostages and their captors. This phenomenon is known as the Stockholm Syndrome, which may be defined as an emotional response on the part of persons held hostage in which they develop strong positive feelings toward the captors and simultaneous negative feelings toward the police (Strentz, 1980). This syndrome was first identified in 1973, following a bank robbery in Stockholm, Sweden, in which four female bank employees were held hostage for 131 hours by a pair of armed robbers. Over the course of this incident, the hostages came to believe that their captors were actually protecting them from the police. Two of the hostages went on to develop romantic attachments to the robbers, with one of them eventually marrying one of her captors.

This phenomenon can be understood as an unconscious reaction to stress in which the victim identifies with the hostage-taker as a way of dealing with stress. It may be considered to be a function of the defense mechanisms of identification with the aggressor and regression. One factor that appears to influence the development of the Stockholm Syndrome is time; the longer the hostages are held, the more likely this phenomenon will be observed. The behavior of the hostage-takers will also influence the development of this syndrome. Hostage-takers who are viewed as relatively benign, or even considerate, will more likely be identified with in a positive manner. The Stockholm Syndrome has been observed in a number of hostage incidents, and may interfere with negotiations because the hostages view police as the real threat and not the hostage-takers. The Stockholm Syndrome is exemplified by the following case.

Case Illustration: *The case of Zvonko Busic best illustrates the Stockholm Syndrome. On Sep-* *tember 10, 1976, a group of Croatian exiles hijacked a TWA Boeing 727 jet bound from New York to Chicago, and forced it to fly to Paris by way of Montreal and London. During the flight, the hijackers dropped leaflets expounding the group's cause of Croatian independence. The hijackers were led by Zvonko Busic, his wife Julienne, Petar Mantanic, Marc Vlassic, and Frane Pesut. The hijackers claimed to possess a bomb, which they threatened to detonate if their demands were not met. In addition, the hijackers stated that they had planted bombs in Chicago and New York which would be detonated if the hijacking was unsuccessful. In reality, a bomb had been planted by one of the group's sympathizers in New York's Grand Central Terminal. This bomb was uncovered by New York police, but exploded as it was being defused, killing a police officer. Subsequently, all other weapons, including that on the plane, were found to be alleged only.*

During this incident, Busic and his accomplices conversed freely with the passengers and crew. They explained the plight of their homeland and assured the hostages that they would not be harmed. Food and alcoholic beverages were also distributed to everyone on board the aircraft. What resulted was a party-like atmosphere in which the terrorists posed for photographs with the hostages.

When the plane finally arrived in Paris and the hijackers agreed to surrender, many passengers and crew members formed a human shield around the hijackers to protect them from the police snipers they feared would shoot Busic and his comrades.

In spite of the dangers associated with hostage situations, negotiations have been remarkably successful in bringing them to a peaceful and successful resolution. This has not only been the case with aircraft hijackings, but also with hostage situations arising out of foiled criminal attempts, domestic disturbances, and suicide attempts.

What to Do In a Hostage Situation

As mentioned earlier, hostages tend to be safest when they do exactly as the hostage-taker orders. In addition to this basic rule, adherence to the following guidelines will increase the chances of surviving a hostage incident (Feldmann & Johnson, 1993):

1. It is essential for a hostage to remain calm during the incident. Although this is admittedly difficult in a highly stressful situation, hostages should make a conscious attempt to remember this important point. A highly emotional display on the part of hostages may only serve to create increased anxiety in the hostage-taker, often leading to an escalation of impulsive, irrational or aggressive behavior. A relatively calm stance, on the other hand, may serve to defuse some of the tension in the situation and allow the hostage-taker to focus on the negotiation process.

2. A related point is not to do anything that would threaten or provoke the hostage-taker. Arguing with the hostage-taker, for example, may only increase negative feelings, increasing the chances of aggressive action against the hostages. As long as the hostage-taker feels relatively safe with his or her captives, chances that they will be harmed decrease. Hostage negotiation specialists at the FBI Academy in Quantico, Virginia, urge that hostages should attempt to "blend into their surroundings" and attract as little attention to themselves as possible (FBI, 1988). This is particularly important in situations where the hostage-takers appear extremely irritable and agitated. As indicated earlier in the chapter, hostages were more likely to be injured during hijackings when they tried to provoke or overpower the hijackers.

3. Hostages are advised to attempt to do whatever the hostage-taker tells them. Refusal or attempts to resist will increase the hostages' risk of harm. It will also introduce doubt into the hostage-taker's mind about whether or not the hostages can be trusted. Any hostage-taker will be more likely to harm hostages he or she views as threatening or uncooperative than those who comply with the hostage-taker's wishes. Furthermore, attempts to resist will also decrease the hostages usefulness to the hostage-taker. It is important to remember that hostages are held because they are perceived as being valuable and because they provide a measure of protection against the police.

4. Another useful tactic is for hostages to try to personalize the situation as much as possible. For example, hostages should give their first names and attempt to talk with their captors. Hostages should share their feelings with the hostage-taker, particularly if those feelings are ones of fear or anxiety. The effect of this is to create a personal relationship between the hostages and the hostage-taker. When the hostage-taker views the hostages as unique individuals, as opposed to nameless/faceless objects, he or she will be much less inclined to do anything that will cause harm.

These basic guidelines will increase the chances of a hostage's release unharmed from any captor. The principles outlined here have been used by law enforcement officers, airline personnel, and others who are at high risk for being taken hostage.

Psychological Profile Of The Aircraft Hijacker

Research into the personality types of aircraft hijackers has been very limited in scope. Efforts have focused mainly on pre-flight identification in order to avoid airline hijacking. Commonly employed techniques for pre-flight passenger screening have focused on demographics and physical description more than personality type. Through the 1960s and 1970s, the profile of most aircraft hijackers consisted of the following: a White male, traveling alone, who purchased his ticket with cash on the day of the hijacking. This person rarely checked any luggage, appeared to be anxious and tense, and preferred to be left alone. The subject often had a small carry-on bag which usually contained a weapon.

Several problems resulted from this profile. The first was the fact that it generated a very large number of false positives. Business travelers making day trips, for example, often buy their tickets at the airport, pay in cash, and have no luggage. Also, as air travel improved and became more accessible, an increasing number of travelers utilized airlines for short, unplanned trips. The increased volume of air travelers also overwhelmed the ability of airline personnel to adequately screen passengers at even the most cursory level. Due to the high false positive rate of the profile, airlines were understandably reluctant to deny seating to passengers simply because they matched the profile.

Another problem with the profile was the assumption that all hijackers were the same. The profile failed to take any subtypes into account. As the data showed, there is great variability among hijackers. By the mid-1970s, however, only the terrorist hijacker had received a more thorough examination. Once again, efforts focused more on developing demographic profiles of the typical terrorist, with an examination of psychopathology left largely unexplored. Studies of terrorists generally revealed them to be young, single, adult males, usually from middle or upper class families, often with at least some college education (Comay, 1976). Many terrorist groups, however, began recruiting women with increasing frequency; examples included Germany's Baader-Meinhoff Gang and the California-based Symbionese Liberation Army. The demographics for women terrorists appeared to be quite similar to those found in their male counterparts (Meyer & Parke, 1991).

Examination of specific terrorist groups, however, may reveal that the above generalizations are incorrect (Johnson & Feldmann, 1992). The composition of many Middle Eastern terrorist

organizations, for example, is clearly different from that cited above. The increasing terrorist activity of many American street gangs will also change the demographic profile. An example of this can be seen in the 1986 arrests of members of the El Rukn gang which had planned to blow up a terminal at O'Hare International Airport in Chicago, an act designed to elicit financial support from the Libyan government. Many right-wing groups in the United States also have clearly different socioeconomic backgrounds. These groups tend to attract members from rural areas who have less formal education and come from blue collar or poverty level settings.

Where psychological profiles do exist, the terrorist is most often viewed as having some degree of paranoia (Soskis, 1983). Other reports have focused on vaguely defined "psychological instability" as influencing the terrorist to seek publicity and media coverage (FBI, 1988). These explanations, however, fail to take into account, or even acknowledge, the stated political goals of terrorists. The constellation of paranoid, narcissistic, antisocial, and borderline personality traits appears readily identifiable in most members of terrorist groups, and also assists in the understanding of an individual's commitment to the group (Johnson & Feldmann, 1992). Self-esteem deficits and issues or conflicts related to personal identity are critical ingredients for membership in the terrorist organization. Finally, terrorist activity has also been described as the outcome of repressed frustrations or the result of neurological dysfunction (Hubbard, 1971, 1986). These studies, however, suffer from being highly speculative and based largely on anecdotal experience.

The Aircraft Hijacking Research Project demonstrated that a single profile of aircraft hijackers is not only inadequate but also incorrect in most instances. Profiles are useful only when they apply to a relatively homogeneous group, such as sexual serial murderers (Ressler, Burgess, & Douglas, 1988). In contrast, aircraft hijackers are a heterogeneous group. Clear characteristic clusters or profiling guidelines emerge only when hijacker motivation is taken into account. In the aircraft hijacking study, motivation was most closely associated with an analysis of demands and the presence of psychiatric disorders.

As discussed earlier, pre-flight passenger screening has obvious limitations in terms of accuracy and practicality. Nevertheless, the training of airline personnel to screen for suspicious or bizarre behavior will assist in preventing some hijackings. More importantly, the categories developed in this study can be used to assist authorities in the management of a hijacking once it occurs. This is particularly true with respect to the development of specific negotiation strategies for each category of hijacker.

Extortionists, for example, have clearly different goals for seizing an aircraft than political terrorists. Based on the data, it can be assumed from the outset that the extortion hijacker is acting alone and has no intention of blowing up the aircraft, and thus killing himself or herself if the extortion demands are not met. This same assumption would be very dangerous to make, however, in terrorist incidents where there are likely to be multiple hijackers on board who are heavily armed and have a strong commitment to die for their cause.

The differences in these profiles lead to quite different negotiation strategies. In dealing with the extortionist, the negotiator must address the hijacker's concerns about payment and escape. With terrorists, on the other hand, the negotiator may be forced to assist the hijackers in finding alternative, non-lethal means of making their political statement known. The means to a negotiated resolution will be vastly different in the latter situation.

Thus, the categories developed in the study will help make negotiation with hijackers more effective. This will serve to decrease the threat to life and property. The information gained about hijacker types can also be applied to the planning of tactical interventions. As a result, law enforcement officers will be better prepared to deal with these unique criminal acts.

Summary: Implications For Future Research

Aircraft hijackings are dramatic events which guarantee widespread media coverage. The publicity, in turn, places great public pressure on law enforcement agencies and governments to resolve the situation peacefully. When loss of life occurs, second-guessing of the handling of the situation, followed by civil litigation, are likely to occur. The impact of instantaneous, global coverage of these events is illustrated by the live broadcast of the French assault on Air France Flight 8969 in Marseille on December 26, 1994. The aircraft had been seized by Algerian terrorists in Algiers and subsequently flown to France. The ultimate goal of the hijackers was to fly to Paris, where they planned to blow up the aircraft. During the raid, four hijackers were killed, six police officers were wounded, and 13 passengers were injured during the evacuation of the plane.

Public pressure, airline industry concerns, and the need of governments to assure the safety of their citizens all make an understanding of hijacking incidents paramount. In spite of the attention focused on the phenomenon of aircraft hijacking, much remains to be learned. Many difficulties also complicate the study of these incidents.

The definition of aircraft hijacking is but one example of the problems encountered. Accurate reporting depends upon a consistent definition of the events. Unfortunately, different agencies categorize hijackings in various ways. The U.S. Department of Transportation (1992), for example, has a narrow definition, with the result that they list fewer incidents per year than the Aircraft Hijacking Research Project revealed. Likewise, the FAA and FBI define these events differently; the present study utilized the FBI definition which also yielded more incidents than the FAA had reported. Sadly, the result is that there is no clear consensus of what constitutes a hijacking or how many have occurred.

Jurisdictional questions also complicate management of the incidents once they occur. While the FBI investigates all hijackings involving American air carriers, it does not manage or negotiate each incident. Various local, state, and federal agencies have all been involved in the direct management of U.S. hijackings. Each jurisdiction has different levels of training and different internal guidelines for crisis management. Thus, some police agencies utilize hostage negotiation strategies extensively, while others refuse to negotiate with hijackers and utilize tactical interventions only. This is quite different from most international incidents, which are handled by designated national special response units whose training and management philosophy are relatively standardized across all incidents.

Given the history of air piracy over the last 30 years and the relative success that hijackers and terrorists have had, it is likely that this form of criminal activity will remain viable. The challenge for law enforcement agencies and forensic behavioral scientists alike is to further refine their understanding of the type of person who seizes an aircraft, and better develop their response and management policies when incidents occur.

ACKNOWLEDGMENT: The authors wish to recognize the assistance of Roger A. Bell, Ed.D., principal investigator of the Aircraft Hijacking Research Project, and special agents William Cheek, Charles Lewis, and Frederick J. Lanceley of the Federal Bureau of Investigation, all of whom were involved in the research activity.

References

American Psychiatric Association. (1968). *Diagnostic and statistical manual of mental disorders* (2nd ed.). Washington, DC: Author.

American Psychiatric Association. (1994). *Diagnostic and statistical manual of mental disorders* (4th ed.). Washington, DC: Author.

Arey, J.A. (1972). *The sky pirates*. New York: Schribner's.

Bell, R.A., Lanceley, F.J., Feldmann, T.B., Johnson, P.W., Cheek, W., Lewis, C., & Worley, T. (1989). Improving hostage negotiation strategies: An empirical study of aircraft hijackers. *American Journal of Preventive Psychiatry and Neurology, 2*, 1-5.

Busby, M.D. (1989). U.S. counterterrorism policy in the 1980's and priorities for the 1990's. *Terrorism, 13*, 7-13.

Comay, M. (1976). Political terrorism. *Mental Health Sociology*, 3, 249-261.

Crenshaw, W.A. (1987). Terrorism and the threat to civil aviation. *Dissertation Abstracts International, 48*, 1007.

Federal Bureau of Investigation Special Operations and Research Unit. (1981). A terrorist organizational profile: A psychological role model. In Y. Alexander & J. Gleason (Eds.), *Behavioral and quantitative perspectives on terrorism.* New York: Pergamon Press.

Federal Bureau of Investigation. (1988). Personal communication with Supervisory Special Agent Frederick J. Lanceley, Special Operations and Research Unit, FBI Academy, Quantico, VA.

Federal Bureau of Investigation. (1988). *Terrorism in the United States: 1987.* Washington, DC: U.S. Government Printing Office.

Federal Bureau of Investigation. (1993). *Uniform crime reports: 1992.* Washington, DC: U.S. Government Printing Office.

Feldmann. T.B. & Johnson, P.W. (1993). Hostage situations and the mental health professional. In P. Blumenreich & S. Lewis (Eds.), *Management of the violent patient: A clinician's guide* (pp. 111-130). New York: Brunner/Mazel.

Feldmann, T.B. & Johnson, P.W. (in press). The dynamics of hostage negotiations. *Journal of the American Academy of Psychoanalysis.*

Fuselier, G.D. (1981). A practical overview of hostage negotiations. *FBI Law Enforcement Bulletin, 50* (6), 2-11.

Gray, O.M. (1981). Hostage negotiations. *Texas Police Journal, 29* (11), 14-18.

Hubbard, D.G. (1971). *The skyjacker: His flights of fantasy.* New York: MacMillan.

Hubbard, D.G. (1986). *Winning back the sky: A tactical analysis of terrorism.* Dallas: Saybrook Publishing.

Jenkins, B., Johnson, J., & Renfeldt, D. (1977). *Numbered lives: Some statistical observations from 77 international hostage episodes.* Santa Monica, CA: The Rand Corporation.

Johnson, P.W. & Feldmann, T.B. (1992). Personality types and terrorism: Self psychology perspectives. *Forensic Reports, 5,* 293-303.

Kupperman, R. & Kamen, J. (1989). *Final warning: Averting disaster in the new age of terrorism.* New York: Doubleday.

Martin, D.C. & Walcott, J. (1989). *Best laid plans: The inside story of America's war against terrorism.* New York: Simon and Shuster.

Meyer, R.G., & Parke, A. (1991). Terrorism: Modern trends and issues. *Forensic Reports, 4,* 51-59.

Moore, K.C. (1976). *Airport, aircraft, and airline security.* Los Angeles: Security World Publishing.

Ressler, R., Burgess, A., & Douglas, J. (1988). *Sexual homicide: Patterns and motives.* Lexington, MA: Lexington Books.

Schrieber, M. (1972). *After-action report of terrorist activities: 20th Olympic games, Munich, West Germany.* Quantico, VA: FBI Academy.

Simon, R.I. & Blum, R.A. (1987). After the terrorist incident: Psychotherapeutic treatment of former hostages. *American Journal of Psychotherapy, 41,* 194-200.

Soskis, D. (1983). Behavioral scientists and law enforcement personnel: Working together on the problem of terrorism. *Behavioral Sciences and the Law, 1,* 47-58.

Stratton, J.G. (1978). The terrorist act of hostage-taking: Exploring the motivation and cause. *Journal of Police Science and Administration, 6* (1), 1-9.

Strentz, T. (1980). The Stockholm syndrome: Law enforcement policy and ego defenses of the hostage. In F. Wright, C. Bahn, & R.W. Rieber (Eds), *Forensic psychiatry and psychology.* New York: New York Academy of Sciences.

Strentz, T. (1983). The inadequate personality as hostage-taker. *Journal of Police Science and Administration, 11* (3), 363-368.

U.S. Department of Transportation (1992). *Criminal acts against civil aviation.* Washington, DC: U.S. Government Printing Office.

Vandiver, J.V. (1981). Hostage situations require preparedness. *Law and Order, 9,* 66-69.

About the Authors

Theodore B. Feldmann, MD, is an Associate Professor in the Department of Psychiatry and Behavioral Sciences at the University of Louisville School of Medicine. He has several clinical positions at local hospitals and clinics and is in private practice in psychotherapy and forensic psychiatry in Louisville, Kentucky. He has been board certified in psychiatry since 1986. He has numerous publications in clinical and forensic psychiatry.

Robert W. Johnson, PhD, is an Assistant Clinical Professor in the Department of Psychiatry and Behavioral Sciences at the University of Louisville School of Medicine. He is also in private practice in clinical-forensic psychology. His interest areas include terrorism, aircraft hijackings, hostage negotiation, and violence in the workplace. He is a Diplomate in Forensic Psychology from the American Board of Professional Psychology.

CHAPTER 16

INSANITY AND MITIGATION TO MURDER

Sandra B. McPherson

Case Illustration: It was early in the summer when R. took his gun into a studio, killed two people, and injured a third. For several days, he eluded the manhunt that was in progress, but he was finally cornered, shot, and taken into custody. News stories detailed his bizarre beliefs and his paranoid thinking. He spoke of cats who warned him of conspiracies. His discussions included government plots, grandiose plans in the stock market, and supernatural events. He had a history of having become violent with his brother and also had some minor drug-related involvements. Signs of maladjustment and psychotic thinking had been evident for many years. In spite of good intelligence, he never completed high school.

After he was shot by the police, R. was paralyzed and found himself facing death penalty charges. He maintained that he remembered nothing of the events surrounding the homicides. It was his conclusion, based on his understanding of himself, that he could not have done it. Among his options for a defense was a plea of Not Guilty by Reason of Insanity (NGRI). The NGRI defense required that he admit to the act and plead that mental illness impaired his ability to know the nature of what he was doing — both of which he was not willing to do. A second alternative would have been a trial, and, upon a finding of guilt, a mitigation hearing. However, given community feeling and the harm done, he was likely to

receive a death sentence in spite of obvious mental illness.

Reluctantly, R. agreed to his defense team's recommendations to accept a prosecutorial offer of a life sentence in return for a guilty plea. He was given 49 years to life by a judge who noted with some emotion that R. had destroyed three families.

Criminal law makes a fundamental assumption that people are responsible for what they do. In narrowly defined arenas, however, exceptions have long been permitted. In the case of murder and its severe penalties, extenuating circumstances may be considered. In England, the case of Daniel M'Naghten (1843) set the original standard for NGRI. It was well before M'Naghten, however, that mental condition was held to remove or reduce the capacity to make competent decisions and be held responsible for them.

In 1700 B.C., the Code of Hammurabi acknowledged that an act could not be punished if an accident was involved, as long as there was no carelessness or neglect. Further, the level of the offense (for example, in modern terms, first degree murder versus a lower homicide) could be reduced where intent was not shown. Similar recognitions of extenuating circumstances and subjective state as factors in responsibility and appropriate punishment are found in such diverse areas and times as Biblical Law, the Code of Dracos, the Roman

Code, and Christian theological expositions (Danesh-Khoshdoo, 1991; Buchanan, 1992). Eastern culture also made similar distinctions with, for example, specifics found in Gautama Buddha's directives of 500 B.C. (Kyokai, 1992).

Criminal responsibility may be partial or total. Guilt, to be a meaningful concept, requires the individual to "appreciate wrongfulness" — to understand what was done and what should have been done.

In any type of mitigation, thinking, perceiving, and emotional states may be important to legal outcomes. Thus, psychological evaluation and testimony may play a pivotal role in a defense. As many of these kinds of evaluations must develop objective information about subjective factors, the task is complex but doable, if the right methods are used and the right precautions are taken in describing results.

Although evaluations are usually undertaken for purposes of preparing testimony, roughly 90% of U.S. cases are handled by plea bargain (Simon, 1995). Psychologists rarely contribute directly to such negotiations, but it is not uncommon for their results to be used by attorneys in these meetings.

Not Guilty by Reason of Insanity

As already indicated, NGRI in some form or another has been around for a long time in the Western world. What NGRI recognizes is that a mentally ill person may commit a punishable act, but due to flawed thinking, not know what he or she is doing. Under such conditions, punishment is withheld.

Mental illness was not always viewed as eliminating criminal responsibility. The treatment of so-called heretics in the medieval period at least partly reflected the notion that mental illness was a by-product of a person's having contracted with the Devil (Mathison, 1958). In much the same way, present laws regarding voluntary intoxication hold people responsible and punishable for acts that come about as a result of an altered state. In effect, contracting with "demon rum" does not excuse behavior. (However, Meloy, 1992, noted a minor exception in California's "settled insanity" concept, where mental illness is defined to include temporary manifestation of an underlying but presumably ongoing psychosis made evident by drug or alcohol abuse.)

In regard to NGRI, as Blau and Pasewark (1994) indicated, there has been a "...periodic expansion or contraction of the aperture of non-culpability in statutes" (p. 70). These authors and others have studied not only the waxing and waning of the opening that the law created for a finding of NGRI, but also the impact of legal changes on the functioning of the legal system.

It is clear that not only the general public, but also presumably sophisticated law enforcement and mental health professionals, believed the NGRI plea to be a loophole which allows significant numbers of criminals who should be held responsible, to escape punishment (Pasewark, Seidenzahl, & Pantle, 1981; Burton & Steadman, 1978).

A number of causes have been identified on the basis of which even sophisticated persons maintain an unwarranted concern about the operation of the NGRI plea. Blau and Pasewark (1994) noted the following:

1. The increasing crime rate has resulted in more people (although not a higher ratio of defendants) being evaluated for NGRI.

2. Mental hospitals are no longer maintaining as many long-term patients and as a result, more mentally disordered persons come to the attention of the courts and are found not competent or NGRI.

3. More mental health professionals endorse a free-will posture than previously and hold people responsible at a higher level.

4. The extensive media coverage of high profile cases has fed a public perception that NGRI is a very common, rather than uncommon, phenomenon.

Interestingly, in looking at media aspects of NGRI, McCutcheon and McCutcheon (1994) evaluated the degree to which certain popular television news shows gave the impression that NGRI was a common occurrence. They found that even news stories that included some accurate statistics still presented information in ways that made NGRI acquittals appear relatively common. They cited a particular program that was ostensibly aired to address the myths of NGRI. At the end, there was some accurate commentary, but the bulk of the program was an emotional discussion of cases that were atypical of NGRI defendants.

McCutcheon and McCutcheon then conducted some experiments to determine whether persons exposed to these distortions could be re-educated. They found that simply providing a contrary media exposure did not change attitudes, but providing written material and assignments to evaluate the material did allow subjects to make changes in their thinking.

One of the more intriguing complexities about the insanity defense is the very old philosophic dilemma between free will and determinism. Law is, and always has been, based on the assumption that people make decisions and can be held responsible for what they do. Psychology, on the other hand, has developed out of a philosophic base where there have been theories and cycles of theories that take a deterministic point of view. To take an extreme position, if all behavior is determined, then no one would be responsible in the sense that the law intends. On the other hand, if people are totally responsible for their acts, then there clearly is no room for even the concept of mitigation or extenuating circumstances in the conduct of human affairs. Neither of those positions would be particularly acceptable to most thoughtful people.

The expert witness faces a dilemma. The psychologist must testify from a scientific viewpoint based on some form of determinism. At the same time, the expert's evaluation answers whether the defendant was or was not (knowingly) acting on the basis of his or her free will. Rychlak and Rychlak (1990) approached this problem by referring to current psychological literature on intentionality and cognition. They suggested that there is no longer the same philosophic conflict because the more mechanistic and automatic versions of determinism have not held up in laboratories or clinics and, therefore, don't have to be held out in the courtroom. Behavior can be viewed scientifically as self-determined and legal responsibility follows.

Statistical Data: As noted, the NGRI plea is infrequently raised and even more infrequently successful as an affirmative defense. (In law, "affirmative" means that the defendant raises the issue and has the burden to substantiate it.)

Two extensive studies were conducted. Pasewark and McGinley (1985) and McGinley and Pasewark (1989) obtained data from all 50 states (but only some of these jurisdictions had figures on frequency and success of the use of NGRI). Wherever there were such figures, findings supported the general rule of highly limited use of the NGRI defense. Using the number of reported crimes as a standard, the authors found a median rate of one NGRI plea per 873 crimes, with a range of 1 in 27 to 1 in 28,594. In looking at the success rate of the use of the plea, the rates were one acquittal for every 6.5 pleas as a median, with a range of 1:1 to 0:64. In general, while different methods of generating rates existed in different studies, the overall finding, regardless of how the figures were calculated, was that the NGRI plea was rarely raised and even more rarely successful.

Another way to "count" this phenomenon is to review in depth evaluations, such as that conducted at a particular Baltimore court for a period of one year. Only 1.2% of 11,497 defendants who were indicted even initially raised an insanity plea. Of these 143 defendants, 16 had charges dropped, 76 withdrew the plea after a medical screening, and 46 dropped the plea after a complete forensic evaluation, leaving 16 cases. In 13 cases, both prosecution and defense agreed to a directed verdict of insanity. The insanity plea was dropped at the trial of one. Only two contested cases remained, with one defendant being found guilty and one achieving an NGRI acquittal (Janofsky, Vandeville, & Rappeport, 1989).

Nonetheless, while statistical studies suggest NGRI is awarded in less than 2% of the cases, the myth of frequency marches on, fed by media hype and fears of crime (Silver, Cirincione, & Steadman, 1994).

Studies have attempted to evaluate the characteristics of insanity acquittees. Findings suggest that the successful NGRI plea involves a psychosis (usually schizophrenia), often extensive prior psychiatric history, and serious offenses (Packer, 1987; Pasewark, Jeffrey, & Bieber, 1987; Steadman, Keitner, Braff, & Arvanites, 1983; Stokman & Heiber, 1984). The same studies, however, have not shown any characteristic age, relationship of victim to offender, or prior criminal history patterns.

In a study by Rice and Harris (1990), a comparison of insanity acquittees with matched and random groups of non-NGRI defendants confirmed the likelihood of psychosis/schizophrenia. The NGRIs in this study had less extensive criminal histories, but seriousness of offense, e.g., murder, was an important discriminator. Also, the figures suggested that a finding of psychosis at some period relatively shortly after the time of the act was of significance in predicting a successful NGRI. (Presumably, the properly conducted sanity evaluation aims to elicit information about cognition at the time of the act, but this finding suggests post event status has practical, if not legally mandated, importance.)

Current Trends: As has already been indicated, the law has changed periodically in response to public perceptions and perhaps also to private agendas. What is intriguing is that regardless of what differences the law seeks to make, the actual way in which cases get processed appears unaffected (Blau & Pasewark, 1994).

In order to address what is apparently a nonproblem, a number of remedies have been sought. The first of these was the guilty but mentally ill (GBMI) statute. In effect, GBMI allows a finding of guilt, but an assignment of the defendant to treatment for mental illness. If the treatment is successful, but time remains on the sentence, the individual is then moved to a standard correctional facility. Depending on the statute, there may be an evaluation of dangerousness and nonresponsiveness to treatment. Such assessments can result in longer sentences than would come from a standard finding of guilt. In some cases, where both NGRI and GBMI options exist, NGRI pleas have not reduced in frequency; in effect, a second category of GBMI verdicts has created a population in addition to that of the NGRI group (Blunt & Stock, 1985; Morgan, McCullough, Jenkins, & White, 1988; Packer, 1955; Smith & Hall, 1982).

Research on GBMI shows that the impact on NGRI is variable, that the potential for increasing vulnerability to longer, rather than shorter, sentences exists, and that there is no reduction of use of the NGRI option. Incidence statistics for GBMI are similar to NGRI — it is a rarely used option (Callahan, McGreevy, Cirincione, & Steadman, 1992; Keilitz, 1987; Mackay & Kopelman, 1988).

Another strategy for dealing with NGRI is that of repeal. Montana, Idaho, and Utah have been cited as repeal states. However, there are still provisions for evaluating the sanity issue through the application of the general criminal definitions of *mens rea* (guilty mind) in their criminal courts. Sometimes, because one of the elements of the crime of murder is the state of mind of the individual, professional testimony has been allowed. There are some apparent contradictions, however. In Idaho, state of mind is not an allowed defense in a criminal charge. At the same time, the Idaho statute permits expert testimony as to *mens rea* where it is part of the definition of the offense (Idaho Code, 1992). The Utah Code (1993) is similar. Not surprisingly, studies of the impact of this so-called repeal movement show no particular change in the actual handling of cases (Heinbecker, 1986; Steadman, Callahan, Robbins, & Morrissey, 1989).

There have been some constitutional questions raised as to whether this repeal strategy can be reconciled with the U.S. Constitution's due process clause or the Eighth Amendment's prohibition against cruel and unusual punishment.

The Montana Supreme Court in *Montana v. Korell* (1984) reasoned that no basic right to an insanity defense existed, and that it was not cruel and unusual punishment because the punishment was for the act. That court said it would only be cruel and unusual if the individual were being punished for mental illness.

The *Korell* case involved a Vietnam veteran with a history of trauma who, after several disputes with a supervisor and a series of stressors in his life, set several fires and then attempted to kill his former boss. The jury was not allowed to consider whether he was mentally ill at the time of the crimes, but only whether such mental illness meant that he did not meet the necessary state of mind set forth in the Code. He was found guilty on that basis.

One mental health expert has advocated the repeal of NGRI defense as a "special defense" (Halpern, 1991, p. 188). Halpern's approach is very much like that of the so-called repeal states. He believes it makes better sense to simply acknowledge that certain crimes require a guilty mind component. Where that is the case, mental health experts can assist the court in substantiating the presence or absence of *mens rea*. If not all aspects of the crime are found to be present, the individual should be acquitted, but then sent into treatment using the civil system. Individuals found guilty but having a mental health compo-

nent to their functioning would be assigned to a treatment facility in the prison system.

Another approach to reduce the use of NGRI has been to change some of the legal technicalities, especially following the Hinckley case. For example, the burden of proof has been shifted from the prosecution to the defense and the so-called volitional prong (irresistible impulse or inability to refrain) has been eliminated. Studies following the Insanity Defense Reform Act (1984) and similarly worded state laws have, however, found no impact from either of these changes (Ogloff, 1991).

Federal and some state laws also changed to disallow expert testimony as to the presence or absence of sanity on the basis that only the jury or judge has this duty. The avoidance of "ultimate issue" testimony is a general concern in the practice of forensic psychology. Some experts suggest that there should never be testimony as to such issues (Goldstein, 1989; Slobogin, 1989). However, some states — Ohio, for example — continue to expect the professional expert to provide an opinion as to sanity.

Where ultimate issue testimony is barred, the defense usually has the expert witness speak to the presence of factors that are part of the legal definition. The defense counsel then makes a legal argument on the basis of those answers. (As discussed below, the same strategy is found in handling death penalty mitigation and sometimes diminished capacity testimony.)

All of these variations notwithstanding, the studies which have been done to measure the effects of barring ultimate issue testimony have shown no particular impact on the process in one direction or another (Fulero & Finkel, 1991; Ogloff, 1991).

Another strategy which has been a part of tinkering with NGRI involves bifurcating — splitting — the trial into two stages. Guilt is determined first, then sanity is considered. Existing studies do not show any differences between one- and two-stage trials in the rate of insanity acquittals (Pasewark, Randolph, & Bieber, 1984).

There have been attempts to mandate institutionalization in mental health, rather than correctional, facilities. These efforts may have decreased institutionalization periods, but no definitive outcome data have been collected (Blau & Pasewark, 1994). Attempts have been made to limit hospitalization time. The NGRI acquittees face rather variable periods of mandatory hospitalization, depending upon the jurisdiction. In some cases, the acquittee may have spent more time in a hospital than he or she would have had in prison, had there been a finding of guilt followed by conventional sentencing. In many cases, however, the offense is so serious that the maximum term would exceed the hospitalization period.

In Oregon, there is a process whereby NGRI acquittees are released if they no longer exhibit active symptoms of mental illness and are not seen as dangerous. They are given close monitoring with evaluation and treatment. If behavioral problems emerge, the conditional release is revoked. This type of program appeared to have some positive impact on recidivism (Blau & Pasewark, 1994).

In appeals decisions, various approaches and concerns have been addressed. The Insanity Defense Reform Act's shifting of the burden of proof has been upheld. One such decision was *United States v. Amos* (1986), in which the defendant, Jeffrey Amos, had raised the insanity defense. Two expert witnesses testified that he was paranoid and delusional. The government's expert indicated that the defendant was capable of understanding wrong from right insofar as the act was concerned. The defendant attempted to resurrect a decision from 1895 (*Davis v. United States*), which had placed the burden of proof on the government. However, the Court did not accept that there was any constitutional mandate involved in that regard.

With regard to bifurcation, the Rhode Island Supreme Court ruled that there was no constitu-
tional requirement for the two-stage trial approach (*Rhode Island v. Smith, 1986*). This case also raised the question of self-incrimination. Again, no constitutional issue was held to be present. On the other hand, there appears to be no constitutional error where states have adopted a bifurcation mode.

Role of the Psychologist: Just as there is little impact on frequency or success of the NGRI plea as a function of tinkering with the statutes, there is also little real impact on the functioning of the psychologist or psychiatrist. In all states, including repeal jurisdictions, the professional addresses the state of mind of the defendant at the time of the act.

NGRI evaluations involve the collection of retrospective data and information that bears upon the functioning of an individual at a point prior to when he or she is being seen. Furthermore, although the subjective account of the defendant plays a significant role in the evaluation, the potential for that account to be viewed as, and in fact to be, self-serving is sufficiently high that it is hazardous to come to conclusions without other data, except where the defendant's story essentially rules out the NGRI defense. For example, in the case of Frank Spisak, the "Cleveland State Killer" (the second death penalty case after capital punishment returned to the State of Ohio in 1981), the initial approach of the defense was NGRI. Spisak had stalked and killed three people and attempted to murder two others. His ultimate diagnosis was Schizotypal Personality Disorder, but there was some basis for an initial impression of Schizophrenia, Paranoid or Mixed Type. His retrospective account as recorded in court documents (Court of Appeals of Ohio, Eighth District, 1984) included the following: (1) that he carried a gun because he had been mugged and wished to have adequate protection; (2) that he killed his first victim, a Black male, because the man offered to have sex with him in a bathroom; (3) that he shot his second victim, also a Black male, after driving back and forth waiting for an opportune time — his reason was to provide retribution for the rape/killing of two White females by a Black man; (4) that he shot at, but missed, a Black female victim in a restroom where he said she had made an anti-Nazi statement; (5) that he killed a White male because that victim was Jewish and seduced young people and also may have seen him kill the first male and might be able to identify him; (6) that he killed his last victim, a Black male, after again riding around and waiting for an opportunity where he would not be caught. (In both of the driving assaults, he had an accomplice.)

Although there were paranoid trends to his thinking and identity issues typical of severe personality disorders, the conditions for NGRI clearly were not met. Spisak understood the wrongfulness of his acts and was able to refrain from such acts when he perceived a danger of arrest.

After interviewing Spisak, the writer suggested to his defense counsel that an NGRI defense would not be successful, even though the statute at that time included both a cognitive and volitional definition. Second and third opinions were obtained. Only one expert was willing to testify that the defendant met the insanity standard, and that testimony was effectively discredited on cross-examination.

The evaluation of defendants for purposes of NGRI defenses includes obtaining information from persons who observed the defendant's behavior close to the time of the act, especially where they could describe the defendant's patterns of thought as revealed in conversations. The more independent these views are and the more disconnected from the crime, the more credible they become. Police reports and interviews, especially when an arrest takes place close to the act, may yield reliable and court-worthy data. In a situation where the defendant is actively psychotic at the time of arrest, it is desirable to begin interviewing the defendant immediately, before there

is any medical treatment of the condition. Defense attorneys need to be cautioned to object to significant psychiatric intervention before the data is collected, unless the defendant's medical condition requires immediate intervention.

Case Illustration: H. was a man with a long history of disturbed behavior. He was unwilling to accept the help his family said he needed. Just prior to the act, he abruptly moved his family to escape from dangerous forces. He began to withdraw more and more from the outside world. He left his family to live on his own. His behavior deteriorated to a point where he began to use the corner of his apartment as a latrine instead of using the bathroom facilities. He spoke with his family periodically, indicating that uniformed assailants were after him. He bought a rifle to protect himself.

Two weeks after the purchase, he was sitting on the street with the weapon. When he was spotted by the police, he shot at them, wounding one of the officers. After a chase, he was apprehended and taken to the city jail. His behavior was obviously peculiar and his conversation did not seem rational to the officers.

A psychologist at the jail was asked to see him and wrote in his report of this contact that the defendant would speak only if given a carrot, at which time he sat cross-legged on the floor and answered some questions.

Subsequent evaluation included the report of the jail psychologist, information from the arrest records, records from his previous hospitalizations, as well as a current psychological evaluation. It was the opinion of the defense expert that H. met the criteria for NGRI. The prosecution expert, however, testified that while H. was NGRI for the shooting, he was sane for the use of a weapon on the basis that he intended to take the law into his own hands when he bought it and knew that was wrong. However, H.'s defense prevailed and he became an insanity acquittee.

While psychological testing is usually a part of

these evaluations, defendants may be too psychotic for psychometrics. Interviews may be taped, preferably on video, to become exhibits in and of themselves of the patient's behavior. The tapes provide the jury with a much more convincing piece of evidence than do the relatively dry descriptive statements of a mental health professional. Where a mental health history includes repeated evaluations and hospitalizations, that data can be integrated into the final report. Such information may illustrate patterns of thinking and acting that are characteristic for the defendant.

Different appellate decisions have importance for NGRI work. *Wyoming v. Zespy* (1986) supported the position that lay testimony can be used to rebut professional testimony. Similarly, in *Arizona v. Bay* (1986), the court allowed a defendant to use only the testimony of himself and his family, rather than requiring that there be expert testimony.

In some cases, defendants have attempted to raise the prohibition against self-incrimination when required to undergo a forensic examination by the state. However, much as the civil client relinquishes any rights to his or her medical record when raising an issue of damage, the defendant who wishes to plead NGRI waives the right to refuse an examination that will focus on his or her state of mind at the time of the act. Because raising this defense acknowledges commission of the act, the defendant and his or her counsel have to make a strategy decision before using the NGRI defense.

From the standpoint of procedure, an Illinois court (*Illinois v. Murphy*, 1986) has indicated that a psychiatrist may testify basing conclusions on the defendant's statements to other mental health professionals. In this case, the other evaluators interviewed Murphy after an assault. An objection on the basis of hearsay was made to keep out testimony based on their reports. The Appeals Court held that the information was not being offered to prove what had occurred, but rather, as a foundation for a psychiatric conclusion relative to state of mind. Furthermore, the Appeals Court felt that the jury was entitled to know the exact basis for the expert's opinion.

Another case, *Illinois v. Littlejohn* (1986), is interesting because of the duplicity of the prosecutor's strategy. A defendant's expert witness was questioned about whether the defendant having given seminars on psychiatric disabilities might affect the expert's conclusions. The notion was that the defendant was something of an expert himself and, therefore, would be able to fool the examiner. The witness properly acknowledged the potential of such an individual manipulating an examination. Subsequently, there was no evidence that the defendant had any special level of mental health knowledge or had ever taught such seminars. Nonetheless, there were three references to his supposed proficiency by prosecution in presenting closing arguments. The murder conviction was overturned on appeal.

Future directions in the case of insanity evaluations include increasing the use of more standardized approaches. There has been significant discussion regarding such measures, notably, the Rogers Criminal Responsibility Assessment Scales (R-CRAS), as well as some others (Rogers & Ewing, 1992). The R-CRAS gives some score-based outcomes which may invite a view of the data that exceeds its true adequacy, giving an illusion of "hard" science that could prejudice the jury. It is also possible that the more tightly drawn or standardized the procedure, the less adequate it may be to assess the realities and vicissitudes of real cases. However, current work is proceeding to collect validity data with some positive outcomes (Borum, 1994).

Testing the Limits

Two disorders raise limit testing questions for the concept of NGRI. Obsessive-Compulsive Disorder (OCD) is defined as "...recurrent obsession (intrusive ideas) or compulsion (repetitive behaviors)...severe enough to be time consuming...or cause marked distress or significant impairment." (American Psychiatric Association, Diagnostic and Statistical Manual of Mental Disorders, Fourth edition, DSM-IV, pp. 417-419). The patient usually recognizes that the symptoms are not reasonable, but during an episode, there may be little insight into the behavior.

In the case of OCD, can there be criminal acts caused by irrational and inappropriate behavior not under the defendant's executive control? Such a question raises the issue as to whether the so-called "volitional prong" should have been eliminated as was done at the federal level (Insanity Defense Reform Act, 1984), then by a number of states which followed suit.

A second condition, Multiple Personality Disorder (MPD), which is now considered a subcategory of Dissociative Disorder, involves "...the presence of two or more distinct identities or personality states that recurrently take control of behavior. [The disorder]...reflects a failure to integrate various aspects of identity, memory, and consciousness" (DSM-IV, 1994, p. 484).

In MPD, the question becomes whether there are psychological conditions in which the defendant has a guilty mind as part of mental function, but not all of the person was aware when the decision to act took place. In effect, was the defendant in a state where he or she could not fully appreciate wrongfulness?

These two conditions have produced both academic discussions and legal issues. In their discussion of OCD and insanity, Rotter and Goodman (1993) took the position that OCD has a combined anxiety-cognition interplay where there is awareness (a) of a rising state of discomfort, and (b) that an irrational repetitious act will reduce that unpleasantness. Given this theory and also given that OCD responds to cognitive therapy approaches, they did not feel the disorder would allow a defendant to meet NGRI criteria with or without the volitional prong.

Clinical experience and a review of the literature by this writer support Rotter and Goodman's position. First of all, murder is not part of a repetitive background mosaic against which the patient's life progresses. Secondly, where there is a compulsive aspect to killing, as in certain serial murders, there is clear capacity to design and carry out acts where discovery is less rather than more likely, and there is an understanding that the fantasies that drive the act are socially unacceptable and morally wrong.

In the case of MPD, the question is not whether there is an irresistible impulse or volitional aspect, but whether there is an absence of the person fully knowing what in fact is occurring in his or her life. If that is so, can the person be held responsible for some dissociated part of the personality which commits a criminal act?

There have been a number of such cases. Slovenko (1993) discussed *State of New Jersey v. Badger* (1988), in which there was alleged to be two personalities, only one of which "knew" what took place. Therefore, only that personality could assist at trial. An attempt was made to find Badger not competent, but the court decided that should any switching of "personalities" take place during the trial, the new personality could be instructed by counsel on what had just occurred. Also relevant are *State of Oregon v. Darnall* (1980) and *State of Hawaii v. Rodriguez* (1984). In both of these cases, the defendant was held responsible. *Rodriguez* involved a directed verdict of acquittal. On appeal, it was held that the jury should have had the opportunity to evaluate the evidence and make the decision as to whether there was criminal responsibility under the statutory definition.

In Ohio, the *Milligan* case, involving 23 personalities (and a great deal of media attention), resulted in an NGRI verdict (Keyes, 1981). This case was the exception, rather than the rule. Most cases are resolved in the direction of finding the person to be capable of determining right from wrong.

Slovenko (1993) ended his discussion in this area with an anecdote in which the judge who had considered an MPD case stated: "The testimony is very interesting. I will send all of you to prison!" (p. 339).

A defendant diagnosed with MPD can be evaluated for criminal responsibility much as are other defendants (Ondrovik & Hamilton, 1990). Where it can be shown that the dissociated act took place without an appreciation of wrongfulness, the NGRI plea might be supported. Obtaining adequate data in such a case, especially data that would withstand a challenge on the basis of malingering, would be extremely difficult. The NGRI plea would rest on the defendant's word. But, the defendant would also maintain an inability to reliably reflect what takes place in his or her thinking. Unless there was very persuasive independent evidence of dissociative function with aggressive or impulsive actions occurring unrelated to the particular crime in question, the simplest explanation would be that the defendant was lying to escape consequences. A prosecution argument to the effect that the defendant was operating on self-serving motives coupled with general skepticism on the part of the jury would more likely than not result in a finding of guilt.

In most cases, this writer would support holding persons with these kinds of disorders responsible at some level. However, OCD and MPD have characteristics that would fit well into some kind of mitigation. Responsibility may not be at the same level that it would be with a non-disordered individual who can more completely control his or her behavior and who is not fragmented in conscious functioning.

Battered Woman Defense

In the typical scenario, a woman lives for some years in a relationship periodically characterized by outbreaks of violence against her person. In a cyclic fashion, there are beatings, periods of remorse and make up, increasing tension between the couple, and then more beatings. The cycle tends to worsen over time, with the beatings becoming more severe and the amount of damage done increasing (Walker, 1984).

Living in a situation like this has been characterized as meeting all of the criteria of destructive cult environments (Boulette & Andersen, 1986). Under such circumstances, perception of options, ability to reason logically, and capacity to engage in planning are impacted. With a heightened sense of fear and an ongoing atmosphere of dread, self-confidence and a sense of efficacy lessen (Walker & Browne, 1986).

It has been argued in various courts in the United States, with varying degrees of success, that an act of murder by the victim of repeated domestic violence can be either self-defense, diminished capacity, or a special case of NGRI. Expert testimony in regard to battered woman syndrome has been used in various ways to establish the necessary state of mind and perception to meet a subjective standard (*Hawthorne v. State of Florida*, 1985; *Fielder v. State of Texas*, 1985; *State of New Jersey v. Kelly*, 1984; *State of Washington v. Allery*, 1984; *Borders v. State of Florida*, 1983; *State of North Dakota v. Leidholm*, 1983; *Buhrle v. State of Wyoming*, 1981; *State of Maine v. Anaya*, 1981; *State of West Virginia v. Dozier*, 1979; *State of Montana v. Grieg*, 1977; *State of Washington v. Wanrow*, 1977; *Ibn-Tamas v. United States*, 1929).

Statistical Factors: Early studies of the incidence of domestic violence have produced results from 16 to 60% of U.S. families (Gelles, 1974; Post, Willett, House, Black, & Weissberg, 1980; Strauss, Gelles, & Steinmetz, 1980; Walker, 1979).

In 1984, a Battered Woman's Hotline presented the following statistics:

1. Every 15 seconds, a woman is battered somewhere in the United States.

2. Six million women will be battered this

year — 4,000 of them, almost 11 a day, will be beaten to death.

3. Two-thirds of all wives will be physically abused during their marriages. Millions more will be mentally abused.

4. Twenty-five percent of all women who attempt suicide cite abuse at home as a factor.

5. Thirty percent of all women murdered in this country are killed by the men they love — a husband or a boyfriend (Women Together, Inc., 1984).

More recently, Follingstad (1994) indicated that research has shown that among 75% of the women who are killed, the assailants are their male partners. However, from a slightly different perspective, a study of female murderers has shown a variety of motives, including the very mundane ones of greed and felony commission (Langley, Crimmens, Brownstein, & Spunt, 1994). The varying figures make it hard to actually determine the extent of battering, and there is a lot of room to view many writings in this field as expressing personal agendas. What is clear, however, is that domestic violence is a significant phenomenon in the United States, and that over time, the experience of victimization can alter the psychological functioning of a human being.

The battered woman defense (BWD) is basically an affirmative defense. It acknowledges the commission of the act but presents evidence that goes to the state of mind of the individual and to the elements of the crime of murder. BWD involves the following:

1. The defendant's psychology is one of learned helplessness, inefficient cognition, significant levels of anxiety, and even reflects a kind of brain-washing.

2. Because of these characteristics, the woman reaches a point where she does not perceive any alternative to her own eventual death than the one of taking action against the person of her tormentor.

Unique legal problems are involved in assert-

ing this defense. Traditional definitions of self-defense have criteria, such as reasonable perception of imminent life-threatening danger, proportionate use of responsive force, non-involvement in initiating the altercation, and the lack of an alternative option, such as escape. It can be hard for a BWD to meet these standards.

Fourteen states allow expert testimony as to the existence of battered woman syndrome, including Georgia, Kansas, Maine, New Hampshire, New York, Pennsylvania, Washington, California, Ohio, Kentucky, West Virginia, Mississippi, Wisconsin, and North Carolina. Canada also allows the admission of testimony. Six states (Florida, Illinois, New Jersey, North Dakota, South Carolina, and Missouri) and Washington, D.C., allow some conditional testimony. These jurisdictions require an examination of the expert and data against existing legal standards. If there is a finding of adequacy, testimony is allowed (Follingstad, 1994).

Psychological Contributions: In these cases, psychological evaluations may be used at the level of the case in chief, may be helpful at pre-sentencing, or may be used for post-conviction relief. As with other areas of mitigatory evidence, the psychological evaluation is both extensive and intensive. Information needs to be obtained as to the total context. Prior adjustment and history of the defendant and of the spouse are needed. Current status of the defendant is equally important. Psychological testing may reveal thought processes typical for victims of chronic abuse. It is desirable to obtain a psychological assessment as close as possible to the time of the act in order to document the more immediate reactive state. It is not uncommon, for example, for the defendant to have called the police immediately following the act and to have presented in a confused state at that point. Obviously, a review of police reports may be helpful.

Neuropsychological issues may be relevant to the syndrome. Many of the women have been victims of repeated head injuries (Gayford, 1975), suffering the kind of impaired neurological functioning that has often been documented in the field of boxing (Strub & Black, 1988). Some of the battered woman syndrome symptoms, including inability to plan, to perceive options, and to initiate action, may be neurologically based (Chitra, Rao, Gangadhar, & Hezck, 1989; McMillan & Glucksman, 1987; Uma & Shobhini, 1987).

Mitigation to Murder

Unlike NGRI or BWD, mitigation to murder or diminished capacity, is a partial, and not complete, defense. It is affirmative in the sense that it raises issues rather than consisting only of a stance of denial. Like NGRI and BWD, it acknowledges the act, although not the requisite mental state.

In the U.S., diminished capacity is defined in terms of intentionality. One of the elements of a criminal offense is the intent of the defendant. If there is evidence of a mental abnormality, a state that interferes in the defendant's forming that intent, or both, diminished capacity allows a reduction in the degree of the offense for which the individual will be held accountable.

There are only a few states in which this defense can be raised and in which expert testimony is allowed. Over a period of time, California has opened, but then narrowed, its door to such testimony (*People v. Wells*, 1949; *People v. Gorshen*, 1959; *People v. Conley*, 1966; and *People v. Wetmore*, 1978). Other states which have allowed this kind of defense include Pennsylvania, Illinois, New Mexico, and Hawaii. New York also has a statute which allows a diminished capacity approach, although the testimony has to be carefully tailored to the requirements of law. By contrast, in Ohio, it is specifically forbidden by existing case law to have any expert testimony as to the elements of the crime (*State of Ohio v. Wilcox*, 1988).

Role of the Psychologist: Hall (1990) has developed criteria for use with Hawaii's mitigation to murder statute. Referencing *State of Hawaii v. Dumlao* (1986), which listed guidelines for the mitigation defense, Hall provided a model as follows: external events have an impact on the defendant which may include developmental experiences, incremental stressors, or immediate provocation. There is a reaction involving the defendant's appraisal or perception of what is going on, which is based in his or her unique psychology. Finally, there is emotional arousal to a point where there is loss of control. In order to develop data to present this defense, there has to be a consideration of the history of the defendant, particularly involving violent behavior. Hall pointed out that it would be absurd to raise as mitigatory that an individual with a long history of wife beating went too far, with the result that she died. Rather, the individual has to have a history that does not show the development of self-controlled violent activity. The situation has to have unique aspects for that person. In the course of assessment, it is important to consider whether or not the individual has had any training for how to deal with stress in making the case as to whether or not there was a true loss of volitional capacity.

Hall (1990) identified two primary types of extreme emotion reactivity. Type 1 involves immobilization and slowing of function. There is psychomotor retardation, numbing of emotional response, delayed reactivity, withdrawal, hypersuggestibility, reduced verbal activity, a sense of confusion and disorientation, and there may be amnesia. Type 2 involves disorganized action, hyperactivity without a specific goal, high reactivity and immediacy, uncontrolled emotional responding, hypo-suggestibility, presence of confusion, disorientation, and sometimes amnesia. The second type is the more usual focus of a mitigatory defense.

In developing mitigation information, the approach is similar to death penalty work in that extensive data regarding the defendant, context, and victim are all obtained. There has to be significant concern for self-serving distortions. There needs to be an assessment of individual base rates for violence. A complete description of the defendant's conduct before, during, and after the act is necessary in order to rate the degree of self-control or dyscontrol.

Similar concerns can be found in the approach of Meloy (1992) and his Systematic Self Report of Violence. Using a 3x3 matrix, Meloy related time (before, during, and after) and psychological mode (thoughts, emotions, and acts) as a way to organize retrospective data. The patient is interviewed, usually more than once, to obtain a detailed report of the event from memory.

Meloy (1988) also noted the importance of differentiating between affective and predatory aggression. Unlike Hall, who focused on different typologies of self-controlled response, Meloy detailed the differences between perpetrators of emotionally based violence and those who operate in a highly cortical and planful fashion. Differentiating characteristics are identified at psychological and neurotransmitter levels. Affective aggression involves the perception of an external or threatening stimulus, a response in terms of threat posturing and verbalization, and an output from neurotransmitters, which includes reduced serotonin and increased norepinephrine, dopamine, and acetylcholine. The resulting intense sympathetic arousal of the autonomic nervous system prepares the individual for a fight or flight response, with sometimes observable concomitants (skin flush, muscle rigidity, pupil dilation, and increased perspiration). Violence tends to occur quickly after the stimulus is presented. The goal is that of threat reduction. There is some potential for third parties to become victims because the defendant is so out of control. There is a heightened awareness with a kind of hyperalert, hyper-vigilant state.

By contrast, predatory aggression involves

minimal overt display. While there is a heightened sensory state, it is focused and selective. Neurotransmitter characteristics also differ, and autonomic arousal is not high. After the act, there may be exhilaration, but there is no sense of building emotion and out-of-control reaction. The violence follows a plan.

The above descriptions clearly call for the development of very precise data about the act and the state at the time of the act, but also more general and comprehensive data about the individual.

Hall and McNinch (1988) detailed the special case of neuropsychological impairment with particular emphasis on frontal lobe dysfunction. A stepwise model was presented, which included obtaining information in the following areas: (a) medical data regarding frontal lobe dysfunction; (b) psychological data associated with frontal lobe dysfunction; (c) evaluation of degree and patterns of self-regulation in evidence in the offense, including issues related to amnesia; (d) assessment of identified deficits and symptoms in relation to their connection with the crime; and (e) assessment of consistency in all defendant produced responses. Results provide a basis for limited and conservative conclusions as to defendant and crime.

Successful development of data bearing on diminished capacity includes clinical interviews, which should be audio taped, video taped, or both, especially when researching the defendant's memory of the sequence of events. There needs to be careful study given of transcripts of the interviews to determine whether the interviewer is a source of suggestion, as well as to analyze the consistency and perspective of the defendant.

Interviewing starts with free recall, then moves to questioning about specific aspects and desired dimensions. Coherence, internal logic, and perspective can be evaluated using a semi-structured format with careful attention to nonsuggestive questioning (Fisher & Geiselman, 1992; Gudjonsson, 1992; Raskin, 1989).

Psychological testing involves both objective and projective data developed at appropriate state-of-the-art levels. While diagnosis may be best achieved through objective personality tests and appropriate intellectual assessments, the use of projectives, such as the Thematic Apperception Test and the Rorschach, may allow the presentation of a sense of the inner workings of the mind of the defendant, which can be important in communicating with the jury.

Ancillary information from other sources (family, friends, unconnected observers of the defendant's behavior, crime scene analyses) may be pivotal to developing final conclusions.

Areas which become a focus of interest include such concepts as reasonable versus unreasonable belief. There may be a question as to whether the individual had a delusion, but the average person would not give credence to such theorizing. Also, a belief may be reasonable but not factual, which can actually become a complete, rather than partial, defense. For example, an individual may assault someone under a mistaken belief that the victim intended harm to the defendant, leading to a self-defense posture.

Belief plays a rather special part in cases where persons have been acting under the influence of hypnosis. While there is disagreement about the likelihood that hypnosis can be used to cause someone to commit a crime, experiments conducted under U.S. government auspices support the possibility (Scheflin, 1978). There are cases on record where the defense has involved hypnotic coercion (Reiser, 1980). Evaluation in such cases focused on the beliefs of the defendant, the presence of a coercive relationship with the hypnotist, and evidence of high dissociative potentials in the defendant.

Another focus of evaluation may be delayed response. A New York statute recognizes that a build up of tension precedes the onset of the extreme emotional state. Delayed response information is obtained through extensive history and ancillary observation data.

A very special situation involves amnesia. The legal system generally views any claim of amnesia as rather suspect (Hermann, 1986). In drug and alcohol related crimes, a blackout state can eliminate the individual's being able to provide any information about the crime, his or her participation in it, or both. However, the degree to which the voluntary state of intoxication may be mitigating is variable and often minimal (Cunnien, 1986; Sweeney, 1990).

One example is found in California, where there is a concept of "diminished actuality," which pertains specifically to the area of intoxication related acts. Evidence regarding a state of intoxication may not be brought forward at the time of the guilt phase but can be provided at the time of sentencing, a different point than is the case in diminished capacity. Testimony must be worded carefully to fit the provisions of the law and must rest on extensive detailed information (Reidy, 1995).

California did have a true diminished capacity law, but it was greatly changed after the *White* case. There was public outrage when Dan White's attorney successfully argued a sugar-induced, temporary mental state as a defense in the killing of the mayor and a councilman in San Francisco (Van Biema, 1985). Subsequently, the acceptability of mental health defenses decreased significantly. At this point, it is still possible to present some mental health facts which may have a bearing on intention aspects, but the professional may not use the word "premeditation" or discuss the capacity for intent. Testimony may include the presence or absence of delusions, which the jury can then use in its assessment as to guilt (Reidy, 1995).

New York State is one of the jurisdictions in which there is a defense of extreme emotional distress (New York State Penal Law 125.25). It is a modified diminished capacity law and involves objective and subjective standards. The charge to the jury is to place themselves in the defendant's situation and look at what happened as the defendant would perceive it. There are references to notions of "reasonable in light of history" (thus, this is an individualized and subjective, rather than an objective or external set of criteria). A man who is always irrational won't qualify under this standard — it has to be a unique state in which something has been simmering in the unconscious and then comes to the forefront as a result of the situation. The person's emotions overwhelm reason; in the heat of the moment, there is loss of control. There has to be an identifiable precipitating cause. The defense has to show why this event occurred.

Assessment is extensive and involves what the defendant was thinking about and feeling. Multiple sources of information must be obtained regarding the act. Dimensions of purpose and knowledge must be assessed (Goldstein, 1995). The following two cases (which have been disguised, but are based on actual events) allow some insight into evaluations focused on diminished capacity.

Case Illustration: A. shot B. in an apparently premeditated fashion. He obtained a weapon in advance and lay waiting for the victim. His history revealed a long-term association with B. Independent observers verified that A. expressed paranoid ideas about B. A.'s behavior in family and business settings over a period of time was consistent with those false beliefs.

Assessment involved not only interviews to obtain A.'s state of mind and his theories, but also included obtaining independent information about his behavior through interviews of several professionals whom A. had earlier consulted. Test data and history supported a long-standing diagnosis of subclinical manic state. A. was given to extreme moods, with alternating periods of high activity and depression. Testimony regarding his state of mind was not at a level which allowed an insanity defense, but it did permit a finding of

murder in the second degree. A. was then sentenced as if he had been found guilty of manslaughter, which was, in effect, a further reduction.

Case Illustration: A woman from another quite different culture, who had the equivalent of a grade school education, violently killed a second woman. The context could be seen as a passion triangle. The degree to which all elements of extreme emotion were met rested entirely upon data from observations of the defendant and interviews of family and associates. A picture emerged of increasing stress and provocation, as well as loss of face. Formal psychological assessment played essentially no part in the data collection, as the defendant was not testable for both reasons of current emotional state (she was mute and physically regressed) and cultural diversity.

Crime scene analysis, however, allowed ample evidence of a sudden severe loss of control. There was an immediate precipitant, in which the woman was publicly shamed. There was a long term build-up of identified crucial factors. An unplanned confrontation between the defendant and victim took place where a weapon happened to be handy. The defendant exploded into action and stabbed the victim to death.

Death Penalty Mitigation

Almost all countries have had capital punishment at some time. Among Western democracies, only the U.S. and South Africa continued in more recent times to do so. South Africa's recent reformation ended its capital punishment use. Generally, homicide is the crime so punished, but the range of offenses has included rape, treason, political incorrectness, and breaking of the food taboo by a wife as the presumed cause of her husband's death. Methods of death have ranged from slow and painful to the contemporary U.S. search for a "humane" procedure, such as lethal injection (Otterbein, 1986).

The death penalty is an ultimate sanction. It is usually reserved for serious crimes, even exceeding "ordinary" murder. The first execution in the United States took place in 1608. Capital crimes at that time included man-stealing. The tension between those who would have the death penalty and those who would not began at almost the same time as the original statutes were drafted. Pennsylvania restricted its use to first degree murder in 1794. Michigan repealed the death penalty, except for treason, in 1846. However, capital punishment was more supported than not. In 1938, the highest number of executions occurred in this country.

The history of capital punishment in the U.S. has been one of diminishing the number of crimes so punished, reducing the cruelty of the process through technology, rationalizing the process, and "sanitizing" executions (Costanzo & White, 1994).

All death penalty statutes in the country were found constitutionally unsound after *Furman v. Georgia* (1972). There was no majority opinion by the United States Supreme Court in *Furman*. Many of the Justices wrote their own reasons for upholding a conclusion of unconstitutionality. Basically, all supported the position that the capricious and arbitrary nature with which the death penalty was imposed violated Eighth Amendment standards. Social science evidence showing clear patterns of racism was an important contributor to this decision.

To address this problem of unfair application, it was mandated that all capital punishment statutes have a provision for mitigation. This defense phase was to be separate from the trial, which determined guilt. In a series of appellate decisions, capital statutes were required to include a process for weighing mitigating versus aggravating factors (*Gregg v. Georgia*, 1976; *Profitt v. Florida*, 1976; *Jurek v. Texas*, 1976; *Lockett v. Ohio*, 1978). However, in the years that followed, the factor of race continued to be prominent. Nonetheless, there have been no fur-

ther Supreme Court decisions in which the issue of racism was the basis for reversal of a death penalty. In *McCleskey v. Kemp* (1987), the United States Supreme Court expressly stated that statistical evidence of discrimination was not relevant because the only question was whether there was discrimination in the case at hand.

Statistical Data: Although the statutes that have been rewritten all contain mitigation procedures, statistical studies show that there has been no particular impact on the racial factor. The Baldus, Woodworth, and Pulaski (1990) studies obtained information on 200 variables for 594 defendants in Georgia murder cases, and on 500 variables in 1,066 homicide prosecutions between 1973 and 1980. Results showed that killers of Whites were 4.3 times as likely to get the death penalty as killers of Blacks. Similarly, a study of the Uniform Crime Reports for 1991 showed that racism and also gender remained important factors in determining death penalty case outcomes. Males constituted 98% of the U.S. death row population. In Ohio, an evaluation of race and gender of the defendant and victim showed a clear pattern of bias:

1. Twenty-nine percent of death row occupants represented Black-on-White crime; the U.S. rate for such crimes is 3%.

2. Thirty-one percent of death row occupants represented Black-on-Black crime, versus the U.S. rate of 49%.

3. One percent (one defendant) involved White-on-Black crime (the U.S. rate was 6%).

4. Forty percent involved White-on-White crime, approximating the 43% U.S. rate. (McPherson, 1992).

Basically, all studies suggested that if a Black male killed a White female, his chances of receiving the death penalty were extremely high; if a White female killed a Black male, her chances of the death penalty were slight to nonexistent. In general, regardless of how the statistics are arranged, it is clear that where the death penalty is the measuring stick, Black life is less valuable than White life.

In spite of this research supporting social factors as strongly influencing outcomes, the mitigation effort is a serious and extensive one with life and death consequences. It is probably one of the few places where psychologists play a role that has an immediate life-involving outcome.

In an ongoing study of the content of death penalty statutes in the United States, the writer has analyzed 24 statutes for aggravating and mitigating factors. The most commonly listed aggravating victim characteristics include being a law enforcement or other government or political official (14). Murder of a child or of a witness and kidnapping are the next most popular (6 and 4, respectively). With respect to crime characteristics, heinous murder and murder for hire are explicitly found in 13 of the statutes, felony murder in 9 of the statutes, and murder to escape prosecution in 9 of the statutes. There are defendant characteristics which are considered aggravating, including a history of violence and a history of murder specifically (12), and committing murder while a prisoner (8). Finally, 11 statutes list "risk to others" as an aggravating factor.

The focus of assessment and testimony is to develop evidence of mitigating factors which will be weighed against those considered aggravating. With regard to the 24 of the 38 death penalty statutes, 16 include the factor of no significant prior history of violence; 17 mention extreme emotion and thus include a concept traditionally mitigating under diminished capacity; 19 include youthfulness of the defendant; 18 reference duress, coercion, or domination of another person; 13 include participation or facilitation by the victim; and 16 include a factor of the defendant being a lesser participant where there are co-defendants.

Although state laws and the United States Supreme Court provide for a weighing of aggravating versus mitigating factors, there is little

research to support the capacity of juries to engage in such a complex task, particularly given the emotional stress of many murder trials. In fact, rather than a dispassionate weighing process, what seems to take place is a more immediate response to evidence as it unfolds, with traditional factors of primacy and recency, as well as emotional importance, being the real determiners of outcome (Costanzo & Costanzo, 1992; Geimer & Amsterdam, 1988; Luginbuhl & Middendorf, 1988; Sandys, 1991). The impact of the defendant as a person had significant importance in determining the jury's ability to return with a life over death recommendation (Diamond, 1989; Stebbins, 1988).

Procedures in Mitigation: In some cases, a psychologist may be called upon by the court in what is essentially a presentence role. That role differs from mitigation. Where a psychologist comes from a court appointment position, everything in the evaluation is delivered to the court and usually to the jury, prosecution, and defense. This puts the psychologist in a neutral posture and is considered desirable in most forensic applications. However, in death penalty work, the question is whether or not the individual or the crime itself has any characteristics that will persuade the jury to recommend life over death. In order to obtain that kind of information, the psychologist needs to be able to offer the security of a confidential relationship. Only when he or she is a member of the defense team can there be protected communication. The ethical requirement that a psychologist only presents scientifically valid and truthful testimony can be upheld by careful decision-making around the testimony phase. In some cases, a psychologist may develop information, then not testify because the data which comes to light will not assist in the mitigation defense. At such a point, the psychologist may function as a consultant, but not as expert witness.

Case Illustration: The defendant was accommodating enough, even jovial at times. He made disparaging remarks directed at the psychologist, but he was cooperative and completed all of the testing asked of him. Unfortunately, not only was his crime particularly heinous (he stalked and killed the only witness against him in a rape case), but the psychological tests allowed only one conclusion: all of the data fit with a diagnosis of Antisocial Personality Disorder and met the Hare (1985) criteria for a psychopath.

When the psychologist and the mitigation specialist, an experienced social worker, attempted to interview the defendant's mother in order to obtain some testimony favorable to his continued existence, she instructed her lawyer to refuse contact. It was rumored that the defendant had been thrown out of a well-known organization of motorcyclists for bad behavior. The result was a foregone conclusion. The final form of the mitigation defense consisted of arguing the nonnecessity of the death penalty because a life sentence would protect society. This argument was not persuasive to the jury.

Case Illustration: In another equally unsuccessful case, a defendant, through his own efforts as well as those of his appeals counsel, obtained a reversal of his original conviction. He was brought back for a second trial several years after the original one. The prosecution had the uphill task of developing the witnesses and evidence of a much earlier event. However, the defendant's personality problems were pervasive. He attempted to be third counsel in his own case, tried to replace his court appointed lawyers with those of his own choosing, filed motions behind his lawyers' backs, took issue with the mitigation expert, and called all the people who might testify for him asking them to neither speak nor cooperate in any way with the defense team. He acceded to some psychological assessment, although not a complete evaluation.

As with the first case cited, the psychological results were not promising and expert testimony would not have been helpful. Following a finding

of guilt the mitigation psychologists acted as consultants, working with members of the family and with the defendant. The goal was to provide testimony about the defendant's good points and to have him express remorse. Unfortunately, but perhaps predictably, the defendant rejected all advice. In the end, he made an unsworn statement pointing out to the jury their inadequacies in having found him guilty. The result was his second trip to death row.

Case Illustration: The combining of psychosocial and psychological data in a case where a robbery related killing was involved, along with some unexpected actions on the part of the defendant, allowed the jury to recommend life imprisonment. In this case, the defendant was the only nondrug using member of his family in three generations. He had established, in spite of significant youthfulness, a stable relationship with the mother of his child. Charts were used to show the family tree, the degree of drug involvement within the immediate family environment, and using color coding, the exceptionality of the defendant's drug free status. To top it off, the defendant, not being particularly bright (which was backed up in testimony regarding his intelligence test results), appeared for his trial during the guilt phase in a powder blue formal suit because this was his best outfit and he wished to respect the court.

When it came time for the mitigation hearing, he donned the same worn jean suit he had on the night of the murder. He said to the jury that they could see that he had not committed the killing because there were no blood stains on this particular suit. His naive and inadequate logic was not lost upon the jury. After his counsel pointed out that certain factors allowed residual doubt and also fit with the psychological testimony as to the defendant's limitations, the jury recommended life imprisonment.

Case Illustration: Amnesia is a problem for the legal system. In one of the early death penalty mitigation investigations conducted by this writer *under the 1981 Ohio Capital Punishment Statute, a defendant had killed his children. He claimed amnesia for the event. He was uncooperative with various aspects of his defense. His behavior gave rise to a theory that he wished to have state assisted suicide, which would be consistent with massive guilt and psychogenic amnesia.*

The Thematic Apperception Test (TAT) is a series of pictures to which the subject responds with a story. On card 5 of the TAT, which shows a woman looking into a room, his story began in third person, but slipped into first person in the following disjointed way: "Here is where I give her better. She's a mother. She looking inside. Coming inside room with cleaning in mind. Room doesn't look like. Here's room. Doesn't look like a bedroom. I don't see a dresser. Nor do I see a headboard. I do see a lamp, a book, shelf, flowers. Coming more to look into the room to clean or see if the children are OK." The defendant's voice tone and facial expression changed when he began to discuss what he didn't see. The murder took place in a bedroom, and the children were in their beds at the time. His demeanor altered a second time when he got to the last line. It was not possible to obtain his cooperation. The issue of competency was raised but did not succeed. The end result found him on death row.

These cases illustrate some of the basic procedures in death penalty mitigation work. Psychological assessment allows some general and particular statements as to the defendant's intelligence, personality, and mental condition. Additionally, there is psychosocial history gathering, family interviewing, evaluation of potential witnesses, and development of a strategy for presentation of the data. Any psychological evidence has to be true in and of itself. Facts cannot be presented where other opposing facts are known. On the other hand, it is entirely legitimate to present testimony as to some distinct, but uncontroverted portion, such as intellectual functioning, instead of opening a discussion of the individual's personality, history, and character.

As the psychologist works with others on the defense team, findings may lead to the recruitment of other experts. For example, there may be a neurological component or a need for specific expertise in drug dependency or the impact of drugs on behavior.

Conclusions

A conservative and cautious mental health expert may contribute to defenses involving criminal responsibility. The focus becomes that of state of mind and matters of intent and guilt are at issue. The approach to psychological investigation may be very specific and focused, but also may include extensive foraging into neighborhoods, employment settings, generations of family history, and the crime scene itself. In testimony, there may be very particular rules as to what can be said by the expert. The work of the psychologist is sometimes independent but also occurs in the context of defense team membership.

Homicide investigators have long approached their task by looking to motive, opportunity, and means. Once they identify a suspect who becomes a defendant, the court process determines whether all elements of guilt are present. In cases where criminal responsibility involves mental health issues, mitigation may be the final arbiter of outcomes.

Annotated Bibliography

Not Guilty By Reason Of Insanity (NGRI)

Gerber, R. S. (1984). *The Insanity Defense*. Port Washington, NY: Associates Faculty Press. In an intriguing and sometimes provocative book, the early as well as contemporary concerns with respect to problems of the sanity defense are explored. Gerber notes that primitive law was based on strict liability — regardless of intent or state of mind, there was responsibility. This extreme position has been replaced by the notion of mitigation and brings with it the dilemmas of how to evaluate and apportion that mitigated responsibility.

Morris, Norval. (1982). *Madness and the Criminal Law*. Chicago: University of Chicago Press. Using fiction, fact, and legal expertise, Morris analyzes the issues that create tension when mental health and law come together over questions of sanity and competency. An iconoclast, he has been able to make people think about the issues, regardless of whether his solutions are accepted.

Multiple Personality Disorder

Keyes, D. (1981). *The Minds of Billy Milligan*. New York: Bantam. One of the few cases where a Multiple Personality Disorder diagnosis allowed a finding of insanity, this extended examination of William Milligan and his various personalities provides information that would support his being found not guilty by reason of insanity. However, the dilemmas of this category and the functioning of mental health professionals are amply illustrated in this exotic case.

Battered Woman Defense

Bauschard, Louise. (1986). *Voices Set Free: Battered Women Speak From Prison*. St. Louis, MO: Women's Self-help Center. This publication reflects the position that battered women who have been convicted of murder continue to suffer abuse as a function of the legal system.

Browne, Angela. (1987). *When Battered Women Kill*. New York: Free Press/London: Collier Macmillan. Browne's book details an empirical study of battered women who have killed or seriously injured their abusers versus women who have not. It includes significant in depth case material.

McNulty, F. (1980). *The Burning Bed*. New York: Hartford, Brace Jovanovich. A battered women gives her own account of her life and her act of setting her husband on fire. Some excerpts from her trial are in the book.

Walker, L. E. (1984). *The Battered Woman Syndrome*. New York: Springer. This book is considered a primary resource and provides the results of an NIMH funded study of the psychology of battered women. It has ample statistical information and can be helpful in preparing testimony, as well as for understanding the phenomenon.

Diminished Responsibility

John Marshall Law Review: Articles by O'Neil (An analysis of Illinois' new offense of second degree murder, 1986, JMLR, 20, 209-233) and Shane (Murder plus mitigation: The lesser mitigated offense, 1993, JMLR, 27, 61-120) provide definitive legal perspectives on the operation, content and some of the potential problems in the newer statutes involving diminished capacity.

Weiner, I. & Hess, A. (Eds.). (1987). *Handbook of Forensic Psychology*. New York: John Wiley & Sons, Ltd. In this well-known handbook, the chapter by Clark, "Specific Intent and Diminished Capacity," provides an excellent discussion of the concept of diminished capacity and diminished responsibility and looks at the ways in which these concepts are interwoven into the legal systems of the United States and in Europe.

Death Penalty Mitigation

Costanzo, M. & White, L. (1994). The death penalty in the United States [Special issue]. *Journal of Social Issues, 50*(2), 1-18. The initial discussion by these editors of this special issue provides legal and social background. Subsequent articles include a focus on attitudes of Americans, trends, evidence on deterrence, Supreme Court acceptance and rejection of social science research, trial issues including a study of attorney persuasion, and a conclusory article on the empirical evidence relative to the death penalty and its implications for the future.

Miller, N. & Radelet, M. (1993). *Executing the Mentally Ill*. Newbury Park: Sage. The case of Alvin Ford illustrates the problems of the death penalty in relation to the mentally ill and mentally retarded. Another aspect of some importance is the negative impact of life on death row on mental function.

Prejean, H. (1993). *Dead Man Walking*. New York: Random House. This volume is the work of a nun and opponent of capital punishment. She spent time as a minister to several prisoners before they were executed. Her book, while proceeding from an advocacy standpoint, illustrates some of the major problems in capital punishment, not the least of which is the possibility of executing the wrong person, and also provides the kind of personal history and detail that is the goal of a mitigation defense — the humanization of the defendant.

White, W. (1987). *The Death Penalty in the '90s*. Ann Arbor: University of Michigan Press. This volume has general information as well as case detail. The first chapter covers the Supreme Court role and points out that before 1968, there was no consideration of the issue of the constitutionality of the death penalty. After that time, the issue of individualized sentencing versus the imposition of even-handed justice became an important focus, given the evidence of racism with respect to the death penalty.

References

American Psychiatric Association (1994). *Diagnostic and statistical manual of mental disorders* (4th ed.). Washington, DC: Author.

Arizona v. Bay, 722 P.2d 280 (Ariz. Sup. Ct. 1986).

Baldus, D. C., Woodworth, G. G., Jr., & Pulaski, C. A. (1990). *Equal justice and the death penalty*. Boston, MA: Northeastern University Press.

Blau, G. L. & Pasewark, R. A. (1994). Statutory changes and the insanity defense: Seeking the perfect insane person. *Law and Psychology Review, 18*, 69-108.

Blunt, L. W. & Stock, H. V. (1985). Guilty but mentally ill: An alternative verdict. *Behavior Sciences and Law, 3*, 49-67.

Borders v. State of Florida, 433 So. 2d 1375 (Fla.App. 3 Dist. 1983).

Borum, R. (1994). *Establishing standards for criminal forensic reports: An empirical analysis*. Paper presented at the annual meeting of the American Psychological Association, New York, NY.

Boulette, T. R. & Andersen, S. M. (1986). "Mind control" of the battering of women. *The Cultic Studies Journal, 3*, 25-35.

Buchanan G. (1992). *Biblical and theological insights*

from ancient and modern civil law. Lewiston, NY: Edwin Mellen Press.

Buhrle v. State of Wyoming, 622 P.2d 1374 (Wyo. 1981).

Burton, N. M. & Steadman, H. J. (1978). Legal professionals' perceptions of the insanity defense. *Journal of Psychiatry and Law, 6*, 175-176.

Callahan, L. A., McGreevy, M. A., Cirincione, C., & Steadman, H. J. (1992). Measuring the effects of the guilty but mentally ill (GBMI) verdict: Georgia's 1982 GBMI reform. *Law and Human Behavior, 16*, 451-562.

Chitra, M., Rao, S., Gangadhar, B., & Hezck, A. (1989). Neuropsychological functioning in post concussion syndrome. *National Institute of Mental Health Journal, 7*(1), 37-41.

Costanzo, M. & Costanzo, F. (1992). Jury decision-making in capital penalty phase, legal assumptions, empirical findings, and a research agenda. *Law and Human Behavior, 16*(2), 185-201.

Costanzo, M. & White, L. (1994). An overview of the death penalty in capital trials: History, current status, legal procedures, and cost in the Unites States. In M. Costanzo & L. White (Eds.), The death penalty in the United States [Special issue]. *Journal of Social Issues, 50*(2), 1-18.

Cunnien, A. (1986). Alcoholic blackouts phenomenology and legal relevance. *Behavioral Sciences and the Law, 4*, 78-85.

Danesh-Khoshdoo, Y. (1991). *The civilization of law: A commentary on the laws of Hammurabi and Magna Carta.* Berrien Springs, MI: Vandevere.

Davis v. United States, 160 U.S. 469 (1985).

Diamond, S. (1989). Using psychology to control law. *Law and Human Behavior, 13*(3), 239-252.

Fielder v. State of Texas, 683 S.W.2d 565 (Tex. Ct. App. 1985).

Fisher, R. & Geiselman, R. (1992). *Memory-enhancing techniques for investigative interviewing: The cognitive interview.* Springfield, IL: Charles C Thomas.

Follingstad, D. R. (1994). Workshop presentation for the American Academy of Forensic Psychology, Santa Fe, NM.

Fulero, S. M., & Finkel, N. J. (1991). Barring ultimate issue testing: An "insane" rule? *Law and Human Behavior, 15*, 495-507.

Furman v. Georgia, 408 U.S. 238 (1972).

Gayford, J. J. (1975). Battered wives: Research on battered wives. *Research on Social Health Journal, 95*(6), 288-289.

Geimer, W. & Amsterdam, J. (1980). Why jurors vote life or death: Operative factors in ten Florida death cases. *American Journal of Criminal Law, 15*(1, 2), 1-54.

Gelles, R. J. (1974). *The violent home: A study of physical aggression between husbands and wives.* Beverly Hills, CA: Sage.

Goldstein, A. (1995). *Personal communication.*

Goldstein, R. L. (1989). The psychiatrist's guide to right and wrong: Part IV: The insanity defense and the ultimate issue rule. *Bulletin of the American Academy of Psychiatry and the Law, 17*, 269-281.

Gregg v. Georgia, 428 U.S. 153 (1976).

Gudjonsson, G. (1992). *Psychology of interrogations,*

confessions and testimony. W. Sussex, England: John Wiley & Sons, Ltd.

Hall, H. (1990). Extreme emotion. *University of Hawaii Law Review, 12*, 39-56.

Hall H. & McNinch, D. (1988). Linking crime specific behavior to neuropsychological impairment. *International Journal of Clinical Neuropsychology*, 113-122.

Halpern, A. L. (1991). The insanity defense in the 21st century. *International Journal of Offender Therapy and Comparative Criminology, 35*(3), 187-189.

Hare, R. D. (1985). *The psychopathy checklist*. Unpublished manuscript. University of British Columbia, Vancouver, Canada.

Hawthorne v. State of Florida, 470 So. 2d 770 (Fla. Dist. Ct. App. 1985).

Heinbecker, P. (1986). Two years' experience under Utah's mens rea insanity law. *Bulletin of the American Academy of Psychiatry and Law, 14*, 185-191.

Hermann, D. (1986). Criminal defenses and pleas in mitigation based on amnesia. *Behavior Science and the Law, 4*(1), 5-26.

House of Lords in Daniel M'Naghten's Case, 10 Cl. & Fin. 200, 8 Eng. Rep. 718 (1843).

Ibn-Tamas v. United States, 407 A.2d 626 (D.C. 1979).

Idaho Code, Art. 18-207 (c) (1992).

Illinois v. Littlejohn, 494 N.E.2d 677 (Ill. 1986).

Illinois v. Murphy, 497 N.E.2d 871 (Ill. 1986).

Insanity Defense Reform Act of 1984, Pub. L., No. 98-473 (1984).

Janofsky, J., Vanderwalle, M. B., & Rappeport, J. R. (1989). Defendants pleading insanity: An analysis of outcome. *Bulletin of the American Academy of Psychiatry and the Law, 17*, 203-210.

Jurek v. Texas, 428 U.S. 262 (1976).

Keilitz, I. (1987). Researching and reforming the insanity defense. *Rutgers Law Review, 39*, 303-306.

Keyes, D. (1981). *The minds of Billy Milligan*. New York: Bantam.

Kyokai, B. D. (1992). *The teaching of Buddha*. Tokyo, Japan: Buddhist Promoting Foundation.

Langley, S., Crimmens, S., Brownstein, H., & Spunt, B. (1994). *Typology of women who kill: Beyond the battered women syndrome*. Paper presented at the annual meeting of the American Psychological Association, Los Angeles, CA.

Lockett v. Ohio, 438 U.S. 586 (1978).

Luginbuhl, J. & Middendorf, K. (1988). Death penalty beliefs and jurors' responses to aggravating and mitigating circumstances in capital trials. *Law and Human Behavior, 12*(3), 263-281.

Mackay, R. D. & Kopelman, J. (1988). The operation of the "guilty but mentally ill (GBMI)" verdict in Pennsylvania. *Journal of Psychiatry and the Law, 16*, 247-262.

Mathison, R. R. (1958). *The eternal search*. New York: G. P. Putnam's Sons.

McCleskey v. Kemp, 481 U.S. 279 (1987).

McCutcheon, Lynn E., & McCutcheon, Lauren E. (1994). Not guilty by reason of insanity: Getting it right or perpetuating the myths? *Psychological*

Reports, 74, 764-766.

McGinley, H. & Pasewark, R. A. (1989). National survey of the frequency and success of the insanity plea and alternate pleas. *Journal of Psychiatry and Law, 17.*

McMillan, T. & Glucksman, E. (1987). The neuropsychology of moderate head injury. *Journal of Neurology, Neurosurgery and Psychiatry, 50*(4), 393-397.

McPherson, S. B. (1992). *Psychosocial investigation in death penalty mitigation: Procedures and pitfalls.* Paper presented at the 3rd European Conference of Law and Psychology, Oxford, England.

Meloy, J. R. (1988). *The psychopathic mind.* Northvale, NJ: Jason Aronson, Inc.

Meloy, J. R. (1992). *Violent attachments.* Northvale, NJ: Jason Aronson, Inc.

Meloy, J. R. (1992). Voluntary intoxication and the insanity defense. *Journal of Psychiatry and the Law, 20* (4), 439-457.

Montana v. Korell, 690 P.2d 992 (1984).

Morgan, D. W., McCullough, T. M., Jenkins, P. L., & White, W. M. (1988). Guilty but mentally ill: The South Carolina experience. *Bulletin of the American Academy of Psychiatry and Law, 16,* 41-48.

New York State Penal Law 125.5.

Ogloff, J. R. P. (1991). A comparison of insanity defense standards in juror decision-making. *Law and Human Behavior, 15,* 509-531.

Ondrovik, J. & Hamilton, D. (1990, April 7). *Multiple personality: Competency and the insanity defense.* Paper presented at Conference on Multiple Personality and Dissociative States. Akron, Ohio.

Otterbein, K. (1986). *The ultimate coercive sanction.* New Haven, CT: Hraf Press.

Packer, I. K. (1987). Homicide and the insanity defense: A comparison of sane and insane murderers. *Behavioral Sciences and the Law, 5,* 25-35.

Packer, I. K. (1985). Insanity acquittals in Michigan 1969-1983: The effects of legislative and judicial changes. *Journal of Psychiatry and Law, 13,* 419-434.

Pasewark, R. A., Jeffrey, R., & Bieber, S. (1987). Differentiating successful and unsuccessful insanity plea defendants in Colorado. *Journal of Psychiatry and Law, 9,* 55-71.

Pasewark, R. A. & McGinley, H. (1985). Insanity plea: National survey of frequency and success. *Journal of Psychiatry and Law, 13,* 101-108.

Pasewark, R. A., Randolph, R. L., & Bieber, S. (1984). Insanity plea: Statutory language and trial procedures. *Journal of Psychiatry and Law, 12,* 399-422.

Pasewark, R. A., Seidenzahl, D., & Pantle, M. L. (1981). Opinions about the insanity plea. *Journal of Forensic Psychology, 8,* 63-72.

People v. Conley, 64 Cal.2d 310, 411 P.2d (1966).

People v. Gorshen, 51 Cal.2d 216, 336 P.2d 491 (1959).

People v. Wells, 202 P.2d 534 (1949).

People v. Wetmore, 22 Cal.3d 318, 583 P.2d 130 (1978).

Post, R. D., Willett, A. R., House, R. M., Black, S. M., & Weissberg, M. P. (1980). A preliminary report of domestic violence among psychiatric inpatients. *American Journal of Psychiatry, 137,* 974-975.

Profitt v. Florida, 428 U.S. 242 (1976).

Raskin, D. (Ed.). (1989). *Psychological methods in criminal investigations and evidence*. New York: Springer.

Reidy, T. (1995). *Personal communication*.

Reiser, M. (1980). *Handbook of Investigative Hypnosis* (pp. 70-74). Los Angeles: Lehi.

Rhode Island v. Smith, 512 A.2d 818 (1986).

Rice, M. E. & Harris, G. T. (1990) The predictors of insanity acquittal. *International Journal of Law and Psychiatry, 13*, 217-224.

Rogers, R. & Ewing, C. P. (1992). The measurement of insanity. *International Journal of Law and Psychiatry, 15*, 113-123.

Rotter, M. & Goodman, W. (1993). The relationship between insight and control in obsessive-compulsive disorder: Implications for the insanity defense. *Bulletin of American Academy of Psychiatric Law, 21*(2), 245-252.

Rychlak, J. F. & Rychlak, R. J. (1990). The insanity defense and the question of human agency. *New Ideas in Psychology, 8*(1), 3-24.

Sandys, M. (1991). *Life or death decisions of capital jurors: Preliminary findings from Kentucky*. Paper presented at the annual meeting of 5th American Society of Criminology, San Francisco, CA.

Scheflin, Alan W. (1978). *The mind manipulators*. Paddington Press.

Silver, E., Cirincione, C., & Steadman, H. J. (1994). Demythologizing inaccurate perceptions of the insanity defense. *Law and Human Behavior, 18*(1), 63-70.

Simon, L. M. I. (1995). A therapeutic jurisprudence approach to the legal processing of domestic violence cases. *Psychology, Public Policy and Law, 1*, 43-79.

Slobogin, D. (1989). The ultimate "issue" issue. *Behavioral Sciences and the Law, 7*, 259-266.

Slovenko, R. (1993). The multiple personality and the criminal law. *Medicine and Law, 12*, 329-340.

Smith, G. A. & Hall, J. A. (1982). Evaluating Michigan's guilty but mentally ill verdict: An empirical study. *Journal of Law Reform, 16*, 77-114.

State of Hawaii v. Dumlao, 715 P.2d 822 (Haw.App. 1986).

State of Hawaii v. Rodriguez, 679 P.2d 615 (Haw. 1984).

State of Maine v. Anaya, 438 A.2d 892 (Me. 1981).

State of Montana v. Grieg, Billings, Montana (Mont. 1977).

State of New Jersey v. Badger, 551 A.2d 207 (N.J. 1988).

State of New Jersey v. Kelly, 478 A.2d 364 (N.J. 1984).

State of North Dakota v. Leidholm, 334 N.W.2d 811 (N.D. 1983).

State of Ohio v. Spisak, Court of Appeals of Ohio, 8th district, July 19, 1984.

State of Ohio v. Wilcox, 70 Ohio St. 2d 192 (1988).

State of Oregon v. Darnall, 614 P.2d 120 (Or.App. 1980).

State of Washington v. Allery, 682 P.2d 312 (Wash. 1984).

State of Washington v. Wanrow, 559 P.2d 548 (Wash. 1977).

State of West Virginia v. Dozier, 255 S.E.2d 511 (W.Va. 1979).

Steadman, H. J., Keitner, L., Braff, J., & Arvanites, M. A. (1983). Factors associated with a successful insanity plea. *American Journal of Psychiatry, 140*, 401-405.

Steadman, H. J., Callahan, L. A., Robbins, P. C., & Morrissey, J. P. (1989). The maintenance of an insanity defense under Montana's abolition. *American Journal of Psychiatry, 146*, 357-360.

Stebbins, D. (1988, April). Psychologist and mitigation: Diagnosis to explanation. *The Champion*, 34-38.

Stokman, C. L. J. & Heiber, P. G. (1984). The insanity defense reform act in New York state, 1980-1983. *International Journal of Law and Psychiatry, 7*, 367-384.

Strauss, M., Gelles, R., & Steinmetz, S. (1980). *Behind closed doors: Violence in the American family.* New York: Doubleday.

Strub, R. L. & Black, F. W. (1988). *Neurobehavioral disorders*. Philadelphia: F. A. Davis Co.

Sweeney, D. (1990). Alcoholic blackouts: Legal implications. *Journal of Substance Abuse Treatment, 7*, 155-159.

Uma, H. & Shobhini, L. (1987). Information processing in patients with closed head injury. *Journal of Psychological Researches, 31*(2), 70-76.

Uniform Crime Reports. (1991). Federal Bureau of Investigation, U.S. Department of Justice, Washington, DC.

United States v. Amos, No. 86-1006 (8th Cir. Oct. 15, 1986).

United States v. Hinckley, 525 F.Supp. 1342 (D.D.C. 1981).

Utah Code, Art. 76-2-305(1), (1992).

Van Biema, D. (1985, November 4). The suicide of Dan White brings a notorious San Francisco murder case to a bizarre end. *People Weekly, 24*, 46.

Walker, L. E. (1979). *The battered woman*. New York: Harper & Row.

Walker, L. E. (1984). *The battered woman syndrome*. New York: Springer.

Walker, L. E. & Browne, A. (1986). Gender and victimization by intimates. *Journal of Personality, 53*(2), 179-195.

Women Together, Inc. (1984). Home is not supposed to hurt. *Flyer*. Cleveland, Ohio.

Wyoming v. Zespy, 723 P.2d 564 (1986).

About the Author

Sandra B. McPherson received her PhD from Case Western Reserve University in Cleveland, Ohio. She has diplomate status in both clinical and forensic psychology. She divides her time between a largely forensic practice in Cleveland and teaching for the Fielding Institute based in Santa Barbara, California. She has developed special expertise in death penalty mitigation, having worked with many defendants currently on Ohio's death row. Her work in this area began with the first case to be brought under the state's revised capital punishment statute. In addition to the other areas of criminal responsibility work, she is particularly active in domestic relations cases, with special emphasis on problems of sexual abuse allegations and the development of court-worthy psychological evaluations. She is a member of the American Psychological Association and the Ohio Psychological Association, of which she has served as president. She is a former president of the State Board of Psychology.

Any correspondence concerning this article should be addressed to Sandra B. McPherson, PhD, 12434 Cedar Road, Suite 15, Cleveland, Ohio 44106.

Part IV
Evaluation and Intervention

CHAPTER 17

INTERVENTION IN LETHAL VIOLENCE

Harold V. Hall

Introduction

Lethal violence in America and the rest of the world will very likely not abate in the next few decades. Trends suggest an increase in the three major types of individual violence — domestic, acquaintance, and stranger — at all levels of society. The prototypic American city of the future may be much like metropolitan murder centers of the United States — Washington D.C., New York City, Detroit, Chicago, New Orleans — and the trend is rapidly spreading to the suburbs. So, what can be done about lethal violence? This brief introduction to the other chapters in this section raises issues associated with intervention and suggests alternative strategies for consideration.

Increasing numbers of individuals in this country are defending themselves with firearms. The National Rifle Association (NRA) presented the following cases (July 1995, p. 8) in support of its position that deadly force is legally justified when one is confronted with imminent threat to life, limb, and in some cases, property:

Buckling his three-year-old daughter into a child restraint seat, Dothan, Alabama resident William Kenneth Long was approached by three masked thugs demanding money. With the barrel of a .38 jabbed into his back, the young father turned around, and instead of handing over his wallet, delivered a single shot into the head of the armed bandit, killing him. The other punks fled the scene and were later arrested. (**The Eagle**, Dothan, AL, 4/19/95)

*A Phoenix, Arizona, gang member thought he had the upper hand as he trained a shotgun on his quarry. But the scattergun was snatched from his hands by his intended victim. Despite aid from another gangster, the first gangbanger was beaten senseless and struck by gunshots, both from his own shotgun and from his mark's .44 Mag. The attack cost the criminal both arms. (**The Republic**, Phoenix, AZ, 4/2/95)*

Is this what we want — killing people, shooting off limbs, shooting robbers with their own guns? Perhaps there are better alternatives than regressing back to the Old West or vigilante law. Yet, more Americans are coming to believe that the police cannot adequately protect them from the increasing violence all around them. Desperate people will take desperate measures, including taking the law into their own hands.

The literature on the control of and intervention against violence is of limited assistance. It may be useful, however, to briefly review primary, secondary, and tertiary prevention strategies. *Primary prevention* focuses on the conditions that foster wide-spread violence and killing (e.g., war and its aftermath, pandemic substance abuse, unemployment, easy accessibility of lethal weapons to violent individuals). *Secondary prevention* involves methods for controlling aggression (e.g., through psychological intervention) in individuals who are at high-risk for committing violence or who have suffered from the effects of violence, and *tertiary prevention* concerns ways to deal with the aftermath of lethal violence once it has occurred. Table 1 shows intervention strategies for the three types of prevention.

Efforts to Reduce Violence

One is struck by the abysmal state of our efforts to reduce violence (e.g., see Bandura,

1973; Baron, 1977; Baron & Richardson, 1994; Eron, Huesmann, Dubow, Romanoff, & Yarmel, 1987; Geen, 1991; Kutash, Kutash, Schlesinger, & Associates, 1978; Megargee, 1966, 1971; Megargee & Bohn, 1979; Yochelson & Samenow, 1976). Whether primary, secondary, or tertiary, most attempts to eliminate or control lethal violence have not been demonstrably effective in reducing overall lethal violence. One reason is because all three prevention strategies depend for their success on openness, visibility, accurate measurement, accountability, and respect for the basic worth of both the perpetrator and the victim. Another reason is the remarkable durability of aggressive behavior over time, regardless of environmental influences, such as intervention (Fromm, 1973; Huesmann, Eron, Lefkowitz, &

TABLE 1
LETHAL VIOLENCE INTERVENTIONS
PREVENTION STRATEGY

Primary	Secondary	Tertiary
Ban firearms	"Red Tag" high-risk individuals for attention	Incarceration
Educate public on substance abuse and violence	Intervention with dysfunctional, violent families	Capital punishment
Eliminate corporal punishment in homes/ schools	Peer group counseling (e.g., youth gangs)	Invasive psychiatric procedures (e.g., brain surgery, castration, chemical approaches)
Decrease media violence; support nonviolent models in media	Psychological intervention (e.g., anger management)	Aversive conditioning strategies (e.g., anectine therapy)
Reduce racism and sexism	Dispute resolution and mediation	Milieu therapy in treatment settings
Develop full employment and educational opportunities	Improve institutions' accountability practices (e.g., police policies on excessive use of force)	Work rehabilitation for murderers
Family values training in violence and prosocial alternatives	Integrate high-risk individual, significant others, and community intervention	Selective incarceration with restitution and risk-analysis

Walder, 1984; Meloy, 1988; Petersilia, Greenwood, & Lavin, 1977).

In the author's experience, most interested parties — from the police officer on the beat, to the forensic psychiatrist or psychologist, to military leaders — deny their own violence potential, tend to excuse or are inattentive to violence which they deem appropriate, support institutions that use lethal violence as a bottom line control strategy, and blame violent perpetrators according to their own judgmental criteria. We view the negativity of fatal aggression according to the nearness of the slaying. If a murder occurs in one's own family, it is a tragedy; if a stranger's family experiences a homicide, we wonder what the victim did wrong. If a country attacks our military personnel or civilians overseas, it is wrong and should be condemned. If our country does the same, there must have been a good reason. Thus, among the reasons intervention strategies across the board have not fared well are those biases and prejudices brought into our individual judgments about violence.

In spite of the fact that they are the least effective in reducing lethal violence, most intervention efforts have focused on tertiary approaches. They may work, but only temporarily, and help us feel that we are being responsive to the problem. The typical procedure with tertiary prevention is to identify perpetrators, then try to control, punish, or incapacitate them. "Throw them in prison and throw away the key," sums up the attitude of the tertiary approach. Helping the perpetrator and victim is usually an afterthought. Only in relatively recent times have victim assistance programs been instituted. In general, no one has ever demonstrated that, as a whole, tertiary approaches, such as imprisonment or capital punishment, reduce more deaths than they directly or indirectly cause.

The high recidivism rates for violence and the volumes of anecdotal accounts suggest that prisons, largely a product of the Industrial Revolution, actually foster violence (e.g., see Hall, 1987). In this real sense, prisons are dangerously obsolete and set the stage for more violence to occur. One cannot change people into nonviolent, productive citizens by placing them in a negative, hostile environment where the name of the game is intimidation and fear. Prison personnel lose much of their humanity as they themselves are affected by the dehumanizing environment.

Most institutions, including police departments, shun being held accountable to outside influences because it reduces their own control. Although held in generally high respect by the community and often equipped with the latest **crime-fighting technology police often overuse their control, including the use of deadly force. Despite the author's work with several police departments and hundreds of police officers and administrators over the last decade, he has yet to see police leadership voluntarily give up control in their methods of conducting business. Police commissioners, often political appointees, usually rubber-stamp the recommendations of the police department.** Open decision-making enhancing processes, so necessary for the success of all intervention approaches, are viewed by police departments as civilian interference. Community-based police approaches, widely hailed as a means of involving ordinary citizens in fighting crime at a grass roots level, are met by resistance from police departments because they diffuse power and control. And, simply placing more police officers on patrol, as provided by the Omnibus Crime Bill of 1994, will not stem the tide of violence now sweeping this country.

Tertiary approaches also do not work because of economics. A vast industry has been built up around the financial aspects of violence and aggression. Prisons, police, and the military have a vested interest in maintaining the status quo, or in increasing their support base. A final reason tertiary approaches cannot deter crime concerns contamination. The system dedicated to controlling violence through violent means has a decidedly negative effect on staff personnel within the system. The institutional person becomes isolated from society and contaminated with the values of power and control at any price, as well as developing the attitude that the people who are served are inferior and not to be trusted. Through the adverse effects on their own mental health, which indirectly influences the behavior of family members and others with whom they come in contact, society as a whole eventually suffers.

Secondary prevention approaches are generally more successful than tertiary approaches, but are applied to fewer individuals. For individuals who are at high-risk for committing violence (e.g., by virtue of their own previous violence), or have been severely traumatized by violence, intervention covers a broad gamut of individual, group, and family strategies. Mental health professionals make their greatest contribution through secondary prevention strategies.

In Chapter 18, Charles Golden and his colleagues examine a wide range of psychometric measures that can be utilized for assessment and therapy with violent individuals. In Chapter 19, Robert Craig demonstrates with several cases how the Megaree system of MMPI classification can be used to good advantage. In Chapter 20, Mary Cerney discusses how the pain associated with a killing within a family can be alleviated. In Chapter 7 on infanticide by women, by Sally Barlow and Claudia Clayton, intervention strategies aimed at individual and group levels are presented. In Chapter 21, Marc Walter addresses cognitive retraining of cerebral deficits associated with violent behavior.

The lack of therapy for perpetrators and victims suffering from violence-related Post-Traumatic Stress Disorder (PTSD) adversely affects not only the quality of their lives, but also the community at large. Untreated persons perpetuate the interlocking cycles of stress and violence that have been well documented in the behavioral science literature. The costs of violence are substantial, particularly if one considers decreased work productivity and the breakup of families as costs. Most victims, left untreated, begin to see the world as a hostile and threatening place and, over time, many become perpetrators themselves through child abuse, spouse battering, or behaviors sanctioned by institutions that allow or support the expression of violence. For both the institution and the individual, violence cycles are initiated and maintained in a neverending pattern of aggression and distress.

A secondary prevention approach developed by the author over the last several decades with several hundred clients illustrates that individuals suffering from severe violence-related PTSD can be helped quickly and effectively. The orchestrated set of interventions is termed the "STOPtrauma" program (Stopping the old pattern of self-defeating behaviors, Thinking about current behavior by measuring baseline function, Opening the person to new interventions, and Phasing out the therapy into adaptive ways of functioning).

The rationale for this intervention is as follows: Persons who have perpetrated, experienced, or witnessed severe violence, including family members who have lost a relative to murder, may exhibit disabling symptoms in the form of flashbacks, nightmares, reduced attention and concentration, guilt, anger, depression and, in general, demoralization and a reduced quality of life. As a result, a chronic syndrome becomes entrenched and generalizes to all aspects of a person's life, the lives of significant others, and even across generations to children. Typically, help from agencies, friends, employers, and others is inadequate, even in their combined efforts, to resolve the PTSD because they do not recognize PTSD, believe the person has adequate resources to cope with the problem of reintegration, or are not aware that methods exist to reduce and redirect PTSD.

The worth of psychotherapeutic and community psychological approaches is just starting to be realized by police departments. A startling statistic is that the majority of police officers who have killed in the line of duty leave the force within several years, primarily because of untreated (and unrecognized) PTSD (Williams, 1987). It has been demonstrated that police departments that recognize and attempt to change their impact on the community at large can do so in substantial ways.

The STOPtrauma therapies that reverse and redirect the PTSD include (a) interventions specific for intrusive memories associated with flashbacks, nightmares, and obsessive-compulsive rumination about events surrounding the trauma (e.g., guided imagery, Eye Movement Desensitization and Reprocessing — EMDR); (b) several Japanese therapies which deepen personal feelings, clarity of thinking and goals, constructive living, and appreciation of others (particularly Morita and Naikan therapies); (c) family/couples therapy which benefits the entire family and resolves secondary PTSD, a common (but seldom diagnosed) condition in which a significant other develops post-trauma symptoms by close psychological proximity to the victim; and (d) assertiveness training which helps redirect the trauma into self-actualization and "win-win" social outcomes. PTSD sufferers, often nonassertive and passive secondary to the trauma, can be taught to express anger at the time irritation occurs instead of a delayed rage reaction. After assertive models are portrayed, learners practice behaviors in mildly stressful but manageable situations that relate to the PTSD (e.g., by role playing).

Eventually, the clients gain highly effective behaviors through modeling. Learners observe their own performances, attitudes, and nonverbal behavior through videotape playback. Logging and homework are an integral part of this intense and effective combination of interventions. Sev-

eral follow-up sessions insure that improvement continues and that the PTSD is eliminated. Treatment can be brief and effective as the following case shows:

Case Illustration. A 35-year-old police officer on a routine domestic call was confronted with a shotgun-wielding drunkard. The officer drew his own firearm, aimed it at the perpetrator and found himself looking into both barrels of a 12-gauge shotgun. At this point, the officer thought he was going to die. The officer eventually cocked his pistol and the perpetrator jerked and fired his shotgun, fortunately missing his target. The officer stood frozen in fear, but was rescued by his fellow policemen.

After the incident, the officer experienced symptoms that rendered him unfit for duty, including seeing the perpetrator's eyes on the highway while he was driving, experiencing flashbacks, nightmares, forgetfulness, and loss of attention and concentration. Post-trauma treatment with the STOPtrauma therapy was initiated with the officer and his wife, who was suffering from secondary PTSD, with marked sleep disturbances and heightened anxiety. The officer's wife learned all of the interventions, which she then applied to her husband at home. In reciprocal fashion, and as he improved, the officer applied the interventions to his wife.

Treatment was completed successfully after 45 days, with the officer returning to unlimited patrol duty a few weeks later. As with similar cases, no exacerbation of symptoms occurred when the officer was exposed to police stresses after treatment. Follow-up after one year revealed that the officer was symptom-free and had recently been promoted to sergeant.

The STOPtrauma method may provide motivated individuals a means of ridding themselves of the disabling effects of PTSD. In most cases, the procedures result in increased behavioral self-control and mastery. Importantly, it is insignificant whether the PTSD sufferer was a perpetrator or a vicim in violence-related activities. The program works on chronic PTSD, as the following case demonstrates:

Case Illustration. A 45-year-old Marine combat veteran, a good-looking and athletic part-Hawaiian male who worked for a local airline, complained of unremitting nightmares and flashbacks following his four years as a Marine sniper in Vietnam, in which he had over 150 confirmed kills and many "probables." Suffering the same pattern for two decades, after about one to one-and-a-half hours of non-REM sleep, he would wake up when he had his first dream, always of an ambush, with him as the victim. He would spend the rest of the night drinking beer and "checking the perimeter" by prowling around the house. After dawn, he would lapse into a deep sleep for one to two hours before preparing for work. He displayed a variety of threatening and violent behaviors over the years since Vietnam, including holding a knife to his wife's throat and threatening to cut off her head, hospitalizing young adult males by provoking them into fights, and ramming his truck into the rear of other vehicles. Surprisingly, he had been arrested only twice for assault and terroristic threatening.

Shortly before intervention, he felt the urge to obtain a deer rifle and ambush the police, envisioning getting killed in the process, thereby dying a hero's death by going out "in a blaze of glory." Intervention consisted of the entire range of STOPtrauma strategies, with an emphasis on meeting with his family, combat rap group treatment, and guided imagery. This last method taught him to reenter his nightmares in a state of relaxation, and to assume "command control" of the dream process and outcome.

As a result of the combined interventions, his nightmares and other PTSD symptoms faded in intensity and frequency. Today, he maintains his job and his family is intact. As happens occasionally with those treated, he became a vigorous advocate of PTSD intervention for other war vet-

erans. He no longer provokes violence.

Five years post-treatment, he has stayed violence-free. He remains, however, an unhappy man with fixated beliefs regarding the basic worthlessness of humans and a chronic dysthymia proving resistent to change. He is nevertheless self-controlled and productive; his family and work colleagues were delighted with his decreased dangerousness.

Secondary approaches to lethal violence, for both perpetrator and victim, the two often later conjoining, are thus known to work in individual cases. The amount of therapeutic time necessary to effect results is considerable and the emotional cost to treatment personnel, many of whom develop secondary PTSD, is substantial. Even with safeguards, such as building in diversity in the workload, clinicians tend to burn out after a few years of continually intense cases.

In the battle between prevention and conditions which create trauma, the latter usually wins out. One rapist can create hundreds of cases of severe PTSD. One organized crime family can create more cases of substance addiction than can be handled by dozens of high-quality drug clinics. On a grander scale, one "small" war, such as in the former Yugoslavia, can create more crippling psychological problems than thousands of superbly trained mental health professionals could possibly treat. For these reasons, secondary approaches are of limited usefulness.

In this volume, several contributors discuss intervention strategies to change the underlying conditions of violence. In Chapter 4, Lita Schwartz and Rosalie Matzkin suggest ways to restructure the media and our lives in order to reduce the media's violent impact on vulnerable individuals. In Chapter 5, on countering social inducements to lethal violence, Leighton Whitaker outlines several needed steps to replace violence with nurturance of life, including caring parenting and education, eliminating corporal punishment in the schools and homes, and eliminating racial and gender discrimination. Lucien Buck makes the fundamentally important observation in Chapter 23 that competition often leads to violence and that cooperation and altruism can be taught. In short, a multitude of good ideas can be applied to a surmountable set of violence-related problems and situations.

An understanding of violence and lethal violence, which is directly relevant to intervention, emerges from the chapters in this volume. Some of these principles of violence are well known, but are ignored in programming. Lethal violence preempts other events for our attention and action, yet we typically are short-sighted or attempt to deny the underlying causes. Violence begets violence. The cycle of injury, death, and revenge continues even as we know the truth of this proposition. Violence, particularly that which is planned, gratifies perpetrators in the short term, yet ultimate aversive consequences in some form are rarely avoidable.

Deception is almost universal in planning or expressing lethal violence. The two basic types of deception — faking good, or denying/minimizing one's negative features, such as concealed dangerousness or exaggerating positive attributes, and faking bad, making up or exaggerating negative characteristics and/or denying positive attributes — are commonly used as manipulations in family, acquaintance, and stranger violence. The self-deception of evaluators is often ignored or denied. Fortunately, the state of the art in deception analysis is progressing. Cross-validation approaches which are discussed in Chapter 1 can counter the effects of deception in lethal violence.

Some less obvious principles of violence are nevertheless pertinent to intervention efforts. As the contributions to this volume make clear, violence almost always is a choice and is subject to cognitive and behavioral control. Interventions ranging from spouse-battering groups to mandatory therapy for police officers who use deadly force benefit all of us when responsibility for making deliberate choices is affirmed.

All successful efforts to reduce violence must thus be based on three essential ingredients: an attitude that change and restructuring society are indeed possible, motivation to involve and dedicate oneself in often unsupported and unheralded efforts to make the world a little safer, and implementation of programs based on what is known about deadly outcomes and conflict. The hope of the contributors to this book is that we can eventually achieve primary prevention of violence.

Annotated Bibliography

Bandura, A. (1973). *Aggression: A social learning analysis*. Englewood Cliffs, NJ: Prentice Hall. This classic and still very relevant textbook probes the origins of aggression, instigators of aggression, and maintaining conditions from a social learning perspective. Modification and control of violence is discussed in terms of modeling principles, differential reinforcement, institutional remedial systems, and changes in social systems. This book should be reviewed by all those who contemplate intervention with violence and aggression.

Jacobson, N. A. (Ed.). (1987). *Psychotherapists in clinical practice: Cognitive and behavioral Perspectives*. New York: Guilford Press. This comprehensive text on cognitive-behavioral approaches to intervention examines conditions and problems which underlie or are associated with violence. The inclusion of multi-model interventions provides the reader with a systematic tool to address violence-related parameters. There is a particularly good treatment of impulsivity and conflict along with self-management strategies for intervention.

Ury, W., Brett, J. M., & Goldberg, S. (1988). *Getting disputes resolved*. San Francisco: Jossey-Bass.

Reflecting the burgeoning literature on dispute resolution, this book points out that struggle may be necessary before relevant parties are ready to resolve the issues. Strategies to keep the struggle within bounds include (l) substitution of posturing for actual violence, (2) fighting only in a limited context wherein relative strength can be assessed (e.g., conflict over an isolated area by small units from both sides), (3) instilling cooling off periods when the conflict threatens to escalate, and (4) the requirement for negotiation (with crisis mediation) during the cooling off periods. The findings can be applied to both individual and collective violence.

References

Bandura, A. (1973). *Aggression: A social learning analysis.* Englewood Cliffs, NJ: Prentice Hall.

Baron, R. A. (1977). *Human aggression.* New York, NY: Plenum Press.

Baron, R. A. & Richardson, D. R. (1994). *Human aggression* (2d ed.). New York: Plenum Press.

Eron, L. D., Huesmann, L. R., Dubow, G., Romanoff, R., & Yarmel, P. (1987). Aggression and its correlates over 22 years. In D. H. Crowell, I. M. Evans, & C. R. O'Donnell (Eds.), *Childhood aggression and violence: Sources of influence, prevention and control* (pp. 249-262). New York: Plenum Press.

Fromm, E. (1973). *The anatomy of human destructiveness.* New York: Holt, Rinehart, & Winston.

Geen, R. G. (1991). *Human aggression.* Pacific Grove, CA: Brooks/Cole.

Hall, H. V. (1987). *Violence prediction: Guidelines for the forensic practitioner.* Springfield, IL: Charles C Thomas.

Huesmann, L. R., Eron, L. D., Lefkowitz, M. M., & Walder, L. O. (1984). Stability of aggression over time and generations. *Developmental Psychology, 20,* 1120-1134.

Kutash, I. L., Kutash, S. B., Schlesinger, L. B., & Associates (1978). *Violence: Perspective on murder and aggression.* San Francisco, CA: Jossey-Bass.

Megargee, E. I. (1966). Undercontrolled and overcontrolled personality types in extreme antisocial aggression. *Psychological Monographs, 80* (Whole No. 611).

Megargee, E. I. (1971). The role of inhibition in the assessment and understanding of violence. In J. L. Singer (Ed.), *The control of aggression and violence* (pp. 242-264). New York: Academic Press.

Megargee, E. & Bohn, M. (1979). *Classifying criminal offenders: A new system based on the MMPI.* Beverly Hills, CA: Sage Publications.

Meloy, R. (1988). *The psychopathic mind: Origins, dynamics, and treatment.* Northvale, NJ: Jason Aronson, Inc.

National Rifleman (July 1995). The armed citizen. *National Rifle Association,* 193, 8.

Williams, T. (Ed.). (1987). *Post-traumatic stress disorders: A handbook for clinicians.* Cincinnati: Disabled American Veterans.

Yochelson, S. & Samenow, S. (1976). *The criminal personality.* New York: Jason Aronson.

About the Author

Harold V. Hall, PhD, is the Director of Psychological Consultants, Inc., and is the President of the Pacific Institute for the Study of Conflict and Aggression in Kamuela, Hawaii. He is a consultant for criminal justice system agencies, including the FBI, the U.S. Secret Service, and National Bureau of Prisons. He has testified more than 100 times as an expert witness in murder trials. He is a Diplomate in both Forensic Psychology and Clinical Psychology from the American Board of Professional Psychology and is a Fellow of the American Psychological Association. He has written or edited five books and numerous articles on forensic-clinical issues.

CHAPTER 18

PSYCHOMETRIC TESTING AND LETHAL VIOLENCE

Charles J. Golden
Michele L. Jackson
Samuel T. Gontkovsky
Angela Peterson-Rohne

Psychometric testing includes general intellectual, neuropsychological, and cognitive testing, along with the projective and objective evaluation of personality disorders. Such testing is used in the analysis of all types of lethal violence in attempts to focus on factors which influence criminal behavior in individuals or to identify common characteristics which may help explain or predict their criminal behavior.

Psychological tests have long been used in the study of individuals who have committed murder, although most of this work is anecdotal. In general, this work has been poorly coordinated and conceived, examining for factors such as dangerousness, impulsivity, mental illness, or retardation without a clear concept of whether or not these disorders were an integral part of the murder sequence or simply unrelated, but associated, conditions.

Some works have attempted to regard all murderers as a single entity, failing to separate out individuals with very different crimes, etiologies, and motivations, while others have focused too much on legal, rather than psychological, classifications. Still others have attempted to develop typologies, but have relied on simplistic classifications which failed to capture the individ-

uality of those who have committed murder. Additional work has attempted to simply generalize from anecdotal evidence to the group as a whole, with predictably unreliable and inconsistent results.

Overview of Psychometric Testing

Psychometric testing itself is a broad field which includes the use of assessment devices to analyze intelligence, personality, attitudes, aptitudes, interests, vocational skills, and brain injury. In general, the scientific work has focused on the areas of intelligence, personality, and brain function, with less reported work in the remaining areas.

Personality assessment represents the study of both enduring, life long traits (such as amorality) which color an individual's perception of the world, as well as shorter term states (such as acute anxiety) which may represent a reaction to current problems. For example, murderers who are incarcerated are more likely to show depression than those who are not incarcerated. As a result, studies of incarcerated murderers may be biased by the reaction of the individual to being in jail.

In many cases, personality problems, such as

anxiety or depression, may be a simultaneous reflection of long-term disorders and a short term reaction to the individual's current status. For example, anxiety may be made up of trait anxiety, a chronic level of anxiety which pervades the person's life regardless of what is happening, and state anxiety, a more acute form which may reflect distress at being charged, jailed, convicted of a crime, or other circumstances of the individual's life.

Objective Evaluation

The scientific evaluation of personality can be accomplished through several avenues. First, "objective" tests, which require the individual to respond to a standard set of questions by answering true or false or by making a specific choice, can be employed. By far, the most commonly used instrument in this area in prisons is the Minnesota Multiphasic Personality Inventory-2 (MMPI-2), a 567-item, true-or-false test which the individual generally reads and answers (although it may be read to individuals unable to read). The MMPI-2 is interpreted by comparing the answers of the individual to the answers of clinical research groups with specific problems and diagnoses, looking for matches which identify specific personality traits or conditions. The original version of the Minnesota Multiphasic Personality Inventory (MMPI) had 566 questions. The bulk of the literature reported on in this chapter consists of work done with the original version of the MMPI.

Projective Evaluation

In contrast to objective tests such as the MMPI-2, other tests are classified as projective tests. These are tests such as the Rorschach or Thematic Apperception Test (TAT).

The Rorschach is the most well known of these tests. This is the standard inkblot test which requires the individual to look at an amorphous inkblot and tell the examiner what he or she sees. The theory behind projective tests is that people see in the inkblots what they bring to the test. Thus, if an individual is obsessed with murder and violence, then he or she will see murder and violence or something which represents murder and violence. Viewing the same inkblot, another person may see flowers, representing quiet and serenity. In another, one may see either a couple dancing or a scene of violence and rape. Some may see red flowers where others see dried blood.

The TAT differs from the Rorschach in that it presents drawings of scenes which show lone individuals in ambiguous settings or characters interacting in unclear ways. The individual is asked to tell a story about the scene, stating who the characters are, what they are doing, and what will happen to them in the future. As with the Rorschach, respondents bring to the test their own conception of reality. They may see a sleeping woman or a dead woman; characters may be angry and fighting, or planning a picnic.

The scoring of projective tests is generally more complex and difficult than the scoring of objective tests. Unlike objective tests, there are no "right" answers or limited number of possible answers. Individuals may have widely different interpretations based on their cultural and ethnic background, intelligence, current preoccupations, environment, and other factors. Thus, any scoring system has the difficult task of separating out these variables to identify those which truly give insight to the individual's personality.

As a result, in many cases, the scoring itself is highly subjective and simply reflects the opinion (and expertise) of the examiner. In other cases, more objective and quantitative scoring systems have been developed to allow for more scientific and replicable study of the results of the test. For the Rorschach, the best known of these scoring systems was developed by Exner (1986). There is no generally used scoring system for the TAT.

Exner's (1986) scoring system used an amalgamation of procedures found in other Rorschach scoring systems, combined with an impressive array of research. This allowed for a more replicable and objective method of analyzing and interpreting data from the Rorschach.

Intelligence Testing

Intelligence tests represent a range of tests which were devised to capture the elusive concept of intelligence. The first of these were the Binet tests, known best in the United States as the Stanford-Binet, but the most frequently used are the Wechsler tests, which have progressed through several similar versions known as the Wechsler Bellevue, the Wechsler Adult Intelligence Scale (WAIS), and the Wechsler Adult Intelligence Scale (Revised; WAIS-R; Wechsler, 1981).

These tests attempt to generate one or more summary scores. These scores measure the general abilities of the individual across intellectual domains. The Stanford-Binet attempts to generate a single score which expresses the individual's ability levels and quantifies his or her ability to do well in school or in life. The Wechsler tests yield three major scores expressed as verbal intelligence, nonverbal (Performance) intelligence, and global (Full Scale) intelligence. Verbal intelligence represents the ability of the individual to answer academic questions, understand verbal situations, find relationships among categories, and perform arithmetic reasoning. Nonverbal (Performance) intelligence represents the ability to copy designs, arrange picture stories sequentially, solve jigsaw puzzle-like tests, identify missing details in pictures, and perform visual-motor copying tasks. Global (Full Scale) intelligence represents a combination of verbal and nonverbal intelligence. Each of the skills included within the more general categories of intelligence can be analyzed separately as well. This can create patterns of results that suggest specific strengths or weaknesses which may, in turn, indicate a specific cognitive approach to problems or specific cognitive deficits.

Shorter tests of intelligence, that attempt to estimate global intelligence, are available. The Revised Beta (Kellogg & Morton, 1957) is a visual-motor, nonverbal test of general intelligence. The Institute of Personality and Ability Testing Culture Free Intelligence Test, or IPAT (Catell & Catell, 1958), is a nonverbal test that measures global intelligence. The Peabody Picture Vocabulary Test (PPVT) is a multiple choice vocabulary test.

Neuropsychological Testing

Neuropsychological testing represents the use of psychological tests to assess the cognitive effects of brain injuries (Golden, Zillmer, & Spiers, 1992). Reviews of the literature have indicated that neuropsychological tests are sensitive to a wide range of deficits from brain damage which cannot be seen on standard neurological or neuroradiological tests (Golden et al., 1992). Thus, such tests are extremely useful in detecting milder and more chronic forms of brain dysfunction which may contribute to lethal violence.

Neuropsychological tests are generally administered as a series of tests that may consist of a standard battery of tests or an individually designed group of tests chosen by the evaluator. The most well known of the test batteries are the Halstead-Reitan Neuropsychological Battery (HRNB; Golden et al., 1992; Halstead, 1947) and the Luria-Nebraska Neuropsychological Battery (LNNB; Golden, Purisch, & Hammeke, 1980, 1985). Individual tests may be chosen from a selection of several hundred tests (Lezak, 1995).

In general, most neuropsychological test batteries include some measure of intelligence; thus, there is an overlap between these areas of investigation.

Goals of this Chapter

Interpretation of personality tests, neuropsychological tests, and intelligence tests are complicated by environmental, gender, and cultural issues. While intelligence tests were originally derived to test a basic level of biological intelligence which was thought to be genetic and immutable, results have shown that past experience, attitude, motivation, education, and culture all affect test results. In the area of personality, responses are also influenced by reading and comprehension skills, motivation, culture, attentiveness, concentration, openness, honesty, rapport with the examiner, and other factors which may distort results. Despite these legitimate concerns, these tests have proven useful in understanding underlying psychological and cognitive processes.

For the purposes of this chapter, we have restricted our examination to studies which focus, at least partially, on the issue of lethal violence, rather than violence or aggression in general. Although some feel that these topics are interchangeable, our goal is to attempt to identify specific factors which may differentiate the murderer from the merely violent individual, the non-violent criminal, or the law-abiding citizen.

The first part of the chapter will examine the literature that has attempted to identify the personality and intellectual variables that distinguish perpetrators of lethal violence from other criminal offenders and the general population. The available literature examines the personality correlates derived from a broad base of projective and objective assessment measures. Much of the research focuses on efforts to identify a single personality trait scale that can be utilized to identify an individual's potential for violent or assaultive behavior. Additional studies have sought to uncover the intellectual deficits and impaired abilities that may be present in violent criminal populations. The work by Megargee and his associates with the

MMPI will not be addressed as it is covered in another chapter in this volume.

Objective Personality Research

One theoretically promising approach to studying lethal violence is to recognize that there is wide psychological heterogeneity among murderers. Thus, it is important to divide lethal murderers along lines where more homogeneous groups can be identified and which can then be studied independently. Most frequently, murderers are defined by their relationship to their chosen victims. The victims are generally classified as a family member or significant other, an acquaintance, or a stranger. The murder of each type of victim tends to have distinct motivations and varied degrees of pre-planning.

Consequently, researchers probe for the perpetrator characteristics that uniquely define the membership of each group of lethal violence offenders. Further work has focused on planning the treatment and institutional needs of murderers based on their inherent characteristics. It is hoped that with increased knowledge of individuals who murder, we will come to be able to identify potential offenders before they commit violent crimes. Predictive identification and early intervention would greatly facilitate the commission of future research and validate the usefulness of previously completed efforts.

Psychologically based typologies have been developed in an effort to classify criminal offenders. The purpose of these taxonomical approaches is to create homogeneous clusters that accurately identify a particular type of criminal offender. These approaches can either classify murderers by the characteristics of their crime or background, then look for psychological differences, or may group them by psychological factors, then look for environmental or crime differences.

A widely used automated classification system is the Eber Diagnostic and Risk Assessment

Profile (DARAP) developed for use in state prisons (Eber, 1974). This is a pencil and paper test with an accompanying computer scoring program. The test produces factor scores, test profiles, and validity checks. The computer program also produces a narrative describing the recommended security requirements, a risk assessment, and appropriate institutional treatment protocol.

Based on inmates in the Georgia Department of Offender Rehabilitation who were administered the DARAP, the regression equations employed by the senior author of this chapter yielded five specific risk prediction measures: escape, violence, suicide, victimization, and recidivism. To date, nearly 10,000 inmates have been tested with this system. The strength of this classification system lies in its ability to predict the behavior of inmates while incarcerated and post-release. It has been utilized in making probation and parole recommendations. A formal written summary of the DARAP results is now required for presentation to the Arizona Board of Pardons and Paroles when an inmate is considered for release (Kennedy, 1986). The DARAP has not, however, been effective in separating lethal violence from violence per se, as is true with all diagnostic instruments.

Few attempts have been made to classify lethal violence offenders as a separate diagnostic entity. One group of researchers, Holcomb, Adams, and Ponder (1985), successfully categorized 80 men charged with premeditated murder based on their MMPI scores. The researchers used the Missouri Mental Status Examination for external validation of the MMPI profile.

Five personality types emerged from this study. Each personality cluster differed significantly from the others across the 13 MMPI scales. The descriptive labels attached to each cluster characterized the predominant psychological make-up of each group. The cluster labels, presented in order from one to five, were Psychotic, Disoriented, Normal, Hostile, and

Depressed. Four of these five groups were found to have thought processes that were described as unstable and unusual. Members of these groups tended to lack control over their lives and lacked adequate planning in most areas of their lives.

This typology is currently the best available for classifying murderers using an automated interpretation of a well-accepted assessment device. Future research should focus on extending the reliability of this typology to other types of murder, and should include women and juveniles in the normative sample. There is no evidence at present, however, that these subtypes distinguish murderers from other prisoners.

A subgroup of lethal violence offenders — serial murderers — was the subject of a typology based on a developmental model (Ansevics & Doweiko, 1991). These authors reviewed popular investigative books and documented the characteristics of 11 serial murderers to develop their descriptive model.

This model examined critical experiences and patterns found in the serial murderers' developmental histories. Commonalities included loss of a mother figure by age five, unusual sexual thoughts or practices in adolescence, and early nonviolent criminal history. Thus far, it appears that its usefulness is limited to potential identification of an individual who may be accused of serial murder, because no research is available to examine the predictive value of the serial murderer typology. Indeed, an examination of the literature as a whole suggests that these characteristics can be seen in many criminals and non-criminals who have not become serial murderers.

Truscott (1990) failed to find any significant differences between extremely assaultive and moderately assaultive groups on the MMPI. This finding was based on a comparison of the groups on the 13 clinical and validity scales of the MMPI. The offender groups differed from the normal controls, but Truscott contended that this difference was not due to assaultiveness, but arose from the antisocial characteristics of the offender groups.

Other studies have attempted to uncover the common personality characteristics of violent offenders. The majority of these efforts have used the MMPI as the primary assessment device. The use of the MMPI continues because of its wide acceptance, ease of administration, well-developed validity scales, and the availability of automated scoring systems. Researchers have focused on different scoring and analytic approaches utilizing the MMPI in attempts to label violent offenders.

The results of these studies are mixed. One set of studies focused on finding "two-point codes." This involves identifying the two highest scales on the MMPI in the hope that this will identify a particular personality type which can be related to violent offenders. Studies focusing on the 4-3 profile type, or peaks on the Psychopathic Deviate and Hysteria Scales, have yielded inconsistent results. This pattern has been of interest because it is believed that individuals with this profile have little regard for traditional morals, a poor response to authority, and a tendency to hold in their emotions until they explode. Davis and Sines (1971) and Persons and Marks (1971) found that subjects who produce the 4-3 profile code are more aggressive and violent than subjects who do not produce this code.

Other efforts (Buck & Graham, 1978; Gynther, Altman, & Warbin, 1973) have not supported the above findings that persons with the 4-3 profile are more hostile and violent than persons producing other two-point codes. Buck and Graham (1978) examined violent criminals convicted of murder, rape, aggravated assault, and robbery. The male inmate sample consisted of 65 offenders who produced the 4-3 profile type and 64 who did not. The groups were further subdivided into "young" and "old" offenders, using 30 years of age as the cutoff. They found that similar aggressive behavior was present in individuals producing other combi-

nations of two-point codes. Their results further indicated that the age of the offender did not account for the failure of the 4-3 profile to identify aggressive behavior. Buck and Graham indicated that this failure to replicate the results of Davis and Sines (1971) and Persons and Marks (1971) could be the result of conducting the study in a medium security penitentiary where the most violent offenders were already selected out.

Fraboni, Cooper, Reed, and Saltstone (1990) also failed to find a significant relationship between the 4-3 code and violent behavior. Their sample was derived from men who had been court-ordered to undergo a psychiatric evaluation. The violent and the nonviolent groups had 35 and 32 subjects, respectively. The groups were matched for age and education. The average age of both groups was 29 years old. The average educational level was nearly 10 years.

None of the violent offenders in this study showed a 4-3 code, although 20% showed either a 4-8 or 8-4 code, another type associated with psychopathic behavior and poor impulse control. Scale 8, the Schizophrenia scale, measures diverse areas such as social alienation, family functioning, and unusual thoughts and perceptions. Fraboni et al. (1990) concluded that these particular code types were extremely unreliable for predicting violence in a criminal population and should not be employed alone in individual assessment.

Efforts to examine the more global MMPI clinical scales profile configurations have also failed to discriminate among groups of criminal offenders (Panton, 1958). Panton separated his sample of 1,313 valid MMPI protocols into six crime classification groups: white collar, aggravated assault, robbery, property theft, aggravated sex, and sexual perversion. The aggravated assault group consisted of men convicted of murder and various types of assault. This group of 157 convicts produced the MMPI two-point code 4-8; however, four of the other five criminal groups also produced this two-point code. Panton's results indicated that the aggravated assault group was indistinguishable from other criminal groups on the MMPI.

Panton's (1958) results were contrary to the findings of a later study (Ingram, Marchioni, Hill, Caraveo-Ramos, & McNeil, 1985) which found a significant main effect of Scale 4 in differentiating violent and nonviolent criminals. Twenty Black males and 32 White males selected from the Nebraska inmate population were used as subjects. Ingram et al.'s finding suggested that criminals incarcerated for violent offenses score higher on the Psychopathic Deviate Scale than their nonviolent counterparts. No racial differences were found for this main effect.

Ingram et al.'s (1985) results suggested a stronger relationship between the MMPI profile and recidivism than aggression. Criminals who were more likely to repeat their crimes were also seen as more impulsive in their criminal behavior. Ingram et al. surmised that recidivism, rather than aggression or violence, may be the variable that moderates the differences between the violent and nonviolent groups on the MMPI.

Overall, the use of objective personality measures to study lethal violence has revealed potentially useful information regarding the underlying personality structure of the murderer. However, this work has not been able to identify distinctive characteristics which discriminate between the murderer and other criminals. Future work using objective personality tests will need to focus on more homogeneous subgroups of murderers, the use of scales developed to study criminal populations, and the association of specific test findings with specific behavioral patterns.

Projective Testing

Research on the use of projective assessment devices for investigating the personality characteristics of perpetrators of lethal violence has pri-

marily utilized the Rorschach inkblot test, along with occasional use of other projective instruments. Due to the extensive time required to administer and score a Rorschach protocol, the studies of murderers' protocols have had small sample sizes (under 40 subjects) or presented detailed single case histories.

As noted earlier, a primary problem in using projective tests such as the Rorschach and the TAT in forensic assessments or in research are the subjective, inconsistent scoring methods. This is more true of the TAT, which has yielded very little usable research. It is less true of the Rorschach, but researchers are still hampered by a proliferation of scoring systems (Beck, 1949; Exner, 1986; Piotrowski, 1957; Schafer, 1954) in the absence of a single universally accepted system of scoring and interpretation.

In a study of men convicted of homicide, Keltikangas-Jarvinen (1978) found that based on combined results from Rorschach and TAT protocols, 63% of the sample of 38 male murderers could be classified as psychopathic, 28% as neurotic, and 9% as psychotic. The author suggested that guilt feelings are contraindicative of future violent assaults. Therefore, it was expected that the neurotic group of murderers would be the least likely to reoffend because of their increased guilt. Further results indicated that the degree of hostility projected on the inkblots was correlated with the commitment of more than one capital murder.

When these results obtained with murderers were supplemented with results from a group of 36 aggravated assault offenders, a profile of a violent offender emerged that was characterized by decreased emotional expression, few meaningful interpersonal relationships, and inability to tolerate negative emotional states, such as depression. Violent offenders were also prone to fusion of the actual and ideal self-concepts, meaning that their self-view is poorly developed and not based entirely on reality (Keltikangas-

Jarvinen, 1978).

Perdue and Lester (1973) differentiated murderers of a family member or a stranger based on Rorschach responses. Each group consisted of 20 male subjects. Murderers of kin were significantly different from murderers of strangers in that they gave more whole (W) responses, fewer animal movement (FM) responses, and had lower F+% and F% scores. Viewed from both the Beck (1949) and Piotrowski (1957) scoring systems for the Rorschach, these differences suggested that individuals who murder family members may be less responsive to emotionally laden material, have less need for physical activity, and have lower levels of depression and anxiety than individuals who murder an unrelated victim (Perdue & Lester, 1973). Perdue and Lester (1973) concluded that murderers of family members are emotionally overcontrolled. They also suggested that the validity of these findings should be interpreted cautiously until the study is replicated.

Gacono and Meloy (1991) found that the protocols of antisocial personality disordered (APD) psychopaths included significantly less T and Y determinants, more personal (PER) responses, and a higher egocentricity ratio when compared to APD individuals who were not characterized as psychopathic. According to Exner (1986), these results indicated an emotional "impoverishment" in which the individual doesn't desire meaningful relationships with others and is indifferent to situations that have little structure. Psychopaths will also tend to focus on their own needs above others and will be callous and cold when involved with others. Gacono's (1992) case presentation of Rorschach results from a sexual murderer was consistent with these hypotheses.

Battered women who have killed a battering spouse presented with a different constellation of response tendencies on the Rorschach (Kaser-Boyd, 1993). The women in Kaser-Boyd's (1993) study ranged in age from 16 to 60. They were all pre-trial detainees referred for a psychiatric eval-

uation to assist in their defense. This group contained 14 White, 12 Black, and 2 Hispanic women. Analyzed using Exner's Comprehensive System (1986), their protocols reflected cognitive constriction, or a reduced level of mental activity; a lack of personal resources and coping strategies to solve problems; and a tendency to vacillate between a passive or an active style when facing problems. Emotionally, they tended to have poor control and were prone to extreme emotional displays. These features manifested themselves in angry, unexpected outbursts. These women were prone to step back when confronted with emotionally charged situations in order to avoid the emotional stimulation (Kaser-Boyd, 1993).

The results obtained with this sample indicated that battered women who kill have a distorted understanding of the world and do not perceive the world as normal individuals do. Consequently, they resemble mentally ill individuals more than normal individuals who kill as a means of escaping danger (Kaser-Boyd, 1993).

Overall, the research involving projective tests has been less productive than the research with objective personality tests. This is due to the lack of a consensus regarding scoring systems, as well as the relatively small sample sizes in most studies using projective tests. Regardless, projective test research and clinical use have generated insights which have been useful in the understanding of the individual murderer. While more extensive research is necessary, these tests have the ability to offer useful psychodiagnostic information about the individual murderer.

Intellectual Assessment

Intellectual assessment with criminal offenders has been used to determine if violent behavior has any cognitive correlates. Alfred Heilbrun completed a series of articles based on prisoners in the Georgia penitentiary system in which he examined the relationship between psychopathy and intelligence (1979, 1990a, 1990b). Psychopathy was defined in the first Diagnostic and Statistical Manual of the Mental Disorders (American Psychiatric Association, 1968) as a personality disorder characterized by a failure of socialization with resulting diminished guilt and frustration tolerance. A psychopathic individual would also lead an impulsive, irresponsible lifestyle with disregard for other individuals. In his initial 1979 study of 76 White male prisoners, Heilbrun found that psychopathy was predictive of violence, but only among less intelligent criminals, as measured by the IPAT. Using the IQ cutoff of 105 to define lower intelligence, Heilbrun found that 90% of this group had committed a violent crime, whereas only 58% of the higher intelligence group had committed a violent crime.

Further findings indicated that the less intelligent psychopaths also committed more impulsive crimes, such as murder or assault. These results are difficult to generalize because the sample consisted of only White males. Additionally, it is unlikely that a "normal" prison population of violent psychopaths would have a mean IQ of 105 to 106. It is the present authors' experience that violent criminal offenders tend to have IQ scores at least one standard deviation below average, while a score of 105 is slightly above average.

In a later study, Heilbrun (1990a) sought to predict dangerousness from personality and intellectual test results. His sample was made up of 275 men who were not subdivided by racial group. Once again, he was able to establish that men who presented as highly antisocial on the MMPI and the California Psychological Inventory (CPI) and who had lower IQ scores were significantly more dangerous and committed more severe crimes, such as murder, when compared to their less antisocial, more intelligent counterparts. Heilbrun (1990b) further differentiated between death-row murderers and those receiving life sentences for murder. His findings indicated that the death-row murderers were significantly more

dangerous than other murderers. Heilbrun (1990b) contended that the combined effect of high antisociality and low intelligence results in serious violence because individuals with this combination of characteristics lack the judgment, cognitive resources, and self-control to prevent themselves from engaging in severely assaultive behavior. Victim resistance may exacerbate the violent behavior in extremely dangerous men (Heilbrun, 1990b). This may be due to the offender's inability to manage the complications created by a noncompliant victim.

The remainder of the literature attempting to connect lowered intelligence with violent behavior has met with disappointing and mixed results. Shawver and Jew (1978) failed to replicate an earlier study (Kunce, Ryan, & Eckelman, 1976) which found that a low ratio of the Similarities subtest to the other subtests of the WAIS was evident in two samples of violent criminal offenders. The significant ratio score was the subject's Similarities score compared to the sum of all of the WAIS subtests multiplied by 100. Both of these studies examined White adult males with psychiatric problems.

These studies were based on the theory advanced by Kahn (1959) that extremely violent behavior is the result of impulsivity derived from poor abstract reasoning ability, which was hypothesized to be measured by the Similarities subtest of the WAIS. These results indicated that either the theory behind the research or the operational definition of the violent criminals' inability to perform mentally abstract verbal tasks was inadequate. The inconsistency may also be due to the extremely small sample sizes of 14 and 26, respectively (Kunce, Ryan, & Eckelman, 1976; Shawver & Jew, 1978).

The failure to differentiate between violent and nonviolent groups also occurred in a study by Tarter, Hegedus, Winsten, and Alterman (1984) when they looked at 101 juvenile delinquents referred for neuropsychological evaluations.

Examination of the Verbal and Performance IQ Scales differential score on the WAIS and WISC-R did not reveal any significant differences between the groups of juvenile criminal offenders.

This was contrary to a later study's finding that Performance IQ Scale (PIQ) scores are greater than Verbal IQ Scale (VIQ) scores in violent offenders and can significantly distinguish violent from nonviolent juvenile offenders (Petee & Walsh, 1986). This sample was made up of 67 White and 58 Black juvenile probationers in Ohio. Other studies have found that the Full Scale IQ scores of violent offenders were lower than the scores for nonviolent criminals (Robertson, Taylor, & Gunn, 1987; Ruff, Templer, & Ayers, 1976; Syverson & Romney, 1985).

The Robertson et al. (1987) study focused on 167 men in pre-trial detention, either in the general prison population or in the psychiatric unit. None of the 76 men in the nonviolent group had any major mental illness, head injury, or chemical dependency. Members of the nonviolent group were then matched with members of a violent, mentally ill group based on age and level of education. They found that no single test in a comprehensive cognitive assessment battery could distinguish between the two groups. The differences lay in areas of social functioning, including higher levels of divorce and unemployment in the violent sample.

The violent men were also more likely to have had a juvenile arrest record and all had previous adult arrests, as opposed to 80% of the nonviolent sample. Despite these promising findings, the Robertson et al. (1987) research failed to find a significantly different mental profile in their violent sample.

In two studies, Holcomb and his colleagues (Holcomb & Adams, 1983; Holcomb, Adams, Ponder, & Anderson, 1984) attempted to find a link between cognitive and personality variables in samples of murderers. In each study, the MMPI was used as the personality measure and the Revised Beta was used as the measure of intelligence. The first study also employed the PPVT.

The results of the first study (Holcomb & Adams, 1983) indicated that the murderers with lower IQ scores tended to have problem-solving difficulties. This inability to see and think through alternatives to aggression may result in increased levels of violence. Another personality variable that was correlated with lower IQ was labeled Introspective Self-Focus. Individuals with this constellation may not use concern for others as an inhibitory force against aggressive behavior.

Holcomb and Adams (1983) also found that a high score on the PPVT indicated that the individuals who had better developed verbal intelligence also possessed the mental constructs necessary to label and analyze their thoughts; thus, they were able to work through troubling emotional states that may lead to aggressive behavior.

Other studies examining the relationship between aggression and intellectual functioning have found lower IQ scores, as measured on the Wechsler Intelligence Scales, in violent groups (Syverson & Romney, 1985; Valliant, Asu, Cooper, & Mammola, 1984). Within the Valliant et al. sample, dangerous offenders had Full Scale IQs on the WAIS-R that were two IQ points less than non-dangerous offenders and 21 IQ points less than a normal group of first-year college students. The members of the dangerous offender group had committed crimes against persons, such as assault, rape, and murder, whereas the non-dangerous group members had committed property crimes, such as theft, breaking and entering, and arson.

In Syverson and Romney's (1985) study, the violent group was differentiated on the basis of having caused bodily harm to the victim. Significant differences were found between the violent and nonviolent groups for WAIS Information, Comprehension, and Object Assembly subtests. Significant differences were also found in the Verbal IQ and the Full Scale IQ scores. These differences showed that the violent offenders had lower IQ scores than the nonviolent sample and also had less well-developed verbal intelligence.

Robertson, Taylor, and Gunn (1987) compared the cognitive functioning of 76 men, subdivided into violent and nonviolent groups, on the WAIS. The violent group tended to have a lower mean Full Scale IQ score, but not significantly lower. No relationship could be found between the pattern of cognitive functioning as measured by the WAIS and a tendency toward violent behavior.

Walsh and Beyer (1986) found that delinquents with a PIQ>VIQ difference of 15 or more IQ points engaged in significantly more violent crimes and property crimes. A later study (Petee & Walsh, 1986) found that significant differences in violent behavior existed between two groups that exhibited a statistically significant PIQ>VIQ difference.

Overall, the intelligence testing results demonstrate a relationship between aggression and intelligence scores. However, this is not a simple relationship, but rather, appears to reflect an interaction among intelligence, personality, and the environment. There is no single consistent pattern of intellectual loss seen in aggressive individuals, although there have been frequent findings of losses in verbal intelligence. Such losses have been associated with early brain injury (Golden et al., 1992). Golden et al. suggested that early brain injury may be related to an inability to tolerate stress or to identify alternate ways out of a stressful situation, leading to the overuse of aggressive impulses. This potential relationship will be discussed in more detail in the next section.

Neuropsychological Testing

Researchers have examined the possible role of brain injury, specifically prefrontal and temporal injuries, in the manifestation of aggressive behavior. Brain dysfunction may account for many of the intellectual and personality findings found in highly aggressive individuals (Golden et al., 1992).

Stuss and Benson (1986) described six specific manifestations of prefrontal damage including the inability to control and monitor personal behavior. These cognitive deficits may occur in an individual with normal or impaired intellectual abilities (Mattson & Levin, 1990).

Aggression due to frontal lobe impairment seems to represent an escape of aggressive behavior because of the brain's lost ability to maintain emotional equilibrium or to control the behavioral expression of changes in mood (Wood, 1987). The most typical form of expression of this impairment is intermittent periods of irritability that escalate into an emotional response, the magnitude of which is quite disproportionate to the eliciting event (Wood, 1987). In contrast to temporal lobe-based explosive disorders (discussed below), the external source of provocation in behavior disorders associated with frontal lobe impairment is almost always clear, and the aggression is usually directed toward that source.

Not only do impaired individuals have less ability to control emotional expression, but they also lack an appreciation for the impact of their behavior. Such individuals are generally highly egocentric and unable to appreciate distress or pain to anyone but themselves. They may show remorse after the fact, as do children, but are unable to show a long-term understanding of what they did. Consequently, they are more likely to repeat their behavior.

In addition, because of their egocentricity, lack of empathy, and lack of planning and anticipation skills, frontally impaired persons are more likely to engage in behaviors which irritate or offend others. When offended individuals respond to these behaviors, the chances for conflict rise dramatically. As a consequence, impaired individuals unnecessarily get themselves into situations which heighten the likelihood of aggression. Such impaired individuals will rarely understand their own role in such conflicts and will see themselves as the aggrieved party.

In the case of many individuals, premorbid tendencies toward aggression or irritability become expanded as frontal lobe controls are lost. In general, individuals who are older when injured and have well-developed internal control systems show less of an impact than those with poorly developed internal controls. Not surprisingly, younger people who have had no chance to develop controls and older individuals who have weak controls are the most likely to show the most full blown versions of this syndrome.

The lack of control over shifts in mood following frontal lobe injury and the rapid shifts in basic drives which direct behavior (Bond, 1984) may be responsible for lowering of the threshold for aggressive behavior (Hart & Jacobs, 1993; Wood, 1987). Although individuals with frontal lobe damage are frequently aware that their aggressive reactions are inappropriate, they have an impaired ability to self-modulate emotions and behaviors in accord with internal need states and the exigencies of the outside world (Luria, 1980).

Temporal lobe impairment is often exhibited by episodes of unprovoked or exaggerated anger, memory and intellectual impairment, auditory or visual hallucinations, delusions, and receptive language impairment. Episodic dyscontrol is most commonly associated with damage to the medial portion of the temporal lobes. The medial temporal lobes contain limbic system structures important for regulating emotion and behavior (Miller, 1990).

Kaplan, in 1899, demonstrated the existence of episodic dyscontrol following head injury. Meninger and Mayman (1956) noted that individuals with a history of illness or injury involving the central nervous system (CNS) are often subject to recurrent acts of rage in response to minor provocation.

The clinical presentation of episodic dyscontrol varies in severity and form. In more severe cases, the aggressive behavior can appear as sudden, unprovoked outbursts which are primitive and poorly organized in nature and are usually directed at the nearest available object or person. Outbursts in less severe cases, however, may appear less out of control, more organized, and more clearly directed against the source of the irritation.

In general, the aggression following temporal lobe damage involves a loss of behavioral control, is unpatterned, is not confined to particular situations, times, and individuals, and occurs with minimal provocation and no premeditation (Barratt, 1993l; Miller, 1990). It does not have the clear antecedents or goals that frontal lobe aggression appears to demonstrate. The research indicates that individuals rarely exhibit organized, directed violence due to ictal phenomena (Elliott, 1992; Lewis & Pincus, 1989; Kaplan, Sadock, & Grebb, 1994; Perrine & Congett, 1994). However, it must be noted that seizures themselves can be set off by physical or psychological stress. As a consequence, the seizures are more likely in threatening and stressful situations. The violent acts committed during seizures are generally very disturbing to the individual because they are unplanned and make little sense, unlike frontal violence, which is more clearly motivated and therefore less disturbing.

The first notable study to utilize a comprehensive neuropsychological battery in the assessment of violent behavior and its relationship to neuropsychological impairments was a study by Bryant, Scott, Golden, and Tori (1984). These authors administered the LNNB-Form I (Golden et al., 1980) to 110 inmate volunteers in California and Nebraska. Violent subjects were those who had committed assaultive crimes against persons. The control group consisted of nonviolent inmates who had been convicted of property crimes. The violent offenders were found to be significantly more impaired on all 14 of the LNNB summary scales. Basic skills in reading, writing, and arithmetic were all lower in the violent group.

To perform additional analyses, the subject LNNB profiles were reclassified according to the Golden et al. (1980) criteria for brain damage. Further analysis indicated that only 28% of the non-brain damaged group had committed violent crimes and that 73% of the brain damaged group had committed violent crimes. These results supported the relationship between organic impairment and the propensity toward violent and aggressive behavior.

The violent group in the Bryant et al. (1984) study demonstrated impaired performance on complex tasks that required integration of sensory information from the auditory, visual, and some esthetic processing systems. The violent group also lacked the ability to create, plan, organize, and execute goal-directed behavior. Sustained concentration and attention were also impaired in the violent offenders. The authors suggested that this constellation of impairment was consistent with Luria's (1980) description of adult-onset frontal lobe syndrome.

Bryant et al. (1984) conducted additional assessments of the 60 inmates from the California facility, using the Wide Range Achievement Test (WRAT) and selected subtests from the WAIS. The analysis of the data failed to find any relationship between the presence of a learning disability and the type of crime that was committed. Both violent and nonviolent groups had deficient performances on the WRAT, indicating similar low levels of educational achievement in both groups.

Langevin, Ben-Aron, Wortzman, Dickey, and Handy (1987) also investigated the relationship between brain damage and criminal aggression. Eighteen homicidal men were compared to 21 men facing nonhomicidal violence charges and to a control group of 16 men with nonviolent and nonsexual offenses. Neuropsychological measures administered to the subjects included the HRNB, the LNNB, and the WAIS-R.

Results, analyzed using univariate analyses of variance, indicated that neuropsychological variables were significant in 20 to 25% of violent offenders and that killers were distinguished by an even higher incidence of neuropathology than the assaulters. The neurological impairment did not relate significantly to diagnosis, drug and alcohol abuse, age, intelligence, or education.

An examination of the physical health of a sample of juvenile delinquents matched to a sample of nondelinquent juveniles found that the delinquents had comparatively more adverse medical histories (Lewis & Shanok, 1977). In a series of later studies, Lewis and his colleagues (Lewis & Shanok, 1979; Lewis, Pincus, & Feldman, 1986; Lewis, Pincus, Bard, Richardson, Prichep, Feldman, & Yeager, 1988) found that trauma to the CNS was commonly seen most frequently among violent juveniles and adults. These CNS trauma included prenatal distress, interpersonal violence, and serious accidents involving head injury. Neurological manifestations of CNS trauma in delinquent and offender populations include the presence of seizures and electroencephalogram abnormalities (Krynicki, 1978; Lewis, Pincus, Shanok, & Glaser, 1982; Mark & Ervin, 1970; Pincus, 1985).

Using a comprehensive neuropsychological battery, Spellacy (1977) sought to differentiate between violent and nonviolent delinquent adolescent males based on the presence of functional impairments indicating brain dysfunction. Each group consisted of 40 boys from a residential treatment school. The mean age for all subjects was 14.6 years.

Of 31 variables used in the statistical analysis, 12 were found to be statistically significant. The nonviolent group had significantly higher Verbal, Performance, and Full Scale IQ scores, as well as superior performance on the Similarities and

Block Design subtests. The violent group had an average of two more errors than expected on the Visual Retention Test and performed significantly worse on the Embedded Figures Test and the WISC Mazes subtest. Impaired performance for the violent group was further evident in sentence repetition and language comprehension tasks.These results indicated that the violent group, characterized by poor impulse control and consistently aggressive behavior, had more group members who manifested neuropsychological impairment than the nonviolent group. Their impaired performance was readily apparent in cognitive, perceptual, and psychomotor abilities. Interestingly, none of the organically impaired violent delinquents had been diagnosed as brain injured prior to or during their institutionalization.

Overall, neuropsychological research has been convincing in demonstrating that many murderers, as well as many chronically aggressive individuals, have brain injury. It is also clear that brain injury is not present in all murderers. Research has yet to focus on differentiating between types of murderers. Such research could determine whether individuals who commit more senseless or impulsive murders are more likely to show brain dysfunction than those who commit less impulsive and more methodical murders. Additional research is also needed on the interaction of neuropsychological and personality variables in murderers, an area which has been largely neglected.

Discussion

Overall, the results of these studies have demonstrated that there are clear differences on personality, intelligence, and neuropsychological testing between violent and nonviolent criminals and the general population. The test outcomes do not differ between lethal violence and general violence but rather, indicate the propensity for violence and aggression in general.

Neuropsychological theories regarding the etiology of violence appear to integrate these findings for a significant portion of the reported studies. As noted above, such theories hypothesize the presence of frontal lobe damage in individuals with multiple violent episodes. In others, there may be temporal lobe damage either alone or in combination with frontal problems, although frontal theories appear to better account for the bulk of the data. Other violent individuals may have additional damage to other parts of the brain as well, but this additional damage does not appear to increase or decrease the likelihood of violent behavior.

Case Illustration 1. Sandra was a 35-year-old woman married to a 63-year-old millionaire. They had been married for a period of three years when she had an apparent stroke. MRI and CT scans revealed that she had a congenital aneurysm at the base of the middle cerebral artery, which had ruptured while she was riding her horse. The subsequent bleeding into the brain caused widespread damage of the left frontal lobe and, to a lesser degree, the parietal and temporal lobes.

Her symptoms included paralysis on the right side of the body, impairment in speaking and understanding, loss of abstract skills, impairment in problem solving, and misperception of events, along with irritability. After the completion of rehabilitation over six months, she remained largely paralyzed, although she could put a small amount of weight on her leg and could perform some limited pincer grasping with her right hand. Her speech was poor and slow, but could be understood with patience.

Her memory was spotty. She was able to retain less than half of what was said to her. Visual memory was much better. Her social skills remained excellent, which was immediately clear when talking to her. However, the content of her speech and her reasoning were extremely limited when dealing with any kind of novel or unusual situation.

Immediately after returning home from the hospital, her husband informed her that he wanted a divorce, as she was no longer a "real woman." He also told her to forget about receiving any money from the divorce as the money was his and he wouldn't give it up. She didn't know what to do, but friends secured a well-known divorce attorney for her. The attorney obtained a court order which temporarily allowed her to remain in their house with a maid while the husband moved elsewhere.

Sandra and her husband continued to occasionally talk to one another, although she had been instructed to refer his calls to her attorney. During these calls, he persisted in making threats that he would kill her before he would let her have any of his money. This scared her, and she confided in the maid. They both agreed she should protect herself, so the maid bought her a small handgun. Sandra was only able to hold the gun in her left hand but she said it made her feel more secure. She believed that its presence would stop anyone from threatening her. She carried it with her at all times.

Sandra reported that one Saturday morning, her husband came over unannounced and demanded that she give up all rights to his money. After she refused, he told her that she'd better reconsider because he could easily choke her and there was nothing she could do to stop him. When she again refused, he started to approach her slowly, stating that she had gone too far and would have to die. She pulled out the gun and shot all six bullets. Only one bullet hit him, striking the clavicle, and ricocheting into the aorta. According to the coroner, he was less than 12 inches from the barrel of the gun when the shot was fired.

The District Attorney prosecuted the case as first degree murder, arguing that it was premeditated, pointing to the purchase of the gun, and suggesting that Sandra had lured her husband

over to the house with the ostensible motive of killing him to get his money, which she might not have gotten in the divorce. By claiming self defense, she was still in line to inherit the money.

Intellectual testing showed that Sandra had a Verbal IQ of 78 and a Performance IQ of 89. Premorbid estimates from the testing suggested her previous Full Scale IQ was 110. Most of her verbal performance stemmed from tests of past learning, rather than showing evidence of current active skills. Neuropsychological testing with the LNNB and the HRNB confirmed extensive brain damage, mostly in the frontal areas of the brain, but extending into the temporal and parietal areas. Higher cognitive skills, reasoning, judgment, logical analysis, insight, and planning and monitoring skills were all substantially impaired, as were receptive and expressive speech skills. Right-sided motor skills were severely impaired. Left-sided motor skills were in the low average range, as were non-verbal tasks which did not require motor speed or dexterity.

Personality testing with the Rorschach indicated limited reality contact (but no evidence of psychosis), poor emotional control, restricted affect, depression, and primitive responses. She tended to overgeneralize from small details and could not integrate the inkblots as "wholes." She was unaware of her misperceptions. The MMPI was read to her. She had some difficulty understanding some of the items, causing an elevation in the F scale (83). While this scale was elevated, it remained within acceptable ranges for a brain injured individual. The remaining validity scales, L and K, were consistent with a valid profile. The MMPI results suggested that she was acutely depressed and anxious, but did not show signs psychopathic signs. There was extensive denial present, as well as a lack of insight.

From the test results and history, the neuropsychologist argued that Sandra had believed that she was in danger of serious harm. While this was a result of misperception, this mispercep-

tion arose from her limited cognitive abilities and inability to integrate information. It was also made worse by her failure to disclose her fears to more responsible people, like her lawyer, rather than relying on a maid with a sixth grade education. Her belief that the gun would protect her from being attacked was also faulty, as was her belief that her husband was doing anything more than threatening her.

This was all consistent with her faulty thinking and personality style following her injury. She was eventually acquitted by a jury on the charge of murder on the grounds that she believed she was defending herself from substantial bodily harm.

Ironically, after his death, her husband was found to have a frontal lobe tumor. We can only speculate on how this may have affected his behavior during the last days of his life.

While neuropsychological theories are attractive for explaining some types of violent behavior, they cannot account for certain specific types of disorders, such as murder for hire, or murder which is planned and calculated for specific gains. Neuropsychological theories cannot explain murder by individuals who are neurologically intact, although improvements in the detection of brain dysfunction (such as Magnetic Resonance Imaging or Positron Emission Tomography) have allowed clinicians to identify brain injury in individuals once thought to be normal.

The neuropsychological theories suggest that several subtypes of violent individuals can be identified, each with a particular pattern of test results across the neuropsychological, intellectual, and personality domains. Individuals with injuries limited to the pre-frontal area of the brain would be expected to show normal intelligence, as the anterior parts of the brain do not directly modulate psychometric intelligence as measured by the Wechsler tests.

On neuropsychological tests, a pattern of deficits on tests measuring higher level cognitive functions would be expected. Generally, such profiles show extended problems in dealing with novelty, abstraction, problem solving, sustained attention, and complex memory functions. However, they also show normal basic abilities in speech and basic construction abilities.

Face to face, such individuals appear normal on the surface. MMPI results may indicate a 49 psychopathic profile or the 43 profile found among many murderers. Some profiles suggestive of schizophrenia are also found among this group. Rorschach profiles are generally impoverished, with the individuals having difficulty seeing anything in the ambiguous inkblots. The answers which are given may have unusual themes, dealing with organic issues or with body parts. In some cases, purely confabulatory responses, which have little or nothing to do with the inkblot itself, may be elicited.

Other violent individuals may show highly focal temporal lobe disorders which result in temporal lobe epilepsy. In these individuals, overall neuropsychological and intellectual profiles are frequently normal. Isolated memory deficits may be present, especially with the formation of new memories. Even EEG profiles will be normal over 50% of the time in temporal lobe epilepsy (Golden et al., 1992). Personality testing on the MMPI may show a relatively normal profile or evidence of hysteria (Scale 3) and hypochondriasis (Scale 1). Over time, such individuals may develop depression and anxiety (Scales 2 and 7) because of the unpredictability of their symptoms and their inability to understand their own behavior.

More common than the violent individual with a highly focal temporal lobe disorder, is the violent individual with a more widespread involvement of the entire temporal lobe. Such disorders may occur after strokes, head traumas, or gun shot wounds. As more of the temporal lobe is involved, there are more widespread and obvious deficits. If the temporal lobe in the left hemisphere is involved, the individual can develop a receptive aphasia, in which he or she is unable to understand speech. Such cases may result in losses in measured intelligence, especially on verbal tests. Verbal memory will be substantially impaired. This will result in substantially reduced Verbal IQ when compared to Performance IQ. Such individuals are unable to complete an MMPI or Rorschach due to their speech disorders.

When the right temporal lobe is involved, the violent individual may show some losses on intellectual testing, especially on the Picture Arrangement subtest of the WAIS-R, which measures the ability of the individual to place pictures from a story in order. Problems are often seen in repeating numbers backwards (Digit Span). Deficits may also arise in the Block Design (organizing block into patterns) and Arithmetic subtests. Some differences may be seen between the Verbal and Performance IQ, with the Verbal IQ being higher.

On neuropsychological tests, difficulties will be seen in novel or complex non-verbal tasks, such as drawing and construction. Non-verbal memory deficits will be evident, sometimes even on short-term, as well as long-term, memory.

In right temporal injuries, MMPI results may reflect little insight into the individual's condition and may even appear to be a "fake good" profile. Profiles may also suggest hysteria and denial and be misinterpreted as suggesting a psychological, rather than an organic, etiology to the problems. On the Rorschach, the individual's answers are basic and primitive because of difficulty dealing with the complexity and ambiguity of the cards. The individual may choose to respond to small parts of the overall picture which suggest concrete simple objects.

Profiles from violent individuals with more diffuse injuries will vary depending on the exact nature and extent of the lesion. The testing profiles will include major aspects of some of the deficits which have already been discussed. Diffuse lesions which arise in early childhood are common, caused by birth problems, genetics, early head trauma, child abuse, early malnutrition, medical disorders (such as encephalitis), and lead poisoning. Such individuals have a history of poor school performance and generally poor skills at adapting to the responsibilities of adulthood.

On intelligence tests, the violent individual may show equally depressed scores on Performance and Verbal IQ or may show higher Performance than Verbal scores. Among the verbal subtests, the Information, Comprehension, and Vocabulary subtests, which tend to be the highest in profiles of individuals injured as adults, are found to be among the lowest scores.

Neuropsychological testing generally shows widespread problems. Although basic skills, such as walking, talking, and seeing may be normal, all higher level skills, including complex language, sustained attention, memory (especially verbal memory), problem solving, judgment, insight, grammar, syntactical skills, spatial relations, reading, writing, and mathematics are generally found to be impaired.

Performance on personality tests are likely to be poor. MMPI items generally cannot be read or understood, causing profiles which appear invalid. Reading the test to the individual may improve the profile, but the overall impression generally remains one of diffuse psychopathology with indications of introversion, psychopathia, schizophrenia, anxiety, and paranoia. If the test is administered in jail, signs of depression are likely as well. Rorschachs are highly variable, but generally abnormal, with difficulty shown in integrating the images from the inkblots.

Neuropsychological test scores are usually substantially impaired with diffuse injuries. These impairments range from all verbally based skills (left hemisphere injuries) to all nonverbally based skills (right hemisphere injuries). A significant number of cerebral injuries will produce motor and sensory deficits, which can be limited to one side or found bilaterally.

Guidelines for Assessment

The major role of these tests is understanding the cognitive and personality factors which may influence the development of lethal violence in a given individual. Thus, any examination must yield a comprehensive assessment of intellectual, personality, and neuropsychological functions. Each area yields a different perspective on the overall functioning of the individual and his or her ability to deal with the stresses and realities of life.

Intelligence testing, primarily the WAIS-R, should be included to give a general level of functioning. Overall, higher IQs are suggestive of more adaptive skills and indicative of more planning skills. The absence of such skills argues against the individual being involved as the primary planner in complex or well-organized criminal activity. IQ scores may indicate longstanding disorders which can be traced back to childhood and require investigation. These scores also add to the overall neuropsychological examination and the personality testing. Personality problems in the presence of low intelligence appear to become more serious.

Personality testing provides insight into an individual's way of perceiving the world. This is important in determining whether an individual's explanation of his or her behavior makes sense psychologically. Thus, if an individual contends that a violent episode was accidental rather than intended, a personality profile suggesting a benign and passive personality would be supportive of such an alibi, while a profile indicating extensive rage and hostility would contradict the explanation. In most cases, personality (and cognitive) correlates can be drawn between various possible scenarios for criminal events which can aid in identifying which alternatives are the most likely.

Neuropsychological testing in conjunction with intelligence testing yields a comprehensive picture of the individual's cognitive status. This generates a picture of the individual's ability to deal with specific stimuli, provides insights into how he or she processes and understands information, and allows us to understand how organic processes can cause increased irritability and aggression or result in an inability to comprehend or understand the consequences of one's behavior. In cases where temporal lobe epilepsy or frontal lobe injuries are alleged, the tests can support or disconfirm such etiologies.

The results of all of the testing must be integrated with the facts of the case generated from the accused, witnesses, police reports, and other sources of data. Final interpretations must include an intensive study of the physical and forensic facts of the case so as to reach conclusions which are consistent with all that is known of the episode of lethal violence. Used in this manner, hypotheses and conclusions can be generated which may be useful in several aspects of the forensic investigation of the case.

This information can be used effectively in determining possible mitigating circumstances in a trial, as well as in making appropriate treatment decisions and prognostic statements. In mitigation to murder, comprehensive testing offers insights into the defendant's behavior and provides methods of explaining such behaviors to a jury and judge. Moreover, such data may provide empirical support for the statements by an accused, so that his or her assertions do not stand alone without support. In cases where the individual is unable to explain his or her behavior, testing can provide insights into understanding the person's motivations and cognitive status.

Testing may also be used in determining such issues as competence to stand trial, although current applications of competency laws in many jurisdictions fail to take neuropsychological deficits into account as factors in such determinations. As a consequence, some individuals with "normal" intelligence but impaired frontal lobe skills resulting in an inability to truly comprehend the effects of their behavior, cooperate with their attorney, and to fully assist in their own defense, are ruled as competent.

Case Illustration 2. *Michael was a 27-year-old Caucasian male with a tenth grade education. His childhood development was unremarkable until he was in an automobile accident at age 15. He was an unrestrained passenger in a head-on collision which resulted in head trauma as well as a broken leg. He was unconscious for 48 hours. He was treated for 10 days in the acute unit of the hospital. He was subsequently released to return home with physical therapy, but no psychological treatment. A neurological assessment at the time of discharge reported no cognitive difficulties. No neuropsychological testing was conducted.*

After returning to school, he performed adequately initially but his performance began to deteriorate within one month. He appeared to students and teachers as impulsive and irritable. Over a 12-month period, he lost most of his friends and his grades declined from a 3.6 average in the semester before his injury to a 1.4 average in the semester after his injury. He was nevertheless promoted to the 11th grade, where his performance showed even more impairment. He was arrested for the first time for shoplifting, and was suspended from school for fighting.

He eventually dropped out of school. He attempted to work, holding a variety of menial jobs. None of the jobs lasted longer than two months. At age 21, he was arrested for assault and battery. He was incarcerated for 18 months and received an additional two-year probationary period. At age 24, while on probation, he was in another automobile accident, in which he was unconscious for 18 hours. In the hospital, he was combative. A psychiatric evaluation indicated a post-concussion syndrome and suggested that his aggressiveness was related to his premorbid aggressive tendencies. He was released with the

suggestion that he seek therapy. As a result of a lack of money and a lack of insight, he never attempted to begin therapy.

After the second accident, his behavior declined in social and occupational activities. He began to drink and get into barroom brawls. He contended that he did not start these fights, but that someone would "persecute" and "attack" him, forcing him to defend himself. He was vague about what he meant by those terms and could not give any clear examples. He was arrested three times for brawls, but no formal charges were filed. Occupationally, his work record declined further. He held fewer jobs and for shorter periods of time. He supported himself through occasional jobs, welfare, and unemployment insurance. He denied getting money from any illegal activities.

At age 27, he was in a bar attempting to converse with a woman. He claimed to have been acting appropriately when "out of nowhere" a man accused him of being rude and attacked him. He stated that he was forced to defend himself. In the process, he struck the man, who fell backward and hit his head on a sharp corner of a table. The table cracked the man's skull and penetrated the brain stem, causing almost instantaneous death.

Witnesses at the scene suggested an alternative scenario. They said that Michael was being rude and irritating to several women in the bar. The witnesses and the bartender agreed that he had not been drinking significantly (one beer), but had been focusing on any woman who looked like she was alone. He had started to inappropriately touch one of the females when a companion asked him to stop. Michael immediately exploded, accusing the man of "following" him and being "out to get him." According to these witnesses, Michael invited the man to settle this dispute "outside." When the man refused and turned his back, Michael attacked him and struck the blow that resulted in the man's death.

After his arrest and being charged with first

degree murder, Michael was seen for a comprehensive neuropsychological examination. Intelligence testing on the WAIS-R indicated a Verbal IQ of 97 and a Performance IQ of 101. Premorbid indicators on the testing estimated that his IQ may have been as high as 105 at one time, suggesting perhaps minimal intellectual loss.

Neuropsychological testing using both the LNNB and HRNB indicated the presence of substantial frontal lobe impairment. On the HRNB, he showed normal performance on the Aphasia Examination (no errors) and on the Sensory Perceptual Examination (three errors overall). He also showed normal motor speed on the Finger Oscillation Test with a tapping speed of 52 for the dominant hand and 48 for the non-dominant hand.

He showed mild deficits on the Speech Sounds Perception Test (9 errors) and the Rhythm Test (7 errors), which appeared related to concentration problems. His performance on the Category Test was extremely impaired (98 errors). This arose from his inability to generate hypotheses and to respond appropriately to feedback. His Tactual Performance Test (TPT) was also impaired, with a Total Time of 18 minutes and 30 seconds. The TPT Memory score (7) was normal, but the Location score (4) was impaired. His performance demonstrated an inability to derive a logical plan for solving the test, as well as perseverative behavior even when he was failing.

Performance on the LNNB showed intact functioning in basic receptive language, basic expressive language, reading, visual-spatial skills, and basic motor skills. He showed elevated scores on Receptive Language (64), due entirely to more complex items requiring verbal analysis. He also showed a mildly elevated score on Expressive Language (66), again due to more complex items which required generation of speech with some intellectual content.

The Memory Scale (72) was also impaired. He generally missed items in which there was extended list learning or interference of some kind. He also showed impairment on Writing (62) and Arithmetic (63), and borderline performance on Tactile (58), Rhythm (56), and Intelligence (59). In all cases, he had difficulty concentrating and solving items with more than one part.

In an individual with normal premorbid intelligence, it is expected that at least 4 to 6 of the scales would show scores below 50. In his case, none of the scores fell below this level. This finding is characteristic of individuals with frontal lobe problems, as is the general difficulty with complex items, generation of speech, problem solving, and flexibility shown during the testing.

Personality testing on the MMPI and Rorschach indicated an individual who was very egocentric, with tenuous controls over his emotions. He had weak contact with reality, and tended to interpret things in a very concrete and highly egocentric manner. He was depressed at the time of the evaluations, probably as a result of what he considered as his unfair confinement. He showed few positive emotions, but a wealth of negative feelings of persecution and unfairness. While he was not psychotic, he frequently misinterpreted the meaning of events around him.

On the basis of these findings, it was indicated that Michael had suffered a frontal lobe injury which caused substantial impairment in his ability to interpret the world around him, in his level of emotional control, and in his insight, and increased his irritability. His history showed that he had been injured at the time of his accident at age 15, which had resulted in an overall decline in the immediate period following the injury. He may have suffered a second injury as well at age 24 from his second accident. After the second accident, there was increased inappropriate behavior and a substantial jump in his aggressive behavior.

While the witnesses' reports suggested that Michael had initiated the fight, his impairments made it impossible for him to recognize his con-

tribution. He believed that he was defending himself and his honor from someone who was persecuting him. It was noted that this was consistent with the eyewitness reports, as well as Michael's overall demeanor in jail.

Alcohol may have played a role in this incident as well, although Michael was not seen at this time or other times as a heavy drinker. His interest in bars arose more from a desire for social interaction than to drink. On the night of the incident, he had reportedly had only one beer. However, we need to recognize that in individuals with brain injury, cognitive processes may be compromised by only a small amount of alcohol. As a result, he may have shown more cognitive compromise at that time than shown later on the testing.

Evaluation by a psychiatrist retained by the prosecution confirmed that the defendant had been involved in several accidents and may have had some minor damage, but generally downplayed the role of cognitive and emotional impairment. An eventual plea bargain to manslaughter was reached on the basis of this data.

Future Research

Heilbrun (1979) has suggested, and we concur, that violence and murder are multidetermined behaviors which do not hinge on any single propensity or attribute. Most of the research to date has been overly simplistic, limiting the number of variables considered and failing to examine their interaction.

Researchers and clinicians should focus on an interactional model which examines the effects of many variables, including intellectual, personality, and neuropsychological factors, in addition to environmental factors. We need a comprehensive approach which examines history, a wide range of personality factors, intelligence, brain function, attitudes, and personal circumstances as well.

Such research would likely need to focus on both the issues of aggression and lethal violence. As has been seen, the patterns of deficits across each of the areas examined in this chapter are quite similar for individuals with many forms of aggressive behavior. Prospective studies of individuals with histories of violence who are returning to society could be especially useful. In such studies, the individual could be examined with a wide array of personality, intellectual, and neuropsychological instruments and then followed over periods of 1, 5, and 10 years. At each measurement point, the individual could be classified by the degree and amount of aggression which had occurred in the interim to determine which factors were predictive of the eventual behavior. Such studies would need to examine the environment of the individual as well as cognitive and personality factors so that the interaction of all of these components could be examined.

In the absence of prospective research, studies need to focus on the interaction of intellectual, personality, and neuropsychological factors in differentiating between violent and nonviolent individuals, as well as between subgroups of violent individuals separated on such dimensions as type of crime, victim, and frequency. While studies with only personality or neuropsychological testing have yielded interesting results, the full understanding of lethal violence can emerge only from understanding all of these influences.

Future research also needs to examine the use of new instrumentation and techniques in measuring these factors. With the MMPI, the continued development of typologies and special scales is a likely area for future success. Neuropsychological measures may need to be refined to take into account the varying cultural and educational levels of individuals who have committed lethal violence.

Psychometric tests offer a powerful tool into the mind and behavior of the lethal offender. More focused and comprehensive research can only add to our understanding and sophistication when working with such individuals. Hopefully, this will not only aid us in forensic activities, but also lead us into new avenues of prevention and treatment.

Annotated Bibliography

Bryant, E., Scott, M., Golden, C., & Tori, C. (1984). Neuropsychological deficits, learning disability, and violent behavior. *Journal of Consulting and Clinical Psychology, 52,* 323-324. One of the earliest comprehensive studies examining the relationship between brain function and violence.

Golden, C. J., Zillmer, E., & Spiers, M. (1992). *Neuropsychological Assessment and Rehabilitation.* Springfield, IL: Charles C Thomas. This book reviews the basic theory and practice of neuropsychology, providing a background for the understanding of the relationships between violence an brain function.

Levin, H. S., Eisenberg, H. M., & Benton, A. L. (Eds.). (1991) *Frontal Lobe Function and Dysfunction.* New York, NY: Oxford University Press. An excellent detailed evaluation of frontal lobe functions.

Luria, A. R. (1980). *Higher Cortical Functions in Man* (2nd ed.). New York, NY: Basic Books. This is a very densely written volume that must be considered a major contribution to the understanding of brain disorders.

Perrine, K. & Congett, S. (1994). Neurobehavioral problems in epilepsy. *Neurologic Clinics, 12,* 129-152. An outstanding summary of the behavioral problems seen with epilepsy including episodes of violence.

References

American Psychiatric Association (1968). *Diagnostic and statistical manual of mental disorders* (1st ed.). Washington, DC: Author.

Ansevics, N. L. & Doweiko, H. E. (1991). Serial murderers: Early proposed developmental model and typology. *Psychotherapy in Private Practice, 9,* 107-122.

Barratt, E. (1993). The use of anticonvulsants in aggression and violence. *Psychopharmacology Bulletin, 29,* 75-81.

Beck, S. J. (1949). *Rorschach's test.* New York: Grune & Stratton.

Bond, M. R. (1984). The psychiatry of closed head injury. In D. N. Brooks (Ed.), *Closed head injury: Psychological, social, and family consequences.* New York: Oxford University Press.

Bryant, E., Scott, M., Golden, C., & Tori, C. (1984). Neuropsychological deficits, learning disability, and violent behavior. *Journal of Consulting and Clinical Psychology, 52,* 323-324.

Buck, J. A. & Graham, J. R. (1978). The 4-3 MMPI profile type: A failure to replicate. *Journal of Consulting and Clinical Psychology, 46,* 344.

Catell, R. B. & Catell, A. K. S. (1958). *IPAT culture free intelligence test.* Champaign, IL: Institute of Personality and Ability Testing.

Davis, K. R. & Sines, J. O. (1971). An antisocial behavior pattern associated with a specific MMPI profile. *Journal of Consulting and Clinical Psychology, 36,* 229-234.

Eber, H. W. (1974). Some psychometric correlates of inmate behavior. *Georgia Journal of Corrections, 1,* 1-14.

Elliott, F. A. (1992). Violence: The neurologic contribution: An overview. *Archives of Neurology, 49,* 595-603.

Exner, J. (1986). *The Rorschach: A comprehensive system: Volume 1: Foundations* (2nd. ed.). New York, NY: John Wiley & Sons.

Fraboni, M., Cooper, D., Reed, T. L., & Saltstone, R. (1990). Offense type and two-point MMPI code profiles: Discriminating between violent and nonviolent offenders. *Journal of Clinical Psychology, 46,* 774-777.

Gacono, C. (1992). Sexual homicide and the Rorschach: A Rorschach case study of sexual homicide. *British Journal of Projective Psychology, 37,* 1-21.

Gacono, C. & Meloy, J. R. (1991). A Rorschach investigation of attachment and anxiety in antisocial personality disorder. *Journal of Nervous and Mental Disease, 179,* 546-552.

Golden, C. J., Hammeke, T., & Purisch, A. (1980). *A manual for the Luria-Nebraska neuropsychological battery (Revised).* Los Angeles, CA: Western Psychological Services.

Golden, C. J., Purisch, A. D., & Hammeke, T. A. (1985). *Luria-Nebraska Neuropsychological Battery: Forms I & II.* Los Angeles, CA: Western Psychological Services.

Golden, C. J., Zillmer, E., & Spiers, M. (1992). *Neuropsychological assessment and rehabilitation.* Springfield, IL: Charles C Thomas.

Gynther, M. D., Altman, A., & Warbin, R. W. (1973). A new actuarial-empirical automated MMPI interpretive program: The 4-3/3-4 code type. *Journal of Clinical Psychology, 29,* 229-231.

Halstead, W. D. (1947). *Brain and intelligence: A quantitative study of the frontal lobes.* Chicago, IL: University of Chicago Press.

Hart, T. & Jacobs, H. (1993). Rehabilitation and management of behavioral disturbances following frontal lobe injury. *Journal of Head Trauma and Rehabilitation, 8,* 1-12.

Heilbrun, A. B. (1979). Psychopathy and violent crime. *Journal of Consulting and Clinical Psychology, 47,* 509-516.

Heilbrun, A. B. (1990a). The measurement of criminal dangerousness as a personality construct: Further validation of a research index. *Journal of Personality Assessment, 54,* 141-148.

Heilbrun, A. B. (1990b). Differentiation of death-row murderers and life-sentence murderers by antisociality and intelligence measures. *Journal of Personality Assessment, 54,* 617-627.

Holcomb, W. R. & Adams, N. (1983). The inner-domain among personality and cognition variables in people who commit murder. *Journal of Personality Assessment, 47,* 524-530.

Holcomb, W. R., Adams, N. A., & Ponder, H. M. (1985). The development and cross-validation of an MMPI typology for murderers. *Journal of Personality Assessment, 49,* 240-244.

Holcomb, W. R., Adams, N. A., Ponder, H. M., & Anderson, W. P. (1984). Cognitive and behavioral predictors of MMPI scores in pretrial psychological evaluations of murderers. *Journal of Clinical Psychology, 40,* 592-597.

Ingram, J. C., Marchioni, P., Hill, G., Caraveo-Ramos, E., & McNeil, B. (1985). Recidivism, perceived problem-solving abilities, MMPI characteristics, and violence: A study of black and white incarcerated male adult offenders. *Journal of Clinical Psychology, 41,* 425-432.

Kahn, M. W. (1959). A comparison of personality, intelligence, and social history of two criminal groups. *Journal of Social Psychology, 49*, 33-40.

Kaplan, H. I., Sadock, B. J., & Grebb, J. A. (1994). *Synopsis of psychiatry* (7th ed.). Baltimore, MD: Williams and Wilkins.

Kaplan, J. (1899). Kopftrauma und psychosen. *Allgemeiner Zeitschrift Fur Psychiatrie, 56*, 292-297.

Kaser-Boyd, N. (1993). Rorschachs of women who commit homicide. *Journal of Personality Assessment, 60*, 458-470.

Kellogg, C. E. & Morton, N. W. (1957). *Revised beta examination* (Rev. ed.). New York, NY: Psychological Corporation.

Keltikangas-Jarvinen, L. (1978). Personality characteristics of homicides and assaulters. *Psychiatria Fennica, 1*, 65-71.

Kennedy, T. (1986). Trends in inmate classification: A status report of two computerized psychometric approaches. *Criminal Justice and Behavior, 13*, 165-184.

Krynicki, V. E. (1978). Cerebral dysfunction in repetitively assaultive adolescents. *Journal of Nervous and Mental Disease, 166*, 59-67.

Kunce, J. T., Ryan, J. J., & Eckelman, C. C. (1976). Violent behavior and differential WAIS characteristics. *Journal of Consulting and Clinical Psychology, 44*, 42-45.

Langevin, R., Ben-Aron, M., Wortzman, G., Dickey, R., & Handy, L. (1987). Brain damage, diagnosis, and substance abuse among violent offenders. *Behavioral Sciences & the Law, 5*, 77-94.

Lewis, D. O. & Pincus, J. H. (1989). Epilepsy and violence: Evidence for a neuropsychotic-aggressive syndrome. *Journal of Neuropsychiatry, 1*, 413-418.

Lewis, D. O., Pincus, J. H., Bard, B., Richardson, E., Prichep, L., Feldman, M., & Yeager, C. (1988). Neuropsychiatric, psychoeducational and family characteristics of 14 juveniles condemned to death in the United States. *American Journal of Psychiatry, 145*, 584-589.

Lewis, D. O., Pincus, J. H., & Feldman, M. (1986). Psychiatric, neurological and psychoeducational characteristics of 15 death row inmates in the United States. *American Journal of Psychiatry, 143*, 838-845.

Lewis, D. O., Pincus, J. H., Shanok, S. S., & Glaser, G. H. (1982). Psychomotor epilepsy and violence in an incarcerated adolescent population. *American Journal of Psychiatry, 139*, 882-887.

Lewis, D. O. & Shanok, S. (1977). Medical histories of delinquent and nondelinquent children: An epidemiological study. *American Journal of Psychiatry, 134*, 1020-1025.

Lewis, D. O. & Shanok, S. (1979). Perinatal difficulties, head, and face trauma and child abuse in the medical histories of seriously delinquent children. *American Journal of Psychiatry, 136*, 419-423.

Lezak, M. (1995). *Neuropsychological assessment* (3rd ed.). New York, NY: Oxford University Press.

Luria, A. R. (1980). *Higher cortical functions in man* (2nd ed.). New York, NY: Basic Books.

Mark, V. H. & Ervin, F. R. (1970). *Violence and the brain*. New York, NY: Harper & Row.

Mattson, A. & Levin, H. (1990). Frontal lobe dysfunction following closed head injury: A review of the literature. *The Journal of Nervous and Mental Disease, 178*, 282-291.

Meninger, K. & Mayman, M. (1956). Episodic dyscontrol: A third order of stress adaptation. *Bulletin of the Meninger Clinic, 20*, 153-160.

Miller, L. (1990). Major syndromes of aggressive behavior following head injury: An introduction to evaluation and treatment. *Cognitive Rehabilitation, 8*, 14-23.

Panton, J. H. (1958). MMPI profile configurations among crime classification groups. *Journal of Clinical Psychology, 14*, 305-308.

Perdue, W. C. & Lester, D. (1973). Those who murder kin: A Rorschach study. *Perceptual and Motor Skills, 36*, 606.

Perrine, K. & Congett, S. (1994). Neurobehavioral problems in epilepsy. *Neurologic Clinics, 12*, 129-152.

Persons, R. W. & Marks, P. A. (1971). The violent 4-3 MMPI personality type. *Journal of Consulting and Clinical Psychology, 36*, 189-196.

Petee, T. A. & Walsh, A. (1986). Violent delinquency, race, and the Wechsler performance-verbal discrepancy. *Journal of Social Psychology, 127*, 353-354.

Pincus, J. H. (1985). Limbic system and violence. In J. H. Pincus & G. J. Tucker (Eds.), *Behavioral neurology* (3rd ed.). Oxford: Oxford University Press.

Piotrowski, Z. A. (1957). *Perceptanalysis.* New York, NY: Macmillan.

Robertson, G., Taylor, P. J., & Gunn, J. C. (1987). Does violence have cognitive correlates? *British Journal of Psychiatry, 151*, 63-68.

Ruff, C. F., Templer, D. I., & Ayers, J. L. (1976). The intelligence of rapists. *Archives of Sexual Behavior, 5*, 327-329.

Schafer, R. (1954). *Psychoanalytic interpretation in Rorschach testing.* New York, NY: Grune & Stratton.

Shawver, L. & Jew, C. (1978). Predicting violent behavior from WAIS characteristics: A replication failure. *Journal of Consulting and Clinical Psychology, 46*, 206.

Spellacy, F. (1977). Neuropsychological differences between violent and nonviolent adolescents. *Journal of Clinical Psychology, 33*, 966-969.

Stuss, D. & Benson, F. (1986). Neuropsychological studies of the frontal lobes. *Psychological Bulletin, 95*, 3-28.

Syverson, K. L. & Romney, D. M. (1985). A further attempt to differentiate violent from nonviolent offenders by means of a battery of psychological tests. *Canadian Journal of Behavioural Science, 17*, 87-92.

Tarter, R. E., Hegedus, A. M., Winsten, N. E., & Alterman, A. I. (1984). Intellectual profiles and violent behavior in juvenile delinquents. *The Journal of Psychology, 119*, 125-128.

Truscott, D. (1990). Assessment of overcontrolled hostility in adolescence. *Journal of Consulting and Clinical Psychology, 2*, 145-148.

Valliant, P. M., Asu, M. E., Cooper, D., & Mammola, D. (1984). Profile of dangerous and non-dangerous offenders referred for pre-trial psychiatric assessment. *Psychological Reports, 54*, 411-418.

Walsh, A. & Beyer, J. A. (1986). Wechsler Performance-Verbal discrepancy and antisocial behavior. *Journal of Social Psychology, 126*, 419-420.

Wechsler, D. (1981). *Wechsler adult intelligence scale.* New York, NY: The Psychological Corporation.

Wood, R. L. (1987). *Brain injury rehabilitation: A neurobehavioral approach.* Rockville, MD: Aspen.

About the Authors

Dr. Charles Golden is Professor of Psychology at Nova Southeastern University in Fort Lauderdale, Florida. He has published over 200 books and articles in the area of psychological and neuropsychological assessment. He is board certified in clinical psychology and clinical neuropsychology and has extensive clinical experience with the evaluation of individuals charged with lethal violence.

Michele Jackson is a student working on her doctorate degree, as well as employed full time as a forensic social worker with the Public Defender's office of Dade County, Florida. Her work primarily involves evaluation of inmates charged with capital crimes.

Samuel T. Gontkovsky and Angela Peterson-Rohne are doctoral students in the clinical psychology program at Nova Southeastern University. Mr. Gontkovsky has strong interests in neuropsychology, while Ms. Peterson-Rohne has specialized in working with men who batter their wives.

CHAPTER **19**

MMPI-BASED PSYCHOLOGICAL ASSESSMENT OF LETHAL VIOLENCE

Robert J. Craig

This chapter deals with a specific type of assessment — psychometric assessment using objective personality tests. While a comprehensive psychological evaluation of an individual defendant recognizes and utilizes all sources of data (e.g., clinical interviews, collateral sources, patient records, forensic and police reports), this chapter only discusses assessment using objective personality tests. Hence, it is more limited than in actual clinical practice, where psychometric test findings are integrated with other sources of information.

By objective psychological tests, we mean standardized instruments or inventories which present the test taker with a limited number of response options. The test taker answers either "true or false," "a, b, or c," "yes, no, or maybe." Hence, these tests are easily scored because one is only required to sum the responses in these few categories. Objective psychological tests tend to be more reliable than personality tests using subjective interpretation, such as the projective tests (i.e., Thematic Apperception Test, TAT; Figure Drawings, etc.). Because of the standardized material, limited response options, and better reliability, objective tests of personality lend themselves to more objective interpretation. Hence, they are often more valid than other types of assessment devices or methodologies.

The most frequently used objective tests for the assessment of personality include the Minnesota Multiphasic Personality Inventory (MMPI; Hathaway & McKinley, 1940), and it's revision, the MMPI-2 (Butcher, Dahlstrom, Graham, Tellegen, & Kaemmer, 1989), the Millon Clinical Multiaxial Personality Inventory-III (MCMI-III; Millon, 1994), the California Psychological Inventory-Revised (CPI-R; Gough, 1987), and the Sixteen Personality Factors (16PF; Cattell, 1989). The MMPI/MMPI-2 has been the most frequently used psychological test with murderers.

Because there is a substantial literature base with this test for this population, and because there have been several assessment refinements, particularly in the area of developing homogeneous patient profiles and in developing special scales from the MMPI item pool, this chapter presents only MMPI-derived studies that have assessed murderers.

Overview and Epidemiology

There are several issues that need to be understood prior to discussing research findings using the MMPI:

1. All of the research has assessed the patient and presented empirical group data after

the commission of the crime and after the perpetrator has been apprehended. The patient's psychological state prior to the commission of the offense is a matter of conjecture, interpolation, and judgment. The offender's psychological state at the time of the assessment is what is actually being measured. The psychological effects of imprisonment itself might also be reflected in test findings (Westermeyer, 1974).

2. Timing of the assessment may affect test results. An offender who is tested in conjunction with a hearing to determine competency to stand trial or while addressing other pretrial evaluation issues in association with an insanity plea, might show different test results than an offender who is tested as part of a research protocol after he or she has been sentenced and is confined in prison for a determined length of time (Finney, Skeeters, Auvenshine, & Smith, 1973; Holcomb, Adams, Nicholas, Ponder, & Anderson, 1984; Panton, 1976).

3. Perpetrators of lethal violence are a heterogeneous population. Intuitively, one would believe that the political assassin or gangland hit man would have different personality traits and motivations than the armed robber who, based on circumstances, goes too far and kills a store employee. The fired employee who returns to the scene of his former employment with a shotgun, killing those in his path, is certainly driven by different psychological forces than the chronically abused housewife who, after sustaining years of physical abuse, engages in a violent and lethal act out of desperation. The drug dealer who was "burned" by a street addict and arranges for a substantial increase in the heroin content of a "bag" which, when injected, results in a lethal overdose, is operating from a different psychological framework than the man who murders while drunk. The point is that these differences must be addressed methodologically and understood psychologically in order for us to have a full accounting of the personality and motives of those who commit murder.

4. Moderator variables are variables which, in themselves, have the capacity to alter scores on tests. The moderator variables that have been most researched are race, gender, and educational level (and its correlates — IQ, social status, and occupational status) (Holcomb & Adams, 1982; Holcomb, Adams, & Ponder, 1984). For example, McDonald and Paitich (1981) found that variables that differentiated murderers from non-murderous felons disappeared when they were compared to people who were unemployed. Researchers and the individual psychologist evaluating an individual patient must consider these variables and how they may have affected scores on the test (Sutker & Moan, 1973).

5. Finally, there are problems with self-report methodology as a method of personality assessment. First, the patient has to have some self-understanding and self-awareness. Second, the patient must be willing to report that knowledge in an unbiased and truthful manner. However, in forensic settings, there are a myriad of motivations that might compel an offender to lie, exaggerate, fake illness, or underreport certain key problems that could be detrimental to the defendant at trial. Malingering, defined as the voluntary production of false or grossly exaggerated physical or psychological symptoms for purposes of secondary gain, may be common among murderers. In fact, a significant number of patients awaiting trial claim amnesia and attribute it to alcohol, drug use, or some emotional block related to the facts of the crime (Parwatikar, Holcomb, & Menninger, 1985). While the MMPI has scales that screen for such tendencies, the psychologist, clinician, or researcher must take such factors into consideration when writing a report or when publishing test findings.

The MMPI as a Measuring Instrument

In this section, a brief history of the MMPI is presented, along with how it purports to measure underlying constructs. The MMPI was originally developed in the late 1930s to assess the major psychopathologies that were then extant and of interest to psychiatrists for both diagnostic and descriptive purposes. Starke R. Hathaway, a psychologist at the University of Minnesota, working in conjunction with J. Charnley McKinley, a neurosurgeon at the University of Minnesota Hospital, began the task by developing an item pool of over 1000 items. Hathaway and McKinley extracted items from then current inventories and added items of interest using a rational approach to item development. A giant step in assessment methodology was achieved when they required patients in clinical groups to show statistical differences in item responses from groups of people considered normal. This has come to be known as the method of empirical criterion keying or the method of group differences, and is now the standard methodology by which scales are developed.

Hathaway and McKinley began with a number of items which tapped areas of interest and then determined which items in the criterion group were endorsed differentially by the criterion group compared to a group of normals. In this methodology, it doesn't matter why the criterion group answered an item in a particular direction; it only matters that they answered it one way and the normals answered it another way. These groups of items then became known as scales. Hathaway and McKinley were initially interested in eight clinical syndromes consisting of Hypocondriasis (Hs), Depression (Dep), Hysteria (Hy), Psychopathic Deviance (Pd), Paranoia (Pa), Psychasthenia (Pt) (an older psychiatric term that referred to nervous anxiety), Schizophrenia (Sc), and Hypomania (Ma). They then tried to develop a scale that would distinguish between normal males and homosexual males without other psychopathology. This was done because, at the time, homosexuality was considered a psychopathology, whereas today, it has been removed from psychiatric nomenclature. Because they were unable to

devise a scale that successfully differentiated a heterosexual male from a homosexual male, they created a scale that measured stereotypic masculine and feminine interests (MF). Validity scales were added that were designed to detect lying, exaggerating, or underreporting actual problems. The test was published in 1940. Shortly thereafter, a special scale, called Social Introversion (Si), was developed by an independent researcher and became attached to the test, thus creating a test with three validity scales and ten clinical scales.

The test became popular immediately, perhaps because of its excellent standardization procedures and, more likely, because of its clinical utility. A spate of research about the test began to be published and, after about ten years of research, strange results began to be reported. The original idea of the test was that a representative member of a clinical group, i.e., a schizophrenic, would score higher on the Sc scale, than would a non-schizophrenic. Similarly, a psychopath would be expected to score in clinically elevated ranges on the Pd scale, but non-psychopaths would not. However, non-schizophrenics were scoring in elevated ranges on the Sc scale and non-psychopaths were scoring higher on the Pd scale than expected. Consequently, researchers began to determine which extra-test traits, symptoms, and characteristics are associated with elevations on each of the clinical scales. Furthermore, certain traits and symptoms were associated with a given scale at one range, but a different set of traits and characteristics were associated at another range of scores. Hence, clinicians who use the MMPI regularly rarely refer to a scale by its original name. Rather, numbers have been assigned to the clinical scales so that clinicians and researchers refer to a scale by its number, as follows: Hypocondriasis (1), Depression (2), Hysteria (3), Psychopathic Deviance (4), Masculinity/Femininity (5), Paranoia (6), Psychasthenia (7), Schizophrenia (8), Hypomania (9), and Social Introversion (10).

Despite its immense popularity, through the

years there developed a number of problems. Some of the test items were outdated, some of the language was sexist, some of the items were considered offensive, particularly items that addressed religious practices and sexual preferences, and items dealing with bowel and bladder functioning were criticized. There was also a debate on whether or not the test was racially biased, because no minorities were used in the original standardization sample.

Additionally, in attempting to adapt the MMPI to other cultures, some items were lost in translation. For example, one MMPI item asked whether the respondent thought that Abraham Lincoln was greater than George Washington. This item, in its literal form, has no equivalent in other cultures. Furthermore, there has been a drastic change in items that are considered "masculine" or "feminine." Due to these and other issues, the original MMPI was considered out of date, even though it continued to be useful clinically.

As a result, a committee of prominent MMPI researchers and clinicians was formed to restandardize the test. The committee went to great efforts to ensure that research knowledge from the original MMPI was applicable to its revision and the current evidence is that they were quite successful in this regard. Thus, much of our knowledge about murderers that was derived from the MMPI should be applicable to research using the MMPI-2.

Psychometric Assessment of Perpetrators of Lethal Violence

There have been three types of studies that have used the MMPI on murderers. The first type of study compares MMPI profiles of murders to some other control group. An offshoot of this type of research is to use multivariate statistics and cluster analysis to discern meaningful subgroups within the larger population. The second type of study utilizes this subgroup methodology in an attempt to find distinct cluster or group profile types, and then determine external characteristics associated with each group profile. The Megargee Classification system is the most elegant and elaborated study of this type and will also be discussed in depth later in this chapter. Finally, special scales have been derived from the MMPI item pool that bear on the question of lethally aggressive behavior. The scale that has been given the most attention by researchers is the Overcontrolled Hostility Scale, which will be discussed later in the chapter.

MMPI Group Profiles of Murderers

Tables 1 and 2 present an overview of studies that have reported MMPI scores for male, female, and adolescent murderers. For males, there were 13 studies and 26 data sets. Sample sizes in these studies ranged from 12 to 137, with a median of 34. Inspection of the data reveals a number of facts: (a) The Pd scale is clinically elevated in almost all profiles. However, this sign is not pathognomonic of murderers. Most people with elevated Pd scores do not commit murder. (b) Among the 26 data sets studies, the Pd and Sc scales were clinically elevated in 10 studies. Pd, Pa, and Sc were elevated in 6 studies; Pd, Pt, and Sc were elevated in 6 studies; and Pa was elevated in 14 studies.

Also, "Within Normal Limits" profiles were found in 4 other subsets. The aggregated median profile of male murderers is a two-point code characterized by elevations in Pd and Pa and is referred to as a 46 codetype. This profile, which appears in Figure 1, suggests persons who are quite hostile, resentful, bitter, angry, argumentative, and irritable. Social maladjustment is likely to be present and they make excessive demands on others for attention, although they resent demands being placed on them by others. They use projection, rationalization, and externalization as primary defenses, and act out impulsively.

TABLE 1
MMPI T Scores of Violent Offenders Emphasizing Murderers

Study	1		2	3	4	5	6	
Scale	White Murderers	Black Murderers	Male Murderers	Death Row	Male/Female Murderers	Male Psych	Sane Murderers	Insane
N	51	51	44	34	61	53	40	12
L	63	64	53	52	50	50	52	51
F	52	51	60	58	68	68	71	74
K	55	56	59	53	50	54	51	53
Hs	60	65	59	61	47	78	69	62
Dep	57	56	63	64	76	63	72	67
Hy	57	56	62	60	68	61	69	64
Pd	76	74	71	72	63	78	79	77
Mf	57	57	57	54	68	68	57	65
Pa	59	64	59	59	69	70	73	68
Pt	60	64	60	61	50	86	75	77
Sc	64	70	65	61	55	92	83	81
Ma	65	70	58	60	59	68	69	70
Si	53	52	50	54	55	58	58	58
Code	4'	489'	4'	4'	2'	8741'	84762'	847'

Study	7					8	9		10				
Scale	Adult Murderers – Cluster Analysis					Males	White	Black	Cluster Analysis				
	Type 1	2	3	4	5				Type 1	2	3	4	5
N	17	26	21	25	21	137	111	49	20	13	18	14	15
L	46	53	53	50	64	50	50	53	45	53	56	50	60
F	96	120	53	68	80	83	85	86	100	115	58	66	76
K	40	45	60	49	56	50	52	53	40	46	62	48	55
Hs	72	90	52	54	77	54	53	49	58	80	31	39	52
Dep	80	95	58	65	80	75	74	68	77	96	64	65	75
Hy	65	82	56	55	73	66	67	65	64	86	60	56	69
Pd	78	90	67	74	81	68	68	65	79	80	50	60	67
Mf	61	68	51	59	61	61	60	62	61	71	60	57	61
Pa	94	105	55	70	83	83	83	80	100	108	59	70	85
Pt	85	97	52	66	77	50	53	45	71	79	21	40	44
Sc	101	130	55	75	88	67	69	67	96	117	23	50	55
Ma	70	85	58	69	63	63	60	65	75	75	50	58	58
Si	67	72	47	54	63	62	63	55	66	71	48	54	62
Code	86724	86724	WNL	8469	8647	6243	62'	6'	6842	8623	WNL	6'	62'

There are paranoid features, such as suspiciousness, a variety of sensitivities, and perhaps problematic thought processes. Aggressive outbursts, substance abuse, antisocial behavior, and

			TABLE 1, CONTINUED			
Study	11		12		13	
Scale	Violent Sober	Violent Drunk	Domestic Murder	Stranger Murder	Violent Homicides	Median T Scores
N	48	41	20	19	35	34
L	53	53	57	56	55	53
F	78	78	55	54	67	68
K	49	53	60	58	53	53
Hs	49	49	56	52	59	56
Dep	70	72	57	53	66	65
Hy	64	65	58	53	63	64
Pd	61	62	59	67	76	72
Mf	62	59	55	53	62	61
Pa	76	76	55	55	69	70
Pt	43	46	56	55	70	60
Sc	61	57	56	57	75	67
Ma	63	58	57	65	66	65
Si	56	60	53	47	57	57
Code	62'	62'	WNL	WNL	48'	

1. Sutker & Moan, 1973
2. Deiker, 1974
3. Panton, 1976
4. McDonald & Paitich, 1981
5. Langevin, Paitich, Orchard, Handy, & Russon, 1982
6. Rogers & Seman, 1983
7. Anderson & Holcolm, 1983
8. Holcolm & Adams, 1983
9. Holcolm, Adams, & Ponder, 1984
10. Holcolm, Adams, & Ponder, 1985
11. Holcolm & Adams, 1985
12. Kalichman, 1988

authority problems may also be present. They are likely to have a history of family and social problems. A personality disorder, either narcissistic, antisocial, or both, is often associated with this profile type. This personality description is considered characterological rather than situational and is reflective of the person's basic personality prior to the act of murder. Keep in mind that an individual murderer may or may not have this prototypic MMPI profile. The only published study reporting on female murderers also found a 46 codetype, but at subclinical levels (Kalichman, 1988a).

It is important to keep in mind that there are a number of variables that can affect test scores. Studies which have addressed these variables are reviewed briefly below.

Race. Holcomb and Adams (1982) reported that Black murderers scored higher than White murderers on Ma and lower on Si. However, when IQ was controlled, earlier differences between Black and White murderers disappeared (Holcomb, Adams, & Ponder, 1984).

Relationship to the Victim. There is some evidence that MMPI scores differ based on the relationship of the murderer to the victim. Women who murdered their domestic partner scored higher on Pa and Si compared to men who murdered either their partner or a stranger. These results suggest that these women had more sensitivity and social withdrawal, perhaps as a result of chronic physical abuse. In fact, their MMPI was

TABLE 2
MMPI T Scores for Female and Adolescent Murderers

Study	1	2
Scale	Female	Adolescents
N	16	18
L	51	47
F	56	86
K	53	46
Hs	52	74
Dep	53	68
Hy	56	68
Pd	65	75
Mf	43	59
Pa	63	76
Pt	53	70
Sc	56	77
Ma	57	68
Si	55	60
Code	WNL	8417

1. Kalichman, 1988
2. Cornell, Miller & Senedek, 1988

"Within Normal Limits." In contrast, men who murdered strangers, compared to men who murdered their domestic partner, had higher levels of social extraversion and impulsivity (low Si). They also had more evidence of sociopathy (Pd) compared to female murderers (Kalichman, 1988a).

Substance Abuse. Holcomb and Adams (1985) compared four groups of murderers and their relationship to substance abuse. Group 1 consisted of 41 men who murdered while intoxicated, Group 2 was made up of 48 men who murdered while sober, Group 3 consisted of 130 male psychiatric patients without histories of substance abuse or violence, and Group 4 consisted of 40 nonviolent patients in a detoxification program. The violent groups scored higher on Pa and lower on Ma, reflecting more suspiciousness and irri-

tability. Men who murdered while sober scored lower on Mf, suggesting lower sensitivity, but more psychopathy (Pd) compared to those who murdered while drunk. The latter group had higher L scores, suggesting psychological naivete.

Amnesia. Inmates undergoing pretrial evaluation were divided into three groups: (a) those who confessed to the crime (N=50), (b) those who denied the crime (N=31), and (c) those who claimed amnesia (N=24). Inmates claiming amnesia scored higher on scales Hs, Dep, and Hy. These claims of more physical problems and depression were interpreted as signs of malingering (Parwatikar, Holcomb, & Menninger, 1985).

Death Row Status. Inmates on Death Row had higher elevations on Pa and Sc. The elevation of scores suggested hopelessness, frustration, alienation, and resentment, rather than psychotic processes, and were most certainly attributed to the effects of possible death rather than to pre-existing personality characteristics (Dahlstrom, Panton, Bain, & Dahlstrom, 1986).

The literature reviewed here suggests that there is no single MMPI profile codetype specific to people who murder. There are certain codetypes that appear more frequently within groups of murderers, but they also appear in those who do not murder. However, any individual patient who has an MMPI profile similar to that of modal types should receive a more thorough scrutiny and evaluation regarding violent tendencies, assaultive behavior, and probability estimates for being at risk for lethal violence.

MMPI Group Classification of Murderers

Edwin Megargee (1977) sought to develop a prisoner taxonomic system that was reliable, economical, valid, and dynamic, possessed clear operational definitions, and which would have treatment implications. His classification system based on this taxonomy now meets the Standards

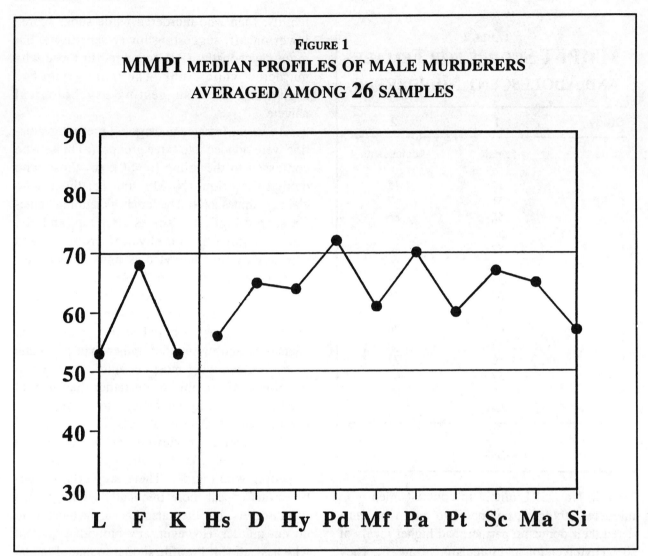

FIGURE 1
MMPI MEDIAN PROFILES OF MALE MURDERERS
AVERAGED AMONG **26** SAMPLES

of the American Correctional Association and satisfies federal court mandates. Using cluster analysis techniques, 10 MMPI "types" were found in a sample of 1,344 males, ages 18 to 27, incarcerated at a Tallahassee federal medium security prison (Megargee & Dorhout, 1977; Meyer & Megargee, 1977). In addition to the MMPI, these prisoners were given other psychological tests. These included the California Psychological Inventory, State-Trait Anxiety Inventory, Adjective Checklist, Personal Opinion Study, Interpersonal Sensitivity Inventory, an Attitudes-Towards-Parents Scale, and a prisonization scale. This battery of tests was given along with a structured clinical interview that was tape recorded and scored on 250 items by independent raters. Additional data included prison investigation reports and Bureau of Prisons demographic data sheets.

Megargee's analysis indicated that these 10 MMPI-based types differed substantially in their family and social history, lifestyle and personality patterns, prison adjustment, and recidivism. In fact, they differed on 140 of 164 variables tested. Modal characteristics of a typical member of the group were then established (Megargee, 1984a, 1984b; Megargee & Bohn, 1977). As of 1983,

TABLE 3
CAPSULE CHARACTERISTICS OF THE TEN TYPES

Name and proportion	MMPI characteristics		Observed model characteristics	Management and treatment recommendations
	Elevation	Pattern		
Able (17%)	Moderate, peak score ca. 70 or less	Bimodal with peaks on 4 and 9	Charming, popular, impulsive, and manipulative. Middle class, achievement oriented, do well in institution but emerge relatively unaffected.	Need change agent with sense of humor and structured setting to deal with their manipulative games and confront them with outcomes of their behavior
Baker (4%)	Moderate; Pd ca 70; D ca. 65	Peaks on 4 and 2, slopes down to right	Inadequate, anxious, defensive, constricted and dogmatic; tends to abuse alcohol but not other drugs	Initial anxiety requires supportive help. Later many will benefit from alcohol treatment and educational programming. Need counseling to stop self-defeating patterns
Charlie (9%)	High; peak scale > 80; several > 70	Peaks on 8, 6, and 4; slopes up to right	Hostile, misanthropic, suspicious with extensive histories of maladjustment, crime, and drug and alcohol abuse. Alienated, aggressive, antagonistic and antisocial	Require secure setting and extensive programming. Consistency, fairness and perseverance needed to avoid further need of drugs and/or acting out when stressed
Delta (10%)	Moderate to high Pd at least 70, often 80 or 90	Unimodal; prominent Pd spike; others below 70	Amoral, hedonistic, egocentric, bright and manipulative. Poor relations with peers and authorities. Impulsive, sensation-seeking leads to frequent infractions	Often have extensive records requiring incarceration. Separate from weaker, more easily exploited inmates Challenging and confronting needed but prognosis poor
Easy (7%)	Low; To scale below 80, often below 70	43 profile; slopes down to right	Bright, stable, well educated middle class, with good adjustment and resources. Underachievers who take easy path, but have good interpersonal relationships	Minimal needs for structure or treatment. Challenge them to take advantage of assets. Respond well to educational programming
Foxtrot (8%)	High Top scale(s) over 80 and others over 70	Slopes up to right; 89 and 4 top three scales	Tough, street-wise, cynical, antisocial. Deprivation and deviance lead to extensive criminal histories, poor prison adjustment. Deficits in all areas	Require structure and strong change agent. Extensive changes needed; peer counseling and program with obvious contingencies required to make behavior more socialized
George (7%)	Moderate; D and Pd ca. 70	Like Baker but scales 1, 2 and 3 more elevated	Hardworking, submissive, anxious from deviant families. Learned criminal values; do their own time and take advantage of educational and vocational opportunities	Need to learn alternatives to crime as livelihood. Supportive treatment at outset, followed by rational-cooperative approach and education and vocational programming
How (13%)	Very high, Top scales >80 or 90	Elevated multimodal profile. No particular code pattern	Unstable, agitated, disturbed, "mental health" cases. Function ineffectively in all areas and have extensive needs	Require further diagnosis and program aimed at overcoming mental health problems. Warm but structured therapeutic environment with mental health resources needed
Item (19%)	Very low, Scales usually under 70	No particular pattern	Stable, effectively functioning well adjusted group with minimal problems, few authority conflicts	Basically normal group with minimal needs for structure, support, or treatment beyond what dictated by legal situation.
Jupiter (3%)	Moderate to high, Peak scales over 70	Slopes up to right with top scores on 8, 9, 7	Overcoming deprived background fairly well but have conflicts with staff and other inmates. Work hard and do better than expected after release.	Change agent supportive of efforts to overcome deficits via educational and/or vocational programming. Counseling and tolerance for setbacks that occur

(From Megargee, E. (1984a). Derivation, validation, and application of an MMPI-based system for classifying criminal offenders. *Medicine and Law*, 3, 109-118. Springer-Verlag Publishers

30,000 federal prisoners have been typed using the Megargee typology (Kennedy, 1986). When the Tallahassee Federal Correctional Institution assigned inmates to living arrangements based on the Megargee classification system, serious assaults dropped by 46% (Megargee, 1984a). Thus, the classification system provides us with a means of distinguishing between potentially violent and nonviolent prisoners.

Megargee chose non-descriptive names for these 10 types in an alphabetized format as follows: Able, Baker, Charlie, Delta, Easy, Foxtrot, George, How, Item, and Jupiter, and the system has been ordered on a continuum from most benign to most pathological (Types I, E, B, A, G, D, J, F, C, and H) (Motiuk, Bonta, & Andrews, 1986). The types, along with their basic characteristics, are presented in Table 3.

The reliability of the Megargee typology has been established by (a) studying the interrater reliability in terms of classifying individual MMPI profiles, (b) using test-retest methodology, and (c) determining the typology's replicability in other populations (Zager, 1988). Research has provided strong support for the validity of the original 10 types. These types have appeared in federal penitentiaries (Bohn, 1979; Edinger, 1979; Edinger & Auerbach, 1978; Edinger, Reuterfors, & Logue, 1982; Hanson, Moss, Hosford, & Johnson, 1983; Johnson, Simmons, & Gordon, 1983; Louscher, Hosford, & Moss, 1983; Megargee, 1986; Megargee & Bohn, 1977; Mrad, Kabacoff, & Cuckro, 1983; Simmons, Johnson, Gouvier, & Muzyczka, 1981; Van Voorhis, 1988; Walters, Mann, Miller, & Chlumsky, 1988), state penitentiary samples (Booth & Howell, 1980; Carey, Garske, & Ginsberg, 1986; Edinger, 1979; Wright, 1988), medium security facilities (Carey, Garske, & Ginsberg, 1986; Johnson, Simmons, & Gordon, 1983), high medium security facilities (Van Voorhis, 1988; Wrobel, Wrobel, & McIntosh, 1988), high security facilities (Louscher, Hosford, & Moss, 1983; Simmons, Johnson,

Gouvier, & Muzyczka, 1981), and in maximum security settings (Louscher, Hosford, & Moss, 1983; Motiuk, Bonta, & Andrews, 1986; Walters, 1986; Wrobel, Wrobel, & McIntosh, 1988). They also appear among death row inmates (Dahlstrom, Panton, Bain, & Dahlstrom, 1986), prison half-way house participants (Motiuk, Bonta, & Andrews, 1986; Mrad, Kabacoff, & Cuckro, 1983) military prisoners (Walters, 1986; Walters, Scrapansky, & Marlow, 1986; Walters et al, 1988), in forensic populations (DiFrancesca & Meloy, 1989; Hutton, Miner, & Langfeldt, 1993; Wrobel, Wrobel, & McIntosh, 1988), in presentencing psychiatric samples (Wrobel, Calovini, & Martin, 1991), and among presidential threateners (Megargee, 1986).

The typology has been documented across a variety of geographic settings and States, including Alabama (Edinger, 1979), California (DiFrancesca & Meloy, 1989; Hanson, Moss, Hosford, & Johnson, 1983; Hutton, Miner, & Langfeldt, 1993; Louscher, Hosford, & Moss, 1983), Kansas (Walters, 1986), Indiana (Van Voorhis, 1988), Kentucky (Johnson, Simmons, & Gordon, 1983), Louisiana (Schaffer, Pettigrew, Blouin, & Edwards, 1983), Missouri (Anderson & Holcolm, 1983; Megargee, 1986; Mrad, Kabacoff, & Cuckro, 1983), North Carolina (Dahlstrom, Panton, Bain, & Dahlstrom, 1986; Edinger, 1979; Edinger, Reuterfors, & Logue, 1982; Megargee, 1986), Ohio (Carey, Garske, & Ginsberg, 1986; Van Voorhis, 1988; Wrobel, Calovini, & Martin, 1991), Tennessee (Simmons, Johnson, Gouvier, & Muzyczka, 1981; Veneziano & Veneziano, 1986), and Utah (Booth & Howell, 1980), as well as in Canada (Motiuk, Bonta, & Andrews, 1986).

While the system has been used with female prisoners (Edinger, 1979; Schaffer, Pettigrew, Blouin, & Edwards, 1983; Wrobel, Calovini, & Martin, 1991), and with adolescent incarcerates (Doren, Megargee, & Schreiber, 1980; Veneziano & Veneziano, 1986), research has not as yet established the utility of the Megargee classification with these groups. Use with adolescents may be particularly problematic because their personality may not have solidified into its adult form. To date, there has been relatively little interest in Megargee's treatment recommendations associated with the typology (Kennedy, 1986).

While not designated specifically as a classification system for murderers, Megargee reported that types Charlie, Foxtrot, and How, the more pathological types, were more prone toward violent behavior. Edinger (1979) independently replicated the typology and found that types Charlie and Jupiter had committed more violent crimes, including murder, and showed more aggressive behavior in prison compared to the other groups. Because type Charlie has been particularly implicated in violence and murder (Anderson & Holcom, 1983; Edinger, 1979; Hanson, Moss, Hosford, & Johnson, 1983; Motiuk, Banta, & Andrews, 1986), a more detailed discussion of this MMPI codetype is presented.

Type Charlie's MMPI profile is characterized by elevations of the scales of Schizophrenia, Paranoia, and Psychopathic Deviance (an 864 three-point codetype), an acting-out aggressive profile type, and suggests a personality style that is sensitive to perceived threats and insults, a hostile and bitter demeanor ready to strike at the slightest provocation, and antisocial traits. Individuals with this profile tend to have authority problems, considerable anxiety, a deviant value system, and poor ego strength. They lack empathy, are cognitively and emotionally constricted, and feel alienated, resentful, bitter, and hostile. Charlie types show poor adjustment histories and tend to have many criminal convictions. On the Adjective Checklist, these men endorsed adjectives which indicated negative affect and described themselves as less stable and irresponsible (Megargee, 1977, 1986). They also tend to have a formal thought disorder, substantial energy, and much anger, and to be quite defensive (DiFrancesca & Meloy, 1989).

Table 4 presents studies which have published T-score information on Type Charlie. Figure 2 presents an MMPI-2 profile with the Charlie classification. This profile is from a 20-year old, single, Black male convicted of first degree murder and attempted murder. He began drinking alcohol in substantial quantities around the eighth grade and drank to intoxication on special occasions on which he chose to celebrate. He denied using illicit drugs. Although he had no serious illness,

TABLE 4
MMPI T SCORES ON TYPE "CHARLIE" PROFILES IN PUBLISHED STUDIES

Author	Year		MMPI Scales											
		L	F	K	Hs	D	Hy	Pd	Mf	Pa	Pt	Sc	Ma	Si
Megargee	1977	50	80	46	60	65	59	77	61	81	72	84	75	57
Edinger	1979	51	79	48	60	65	59	77	61	79	73	90	75	56
	M	50	76	44	60	65	58	75	61	78	75	89	74	60
	F	48	76	49	57	61	52	74	51	80	74	88	68	62
Edinger et al.	1982	52	77	50	60	64	61	79	61	79	70	84	75	53
		47	76	48	59	65	58	78	64	75	71	84	70	61
Mrad et al.	1983	49	79	46	57	63	53	70	62	73	70	86	74	58
Hutton	1993	52	79	49	59	68	59	76	67	78	73	88	69	59

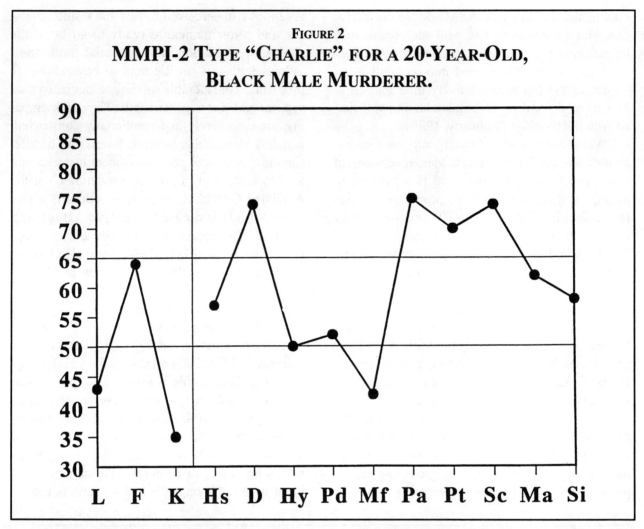

FIGURE 2

MMPI-2 TYPE "CHARLIE" FOR A 20-YEAR-OLD, BLACK MALE MURDERER.

he had received a gunshot wound to the head a few years ago, resulting in a three-day hospitalization. Subsequent to this incident, he reported migraine headaches, jaw pain, and non-specific memory problems, although he showed no apparent memory disorders.

This inmate had argued with his eventual victims on a previous occasion and, upon seeing them on the street, left the area to find a means to kill them. He returned to the area, shot and killed one of the victims, and shot the other victim with the intent to kill him, but the victim recovered from his wounds. The inmate would not provide any other details, but stated that he was involved in a gang, both prior to his arrest and subsequent

to his imprisonment. He later received his GED in prison.

The profile suggests an individual who is quite angry, depressed, and sullen. He gets upset with people whom he believes have harmed him and blames other people for his difficulties. He appears tense, irritable, pessimistic, and preoccupied with his problems. Projection and acting out are his major defenses and he seems prone to misunderstand the motives of other people. Paranoid features to his personality are likely. He has numerous somatic complaints with much anxiety, worry, and ruminations. Thinking is likely to be permeated by an obsessive quality. He views the world as a threatening place, feels he's getting a raw deal out of life, and sees little wrong in violating societal rules and conventions because of the perceived injustices that have been perpetuated upon him. He is high-strung, reports some bizarre perceptions, unusual thinking, a sense of alienation, and a lack of warm relationships, especially because he views others as potentially threatening and harmful. This inmate shows suspicious attitudes and an ingrained hostility, combined with malevolent projections. One can imagine that such a psychological state would put him at risk for lethal violence.

With the revision of the MMPI-2, Megargee has been studying the impact of the restandardization on his classification system. He has determined that a new set of classification rules will be required when using the MMPI-2 and is presently conducting research to determine if the empirical correlates established for the MMPI will be similar to those found with the MMPI-2 (Megargee, 1993, 1994). Readers interested in using the Megargee Classification System for MMPI/MMPI-2 profiles should contact the test's publisher, National Computer Systems, which can score the MMPI-2 and classify the profile according to the Megargee system for a nominal fee. Of course, the system has not been cross-validated for the MMPI-2; thus, any use the readers make of the system is at their own risk, so to speak. Another option is to use the original MMPI and have NCS classify the profile according to the old Megargee rules. One final option is to obtain Megargee's original monograph (which is out of print) through inter-library loan and classify the profiles yourself according to the specified rules.

In summary, research on the Megargee classification system has found the following: (a) An individual in the group code may not show all of the characteristics of the group itself and may show variability around the prototype characteristics; (b) The system is dynamic and an individual may change group membership over the course of his or her sentence; (c) The ten types have

appeared across multiple prison settings, although the prevalence of each type within each setting shows considerable variability. Types Able, Charlie, Foxtrot, and How show exceptional validity; (d) It is possible that different sorting rules may be required for Black and White inmates, and there is little justification for using the system with females or adolescents due to a paucity of research with these populations; (e) While the types have been replicated across many settings, there is less research verifying the correlates associated with each type; and (f) Type Charlie is particularly associated with poor adjustment and violent behavior, but this type is not specific to murderers per se.

MMPI Special Scales

Early research sought to develop scales derived from the MMPI item pool that might be able to detect meaningful differences between criminal classification groups. Results were mixed. For example, Panton (1958), using the Prison Adjustment Scale (PAS), reported that the PAS was unable to distinguish among six crime classification groups, while Christensen and Le Unes (1974) found that the PAS, along with the Lie and Psychopathic Deviance scales, did differentiate among crime classification groups.

The MMPI-derived Overcontrolled Hostility Scale (OH) was an outgrowth of previous attempts to measure differences on hostility and impulse control between assaultive and nonassaultive criminals (Megargee, 1966; Megargee, Cook, & Mendelsohn, 1967). Megargee and his colleagues reasoned that there may be at least two distinct personality types among assaultive individuals, which were labeled "chronically overcontrolled" and "undercontrolled" aggressive types. The former type is characterized by excessive inhibitions against the expression of aggression in any form. Individuals of this type are extremely frustrated because their anger and hostility build up over time, until suddenly, they commit an aggressive act of homicidal intensity.

Megargee conducted an item analysis of MMPI test responses of four groups consisting of extremely assaultive, moderately assaultive, non-assaultive, and normals, and developed a 31-item scale that was able to differentiate successfully among groups. This scale was cross-validated using independent samples. Surprisingly, the types of items that successfully differentiated between overcontrolled and undercontrolled types were passive and non-aggressive in quality (e.g., answering "True" to the statement, "I do not mind being made fun of"). The scale correlated positively with MMPI scales L, K, and Hy, suggesting rigidity, repression of conflicts, and a self-presentation of positive adjustment; it correlated negatively with Pt, Pd, Sc, & Ma scales, suggesting inhibition of acting out rebelliousness and authority conflicts. Megargee suggested that the OH scale is measuring impulse control and hostile alienation. Megargee set a raw score of > 18 (T 70) on the OH scale as indicating people who are highly overcontrolled, and a raw score of < 11 (T 40) as reflecting undercontrolled hostility. Scores in the mid-range could reflect either hostility or control.

A substantial amount of research has been conducted on the OH scale. Much of this research has studied the scale's construct validity and its ability to distinguish between highly, moderately, and infrequently or non-assaultive inmates. Research has supported the construct validity of the OH Scale (du Toit & Duckitt, 1990; Gudjonsson, Petursson, & Sigurdardottir, 1991; Quinsey, Maguire, & Varney, 1983; White, 1975; White, McAdoo, & Megargee, 1973). These studies demonstrated that patients with high OH scores, when given other tests, have personality dimensions reflecting higher degrees of control, inhibition of aggression, and social adjustment.

In general, most studies have generally validated the OH scale, with high scores on the scale

reflecting rigid control of aggression (Deiker, 1974; Henderson, 1983; Lane & Kling, 1979; Quinsey, Maguire, & Varney, 1983; Walters, Solomon, & Greene, 1982). Studies which failed to support the Megargee typology have typically administered it apart from the MMPI — removing the 31 items from the MMPI and giving the scale as a single test (Hoppe & Singer, 1976; Rawlings, 1973).

Only three published studies, which are discussed below, have reported on OH scores with a criterion group of exclusively murderers. Many other studies have used inmate populations in which murderers were included in the assaultive group and also included non-lethal violent inmates. These studies will not be reviewed because inclusion of non-lethal violent assaulters contaminates the groups for our purposes.

Deiker (1974) studied a sample of 44 homicidal males in Massachusetts. These inmates had an average OH score of 14.5. They would be rated as "moderately overcontrolled." Quinsey, Arnold, and Pruesse (1980) reported that 25 murderers of family members had a mean score of 13.5 on the OH scale, while non-family murderers had a mean score of 14.0. Once again, these scores were in the moderate range. Finally, Quinsey, Maguire, and Varney (1983) found that inmates who were classified as overcontrolled murderers attained a mean score of 18.5 on the OH scale, while inmates classified as undercontrolled murderers had a mean score of 12.5. Thus, two studies were viewed as not supporting the scale's ability to differentiate violent from nonviolent murderers, while the last study supported the typology of overcontrolled and undercontrolled hostile personalities.

Research has largely substantiated the validity of the Megargee typology of the overcontrolled and undercontrolled hostility personality types. However, Megargee never asserted that these are the only two types who commit murder and never developed the scale to distinguish murderers from nonviolent inmates. The OH scale was designed to detect one type of murderer — the overcontrolled type — and the scale seems to function well in this area. There certainly are many other types of murderers and motivations for the murders themselves, such that the OH scale would not be appropriate for these types. For example, some murderers have been socialized into a deviant subculture with norms that approve and reward aggression and violence in certain circumstances because of its instrumental value to the subgroup (du Toit & Duckitt, 1990). Researchers have sought to extend the OH scale beyond its original intent and we now know some of its limitations.

Case Presentation and Analysis

Case Illustration:The inmate is a 45-year-old Black male who was admitted to the medical clinic of a correctional facility for treatment of recurrent depression. He had an extensive psychiatric history since his early teens and had 40 psychiatric admissions to public and private psychiatric hospitals. He had a history of self-mutilation and had made five suicide attempts since the age of 18. At age 7, he began swallowing marbles and rocks whenever he became angry at his parents.

In his most recent attempt, he tried to kill himself by swallowing wire and bedsprings. During his incarceration, he swallowed broken glass, wire, and bedsprings to cope with his anger. The precipitant to his most recent attempt was a threat from a correctional officer to transfer him from the psychiatric residential wing to the general population.

His diagnoses at the time of the evaluation were Major Depression, Recurrent; Opiate and Cocaine Dependence, by history; and Antisocial and Borderline Personalty Disorders. Psychiatric medications included Lithium and Prozac. He had a period of opiate addiction and was treated with Methadone maintenance. He was also HIV positive and was taking AZT.

The inmate's mother had died when he was a

young child and his father had died of a gunshot wound when the inmate was in his teens. He had never married, but had fathered two children from two different females. Both his current girlfriend and their infant were HIV positive. He contracted the disease from a former girlfriend who later committed suicide.

This inmate had a long history of violence and was convicted of murder and armed robbery on five separate occasions. He was awaiting trial for charges of arson and murder. He became involved with gangs early in life and started selling drugs at age 14. He reported difficulty in controlling his anger since age 8, when he stabbed his grammar school teacher in the back with a pair of scissors. He admitted to having a nasty temper and problems with authority. His temper emerges whenever he believes that someone is trying to control him. During the elementary grades, he was placed in behavior disordered programs. He didn't go to high school and supported himself by selling drugs and by pimping. His IQ is in the Average range.

Figure 3 presents the inmate's MMPI-2 Profile. The Megargee classification of this profile is type "Charlie."

The profile suggests exaggeration in which the inmate reported more symptoms than would be established by an objective review. This response set is understandable, given his motivation to remain in the psychiatric wing and his desire not to return to the general population. This circumstance nicely illustrates the effects of the context of testing discussed earlier in this chapter. However, by scrutinizing his current situation and with his extensive psychiatric history, we can interpret a "scaled-down" version of this profile.

The profile suggests the presence of delusions, but not hallucinations (Scales Pa and Sc), hyperactivity (Ma), and antisocial behavior and traits (Pd). His content scales were not systematically elevated, as would be the case in a random response set, but were specifically elevated, con-

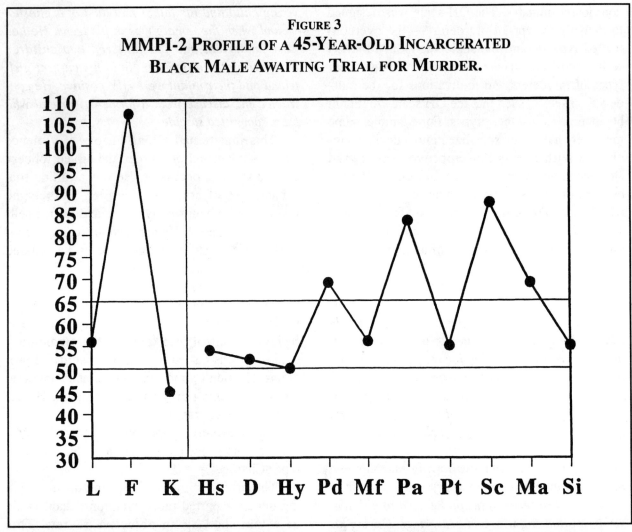

FIGURE 3
MMPI-2 PROFILE OF A 45-YEAR-OLD INCARCERATED
BLACK MALE AWAITING TRIAL FOR MURDER.

sistent with his history. He reported Family Problems (FAM), Antisocial Practices (ASP), Anger (ANG), and Bizarre Mentation (BIZ).

Interestingly, both the Clinical Scale and the Content Scale, suggesting depression, were not significantly elevated. This may reflect a positive treatment response to the antidepressant drug, Prozac.

This inmate has problems in controlling his anger, is hyperactive, tends to act out, has a low frustration tolerance, is emotionally labile, shows evidence of a thought disorder, is narcissistic, and is prone toward sexual acting out, lying, stealing, aggressive outbursts, and assaultive behaviors.

His OH scale is a T Score of 55, and suggests that he is not an overcontrolled hostility type. He has a number of persecutory ideas, lacks control, has problems with authority, and has a defensive structure characterized by projection and acting out. He is at extremely high risk for continued adjustment problems within the correctional facility. If this inmate is to receive psychological treatment, goals need to be directed at anger management. It seems that this person would not be able to function in society at the time of the evaluation and that long-term prognosis is poor. Confinement with humane care seemed to be the appropriate treatment plan for him.

Group Differences and Individual Prediction

Until recently, the psychological literature has focused on group differences and has ignored the predictability of the criterion for any individual member of the group. This issue pertains to actuarial versus clinical prediction. Actuarial prediction tends to be accurate for the group, but is unable to successfully predict which member of the group will demonstrate the criterion behavior — in this case, lethal violence. Clinical prediction from psychological tests relies on the test properties of sensitivity and specificity. Test sensitivity is defined as the probability that the person has the trait in question, given a test score that suggests he or she should have the trait. Test specificity is the probability that a person does not have the trait if the test score suggests that he or she does not have it.

In order for psychologists to make individual predictions from psychological tests, information must be available on the test's sensitivity and specificity. Statistically, these values should be above 70%, but base rates affect the social value of our predictions. By base rates, we mean the rate of occurrence of the criterion in the general population. If all patients with an affective disorder show depression, then the base rate for depression is 100% and we do not need any other information to make a prediction about depression once we know that a patient has an affective disorder. If the rate of lethal violence in the general population is 1%, then we know that 99% of the people we evaluate, in general, for lethal violence will not become violent. Of course, the rate of occurrence of violence in a forensic population is higher than 1%. Individual prediction is most reliable when the base rate of the behavior is 50%, but it becomes inordinately difficult when the base rate is less than 5%. Needless to say, there has been no information published to date on the sensitivity or specificity on any MMPI

scale in the prediction of lethal violence, and this information is available neither for the Megargee classification system nor for the Overcontrolled Hostility scale.

Guidelines for Assessment Using Psychological Tests in the Assessment of Lethal Violence

1. Objective personality tests have their highest validity when used to determine present symptoms, problems, traits, and disorders. Various degrees of inference are required to postdict psychological states retrospectively.

2. Consider the possible effects of the context of testing on test scores. Also, evaluate whether certain moderator variables have affected test scores.

3. Use both objective and projective psychological tests in the evaluation and integrate test results with other sources of information, such as arrest records and collateral information, to produce a comprehensive report. Never use psychological tests alone to make final recommendations.

4. When selecting an objective personality test, the MMPI/MMPI-2 has been the most frequently used and most frequently researched personality test with perpetrators of lethal violence and should be the instrument of choice.

5. Maintain an adequate level of knowledge of the professional literature regarding how murderers tend to score on the MMPI. Also, consider local base rates, or how particular patients tend to score on an instrument, such as the MMPI, in your particular setting.

6. Understand and appreciate the limitations of your assessment instruments, as well as the limitations of other sources of data.

7. Render a professional evaluation based on all known sources of information, adhering to data, rather than speculation, hunches, intuition, guesses, and theoretical proclamations.

8. Make affirmative statements (either posi-

tive or negative) and don't be afraid to say "I don't know." Others will afford you greater respect.

Final Comments

The assessment, evaluation, and prediction of lethal violence requires the highest degree of professional acumen and is one of society's most important functions. Patients have the right to the most competent assessment with validated measures and reliable and empirically determined predictors. This is our science and this is our mission.

References

Anderson, W. & Holcomb, W. R. (1983). Accused murderers: Five MMPI personality types. *Journal of Clinical Psychology, 39*, 761-768.

Bohn, M. J. (1979). Management classification for young adult inmates. *Federal Probation, 43*, 53-59.

Booth, R. J. & Howell, R. J. (1980). Classification of prison inmates with the MMPI: An extension and validation of the Megargee typology. *Criminal Justice and Behavior, 7*, 407-422.

Butcher, J. N., Dahlstrom, W. G., Graham, J. R., Tellegen, A., & Kaemmer, B. (1989). *Minnesota Multiphasic Personality Inventory-2: Manual for administration and scoring*. Minneapolis: University of Minnesota Press.

Carey, R. J., Garske, J. P., & Ginsberg, J. (1986). The prediction of adjustment to prison by means of an MMPI-based classification. *Criminal Justice and Behavior, 13*, 347-365.

Cattell, R. B. (1989). *The 16 PF: Personality in depth*. Champaign, IL: Institute for Personality and Ability Testing.

Christensen, L. & LeUnes, A. (1974). Discriminating criminal types and recidivism by means of the MMPI. *Journal of Clinical Psychology, 30*, 192-193.

Cornell, D. G., Miller, C., & Benedek, E. P. (1988). MMPI profiles of adolescents charged with homicide. *Behavioral Sciences and the Law, 6*, 401-407.

Dahlstrom, W. G., Panton, J. H., Bain, K. P., & Dahlstrom, L. E. (1986). Utility of the Megargee-Bohn MMPI typological assignments: Study with a sample of death row inmates. *Criminal Justice and Behavior, 13*, 5-17.

Deiker, T. E. (1974). A cross-validation of MMPI scales of aggression on male criminal criterion groups. *Journal of Consulting and Clinical Psychology, 42*, 196-202.

DiFrancesca, K. R., & Meloy, J. R. (1989). A comparative clinical investigation of the "How" and "Charlie" MMPI subtypes. *Journal of Personality Assessment, 53*, 396-403.

Doren, D. M., Megargee, E. I., & Schreiber, H. A. (1980). The MMPI criminal classifications applicability to a juvenile population. *The Differential View: A Publication of the International Differential Treatment Association, 9*, 42-47.

du Toit, L. & Duckitt, J. (1990). Psychological characteristics of over- and undercontrolled violent offenders. *Journal of Psychology, 124*, 125-141.

Edinger, J. D. (1979). Cross validation of the Megargee MMPI typology for prisoners. *Journal of Consulting and Clinical Psychology, 47*, 234-242.

Edinger, J. D. & Auerbach, S. M. (1978). Development and validation of a multidimensional multivariate model for accounting for infractionary behavior in a correctional setting. *Journal of Personality and*

Social Psychology, 36, 1472-1489.

Edinger, J. D., Reuterfors, D., & Logue, P. (1982). Cross validation of the Megargee MMPI typology. *Criminal Justice and Behavior, 9,* 184-203.

Finney, J. C., Skeeters, D. E., Auvenshine, C. D., & Smith, D. F. (1973). Phases of psychopathology after assassination. *American Journal of Psychiatry, 130,* 1379-1380.

Fraboni, M., Cooper, D., Reed, T. L., & Saltstone, R. (1990). Offense type and two-point MMPI code profiles: Discriminating between violent and nonviolent offenders. *Journal of Clinical Psychology, 46,* 774-777.

Gough, H. G. (1987). *The California Psychological Inventory: Administrator's guide.* Palo Alto, CA: Consulting Psychologists Press.

Gudjonsson, G. H., Petursson, H., & Sigurdardottir, H. (1991). Overcontrolled hostility among prisoners and its relationship with denial and personality scores. *Personality and Individual Differences, 12,* 17-20.

Hanson, R. W., Moss, C. S., Hosford, R. E., & Johnson, M. E. (1983). Predicting inmate penitentiary adjustment: An assessment of four classificatory methods. *Criminal Justice and Behavior, 10,* 293-309.

Hathaway, S. R. & McKinley, J. C. (1940). *Minnesota Multi-Phasic Personality Inventory.* Minneapolis, MN: University of Minnesota Press.

Henderson, M. (1983). Self-reported assertion and aggression among violent offenders with high or low levels of over-controlled hostility. *Personality and Individual Differences, 4,* 113-115.

Holcolm, W. R. & Adams, N. A. (1982). Racial influences on intelligence and personality of people who commit murder. *Journal of Clinical Psychology, 38,* 793-796.

Holcomb, W. R. & Adams, N. A. (1983). The inner-domain among personality and cognition variables in people who commit murder. *Journal of Personality Assessment, 47,* 524-530.

Holcomb, W. R. & Adams, N. A. (1985). Personality mechanisms of alcohol-related violence. *Journal of Clinical Psychology, 41,* 714-722.

Holcomb, W. R., Adams, N. A., & Ponder, H. M. (1984). Are separate black and white norms needed? An IQ-controlled comparison of accused murderers. *Journal of Clinical Psychology, 40,* 189-193.

Holcomb, W. R., Adams, N. A., Nicholas, A., Ponder, H. M., & Anderson, W. (1984). Cognitive and behavioral predictors of MMPI scores in pretrial psychological evaluations of murderers. *Journal of Clinical Psychology, 40,* 592-597.

Holcomb, W. R., Adams, N. A., Nicholas, A., & Ponder, H. M. (1985). The developmental and cross-validation of an MMPI typology of murders. *Journal of Personality Assessment, 49,* 240-244.

Hoppe, C. M. & Singer, R.D. (1976). Overcontrolled hostility, empathy, and egocentric balance in violent and non-violent psychiatric offenders. *Psychological Reports, 39,* 1303-1308.

Hutton, H. E., Miner, M. H., & Langfeldt, V. C. (1993). The utility of the Megargee-Bohn typology in a forensic psychiatric hospital. *Journal of Personality Assessment, 60,* 572-587.

Johnson, D. A., Simmons, J. D., & Gordon, D. C. (1983). Temporal consistency of the Meyer-Megargee inmate typology. *Criminal Justice and Behavior, 10,* 263-268.

Kalichman, S. C. (1988a). MMPI profiles of women and men convicted of domestic homicide. *Journal of Clinical Psychology, 44*, 847-853.

Kalichman, S. C. (1988b). Empirically derived MMPI profile subgroups of incarcerated homicide offenders. *Journal of Clinical Psychology, 44*, 733-738.

Kennedy, T. D. (1986). Trends in inmate classification: A status report on two computerized psychometric approaches. *Criminal Justice and Behavior, 13*, 165-184.

Lane, P. J. & Kling, J. S. (1979). Construct validation of the Overcontrolled Hostility scale of the MMPI. *Journal of Consulting and Clinical Psychology, 47*, 781-782.

Langevin, R., Paitich, D., Orchard, B., Handy, L., & Russon, A. (1982). Diagnosis of killers seen for psychiatric assessment: A controlled study. *Acta Psychiatrica Scandinavica, 66*, 216-228.

Louscher, P. K., Hosford, R. E., & Moss, C. S. (1983). Predicting dangerous behavior in a penitentiary using the Megargee typology. *Criminal Justice and Behavior, 10*, 269-284.

McDonald, A. & Paitich, D. (1981). A study of homicide: The validity of predictive test factors. *Canadian Journal of Psychiatry, 26*, 549-554.

Megargee, E. I. (1966). Undercontrolled and overcontrolled personality types in extreme antisocial aggression. *Psychological Monographs, 80*, (Whole No. 611).

Megargee, E. I. (1977). A new classification system for criminal offenders, I: The need for a new classification system. *Criminal Justice and Behavior, 4*, 107-114.

Megargee, E. I. (1984a). Derivation, validation and application of an MMPI-based system for classifying criminal offenders. *Medicine and Law, 3*, 109-118.

Megargee, E. I. (1984b). A new classification system for criminal offenders: VI. Differences among the types on the Adjective Checklist. *Criminal Justice and Behavior, 11*, 349-376.

Megargee, E. I. (1986). A psychometric study of incarcerated presidential threateners. *Criminal Justice and Behavior, 13*, 243-260.

Megargee, E. I. (1993). Using the MMPI-2 with criminal offenders: A progress report. *MMPI-2 & MMPI-A News & Profiles, 4*, 2-3.

Megargee, E. I. (1994). Using the Megargee MMPI-based classification system with MMPI-2s of male prison inmates. *Psychological Assessment, 6*, 337-344.

Megargee, E. I. & Bohn, M. J., Jr. (1977). A new classification system for criminal offenders, IV: Empirically determined characteristics of the ten types. *Criminal Justice and Behavior, 4*, 149-210.

Megargee, E. I., Cook, P. E., & Mendelsohn, G. A. (1967). Development and validation of an MMPI scale of assaultiveness in overcontrolled individuals. *Journal of Abnormal Psychology, 72*, 519-528.

Megargee, E. I. & Dorhout, B. (1977). A new classification system for criminal offenders, III: Revision and refinement of the classificatory rules. *Criminal Justice and Behavior, 4*, 125-148.

Meyer, J., Jr. & Megargee, E. I. (1977). A new classification system for criminal offenders, II: Initial development of the system. *Criminal Justice and Behavior, 4*, 115-124.

Millon, T. (1994). Millon Clinical Multiphasic Personality Inventory-III. Minneapolis, MN: National Computer Systems.

Motiuk, L. L., Bonta, J., & Andrews, D. A. (1986). Classification in correctional halfway houses: The relative and incremental predictive criterion validities of the Megargee-MMPI and LSI systems. *Criminal Justice and Behavior, 13*, 33-46.

Mrad, D. F., Kabacoff, R. A., & Cuckro, P. (1983). Validation of the Megargee typology in a halfway house setting. *Criminal Justice and Behavior, 10*, 252-262.

Panton, J. H. (1958). MMPI profile configurations among crime classification groups. *Journal of Clinical Psychology, 14*, 308-312.

Panton, J. H. (1976). Personality characteristics of death-row inmates. *Journal of Clinical Psychology, 32*, 306-309.

Parwatikar, S. D., Holcomb, W. R., & Menninger, K. A. (1985). The detection of malingered amnesia in accused murders. *Bulletin of the American Academy of Psychiatry and the Law, 13*, 97-103.

Quinsey, V. L., Arnold, L. S., & Pruesse, M. G. (1980). MMPI profiles of men referred for a pretrial psychiatric assessment as a function of offense type. *Journal of Clinical Psychology, 36*, 410-417.

Quinsey, V. L., Maguire, A., & Varney, G. W. (1983). Assertion and overcontrolled hostility among mentally disordered murderers. *Journal of Consulting and Clinical Psychology, 51*, 550-556.

Rawlins, M. D. (1973). Self-control and interpersonal violence. *Criminology, 11*, 23-48.

Rogers, R. & Seman, W. (1983). Murder and criminal responsibility: An examination of MMPI profiles. *Behavioral Sciences and the Law, 1*, 89-95.

Schaffer, C. E., Pettigrew, C. G., Blouin, D., & Edwards, D. W. (1983). Multivariate classification of female offender MMPI profiles. *Journal of Crime and Justice, 6*, 57-66.

Simmons, J. G., Johnson, J. L., Gouvier, W. D., & Muzyczka, M. J. (1981). The Meyer-Megargee inmate typology: Dynamic or unstable? *Criminal Justice and Behavior, 15*, 49-55.

Sutker, P. & Moan, C. E. (1973). A psychosocial description of penitentiary inmates. *Archives of General Psychiatry, 29*, 663-667.

Van Voorhis, P. (1988). A cross classification of five offender typologies: Issues of construct and predictive validity. *Criminal Justice and Behavior, 15*, 109-124.

Veneziano, C. A. & Veneziano, L. (1986). Classification of adolescent offenders with the MMPI: An extension and cross-validation of the Megargee typology. *International Journal of Offender Therapy and Comparative Criminology, 30*, 11-23.

Walters, G. D. (1986). Correlates of the Megargee criminal classification system: A military correctional setting. *Criminal Justice and Behavior, 13*, 19-32.

Walters, G. D., Mann, M. F., Miller, M. P., Hemphill, L., & Chlumsky, M. L. (1988). Emotional disorder among offenders: Inter- and intrasetting comparisons. *Criminal Justice and Behavior, 15*, 433-453.

Walters, G. D., Scrapansky, T. A., & Marlow, G. A. (1986). The emotionally disturbed military offender: Identification, background and institutional adjustment. *Criminal Justice and Behavior, 13*, 261-285.

Walters, G. D., Solomon, G. S., & Greene, R. J. (1982). The relationship between the Overcontrolled Hostility scale and the MMPI 4-3 high point pair. *Journal of Clinical Psychology, 38*, 613-615.

Westermeyer, J. (1974). Caveats on diagnosing assassins. *American Journal of Psychiatry, 131*, 722-723.

White, W. C. (1975). Validity of the Overcontrolled-

Hostility scale: A brief report. *Journal of Personality Assessment, 39*, 587-590.

White, W. C., McAdoo, W. G., & Megargee, E. I. (1973). Personality factors associated with over- and undercontrolled offenders. *Journal of Personality Assessment, 37*, 473-478.

Wright, K. N. (1988). The relationship of risk, needs, and personality classification systems and prison adjustment. *Criminal Justice and Behavior, 15*, 454-471.

Wrobel, T. A., Calovini, P. K., & Martin, T. O. (1991). Application of the Megargee MMPI typology to a population of defendants referred for psychiatric evaluation. *Criminal Justice and Behavior, 18*, 397-405.

Wrobel, N. H., Wrobel, T. A., & McIntosh, J. W. (1988). Application of the Megargee typology to a forensic psychiatric population. *Criminal Justice and Behavior, 15*, 247-254.

Zager, L. D. (1988). The MMPI-based criminal classification system: A review, current status, and future directions. *Criminal Justice and Behavior, 15*, 39-57.

About the Author

Robert James Craig, PhD, is the Director of the Drug Abuse Program at the West Side Veterans Administration Medical Center in Chicago and teaches at the School of Public Health at the University of Illinois at Chicago. He is a Diplomate in Clinical Psychology from the American Board of Professional Psychology. He has written or edited five books and numerous articles in the areas of substance abuse, diagnostic evaluation, and intervention.

CHAPTER 20

HEALING THE WOUNDS OF SIBLING SURVIVORS OF VIOLENCE

Mary S. Cerney

Introduction:

Violence has become a national preoccupation. As awareness of its presence has heightened, so has recognition of its consequences, not only for the victims, but also for the victims' survivors.

Although acts of violence take many forms, homicide or murder is probably its most extreme expression. Murder and its consequences are far-reaching, going well beyond the confines of the murder scene. Touching and leaving its mark on countless innocent victims, some of whom may not have even been born at the time of the murder, its effects can radiate and impact for generations.

Numerous considerations enter into an examination of an individual's reaction to violence. Persons of all ages are impacted by all or some of these considerations, while others may be peculiar only to a specific age or relationship group. Siblings — the subject of this chapter — span all age groups, and are characterized by certain specified variables not shared by other victims of violence. This chapter explores siblings' reactions to a particular kind of violence — that of homicide or murder.

There is a paucity of information regarding the reaction of siblings to the homicide of a brother or sister. What is found is usually embed-ded in a description of family interventions for survivors of homicide victims. Consequently, much of the data used in this chapter are excerpted from my clinical experience.

Overview and Epidemiology

Violence in today's society is reaching epidemic proportions. Increased violence and the easy accessibility to guns, along with the devaluing of human life, have generated a critical situation. In former times, a crime of violence was front page news and was talked about for days, if not weeks, afterwards. Today, such an event is lost in the folds of ensuing pages, perhaps merely a notation in a police report. Only something as shocking, frightening, and senseless as the Oklahoma City bombing on April 19, 1995 can command the nation's front page for any length of time.

Children — particularly small children — tug at the heart strings of all but the most hardened individuals. Who can forget the picture of the fireman holding the bleeding child after the Oklahoma City bombing featured on the front page of the nation's newspapers? Classmates and close friends frequently experience reactions similar to siblings in their experience of tragedy. What about the children who saw that picture or lost their siblings or classmates in that bombing!

Other pictures, too, spoke to the wide-spread pain, as husbands, wives, children — someone's siblings — were lost in the rubble that was once the Federal Building in Oklahoma City. What about these victim survivors? What about the siblings and friends of the victims lost?

Individuals of any age can suffer painful sequelae to violence regardless of their blood relationship or lack of it. Friends — sibling substitutes — may be more acutely affected, but there is little consideration or help for them unless they obtain it on their own. Their statistics rarely enter into any study. They become visible only in the consulting room, sometimes only many years after the fact.

Today's citizens are exposed to violence in every aspect of their lives. Television has become more raw and revealing in its episodes of violence; families, torn apart by financial and other concerns, lash out and hurt the most vulnerable; drugs and alcohol confuse judgment and thinking, while numbing the usual controls that inhibit erratic behavior. As controls disappear along with respect for authority and rules, it is no wonder that we see an increase in violence. News reports of drive-by shootings occurring not only in the crowded ghettos of cities and towns, but also in up-scale neighborhoods, make us pause and reflect: No neighborhood is safe.

Review of the Literature

After an extensive review of the literature, Amick-McMullan, Kilpatrick, Veronen, and Smith (1989) noted that "the indirect victims, those who have lost a loved one to homicide, are nearly invisible in the existing literature. We have no information concerning the number of survivors, and have only scant information about the impact of homicide on their psychological adjustment" (p. 22). They found a "striking relationship between psychological adjustment and satisfac-

tion with how the criminal justice system handled the homicide cases" (p. 32). This study, however, did not segregate the sample into discrete categories according to blood relationship. It was a small preliminary study involving only "19 survivors recruited through a victim witness program and a victim rights organization" (p. 21).

In their initial study, Masters, Friedman, and Getzel (1988) found that "recovery is prolonged by knowledge that the perpetrator is usually alive and in some cases unpunished, by repetitive confrontations with the criminal justice system, and by the multiple losses endured: loss of a family member, loss of illusions of safety and invulnerability, loss of a sense of trust in the surrounding community, and loss of a belief system" (p. 109). This study also dealt with the family as a whole unit, not as individual members.

Burgess (1975), in her pilot study of family reaction to homicide, identified a two-phased homicide-trauma syndrome experienced by families of homicide victims. She defined the first phase as an acute process that includes the immediate reactions to the homicide, the funeral details, and the police investigation. The second, or long-term reorganization, phase includes the psychological issues of bereavement and the sociolegal issues of the criminal justice process.

Rynearson and McCreery (1993) examined the intensity and relationship of trauma and responses to bereavement in family members following homicide. They used a standardized evaluation protocol consisting of the Texas Revised Inventory of Grief, Impact of Event Scale, and Dissociative Experiences Scale. They concluded that a combination of intense grief and intense traumatic imagery should alert the clinician to the potential for a dysfunctional bereavement response.

Summarizing previous research studying the family's response to the murder of one of its members, Parkes (1993) noted that "any or all of the following factors (which are likely to be present after a murder) can increase the prevalence of psychosocial problems in the wake of bereavement:

  (a) sudden, unexpected deaths

  (b) untimely deaths

  (c) witnessing of horrific circumstances

  (d) threat to the life of the survivor or other loss of personal security

  (e) guilt at having survived

  (f) intense anger or ambivalence

  (g) deaths by human agency, particularly when compensation is involved" (p. 49).

In 1964, Cain, Fast, and Erickson wrote: "the investigation of children's reactions to the death of siblings remains in an early stage" (p. 741). More than 30 years later, it still remains in an early stage.

Cain et al. (1964) found no credence for the theory of a child's belief that rivalry-bred hostile wishes might be solely responsible for the sibling's death. Rather, they emphasized the importance of multiple-based sibling tensions, rivalries, and hostilities as playing an important role in the overall analysis of the child's response to the death of a sibling. Whenever a child dies, there is usually blame leveled all around. Some families focus the blame externally, while others do so internally. It is no wonder that surviving children feel that they, too, are to blame for the death. I have found that surviving siblings suffer intense feelings of guilt, particularly when the parents are obviously preoccupied and devastated by their grief and fail to discuss the situation with surviving children.

A frequent effect on a child of the death of a sibling is a disturbed attitude toward doctors, hospitals, and religion. Not only can doctors be seen as impotent in the face of illness, but they may also be seen as directly responsible for the death. Cain et al. (1964) suggested that these feelings expressed by the parents are then shared by the children. Surviving children may construe the hospital as the place where people die, and conse-

quently, if they or one of their parents must go there, they fear that they will never see each other again.

God, too, falls victim to the blame cycle. How can a God, who is supposed to be kind and loving, take a child from his or her family? Many children are puzzled and confused about why God would "kill," "murder," or "take" their sibling from them.

Other fears generated include an awareness of death and that "you don't wake up," making it hard to go to sleep. Some children counterphobically state "I can't die," or "I won't die," to cover the intensity of this fear.

Although the literature contains embedded references to the reactions of siblings to disaster, a search revealed no specific study of children's responses to the *murder* of their siblings. This area needs to be expanded in the research literature.

Violence

Homicide, the most violent of violent crimes, is the end product of the predisposition to violence. Violent crime statistics show an ominous increase compared with those of 1983. And not all crimes are reported. The concern regarding violence is growing in the nation as more and more individuals are victimized in ways of cruelty that never enter the national statistics.

Description of the Stages of Grief Response

As E. K. Rynearson (1984) noted, "it is the manner of dying rather than the event of death that determines the meaning of death, which in turn influences the form and course of subsequent bereavement" (p. 1452). Confrontation with homicide or murder immediately spawns terror. This type of death is condemned. In homicide, not only is the death by definition a violent one, it transgresses the bereaved one's need for privacy.

Murders are usually widely publicized, with investigations not only of the perpetrator, but also of the deceased and the family of the deceased, thus causing increased pain to the bereaved. There is no respect for privacy.

Murder is, by definition, a traumatic death. T. Rynearson (1994) noted that such a death produces "syndromal effects...(1) posttraumatic stress disorder((PTSD) experiences of intrusive reenactment and avoidance), (2) victimization (rage and a sense of defilement), and (3) compulsive inquiry (a social and psychological need for investigation and punishment of the murderer)" (p. 341).

Webster's New Universal Unabridged Dictionary (McKechnie et al., 1983) defines trauma in psychiatry as "an emotional experience, or shock, which has a lasting psychic effect" (p. 1942). The Diagnostic and Statistical Manual of Mental Disorders, Fourth Edition (American Psychiatric Association, 1994, DSM-IV) poses more elaborate descriptive criteria to satisfy the diagnosis of PTSD. (See Table 1).

Siblings can experience affect that could be more painful than the actual occurrence as they go over and over the details of their sibling's death. The reenactment, which they create in their minds, can grow in such painful detail that the actual torture can be experienced as occurring to the survivor. For example, Janet and Jean were 18-year-old twins. Jean was murdered by her boyfriend in a fit of rage and entitlement because she was ending their relationship. One day, Janet exclaimed, "I sometimes actually feel the knife as it plunged into Jean's throat."

The sense of victimization produces rage toward the perpetrator. This rage can lead to actually hunting for the murderer and killing in revenge. Although the revenge is not usually carried out, the desire for it can remain, thus interrupting and precluding grief resolution. When there is an investigation and intense questioning, as is frequently the case, patients report that the

wound inflicted by the sibling's death remains open and raw, ever irritated anew. Younger children usually do not get involved in the questioning unless they have witnessed the murder, but they suffer the consequences by absorbing much grief and uncertainty from their parents and older siblings. Older siblings are more likely to become involved in the investigation and questioning, particularly if there is even the remotest suspicion that they might have been involved in the murder. Being a suspect when suffering so intensely can seriously impair a surviving sibling.

An almost sadomasochistic tendency can be seen in the compulsive rumination and searching for the details of what happened. Each exploration deepens the wound, yet the surviving sibling seems unable to interrupt the process and often cannot do so without professional help.

Case Illustration: Patrice was a social worker in a nearby city when she received word that her sister had been murdered. Her sister had lived with her husband and three young children in a small, deeply religious settlement. The sister was found when the oldest daughter, age eight, could not get into her home because all doors were locked when she returned from school. She went to a neighbor, who called the child's father and the police. The father arrived within minutes. Finding the back door now open, he went through the house and found his wife face down on their bed with a cord around her neck and her jeans on backwards. He then heard some whimpering and opening the closet door in the children's room, found his five-year-old daughter and her playmate crouched in fear in the darkened closet. "The bad man" had told them that if they made any noise, he would kill them. The three-year-old was still with the baby sitter, who had been attempting to call the home.

Patrice seemed obsessed with the details of the case. She continued to go over each item, reading and rereading the police report, and investigating on her own. She questioned every-

---

TABLE 1
DIAGNOSTIC CRITERIA FOR 309.81 POSTTRAUMATIC STRESS DISORDER

A. The person has been exposed to a traumatic event in which both of the following were present:
    (1) the person experienced, witnessed, or was confronted with an event or events that involved actual or threatened death or serious injury, or a threat to the physical integrity of self or others
    (2) the person's response involved intense fear, helplessness, or horror
Note: In children, this may be expressed instead by disorganized or agitated behavior.

B. The traumatic event is persistently reexperienced in one (or more) of the following ways:
    (1) recurrent and intrusive distressing recollections of the event, including images, thoughts, or perceptions
Note: In young children, repetitive play may occur in which themes or aspects of the trauma are expressed.
    (2) recurrent distressing dreams of the event.
Note: In children, there may be frightening dreams without recognizable content.
    (3) acting or feeling as if the traumatic event were recurring (includes a sense of reliving the experience, illusions, hallucinations, and dissociative flashback episodes, including those that occur on awakening or when intoxicated).
Note: In young children, trauma-specific reenactment may occur.
    (4) intense psychological distress at exposure to internal or external cues that symbolize or resemble an aspect of the traumatic event
    (5) physiological reactivity on exposure to internal or external cues that symbolize or resemble an aspect of the traumatic event

C. Persistent avoidance of stimuli associated with the trauma and numbing of general responsiveness (not present before the trauma), as indicated by three (or more) of the following:
    (1) efforts to avoid thoughts, feelings, or conversations associated with the trauma
    (2) efforts to avoid activities, places, or people that arouse recollections of the trauma
    (3) inability to recall an important aspect of the trauma.
    (4) markedly diminished interest or participation in significant activities
    (5) feeling of detachment or estrangement from others
    (6) restricted range of affect (e.g., unable to have loving feelings)
    (7) sense of a foreshortened future (e.g., does not expect to have a career, marriage, children, or a normal life span)

D. Persistent symptoms of increased arousal (not present before the trauma), as indicated by two (or more) of the following:
    (1) difficulty falling or staying asleep
    (2) irritability or outbursts of anger
    (3) difficulty concentrating
    (4) hypervigilance
    (5) exaggerated startle response

E. Duration of the disturbance (symptoms in Criteria B, C, and D for more than 1 month)

F. The disturbance causes clinically significant distress or impairment in social, occupational, or other important areas of functioning

Specify if:
    Acute: if duration of symptoms is less than 3 months
    Chronic: if duration of symptoms is 3 months or more

Specify if:
    With Delayed Onset: onset of symptoms is at least 6 months after the stressor

---

American Psychiatric Association (1994). *Diagnostic and Statistical Manual of Mental Disorders* (4th ed.). Washington, DC: American Psychiatric Association, pp. 427-429. Reprinted with permission.

one who was even remotely involved with her sister that afternoon. There were many individuals to speak with because her sister had been very active in her church and in the community and was highly respected. The entire family was quite close knit, with many family members and relatives within the area. They were very supportive of one another, the husband, and the children. Patrice contemplated quitting her job to care for her nieces, and she visited their home frequently to be with them. When questioned during a therapy session, she admitted that a partial reason for visiting the home was to go through the rooms seeking more information about what had happened and how it had happened, hoping to gain some insight into how her sister might have felt and some clue to the murderer, who was never convicted, although a prime suspect was identified. This state continued for three years, until Patrice sought help because obsessiveness with the details was interfering with her work, her family relationships, and her life in general.

Excessive rumination such as that experienced by Patrice may indicate the presence of underlying guilt that is not being addressed. That guilt may be related to the early childhood wish that the sibling be gone. Sometimes an older or younger sibling may have actually stated, "I wish you were dead!" It is not uncommon when children are young, before age 10 (give or take a year or so), when they are still locked into a concrete mode of thinking, that they wish, in their omnipotent stance, to rid themselves of the competition or annoyance of the sibling. Those comments, uttered in moments of desperation, come back to haunt them when the victim sibling is indeed gone, and gone by means of violence.

Two kinds of reactions frequently occur, depending on the sibling positions of the survivor and the deceased. In my experience with grieving siblings, I have found a similarity to two Bible stories: Cain and Abel, and Esau and Jacob. Although I have not as yet found any reference in the literature to the latter pair, Masters et al. (1988) cited the Genesis 4:8 reference to Cain inviting his brother Abel to go with him into the field to kill him. The authors did not pursue that reference except to link it to history, literature, and the modern mystery thriller. They use the tale to illustrate the fascination humankind seems to entertain toward the deliberate killing of one human being by another.

In the biblical story, Cain saw that his brother, Abel, seemed to be favored by God, which was also true of another biblical story, that of Joseph and his brothers. Cain actually killed his brother, whereas Joseph — who was supposed to die — was saved by one of the brothers, who suggested that they sell Joseph into slavery instead. Both stories contain the familiar theme of envy of the attention and love that parents and God appeared to bestow on a younger brother.

Children who have difficulty with sharing continue to function on a less malevolent level by attempting to get their younger siblings into trouble, which usually backfires on them. In listening to little children whose sovereign domain has been invaded by the birth of a newborn sibling, one hears some devastating sentences. Philip, age 4, had listened to his new baby sister cry for some time before he exclaimed, "Throw her into the garbage disposal. She makes too much noise!" It is difficult for a monarch to give up his sovereign domain where all others are his servants. Sharing is not an easy skill to learn. These are the forgotten thoughts that come back to haunt a sibling at moments of tragedy.

When the murdered sibling is younger than the survivor, there may be underlying guilt and fear that the wish the child uttered many years ago — to be rid of the offending sibling — has finally been fulfilled — that is, the annihilation of the usurper of the throne. An oldest child is ruler of the domain until another child arrives to give him or her competition. That competition can readily be observed in very young children, who are frequently quite open in their dislike of the new baby.

With murdered siblings who are older, there is what I have called the Esau and Jacob phenomenon — that is, the stealing of the birthright, the privileges of the oldest or older child. Younger children frequently want to do what the older child can do and feel underprivileged in that they seem to be denied the opportunities that the older one has. Like Jacob of the Old Testament, the younger sibling wants the rights of the older brother (Esau) and often will do everything possible to get them. If something happens to the older sibling, there is the questioning of what should have been done. "Have I earned the right to be the 'oldest' child legitimately?" Many become reluctant to assume the coveted position and subsequently act out their guilt through irresponsible behavior.

Both of these reactions, whether to the death of a younger sibling or of an older sibling, speak to the surviving sibling's underlying guilt and will generally be expressed in terms of "If only...." "If only" I had called; "if only" I had died in his or her place; "if only" I had called him or her as I had planned.

Dealing with the fantasies and realities of the murderer and the murder scene, complicated as they are by one's internal agenda, generally is most difficult for the majority of surviving siblings. *These issues, however, are not the only cause of the sibling's grief. The response to the death of a sibling is multidetermined.*

Very young children do not have the cognitive ability to formulate in words their intense inner conflicts. They will express their feelings and guilt through their behavior. Their limited understanding convinces them that everyone knows that they are guilty and are thus to blame for the tragic death of their sibling. Consequently, they may tend to act out in negative ways, such as irritating one and all and getting into all kinds of mischief; or they may be extra good and become

extremely perfectionistic, as if attempting to prove to the world that their sibling's death could not have been their fault. After all, how could one so very good do such an evil thing as murder! The real tragedy is that little children are often overlooked in the grief process because they are "too young to understand," with consequent misbehavior or the beginning of a perfectionism that can continue well into adulthood.

Strange as it may seem, individuals in all stages of development may evidence behaviors similar to those of very young children described above. These reactions, however, appear to be seen in parents more often when they have lost a child, but not as frequently when they have lost a sibling — at least it is not so reported in the surveyed literature.

Individuals well into middle age may not have experienced the death of a close relative. They are, therefore, ill prepared to deal with the loss, especially the murder, of a sibling. Parents most often cannot help them much in dealing with their grief. Devastated by their loss of a child, the parents tend to overlook the deep pain of their surviving children. Meanwhile, the children feel left out, unwanted, and unable to understand their own pain. Observing the all-absorbing grief of their parents, these children report feeling as if their parents might wish that the surviving children had died instead. Regardless of the previous behavior of the murdered sibling, the parents tend to dwell on how that child did not deserve to be murdered. In desperation, burdened by their own pain, feeling guilty and responsible for their parents pain, many of these children resort to delinquent or self-destructive behavior to shock their parents out of their grief and force them to deal with something other than the loss of their child.

Many children are quite conscious of the motivation underlying their behavior. Seventeen-year-old Jennifer reported in a grief therapy session:

You would think Erin was the most perfect daughter in the whole world. But she was a pain. She sassed Mom and Dad, moved out into the apartment of a girl Mom and Dad didn't like, and when they cut off supporting her, she moved back home, but her behavior didn't change much. She continued to date the creep who killed her despite what Mom and Dad said. That night, the night of the murder, they told her not to go out, but she went out anyway. Now I feel guilty. Perhaps if I had added my voice to theirs, it might have made a difference. Now I'm the oldest. What a drag! What am I to do? I'm mad at Mom and Dad because it's as if the rest of us don't exist. Yet I feel I should do something to snap them out of their depression.

Death of a sibling may be more traumatic when both siblings are still quite young and living in the home. After siblings leave the parental home, many tend to grow apart and become absorbed in their own families, their own friends, and their own interests. The loss of a sibling may not be as traumatic later in life, although this is not necessarily the case. Some siblings grow even closer as they age. They may live in the same vicinity, socialize together, and share many other aspects of their lives.

Case Illustration: Sara and Beth were sisters who seemed to grow closer through the years. Both were in their 60s when Sara died of breast cancer. This death was especially difficult for Beth, who had lost her oldest son to colon cancer just months before her sister's diagnosis. Her son had been an oncology doctor and director of the oncology unit at a hospital in another city and state. The two sisters had entertained together and shared so much throughout the years. Because Beth's son had been out of the home for many years, it was difficult to determine whose death affected her more, although cancer had killed them both.

Although the above example does not involve the murder of a sibling, it illustrates a common

cognitive-affective-behavioral process experienced by a surviving sibling. It generally takes about two to four weeks for the initial shock resulting from sudden death to wear off — sometimes even longer. In cases of death due to violence, it may take considerably longer. Dealing with the shock, the trauma of the initial confrontation with the death of a sibling, tends to numb an individual. This numbness can be confusing for the onlooker who might mistake it for indifference.

Masters et al. (1988) emphasized the problems created by the justice system. Repeated confrontations with the criminal justice system, pretrial hearings, the trial itself if the murderer is caught, the recital of the details of the murder, the sentencing, and later, the parole hearing or the freeing of the defendant tend to reopen wounds that may have begun to heal. Frequently, the murderer is not caught, and the family members — especially the siblings — may live in fear for their own lives. Even after the defendant is sentenced, there is always the possibility that he or she will someday be freed. Healing for the sibling and other members of the family will come only when they can let go of their anger — an extremely difficult task in these circumstances.

Treatment

Initial interventions must take into consideration that surviving siblings have been severely traumatized by the suddenness and the brutality of the death of the sibling. As T. Rynearson (1994) stated, "If the patient presents in a flooded state of reenactment imagery, then restructuring this traumatic fantasy will be the initial goal of therapy" (p. 343). Children, adolescents, and adults alike must first be calmed and helped to gain some resiliency, stability, and a sense of self separate and apart from the deceased sibling before work with the loss of that sibling can be initiated. Losing a sibling also brings to mind the possibility of one's own death, a concept that in the busyness of everyday life is conveniently avoided.

Terr (1981) reported on her study that included the "25 youngsters who had been kidnapped from their Chowchilla, Calif., school bus in July 1976 and of one child who had left the bus before its capture" (p. 1543). According to reports, three young kidnappers, for unknown reasons, boarded the bus at gun point, forced the driver and the children into two blackened vans, drove them around for about 11 hours, and then buried them alive for 16 hours in a truck-trailer. Eventually, two of the kidnapped boys managed to dig their way out of the trailer and helped the entire group to escape.

Later, Terr (1983) reported on her 4- to 5-year follow-up of these children, noting that their posttraumatic play represented attempts to cope with feelings they were unable to verbalize. Adults, in their behavior, can do the same. Terr found 11 characteristics in her study of these children, as follows:

compulsive repetitiveness, unconscious link to the traumatic event, literalness, failure to relieve anxiety, wide age range of players, varying lag time prior to its development, carrying power to involve nontraumatized children, contagion to new generations, danger, art, and talk as alternative modes of playing, and usefulness of tracing post-traumatic play to an earlier trauma (p. 741).

Terr (1983) also found that many of the children did not want others to know that they were part of the Chowchilla kidnapping. They were embarrassed by what had been their early vulnerability, even though they had effected their own release without injury or death. Although half (13) of the 26 original children involved in the kidnapping volunteered to participate in the follow-up study, the others joined the study only when it was decided to offer each child $100 for participating.

Terr (1983) found that each of these children

continued to exhibit posttraumatic effects 4 to 5 years after the experience. The severity of their symptoms depended on their prior vulnerability, the family pathology, and the community bonding. A new finding not evident in her previous work with these children was profound pessimism about the future. They did not expect to live very long and expected some future disaster. They also reported a belief in omens and predictions, suggesting that they believed they may have been given a warning sign that they did not recognize and did not follow through on. At this follow-up, they had developed memories that were inaccurate. Generally, the children did not want to think about what had happened. They experienced considerable shame and avoided telling others about what had happened. These children continued to suffer repeated nightmares and dreams of their death. Clearly, the brief treatment given to these children 5 to 13 months after the experience did not prevent the symptoms and signs from surfacing four years later.

The reactions of the children, however, were different from those of the adults. Terr (1983) noted that

there were significant differences between the long-term responses of children and adults to trauma: (1) The children did not become fully or partly amnesic, (2) 'psychic numbing' was not observed..., (3) intrusive, dysphoric flashbacks were not evident..., (4) decline in school performance was relatively infrequent..., (5) posttraumatic play and reenactment were more frequently observed...and were more important to their personality development, (6) time skew was a more frequent posttraumatic manifestation..., and (7) a limited view of the future was particularly striking (p. 1550).

Terr (1983) concluded from her work with these children over a 4- to 5-year period that children are not more flexible than adults following a pure psychic trauma. They were still vulnerable to reexperiencing the kidnapping trauma and its sequelae. Although Terr's work did not deal directly with the murder of a sibling, the information on the trauma response would be helpful in working with a sibling traumatized by the murder of a brother or sister.

If Terr (1983) found the above reactions where no death had occurred, what would be the impact of death on the victim's survivors? In any work with sibling survivors, these issues must not be forgotten.

Pynoos, Nader, Frederick, Gonda, and Stuber (1987) followed the children who attended an elementary school where a sniper attack resulted in the death of a schoolmate. Shortly after the school dismissal bell rang on February 24, 1984, a sniper concealed behind a second-story window across the street, opened fire on the children still in the school yard. "One ten-year-old, fifth-grade girl was killed, and more than 13 other children, and one playground supervisor, were wounded" (p. 54). This siege did not end until police stormed the room from which the sniper had fired and found him dead.

At a one-year follow-up, Pynoos et al. (1987) found that "children respond similarly to adults in the nature and frequency of grief reactions" (p. 60) and that grieving continues after one year. Children, however, find it more difficult to deal with their grief because neither their cognitive nor psychological capacities are sufficiently developed to comprehend what has happened and may continue to happen. In the event of severe trauma, as in the school incident, the nearer one is to the actual event, the more intense the trauma.

A significant contributing factor found by Pynoos et al. (1987) was the depth of the relationship between the individual and the one murdered. Adults may have difficulty in assessing their children's reaction to such trauma because children do not show a recognizable sadness. That capacity develops slowly and is rarely reached before adulthood, if then, as clinicians who work in this area will testify from their clinical practice.

Children and adults involved in the loss of a loved one, sibling or otherwise, are faced with the dual demands of trauma mastery and grief work. The trauma complicates the bereavement process and, if not addressed and worked through first, appears to increase the likelihood of pathological grief (Pynoos et al., 1987; Pynoos & Nader, 1988).

Pynoos and Nader (1988) proposed a detailed early intervention and psychological first-aid program for children of all ages. Much of what they proposed is also applicable to adults. No outline can include all factors that might affect an individual's response, particularly to the murder of a sibling. Therefore, therapists should remember that when the individual's response is out of proportion to what would normally be expected under the circumstances, they should look for other risk factors that might be known only to the individual.

The first area to explore, according to Pynoos and Nader (1988), is that of exposure. Did the victim survivor witness the murder? Was he or she on site but unable to observe what happened? Was he or she in the neighborhood or out of the vicinity? Other factors can affect an individual's response to trauma, and they need to be explored: (1) individual psychopathology; (2) family response, psychopathology, or both; (3) relationship with the victim; (4) experience of previous trauma, particularly during the previous year; and (5) worry about the safety of a family member or another significant other.

In working with children, many treaters make the mistake of accepting the parents' description of their children's grief. Parents, because of the depth of their own grief, may be poor observers of their children's grief and may be unable to differentiate "between symptom increase because of a previous life experience versus specific reactions to the current violent event" (Pynoos & Nader, p. 455). Pynoos and Eth (1986) presented what they described as "a widely applicable technique of interviewing the traumatized child who has recently witnessed an extreme act of violence" (p. 306). Their child interviewing techniques can be used with children ages 3 to 16. They have used it with more than 200 children and have taught it to other mental health professionals who also have used it in a variety of clinical settings, including homicide, suicide, rape, aggravated assault, accidental death, kidnapping, and school and community violence. They suggested that the method is "easily learned and involves a three-stage approach [that] allows for proper exploration, support and closure within a 90-minute initial interview" (p. 306). Pynoos and Eth reported that they do not find it necessary to have others present. They meet with each child alone in a quiet room. After some preliminary remarks, they give the child a pencil and a paper and ask the child to "draw whatever you'd like but something you can tell a story about" (p. 307). After they assure the child that the quality of the drawing is of no concern, the child is permitted to approach the task without distraction or interference. From that simple task, the rest of the interview proceeds.

One of the more subtle ways in which exposure to extreme violence may affect children is through traumatic influences on the ongoing developmental process. Terr (1989) reported that the children in her study tended to close in their vision of the future and did not expect to live long. Pynoos and Nader (1988) found that the children were frightened of the future and tended to avoid intimate interpersonal relationships, including marriage.

Pynoos and Nader's program for children exposed to violence and traumatic death, described in great detail in their 1988 article and more succinctly in their 1990 article, summarizes a well-rounded approach involving the community, the family, and the classroom to deal with this problem. The authors briefly discuss variant forms of violence witnessed by children —

domestic violence, suicide, homicide, rape, community violence, juvenile gang violence, and hit-and-run and vehicular manslaughter — and follow each with a vignette giving an example of that particular form of violence.

The symptom groupings listed by Pynoos and Nader (1990) state the violent event and list what can be expected to result from that event. For example, if the child experiences a life threat or is a witness to injury, then one must be concerned about PTSD; if there is a loss, then consider grief reactions; if the child expresses some worry about another, be alert to separation anxiety symptoms; and finally, a caution that a reminder of previous life experience could bring about an exacerbation or renewal of symptoms.

The treatment outlines created by Pynoos and Nader (1990) take the behaviors that follow a traumatic experience as listed above and succinctly give a treatment plan for the classroom, the family, and the individual working with the child. They include goals to be achieved with each plan. For example, if the child is exhibiting symptoms that suggest PTSD, the classroom should address the fears that the event could reoccur. The first goal is to minimize contagion of fear and its interference with daily activities and tasks. Goal two is to normalize the recovery process. The family would address the child's feelings of vulnerability. Their goal is to restore a sense of security. The individual treatment would be aimed at restoring the child's personal integrity. Goal one: thoroughly explore the child's subjective experience. Goal two: integrate the experience into the continuity of the child's life.

Although the previous references suggest ways of dealing with the PTSD symptoms, they do not speak directly to the trauma caused by the legal system. Families, as suggested by Getzel and Masters (1984), generally experience the legal system as uncaring and cold, with little concern for what the family is experiencing. The court system may appear to favor the criminal if one is caught.

Sprang, McNeil, and Wright (1989) illustrated the problems confronted by the victim survivors whose significant other has been murdered. Not only are they victimized by the criminal, but also by the legal system, including the press, which may hound them for reactions, comments, and stories about how they feel, especially during the trial. Sprang et al. suggested that "mourning for families of murder victims is more profound, more lingering, and more complex than normal grief" (p. 159). Complications inherent in the legal system prolong the grief. Often, the grief cannot be resolved until after the trial — if there is one — and even then, periodic reviews for parole can reactivate the pain of the original trauma.

Terr (1989) concluded that no accepted research study has established that a particular treatment is best for everyone. The possibilities for treatment are family, group, and individual psychotherapy. Usually, with siblings, any individual case and situation may require more than one type of treatment. Within the individual treatment group, a variety of modalities are possible, depending on the sibling survivor. These modalities include play therapy, psychodynamic psychotherapy, cognitive and behavioral therapies, and medication. Most therapists agree that a combination of these possibilities offers the most effective treatment.

This chapter has been devoted primarily to discussing ways to deal with the trauma of a lost family member. Although the literature speaks mainly to the impact on families and others, it does contain some references to the impact of such loss on a sibling.

As stated earlier, the first stage in the therapeutic work with these individuals will be to enable them to gain some resiliency, to establish some groundedness in dealing with the trauma. This phase may take a year or more, depending on the relationship that existed between the concerned parties, their age difference, their role in the family, and whether or not they were living at home or close to home. Other factors specific to the particular individual, such as the circumstances surrounding the murder and who committed it, will also impact on the grieving process.

Once the surviving sibling has established some equilibrium, the time may be appropriate to deal with the resolution of grief. Therapists must remember, however, that aspects of PTSD may interrupt the grieving process and prevent its resolution. In those cases, it is important to attend to the PTSD and what caused it to resurface before continuing with the resolution of grief.

There are many techniques to enable an individual to resolve matters left unresolved by the untimely death of the sibling. Some individuals are helped by writing a letter or letters to the victim sibling. Others may be helped through the use of imagery to clarify those unresolved issues and to come to some amicable resolution to problems, if they existed, within the relationship. Imagery that allows the individual to tap into the level of concrete thinking where there is no difference between what is real and what is unreal has proven very effective in relieving guilt and completing the unfinished business that prevents a satisfying ending (Cerney, 1989; Cerney & Buskirk, 1991). "From a fringe, even questionable existence," stated Block (1981), "imagery has risen to be one of the hottest topics in cognitive science" (p. 1). Eye movement desensitization and reprocessing (EMDR), pioneered by Shapiro (1989a; 1989b) and clinicians she has trained (Lipke & Botkin, 1992), shows promise in facilitating the working through of PTSD symptoms. Although somewhat controversial, this relatively recent technique on the PTSD scene involves the use of saccadic eye movements while holding in mind the most salient aspect of a traumatic memory. Following the procedures, which require the clinician to be trained by a qualified trainer, reported results include "(1) a lasting reduction of anxiety, (2) changes in the cognitive assessment of the memory, and (3) cessation of flashbacks, intrusive thoughts, and sleep disturbances" (Shapiro, 1989a, p. 211). Results have been reported after only one session.

Other techniques used by individual therapists have proven markedly effective depending on the individuals involved (both patient and treater), and on where the patient is in the grief process at the time of the intervention. Much depends on the sensitivity of the clinician and the timing of the intervention.

Summary

Surviving siblings of murder victims present a unique situation to the treater. These individuals share many, if not most, of the characteristics of other persons who have lost a family member to murder. They, however, share some other characteristics that may be peculiar only to siblings. Siblings are on the same level with each other, which raises many uncomfortable questions for the survivor. Death, something to be considered in the distant future and not at the present time, now becomes an immediate possibility.

The relationship with siblings can be quite complicated, depending on the psychopathology or health of the parents and the psychopathology of the individuals involved. Many factors will enter into the consciousness of the surviving sibling regarding the victim sibling. Now that the sibling is indeed dead, guilt can surface about having wished the other dead at some time in one's life. Other sources of guilt may relate to how the rivalries and expectations of each of them were handled.

There is a paucity of material devoted specifically to the understanding of the problems encountered by siblings when one of their own is murdered. Many of the problems are similar in nature to what families experience when a non-sibling member is murdered. When a sibling is murdered, the parents lose a child, regardless of

the age of the individual. How they handle the loss will impact on what happens to the sibling who has lost a brother or sister. Parents can become hostile to one another, blaming each other for what happened; frequently, the father becomes very stoical and the mother handles the grief for the family. Children, in desperation, may act out to distract their parents and to alert them to the existence of other children within their family. At times, the children may feel that they cease to exist because their parents are preoccupied with only one individual — the murdered child. For many children, when they lose a sibling, they also lose their parents. Their grief is multiplied and made an almost impossible task. When one is very young, the sense of self and one's capacity to handle the stress of daily living is insufficient to deal not only with the heavy loss encountered by the death of a sibling, but the additional enormous loss of the parents.

In working with individuals who have lost a sibling, one may encounter symptoms characteristic of PTSD. Before the actual grieving can be processed, the issue of the PTSD must first be addressed. This chapter suggests some issues that must be considered and addressed in the process of a total grief resolution process.

Annotated Bibliography

Jarratt, C. J. (1994). *Helping Children Cope with Separation and Loss* (Rev. ed.). Boston: Harvard Common Press. Although this book is not related to sibling loss resulting from murder, it does offer the clinician and caregiver some understanding of the problems children face in coping with loss. How children deal with these early losses or any of the multiple losses that they are currently facing will affect their development and their functioning in years to come. Grief resolution is not accomplished in a few sessions. Even children who receive help in the early stages of their grief may be left without help in the latter stages of grief. A good experience may be the main benefit of early intervention so that the child may be able to ask again for such an experience when the need arises.

van der Hart, O. (Ed.). (1988). *Coping with Loss: The Therapeutic Use of Leave-Taking Rituals* (C. L. Stennes, Trans.). New York: Irvington Publishers. The contributors to this book illustrate a variety of leave-taking rituals that can serve as therapy for individuals who have suffered the loss of a loved one. Therapists are shown how and when to use rituals with individuals who have experienced abuse or who have been divorced, individuals who remain preoccupied emotionally with a bad interpersonal relationship that has ended, and individuals suffering from posttraumatic stress. The underlying theme is to help the therapist work with patients whose difficulty in "letting go" of a person or situation prevents them from beginning a new life on their own.

Webb, N. B. (Ed.). (1993). *Helping Bereaved Children: A Handbook for Practitioners.* New York: Guilford Press. This book is helpful not only for its content but for the resource material included in its appendix: lists of suppliers of play therapy materials, bereavement resources, and references about different religious, cultural, and ethnic practices that can help the clinician and caretaker better understand an individual child's reaction to death.

Part 1 concretizes a variety of counseling techniques and therapeutic interventions for helping children who have suffered different kinds of losses. Part 2 focuses on family members, with topics ranging from the death of a grandparent to the traumatic death by murder-suicide of both parents. Part 3 looks at other deaths that can affect the child, such as the death of a neighbor, a classmate, or a teacher.

Acknowledgment: The author wishes to express her appreciation to Eleanor Bell for her editing of this manuscript.

References

American Psychiatric Association (1994). *Diagnostic and statistical manual of mental disorders* (4th ed.). Washington, DC: Author.

Amick-McMullan, A., Kilpatrick, D. G., Veronen, L. J., & Smith, S. (1989). Family survivors of homicide victims: Theoretical perspectives and an exploratory study. *Journal of Traumatic Stress, 2,* 21-35.

Block, N. J. (Ed.). (1981). *Imagery.* Cambridge, MA: M.I.T. Press.

Burgess, A. W. (1975). Family reaction to homicide. *American Journal of Orthopsychiatry, 45,* 391-398.

Cain, A. C., Fast, I., & Erickson, M. E. (1964). Children's disturbed reactions to the death of a sibling. *American Journal of Orthopsychiatry, 34,* 741-752.

Cerney, M. S. (1989). "If only..." Remorse in grief therapy. In E. M. Stern (Ed.), *The psychotherapy patient: The remorseful patient* (pp. 235-248). New York: Haworth.

Cerney, M. S. & Buskirk, J. R. (1991). Anger: The hidden part of grief. *Bulletin of the Menninger Clinic, 55,* 228-237.

Getzel, G. S. & Masters, R. (1984, March). Serving families who survive homicide victims. *Social Casework: The Journal of Contemporary Social Work*, 138-144.

Lipke, H. J. & Botkin, A. L. (1992). Case studies of eye movement desensitization and reprocessing (EMDR) with chronic post-traumatic stress disorder. *Psychotherapy, 29*, 591-595.

Masters, R., Friedman, L. N., & Getzel, G. (1988). Helping families of homicide victims: A multidimensional approach. *Journal of Traumatic Stress, 1*, 109-125.

McKechnie, J. L., et al. (Eds.). (1983). *Webster's new universal unabridged dictionary* (2nd ed.). New York: Simon & Schuster.

Parkes, C. M. (1993). Psychiatric problems following bereavement by murder or manslaughter. *British Journal of Psychiatry, 162*, 49-54.

Pynoos, R. S. & Eth, S. (1986). Witness to violence: The child interview. *Journal of the American Academy of Child Psychiatry, 25*, 306-319.

Pynoos, R. S. & Nader, K. (1988). Psychological first aid and treatment approach to children exposed to community violence: Research implications. *Journal of Traumatic Stress, 1*, 445-473.

Pynoos, R. S. & Nader, K. (1990). Children's exposure to violence and traumatic death. *Psychiatric Annals, 20*, 334-344.

Pynoos, R. S., Nader, K., Frederick, C., Gonda, L., & Stuber, M. (1987). Grief reactions in school age children following a sniper attack at school. *Israeli Journal of Psychiatry and Related Sciences, 24*(1-2), 53-63.

Rynearson, E. K. (1984). Bereavement after homicide: A descriptive study. *American Journal of Psychiatry, 141*, 1452-1454.

Rynearson, E. K. & McCreery, J. M. (1993). Bereavement after homicide: A synergism of trauma and loss. *American Journal of Psychiatry, 150*, 258-261.

Rynearson, T. (1994). Psychotherapy of bereavement after homicide. *Journal of Psychotherapy Practice and Research, 3*, 341-347.

Shapiro, F. (1989a). Efficacy of the eye movement desensitization procedure in the treatment of traumatic memories. *Journal of Traumatic Stress, 2*, 199-223.

Shapiro, F. (1989b). Eye movement desensitization: A new treatment for post-traumatic stress disorder. *Journal of Behavioral Therapy and Experimental Psychiatry, 20*, 211-217.

Sprang, M. V., McNeil, J. S., & Wright, R. (1989, March). Psychological changes after the murder of a significant other. *Social Casework: The Journal of Contemporary Social Work*, 159-164.

Terr, L. C. (1981). "Forbidden games": Post-traumatic child's play. *Journal of the American Academy of Child Psychiatry, 20*, 741-760.

Terr, L. C. (1983). Chowchilla revisited: The effects of psychic trauma four years after a school-bus kidnapping. *American Journal of Psychiatry, 140*, 1543-1550.

Terr, L. C. (1989). Treating psychic trauma in children: A preliminary discussion. *Journal of Traumatic Stress, 2*, 3-20.

About the Author

Dr. Mary S. Cerney is a clinical psychologist in private practice in Topeka and Kansas City, Kansas. She had been a Section Psychologist at the C. F. Menninger Memorial Hospital for 23 years until she took early retirement and went into private practice on March 1, 1993. Dr. Cerney is a Diplomate in Clinical Psychology of The American Board of Professional Psychology and is certified in Psychoanalysis by the American Psychoanalytic Association. Dr. Cerney is a clinical and didactic faculty member of the Karl Menninger School of Psychiatry and the Postdoctoral Program in Clinical Psychology. Currently, she is President of the Society for Personality Assessment.

CHAPTER 21

COGNITIVE RETRAINING OF CEREBRAL DEFICITS ASSOCIATED WITH VIOLENT BEHAVIOR

Marc S. Walter

Introduction

Although treatment of brain injury dates back to the First World War, it was not until the 1970s that cognitive retraining (and cognitive rehabilitation) were referred to as such (Boake, 1991). Since the 1970s, numerous programs have been established in medical centers and outpatient settings designed to help individuals with brain dysfunction return to premorbid levels of ability, if possible, or at least to help them increase their level of functional independence (Kreutzer & Wehman, 1991; Meier, Benton, & Diller, 1987; Uzzell & Gross, 1986). The retraining strategies differ depending upon the acuteness of the injury, the age and educational background of the individual, and the specificity (versus generality) of the brain dysfunction or behavioral disturbance to be treated.

In an inpatient setting, such as a neurorehabilitation unit, the treatment will be team oriented and focus on general cognitive variables, such as maintenance of basic alertness, attention, and orientation. The outpatient rehabilitation setting may focus more on practical areas, such as community reintegration and increased independence, in addition to specific problem areas, including memory and learning, visuospatial processing, or executive function.

It goes without saying that a vital part of cognitive retraining is to address psychological adjustment and reintegration. This, in turn, must take into account premorbid personality functioning, the direct effects of brain damage on personality and psychological functioning, as well as the psychological reaction of the individual to the trauma (Gordon & Hibbard, 1991).

In that damage to many areas of the brain can result in violent behavior both in animals and humans (Volavka, 1995), it would be expected that the principles and methodologies of cognitive retraining/rehabilitation would have been used to retrain violent offenders in prison populations. However, a Medline and PsychINFO search in February of 1995 found no published articles specifically related to this topic. Undoubtedly, many reasons for this lack exist, such as funding and philosophical issues. As will be pointed out, however, there are many good reasons to set up such programs for both the individual offender and society as a whole.

It is assumed that criminal violent behavior is multifactorial in nature. In a transactional model (see Volavka, 1995), an individual may have certain diatheses (for example, genetic abnormalities or cerebral dysfunction caused by prenatal or perinatal complications) which could interact with the environment to further reward or extinguish certain behaviors or create further cerebral dysfunction; this is reflected back upon the environment (e.g., the child's caretakers) and causes it to react back onto the individual. A specific instance of this process might be that of the "crack baby" whose irritability elicits physical abuse and neglect from his or her drug addicted mother. As a result, the infant suffers further brain damage and additionally learns inappropriate coping skills to deal with his or her environment. Subsequently, in school, the child's brain damage and aberrant behavior cause him or her to be selected out by teachers and other students as abnormal and, if not handled appropriately, the child may learn to use violent behavior to obtain his or her goals. The child may then be placed in a separate classroom with other behaviorally abnormal individuals or may "bond" with them through other means, thus providing the child with a peer group of violence prone individuals. Without adequate intervention strategies, this scenario only worsens as the child grows up.

Although not dealt with in any detail in this chapter, there are other behaviorally oriented techniques for dealing with violent behavior secondary to brain damage. For example, Novaco (1975) has written extensively on anger control, although he has not specifically applied this to individuals with brain damage. There is no reason, however, why this could not be done. Others (see, for example, Jacobs, 1993) have applied behavior analytic techniques to modifying inappropriate behaviors, including violent acting out in brain damaged individuals. Although it can be argued that behavior modification or cognitive behavior modification should be considered as part of the cognitive retraining process, especially when maladaptive behaviors are involved, it is a separate treatment modality and as such will not be discussed in this chapter.

Psychotherapy is also a critical component of the rehabilitation of brain injured individuals (Prigatano, 1994; Prigatano & Klonoff, 1990), but because it is an adjunct to cognitive retraining, it will not be discussed in this chapter. An important point in this regard is that cognitive retraining of violent offenders does not take place in a vacuum. Such individuals need to have a rationale for changing their behavior as well as sufficient motivation to do so. Individual, group, or family psychotherapy may be instrumental in helping them put their cognitive or neurocognitive gains into the necessary perspective so that they can use their new cognitive skills to refrain from violent outbursts.

Cognitive and behavioral deficits subsequent to brain injury are also subject to modification by numerous psychopharmacologic agents (Stein, Glasier, & Hoffman, 1994). Drugs such as lithium, propranolol, and carbamazepine (Tegretol) have been found to be effective in some instances for the control of aggressive behavior (Workman & Tellian, 1994). Furthermore, much research points to the relationship of low levels of brain serotonin and impulsive aggressive behavior in humans (see Volavka, 1995, pp. 49-58, for a summary). This suggests that coincident treatment of violent offenders with selective serotonin re-uptake inhibitors (SSRs), such as fluoxetine (Prozac), while they are in cognitive retraining, will be of value in their ultimate rehabilitation.

Brain Dysfunction and Violent Behavior

Although it has been amply demonstrated in animal research that brain damage in certain cerebral structures, such as the limbic system and the frontal lobes, can result in increased aggressive and violent behaviors, there is far from a one-to-one correlation of brain injury and aggressive behaviors in humans. In this author's experience, for example, working as a neuropsychologist in both inpatient and outpatient settings, I have never been physically attacked by a patient with brain damage and have been threatened verbally on relatively few occasions, despite having worked with several thousand individuals with brain dysfunction over a period of 15 years. Violent behavior on the part of brain damaged individuals is probably seen more in locked wards and forensic units and may be experienced to a much greater extent by the families of such persons (Brooks, Campsie, & Symington, 1986).

Head injury, presumably resulting in brain damage, is probably found much more often in violent offenders than in the normal population or even in the nonviolent offender population. For example, in a workups of 15 death row inmates "chosen for examinations because of the imminence of their executions and not for evidence of neuropsychopathology," all evidenced histories of "severe head injury" (Lewis, Pincus, Bard, Richardson, Prichep, Feldman, & Yeager, 1986, p. 840).

For the purposes of this chapter, there are two general types of brain injury which may result in or be correlated with violent behavior: diffuse injury and localized injury. Diffuse injury refers to damage to large expanses of the brain and may include injury to cortical or subcortical areas, or both. Typical causes of diffuse brain injury include perinatal hypoxia, moderate to severe closed head injury (e.g., as a result of motor vehicle accident head trauma), and dementing illnesses, such as senile dementia of the Alzheimer type (SDAT). With regard to specific structures in humans, the areas most likely, if injured, to result in violent behavior would be the frontal lobes and the temporal lobes/limbic system. Although it has been possible in animal studies to selectively damage discrete areas of the brain and correlate these areas with violent behavior syndromes, such specific lesion localization studies are not possible in humans. Furthermore, appropriately sensitive neuroanatomic measurement techniques have only recently become available to "map the brains" of violent individuals (Raine, 1993). It is likely, however, that these new technologies will allow much more specific "behavioral mapping" of the brain within the next decade.

Diffuse injury. A number of studies employing neuropsychological test batteries have found diffuse brain dysfunction among violent offenders as opposed to nonviolent offenders or other control groups. For example, Spellacy (1977) noted this trend for violent adolescents, as did Lewis, Pincus, Feldman, Jackson, and Bard (1988). A more diffuse pattern was also seen among adult violent offenders by Yeudall and Fromm-Auch (1979) and Spellacy (1978).

Diminished intellectual ability, as evidenced by low IQ, is often found after a significant brain injury; individuals with mental retardation, for example, often are found to have abnormalities in neurocognitive functioning (Skoff, 1988). In practice, the correlation between intellectual ability, as estimated by years of education, and neurocognitive functioning was well illustrated by Heaton, Grant, and Matthews (1991), for example. In two of the studies cited above (Lewis et al., 1988; Spellacy, 1978), the violent offenders had lower full scale IQs than the nonviolent ones. High levels of intellectual functioning may, in fact, correlate negatively with criminal behavior (Kandel, Mednick, Kirkegaard-Sorensen, Hutchings, Knop, Rosenberg, & Schulsinger, 1988).

Localized brain dysfunction. Inasmuch as the frontal lobes, specifically the prefrontal areas of the brain in humans, control executive functioning, it would not be unexpected to find an increased correlation between criminality, including lethal violence, among individuals with frontal lobe disturbance. Given that even in mild to moderate head injury (e.g., secondary to motor vehicle accidents) there may often be significant injury to the frontal lobe (Gennarelli, 1986), and that there are 3 million closed head injuries per year in the United States (Beers, 1992), it is fortunate that there is not a one-to-one mapping between frontal lobe disturbance and violent behavior.

In clinical practice with head injured individuals, one is not usually presented with a discrete lesion. Rather, a substantial area, such as the prefrontal cortex, the temporal lobe(s), or both, has sustained blunt trauma; often, diffuse injury to other sections of the brain is additionally present. The prefrontal lobes have, for example, been parcelled out, using animal and human studies, into three regions: the dorsolateral, medial, and the orbitofrontal. Injury primarily to the dorsolateral area may result in a condition called "pseudodepression," in which an individual appears to be motorically slowed, with flat affect and poor initiation. Injury to the orbitofrontal area may result in a condition termed "pseudopsychopathic," in which the individual is irritable and impulsive. Medial frontal injuries may result in an almost akinetic state (Parker, 1990). One of the most interesting studies in this area was conducted by Raine (Raine, Lencz, & Scerbo, 1995), in which 20 charged murderers and two charged with attempted murder were given positron emission tomographic (PET) scans while carrying out a continuous performance task (CPT). The CPT is felt to primarily engage the prefrontal lobes, so alterations in activity during this task would emphasize impairment in the subjects' brains compared to normal controls. Underutilization of the radioisotope-labelled deoxy-glucose was consistently seen in most of the murderers' prefrontal areas compared to controls. Similar reductions in premotor frontal areas were not noticed nor was reduction seen in other areas of the brain.

Several neuropsychological studies involving violent offenders have also localized dysfunction to the anterior brain, which would include the frontal lobes (Yeudall, 1977; Yeudall & Fromm-Auch, 1979; Yeudall, Fromm-Auch, & Davies, 1982); it might also include the anterior portions of the temporal lobes, however.

For temporal lobe dysfunction and violent behavior, there is more evidence of a correlation. In animal studies, injury to various limbic and temporal cortical lobe structures can result in violence (see Volavka, 1995, pp. 29-31, for summary). Limbic system functioning is quite complex,

given the number of structures involved, but it generally includes analysis, integration, modulation, and storage of affective material (and noneffective material to some degree). Subcortically implanted electrodes in violent humans have picked up abnormal electrical activity in such limbic structures as the amygdala (Mark & Ervin, 1970), and stimulation of these structures appeared to trigger rage reactions. The elicitation of rage behavior occurred at a significant time after stimulation of the amygdala, however, which weakens the correlation.

Psychosurgery for violent behavior was popular up until at least the early 1980s and limbic structures were often selected for ablation or interruption. The efficacy of such surgeries has been questioned, however (Valenstein, 1986).

Using functional neuroimaging techniques (PET), Volkow and Tancredi (1987) examined four violent psychiatric inpatients. The most consistent finding was decreased blood flow in the left temporal region of the brain, especially the cortex; in two of the four, glucose metabolism was decreased in the left temporal area; in two of the patients, frontal lobe abnormalities were noted. In addition, three out of the four patients had left temporal EEG abnormalities. Two of the patients had CAT scan abnormalities as well.

Yeudall and his group (Yeudall & Fromm-Auch, 1979; Yeudall et al., 1982) elaborated a left fronto-temporal-limbic damage theory based on their neuropsychological testing of aggressive criminals. Their theory maintained that injury along this axis in the left cerebral hemisphere facilitates the emergence of aggression.

Raine (1993) attempted to integrate the findings from various brain imaging and other types of studies of violent offenders as follows: He hypothesized that violent offenders tend to have more frontal lobe dysfunction, while sexual offenders have more deficits in the temporal lobe. Combined temporal and frontal lobe disturbance would characterize violent sexual offenders.

Cognitive Retraining

For the sake of argument, let us assume that violent offenders fall into one of the following three groups in terms of brain dysfunction: localized frontal, localized temporal, or diffuse. If we were given the opportunity to retrain such individuals, how would we go about doing so? There are a variety of approaches, but recent developments in the field of cognitive retraining suggest that the first step would be to ensure that the individuals are ready and sufficiently prepared to participate. At a minimum, they should have complete medical, neuropsychiatric, and neuropsychological workups, and be medically stable. For example, an individual with an uncontrolled seizure disorder would not be appropriate for cognitive retraining in that the person's periodic seizures would interfere with the learning of new skills. An individual whose behavior is unmanageable would not be ready to start cognitive retraining until completing appropriate cognitive-behavioral treatment. An acutely depressed, anxious, or psychotic individual would not be appropriate to retrain until his or her psychiatric disturbance had been brought under control. The person might require a significant period of psychiatric/psychologic treatment before the commencement of cognitive retraining.

Basic selection criteria should also be considered. In addition to medical and psychiatric considerations, intellectual functioning and intactness of the learning apparatus of the brain would be important in selecting out the individuals who would do best. The selection criteria, of course, would be based upon the type of program that is set up. In individual cognitive retraining, the goals and objectives are set for the individual and modified with the rate of progress. Therefore, persons of even significantly limited cognitive ability can be retrained to some degree; whether their ultimate level of retraining is going to be clinically meaningful or significant in "real

world" situations is a relevant consideration. For example, although we may never be able to rehabilitate an impulsive, irritable, and aggressive inmate with an IQ of 65 to live independently, the inmate may be able to be trained to channel his or her aggressive impulses into crafts or use self-talk to prevent acting out in stressful situations. Even persons with severe memory disturbances can be retrained to a limited degree (Gianutsos & Matheson, 1987), although therapeutic goals would be limited and they would probably need environmental cues to maintain optimal function.

On the other hand, in group cognitive retraining, selection criteria would be more important. For example, an individual with severely impaired new learning ability is going to be potentially disruptive in a memory group where most of the members are higher functioning. In certain group activities, however, such as those which place demands on frontal lobe functioning, an individual who is more impaired than the rest of the group may help the other participants gain perspective and illustrate many therapeutic points.

As mentioned above, there are two levels of cognitive retraining: general and specific. The general techniques of cognitive retraining involve such areas as basic attention (see, for example, Attention Process Training, APT, described in Sohlberg & Mateer, 1989), and abstracting ability (see, for example, the Reitan Evaluation of Hemispheric Abilities and Brain Improvement Training program, REHABIT, described in Reitan & Wolfson, 1988, Chapter VI). It should be noted, however, that both the APT and REHABIT programs can be used for lower and higher functioning individuals.

Other investigators (Bradley, Welch, & Skilbeck, 1993) have advocated using computer assisted cognitive retraining to improve "foundation" neurocognitive abilities before attempting to retrain "higher level" neurocognitive functioning. In some instances, in fact, Bracy (1983) has had success in sending patients home with computers and cognitive retraining software, which they used on a daily basis. The patients followed up with him on a weekly or bi-weekly basis, at which time he assessed their gains and reformulated the therapeutic goals as necessary.

As a practical matter, if an offender, in order to be retrained, needs initial extensive work in basic attentional and alerting areas, this would probably indicate that the individual had so much neurocognitive dysfunction that he or she would require a neuropsychiatrically oriented facility rather than a criminal one.

General cognitive retraining. The type of stimuli that one would use in a general stimulation program typically starts out simple, for example, flashes to one part of a video monitor, single target letters or numbers interspersed among others on a piece of paper or played on a tape, and progresses to more complex tasks, with the addition of multiple targets, distractor stimuli, increased background "noise," and multitasking demands. This discussion of generalized attention training raises an important issue among the offender population, namely that attention deficit disorder with and without hyperactivity (ADD/ADHD) is probably much more in evidence (Volavka, 1995) than in the general population. Thus, this type of cognitive retraining might be much more useful in the offender population, especially given that there may be hesitancy to administer psychostimulants because of their abuse potential.

Sohlberg and Mateer (1989) designed APT to retrain individuals across a variety of specific attentional modalities. These areas include focused, sustained, selective, alternating, and divided attention. In evaluating the efficacy of APT, they administered over 60 exercises in a hierarchical fashion over an average of six weeks, with an average of eight sessions per week, and found improvements in various attention measures and visual task measures, as well as some

transfer to memory function (Mateer, Sohlberg, & Youngman, 1990). The authors pointed out that transference effects (i.e., from improvement in attention to improvement in memory) occur because memory is so dependent upon initial attention to the stimuli to be remembered. In other words, if the stimulus material is not attended to, it is not going to be encoded and thus, is not going to be remembered.

The authors noted, however, that although attention training may improve memory function, it often does not improve it to premorbid levels, so that other methodologies will need to be used. They teach their memory impaired patients to use prospective memory techniques, for example, a highly structured appointment book, such as a Day Runner or Day Timer. An important part of their program is getting their patients to write down all necessary information under the appropriate category and date; it is also important to train the patients to consult their appointment books frequently. In addition, they advocated the use of other "external memory aids," such as alarm watches, timers, and computerized appointment books. This type of program can be adapted for individuals with diffuse, frontal, temporal, or other cortical (or subcortical) focalized dysfunction.

Attention can be affected by lesions to a variety of brain regions (Mesulam, 1985, Chapter 3), although lesions to different areas of the brain tend to produce different types of attentional disturbances. For example, lesions to the right posterior cortex may produce left spatial inattention or even left hemisensory neglect. In any case, some of the more complex types of attention, such as divided attention, are good examples of executive functions, and their presence reflects integrity of the prefrontal lobe. Divided attention, for example, is the basis for the ability to carry out multitasking activities, that is, the ability to switch from one activity to another without losing track of where one is.

It was pointed out above that individuals diagnosed with ADD or ADHD are overrepresented in the offender population. This brings up the interesting point that so-called attention deficit disorders probably are caused as much by disturbance in prefrontal lobe function as by disturbance in other attentional centers (Ratey, Middeldorp-Crispijn, & Leveroni, 1995). Individuals with ADD/ADHD often have difficulty not only with attention-related behaviors, such as the five types of attention discussed by Sohlberg and Mateer (1989), but also with such typical frontal lobe functions as learning from experience, adapting their behavior to the environment, delaying their impulses and gratifications, and "attending to" the long-term consequences of their actions. Thus, a connection is made between various aspects of attention and frontal lobe dysfunction in the ADD/ADHD population, just as might be expected from the connection seen in APT discussed above.

As a corollary, one would expect that APT (or a similarly styled treatment modality) would be effective for ADD/ADHD offenders. It is speculated that an important side effect of this type of treatment would be to teach the offender to pay attention to his or her own behavior and that this would be an important first step in enabling the individual to analyze the behavior and ultimately control his or her impulses.

Drawing from the well-known principle that "abstraction" is impaired by brain injury, either of localized or diffuse character, Reitan and Wolfson (1988) devised the REHABIT program. They utilized a five-track program, with track A being more language-based and track E being more visuospatially based. Track C is relatively free of spatial- or language-based stimuli, but depends more on "reasoning, organization, planning and abstraction skills." (Reitan & Wolfson, 1988, p. 186). Tracks B and D reference language-related and visuospatial-related abstraction, respectively.

Reitan and Wolfson noted that in many cases, cognitive retraining is initiated with Track C, inasmuch as impairment in relatively pure abstractive abilities is so frequent among brain injured individuals. Parenthetically, they pointed out that often times, attention variables need to be addressed in the course of retraining. Their tracks, however, do not routinely include specific attention training modules as such. However, Module C contains several attention tasks which can be used in different sensory modalities in individuals with attention problems. For example, one of the exercises is to underline the number "4" throughout a page of numbers. Other stimulus material, including geometric designs, letters, and words is also available. Various other activities in Track C involve physically (and visually) sorting objects and organizing different types of material. For example, the authors described a bead stringing task with five different shapes of beads in five different colors; the retrainer is encouraged to request the patient to sort at a level of complexity appropriate to that patient's needs and abilities. Thus, there appears to be a fair amount of flexibility built into this retraining system. Although Reitan and Wolfson (1988) disavowed it, many of the "abstraction" activities in Track C could be considered related to or dependent upon prefrontal cerebral functioning. This track then might be especially helpful in remediation of deficits for frontal lobe disordered offenders.

Temporal lobe retraining. Injury to the right cerebral hemisphere, including the right temporal lobe, often causes deficits in visual spatial and visual perceptual processing. In the case of the violent offender, he or she may have suffered an insult to the brain, such as a head injury or a stroke, which produced focal right cerebral damage and resulted in impairment in his or her ability to correctly analyze (and express) affective environmental stimuli. This may cause the individual to perceive and interpret others' behavior in a paranoid fashion, and, as a result, overreact violently. Injury to the right hemisphere may also cause an offender to underexpress emotions so that other people have difficulty reading his or her affect.

Various groups have designed rehabilitation programs specifically for visual perceptual disturbances (Diller & Weinberg, 1986; Gianutsos & Matheson, 1987). These groups focused on basic visual perceptual processes, such as visual scanning, which is often interrupted after injury to the right brain. Specifically, scanning to the left visual space is affected adversely; various other sensory modalities may be impacted (the ultimate result, for example, of a right middle cerebral artery accident results in paralysis of the left side of the body, as well as complete sensory neglect to the left side of personal and extra personal space). To retrain visual scanning, stimuli are usually presented via computer on a video monitor. More complex visual perceptual dysfunctions are retrained through various techniques; for example, deficits in affective perception and expression might be addressed in either individual or group settings.

Feedback from a therapist or other individuals in a group is very important to help the individual readjust his or her perceptions. Even if an offender continues to perceive in a distorted fashion, if the individual can be taught to check his or her hypotheses before acting on them, then he or she could become much less of a threat.

Disturbances in either verbal-semantic or visual-figural memory and learning may ensue from damage to the left or right temporal lobes, respectively. Numerous cognitive retraining programs on memory have been established; for example, see O'Connor and Cermak (1987), and Wilson and Moffat (1992). Without adequate memory, the offender will be unable to learn from experience, which will limit the individual's ability to benefit from treatment in general and may even limit the impact of punishment for his or her crime. Depending on the type of memory disturbance, there are a variety of techniques which

have been employed. O'Connor and Cermak (1987) discussed three types of memory retraining programs: imagery, mnemonic techniques, and organization strategies; behavioral techniques using reinforcers are also helpful. In the end, however, use of external memory aids, such as appointment books and alarm watches may be necessary. Therapy may be conducted on an individual or group basis; microcomputers are often used in the presentation of stimuli.

In discussing the rehabilitation of deficits associated with damage to temporal lobe structures, affective regulation/impulse control also needs to be mentioned. Problem behaviors initiated by distorted analyses of the environment have been discussed above under visual perceptual training. Not only must perception be retrained, but the individual must also be retrained to control his or her impulses before acting them out. Retraining in this area can either be in an individual or a group setting. It tends to be more "psychological" in its focus, in order to relate more to the development of self-insight to behavior, motivation, and the results or effects of one's actions. (This area can also be rehabilitated using "frontal lobe" techniques which will be discussed below.) Video feedback of behavior may play an important role in improving self-awareness and ultimately self-control.

Right-handed individuals with developmental or acquired injury to the left temporal lobe (the situation in left-handers is somewhat different) may have disturbances in speech/language function and may require cognitive retraining in this area. The type and intensity of therapy will, of course, be predicated upon the severity of the condition. In a survivor of a left middle cerebral stroke with both receptive and expressive aphasia (i.e., global aphasia), intensive individual and group treatment will be required and the outcome may still be poor. On the other hand, language disturbances acquired after a head injury may be bothersome but mild and readily amenable to treatment (Milton & Wertz, 1986).

As a rule, violent offenders would not show severe language disturbance unless they suffered stroke or focal head injury after incarceration. Rather, they would present with the residual language problems associated with developmental delays or head injuries acquired in childhood. They may have been in special education or had speech/language therapy as children. The focus of cognitive treatment as adults would best address areas such as appropriate use of language to express their emotions, verbal self-control, and use of "metacognitive" strategies to guide their behavior (see Ylvisaker, 1985, Chapter 12).

Frontal lobe retraining. As noted above, when individuals suffer head injury in motor vehicle accidents, both the frontal lobes and the temporal lobes are often injured. Thus, in practice, it is hard to separate frontal from temporal lobe patterns of injury; successful programs which specialize in rehabilitating head injury survivors incorporate modalities which treat both frontal and temporal patterns of deficits (Prigatano, 1990). Such patterns include both the memory and impulse control dysfunctions seen often when the temporal lobe is injured (see above), as well as the deficits in executive functions seen after injuries to the frontal lobe.

One of the more interesting and problematic neurocognitive disturbances typically experienced after frontal lobe injury is lack of awareness of a deficit (see Prigatano & Schacter, 1991, for a detailed analysis of diminished awareness syndromes occurring after insults to a variety of brain regions). Obviously, if an individual is not aware of a cognitive dysfunction, he or she will not be motivated to engage in rehabilitation, nor understand why therapists are trying to engage him or her. Depending upon premorbid personality factors, the individual may actually become hostile to therapeutic initiatives. As discussed previously, in violent offenders this hostility may erupt into aggression; thus, improving their levels

of awareness is critical.

The treatment of impaired awareness is varied, depending upon the degree of impairment, associated brain damage in other neurocognitive areas, premorbid (and postmorbid) personality characteristics, and setting. Barco, Crosson, Bolestra, Werts, and Stout (1991) discussed assessment and intervention strategies for three levels of awareness: intellectual, emergent, and anticipatory. It should be noted that each level includes the prior level(s). Intellectual awareness refers to the insight that a deficit exists in a general sense. In emergent awareness, the individual is aware of a difficulty as it occurs. Anticipatory awareness refers to the anticipation of difficulties due to a particular deficit. Barco et al.'s interventions include both facilitation and compensation strategies geared to specific degrees of impairment. For example, in retraining intellectual awareness, they use various feedback approaches (including video feedback, which they find quite effective) and self-rating scales.

As von Cramon and Mathes-von Cramon (1990) pointed out, there are relatively few controlled studies of treatments specifically designed to retrain frontal lobe dysfunction. They devised a technique called Problem Solving Training (PST), consisting of four modules presented in group format. The first module involved "generating goal-directed ideas," the second involved "a systemic and careful comparison of information," the third "consisted of tasks where multiple information needed to be processed simultaneously," and the fourth "focused on the patients' difficulties in drawing inferences" (von Cramon & Mathes-von Cramon, 1990, p. 173). They found that PST improved performance in several tasks dependent upon frontal lobe functioning, but that training in a placebo memory improvement technique did not.

In her seminal book on neuropsychological assessment, Lezak (1995) presented a four-component model of executive functions. These components are volition, planning, purposive action, and effective performance. Although it was not her purpose to present cognitive retraining approaches for retraining these executive functions, some representative interventions will be discussed in this chapter. In Lezak's view, volition "requires the capacity to formulate a goal or, at a less well conceptualized level, to form an intention. Motivation, including the ability to initiate activity, is one necessary precondition for volitional behavior. The other is awareness of oneself psychologically, physically, and in relation to one's surroundings" (Lezak, 1995, p. 651). It is important to note that the degree of impairment in each of these and the following executive behaviors will depend upon the specific area of brain damage and the degree of brain damage in the individual. One might, for example, see an individual in a criminal setting with almost complete lack of volition and inability to form almost any intent. Such an individual would probably be extremely apathetic and would most properly be confined to a custodial psychiatric forensic facility. The more typical individual would not have a severe deficit in volition (or, for that matter, other executive function areas), and the following interventions will be directed toward such persons. To retrain volition only, the therapist will need to investigate the patient's reinforcement system, examining for both internal and external reinforcers. When such an analysis is complete, the therapist will have a tool to initially manipulate motivational levels externally and ultimately teach the patient to manipulate such levels internally. At a more concrete level, the therapist is helping the patient verbalize, if possible, what he or she wants in a variety of situations, ranging from short-term concrete choices, such as food preferences, to long-term, more abstract choices, such as career decisions. It is likely that the patient will have some degree of lack of awareness along the dimensions listed above. The patient may, for example, offer his or her own

emotional responses to certain stimuli; for example, the patient may not be aware that he or she tolerates one guard while disliking another guard. The patient may only be aware that he or she periodically becomes agitated and not know why. First of all, however, the specific aversive stimulus would have to be identified. It is unlikely that the patient would know spontaneously that it was a particular guard whom he or she disliked. Rather, the therapist would need to take the patient through each aspect of the patient's daily routine and ascertain the individual's likes and dislikes. This would increase the patient's level of self-awareness, although such an intervention might need to be done on a regular basis as conditions change for the individual. The therapist could use a "self-talk" intervention, namely, the therapist could teach the patient to ask himself or herself in each situation what feelings were experienced, what he or she wanted to happen, and how important the outcome was, for example. Awareness of the physical, psychological, and social aspects of the patient's environment and how they impact the individual are also critical. The therapist will train the patient to attend to and then evaluate each relevant stimulus in his or her environment and then express a feeling in an emotionally neutral situation, or at least a thought reflecting its lack of relevance to the patient. Some of the treatment approaches discussed under attention training above may be useful in this case. Helping the patient understand and be aware of the impact of his or her behavior on others is crucial. This is best approached using role play, preferably in a group, although individual role play with video feedback can be helpful. Auditory feedback alone may be indicated if the issue is a patient's threatening or otherwise abnormal tone of voice, of which the patient is unaware.

Assuming that volition or volitional behavior has been sufficiently rehabilitated (or was not at issue), the planning component of executive functioning should be addressed next. Lezak (1995, p. 654) noted that,

> *in order to plan, one must be able to conceptualize changes from present circumstances (i.e., look ahead), deal objectively with oneself in relation to the environment and view the environment objectively (i.e., take the abstract attitude...). The planner must also be able to conceive of alternatives, weigh and make choices, and entertain both sequential and hierarchical ideas necessary for the development of a conceptual framework or structure that will give direction to the carrying out of a plan. Good impulse control and reasonably intact memory functions are also necessary. Moreover, all of this conceptual activity requires a capacity for sustained attention.*

Lezak (1995) pointed out that planning can be assessed using such tests as the Porteus Mazes, the WISC-R (WISC-III) Mazes subtest, or the Tower of London. (The latter test is based on the similar Tower of Hanoi paradigm, in which beads of different colors have to be moved from one upright to another to match a target pattern in the least number of moves.) These types of tests can easily be adapted for use as cognitive retraining instruments. In the cognitive retraining of planning, the therapist would start with a structured exercise, perhaps set out in a flow sheet format, with beginning and end conditions specified and alternative choices presented. A task readily adaptable to most situations and levels of functioning is map reading/route finding. One can start out with relatively few points on the map and a simple exercise to carry out, such as finding the shortest route from the video store to the bank. At a more complex level, the patient can be asked to make a dozen deliveries, scattered in different parts of town, in the most efficient manner. As the patient masters these types of exercises, more abstract and complex ones may be introduced. Presumably, in order to tap the patient's motivational system, it would be important for subsequent scenarios to be relevant to the

patient's needs; for example, planning ways to stay out of lock down, planning an appeal process, or devising ways to deal with other abrasive inmates or guards. In choosing a specific scenario, the therapist would initially present it to the patient and obtain his or her responses in order to establish a pretreatment baseline. The therapist would then perform a posttreatment test involving a similar situation to check for generalization. Optimally, by the end of treatment for this executive component, the patient would be able to generate his or her own scenarios and best responses to reach the goal.

As Lezak (1995) pointed out, purposive action involves "the translation of an intention or plan into a productive, self-serving activity requiring the actor to initiate, maintain, switch, and stop sequences of complex behavior in an orderly and integrated manner" (p. 658). Other key areas to be remediated in this executive component include self-regulatory behavior and inhibition of impulses. Impairment of productivity may need to be remediated if there is a "disassociation between intention and action..." (Lezak, p. 665). Patients displaying this problem will benefit from being cued through the execution of self-made plans as needed. Ultimately, the cues will be faded as much as possible. The plans would start out relatively simply, involving, for example, Tinkertoy Test constructions (which also make an excellent initial test for a variety of executive functions; Lezak, 1995), and progress to more complex work and social plans or goals which may need to be replicated in a group setting or in a work environment.

Also influencing productivity is flexibility of thinking, which involves starting and stopping a task at the right time and shifting cognitive (or behavioral) set as appropriate. Most often, the types of behaviors which will need to be remediated will involve perseveration or impulsivity. Perserverative behavior can range from perseveration of discreet physical acts or words, to more subtle perseveration of ideas or even problem solving strategies. Assuming that the patient is not showing perseverative behaviors indicative of more severe frontal lobe dysfunction, such as utilization behavior (in which he or she has no conscious control over his or her need to grasp objects placed in his or her hand), the patient should first be made aware of his or her perseverations using the techniques discussed above. Then the therapist can work with the patient on tasks pertinent to the particular area of perseveration. For example, a variety of Lurian Tasks (Lezak, 1995, pp. 671-672), such as copying alternating figures or letters, or rapid written naming of objects, are available. The therapist can work with the patient to moderate the patient's speed of responding and attention to the stimulus material to the point where the perseverations will drop out. At a higher conceptual level, the therapist has the patient "brainstorm," that is, generate as many alternatives as possible. The patient would then choose the best alternative. The treatment goal is, however, to increase flexibility of thinking so that the patient will not get "stuck" in a routinized response pattern.

As for the remediation of impulsivity, the approach is similar to that taken for the treatment of perseveration. More focus on maintaining sustained attention and awareness of what is motivating about the task may be needed. Once again, at higher levels of conceptual and behavioral complexity, "self-talk" strategies will be presented to the patient. The patient will ultimately cue himself or herself to stop and think before acting and, on a continuing basis reexamine his or her behaviors in light of shifting stimulus characteristics.

Achieving effective performance, which is the last executive component discussed by Lezak (1995), involves "the performer's ability to monitor, self-correct, and regulate the intensity, tempo, and other qualitative aspects of delivery" (p. 674). In many ways, the task of the therapist will be to get the patient to fine tune his or her behaviors. That is, the therapist will encourage self-correction in a variety of tasks and, in a group format, will encourage the participants to give each other feedback about the efficacy of their behavior or performance. The Random Generation Task of Baddeley (see Lezak, p. 674), in which an individual attempts to give a sequence of letters in random order, can be adapted nicely as a therapeutic exercise.

There are numerous other individualized retraining approaches that are based upon the relatively new specialty area of cognitive neuropsychology which are of interest, but will not be detailed here (see, for example, Burgess & Aldermann, 1990; Riddoch & Humphreys, 1994).

For illustrative purposes, a composite (but hypothetical) case is presented:

Case Illustration: Mr. R.K. is a 35-year-old, right-handed, divorced, White male with a high school education. History is remarkable for an alcoholic, verbally abusive father who left the home when R.K. was five; he was raised by his mother, who did not remarry, although she had one other child, a girl, when R.K. was nine. He developed normally, was an average student, and participated in athletics, being especially good in baseball until high school, when he started to experiment with drugs and alcohol. At that time, he began to "street fight" on a regular basis while "high" on alcohol, amphetamines, or both, and was knocked out briefly on at least 10 occasions. He never went to the hospital for these concussions and denied that they had any impact on him whatsoever. As a juvenile, he was arrested three times: once for drinking, once for simple assault, and once for shoplifting (of liquor).

As an adult, prior to the instant offense, he had been arrested twice for driving while intoxicated. He had been able to maintain steady employment in the construction trades, primarily as a non-union carpenter, although he had been fired from several job sites for intoxication, fight-

ing with coworkers, and "mouthing off" to supervisors.

He was convicted of second degree murder after beating to death an "old friend" with whom he was playing pool. He had been drinking prior to the offense (his blood alcohol was found to be .09 about three hours after the crime). He claimed that he had a "black out" and remembered nothing after meeting his friend at the bar. Witnesses reported that R.K. became enraged after missing an easy shot and attacked his friend with a cue stick when he made a sarcastic remark. He was apprehended at the scene and did not try to escape.

Neuropsychological evaluation was requested by the court prior to sentencing. The Wechsler Adult Intelligence Scale-Revised (WAIS-R) results were as follows: Verbal IQ 105, Performance IQ 98, and Full Scale IQ 102. The Impairment Index from the Halstead Reitan Neuropsychological Test Battery was .3, which is within normal limits (WNL). His left non-dominant hand performance on various motor and strength tests was worse than expected and he made slightly more left-sided sensory errors than right-sided ones. Naming and verbal fluency were WNL. Memory for verbal material was intact on a supraspan word list (California Verbal Learning Test), although he used serial position rather than semantic clustering to learn the list. Delayed recall of the Rey-Osterrieth Complex Figure was impaired, as was the copy; his copy was also segmentally, rather than holistically, organized. Speed in completing the Trail Making Test Part A was WNL; he was moderately slowed on Trails B, however. On the Wisconsin Card Sorting Test (WCST) he was borderline in number of perseverative responses and made four failures to maintain set, which is quite abnormal. Overall, the test results were consistent with right cerebral dysfunction, probably localized to the frontotemporal area.

Psychological evaluation, including projectives and an MMPI-2, showed mild defensiveness and concreteness. MMPI-2 elevations in Scales 3, 4, and 9 suggested diminished awareness in an antisocial individual.

During the first two years of his sentence, he attended substance abuse and anger control groups, which seemed to improve his insight in that a repeat MMPI-2 showed drops in Scales 3 and 9. He subsequently started a cognitive retraining program with two primary components: a group which focused on training interpersonal skills using a variety of psychological and cognitive exercises and individual cognitive retraining. The latter was geared toward improving "right hemisphere" skills, including visual memory, as well as executive functioning.

Initially, the cognitive retraining program involved increasing his awareness of his feelings about other individuals; it was noted, for example, that he responded in a distorted, and at times paranoid, fashion to a particular tone of voice of one of the other members of his group. This observation served as a basis for a training program that helped him realistically perceive and evaluate such behaviors. Video monitoring of him in individual and group treatment was also used to increase his awareness of his own interpersonal presentation. One of the results was that he was able to change his facial appearance in a better modulated way so that he did not always appear to be threatening to others. This change, in turn, helped him get along better with the guards who had felt that he was a "hard case" because of his facial expression.

As his self-awareness increased, he spontaneously showed improvement in his impulse control. This improvement was facilitated in therapy by helping him maintain sustained attention in a variety of complex cognitive and social situations. Furthermore, he was trained in generating alternative conceptualizations or responses to a variety of situations. Ultimately, the training in these areas enabled him to participate in the therapy group in a more creative and pertinent way.

Repeat neuropsychological evaluation after two years of cognitive retraining showed moderate, but significant, improvement in the Complex Figure, WCST, and the CVLT. His behavior in prison has been exemplary.

Future Directions. Because the area of cognitive retraining is relatively young, there is as yet no one-to-one mapping of treatment modality to symptom-complex in most instances. This is probably seen to the greatest extent for the executive function disorders. As the field matures, however, there will undoubtedly continue to be numerous single case studies of a variety of cognitive remediation techniques and ultimately more group designs. Additionally, novel uses of current psychotropics or the development of new agents may facilitate the ability of cognitive retraining in such areas as attention and memory. Continuing research using in vivo techniques, such as PET or SPECT scans, will undoubtedly change our conception of the schema of the brain-behavior interface, which, in turn, will remold many of our treatment approaches.

However, as stated at the beginning of this chapter, there have been no published studies of cognitive retraining in the criminal justice system. There is no question but that this represents a tremendous gap in that system. Although cognitive retraining would appear to be a labor intensive intervention, in fact, one could conceivably use inmates who had mastered one level of a particular executive function hierarchy to train others in that level. It is hoped that by conducting cognitive retraining in this fashion, the negative response to previously attempted systematized psychological intervention, namely "behavioral modification," will be avoided.

At a more basic level, however, it is hoped that as the criminal justice system becomes more aware of and takes into account the effects of brain damage on behavior and response to punishment, it will modify sentencing, incarceration, and rehabilitation procedures appropriately. A simple example of this could be to have a section of the prison for the neurologically impaired where even the guards had some specialized training in how to work with brain damaged individuals. Within this context, it would be a relatively straightforward process to place the prisoners in appropriate "classes" and treatment groups.

References

Alderman, N. & Burgess P. W. (1990). Integrating cognition and behaviour: A pragmatic approach to brain injury rehabilitation. In R. L. Wood & I. Fussey (Eds.), *Cognitive rehabilitation in perspective* (pp. 204-228). London: Taylor & Francis.

Barco, P. P., Crosson, B., Bolestra, M. M., Werts, D., & Stout, R. (1991). Training awareness and compensation in postacute head injury rehabilitation. In J. S. Kreutzer & P. H. Wehman (Eds.), *Cognitive rehabilitation for persons with traumatic brain injury* (pp. 129-146). Baltimore: Brookes.

Beers, S. R. (1992). Effects of mild head injury in children and adolescents. *Neuropsychology Review, 3*, 281-320.

Boake, C. (1991). History of cognitive rehabilitation following head injury. In J. S. Kreutzer & P. H. Wehman (Eds.), *Cognitive rehabilitation for persons with traumatic brain injury* (pp. 3-12). Baltimore: Brookes.

Bracy, O. (1983). Computer based cognitive rehabilitation. *Cognitive Rehabilitation, 1*, 7-8, 18.

Bradley, V. A., Welch, J. L., & Skilbeck, C. E. (1993). *Cognitive retraining using microcomputers.* Hillsdale, NJ: Erlbaum.

Brooks, N., Campsie, L., & Symington C. (1986). The five year outcome of severe blunt head injury: A relative's view. *Journal of Neurology, Neurosurgery and Psychiatry, 49*, 764-770.

Burgess, P. W. & Alderman, N. (1990). Rehabilitation of dyscontrol syndromes following frontal lobe damage: A cognitive neuropsychological approach. In R. L. Wood & I. Fussey (Eds.), *Cognitive rehabilitation in perspective* (pp. 183-203). London: Taylor & Francis.

Diller, L. & Weinberg, J. (1986). Learning from failures in perceptual cognitive retraining in stroke. In B. P. Uzzell & Y. Gross (Eds.), *Clinical neuropsychology of intervention* (pp. 283-293). Boston: Nijhoff.

Gennarelli, T. A. (1986). Mechanisms and pathophysiology of cerebral concussion. *Journal of Head Trauma Rehabilitation, 1*, 23-29.

Gianutsos, R. & Matheson, P. (1987). The rehabilitation of visual perceptual disorders attributable to brain injury. In M. J. Meier, A. L. Benton, & L. Diller (Eds.), *Neuropsychological rehabilitation* (pp. 202-241). New York: Guilford.

Gordon, W. A. & Hibbard, M. R. (1991). The theory and practice of cognitive remediation. In J. S. Kreutzer & P. H. Wehman (Eds.), *Cognitive rehabilitation for persons with traumatic brain injury* (pp. 13-22). Baltimore: Brookes.

Heaton, R. K., Grant, I., & Matthews, C. G. (1991). *Comprehensive norms for an expanded Halstead-Reitan battery*. Odessa, FL: PAR.

Jacobs, H. E. (1993). *Behavior analysis guidelines and brain injury rehabilitation*. Gaithersburg, MD: Aspen.

Kandel, E., Mednick, S. A., Kirkegaard-Sorense, L., Hutchings, B., Knop, J., Rosenberg, R., & Schulsinger, F. (1988). IQ as a protective factor for subjects at high risk for antisocial behavior. *Journal of Consulting and Clinical Psychology, 56*, 224-226.

Kreutzer, J. S. & Wehman, P. H. (Eds.), (1991). *Cognitive rehabilitation for persons with traumatic brain injury*. Baltimore: Brookes.

Lewis, D. O., Pincus, J. H., Bard, B., Richardson, E., Prichep, L. S., Feldman, M., & Yeager, C. (1986). Psychiatric, neurological, and psychoeducational characteristics of 15 death row inmates in the United States. *American Journal of Psychiatry, 143*, 838-845.

Lewis, D. O., Pincus, J. H., Feldman, M., Jackson, L., & Bard, B. (1988). Neuropsychiatric, psychoeducational, and family characteristics of 14 juveniles condemned to death in the United States. *American Journal of Psychiatry, 145*, 584-589.

Lezak, M. D. (1995). *Neuropsychological assessment*. (3rd ed). New York: Oxford University Press.

Mark, V. H. & Ervin, F. R. (1970). *Violence and the brain*. New York: Harper.

Mateer, C. A., Sohlberg, M. M., & Youngman, P. K. (1990). The management of acquired attention and memory deficits. In R. L. Wood & I. Fussey (Eds.), *Cognitive rehabilitation in perspective* (pp. 68-96). London: Taylor & Francis.

Meier, M. J., Benton, A. L., & Diller, L. (1987). *Neuropsychological rehabilitation*. New York: Guilford.

Mesulam, M. M. (1985). *Principles of behavioral neurology*. Philadelphia, PA: Davis.

Novaco, R. W. (1975). Anger and coping with stress. In J. Foreyt & D. Rathjen (Eds.), *Cognitive behavior therapy: Therapy, research and practice*. New York, NY: Plenum.

O'Connor, M. & Cermak, L. S. (1987). Rehabilitation of organic memory disorders. In M. J. Meier, A. L. Benton & L. Diller (Eds.), *Neuropsychological rehabilitation* (pp. 260-279). New York: Guilford.

Parker, R. S. (1990). *Traumatic brain injury and neuropsychological impairment*. New York: Springer-Verlag.

Prigatano, G. P. (1990). Effective traumatic brain injury rehabilitation: Team/patient interaction. In E. D. Bigler (Ed.), *Traumatic brain injury* (pp. 297-312). Austin, TX: Pro-Ed.

Prigatano, G. P. (1994). Individuality, lesion location, and psychotherapy after brain injury. In A. L. Christensen & B. P. Uzzell (Eds.), *Brain injury and neuropsychological rehabilitation* (pp. 173-186). Hillsdale, NJ: Erlbaum.

Prigatano, G. P. & Klonoff, P. S., (1990). Psychotherapy and neuropsychological assessment after brain injury. In E. D. Bigler (Ed.), *Traumatic brain injury* (pp. 313-330). Austin, TX: Pro-Ed.

Prigatano, G. P. & Schacter, D. L. (1991). *Awareness of deficit after brain injury*. New York: Oxford.

Raine, A. (1993). *The psychopathology of crime*. San Diego, CA: Academic.

Raine, A., Lencz, T., & Scerbo, A. (1995). Neuroimaging, neuropsychology, neurochemistry and psychophysiology. In J. J. Ratey (Ed.), *Neuropsychiatry of personality disorders* (pp. 50-78). Cambridge, MA: Blackwell.

Ratey, J. J., Middeldorp-Crispijn, C. W., & Leveroni, C. L. (1995). Influence of attention problems on the development of personality. In J. J. Ratey (Ed.), *Neuropsychiatry of personality disorders* (pp. 79-119). Cambridge, MA: Blackwell.

Reitan, R. M. & Wolfson, D. (1988). *Traumatic brain injury*. Volume II. Tucson, AZ: Neuropsychology Press.

Riddoch, M. J., & Humphreys, G. W. (Eds.). (1994). *Cognitive neuropsychology and cognitive rehabilitation*. Hillsdale, NJ: Erlbaum.

Skoff, B. F. (1988). The utility of neuropsychological assessments of mentally retarded individuals. In D. C. Russo & J. H. Kedesdy (Eds.), *Behavioral medicine with the developmentally disabled* (pp. 161-170). New York: Plenum.

Sohlberg, M. M. & Mateer, C. A. (1989). *Introduction to cognitive rehabilitation*. New York: Guilford.

Spellacy, F. (1977). Neuropsychological differences between violent and nonviolent adolescents. *Journal of Clinical Psychology, 33*, 966-969.

Spellacy, F. (1978). Neuropsychological discrimination between violent and nonviolent men. *Journal of Clinical Psychology, 34*, 49-52.

Stein, D. G., Glasier, M. M., & Hoffman, S. W. (1994). Pharmacological treatments for brain-injury repair: Progress and prognosis. In A. L. Christensen & B. P. Uzzell (Eds.), *Brain injury and neuropsychological rehabilitation* (pp.17-40). Hillsdale, NJ: Erlbaum.

Uzzell, B. P. & Gross, Y. (Eds.). (1986). *Clinical neuropsychology of intervention*. Boston: Nijhoff.

Valenstein, E. S. (1986). *Great and desperate cures*. New York: Basic.

Volavka, J. (1995). *Neurobiology of violence*. Washington, DC: American Psychiatric Press.

Volkow, N. D. & Tancredi, L. (1987). Neural substrates of violent behaviour: A preliminary study with positron emission tomography. *British Journal of Psychiatry, 151*, 668-673.

von Cramon, D. Y. & Mathes-von Cramon, G. (1990). Frontal lobe dysfunctions in patients—therapeutical approaches. In R. L. Wood & I. Fussey (Eds.), *Cog-

nitive rehabilitation in perspective (pp. 164-180). London: Taylor & Francis.

Wilson, B. & Moffat, N. (Eds.). (1992). *Clinical management of memory problems*. San Diego: Singular.

Workman, E. A. & Tellian, F. F. (1994). *Practical handbook of psychopharmacology*. Boca Raton, FL: CRC.

Yeudall, L. T. (1977). Neuropsychological assessment of forensic disorder. *Canada's Mental Health, 25,* 7-15.

Yeudall, L. T. & Fromm-Auch, D. (1979). Neuropsychological impairments in various psychopathological populations. In J. Gruzelier & P. Flor-Henry (Eds.), *Hemisphere asymmetries of function in psychopathology* (pp. 401-428). Amsterdam: Elsevier.

Yeudall, L. T., Fromm-Auch, D., & Davies, P. (1982). Neuropsychological impairment of persistent delin-

quency. *Journal of Nervous and Mental Disorders, 170,* 257-265.

Ylvisaker, M. (Ed.). (1985). *Head injury rehabilitation: Children and adolescents*. San Diego: College-Hill.

About the Author

Marc Walter, PhD, is a clinical neuropsychologist practicing in Phoenix, Arizona. He is a Diplomate of the American Board of Clinical Neuropsychology and the American Board of Professional Psychology. He graduated from Swarthmore College before obtaining an MA from Johns Hopkins University Medical School in pharmacology. He subsequently achieved his PhD in clinical psychology from the University of Miami in 1980. His current practice focuses on evaluating and treating head injured individuals. Criminal forensic evaluation of offenders with brain dysfunction is an area of special interest to him.

CHAPTER 22

THE HOSTAGE TRIAD:
TAKERS, VICTIMS, AND NEGOTIATORS

John A. Call

Introduction

To many, hostage taking is a new and shocking phenomenon, something that has developed in the last quarter of the 20th century. In truth, hostage taking has a history as old as humankind. In Greek mythology, there is perhaps the first documented use of a hostage negotiator and of the Stockholm Syndrome (Rahe, Karson, Howard, Rubin, & Poland, 1990). Persephone, daughter of the goddess Demeter, was kidnapped by Hades, king of the underworld. Intense and lengthy negotiations ensued involving the Greek state and Olympian deities. Demeter, in her anger, caused all the crops on Earth to die. This forced Zeus to send Eros as his "hostage negotiator" to seek a compromise with Hades. Following the negotiations, Hades allowed Persephone to return to Earth once a year, during the Spring. Demeter relented and permitted Earth's crops to grow when Persephone returned but then caused them to die in the Fall when her daughter reentered the underworld. The hostage, Persephone, at first rejected Hades' advances, but later came to love and marry him (Hamilton, 1942), thus reacting similarly to the more recent female hostage who divorced her husband to marry Jan-Erik Olsson, the Swedish bank robber who held her and three others hostage for 131 hours in the vault of Sveriges Kreditbank in Stockholm, Sweden, in August 1973 (Strentz, 1980).

Human history is replete with other examples of hostage taking. The Romans regularly exchanged hostages with other nations as part of treaties to ensure that each party would fulfill their obligations. In the Middle Ages, soldiers took hostages to sell for ransom. A notable example is the English king, Richard Coeur-de-Lion, who was captured and held hostage for ransom by Emperor Henry VI on his way home from the third Crusade (Montgomery, 1983). Other famous hostages of that era were Joan of Arc and Miguel de Cervantes. As late as the 17th century, there existed Christian religious orders, such as the Mercedarians and Trinitarians, which were dedicated to the rescue of hostages held as slaves in Islamic countries surrounding the Mediterranean Sea (Allondi, 1994).

Sea pirates, as well as renegade governments, have captured and used hostages to obtain money or goods from those third parties who valued the hostages' lives. From 1801 through 1805, the United States employed its most powerful warships, including the heavy frigates *President*, 44; *Philadelphia*, 36; *Constellation*, 36; *Chesapeake*, 36; and the *Constitution*, 44, in the War with

Tripoli. This war was fought, in part, to stop hostage taking on the part of Yseuf Karamanli, Pasha of Tripoli. Interestingly, the war ended on June 3, 1805, when the United States agreed to pay $60,000 for the release of American hostages and to evacuate the captured city of Derna, and Tripoli agreed to waive all claims to future tribute (Sweetman, 1984).

Air piracy began with the advent of air travel. One of the first documented "skyjackings" took place in Peru in the early 1930s (Phillips, 1973). A group of revolutionaries took command of a plane and dropped leaflets promoting its cause. At the time, the event received little media attention. Skyjackings began to catch the public's eye in the late 1940s, when armed individuals began to capture Eastern bloc airplanes in an effort to escape to the West. There were approximately 15 successful attempts over a three-year period, with the hostage takers forcing the captured planes to land in the American zone in West Germany. These hostage takers were hailed as freedom fighters and heroes rather than criminals or crazed terrorists (Phillips).

There were 32 skyjackings between 1948 and 1960 (Head, 1990). Not one plane captured was American. Then, in May of 1961, an armed man forced a National Airlines plane to fly from the U.S. to Castro's Cuba. The Western public did not perceive this hostage taker as a hero, nor the ones that followed. Skyjackings increased over the next decade, culminating in the dramatic capture of four planes over a three-day period by Arab terrorists in September 1970. By January 1973, the U.S. government required all passengers on U.S. airlines to be screened for weapons and explosives.

Most writers in the area of hostage taking and hostage negotiations mark 1972 as the watershed year in the modern history of hostage incidents. In March of that year, Palestinian terrorists took hostage 11 Israeli athletes participating in the 1972 Olympic Games in Munich. The terrorists'

demands were refused and the Munich police opened fire. An hour and a half later, 22 people were dead — a policeman, 10 terrorists, and all the hostages (Soskis & Van Zandt, 1986).

Following this incident, the governments and police forces of much of the Western world began to reconsider policy. For example, by January 1973, the New York City Police Department had in place a Hostage Recovery Program which included not only special weapon and action teams but also police detectives trained as hostage negotiators (Bolz & Hershey, 1979; Schlossberg, 1980). The success of police psychologist, Harvey Schlossberg, and police captain, Frank Bolz, in designing and managing this program garnered the interest of the Federal Bureau of Investigation (FBI). The FBI, following Schlossberg's and Bolz's lead, developed the Special Operations and Research Unit (SOARU), based at the FBI Academy located in the wooded hills of northern Virginia, southwest of Washington, D.C. Members of this unit are responsible for research and the training of FBI negotiators (Soskis & Van Zandt, 1986). Each FBI field office has at least one special agent trained as a negotiator. SOARU personnel likewise provide negotiation schools for state and local law enforcement agencies as well as work with the 51-member Hostage Rescue Team, also based at the Academy (Kessler, 1993).

Since 1973, the use of trained personnel designated as hostage negotiators has steadily increased in the United States. In 1989, a survey of all state police (n = 50), large municipal police agencies (n = 191), and a random sample of each state's small municipal agencies (n = 1169) was initiated. Of the law enforcement agencies that responded, 68% (17) of the state police agencies, 96% (125) of the large municipal agencies, and 30% (158) of the small municipal law enforcement agencies had a designated negotiator (Butler, Leitenberg, & Fuselier, 1993).

Hostage taking is a diverse and inadequately

studied phenomenon. Hostage takers may act alone or in groups. There may be one hostage, such as Patty Hearst, or hundreds. There were 450 hostages in the October 3, 1985 *Achille Lauro* incident and approximately 350 hostages in the September 5, 1986 Pan Am Flight 73 incident (McDuff, 1992). The motivations of hostage takers can vary, ranging from the trapped criminal to the political terrorist to the emotionally disturbed husband holding a weapon to his wife's head. Thus, the hostages may or may not be personally known to the hostage taker. Also, the location of the hostages may or may not be known to law enforcement. Furthermore, hostage incident locations can be mobile, such as an airplane, train, bus, or ship, or stationary, as in a barricade situation. Hostage incidents may be of short duration, spanning only a few hours (16 hours in the case of the "Munich Massacre"), or may last for weeks, months, or even years (444 days in the case of the U.S. embassy hostages held in Iran). Finally, although most people think of hostages as being people, there are many incidents of property being held hostage, such as the 1971 seizure of the Statue of Liberty by the Vietnam Veterans Against the War.

There has been little systematic study of hostage incidents, with almost all scholarly articles focusing on anecdotal information, developing concepts based on personal experiences, or both (Fuselier, 1988). Thus, a primary goal of this chapter is, for the first time, to compile and present in one place a summary of all, or almost all, statistical information related to hostage incidents accessible in the public domain. Frankly, this endeavor has been made manageable by the fact that there is so little information available. Besides the presentation and analyses of the statistical research, the literature regarding hostage taker typology, the dynamics, phases, and negotiator techniques related to a hostage event, as well as an analysis of the hostage experience, both during and after the event, are presented.

The Hostage Taker

Hostage taking is a triadic event (Soskis & Van Zandt, 1986). It involves the hostage taker, the hostage, and some third person or entity. Typically, the hostage has no value for the hostage taker except as a tool to influence or gain the attention of the third person (Schlossberg, 1980). What types of people take hostages? This question and its answer are a logical beginning place in developing an understanding of the hostage taking incident.

When exploring this question, one notes that most authors focus in some way on the hostage taker's motivation. Miron and Goldstein (1979) wrote that hostage takers can be categorized as having one of two motivating purposes. They term these as either instrumental or expressive. Instrumental hostage taking occurs when the hostage taker is attempting to achieve a goal or change some aspect of society. Expressive hostage taking is motivated by internal emotions and impulses which are often quite personal and obscure. Wesselius and DeSarno (1983) noted that probably most hostage takers have mixed instrumental and expressive motivations.

Strentz (1986) wrote that there are five types of hostage takers in the United States: the antisocial personality disorder, the inadequate personality disorder, the psychotically depressed, the paranoid schizophrenic, and the political assassin motivated by political-religious ideology. Hacker (1976) made note of three types: the crusader, the criminal, and the crazies. The crusader is that individual motivated by political-religious ideology. Crazies are people who are emotionally disturbed. Middendorf (1975) also noted three categories of hostage takers: political, escape, and personal gain. Cooper (1981) enumerated six categories. These are political extremists, fleeing criminals, institutionalized persons, wronged persons, religious fanatics, and mentally disturbed persons. Kobetz (1975) enumerated five types.

These are prison takeovers and/or escape attempts, aircraft hijackings, seizure of VIPs, interrupted armed robbery, and mentally unbalanced persons.

Fuselier (1988) and Soskis and Van Zandt (1986) promoted the four categories espoused by SOARU. These are the emotionally disturbed, the trapped criminal, the political terrorist, and the prison inmate. Butler et al. (1993) made note of these four types but also included a fifth category titled combination.

Table 1 suggests that there is a growing consensus regarding hostage taker typologies. The present author suggests six general categories. These are (a) Emotionally Disturbed, (b) Political Extremist, (c) Religious Fanatic, (d) Criminal, (e) Prison Inmate, and (f) Combination. The latter category is required because it is believed that

many of the others are not necessarily mutually exclusive. Furthermore, a thorough reading of the literature indicates that there are relevant sub-categories for several of the six general categories enumerated above.

Starting with the Emotionally Disturbed category, Fuselier (1988), following Strentz (1986), noted four subtypes. These are (a) paranoid, various types, (b) depressed, various types, (c) inadequate personality, and (d) antisocial personality. The use of the latter subtype is questionable in the context of the Emotionally Disturbed category. This subtype is descriptive of a personality disorder, not an emotional disorder. Logically, it is much more likely that individuals with this personality disorder will be involved in hostage incidents with instrumental motivations, such as a trapped criminal or terrorist skyjacking, rather

TABLE 1
EXISTING TYPOLOGIES OF HOSTAGE TAKING

RESEARCHER	YEAR	HOSTAGE TAKER CATEGORIES
Middendorf	1975	1. Political 2. Escape 3. Personal Gain
Kobetz	1975	1. Prison Takeovers/Escape Attempts 2. Aircraft Hijackings 3. Seizure of VIPs 4. Interrupted Armed Robbery 5. Mentally Unbalanced Persons
Hacker	1976	1. Crusaders 2. Criminals 3. Crazies
Miron & Goldstein	1979	1. Instrumental 2. Expressive
Cooper	1981	1. Political Extremists 2. Fleeing Criminals 3. Institutionalized Persons 4. Wronged Persons 5. Religious Fanatics 6. Mentally Disturbed Persons
Wesselius & DeSarno	1983	1. Instrumental 2. Expressive 3. Combination
Strentz	1986	1. Anti-social Personality Disorder 2. Inadequate Personality Disorder 3. Psychotically Depressed 4. Paranoid Schizophrenic 5. Political Assassin
Soskis & Van Zandt	1986	1. Emotionally Disturbed 2. Trapped Criminal 3. Political 4. Prison Inmate
Fuselier	1988	1. Emotionally Disturbed 2. Trapped Criminal 3. Political 4. Prison Inmate
Butler et al.	1993	1. Emotionally Disturbed 2. Trapped Criminal 3. Political 4. Prison Inmate 5. Combination

than the expressive acts of the emotionally disabled.

Likewise, the concept of inadequate personality disorder is believed to be of limited value as a subtype. Inadequate personality disorder is no longer a diagnostic classification as noted in the Diagnostic and Statistical Manual of Mental Disorders, Fourth Edition (American Psychiatric Association, 1994). Previously, this personality disorder described an individual whose day-to-day responses to emotional, intellectual, social, and physical demands fell short of the expectations of others. Early skyjacker profile work done by Hubbard (1973) suggested that a certain subset of these individuals did display inadequate personality traits. However, other diagnostic criteria were just as relevant.

Hubbard's composite profile of approximately 50 North American skyjackers suggested that these individuals were White males, approximately 29 years old, with a lower socio-economic background. Most were significantly mentally disturbed, physically weak, narcissistic, depressed, and paranoid. Many were diagnosed as suffering from paranoid schizophrenia. Interestingly, they were not really interested in politics and did not keep up with current events.

In his analysis of the Emotionally Disturbed category of hostage taker, Pearce (1977) described the following subtypes: (a) the brain damaged individual; (b) the elderly/senile individual; (c) the retarded, depressed person; (d) the agitated, depressed person; (e) the schizophrenic; and (f) the barricaded person as an equivalent to attempted suicide (suicide by cop). The dynamics of the first two subtypes involve a person who is brain damaged, either through traumatic brain injury or senility, who then experiences a loss of inhibition or control, as well as develops paranoid ideation. This sets the stage for a hostage/barricade situation. The retarded, depressed person is a descriptive term for an individual whose depression is, in part, experienced with significant

lethargy, fatigue, and motor slowing. It does not refer to a person with subnormal intelligence who is also depressed.

Kennedy and Dyer (1992), discussing a small sample of men who took their own children hostage, noted that each had a history of alcohol abuse, drug abuse, or both, and a family history and ethos of violent and unstable relationships. The hostage taking was initiated by situational stress within the family. A similar phenomenon was reported by Gist and Perry (1985). They described a group of hostage takers who did not appear to be motivated by severe emotional disturbance, criminal involvement, or political extremist activities. Instead, the hostage situations revolved around domestic incidents, suicidal gestures (as opposed to attempts), neighborhood conflicts, and alcohol related incidents. Finally, using Miron and Goldstein's (1979) typology of instrumental versus expressive, it can logically be assumed that the latter motivational label is probably more appropriate for the emotionally disturbed hostage taker.

With respect to the Political Extremist, Knutson (1980) described two subtypes: the reluctant captor and the deliberate hostage taker. Her research suggested that the majority of American politically motivated hostage takers, at least until 1980, can be classified as the former subtype. Her interviews with these individuals indicated that they were unwilling, if not unable, to kill their hostages. Importantly, they did not attempt to dehumanize their hostages but rather, before, during, and after the hostage event, experienced their captives as people and not things. The reluctant captors spent time trying to win over the hearts and minds of their hostages, some handing out pamphlets and other written material explaining their cause. They usually did not have a past criminal record. As hostage takers, they often acted in a naive or "dumb" manner in comparison to the deliberate hostage taker. For example, if a hostage asked to leave the hijacked plane, the reluctant captor might just let them go. Knutson summed up their personality style as dreamers and philosophers whose violent act was part of an attempt to right a wrong or a perceived injustice.

Deliberate hostage takers, on the other hand, are perfectly willing to execute their captives. The hostages are discardable implements to be used as long as needed by the hostage taker. They are supremely goal oriented but unfeeling, like a shark seeking a meal. Although uncaring, they are well aware of the hostages' emotions but use them to their own ends. They will terrorize one minute and act friendly the next in their effort to control the situation. However, they are constantly aware that it is their ability to kill that provides them ultimate control. Interestingly, Knutson found in her sample that, as children, both subtypes of hostage takers were likely to have experienced a close brush with death.

There have been other attempts to explain the political extremist from a psychological point of view. Ferracuti (1982) concluded that the best approach to understanding these individuals is to use what he termed "the subcultural theory." In simple terms, political extremists live in their own sealed communities or subcultures with their own unique self-imposed value systems. What may be relevant for the culture at large may be meaningless for the political extremist's subculture and vice versa. To understand a particular subtype of Political Extremist, one must first understand the values and mores of that subculture. Global theories applicable to all political extremists may be unobtainable. Thorough understanding may come only via investigation of each subculture.

Frankly, this makes sense. As an example of what this may entail from a scientist's point of view, Ferracuti and Bruno (1981) studied right-wing Italian terrorists and then conceptualized a set of traits which they termed the "authoritarian-extremist personality." These traits are only relevant to the political extremists studied, i.e., the right-wing Italian terrorist. This personality style or subtype is described in the following manner:

1. Ambivalent feelings towards authority.
2. Lack of psychological insight.
3. Conventional behavior patterns.
4. Emotionally detached from the consequences of their actions.
5. Sexual identity disturbances.
6. Superstitious and magical thinking.
7. Self-destructive.
8. Below normal educational experiences.
9. Perceives weapons as fetishes and follows violent subcultural norms.

Only Cooper (1981) enumerated the general hostage taker category of the Religious Fanatic. SOARU personnel do not, as yet, use this category. Nevertheless, the FBI hostage negotiators have had some experience with this type of hostage taker. One of the best known incidents resulted in the April 19, 1993 deaths of 96 Branch Davidians in Waco, Texas. Some may argue that the Waco incident was a barricade situation without hostages. However, there were 17 children who died in the fire who could only be considered hostages, even if they would have disagreed with that label. Unlike what was reported in the media, the FBI had a full complement of negotiators who were trained, experienced, rested, and well managed. It is this author's opinion that this group of potential barricade incident participants or hostage takers is worth labeling separately from the other general categories.

With respect to understanding possible subtypes of this category, the advice of Ferracuti (1982) concerning understanding political extremists probably applies. A thorough understanding of Religious Fanatics will likely require analysis of a particular cult's internal mores and values.

The Criminal category is usually thought of as consisting of the trapped criminal. For example, the bank robber who is unable to make his escape before the police arrive. However, from the victims' point of view, i.e., the hostage and the third party the hostage taker is trying to influence, the kidnapping situation is just as traumatic. Corsi (1981) developed a typology of terrorism that involved analysis of terrorist activity along two dimensions. His analysis is appropriate to not only terrorist hostage takers but to others as well. What are relevant to the present discussion are Corsi's Type 1 and Type 2 events. Both events are similar in that the perpetrators are intending to take hostages. They differ in that the hostage takers intend to hold the hostages at a known site in a Type 1 event and at an unknown site in a Type 2 event. This difference in location impacts most on negotiator style. However, the hostage experience remains the same (Siegel, 1984).

The major subtype in the Criminal category is the criminal psychopath. The criminal psychopath is also believed to be a major subtype in the Prison category of hostage taker. However, other subtypes also occur. For example, in the November 23, 1987 Oakdale, Louisiana, riot where 200 Cuban inmates held 26 people hostage at a Federal Detention Center, the only hostage seriously physically injured was stabbed by an emotionally disturbed inmate. This occurrence is also an example of a Combination hostage taker.

In summary, this author presents, in Table 2, a hostage taker typology. More extensive detailing of all possible subtypes awaits further research effort.

Hostage Incident Database Analyses

Ongoing systematic nationwide collection of hostage incident information is not being done. The fact that hostage taking is not a separate criminal offense may be one reason for this lack of data gathering. In other words, hostage taking occurs in the context of other criminal offenses, such as bank robbery or kidnapping, and it is these crimes that are reported and statistically analyzed, not the hostage incident. This lack of systematic research is unfortunate. However, a small sample of relevant databases exists in the public domain. The information contained in these databases is enlightening and confirms the need to develop and maintain a nationwide data collection effort. However, when analyzing these databases one must keep in mind the definitional structure of the data (i.e., international versus national hostage incidents, political extremist versus prison inmate hostage takers, etc.) as well as the time frame during which the data was collected.

Edward Mickolus (1976), while a Yale graduate student and later as a policy analyst with the Central Intelligence Agency, developed a comput-

TABLE 2 HOSTAGE TAKER TYPOLOGIES	
General Category	**Possible Subtypes**
Emotionally Disturbed	1. Brain Damaged 2. Elderly/Senile 3. Depressed, Various Types 4. Paranoid, Various Types 5. Schizophrenic 6. Substance Abuser 7. Family Disputes
Political Extremists	1. Reluctant Captors 2. Deliberate Hostage Takers
Religious Fanatics	
Criminals	1. Antisocial Personality Disorder/Trapped Criminal 2. Antisocial Personality Disorder/Kidnapper
Prison Inmates	1. Antisocial Personality Disorder
Combination	

erized database of over 3,329 international terrorist incidents from 1968 through 1977. This database is termed ITERATE which stands for International Terrorism: Attributes of Terrorist Events. Note that the ITERATE data excludes all hostage taking incidents which occurred in the United States.

In 1981, Corsi published an analysis of ITERATE data which covered 539 events of international terrorism occurring between January 1970 and July 1974. In part, Corsi studied (a) the type of hostage target (people versus property) in relation to whether the hostage location was known or unknown (Type 1 versus Type 2 event); (b) the purpose of the hostage taking; (c) the attitude of the hostage takers toward their own death; and (d) the duration of the hostage event.

Analysis of the data tells us that for a four-and-half-year period in the early 1970s, the most favored hostage taking scenario by Political Extremists was hijacking airplanes, followed by kidnapping. Overall, the most frequent purpose was the forcing of specific demands on a third party. The majority of Political Extremist hostage takers were not suicidal. In fact, the kidnappers developed elaborate escape plans. The duration of

a Type 1 incident was usually one day, while the duration of a Type 2 incident was usually five days or more.

A more thorough analysis of the ITERATE data was performed by Head (1990). Head used the full database of 3,329 international terrorist incidents from 1968 through 1977 in his study. During this time frame, a total of 6,042 hostages were held. Head was specifically interested in hostage taking situations and rearranged the ITERATE into three sub-categories of political extremist hostage incidents. These were hijacking, kidnapping, and barricade situations. In part, Head studied the number of hostage takers in terrorist hostage taking incidents and the number and types of casualties in such incidents. A review of his analysis, presented in Table 3, suggests that, from 1968 through 1977, international political extremist hostage takers preferred to work in groups of three or more.

Table 4 provides some very significant information about casualty rates in Political Extremist hostage incidents. First, it is apparent that, from 1968 through 1977, Political Extremist hostage situations were not particularly lethal to either the hostage or the hostage taker. For example, in only

TABLE 3
NUMBER OF POLITAL EXTREMIST HOSTAGE TAKERS BY INCIDENT
1970-1974 INTERNATIONAL TERRORISM:
ATTRIBUTES OF TERRORIST EVENTS DATABASE

Number of Hostage Takers	1	2	3	4	5 or more
	n %	n %	n %	n %	n %
Hijacking	15 (45.5)	17 (56.7)	21 (50.0)	14 (36.8)	21 (25.3)
Kidnapping	3 (9.1)	8 (26.7)	11 (26.2)	16 (42.1)	41 (49.4)
Barricade	8 (24.2)	5 (16.7)	10 (23.8)	8 (21.1)	21 (25.3)
Total	33	30	42	38	83

Note. *From The Hostage Response: An Examination of the U.S. Law Enforcement Practices Concerning Hostage Incidents* (p. 107a), by W. B. Head, 1990, Doctoral Dissertation, State University of New York at Albany, Dissertation Abstracts International. Copyright 1990 by W. B. Head. Adapted with permission.

TABLE 4
CASUALTY RATES IN POLITICAL EXTREMIST HOSTAGE INCIDENTS 1970-1974 INTERNATIONAL TERRORISM:
ATTRIBUTES OF TERRORIST EVENTS DATABASE

Casualty Rate	0	1	2	3	4 or more	0 v 1 or more
	n %	n %	n %	n %	n %	%
HOSTAGES WOUNDED						
Hijacking	66 (20.6)	4 (23.5)	6 (50)	1 (12.5)	10 (37.0)	76% v 24%
Kidnapping	220 (68.8)	10 (58.8)	4 (33.3)	5 (62.5)	3 (11.1)	91% v 9%
Barricade	34 (10.6)	3 (17.6)	2 (16.6)	2 (25.0)	14 (51.8)	62% v 38%
Total	320	17	12	8	27	83% v 17%
HOSTAGE TAKER WOUNDED						
Hijacking	77 (21.2)	8 (53.3)	2 (40.0)	2 (50.0)	0 (0.0)	87% v 13%
Kidnapping	237 (65.2)	2 (13.3)	1 (20.0)	2 (50.0)	0 (0.0)	98% v 2%
Barricade	49 (13.4)	5 (33.3)	2 (40.0)	0 (0.0)	0 (0.0)	88% v 12%
Total	363	15	5	4	0	94% v 6%
HOSTAGE TAKER KILLED						
Hijacking	75 (21.3)	7 (46.7)	3 (37.5)	2 (66.6)	2 (22.2)	84% v 16%
Kidnapping	234 (66.5)	5 (33.3)	1 (12.5)	0 (0.0)	2 (22.2)	97% v 3%
Barricade	43 (12.2)	3 (20.0)	4 (50.0)	1 (33.3)	5 (55.5)	77% v 23%
Total	352	15	8	3	9	91% v 9%
TOTAL DEATHS						
Hijacking	71 (22.7)	8 (24.2)	2 (15.3)	3 (50.0)	5 (23.8)	80% v 20%
Kidnapping	205 (65.0)	22 (66.6)	8 (61.5)	0 (0.0)	6 (28.6)	85% v 15%
Barricade	37 (11.9)	3 (9.1)	3 (23.1)	3 (50.0)	10 (47.6)	66% v 34%
Total	313	33	13	6	21	81% v 19%

Note. *From The Hostage Response: An Examination of the U.S. Law Enforcement Practices Concerning Hostage Incidents* (p. 108a), by W. B. Head, 1990, Doctoral Dissertation, State University of New York at Albany, Dissertation Abstracts International. Copyright 1990 by W. B. Head. Adapted with permission.

about 17% of the incidents were one or more hostages wounded and in only about 19% of the incidents were there one or more deaths. It is also striking to note that barricade situations were the most dangerous (more so for the hostage than for the hostage taker in terms of being wounded) and kidnapping incidents were the least dangerous. Explosives were the most frequent type of weapon used. Likewise, analyses of ITERATE data indicate that hostage situations where negotiation was used were generally less lethal than those where a government refused to acknowledge the hostage takers' demand (Miller, 1980).

A more recent analysis of Political Extremist hostage taking was performed by Friedland and Merari (1992). They developed a small database of 69 incidents of international and domestic politically motivated hostage taking incidents between the years of 1979 and 1988. Specifically, the incidents were either a barricade situation or a hijacking of transport, i.e., airplanes, buses, trains, etc. Kidnap cases were excluded from their database. These researchers were interested in developing a descriptive profile of the hostage incidents as well as identifying the factors that determine the outcome of the hostage incident.

Friedland and Merari's results indicated that in their sample, hijacking of airplanes and barricade incidents occurred with equal frequency (46.4% each). The majority of the hostages were civilian (59.4%) and did not possess a symbolic meaning for the hostage taker. The average number of hostages in a barricade incident was 35, with a range from 1 to 156. The average number of hostages in a hijacking incident was 131, with a range from 3 to 434. In 63.3% of the cases, there were five or fewer hostage takers, but the use of larger teams was also observed. For example, in 15% of the cases, the hostage takers used teams of between 6 and 10, and in 23.2% of the cases, teams of 10 or more were used.

In 43.8% of the incidents, the hostage situation lasted 24 hours or less. The remainder were fairly evenly distributed along the time line: 1 to 2 days — 17.5%; 2 to 5 days — 14%; 6 to 10 days — 7.2%; and 10 days or more — 17.5%.

In terms of outcome, the most frequent conclusion was violent, i.e., assault by the authorities (31.1%). It is unclear if this signifies a trend away from the low casualty rates reported in the decade-old ITERATE data. If it does, then Political Extremist hostage situations are becoming more dangerous.

The next most frequent outcome was unconditional surrender by the hostage takers (19.7%). In 36% of the incidents, the authorities gave the hostage takers full or partial concessions. A violent conclusion to the hostage situation was more probable if the hostage incident was a barricade situation, a trained rescue team was available, and no attempts at mediation or negotiation were made. This last result is consistent with the research of Miller (1980) mentioned above.

In his research efforts, Head (1990) developed two other databases. The first he termed the Hostage Event Analytic Database (HEAD). This database included 3,330 accounts of hostage taking, with the primary focus being on any hostage incident that occurred in the United States between 1973 and 1982. The second database was developed from the files of the New York Police Department Hostage Recovery Program and included 137 hostage taking incidents for the same time period.

A synopsis of some of the significant findings from the HEAD database are presented in Tables 5 through 9. The HEAD data represent a more random sample of hostage incidents in comparison to the ITERATE data, which dealt only with international political extremist hostage takers. Of note is the fact that the HEAD data suggest that homes, either of the hostage taker or the hostage, are one of the most frequent scenes of hostage taking, second only to various forms of transportation. This fact coincides with data from Strentz (1985) and Butler, Leitenberg, and Fuselier (1993) which suggested that the most frequent category of hostage taker in the United States is the Emotionally Disturbed. It is hypothesized that many of these individuals are taking family members, relatives, or acquaintances hostage in the home. Within the transportation category, aircraft had the highest frequency, making up 201 incidents. Head also noted that about 12.5% of the hostages were captured and held in their work place.

Seventy percent of the hostage takers in the HEAD data were categorized as criminals, prison inmates, or emotionally disturbed individuals. This may account for some of the differences noted in the HEAD data in comparison to the information reported from databases made up solely of Political Extremist hostage takers. For example, in the HEAD database, the hostage taker was more often a young, White male, acting alone, who took only one or two hostages. The most frequent type of weapon used by the hostage taker was a handgun (31%). Generally, the hostage event lasted no more than one day (approximately 31% ended within 6 hours) and the incident usually concluded with no one wounded or killed. However, hostages appeared more at risk for injury in com-

TABLE 5

HOSTAGE SCENE CHARACTERISTICS
1973-1982 HOSTAGE EVENT ANALYTIC DATABASE

Hostage Scene	Number of Incidents
	n %
Home	164 (20.4)
Public place	125 (15.6)
Office, school, place of employment of the hostage	100 (12.5)
Transportation i.e., motor vehicle, aircraft, other transportation, embarkation area	282 (35.2)
Prison	64 (8.0)
Other/Unknown	66 (8.2)
Total	801

Note. From *The Hostage Response: An Examination of the U.S. Law Enforcement Practices Concerning Hostage Incidents* (p. 112a), by W. B. Head, 1990, Doctoral Dissertation, State University of New York at Albany, Dissertation Abstracts International. Copyright 1990 by W. B. Head. Adapted with permission.

TABLE 6

HOSTAGE CHARACTERISTICS
1973-1982 HOSTAGE EVENT ANALYTIC DATABASE

NUMBER OF HOSTAGES	1	2	3 or 4	5-9	10 or more	Unknown
	301 (38%)	92 (11%)	68 (8%)	70 (9%)	184 (23%)	86 (11%)
GENDER OF HOSTAGES	Male	Female	Male & Female	Unknown		
	261 (33%)	146 (18%)	326 (41%)	68 (8%)		
TYPE OF HOSTAGES	Government Employee	Comm/Bus & Family	Bystander	Empl. & Bystander	Other	Unknown
	59 (7%)	240 (30%)	148 (18%)	205 (26%)	102 (13%)	47 (6%)

Note. From *The Hostage Response: An Examination of the U.S. Law Enforcement Practices Concerning Hostage Incidents* (p. 114a), by W. B. Head, 1990, Doctoral Dissertation, State University of New York at Albany, Dissertation Abstracts International. Copyright 1990 by W. B. Head. Adapted with permission.

ally concluded with no one wounded or killed. However, hostages appeared more at risk for injury in comparison to hostage takers. Perhaps one reason for such a high survival rate amongst the hostage incident participants resides in the fact that some form of negotiation was used in 64% of the hostage incidents (463 incidents used a trained or untrained negotiator versus 270 incidents which did not have a negotiator of any sort present).

In 1989, Butler et al. (1993) surveyed all state police (n = 50), large municipal police agencies (n = 191), and a random sample of each state's small municipal agencies (n = 1,169) with respect

TABLE 7
HOSTAGE TAKER CHARACTERISTICS
1973-1982 HOSTAGE EVENT ANALYTIC DATABASE

Number of hostage takers	1	2	3	4	5 or more	Unknown
	373 (47%)	123 (15%)	75 (9%)	54 (7%)	93 (12%)	83 (10%)
Gender of hostage takers	Male	Female	Male & Female	Unknown		
	635 (80%)	25 (3%)	82 (10%)	59 (7%)		
Race of hostage takers	Black	Hispanic	Asian	Caucasian	Other	Unknown
	35 (4%)	77 (10%)	41 (5%)	490 (61%)	41 (5%)	117 (15%)
Age of hostage takers	Less than 20	20-29	30-49	50 & over	Mixed	Unknown
	47 (6%)	152 (19%)	157 (20%)	18 (2%)	97 (12%)	330 (41%)
Motive of hostage takers	Family Dispute	Unintentional	Political/ Publicity	Money	Other	Unknown
	36 (4%)	30 (4%)	270 (33%)	181 (23%)	117 (15%)	102 (13%)
Typology of hostage takers	Political Extremist/ Religious Fanatic	Criminal/ Prison Inmate	Emotionally Disturbed	Other		
	165 (21%)	419 (52%)	147 (18%)	70 (9%)		

Note. From *The Hostage Response: An Examination of the U.S. Law Enforcement Practices Concerning Hostage Incidents* (p. 113b), by W. B. Head, 1990, Doctoral Dissertation, State University of New York at Albany, Dissertation Abstracts International. Copyright 1990 by W. B. Head. Adapted with permission.

TABLE 8
HOSTAGE INCIDENT DURATION
1973-1982 HOSTAGE EVENT ANALYTIC DATABASE

INCIDENT DURATION	NUMBER OF INCIDENTS
	n (%)
24 hours or less	426 (53.2)
1-5 days	122 (15.2)
6 days or more	86 (10.7)
Unknown	167 (20.8)
Total	801

Note. From *The Hostage Response: An Examination of the U.S. Law Enforcement Practices Concerning Hostage Incidents* (p. 113a), by W. B. Head, 1990, Doctoral Dissertation, State University of New York at Albany, Dissertation Abstracts International. Copyright 1990 by W. B. Head. Adapted with permission.

TABLE 9
CASUALTY RATES IN HOSTAGE INCIDENTS
1973-1982 HOSTAGE EVENT ANALYTIC DATABASE

NUMBER OF HOSTAGE TAKERS	1	2	3	4	5 or more
CASUALTY RATE	0	1	2	3 or more	Unknown
	n %	n %	n %	n %	n %
Hostages wounded	672 (83)	71 (9)	21 (3)	29 (4)	8 (1)
Hostage taker wounded	746 (93)	34 (4)	6 (1)	10 (1)	5 (1)
Responding official wounded	765 (96)	12 (1)	7 (1)	12 (1)	5 (1)
Hostages killed	704 (87)	55 (7)	16 (2)	21 (3)	5 (1)
Hostage taker killed	703 (87)	71 (9)	7 (1)	15 (2)	5 (1)
Responding official killed	781 (98)	7 (1)	4 (0)	5 (1)	4 (0)

Note. From *The Hostage Response: An Examination of the U.S. Law Enforcement Practices Concerning Hostage Incidents* (p. 115a), by W. B. Head, 1990, Doctoral Dissertation, State University of New York at Albany, Dissertation Abstracts International. Copyright 1990 by W. B. Head. Adapted with permission.

police agencies, and 45% (n = 529) of the small municipal law enforcement agencies responded. As noted in the Introduction, 68% (n = 17) of the state police agencies, 96% (n = 125) of the large municipal agencies, and 30% (n = 158) of the small municipal law enforcement agencies had a designated negotiator. These researchers, using this sample of 300 agencies which employed a designated negotiator, then studied various hostage situation characteristics.

Butler et al. (1993) found that negotiated surrender was the most common outcome (65% of the 410 incidents studied), with assault by the authorities the next most common (17%). Also, the data indicated that domestic law enforcement deals primarily with hostage situations that are not politically motivated. Of these, the most frequent hostage taker typology is Emotionally Disturbed. The next most frequent is the Criminal. The data also indicated that the lethality of the domestic hostage incident is much less than that observed in the politically motivated hostage incidents observed in the prior databases. With

respect to hostage taker deaths, the data indicated that the hostage taker was killed in 6% of the incidents during assaults and that the hostage taker committed suicide in 4% of the incidents.

Head (1990) provided an in-depth view of a large municipal law enforcement agency's experience in his analysis of 137 hostage incidents worked by members of the New York Police Department (NYPD) Hostage Recovery Program from 1973 through 1982. A synopsis of the significant findings is presented in Tables 10 through 14.

The data shown in Table 10 indicate that the home, either of the hostage taker or the hostage, is the primary hostage incident scene. This is followed by public places and the work place of the hostage. Hostage situations that involve transportation declined significantly in comparison to the previous databases. Most likely, this is due to the fact that the majority of the NYPD hostage takers were not Political Extremists, perpetrators who appear to favor mobile hostage situations.

Eighty-four percent of the hostage takers in the NYPD data were categorized as criminals,

TABLE 10
HOSTAGE SCENE CHARACTERISTICS
1973-1982 NEW YORK POLICE DEPARTMENT DATABASE

HOSTAGE SCENE	NUMBER OF INCIDENTS
	n %
Home	55 (41)
Public place	39 (28)
Office, school, place of employment of the hostage	19 (14)
Transportation i.e., motor vehicle, aircraft, other transportation, embarkation area	10 (7)
Prison	1 (1)
Other/Unknown	12 (9)
Total	137

Note. *From The Hostage Response: An Examination of the U.S. Law Enforcement Practices Concerning Hostage Incidents* (p. 140a), by W. B. Head, 1990, Doctoral Dissertation, State University of New York at Albany, Dissertation Abstracts International. Copyright 1990 by W. B. Head. Adapted with permission.

TABLE 11
HOSTAGE CHARACTERISTICS
1973-1982 NEW YORK CITY POLICE DEPARTMENT DATABASE

NUMBER OF HOSTAGES	1	2	3 or 4	5-9	10 or more	Unknown
	59 (43%)	35 (26%)	15 (11%)	13 (9%)	10 (5%)	8 (6%)
GENDER OF HOSTAGES	Male	Female	Male & Female	Unknown		
	43 (31%)	47 (35%)	37 (27%)	1 (7%)		
TYPE OF HOSTAGES	Government Employees	Comm/Bus & Family	Bystander	Empl. & Bystander	Other	Unknown
	5 (4%)	52 (38%)	36 (26%)	14 (10%)	23 (17%)	7 (5%)

Note. From *The Hostage Response: An Examination of the U.S. Law Enforcement Practices Concerning Hostage Incidents* (p. 114c), by W. B. Head, 1990, Doctoral Dissertation, State University of New York at Albany, Dissertation Abstracts International. Copyright 1990 by W. B. Head. Adapted with permission.

prison inmates, or emotionally disturbed individuals (see Table 12). This is consistent with the data produced by Butler et al. (1993). However, unlike these later research findings, the majority of the NYPD hostage takers were typed as Criminals, including some Prison Inmates, not Emotionally Disturbed. The data also indicated that, more often than not, the hostage taker was a young, White male (35%) or Black male (26%), acting alone, who took only one or two hostages. Again, the most frequent type of weapon used by the hostage taker was a handgun (41%). Generally, the hostage event lasted no more than one day (approximately 61% ended within 6 hours) and the incident usually concluded with no one wounded or killed (see Table 13). However, the

TABLE 12						
HOSTAGE TAKER CHARACTERISTICS						
1973-1982 NEW YORK POLICE DEPARTMENT DATABASE						
Number of hostage takers	1	2	3	4	5 or more	Unknown
	75 (56%)	32 (23%)	14 (10%)	6 (4%)	7 (10%)	3 (2%)
Gender of hostage takers	Male	Female	Male & Female	Unknown		
	119 (87%)	7 (5%)	7 (5%)	4 (3%)		
Race of hostage takers	Black	Hispanic	Asian	Caucasian	Other	Unknown
	35 (26%)	14 (10%)	2 (1%)	47 (35%)	7 (5%)	32 (23%)
Age of hostage takers	Less than 20	20-29	30-49	50 & over	Mixed	Unknown
	13 (9%)	50 (37%)	34 (26%)	2 (1%)	10 (7%)	28 (20%)
Motive of hostage takers	Family Dispute	Unintentional	Political/ Publicity	Money	Other	Unknown
	22 (16%)	8 (6%)	14 (10%)	53 (39%)	22 (16%)	18 (13%)
Typology of hostage takers	Political Extremist/ Religious Fanatic	Criminal/ Prison Inmate	Emotionally Disturbed	Other		
	4 (3%)	78 (58%)	35 (26%)	18 (13%)		

Note. From *The Hostage Response: An Examination of the U.S. Law Enforcement Practices Concerning Hostage Incidents* (p. 141b), by W. B. Head, 1990, Doctoral Dissertation, State University of New York at Albany, Dissertation Abstracts International. Copyright 1990 by W. B. Head. Adapted with permission.

hostages appeared more at risk for injury than the hostage taker (see Table 14).

The Dynamics of Hostage Taking and Negotiation

In some ways, hostage taking is analogous to theater, but a theater of terror instead of amusement. The hostage taker is the star, the hostages the supporting cast, and the public and law enforcement the audience. However, another way to conceptualize hostage taking, and perhaps a way that is more practical, is to understand hostage taking as an attempt by the hostage taker to solve a problem. In this light, hostage taking is a behavior designed and implemented by the captor in an effort to meet his or her needs, whether instrumental or expressive. Obviously, to initiate such a desperate act, the hostage taker must be experiencing extreme frustration.

Three different participants are linked in a hostage taking situation. The hostage taker is attempting to influence a third person or entity to meet his or her needs by threatening the well being of the hostages. Seemingly, the hostage taker has the upper hand. The hostage taker creates a crisis and either his or her demands are met or the hostages are killed. This childlike simplicity colors all hostage incidents and marks hostage taking as the ultimate narcissistic act.

The key question in any hostage situation is whether or not there exists a bargaining range. Can a bargaining model be implemented or will the incident be controlled by the concept of

TABLE 13
HOSTAGE INCIDENT DURATION
1973-1982 NEW YORK CITY POLICE DEPARTMENT DATABASE

INCIDENT DURATION	NUMBER OF INCIDENTS
	n (%)
24 hours or less	102 (74.5)
1-5 days	14 (10.2)
6 days or more	5 (3.6)
Unknown	16 (11.6)
Total	137

Note. From *The Hostage Response: An Examination of the U.S. Law Enforcement Practices Concerning Hostage Incidents* (p. 141a), by W. B. Head, 1990, Doctoral Dissertation, State University of New York at Albany, Dissertation Abstracts International. Copyright 1990 by W. B. Head. Adapted with permission.

TABLE 14
CASUALTY RATES IN HOSTAGE INCIDENTS
1973-1982 NEW YORK CITY POLICE DEPARTMENT DATABASE

CASUALTY RATE	0	1	2 or more	Unknown
	n %	n %	n %	n %
Hostages wounded	111 (81)	21 (15)	4 (3)	1 (1)
Hostage taker wounded	128 (94)	8 (6)	0 (0)	1 (1)
Responding official wounded	130 (95)	6 (4)	1 (1)	0 (0)
Hostages killed	126 (91)	9 (7)	1 (1)	15 (1)
Hostage taker killed	125 (91)	10 (7)	1 (1)	1 (1)
Responding official killed	125 (91)	10 (7)	1 (1)	1 (0)

Note. From *The Hostage Response: An Examination of the U.S. Law Enforcement Practices Concerning Hostage Incidents* (p. 143b), by W. B. Head, 1990, Doctoral Dissertation, State University of New York at Albany, Dissertation Abstracts International. Copyright 1990 by W. B. Head. Adapted with permission.

"brinkmanship?" Brinkmanship may be defined as the deliberate creation of risk, designed to be sufficiently intolerable to one's opponent so as to induce that person to meet one's demands. The brink is not a sharp precipice, but a slippery slope, gradually getting steeper, out of the control of either party (Dixit & Nalebuff, 1991). In brinkmanship, the winner takes all; there are no 50-50 solutions. Initially, the hostage taker attempts to predefine the situation as one in which brinkmanship, or crisis bargaining, is the rule. It is the negotiator's role to redefine the rules of communication, if he or she can, from one where crisis bargaining techniques are employed to one where normative bargaining techniques are used (Donohue, Ramesh, Kaufmann, & Smith, 1991).

Normative bargaining may be defined as that style of negotiation most commonly observed in the everyday world, where the parties attempt to develop a mutually satisfying agreement based upon the concept of quid pro quo.

Crisis bargaining is characterized by several features. These are (a) the use of coercion, (b) bargaining for high stakes, (c) focusing on one alternative, (d) high degree of emotional content, (e) preponderance of face or ego issues, (f) the feeling of urgency, (g) the lack of complete information, and (h) failure to work out detailed implementation and monitoring plans. Looking at these in more detail, the hostage taker believes that accommodation is not possible. Thus, the hostage taker feels compelled to coerce or force his or her opponent to act in the way the hostage taker desires. The stakes are high for the hostage taker, the hostage, and the negotiator. At the very least, someone's life is at risk. The hostage taker has one position or desire and focuses on that without considering other alternatives. In contrast, during normative bargaining, where the disputants are not actively attempting to coerce each other, where the stakes are not life and death, the parties are usually more willing to develop and consider alternative proposals.

Bargaining in a crisis situation is usually highly emotional, with the predominant feelings displayed being anger, hostility, and fear. Likewise, where bargainers use coercive strategies and tactics, "face" issues enter into the process. Substantive issues are thus left undiscussed while communication escalates into conflict. Crisis bargaining is rife with feelings of urgency, as well as a lack of complete information. In part, the lack of information is determined situationally in that there may not be enough time to acquire sufficient facts. However, the lack of information is also determined internally. Because of the very nature of crisis bargaining, which focuses on the use of coercion, face, and one alternative, the parties experience difficulty performing possibility think-

ing and seeking complete information and understanding. Finally, crisis bargainers tend to not work out detailed implementation and monitoring plans for their agreements. The stress of a crisis limits the disputants' abilities to control their emotions, think creatively, and develop contingency plans in the event the agreement breaks down.

No matter if the hostage taking incident is a well organized and executed act by political extremists or a haphazard act by a jewelry store robber, the stress of the crisis erodes higher level thought processes and exposes the more primitive, and dangerous emotions and impulses of the "lizard" brain. This is where the trained negotiator fits into the puzzle. It is the main role of the negotiator to move the bargaining away from brinkmanship toward more rational problem solving. To do this, negotiators face three key issues. These are (a) relational issues, (b) content issues, and (c) strategic issues.

One of the first things a negotiator must do is develop a relationship with the hostage taker. Schlossberg (1980) noted that the negotiator should "establish himself as a significant other" (p. 115). Rogan, Donohue, and Lyles (1990) stated that the negotiator must "communicate support for the hostage-taker's plight to make that person receptive to the negotiator's demands. The role of the negotiator is therefore dualistic; being both trusted friend and hated adversary of the hostage-taker" (p. 77). Donohue et al. (1991) outlined four relational parameters that are crucial in turning crisis bargaining into more normative bargaining. These are (a) trust, (b) attraction, (c) formality, and (d) control. By attending and empathizing, the negotiator attempts to build trust. Establishing trust in himself or herself makes the negotiator more attractive psychologically to the hostage taker. Manipulating the formality of communication, as well as the hostage taker's perceived control over the communication, helps to de-escalate the need for coercion and threats and foster a working relationship between the parties.

As the negotiator develops a relational base, he or she is also analyzing the content of the hostage taker's messages. Specifically, three content issues are crucial. These are (a) the problem, (b) the feelings, and (c) information integration. Remember that the hostage incident is an attempt by the hostage taker to solve a problem. Thus, it is crucial for the negotiator to understand the hostage taker's problem and feelings about the problem. Then, via reflective listening and other techniques, the negotiator attempts to guide the hostage taker to explore and develop other, more rational, solutions.

Strategic issues are those strategies and tactics that the hostage taker and negotiators use to gain concessions from each other. They include (a) position adjustment, (b) compliance gaining, and (c) proposal development. Recognizing the hostage taker's techniques and then countering them helps move crisis bargaining toward normative bargaining.

Hostage negotiation does not take place in a vacuum and the negotiator is not alone or, usually, in a face-to-face conversation with the hostage taker. Typically, the negotiator is part of a team and is a member of a law enforcement agency. The typical team for most large municipal law enforcement agencies is made up of the primary negotiator, the secondary negotiator, and the behavioral scientist consultant. When possible, the FBI utilizes a more elaborate seven-person team. This includes the primary negotiator, the secondary negotiator, the negotiation team leader, the negotiation recorder, the status coordinator, the tactical liaison, and the behavioral science expert (Fuselier & Van Zandt, 1987).

Only the primary negotiator talks to the hostage taker. The secondary negotiator can relieve the primary, but his or her most important purpose is to "act as negotiator to the negotiator. In effect, the backup permits the primary negotiator to ventilate and share some of the stress"

(Schlossberg, 1980, p. 115). The negotiation team leader communicates with the on-scene commander. The tactical liaison channels information between the tactical team and the negotiators. The negotiation recorder maintains a negotiations log and monitors the audio probe if one is in place. The status coordinator maintains the critical incident board and acts as a resource person. The behavioral science expert constantly assesses the mental status of the hostage taker and recommends negotiation techniques and approaches (Fuselier & Van Zandt, 1987).

According to Butler et al. (1993), 55% of the large municipal agencies in their sample employed a professional consultant, 76% of whom were doctoral level psychologists. With respect to the state police, 59% employed a consultant, while only 25% of the small municipal agencies employed a professional consultant. The three major roles of the behavioral scientist consultant are hostage taker assessment (82%), consultation on negotiation techniques (59%), and post-incident counseling (64%). Significantly, Butler et al. (1993) found that those organizations which employed mental health professionals as consultants were much more successful in concluding hostage situations without bloodshed in comparison to those that did not.

Rueth (1993) noted that the behavioral science expert collects data from several sources, including listening to the hostage taker's conversations with the negotiator, as well as interviewing relevant third persons. The consultant attempts to develop a dynamic diagnosis of the hostage taker. That is a description of the hostage taker's thoughts, mood, sensorium, cognition, suicide potential, and reality contact. This information can then be used to alter negotiation style. For example, Pearce (1977) suggested that with elderly/senile hostage takers, negotiations should take place during the daylight hours because their level of consciousness fluctuates at night. Also, with these individuals, the negotiator should initially focus on happy experiences from the past because their recent memory is often quite impaired. Fuselier (1986) noted that, with psychotically depressed individuals, understanding and support should be provided, but without telling the individual that "things will be okay" because the person will believe that the negotiator does not really understand. The negotiator should "gently interrupt [the hostage taker's] long statements about 'sins' or death and convince him to talk about interests, hobbies, or anything positive, relating to his self-worth" (Fuselier, p. 3).

Likewise, Fuselier (1986) recommended interacting with a paranoid schizophrenic differently than with a paranoid personality disorder. The first type of hostage taker is experiencing a thought disorder and manifests hallucinations and delusions. The second type of hostage taker has adequate reality contact, but demonstrates a life long history of suspicion and distrust.

The paranoid personality can be involved in a spontaneous hostage incident provoked by jealousy centering around a spouse or lover. With the paranoid personality, a business-like negotiation focusing on problem solving is recommended. The paranoid schizophrenic often purposefully initiates a hostage situation for bizarre reasons.

A case example is presented by Strentz (1986). In May 1982, a 28-year-old, White male, armed with a handgun, entered a television station in Phoenix, Arizona. He fired a shot, took hostages, and demanded to read a lengthy statement over the television. Recommended negotiation guidelines were followed, which included (a) encouraging the hostage taker to talk, (b) not confronting or arguing, (c) stalling for time, (d) interacting in a sincere manner, but not being overly friendly, and (e) continually assessing the hostage taker's dangerousness.

Of note is the recommendation to stall for time. Specifically, this means not giving in to the hostage taker's demands too soon. It would have been easy for the Phoenix police to immediately let the hostage taker read his rambling statement over the air. But Strentz noted that if a hostage taker's instrumental needs are met too soon (reading the statement), before the hostage taker is fatigued, he or she may violently act out his or her expressive needs. In this case example, the negotiator stalled from 5:00 p.m. until 10:00 p.m. before permitting the statement to be read. "By this time, the subject was fatigued and the initial excitement had dissipated sufficiently so that he surrendered when his instrumental demand was met. Clearly, his expressive demand for attention had been satisfied by the hours of negotiating" (Strentz, p. 14).

Another episode of a paranoid schizophrenic hostage taker is reported by Wesselius and DeSarno (1983). In their case report, a 24-year-old, single, White male, armed with several pistols, a sawed-off shotgun, a machine gun, ammunition, a sandwich, and a carton of cigarettes took over a law enforcement agency on a Saturday, capturing seven hostages. The hostage taker demanded to see five specific law enforcement officers and a chaplain. During the incident, the hostage taker's mood fluctuated from calm to agitated to violent, seemingly in random fashion. His paranoid irrationality was marked.

[Standard negotiations began. However,] the negotiator reported only fleeting moments of rapport with HT. Any noise or event in the hostage-holding area disrupted his ability to relate to the negotiator. He required frequent reassurance from the negotiator in order not to be overwhelmed with feelings of being trapped and out of control or that he was being tricked. An on-site psychiatric advisor assessed HT as erratic and homicidal. The hostages were considered to be in high risk of being harmed. Officials in the command post made the decision that HT was to be stopped tactically when an opportunity arose. Soon after, when HT's gun barrel was pointed away from the hostages and there was minimal risk to the hostages from ricocheting bullets, HT

was killed by a police sniper and the siege ended (p. 36).

Donohue et al. (1991) wrote that hostage negotiation is a five-stage process. These stages are termed (a) Intelligence Gathering, (b) Introduction and Relationship Development, (c) Problem Clarification and Relationship Development, (d) Problem Solving, and (e) Resolution. The goal of negotiations is the surrender of the hostage taker and the release of the hostages.

During the first stage, the negotiators gather intelligence, develop a negotiation strategy, and attempt to predict any problems or difficulties that may arise. The negotiators typically do not make contact with the hostage taker until the tactical teams have secured the area. Stage two starts when the primary negotiator makes contact with the hostage taker and begins to structure the communications between them. The negotiator attempts to build a relationship, uses an informal tone, and attempts to defer action on demands until a modicum of trust and attraction is developed. During stage three, the negotiator continues to build a relationship and at the same time attempts to understand the problem from the hostage taker's point of view. A goal for the end of stage three is a tacit agreement between hostage taker and negotiator to bargain normatively, rather than using brinkmanship. Thus, stage four is taken up with the negotiator and hostage taker attempting to problem solve a more rational solution to the situation. The negotiator, while continuing to build trust, becomes more directive in his communications. He or she develops proposals and seeks compliance. During the final stage of negotiations, a key point is to slow down the pace of communication to ensure that no mistakes are made. The negotiator carefully implants the specifics of the hostages' release and the hostage taker's surrender by replaying the proposed scenario over and over in his or her conversation with the perpetrator. Likewise, the negotiator continually assesses the strength of the fragile bond of trust that he or she has developed to make sure that the working relationship remains intact with the hostage taker.

Schlossberg (1980) wrote that the negotiating team, or members of the team, perform five important functions during the hostage incident. These are (a) gathering intelligence, (b) organizing the intelligence, (c) coordinating with the containment team, (d) analyzing the intelligence, and (f) developing strategy.

Of course, the above negotiation models highlight the perfect situation when everything goes as planned. In the real world, this does not always happen. According to Fuselier and Van Zandt (1987), the negotiator can measure his or her progress in negotiating, or lack thereof, using the following seven guidelines: (a) no one has been killed since the negotiations started; (b) there has been a decrease in the number of verbal threats; (c) the hostage taker's tone of voice is less emotional, that is slower and lower; (d) the hostage taker talks more; (e) the hostage taker talks about personal things, i.e., expressive goals; (f) some hostages have been freed; and (g) deadlines that were initially set by the hostage taker have passed without crisis.

Besides the above seven factors Soskis and Van Zandt (1986) noted that negative signs for successful negotiation include: (a) the hostage taker has killed an important person in his life, i.e., his spouse or child; (b) the hostage taker states that he wants the police to kill him; (c) the hostage taker has set a deadline for his death; and (d) the hostage taker refuses to negotiate.

The Hostage Experience

Being a hostage is a traumatic event with severe psychological and behavioral repercussions, both for the short term as well as the long term. The hostage experience has been tagged with several names: (a) the Stockholm Syndrome (Hacker, 1976); (b) the Common Sense Syndrome (Strentz, 1977); (c) the Survivor Identification Syndrome (Schlossberg, 1980); (d) the Hostage Response Syndrome (Wesselius & DeSarno, 1983); and (e) the Hostage Identification Syndrome (Turner, 1985). Whatever one calls the experience, the phenomenon is not well understood by the public or the media and surviving hostages often receive "secondary injuries" from rescuers, friends, family, or the public (Allondi, 1994; Hillman, 1981; McDuff, 1992; Simon & Blum, 1987; Symonds, 1980a; Symonds, 1980b).

The initial psychological phases experienced by the hostage are usually (a) denial, (b) delusions of immediate rescue, (c) "busywork," and (d) taking stock of one's life (Strentz, 1980). Generally, a person is not prepared psychologically for being captured and threatened with death. Thus, a typical first reaction is denial. Phrases such as, "This can't be happening...it must be some sort of joke," run through the captives' minds. These thoughts are then followed by wish/need statements, magical in content, such as "the police will get here any minute and save us." As the reality of the situation sets in, many hostages seek to avoid thinking about their plight with "busywork." This can include counting objects or persons, thinking snatches of song over and over in their mind, etc. Strentz (1980) also noted that most of the hostages he interviewed admitted to thinking about their lives, taking stock of the pluses and minuses, and considering things they might do differently if they survived.

Likewise associated with the initial phases is the phenomenon of "frozen fright" (Symonds, 1980a; Symonds, 1980b). Symonds wrote that few hostages run around in a panic, screaming. They are not allowed to do so by the hostage taker. Rather, the hostages' complete beings become focused on the hostage taker — the giver of life or death. This focus is reinforced by the hostage taker who wants the hostages to know that the hostage taker thoroughly controls their existence.

In this context, the hostages experience a dissociation of affect from thought and behavior. They display pseudo-calmness as well as cooperative behavior. Existing within this hostile environment, feeling isolated, and helpless, the hostages lose the ability to think calmly and rationally. They develop what Symonds terms "traumatic psychological infantilism" (1980b, p. 40). They have to comply, obey, placate, and submit or they will be killed.

The hostages may or may not develop a positive bond with the hostage taker. This aspect of the hostage experience depends upon two basic factors: (a) time and, more importantly, (b) lack of negative contact between the hostage and hostage taker. Time by itself does not insure that a positive bond will develop. More specifically, if the hostages are beaten or raped, the odds that positive feelings will develop are unlikely. Rather, the positive bonding is fostered by a "pathological transference" (Symonds, 1980b, p. 41). When the hostage taker, who clearly can torture or kill the hostages does not do so, then the captives feel a sense of gratitude for being granted the favor of life.

Law enforcement personnel and the public must understand that this bonding experience can occur in almost any individual, not just naive citizens. Symonds reported several examples of experienced police officers who were held captive and manifested the phenomena (Symonds, 1980a; Symonds, 1980b). One was an off duty detective who was held captive after he walked in on a robbery. He was tied and a bag was placed over his head. He listened as the robbers argued amongst themselves about killing him. Eventually they left, letting him live. Sometime later, after two of the criminals were apprehended, one of them told the detective, "You owe me something — I saved your life" (Symonds 1980b, p. 41). The detective agreed, visited the man in prison, and over time, developed a close relationship with him.

The positive feeling can also develop within the hostage taker. Ochberg (1978) reported the experience of Gerald Vaders, who was held hostage by South Moluccans in December 1975 on a train in Holland. Mr. Vaders was selected to be executed. Before his execution, he asked to speak with a fellow hostage. With the hostage takers listening, Mr. Vaders talked of various problems in his family life and left instructions for his wife regarding how to deal with a foster child. After he was through, Mr. Vaders indicated he was ready to die. His captors refused to kill him. Rather, they quickly selected another man and shot him instead. Mr. Vaders had ceased to be a nonentity and had become a person.

Strentz (1980) suggested that one duty of the negotiator is to foster the positive transference between hostage taker and hostage. This can be done by asking the hostage taker to ask his captives about their health situation and to provide messages for the hostages' families. Hostage takers who are psychopaths do not care, however, and never will. Also, hostage takers who isolate the hostages by placing them in another room or blindfolding and gagging them will likely continue to dehumanize the hostages, making it much easier for the hostage takers to kill them.

Likewise, different cultural values; preexisting racial, ethnic, religious, or ideological stereotypes; and the lack of a common language can work against the development of a positive bond between hostage taker and hostage. In these cases, it is possible that the passage of time will, in fact, work against the hostages' survival as the hostage taker's negative view of his or her hostages is selectively reinforced (Turner, 1985). An excellent example is documented by Jacobson (1973). Jacobson was herself a hostage, along with 148 other airline passengers, held for seven days in September 1970 by members of the Popular Front for the Liberation of Palestine. The passengers were mainly Americans or Europeans of Jewish ancestry. As the days progressed, Jacob-

son observed that the initially helpful Arab physician assigned by the hostage takers to take care of them became increasingly hostile and rejecting.

Another phenomena of the hostage experience which appears to occur with great frequency, even in the absence of positive feelings for the hostage taker, is the development of negative feelings for the authorities. The hostages do not care about the demands of the hostage takers; they want to be set free unharmed, and they want their freedom now. As the negotiations drag out, the hostages come to resent the authorities' seeming indifference to their plight.

Because of the hostage experience, the hostage recovery team can never rely on help from the hostages to effect their own rescue. For example, case after case has shown that hostages are more likely to obey the hostage taker during a rescue attempt rather than members of the special weapons and action teams (SWAT).

Following rescue, hostages continue to suffer psychological difficulties. It is clear that they are experiencing posttraumatic stress disorder (Allondi, 1994; Wesselius & DeSarno, 1983). Symptoms include an exaggerated startle response; nightmares; sleep disturbance; guilt; problems with memory and concentration; withdrawal from previously enjoyed activities, behaviors, and relationships; and exacerbation of symptoms when events occur that in some way resemble the traumatic event. Interestingly, this has been documented even in those hostages who developed strong positive feelings for their captors. Hillman (1981) and Jessee, Strickland, and Ladewig (1992) observed these symptoms in adults and children even a year post-event. In fact, Allondi (1994) reported that nine years after the Moluccan hostage incident, approximately one-half of the hostages and their families continued to have symptoms of post traumatic stress disorder, with treatment being required by 10 to 12% of the hostages and their families.

Rescued hostages require special care.

McDuff (1992) suggested that special intervention teams need to interact with hostage victims after their release and before they reenter their normal world. These teams can help in the following ways: (a) foster the development of a supportive internal social network amongst the victims designed to foster adaptation and rehabilitation; (b) act as gatekeepers between the victims and others, thus controlling the potentially intrusive impact of media and authorities; and (c) educate the victims and their families with respect to the psychological consequences of their hostage experience, as well as give special attention to the not infrequent destructive, blaming attitude the public often adopts towards hostage victims.

Simon and Blum (1987) noted that unlike neurotic patients who must remember and work through past psychological trauma, hostage victims need to overcome their trauma and learn to forget it. To achieve this goal, Symonds (1980b) noted that the hostages must be shown how to restore their sense of power. This is accomplished therapeutically by helping the victims reduce their perception of helplessness, isolation, and domination.

Can anything be done to inoculate potential hostages against the stress of the hostage experience? This is a controversial question. Hillman (1981) studied 14 prison guards who were held hostage during the February 1980 Santa Fe prison riot. During this riot, the guards suffered extreme helplessness, fear, and sensory overload. Each one decided he was going to die as they listened to the torture deaths of other victims around them. Hillman concluded that "no amount of preparation can adequately anticipate what the hostage experience will be like" (p. 1195). Hillman pointed out that "even experienced pilots captured during the Viet Nam war manifested some hysterical reactions, as well as psychotic reactions during their capture" (p. 1195).

However, Strentz and Auerbach (1988) and Auerbach, Kiesler, Strentz, Schmidt, and Serio

(1994) concluded that perhaps potential hostages can be trained to better cope with the hostage experience. These researchers reported an experiment in which 57 subjects were divided into three groups. One group received training in emotion-focused stress coping techniques such as deep breathing, deep muscle relaxation, thought stopping, and self-directed fantasy. A second group received training in problem-focused stress coping techniques, such as prisoner of war tap codes, ways of maintaining personal dignity, and methods of aiding as well as projecting a willingness to aid each other. The third group received no special education. The subjects were then subjected to a simulated four-day hostage situation.

Results suggested that those subjects who received training in emotion-focused stress coping techniques were more successful in controlling anxiety and exhibited less behavioral disturbance during the hostage simulation. Also, these same subjects reported perceiving the simulated hostage takers as less dominant and more friendly and were themselves perceived in the same light by the hostage takers. This research is interesting but, as with all simulation studies, the conclusions that can be drawn to the real world must be done so with care.

Conclusion

Although hostage taking has been in existence for over a thousand years, the phenomenon has not been studied systematically until the latter quarter of this century. Through this recent research, progress has been made in developing hostage taker typologies and understanding the motivations of different hostage takers. Likewise, the dynamics of the hostage incident are beginning to be investigated. This research has increased our understanding of the hostage taking event, including its phases, and applicable negotiator techniques, as well as analyses of the hostage experience both during and after the event.

Much of this early work has been performed by law enforcement personnel and the few behavioral scientists who work with them. Likewise, most of this work is anecdotal and theoretical in nature. Almost no empirical research has been performed. The databases discussed above represent the majority of statistical research that exists in the public domain. Thus, much work remains for future investigators.

Areas ripe for further research are (a) the systematic documentation and analysis of hostage events, (b) analysis and development of effective negotiation techniques, (c) analysis and development of effective hostage victim treatment techniques, and (d) understanding the impact of media on hostage events and their resolution. First, it would be appropriate that a national database of hostage incidents be created similar to that developed for violent crimes at the National Center for the Analysis of Violent Crime. Even though there is presently no systematic collection and review of hostage incidents on a national level, this does not preclude hostage recovery programs associated with local law enforcement and state police from developing and maintaining their own databases. After a period of time, these local databases could well be crucial storehouses of information relevant to understanding local hostage incidents.

Presently, hostage negotiation is taught more as an art form, with little scientific analysis of technique effectiveness or lack thereof. However, programs are available which can be used to understand, critique, and educate negotiators. One excellent example is the verbal interactional analysis technique developed by Fowler, DiVivo, and Fowler (1985). Coupling the use of databases with a systematic analysis of negotiation techniques would result in the ability to empirically validate negotiation style and effectiveness.

Anecdotal evidence suggests that relatively few hostage victims seek post incident treatment although it has been empirically demonstrated that most victims will suffer from post traumatic stress disorder. Why might this be true? Is it because current therapies are ineffective, because hostage victims feel publicly stigmatized, or is there some other reason or set of reasons? Longitudinal studies of hostage victims need to be performed in an effort to document the most effective treatment modalities, as well as gain a better understanding of the effects of being held hostage.

In those hostage situations lasting one day or less, the media probably has minimal impact. This probably is not true for longer term hostage events. What effect does the media play in hostage situations? To what extent do news stories influence future hostage takers? Can media stories have a negative impact on the recovery of hostage victims? Should ethical guidelines be developed for news reporters regarding the way in which they conduct themselves during and after a hostage situation? These are just a few questions that require thought and consideration by researchers.

In conclusion, although much has been accomplished, more remains to be done.

References

Allondi, F. A. (1994). Post-traumatic stress disorder in hostages and victims of torture. *Psychiatric Clinics of North America, 17,* 279-288.

American Psychiatric Association (1994). *Diagnostic and statistical manual of mental disorders (4th ed.).* Washington, DC: American Psychiatric Association.

Auerbach, S. M., Kiesler, D. J., Strentz, T., Schmidt, J. A., & Serio, C. D. (1994). Interpersonal impacts and adjustment to the stress of simulated captivity: An empirical test of the Stockholm Syndrome. *Journal of Social and Clinical Psychology, 13,* 207-221.

Bolz, F. & Hershey, E. (1979). *Hostage cop.* New York: Rawson, Wade.

Butler, W. M., Leitenberg, H., & Fuselier, G. D. (1993). The use of mental health professional consultants to police hostage negotiation teams. *Behavioral Sciences & the Law, 11*, 213-221.

Cooper, H. H. A. (1981). *The hostage takers.* Boulder, CO: Paladin Press.

Corsi, J. R. (1981). Terrorism as a desperate game. *Journal of Conflict Resolution, 25*, 47-85.

Dixit, A. K. & Nalebuff, B. J. (1991). *Thinking strategically.* New York: W. W. Norton and Company.

Donohue, W. A., Ramesh, C., Kaufmann, G., & Smith, R. (1991). Crisis bargaining in intense conflict situations. *International Journal of Group Tensions, 21*, 133-153.

Ferracuti, F. (1982). A sociopsychiatric interpretation of terrorism. *The Annals of the American Academy of Political and Social Sciences, 463*, 129-140.

Ferracuti, F. & Bruno, F. (1981). Psychiatric aspects of terrorism in Italy. In I. L. Barak-Glantz & C. R. Huff (Eds.), *The mad, the bad and the different: Essays in honor of Simon Dinitz* (pp. 199-213). Lexington: Lexington Books.

Fowler, R., DiVivo, P. P., & Fowler, D. J., (1985). Analyzing police hostage negotiations: The verbal interactional analysis technique. *Emotional First Aid, 2*, 16-28.

Friedland, N. & Merari, A. (1992). Hostage events: Descriptive profile and analysis of outcomes. *Journal of Applied Social Psychology, 22*, 134-156.

Fuselier, G. D. (1986, September) *A practical overview of hostage negotiations.* Federal Bureau of Investigation, U.S. Department of Justice.

Fuselier, G. D. (1988). Hostage negotiation consultant: Emerging role for the clinical psychologist. *Professional Psychology: Research and Practice, 19*, 175-179.

Fuselier, G. D. & Van Zandt, C. R. (1987). *A practical overview of hostage negotiations.* Unpublished manuscript, FBI Academy, Quantico, VA.

Gist, R. G. & Perry, J. D. (1985). Perspectives on negotiation in local jurisdictions: Part I. A different typology of situations. *FBI Law Enforcement Bulletin, November*, 21-24.

Hacker, F. J. (1976). *Crusaders, criminals, crazies: Terror and terrorism in our time.* New York: W. W. Norton Company.

Hamilton, E. (1942). *Mythology.* Boston: Little, Brown and Company.

Head, W. B. (1990). *The hostage response: An examination of the U.S. law enforcement practices concerning hostage incidents.* (Doctoral dissertation, State University of New York at Albany). Dissertation Abstracts International, 50, 4111-A. University Microfilms International No. DA9013316.

Hillman, R. G. (1981). The psychopathology of being held hostage. *American Journal of Psychiatry, 138*, 1193-1197.

Hubbard, D. G. (1973). *The skyjacker: His flights of fantasy.* New York: Collier Books.

Jacobson, S. R. (1973). Individual and group responses to confinement in a skyjacked plane. *American Journal of Orthopsychiatry, 43*, 459-469.

Jessee, P. O., Strickland, M. P., & Ladewig, B. H. (1992). The after effects of a hostage situation on children's behavior. *American Journal of Orthopsychiatry, 62*, 309-312.

586 *Lethal Violence*

Kennedy, H. G. & Dyer, D. E. (1992). Parental hostage takers. *British Journal of Psychiatry, 160,* 410-412.

Kessler, R. (1993). *The FBI.* New York: Pocket Books.

Knutson, J. N. (1980). The dynamics of the hostage taker: Some major variants. *Annals New York Academy of Sciences, 347,* 117-128.

Kobetz, R. W. (1975, May). Hostage incidents — The new police priority. *The Police Chief,* 32-35.

McDuff, D. R. (1992). Social issues in the management of released hostages. *Hospital and Community Psychiatry, 43,* 825-828.

Mickolus, E. (1976). Negotiating for hostages: A policy dilemma. *Orbis, 19,* 1309-1325.

Middendorf, W. (1975). New developments in the taking of hostages and kidnapping — a summary. *National Criminal Justice Reference Service Translation.*

Miller, A. H. (1980). *Terrorism and hostage negotiations.* Boulder, CO: Westview Press.

Miron, M. & Goldstein, A. (1979). *Hostage.* New York: Pergamon Press.

Montgomery, B. (1983). *A history of warfare.* New York: William Morrow and Company.

Ochberg, F. (1978). The victim of terrorism: Psychiatric considerations. *Terrorism, 1,* 147-168.

Pearce, K. I. (1977). Police negotiations: A new role for the community psychiatrist. *Canadian Psychiatric Association Journal, 22,* 171-175.

Phillips, D. (1973). *Skyjack: The story of air piracy.* London: Harrap and Company.

Rahe, R. H., Karson, S., Howard, N. S., Rubin, R. T., &

Poland, R. E. (1990). Psychological and physiological assessments on American hostages freed from captivity in Iran. *Psychosomatic Medicine, 52,* 1-16.

Rogan, R. G., Donohue, W. A., & Lyles, J. (1990). Gaining and exercising control in hostage negotiations using empathic perspective-taking. *International Journal of Group Tensions, 20,* 77-91.

Rueth, T. W. (1993). On site psychological evaluation of a hostage taker. *Psychological Reports, 73,* 659-664.

Schlossberg, H. (1980). Values and organization in hostage and crisis negotiation teams. *Annals of the New York Academy of Sciences, 347,* 113-116.

Siegel, R. K. (1984). Hostage hallucinations: Visual imagery induced by isolation and life-threatening stress. *The Journal of Nervous and Mental Disease, 172,* 264-272.

Simon, R. I. & Blum, R. A. (1987). After the terrorist incident: Psychotherapeutic treatment of former hostages. *American Journal of Psychotherapy, 41,* 194-200.

Soskis, D. A. & Van Zandt, C. R. (1986). Hostage negotiation: Law enforcement's most effective nonlethal weapon. *Behavioral Sciences & the Law, 4,* 423-435.

Strentz, T. (1977). *Survival adaptation...the common sense syndrome.* Unpublished manuscript, FBI Academy, Quantico, VA.

Strentz, T. (1980). The Stockholm Syndrome: Law enforcement policy and ego defenses of the hostage. *Annals of the New York Academy of Sciences, 347,* 137-150.

Strentz, T. (1985). *A statistical analysis of American hostage situations.* Unpublished manuscript, FBI Academy, Quantico, VA.

Strentz, T. (1986). Negotiating with the hostage-taker exhibiting paranoid-schizophrenic symptoms. *Journal of Police Science and Administration, 14*, 12-17.

Strentz, T. & Auerbach, S. M. (1988). Adjustment to the stress of simulated captivity: Effects of emotion-focused versus problem-solving preparation on hostages differing in locus of control. *Journal of Personality and Social Psychology, 55*, 652-660.

Sweetman, J. (1984). *American naval history: An illustrated chronology of the U.S. Navy and Marine Corps 1775-present.* Annapolis: Naval Institute Press.

Symonds, M. (1980a).Victims' responses to terror. *Annals New York Academy of Sciences, 347*, 129-136.

Symonds, M. (1980b). Acute responses of victims' to terror. *Evaluation and Change*, Special Issue, 39-41.

Turner, J. T. (1985). Factors influencing the development of the hostage identification syndrome. *Political Psychology, 6*, 705-711.

Wesselius, C. L. & DeSarno, J. V. (1983). The anatomy of a hostage situation. *Behavioral Sciences & the Law, 1*, 33-45.

About the Author

John A. Call, PhD, JD, is a psychologist, attorney, and a Diplomate in Forensic Psychology of the American Board of Professional Psychology and the American Board of Forensic Psychology. Dr. Call has received special training in hostage negotiations. He is a graduate of the FBI Police Seminar on Hostage Negotiations and the FBI Advanced Seminar on Hostage Negotiations. Dr. Call is the police psychologist for the Oklahoma City Police Department and has taught at the Oklahoma City Police Department Training Academy. Dr. Call is in private practice as a clinical and forensic psychologist in the Oklahoma City area.

HOSTAGE NEGOTIATOR'S COMPUTER DATABASE

Because there is no national systematic collection and review of hostage incidents, it is incumbent upon local law enforcement authorities to develop and maintain their own hostage incident databases. With the development of such databases, local hostage recovery programs are better able to obtain relevant information regarding hostage incidents in their community and analyze negotiation style and effectiveness. Dr. Call has developed a computer database model for use by hostage recovery programs. Those interested in obtaining further information regarding the HOSTAGE NEGOTIATOR'S COMPUTER DATABASE are invited to contact Dr. Call at 5100 N. Brookline, Suite 700, Oklahoma City, Oklahoma, 73112.

CHAPTER 23

BEYOND CONFLICT AND COMPETITION: DIVERSITY, COOPERATION, AND LIFE AFFIRMATION AS ALTERNATIVES TO VIOLENCE

Lucien A. Buck

While it is clear that violence is derived from multiple causes, the purpose of this chapter is to examine the conflict-competition-violence cycle promoted within Western civilization. Differences between people are inevitable and desirable, but conflict is not. A conflict view is derived from the conviction that variance is equivalent to opposition and struggle. Competition is an orientation that converts opposition — conflict — into a position of being against others in a win-lose contest. Competition — in order to avoid losing — fosters destructiveness.

While conflict, competition, and violence have been idealized within Western society, diversity (an acceptance of the legitimacy of different points of view), cooperation (an orientation that works to enhance the position of all parties), and life affirmation offer alternatives to violence. There is considerable evidence in support of human potential for prosocial and altruistic attitudes and behaviors as a basis for choice.

Conflict, as the inherent nature of human beings and of the universe, is so basic to the thought of Western Civilization that it seems unnecessary to justify its pervasive influence. Discussion of alternatives to a conflict view generally leads to a response of surprise or disbelief. This unquestioned assumption, however, is

reflected in the earliest stages of Western culture. Fine (1985), for example, described hate cultures in terms that reflect their conflict foundations, e.g., emotional conflict, antagonism, discord, and conquest. While there are other hate societies, Western Civilization has advocated a conflict perspective throughout its recorded history. Early Greek, Roman, and Jewish societies promoted an expansionistic, warlike tradition. Christianity, originally based upon principles of love and harmony, was converted to a conflict view by the acceptance of the "justified war" and the "holy war." Fromm (1973) similarly pointed out the typical way in which differences are converted into perspectives of opposition within destructive societies; Western Civilization fits Fromm's definition of this type of culture.

The history of warfare within the West is clearly based upon a conflict orientation: "The view of the clash of arms as the regulator of human affairs, the legitimate arbiter of conflicting state interest, and the instrument for eliminating the decadent, the feeble, and the corrupt influenced thinking about war from classical times to the First World War" (Craig, 1989, p. 31). This conclusion reflects an admiration of conflict in addition to accepting it as natural to human relationships. The power of conflict to distort rational argument is exemplified by Zuckerman's (1989) analysis of NATO's supreme command: "But the plans have always been so unrealistic that they defy all imagination...the planned use of nuclear weapons would utterly destroy the battlefield itself and everything on it, including NATO's own armies" (pp. 30-31). This irrationality is derived from the traditional conflict perspective of Western Civilization and an adherence to the illusion of warfare as a decisive solution.

Weigley's (1991) analysis of the roots of modern warfare, however, provided little support for the value of battle: "If wars remained incapable of producing decisions at costs proportionate to their objects...the whole history of war must be regarded as a history of almost unbroken futility" (p. 13). Convictions regarding the merit of conflict are not supported by the historical record, and this applies equally to the most recent example — the Gulf War (Draper, 1992).

Belief in the value of conflict within the fields of biology, psychology, sociology, and anthropology also lacks validation. The recent volume, *Aggression: The Myth of the Beast Within* (Klama, 1988), illustrates the conflict bias that has existed in many scientific spheres and attempts to counter this tradition with alternative views. Psychological analysis of nuclear policy has pointed out that "deterrence theory takes conflict for granted" (Tetlock, McGuire, & Mitchell, 1991, p. 244). This same assumption underlies a great deal of psychological research and theory. Psychological analysis, of course, is predominantly an outgrowth of Western scientific and philosophical traditions. The field of conflict resolution, for example, is not balanced by a parallel effort to examine the implications of diversity. The general study of family dynamics has emphasized an analysis of dysfunction, and the individual relationships between men and women have often been interpreted as a war, e.g., Lewis (1976), *Psychic War in Men and Women*; Tavris and Offir (1977), *The Longest War*; and Lewontin

(1994), *Women Versus the Biologists*.

The unquestioned assumption that conflict is inherent in the human condition is also basic to the study of violence. Gelles and Cornell's (1990) evaluation of violence within the family emphasized this focus, e.g., "Many interactions in the family are inherently conflict-structured." (p. 109). This view of the centrality of conflict to the study of violence has a long history (e.g., Coleman & Weinman, 1981; Saul, 1976; Spiegal, 1972; Storr, 1970; Straus, Gelles, & Steinmetz, 1980; Toch, 1992; Wertham, 1969).

A conflict view typically leads to competitiveness — once difference is interpreted within an oppositional framework, the selection of a style based upon winning or losing seems to be the only choice. As a result, Western Civilization has extended its bias in favor of conflict to include competition as an essential and natural characteristic of homo sapiens. Hate cultures, consistent with their conflict orientation, are highly competitive (Fine, 1985). War is, of course, a competitive solution to the conflict interpretation of group or national relationships; it is the epitome of societies' admiration of competitiveness. This veneration has been pointed out by Craig (1989) in terms of the assessment that war promotes superiority by "eliminating the decadent, the feeble, and the corrupt" (p. 31).

As with all forms of competitiveness, however, war is an unsatisfactory (Weigley, 1991; Zukerman, 1989), as well as irrational, solution. The advocates of war have implicitly acknowledged its ineffectiveness by attempting to restrain its destructiveness by means of rules — an effort that fails at all levels of competition. The absurdity of such regulation, however, is best captured by the oxymoron of "civilized" warfare.

Belief in the desirability and unavoidability of competitiveness extends throughout the natural and social sciences. The interdisciplinary examination of Western scientific traditions in the volume, *Aggression: The Myth of the Beast Within*

(Klama, 1988), has provided clear evidence of the bias that "human nature is fundamentally competitive" (p. 33). This analysis implicitly links competitiveness to the conflict focus of Western culture, a connection also evident in the psychological study of deterrence theory, family violence, and female-male relationships (Gelles & Cornell, 1990; Lewis, 1976; Tavris & Offir, 1977; Tetlock, McGuire, & Mitchell, 1991).

Kohn (1986), however, is one of the few authors to attempt a comprehensive analysis of competition. He confirmed the ubiquitousness of the belief in competitiveness as an inherent human characteristic in the United States and challenged the near universal agreement that it is unavoidable, an effective motivator, enjoyable, and a promoter of self-confidence. May (1953) summarized the consequences of competition as follows: "It makes every man the potential enemy of his neighbor, it generates much interpersonal hostility and resentment, and increases greatly our anxiety and isolation from each other" (p. 48). The contribution of competition to violence has often been cited by specialists in this area of study (e.g., Coleman & Weinman, 1981; Frank, 1972; Kolb, 1972; Roberts, Mock, & Johnstone, 1981; Saul, 1976; Storr, 1970; Toch, 1992; Wertham, 1969; Wolfgang, 1981).

As competition reflects a win-lose conflict, it is difficult to prevent this process from ending in violence. Kohn (1986) stated the connection succinctly: "competition is a kind of aggression" (p. 143). As a result, Western thinkers view human destructiveness as inescapable, both as an outcome of competition and as an inherent characteristic of human nature in its own right. Violence is a central preoccupation of hate cultures in general and in Western Civilization in particular (Fine, 1985).

Inasmuch as war is, by definition, the pitting of forces against other groups, it is an obvious example of competition as violence (e.g., Craig, 1989; Weigly, 1991; Zuckerman, 1989). In addi-

tion, there is a long history of scientific effort to substantiate violence as a fundamental attribute of human beings and this bias continues to exist in contemporary science (Klama, 1988). Gelles and Cornell (1990) substantiated the pervasiveness of "intimate violence" within the West: "The history of Western society is one in which children have been subjected to unspeakable cruelties" (p. 26). The abuse observed in the family "exists within a cultural context where violence is tolerated, accepted and even mandated" (Gelles & Cornell, p. 110)." This behavior is a logical result of the war between the sexes (Lewis, 1976; Tavris & Offir, 1977) and the casualties are clear. For example, in 1984, "806 husbands were killed by their wives, while 1,310 wives were slain by their husbands" (Gelles & Cornell, p. 67).

The primary implication of the data presented above involves evidence supporting the extent to which violence exists and can be encouraged within normal human beings. Some of the primary sources of this violence are the values approved of and admired by society, i.e., conflict and competition. The view that difference is always to be interpreted from a conflict perspective predisposes people within Western culture to a process that ends in violence. If people are "naturally" in conflict with each other, competition becomes a valuable, perhaps inevitable, choice. When this idealized social option can be confined within the "rules of fair play," violence can be avoided or partially controlled. When competitiveness is interpreted within a framework of "winning at any cost," rules are abandoned and violence is inevitable. Some individuals have been captured more effectively by these values, or exhibit other personal vulnerabilities to violent behavior. The main focus of this discussion, however, is not an examination of individual proneness to violence, but rather, an analysis of the conflict-competition-violence cycle. If violence is to be controlled, attention cannot be limited to a psychological analysis of individuals.

The Conflict, Competition, Violence Cycle

A good starting point for analyzing the cycle of violence is Toch's (1992) discussion of *Violent Men*, in which he stated, "violence is viewed as interpersonal, as a form of social conduct comparable to other forms of social conduct" (p. 13). More specifically, Toch pointed out that "violence is often a two-person game" (p. 7). While he perceived some people as violence prone, "even where the victim does no more than appear at the wrong time and place, his or her contribution is essential for the consummation of his or her destruction" (p. 7). This is not an attempt to blame the victim, but rather an emphasis upon the conception that violence often grows out of a sequence of events on the part of at least two people which ends with one individual feeling "that he or she must resort to a physical act, that a problem he or she faces calls for a destructive solution" (p. 7).

The appropriate unit of study, therefore, is the violent incident. Toch (1992) proposed that violence grows out of "a sequence beginning when two or more players make their opening move and ending when one player proceeds to hurt another" (pp. 35-36). He provided a number of specific examples which indicate that police-civilian interactions are often viewed as conflict. Even when an individual attempts to comply with a police officer's order, the officer may convert "the situation (as the person sees it) into a confrontation between two hostile parties" (p. 48). However, regardless of who takes such a step, an interaction involving a difference of opinion changes into a conflict because at least one of the actors interprets events in this fashion. Even if one person lacks an initial conflict view, it is difficult to avoid this outcome in a society that seldom provides any alternative. Once the interaction is defined as a conflict, both participants easily move on to compete with one another. As stated by Toch, "The civilian warns the officer of the fact that he intends to resist if the action is escalated. The officer must face the showdown, however, because his only perceived alternative would be to admit defeat" (p. 47). Many examples of this type of sequence are provided by Toch and are often described as "man to man" confrontations (pp. 48-49) — a synonym for competition.

While the specific words "conflict" and "competition" are not always used by Toch (1992), the sequence is clear: "The initial stance of the violence-prone person makes violence probable; his first moves increase the probability of violence; the reaction of the victim converts probability into certainty" (p. 180). While he conceded that some people are violence-prone, it is clear that individuals with less potential for violence are easily drawn into a violent incident. In addition, Toch interpreted other forms of violence in a similar fashion: "every riot is...a violent incident....The game is played between members of a frustrated group and the agents of white society" (p. 199).

It is of central importance, however, to clarify that the steps of the violent incident are built upon culturally promoted concepts of conflict and competition, as this ties violence to the "normal" population rather than to some type of exceptional, perhaps abnormal, person. While such people exist, they cannot be held responsible for the general problem of violence or for socially approved violence.

A variety of other investigators have provided evidence consistent with Toch's perspective. Wertham (1969), for example, proposed that violence cannot be understood in terms of "human nature" alone. According to Wertham, "Violence and violence-mindedness are deeply embedded in our whole social life" (p. 20). Similar to Toch, Wertham viewed violence as growing out of an interpersonal interaction. Wertham stated, "We always have to visualize the potential influence on one another of first, the perpetrator; second, the victim; third, the reaction of other people in a smaller or wider circle" (p. 47). Thus, the response of other people is added as an important influence to the escalation characteristic of a violent incident.

A comparable sequence of events was proposed by Tedeschi and Felson (1994) in terms of social interactionist theory. From this perspective, violence is the end result of a series of behaviors and interpretations of events between two individuals. At various stages, a grievance may be resolved or forgiven, otherwise the interaction escalates into a violent encounter. Third parties, however, can intervene in this sequence (Tedeschi & Felson, pp. 247-248). Tedeschi and Felson provided extensive research support for coercive action in a variety of contexts; one of the most reliable elicitors of retaliation is "perceived intentional attack" (pp. 256-257).

Consistent with Toch and Wertham, Sargent (1972) discussed "the lethal situation" (p. 105). Roberts, Mock, and Johnstone (1981) provided evidence of homicide growing out of a relationship that "can no longer be sustained but cannot be given up" (p. 24). Wolfgang (1981) analyzed violence that grows out of social situations which "escalate arguments to altercations" (p. 109). Meloy (1992) concluded that most violence is perpetrated within a bond or attachment. Campbell (1993) proposed a sequence of escalation in criminal and domestic violence, and Walker (1968) interpreted the 1968 Chicago riots as growing out of reciprocal provocations between the police and some of the demonstrators at the Democratic National Convention, although the police were described as the primary aggressors.

In addition, Rappaport and Holden (1981) attacked the prevalence of "person blame" interpretations. This focus upon deviant individuals leads to a preoccupation with violence among the powerless and ignores the violence of the powerful. As a result, "person-blame ideology" leads to

the inability to predict individual violence and to develop adequate prevention strategies (p. 425).

Rappaport and Holden (1981) concluded that violence is rooted in the general society. They stated, "more individual violence is perpetuated among people known to one another than between strangers, unless of course one wants to include organized violence such as wars, or recreational violence such as football games...(p. 413)." The primary implication consistent with this chapter is that violence is rooted in the socialization of people within Western Civilization, and these roots are importantly derived from conflict-competition values.

Toch (1992) and Wertham (1969), for example, discussed the competitive, aggressive childhood games and toys that prepare children for the adult cycle, leading to violence and war. "The American family and the American home are perhaps as or more violent than any other single American situation..." (Straus, Gelles, & Steinmetz, 1980, p. 4). One of the primary consequences of this education within the family is to promote "the idea that violence can be and should be used to secure good ends — the moral rightness of violence" (Straus, Gelles, & Steinmetz, p. 103).

Violence increases in direct proportion to the amount of conflict (Straus, Gelles, & Steinmetz, 1980), and occurs least within noncompetitive relationships — democratic or equal households. These conclusions continue to be supported by the more recent analyses of Friedman (1993) and Gelles and Cornell (1990). However, Gelles and Cornell more clearly emphasized that the idealization of these values can be found throughout the history of Western Civilization. While Gelles and Cornell concluded that "people learn to be violent when they grow up in violent homes" (p. 113), the present analysis extends the principle to the learning of a conflict-competition ideology within the home.

The home as a context for learning violence

has been pointed out by other investigators, such as Wolfgang (1981), who also emphasized the particular efforts to instill competitiveness and violence in males within this culture. Friedman (1993) discussed violence as a "macho sport" that has gone haywire (p. 454). This position is supported by Coleman and Weinman (1981), who stated that conjugal violence is enhanced by a concept of masculinity that places demands on men to be "strong, dominant and superior" (p. 237). While male gender roles promote competitiveness-violence, Coleman and Weinman concluded that violence must be understood within an interactional framework.

Sonkin and Auerbach-Walker (1985) took a similar position, stating that "battering men are only an extreme on the continuum of being 'a man' in this society" (pp. 4-5). As Kilmartin (1994) summarized, competitiveness and aggressiveness are basic characteristics of a "real man," and lack of proper masculinity is punished. Masculine ideology results in participation in dangerous sports that lead to "debilitating injuries" and "death," a belief in "heroic" behavior during wartime that ends in "victimization," and participation in unsafe sexual practices in the time of AIDS (Kilmartin, pp. 160-162). Masculine violence often fits an interactional pattern: "37% of the cases in which a male murdered another male were precipitated by trivial events, such as the killer's 'saving face' when another man had insulted him" (pp. 212-213).

Farrell (1993) promoted a parallel perspective in terms of the roots of male competitiveness, but emphasized that "men's focus on winning was, historically, a focus on protection — even at the expense of themselves" (p. 69). Society has trained men to push competitiveness into violence, then people are surprised by the destructiveness of men. In Farrell's (1993) words, "The tragedy of the warrior is that the more he fights the enemy, the more he begins to be like the enemy" (p. 71).

If a major source of violence in Western Civilization is derived from the socially approved or even idealized values of conflict and competition, control of destructive behavior requires a reassessment of the bias inherent in these concepts. This means confronting the fact that violence is primarily a consequence of the normal socialization of men, but is also pervasively supported by, and participated in, by women, either directly or indirectly. Violence cannot be reduced substantially by the imprisonment or treatment of individuals as long as there is widespread encouragement of assaultive behavior by means of the conflict-competition-violence cycle. Society must reflect carefully upon some of its cherished beliefs, and must discover alternatives to behavior that is considered "the only way."

In order, however, to confront other possibilities, an additional bias of Western Civilization must be questioned — the pervasive belief that self-interest drives all behavior. If selfishness is inherent, conflict is inevitable, competition is desirable, and violence is unavoidable. As the volume *Aggression: The Myth of the Beast Within* (Klama, 1988) has shown, the conception of fundamental selfishness has a long history within Western Civilization and continues to be a cornerstone of sociobiology. The epitome of these efforts is represented by the attempt to interpret the altruistic behavior observed in many species as evidence of "selfish genes" (Klama, p. 13). Even the "cooperativeness and altruism" necessary for the maintenance of complex, human societies has to be viewed as based upon a reaction against biological selfishness (Klama, p. 31).

Mutualism, Cooperation, Diversity, and Prosocial Behavior

In spite of the prejudice that interprets all human behavior from the perspective of basic selfishness, there is growing and extensive evidence which contradicts this bias. While it is clear that human beings have considerable capacity for egoistic behavior, it is equally apparent that other potentials are an inherent part of human nature. In fact, there is a long history of scientific efforts to contradict the cultural prejudice that self-interest is the fundamental animal or human potential (e.g., Allee, *The Social Life of Animals*, 1958). Allee proposed "that a general principle of automatic cooperation is one of the fundamental biological principles" (p. 30), and provided evidence to support the conception "that the drift toward natural cooperation is somewhat stronger than the opposing tendency toward disoperation" (p. 203). The term "disoperation" was used to refer to "harmful effects," such as "intense competition," that can result from undesirable conditions — e.g., overcrowding. Similarly, Saul (1976) and Kohn (1986) provided evidence that prosocial behavior is as characteristic of human nature as the traditionally promoted views of conflict, competition, or violence.

Wilson's (1992) discussion of the present crisis of mass extinction implicated the human conflict-competition-violence cycle. Wilson stated, "Human hunters help no species" (p. 253). According to Wilson, mutualism is a central facilitator of the biodiversity necessary for maintaining the world's ecology (p. 178). Mutualism represents "an intimate coexistence of two species benefiting both" (p. 178). Wilson went even further by proposing that mutualism is a fundamental foundation for life. "Most life on land depends ultimately on one such relationship...the intimate and mutually dependent coexistence of fungi and the root systems of plants" (p. 178).

These general perspectives regarding the relationships among life forms provide a picture quite different from the self-interest, conflict-competition bias which has dominated Western thought. Evidence of mutualism, diversity, and cooperation provides support for this perspective as fundamental to all life forms. Bertness (1992), for example, recently emphasized the critical role of cooperation in the ecology of the seaward edge of the salt marsh. Honeycutt (1992) provided evidence not only of cooperativeness, but of altruistic behavior in mole-rats, stating that "apparent acts of altruism are common in many animal species" (p. 43). Weiner (1994), in his review of variations in the finch, concluded that mutualism, as well as competition, is basic to evolutionary change. Even further, Heinrich (1989) observed altruistic behavior in ravens — actively helping each other find food, and Chadwick (1991) reported supportive and nurturant behavior toward sick and wounded herd members among elephants. Finally, de Waal (1988) analyzed "peacemaking" among a variety of primate species — chimpanzees, rhesus monkeys, stump-tailed monkeys, pygmy chimps, and great apes.

If mutualism is fundamental to all life, prosocial behavior is an inherent human potential. The early hominid species have been viewed by Leakey and Lewin (1992) as demonstrating "a significant degree of cooperation" (pp. 116-117). Rather than supporting the "hunting ape hypothesis," these authors proposed that "evolutionary history has endowed our species with an inclination to cooperate" (p. 18). Further, they concluded that "[t]here is no evidence of frequent violence or warfare in human prehistory until about ten thousand years ago, when humans began to practice food production" (p. 18). Similarly, Zur (1989) reviewed evidence which supports the conclusion that "for the last 200,000 years humans have had the technical and physical capability to create and use weapons against each other, but only in the last 13,000 years have humans begun to design and use weapons to defend against and attack other human beings."

Leakey and Lewin (1992) interpreted prosocial behavior as essential to the rise of technology, and proposed that altruism must have been highly developed in "intelligent and intensely social animals, like our human ancestors" (p. 350). Johanson and Johanson (1994) supported the concept that cooperation among social hominids was the foundation for "the dramatic growth in brain size" characteristic of Homo (p. 81). Consistent with Leakey and Lewin (1992), these investigators found no evidence of skilled hunting ability in homo habilis or homo erectus. Johanson and Johanson (pp. 300-302) concluded that culture has "propelled the human species." Rather than competitive-violent skills, art — appearing 40,000 to 50,000 years ago — was the foundation for the transition to fully modern human beings.

The pervasiveness of prosocial behavior continues to be supported by evidence regarding contemporary human functioning. Buck and Ginsburg (1991) argued that "altruism and other kinds of social behaviors involve species specific behavior systems" (p. 150). They provided evidence of a biological basis for altruism, and argued that the need to "dehumanize" the enemy during warfare indicates "that there is something about human qualities per se that tends to discourage killing and promote bonding" (p. 162). This is consistent with Kelman and Hamilton's (1989) conclusion that, in spite of the frequency of crimes of obedience, "more than one enlisted man avoided carrying out...orders, and more than one, by sworn oath, directly refused to obey them" at the My Lai Massacre (p. 7), and even the hardened Nazi Einsatzgruppen troops showed symptoms of "psychological decompensation" as a result of "face-to-face shooting" (Lifton, 1986, p. 15).

Prosocial attitudes and feelings, therefore, need to be overcome in order to promote violence. Batson and Oleson (1991) reported that "[t]he relatively high rate of helping by high-empathy individuals, even when justification for not helping was high, is precisely what we would expect if feeling empathy for the person in need evokes altruistic motivation to have that person's need reduced" (p. 70). In addition, these investigators found no evidence that altruistic responses were related to specific rewards or punishments (p. 72). This supports the empathy-altruism hypothesis that human beings are "capable of caring about the welfare of others for their sakes and not simply for our own" (p. 63). Batson and Oleson concluded that people continue to get involved in spite of pressures that oppose empathy, and that altruism is likely to be more resilient when related to strong attachments (pp. 81-82).

Consistent with this, Fogelman and Wiener (1985) provided examples of the altruism of seemingly ordinary people who helped victims of Nazi oppression. Some of these rescuers helped people with whom they had developed strong attachments, but others saved people they did not know and sometimes individuals they did not like. While a variety of factors were involved, these "ordinary" people acted altruistically under conditions that involved great personal risk. Such behavior is difficult to interpret within the context of self-interest.

Many similar examples can be found that exhibit varying degrees of prosocial concern and personal risk. Buck (1991) discussed the courage and altruism of a number of noteworthy individuals, many of whom put their lives on the line in support of their actions: Liu Binyan, Mohandas K. Gandhi, Vaclav Havel, Martin Luther King, Nelson Mandela, Andrei Sakarov, and Anatol Shcharansky. This list is not exhaustive and could be updated with many additional figures, such as Aung San Suu Kyi, who challenged the dictators of Myanmar or the Brazilian union organizer, Chico Mendes. Nevertheless, any such list leaves out thousands of other less prominent people who have fought for others' rights with little recognition, e.g., the extensive list cited by Branch (1988) as participants in the American Civil Rights movement or the whistleblowers discussed by Glazer and Glazer (1986).

Fiske (1991) provided cross-cultural support for altruism. Fiske stated, "What the ethnographic evidence shows is that prosocial behavior is universal, helping is the mode, and altruism is very common" (p. 177). Defining altruism as "a genuine concern for some good beyond the self, motivated by a deep sense of personal connection or moral obligation to others" (p. 177), Fiske concluded that it is an inherent characteristic of human nature. Fiske (pp. 177-178) proposed four types of relationships that represent most human interaction: (a) communal sharing (kindness and sharing with no expectation of reciprocation); (b) authority ranking (interactions that include the provision of services or goods to the authority out of a sense of respect, and protection and other services to subordinates resulting from a sense of responsibility); (c) equality matching (the distribution of goods among peers seeking a balanced exchange as a result of a desire to share equally); and (d) market pricing (exchanges derived from bargaining with reference to prices or some other standard). Fiske interpreted all of these modes of interaction as prosocial — growing out of "compassion and concern for others" because the social relationships involved are "intrinsically motivating" (pp. 178-179).

Even market pricing, which is often viewed as selfish, competitive, or antisocial, can be successful only within some "culturally specific social form" (pp. 181-182). The pervasiveness of working together — prosocial interaction — is also supported by Fine's (1985) description of love cultures and Fromm's (1973) category of life-affirmative societies.

The Diversity, Cooperation, and Life Affirmation Cycle

Violence can be reduced by revising the assumptions we promote as basic to human nature. If human beings are prosocial and altruistic, the behavior of others cannot be automatically viewed as driven by self-interest. If human beings have considerable capacity for empathy, conflict is not inevitable. It is, in fact, the concept of

inherent conflict that often produces an expectation of opposition, and this forces relationships toward struggle. It is differences that are inevitable, not conflict. Differences may be compatible and allow for easy acceptance, but they may also be incompatible, making it extremely difficult to achieve a working relationship. All differences, however, can be considered within a perspective of diversity, rather than conflict. Diversity accepts the inevitability of differences, and works to honor the legitimacy of all points-of-view.

Wilson (1992) proposed that biological diversity "is the key to the maintenance of the world as we know it" (p. 15). It is the unwillingness of modern technological society to tolerate different life forms that has created a crisis of biodiversity; that is, "we are in one of the great extinction spasms of geological history" (p. 280). The survival of human beings is interdependent with that of other species. Diversity at the psychological, sociological, and political levels may also relate to survival, but certainly provides an alternative to conflict-violence relationships.

May's (1972) conception of integrative power is based upon a diversity perspective; it is the power to seek solutions that foster the growth of all parties. Within this form of problem solving, it is assumed that those on the other side can be trusted and are seeking a justifiable purpose, given their values. This is also the framework that Fromm (1963) described as essential to loving, and Maslow (1971) proposed for the "Being-cognition" characteristic of self-actualizing people (pp. 251-266).

Similarly, while Erikson (1987) recognized difference as a foundation for the individuality required for a healthy ego-identity, he also saw the need for the growth that is reflected in a wider identity. He defined a wider identity as "...the capacity for empathic identification with other people...the willingness to understand the otherness as well as the all-too-familiar in ourselves"

(p. 502). A wider identity promotes integrative power.

In addition to these authors, Gandhi's writings are derived from a diversity perspective (Buck, 1992a, 1994). For example, his conception of the ideal social order is reflected in "Sarvodaya" — "the welfare of all" (Gandhi, 1954, p. 3). In order to protect the welfare of all, the rights of individuals need to be shielded against encroachment by all authorities, e.g., the state, majoritarian abuse, and centralization (Gandhi, 1961, pp. 45, 70). Gandhi focused upon equality as a context for sexual, economic, social, and international diversity (Buck, 1994). This emphasis was most clearly expressed in his statements relevant to religion: "In reality there are as many religions as there are individuals" (Gandhi, 1954, p. 25).

Gandhian synthesis is an orientation directed toward the enhancement of the desires of the other — including an "opponent" — even as one advances one's own position (Buck, 1994). This requires an open-ended, creative solution to problems where the focus is upon the means. Therefore, success is determined by utilizing the proper approach, rather than the achievement of a particular goal. The process of moving toward creative solutions involves a sequence of steps (Buck, 1994). The first effort is the persistent search for avenues of cooperation. The pursuit of mutuality begins with a reduction of demands to a minimum consistent with "truth," but this is combined with refusing to surrender essentials.

However, cooperation is not compromise in the Western tradition; a new synthesis is found where there is no victory or concession. If initial problem solving efforts fail, an attempt is made to find a solution through reason. When cooperation and reason fail, self-suffering may be initiated. Self-suffering is an attempt to touch the humane potential present in all human beings; however, Gandhi left open the possibility that it is impossible to reach this capacity in some individuals. At each step, it is necessary to seek a return to cooperative efforts. When cooperation, reason, or self-suffering have not resolved the situation, direct action is required — noncooperation.

Diversity provides fertile soil for the cultivation of cooperation. Within this framework, harmony represents a rational, effective mode of action. For example, listening carefully to the other person's version of an automobile accident, and accepting that position as an honest interpretation sets the stage for an amiable solution. Cooperation is a means of interacting that is an alternative to competition; it reflects an attempt to work with others and often to unite in a mutual effort toward a joint goal.

The central issue is the attitude and intent to work with, rather than having a unified purpose. In this way, cooperation can serve as a means for moving toward a single goal, or for developing creative solutions to diverse goals. Therefore, accepting the legitimacy of the other person's view of an accident does not mean agreeing with it. The cooperative response can be to work harmoniously to collect the relevant information necessary to provide separate versions to the insurance companies.

Competition is a means of working against others, whether there is a single end or a multiplicity of ends. The central feature is the intent to win and avoid losing. A competitive response to an accident is likely to result in the loss of valuable information and possibly an escalation of anger into a violent interaction. The opposite of competition involves not moving against, but this is not the same as working with. There are many forms of noncompetitiveness that do not include cooperation, e.g., avoidance, conformity, and surrender.

The primary focus of these definitions is on internal events, rather than on behavior or conditions of the environment. At the behavioral level, cooperation and competition are often confused, and some behaviors can serve either alternative.

Environments can be arranged to enhance both modes, but a cooperative or competitive structure can be subverted by contrary intentions. This does not mean that such structural arrangements are irrelevant; they can provide a context for learning cooperative or competitive attitudes.

Cooperation is relatively independent of external events; one can successfully cooperate independent of the behavior of others. The cooperativeness of others enhances the ease with which solutions can be reached, but one can cooperate even with a competitor, making it impossible for the competitor to win or lose. For example, one can play tennis cooperatively with a competitor. This requires an effort to place the ball close to the other person so they can make an effective return. Competitive scoring will guarantee more points for the other player, but little satisfaction that he or she has won. This approach may also convert the game into a cooperative interaction where winning is no longer important to either player.

Cooperation requires the growth of independence; it is derived from an internal locus of choice and the sense of self-worth that comes from competence. It takes as much competence to place a ball near a player as it does to aim far away.

Cooperation cannot be coerced; duty and subservience can provide a surface imitation, but they lack the intent and capacity to *work with*. Equality is the necessary context for cooperative efforts. Competition is inherently a relationship between superior and inferior. It is goal- and achievement-oriented — winning and losing. Within this context, the goal must be constantly reachieved — there can be no enduring satisfaction. The temporary gloating derived from winning is often converted into guilt over the subjugation of another person, particularly when the opponent is also a friend or intimate. While cooperation can be evaluated relative to a goal, this represents a superficial level. It can become

entirely independent of goals; it is best understood as a process, rather than an achievement.

Cooperative tennis is not concerned with scores. Exercise and the enhancement of the skill necessary for mutual play provides the satisfaction. As a process, cooperation is the means and the goal — they are the same. In this fashion, as long as one attempts to work with others, "success" is guaranteed. If "success" comes from the effort, failure can only result from an unwillingness or inability to try.

Competition, while primarily reflecting an attitude, is dependent upon events outside of the person. In order to compete, a competitor is required. It is hard to win without another who is willing to put himself or herself in the position of losing. Competition leads to dependence upon the actions of others and diminishes self-control and self-worth, regardless of winning or losing. The effort to be number one is based on comparing oneself to others, and the individual is defined by this comparison, rather than by an internalized sense of competence. Most people can never become number one, and the few who do succeed, experience failure most of the time. Those rare individuals who reach the top know, or will soon know, that they are easily and inevitably replaced. Competitiveness opens one to permanent and unavoidable vulnerability, which promotes fear of failure and conformity rather than individuality.

Cooperativeness requires the courage of self-choosing, where courage is defined as the willingness to act in spite of fear or despair. All choices require the courage to accept responsibility for the consequences of one's actions. Cooperative choices involve the courage to give up previously learned aggressive methods. As cooperativeness is used and tested, and self-confidence in its application is enhanced, faith in its strength is experienced. A capacity for working with requires growth of the total person. In order to grasp the strength derived from this orientation, the individual must become aware of cooperative options and be able to apply them. Cooperation blends individuality with community; competition denies community.

Competitiveness leads to internal change — secretiveness, deceptiveness, manipulativeness, and exploitiveness. These natural consequences of an intense desire to win must be moderated by the establishment of rules. While rules can be added to cooperative games and are required in order to guarantee "fair competition," there is no parallel need to insure fair cooperation. It is evident, however, that within the context of a struggle, rules are made to be broken and winning is everything. If rules are incorporated within a cooperative venture, there is no desire to break rules, except for remnants of competitiveness or a desire for an advantage. A cooperative tennis game does not need to provide a rule that it is necessary to place the ball close to the other person. As the players increase their ability to work with each other, they will move in this direction.

One alternative to competition is compromise — giving up on, or giving in to, some important concerns. This resolution of conflict-competition results in some degree of dissatisfaction for everyone involved, but deescalates the movement toward destructiveness.

A diversity-cooperation stance allows for creative solutions that incorporate the essential needs of all participants, leaving no winners or losers. The respect central to this framework allows for the legitimacy of positions not previously considered. If there is a disagreement about competitive tennis, there are many options in addition to compromise, e.g., cooperative tennis. In order for this to be a creative solution, both people need to find this option desirable, and neither can feel that they have given up something important. Creativity flourishes more openly in an environment that minimizes a fear of failure and enhances a willingness to risk.

Competitiveness represents a common mode for people within Western culture, but it provides little opportunity for healthy growth. It may be more effective than inaction or escape, but is almost universally inferior to cooperation for dealing with important human issues, such as child rearing, education, intimacy, work, creativity, social relationships, international affairs, and the relationship to the environment. A marriage based upon competition must end with the defeat of the husband or the wife, or both.

Competition is best viewed as culturally promoted pathology. It is related to a deficit view of life based upon a belief in, or the actuality of, limited resources. Harmony is more consistent with sufficiency or even inexhaustibility of wealth. Competition leads to scarcity, even where there is none; cooperation provides the creative opportunity for expanding assets. In a cooperative relationship, the partners can share skills, such as political science or mathematics, with one another with the result that both enlarge their competence.

Many of the characteristics of cooperation are supported by Kohn's (1986) review of the literature. According to Kohn, cooperative efforts lead to superior performance, as measured by a variety of characteristics. Collaboration produces greater enjoyment, more self-esteem, less anxiety, less conformity, more creativity, greater empathy, and less violence. Given the strenuous efforts to teach competition within Western society (Kohn), the greater frequency of collaboration provides strong support for the conclusion that cooperation is more fundamental or more powerful than competition.

Further evidence supporting the value of cooperation was provided by Levine and Moreland (1990) in regard to small group process. They offered evidence of serious negative consequences of conflict "including interpersonal hostility, reduced performance, and even group dissolution" (p. 605). They found that on the other hand cooperation fosters togetherness, mutual attentiveness, affection, self-disclosure, and coordinated behavior.

Similarly, Weinstein (1991) supported the effectiveness of a variety of forms of cooperative education. Educational practices that encourage or require students to work together for common goals are superior to competitive situations at producing positive race relations, prosocial development, and improved interactions between academically handicapped and other students. Snow and Swanson (1992) also found evidence supporting the effectiveness of cooperation for cognitive achievement and for producing more positive attitudes toward school, improved self-esteem, and better relationships among students.

Deutsch (1993) concluded that students can learn "that it is to their advantage if other students learn well and that it is to their disadvantage if others do poorly" (p. 510). This cooperative attitude can be fostered while simultaneously requiring "individual accountability" (p. 510). Cooperative learning approaches consistently demonstrated greater commitment, helpfulness, and caring; more skill in empathizing with others; higher self-esteem; more positive attitudes toward learning; and greater competence with and improved attitudes for effective collaboration. Deutsch also emphasized that high-achieving students learn "at least as much" in cooperative classrooms (p. 511).

Support for the effectiveness of cooperative alternatives has been found in other situations. Tetlock, McGuire, and Mitchell (1991) argued that there are more effective approaches to international relations than classical deterrence theory, which is based upon a competitive-violence perspective. While conceding that it is difficult to judge the success or failure of deterrence in many situations, some dramatic failures are clear. The effectiveness of a cooperative strategy was exemplified by the Cuban Missile Crisis. Kennedy's policy can be viewed as sending implicit cooperative signals to the Soviets (p. 262).

In addition, Tetlock et al. (1991) provided evidence in support of graduated and reciprocated initiatives in tension-reduction (GRIT) strategy. This policy is based upon a cooperative spiral — unilateral reduction of tension is announced and specific actions taken. Cooperative efforts continue in the face of defection or the apparent lack of response by the other party. This action is taken without any sense or actuality of weakening one's own position. GRIT is highly consistent with Gandhi's orientation, and has been demonstrated to be more effective than "tit-for-tat" approaches in which initial cooperation is followed by repeating the opponents move — including competition or failure to respond (p. 262). GRIT is particularly effective when "repeated and rephrased" (p. 263) — that is when cooperation is persistently pursued. Cooperative alternatives can obstruct violent consequences because the initiative remains in one's own hands, rather than allowing the other side the determination of the next step.

Carneval and Pruitt (1992) recently argued for the advantages of win-win negotiation "in which parties achieve higher joint benefit than they could with a compromise agreement" (p. 535). They also emphasized the readiness of people to cooperate and described a variety of win-win solutions, such as each party winning on the issues it finds important, expanding the pie, compensating the loser, and developing new options. Similar to Gandhi, they recommended that effective problem solving be firm and flexible, but they differed in stating that concern for the other party's outcome can be genuine or strategic. For Gandhi, genuine acceptance of the legitimacy of the other's goal is most effective.

It is impossible to provide, within this context, a detailed analysis of the hundreds of applications of Gandhian synthesis, but the reviews of Bondurant (1965), Malik (1986), Shepard (1987), and Oza (1991) have provided extensive examples. The effectiveness of Gandhian cooperation has also been demonstrated in the United States within King's civil rights movement (Branch, 1988). In addition, Buck (1992a) proposed that the centrality of cooperativeness in the approaches of Mandela, Havel, Sakarov, and Scharansky parallel the Gandhian position.

According to Gandhi, when cooperation, reason, or self-suffering have not resolved the situation, direct action is required (Buck, 1994). There are a multitude of possibilities, but the group of methods called "Satyagraha" are most central to Gandhian synthesis. Gandhi (1950) defined the core of Satyagraha as an autonomous, loving search for truth. In practice, this search is not easy to implement, as it requires the simultaneous application of noncooperation and nonviolence (Buck, 1994). The fullest utilization of Satyagraha requires changing oneself — initiating a process of self-realization. The most difficult of these changes is to learn the self-discipline required for nonviolence. While violence can never be completely removed from life or from social interaction, it can be reduced radically and all choices can aim toward the "least violence" (Buck, p. 240).

The Salt Satyagraha, which began on March 12, 1930, reflects all of the components of a successful campaign (Bondurant, 1965). This action started with extensive public planning, training participants to resist a violent response when attacked by the police, and a letter by Gandhi to the Viceroy Lord Irwin informing him of the details of the action. In spite of jailing thousands and violent attacks by the police, the English capitulated. Creatively, however, Gandhi allowed the Viceroy to avoid the appearance of capitulation. The salt laws were not repealed, but in practice, the British salt monopoly ended. This campaign did not begin until cooperative negotiations broke down, and it did not avoid violence. However, almost all of the violence was initiated by the British, and there was less destruction than during hostile Indian uprisings.

The most important implications of Gandhian synthesis are that extensive control over violence is possible, and that cooperation and nonviolent noncooperation represent powerful alternatives for solving differences — noncooperative means lead to noncompetitive alternatives (Buck, 1994). In addition, Satyagraha requires a comprehensive program of planning and training. The requirement for independence — the capacity to act alone — must be balanced with the social responsiveness basic to service to the community. This prosocial focus is built upon the value of equality.

Courage is the crucial virtue required for nonviolence; it is part of a total process of growth which avoids seeking authority over others even as it resists external coercion. Courage includes the force of loving and, therefore, the strength to resist violence. The courage of the Satyagrahi is the bravery of the gentle and the nonviolent; it is not the competitive-violence of the Western ideal. Satyagraha requires complete openness and honesty. The "other" is told all of the details of a planned action, and the exact demands are specified and kept to the essential minimum, contrary to ordinary principles of negotiation. Rejection of conflict-competition perspectives diminishes the likelihood of violence, but the least violence is derived from alternatives that utilize cooperation or noncooperation.

Gandhian synthesis is derived from the conception that violence can never be solved by counter violence, only by nonviolent means. When the Satyagahi is attacked, the appropriate response is to reject any self-protection or violent response, and continue with the planned action, e.g., unauthorized march. This requires extensive discipline and the courage to give up violent methods. It is not possible to avoid violence by others, but it is possible to reject one's own. This will result in less likelihood of assault or death than when both sides resort to violence.

The obsession with interpreting human behavior from a violence perspective has been coupled with a strange neglect of the psychological study of love, one of the central defining characteristics of human beings. Freud (1949) proposed two basic instincts — eros and the destructive instincts — as central to human functioning. According to Freud, "[t]he aim of the first of these basic instincts is to establish ever greater unities and to preserve them — in short to bind together; the aim of the second...is to undo connections and so to destroy things" (p. 20). This represents Freud's conception, in one of his last works, that there are inherent forces toward unification within human beings, as well as destructive ones. The centrality of loving, to Freud's thought, has been demonstrated by Bergman (1987) and Lear (1990).

Fromm (1964) accepted the forces of eros and destruction, but revised the Freudian perspective to suggest that "[t]he life instinct thus constitutes the primary potentiality in man; the death instinct a secondary potentiality" (p. 50). Fromm added to this the distinction between the necrophilous — attraction to "all that is not alive, all that is dead" — and the biophilous — "reverence for life" — orientations (pp. 37-61). The nechrophiliac believes in force, the power to kill; the biophiliac "loves the adventure of living," wants to "influence by love" (Fromm, pp. 40-47). Love of life grows out of interpersonal and social forces rather than biological ones. Whether inherent in the biological system or learned, loving is as fundamental to human nature as violence.

Gandhi (1940) and May (1972) also agreed that good and evil are inseparable in life. As stated by Gandhi (1940):

Ahimsa is a comprehensive principle. We are helpless mortals caught in the conflagration of himsa. Man cannot for a moment live without consciously or unconsciously committing outward himsa. The very fact of his living — eating, drinking, moving about — necessarily involves some himsa, destruction of life, be it ever so minute (p. 257).

Ahimsa, therefore, needs to be understood as a principle of *least* violence rather than nonviolence. Ahimsa is equivalent to love. "In its positive form, *Ahimsa* means the largest love, the greatest charity" (Gandhi, 1970, pp. 13-14). The process of working toward least violence is endless, and Gandhi readily acknowledged his own imperfections.

The essence of Gandhi's contribution lies in his demonstration of the extent to which people can rise above destructiveness (Buck, 1984, 1994, in press). This process requires changing one's whole orientation toward life (Gandhi, 1940). Similarly to Gandhi, King grasped the importance of Ahimsa, and saw the necessity of training in nonviolent methods. According to Branch (1988), King promoted a nonviolent approach in the South. King balanced nonviolence with an orientation intended to enhance the humanity of the opponent as well as one's own interests.

Acceptance of diversity, an openness and capacity for cooperation, and an affirmation of life are possible, and are as solidly founded in human beings as conflict-competition-violence. Both perspectives are utilized by people in varying degrees, but this chapter proposes diversity-cooperation-life affirmation as a more effective means of living — as more compatible with health. Health, as has previously been proposed (Buck, 1990, 1992b), is best characterized as a group of adaptations built upon considerable autonomy. Healthy people fit in with social expectations to varying degrees or radically dissent. Personal values and a sense of community are united in a fashion that facilitates "free assent." Values are internalized as one's own, based on their relevance to the unique potential for growth within the person, and the individual's connectedness to significant others. As a result, people who have moved reasonably in the direction of health have a greater capacity for dealing with differences by respecting the legitimacy of multiple points of view while holding solid self-values.

In addition, such individuals are open to the choice of working *with* others and are receptive to life-affirming solutions. Choice, for the healthy, includes maximizing the alternatives available to the person. The necessity of developing autonomy in order to enhance respect and nonviolence was advocated by Gandhi in his analysis of the term "Swaraj" — self rule. The focus of freedom is on each individual. Swaraj, as with all Gandhian concepts, is a process requiring continuous effort and self-discipline for which Gandhi has used the term "Brahmacharya." Swaraj, however, is always integrated with, but not controlled by, social responsiveness (Buck, 1994).

Loving, like choice, is promoted by the degree of independence reached by each person. Loving is, by definition, life-affirming. It represents a relationship between equals who have the security to engage in a process of exchange, characterized by *giving to* rather than *giving up*, by empathic knowing, by respecting the unique individuality of others, by caring in the sense of active concern for the self-actualization of other people, and by voluntary responsiveness to that growth. This is a process consistent with Fromm's (1963) "art of loving," Maslow's (1968) "transition from D-love to B-love," and May's (1969) "process of loving." Advanced phases of this process reflect complementarity — a fitting together that enlarges each person even as it respects the individuality of both. The mutuality promoted — the ability to share in the satisfactions derived from the other person's growth — enhances a new unity, a consenting harmony (Arieti & Arieti, 1977), a process partnership (Rogers, 1972).

Success within a two-person union prepares one for a capacity to surpass this boundary and embrace a new generation, eventually extending to an understanding and respect for all of humanity. Erikson's (1982) epigenetic process integrated the intertwining issues of intimacy, generativity, and integrity representative of the life-affirming accomplishments possible within a receptive culture. Generativity expands intimacy to include a more "universal care" (p. 68), even as integrity culminates in "a sense of coherence and wholeness" (p. 65). Integrity unifies "a comradeship with the ordering ways of distant times and different pursuits" (p. 65). It is built from the widening of identity to include the commonality reflected in the experience of otherness in oneself and sameness in others (Erikson, 1987).

The possibilities of love for serving the affirmation of life are also central to Gandhi's (1970) thinking. Gandhi summarized love's potential for enhancing the other by stating: "Love is reckless in giving away, oblivious as to what it gets in return" (p. 2). The culmination of Gandhi's life-affirming directions is included within his interpretation of "Advaita." Advaita is based upon a respect for all people (Gandhi, 1967), unity with all human beings, and unity with all life.

Education for Nonviolence

If a great deal of violence grows out of the context of an escalating sequence of conflict-competition, part of the solution can be found in diversity-cooperation socialization. A focus upon individuals, whether from a punishment or rehabilitation perspective, cannot succeed as long as society continues to admire and promote combative, win-lose alternatives for solving problems. As Toch (1992) has concluded, violence takes place within "violence-prone games." "The violence-prone person invites violence-prone interactions with other people" (p. 225). While Toch (pp. 223-231) at times focused upon the "subculture of violence" and the rehabilitation of violent men, he proposed that the first step toward nonviolence is tied to self-knowledge.

Self-knowledge includes an understanding of "one's conduct in its social context" (p. 231). Toch went even further in tying violence to the general culture by discussing the focus of children's games as promoters of "competitive, retaliatory and aggressive" solutions, and proposed that "equity, justice and fairness" could be built into games (pp. 234-235). He also discussed the Oakland Police Department's violence reduction project, which has successfully helped officers gain insight into their own violence-promoting behavior. This demonstrated that it is possible to teach people to avoid the challenges that usually provoke an escalation of aggression, and to eliminate their own tendencies to threaten others. As a result, he concluded that "individual change can go hand in hand with group-based change and organizational change and even with community change" (p. 254).

Toch concluded that, in the final analysis, violent individuals are educated in destructiveness. He stated: "Our Violent Men, after all, are basically children who have learned to use force as a compensatory tool" (p. 257). Violence is, to a considerable degree, learned as a means of problem solving, but even those who have learned well can be socialized with nonviolent alternatives.

Wertham (1969) also discussed the extensive indoctrination in violence that this society provides for its children, particularly boys. He proposed that violence "is not a thing apart but is linked by a thousand threads to the present fabric of our social and institutional life" (p. 338). One of the most important of these threads is what Wertham has called "violence-thinking," the tendency to think only of violent solutions to problems and to use all sorts of rationalizations to defend these choices. As noted by Wertham, "We say freedom and mean power, we say power and mean violence" (p. 346).

One of the clearest results of the study of violence is that violence leads to violence. As a result, Gandhi concluded that we can never solve violence through violent means (Buck, 1994). Straus, Gelles, and Steinmetz (1980) tied the education of violence to the family, stating, "the American family and the American home are perhaps as or more violent than any other single American institution" (p. 4). They emphasized the need for "long-term changes in the fabric of society," and an alteration of the toleration, acceptance and even encouragement of beliefs that "create a cycle of violence" (p. 244). As an alternative to violence, they provided evidence that demonstrated considerably lower rates of spouse abuse within families that share decision making, i.e., cooperative families. The reduction of violence requires the elimination of norms that "legitimize and glorify" violence, such as beliefs in the value of physical punishment; the mobilization of extended family and community support systems that utilizes prosocial, altruistic means; and the reduction of inequality between the sexes that can solve "the battle of the sexes" (pp. 237-243). Essentially, Strauss, et al. promoted nonviolent-cooperative alternatives to child rearing that are consistent with Gandhian synthesis.

Their conclusions were recently updated and extended by Gelles and Cornell (1990). Gelles and Cornell found that, in regard to wife abuse, women who chose to stay with their husbands were least effective when they struck back — an escalation of violence — and most effective when they became convinced and determined that "the violence must stop now" (p. 81). This is consistent with the Gandhian refusal to accept violence from others, even as it is rejected as a means of solving differences.

While Tedeschi and Felson (1994) seemed to accept coercive behavior as an inevitable aspect of human interactions, they suggested that "[p]eople who can state grievances and criticize without offending the target and who can give adequate accounts for their own misbehavior are less likely to become involved in coercive episodes" (p. 362). Further, they proposed that "empathy with others inhibits the use of coercion" (p. 363). Parallel to this is research summarized by Adams (1989), which indicated that a belief in the conception that war is inherent in human nature makes it less likely that students will believe in nonviolent alternatives or participate in actions promoting peace.

Western conflict-violence values obstruct the awareness of nonviolent possibilities. However, there is evidence supporting Tedeschi and Felson's position (1994) that the capacity to take the perspective of others reduces violence (Miller & Eisenberg, 1988). Not only did abusive parents score lower on indexes of empathic responsiveness, but abused children also exhibited less empathy. Similarly, Koss, Goodman, Browne, Fitzgerald, Keita, and Russo (1994) provided data indicating that men who lack empathy in their gender schema are more sexually aggressive, more supportive of rape, and more likely to use violence for "resolving conflict" (pp. 30-31).

Violence may promote violence by stifling empathy. Empathy requires taking the perspective of the other, and therefore, to some degree, grants legitimacy to the other person's point-of-view. This is, of course, basic to Gandhian cooperativeness — the acceptance of difference without translating it into conflict.

Kohn (1986) also questioned the competition-violence represented in the athletic games of childhood. He pointed out that many cooperative games have been proposed. The "cooperative conflict" advocated by Kohn (p. 157) is, in fact, simply cooperation built upon discussion and debate that is necessary to reveal each person's point-of-view — the disclosure necessary for empathy. For Kohn, a noncompetitive society is possible, but will require the modification of fundamental aspects of the economic and political system. Kohn proposed that education for a noncompetitive society requires the "affirmation of an alternative vision" (p. 194). Alternatives that break the connection among self-interest, conflict, and competition, have the best chance of avoiding the cycle of violence.

Conclusions

Violence is caused by a variety of factors, but one of its primary sources is derived from the culturally promoted values of conflict and competition. Justification of conflict-competition as essential human characteristics is typically related to innate self-interest. Destructiveness is, therefore, rooted in basic values of Western Civilization. The conflict-competition-violence cycle is taught to children within the family environment (Gelles & Cornell, 1990) as part of normal socialization, but is particularly characteristic of masculine education (Farrell, 1993; Kilmartin, 1994). As a consequence of this training, violence is promoted as a preferred solution to relationship problems. The pervasiveness of violence within society, therefore, cannot be adequately reduced by techniques oriented toward particular individuals in terms of either rehabilitation or punishment.

A comprehensive solution to violence must come from the reeducation of society, and from questioning the self-interest-conflict-competition-violence bias that is promoted both generally and by much of the scientific community. Alternative perspectives must be given clearer recognition, and must become a regular part of the socialization of children. Human beings have potential for prosocial and altruistic behavior that is equal to their potential for selfishness and competitiveness. While all of these possibilities are available to human beings, none are more fundamental. It is proposed here, however, that altruism, diversity, cooperation, and life affirmation are more effective perspectives for dealing with human interactions.

Children need to be educated and adults reeducated in terms of the multiple options available for solving life's problems. The best means for avoiding violence is to refuse to join the conflict-competition cycle that escalates into assault or homicide. People need to get in touch with a sense of community and with prosocial capacity, and develop an awareness of the effectiveness of coping styles consistent with these sources. Differences among people are inevitable and desirable within democratic societies. However, difference can be understood within the perspective of diversity — respect for the legitimacy of alternative points of view.

Diversity enhances empathic understanding, and thereby encourages mutual disclosure and honesty. Tolerance of diversity makes cooperation more effective, and cooperative solutions are not dependent upon the initial stance of the other person. What is necessary is to give up efforts toward victory, defeat, or compromise in order to seek win-win solutions. In view of the intense socialization in competitiveness, training will be necessary in order to learn to work toward a creative synthesis that provides for the essential needs of both parties.

As cooperativeness is never passivity or conformity, it requires the courage necessary to persist with deeply held beliefs, and also the flexibility that comes from strength. Cooperation maintains self-control and choice; it does not depend upon the behavior of others. Cooperativeness is primarily a reflection of the attitude of working with others — even those initially defined as enemies. It includes a willingness to change, to grow. Techniques are valuable as part of learning cooperativeness as long as they are used within the context of working together, but they are meaningless if there is a conscious, or even unconscious, desire to win.

Practice with situations that require cooperation for the success of both participants can exemplify the positive feelings and the creative levels of achievement that occur within this atmosphere. Tasks can be arranged to demonstrate the value of unilateral cooperation, i.e., while one persists at achieving one's own goals, each move of the other person (competitive, manipulative, etc.) is responded to cooperatively. A variety of additional techniques can be taught, such as practicing tasks that can only be solved by achieving higher benefits for both parties, or using cooperative games and athletic events that counter the usual situation of pitting people against each other.

In addition to education in cooperative approaches, noncooperation can be taught as a means of returning a deadlocked situation to a context of working with the other party for mutual gain. Noncooperation includes a variety of techniques that always seeks to avoid conflict and never includes competitiveness. This is consistent with Gandhi's Satyagraha, which is based upon the altruistic principle of a loving search for truth. Noncooperation is always in the service of cooperation, and is restricted to the use of nonviolent options. As violence is difficult to eliminate or even reduce, advance planning, honesty, and self-discipline must be pursued. Ideally, noncooperative approaches are built upon self-awareness and self-growth — a balance between one's conscience and a sense of community, and a striving for equality.

Violence maximizes violence; nonviolence leads to least violence. It is clear that people can change, even in a violence-promoting society. Most people already resist the entrapment of the conflict-competition cycle sufficiently to avoid extreme violence. Noncooperation provides an active means of coping that is an alternative to either violence or passivity.

The primary problem of violence can be reduced only by changing society — cooperative-nonviolent games and athletic events must be promoted; education in violent problem solving rooted in physical punishment must be abandoned; training in competition-violence that is called masculinity must be modified; and the admiration and allure of violence, represented by the death penalty or war, must be confronted openly. Cooperation guarantees success as long as one maintains the cooperative stance, but it is a process that one must continuously work toward achieving.

References

Adams, D. (1989). The Seville statement on violence and why it is important. *Journal of Humanistic Psychology, 29,* 328-337.

Allee, W. C. (1958). *The social life of animals.* Boston: Beacon.

Arieti, S. & Arieti, J. A. (1977). *Love can be found.* New York: Harcourt, Brace & Jovanovich.

Batson, C. D. & Oleson, K. C. (1991). Current status of the empathy-altruism hypothesis. In M. S. Clark (Ed.), *Prosocial behavior.* Newbury Park, CA: Sage.

Bergman, M. S. (1987). *The anatomy of loving.* New York: Columbia University Press.

Bertness, M. D. (1992). The ecology of a New England salt marsh. *American Scientist, 80,* 260-268.

Bondurant, J. V. (1965). *Conquest of violence* (Rev. ed.). Berkeley: University of California Press.

Branch, T. (1988). *Parting the waters: America in the King years 1954-63.* New York: Simon & Schuster.

Buck, L. A. (1984). Nonviolence and Satyagraha in Attenborough's Gandhi. *Journal of Humanistic Psychology, 24,* 130-141.

Buck, L. A. (1990). Abnormality, normality and health. *Psychotherapy, 27,* 187-194.

Buck, L. A. (1991). *Courage, autism and schizophrenia.* Paper presented at the 49th Ann. Conv., International Council of Psychologists, San Francisco, CA.

Buck, L. A. (1992a). *Diversity-cooperation-life affirmation as a context for health.* Paper presented at the 50th Ann. Convention, International Council of Psychologists, Amsterdam, The Netherlands.

Buck, L. A. (1992b). The myth of normality: Consequences for the diagnosis of abnormality and health. *Social Behavior and Personality, 20,* 251-262.

Buck, L. A. (1994). Gandhian synthesis. *Journal of Developing Societies, 11,* 112-119.

Buck, L. A. (in press). Gandhi and Jefferson: Democracy and humanism. *Gandhi Marg.*

Buck, R. & Ginsburg, B. (1991). Spontaneous communication and altruism: The communicative gene hypothesis. In M. S. Clark (Ed.), *Prosocial behavior.* Newbury Park, CA: Sage.

Campbell, A. (1993). *Men, women and aggression.* New York: Basic Books.

Carneval, P. J. & Pruitt, D. G. (1992). Negotiation and mediation. In M. R. Rosenzweig & L. W. Porter (Eds.), *Annual review of psychology.* Palo Alto, CA: Annual Reviews.

Chadwick, D. H. (1991). Elephants — Out of time, out of space. *National Geographic, 179,* 2-49.

Coleman, K. H. & Weinman, M. (1981). Conjugal violence. In J. R. Hays, T. K. Roberts, & K. S. Solway (Eds.), *Violence and the violent individual.* New York: Spectrum.

Craig, G. A. (1989). The grand decider. *New York Review of Books, 36,* 31-36.

Deutsch, M. (1993). Educating for a peaceful world. *American Psychologist, 48,* 510-517.

deWaal, F. (1988). *Peacemaking among primates.* Cambridge: Harvard University Press.

Draper, T. (1992). The true history of the gulf war. *New York Review of Books, 39*, 38-45.

Erikson, E. H. (1982). *The life cycle completed.* New York: Norton.

Erikson, E. H. (1987). Remarks on the "wider identity." In E. H. Erikson, *A way of looking at things.* New York: Norton.

Farrell, W. (1993). *The myth of male power.* New York: Simon & Schuster.

Fine, R. (1985). *The meaning of love in human experience.* NewYork: Wiley.

Fiske, A. P. (1991). Cultural relativity of selfish individualism. In M. S. Clark (Ed.), *Prosocial behavior.* Newbury Park, CA: Sage.

Fogelman, E. & Wiener, V. L. (1985). The few, the brave, the noble. *Psychology Today, 19*, 60-65.

Frank, J. D. (1972). Psychological aspects of international violence. In J. Fawcett (Ed.), *Dynamics of violence.* Chicago: AMA.

Freud, S. (1949). *An outline of psychoanalysis.* New York: Norton.

Friedman, L. M. (1993). *Crime and punishment in American history.* New York: Basic Books.

Fromm, E. (1963). *The art of loving.* New York: Bantam.

Fromm, E. (1964). *The heart of man.* New York: Harper & Row.

Fromm, E. (1973). *The anatomy of human destructiveness.* New York: Holt, Rinehart & Winston.

Gandhi, M. K. (1940). *An autobiography; or the story of my experiments with truth* (2d ed.). Ahmedabad: Navajivan.

Gandhi, M. K. (1950). *Satyagraha in South Africa* (**2nd** ed.). Ahmedabad: Navajivan.

Gandhi, M. K. (1954). In B. Kumarappa (Ed.), *Sarvodya.* Ahmedabad: Navajivan.

Gandhi, M. K. (1961). In R. K. Prabhu (Ed.), *Democracy: Real and deceptive.* Ahmedabad: Navajivan.

Gandhi, M. K. (1967). In R. K. Prabhu, & U. R. Rao (Eds.), *The mind of Mahatma Gandhi.* Ahmedabad: Navajivan.

Gandhi, M. K. (1970). In A. T. Hingorani (Ed.), *The law of love.* Bombay: Bharatiya Vidya Bhavan.

Gelles, R. J. & Cornell, C. P. (1990). *Intimate violence in families* (2d ed.). Newburg Park: Sage.

Glazer, M. P. & Glazer, P. M. (1986). Whistleblowing. *Psychology Today, 20*, 36-43.

Heinrich, B. (1989). *Ravens in winter.* New York: Summit.

Honeycutt, R. L. (1992). Naked mole-rats. *American Scientist, 80*, 43-53.

Johanson, D. & Johanson, L. (1994). *Ancestors.* New York: Villard.

Kelman, H. C. & Hamilton, V. L. (1989). *Crimes of obedience.* New Haven: Yale University Press

Kilmartin, C. T. (1994). *The masculine self.* New York: Macmillan.

Klama, J. (1988). *Aggression: The myth of the beast within.* New York: Wiley.

Kohn, A. (1986). *No contest: The case against competition*. Boston: Houghton-Mifflin.

Kolb, L. C. (1972). Violence and aggression: An overview. In J. Fawcett (Ed.), *Dynamics of violence*. Chicago: AMA.

Koss, M. P., Goodman, L. A., Browne, A., Fitzgerald, L. F., Keita, G. P., & Russo, N. F. (1994). *No safe haven*. Washington, DC: APA.

Leaky, R. & Lewin, R. (1992). *Origins reconsidered*. New York: Doubleday.

Lear, J. (1990). *Love and its place in nature*. New York: Farrar, Straus & Giroux.

Levine, J. M. & Moreland, R. L. (1990). In M. R. Rosenzweig, & L. W. Porter (Eds.), *Annual review of psychology*. Palo Alto, CA: Annual Reviews.

Lewis, H. B. (1976). *Psychic war in men and women*. New York: New York University Press.

Lewontin, R. C. (1994). Women versus the biologists. *New York Review of Books, 41*, 31-35.

Lifton, R. J. (1986). *The Nazi doctors*. New York: Basic Books.

Malik, S. (1986). *Gandhian satyagraha and contemporary world*. Rohtak, India: Manthan.

Maslow, A. H. (1968). *Toward a psychology of being* (2d ed.). New York: Van Nostrand Reinhold.

Maslow, A. H. (1971). *The farther reaches of human nature*. NewYork: Viking.

May, R. (1953). *Man's search for himself*. New York: Delta.

May, R. (1969). *Love and will*. New York: Norton.

May, R. (1972). *Power and innocence*. New York: Norton.

May, R. (1981). *Freedom and destiny*. New York: Norton.

Meloy, J. R. (1992). *Violent attachments*. Northvale, NJ: Aronson.

Miller, P. A. & Eisenberg, N. (1988). The relation of empathy to aggressive and externalizing/antisocial behavior. *Psychological Bulletin, 103*, 324-344.

Oza, D. K. (1991). *Voluntary action and Gandhian approach*. New Delhi: National Book Trust.

Rappaport, J. & Holden, K. (1981). Prevention of violence. In J. R. Hays, T. K. Roberts, & K. S. Soloway (Eds.), *Violence and the violent individual*. New York: Spectrum.

Roberts, T. K., Mock, L. T., & Johnstone, E. E. (1981). Psychological aspects of the etiology of violence. In J. R. Hays, T. K. Roberts, & K. S. Soloway (Eds.), *Violence and the violent individual*. New York: Spectrum.

Rogers, C. R. (1972). *Becoming partners*. New York: Delacourte.

Sargent, D. A. (1972). The lethal situation: Transmission of urge to kill from parent to child. In J. Fawcett (Ed.), *Dynamics of violence*. Chicago: AMA.

Saul, L. J. (1976). *The psychodynamics of hostility*. New York: Aronson.

Shepard, M. (1987). *Gandhi today*. Arcata, CA: Simple Productions Press.

Snow, R. E. & Swanson, J. (1992). Instructional psychology: Aptitude, adaptation, and assessment. In M. R.

Rosenzweig, and L. W. Porter (Eds.), *Annual review of psychology*. Palo Alto, CA: Annual Review.

Sonkin, D. J. & Auerbach-Walker, L. E. (1985). *The male batterer*. New York: Springer.

Spiegal, J. P. (1972). Toward a theory of collective violence. In J. Fawcett (Ed.), *Dynamics of violence*. Chicago: AMA.

Storr, A. (1970). *Human aggression*. New York: Bantam.

Straus, M. A., Gelles, R. J., & Steinmetz, S. K. (1980). *Behind closed doors*. Garden City, NY: Anchor.

Tavris, C. & Offir, C. (1977). *The longest war*. New York: Harcourt, Brace & Jovanovich.

Tedeschi, J. T. & Felson, R. B. (1994). *Violence, aggression, and coercive actions*. Washington, DC: APA.

Tetlock, P. E., McGuire, C. B., & Mitchell, G. (1991). Psychological perspectives on nuclear deterrence. In M. R. Rosenzweig, & L. W. Porter (Eds.), *Annual Review of Psychology*. Palo Alto, CA: Annual Reviews.

Toch, H. (1992). *Violent men*. Washington, DC: APA.

Walker, D. (1968). *Rights in conflict*. New York: Signet.

Weigley, R. F. (1991). *The age of battles*. Bloomington, IN: Indiana University Press.

Weiner, J. (1994). *The beak of the finch*. New York: Knopf.

Weinstein, C. S. (1991). The classroom as a social context for learning. In M. R. Rosenzweig, & L. W. Porter (Eds.), *Annual Review of Psychology*, Palo Alto, CA: Annual Reviews.

Wertham, F. (1969). *A sign for Cain*. New York: Warner.

Wilson, E. O. (1992). *The diversity of life*. Cambridge, MA: Belknap.

Wolfgang, M. E. (1981). Sociocultural overview of criminal violence. In J. R. Hays, T. K. Roberts, & K. S. Soloway (Eds.), *Violence and the violent individual*. New York: Spectrum.

Zuckerman, L. (1989). Converging on peace? *New York Review of Books, 36*, 26-32.

Zur, O. (1989). War myths: Exploration of the dominant collective beliefs about warfare. *Journal of Humanistic Psychology, 29*, 297-327.

About the Author

Lucien A. Buck, PhD, is a Professor of Psychology at Dowling College in Oakdale, New York. He is a Diplomate in Clinical Psychology from the American Board of Professional Psychology. He has numerous publications and presentations in the areas of conflict, competitiveness and violence, perception, altered consciousness, and psychotherapy. He has presented at several international conferences on Gandhian concepts as they apply to democracy, humanism, and life affirmation.

Reference List

Abel, E. L. (1986). Guns and blood alcohol levels among homicide victims. *Drug and Alcohol Dependence, 18*, 253-257.

Abel, E. L. (1987). Drugs and homicide in Erie County, New York. *International Journal of Addictions, 22*(2), 195-200.

Abel, E. L. & Zeidenberg, P. M. (1985). Age, alcohol and violent death: A postmortem study. *Journal of Studies on Alcohol, 46*(3), 228-231.

Abel, E. L. & Zeidenberg, P. M. (1986). Alcohol and homicide: A comparison between Erie County, New York and Los Angeles County, California. *American Journal on Drug and Alcohol Abuse, 12*, 121-129.

Abel, G. G., Becker, I., Mittleman, M., Cunningham-Rathner, J., Rouleau, J., & Murphy, W. (1987). Self-reported sex crimes of nonincarcerated paraphiliacs. *Journal of Interpersonal Violence, 2*(1), 3-25.

Abel, G. G., Becker, J. V., Mittleman, J., Cunningham-Rathner, J., Rouleau, J. U., & Murphy, W. (1987, March). Self-reported sex crimes of non-incarcerated paraphiliacs. *Journal of Interpersonal Violence*, pp. 3-25.

Abel, G. G., Becker, J. V., & Skinner, L. J. (1981). Aggressive behavior and sex. *Psychiatric Clinics of North America, 3*, 133-151.

Abel, G. G., Levis, D. J., & Clancy, J. (1970). Aversion therapy applied to taped sequences of deviant behavior in exhibitionism and other sexual deviations: A preliminary report. *Journal of Behavior Therapy and Experimental Psychiatry, 1*, 59-66.

Abel, G. G., Mittleman, M., Becker, J. V., Rathner, J., & Rouleau, J. (1988). Predicting child molester's response to treatment. *Annals of the New York Academy of Science, 528*, 223-234.

Abel, G. G. & Osborn, C. (1992). The paraphilias: The extent and nature of sexually deviant and criminal behavior. *Psychiatric Clinics of North America, 15*(3), 675-687.

Abikoff, H. & Klein, R. G. (1992). Attention-deficit hyperactivity and conduct disorder: Comorbidity and implications for treatment. *Journal of Consulting and Clinical Psychology, 60*(6), 881-892.

Achenbach, T. (1993). Taxonomy and comorbidity of conduct problems: Evidence from empirically based approaches. *Development and Psychopathology, 5*, 51-64.

Adams, D. (1989). The Seville statement on violence and why it is important. *Journal of Humanistic Psychology, 29*, 328-337.

Adams, H. E. & Chiodo, J. (1984). Sexual deviations. In H. E. Adams & P. Sutker (Eds.), *Comprehensive handbook of psychopathology* (pp. 777-806). New York: Plenum.

Adams, K. (1976). Behavioral treatment of reflex or sensory-evoked seizures. *Journal of Behavior Therapy and Experimental Psychiatry, 7*, 123-127.

Adelman, L. (1993). Violence on television: Teach the children. American Educational Research Association, Division E (Counseling and Human Development) *Newsletter, 12* (1), p. 3.

Alderman, N. & Burgess P. W. (1990). Integrating cognition and behaviour: A pragmatic approach to brain injury rehabilitation. In R. L. Wood & I. Fussey (Eds.), *Cognitive rehabilitation in perspective* (pp. 204-228). London: Taylor & Francis.

Allee, W. C. (1958). *The social life of animals*. Boston: Beacon.

Allen, N. (1983). Homicide followed by suicide: Los Angeles, 1970-1979. *Suicide and Life-Threatening Behavior, 13*(3).

Allen, N. H. (1983, Fall). Homicide followed by suicide: Los Angeles, 1970-1979. *Suicide and Life-Threatening Behavior*, pp. 155-564.

Allondi, F. A. (1994). Post-traumatic stress disorder in hostages and victims of torture. *Psychiatric Clinics of North America, 17*, 279-288.

American Medical Association (1992). *Diagnostic and treatment guidelines in elder abuse and neglect*. Chicago: Author.

American Psychiatric Association (1968). *Diagnostic and statistical manual of mental disorders* (1st ed.). Washington, DC: Author.

American Psychiatric Association. (1968). *Diagnostic and statistical manual of mental disorders* (2nd ed.). Washington, DC: Author.

American Psychiatric Association. (1980). *Diagnostic and statistical manual of mental disorders* (3rd ed.). Washington, DC: Author.

American Psychiatric Association. (1987). *Diagnostic and statistical manual of mental disorders* (3rd ed., revised). Washington, DC: Author.

American Psychiatric Association. (1994). *Diagnostic and statistical manual of mental disorders* (4th ed.). Washington, DC: Author.

American Psychological Association Commission on Violence and Youth (1993). *Violence & youth: Psychology's response*, Vol. I. Washington, DC: American Psychological Association.

Amick-McMullan, A., Kilpatrick, D. G., Veronen, L. J., & Smith, S. (1989). Family survivors of homicide victims: Theoretical perspectives and an exploratory study. *Journal of Traumatic Stress, 2*, 21-35.

Amighi, J. (1990). Some thoughts on the cross-cultural study of maternal warmth and detachment. *Pre and Perinatal Psychology Journal, 5*(2), 131-146.

Anastasi, A. (1979). Sex differences: Historical perspectives and theoretical implications. *Catalogue of Selected Documents in Psychology, 10* (2), Ms. No. 1999.

Anderson, W. & Holcomb, W. R. (1983). Accused murderers: Five MMPI personality types. *Journal of Clinical Psychology, 39*, 761-768.

Ansevics, N. L. & Doweiko, H. E. (1991). Serial murderers: Early proposed developmental model and typology. *Psychotherapy in Private Practice, 9*, 107-122.

Appleby, L. & Dickens, C. (1993). Mothering skills of women with mental illness: Not enough known about the postpartum period. *British Medical Journal, 306*(6874), 348.

Archer, J. (1995). What can ethology offer the psychological study of human aggression? *Aggressive Behavior, 21,* 243-255.

Arey, J.A. (1972). *The sky pirates.* New York: Schribner's.

Arieti, S. & Arieti, J. A. (1977). *Love can be found.* New York: Harcourt, Brace & Jovanovich.

Arizona v. Bay, 722 P.2d 280 (Ariz. Sup. Ct. 1986).

Ashbach, C. (1994). Media influences and personality development: The inner image and the outer world. In D. Zillmann, J. Bryant, & A. C. Huston, (Eds.), *Media, children, and the family: Social scientific, psychodynamic, and clinical perspectives* (pp. 117-128). Hillsdale, NJ: Lawrence Erlbaum Associates.

Ashe, A. & Rampersad, A. (1993). *Days of grace: A memoir.* New York: Knopf.

Ashford, J. W., Schulz, S. C., & Walsh, G. O. (1980). Violent automatism in a partial complex seizure, *Archives of Neurology, 37,* 120-122.

Asimov, I. (1981). *Isaac Asimov's book of facts.* New York: Bell Publishing Co.

Associated Press (1994, November 4). Police seize suspect obsessed by a movie. *The New York Times,* p. A25.

Auerbach, S. M., Kiesler, D. J., Strentz, T., Schmidt, J. A., & Serio, C. D. (1994). Interpersonal impacts and adjustment to the stress of simulated captivity: An empirical test of the Stockholm Syndrome. *Journal of Social and Clinical Psychology, 13,* 207-221.

Auletta, K. (1991). *Three blind mice: How the networks lost their way.* New York: Random House.

Avis, J. M. (1994). Advocates versus researchers—a false dichotomy? A feminist, social constructionist response to Jacobson. *Family Process, 33,* 87-91.

Bach, S. (1991). On sadomasochistic object relations. In G. Fogel & W. Myers (Eds.), *Perversions and near-perversions in clinical practice* (pp. 75-92). New Haven: Yale University.

Bachman, R. (1992). *Elderly victims* [NCJ-138330]. Washington, DC: U.S. Department of Justice.

Bachman, R. (1994a, January). *Violence against women* [NCJ-145325]. A national crime victimization survey report. Washington, DC: U.S. Department of Justice.

Bachman, R. (1994b, July). *Violence against women* [A National Crime Victimization Survey Report]. Washington, DC: U.S. Department of Justice.

Bachman, R. & Pillemer, K. A. (1992). Epidemiology and family violence involving adults. In R. T.

Ammerman & M. Hersen (Eds.), *Assessment of family violence A clinical and legal sourcebook* (pp. 108-120). New York: John Wiley & Sons, Inc.

Bach-Y-Rita, G., Lion, F., Clement, C., & Ervin, F. (1971). Episodic dyscontrol: A study of 130 violent patients. *American Journal of Psychiatry, 127,* 49-54.

Bach-Y-Rita, G., Lion, J. R.,Clement, C. E., & Ervin, F. R., (1971). Episodic dyscontrol: Study of 130 violent patients. *American Journal of Psychiatry, 127,* 1473-1478.

Bach-Y-Rita, G. & Veno, A. (1974). Habitual violence: A profile of 62 men. *American Journal of Psychiatry, 131,* 154-217.

Baik, S. & Uku, J. (1988). Ligature strangulation of a woman during sadomasochistic sexual activity. *The American Journal of Forensic Medicine and Pathology, 9*(3), 249-251.

Baldus, D. C., Woodworth, G. G., Jr., & Pulaski, C. A. (1990). *Equal justice and the death penalty.* Boston, MA: Northeastern University Press.

Ballentine, J. (1969). *Ballentine's law dictionary* (3rd ed.). San Francisco: Bancroft-Whitney Co.

Banay, R. S. (1969). Unconscious motivation in crime. *Medical Aspects of Human Sexuality, 3,* 91-102.

Bandler, R. (1988). Brain mechanisms of aggression as revealed by electrical and chemical stimulation: Suggestion of a central role for the midbrain periaqueductal grey region. *Progress in Psychobiology, Physiology, and Psychology, 13,* 67-154.

Bandura, A. (1965). Influence of models reinforcement contingencies on the acquisition of imitative responses. *Journal of Personality and Social Psychology, 1,* 585-595.

Bandura, A. (1973). *Aggression: A social learning analysis.* Englewood Cliffs, NJ: Prentice Hall.

Bandura, A. (1977). *Social learning theory.* Englewood Cliffs, NJ: Prentice-Hall.

Bandura, A. (1983). Psychological mechanisms of aggression. In R. G. Geen & E. I. Donnerstein (Eds.), *Aggression: Theoretical and empirical reviews,* (Vol. 1, pp. 1-40). San Diego, CA: Academic Press.

Bandura, A. (1986). *Social foundations of thought and action:* A social cognitive theory. Englewood Cliffs, NJ: Prentice Hall.

Bandura, A., Ross, D., & Ross, S. A. (1961). Transmission of aggression through imitation of aggressive models. *Journal of Abnormal and Social Psychology, 63,* 575-582.

Bandura, A., Ross, D., & Ross, S. A. (1963). Imitation of film-mediated aggressive models. *Journal of Abnormal and Social Psychology, 66,* 3-11.

Bandura, A. & Walters, R. H. (1959). *Adolescent aggression.* New York, NY: Ronald Press.

Bandura, A. & Walters, R. H. (1963). *Social learning and personality development.* New York: Holt, Rinehart, & Winston.

Barco, P. P., Crosson, B., Bolestra, M. M., Werts, D., & Stout, R. (1991). Training awareness and compensation in postacute head injury rehabilitation. In J. S. Kreutzer & P. H. Wehman (Eds.), *Cognitive rehabilitation for persons with traumatic brain injury* (pp. 129-146). Baltimore: Brookes.

Barefoot v. Estelle, 463 U.S. 880 (1983).

Barkley, R. (1994). Impaired delayed responding. In D. Routh (Ed.), *Disruptive behavior disorders in childhood.* New York: Plenum Press.

Barkley, R. A. (1990). *Attention deficit hyperactivity disorder.* New York: Guilford Press.

Barkley, R. (1995). Sex differences in ADHD. *The ADHD Report, 3*(1), 1-5.

Barlow, D. H. (1974). The treatment of sexual deviation: Toward a comprehensive behavioral approach. In K. S. Calhoun, H. E. Adams, & K. M. Mitchell (Eds.), *Innovative treatment methods in psychopathology* (pp. 121-147). New York: Wiley.

Barlow, D. H. & Agras, W. S. (1973). Fading to increase sexual responsiveness in homosexuals. *Journal of Applied Behavioral Analysis, 6,* 355-367.

Barlow, D. H., Agras, W. S., Abel, G. G., Blanchard, E. B., & Young, L. D. (1977). A heterosocial skills behavior checklist for males. *Behavior Therapy, 8,* 229-239.

Baron, R. A. (1977). *Human aggression.* New York, NY: Plenum Press.

Baron, R. A. & Richardson, D. R. (1994). *Human aggression* (2d ed.). New York: Plenum Press.

Barnard, G. W., Vera, H., Vera, M., & Newman, G. (1982). Till death do us part: A study of spouse murder. Bulletin of the American *Academy of Psychiatry and Law, 10,* 271-280.

Barnett, A. & Schwartz, E. (1989). Urban homicide: Still the same. *Journal of Quantitative Criminology, 5,* 83-100.

Barnett, O. W. & Hamberger, L. K. (1992). The assessment of maritally violent men on the California Psychological Inventory. *Violence and Victims, 7,* 15-22.

Baron, R. A. (1977). *Human aggression.* New York, NY: Plenum Press.

Baron, R. A. (1984). Reducing organizational conflict: An incompatible response approach. *Journal of Applied Psychology, 69,* 272-279.

Baron, R. A. & Bell, P. A. (1975). Aggression and heat: Mediating effects of prior provocation and exposure to an aggressive model. *Journal of Personality and Social Psychology, 31,* 825-832.

Baron, R. A. & Bell, P. A. (1976). Aggression and heat: The influence of ambient temperature, negative affect, and a cooling drink on physical aggression. *Journal of Personality and Social Psychology, 33,* 245-255.

Baron, R. A. & Lawton, S. F. (1972). Environmental influences on aggression: The facilitation of modeling effects by high ambient temperatures. *Psychonomic Science, 26,* 80-83.

Baron, R. A. & Richardson, D. R. (1994). *Human aggression* (2d ed.). New York: Plenum Press.

Barratt, E. (1993). The use of anticonvulsants in aggression and violence. *Psychopharmacology Bulletin, 29,* 75-81.

Barrett, R. K. (1993). Urban adolescent homicidal violence: An emerging public health concern. *Urban League Review, 16,* 67-76.

Bartol, C. (in press). Police psychology: Then, now, and beyond. *Criminal Justice and Behavior*.

Bates, J. E. (1994). Introduction. In J. E. Bates & T. D. Wachs (Eds.), *Temperament: Individual differences at the interface of biology and behavior* (pp. 1-6). Washington, DC: American Psychological Association.

Batson, C. D. & Oleson, K. C. (1991). Current status of the empathy-altruism hypothesis. In M. S. Clark (Ed.), *Prosocial behavior*. Newbury Park, CA: Sage.

Bauer, C. & Ritt, L. (1988). A Victorian indictment of wife beating. In G. W. Russell (Ed.), *Violence in intimate relationships*. New York: PMA Publishing.

Bauers, S. (1995, March 6). Slain couple's son arrested in Missouri. *The Philadelphia Inquirer*, pp. A1, A10.

Baughman, Jr., F. A. (1993, May 12). Treatment of attention-deficit hyperactivity disorder. *Journal of the American Medical Association, 269*: 2368.

Baum, C. (1989). Conduct disorders. In T. Ollendick & M. Hansen (Eds.), Handbook of child psychopathology (2nd ed.), (pp. 171-196). New York: Plenum Press.

Baumeister, R. F., Stillwell, A., & Wotman, S. R. (1990). Victim and perpetrator accounts of interpersonal conflict: Autobiographical narratives about anger. *Journal of Personality and Social Psychology, 59*, 994-1005.

Baydar, N. & Brooks-Gunn, J. (1991). Effects of maternal employment and child-care arrangements on preschoolers' cognitive and behavioral outcomes: Evidence from the children of the national longitudinal survey of youth. *Developmental Psychology, 27*(6), 932-945.

Beck, S. J. (1949). *Rorschach's test*. New York: Grune & Stratton.

Beers, S. R. (1992). Effects of mild head injury in children and adolescents. *Neuropsychology Review, 3*, 281-320.

Bell, R.A., Lanceley, F.J., Feldmann, T.B., Johnson, P.W., Cheek, W., Lewis, C., & Worley, T. (1989). Improving hostage negotiation strategies: An empirical study of aircraft hijackers. *American Journal of Preventive Psychiatry and Neurology, 2*, 1-5.

Belsky, J. (1988). The "effects" of infant day care reconsidered. *Early Childhood Research Quarterly, 3*, 235-272.

Belsky, J. (1990). Parental and nonparental child care and children's socioemotional development: A decade in review. *Journal of Marriage and the Family, 52*, 885-903.

Belsky, J. & Braungart, J. M. (1991). Are insecure-avoidant infants with extensive day-care experience less stressed by and more independent in the strange situation? *Child Development, 62*, 567-571.

Benedikt, M. (1881). *Brains of criminals*. New York: Wm. Wood & Company.

Benson, D. F. (1986). Interictal behavior disorders in epilepsy. *Psychiatric Clinics of North America, 9*(2), 283-292.

Benton, D., Kumari, N., & Brain, P. F. (1982). Mild hypoglycemia and questionnaire measures of aggression. *Biological Psychology, 14*, 129-135.

Berenbaum, S. A. & Hines, M. (1992). Early androgens are related to childhood sex-typed toy preferences. *Psychological Science, 3*(3), 203-206.

Bergman, M. S. (1987). *The anatomy of loving*. New York: Columbia University Press.

Berkowitz, L. (1965). The concept of aggressive drive: Some additional considerations. In L. Berkowitz (Ed.), *Advances in experimental psychology* (Vol. 2, pp. 301-329). New York: Academic Press.

Berkowitz, L. (1969). The frustration-aggression hypothesis revisited. In L. Berkowitz (Ed.), *Roots of aggression* (pp. 1-28). New York: Atherton Press.

Berkowitz, L. (1984). Some effects of thoughts on anti- and prosocial influences of media events: A cognitive-neoassociation analysis. *Psychological Bulletin, 95*, 410-427.

Berkowitz, L. (1988). Frustrations, appraisals, and aversively stimulated aggression. *Aggressive Behavior, 14*, 3-11.

Berkowitz, L. (1989). Frustration-aggression hypothesis: Examination and reformulation. *Psychological Bulletin, 106*(1), 59-73.

Berkowitz, L. (1992). *Aggression: Its causes, consequences and control*. New York: McGraw Hill.

Berkowitz, L. & LePage, A. (1967). Weapons as aggression-eliciting stimuli. *Journal of Personality and Social Psychology, 7*, 202-207.

Berman, A. (1979). Dyadic death: Murder-suicide. *Suicide and Life Threatening Behavior, 9* (1).

Berman, A. L. (1979, Spring). Dyadic death: Murder-suicide. *Suicide and Life-Threatening Behavior*, pp. 15-23.

Berry, C. A., Shaywitz, S. E., & Shaywitz, B. A. (1985). Girls with attention deficit disorder: A silent minority? A report on behavioral and cognitive characteristics. *Pediatrics, 76*, 801-809.

Bertness, M. D. (1992). The ecology of a New England salt marsh. *American Scientist, 80*, 260-268.

Bezirganian, S. & Cohen, P. (1992). Sex differences in the interaction between temperament and parenting. *Journal of the American Academy of Child & Adolescent Psychiatry, 31*(5), 790-801.

Bianculli, D. (1992). *Teleliteracy: Taking television seriously*. New York: Continuum.

Biblow, E. (1973). Imaginative play and the control of aggressive behavior. In J. L. Singer, (Ed.), *The child's world of make-believe* (pp.104-128). New York: Academic Press.

Binder, L. (1983). Persisting symptoms after mild head injury. *Journal of Clinical and Experimental Neuropsychology, 8*, 323-346.

Birns, B. (1976). The emergence and socialization of sex differences in the earliest years. *Merrill-Palmer Quarterly, 22*, 229-250.

Black, H. (1990). *Black's law dictionary: Definitions of the terms and phrases of American and English jurisprudence ancient and modern* (6th ed.). St. Paul: West Publishing Co.

Blanchard, D.C. (1984). Applicability of animal models

to human aggression. In K. J. Flannelly (Ed.), *Biological perspectives on aggression.* New York: Alan R. Liss, Inc.

Blanchard, R. & Hucker, S. (1991). Age, transvestism, bondage, and concurrent paraphilic activities in 117 cases of autoerotic asphyxia. *British Journal of Psychiatry, 159,* 371-377.

Blankenhorn, D. (1995). *Fatherless America: Confronting our most urgent social problem.* New York: Basic Books.

Blass, T. (1991). Understanding behavior in the Milgram obedience experiment: The role of personality, situations, and their interactions. *Journal of Personality and Social Psychology, 60,* 398-413.

Blau, G. L. & Pasewark, R. A. (1994). Statutory changes and the insanity defense: Seeking the perfect insane person. *Law and Psychology Review, 18,* 69-108.

Bloch, B. & Zemring, R. E. (1973). Homicide in Chicago. *Journal of Research in Crime and Delinquency, 10,* 1-12.

Block, J. (1976). Issues, problems and pitfalls in assessing sex differences: A critical review of "the psychology of sex differences." *Merrill-Palmer Quarterly, 22,* 283-308.

Block, J. (1978). Another look at differentiation in the socialization behaviors of mothers and fathers. In F. Denmark & J. Sherman (Eds.), *Psychology of women: Future direction of research.* New York: Psychological Dimensions.

Block, J. (1979, September). *Socialization influences on personality development in males and females.* Paper presented at the meeting of the American Psychological Association, New York.

Block, J. H. (1973). Conceptions of sex role: Some cross-cultural and longitudinal perspectives. *American Psychologist, 28,* 512-526.

Block, N. J. (Ed.). (1981). *Imagery.* Cambridge, MA: M.I.T. Press.

Blount, W. R., Silverman, I. J., Sellers, C. S., & Seese, R. A. (1994). Alcohol and drug use among abused women who kill, abused women who don't and their abusers. *Journal of Drug Issues, 24*(2), 165-177.

Blum, R. (1981). Violence, alcohol and setting: An unexplored nexus. In J. J. Collins (Ed.), *Drinking and crime* (pp. 110-142). New York: Guilford Press.

Blumler, J. & Katz, E. (Eds.). (1974). *The uses of mass communication: Current perspectives on gratification research.* Beverly Hills: Sage Publications.

Blunt, L. W. & Stock, H. V. (1985). Guilty but mentally ill: An alternative verdict. *Behavior Sciences and Law, 3,* 49-67.

Boake, C. (1991). History of cognitive rehabilitation following head injury. In J. S. Kreutzer & P. H.

Wehman (Eds.), *Cognitive rehabilitation for persons with traumatic brain injury* (pp. 3-12). Baltimore: Brookes.

Bohn, M. J. (1979). Management classification for young adult inmates. *Federal Probation, 43*, 53-59.

Boll, T. (1985). Developing issues in neuropsychology. *Journal of Clinical and Experimental Neuropsychology, 7*, 473-484.

Bolz, F. & Hershey, E. (1979). *Hostage cop*. New York: Rawson, Wade.

Bond, M. R. (1984). The psychiatry of closed head injury. In D. N. Brooks (Ed.), *Closed head injury: Psychological, social, and family consequences*. New York: Oxford University Press.

Bondurant, J. V. (1965). *Conquest of violence* (Rev. ed.). Berkeley: University of California Press.

Booth, R. J. & Howell, R. J. (1980). Classification of prison inmates with the MMPI: An extension and validation of the Megargee typology. *Criminal Justice and Behavior, 7*, 407-422.

Borders v. State of Florida, 433 So. 2d 1375 (Fla.App. 3 Dist. 1983).

Borum, R. (1994). *Establishing standards for criminal forensic reports: An empirical analysis*. Paper presented at the annual meeting of the American Psychological Association, New York, NY.

Boulette, T. R. & Andersen, S. M. (1986). "Mind control" of the battering of women. *The Cultic Studies Journal, 3*, 25-35.

Bourdouris, J. (1971). Homicide and the family. *Journal of Marriage and the Family, 33*, 667-676.

Bourget, D. & Bradford, J. M. W. (1987). Affective disorder and homicide: A case of familial filicide, theoretical and clinical considerations. *Canadian Journal of Psychiatry, 32*, 222-225.

Bourget, D. & Bradford, J. M. W. (1990). Homicidal parents. *Canadian Journal of Psychiatry, 35*(3), 233-237.

Bouvier, J. (1914). *Bouvier's law dictionary and concise encyclopedia* (Vol. 1). St. Paul: West Publishing Co.

Boy, 5, is killed for refusing to steal candy. (1994, October 15). *The New York Times*, p.9.

Bracy, O. (1983). Computer based cognitive rehabilitation. *Cognitive Rehabilitation, 1*, 7-8, 18.

Bradford, J. (1989). The organic treatment of violent sex offenders. In A. J. Stunkard & A. Baum (Eds.), Perspectives in behavioral medicine: *Eating, sleeping, and sex* (pp. 203-221). Hillsdale: Erlbaum.

Bradford, J., Boulet, J., & Pawlak, A. (1992). The paraphilias: A multiplicity of deviant behaviors. *Canadian Journal of Psychiatry, 37*, 104-108.

Bradford, J. W. & Smith, S. M. (1979). Amnesia and homicide: The Padola case and a study of thirty cases. *Bulletin of the American Academy of Psychiatry and the Law*, 7, 219-231.

Bradley, V. A., Welch, J. L., & Skilbeck, C. E. (1993). *Cognitive retraining using microcomputers*. Hillsdale, NJ: Erlbaum.

Bradsher, K. (1995, April 17). Gap in wealth in U.S. called widest in west. *New York Times*, pp. A1, D4.

Brain, P. F. (1979). Dividing up aggression and considerations in studying the physiological substrates of these phenomenon. *The Behavioral and Brain Sciences, 2,* 216.

Brain, P. F. & Haug, M. (1992). Hormonal and neurochemical correlates of various forms of animal aggression. *Psychoneuroendocrinology, 17*(6), 537-551.

Brancale, R. (1955). Problems of classification. *National Probation and Parole Association Journal, 1,* 118-125.

Branch, T. (1988). *Parting the waters: America in the King years 1954-63*. New York: Simon & Schuster.

Braucht, G. N., Loya, F., & Jamieson, K. J. (1980). Victims of violent death: A critical review. *Psychological Bulletin, 87*(2), 309-333.

Breedlove, S. (1994). Sexual differentiation of the human nervous system. In L. Porter & M. Rosenzweig (Eds.), *Annual review of psychology*. Palo Alto, CA: Annual Reviews Inc.

Breggin, P. R. (1975). Psychosurgery for the control of violence: A critical review. In W. Fields & W. Sweet (Eds.), *Neural basis of violence and aggression* (pp. 350-391). St Louis: Warren H. Green.

Breggin, P. R. (1995, April 13). Personal communication.

Breggin, P. R. & Breggin, G. R. (1994). *The war against children*. New York: St. Martins Press.

Brennan, P., Mednick, S., & Kandel, E. (1991). Congenital determinants of violent and property offending. In D. J. Peppler & K. H. Rubin (Eds.), *The development and treatment of childhood aggression* (pp. 81-92). NJ: Lawrence Earlbaum Associates.

Brenner, M. (1977). Does employment cause crime? *Criminal Justice Newsletter, 5,* 10/24, 5.

Breslau, N. (1990). Does brain dysfunction increase children's vulnerability to environmental stress? *Archives of General Psychiatry, 47,* 15-20.

Breslau, N., Davis, G. C., & Andreski, P. (1995). Risk factors for PTSD-related traumatic events: A prospective analysis. *American Journal of Psychiatry, 152*(4), 529-534.

Brewer. C. (1971). Homicide during a psychomotor seizure: The importance of air-encephalography in establishing insanity under the McNaughten rules. *The Medical Journal of Australia, 1,* 857-859.

Brody, J. (1994, November 6). Battling the baby blues: Research brings understanding, help for postpartum depression. *Star Tribune*, p. 3E.

Bromberg, W. (1961). *The mold of murder*. New York, NY: Grune & Stratton.

Brooks, N., Campsie, L., & Symington C. (1986). The five year outcome of severe blunt head injury: A relative's view. *Journal of Neurology, Neurosurgery and Psychiatry, 49*, 764-770.

Brooks, S. & Harford, T. (1992). Occupation and alcohol-related causes of death. *Drug and Alcohol Dependence, 29*, 245-251.

Browne, A. (1987). *When battered women kill*. New York: The Free Press.

Browne, A. (1987). *When battered women kill*. New York: Macmillan.

Browne, A. & Williams, K. R. (1989). Exploring the effect of resource availability and the likelihood of female-perpetrated homicides. *Law and Society Review, 23*, 71-94.

Browne, A. & Williams, K. R. (1993). Gender, intimacy, and lethal violence: Trends from 1976 through 1987. *Gender & Society, 7*(1), 78-98.

Bruni, F. (1994, September 4). Hack by popular demand: Serial killers are hot in fiction, films. *Tallahassee Democrat*, p. 4E.

Brunner, H., Nelen, X., Ropers, H., & van Oost (1993). Abnormal behavior associated with a point mutation in the structural gene for monoamine Oxidase A. *Science, 262*, 578-580.

Brush, L. D. (1990). Violent acts and injurious outcomes in married couples: Methodological issues in the National Survey of Families and Households. *Gender & Society, 4*, 56-67.

Brush, L. D. (1993). Violent acts and injurious outcomes in married couples: Methodological issues in the national survey of families and households. In P. B. Bart & E. G. Moran (Eds.), *Violence against women* (pp. 240-251). Newbury Park: Sage.

Bryant, E., Scott, M., Golden, C., & Tori, C. (1984). Neuropsychological deficits, learning disability, and violent behavior. *Journal of Consulting and Clinical Psychology, 52*, 323-324.

Buchanan, C. M., Eccles, J. S., & Becker, J. B. (1992). Are adolescents the victims of raging hormones? *Psychological Bulletin, 111*(1), 62-107.

Buchanan G. (1992). *Biblical and theological insights from ancient and modern civil law*. Lewiston, NY: Edwin Mellen Press.

Buck, L. A. (1984). Nonviolence and Satyagraha in Attenborough's Gandhi. *Journal of Humanistic Psychology, 24*, 130-141.

Buck, L. A. (1990). Abnormality, normality and health. *Psychotherapy, 27*, 187-194.

Buck, L. A. (1991). *Courage, autism and schizophrenia.* Paper presented at the 49th Ann. Conv., International Council of Psychologists, San Francisco, CA.

Buck, L. A. (1992a). *Diversity-cooperation-life affirmation as a context for health.* Paper presented at the 50th Ann. Convention, International Council of Psychologists, Amsterdam, The Netherlands.

Buck, L. A. (1992b). The myth of normality: Consequences for the diagnosis of abnormality and health. *Social Behavior and Personality, 20,* 251-262.

Buck, L. A. (1994). Gandhian synthesis. *Journal of Developing Societies, 11,* 112-119.

Buck, L. A. (in press). Gandhi and Jefferson: Democracy and humanism. *Gandhi Marg.*

Buck, R. & Ginsburg, B. (1991). Spontaneous communication and altruism: The communicative gene hypothesis. In M. S. Clark (Ed.), *Prosocial behavior.* Newbury Park, CA: Sage.

Buck, J. A. & Graham, J. R. (1978). The 4-3 MMPI profile type: A failure to replicate. *Journal of Consulting and Clinical Psychology, 46,* 344.

Budd, R. D. (1982). The incidence of alcohol use in Los Angeles County homicide victims. *American Journal of Drug & Alcohol Abuse, 9*(1), 105-11.

Buhrle v. State of Wyoming, 622 P.2d 1374 (Wyo. 1981).

Bundy says porn fueled violent fantasies. (1989, January 25). *Philadelphia Inquirer,* p. 4A.

Bureau of Justice. (1985, March). *The crime of rape* (NCJ-96777). Washington, DC: U.S. Department of Justice.

Bureau of Justice. (1988, March). *Report to the nation,* 2nd edition [Bureau of Justice Statistics]. Washington, DC: U.S. Department of Justice.

Bureau of Justice Statistics. (1989). *Criminal victimization in the United States, 1987.* Washington, DC: U.S. Department of Justice.

Bureau of Justice. (1992a, December). *Criminal Victimization in the United States* [Bureau of Justice Statistics]. Washington, DC: U.S. Department of Justice.

Bureau of Justice. (1992b, December). *Criminal victimization in the United States: 1973-1990 trends* [Bureau of Justice Statistics]. Washington, DC: U.S. Department of Justice.

Bureau of Justice. (1992c). *Criminal victimization in the United States, 1990.* Washington, DC: U.S. Department of Justice.

Bureau of Justice. (1993). *Highlights from 20 Years of Surveying Crime Victims* [Bureau of Justice Statistics]. Washington, DC: U.S. Department of Justice.

Bureau of Justice Statistics. (1994b, July). *Criminal victimization in the United States: 1972-92* (NCJ-147006). Washington, DC: U.S. Department of Justice.

Bureau of Justice Statistics. (1994a, March). *Criminal victimization in the United States: 1992* (NCJ-145125). Washington, DC: U.S. Department of Justice.

Bureau of Labor Statistics. (1993). Washington, DC: U.S. Department of Labor.

Burgess, A., Hartman, C., Ressler, R., Douglas, J., & McCormack, A. (1986). Sexual homicide: A motivational model. *Journal of Interpersonal Violence, 1*(3), 251-272.

Burgess, A. W. (1975). Family reaction to homicide. *American Journal of Orthopsychiatry, 45,* 391-398.

Burgess, P. W. & Alderman, N. (1990). Rehabilitation of dyscontrol syndromes following frontal lobe damage: A cognitive neuropsychological approach. In R. L. Wood & I. Fussey (Eds.), *Cognitive rehabilitation in perspective* (pp. 183-203). London: Taylor & Francis.

Burgess, R. L. & Youngblood, L. M. (1988). *Social incompetence and the interpersonal transmission of abusive parental practices.* In G. T. Hotaling, D. Finklehor, J. T. Kirkpatrick, & M. A. Straus (Eds.), *Family abuse and its consequences: New directions in research* (pp. 38-60). Newbury Park, CA: Sage.

Burke, B. (1984). Infanticide: Why does it happen in monkeys, mice, and men? *Science, 84*(5), 26-31.

Burrowes, K. L., Hales, R. E., & Arrington, E. (1988). Research on the biological aspects of violence. Psychiatric Clinics of North America, *11*(4), 499-509.

Burton, N. M. & Steadman, H. J. (1978). Legal professionals' perceptions of the insanity defense. *Journal of Psychiatry and Law, 6,* 175-176.

Busby, M.D. (1989). U.S. counterterrorism policy in the 1980's and priorities for the 1990's. *Terrorism, 13,* 7-13.

Buss, A. H. (1961). *The psychology of aggression.* New York, NY: Wiley.

Butcher, J. N., Dahlstrom, W. G., Graham, J. R., Tellegen, A., & Kaemmer, B. (1989). *Minnesota Multiphasic Personality Inventory-2: Manual for administration and scoring.* Minneapolis: University of Minnesota Press.

Buteau, J. M., Lesage, A. D., & Kiely, M. C. (1993, October). Homicide followed by suicide: A Quebec case series, 1988-1990. *Canadian Journal of Psychiatry,* pp. 552-556.

Butler, W. M., Leitenberg, H., & Fuselier, G. D. (1993). The use of mental health professional consultants to police hostage negotiation teams. *Behavioral Sciences & the Law, 11,* 213-221.

Butterfield, F. (1994, October 14). Teen-age homicide rate has soared. *New York Times,* p. A22.

Butterfield, F. (1995a, March 10). Justice department awarding grants to develop gun detectors. *New York Times,* p. A22.

Butterfield, F. (1995b, April 12). New prisons cast shadow over higher education. *New York Times,* p. A21.

Cain, A. C., Fast, I., & Erickson, M. E. (1964). Children's disturbed reactions to the death of a sibling. *American Journal of Orthopsychiatry, 34,* 741-752.

Cairns, R. B. & Cairns, B. D. (1991). Social cognition and social networks: A developmental perspective. In D. J. Pepler & K. H. Rubin (Eds.), *The development and treatment of childhood aggression* (pp. 249-278). NJ: Lawrence Erlbaum Associates.

Callahan, C. & Rivara, F. (1992). Urban high school youth and handguns: A school-based survey. *Journal of the American Medical Association, 267,* 3038-3042.

Callahan, L. A., McGreevy, M. A., Cirincione, C., & Steadman, H. J. (1992). Measuring the effects of the guilty but mentally ill (GBMI) verdict: Georgia's 1982 GBMI reform. *Law and Human Behavior, 16,* 451-562.

Campbell, A. (1993). *Men, women and aggression.* New York: Basic Books.

Campbell, A., Muncer, S., & Coyle, E. (1992). Social representation of aggression as an explanation of gender differences: A preliminary study. *Aggressive Behavior, 18,* 95-108.

Campbell, J. (1995). *Assessing dangerousness: Violence by sexual offenders, batterers and child abusers.* Interpersonal Violence: The Practice Series. Thousand Oaks, CA: Sage.

Campbell, J. C. (1992). "If I can't have you, no one can:" Power and control in homicide of female partners. In J. Radford & D. E. H. Russell (Eds.), *Femicide: The politics of woman killing.* New York: MacMillan.

Campbell, J. C. (1993). The Danger Assessment Instrument. Risk factors of homicide of mate by battered women. In C. Block & R. L. Block (Eds.), *Questions and answers in lethal and non-lethal violence. Proceedings of the first annual Workshop of the Homicide Research Working Group.* Washington, DC: U.S. Department of Justice, National Institute of Justice Research Report.

Cantos, A. L., Neidig, P. H., & O'Leary, K. D. (1994). Injuries of women and men in a treatment program for domestic violence. *Journal of Family Violence, 9,* 113-124.

Caprara, G. V., Renzi, P., Alcini, G., D'Imperio, G., & Travaglia, G. (1983). Instigation to aggress and escalation of aggression examined from a personological perspective: The role of irritability and of emotional susceptibility. *Aggressive Behavior, 9,* 345-351.

Caprara, G. V., Renzi, P., Amolini, P., D'Imperio, G., & Travaglia, G. (1984). The eliciting cue value of aggressive slides reconsidered in a personological perspective: The weapons effect and irritability. *European Journal of Social Psychology, 14,* 313-322.

Carey, R. J., Garske, J. P., & Ginsberg, J. (1986). The prediction of adjustment to prison by means of an MMPI-based classification. *Criminal Justice and Behavior, 13,* 347-365.

Carlson, V., Cicchetti, D., Barnett, D., & Braunwald, K. (1989). Disorganized/disoriented attachment relationships in maltreated infants. *Developmental Psychology, 27*(1),108-118.

Carneval, P. J. & Pruitt, D. G. (1992). Negotiation and mediation. In M. R. Rosenzweig & L. W. Porter (Eds.), *Annual review of psychology.* Palo Alto, CA: Annual Reviews.

Cases, O., Seif, I., Grimsby, J., Gaspar, P., Chen, K., Pournin, S., Muller, U., Aguet, M., Babinet, C., Shih, J., & De Maeyer, E. (1995). Aggressive behavior and altered amounts of brain serotonin and norepinephrine in mice lacking MAOA. *Science, 268,* 1763-1766.

Caspi, A., Henry, B., McGee, R.O., Moffitt, T.E., & Silva, P.A. (1995). Temperamental origins of child and adolescent behavior problems: From age three to age fifteen. *Child Development, 66,* 55-68.

Caspi, A., Lynam, D., Moffitt, T. E., & Silva, P. A. (1993). Unraveling girls' delinquency: Biological, dispositional, and contextual contributions to adolescent misbehavior. *Developmental Psychology, 29*(1), 19-30.

Cattell, R. B. (1989). *The 16 PF: Personality in depth.* Champaign, IL: Institute for Personality and Ability Testing.

Catell, R. B. & Catell, A. K. S. (1958). *IPAT culture free intelligence test.* Champaign, IL: Institute of Personality and Ability Testing.

Cautela, J. (1967). Covert sensitization. *Psychological Reports, 20*, 459-468.

Cazenave, N. A. & Zahn, M. A. (1992). Women, murder, and male domination: Police reports of domestic violence in Chicago and Philadelphia. In E. C. Viano (Ed.), *Intimate violence: Interdisciplinary perspective.* Washington, DC: Hemisphere Publishing Corp.

Centers for Disease Control (1992, October 16). Behaviors related to unintentional and intentional injuries among high school students — United States, 1991. *MMWR 41*(41), 760-772.

Centerwall, B. S. (1989). Exposure to television as a cause of violence. In G. Comstock (Ed.), *Public communication and behavior*, Vol. 2, (pp. 1-58). New York: Academic Press.

Cerney, M. S. (1989). "If only..." Remorse in grief therapy. In E. M. Stern (Ed.), *The psychotherapy patient: The remorseful patient* (pp. 235-248). New York: Haworth.

Cerney, M. S. & Buskirk, J. R. (1991). Anger: The hidden part of grief. *Bulletin of the Menninger Clinic, 55*, 228-237.

Chadwick, D. H. (1991). Elephants — Out of time, out of space. *National Geographic, 179*, 2-49.

Chandola, C. A., Robling, M. R., Peters, T. J., Melville-Thomas, G. & McGuffin, P. (1992). Pre- and perinatal factors and the risk of subsequent referral for hyperactivity. *Journal of Child Psychology & Psychiatry, 33*(6), 1077-1090.

Charters, W. W., Ed. (1993). *Motion pictures and youth: The Payne Fund Studies.* New York: Macmillan.

Cherland, E. & Matthews, P. C. (1989). Attempted murder of a newborn: A case history. *Canadian Journal of Psychiatry, 34*, 337-339.

Chi, C. & Flynn, J. (1971). Neural pathways associated with hypothalamically elicited attack behavior in cats. *Science, 171*, 703-706.

Childs, R. E. (1985). Maternal psychological conflicts associated with the birth of a retarded child. *Maternal-Child Nursing Journal*, 175-182.

Chimbos, P. D. (1978). *Marital violence: A study of interspousal homicide.* San Francisco, CA: R & E Research Associates.

Chitra, M., Rao, S., Gangadhar, B., & Hezck, A. (1989). Neuropsychological functioning in post concussion syndrome. *National Institute of Mental Health Journal, 7*(1), 37-41.

Christensen, L. & LeUnes, A. (1974). Discriminating

criminal types and recividism by means of the MMPI. *Journal of Clinical Psychology, 30,* 192-193.

Christy, P. R., Gelfand, D. M., & Hartman, D. P. (1971). Effects of competition-induced frustration on two classes of modeled behavior. *Development Psychology, 5,* 104-111.

Chusid, J. & McDonald, J. (1962). *Correlative neuroanatomy and functional neurology.* Los Altos, CA: Lange Medical Publication.

Ciccone, J.R., (1992). Murder, insanity, and medical expert witnesses. *Archives of Neurology, 49,* 608-611.

Claire, I. C. (1993). Issues in the assessment and treatment of male sex offenders with mild learning disabilities. *Sexual and Marital Therapy, 8*(2), 167-180.

Clark, R. (1971). *Crime in America.* New York: Pocket Books.

Clarke-Stewart, K. A. (1989). Infant day care. *American Psychologist, 44,* 266-273.

Coates, C. J. (1988). A psychosocial approach to family violence: Application of Conceptual Systems Theory. In G. W. Russell (Ed.), *Violence in intimate relationships.* New York: PMA Publishing.

Cocozza, J. J. & Steadman, H. J. (1976). The failure of psychiatric prediction of dangerousness: Clear and convincing evidence. *Rutgers Law Review, 29,* 1084-1101.

Cohn, D. (1990). Child-mother attachment of six-year-olds and social competence at school. *Child Development, 61,* 152-162.

Coid, J. (1982). *Homicide in Bermuda.* M. Phil. Thesis: University of London.

Coid, J. (1983). The epidemiology of abnormal homicide and murder followed by suicide. *Psychological Medicine, 13,* 855-860.

Cole, M. & Cole, S. (1993). *The development of children.* New York: W. H. Freeman and Company.

Coleman, K. H. & Weinman, M. (1981). Conjugal violence. In J. R. Hays, T. K. Roberts, & K. S. Solway (Eds.), *Violence and the violent individual.* New York: Spectrum.

Collaer, M. & Hines, M. (1995). Human behavioral sex differences: A role for gonadal hormones during early development? *Psychological Bulletin, 118,* 55-107.

Collins, J. J. (1981). *Drinking and Crime.* New York: Guilford Press.

Collins, J. J. & Messerschmidt, P. M. (1993). Epidemiology of alcohol-related violence. *Alcohol Health & Research World, 17*(2), 92-100.

Comay, M. (1976). Political terrorism. *Mental Health Sociology, 3,* 249-261.

Combs-Orme, T. P., Taylor, J. R., Scott, E. B., & Holmes, S. J. (1983). Violent deaths among alcoholics: A descriptive study. *Journal of Studies on Alcohol, 44*(6), 938-949.

Compas, B., Hinden, B., & Gerhardt, C. (1995). Adolescent development: Pathways and processes of risk and resilience. In L. W. Porter & M. R. Rosenzweig (Eds.), *Annual Review of Psychology* (Vol. 46, pp. 65-93). Palo Alto, CA: Annual Reviews Inc.

Comstock, G. (1989). *The evolution of American television.* Newbury Park, CA: Sage Publications.

Conn, C. & Silverman, I. (Eds.). (1991). *What counts: The complete Harper's index.* New York: Henry Holt & Co.

Constantino, J., Grosz, D., Saenger, P., Chandler, D., Nandi, R., & Earls, F., (1993). Testosterone and aggression in children. *Journal of the American Academy of Child and Adolescent Psychiatry, 32,* 1217-1222.

Cook, D. (1991). *A history of narrative film* (2nd ed.). New York: W. W. Norton.

Coon, H., Carey, G., Fulker, D., & DeFries, J. (1993). Influences of school environment on the academic achievement scores of adopted and nonadopted children. *Intelligence, 17,* 79-104.

Cooper, H. H. A. (1981). *The hostage takers.* Boulder, CO: Paladin Press.

Copeland, L. (1995, March 10). Caning criminals? It gains advocates. *Philadelphia Inquirer*, pp. A1, A20.

Cornell, D. G. (1993). Juvenile homicide: A growing national problem. *Behavioral Sciences and the Law, 11,* 389-396.

Cornell, D. G., Miller, C., & Benedek, E. P. (1988). MMPI profiles of adolescents charged with homicide. *Behavioral Sciences and the Law, 6,* 401-407.

Cornwall, A. & Bawden, H. N. (1992). Reading disabilities and aggression: A critical review. *Journal of Learning Disabilities, 25*(5), 281-288.

Corsi, J. R. (1981). Terrorism as a desperate game. *Journal of Conflict Resolution, 25,* 47-85.

Costanzo, M. & Costanzo, F. (1992). Jury decision-making in capital penalty phase, legal assumptions, empirical findings, and a research agenda. *Law and Human Behavior, 16*(2), 185-201.

Costanzo, M. & White, L. (1994). An overview of the death penalty in capital trials: History, current status, legal procedures, and cost in the Unites States. In M. Costanzo & L. White (Eds.), The death penalty in the United States [Special issue]. *Journal of Social Issues, 50*(2), 1-18.

Courtois, C. A. (1988). *Healing the incest wound: Adult survivors in therapy.* New York: Norton.

Cousy, R. (1975). *The killer instinct.* New York: Random House.

Craig, G. A. (1989). The grand decider. *New York Review of Books, 36,* 31-36.

Crenshaw, W.A. (1987). Terrorism and the threat to civil aviation. *Dissertation Abstracts International, 48,* 1007.

Crichton, M. (1972). *Terminal man.* New York: Alfred Knopf.

Crick, N. & Dodge, K. (1994). A review and reformulation of social information-processing mechanisms in children's social adjustment. *Psychological Bulletin, 115,* 74-101.

Criminal Statistics England & Wales (1980). CMND, HMSO: London.

Crittenden, P. Claussen, A., & Sugarman, D. (1994). Physical and psychological maltreatment in middle childhood and adolescence. *Development and Psychopathology, 6,* 145-164.

Cummings, E. M., Davies, P. T., & Simpson, K. S. (1994). Marital conflict, gender, and children's appraisals and coping efficacy as mediators of child adjustment. *Journal of Family Psychology, 8*(2), 141-149.

Cummings, E., Hennessy, K., Rabideau, G., & Cicchetti, D. (1994). Responses of physically abused boys to interadult anger involving their mothers. *Development and Psychopathology, 6,* 31-41.

Cunnien, A. (1986). Alcoholic blackouts phenomenology and legal relevance. *Behavioral Sciences and the Law, 4,* 78-85.

Currie, S., Heathfield, K. W. G., Hensen, R. A., & Scott, D. F. (1971). Clinical course and prognosis of temporal lobe epilepsy. *Brain, 94,* 173-190.

Curtis, L. A. (1974). Victim precipitation and violent crime. *Social Problems, 21,* 594-605.

Dabbs, J. M., Jr., Ruback, R. B., Frady, R. L., Hopper, C. H., & Sgoutas, D. D. (1988). Saliva testosterone and criminal violence among women. *Personality and Individual Differences, 9,* 269-275.

Dahlstrom, W. G., Panton, J. H., Bain, K. P., & Dahlstrom, L. E. (1986). Utility of the Megargee-Bohn MMPI typological assignments: Study with a sample of death row inmates. *Criminal Justice and Behavior, 13,* 5-17.

Dalton, K. (1964). *The premenstrual syndrome.* Springfield, IL: Charles C Thomas.

Daly, M. & Wilson, M. (1980). Discriminative parental solicitude: A biological perspective. *Journal of Marriage and Family, 42,* 277-288.

Daly, M. & Wilson, M. (1983). *Sex, evolution and behavior* (2nd ed.). Boston: Willard Grant Press.

Daly, M. & Wilson, M. (1984). A sociobiological analysis of human infanticide. In G. Hausfater & S. B. Hrdy, (Eds.), *Infanticide: Comparative and evolutionary perspectives* (pp. 487-502). Hawthorne, NY: Aldine de Gruyter.

Daly, M. & Wilson, M. (1988). *Homicide.* Hawthorne, NY: Aldine de Gruyter.

Danesh-Khoshdoo, Y. (1991). *The civilization of law: A commentary on the laws of Hammurabi and Magna Carta.* Berrien Springs, MI: Vandevere.

Daniel, A. E. & Harris, P. W. (1982). Female homicide offenders referred for pretrial psychiatric examination: A descriptive study. *Bulletin of the American Academy of Psychiatry and Law, 10,* 261-269.

Daniel, A. E. & Robins, A. J. (1985, September). Violent women. *Psychiatry in Family Practice,* pp. 96-108.

Daniell, R. (1984). *Sleeping with soldiers.* New York: Holt, Rinehart, and Winston.

Danto, B. L. (1978). Suicide among murderers. *International Journal of Offender Therapy & Comparative Criminology, 22*(2), 140-143.

Danto, B. L. (1982). A psychiatric view of those who kill. In B. L. Danto, J. Bruhns, & A. H. Kutsher (Eds.), *The human side of homicide.* New York: Columbia University Press.

Dao, J. (1995, March 8). Death penalty in New York restored after 18 years; Pataki sees justice served. *New York Times,* pp. A1, B5.

Davidson, T. (1978). *Conjugal crime.* New York: Hawthorn Books.

Davies, K. (1993, February 27). Two young suspects in a toddler's slaying have had tough lives. *The Philadelphia Inquirer,* p. A5.

Davis v. United States, 160 U.S. 469 (1985).

Davis, K. R., & Sines, J. O. (1971). An antisocial behavior pattern associated with a specific MMPI profile. *Journal of Consulting and Clinical Psychology, 36,* 229-234.

Davis, M. & Emory, E. (1995). Sex differences in neonatal stress reactivity. *Child Development, 66,* 14-27.

Davis, T. (1995). Gender differences in masking negative emotions: Ability or motivation. *Developmental Psychology, 31,* 660-667.

Davison, W. P. & Yu, F. T. C. (Eds.). (1974). Mass communication research: Major issues and future directions. New York: Praeger.

Dawson, J. M. & Boland, B. (1993). Murder in large urban counties, 1988. *Bureau of Justice Statistics Special Report,* U.S. Department of Justice (NCJ-140614). Washington, DC: Supt. Docs.

Dawson, J. M. & Langan, P. A. (1994). *Murder in Families* [Special Report]. Washington, DC: Bureau of Justice Statistics.

Dawson, J. M. & Langan, P. A. (1994, July). *Murder in Families* [Bureau of Justice Special Report]. Washington, DC: U.S. Department of Justice.

DeFleur, M. D., & Dennis, E. E. (1991). *Understanding mass communication,* (4th ed.). Boston: Houghton Mifflin.

DeFries, J. (1991). Discussion. In E. E. Duane & D. B. Gray (Eds.), *The reading brain: The biological basis of dyslexia* (p. 163). Parkton, MD: York Press.

DeFries, J., Olson, R. K., Pennington, B. F., & Smith, S. D. (1991). Colorado reading project: An update. In D. D. Duane & D. B. Gray (Eds.), *The reading brain: The biological basis of dyslexia* (pp. 53-63). Parkton, MD: York Press.

Deiker, T. E. (1974). A cross-validation of MMPI scales of aggression on male criminal criterion groups. *Journal of Consulting and Clinical Psychology, 42,* 196-202.

Deikman, A. J. (1990). *The wrong way home.* Boston: Beacon Press.

Dekker, J., Everaerd, W., & Verhelst, N. (1985). Attending to stimuli or images of sexual feelings: Effects on sexual arousal. *Behavior Research and Therapy, 23*(2), 139-149.

DeMaris, A. (1992). Male versus female initiation of aggression: The case of courtship violence. In E. C. Viano (Ed.), *Intimate violence: Interdisciplinary perspective.* Washington, DC: Hemisphere Publishing Corp.

Demaris, O. & Wills, G. (1968). *Jack Ruby* (pp. 125-126). New York: The New American Library, Inc.

DeMause, L. (1976). *The history of childhood.* London: Souvenir Press.

DeMause, L. (1990). The history of child assault. *The Journal of Psychohistory, 18*(1), 1-28.

De Pauw, K. W. & Szulecka, T. K. (1988). Dangerous delusions: Violence and the misidentification syndrome. *British Journal of Psychiatry, 152,* 91-96.

Depression, stress can trigger moms to kill. (1994, November 5). *Star Tribune,* p. 14A.

Depue, R. L. (1993). *Violence in America: In our communities and in our workplaces.* Paper presented at the FBI National Academy Conference, Birmingham, AL.

Derogatis, L. R. & Melisaratos, N. (1979). The DSFI: A multidimensional measure of sexual functioning. *Journal of Sex and Marital Therapy, 5,* 244-281.

Dershowitz, A. M. (1973). Dangerousness as a criterion for confinement. *Bulletin of the American Academy of Psychiatry and the Law, 11,* 172-179.

De Silva, P. (1993). Fetishism and sexual dysfunction: Clinical presentation and management. *Sexual and Marital Therapy, 8*(2), 147-155.

Deutsch, M. (1993). Educating for a peaceful world. *American Psychologist, 48,* 510-517.

Devinsky, O. & Bear, D.M. (1984). Varieties of aggressive behavior in temporal lobe epilepsy. *American Journal of Psychiatry, 141,* 651-656.

deWaal, F. (1988). *Peacemaking among primates.* Cambridge: Harvard University Press.

deWaal, F. (1989). *Peacemaking among primates.* Cambridge, MA: Harvard University Press.

Diamond, S. (1989). Using psychology to control law. *Law and Human Behavior, 13*(3), 239-252.

Dickstein, L. J. & Nadelson, C. C. (1989). Conclusion. In L. J. Dickstein & C. C. Nadelson (Eds.), *Family Violence: Emerging Issues of a National Crisis.* Washington, DC: American Psychiatric Press.

Dietz, P. E. (1987). Patterns in human violence. In R. E. Hales & A. J. Frances (Eds.), *American Psychiatric Association Annual Review, Vol. 6* (pp. 465-490). Washington, DC: American Psychiatric Press, Inc.

Dietz, P. E. (1992). Mentally disordered offenders: Patterns in the relationship between mental disorder and crime. *Psychiatric Clinics of North America, 15,* 539-551.

Dietz, P. E., Hazelwood, R. R., & Warren, J. (1990). The sexually sadistic criminal and his offenses. *Bulletin of the American Academy of Psychiatry and Law,* 18(2), 71-86 and 163-178.

DiFrancesca, K. R. & Meloy, J. R. (1989). A comparative clinical investigation of the "How" and "Charlie" MMPI subtypes. *Journal of Personality Assessment, 53,* 396-403.

Diller, L. & Weinberg, J. (1986). Learning from failures in perceptual cognitive retraining in stroke. In B. P. Uzzell & Y. Gross (Eds.), *Clinical neuropsychology of intervention* (pp. 283-293). Boston: Nijhoff.

Dix, G. E. (1976). "Civil" commitment of the mentally ill and the need for data on the prediction of dangerousness. *American Behavioral Scientist, 19*(3), 318-334.

Dixit, A. K. & Nalebuff, B. J. (1991). *Thinking strategically.* New York: W. W. Norton and Company.

Dobash, R. E. & Dobash, R. P. (1990) How theoretical definitions and perspectives affect research and policy. In D. J. Besharov (Ed.), *Family violence: Research and public policy issues.* Washington, DC: The AEI Press.

Dobash, R. P., Dobash, R. E., Wilson, M., & Daly, M. (1992). The myth of sexual symmetry in marital violence. *Social Problems, 39,* 71-91.

Dobbin, B. (1994, October 8). Jail term for teen in boy's slaying. *The Philadelphia Inquirer,* p. A3.

Dodge, K. A. (1986). A social information processing model of social competence in children. In M. Perlmutter (Ed.), *Eighteenth Annual Minnesota Symposium on Child Psychology,* (pp. 77-125). Hillsdale: Lawrence Erlbaum Associates.

Dodge, K. A. (1993). Social-cognitive mechanisms in the development of conduct disorder and depression. In L. W. Porter & M. R. Rosenzweig (Eds.), *Annual review of psychology* (Vol. 44, pp. 559-580). Palo Alto, CA: Annual Reviews Inc.

Dodge, K. A., Bates, J. E., & Pettit, G. S. (1990). Mechanisms in the cycle of violence. *Science, 250,* 1678-1683.

Dodge, K., Pettit, G., & Bates, J. (1994). Socialization mediators of the relations between socioeconomic status and child conduct problems. *Child Development, 65,* 649-665.

Dohrenwend, B. P., Levav, I., Shrout, P. E., Schwartz, S., Naveh, G., Link, B. G., Skodol, A. E., & Stueve, A. (1992). Socioeconomic status and psychiatric disorders: The causation-selection issue. *Science, 255,* 946-951.

Dollard, J., Doob, L., Miller, N., Mowrer, O. H., & Sears, R. R. (1939). *Frustration and aggression.* New Haven, CT: Yale University Press.

Donohue, W. A., Ramesh, C., Kaufmann, G., & Smith,

R. (1991). Crisis bargaining in intense conflict situations. *International Journal of Group Tensions, 21,* 133-153.

d'Orban, P. T. (1979). Women who kill their children. *British Journal of Psychiatry, 134,* 560-571.

Doren, D. M., Megargee, E. I., & Schreiber, H. A. (1980). The MMPI criminal classifications applicability to a juvenile population. *The Differential View: A Publication of the International Differential Treatment Association, 9,* 42-47.

Dorland, W.A., (Ed.). (1988). *Dorland's illustrated medical dictionary* (25th ed.). Philadelphia: W. B. Saunders Co.

Dormanen, S. (1980). Statistical patterns of victimization. *Evaluation* (Special issue), 12-13.

Douglas, J. E. & Burgess, A. W. (1986). Criminal profiling: A viable investigative tool against violent crime. *FBI Law Enforcement Bulletin, 55,* 9-13.

Douglas, J. E., Burgess, A. W., Burgess, A. G., & Ressler, R. K. (1992). *Crime classification manual: A standard system for investigating and classifying violent crimes.* New York: Lexington Books.

Douglas, J. E., Ressler, R. K., Burgess, A. W., & Hartman, C. R. (1986). Criminal profiling from crime scene analysis. *Behavioral Sciences and the Law, 4*(4), 401-421.

Douglas, M. (1987). The battered woman syndrome. In D. J. Sonkin (Ed.), *Domestic violence on trial* (pp. 6-39). New York: Springer Publishing.

Douglas, V. (1989). Can Skinnerian theory explain attention deficit disorder? A reply to Barkley. In L. Bloomingdale & J. Swanson (Eds.), *Attention deficit disorder: Current concepts and emerging trends in attentional and behavioral disorders of childhood* (Vol. IV, pp. 235-254). Oxford: Pergamon Press.

Drake, M. E., Hietter, S. A., & Pakalnis, A. (1992). EEG and evoked potentials in episodic-dyscontrol syndrome. *Neuropsychobiology, 26,* 125-128.

Draper, T. (1992). The true history of the gulf war. *New York Review of Books, 39,* 38-45.

Dubonowsky, W. (February 1980). Pain cues as maintainers of human violence. *Presented at Symposium on Dangerousness Prediction.* Honolulu, HI.

Duncan, A., Durstan, G., & Wellbourn, E. (Eds.) (1977). *Dictionary of medical ethics.* London: Darton, Longman & Todd Pub.

Duncan, T. S. (1995). Death in the office: Workplace homicides. *FBI Law Enforcement Bulletin, 64*(4), 20-25.

Dunlap, D. W. (1995, March 8). June '94 produced a record for antigay attacks. *New York Times,* p. B2.

du Toit, L. & Duckitt, J. (1990). Psychological characteristics of over- and undercontrolled violent offenders. *Journal of Psychology, 124,* 125-141.

Dutton, D. G. (1994). Behavioral and affective correlates of borderline personality organization in wife assaulters. *International Journal of Law and Psychiatry, 17*(3), 265-277.

Dutton, D. G. (1995). *The domestic assault of women.* Vancouver: University of British Columbia Press.

Eagly, A. (1993). Sex differences in human social behavior: Meta-analytic studies of social psychological research. In M. Haug, R. Whalen, C. Aron, & K. Olsen (Eds.), *The development of sex differences and similarities in behavior* (pp. 421-436). Boston: Kluwer Academic Publishers.

Eagly, A. (1995). The science and politics of comparing men and women. *American Psychologist, 50,* 145-158.

Eagly, A. H. & Steffen, V. J. (1986). Gender and aggressive behavior: A meta-analytic review of the social psychological literature. *Psychological Bulletin, 100,* 309-330.

Earls, F. (1987). Sex differences in psychiatric disorders: Origins and developmental influences. *Psychiatric Developments, 1,* 1-23.

Eber, H. W. (1974). Some psychometric correlates of inmate behavior. *Georgia Journal of Corrections, 1,* 1-14.

Eccles, A., Marshall, W. L., & Barbaree, H. E. (1988). The vulnerability of erectile measures to repeated assessments. *Behavior Research and Therapy, 26*(2), 179-183.

Eckert, W., Katchis, S., & Donovan, W. (1991). The pathology and medicolegal aspects of sexual activity. *The American Journal of Medicine and Pathology, 12*(1), 3-15.

Eckholm, E. (1995, February 24). Studies find death penalty tied to race of the victims. *New York Times,* pp. B1, B4.

Edinger, J. D. (1979). Cross validation of the Megargee MMPI typology for prisoners. *Journal of Consulting and Clinical Psychology, 47,* 234-242.

Edinger, J. D. & Auerbach, S. M. (1978). Development and validation of a multidimensional multivariate model for accounting for infractionary behavior in a correctional setting. *Journal of Personality and Social Psychology, 36,* 1472-1489.

Edinger, J. D., Reuterfors, D., & Logue, P. (1982). Cross validation of the Megargee MMPI typology. *Criminal Justice and Behavior, 9,* 184-203.

Edleson, J. L. (1990). Judging the success of intervention with men who batter. In D. J. Besharov (Ed.), *Family violence: Research and public policy issues.* Washington, DC: The AEI Press.

Egeland, A., Stroufe, & Ericson, M. (1983). The developmental consequences of different patterns of maltreatment. *Child Abuse and Neglect, 7,* 299-305.

Egger, S. A. (1990a). Serial murder: A synthesis of literature and research. In S. A. Egger (Ed.), *Serial murder: An elusive phenomenon.* New York: Praeger.

Egger, S. A. (1990b). Linkage blindness: A systemic myopia. In S. A. Egger (Ed.), *Serial murder: An elusive phenomenon.* New York: Praeger.

Ehrhardt, A. (1979, September). *Biological sex differences: A developmental perspective.* Paper presented at the meeting of the American Psychological Association, New York.

Ehrhardt, A. & Meyer-Bahlburg, F. (1979). Prenatal sex hormones and the developing brain: Effects on psychosexual differentiation and cognitive functioning. In W. Creger (Ed.), *Annual review of medicine* (Vol. 30). Palo Alto, CA: Annual Reviews Inc.

Ehrhardt, A. & Meyer-Bahlburg, F. (1981). Effects of prenatal sex hormones on gender-related behavior. *Science, 177*, 1312-1318.

Eibl-Eibesfeldt, I. (1989). *Human ethology.* Hawthorne, NY: Aldine de Gruyter.

Eichelman, B. (1983). The limbic system and aggression in humans. *Neuroscience and Biobehavioral Reviews, 7*, 391-394.

Eichelman, B. (1992). Aggressive behavior: From laboratory to clinic. *Archives of General Psychiatry, 49*, 448-492.

Eichelman, B. S. (1990). Neurochemical and psychopharmacologic aspects of aggressive behavior. *Annual Review of Medicine, 41*, 149-158.

Elliott, F. A. (1982). Neurological findings in adult minimal brain dysfunction and the dyscontrol syndrome. *Journal of Nervous and Mental Disease, 170*, 680-687.

Elliott, F. A. (1992). Violence: The neurologic contribution: An overview. *Archives of Neurology, 49*, 595-603.

Ellis, D. (1992). Woman abuse among separated and divorced women: The relevance of social support. In E. C. Viano (Ed.), Intimate violence: *Interdisciplinary perspective.* Washington, DC: Hemisphere Publishing Corp.

Elms, A. C. & Milgram, S. (1966). Personality characteristics associated with obedience and defiance toward authoritative command. *Journal of Experimental Research in Personality, 1*, 282-289.

Eme, R. (1979). Sex differences in childhood psychopathology: A review. *Psychological Bulletin, 86*, 574-595.

Eme, R. F. (1984). Sex-related differences in the epidemiology of child psychopathology. In C. S. Widom (Ed.), *Sex roles and psychopathology* (pp. 279-308). New York: Plenum Press.

Emery, R. R. (1982). Interparental conflict and the children of discord and divorce. *Psychological Bulletin, 92*, 310-330.

Engel, J., Caldecott-Hazard, S., & Bandler, R. (1986). Neurobiology of behavior: Anatomic and physiological implications related to epilepsy. *Epilepsia, 27* (Suppl. 2), S3-13.

Erikson, E. H. (1950). *Childhood and society.* New York: W.W. Norton.

Erikson, E. H. (1982). *The life cycle completed.* New York: Norton.

Erikson, E. H. (1987). Remarks on the "wider identity." In E. H. Erikson, *A way of looking at things.* New York: Norton.

Eron, L. D., Walder, L. O., & Lefkowitz, M. M. (1971). *Learning of aggression in children.* Boston: Little, Brown.

Eron, L. D., Huesmann, L. R., Dubow, G., Romanoff, R., & Yarmel, P. (1987). Aggression and its correlates over 22 years. In D. H. Crowell, I. M. Evans, & C. R. O'Donnell (Eds.), *Childhood aggression and violence: Sources of influence, prevention and control* (pp. 249-262). New York: Plenum Press.

Eron, L. D. & Huesmann, L. R. (1990). The stability of aggressive behavior — even unto the third generation. In M. Lewis & S. M Miller (Eds.), *Handbook of developmental psychopathology* (pp. 147-156). New York: Plenum Press

Eron, L. D., Huesmann, L. R., & Zelli, A. (1991). The role of parental variables in the learning of aggression. In D. J. Pepler & K. H. Rubin (Eds.), *The development and treatment of childhood aggression* (pp. 169-188). NJ: Lawrence Earlbaum Associates.

Estell, K. (Ed.). (1994). *The African American Almanac.* Detroit, MI: Gale Research Inc.

Ewing, C. P. (1987). *Battered women who kill: Psychological self-defense as legal justification.* Lexington, KY: D. C. Heath.

Exner, J. (1986). *The Rorschach: A comprehensive system: Volume 1: Foundations* (2nd. ed.). New York, NY: John Wiley & Sons.

Fagan, J. (1988). Contributions of family violence research to criminal justice policy on wife assault: Paradigms of science and social control. *Violence and Victims, 3*(3), 159-186.

Famigetti, R. (1994). *The world almanac and book of facts: 1995.* Mahwah, NJ: Funk and Wagnalls.

Family Violence Working Group. (1994, June). *A report to the Assistant Attorney General for the Office of Justice Programs* [Justice Programs on Family Violence]. Washington, DC: National Institute of Justice.

Farley, F. (1991). The type-t personality. In L. Lipsitt & L. L. Mitkin (Eds.), *Self-regulatory behavior and risk taking: Causes and consequences* (pp. 371-382). Norwood, NJ: Ablex.

Farley, R. (1986). Homicide trends in the United States. In D. F. Hawkins (Ed.), *Homicide among Black Americans.* New York: University Press of America.

Farrell, W. (1993). *The myth of male power.* New York: Simon & Schuster.

Farrington, D. P. (1984). Childhood, adolescent, and adult features of violent males. In L. R. Huesman (Ed.), *Aggressive behavior: Current perspectives* (pp. 215-240). New York: Plenum Press.

Federal Bureau of Investigation Special Operations and Research Unit. (1981). A terrorist organizational profile: A psychological role model. In Y. Alexander & J. Gleason (Eds.), *Behavioral and quantitative perspectives on terrorism.* New York: Pergamon Press.

Federal Bureau of Investigation. (1988). Personal communication with Supervisory Special Agent Frederick J. Lanceley, Special Operations and Research Unit, FBI Academy, Quantico, VA.

Federal Bureau of Investigation. (1988). *Terrorism in the United States: 1987.* Washington, DC: U.S. Government Printing Office.

Federal Bureau of Investigation (1989). *Uniform Crime Reports for the United States*. Washington, DC: Department of Justice.

Federal Bureau of Investigation. (1993). *Crime in the United States: Canadian Crime Statistics, 14*, 6-11.

Federal Bureau of Investigation (1993). *Response and Management of Critical Incidents*. Special Operations and Research Unit. FBI Academy. Quantico, VA.

Federal Bureau of Investigation. (1993). *Uniform crime reports: 1992*. Washington, DC: U.S. Government Printing Office.

Federal Bureau of Investigation (1994). *Crime in America. Uniform Crime Reports 1993*. Washington, DC: U.S. Government Printing Office.

Fedora, O. & Fedora, S. (1983). Some neuropsychological and psychophysiological aspects of psychopathic and nonpsychopathic criminals. In P. Flor-Henry & J. H. Gruzelier (Eds.), *Laterality and psychopathology*. Amsterdam: Elsevier.

Fedora, O., Reddon, J., Morrison, J., Fedora, S., Pascoe, H., & Yeudall, L. (1992). Sadism and other paraphilias in normal controls and aggressive and nonaggressive sex offenders. *Archives of Sexual Behavior, 21*(1), 1-15.

Feingold, A. (1994). Gender differences in personality: A meta-analysis. *Psychological Bulletin, 116*, 429-456.

Feldmann, T. B. (1995a). *Workplace violence: An examination of 240 incidents*. Paper presented at the annual meeting of the American College of Forensic Psychiatry, San Francisco.

Feldmann, T. B. (1995b). Workplace violence: Origins and interventions. *Clinical Advances in the Treatment of Psychiatric Disorders, 9*(1), 6-12.

Feldmann, T. B. & Johnson, P. W. (1993). Hostage situations and the mental health professional. In P. Blumenreich & S. Lewis (Eds.), *Management of the violent patient: A clinician's guide*. New York: Brunner/Mazel.

Feldmann, T.B. & Johnson, P.W. (in press). The dynamics of hostage negotiations. *Journal of the American Academy of Psychoanalysis*.

Felson, R. B., Ribner, S. A., & Siegel, M. A. (1984). Age and the effect of third parties during criminal violence. *Sociology and Social Research, 68*(4), 452-562.

Fenton, G. W. & Udwin, E. L. (1965). Homicide, temporal lobe epilepsy and depression: A case report. *British Journal of Psychiatry, 111*, 304-306.

Fenwick, P. (1986). Murdering while asleep. *British Medical Journal, 293*, 574-575.

Fenwick, P. (1989). Dyscontrol. In E. H. Reynolds & M. R. Trimble (Eds.), *The bridge between neurology and psychiatry*. New York, NY: Churchill Livingston Inc.

Ferracuti, F. (1982). A sociopsychiatric interpretation of

terrorism. *The Annals of the American Academy of Political and Social Sciences, 463*, 129-140.

Ferracuti, F. & Bruno, F. (1981). Psychiatric aspects of terrorism in Italy. In I. L. Barak-Glantz & C. R. Huff (Eds.), *The mad, the bad and the different: Essays in honor of Simon Dinitz* (pp. 199-213). Lexington: Lexington Books.

Feshbach, S. (1970). Aggression. In P. H. Mussen (Ed.), *Carmichael's manual of child psychology* (pp. 159-259). New York: Wiley.

Fielder v. State of Texas, 683 S.W.2d 565 (Tex. Ct. App. 1985).

Filskov, S. & Boll, T. (Eds.). (1981). *Handbook of clinical neuropsychology* (Vol. 1). New York: John Wiley & Sons.

Fincham, F. D. & Osborne, L. N. (1993). Marital conflict and children: Retrospect and prospect. *Clinical Psychology Review, 13*, 75-88.

Fincham, F. D., Grych, J. H., & Osborne, L. N. (1994). Does marital conflict cause child maladjustment? Directions and challenges for longitudinal research. *Journal of Family Psychology, 8*(2), 128-140.

Fine, P., Roseman, J. M., Constandinou, C. M., Brissie, R. M., Glass, J. M., & Wrigley, J. M. (1994, May). Homicide among Black males in Jefferson County, Alabama 1978-1989. *Journal of Forensic Sciences*, pp. 674-684.

Fine, R. (1985). *The meaning of love in human experience*. New York: Wiley.

Fingerhut, L. A. & Kleinman, J. C. (1990). International and interstate comparisons of homicide among young males. *Journal of the American Medical Association, 226*, 2342.

Finkelhor, D. (1983). Common features of family abuse. In E. D. Finkelhor & R. J. Gelles (Eds.), *The dark side of families: Current family violence research*. Beverly Hills: Sage.

Finkelhor, D. (1984). *Child sexual abuse: New theory and research*. New York: Free Press.

Finklehor, D. & Baron, L. (1986). *Risk factors for child sexual abuse*. Beverly Hills, CA: Sage.

Finklehor, D. & Browne, A. (1985). The traumatic impact of child sexual abuse: A conceptualization. *American Journal of Orthopsychiatry, 55*, 530-541.

Finkelhor, D. & Hotaling, G. (1983). *Sexual abuse in the national incidence study of child abuse and neglect* [Report to the National Center on Child Abuse and Neglect].

Finklehor, D. & Pillemar, K. (1988). Elder abuse: Its relationship to other forms of domestic violence. In G. T. Hotaling, D. Finkelhor, J. Kirkpatrick, & M. D. Straus (Eds.), *Family abuse and its consequences: New directions in research* (pp. 244-254). Newbury Park, CA: Sage.

Finkelhor, D. & Yllö, K. (1983a). *License to rape: Sexual abuse of wives*. New York: Holt, Rinehart & Winston.

Finkelhor, D. & Yllö, K. (1983b). Rape in marriage: A sociological view. In D. Finkelhor, R. Gelles, G. Hotaling, & M. A. Straus (Eds.), *The dark side of families*. Beverly Hills, CA: Sage.

Finkelhor, D., Araji, S., Baron, L., Browne, A., Peters, S. D., & Wyatt, G. E. (1988). *Sourcebook on child sexual abuse*. Beverly Hills, CA: Sage.

Finkelhor, D., Hotaling, G., & Yllö, K. (1988). *Stopping family violence: Research priorities for the coming decade*. Newbury Park, CA: Sage.

Finney, J. C., Skeeters, D. E., Auvenshine, C. D., & Smith, D. F. (1973). Phases of psychopathology after assassination. *American Journal of Psychiatry, 130*, 1379-1380.

Fisher, D. & Howells, K. (1993). Social relationships in sexual offenders. *Sexual and Marital Therapy, 8*(2), 123-136.

Fisher, R. & Geiselman, R. (1992). *Memory-enhancing techniques for investigative interviewing: The cognitive interview.* Springfield, IL: Charles C Thomas.

Fiske, A. P. (1991). Cultural relativity of selfish individualism. In M. S. Clark (Ed.), *Prosocial behavior.* Newbury Park, CA: Sage.

Flavin, D. K., Franklin, J. E., & Frances, R. J. (1990). Substance abuse and suicidal behavior. In S. J. Blumenthal & D. J. Kubfer (Eds.), *Suicide over the life cycle* (pp. 177-204). Washington, DC: American Psychiatric Press.

Flor-Henry, P. (1976). Lateralized temporal-limbic dysfunction and psychopathology. In H. R. Harnad, H. D. Steklis, & J. Lancaster (Eds.), *Origins and evolutions of language and speech.* New York: New York Academy of Sciences.

Florance, E. C. (1955). The neurosis of Raskolnikov: A study in incest and murder. *Archives of Criminal Psychodynamics, 1*, 344-396.

Floud, J. & Young, W. (1981). *Dangerousness and criminal justice.* London: Heinemann.

Fogelman, E. & Wiener, V. L. (1985). The few, the brave, the noble. *Psychology Today, 19*, 60-65.

Follingstad, D. R. (1994). Workshop presentation for the American Academy of Forensic Psychology, Santa Fe, NM.

Ford, C. & Beach, F. (1951). *Patterns of sexual behavior.* New York: Harper & Row.

Fornell, P. (1994, October 18). 6-year-olds suspected in death of girl, 5. *The Philadelphia Inquirer*, p. A-16.

Fowler, R., DiVivo, P. P., & Fowler, D. J., (1985). Analyzing police hostage negotiations: The verbal interactional analysis technique. *Emotional First Aid, 2*, 16-28.

Fowler, S. C., Johnson, J. S., Kallman, M. J., Liou, J. R., Wilson, M. C., & Hikal, A. H. (1993). In a drug discrimination procedure isolation-reared rats generalize to lower doses of cocaine and amphetamine than rats reared in an enriched environment. *Psychopharmacology, 110*, 115-118.

Fox, J. A. & Levin, J. (May 12, 1993). Postal violence cycle of despair turns tragic. *USA Today*, 13a.

Fox, J. A. & Levin, J. (1993, November 30). Firing back: The growing threat of workplace homicide. *The Annals of the American Academy of Political and Social Sciences.*

Fraboni, M., Cooper, D., Reed, T. L., & Saltstone, R. (1990). Offense type and two-point MMPI code profiles: Discriminating between violent and nonviolent offenders. *Journal of Clinical Psychology, 46*, 774-777.

Fraiberg, S. (1987). The mass media: New schoolhouses for children. In L. Fraiberg (Ed.), *Selected writings of Selma Fraiberg* (pp. 573-587). Columbus: Ohio State University Press.

Frank, J. D. (1972). Psychological aspects of international violence. In J. Fawcett (Ed.), *Dynamics of violence*. Chicago: AMA.

Frank, M. G.. & Gilovich, T. (1988). The dark side of self- and social perception: Black uniforms and aggression in professional sports. *Journal of Personality and Social Psychology, 54*, 74-85.

Frederick, J. C. (1976). Determining dangerousness. In *Paper victories and hard realities*. Washington, DC: Health Policy Center, Georgetown University.

Freed, R. S. & Freed, S. A. (1989). Beliefs and practices resulting in female deaths and fewer females than males in India. *Population and Environment: A Journal of Interdisciplinary Studies, 10*(3), 144-161.

Freedman, J. L. (1992). Television violence and aggression: What psychologists should tell the public. In P. Suedfeld & P. E. Tetlock (Eds.), *Psychology and social policy* (pp. 179-189). New York: Hemisphere.

Freeman, L. (1956). *Catch me before I kill more*. New York: Pocket Books.

Freud, S. (1930/1989). From Civilization and its discontents. In P. Gay (Ed.), *The Freud reader*, p. 772.

Freud, S. (1938). Three contributions to a theory of sex. In *The basic writings of Sigmund Freud*, trans. A. Brill. New York: Modern Library, 1938. (Original work published 1905.)

Freud, S. (1949). *An outline of psychoanalysis*. New York: Norton.

Frick, P. (1994). Family dysfunction and the disruptive behavior disorders. In T. Ollendick & R. Prinz (Eds.), *Advances in clinical child psychology* (Vol. 16, pp. 203-226). New York: Plenum Press.

Frick, P., Lahey, B., Loeber, R., Tannenbaum, L., Van Horn, Y., Christ, M., Hart, E., & Hanson, K. (1993). Oppositional defiant disorder and conduct disorder: A meta-analytic review of factor analyses and cross-validation in a clinic sample. *Clinical Psychology Review, 13*, 319-340.

Friedland, N. & Merari, A. (1992). Hostage events: Descriptive profile and analysis of outcomes. *Journal of Applied Social Psychology, 22*, 134-156.

Friedlander, B. (1993). Community violence, children's development, and mass media: In pursuit of new insights, new goals, and new strategies. In D. Reiss, J. E. Richters, M. Radke-Yarrow, & D. Scharff (Eds.), *Children and violence* (pp. 66-81). New York: Guilford.

Friedlander, B. Z. (1993). Community violence, children's development and mass media: In pursuit of new insights, new goals, and new strategies. Special issue: Children and violence. *Psychiatry: Interpersonal and Biological Processes, 56*, 66-81.

Friedman, L. (1994, November). Adopting the health care model to prevent victimization. *National Institute of Justice Journal*, pp. 16-19.

Friedman, L. M. (1993). *Crime and punishment in American history*. New York: Basic Books.

Fromm, E. (1963). *The art of loving*. New York: Bantam.

Fromm, E. (1964). *The heart of man.* New York: Harper & Row.

Fromm, E. (1969). *Escape from freedom.* New York: Avon Books. (Original work published 1941).

Fromm, E. (1973). *The anatomy of human destructiveness.* New York: Holt, Rinehart, & Winston.

Fulero, S. M., & Finkel, N. J. (1991). Barring ultimate issue testing: An "insane" rule? *Law and Human Behavior, 15,* 495-507.

Furby, L., Weinrott, M., & Blackshaw, L. (1989). Sex offender recidivism: A review. *Psychological Bulletin, 105*(1), 3-30.

Furman v. Georgia, 408 U.S. 238 (1972).

Fuselier, G. D. (1981). A practical overview of hostage negotiations. *FBI Law Enforcement Bulletin, 50*(6), 2-11.

Fuselier, G. D. (1986, September) *A practical overview of hostage negotiations.* Federal Bureau of Investigation, U.S. Department of Justice.

Fuselier, G. D. (1988). Hostage negotiation consultant: Emerging role for the clinical psychologist. *Professional Psychology: Research and Practice, 19,* 175-179.

Fuselier, G. D., & Van Zandt, C. R. (1987). *A practical overview of hostage negotiations.* Unpublished manuscript, FBI Academy, Quantico, VA.

Gacono, C. (1992). Sexual homicide and the Rorschach: A Rorschach case study of sexual homicide. *British Journal of Projective Psychology, 37,* 1-21.

Gacono, C., & Meloy, J. R. (1991). A Rorschach investigation of attachment and anxiety in antisocial personality disorder. *Journal of Nervous and Mental Disease, 179,* 546-552.

Gammage, J., Gibbons, T. J., Jr., & Marder, D. (1994, November 16). Three charged in mob beating death of Fox Chase teen. *The Philadelphia Inquirer,* pp. A1, A12.

Gandhi, M. K. (1940). *An autobiography; or the story of my experiments with truth* (2d ed.). Ahmedabad: Navajivan.

Gandhi, M. K. (1950). *Satyagraha in South Africa* (**2nd ed.**). Ahmedabad: Navajivan.

Gandhi, M. K. (1954). In B. Kumarappa (Ed.), *Sarvodya.* Ahmedabad: Navajivan.

Gandhi, M. K. (1961). In R. K. Prabhu (Ed.), *Democracy: Real and deceptive.* Ahmedabad: Navajivan.

Gandhi, M. K. (1967). In R. K. Prabhu, & U. R. Rao

(Eds.), *The mind of Mahatma Gandhi*. Ahmedabad: Navajivan.

Gandhi, M. K. (1970). In A. T. Hingorani (Ed.), *The law of love*. Bombay: Bharatiya Vidya Bhavan.

Garai, J. & Scheinfeld, A. (1968). Sex differences in mental and behavioral traits. *Genetic Psychology Monographs, 77*, 169-229.

Gayford, J. J. (1975). Battered wives: Research on battered wives. *Research on Social Health Journal, 95*(6), 288-289.

Gayral, L., Millet, G., Moron, P., & Turnin, J. (1956). Crises et paroxysmes catathymiques. *Annales Medico-Psychologiques, 114*, 25-50.

Geberth, V. G. (1990a, May). The serial killer and the revelations of Ted Bundy. *Law and Order*, 72-75.

Geberth, V. G. (1990b). *Practical homicide investigation: Tactics, procedures, and forensic techniques (2nd ed.)*. New York: Elsevier.

Geberth, V. (1993, July). *Suicide by cop*. Law and Order, pp. 105-108.

Geen, R. G. (1978). Effects of attack and uncontrollable noise on aggression. *Journal of Research in Personality, 12*, 15-29.

Geen, R. G. (1991). *Human aggression*. Pacific Grove, CA: Brooks/Cole.

Geen, R. G. & Berkowitz, L. (1967). Some conditions facilitating the occurrence of aggression after the observation of violence. *Journal of Personality, 35*, 666-676.

Geffner, R. & Pagelow, M. D. (1990). Victims of spouse abuse. In R. T. Ammerman & M. Herson (Eds.), *Treatment of family violence: A sourcebook* (pp.113-135). New York: John Siley & Sons.

Geimer, W. & Amsterdam, J. (1980). Why jurors vote life or death: Operative factors in ten Florida death cases. *American Journal of Criminal Law, 15*(1, 2), 1-54.

Gelles, R. (1987). *Family violence*. Newbury Park, CA: Sage.

Gelles, R. J. (1974). *The violent home: A study of physical aggression between husbands and wives*. Beverly Hills, CA: Sage.

Gelles, R. J. & Cornell, C. P. (1990). *Intimate violence in families* (2d ed.). Newburg Park: Sage.

Gelles, R. J. & Pedrick, C. C. (1985). *Intimate violence in families*. Beverly Hills CA: Sage.

Gelles, R. J. & Straus, M. A. (1988). *Intimate violence*. New York: Simon & Schuster.

Gennarelli, T. A. (1986). Mechanisms and pathophysiology of cerebral concussion. *Journal of Head Trauma Rehabilitation, 1*, 23-29.

Genthner, R. W., Shuntich, R., & Bunting, K. (1975). Racial prejudice, belief similarity, and human aggression. *Journal of Psychology, 91*, 229-234.

Gerbner, G., Gross, L., Morgan, M., & Signorielli, N. (1980). The "mainstreaming" of America: Violence profile No. 11. *Journal of Communication, 30* (3), 10-29.

Gerzon, M. (1992). *A choice of heroes: The changing faces of American manhood*. Boston: Houghton Mifflin Co.

Geschwind, N. & Galaburda, A. M. (1987). *Cerebral lateralization: Biological mechanisms, associations, and pathology*. Cambridge: The MIT Press.

Getzel, G. S. & Masters, R. (1984, March). Serving families who survive homicide victims. *Social Casework: The Journal of Contemporary Social Work*, 138-144.

Ghosdian-Carpey, J., & Baker, L. A. (1987). Genetic and environmental influences on aggression in 4- to 7-year old twins. *Aggressive Behavior, 13*, 173-186.

Gianutsos, R. & Matheson, P. (1987). The rehabilitation of visual perceptual disorders attributable to brain injury. In M. J. Meier, A. L. Benton, & L. Diller (Eds.), *Neuropsychological rehabilitation* (pp. 202-241). New York: Guilford.

Gibb, W. (1995, March). Seeking the criminal element. *Scientific American*, 101-107.

Gibbons, D. C. (1968). *Society, crime and criminal careers*. Englewood Cliffs, NJ: Prentice Hall.

Gibson, E. & Klein, S. (1969). Murder 1957 to 1968. HMSO: London.

Gillespie, C. (1989). *Justifiable homicide: Battered women, self defense and the law*. Columbus, OH: Ohio State University Press.

Gist, R. G. & Perry, J. D. (1985). Perspectives on negotiation in local jurisdictions: Part I. A different typology of situations. *FBI Law Enforcement Bulletin, November*, 21-24.

Glazer, M. P. & Glazer, P. M. (1986). Whistleblowing. *Psychology Today, 20*, 36-43.

Goetting, A. (1989). Men who kill their mates: A profile. *Journal of Family Violence, 4*, 285-296.

Goetting, A. (1989a). Patterns of homicide among children. *Criminal Justice and Behavior, 16*(1), 63-80.

Goetting, A. (1989b). Patterns of marital homicide: A comparison of husbands and wives. *Journal of Comparative Family Studies*, 341-354.

Golden, C. J., Hammeke, T., & Purisch, A. (1980). *A manual for the Luria-Nebraska neuropsychological battery (Revised)*. Los Angeles, CA: Western Psychological Services.

Golden, C. J., Purisch, A. D., & Hammeke, T. A. (1985). *Luria-Nebraska Neuropsychological Battery: Forms I & II*. Los Angeles, CA: Western Psychological Services.

Golden, C. J., Zillmer, E., & Spiers, M. (1992). *Neuropsychological assessment and rehabilitation*. Springfield, IL: Charles C Thomas.

Goldstein, A. (1995). *Personal communication.*

Goldstein, R. (1974). Brain research and violent behavior. *Archives of Neurology, 30,* 1-18.

Goldstein, R. L. (1989). The psychiatrist's guide to right and wrong: Part III: Postpartum depression and the "appreciation" of wrongfulness. *Bulletin of the American Academy of Psychiatry and Law, 17*(2), 121-128.

Goldstein, R. L. (1989). The psychiatrist's guide to right and wrong: Part IV: The insanity defense and the ultimate issue rule. *Bulletin of the American Academy of Psychiatry and the Law, 17,* 269-281.

Gomes-Schwartz, B., Horowitz, J., & Cardareli, A. P. (1988, July). *Child sexual abuse victims and their treatment* [National Institute of Juvenile Justice and Delinquency Prevention]. Washington, DC: U.S. Department of Justice.

Good, M.I. (1978). Primary affective disorder, aggression and criminality: A review and clinical study. *Archives of General Psychiatry, 35,* 954-960.

Goodall, J. (1986). *The chimpanzee of Gombe: Patterns of behavior.* Cambridge, MA: The Belknap Press of Harvard University Press.

Goodin, D. S. & Aminoff, M. J. (1984). Does interictal EEG have a role in the diagnosis of epilepsy? *Lancet, 8281,* 837-839.

Goodman, R. (1991). Developmental disorders and structural brain development. In M. Rutter & P. Casaer (Eds.), *Biological risk factors for psychosocial disorders* (pp. 26-44). New York: Cambridge University.

Goodwin, D. W. (1973). Alcohol in suicide and homicide. *Quarterly Journal for the Study of Alcoholism, 34,* 144-1-56.

Gordon, W. A. & Hibbard, M. R. (1991). The theory and practice of cognitive remediation. In J. S. Kreutzer & P. H. Wehman (Eds.), *Cognitive rehabilitation for persons with traumatic brain injury* (pp. 13-22). Baltimore: Brookes.

Gorenstein, E. E. & Newman, J. P. (1980). Disinhibitory psychopathology: A new perspective and a model for research. *Psychological Review, 87*(3), 301-315.

Gottesman, I., & Goldsmith, H. (1994). Developmental psychopathology of antisocial behavior: Inserting genes into its ontogenesis and epigenesis. In C. Nelson (Ed.), *Threats to optimal development* (Vol. 27, pp. 69-104). Hilldale, NJ: Lawrence Erlbaum Associates.

Gough, H. G. (1987). *The California Psychological Inventory: Administrator's guide.* Palo Alto, CA: Consulting Psychologists Press.

Gray, O.M. (1981). Hostage negotiations. *Texas Police Journal, 29* (11), 14-18.

Greenbaum, S. (1994). Drugs, delinquency, and other data. *Juvenile Justice, 2* (1), 2-8.

Greenberg, M., Speltz, M., & DeKlyen, M. (1993). The role of attachment in the early development of disruptive behavior problems. *Development and Psychopathology, 5*, 191-213.

Greenfield, L. A. (1995). *Prison sentences and time served for violence.* U.S. Department of Justice (NCJ-153858). Washington DC: Supt. Documents.

Greenland, C. (1971). Evaluation of violence and dangerous behavior associated with mental illness. *Seminars in Psychiatry, 3*, 345-356.

Gregg v. Georgia, 428 U.S. 153 (1976).

Griffitt, W. & Veitch, R. (1971). Hot and crowded: Influence of population density and temperature on interpersonal affective behavior. *Journal of Personality and Social Psychology, 17*, 92-98.

Grimshaw, G., Bryden, M., & Finegan, J. (1995). Relations between prenatal testosterone and cerebral lateralization in children. *Neuropsychology, 9*, 68-79.

Grosz, H. & Zimmerman, J. (1965). Experimental analysis of hysterical blindness: A follow-up report and new experiment data. *Archives of General Psychiatry, 13*, 255-260.

Grubin, D. (1994). Sexual murder. *British Journal of Psychiatry, 165*, 624-629.

Grych, J. H. & Fincham, F. D. (1992). Interventions for children of divorce: Toward greater integration of research and action. *Psychological Bulletin, 111*(3), 434-454.

Gualtieri, T. & Hicks, R. E. (1985). An immunoreactive theory of selective male affliction. *The Behavioral and Brain Sciences, 8*, 427-441.

Gudjonsson, G. (1992). *Psychology of interrogations, confessions and testimony.* W. Sussex, England: John Wiley & Sons, Ltd.

Gudjonsson, G. & Petursson, H. (1982). Some criminological and psychiatric aspects of homicide in Iceland. *Medicine, Science and the Law, 22*, 91-98.

Gudjonsson, G. H., Petursson, H., & Sigurdardottir, H. (1991). Overcontrolled hostility among prisoners and its relationship with denial and personality scores. *Personality and Individual Differences, 12*, 17-20.

Gulotta, G. (1980). Victimization and interpersonal misunderstandings in dyadic systems. *Victimology: An International Journal, 5*, 110-114.

Gunn, J. (1978). Epileptic homicide: A case report. *British Journal of Psychiatry, 132*, 510-513.

Gunn, J. (1981). *Neurology, 31*, 1204-1205.

Gunn J. & Fenton, G. (1971). Epilepsy, automatism and crime. *Lancet, 1*, 1173-6.

Gynther, M. D., Altman, A., & Warbin, R. W. (1973). A new actuarial-empirical automated MMPI interpretive program: The 4-3/3-4 code type. *Journal of Clinical Psychology, 29*, 229-231.

Hachinski, V. (1993). Brain damage and violence. *Archives of Neurology, 50*, 871.

Hacker, F. J. (1976). *Crusaders, criminals, crazies: Terror and terrorism in our time.* New York: W. W. Norton Company.

Haeberle, E. (1978). *The sex atlas.* New York: Seabury.

Haig, D. (1993). Genetic conflicts in human pregnancy. *The Quarterly Journal of Biology, 68*, 495-525.

Hall, G. C., Proctor, W. C., & Nelson, G. M. (1988). Validity of physiological measures of pedophilic sexual arousal in a sexual offender population. *Journal of Consulting and Clinical Psychology, 56*, 118-122.

Hall, H. V. (1982). Dangerousness predictions and the maligned forensic professional: Suggestions for detecting distortion of true basal violence. *Criminal Justice and Behavior, 9*, 3-12.

Hall, H. V. (1984). Predicting dangerousness for the courts. *American Journal of Forensic Psychology, 4*, 5-25.

Hall, H. V. (1985). Cognitive and volitional capacity assessment: A proposed decision tree. *American Journal of Forensic Psychology, 3*, 3-17.

Hall, H. V. (1986). The forensic distortion analysis: A proposed decision tree and report format. *American Journal of Forensic Psychology, 4*, 31-59.

Hall, H. V. (1987). *Violence prediction: Guidelines for the forensic practitioner.* Springfield, IL: Charles C Thomas.

Hall, H. V. (1990). Extreme emotion. *University of Hawaii Law Review, 12*, 39-82.

Hall, H. V. & McNinch, D. (1988). Linking crime-specific behavior to neuropsychological impairment. *International Journal of Clinical Neuropsychology, 10*, 113-122.

Hall, H. V. & Pritchard, D. (1996). *Detecting malingering and deception: The forensic distortion analysis.* Winter Park, FL: GR Press.

Hall, H. V. & Sbordone, R. J. (1993). *Disorders of executive function: Civil & criminal law applications.* Winter Park, FL: Paul M. Deutsch.

Hall, H. V., & Shooter, E. (1989). Explicit alternative testing for feigned memory deficits. *Forensic Reports, 2*, 277-286.

Hall, H. V., Catlin, E., Boissevain, A., & Westgate, J. (1984). Dangerous myths about predicting dangerousness. *American Journal of Forensic Psychology, 2*, 173-193.

Hall, H. V., Shooter, E. A., Craine, A., & Paulsen, S. (1991). Explicit alternative testing: A trilogy of studies on faked memory deficits. *Forensic Reports, 4*, 259-279.

Hall, R. C. (1980). Depression. In R. C. Hall (Ed.), *Psychiatric presentations of medical illness: Somatopsychic disorders* (pp. 37-63). New York: SP Medical and Scientific Books.

Halleck, S. (1971). *Psychiatry and the dilemmas of crime.* Los Angeles: University of California Press.

Halliwell, S. (1987). *The poetics of Aristotle: Translation and commentary.* Chapel Hill: University of North Carolina Press.

Halpern, A. L. (1991). The insanity defense in the 21st century. *International Journal of Offender Therapy and Comparative Criminology, 35*(3), 187-189.

Halpern, D. F. (1992). *Sex differences in cognitive abilities* (2nd ed.). NJ: Lawrence Earlbaum Associates.

Halstead, W. D. (1947). *Brain and intelligence: A quantitative study of the frontal lobes.* Chicago, IL: University of Chicago Press.

Hamai, M., Nishida, T., Takasaki, H., & Turner, L. (1992). New records of within-group infanticide and cannibalism in wild chimpanzees. *Primates, 33*, 151-162.

Hamberger, L. K. & Hastings, J. (1988). Characteristics of male spouse abusers consistent with personality disorders. *Hospital and Community Psychiatry, 39,* 763-770.

Hamilton, E. (1942). *Mythology.* Boston: Little, Brown and Company.

Hampton, R. L. & Gelles, R. J. (1994). Violence toward Black women in a national representative sample of Black families. *Journal of Comparative Family Studies, 25,* 105-119.

Hanawalt, B. (1977). Childrearing among the lower classes of late medieval England. *Journal of Interdisciplinary History, 8*(1), 1-22.

Haney, C., Banks, C., & Zimbardo, P. G. (1973). International dynamics in a simulated prison. *International Journal of Criminology and Penology, 1,* 69-97.

Hanks, S. E. (1992). Translating theory into practice: A conceptual framework for clinical assessment, differential diagnosis, and multi-modal treatment of maritally violent individuals, couples, and families. In E. C. Viano (Ed.), *Intimate violence: Interdisciplinary perspective.* Washington, DC: Hemisphere Publishing Corp.

Hansen, J. & Bjarnason, O. (1974). Homicide in Iceland, 1946 1970. *Forensic Science, 4,* 107-117.

Hanson, R. W., Moss, C. S., Hosford, R. E., & Johnson, M. E. (1983). Predicting inmate penitentiary adjustment: An assessment of four classificatory methods. *Criminal Justice and Behavior, 10,* 293-309.

Harder, D. W. & Lewis, S. J. (1986). The assessment of shame and guilt. In J. N. Butcher & C. D. Spielberger (Eds.), *Advances in personality assessment* (Vol. 6, pp. 89-114). Hillsdale, NJ: Erlbaum.

Hare, R. D. (1978). Electrodermal and cardiovascular correlates of sociopathy. In R. D. Hare & D. Schalling (Eds.), *Psychopathic behavior: Approaches to research.* New York: Wiley.

Hare, R. D. (1985). *The psychopathy checklist.* Unpublished manuscript. University of British Columbia, Vancouver, Canada.

Harlow, C. (1991). *Female victims of crime* [Bureau of Justice Statistics]. Washington, DC: U.S. Department of Justice.

Harlow, H. & Harlow, M. (1962). The effect of rearing conditions on behavior. *Bulletin of the Menninger Clinic, 26,* 213-224.

Harris, T. (1988). *Silence of the lambs.* New York: St. Martin's Press.

Hart, B. (1974). Gonadal androgen and sociosexual behavior of male mammals. *Psychological Bulletin, 81,* 383-400.

Hart, T. & Jacobs, H. (1993). Rehabilitation and management of behavioral disturbances following frontal lobe injury. *Journal of Head Trauma and Rehabilitation, 8,* 1-12.

Hartup, W. W. (1983). Peer relations. In P. H. Mussen & E. M. Hetherington (Eds.), *Handbook of child psychology* (Vol. 4, pp. 104-174). New York: Wiley.

Hastings, J. & Hamberger, L. K. (1988). Personality characteristics of spouse abusers: A controlled comparison. *Violence and Victims, 3,* 31-48.

Hathaway, S. R., & McKinley, J. C. (1940). *Minnesota Multi-Phasic Personality Inventory.* Minneapolis, MN: University of Minnesota Press.

Haughton, P. M., Lewsley, A., Wilson, M., & Williams,

R. G. (1979). A forced-choice procedure to detect feigned or exaggerated hearing loss. *British Journal of Audiology, 13*, 135-138.

Hauser, W. A. & Kurland, L. T. (1975). The epidemiology of epilepsy in Rochester, Minnesota, 1953 through 1967. *Epilepsia, 16*, 1-66.

Hausfater, G. & Hrdy, S. B. (Eds.). (1984). *Infanticide: Comparative and evolutionary perspectives.* New York: The Aldine Publishing Company.

Hawkes, K. (1981). A third explanation for female infanticide. *Human ecology, 9*(1), 79-96.

Hawkins, D. F. (1986a). Black homicide: The adequacy of existing research for devising prevention strategies. In D. F. Hawkins (Ed.), *Homicide among Black Americans.* New York: University Press of America.

Hawkins, D. F. (1986b). Black and White homicide differentials: Alternatives to an inadequate theory. In D. F. Hawkins (Ed.), *Homicide among Black Americans.* New York: University Press of America.

Hawthorne v. State of Florida, 470 So. 2d 770 (Fla. Dist. Ct. App. 1985).

Hayes, S. C., Brownell, K. D., & Barlow, D. H. (1978). The use of self-administered covert desensitization in the treatment of exhibitionism and sadism. *Behavior Therapy, 9*, 283-289.

Hayes, S. C., Brownell, K. D., & Barlow, D. H. (1983). Heterosocial skills training and covert desensitization effects on social skills and sexual arousal in sexual deviants. *Behavior Therapy, 21*(4), 383-392.

Hazelwood, R., Dietz, P., & Burgess, A. (1982). Equivocal deaths: Accident, suicide or homicide? In R. Hazelwood, P. Dietz, & A. Burgess (Eds.), *Auto-erotic fatalities* (pp. 139-153). Lexington, MA: Heath.

Hazelwood, R. R., & Douglas, J. E. (1980, April). The lust murderer. *FBI Law Enforcement Bulletin*, 103-107.

Hazelwood, R. R., Warren, J., & Dietz, P. E. (1993). Compliant victims of the sexual sadist. *Australian Family Physician, 22*(4), 474-479.

Head, W. B. (1990). *The hostage response: An examination of the U.S. law enforcement practices concerning hostage incidents.* (Doctoral dissertation, State University of New York at Albany). Dissertation Abstracts International, 50, 4111-A. University Microfilms International No. DA9013316.

Heaton, R. K., Grant, I., & Matthews, C. G. (1991). *Comprehensive norms for an expanded Halstead-Reitan battery.* Odessa, FL: PAR.

Heilbroner, D. (1993, August). Serial murder and repression. *Playboy, 78*, 147-150.

Heilbrun, A. B. (1979). Psychopathy and violent crime. *Journal of Consulting and Clinical Psychology, 47*, 509-516.

Heilbrun, A. B. (1990a). The measurement of criminal dangerousness as a personality construct: Further validation of a research index. *Journal of Personality Assessment, 54*, 141-148.

Heilbrun, A. B. (1990b). Differentiation of death-row murderers and life-sentence murderers by antisociality and intelligence measures. *Journal of Personality Assessment, 54*, 617-627.

Heinbecker, P. (1986). Two years' experience under Utah's mens rea insanity law. *Bulletin of the American Academy of Psychiatry and Law, 14*, 185-191.

Heinrich, B. (1989). *Ravens in winter*. New York: Summit.

Hellman, D. & Blackman, N. (1966). Enuresis, firesetting, and cruelty to animals: A triad predictive of adult crime. *American Journal of Psychiatry, 26*, 9-16.

Hellman, D. S. & Blackman, N. (1966). Enuresis, firesetting and cruelty to animals: A triad predictive of adult crime. *American Journal of Psychiatry, 122*, 1431-1435.

Helmholtz, R. H. (1975). Infanticide in the province of Canterbury during the fifteenth century. *History of Childhood Quarterly, 2*, 379-90.

Henderson, M. (1983). Self-reported assertion and aggression among violent offenders with high or low levels of over-controlled hostility. *Personality and Individual Differences, 4*, 113-115.

Hendricks, S. E., Fitzpatrick, D. F., Hartmann, K., Quaife, M. A., Stratbucker, R. A., & Graber, B. (1988). Brain structure and function in sexual molesters of children and adolescents. *Journal of Clinical Psychiatry, 49*, 108-112.

Henkoff, R. (1992, August 10). Kids are killing, dying, bleeding. *Fortune*, pp. 62-69.

Herbert, B. (1994, December 7). Targeting women for guns. *The New York Times*, p. A23.

Herjanic, M. & Meyer, D. A. (1976, June). Psychiatric illness in homicide victims. *American Journal of Psychiatry*, pp. 691-693.

Hermann, B. P., Schwartz, M. S., Whitman, S., & Karnes, W. E. (1980). Aggression and epilepsy: Seizure type comparisons and high risk variables. *Epilepsia, 22*, 691-698.

Hermann, D. (1986). Criminal defenses and pleas in mitigation based on amnesia. *Behavior Science and the Law, 4*(1), 5-26.

Herzog, E. & Sudia, C.E. (1973). Children in fatherless families. In B. M. Caldwell & H. N. Ricciuti (Eds.), *Review of child development research* (Vol. 3, pp. 141-232). Chicago: The University of Chicago Press.

Hetherington, M. & Camara, K. (1984). Families in transition: The processes of dissolution and reconstitution. In R. Parke (Ed.), *Review of child development research* (Vol. 7, pp. 398-439). Chicago: The University of Chicago Press.

Hetherington, M., Stanley-Hagan, M., & Anderson, E. R. (1989). Marital transitions: A child's perspective. *American Psychologist, 44*(2), 303-312.

Higginbotham, A. R. (1989, Spring). Sin of the age: Infanticide and illegitimacy in Victorian London. *Victorian Studies*, 319-337.

Hillard, J. R., Zung, W. W., Holland, J. M., & Johnson, M. M. (1985). Accidental and homicidal death in a psychiatric emergency room population. *Hospital and Community Psychiatry, 36*(6), 640-643.

Hillman, R. G. (1981). The psychopathology of being held hostage. *American Journal of Psychiatry, 138*, 1193-1197.

Hines, M. (1993). Hormonal and neural correlates of sex-typed behavioral development in human beings. In M. Haug, R. E. Whalen, C. Aron, & K. L. Olsen (Eds.), *The development of sex differences and simi-*

Reference List 651

larities in behavior (pp. 131-149). Dordrecht: Kluwer Academic Publishers.

Hines, M.. & Green, R. (1991). Human hormonal and neural correlates of sex-typed behaviors. *Review of Psychiatry, 10,* 536-555.

Hines, M.. & Kaufman, F. (1994). Androgen and the development of human sex-typical behavior: Rough-and-tumble play and sex of preferred playmates in children with Congenital Adrenal Hyperplasia (CAH). *Child Development, 65,* 1042-1053.

Hinshaw, S. P. (1992a). Academic underachievement, attention deficits, and aggression: Comorbidity and implications for intervention. *Journal of Consulting and Clinical Psychology, 60*(6), 893-903.

Hinshaw, S. P. (1992b). Externalizing behavior problems and academic underachievement in childhood and adolescence: Causal relationships and underlying mechanisms. *Psychological Bulletin, 111*(1), 127-155.

Hinshaw, S. P. (1994). *Attention deficits and hyperactivity in children.* Thousand Oaks, CA: Sage Publications.

Hinshaw, S., Lahey, B., & Hart, E. (1993). Issues of taxonomy and comorbidity in the development of conduct disorder. *Development and Psychopathology, 5,* 31-49.

Hinton, J. W. (Ed.). (1983). *Dangerousness: Problems of assessment and prediction.* London: Allen and Unwin.

Hiraiwa-Hasegawa, M. (1987). Infanticide in primates and a possible case of male-biased infanticide in chimpanzees. In Y. Itso, J. L. Brown, & J. Kikkawa (Eds.), *Animal Societies: Theories and Facts* (pp. 125-139). Tokyo: Japan Scientific Societies Press.

Hirschel, D. & Hutchison & Dean, C. (1992, February). The failure of arrest to deter spouse abuse. *Journal of Research in Crime and Delinquency.*

Hirschi, T. & Hindelang, M. (1977). Intelligence and delinquency: A revisionist review. *American Sociological Review, 42,* 571-587.

Hoffer, P. & Hull, N. E. H. (1981). *Murdering mothers: Infanticide in England and New England.* New York: New York University Press.

Hoffman, L. (1991). The influence of the family environment on personality: Accounting for sibling differences. *Psychological Bulletin, 110,* 187-203.

Hoffman, L. W. (1989). Effects of maternal employment in the two-parent family. *American Psychologist, 44*(2), 283-292.

Hoffman, M. (1960). Power assertion by the parent and its impact on the child. *Child Development, 31,* 129-143.

Holcolm, W. R. & Adams, N. A. (1982). Racial influences on intelligence and personality of people who commit murder. *Journal of Clinical Psychology, 38,* 793-796.

Holcomb, W. R. & Adams, N. A. (1983). The inner-domain among personality and cognition variables in people who commit murder. *Journal of Personality Assessment, 47,* 524-530.

Holcomb, W. R. & Adams, N. A. (1985). Personality mechanisms of alcohol-related violence. *Journal of Clinical Psychology, 41,* 714-722.

Holcomb, W. R., Adams, N. A., Nicholas, A., Ponder, H.

M., & Anderson, W. (1984). Cognitive and behavioral predictors of MMPI scores in pretrial psychological evaluations of murderers. *Journal of Clinical Psychology, 40,* 592-597.

Holcomb, W. R., Adams, N. A., Nicholas, A., & Ponder, H. M. (1985). The developmental and cross-validation of an MMPI typology of murders. *Journal of Personality Assessment, 49,* 240-244.

Holcomb, W. R., Adams, N. A., & Ponder, H. M. (1984). Are separate black and white norms needed? An IQ-controlled comparison of accused murderers. *Journal of Clinical Psychology, 40,* 189-193.

Holden, S. (1995, March 17). Mutilating, murderous lesbians, with a light side. *New York Times,* p. C8.

Holinger, P.C. (1980). Violent deaths as a leading cause of mortality: An epidemiological study of suicide, homicide and accidents. *American Journal of Psychiatry, 137*(4), 472-475.

Holinger, P. C., Luke, K. W., Montes, P., Perez, S., & Sandlow, J. (1987). Synthesis: Violent deaths in aggregate. In P. C. Holinger (Ed.), *Violent deaths in the United States* (pp. 138-158). New York: Guilford Press.

Hollman, L. & McCoy, C. (1992, August 2). The growing urban arsenal: Are rising handgun sales only a reflection of the problem, or a cause too? *The Philadelphia Inquirer,* pp. E1, E4.

Holmes, R. K. & DeBurger, J. E. (1985). Profiles in terror: The serial murderer. *Federal Probation, 49*(3), 29-34.

Holmes, R. M. (1989). *Profiling serial murders.* Newbury Park, CA: Sage Publications.

Holmes, S. A. (1995, October 28). Ranks of inmates reach one million in a 2-decade rise. *New York Times,* pp. A1, A25.

Honeycutt, R. L. (1992). Naked mole-rats. *American Scientist, 80,* 43-53.

Hoppe, C. M. & Singer, R.D. (1976). Overcontrolled hostility, empathy, and egocentric balance in violent and non-violent psychiatric offenders. *Psychological Reports, 39,* 1303-1308.

Horan, D. & Delahoyde, M. (1982). *Infanticide and the handicapped infant.* Provo: BYU Press.

Horsfals, J. (1991). *The presence of the past: Male violence in the family.* North Sydney, Australia: Allen & Unwin.

Hotaling, G. T., Finkelhor, D., Kirkpatrick, J. T., Straus, M. A., (Eds.) (1988). *Family abuse and its consequences: New directions in research.* Newbury Park, CA: Sage.

Hotaling, G. T. & Sugarman, D. B. (1986). An analysis of risk markers in husband to wife violence: The current state of knowledge. *Violence and Victims, 1,* 101-124.

Hotaling, G. T. & Sugarman, D. B. (1990). Prevention of wife assault. In R. T. Ammerman & M. Hersen (Eds.), *Treatment of family violence: A sourcebook.* New York: John Wiley & Sons.

House, E.. & Pansky, B. (1967). *A functional approach to neuroanatomy.* New York: McGraw-Hill.

House of Lords in Daniel M'Naghten's Case, 10 Cl. & Fin. 200, 8 Eng. Rep. 718 (1843).

Howe, M. (1992, June 17). M.T.A. panel approves cut in cigarette advertisements. *New York Times Metro,* p. B3.

Hrdy, S. B. (1976). The care and exploitation of nonhuman primate infants by conspecifics other than the mother. *Advances in the Study of Behavior, 6,* 101-158.

Hrdy, S. B. (1977). The puzzle of langur infant-sharing. In *The langurs of Abu: Female and male strategies of reproduction.* Cambridge: Harvard University Press.

Hrdy, S. B. (1979). Infanticide among animals: A review, classification, and examination of the implications for the reproductive strategies of females. *Ethology and Sociobiology, 1,* 13-40.

Hrdy, S. B. (1987). Sex-biased investment in primates and other mammals. In R. Gelles & J. Lancaster (Eds.), *Child abuse and neglect* (pp. 97-147). Hawthorne, NY: Aldine de Gruyter.

Hrdy, S. B. (1990). Sex bias in nature and in history: A late 1980's re-examination of the "biological origins" argument. *Yearbook of Physical Anthropology, 33,* 25-37.

Hrdy, S. B. (1992). Fitness tradeoffs in the history and evolution of delegated mothering with special reference to wet-nursing, abandonment, and infanticide. *Ethology and Sociobiology, 13,* 409-442.

Hsieh, C. & Pugh, M. (1993, Autumn). Poverty, income inequality, and violent crime: A meta-analysis of recent aggregate data studies. *Criminal Justice Review,* pp. 182-202.

Hubbard, D.G. (1971). *The skyjacker: His flights of fantasy.* New York: MacMillan.

Hubbard, D.G. (1973). *The skyjacker: His flights of fantasy.* New York: Collier Books.

Hubbard, D.G. (1986). *Winning back the sky: A tactical analysis of terrorism.* Dallas: Saybrook Publishing.

Hucker, S. & Stermac, L. (1992). The evaluation and treatment of sexual violence, necrophilia, and asphyxiophilia. *Psychiatric Clinics of North America, 15*(3), 703-719.

Huesmann, L. R. (1986). Psychological processes promoting the relation between media violence and aggressive behavior by the viewer. *Journal of Social Issues, 42,* 125-139.

Huesmann, L. R. & Eron, L. D. (1986). The development of aggression in American children as a consequence of television violence viewing. In L. R. Huesmann & L. D. Eron (Eds). *Television and the aggressive child: A cross national comparison.* Hillsdale, NJ: Lawrence Erlbaum Associates

Huesmann, L. R., Eron, L. D., Lefkowitz, M. M., & Walder, L. O. (1984). Stability of aggression over time and generations. *Developmental Psychology, 20*, 1120-1134.

Hull, J. D. (1995, January 30). The state of the union. *Time*, 53-62.

Humes, J. C. (1994). *The wit and wisdom of Winston Churchill*. New York: Harper Perennial.

Humphrey, J. A. & Palmer, S. (1986). Race, sex, and criminal homicide offender-victim relationship. In D. F. Hawkins (Ed.), *Homicide among Black Americans*. New York: University Press of America.

Huston, A., Donnerstein, E., Fairchild, H., et al. (1992). *Big screen, small world*. Lincoln: University of Nebraska Press.

Huston, A., Zillmann, D., & Bryant, J. (1994). Media influence, public policy, and the family. In A. Huston, D. Zillmann, & J. Bryant (Eds.), *Media, children, and the family: Social scientific, psychodynamic, and clinical perspectives* (pp. 3-18). Hillsdale, NJ: Lawrence Erlbaum Associates.

Huston, A. C. (1983). Sex typing. In P. H. Mussen & E. M. Hetherington (Eds.), *Handbook of child psychology* (Vol. 4, pp. 388-432). New York: Wiley.

Hutton, H. E., Miner, M. H., & Langfeldt, V. C. (1993). The utility of the Megargee-Bohn typology in a forensic psychiatric hospital. *Journal of Personality Assessment, 60*, 572-587.

Hyde, J. S. (1984). How large are gender differences in aggression? A developmental meta-analysis. *Developmental Psychology, 20*, 722-736.

Hyde, J. S. (1986). Gender differences and aggression. In J. S. Hyde & M. C. Linn (Eds.), *The psychology of gender: Advances through meta-analysis* (pp. 51-66). Baltimore: The Johns Hopkins University Press.

Ibn-Tamas v. United States, 407 A.2d 626 (D.C. 1979).

Idaho Code, Art. 18-207 (c) (1992).

Illinois v. Littlejohn, 494 N.E.2d 677 (Ill. 1986).

Illinois v. Murphy, 497 N.E.2d 871 (Ill. 1986).

Ingram, J. C., Marchioni, P., Hill, G., Caraveo-Ramos, E., & McNeil, B. (1985). Recidivism, perceived problem-solving abilities, MMPI characteristics, and violence: A study of black and white incarcerated male adult offenders. *Journal of Clinical Psychology, 41*, 425-432.

Insanity Defense Reform Act of 1984, Pub. L., No. 98-473 (1984).

Insanity defense work group: American Psychiatric Association statement on the insanity defense (1982). *American Journal of Psychiatry, 140*, 681-688.

International Reference Organization (1981). *Forensic Medicine and Science, 2*, 227-230.

Issues for the September 1994 United Nations international conference on population and development (1994). *Audubon, 96*(4), 56.

Jacklin, C. H. (1989). Female and male: Issues of gender. *American Psychologist, 44*(2), 127-133.

Jacobs, H. E. (1993). *Behavior analysis guidelines and brain injury rehabilitation.* Gaithersburg, MD: Aspen.

Jacobsen, C. F. (1936). Studies of cerebral function in primates: I. The functions of the frontal association areas in monkeys. *Comprehensive Psychology Monographs, 13*, 3-60.

Jacobson, E. (1964). *The self and the object world.* New York: International Universities Press.

Jacobson, N. S. & Addis, M. E. (1993). Research on couples and couple therapy: What do we know? Where are we going? *Journal of Counseling and Clinical Psychology, 61*, 85-93.

Jacobson, S. R. (1973). Individual and group responses to confinement in a skyjacked plane. *American Journal of Orthopsychiatry, 43*, 459-469.

Jaffe, P. A., Wolfe, D. A., & Wilson, S. K. (1990). *Children of battered women.* Newbury Park, CA: Sage.

Janofsky, J., Vanderwalle, M. B., & Rappeport, J. R. (1989). Defendants pleading insanity: An analysis of outcome. *Bulletin of the American Academy of Psychiatry and the Law, 17*, 203-210.

Jenkins, B., Johnson, J., & Renfeldt, D. (1977). *Numbered lives: Some statistical observations from 77 international hostage episodes.* Santa Monica, CA: The Rand Corporation.

Jenkins, P. (1989). Serial murder in the United States 1900-1940: A historical perspective. *Journal of Criminal Justice, 17*, 377-392.

Jenkins, P. (1992). A murder "wave"? Trends in American serial homicide 1940-1990. *Criminal Justice Review, 17*(1), 1-19.

Jenkins, P. (1992). Murder "wave"? Trends in American Serial Homicide, 1940-1990. *Criminal Justice Review, 17*, 1-19.

Jenkins, R. L. (1991). Socializing the unsocialized delinquent. In W. A. Rhodes & W. K. Brown (Eds.), *Why some children succeed despite the odds* (pp. 141-148). New York: Praeger.

Jessee, P. O., Strickland, M. P., & Ladewig, B. H. (1992). The after effects of a hostage situation on children's behavior. *American Journal of Orthopsychiatry, 62*, 309-312.

Jessor, R. (1992). Risk behavior in adolescence: A psychosocial framework for understanding and action. In D. E. Rogers & E. Ginzburg (Eds.), *Adolescents at risk: Medical and social perspectives*. Boulder, CO: Westview Press.

Jhally, S. (Writer, Director, Producer) (1990). *Dreamworlds: Desire/sex/power* (video). Northampton, MA: Media Education Foundation.

Johanson, D. & Johanson, L. (1994). *Ancestors*. New York: Villard.

John, H. W. (1977). Alcoholism and criminal homicide: Overview. *Alcohol Health and Research World*, 8-13.

Johnson, D. A., Simmons, J. D., & Gordon, D. C. (1983). Temporal consistency of the Meyer-Megargee inmate typology. *Criminal Justice and Behavior, 10*, 263-268.

Johnson, I. M., Crowley, J., & Sigler, R. T. (1992). Agency response to domestic violence: Services provided to battered women. In E. C. Viano (Ed.), *Intimate violence: Interdisciplinary perspective*. Washington, DC: Hemisphere Publishing Corp.

Johnson, J. H. & Fennell, E. B. (1992). Aggressive, antisocial, and delinquent behavior in childhood and adolescence. In C. E. Walker & M. C. Roberts (Eds.), *Handbook of clinical child psychology* (2nd ed., pp. 341-358). New York: Wiley.

Johnson, P.W. & Feldmann, T.B. (1992). Personality types and terrorism: Self psychology perspectives. *Forensic Reports, 5*, 293-303.

Johnson, T. E. & Rule, B. G. (1986). Mitigating circumstances information, censure and aggression. *Journal of Personality and Social Psychology, 50*, 537-542.

Jones, A. (1980). *Women who kill*. New York: Fawcett Crest.

Joynt, R. J. (1992). Make my day. *Archives of Neurology, 49*, 591.

Jurek v. Texas, 428 U.S. 262 (1976).

Justice, B., Justice, R., & Kraft, J. (1974). Early warning signs of violence: Is a triad enough? *American Journal of Psychiatry, 131*, 457-459.

Kagan, J. (1994). *Galen's prophecy*. New York: Basic Books.

Kahn, M. W. (1959). A comparison of personality, intelligence, and social history of two criminal groups. *Journal of Social Psychology, 49*, 33-40.

Kaimowitz v. Dept. of Mental Health, 42 U.S.L.W. Suppl. 2063, (D. Michigan, 1973).

Kalichman, S. C. (1988a). MMPI profiles of women and men convicted of domestic homicide. *Journal of Clinical Psychology, 44*, 847-853.

Kalichman, S. C. (1988b). Empirically derived MMPI profile subgroups of incarcerated homicide offenders. *Journal of Clinical Psychology, 44*, 733-738.

Kamphi, A. (1992). Response to historical perspective: A

developmental language perspective. *Journal of Learning Disabilities, 25*, 48-52

Kandel E., & Freed, D. (1989). Frontal lobe dysfunction and antisocial behavior: A review. *Journal of Clinical Psychology, 45*, 404-413.

Kandel, E., Mednick, S. A., Kirkegaard-Sorense, L., Hutchings, B., Knop, J., Rosenberg, R., & Schulsinger, F. (1988). IQ as a protective factor for subjects at high risk for antisocial behavior. *Journal of Consulting and Clinical Psychology, 56*, 224-226.

Kaplan, H. I., Sadock, B. J., & Grebb, J. A. (1994). *Synopsis of psychiatry* (7th ed.). Baltimore, MD: Williams and Wilkins.

Kaplan, J. (1899). Kopftrauma und psychosen. *Allgemeiner Zeitschrift Fur Psychiatrie, 56*, 292-297.

Kaplan, J. (Gen. Ed.). (1992). Adolph Hitler. In *Familiar quotations*, 16th edition, John Bartlett, p. 676. Boston: Little, Brown and Company.

Kaplan, M. S., Abel, G. G., Cunningham-Rathner, J., & Mittleman, M. (1990). The impact of parolees' perception of confidentiality of their self-reported sex crimes. *Annals of Sex Research, 3*, 292-303.

Kaser-Boyd, N. (1993). Rorschachs of women who commit homicide. *Journal of Personality Assessment, 60*, 458-470.

Kashani, J. H., Daniel, A. F., Dandoy, A. C., & Holcomb, W. R. (1992, March). Family violence: Impact on children. *Journal of the American Academy of Child and Adolescent Psychiatry*, pp. 181-189.

Kazdin, A. E. (1992). Child and adolescent dysfunction and paths toward maladjustment: Targets for intervention. *Clinical Psychology Review, 12*, 795-817.

Kazdin, A. E. (1995). Conduct disorder. In F. Verhulst & H. Koot (Eds.), *The epidemiology of child and adolescent psychopathology*. Oxford: Oxford University Press.

Keehn, R. J., Goldberg, I. D., & Beebe, G. W. (1974). Twenty-four year mortality follow-up of Army veterans with disability separations for psychoneurosis in 1944. *Psychosomatic Medicine, 36*(1), 27-46.

Keilitz, I. (1987). Researching and reforming the insanity defense. *Rutgers Law Review, 39*, 303-306.

Kellermann, A. L., Rivara, F. P., Rushforth, N. B., Banton, J. G., Reay, D. T., Francisco, J. T., Locci, A. B., Prodzinski, J. B., Hackman, B. B., & Somes, G. P. (1993). Gun ownership as a risk factor for homicide in the home. *The New England Journal of Medicine, 329*(15), 1084-1091.

Kellogg, C. E. & Morton, N. W. (1957). *Revised beta examination* (Rev. ed.). New York, NY: Psychological Corporation.

Kelly, C. (1976). *Crime in the United States: Uniform Crime Reports*. Washington DC: Supt. of Documents, U.S. Government Printing Office.

Kelman, H. C. & Hamilton, V. L. (1989). *Crimes of obedience*. New Haven: Yale University Press

Keltikangas-Jarvinen, L. (1978). Personality characteristics of homicides and assaulters. *Psychiatria Fennica, 1*, 65-71.

Kemper, C., Silverman, F., & Steels, B. (1962). The battered child syndrome. *Journal of the American Medical Association, 181,* 1.

Kennedy, H. G., & Dyer, D. E. (1992). Parental hostage takers. *British Journal of Psychiatry, 160,* 410-412.

Kennedy, T. D. (1986). Trends in inmate classification: A status report on two computerized psychometric approaches. *Criminal Justice and Behavior, 13,* 165-184.

Kerig, P., Cowan, P., & Cowan, C. (1993). Marital quality and gender differences in parent-child interaction. *Developmental Psychology, 29,* 931-939.

Kernberg, O.F. (1975). *Borderline conditions and pathological narcissism.* New York: Aronson.

Kernberg, O.F. (1984). *Severe personality disorders: Psychotherapeutic strategies.* New Haven: Yale University Press.

Kernberg, O.F. (1989). The Narcissistic Personality Disorder and the differential diagnosis of antisocial behavior. *The Psychiatric Clinical of North America, 12,* 553-570.

Kessler, R. (1993). *The FBI.* New York: Pocket Books.

Keyes, D. (1981). *The minds of Billy Milligan.* New York: Bantam.

Kgachaturyan, A. A. (1951). *Neuropatologiya i Psichiatriya, 20,* 18-22. Microfilmed English translation, Library of Congress, TT60-13724.

Kiersch, T. A. (1962). Amnesia: A clinical study of ninety-eight cases. *American Journal of Psychiatry, 119,* 57-60.

Kiger, K. (1990). The darker figure of crime: The serial murder enigma. In S. A. Egger (Ed.), *Serial murder: An elusive phenomenon.* New York: Praeger.

Killer women on TV (1992, October 12). *New York Times,* p. C20.

Killings said to rise after gun laws are relaxed (March 15, 1995). *New York Times,* p. A23.

Kilmartin, C. T. (1994). *The masculine self.* New York: Macmillan.

Kim, K., & Cho, Y. (1992). Epidemiological survey of spousal abuse in Korea. In E. C. Viano (Ed.), *Intimate violence: Interdisciplinary perspective.* Washington, DC: Hemisphere Publishing Corp.

King, A., Lancaster, J., & Benitone, J. (1970). Amygdalectomy in the free-ranging vervet (ceropithecusalthiops). *Journal of Psychiatric Research, 7,* 191-199.

King, D., & Ajmone, M. (1977). Clinical features and ictal patterns of epileptic patients with EEG temporal lobe foci. *Annals of Neurology, 2,* 138-147.

Kinzel, A. (1970). Body-buffer zones in violent prisoners. *American Journal of Psychiatry, 127,* 59-64.

Klama, J. (1988). *Aggression: The myth of the beast within.* New York: Wiley.

Klatsky, A. L. & Armstrong, M. A. (1993). Alcohol use, other traits, and risk of unnatural death: A prospective study. *Alcoholism: Clinical and Experimental Research, 17*(6), 1156-1162.

Knutson, J. (1995). Psychological characteristics of maltreated children: Putative risk factors and consequences. In J. Spence, J. Darley, & D. Foss (Eds.), *Annual review of psychology,* (pp. 401-431). Palo Alto, CA: Annual Reviews Inc.

Knutson, J. N. (1980). The dynamics of the hostage taker: Some major variants. *Annals New York Academy of Sciences, 347*, 117-128.

Kobetz, R. W. (1975, May). Hostage incidents — The new police priority. *The Police Chief*, 32-35.

Kohn, A. (1986). *No contest: The case against competition*. Boston: Houghton-Mifflin.

Kohut, H. (1978). *The search for the self*. New York: International Universities Press.

Kohut, H. (1978). Thoughts on narcissism and narcissistic rage. In P. Ornstein (Ed.), *The search for the self*, Vol. 2. New York: International Universities Press.

Kolb, L. C. (1972). Violence and aggression: An overview. In J. Fawcett (Ed.), *Dynamics of violence*. Chicago: AMA.

Kolbert, E. (1993, December 26). The remote control avenger. *The New York Times*, Sec. 9 (Styles of the Times), p. 8.

Kopp, C. B. & Kaler, S. R. (1989). Risk in infancy: Origins and implications. *American Psychologist, 44*(2), 224-230.

Koss, M. P., Goodman, L. A., Browne, A., Fitzgerald, L. F., Keita, G. P., & Russo, N. F. (1994). *No safe haven: Male violence against women at home, at work, and in the community*. Washington, DC: American Psychological Association.

Koss, M. P. & Haslet, L. (1992). Somatic consequences of violence against women. *Archives of Family Medicine, 1*, 53-59.

Kozol, H., Boucher, R., & Garofalo, R. (1972). The diagnosis and treatment of dangerousness. *Crime and Delinquency, 18*, 371-391.

Kozol, H. L., Cohen, M. I., & Garafolo, R. F. (1966). The criminally dangerous sex offenders. *New England Journal of Medicine, 275*, 79-84.

Krafft-Ebing, R. von. (1934). *Psychopathia sexualis*, trans. F. J. Rebman. Brooklyn, NY: Physicians and Surgeons Book Co., 1934. (Original work published 1886.)

Krafft-Ebing, R. von (1965). *Psychopathia sexualis*. (E. S. Klaf, Trans.). New York: Stein & Day. (Original work published 1886).

Kratcoski, P. C. (1988). Families who kill. *Marriage and the Family Review, 12*, 47-70.

Kreutzer, J. S. & Wehman, P. H. (Eds.), (1991). *Cognitive rehabilitation for persons with traumatic brain injury*. Baltimore: Brookes.

Kreuz, L. E. & Rose, R. M. (1972). Assessment of aggressive behaviors and plasma testosterone in a young criminal population. *Psychosomatic Medicine, 34*, 321-332.

Krishnaswamy, S. (1984). A note on female infanticide: An anthropological inquiry. *The Indian Journal of Social Work, 45*(3), 297-302.

Kristof, N. D. (1995, April 4). With cult under cloud, its still his guiding star. *New York Times*, p. A4.

Kruttschnitt, C. (1993). Violence by and against women: A comparative and cross-national analysis. *Violence and Victims, 8*, 253-270.

Krynicki, V. E. (1978). Cerebral dysfunction in repetitively assaultive adolescents. *Journal of Nervous and Mental Disease, 166*, 59-67.

Kubey, R. (1990). Media implications for the quality of family life. In D. Zillmann, J. Bryant, & A. C. Huston, Eds. (1994). *Media, children, and the family: Social scientific, psychodynamic, and clinical perspectives* (pp. 61-69). Hillsdale, NJ: Lawrence Erlbaum Associates.

Kubey, R. & Czikszentmihalyi, M. (1990). *Television and the quality of life: How viewing shapes everyday experience.* New York: Lawrence Erlbaum Associates.

Kunce, J. T., Ryan, J. J., & Eckelman, C. C. (1976). Violent behavior and differential WAIS characteristics. *Journal of Consulting and Clinical Psychology, 44*, 42-45.

Kupperman, R. & Kamen, J. (1989). *Final warning: Averting disaster in the new age of terrorism.* New York: Doubleday.

Kuralt, C. (1985). *On the road with Charles Kuralt.* New York: Ballantine Books.

Kurland, H. D., Yeager, C. T., & Arthur, R. J. (1963). Psychophysiologic aspects of severe behavior disorders. Archives of *General Psychiatry, 8*, 599-604.

Kusum, (1993). The use of pre-natal diagnostic techniques for sex selection: The Indian scene. *Bioethics, 7*(2/3), 149-165.

Kutash, I. L., Kutash, S. B., Schlesinger, L. B. & Associates (1978). *Violence: Perspective on murder and aggression.* San Francisco, CA: Jossey-Bass.

Kyokai, B. D. (1992). *The teaching of Buddha.* Tokyo, Japan: Buddhist Promoting Foundation.

Lagaipa, S. J. (1990). Suffer the little children: The ancient practice of infanticide as a modern moral dilemma. *Issues in Comprehensive Pediatric Nursing, 13*, 241-251.

Lahey, B., Hart, E., Pliszka, S., Applegate, B., & McBurnett, K. (1993). Neurophysiological correlates of conduct disorder: A rationale and a review of the research. *Journal of Clinical Child Psychology, 22*, 141-153.

Lahey, B. B. & Loeber, R. (1994). Framework for a developmental model of oppositional defiant disorder and conduct disorder. In D. K. Routh (Ed.), *Disruptive behavior disorders in childhood* (pp. 139-180). New York: Plenum Press.

Landau, S.F. (1975). Pathologies among homicide offenders: Some cultural profiles. *British Journal of Criminology, 15*, 157 166.

Landers, A. (1986, May 22). Letter from the bear facts in Bayside. *Philadelphia Inquirer.*

Lane, P. J. & Kling, J. S. (1979). Construct validation of the Overcontrolled Hostility scale of the MMPI. *Journal of Consulting and Clinical Psychology, 47*, 781-782.

Lang, R. (1993). Neuropsychological deficits in sexual offenders: Implications for treatment. *Sexual and Marital Therapy, 8*(2), 181-200.

Langan, P. A.. & Innes, C. A. (1986 August). *Preventing domestic violence against women.* Washington, DC: U.S. Department of Justice.

Langer, W. (1974). Infanticide: A historical survey. *History of Childhood Quarterly, 1,* 353-365.

Langevin, R., Bain, J., Wortzman, G., Hucker, S., Dickey, R., & Wright, P. (1988). Sexual sadism: Brain, blood, and behavior. *Annals of the New York Academy of Science, 528,* 163-171.

Langevin, R., Ben-Aron, M., Wortzman, G., Dickey, R., & Handy, L. (1987). Brain damage, diagnosis, and substance abuse among violent offenders. *Behavioral Sciences & the Law, 5*(1), 77-94.

Langevin, R., Handy, L., Paitich, D., & Russon, A. (1983). A new version of the Clarke Sexual History Questionnaire for Males. In R. Langevin (Ed.), *Erotic preference, gender identity, and aggression* (pp. 287-305). Hillsdale: Erlbaum.

Langevin, R., Paitich, D. O., B, Handy, L., & Russon, A. (1982). The role of alcohol, drugs, suicide attempts and situational strains in homicides committed by offenders seen for psychiatric assessment. *ACTA Psychiatry of Scandinavia, 66,* 229-242.

Langevin, R., Paitich, D., Orchard, B., Handy, L., & Russon, A. (1982). Diagnosis of killers seen for psychiatric assessment: A controlled study. *Acta Psychiatrica Scandinavica, 66,* 216-228.

Langley, S., Crimmens, S., Brownstein, H., & Spunt, B. (1994). *Typology of women who kill: Beyond the battered women syndrome.* Paper presented at the annual meeting of the American Psychological Association, Los Angeles, CA.

Lanzkron, J. (1963). Murder and insanity. *American Journal of Psychiatry, 119,* 754-758.

Larson, E. (1993). The story of a gun. *The Atlantic Monthly, 271,* 48-78.

Law Firm of Littler, Mendelson, Fastiff, Tichy, & Mathiason. (1994). *Terror and violence in the workplace.* San Francisco: Author.

Laws, D. R., Meyer, J., & Holmen, M. L. (1978). Reduction of sadistic sexual arousal by olfactory aversion: A case study. *Behavior Research and Therapy, 16,* 281-285.

Leaky, R. & Lewin, R. (1992). *Origins reconsidered.* New York: Doubleday.

Lear, J. (1990). *Love and its place in nature.* New York: Farrar, Straus & Giroux.

Leary, W. E. (1995, April 21). Young people who try suicide may be succeeding more often. *New York Times,* p. A15.

Ledingham, J. E. (1991). Social cognition and aggression. In D. J. Pepler & K. H. Rubin (Eds.), *The development and treatment of childhood aggression* (pp. 279-285). NJ: Lawrence Erlbaum Associates.

Lefkowitz, M. M., Eron, L., Walder, L., & Huesmann, L. R. (1977). *Growing up to be violent: A longitudinal study of the development of aggression.* New York: Pergamon.

Lester, D. (1977). The prediction of suicide and homicide rates cross-nationally by means of stepwise multiple regression. *Behavior Science Research, 1,* 61-69.

Lester, D. (1985). The relation of twin infanticide to status of women, societal aggression, and material well-being. *The Journal of Social Psychology, 126*(1), 57-59.

Lester, D. (1993). Restricting the availability of alcohol and rates of personal violence (suicide and homicide). *Drug and Alcohol Dependence, 31*, 215-217.

Levine, J. M. & Moreland, R. L. (1990). In M. R. Rosenzweig, & L. W. Porter (Eds.), *Annual review of psychology.* Palo Alto, CA: Annual Reviews.

Levine, S., Risen, C., & Althof, S. (1990). Essay on the diagnosis and nature of paraphilia. *Journal of Sex and Marital Therapy, 16*(2), 89-102.

Lewin, J. & Sumners, D. (1992). Successful treatment of episodic dyscontrol with carbamazepine. *British Journal of Psychiatry, 161*, 261-262.

Lewis, C., Hitch, G., & Walker, P. (1994). The prevalence of specific arithmetic difficulties and specific reading difficulties in 9- to 10-year old boys and girls. *Journal of Child Psychology and Psychiatry, 35*, 283-292.

Lewis, D.O., Pincus, J., Bard, B., Richardson, E., Prichep, L., Feldman, M., & Yeager, C. (1988). Neuropsychiatric, psychoeducational, and family characteristics of 14 juveniles condemned to death in the United States. *American Journal of Psychiatry, 145*, 584-589.

Lewis, D. O. & Pincus, J. H. (1989). Epilepsy and violence: Evidence for a neuropsychotic-aggressive syndrome. *Journal of Neuropsychiatry, 1*, 413-418.

Lewis, D. O., Pincus, J. H., & Feldman, M. (1986). Psychiatric, neurological and psychoeducational characteristics of 15 death row inmates in the United States. *American Journal of Psychiatry, 143*, 838-845.

Lewis, D. O., Pincus, J. H., Shanok, S. S., & Glaser, G. H. (1982). Psychomotor epilepsy and violence in an incarcerated adolescent population. *American Journal of Psychiatry, 139*, 882-887.

Lewis, D. O., & Shanok, S. (1977). Medical histories of delinquent and nondelinquent children: An epidemiological study. *American Journal of Psychiatry, 134*, 1020-1025.

Lewis, D. O. & Shanok, S. (1979). Perinatal difficulties, head, and face trauma and child abuse in the medical histories of seriously delinquent children. *American Journal of Psychiatry, 136*, 419-423.

Lewis, H. B. (1976). *Psychic war in men and women.* New York: New York University Press.

Lewis, M., Feiring, C., McGuffog, C., & Jaskir, J. (1984). Predicting psychopathology in six-year-olds from early social relations. *Child Development, 55*, 123-136.

Lewontin, R. C. (1994). Women versus the biologists. *New York Review of Books, 41*, 31-35.

Lezak, M. (1983). *Neuropsychological assessment* (2nd ed.). New York: Oxford Press.

Lezak, M. (1995). *Neuropsychological assessment* (3rd ed.). New York, NY: Oxford University Press.

Liebert, R. M. & Sprafkin, J. (1988). *The early window: Effects of television on children and youth* (3rd ed.). New York: Pergamon Press.

Liederman, J. & Flannery, K. A. (1995). The sex ratios

of families with a neurodevelopmentally disordered child. *Journal of Child Psychology and Psychiatry, 36*(3), 511-517.

Lifton, R. J. (1986). *The Nazi doctors.* New York: Basic Books.

Lipke, H. J. & Botkin, A. L. (1992). Case studies of eye movement desensitization and reprocessing (EMDR) with chronic post-traumatic stress disorder. *Psychotherapy, 29*, 591-595.

Litman, R. (1967). Sigmund Freud on suicide. *Psychoanalytic Forum, 1*, 205-221.

Litman, R. L. (1995). Suicide prevention in a treatment setting. *Suicide and Life-Threatening Behavior, 25*, 134-142.

Lloyd, S. A. (1990). Asking the right questions about the future of marital violence research. In D. J. Besharov (Ed.), *Family violence: Research and public policy issues.* Washington, DC: The AEI Press.

Lockett v. Ohio, 438 U.S. 586 (1978).

Loeber, R. (1990). Development and risk factors of juvenile antisocial behavior and delinquency. *Clinical Psychology Review, 10*, 1-41.

Loeber, R. & Keenan, K. (1994). Interaction between conduct disorder and its comorbid conditions: Effects of age and gender. *Clinical Psychology Review, 14*(6), 497-523.

Loeber, R., Wung, P., Keenan, K., Giroux, B., Stouthamer-Loeber, M., Van Kammen, W., & Maughan, B. (1993). Developmental pathways in disruptive child behavior. *Development and Psychopathology, 5*, 103-133.

Loew, C. A. (1967). Acquisition of a hostile attitude and its relationship to aggressive behavior. *Journal of Personality and Social Psychology, 5*, 335-341.

Lore, R. K. & Schultz, L. A. (1993). Control of human aggression. *American Psychologist, 48*, 1, 16-25.

Lourie, R. (1993). *Hunting the devil.* New York: Harper.

Louscher, P. K., Hosford, R. E., & Moss, C. S. (1983). Predicting dangerous behavior in a penitentiary using the Megargee typology. *Criminal Justice and Behavior, 10*, 269-284.

Luckenbill, D. F. (1977, December). Criminal homicide as a situated transaction. *Social Problems*, pp. 176-186.

Luginbuhl, J. & Middendorf, K. (1988). Death penalty beliefs and jurors' responses to aggravating and mitigating circumstances in capital trials. *Law and Human Behavior, 12*(3), 263-281.

Luria, A. R. (1980). *Higher cortical functions in man* (2nd ed.). New York, NY: Basic Books.

Lyon, B. (1986, May 22). The selling of Mike Tyson. *Philadelphia Inquirer*, pp. 1D, 4D.

Lytton, H. (1990a). Child and parent effects in boys' conduct disorder: A reinterpretation. *Developmental Psychology, 26*(5), 683-697.

Lytton, H. (1990b). Child effects — still unwelcome? Response to Dodge and Wahler. *Developmental Psychology, 26*(5), 705-709.

Lytton, H. & Romney, D. M. (1991). Parent's differential socialization of boys and girls: A meta-analysis. *Psychological Bulletin, 109*(2), 267-296.

Maccoby, E. (1983). Socialization in the context of the family: Parent-child interaction. In P. H. Mussen & E. M. Hetherington (Eds.), *Handbook of child psychology* (Vol. 4, pp. 1-87). New York: Wiley.

Maccoby, E. (1986). Social groupings in childhood: Their relationship to prosocial and antisocial behavior in boys and girls. In D. Olweus, J. Block, & M. Radke-Yarrow (Eds.), *Development of antisocial behavior in boys and girls* (pp. 263-284). New York: Academic Press.

Maccoby, E. (1988). Gender as a social category. *Developmental Psychology, 24*(6), 755-765.

Maccoby, E. (1990). Gender and relationships: A developmental account. *American Psychologist, 45*(4), 513-520.

Maccoby, E. E. (1991). Gender and relationships: A reprise. *American Psychologist, 46,* 538-539.

Maccoby, E. (1992). The role of parents in the socialization of children: An historical overview. *Developmental Psychology, 28*(6), 1006-1017.

Maccoby, E. & Jacklin, C. (1974). *The psychology of sex differences.* Stanford, CA: Stanford University Press.

Maccoby, E. & Jacklin, C. (1980). Sex differences in aggression: A rejoinder and reprise. *Child Development, 51,* 964-980.

Maccoby, E. & Martin, J. A. (1983). Socialization in the context of the family: Parent-child interaction. In E. M. Hetherington (Ed.), *Handbook of child psychology* (Vol. 4, pp. 1-87). New York: Wiley.

MacCulloch, M., Snowden, P., Wood, P., & Mills, H. (1983). Sadistic fantasy, sadistic behavior, and offending. *British Journal of Psychiatry, 143,* 20-29.

MacDonald, J. (1968). *Homicidal threats.* Springfield, IL: Charles C Thomas.

Mackay, R. D. & Kopelman, J. (1988). The operation of the "guilty but mentally ill (GBMI)" verdict in Pennsylvania. *Journal of Psychiatry and the Law, 16,* 247-262.

MacLean, P. D. (1962). New findings relevant to the evolution of the psychosexual functions of the brain. *Journal of Nervous and Mental Disorders, 135,* 289-301.

Maguire, K. & Pastore, A. (Eds). (1994). *Sourcebook of criminal justice statistics, 1993.* U.S. Department of Justice, Bureau of Justice Statistics, Washington, DC: U.S. Government Printing Office.

Maguire, K., Pastore, A., & Flanagan, T. (Eds.). (1993). *Sourcebook of criminal justice statistics, 1992.* U.S. Department of Justice, Bureau of Justice Statistics, Washington, DC: U.S. Government Printing Office.

Maguire, K., Pastore, A., & Flanagan, T. J. (1993). *Bureau of Justice Statistics Sourcebook of Criminal Justice Statistics — 1992.* Washington: U. S. Department of Justice.

Mahowald, M. W., Bundlie, S. R., Hurwitz, T. D., & Schenck, C. H. (1990). Sleep, violence-forensic science implications: Polygraph and video documentation. *Journal of Forensic Sciences, 35,* 413-432.

Mahowald, M. W., Schenck, C. H., Rosen, G. M., & Hurwitz, T. D. (1992). The role of a sleep disorder center in evaluating sleep violence. *Archives of Neurology, 49,* 604-607.

Maier, H. (1912). Ueber einige arten catathyme wahnbildung und paranoia [On types of catathymic formations in psychosis and paranoia]. *Ztschr F.d. Ges. Neurol U Psychiat., 13,* 555.

Maier, H. (1923). Ueber einige arten der psychogenen mechanismen [On types of psychogenetic mechanisms]. *Ztschr F.d. ges Neurol U Psychiat, 39*, 116-120.

Maier, H. W. (1912). Uber katathyme Wahnbildung und Paranoia. *Zeitschrift fur die gesamte Neurologie und Psychiatrie, 13*, 555-610.

Mailer, N. (1984). *Tough guys don't dance.* New York: Random House.

Malamud, N. (1967). Psychiatric disorders with intracranial tumors of the limbic system. *Archives of Neurology, 17*, 113-123.

Malamuth, N. & Spinner, B. (1980). A longitudinal content analysis of sexual violence in the best-selling erotic magazines. *Journal of Sex Research, 17*, 226-237.

Malik, S. (1986). *Gandhian satyagraha and contemporary world.* Rohtak, India: Manthan.

Mancuso, P. J., Jr. (1989). Domestic violence and the police: Theory, policy, and practice. In L. J. Dickstein & C. C. Nadelson (Eds.), *Family violence: Emerging issues of a national crisis.* Washington, DC: American Psychiatric Press.

Mann, C. R. (1989). Getting even? Women who kill in domestic encounters. In S. L. Johann & F. Osanka (Eds.), *Representing...battered women who kill* (pp. 8-26). Springfield, IL: Charles C Thomas.

Mann, C. R. (1990). Black female homicide in the United States. *Journal of Interpersonal Violence, 5*, 176-201.

Mann, C. R. (1992). Female murderers and their motives: A tale of two cities. In E. C. Viano (Ed.), *Intimate violence: Interdisciplinary perspective.* Washington, DC: Hemisphere Publishing Corp.

Mark, V. H. & Ervin, F. R. (1970). *Violence and the brain.* New York, NY: Harper & Row.

Markman, H. J., Renick, M. J., Floyd, F. J., Stanley, S. M., & Clements, M. (1993). Preventing marital distress through communication and conflict management training: A 4- and 5-year follow-up. *Journal of Counseling and Clinical Psychology, 61*, 70-77.

Marlatt, G. A. (1985). Cognitive factors in the relapse process. In G. A. Marlatt & J. R. Gordon (Eds.), *Relapse prevention* (pp. 128-200). New York: Guilford Press.

Marquis, J. (1970). Orgasmic reconditioning: Changing sexual choice through controlling masturbatory fantasies. *Journal of Behavior Therapy and Experimental Psychology, 1*, 263-271.

Marshall, W. L. (1979). Satiation therapy: A procedure for reducing deviant arousal. *Journal of Applied Behavioral Analysis, 12*, 10-22.

Marshall, W. L. (1993). The role of attachments, intimacy, and loneliness in the etiology and maintenance of sex offending. *Sexual and Marital Therapy, 8*(2), 109-121.

Marshall, W. L. & Barbaree, H. E. (1988). The long-term evaluation of a behavioral treatment program for child molesters. *Behavior Research and Therapy, 26*(5), 499-511.

Marshall, W. L., Barbaree, H. E., & Butt, J. (1988). Sexual offenders against male children: Sexual preferences. *Behavior Research and Therapy, 26*(5), 283-391.

Martell, D. A. (1992a). Estimating the prevalence of

organic brain dysfunction in maximum-security forensic patients. *Journal of Forensic Sciences, JFS-CA, 37*(3), 878-893.

Martell, D. A. (1992b). Forensic neuropsychology and the criminal law. *Law and Human Behavior, 16,* 313-336.

Martin, B.. & Hoffman, J. A. (1990). Conduct disorders. In M. Lewis & S. M. Miller (Eds.), *Handbook of developmental psychopathology* (pp. 109-116). New York: Plenum Press.

Martin, D.C. & Walcott, J. (1989). *Best laid plans: The inside story of America's war against terrorism.* New York: Simon and Shuster.

Maruyama, M. (1963). The second cybernetics: Deviation-amplifying mutual causal processes. *American Scientist, 51,* 164-179.

Maslow, A. H. (1968). *Toward a psychology of being* (2d ed.). New York: Van Nostrand Reinhold.

Maslow, A. H. (1971). *The farther reaches of human nature.* NewYork: Viking.

Maslow, A. H. (1987). *Motivation and personality.* New York: Harper & Row.

Massey, C. R. & McKean, J. (1985). The social ecology of homicide: A modified lifestyle/routine activities perspective. *Journal of Criminal Justice, 13,* 417-428.

Mast, G. (1986). *A short history of the movies* (4th ed.). New York: Macmillan.

Masten, A., Best, K., & Garmezy, N. (1990). Resilience and development: Contributions from the study of children who overcome adversity. *Development and Psychopathology, 49,* 547-555.

Mateer, C. A., Sohlberg, M. M., & Youngman, P. K. (1990). The management of acquired attention and memory deficits. In R. L. Wood & I. Fussey (Eds.), *Cognitive rehabilitation in perspective* (pp. 68-96). London: Taylor & Francis.

Mathison, R. R. (1958). *The eternal search.* New York: G. P. Putnam's Sons.

Matter of Torsney, 412 N.Y.S.2d 914, reh'g ordered, 417 N.Y.S.2d 467, rev'd, 420 N.Y.S.2d 192 (Ct. App. N.Y. 1979).

Mattson, A. & Levin, H. (1990). Frontal lobe dysfunction following closed head injury: A review of the literature. *The Journal of Nervous and Mental Disease, 178,* 282-291.

Masters, A. L. (1990). Infanticide: The primate data. *The Journal of Psychohistory, 18,* 99-108.

Masters, R., Friedman, L. N., & Getzel, G. (1988). Helping families of homicide victims: A multidimensional approach. *Journal of Traumatic Stress, 1,* 109-125.

Matzkin, R. G. (1985). The film encounter in the life-world of urban couples: A uses and gratifications study. (Doctoral dissertation, Teachers College, Columbia University).

Maxim, P. S. & Keane, C. (1992). Gender, age, and the risk of violent death in Canada, 1950-1986. *Canadian Review of Sociology and Anthropology, 29*(3), 329-354.

May, R. (1953). *Man's search for himself.* New York: Delta.

May, R. (1969). *Love and will.* New York: Norton.

May, R. (1972). *Power and innocence.* New York: Norton.

May, R. (1981). *Freedom and destiny.* New York: Norton.

Mayo, D.L. (1992). What is being predicted? Definitions of "suicide." In R. W. Maris, S. L. Berman, J. T. Maltsberger, & R. I. Yufit (Eds.), *Assessment and Prediction of Suicide.* (pp. 88-101). New York: Guilford Press.

Mays, S. (1993). Infanticide in Roman Britain. *Antiquity, 67,* 883-888.

Maziade, M., Caron, C., Cote, R., Boutin, P., & Thivierge, J. (1990). Extreme temperament and diagnosis: A study in a psychiatric sample of consecutive children. *Archives of General Psychology, 47,* 477-484.

McAnulty, R. D. & Adams, H. E. (1992). Behavior therapy with paraphilic disorders. In S. M. Turner, K. S. Calhoun, & H. E. Adams (Eds.), *Handbook of behavior therapy* (2nd ed.) (pp. 175-201). New York: Wiley.

McCay, M. M. (1994, January/February). The link between domestic violence and child abuse. *Child Welfare,* pp. 29-39.

McCleskey v. Kemp, 481 U.S. 279 (1987).

McCully, R. S. (1964). Vampirism: Historical perspective and underlying process in relation to a case of auto-vampirism. *Journal of Nervous and Mental Disease, 139,* 440-452.

McCurdy, K. & Daro, D. (1993). *Current trends in child abuse reporting and fatalities: The results of the 1992 annual fifty state survey* (Working paper number 808). Chicago, IL: National Center on Child Abuse Prevention Research.

McCurdy, K. & Daro, D. (1994, April). *Current trends in child abuse reporting and fatalities: The results of the 1993 annual fifty states survey* [(Working paper number 808)]. Chicago, IL: National Center on Child Abuse Research.

McCutcheon, Lynn E., & McCutcheon, Lauren E. (1994). Not guilty by reason of insanity: Getting it right or perpetuating the myths? *Psychological Reports, 74,* 764-766.

McDonald, A. & Paitich, D. (1981). A study of homicide: The validity of predictive test factors. *Canadian Journal of Psychiatry, 26,* 549-554.

McDuff, D. R. (1992). Social issues in the management of released hostages. *Hospital and Community Psychiatry, 43,* 825-828.

McGinley, H. & Pasewark, R. A. (1989). National survey of the frequency and success of the insanity plea and alternate pleas. *Journal of Psychiatry and Law, 17.*

McGowan, J. (1991). Little girls dying: An ancient and thriving practice. *Commonweal, 118*(14), 481-482.

McIntosh, J. L. (1992). Methods of Suicide. In R. W.

Maris, A. L. Berman, J. T. Maltsberger, & R.I. Yufit (Eds.), Assessment and Prediction of Suicide. (pp. 381-397). New York: Guilford Press.

Meloy, R. (1988). *The psychopathic mind: Origins, dynamics and treatment*. Northvale, NJ: Aronson.

McKechnie, J. L., et al. (Eds.). (1983). *Webster's new universal unabridged dictionary* (2nd ed.). New York: Simon & Schuster.

McLuhan, M. (1989). *The global village: Transformations in world life and media*. New York: Oxford University Press.

McManus, I. C. & Bryden, M. P. (1991). Geschwind's theory of cerebral lateralization: Developing a formal, causal model. *Psychological Bulletin, 110*(2), 237-253.

McMillan, T. & Glucksman, E. (1987). The neuropsychology of moderate head injury. *Journal of Neurology, Neurosurgery and Psychiatry, 50*(4), 393-397.

McMillen, M. (1979). Differential mortality by sex in fetal and neonatal deaths. *Science, 204,* 89-91.

McPherson, S. B. (1992). *Psychosocial investigation in death penalty mitigation: Procedures and pitfalls.* Paper presented at the 3rd European Conference of Law and Psychology, Oxford, England.

Megargee, E. I. (1966). Undercontrolled and overcontrolled personality types in extreme antisocial aggression. *Psychological Monographs, 80,* (Whole No. 611).

Megargee, E. I. (1971). The role of inhibition in the assessment and understanding of violence. In J. L.

Singer (Ed.), *The control of aggression and violence* (pp. 242-264). New York: Academic Press.

Megargee, E. I. (1977). A new classification system for criminal offenders, I: The need for a new classification system. *Criminal Justice and Behavior, 4,* 107-114.

Megargee, E. I. (1984a). Derivation, validation and application of an MMPI-based system for classifying criminal offenders. *Medicine and Law, 3,* 109-118.

Megargee, E. I. (1984b). A new classification system for criminal offenders: VI. Differences among the types on the Adjective Checklist. *Criminal Justice and Behavior, 11,* 349-376.

Megargee, E. I. (1986). A psychometric study of incarcerated presidential threateners. *Criminal Justice and Behavior, 13,* 243-260.

Megargee, E. I. (1993). Aggression and violence. In H. E. Adams & P. B. Sutker (Eds.), *Comprehensive handbook of psychopathology (2nd ed.).* New York: Plenum.

Megargee, E. I. (1993). Using the MMPI-2 with criminal offenders: A progress report. *MMPI-2 & MMPI-A News & Profiles, 4,* 2-3.

Megargee, E. I. (1994). Using the Megargee MMPI-based classification system with MMPI-2s of male prison inmates. *Psychological Assessment, 6,* 337-344.

Megargee, E. I. & Bohn, M. J., Jr. (1977). A new classification system for criminal offenders, IV: Empirically determined characteristics of the ten types. *Criminal Justice and Behavior, 4,* 149-210.

Megargee, E. & Bohn, M. (1979). *Classifying criminal offenders: A new system based on the MMPI.* Beverly Hills, CA: Sage Publications.

Megargee, E. I., Cook, P. E., & Mendelsohn, G. A. (1967). Development and validation of an MMPI scale of assaultiveness in overcontrolled individuals. *Journal of Abnormal Psychology, 72,* 519-528.

Megargee, E. I. & Dorhout, B. (1977). A new classification system for criminal offenders, III: Revision and refinement of the classificatory rules. *Criminal Justice and Behavior, 4,* 125-148.

Meier, M. J., Benton, A. L., & Diller, L. (1987). *Neuropsychological rehabilitation.* New York: Guilford.

Meiselman, K. (1978). *Incest.* San Francisco: Jossey-Bass.

Mellgren, D. (1994, October 19). Horrified Scandinavians react to killing. *The Philadelphia Inquirer,* pp. A1, A9.

Meloy, J. R. (1988). *The psychopathic mind: Origins, dynamics, and treatment.* Northvale, NJ: Jason Aronson, Inc.

Meloy, J. R (1992). *Violent attachments.* Northvale, NJ: Jason Aronson, Inc.

Meloy, J. R. (1992). Voluntary intoxication and the insanity defense. *Journal of Psychiatry and the Law, 20* (4), 439-457.

Meloy, J. R., Gacono, L. B., & Kenney, L. (1994). A Rorschach investigation of sexual homicide. *Journal of Personality Assessment, 62,* 58-67.

Meloy, R. (1988). *The psychopathic mind: Origins, dynamics, and treatment.* Northvale, NJ: Jason Aronson, Inc.

Melton, G., Petrila, J. Poythress, N., & Slobogin, C. (1987). *Psychological evaluations for the courts.* New York: Guilford.

Meninger, K. & Mayman, M. (1956). Episodic dyscontrol: A third order of stress adaptation. *Bulletin of the Meninger Clinic, 20,* 153-160.

Menken, M. (1992). Grappling with the enigma of violence. *Archives of Neurology, 49,* 592-594.

Merchandising murder (1995, March 31). "Arts and entertainment" channel of cable television. (Philadelphia area channel 29, 9-10 p.m. EST)

Merrill, J. C., Lee, J., & Friedlander, E. J., (1994). *Modern mass media,* (2nd ed.). New York: Harper Collins.

Mesulam, M. M. (1985). *Principles of behavioral neurology.* Philadelphia, PA: Davis.

Meyer, J., Jr. & Megargee, E. I. (1977). A new classification system for criminal offenders, II: Initial development of the system. *Criminal Justice and Behavior, 4,* 115-124.

Meyer, R.G. & Parke, A. (1991). Terrorism: Modern trends and issues. *Forensic Reports, 4,* 51-59.

Meyer-Bahlburg, H. & Ehrhardt, A. (1982). Prenatal sex

hormones and human aggression. *Aggressive Behavior, 8,* 39-62.

Meyers, W. C. (1994). Sexual homicide by adolescents. *Journal of the American Academy of Child and Adolescent Psychiatry, 33,* 962-969.

Michener, J. (1992). *The world is my home: A memoir.* New York: Random House.

Michigan Corrections Department. (1978). Reported in Monahan, J., *The Clinical Prediction of Violent Behavior.* National Institute of Mental Health, DHHS Publication Number (ADM) 81-92. Washington, DC: Supt. Docs.

Mickolus, E. (1976). Negotiating for hostages: A policy dilemma. *Orbis, 19,* 1309-1325.

Middendorf, W. (1975). New developments in the taking of hostages and kidnapping — a summary. *National Criminal Justice Reference Service Translation.*

Miedzian, M. (1991). *Boys will be boys: Breaking the link between masculinity and violence.* New York: Doubleday.

Milavsky, J. R., Stipp, H. H., Kessler, R. C., & Rubens, W. S. (1982). *Television & aggression: A panel study.* New York: Academic Press.

Milgram, S. (1963). Behavioral study of obedience. *Journal of Abnormal and Social Psychology, 67,* 371-378.

Milgram, S. (1965). Some conditions of obedience to authority. *Human Relations, 18,* 57-76.

Miller, A. H. (1980). *Terrorism and hostage negotiations.* Boulder, CO: Westview Press.

Miller, B. D. (1981). *The endangered sex: Neglect of female children in rural North India.* Ithaca, NY: Cornell University.

Miller, D., & Looney, J. (1974). The prediction of adolescent homicide: Episodic dyscontrol and dehumanization. *American Journal of Psychoanalysis, 34,* 187-198.

Miller, K. E. Q. (1995, March 6). Mother's love was not enough to save family. *The Philadelphia Inquirer,* pp. A1, A10.

Miller, L. (1990). Major syndromes of aggressive behavior following head injury: An introduction to evaluation and treatment. *Cognitive Rehabilitation, 8,* 14-23.

Miller, N. E. (1948). Theory and experiment relating psychoanalytic displacement to stimulus-response generalization. *Journal of Abnormal and Social Psychology, 43,* 155-178.

Miller, P. A., & Eisenberg, N. (1988). The relation of empathy to aggressive and externalizing/antisocial behavior. *Psychological Bulletin, 103,* 324-344.

Millon, T. (1994). Millon Clinical Multiphasic Personality Inventory-III. Minneapolis, MN: National Computer Systems.

Milne, H. B. (1979). Epileptic homicide: Drug-induced. *British Journal of Psychiatry, 134,* 547-552.

Milner, J. S. (1995). Physical child abuse assessment: Perpetrator evaluation. In J. T. Campbell (Ed.), *Assessing dangerousness: Violence by sexual offenders, batterers and child abusers* (pp. 41-67). Thousand Oaks, CA: Sage.

Miron, M. & Goldstein, A. (1979). *Hostage.* New York: Pergamon Press.

Misery in the maternity wards. (1990, January 20). *The Economist, 52.*

Mishima, Y. (1956). *Temple of the golden pavilion.* Berkeley: University of California Press.

Mock, L. F. & Crawford, C. A. (1994, November). Health and criminal justice: Strengthening the partnership. *National Institute of Justice Journal,* pp. 2-7.

Moffitt, T. (1993a). Adolescent-limited and life-course-persistent antisocial behavior: A developmental taxonomy. *Psychological Review, 100,* 674-701.

Moffitt, T. (1993b). The neuropsychology of conduct disorder. *Development and Psychopathology, 5,* 135-151.

Mohnot, S. M. (1971). Some aspects of social changes and infant-killing in the Hanuman langur *Presbytis entellus* (Primates: Cercopithecidae) in Western India. *Mammalia, 35,* 175-198.

Monahan, J. (1978). The prediction and control of violent behavior. In *Research into violent behavior: Overview and sexual assaults.* Hearings before the Subcommittee on Domestic and International Science Planning, Analysis, and Cooperation of the Committee on Science and Technology, U.S. House of Representatives. 95th Congress, Second session.

Monahan, J. (1981). *Predicting violent behavior: An assessment of clinical techniques.* Beverly Hills, CA: Sage.

Monahan, J. (1981). *The clinical prediction of violent behavior.* National Institute of Mental Health, DHHS Publication Number (ADM) 81-92. Washington, DC: Supt. Docs.

Monahan, J. (Ed.). (1983). *Who is the client?* Washington, DC: American Psychological Association.

Monahan, J. (1988). Risk assessment of violence among the mentally disordered: Generating useful knowledge. *International Journal of Law and Psychiatry, 11,* 249-257.

Monahan, J. (1992). Mental disorder and violent behavior: Perceptions and evidence. *American Psychologist, 47*(4), 511-521.

Monahan, J. (1992). Risk assessment: Commentary on Poythress and Otto. *Forensic Reports, 5,* 151-154.

Monahan, J. & Cummings, L. (1975). Social policy implications of the inability to predict violence. *Journal of Social Issues, 31,* 153-164.

Monahan, J. & Klassen, D. (1982). Situational approaches to understanding and predicting individual violent behavior. In M. E. Wolfgang & N. A. Weiner (Eds.), *Criminal violence* (pp. 292-319). Beverly Hills, CA: Sage Publications.

Money, J. (1984). Paraphilias: Phenomenology and classification. *American Journal of Psychotherapy, 38*(2), 164-179.

Money, J. & Ehrhardt, A. (1972). *Man and women, boy and girl.* Baltimore, MD: Johns Hopkins University.

Monroe, R. R. (1985). Episodic behavioral disorders and limbic ictus. *Comprehensive Psychiatry, 26*, 466-479.

Montana v. Korell, 690 P.2d 992 (1984).

Montgomery, B. (1983). *A history of warfare.* New York: William Morrow and Company.

Moore, K.C. (1976). *Airport, aircraft, and airline security.* Los Angeles: Security World Publishing.

Moran, R. (1995, February 24). Hate crimes increasing in Pa. *New York Times*, p. B2.

Morgan, D. W., McCullough, T. M., Jenkins, P. L., & White, W. M. (1988). Guilty but mentally ill: The South Carolina experience. *Bulletin of the American Academy of Psychiatry and Law, 16*, 41-48.

Morris, T. & Blom-Cooper, L. (1976). Homicide in England. In M. E. Wolfgang (Ed.), *Studies in Homicide* (pp. 24-35). Harper & Row: New York.

Morton, J. H., Addison, H., & Addison, R.G. (1953). Clinical study of pre-menstrual tension. *American Journal of Obstetrics and Gynecology, 65*, 1182-1191.

Moscicki, E. K. (1995). Epidemiology of suicidal behavior. *Suicide and Life Threatening Behavior, 25*(1), 22-35.

Moseley, K. L. (1978). The history of infanticide in Western society. *Issues in Law and Medicine, 1*(5), 345-361.

Moss, D. (1995, March 3). Md. snuffs out smoking in nearly every workplace. *USA Today*, p. 3A.

Motiuk, L. L., Bonta, J., & Andrews, D. A. (1986). Classification in correctional halfway houses: The relative and incremental predictive criterion validities of the Megargee-MMPI and LSI systems. *Criminal Justice and Behavior, 13*, 33-46.

Motto, J. A. (1992). An integrated approach to estimating suicide risk. In R. W. Maris, A. L. Berman, J. T. Maltsberger, & R. I. Yufit (Eds.), *Assessment and Prediction of Suicide* (pp. 625-239). New York: Guilford Press.

Moyer, K. E. (1968). Kinds of aggression and their physiological basis. *Community, Behavior, and Biology, 2*, 65-87.

Mrad, D. F., Kabacoff, R. A., & Cuckro, P. (1983). Validation of the Megargee typology in a halfway house setting. *Criminal Justice and Behavior, 10*, 252-262.

Mueller, C. W. (1983). Environmental stressors and aggressive behavior. In R. G. Geen & E. I. Donnerstein (Eds.), *Aggression: Theoretical and empirical reviews* (Vol. 2, pp. 51-76). New York: Academic Press.

Mungus, D. (1983). An empirical analysis of specific syndromes of violent behavior. The *Journal of Nervous and Mental Disease, 171*, 354-361.

Murphy, C. M., Meyer, S., & O'Leary, K. D. (1993). Family of origin violence and MCMI-II psychopathology among partner assaultive men. *Violence and Victims, 8*, 165-176.

Murphy, C. M., Meyer, S., & O'Leary, K. D. (1994). Dependency characteristics of partner assaultive men. *Journal of Abnormal Psychology, 103*(4), 729-735.

Murphy, J., Jellinek, M., Quinn, D., Smith, G., Poitrast, F., & Goshko, M. (1991). Substance abuse and serious child mistreatment: Prevalence, risk, and outcome in a court sample. *Child Abuse and Neglect, 15*, 197-211.

Murphy, W.D. (1990). Assessment and modification of cognitive distortions in sexual offenders. In W. Marshall, H. E. Barbaree, & D. R. Laws (Eds.), *Handbook of sexual assault: Issues, theories, and treatment of the offender* (pp. 331-430). New York: Plenum.

Murray, C. & Herrnstein, R. J. (1994). *The bell curve.* New York: Free Press.

Murray, J. P. (1988, Summer). On tv violence. American Psychological Association Div. 29 (Child, Youth, and Family Services) *Newsletter, 16* (3), pp. 1, 12.

Myers, E., Bays, J., Becker, J., Berliner, L., Corwin, D., & Sawitz, K. (1989). Expert testimony in child sexual abuse litigation. *Nebraska Law Review, 68*(1 & 2), 1-145.

Myers, J. K., Weissman, M. M., Tischler, G. L., Holzer, C. E., III, Leaf, P. J., Orvaschel, H., Anthony, J. C., Boyd, J. H., Burke, J. D., Kramer, M., & Stoltzman, R. (1984). Six-month prevalence of psychiatric disorders in three communities. *Archives of General Psychiatry, 41*, 959-967.

Nachshon, I. & Denno, D. (1987). Violent behavior and cerebral hemisphere function. In S. A. Mednick, T. E. Moffitt, & S. A. Stack (Eds.), *The causes of crime: New biological approaches* (pp. 185-217). New York: Cambridge University Press.

National Center for the Analysis of Violent Crime (1994). *Serial, mass and spree murderers in the United States: Search of major wire services and publications: Offenders operating from 1960 to present.* Quantico, VA: FBI Academy.

National Committee for Prevention of Child Abuse. (1986, September). *Child abuse: Prelude to delinquency? Findings of a Research Conference Conducted by the National Committee for Prevention of Child Abuse.* Washington, DC: Office of Juvenile Justice and Delinquency Prevention.

National Institute of Justice (1989, January). Stranger abductive homicides of children. Washington, DC: Office of Juvenile Justice and Delinquency Prevention.

National Institute for Occupational Safety and Health (1992). *Report on traumatic occupational fatalities.* Washington, DC: U.S. Department of Health and Human Services.

National Rifleman (July 1995). The armed citizen. *National Rifle Association*, 193, 8.

National Safe Workplace Institute (1993). *Breaking point: The workplace violence epidemic and what to do about it*. Washington, DC: Author.

National Victims Center. (1992). *Rape in America: A report to the nation*. Arlington, VA: Author.

New York State Penal Law 125.5.

Newman, M. (1995, March 10). Weapons at school: Box cutters escape detection. *New York Times*, pp. A1, B4.

Newton, M. (1990). *Hunting humans: The encyclopedia of serial killers* (Vol. 1). New York: Avon Books.

Ney, P. G. (1992). Transgenerational triangles of abuse: A model of family violence. In E. C. Viano (Ed.), *Intimate violence: Interdisciplinary perspective*. Washington, DC: Hemisphere Publishing Corp.

Nielsen Media Research. (1990). *Report on television*. New York: A. G. Nielsen Co.

Northwestern National Life Insurance Company (1993). *Fear and violence in the workplace*. Minneapolis, MN: Author.

Nousiainen, U., Suomalainen, T., & Mervaala, E. (1992). Clinical benefits of scalp EEG studies in intractable seizure disorders. *Acta Neurologic Scandanavia, 85*, 181-186.

Novaco, R. (1975). *Anger control: The development and evaluation of an experimental treatment*. Lexington, MA: Lexington Books.

Novaco, R. W. (1975). Anger and coping with stress. In J. Foreyt & D. Rathjen (Eds.), *Cognitive behavior therapy: Therapy, research and practice*. New York, NY: Plenum.

Novello, A. (1992, June). From the Surgeon General, U.S. Public Health Service, a medical response to domestic violence. *Journal of the American Medical Association*, p. 3132.

Novello, A., Shosky, J., & Froehlke, R. (1992). A medical response to violence. *Violence, 21*, American Medical Association.

Novick, K. K. & Novick, J. (1987). The essence of masochism. *Psychoanalytic Study of the Child, 42*, 353-384.

O'Brien, R. M. (1987). The interracial nature of violent crimes: A reexamination. *American Journal of Sociology, 4*, 817-835.

O'Carroll, P. W. (1986). Patterns and recent trends in black homicide. In D. F. Hawkins (Ed.), *Homicide among Black Americans*. New York: University Press of America.

Ochberg, F. (1978). The victim of terrorism: Psychiatric considerations. *Terrorism, 1*, 147-168.

O'Connor, M. & Cermak, L. S. (1987). Rehabilitation of organic memory disorders. In M. J. Meier, A. L. Benton & L. Diller (Eds.), *Neuropsychological rehabilitation* (pp. 260-279). New York: Guilford.

Office of Youth Services (1994). *Youth Gang Response System*. Report submitted to the Seventeenth Legislature, Hawaii, pp. 1-22.

Offord, D. R., Boyle, M. H., & Racine, Y. A. (1991). In D. J. Pepler & K. H. Rubin (Eds.), *The development and treatment of childhood aggression* (pp. 31-54). Hillsdale, NJ: Lawrence Earlbaum Associates.

Ogloff, J. R. P. (1991). A comparison of insanity defense standards in juror decision-making. *Law and Human Behavior, 15*, 509-531.

O'Halloran, R., & Dietz, P. (1993). Autoerotic fatalities with power hydraulics. *Journal of Forensic Sciences, 38*(2), 359-364.

O'Leary, K. D. (1993). Through a psychological lens: Personality traits, personality disorders, and levels of violence. In R. J. Gelles & D. R. Loseke (Eds.), *Current controversies on family violence*. Newbury Park, CA: Sage.

Ondrovik, J., & Hamilton, D. (1990, April 7). *Multiple personality: Competency and the insanity defense.* Paper presented at Conference on Multiple Personality and Dissociative States. Akron, Ohio.

Oreskes, M. (1990, June 28). Profiles of today's youth: they couldn't care less. *The New York Times*, p. A1.

Otterbein, K. (1986). *The ultimate coercive sanction.* New Haven, CT: Hraf Press.

Ounstead, C., & Taylor, D. (1972). The Y chromosome message: A point of view. In C. Ounstead & D. Taylor (Eds.), *Gender differences: Their ontogeny and significance* (pp. 241-261). London: Churchill Livingstone.

Oza, D. K. (1991). *Voluntary action and Gandhian approach.* New Delhi: National Book Trust.

Packer, I. K. (1985). Insanity acquittals in Michigan 1969-1983: The effects of legislative and judicial changes. *Journal of Psychiatry and Law, 13*, 419-434.

Packer, I. K. (1987). Homicide and the insanity defense: A comparison of sane and insane murderers. *Behavioral Sciences and the Law, 5*, 25-35.

Pagelow, M. D. (1984). *Family violence.* New York: Praeger.

Palmer, S., & Humphrey, J. A. (1980, Summer). Offender-victim relationships in criminal homicide followed by offender's suicide, North Carolina, 1972-1977. *Suicide and Life-Threatening Behavior, 10*, pp. 106-118.

Pan, H. S., Neidig, P. H., & O'Leary, K. D. (1994). Predicting mild and severe husband-to-wife physical aggression. *Journal of Consulting and Clinical Psychology, 62*, 975-981.

Pankratz, L. (1979). Symptom validity testing and symptom retraining: Procedures for the assessment and treatment of functional sensory deficits. *Journal of Consulting and Clinical Psychology, 47*, 409-410.

Pankratz, L. (1983). A new technique for the assessment and modification of feigned memory deficit. *Perceptual and Motor Skills, 57*, 367-372.

Pankratz, L. (1988). Malingering on intellectual and neuropsychological measures. In R. Rogers (Ed.), *Clinical assessment of malingering and deception* (pp. 169-182). New York: Guilford Press.

Pankratz, L., Fausti, S., & Peed, S. (1975). A forced-choice technique to evaluate deafness in the hysterical or malingering patient. *Journal of Consulting and Clinical Psychology, 43*, 421-422.

Panton, J. H. (1958). MMPI profile configurations

among crime classification groups. *Journal of Clinical Psychology, 14*, 305-312.

Panton, J. H. (1976). Personality characteristics of death-row inmates. *Journal of Clinical Psychology, 32*, 306-309.

Paradis, C. M., Horn, L., Lazar, R. M., & Schwartz, D. W. (1994). Brain dysfunction and violent behavior in a man with a congenital subarachnoid cyst. *Hospital and Community Psychiatry, 45*, 714-716.

Parke, R. D., & Slaby, R. G. (1983). The development of aggression. In P. H. Mussen & E. M. Hetherington (Eds.), *Handbook of child psychology* (Vol. 4, pp. 548-605). New York: Wiley.

Parker, R. N., & Toth, A. M. (1990). Family intimacy and homicide: A macro-social approach. *Violence and Victims, 5*, 195-210.

Parker, R. S. (1990). *Traumatic brain injury and neuropsychological impairment*. New York: Springer-Verlag.

Parkes, C. M. (1993). Psychiatric problems following bereavement by murder or manslaughter. *British Journal of Psychiatry, 162*, 49-54.

Parwatikar, S. D., Holcomb, W. R., & Menninger, K. A. (1985). The detection of malingered amnesia in accused murders. *Bulletin of the American Academy of Psychiatry and the Law, 13*, 97-103.

Pasewark, R. A., & McGinley, H. (1985). Insanity plea: National survey of frequency and success. *Journal of Psychiatry and Law, 13*, 101-108.

Pasewark, R. A., Jeffrey, R., & Bieber, S. (1987). Differentiating successful and unsuccessful insanity plea defendants in Colorado. *Journal of Psychiatry and Law, 9*, 55-71.

Pasewark, R. A., Randolph, R. L., & Bieber, S. (1984). Insanity plea: Statutory language and trial procedures. *Journal of Psychiatry and Law, 12*, 399-422.

Pasewark, R. A., Seidenzahl, D., & Pantle, M. L. (1981). Opinions about the insanity plea. *Journal of Forensic Psychology, 8*, 63-72.

Patterson, G. (1993). Orderly change in a stable world: The antisocial trait as a chimera. *Journal of Consulting and Clinical Psychology, 61*, 911-919.

Patterson, G., Cobb, J., & Ray, R. (1972). A social engineering technology for retraining the families of aggressive boys. In H. Adams & I. Unikel (Eds.), *Issues in transient behavior therapy*. Springfield, IL: Charles C Thomas.

Patterson, G., Littman, R., & Bricker, W. (1967). Assertive behavior in children: A step towards a theory of aggression. *Monographs of the Society for Research in Child Development, 44*(4, Serial No. 113).

Patterson, G., Reid, J., & Dishion, T. (1992). *Antisocial boys*. Eugene, OR: Castalia.

Patterson, G. R., Capaldi, D., & Bank, L. (1991). An early starter model for predicting delinquency. In D. J. Pepler & K. H. Rubin (Eds.), *The development and treatment of childhood aggression* (pp. 390-410). Hillsdale, NJ: Lawrence Erlbaum Associates.

Patterson, G. R., DeBaryshe, B. D., & Ramsey, E. (1989). A developmental perspective on antisocial behavior. *American Psychologist, 44*(2), 329-335.

Paulsen, S., & Hall, H. V. (1991). Common sense clinical process factors in deception analysis. *Forensic Reports, 4*, 37-39.

Pearce, K. I. (1977). Police negotiations: A new role for

the community psychiatrist. *Canadian Psychiatric Association Journal, 22*, 171-175.

People v. Conley, 64 Cal.2d 310, 411 P.2d (1966).

People v. Gorshen, 51 Cal.2d 216, 336 P.2d 491 (1959).

People v. Wells, 202 P.2d 534 (1949).

People v. Wetmore, 22 Cal.3d 318, 583 P.2d 130 (1978).

Perdue, W. C., & Lester, D. (1973). Those who murder kin: A Rorschach study. *Perceptual and Motor Skills, 36*, 606.

Perkins, D. (1991). Clinical work with sex offenders in secure settings. In C. R. Hollins & K. Howell (Eds.), *Clinical approaches to sex offenders and their victims* (pp. 151-177). West Sussex: Wiley.

Perkinson, H. (1995). Getting better: Television and moral progress. In A. Alexander & J. Hanson (Eds.), *Taking sides: Clashing views on controversial issues in mass media and society* (3rd ed.) (pp. 9-16). Guilford, C T: Dushkin Publishing.

Pernanen, K. (1991). *Alcohol in human violence.* New York: Guilford Press.

Perog-Good, M. A. (1992). Sexual abuse in dating relationships. In E. C. Viano (Ed.), *Intimate violence: Interdisciplinary perspective.* Washington, DC: Hemisphere Publishing Corp.

Perr, I. N. (1975). Psychiatric testimony and the Rashomon phenomenon. *Bulletin of the American Academy of Psychiatry and the Law, 3*, 83-98.

Perrine, K., & Congett, S. (1994). Neurobehavioral problems in epilepsy. *Neurologic Clinics, 12*, 129-152.

Perry, D. G., Perry, L. C., & Boldziar, J. P. (1990). Learning of aggression. In M. Lewis & S. M. Miller (Eds.), *Handbook of developmental psychopathology* (pp. 135-142). New York: Plenum Press.

Persons, R. W., & Marks, P. A. (1971). The violent 4-3 MMPI personality type. *Journal of Consulting and Clinical Psychology, 36*, 189-196.

Petee, T. A., & Walsh, A. (1986). Violent delinquency, race, and the Wechsler performance-verbal discrepancy. *Journal of Social Psychology, 127*, 353-354.

Petersilia, J., Greenwood, P., & Lavin, M. (1977). *Criminal careers of habitual felons.* Santa Monica, CA: Rand.

Peterson, R. C., & Stillman, R. C. (1979). Phencyclidine: A review. *Journal of the Medical Society of New Jersey, 76*, 139-144.

Phillips, D. (1973). *Skyjack: The story of air piracy.* London: Harrap and Company.

Piaget, J. (1936). *The language and thought of the child.* New York: Harcourt, Brace, and World.

Piaget, J. (1952). *The origin of intelligence in children.* New York: International Universities Press.

Piers, M. (1978). *Infanticide.* New York: W. W. Norton & Co.

Pillemar, K., & Finkelhor, D. (1988). The prevalence of

elder abuse: A random sample survey. *The Gerontologist, 28*(1), 51-57.

Pincus, J. H. (1985). Limbic system and violence. In J. H. Pincus & G. J. Tucker (Eds.), *Behavioral neurology* (3rd ed.). Oxford: Oxford University Press.

Piotrowski, Z. A. (1957). *Perceptanalysis.* New York, NY: Macmillan.

Plass, P. (1993, June). African American family homicide: Patterns in partner, parent, and child victimization, 1985-1987. *Journal of Black Studies, 23,* pp. 515-538.

Pleck E., Pleck, J. H., Grossman, M., & Bart, P. B. (1978). The battered data syndrome: A comment on Steinmetz' article. *Victimology, 2*(3-4), 680-684.

Poirier, J. (1991). Disputed custody and concerns of parental violence. *Psychotherapy in Private Practice, 9*(3), 7-23.

Pokorny, A. D. (1965). A comparison of homicides in two cities. *Journal of Criminal Law, Criminology and Police Science, 56,* 479-487.

Police Chief. (1995, January). IACP summit: Murder. *Police Chief,* Vol. LXII, pp. 30-31.

Pollack, L. (1983). *Forgotten children: Parent-child relations from 1500-1900.* Cambridge: Cambridge University Press.

Pontius, A. A. (1973). Conceptual model of minimal brain dysfunction. General Discussion, Proceedings of the MBD Conference, 1972. *Annals of the New York Academy of Sciences, 205,* 61-63.

Pontius, A. A. (1974). Basis for a neurological test of frontal-lobe system maturational lag in juvenile delinquents shown in narratives test. *Adolescence, 44,* 509-518.

Pontius, A. A. (1987). "Psychotic trigger reaction": Neuro-psychiatric and neuro-biological (limbic?) aspects of homicide, reflecting on normal action. *Integrative Psychiatry, 5,* 116-139.

Pontius, A. A. (1993). Neuropsychiatric update of the crime "profile" and "signature" in single or serial homicides: Rule out limbic psychotic trigger reaction. *Psychological Reports, 73,* 875-892.

Porter, B. (1983, April). Mind hunters: Tracking down killers with the FBI's psychological profiling team. *Psychology Today,* 162-170.

Post, R. D., Willett, A. R., House, R. M., Black, S. M., & Weissberg, M. P. (1980). A preliminary report of domestic violence among psychiatric inpatients. *American Journal of Psychiatry, 137,* 974-975.

Postman, N. (1986). *Amusing ourselves to death: Public discourse in the age of show business.* New York: Penguin Books.

Poussaint, A. F. (1983). Black-on-Black homicide: A psychological-political perspective. *Victimology, 8*(3-4), 161-169.

Prentice-Dunn, S., & Rogers, R.W. (1983). Deindividuation in aggression. In R. G. Geen & E. I. Donnerstein (Eds.), *Aggression, theoretical and empirical reviews,* Vol. 2, pp. 155-171. NY: Academic Press.

Prigatano, G. P. (1990). Effective traumatic brain injury

rehabilitation: Team/patient interaction. In E. D. Bigler (Ed.), *Traumatic brain injury* (pp. 297-312). Austin, TX: Pro-Ed.

Prigatano, G. P. (1994). Individuality, lesion location, and psychotherapy after brain injury. In A. L. Christensen & B. P. Uzzell (Eds.), *Brain injury and neuropsychological rehabilitation* (pp. 173-186). Hillsdale, NJ: Erlbaum.

Prigatano, G. P. & Klonoff, P. S., (1990). Psychotherapy and neuropsychological assessment after brain injury. In E. D. Bigler (Ed.), *Traumatic brain injury* (pp. 313-330). Austin, TX: Pro-Ed.

Prigatano, G. P. & Schacter, D. L. (1991). *Awareness of deficit after brain injury.* New York: Oxford.

Prins, H. (1985). Vampirism: A clinical condition. *British Journal of Psychiatry, 146,* 666-668.

Prior, M. (1992). Childhood temperament. *The Journal of Child Psychology and Psychiatry and Allied Disciplines, 33*(1), 249-279.

Prior, M. (1993). Sex differences in psychological adjustment from infancy to 8 years. *Journal of the American Academy of Child and Adolescent Psychiatry, 32*(2), 291-304.

Pritchard, D. (1977). Stable predictors of recidivism. *Journal Supplement Abstract Service, 7,* 72.

Pritchard, D. (1990). *Tests of Neuropsychological Malingering.* Manual and software available directly through David Pritchard, PhD, ABPP, Atlanta, Georgia.

Pritchard, D. (1995). Personal communication.

Prochaska, J., DiClemente, C., & Norcross, C. (1992). In search of how people change: Applications to addictive behaviors. *American Psychologist, 47*(9), 1102-1114.

Profitt v. Florida, 428 U.S. 242 (1976).

PROMIS Research Project (1977). *Highlights of Interim Findings and Implications.* Washington, DC: Institute for Law and Social Research.

Pynoos, R. S. & Eth, S. (1986). Witness to violence: The child interview. *Journal of the American Academy of Child Psychiatry, 25,* 306-319.

Pynoos, R. S. & Nader, K. (1988). Psychological first aid and treatment approach to children exposed to community violence: Research implications. *Journal of Traumatic Stress, 1,* 445-473.

Pynoos, R. S. & Nader, K. (1990). Children's exposure to violence and traumatic death. *Psychiatric Annals, 20,* 334-344.

Pynoos, R. S., Nader, K., Frederick, C., Gonda, L., & Stuber, M. (1987). Grief reactions in school age children following a sniper attack at school. *Israeli Journal of Psychiatry and Related Sciences, 24*(1-2), 53-63.

Quadagno, D., Briscoe, R., & Quadagno, J. (1977). Effect of perinatal gonadal hormones on selected non-sexual behavior patterns: A critical assessment of the non-human and human literature. *Psychological Bulletin, 84,* 62-80.

Quay, H. (1986). Conduct disorders. In H. Quay & J. Nerry (Eds.), *Psychopathological disorders of childhood* (3rd ed.) New York: John Wiley & Sons.

Quinsey, V. L., Arnold, L. S., & Pruesse, M. G. (1980). MMPI profiles of men referred for a pretrial psychiatric assessment as a function of offense type. *Journal of Clinical Psychology, 36,* 410-417.

Quinsey, V. L., Maguire, A., & Varney, G. W. (1983). Assertion and overcontrolled hostility among mentally disordered murderers. *Journal of Consulting and Clinical Psychology, 51*, 550-556.

Rahe, R. H., Karson, S., Howard, N. S., Rubin, R. T., & Poland, R. E. (1990). Psychological and physiological assessments on American hostages freed from captivity in Iran. *Psychosomatic Medicine, 52*, 1-16.

Raine, A. (1993). *The psychopathology of crime.* San Diego, CA: Academic.

Raine, A., Buchsbaum, M. S., Stanley, J., Lottenberg, S., Abel, L., & Stoddard, J. (1994). Selective reductions in prefrontal glucose metabolism in murderers. *Biological Psychiatry, 36*, 365-373.

Raine, A., Lencz, T., & Scerbo, A. (1995). Neuroimaging, neuropsychology, neurochemistry and psychophysiology. In J. J. Ratey (Ed.), *Neuropsychiatry of personality disorders* (pp. 50-78). Cambridge, MA: Blackwell.

Raine, A. & Scerbo, A. (1991). Biological theories of violence. In J. S. Milner (Ed.), *Neuropsychology of Aggression* (pp. 1-26). Boston: Kluwer.

Ramani, V. & Gumnit, R.J. (1981). Intensive monitoring of epileptic patients with a history of episodic aggression. *Archives of Neurology, 38*, 570-571.

Rankin, R. (1995, March 16). No crusade by Clinton on violence in the movies. *The Philadelphia Inquirer*, pp. E1, E8.

Rappaport, J. & Holden, K. (1981). Prevention of violence. In J. R. Hays, T. K. Roberts, & K. S. Soloway (Eds.), *Violence and the violent individual.* New York: Spectrum.

Raskin, D. (Ed.). (1989). *Psychological methods in criminal investigations and evidence.* New York: Springer.

Ratey, J. J., Middeldorp-Crispijn, C. W., & Leveroni, C. L. (1995). Influence of attention problems on the development of personality. In J. J. Ratey (Ed.), *Neuropsychiatry of personality disorders* (pp. 79-119). Cambridge, MA: Blackwell.

Rawlins, M. D. (1973). Self-control and interpersonal violence. *Criminology, 11*, 23-48.

Reich, W. T. (1995). *Encyclopedia of bioethics.* New York: Macmillan Publishing Co.

Reid, J. (1993). Prevention of conduct disorder before and after school entry: Relating interventions to developmental findings. *Development and Psychopathology, 5*, 243-262.

Reidy, T. (1995). *Personal communication.*

Reinisch, J. M. (1981). Prenatal exposure to synthetic progestin increases potential for aggression in humans. *Science, 211*, 1171-1173.

Reinisch, J. & Karow, W. (1977). Prenatal exposure to synthetic progestins and estrogens: Effect on human development. *Archives of Sexual Behavior, 6*, 257-288.

Reis, D. (1974). Central neurotransmitters in aggression. *Research Publication of the Association for Research of Nervous Mental Disease, 52*, 119-148.

Reiser, M. (1980). *Handbook of Investigative Hypnosis* (pp. 70-74). Los Angeles: Lehi.

Reiss, A. J., Jr. & Roth, J. A. (1993). *Understanding and preventing violence.* Washington, DC: National Academy Press.

Reitan, R. M. & Wolfson, D. (1988). *Traumatic brain injury.* Volume II. Tucson, AZ: Neuropsychology Press.

Reitan, R. M. & Wolfson, D. (1993). *The Halstead-Reitan neuropsychological test battery* (2d ed.) (pp. 85-92). Tucson, AZ: Neuropsychology Press.

Renken, B., Egeland, B., Marvinney, D., Mangelsdorf, S., & Sroufe, A. (1989). Early childhood antecedents of aggression and passive-withdrawal in early elementary school. *Journal of Personality, 57,* 274-284.

Resnick, P. J. (1969). Child murder by parents: A psychiatric review of filicide. *American Journal of Psychiatry, 126*(3), 325-334.

Resnick, P. J. (1970). Murder of the newborn: A psychiatric review of neonaticide. *American Journal of Psychiatry, 126,* 1414-1420.

Ressler, R., Burgess, A., & Douglass, J. (1988). *Sexual homicide: Patterns and motives.* Lexington, MA: Lexington Books.

Ressler, R., Burgess, A., Douglas, J., Hartman, C., & D'Agostino, R. (1986). Sexual killers and their victims. *Journal of Interpersonal Violence, 1*(3), 288-308.

Ressler, R. K., Burgess, A. W., Douglas, J. E., Hartman, C., & D'agostino, R. (1986). Sexual killers and their victims. *Journal of Interpersonal Violence, 1*(3), 288-308.

Ressler, R. K., Douglas, J. E., Groth, A. N., & Burgess, A. W. (1980, September). Offender profiles: A multidisciplinary approach. *FBI Law Enforcement Bulletin,* 157-161.

Restak, R. (1993). The neurological defense of violent crime. *Archives of Neurology, 50,* 869-871.

Revitch, E. (1957). Sex murder and sex aggression. *Journal of the Medical Society of New Jersey, 54,* 519-524.

Revitch, E. (1964). Paroxysmal manifestations of non-epileptic origin: Catathymic attacks. *Diseases of the Nervous System, 25,* 662-669.

Revitch, E. (1975). Psychiatric evaluation and classification of antisocial activities. *Diseases of the Nervous System, 36,* 419-421.

Revitch, E. (1977). Classification of offenders for prognosis and dispositional evaluation. *Bulletin of the Academy of Law and Psychiatry, 5,* 1-11 and 41-50.

Revitch, E. & Schlesinger, L. B. (1978). Murder: Evaluation, classification and prediction. In I. L. Kutash, S. B. Kutash, & L. B. Schlesinger (Eds.), *Violence: Perspectives on murder and aggression.* San Francisco: Jossey-Bass.

Revitch, E. & Schlesinger, L. B. (1981). *Psychopathology of homicide.* Springfield, IL: Charles C Thomas.

Revitch, E. & Schlesinger, L. B. (1989). *Sex murder and sex aggression.* Springfield, IL: Charles C Thomas.

Rhode Island v. Smith, 512 A.2d 818 (1986).

Rice, M. E. & Harris, G. T. (1990) The predictors of insanity acquittal. *International Journal of Law and Psychiatry, 13,* 217-224.

Richters, J. & Cicchetti, D. (1993). Mark Twain meets DSM-III-R: Conduct disorder, development, and the concept of harmful dysfunction. *Development and Psychopathology, 5,* 5-29.

Richters, J. E. & Martinez, P. (1993). The NIMH community violence project: I. Children as victims of, and witnesses to violence. In D. Reiss, J. E. Richters, M. Radke-Yarrow, & D. Scharff (Eds.), *Children and violence* (pp. 7-21). New York: Guilford Press.

Rickey, C. (1995, April 2). Once an adult movie, now a hoot. *Philadelphia Inquirer*, pp. 5, 14.

A riddle wrapped in a mystery inside an enigma (1994). *New Yorker, 70*(41), 45-46.

Riddoch, M. J. & Humphreys, G. W. (Eds.). (1994). *Cognitive neuropsychology and cognitive rehabilitation.* Hillsdale, NJ: Erlbaum.

Ritz Film Bill (1995, March/April). John Sayles changes course. Philadelphia: Entropy Design, pp. 15-17.

Rivinus, T. M. & Larimer, M. E. (1993). Violence, alcohol, other drugs, and the college student (Chapter 4, pp.71-119). In L. C. Whitaker & J. W. Pollard (Eds.), *Campus violence: Kinds, causes, and cures.* New York: The Haworth Press. Published simultaneously in *Journal of College Student Psychotherapy, 8,* 1/2, 3, 1993.

Rizzo, N. D. (1982). Murder in Boston: Killers and their victims. *International Journal of Offender Therapy and Comparative Criminology, 26*(1), 36-42.

Roberts, J. V. & Grossman, M. G. (1993). Sexual homicide in Canada: A descriptive analysis. *Annals of Sex Research, 6,* 5-25.

Roberts, T. K., Mock, L. T., & Johnstone, E. E. (1981). Psychological aspects of the etiology of violence. In J. R. Hays, T. K. Roberts, & K. S. Soloway (Eds.), *Violence and the violent individual.* New York: Spectrum.

Robertson, G., Taylor, P. J., & Gunn, J. C. (1987). Does violence have cognitive correlates? *British Journal of Psychiatry, 151,* 63-68.

Robins, L. N. (1966). *Deviant children grow up.* Baltimore: Williams & Wilkins.

Robins, L. N. (1991). Conduct disorder. *The Journal of Child Psychology and Psychiatry and Allied Disciplines, 32,* 193-209.

Rodin, E. (1973). Psychomotor epilepsy and aggressive behavior. *Archives of General Psychiatry, 28,* 210-213.

Rogan, R. G., Donohue, W. A., & Lyles, J. (1990). Gaining and exercising control in hostage negotiations using empathic perspective-taking. *International Journal of Group Tensions, 20,* 77-91.

Rogers, C. (1993). Gang-related homicides in Los Angeles County. *Journal of Forensic Sciences, 38*(4), 831-834.

Rogers, C. R. (1972). *Becoming partners*. New York: Delacourte.

Rogers, R. (1984). *R-CRAS: Rogers Criminal Responsibility Assessment Scales*. Odessa, FL: Psychological Assessment Resources.

Rogers, R. (Ed.). (1988). *Clinical assessment of malingering and deception*. New York: Guilford Press.

Rogers, R. & Ewing, C. P. (1992). The measurement of insanity. *International Journal of Law and Psychiatry, 15*, 113-123.

Rogers, R. & Seman, W. (1983). Murder and criminal responsibility: An examination of MMPI profiles. *Behavioral Sciences and the Law, 1*, 89-95.

Rose, H. M. & McClain, P. D. (1990). *Race place and risk: Black homicide in urban America*. Albany, NY: SUNY Press.

Rose, L. (1986). *The massacre of the innocents: Infanticide in Britain 1800-1939*. London: Routledge & Kegan Paul.

Rose, R. (1995). Genes and human behavior. *Annual Review of Psychology, 46*, 625-54.

Rosenbaum, A. & Mauero, R. D. (1990). Perpetrators of spouse abuse. In R. T. Ammerman & M. Hersen (Eds.), *Treatment of family violence: A sourcebook*. New York: John Wiley & Sons.

Rosenbaum, M. (1990). The role of depression in couples involved in murder-suicide and homicide. *American Journal of Psychiatry, 147*(8), 1036-1039.

Rosenbaum, M. & Bennett, B. (1986). Homicide and depression. *American Journal of Psychiatry, 143*, 367-370.

Rosenfield, R., Decker, S., & Kohfield, C. (1993). Different levels, common causes: St. Louis homicide rates in national perspective. In C. R. Block & R. L. Block (Eds.), *Questions and answers in lethal and non-lethal violence. Proceedings of the first annual Workshop of the Homicide Research Working Group*. Washington, DC: U.S. Department of Justice, National Institute of Justice Research Report.

Rosman, J. & Resnick, P. (1989). Sexual attraction to corpses: A psychiatric review of necrophilia. *Bulletin of the American Academy of Psychiatry and Law, 17*(2), 153-163.

Roth, J. (1994, February). Understanding and preventing violence. *National Institute of Justice Research in Brief*, 1-20.

Roth, J. A. (1994a, February). *Psychoactive substances and violence* [Research in Brief]. Washington, DC: U.S. Department of Justice.

Roth, J. A. (1994b, February). *Understanding and preventing violence* [Research in Brief]. Washington, DC: U.S. Department of Justice.

Rothbaum, F. & Weisz, J. (1994). Parental caregiving and child externalizing behavior in nonclinical samples: A meta-analysis. *Psychological Bulletin, 116*, 55-74.

Rotter, M. & Goodman, W. (1993). The relationship between insight and control in obsessive-compulsive disorder: Implications for the insanity defense. *Bulletin of American Academy of Psychiatric Law, 21*(2), 245-252.

Rotton, J., Barry, T., Frey, J., & Soler, E. (1978). Air pollution and interpersonal attraction. *Journal of Applied Social Psychology, 8,* 57-71.

Rubin, B. (1972). Prediction of dangerousness in mentally ill criminals. *Archives of General Psychiatry, 27,* 397-409.

Rueth, T. W. (1993). On site psychological evaluation of a hostage taker. *Psychological Reports, 73,* 659-664.

Ruff, C. F., Templer, D. I., & Ayers, J. L. (1976). The intelligence of rapists. *Archives of Sexual Behavior, 5,* 327-329.

Rule, A. (1988). *Small sacrifices: A true story of passion and murder.* London: Corgi Press.

Rule, B. G., Taylor, B. R., & Dobbs, A. R. (1987). Priming effects of heat on aggressive thoughts. *Social Cognition, 5,* 131-143.

Ruotolo, A. (1968). Dynamics of sudden murder. *American Journal of Psychoanalysis, 28,* 162-176.

Rushforth, N. B., Ford, A., Hirsch, C., Rushforth, N. M., & Adelson, L. (1977). Violent death in a metropolitan county. *New England Journal of Medicine, 297,* 531-538.

Rushton, P. (1988). Epigenetic rules in moral development: Distal-proximal approaches to altruism and aggression. *Aggressive Behavior, 14,* 35-50.

Russel, D. (1986). *The secret trauma: Incest in the lives of girls and women.* New York: Basic Books.

Russel, D. E. (1982). The prevalence and incidence of forcible rape and attempted rape of females. *Victimology: An International Journal, 7,* 81-93.

Russell, D. E. H. (1984). *Sexual exploitation: Rape, child sexual abuse, and workplace harassment.* Beverly Hills: Sage.

Rutter, M. (1970). Sex differences in children's responses to family stress. In E. Anthony & C. Koupernik (Eds.), *The child in his family.* New York: Wiley.

Rutter, M. (1985). Resilience in the face of adversity. *British Journal of Psychiatry, 147,* 598-611.

Rutter, M. (1989). Isle of Wight revisited: Twenty-five years of child psychiatric epidemiology. *Journal of the American Academy of Child & Adolescent Psychiatry, 28,* 633-653.

Rutter, M. (1994). Family discord and conduct disorder: Cause, consequence, or correlate? *Journal of Family Psychology, 8,* 170-186.

Rutter, M. & Mawhood, L. (1991). The long-term psychosocial sequelae of specific developmental disorders of speech and language. In M. Rutter & P. Casaer (Eds.), *Biological risk factors for psychosocial disorders* (pp. 233-259). New York: Cambridge University Press.

Rutter, M., Macdonald, H., Le Couteur, A., Harrington, R., Bolton, P., & Bailey, A. (1990). Genetic factors in child psychiatric disorder-II. Empirical findings. *Journal of Child Psychiatry and Psychology, 31,* 39-83.

Rychlak, J. F. & Rychlak, R. J. (1990). The insanity defense and the question of human agency. *New Ideas in Psychology, 8*(1), 3-24.

Rynearson, E. K. (1984). Bereavement after homicide: A descriptive study. *American Journal of Psychiatry, 141,* 1452-1454.

Rynearson, E. K. & McCreery, J. M. (1993). Bereavement after homicide: A synergism of trauma and loss. *American Journal of Psychiatry, 150,* 258-261.

Rynearson, T. (1994). Psychotherapy of bereavement after homicide. *Journal of Psychotherapy Practice and Research, 3,* 341-347.

Sagan, C. (1980). *Cosmos.* New York: Random House.

Salinsky, M., Kanter, R., & Dasheiff, R. (1987). Effectiveness of multiple EEGs in supporting the diagnosis of epilepsy: An operational curve. *Epilepsia, 28,* 331-334.

Sally Jesse Raphael (1995, March 3). National Broadcasting Company (Philadelphia area Channel 2, 10 a.m.)

Sanders, B. (1994). *A is for ox: Violence, electronic media, and the silencing of the written word.* New York: Pantheon Books.

Sandys, M. (1991). *Life or death decisions of capital jurors: Preliminary findings from Kentucky.* Paper presented at the annual meeting of 5th American Society of Criminology, San Francisco, CA.

Sanson, A., Smart, D., Prior, M., and Oberklaid, F. (1993). Precursors of hyperactivity and aggression. *Journal of the American Academy of Child and Adolescent Psychiatry, 32,* 1207-1216.

Sargent, D. A. (1972). The lethal situation: Transmission of urge to kill from parent to child. In J. Fawcett (Ed.), *Dynamics of violence.* Chicago: AMA.

Satten, J., Menninger, K. A., & Mayman, M. (1960). Murder without apparent motive: A study in personality disorganization. *American Journal of Psychiatry, 117,* 48-53.

Saul, L. J. (1976). *The psychodynamics of hostility.* New York: Aronson.

Saunders, E. (1989). Neonaticides following "secret" pregnancies: Seven case reports. *Public Health Reports, 104*(4), 368-372.

Scarr, S. & Eisenberg, M. (1993). Childcare research: Issues, perspectives, and results. In L. W. Porter & M. R. Rosenzweig (Eds.), *Annual review of psychology* (Vol. 44, pp. 613-644). Palo Alto, CA: Annual Reviews Inc.

Schacter, D. L. (1986). Amnesia and crime: How much do we really know? *American Psychologist, 41,* 286-295.

Schafer, R. (1954). *Psychoanalytic interpretation in Rorschach testing.* New York, NY: Grune & Stratton.

Schaffer, C. E., Pettigrew, C. G., Blouin, D., & Edwards, D. W. (1983). Multivariate classification of female offender MMPI profiles. *Journal of Crime and Justice, 6,* 57-66.

Schalling, D. (1978). Personality correlates of plasma testosterone levels in young delinquents: An example of person-situation interaction? In S. A. Mednick, T. E. Moffitt, and S. A. Stack (Eds.), *The causes of crime: New biological approaches* (pp. 283-291). New York: Cambridge University Press.

Schatzman, M. (1986). To sleep perchance to kill. *New Scientist, 26*, 60-62.

Scheflin, Alan W. (1978). *The mind manipulators*. Paddington Press.

Scheper-Hughes, N. (1989, October). Death without weeping: Has poverty ravaged mother love in the shantytowns of Brazil? *Natural History*, 8-16.

Schiffer, R. B., & Babigian, H. M. (1984). Behavioral disorders in multiple sclerosis, temporal lobe epilepsy, and amyotrophic lateral sclerosis. *Archives of Neurology, 41*, 1067-1069.

Schlain, B. (1993, April). Channel surfing — strictly male turf: Overuse of the television's remote control. *Cosmopolitan*, p. 110.

Schlesinger, L. B. (1980). Distinctions between psychopathic, sociopathic, and anti-social personality disorders. *Psychological Reports, 47*, 15-21.

Schlesinger, L.B. (1996). The catathymic process: Psychopathology and psychodynamics of extreme aggression. In L. B. Schlesinger (Ed.), *Explorations in criminal psychopathology: Clinical syndromes with forensic implications*. Springfield, IL: Charles C Thomas.

Schlesinger, L. B., & Kutash, I. L. (1981). The criminal fantasy technique: A comparison of sex offenders and substance abusers. *Journal of Clinical Psychology, 37*, 210-218.

Schlesinger, L. B., & Revitch, E. (1980). Stress, violence, and crime. In I. L. Kutash & L. B. Schlesinger (Eds.), *Handbook on stress and anxiety*. San Francisco: Jossey-Bass.

Schlesinger, L. B., & Revitch, E. (1990). Outpatient treatment of the sexually motivated murderer and potential murderer. *Journal of Offender Counseling, Services, and Rehabilitation, 15*, 163-178.

Schloesser, P., Pierpont, J., & Poertner, J. (1992). Active surveillance of child abuse fatalities. *Child Abuse and Neglect, 16*, 3-10.

Schloss, B., & Giesbrecht, N. (1972). *Murder in Canada. A report on capital and non-capital murder statistics, 1961-1970*. Centre of Criminology: University of Toronto.

Schlossberg, H. (1980). Values and organization in hostage and crisis negotiation teams. *Annals of the New York Academy of Sciences, 347*, 113-116.

Schmidt, W. E. (1993, February 23). 2 boys arraigned in abduction and killing of British toddler. *The New York Times*, p. A3.

Schneider, K. (1995, March 13). Hate groups use tools of the electronic trade. *New York Times*, p. A12.

Schonert-Reichl, K., & Offer, D. (1992). Gender differences in adolescent symptoms. In B. B. Lahey & A. E. Kazdin (Eds.), *Advances in clinical psychology* (Vol. 14, pp. 27-54). New York: Plenum Press.

Schrieber, M. (1972). *After-action report of terrorist activities: 20th Olympic games, Munich, West Germany*. Quantico, VA: FBI Academy.

Schut, E. (1995, March/April). Faster, Pussycat! Kill! Kill! *Ritz Film Bill*, p. 30. Philadelphia: Entropy Design.

Schwartz, A. J. (1990). The epidemiology of suicide among students at colleges and universities in the United States (Chapter 2, pp. 25-44). In L. Whitaker & R. Slimak (Eds.), *College student suicide*. New York: The Haworth Press. Published simultaneously in *Journal of College Student Psychotherapy, 4*, 3/4, 1990.

Schwartz, A. J. & Whitaker, L. C. (1990). Suicide among college students: Assessment, treatment, and intervention (Chapter 12, pp. 303-340). In S. Blumenthal & D. Kupfer (Eds.), *Suicide across the life cycle: Risk factors, assessment, and treatment of suicidal patients.* Washington, DC: American Psychiatric Press.

Schwartz, L. L. & Matzkin, R. G. (1993) [Transcripts of proceedings in cases of *Comm. of Penn. vs. Tabitha Buck, Lisa Michelle Lambert, and Lawrence Yunkin* for the murder of Laurie Show.] Unpublished raw data.

Selkin, J. (1976). Rescue fantasies in homicide-suicide. *Suicide Life-Threatening Behavior, 6,* (2).

Selling to school kids. (1995, May). *Consumer Reports,* pp. 327-329.

Sendi, I. B. & Blomgren, P. G. (1975). A comparative study of predictive criteria in the predisposition of homicidal adolescents. *American Journal of Psychiatry, 132,* 423-427.

Seplow, S. (1994, December 2). The more they watch, the more they fear. *The Philadelphia Inquirer,* pp. A1, A21.

Serber, M. (1970). Shame aversion therapy. *Journal of Behavior Therapy and Experimental Psychiatry, 1,* 213-215.

Serbin, L., Sprafkin, C., Elman, M., & Doyle, A. (1984). The early development of sex differentiated patterns of social behavior. *Canadian Journal of Social Science, 14,* 350-363.

Seventy-six in law enforcement slain in '94 F.B.I. says.

(1995, April 3). *New York Times,* p. A14.

Sgroi, S. (1982). *Handbook of clinical intervention in child sexual abuse.* Lexington, MA: Lexington Books.

Shalinsky, A. & Glascock, A. (1988). Killing infants and the aged in nonindustrial societies: Removing the liminal. *The Social Science Journal, 25*(3), 277-287.

Shapiro, D. (1965). *Neurotic styles.* New York: Basic Books, Inc.

Shapiro, F. (1989a). Efficacy of the eye movement desensitization procedure in the treatment of traumatic memories. *Journal of Traumatic Stress, 2,* 199-223.

Shapiro, F. (1989b). Eye movement desensitization: A new treatment for post-traumatic stress disorder. *Journal of Behavioral Therapy and Experimental Psychiatry, 20,* 211-217.

Shaw, D., Emery, R., & Tuer, M. (1993). Parental functioning and children's adjustment in families of divorce: A prospective study. *Journal of Abnormal Child Psychology, 21,* 119-134.

Shawver, L. & Jew, C. (1978). Predicting violent behavior from WAIS characteristics: A replication failure. *Journal of Consulting and Clinical Psychology, 46,* 206.

Shaywitz, S. & Shaywitz, B. (1988). Attention deficit disorder: current perspectives. In J. F. Kavanagh & T. J. Truss, Jr. (Eds.), *Learning disabilities: Proceedings of the national conference* (pp. 369-389). Parkton, NJ: York Press.

Shaywitz, S., Shaywitz, B., Fletcher, J., & Escobar, M. (1990). Prevalence of reading disability in boys and girls. *Journal of the American Medical Association, 264,* 998-1002.

Shaywitz, B., Shaywitz, S., Pugh, K., Constable, R., Skudlarski, P., Fulbright, R., Bronem, R., Fletcher, J., Shankweller, D., Katz, L., & Gore, J. (1995). Sex differences in the functional organization of the brain for language. *Science, 373*, 607-609.

Shepard, M. (1987). *Gandhi today.* Arcata, CA: Simple Productions Press.

Sherman, L., & Berke, R. (1989). The specific deterrent effects of arrest for domestic assault. *American Sociological Review, 49*, 261-272.

Sherman, L. W., Schmidt, J. D., Rogan, D., & Deriso, C. (1991). Predicting domestic homicide: Prior police contact and gun threats. In Steinman, M. (Ed.), *Woman battering: Policy responses* (pp. 73-93). Cincinnati: Anderson Publishing Company.

Shooter, E., & Hall, H. V. (1990). Explicit alternative testing for deliberate distortion: Toward an abbreviated format. *Forensic Reports, 3*, 115-119.

Short, J. F. (Ed.). (1968). *Gang delinquency and delinquent subcultures.* New York: Harper & Row.

Showalter, C. R., Bonnie, R. J., & Roddy, V. (1980). The spousal-homicide syndrome. *International Journal of Law and Psychiatry, 3*, 117-141.

Shuman, S. I. (1977). *Psychosurgery and the medical control of violence* (pp. 240-241). Detroit: Wayne State Press.

Siano, B. (1995). Frankenstein must be destroyed: Chasing the monster of television violence. In *Taking sides: Clashing views on controversial issues in mass media and society* (3rd ed.) (pp. 28-35). Guilford, C T : Dushkin Publishing.

Siegel, R. K. (1984). Hostage hallucinations: Visual imagery induced by isolation and life-threatening stress. *The Journal of Nervous and Mental Disease, 172*, 264-272.

Signorielli, N. (1991). *A sourcebook on children and television.* Westport, CT: Greenwood Publishing.

Signorielli, N., & Morgan, M. (1990). *Cultivation analysis: New directions in media effects research.* Newbury Park, CA: Sage Publications.

Silver, E., Cirincione, C., & Steadman, H. J. (1994). Demythologizing inaccurate perceptions of the insanity defense. *Law and Human Behavior, 18*(1), 63-70.

Silver, J. M., & Yudofsky, S. C. (1987). Aggressive

behavior in patients with neuropsychiatric disorders. *Psychiatric Annals, 17*(6), 367-370.

Silverman, R. & Mukherjee, S.K. (1987). Intimate homicide: An analysis of violent social relationships. *Behavioral Sciences and the Law, 5*(1), 37-47.

Silverman, R. A. & Kennedy, L. W. (1988). Women who kill their children. *Violence and Victims, 3*(2), 113-127.

Silverstein, L. B. (1991). Transforming the debate about child care and maternal employment. *American Psychologist, 46*(10), 1025-1032.

Sima, A. A. F., D'Amato, C., Defendini, R. F., Jones, M. Z., Foster, N. L., Lynch, T., & Wilhelmsen, K. C. (1994). Primary limbic gliosis familial and sporadic cases. *Brain Pathology, 4*, 538.

Simmons, J. G., Johnson, J. L., Gouvier, W. D., & Muzyczka, M. J. (1981). The Meyer-Megargee inmate typology: Dynamic or unstable? *Criminal Justice and Behavior, 15*, 49-55.

Simon, L. M. I. (1995). A therapeutic jurisprudence approach to the legal processing of domestic violence cases. *Psychology, Public Policy and Law, 1*, 43-79.

Simon, R. I. & Blum, R. A. (1987). After the terrorist incident: Psychotherapeutic treatment of former hostages. *American Journal of Psychotherapy, 41*, 194-200.

Singer, D. G. & Singer, J. L. (1990). *The house of make-believe: Children's play and the developing imagination.* Cambridge, MA: Harvard University Press.

Skoff, B. F. (1988). The utility of neuropsychological assessments of mentally retarded individuals. In D. C. Russo & J. H. Kedesdy (Eds.), *Behavioral medicine with the developmentally disabled* (pp. 161-170). New York: Plenum.

Skorneck, C. (1994, July 25). Serious crimes up among juveniles. *Chicago Sun Times*, p. 9.

Slobogin, D. (1989). The ultimate "issue" issue. *Behavioral Sciences and the Law, 7*, 259-266.

Slovenko, R. (1977). Criminal justice procedures in civil commitment. *Hospital and Community Psychiatry, 28*, 817-826.

Slovenko, R. (1993). The multiple personality and the criminal law. *Medicine and Law, 12*, 329-340.

Smith, D. & Over, R. (1987). Does fantasy-induced sexual arousal habituate? *Behavior Research and Therapy, 25*(6), 477-485.

Smith, G. A. & Hall, J. A. (1982). Evaluating Michigan's guilty but mentally ill verdict: An empirical study. *Journal of Law Reform, 16*, 77-114.

Smith, J. T. & English, M. J. (1978). Alternatives in psychiatric testimony on dangerousness. *Journal of Forensic Science, 23*, 588-595.

Smith, L. & Mehren, E. (1994, November 5). Why does a mother kill her child? *Los Angeles Times*, pp. A1, A4.

Smith, M. D., Devine, J. A., & Sheley, J. F. (1992). Crime and unemployment: Effects across age and race categories. *Sociological Perspectives, 35*(4), 551-572.

Smith, S. N. & Brown, E. (1978). Necrophilia and lust murder. *Bulletin of the American Academy of Psychiatry and Law, 6,* 259-268.

Snow, R. E. & Swanson, J. (1992). Instructional psychology: Aptitude, adaptation, and assessment. In M. R. Rosenzweig, and L. W. Porter (Eds.), *Annual review of psychology.* Palo Alto, CA: Annual Review.

Snowling, M. (1991). Developmental reading disorders. *Journal of Child Psychology and Psychiatry, 32,* 49-73.

Sohlberg, M. M. & Mateer, C. A. (1989). *Introduction to cognitive rehabilitation.* New York: Guilford.

Solzhenitsyn, A. I. (1978, June 8). *Solzhenitsyn on Western decline* (Harvard University commencement address).

Sonkin, D., Martin, D., & Walker, L., (Eds.). (1985). *The male batterer: A treatment approach.* New York: Springer.

Sonkin, D. J. & Auerbach-Walker, L. E. (1985). *The male batterer.* New York: Springer.

Sonuga-Barke, E. J. S., Lamparelli, M., Stevenson, J., Thompson, M., & Henry, A. (1994). Behaviour problems and pre-school intellectual attainment: The association of hyperactivity and conduct problems. *Journal of Child Psychology & Psychiatry, 35*(5), 949-960.

Soskis, D. (1983). Behavioral scientists and law enforcement personnel: Working together on the problem of terrorism. *Behavioral Sciences and the Law, 1,* 47-58.

Soskis, D. A. & Van Zandt, C. R. (1986). Hostage negotiation: Law enforcement's most effective nonlethal weapon. *Behavioral Sciences & the Law, 4,* 423-435.

Speece, M. W. & Brent, S. B. (1992). The acquisition of a mature understanding of three components of the concept of death. *Death Studies, 16,* 211-229.

Spellacy, F. (1977). Neuropsychological differences between violent and nonviolent adolescents. *Journal of Clinical Psychology, 33,* 966-969.

Spellacy, F. (1978). Neuropsychological discrimination between violent and nonviolent men. *Journal of Clinical Psychology, 34,* 49-52.

Speltz, M., Greenberg, M., & DeKlyen, M. (1990). Attachment in preschoolers with disruptive behavior: A comparison of clinic-referred and non-problem children. *Development and Psychopathology, 2,* 31-46.

Spiegal, J. P. (1972). Toward a theory of collective violence. In J. Fawcett (Ed.), *Dynamics of violence.* Chicago: AMA.

Spindler, A. M. (1995, March 16). In Paris, clothes that

look tough, masculine and dangerous. *New York Times*, p. C13.

Sprang, M. V., McNeil, J. S., & Wright, R. (1989, March). Psychological changes after the murder of a significant other. *Social Casework: The Journal of Contemporary Social Work*, 159-164.

Stacey, W. A., Hazlewood, L. R., & Shupe, A. (1994). *The violent couple*. Westport, CN: Praeger.

Stanovich, K. (1994). Annotation: Does dyslexia exist? *Journal of Child Psychology and Psychiatry, 35*, 579-595.

Staples, R. (1986). The masculine way of violence. In D. F. Hawkins (Ed.), *Homicide among Black Americans*. New York: University Press of America.

Stark, E. & Flitcraft, A. (1988). Violence among intimates: An epidemiological review. In V. B. Van Hasselt, R. L. Morrison, A. S. Bellack, & M. Hersen (Eds.), *Handbook of family violence* (pp. 293-317). New York: Plenum.

Stark, E., Flitcraft, A., Zuckerman, D., Grey, A., Robinson, J., & Frazier, W. (1981). *Wife abuse in the medical setting: An introduction for health personnel* [monograph series no. 7]. Washington, DC: U.S. Government Printing Office.

State of Hawaii v. Dumlao, 715 P.2d 822 (Haw.App. 1986).

State of Hawaii v. Rodriguez, 679 P.2d 615 (Haw. 1984).

State of Maine v. Anaya, 438 A.2d 892 (Me. 1981).

State of Montana v. Grieg, Billings, Montana (Mont. 1977).

State of New Jersey v. Badger, 551 A.2d 207 (N.J. 1988).

State of New Jersey v. Kelly, 478 A.2d 364 (N.J. 1984).

State of North Dakota v. Leidholm, 334 N.W.2d 811 (N.D. 1983).

State of Ohio v. Spisak, Court of Appeals of Ohio, 8th district, July 19, 1984.

State of Ohio v. Wilcox, 70 Ohio St. 2d 192 (1988).

State of Oregon v. Darnall, 614 P.2d 120 (Or.App. 1980).

State of Washington v. Allery, 682 P.2d 312 (Wash. 1984).

State of Washington v. Wanrow, 559 P.2d 548 (Wash. 1977).

State of West Virginia v. Dozier, 255 S.E.2d 511 (W.Va. 1979).

Steadman, H. & Cocozza, J. (1974). *Careers of the criminal insane*. Lexington, MA: Lexington Books.

Steadman, H. J., Keitner, L., Braff, J., & Arvanites, M. A. (1983). Factors associated with a successful insanity plea. *American Journal of Psychiatry, 140*, 401-405.

Steadman, H. J., Callahan, L. A., Robbins, P. C., & Morrissey, J. P. (1989). The maintenance of an insanity defense under Montana's abolition. *American Journal of Psychiatry, 146*, 357-360.

Steadman, H. S. (1982). A situational approach to violence. *International Journal of Psychiatry and Law, 5*, 171-186.

Stebbins, D. (1988, April). Psychologist and mitigation: Diagnosis to explanation. *The Champion*, 34-38.

Stein, D. G., Glasier, M. M., & Hoffman, S. W. (1994). Pharmacological treatments for brain-injury repair: Progress and prognosis. In A. L. Christensen & B. P. Uzzell (Eds.), *Brain injury and neuropsychological rehabilitation* (pp. 17-40). Hillsdale, NJ: Erlbaum.

Stein, D. J., Hollander, E., Cohen, L., Frenkel, M., Saoud, J. B., Decaria, C., Aronowitz, B., Levin, A., Liebowitz, M., & Cohen, L. (1993). Neuropsychiatric impairment in impulsive personality disorder. *Psychiatric Research, 48*, 257-266.

Stein, K. F. (1991). A national agenda for elder abuse and neglect research: Issues and recommendations. *Journal of Elder Abuse and Neglect, 3*(3), 91-108.

Steinhausen, H., Willms, J., & Spohr, H. (1994). *Journal of Child Psychology and Psychiatry, 35*, 323-331.

Steinmetz, S. (1978). The battered husband syndrome. *Victimology, 2*(3-4), 499-509.

Stephen, J. & Brien, P. (1994, December). *Capital Punishment 1993*. U. S. Department of Justice (NCJ-150042). Washington, DC: Supt. Docs.

Stets, J. & Straus, M. (1990). Gender differences in reporting marital violence and its medical and psychological consequences. In M. A. Straus & R. J. Gelles (Eds.), *Physical violence in American families*. New Brunswick, NJ: Transaction Publishers.

Stokman, C. L. J. & Heiber, P. G. (1984). The insanity defense reform act in New York state, 1980-1983. *International Journal of Law and Psychiatry, 7*, 367-384.

Stone, B. S. (1990). *Mental health and the law: A system in transition.* National Institute of Mental Health,

DHEW Publication No. ADM 76-176. Washington, DC: U.S. Government Printing Office.

Stone, J. L., McDaniel, K. D., Hughes, J. R., & Hermann, B. O. (1986). Episodic dyscontrol disorder and paroxysmal EEG abnormalities: Successful treatment with carbamazepine. *Biological Psychiatry, 21*, 208-212.

Storr, A. (1970). *Human aggression.* New York: Bantam.

Stout, K. D. (1992). "Intimate femicide" Effect of legislation and social services. In J. Radford & D. E. H. Russell (Eds.), *Femicide: The politics of woman killing.* New York: MacMillan.

Stout, K. D. (1993). Intimate femicide: A study of men who have killed their mates. *Journal of Offender Rehabilitation, 19*, 81-94.

Stratton, J.G. (1978). The terrorist act of hostage-taking: Exploring the motivation and cause. *Journal of Police Science and Administration, 6* (1), 1-9.

Straus, M. A. (1990). The national family violence surveys. In M.A. Straus & R. J. Gelles (Eds.), *Physical violence in American families: Risk factors and adaptation to violence in 8,145 families* (pp. 3-16). New Brunswick, NJ: Transaction.

Straus, M. A. & Gelles, R. (1986). Societal change and change in family violence from 1975 to 1985 as revealed by two national surveys. *Journal of Marriage and the Family, 48*, 465-479.

Straus, M. A. & Gelles, R. J. (1988). How violent are American families? Estimates from the National Family Violence Resurvey and other Studies. In G. T. Hotaling, D. Finklehor, J. T. Kirkpatrick, & M. A. Straus (Eds.), *Family abuse and its consequences: New directions in research* (pp. 1-35). Newbury Park, CA: Sage.

Straus, M. A., & Gelles, R. J. (1990). *Physical violence in American families.* New Brunswick, NJ: Transaction Publishers.

Straus, M. A., Gelles, R. J., & Steinmetz, S. (1980). *Behind closed doors: Violence in the American family.* Garden City, NY: Anchor.

Strauss, M., Gelles, R., & Steinmetz, S. (1980). *Behind closed doors: Violence in the American family.* New York: Doubleday.

Strentz, T. (1977). *Survival adaptation...the common sense syndrome.* Unpublished manuscript, FBI Academy, Quantico, VA.

Strentz, T. (1980). The Stockholm syndrome: Law enforcement policy and ego defenses of the hostage. In F. Wright, C. Bahn, & R.W. Rieber (Eds), *Forensic psychiatry and psychology.* New York: New York Academy of Sciences.

Strentz, T. (1980). The Stockholm Syndrome: Law enforcement policy and ego defenses of the hostage. *Annals of the New York Academy of Sciences, 347,* 137-150.

Strentz, T. (1983). The inadequate personality as hostage-taker. *Journal of Police Science and Administration, 11* (3), 363-368.

Strentz, T. (1985). *A statistical analysis of American hostage situations.* Unpublished manuscript, FBI Academy, Quantico, VA.

Strentz, T. (1986). Negotiating with the hostage-taker exhibiting paranoid-schizophrenic symptoms. *Journal of Police Science and Administration, 14,* 12-17.

Strentz, T., & Auerbach, S. M. (1988). Adjustment to the stress of simulated captivity: Effects of emotion-focused versus problem-solving preparation on hostages differing in locus of control. *Journal of Personality and Social Psychology, 55,* 652-660.

Strub, R. L., & Black, F. W. (1988). *Neurobehavioral disorders.* Philadelphia: F. A. Davis Co.

Strube, M. J., Turner, D. W., Cerro, D., Stevens, J., & Hinchey, F. (1984). Interpersonal aggression and the Type A coronary-prone behavior pattern: A theoretical distinction and practical implications. *Journal of Personality and Social Psychology, 47,* 839-847.

Strube, R., & Black, F. (1981). *Organic brain syndromes.* Philadelphia, PA: F. A. Davis Company.

Sturup, G. K. (1968). Treatment of sexual offenders in Herstedvester, Denmark. *Acta Psychiatrica Scandinavia,* Supp. 204, 44.

Stuss, D., & Benson, F. (1986). Neuropsychological studies of the frontal lobes. *Psychological Bulletin, 95,* 3-28.

Summit, R. (1983). The child sexual abuse accommodation syndrome. *Child Abuse and Neglect, 7,* 177-193.

Surgeon-General's Scientific Advisory Committee on Television and Social Behavior (1972). *Television and growing up: The impact of television violence.* Washington: United States Government Printing Office.

Sutherland, E. H. (1947). *Principles of criminology.* Philadelphia: Lippincott.

Sutker, P., & Moan, C. E. (1973). A psychosocial description of penitentiary inmates. *Archives of General Psychiatry, 29,* 663-667.

Swanson, D. W., Bonhert, P. J., & Smith, J. A. (1970). *The paranoid.* Boston: Little, Brown.

Swanson, J. W., Holzer, C. E., Ganju, V. H., & Jono, R. T. (1990). Violence and psychiatric disorders in the community: Evidence from the epidemiologic catchment area surveys. *Hospital & Community Psychiatry, 41,* 761-777.

Sweeney, D. (1990). Alcoholic blackouts: Legal implications. *Journal of Substance Abuse Treatment, 7,* 155-159.

Sweetman, J. (1984). *American naval history: An illustrated chronology of the U.S. Navy and Marine Corps 1775-present.* Annapolis: Naval Institute Press.

Symonds, M. (1980a). Victims' responses to terror. *Annals New York Academy of Sciences, 347,* 129-136.

Symonds, M. (1980b). Acute responses of victims to terror. *Evaluation and Change,* Special Issue, 39-41.

Syverson, K. L., & Romney, D. M. (1985). A further attempt to differentiate violent from nonviolent offenders by means of a battery of psychological tests. *Canadian Journal of Behavioural Science, 17,* 87-92.

Tanay, E. (1969). Psychiatric study of homicide. *American Journal of Psychiatry, 125,* 1252-1258.

Tanay, E. (1975). Dangerousness and psychiatry. *Current Concepts in Psychiatry, 1,* 17-26.

Tancredi, L. R., & Volkow, N. (1988). Neural substrates of violent behavior: Implications for law and public policy. *International Journal of Law and Psychiatry, 11,* 13-49.

Tangney, J. P. (1990). Assessing individual differences in proneness to shame and guilt: Development of the Self-conscious Affect and Attribution Inventory. *Journal of Personality and Social Psychology, 59,* 102-111.

Tanner, J. (1978). *Fetus into man: Physical growth from conception to maturity.* Cambridge: Harvard University Press.

Tarasoff v. Regents of University of California, 131 Cal. Rptr. 14 (1976).

Tardiff, K. (1992, June). The current state of psychiatry in the treatment of violent patients. *Archives of General Psychiatry,* pp. 493-499.

Tardiff, K. M. (1985). Patterns and major determinants of homicide in the United States. *Hospital and Community Psychiatry, 36*(6), 632-639.

Tarsh, M. J. (1986). On serious violence during sleep walking. *British Journal of Psychiatry, 148,* 476.

Tarter, R. E., Hegedus, A. M., Winsten, N. E., & Alterman, A. I. (1984). Intellectual profiles and violent behavior in juvenile delinquents. *The Journal of Psychology, 119,* 125-128.

Tavris, C., & Offir, C. (1977). *The longest war.* New York: Harcourt, Brace & Jovanovich.

Taylor, D. (1985). Developmental rate is the major differentiator between the sexes. *The Behavioral and Brain Sciences, 8,* 459-460.

Taylor, P., & Kopelman, M. (1984). Amnesia for criminal offenses. *Psychological Medicine, 14,* 581-588.

Taylor, S. P., & Pisano, R. (1971). Physical aggression as a function of frustration and physical attack. *Journal of Social Psychology, 84,* 261-267.

Tedeschi, J., & Felson, R. (1994). *Violence, aggression & coercive actions.* Washington DC: American Psychological Association.

Teltsch, K. (1992, August 18). Keeping teenagers smokeless. *New York Times*, Metro Section, pp. B1, B4.

Terr, L. C. (1981). "Forbidden games": Post-traumatic child's play. *Journal of the American Academy of Child Psychiatry, 20,* 741-760.

Terr, L. C. (1983). Chowchilla revisited: The effects of psychic trauma four years after a school-bus kidnapping. *American Journal of Psychiatry, 140,* 1543-1550.

Terr, L. C. (1989). Treating psychic trauma in children: A preliminary discussion. *Journal of Traumatic Stress, 2,* 3-20.

Tetlock, P. E., McGuire, C. B., & Mitchell, G. (1991). Psychological perspectives on nuclear deterrence. In M. R. Rosenzweig, & L. W. Porter (Eds.), *Annual Review of Psychology.* Palo Alto, CA: Annual Reviews.

Thearle, M. J., & Gregory, H. (1988). Child abuse in nineteenth century Queensland. *Child Abuse and Neglect, 12,* 91-101.

Theodor, L. H., & Mandelcorn, M. S. (1973). Hysterical blindness: A case report and study using a modern psychophysical technique. *Journal of Abnormal Psychology, 82,* 552-553.

Thompson, A. (1988, May 1). Action! The films that win audiences. *Philadelphia Inquirer*, p. 1F.

Thurer, S. L. (1994). *The myths of motherhood: How culture reinvents the good mother.* Boston: Houghton Mifflin.

Tieger, T. (1980). On the biological basis of sex differences in aggression. *Child Development, 51,* 943-963.

Tifft, L. L. (1993). *Battering of women: The failure of intervention and the case for prevention.* Boulder, CO.: Westview Press.

Time-Life Editors. (1992). *Mass Murderers.* New York: Time-Life Books.

Toch, H. (1969). *Violent men.* Chicago: Aldine.

Toch, H. (1975). *Men in crisis: Human breakdowns in prison.* Chicago, IL: Aldine.

Toch, H. (1980). The catalytic situation in the violence equation. *Journal of Applied Social Psychology, 15,* 105-123.

Toch, H. (1992). *Violent men.* Washington, DC: APA.

Tollison, C. D., & Adams, H. E. (1979). *Sexual disorders: Treatment, theory and research.* New York: Gardener.

Tolman, R. M., & Bhosley, G. (1991). The outcome of participation in a sheltered-sponsored program for men who batter. In D. Knudsen & J. Miller (Eds.), *Abused and battered: Social and legal responses to family violence.* New York: Aldine de Gruyter.

Totman, J. (1978). *The murderess: A psychosocial study of criminal homicide*. San Francisco, CA: R and E Research Associates.

Toufexis, A. (1988, June 20). Why mothers kill their babies. *Time, 131,* 81-83.

Treiman, D. M. (1986). Epilepsy and violence: Medical and legal issues. *Epilepsia, 27,* (Suppl. 2), S77-104.

Truscott, D. (1990). Assessment of overcontrolled hostility in adolescence. *Journal of Consulting and Clinical Psychology, 2,* 145-148.

Tuckman, C. (1994, November 17). The legacy of Susan Smith. *The Denver Post,* B-11.

Tsuang, P. (1994). Genetics, epidemiology, and the search for causes of schizophrenia. *American Journal of Psychiatry, 151,* 3-6.

Turner, J. T. (1985). Factors influencing the development of the hostage identification syndrome. *Political Psychology, 6,* 705-711.

Turner, P. J. (1991). Relations between attachment, gender, and behavior with peers in preschool. *Child Development, 62,* 1475-1485.

Twentyman, C. T., & McFall, R. M. (1975). Behavioral training of social skills in shy males. *Journal of Consulting and Clinical Psychology, 43,* 384-395.

Tzeng, O., Jackson, J., & Karlson, H. (1991). *Theories of child abuse and neglect: Differential perspectives, summaries and evaluations.* New York: Praeger.

Ullah, P. (1988). Unemployment and psychological well-being. In J. G. Howells (Ed.), *Modern perspectives in psychosocial pathology* (pp. 247-267). New York: Brunner/Mazel.

Uma, H., & Shobhini, L. (1987). Information processing in patients with closed head injury. *Journal of Psychological Researches, 31*(2), 70-76.

Uniform Crime Reports. (1991). Federal Bureau of Investigation, U.S. Department of Justice, Washington, DC.

Uniform Crime Reports for the United States, 1993. Federal Bureau of Investigation, U.S. Department of Justice, Washington, DC: U.S. Government Printing Office.

United States v. Amos, No. 86-1006 (8th Cir. Oct. 15, 1986).

United States v. Hinckley, 525 F.Supp. 1342 (D.D.C. 1981).

Uriquiza, A. J., Wirtz, S. J., Peterson, M. S., & Singer, V. A. (1994). Screening and evaluating abused and neglected children entering protective custody. *Child Welfare, 73*(2), 155-171.

U.S. Department of Health and Human Services (1993). *Preventing Homicide in the Workplace* (NIOSH Publication No. 4-5). Rockville, MD: Author.

U.S. Department of Justice (1983, October). *Report to the Nation on Crime and Justice* (NCJ-87068). Washington, DC: U.S. Government Printing Office, Supt. Docs.

U.S. Department of Justice. (1984). *Family violence: interventions for the justice system* [Program Brief]. Washington, DC: U.S. Department of Justice.

U.S. Department of Justice (1985, June). *National survey of crime severity* (NCJ-96017), Washington, DC: U.S. Government Printing Office, Supt. Docs.

U. S. Department of Justice (1993, May). *Felony defendants in large urban counties* (NCJ-141872), Washington, DC: U.S. Government Printing Office, Supt. Docs.

U.S. Department of Justice (1994). *Violence between intimates* (NIJ-149259). Washington, DC: U.S. Government Printing Office, Supt. Doc.

U.S. Department of Justice (1994, April). *Murder in the family* (NCJ-143498), Washington, DC: U.S. Government Printing Office, Supt. Docs.

U.S. Department of Justice (1995, April). *Correctional populations in the United States* (NCJ-153849), Washington, DC: U.S. Government Printing Office, Supt. Docs.

U.S. Department of Transportation (1992). *Criminal acts against civil aviation.* Washington, DC: U.S. Government Printing Office.

Utah Code, Art. 76-2-305(1), (1992).

Uzzell, B. P., & Gross, Y. (Eds.). (1986). *Clinical neuropsychology of intervention.* Boston: Nijhoff.

Valenstein, E. S. (1980). *The psychosurgery debate: Scientific, legal and ethical perspectives.* San Francisco: W. H. Freeman.

Valenstein, E. S. (1986). *Great and desperate cures.* New York: Basic.

Valliant, P. M., Asu, M. E., Cooper, D., & Mammola, D.

(1984). Profile of dangerous and non-dangerous offenders referred for pre-trial psychiatric assessment. *Psychological Reports, 54,* 411-418.

Van, J. (1995, February 18). Murderous statistic: Teens blamed for soaring U. S. homicide rate. *Chicago Tribune,* p. 15.

Van Biema, D. (1985, November 4). The suicide of Dan White brings a notorious San Francisco murder case to a bizarre end. *People Weekly, 24,* 46.

Van Biema, D. (1994, November 14). Parents who kill. *Time, 50.*

Van Voorhis, P. (1988). A cross classification of five offender typologies: Issues of construct and predictive validity. *Criminal Justice and Behavior, 15,* 109-124.

Van Zandt, C. R. (1993). Suicide by cop. *The Police Chief, LX*(7), 24-30.

Vandiver, J.V. (1981). Hostage situations require preparedness. *Law and Order, 9,* 66-69.

Vaselle-Augenstein, R., & Ehrlich, A. (1992). Male batterers: Evidence for psychopathology. In E. C. Viano (Ed.), *Intimate violence: Interdisciplinary perspective.* Washington, DC: Hemisphere Publishing Corp.

Venables, P. H. (1987). Autonomic nervous system factors in criminal behavior. In S. A. Mednick, T. E. Moffitt, & S. A. Stack, (Eds.), *The causes of crime: New biological approaches* (pp. 110-136). Cambridge, UK: Cambridge University Press.

Veneziano, C. A., & Veneziano, L. (1986). Classification of adolescent offenders with the MMPI: An extension and cross-validation of the Megargee typology. *International Journal of Offender Therapy and Comparative Criminology, 30,* 11-23.

Verhovek, S. H. (March 6, 1995). States seek to let citizens carry concealed weapons. *New York Times,* p. A1.

Verloove-Vanhorick, S., Veen, S., Ens-Kokkum, M., Schreuder, A., Brand, R., & Ruys, J. (1994). Sex difference in disability and handicap at five years of age in children born at very short gestation. *Pediatrics, 93,* 576-579.

Vetch, M. R., & Garrett, R. R. (1992, September). Elder and child abuse. *Journal of Interpersonal Violence,* 418-428.

Virkkunen, M. (1974). Suicide linked to homicide. *Psychiatric Quarterly, 48,* 276-282.

Vogel, C. H. (1979). Der Hanuman-Langur (*Presbytis entellus*), ein Paradeexemplar fur die theoretischen Konsepte der "Soziobiologie"? Verhandl. *Deut. Zool Ges.,* 73-89.

Vogel, C. H., & Loch, H. (1984). Reproductive parameters, adult-male replacements, and infanticide among free-ranging langurs (*Presbytis entellus*) at Jodhpur (Rajasthan), India. In G. Hausfater & S. B. Hrdy (Eds.), *Infanticide: Comparative and evolutionary perspectives* (pp. 237-255). New York: Aldine.

Vogel, S. A. (1990). Gender differences in intelligence, language, visual-motor abilities, and academic achievement in males and females with learning disabilities: A review of the literature. *Journal of Learning Disabilities, 23,* 44-52.

Volavka, J. (1995). *Neurobiology of violence.* Washington, DC: American Psychiatric Press.

Volkow, N. D., & Tancredi, L. (1987). Neural substrate of violent behavior: A preliminary study with positron emission tomography. *British Journal of Psychiatry, 151,* 668-673.

Volkow, N. D., & Tancredi, L. (1987). Neural substrates of violent behaviors: A preliminary study with positron emission tomography. *British Journal of Psychiatry, 151,* 668-673.

von Cramon, D. Y., & Mathes-von Cramon, G. (1990). Frontal lobe dysfunctions in patients—therapeutical approaches. In R. L. Wood & I. Fussey (Eds.), *Cognitive rehabilitation in perspective* (pp. 164-180). London: Taylor & Francis.

von Hentig, H. (1940). Remarks on the interaction of perpetrator and victim. *Journal of Criminal Law and Criminology, 31,* 303-309.

Voss, H. L., & Hepburn, J. R. (1968). Patterns of criminal homicide in Chicago. *Journal of Criminal Law, Criminology and Police Science, 59,* 499-508.

Wadsworth, S. J., DeFries, J. C., Stevenson, J., Gilger, J. W., & Pennington, B. F. (1992). Gender ratios among reading-disabled children and their siblings as a function of parental impairment. *Journal of Child Psychology & Psychiatry, 33*(7), 1229-1239.

Waldo, M. (1987). Also victims: Understanding and treating men arrested for spouse abuse. *Journal of Counseling and Development, 65,* 385-388.

Walker, D. (1968). *Rights in conflict.* New York: Signet.

Walker, E. A. (1961). Murder or epilepsy? *Journal of Nervous and Mental Disorders, 133,* 430-437.

Walker, L. E. (1979). *The battered woman.* New York: Harper & Row.

Walker, L. E. (1984). *The battered woman syndrome.* New York: Springer.

Walker, L. E., & Browne, A. (1986). Gender and victimization by intimates. *Journal of Personality, 53*(2), 179-195.

Walker, L. E. (1988). The battered woman syndrome. In G. Hotaling, D. Finkelhor, J. Kirkpatrick, & M. A. Straus (Eds.), *Family abuse and its consequences: New directions in research* (pp. 139-147). Newbury Park, CA: Sage.

Walker, L. E. (1989). *Terrifying love: Why battered women kill and how society responds.* New York: Harper & Row.

Walker, L. E. (1989a). *Terrifying love: Why battered woman kill and how society responds.* New York: Harper & Row.

Walker, L. E. (1989b). Psychology and violence against women. *American Psychologist, 44,* 695-702.

Walsh, A., & Beyer, J. A. (1986). Wechsler Performance-Verbal discrepancy and antisocial behavior. *Journal of Social Psychology, 126,* 419-420.

Walters, G. D. (1986). Correlates of the Megargee criminal classification system: A military correctional setting. *Criminal Justice and Behavior, 13,* 19-32.

Walters, G. D., Mann, M. F., Miller, M. P., Hemphill, L., & Chlumsky, M. L. (1988). Emotional disorder among offenders: Inter- and intrasetting comparisons. *Criminal Justice and Behavior, 15,* 433-453.

Walters, G. D., Scrapansky, T. A., & Marlow, G. A. (1986). The emotionally disturbed military offender: Identification, background and institutional adjustment. *Criminal Justice and Behavior, 13,* 261-285.

Walters, G. D., Solomon, G. S., & Greene, R. J. (1982). The relationship between the Overcontrolled Hostility scale and the MMPI 4-3 high point pair. *Journal of Clinical Psychology, 38*, 613-615.

Ward, A. A. (1948). The cingulate gyrus: Area 24. *Journal of Neurophysiology, 11*, 13-23.

Wass, H., Raup, J. L., & Sisler, H. H. (1989). Adolescents and death on television: A follow-up study. *Death Studies, 13*, 161-173.

Watts, D. P. (1989). Infanticide in mountain gorillas: New cases and a reconsideration of the evidence. *Ethology, 81*, 1-18.

Webster, C., Slomen, D., Sepejak, D., Butler, B., Jensen, F., & Turral, G. (1979). *Dangerous Behavior Rating Scheme (DBRS): Construction and Inter-Rater Reliability*. Unpublished manuscript, Toronto, Ontario.

Webster, M. (1991). *Webster's ninth collegiate dictionary*. Springfield, MA: Merriam Webster, Inc.

Wechsler, D. (1981). *Wechsler adult intelligence scale*. New York, NY: The Psychological Corporation.

Wedgwood, C. V. (1957). *The Thirty Years War*. Harmondsworth, Middlesex, England: Penguin Books.

Weiger, W. A., & Bear, D. M. (1988). An approach to the neurology of aggression. *Journal of Psychiatric Research, 22*, 85-98.

Weigley, R. F. (1991). *The age of battles*. Bloomington, IN: Indiana University Press.

Weiner, J. (1994). *The beak of the finch*. New York: Knopf.

Weinstein, C. S. (1991). The classroom as a social context for learning. In M. R. Rosenzweig, & L. W. Porter (Eds.), *Annual Review of Psychology*, Palo Alto, CA: Annual Reviews.

Weisheit, R. (1986). When mothers kill their children. *The Social Science Journal, 23*(4), 439-448.

Weiss, B., Dodge, K. A., Bates, J. E., & Pettit, G. S. (1992). Some consequences of early harsh discipline: Child aggression and a maladaptive social information processing style. *Child Development, 63*, 1321-1335.

Welte, J. W., & Abel, E. L. (1989). Homicide: Drinking by the victim. *Journal of Studies on Alcohol, 50*(3), 197-201.

Wender, P. H. (1972). The minimal brain dysfunction syndrome in children. *The Journal of Nervous and Mental Disease, 155*, 55-71.

Wertham, F. (1937). The catathymic crisis: A clinical entity. *Archives of Neurology and Psychiatry, 37*, 974-978.

Wertham, F. (1969). *A sign for Cain*. New York: Warner.

Wertham, F. (1978). The catathymic crisis. In I. L. Kutash, S. B. Kutash, L. B. Schesinger & Associates (Eds.), *Violence* (pp. 165-170). San Francisco, CA: Jossey-Bass, Inc.

Wesselius, C. L., & DeSarno, J. V. (1983). The anatomy of a hostage situation. *Behavioral Sciences & the Law, 1*, 33-45.

West, D.J. (1966). *Murder followed by suicide*. Cambridge: Harvard University Press.

West, I. (1988). *Study findings: Study of national incidence and prevalence of child abuse and neglect*. Washington, DC: U.S. Department of Health and Human Services.

Westermeyer, J. (1974). Caveats on diagnosing assassins. *American Journal of Psychiatry, 131*, 722-723.

Whalen, C. (1989). Attention deficit and hyperactivity disorders. In T. Ollendick & M. Hersen (Eds.), *Handbook of child psychopathology* (2nd ed.). New York: Plenum Press.

Wheeler, D., & Rubin, H. B. (1987). A comparison of volumetric and circumferential measures of penile erection. *Archives of Sexual Behavior, 16*, 289-299.

Whitaker, L. C. (1980). *Objective measurement of schizophrenic thinking: A practical and theoretical guide to the Whitaker Index of Schizophrenic Thinking.* Los Angeles: Western Psychological Services.

Whitaker, L. C. (1987). Macho and morbidity: The emotional need vs. fear dilemma in men. *Journal of College Student Psychotherapy, 1*, 4, 33-47.

Whitaker, L. C. (1990). Myths and heroes: Visions of the future. *Journal of College Student Psychotherapy, 4*, 2, 13-33.

Whitaker, L. C. (1992). *Schizophrenic disorders: Sense and nonsense in conceptualization, assessment, and treatment.* New York: Plenum Press.

Whitaker, L. C. (1993a). Violence is golden: Commercially motivated training in impulsive cognitive style and mindless violence. *Journal of College Student Psychotherapy, 8*, 1/2, 45-69. Published simultaneously in L. C. Whitaker and J. W. Pollard (Eds.), *Campus violence: Kinds, causes, and cures.* New York: The Haworth Press.

Whitaker, L. C., & Pollard, J. W. (Eds.). (1993b). *Campus violence: Kinds, causes, and cures.* New York: The Haworth Press. Published simultaneously in *Journal of College Student Psychotherapy, 8*, 1/2, 3.

Whitcomb, D. (1992, March). *When the victim is a child* (2d ed.). [Issues and Practices in Criminal Justice]. Washington, DC: U.S. Department of Justice, National Institute of Justice.

White, S., & Hatcher, C. (1988). Violence and trauma response. In *Occupational medicine: State of the art reviews*, Vol. 4. Philadelphia: Handley and Belfus.

White, W. C. (1975). Validity of the Overcontrolled-Hostility scale: A brief report. *Journal of Personality Assessment, 39*, 587-590.

White, W. C., McAdoo, W. G., & Megargee, E. I. (1973). Personality factors associated with over- and undercontrolled offenders. *Journal of Personality Assessment, 37*, 473-478.

Wickramasekera, I. (1976). Aversive behavior rehearsal for sexual exhibitionism. *Behavior Therapy, 7*, 167-176.

Widom, C. S. (1989). Child abuse, neglect, and adult behavior: Research design and findings on criminality, violence, and child abuse. *American Journal of Orthopsychiatry, 59*, 355-367.

Widom, C. S. (1989). Does violence beget violence? A critical examination of the literature. *Psychological Bulletin, 106* (1), 3-28.

Widom, C. S. (1989). The intergenerational transmission of violence. In N. A. Weiner & M. E. Wolfgang (Eds.), *Pathways to criminal violence.* (pp.137-201). Newbury Park, CA: Sage.

Widom, C. S. (1992, October). *The cycle of violence* [Research in Brief]. Washington, DC: National Institute of Justice.

Widom, C. S. (1992, October). The cycle of violence. U.S. Department of Justice (NCJ136607), Washington DC, Supt. Docs.

Wilbanks, W. (1983). Female homicide offenders in the U.S. *International Journal of Women's Studies, 6*(4), 302-310.

Wilbanks, W. (1983). The female homicide offender in Dade County, Florida. *Criminal Justice Review, 8,* 9-14.

Wilbanks, W. (1986). Criminal homicide offenders in the U.S.: Black vs. White. In D. F. Hawkins (Ed.), *Homicide among Black Americans.* New York: University Press of America.

Wilber, C. G. (1985). A case of lust murder. *The American Journal of Forensic Medicine and Pathology, 6*(3), 226-232.

Wilhelmsen, K. C., Lynch, T., Neystat, M., Nygaard, T. G., Bernstein, M., Marder, K., Mayeux, R., Fahn, S., Rowland, L. P., Foster, N. L., Wszolek, Z., Koehan, K., Sima, A. A. F., & Deffendini, R. (August, 1994). *Clinical, pathologic and genetic analysis of familial disinhibition-dementia-Parkinsonism-amyotrophy-complex: A possible clue to the etiology of atypical dementias.* Fourth International Conference on Alzheimer's Disease, Minneapolis, MN.

Wilkie, I., Pearn, J., & Petrie, G. (1982). Neonaticide, infanticide and child homicide. *Medicine, Science and the Law, 22,* 31-34.

Willerman, L. (1979). The effects of families on intellectual development. *American Psychologist, 34,* 923-929.

Williams, D. (1969). Neural factors related to habitual aggression. *Brain, 92,* 503-520.

Williams, S., & McGee, R. (1994). Reading attainment and juvenile delinquency. *Journal of Child Psychology and Psychiatry, 35,* 441-459.

Williams, T. (Ed.). (1987). *Post-traumatic stress disorders: A handbook for clinicians.* Cincinnati: Disabled American Veterans.

Wilson, A. (1993). Introduction. In A. Wilson (Ed.), *Homicide: The victim/offender* (p. 3). Cincinnati, OH: Anderson Publishing Co.

Wilson, B., & Moffat, N. (Eds.). (1992). *Clinical management of memory problems.* San Diego: Singular.

Wilson, C., & Pitman, P. C. (1962). *Encyclopedia of murder.* New York: Putnam.

Wilson, E. O. (1992). *The diversity of life.* Cambridge, MA: Belknap.

Wilson, J. Q. (1993). The moral sense. *American Political Science Review, 87*(1), 1-10.

Wilson, L., & Rogers, R. W. (1975). The fire this time: Effects of race of target insult, and potential retaliation on black aggression. *Journal of Personality and Social Psychology, 32,* 857-864.

Wilson, M., & Daly, M. (1993). Spousal homicide risk and estrangement. *Violence and Victims, 8,* 3-16.

Wines, M. (1993, October 21). Reno chastises TV networks on violence in programming. *The New York Times,* p. A1.

Witkin, G. (1991, April 8). Kids who kill. *Newsweek,* pp. 26-32.

Witwer, M. (1994, November). Doctors focus on the threat to health from violence. *National Institute of Justice Journal,* p. 8.

Woenstendiek, J. (1993, March 28). Grim data on teens in U.S. *The Philadelphia Inquirer*, pp. A1, A6.

Wolfe, D., & McGee, R. (1994). Dimensions of child maltreatment and their relationship to adolescent adjustment. *Development and Psychopathology, 6*, 165-181.

Wolfgang, M. (1958). *Patterns in criminal homicide.* London: University of Oxford Press.

Wolfgang, M. (1958). An analysis of homicide-suicide. *Journal of Clinical and Experimental Psychopathology, 19*, 208-217.

Wolfgang, M. (1959). Suicide by means of victim-precipitated homicide. *Journal of Clinical and Experimental Psychopathology, 20*, 335-349.

Wolfgang, M. (1977). From boy to man – From delinquency to crime. *National symposium on the serious juvenile offender.* Minneapolis, MN.

Wolfgang, M. (1978). An overview of research into violent behavior. *Testimony before the U.S. House of Representatives Committee on Science and Technology.*

Wolfgang, M. E. (1958). *Patterns in criminal homicide.* Philadelphia: University of Pennsylvania Press.

Wolfgang, M. E. (1978). Overview of research into violent behavior. In *Research into violent behavior: Overview and sexual assaults.* Hearings before the Subcommittee on Domestic and International Science Planning, Analysis, and Cooperation of the Committee on Science and Technology, U.S. House of Representatives. 95th Congress, Second session.

Wolfgang, M. E. (1981). Sociocultural overview of criminal violence. In J. R. Hays, T. K. Roberts, & K. S. Soloway (Eds.), *Violence and the violent individual.* New York: Spectrum.

Wolpe, J. (1958). *Psychotherapy by reciprocal inhibition.* Stanford: Stanford University Press.

Women Together, Inc. (1984). Home is not supposed to hurt. *Flyer.* Cleveland, Ohio.

Wong, M. & Singer, K. (1973). Abnormal homicide in Hong Kong. *British Journal of Psychiatry, 123*, 295-298.

Wood, R. L. (1987). *Brain injury rehabilitation: A neurobehavioral approach.* Rockville, MD: Aspen.

Workers who fight firing with fire (1994, April 25). *Time Magazine, 144*, pp. 35-37.

Workman, E. A., & Tellian, F. F. (1994). *Practical handbook of psychopharmacology.* Boca Raton, FL: CRC Press.

Wright, K. N. (1988). The relationship of risk, needs, and personality classification systems and prison adjustment. *Criminal Justice and Behavior, 15*, 454-471.

Wrightson, K. (1975). Infanticide in early seventeenth-century England. *Local Population Studies, 15*, 10-21.

Wrobel, N. H., Wrobel, T. A., & McIntosh, J. W. (1988). Application of the Megargee typology to a forensic psychiatric population. *Criminal Justice and Behavior, 15*, 247-254.

Wrobel, T. A., Calovini, P. K., & Martin, T. O. (1991). Application of the Megargee MMPI typology to a population of defendants referred for psychiatric evaluation. *Criminal Justice and Behavior, 18*, 397-405.

Wyoming v. Zespy, 723 P.2d 564 (1986).

Yarvis, R. M. (1990). Axis I and axis II diagnostic parameters of homicide. *Bulletin of the American Academy of Psychiatry and Law, 18,* 249-269.

Yeudall, L. T. (1977). Neuropsychological assessment of forensic disorders. *Canada's Mental Health, 25,* 7-15.

Yeudall, L. T., & Fromm-Auch, D. (1979). Neuropsychological impairments in various psychopathological populations. In J. Gruzelier & P. Flor-Henry (Eds.), *Hemisphere asymmetrics of function and psychopathology* (pp. 5-31). New York: Elsevier/ North Holland.

Yeudall, L. T., Fromm-Auch, D., & Davies, P. (1982). Neuropsychological impairment of persistent delinquency. *Journal of Nervous and Mental Disorders, 170,* 257-265.

Yllo, K., & Straus, M. A. (1981). Interpersonal violence among married and cohabiting couples. *Family Relations, 30,* 339-347.

Yeudall, L. T., & Fromm-Auch, D. (1979). Neuropsychological impairment in various psychopathological populations. In J. Gruzelier & P. Flor-Henry (Eds.), *Hemisphere asymmetrics of function in psychopathology*. Amsterdam, Elsevier/North-Holland.

Yeudall, L. T., Fedora, O., & Fromm, D. (1987). A neuropsychosocial theory of persistent criminality: Implications for assessment and treatment. In R. W. Rieber (Ed.), *Advances in forensic psychology and psychiatry* (Vol. 2). Norwood, NJ: Ablex.

Ylvisaker, M. (Ed.). (1985). *Head injury rehabilitation: Children and adolescents*. San Diego: College-Hill.

Yochelson, S., & Samenow, S. (1976). *The criminal personality*, Vols. I, II, & III. New York: Jason Aronson.

Yochelson, S., & Samenow, S. (1976). *The criminal personality*. New York: Jason Aronson.

Zager, L. D. (1988). The MMPI-based criminal classification system: A review, current status, and future directions. *Criminal Justice and Behavior, 15,* 39-57.

Zahn-Waxler, C. (1993). Warriors and worriers: Gender and psychopathology. *Development and Psychopathology, 5,* 79-90.

Zahn-Waxler, C., Radke-Yarrow, M., & Wager, E. (1992). Development of concern for others. *Developmental Psychology, 28,* 126-136.

Zaslow, M. J. (1988). Sex differences in children's response to parental divorce: Research methodology and postdivorce family forms. *American Journal of Orthopsychiatry, 58*(3), 355-378.

Zaslow, M. J. (1989). Sex differences in children response to parental divorce: Samples, variabl ages, and sources. *American Journal of Orthopsyc. atry, 59,* 118-141.

Zaslow, M. J., & Hayes, C. D. (1986). Sex differences in children's response to psychosocial stress: Toward a cross-context analysis. In M. E. Lamb, A. L. Brown, & B. Rogoff (Eds.), *Advances in developmental psychology* (Vol. 4, pp. 285-333). London: Lawrence Erlbaum Associates.

Zawitz, M. W., Klaus, P., Bachman, R., Bastian, L. D., DeBerry, M., Rand, M., & Taylor, B. (1993, October). *Highlights from 20 years of surveying crime victims: The National Crime Victimization Survey, 1973-92* [NCJS-144525]. Washington, DC: U.S. Department of Justice.

Zillman, D., Katcher, A. H., & Milavsky, B. (1972). Excitation transfer from physical exercise to subsequent aggressive behavior. *Journal of Experimental Social Psychology, 8*, 247-259.

Zillmann, D. (1982). Television viewing and arousal. In D. Pearl, L. Bouthilet, & J. Lazar (Eds.), *Television and behavior: Ten years of scientific progress and implications for the eighties*, Vol. 2, Technical reports (pp. 53-67). Washington: United States Government Printing Office.

Zillmann, D., & Johnson, R. C. (1973). Motivated aggressiveness perpetuated by exposure to aggressive films and reduced exposure to nonaggressive films. *Journal of Research in Personality, 7*, 261-276.

Zillmann, D., J. Bryant, & A. C. Huston, Eds. (1994). *Media, children, and the family: Social, scientific, psychodynamic, and clinical perspectives*. Hillsdale, NJ:Lawrence Erlbaum Associates.

Zoccolillo, M. (1993). Gender and the development of conduct disorder. *Development and Psychopathology, 5*, 65-78.

Zuckerman, L. (1989). Converging on peace? *New York Review of Books, 36*, 26-32.

Zuckerman, M. (1994). Impulsive unsocialized sensation seeking: the biological foundations of a basic dimension of personality. In J. E. Bates & T. D. Wachs (Eds.), *Temperament: Individual differences at the interface of biology and behavior* (pp. 219-245). Washington, DC: American Psychological Association.

Zur, O. (1989). War myths: Exploration of the dominant collective beliefs about warfare. *Journal of Humanistic Psychology, 29*, 297-327.

Subject Index